30p

G000146462

LE

The Budget Guide to

MEXICO

1991

Zanley F. Galton III
Editor

Jennifer C. Bernstein
Assistant Editor

Written by Harvard Student Agencies, Inc.

PAN BOOKS
London, Sydney and Auckland

Helping Let's Go

If you have suggestions or corrections, or just want to share your discoveries, drop us a line. We read every piece of correspondence, whether a 10-page letter, a postcard, or, as in one case, a collage. All suggestions are passed along to our researcher/writers. Please note that mail received after June 1, 1991 will probably be too late for the 1992 book, but will be retained for the following edition. Address mail to: *Let's Go: Mexico;* Harvard Student Agencies, Inc.; Thayer Hall-B; Harvard University; Cambridge, MA 02138; USA.

In addition to the invaluable travel advice our readers share with us, many are kind enough to offer their services as researchers or editors. Unfortunately, the charter of Harvard Student Agencies, Inc. enables us to employ only currently enrolled Harvard students.

Published in Great Britain 1991 by Pan Books Ltd
Cavaye Place, London SW10 9PG
9 8 7 6 5 4 3 2 1

Published in the United States of America
by St. Martin's Press, Inc.

ISBN: 0 330 31712 1

Let's Go: Mexico is written by Harvard Student Agencies, Inc., Harvard University, Thayer Hall-B, Cambridge, Mass. 02138, USA.

Publishing Manager   Ravi Desai
Managing Editors   Jessica V.V. Avery
Michael Scott Krivan
Alexandra M. Tyler

Production/Communication Coordinator   C. W. Cowell
Editor   Zanley F. Galton III
Assistant Editor   Jennifer Bernstein

Researcher/Writers

Aguascalientes, The Bajío, Colima, Durango, Jalisco, Mazatlán, Michoacán, Nayarit, Zacatecas — Chris M. Brown

Belize, C. Chetumal, Chiapas, Guatemala, Oaxaca Coast — Sue M. Johnson

Oaxaca de Juárez and environs, Teapa, Villahermosa, The Yucatán (except C. Chetumal) — Julie Mallozzi

Guerrero, La Venta, Morelos, Puebla, southern Veracruz, Tuxtepec, Tlaxcala — Courtney T. Pyle

Baja California, Chihuahua, Los Mochis, Sonora — Kenneth A. Smith

Brownsville, Hidalgo, Mexico City, northern Veracruz, Nuevo Leon, Tamaulipas — David Sorola

Sales Group Manager   Robert D. Frost
Sales Representatives   Christine J. Hahn
Cristina D. Toro-Hernandez
David R. Tunnell

Legal Counsel   Pasternak, Blankstein, and Lund

ACKNOWLEDGMENTS

How sweet it is.

After countless hours of dungeon-based summer toil, to be only these few words away from completing the book is to be as proud as a *poblano* on the 5th of May.

A lion's share of the credit for this book goes to Jennifer Bernstein, who cranked through a hellish production schedule, endured editorial gibes from yours truly with polite laughter, and produced verbs to raise the dead when mine couldn't move a sycophant to flattery. Her crunch-time late-night work more than made this book better; her labors made this book. I thank you deeply, JB.

I am deeply indebted to whichever Travel Guide God it was that blessed me with a crack research team of six intrepid souls. Chris Brown added laughter to my summer with his comic style and wry commentary, and more than a few of his city introductions will go down in history; long live Bugle Boy jeans and the Earl of Sandwich! Sue Johnson trekked through Belize and Guatemala, garnering marriage proposals along the way. Her thoroughness was unsurpassed, and the areas she added to the book will pave the way for further expansion next year. Julie Mallozzi covered the Yucatán with a skill that the region both needed and deserved. Upon arrival of each JM copybatch, I sent a prayer of thanks to Chac for her prose and clear handwriting. Courtney Pyle discoed through southern-central Mexico, pausing long enough to send home copy that proved her unbending dedication to the cause. To top it all of, she furnished the office with some damn good brownies when she returned to Cambridge. Successful completion of Ken Smith's difficult route required a firmness of purpose and a willingness to test the upper envelope of his credit card limit. All Baja-bound travelers should utter a profound "Yay" for Ken's demonstration of both those characteristics. And David Sorola did a fantastic job canvassing Mexico City (with style and on time), adding to the text stories of historical note and personal interest.

This turquoise tome reads as smoothly as it does thanks to one man: Michael Krivan, Managing Editor *extraordinaire.* Extracting the seeds of ideas from my mostly mis-directed sputterings and transforming them into well-written passages, Mikey proved his editing prowess time and time again throughout the summer. There is no boss more eagle-eyed, no grocery shopper more enthusiastic, and no partner more willing to Aerobie at any time of day or night. Yeah, Mike: this book is as much yours as mine.

Although Ravi Desai had no specific contact with this book, *el jefe* did a fine job of controlling the whole mess and, more importantly, showed a deep understanding of the proper construction of a G&T.

I'm fond of saying that this is the best job in the world, and it's sure not because of the hours: Kevin "Big Guy" Young, possibly the funniest man on campus, kept at least one of us laughing at all times (*really* sorry about those dogs); Steve Glick always let me cry on his shoulder during his brief dungeon visits; Darcy Tromanhauser never stopped reminding me of my fantastically fine singing ability; and Andrew Kaplan provided a healthy dose of weirdness every day. Jenny Lyn, Jenny S., Jody, Ian, Liane, Jessica, and Alex (goblazersgoblazersgoblazers) all made the summer more enjoyable.

As co-inhabitants of the Gables, Chris Cowell and Jamie Rosen provided extra-office relief: among everything else, Chris listened attentively during those times when I chose to spill my heart, and Jamie's consummate skill as a chef proved to be an invaluable asset to the rooming group. Lara atoned for the theft of my typists and toilet paper with the pleasure of her company in the Gables's late-night swimming class; God willing, she will think small forevermore. To schoolyear roommates Pete Wardle and Alejandro Canelos, I'd like to propose a toast: to two awesome years, with two more on the way.

During the spring, Amy Savel's welcoming smile made doing tearsheets in the office that much less painful. May she continue to do an incredible job of organizing the office's mail for years to come.

Finally, I'd like to thank my parents for showing me the far corners of the world at a young age; this book is dedicated to my mother and father, as well as the rest of my family, with love.

Jack Atimak lives. Forever.

—ZFG

About Let's Go

In 1960, Harvard Student Agencies, a three-year-old nonprofit corporation established to provide employment opportunities to Harvard and Radcliffe students, was doing a booming business selling charter flights to Europe. One of the extras HSA offered passengers on these flights was a 20-page mimeographed pamphlet entitled *1960 European Guide,* a collection of tips on continental travel compiled by the staff at HSA. The following year, students traveling to Europe researched the first full-fledged edition of *Let's Go: Europe,* a pocket-sized book with a smattering of tips on budget accommodations, irreverent write-ups of sights, and a decidedly youthful slant. The first editions proclaimed themselves to be the companions of the "adventurous and often impecunious student."

Throughout the 60s, the series reflected its era: a section of the 1968 *Let's Go: Europe* was entitled "Street Singing in Europe on No Dollars a Day;" the 1969 guide to America led off with a feature on drug-ridden Haight-Ashbury. During the 70s, *Let's Go* gradually became a large-scale operation, adding regional European guides and expanding coverage into North Africa and Asia. In 1981, *Let's Go: USA* returned after an eight-year hiatus, and in the next year HSA joined forces with its current publisher, St. Martin's Press. Now in its 31st year, *Let's Go* publishes 13 titles covering more than 40 countries.

Each spring, over 150 Harvard-Radcliffe students compete for some 70 positions as *Let's Go* researcher/writers. Those hired possess a rare combination of budget travel sense, writing ability, stamina, and courage. Each researcher/writer travels on a shoestring budget for seven weeks, researching seven days per week, and overcoming countless obstacles in the quest for better bargains.

Back in a basement in Harvard Yard, an editorial staff of 25, a management team of five, and countless typists and proofreaders—all students—spend four months poring over more than 50,000 pages of manuscript as they push the copy through 12 stages of intensive editing. In September the efforts of summer are converted from computer diskettes to nine-track tapes and delivered to Com Com in Allentown, Pennsylvania, where their computerized typesetting equipment turns them into books in record time. And even before the books hit the stands, next year's editions are well underway.

A Note to our Readers

The information for this book is gathered by Harvard Student Agencies' researchers during the late spring and summer months. Each listing is derived from the assigned researcher's opinion based on his or her visit at a particular time. The opinions are expressed in a candid and forthright manner. Other travelers might disagree. Those traveling at a different time may have a different experience since prices, dates, hours, and conditions are always subject to change. You are urged to check beforehand to avoid inconvenience and surprises. Travel always involves a certain degree of risk, especially in low cost areas. When traveling, especially on a budget, you should always take particular care to ensure your safety.

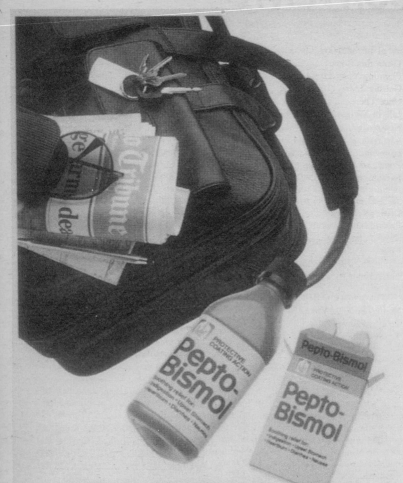

CARRY-ON RELIEF.

CONTENTS

LIST OF MAPS

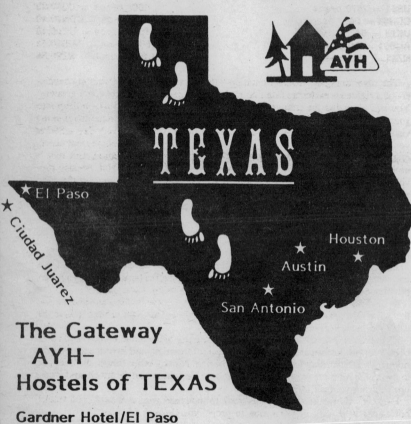

LET'S GO: MEXICO

General Introduction

US$1 = 2872 pesos	1000 pesos = US$0.35
CDN$1 = 2498 pesos	1000 pesos = CDN$0.40
UK£1 = 5485 pesos	1000 pesos = UK£0.18
AUS$1 = 2441 pesos	1000 pesos = AUS$0.41
NZ$1 = 1782 pesos	1000 pesos = NZ$0.56

The silver lining of Mexican inflation—though tragic for the domestic consumer—is a righteous exchange rate that makes the Republic a perfect budget getaway. You will marvel at the culinary, recreational, and wearable gems which drop into your lap at the slightest financial provocation. It follows that Mexico moves many visitors to decadence. Sensory indulgence is the order of the day, every day: whether you prefer to reel with tequila on your tongue, fuse with the phosphorescent ocean, or resonate with a *marimba* groove, your body is in for a revelation. But that is no excuse to leave your mind behind, no matter who recommends it. Mexico provides ample food for thought. Assimilating the massive contradictions of the present, meditating on an operatic history, and anticipating a multifarious future will challenge your intellect and engage your compassion.

Using this Book

Let's Go suggests accommodations and restaurants for the most value-conscious traveler and provides helpful hints for packing, crossing the border, eating a mango, hitching a ride, bargaining for sandals, snorkeling safely—you name it.

We'll help you plan your trip, give you a crash course in Mexican history and literature, acquaint you with the unwritten rules, and get you around Mexico as efficiently and inexpensively as possible.

Within each regional section, you'll find write-ups of the notable towns and cities, complete with historical anecdotes, practical information, and lists of accommodations ranked according to our recommendation. Among other things, we'll let you know which ruins are worth the five-hour bus ride, what to eat for lunch, and where not to drink yourself into a stupor.

Use *Let's Go* for its advice. This book cannot bind you, as would train tracks, but can serve as sails of suggestion to propel you through Mexico.

Planning Your Trip

A vacation is like a hot date. If you want to script your moves, read this book cover to cover right now, and write the Mexican Government Tourism Office to mine their travel information (see Useful Addresses below and the Practical Information section for each city). If you like playing it by ear, just take off and enjoy Mexico in all its spontaneity.

Mexico lies in the great desert belt of the Americas and is bounded by seas in all directions except north, where it runs into the U.S., and the extreme southeast, where Guatemala borders the states of Chiapas and Tabasco. High mountain ranges and mesas disrupt the flow of most of the country's land, but on the coasts, the Sierra Madres plunge down to sea-level lowlands in the space of a few miles. Need-

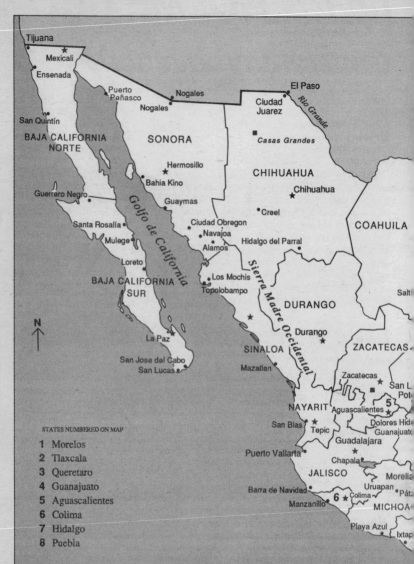

Tijuana
★ Mexicali
Ensenada
Puerto Peñasco
Nogales
El Paso
Ciudad Juarez
Rio Grande
San Quintín
BAJA CALIFORNIA NORTE
Nogales
SONORA
Casas Grandes
CHIHUAHUA
Hermosillo ★
Bahia Kino
Chihuahua ★
Guerrero Negro
Guaymas
Creel
Santa Rosalía
Ciudad Obregon
Navajoa
Alamos
Hidalgo del Parral
COAHUILA
Mulege
Golfo de California
Loreto
Los Mochis
BAJA CALIFORNIA SUR
Topolobampo
Sierra Madre Occidental
DURANGO
Salt
La Paz
Durango ★
ZACATECAS
San Jose del Cabo
San Lucas
SINALOA
Mazatlan
Zacatecas ★
San L Pot
NAYARIT
Aguascalientes ★
5
San Blas
Tepic ★
Dolores Hid
Guanajuat
Puerto Vallarta
Guadalajara ★
Chapala
JALISCO
Morelia
Barra de Navidad
Uruapan
Pátz
Manzanillo
6 ★ Colima
MICHOA
Playa Azul
Ixtap

STATES NUMBERED ON MAP

1 Morelos
2 Tlaxcala
3 Queretaro
4 Guanajuato
5 Aguascalientes
6 Colima
7 Hidalgo
8 Puebla

OCEANO PACIFICO

N
↑

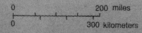

0 ———————— 200 miles
0 ———————— 300 kilometers

Mexico

UNITED STATES OF AMERICA

Golfo de Mexico

as Negras

Laredo

Nuevo Laredo

McAllen   Brownsville

Reynosa   Matamoros

nterrey

O

N

TAMAULIPAS

Tampico

N LUIS
OTOSI

guel
nde
aretaro
Chicomoztóc
Pachuca

7

ico
City

2
Tlaxcala

8   Puebla

1

Cuernavaca

xco   Tehuacan

RRERO

Chilpancingo

Acapulco

Tuxpan

Papantla

VERACRUZ

Jalapa

Veracruz

San Andrés
Tuxtla   TABASCO

Catemaco   Villahermosa

Tuxtepec

OAXACA

Oaxaca

Mitla   Tuxtla Gutierrez

Tehuantepec

Puerto Escondido

Puerto Angel

Palenque

San Cristobal   Bonampak
de las Casas

Comitan

CHIAPAS

Tonalá

Tapachula

Mérida   Valladolid

YUCATAN   Chichen Itza

Cobá

Uxmal

Campeche

CAMPECHE   QUINTANA ROO

Chetumal

Escarcega

Tikal

Ciudad
Cuauhtémoc

GUATEMALA

Guatemala City

Antigua

Isla
Mujeres

Cancun

Isla
Cozumel

Belize City

Belmopan

BELIZE

less to say, the country has experienced and continues to experience dramatic tectonic movements.

The Tropic of Cancer bisects Mexico into a temperate north and tropical south, but the climate varies considerably even within these belts. The Baja desert heats up to 100°F (40°C), and the Yucatán remains hot and humid year-round; winters in northern and central Mexico can chill even the most hot-blooded traveler.

Although slick tourist beaches and Acapulco's high-priced resort hotels are the loudest promoters of Mexico, they do not represent Mexico at its most compelling. Secluded, undeveloped coastal towns line the Pacific coast, and 11,000 archeological sites bridge the centuries between modern Mexico and its ancient civilizations. Especially in the central and southern areas, ruins are plentiful and beaches are unspoiled by the oil wells of the northern shores.

Central Mexico, the area around Mexico City, combines the architectural and cultural traditions of ancient Aztec, colonial Spanish, and contemporary *mestizo* civilizations. Mexico City serves as a base for excursions to Teotihuacán, Cuernavaca, Taxco, and Puebla. Slightly longer trips reach Oaxaca, Veracruz, and Morelia. If you have more money than time to spare, take advantage of the cheap air service between cities.

To the east, the humid Yucatán Peninsula is swathed in tropical jungle and dotted with important archeological sites. The largest numbers of *indígenas* in the Republic live in the southern states of Oaxaca and Chiapas. In southwestern Mexico—Morelos, Jalisco, and Colima—Old World culture lingers. The southern coast, from Jalisco to the Istmo de Tehuantepec, runs the gamut from dry to tropical to, just inland, extremely mountainous. Baja California is mostly arid, less developed than the rest of Mexico, and best suited for travelers who like it rough.

Northern Mexico lives on industry and agriculture, and lacks compelling tourist attractions. If you enter Mexico from the northwest, consider taking the train ride through the beautiful Barranca del Cobre (Copper Canyon) before heading farther south. Those arriving from the northeast may find little of interest before the cities of San Luis Potosí and Zacatecas.

The rainy season lasts from May until October (with a hurricane season in the south Aug.-Oct.). The southern half of the country averages over 100 in. per year (75% of that during the rainy season), so a summer vacation is likely to be on the damp side. Write to IAMAT for a comprehensive and up-to-date climate chart (see Health below).

Festivals celebrate the weave of independent strands that make up Mexican culture. Fairs, on the other hand, serve the needs of commerce more directly and last for a number of days. For more complete information, write the Mexican Government Tourism Office (see Useful Addresses below), or the tourist office specific to the city or state you are interested in visiting.

Calendar of Fiestas

Winter

Dec. 18: Día de la Virgen de la Soledad, patron saint of Oaxaca.

Dec. 23: Fiesta de los Rábanos. Carved radish contest in Oaxaca, Oax.

Dec. 25: Christmas. National holiday.

Dec. 30-Jan. 6: Feria del Bastón. Beautiful carved wood. Tlaxcala, Tlax.

Dec. 31: New Year's Eve. Midnight supper.

Jan. 6: Día de Los Reyes (Day of the Kings).

Jan. 16-22: Fiesta de San Sebastian. Chenalhó, Chis.

Jan. 17: A *pastorela* to salute St. Anthony of Abad in Patzcuaro, Mich.

Jan. 26-Feb. 2: Fiesta de la Candelaria. Vallodolid, Yuc.

Feb. 1: Día de Nuestro Señor del Rescate. Tzintzuntzan, Mich.

One week before Ash Wed.: Carnival. Mardi Gras meets the Maya across the country.

Feb. 5: Fiesta Brava. Bullfights in Colima, Col.

March 10-17: Fiesta de San Patricio. Melaque, Jal.

March 10-April 15: Feria de San Marcos. Aguascalientes, Ags.

Spring

March 16-26: Feria de la Primavera. Cuernavaca, Mor.

March 19: Día del Señor San José. San José del Cabo, B.C.

March 21: Birthday of former president Benito Juárez. National holiday.

March 29: Fiesta de San Pedro Martír. Chamula, Chis.

Palm Sunday: Domingo de Ramos. A movable feast. San Miguel de Allende, Gto.

Week before Easter: Semana Santa (Holy Week). Ubiquitous.

Third week of April: Livestock and crafts fair. Villahermosa, Tab.

May 1: Labor Day. National holiday.

May 2-8: Festival de las Flores. Cuernavaca, Mor.

May 3: Day of the Cross.

May 5: Defeat of the French at Puebla in 1862. National holiday.

May 18: Anniversary of the founding of Morelia, Mich.

Summer

All June: Expo Fair in Ciudad Juárez, Chih.

June 6: Fiesta del Aniversario de los Padres. The Republic pays homage to 25 years of sheer perfection, wishing Señor y Señora Galton many more.

June 22-25: Fiesta de San Juan Bautista. Chamula, Chis.

June 23: Festival of La Olla dam. Guanajuato, Gto.

June 27-30: Fiesta de San Pedro. Chenalhó, Chis.

June 30: Día de San Pedro. Tehuantepec, Oax.

First week of July: Feria del Pan de San Juan Totolaca. Tlaxcala, Tlx.

July 7: Fiesta de las Luces. Comitan, Chis.

Second week of July: Feria Nacional. Durango, N.L.

Last two Mondays of July: Guelaguetza. Oaxaca, Oax.

July 17-25: Festival of San Cristóbal. San Cristóbal de las Casas, Chis.

July 24-26: Fiesta de Santiago Apóstol. San Andrés Larráinzar, Chis.

Sometime in August: Running of the bulls. Huamantla, Tlx.

August 8: *Pulque* worship. Tepoztlan, Mor.

August 8-11: Fiesta de San Lorenzo. Zinacantán, Chis.

Aug. 13: Commemoration of the defense of Mexico against the Spaniards, not to mention of the fortuitous birth of S-bu, patron saint of Charlottesville, VA. After *Santa Barbara*, celebrants eat hearts of palm, play Liverpool rummy, and pop their mouths roundly all night long.

Aug. 15: Día de la Asunción de la Virgen María.

Aug. 25: Día de San Luis Rey, patron saint of San Luis Potosí, S.L.P.

Aug. 27: Día de la Morisma. Reenactment of battle between Moors and Christians. Zacatecas, Zac.

Sept. 5: Cumpleaños de la Señorita Amanda. Thousands crowd the beaches of western Mexico, to dance deliriously under the brilliant heavens.

Sept. 8: Día de la Virgen de los Remedios. Great fireworks. Cholula, Pue.

Sept. 14: Charro Day. Gentlemen cowboys ho!

Sept. 15-30: Fair of St. Roman, the city's patron, in Campeche, Camp.

Sept. 15: Noche del Grito. In Mexico City, the president gives the Cry of Dolores that heralded independence.

Sept. 16: Día de la Independencia. National holiday.

Autumn

Sept. 29: Día de San Miguel Arcángel. Chalma, Mex., and Taxco, Gro.

Sept. 30: Birthday of José Moría Morelos de Pavón. Morelia, Mich.

Oct. 12: Día de la Raza (Columbus Day). National holiday.

Oct. 12: Día de la Virgen de Zapopan. Massive procession through the streets of Guadalajara, Jal.

Oct. 24: Dance and choir contest for people of Tarascan extraction. Uruapan, Mich.

Nov. 1-2: Días de la Muerta (Days of the Dead). Parties everywhere. Especially raucous in Comitan, Chis. and in Tarascan communities such as Pátzcuaro, Mich.

Sunday after Nov. 14: Festival for St. Inocencia Martir. Guadalajara, Jal.

Nov. 20: Anniversary of the 1910 Revolution. National holiday.

Nov. 28: Fiesta de San Andrés. San Andrés Larráinzar, Chis.

Dec. 1: Feria de la Plata. Silversmiths ply their wares in Taxco, Gro.

Early Dec.: Agriculture and crafts fair in honor of the Virgin de la Salud. Pátzcuaro, Mich.

Dec. 12: Día de Nuestra Señora de Guadalupe, patron saint of Mexico. Marks the beginning of the Christmas festivities which continue into January.

Useful Addresses

Government Agencies

Embassy of Mexico, 1019 19th St. NW #810, Washington, DC, 20036 (tel. (202) 293-1711); in the **U.K.,** 8 Halkin St., London SW1 X7DW (tel. (071) 235 63 93); in **Canada,** 130 Albert St. #1800, Ottawa, Ont. K1P 5G4 (tel. (613) 233-8988); in **Australia,** 14 Perth Ave., Yarralumla, Canberra, A.C.T. 2600 (tel. 73 39 05).

Consulate of Mexico, 8 E. 41st St., New York, NY 10017 (tel. (212) 689-0456); in the **U.K.,** 8 Halkin St., London SW1 X7DW (tel. (071) 235 63 93); in **Canada,** 60 Bloor St. W #203, Toronto, Ont. M4W 3B8 (tel. (416) 922-2718); in **Australia,** 232 South Rd., Mile End, Adelaide 5031 (tel. 43 80 11).

Mexican Government Tourism Office, 405 Park Ave. #1002, New York, NY 10022 (tel. (212) 755-7263; fax (212) 753-2874; 24-hr. information tel. (800) 262-8900); in the **U.K.,** Mexican Ministry of Tourism, 60/61 Trafalgar Sq., 3rd floor, London WC2N 5DS (tel. (071) 734 10 50); in **Canada,** 2 Bloor St. W #1801, Toronto, Ont. M4W 3E2 (tel. (416) 925-0704 or 925-1876). Provides maps, information, and tourist cards. Check your phone book for local offices. Also operates a 24-hr. hotline out of Mexico City (tel. (5) 250 01 23) for complaints, emergencies, and less urgent information.

Embassy and Consulate of Belize, 3400 International Dr. NW #2J, Washington, DC 20008 (tel. (202) 363-4505).

Embassy and Consulate of Guatemala, 2220 R St. NW, Washington, DC 20008 (tel. (202) 745-4952); in the **U.K.,** 13 Fawcett St., London SW10 (tel. (071) 351 30 42); in **Canada,** 294 Albert St. #249, Ottawa, Ont. K1P 6E6 (tel. (613) 237-3941).

Travel Organizations

Council on International Educational Exchange (CIEE), 205 E. 42nd St., New York, NY 10017 (tel. (212) 661-1414; for charter flights tel. (800) 223-7402). Information on overseas education, voluntary service, and work opportunities. Issues the ISIC, other international ID cards, and IYHF memberships. Write for their free annual *Student Travel Catalogue.* See Alternatives to Tourism below for other publications. Council Travel, the budget travel division of CIEE, operates 30 offices throughout the U.S.

Federation of International Youth Travel Organizations (FIYTO), Islands Brygge 81, DK-2300 Copenhagen S, Denmark (tel. (31) 54 50 80). Issues the International Youth Card to anyone under 26. Free annual catalogue lists over 4000 discounts for cardholders, including airfares. Free brochure, *Youth Travel Services,* lists organizations that provide free services to those with the International Youth Card or the ISIC.

International Student Travel Confederation (ISTC), Gothersgade 30, 1123 Copenhagen K, Denmark (tel. (33) 93 93 03). Umbrella for the following organizations: in the **U.S.,** CIEE/Council Travel (see address above); in **Canada,** Travel CUTS (see address below); in the U.K., STA Travel (see address below); in **Ireland,** USIT, Aston Quay, O'Connell Bridge, Dublin (tel. (01) 679 88 33); in **Australia,** STA Travel (see address below); in **New Zealand,** Student Travel, 10 High St., Auckland (tel. (09) 39 97 23).

International Youth Hostel Federation (IYHF), 9 Guessens Rd., Welwyn Garden City, Herts, England AL8 6QW (tel. (0707) 33 24 87). In the U.S., American Youth Hostels (AYH), P.O. Box 37613, Washington, DC 20013 (tel. (202) 783-6161). IYHF memberships, hostel handbooks, information on budget travel. In **Canada,** Canadian Hostelling Association (CHA), National Office, 1600 James Naismith Dr. #608, Gloucester, Ont. K1B 5N4 (tel. (613) 748-5638). IYHF memberships and hostel handbooks. In the U.K., Youth Hostels Association of England and Wales (YHA), 14 Southampton St., Covent Gardens, London WC2E 7HY (tel. (071) 836 10 36). In **Australia,** Australian Youth Hostels Association (AYHA), 60 Mary St., Surry Hills, Sydney, New South Wales 2010 (tel. (02) 212 11 51). In **New Zealand,** Youth Hostels Association of New Zealand, P.O. Box 436, Manchester and Gloucester St., Christchurch, 1 (tel. 79 99 70, fax 65 44 76).

Let's Go Travel Services, Harvard Student Agencies, Inc., Thayer Hall-B, Harvard University, Cambridge, MA 02138 (tel. (617) 495-9649 or 1-800-5LETSGO). Managed by the same uppity Harvard students who write these books. Sells railpasses, AYH memberships (valid at all IYHF hostels), international student and teacher ID cards, International Youth Cards for nonstudents, travel guides (including the *Let's Go* series) and maps, discount airfares, and a complete line of budget travel gear. All items available by mail. Call or write for a catalogue.

Servicio Educativo de Turismo de los Estudiantes y la Juventud de México (SETEJ), Hamburgo 301, Colonia Juárez, México D.F. 06600 (tel. (5) 211-07-43 or 211-28-59). Sells student ID cards. Arranges group tours with Mexican students. See Accommodations below for hostel information.

STA Travel, 74 and 86 Old Brompton Rd., London SW7 3LQ (for intercontinental travel tel. (071) 937 99 62, for European 937 99 21, for North American 937 99 71). In the **U.S.,** 7202 Melrose Ave., Los Angeles, CA 90046 (tel. (800) 777-0112 or (213) 934-8722). In **Australia,** 220 Faraday St., Melbourne, Victoria 3053 (tel. (03) 347 69 11). In **New Zealand,** 64 High St., Auckland (tel. (09) 39 04 58). Provides bargain flights, railpasses, accommodations, insurance, and international ID cards.

Travel CUTS (Canadian Universities Travel Service), 187 College St., Toronto, Ont. M5T 1P7 (tel. (416) 979-2406). Discount transatlantic flights from Canadian cities. Sells international ID cards, hostel memberships, and railpasses. Administers the Canadian Student Work Abroad Programme. Publishes the *Canadian Student Traveler,* a free student newspaper available at their offices and on campuses across Canada.

U.S. Servas Committee, 11 John St. #706, New York, NY 10038 (tel. (212) 267-0252). Devoted to international understanding. Worldwide network of people willing to host visitors.

U.S. Travel and Tourism Administration, Dept. of Commerce, 14th and Constitution Ave. NW, Washington, DC 20230 (tel. (202) 377-4003 or 377-3811). Abundant free literature. Branch in Mexico.

Transportation Services

American Automobile Association (AAA), 1000 AAA Dr., Heathrow, FL 32746 (tel. (407) 444-7000). Sells road maps and travel guides. American Express traveler's checks commission-free for members. Issues Mexican auto insurance (see Getting There By Car below). No routing service for Mexico.

Canadian Automobile Association, 2 Carlton St., Toronto, Ont. M5B 1K4 (tel. (416) 964-3170). Maps of Mexico for members. Will highlight routes directly on the maps.

Asociación Mexicana Automovilísticas, A.C., Av. Orizaba 7, 2° piso, México D.F. 06700 (tel. (5) 208-83-29). Write for up-to-date road maps and information about car travel in Mexico.

Asociación Nacional Automovilística, Edificio ANA, Calle M. Shultz 136, México D.F. 06470 (tel. (5) 705-08-76 or 705-16-32).

Mexican Government Railway System, Buenavista Gran Central Estación, Departamento de Tráfico de Pasajeros, México D.F. 06358 (tel. (5) 547-89-72).

Publications

Adventures in Mexico (AIM), Apdo. Postal 31-70, Guadalajara, Jalisco, 45050 México. Newsletter on retirement and travel in Mexico. Endearing approach to the country's quirks. Annual subscription (6 issues) costs US$15 or CDN$18. Personal checks accepted. Back issues, most of which are devoted to a single city or region, available for US$2 each.

Animal and Plant Health Inspection Service, U.S. Department of Agriculture, Washington, DC 20250 (tel. (202) 436-8413). Write "Attn: Public Information" on the envelope for free pamphlet entitled *Visiting Mexico.*

Forsyth Travel Library, 9154 W. 57th St., P.O. Box 2975, Shawnee Mission, KS 66201 (tel. (800) FORSYTH (367-7984) or (913) 384-3440). Mail-order maps and travel guides for Mexico. Write for free newsletter and catalogue.

John Muir Publications, P.O. Box 613, Santa Fe, NM 87504 (tel. (800) 888-7504 or (505) 982-4078). Publishes the *Shopper's Guide to Mexico* (US$9.95) on the subject of folk art, the *People's Guide to Mexico* (US$17.95), which includes Belize and Guatemala, and the *People's Guide to RV Camping in Mexico* (US$13.95). Add US$2.75 shipping and handling for one book, 50¢ for each additional book.

México Desconocido, Monte Pelvoux 110-104, Lomas de Chapultepec, México D.F. 11000 (tel. (5) 540-40-40 or 259-09-39). Monthly travel magazine in Spanish and English describing little-known areas of Mexico. Write for information.

Rand McNally Book Manufacturing Sales Office, 10 Tower Office Pk., Woburn, MA 01801 (tel. (617) 938-1651). Mexico atlas (US$15).

Superintendent of Documents, U.S. Government Printing Office, Washington, DC 20402 (tel. (202) 783-3238). Prints the budget of the U.S. and the *Congressional Record,* both of which should dissuade pesky cockroaches. Also publishes *Your Trip Abroad* (US$1), *Safe Trip Abroad* (US$1), *Health Information for International Travel* (US$5), and *Tips for Travelers to Mexico* (ask for #9309; US$1).

Wide World Books and Maps, 401 N.E. 45th St., Seattle, WA 98105 (tel. (206) 634-3453). Wide selection of books about Mexico as well as hard-to-find maps of the country.

Documents and Formalities

Tourist Cards

All foreigners in Mexico must carry a **tourist card** (FMT in Spanish). Although cards are available at Mexican embassies, consulates, and tourist offices (see Useful Addresses above), most people pick them up when they cross the border or on their flight into Mexico (make sure to get one when you check in). On it, you must indicate your intended destination and expected length of stay. If your financial condition looks suspect, you will be asked to prove that you have enough money to last your whole visit. Finally, proof of citizenship is a necessity. Travelers from outside North America must present a passport. U.S. and Canadian citizens can obtain a tourist card with an original birth certificate or naturalization papers, plus some type of photo ID. But be forewarned: traveling in Mexico without a passport is asking for trouble. A passport carries much more authority with local officials than does a birth certificate. U.S. and Canadian citizens spending no more than three days in Mexico, if they remain in duty-free border towns or ports, do not need tourist cards but still must carry proof of citizenship.

Tourist cards are valid for 90 or 180 days. Try to get a card that will be valid longer than your projected stay. It is easier to obtain a 180-day tourist card at the border than to extend a 90-day card or validate an expired card (which requires that you leave the country temporarily); if you do need an extension, visit a local office of the Delegación de Servicios Migratorios several weeks before your card expires. (They also take care of lost cards.) Theoretically the 180-day card permits multiple entries into Mexico but may not in practice.

While in Mexico, you are required by law to carry your tourist card at all times. Make a photocopy and keep it in a separate place; although it won't replace a lost or stolen tourist card, a copy should facilitate replacement. If you do lose your card, expect long delays and bureaucratic inconvenience when you attempt to convince border officials to let you leave the country.

Passports

U.S. citizens may apply for passports at a U.S. passport agency or at any of the several thousand federal and state courthouses and U.S. post offices authorized to accept passport applications. Old passports may be renewed if issued less than 12 years ago and after the holder's sixteenth birthday; otherwise, a new one must be ordered. A traveler returning to the U.S. with an expired passport is subject to a US$80 fine. If you lose your passport or if it is stolen, report the loss to the nearest U.S. embassy or consulate and to the local police. In the U.S., report it to Passport Services, Department of State, 1425 K St. NW, Washington, DC 20522.

New and replacement passport applications must be made in person unless the applicant is less than 13 years old, in which case either parent can take care of it. Passport renewals may be made by mail. All walk-in applicants must submit an application form (available at the above locations and in travel agencies); proof of U.S. citizenship (a birth certificate or certified copy, naturalization papers, or a previous passport); one piece of identification bearing the applicant's signature and either a photo or a description (e.g. a valid driver's license); and two identical black-and-white or color photographs (maximum 2 in. square on a white background) taken less than six months before the application date. If eligible to apply by mail, the applicant has only to submit the photos and an old passport along with "Form DSP 82." When requested in person, a passport costs US$42 (valid for 10 years), US$27 for those under 18 (valid for 5 years); by mail a passport costs US$35, US$20 for those under 18. Do not send cash in the mail; checks should be made out to Passport Services. Bring exact change if paying cash at a passport agency. Doubl-Dollar Days coupons are not accepted.

Processing usually takes about two weeks, but may take longer during the busier months (Jan.-July); the U.S. government recommends applying between August and December, when Passport Services is least busy. Express-mail return of the passport is also possible. If the applicant has proof that she or he is leaving soon (such as a plane ticket), the agency will process the application immediately; call your local office to find out what time to arrive for rush service. For more information, write to Passport Services or call (202) 326-6060 (202-647-0518 for a recording).

Canadian citizens may apply for a five-year, renewable passport by mail: write to the Passport Office, Department of External Affairs, Ottawa, Ont. K1A 0G3. Applications may be made in person at one of the 23 regional offices or, if abroad, at the nearest embassy/consulate. The necessary forms are available from passport offices, post offices, and most travel agencies. Evidence of Canadian citizenship (original documents only), certification of identity (a previous passport or refugee travel document issued within the past 5 years works), and two identical photographs (maximum 50×70mm, black-and-white preferred) must be submitted with the completed application. Both photographs must be signed by the applicant, and one photograph and the application itself must be countersigned by a "guarantor"—someone who has known the applicant for at least two years and whose profession falls into one of a number of categories listed on the application (including clergy member, roadkill collector, medical doctor, police officer, and notary public). The passport costs CDN$25; payment by mail must be made with a check written to the Receiver General for Canada or to the nearest embassy/consulate if the applicant is abroad. In-person applications receive much faster service (3-5 days) than applications by mail (about 2 weeks), and no rush service is available. For more information, request the brochure *Bon Voyage, But*— from the Passport Office.

British citizens can apply for a full passport at main post offices or regional passport offices in Belfast, Glasgow, Liverpool, London, Newport, and Peterborough. In addition to the application (which must be countersigned by someone who practices a "respected profession" and who has known the applicant for at least 2 years), the applicant will have to present an original birth certificate and/or marriage certificate, and two identical copies of a recent photograph (maximum 63×50mm, minimum 50×38mm), one countersigned by the same person who verified the application. Passports cost £15; they are valid for 10 years, five years for people under 16. If the applicant already has a passport, on which the details and likeness remain true, documentation is often waived for renewal. The application process usually takes four weeks; it can drag on during the busy season between February and August, or be cut short during November and December. If the applicant is leaving soon, the process can be accelerated.

Australian citizens must apply for a passport in person at a local post office, where an appointment may be necessary, or through a passport office. A parent may file for an applicant who is under 18 and unmarried. The passport application should be countersigned by someone who practices a "respected profession" and has known the applicant for at least one year, and should be accompanied by: two black-and-white or color photographs (45×35mm), one of which has been countersigned by that vaunted friend; proof of citizenship (a passport issued after July 1, 1983, naturalization or citizenship papers, or an original birth certificate); proof of present name and/or evidence of change of name (e.g. a marriage certificate); and another form of identification. Application fees are adjusted every three months; in the summer of 1990, an Australian passport cost AUS$76 (valid for 10 years), AUS$31 for those under 18 (valid for 5 years). There is also a departure tax of AUS$10 when a citizen over 11 years old leaves the country.

The applicant should expect to wait two weeks for a passport, but rush service is available. If you live too far away to file in person or have any other questions, call toll-free Monday through Friday during working hours (tel. (008) 02 60 22).

New Zealand citizens can either apply for passports in person at a local passport office or write to the Department of Internal Affairs (Passports Head Office), Private Bag, Wellington (tel. 73 86 99). Apart from the application, two recent, passport-sized photos (1 certified by a "friend"; this just gets easier and easier), proof of identity (in the form of testimony by the same friend), and proof of New Zealand citizenship (an old passport is usually acceptable) are necessary. The passport costs NZ$50 and is valid for 10 years; people under 18 need to extend their passports after five years have passed. In an emergency, the office will provide speedy processing; otherwise, expect a three-week wait.

Before you leave, record your passport number and keep it separate from the passport. If you lose your passport in Mexico, notify the local police and the nearest consulate. Consulates recommend that you carry an expired passport or a copy of your birth certificate in a separate part of your baggage. You should also carry a few passport-type photos. Your consulate can issue a new passport or temporary traveling papers.

A **visa** is an endorsement or stamp placed in your passport. Visas are not necessary for U.S., Canadian, or British citizens unless they will be in Mexico for more than six months. Australians and New Zealanders, however, do need visas regardless of the length of stay. Businesspeople, missionaries, and students who expect to earn a diploma in Mexico also must obtain a visa. Applications require a valid passport, six frontal photos, and five profile photos. Consulates claim to have 24-hr. visa service if you apply in person; by mail, however, they may take weeks.

Student and Youth Identification

It's not worth your while to buy a student ID card if you plan to travel only in Mexico; foreign students are only rarely entitled to special discounts on accommodations, long-distance bus and train fares, and admission to archeological sites, theatrical performances, and museums. Where a student rate is advertised, a current university ID card is generally sufficient proof of student status.

Still, you might consider spending your hard-earned money on an International Student Identity Card (ISIC), available at many student travel offices. It includes repatriation insurance of US$3000, US$3000 of accident-related coverage, and US$100 per day for up to 60 days of in-hospital illness (if issued in the U.S., this insurance covers only foreign travel). To get an ISIC, you must supply dated proof of student status; proof of birthdate and nationality; and a $1\frac{1}{2} \times 2$ in. photo signed on the back. The card costs US$14 and is valid for 16 months, from September 1 of one year until the end of the following year. You cannot purchase a new card in January unless you were in school during the fall semester; if you are about to graduate, buy a card now.

If you are ineligible for the ISIC but are under 26, you can take advantage of the International Youth Card, issued by the Federation of International Youth Travel Organizations (FIYTO), which entitles you to some price reductions in Mexico. To get the card, you must submit proof of birthdate, a $1\frac{1}{2} \times 2$ in. photo signed on the back, and US$15. For further information, write to FIYTO (see Useful Addresses above).

Once in Mexico, those under 27 may purchase a SETEJ card, which provides discounts in hostels, hotels, restaurants, and museums. (See Useful Addresses and the Practical Information section of Mexico City for addresses.) Even if you don't

have student identification, never hesitate to ask about youth discounts, and carry proof of age with you.

Driver's License and Vehicle Permits

An international driver's license is not necessary for driving in Mexico; any valid driver's license is acceptable. You will, however, need a Mexican **vehicle permit**, issued as you cross the border. You must be able to prove ownership of your car, trailer, or motorcycle. Bring the title with you, or, if the car is rented or not fully paid for, a notarized letter from the bank or other owner authorizing you to take the vehicle into Mexico. To extend a vehicle permit beyond its original expiration date, contact the temporary importation department of Mexican customs. Permits are not required for Baja California or places near the border.

Resist the temptation to abandon, sell, or give away your car in Mexico. Once you enter the country with a car, your tourist card will be marked such that you will not be allowed to leave without the vehicle. Even if your car disintegrates somewhere in Mexico, you must get permission to leave without it; permission can be obtained (for a fee) at either the federal registry of automobiles in Mexico City or a local office of the *hacienda* (treasury department). If you have received permission to leave your broken-down car behind in Mexico, you have up to 45 days after the expiration of your vehicle permit to reclaim the car before the Mexican government disposes of it.

A vehicle permit is valid only for the person to whom it was issued unless another driver is approved by the federal registry. Violation of this law can result in confiscation of the vehicle or heavy fines. Furthermore, only legitimate drivers may purchase car-ferry tickets.

Fishing Licenses

If you plan to fish in Mexico, you will need a license. The fee is US$7.50 per week, US$10 per month, or US$20 per year. Licenses are available in port cities at any Mexican *Oficina de Pesca*.

Customs—Entering Mexico

You must have the right documents on hand to get into the country. A clean, neat appearance will help. Don't pass out *mordidas* (bribes; literally, "little bites"); they are often inappropriate, and may do more harm than good.

Entering Mexico overland, you'll first see the border guards. They will direct travelers to the immigration office, where a new batch of officials will issue a tourist card to those who don't have one already and a car permit to auto drivers. Customs officials will then inspect luggage and stamp papers. If there is anything amiss when you arrive at the immigration checkpoint 32km into the interior, you'll have to turn back.

Entering Mexico by air is somewhat easier. Agents process forms and examine luggage right in the airport. Because air passengers rarely are penniless hippies, immigration officials are less strict than at the border. If your papers are out of order at any official location, however, count on a long wait. Keep some form of picture ID with you at all times, since customs officials stop buses all over Mexico, not just at the border. Lacking the proper documentation is an invitation for painful confrontations with bureaucrats.

Each visitor may enter with up to 110 pounds of luggage (140 lbs. on Mexicana). Adults may carry 50 cigars, 200 cigarettes, and 250 grams of tobacco with them. One camera and one 8mm motion picture camera, with 12 rolls of film for each, are also allowed. To use flashes or a tripod at archeological sites, you must get permission from the Instituto Nacional de Antropología e Historia, Director de Asuntos Jurídicos, Cordoba No. 45, 2° piso, México D.F. 06700 (tel. (5) 511-08-44 or 511-61-67).

A dog or cat may accompany you into the country if the little critter has proof of vaccination for rabies, hepatitis, pip, and letospirosis, and a health certificate issued by a veterinarian less than 72 hours before entry and stamped by a local office of the U.S. Department of Agriculture and a Mexican consulate. The consulate pet visa fee is US$15.80. Keep in mind that bringing a pet to Mexico will try your patience; more significantly, animals will be unwelcome at most hotels.

Customs—Leaving Mexico

Crossing the border can take five minutes or five hours; the better your paperwork, the shorter your encounter with customs should be. When reëntering your home country, you must declare all articles acquired abroad and pay a duty on those which exceed your country's customs allowance. To establish value when you return home, keep receipts for items purchased abroad. Since you pay no duty on goods brought from home, record the serial numbers of any expensive items (cameras, computers, radios, etc.) you are taking on vacation before you leave. Check with your country's customs office to see if it has a special form for registering these valuables and turn in your list to the airport customs office before you depart.

Most countries object to the importation of firearms, explosives, ammunition, obscene literature and films, fireworks, and lottery tickets. Do not try to take drugs out of Mexico. To avoid problems when carrying prescription drugs, label bottles clearly and have the prescription or a doctor's certificate ready to show the customs officer.

Crossing the border with live animals is usually prohibited. For information on wildlife and wildlife products, contact TRAFFIC (U.S.A.), World Wildlife Fund, 1250 24th St. NW, Washington, DC 20037 (tel. (202) 293-4800), or the Animal and Plant Health Inspection Service, U.S. Department of Agriculture, 700 Federal Bldg. 1, 6505 Belcrest Rd., Hyattsville, MD 20782 (tel. (301) 436-8013).

U.S. citizens may bring back US$400 worth of goods duty-free; the next US$1000 worth is subject to a 10% tax. Duty-free goods must be for personal or household use, and cannot include more than 100 cigars, 200 cigarettes (1 carton), and one liter of alcohol (you must be 21 years old to carry liquor into the U.S.). If you have claimed an exemption within the last 30 days or have been out of the country less than 48 hours, then you can bring back only US$25 worth of duty-free goods, including no more than 50 cigarettes, 10 cigars, 150 milliliters of alcohol, and 150 milliliters of perfume. All duty-free goods must accompany you; they cannot be shipped separately. Since the U.S. considers Mexico a developing country, many Mexican imports enjoy favored status, and about 2700 items, mostly handicrafts, are exempt from the US$400 limit. For more information, call a U.S. consulate in Mexico. You may mail unsolicited gifts worth less than US$50 back to the U.S. from Mexico duty-free, but you may not send any liquor, tobacco, or perfume. Mark the accurate price and nature of the gift as well as the words "Unsolicited Gift" on the package (see Mail below). Spot checks are occasionally made. The U.S. Postal Service will charge duty plus a handling charge on parcels worth over US$50. It is illegal to send "gifts" to yourself. There is no duty on unaltered, personal goods of U.S. origin mailed back to the States. Be sure to write "American goods returned" on the parcel. For more information, get a free copy of *Know Before You Go* from the U.S. Customs Service, 1301 Constitution Ave., Washington, DC 20229 (tel. (202) 566-8195).

Canadian citizens abroad for 48 hours or more may bring back CDN$100 of duty-free goods. Once every calendar year, after you have been abroad at least seven days, you may bring in articles worth up to CDN$300. Duty-free goods can include no more than 200 cigarettes, 50 cigars, and 1kg of tobacco if you are over 15 years old, one 40-ounce bottle or up to 24 12-ounce bottles or cans of alcohol if you meet the age requirements of your port of entry, generally age 19. Anything above the duty-free allowance is taxed: 20% for goods that accompany you, more for shipped items. You can send gifts worth up to CDN$40 duty-free, except alcohol or tobacco. For more information and the brochure *I declare/Je Declare,* write or call the Revenue Canada Customs and Excise Department, Communications Branch, Mackenzie Ave., Ottawa, Ont. K1A OL5 (tel. (613) 957-0275).

British citizens may return home with £32 of duty-free goods purchased abroad, including two liters of still table wine plus one liter of alcohol (over 22% by volume) or two liters of alcohol (not over 22% by volume) and (for those over 17) 100 cigarettes, 50 cigars, and 250 grams of tobacco. For more information contact Her Majesty's Customs and Excise Office, New King's Beam House, 22 Upper Ground, London SE1 9PJ (tel. (071) 382 54 68).

Australian citizens may return home with up to AUS$400 worth of goods duty-free, AUS$200 for those under 18; the next AUS$160 worth will be taxed at 20%. These goods may include no more than 250 cigarettes and one liter of alcohol (for those 18 and over), and must be carried into the country by the declarer. If you mail back personal property, mark it "Australian goods returned" to avoid duty. You may not mail unsolicited gifts duty-free. These and other restrictions can be found in *Customs Information for All Travelers,* available from local offices of the Collector of Customs and Australian consulates.

New Zealand citizens may bring back NZ$500 of duty-free goods. Those over 16 may bring back 200 cigarettes, 50 cigars, 250 grams of tobacco, or any mixture of the three not to exceed 250 grams; 4.5 liters of wine or beer; and one 1125-milliliter bottle of liquor. For more information, contact the nearest customs office, embassy, or consulate. Ask for the brochures *New Zealand Customs Guide for Travelers* and *If You're Not Sure About It, DECLARE IT.*

Money

Currency and Exchange

This book was researched in the summer of 1990. The skyrocketing prices and fluctuating peso value that characterized the Mexican economy during the 1980s began to stabilize in December of 1988. The steady devaluation of the peso will probably continue at least through 1990. Nonetheless, prices are always subject to change. Therefore, if you find that *Let's Go* prices are consistently high or low by a certain amount, let that be your guide in calculating recent changes in cost.

Be sure to buy approximately US$50 worth of pesos before leaving home, especially if you will arrive in the afternoon or on a weekend. This will save you time at the airport and help you avoid the predicament of having no cash after bank hours. Acquaint yourself with Mexican money: you'll encounter five-, 10-, 50-, and 100-peso coins, and bills in denominations of 500, 1000, 2000, 5000, and on up. (The 500- and 2000-peso bills look a lot alike; try not to confuse them.) You may want to keep 2000 pesos or so in change in your pockets for panhandlers, subways, or kids who offer to watch your parked car. In addition, some Mexican pay phones require a one-peso coin, which, because of its utter lack of value, may be hard to find when you need it. Hoard accordingly. The symbol for pesos is the same as for U.S. dollars. The common abbreviation "M.N." (*Moneda Nacional*) also stands for the peso.

Changing money in Mexico can be inconvenient. Some banks won't exchange until noon, when the daily peso quotes come out, and then stay open only until 1:30pm. You can switch U.S. dollars for pesos anywhere, but some banks refuse to deal with other foreign currencies.

Banks use the official exchange rates, but they sometimes extract a flat commission as well. Therefore, the more money you change at one time, the less you will lose in the transaction. The lineup of national banks in Mexico includes Bánamex, Bancomer, Comermex, and Serfin.

Casas de cambio may offer better exchange rates than banks and are usually open as long as the stores near which they do business. In most towns, the exchange rates at restaurants and hotels are extremely unfavorable; avoid them unless it's an emergency and the banks are closed.

Don't forget to write.

If your American Express® Travelers Cheques are lost or stolen, we can hand-deliver a refund virtually anywhere you travel. Just give us a call. You'll find it's a lot less embarrassing than calling home.

Traveler's Checks

If money makes your world go round, then a pickpocket could bring the world to a screeching halt. Traveler's checks will take the sting out of theft, but there are places (especially in northern Mexico) accustomed to the real, green dollar that will not accept any substitute. To avoid problems, always have your passport with you (not just the number); it often means the difference between apologetic refusal and grudging acceptance. Carry traveler's checks in busy towns and cities, but stick to cash, risky though it may be, when traveling through the less touristed spots.

Many banks and companies sell traveler's checks, usually for the face value of the checks plus a 1-2% commission. Bank of America WorldMoney traveler's checks are sold commission-free in California, and AAA supplies American Express traveler's checks to its members *sans* commission.

Toll-free numbers provide information about purchasing traveler's checks and obtaining refunds.

American Express: Tel. (800) 221-7282 in the U.S.; from elsewhere, call collect (44 27) 357 16 00. There is also a specific number for each country. Checks available in seven currencies. American Express charges no commission, but banks may expect something for their trouble.

Bank of America: Tel. (800) 227-3460 in the U.S.; elsewhere, call collect (415) 624-5400. Checks available in U.S. dollars only. Commission of 1% per US$100 unless you have an account with Bank of America. Checkholders may use the Travel Assistance hotline (see Insurance below).

Barclays: Tel. (800) 221-2426 in the U.S. or Canada; elsewhere, call collect (415) 574-7111 or (212) 406-4200. Associated with Visa. Checks available in three currencies. 1% commission charged. Representative banks in many locations throughout Mexico.

Citicorp: Tel. (800) 645-6556 in the U.S. and Canada; from Latin America, call toll-free (800) 901-05 or collect (5) 525-43-80; elsewhere, call collect (813) 623-1709. Four currencies available. Checkholders are automatically enrolled in Travel Assist Hotline (tel. (800) 523-1199) for 45 days after purchase.

MasterCard: Tel. (800) 223-9920 in the U.S. and Canada; elsewhere, call collect (212) 974-5696. Checks available in 11 currencies. MasterCard itself charges no commission, but depending on the bank where you purchase the checks, you may have to pay 1-2%.

Thomas Cook: Tel. (800) 223-4030 or (800) 223-7373 in the U.S.; elsewhere, call collect (212) 974-5696. Associated with Mastercard. Eleven currencies available. Commission of 1%, plus the seller's fee if purchased from a bank.

Visa: Tel. (800) 227-6811 in the U.S. and Canada; from the U.K., call collect (071) 937 80 91; elsewhere, call collect (415) 574-7111. Thirteen currencies available. No commission through Visa but individual banks might charge 1%.

Each agency refunds lost or stolen traveler's checks, but expect hassles if you lose track of them. When buying checks, get a list of refund centers. To expedite the refund process, separate your check receipts and keep them in a safe place. Record check numbers as you cash them to help identify exactly which checks might be missing. As an additional precaution, leave a list of the numbers with someone at home. Even with the check numbers in hand, you will probably find that getting a refund involves hours of waiting and spools of red tape.

It's best to buy most of your checks in small denominations (US$20) to minimize your losses at times when you need cash fast and can't avoid a bad exchange rate. Don't keep all your money in the same place: split it up among pockets and bags, or better yet, use a money belt. If possible, purchase checks in U.S. dollars, since many *casas de cambio* refuse to change other currencies.

Credit Cards

Most of the banks that cash traveler's checks will make cash advances on a credit card as well. Be prepared to flash your passport. Major credit cards—Visa, Master-Card, and American Express—can prove invaluable in a financial emergency. Not only are they accepted by many Mexican businesses, especially in tourist areas, but they can also work in Automatic Teller Machines. And if you lose your airline ticket, you can always charge a new one.

All major credit card companies have some form of worldwide lost card protection service, and most offer a variety of additional travel services to cardholders—make sure to inquire before you leave home. Students or low-income travelers may have difficulty procuring a credit card, but family members can sometimes obtain a joint-account card. American Express will issue an extra green card for US$25 per year or an extra gold card for US$30 (bills go to the main cardholder). Visa also issues extra cards on accounts, but the fee varies. For more information, write Chase Visa, P.O. Box 5111, 1400 Union Turnpike, New Hyde Park, NY 11042. Call them at (800) 645-7352 or (800) THE-PLUS (843-7587) for ATM locations all over the U.S. and Mexico.

Sending Money

Sending money to Mexico should be approached with the same hesitation as drinking from a brackish pond downstream from a sewage plant. The cheapest way to receive emergency money is to have it sent through a large commercial bank that has associated banks within Mexico. The sender must either have an account with the bank or bring in cash or a money order, and some banks cable money only for regular customers. The sender can specify whether the money is to be disbursed in pesos or U.S. dollars. The service costs US$25-80, depending on the amount sent. Cabled money should arrive in one to three days if the sender can furnish exact information (i.e. recipient's passport number and the Mexican bank's name and address); otherwise, there will be significant delays. To pick up money, you must show some form of positive identification, such as a passport. The sender will receive no confirmation that the money has reached you, and you will receive no confirmation that the sender has received no confirmation.

A local bank will probably work through a larger one, so cabling will be slower and more expensive. It is possible to have your local bank send money at specified periods, but most banks will be as reluctant as an astronaut approaching a black hole.

Western Union offers a convenient service for cabling money. The sender can call (800) 325-6000 or (800) 325-4176, recite a credit card number (Visa or Master-Card only), and send any amount of money that the sender's credit limit can sustain. If the sender has no credit card, he or she must go in person to one of Western Union's offices with cash or a cashier's check—no money orders accepted. The money will arrive at the central telegram office or post office of the designated city, where the recipient can obtain it upon presentation of suitable identification. If you are in a major Mexican city, the money should arrive within 24 hours. In a smaller city, it could take 48 hours, and if you are out on a donkey trail somewhere, the time frame is indefinite. The money will arrive in pesos and will be held for 30 days. If no one picks it up, it will be returned to the sender minus the transaction cost. Cabling costs run up to to US$45 for sending as much as US$1000.

Sending money through American Express costs about as much as using a bank, and the sender need not have an American Express card. Money will arrive immediately at any of the 41 international offices in Mexico, or in three to five days at other designated offices, where it will be held until further notice. Money is disbursed in traveler's checks (U.S. dollars) to the international offices and in peso form to other locations. It costs about US$45 to send US$500 to one of the international offices, although in some parts of the U.S. the same transaction can cost as little as US$10. When sending money to Mexico, you are limited to US$1000 per day.

Finally, if you are a U.S. citizen and suddenly find yourself in an extreme emergency, you can have money sent via the State Department's Citizen Emergency Center (tel. (202) 647-5225). The center will need to know the sender's name and address, the recipient's name, and the reason for sending the money. The quickest way to get the money (preferably less than US$500) to the State Department is to cable it through Western Union or else to drop off cash, certified check, bank draft, or money order at the center itself. It takes longer to send the money through your own bank. Once they receive it, the State Department will cable the money, for a fee of US$15, to the nearest embassy or consulate, which will then release the cash according to the sender's instructions. The money should arrive within 24 hours. If you want to, you can send a short telegraphic message along with the money. The center's address is: Dept. of State #4811, 2201 C St. NW, Washington, DC 20520.

Packing

Pack light.

Set out everything you'll need, and then take half of that plus more money. One New York Times correspondent recommends that you "take no more than you can carry for half a mile at a dead run." This advice may be extreme (unless you expect to be pursued by *federales*), but the gist is clear.

Decide whether a light suitcase, shoulder bag, backpack, or shoebox is best for the kind of traveling you'll be doing. A convertible pack could spare you this difficult decision. If you will be staying in one city or town for a while, a light suitcase ought to suffice. Those striving for the more casual, unobtrusive look should take a large shoulder bag that closes securely. If you will be riding a lot of buses or covering a lot of ground by foot, a backpack may be the best choice. An internal-frame model is less bulky and can't be broken as easily by baggage handlers. For hiking, an external frame lifts weight off the back and distributes it more evenly, allows for some ventilation, and is more pleasant to carry over uneven terrain; internal frames mold to the back better, keep a lower center of gravity, and are more comfortable for long-distance hiking on the level. If you're taking a sleeping bag, keep in mind that you can strap it onto the outside of an external frame, while you usually must allow room for bedding inside an internal frame pack. A pack that loads from the front rather than the top saves you from having to grope at the bottom for hidden items, but the greater stress on a larger zipper area makes this a weaker design. Packs with several compartments are convenient, but outside zippers and flaps make easy targets for pickpockets. When choosing a backback, consider how much more cumbersome it will be with 50 pounds of gear stuffed inside. Decent packs start at about US$100.

In addition to your main bag, bring a smaller day-pack for sightseeing or carry-on; it is a good idea to keep some of your valuables with you. A small purse, neck pouch, or moneybelt will guard your money, passport, and other important articles. Moneybelts are available at most camping supply stores and through the Forsyth Travel Library (see Useful Addresses above).

To get an idea of what clothing to pack, check a newspaper or IAMAT climate chart (see Health below) for the places you plan to visit. Shorts, on either sex, are appropriate only at the beach and in the more cosmopolitan parts of Mexico.

Many Mexican cities have no public places to do laundry. One solution is to give your clothes to the hotel cleaning person, who is often more than eager to earn some extra money, and will do a much better job than a washing machine would. Make sure that whoever you approach is a permanent employee of the hotel, and establish a price in advance. Another possibility is to carry a mild laundry soap and do laundry by hand in hotel sinks.

Footwear is not the place to cut costs. Comfortable walking shoes or a good pair of running shoes is essential. Save your sandals and other non-utilitarian shoes for short walks and evenings out. If you plan to hike or climb over pyramids and ruins, bring a pair of sturdy hiking boots. Break in all your shoes before you go, but if you do get plagued by blisters, moleskin (available at most drugstores and wherever camping/sporting goods are sold) helps protect the tender areas.

Most toiletries such as aspirin and razor blades are available in Mexican pharmacies, but some items—tampons, prescription drugs, and contraceptives—are best brought from home. Even when these items are available over the counter, their ingredients may differ from the same-named product in the U.S. Toilet paper is often elusive; always carry some for those out-of-the way places and cheap hotels.

Bring some plastic bags and rubber bands. They will make separating dirty and clean clothes much easier, and can keep a wet swimsuit from transforming your entire suitcase into a festering mess. Other handy items to bring along are a flashlight, water bottle, travel alarm clock or noisy watch, needle and thread, British squash ball (as a sink stopper), sheet sack (required by many hostels), an amazing Aerobie, and safety pins.

If your Spanish is not fluent, buy a good Spanish-English dictionary before you leave, because language dictionaries are scarce and expensive in Mexico. A compass may come in handy for orienting yourself in new places—and for following the directions in *Let's Go* listings. You should also bring film and batteries from home, since the quality and variety of such goods are poorer in Mexico.

Safety and Security

Contrary to what you've probably heard about *bandidos,* squalor, and other perils, Mexico is relatively safe, although large cities (especially Mexico City) demand extra caution. After dark, keep away from bus and train stations, subways, and public parks. Shun empty train compartments; many travelers avoid the theft-ridden Mexican train system altogether. When on foot, stay out of trouble by sticking to busy, well-lit streets, and conducting yourself as the local people do. Act as if you know exactly where you are going: an obviously bewildered bodybuilder is more likely to be harassed than a stern and confident 98-lb. weakling. Ask the manager of your hotel or hostel for advice on specific areas.

To protect belongings, buy small luggage locks and keep your bags locked when storing them in your hotel room or in a bus or train station. Checking baggage on trains is akin to kissing them good-bye. Keep your money and valuables near you at all times: under the pillow at night and in the bathroom while you shower. A money belt is probably the best idea. A neck pouch, although less accessible, is equally safe. In city crowds and especially on public transportation, pickpockets are amazingly deft at their craft. Hold your bags tightly. Fanny packs worn loosely outside clothing scream "steal me!" to thieves. If you must keep money in a pocket, place it in the front pocket with your hand over it. Make two photocopies of all important documents; keep one copy with you (separated from the original), and leave one with someone at home.

Insurance

You may wish to purchase travel insurance before you leave, but watch out for unnecessary coverage. Your homeowner's insurance or family's coverage may very well protect against theft during travel; generally, it covers up to US$500 for loss of passports, plane tickets, and tourist cards.

Find out before leaving if you have health insurance which reimburses costs incurred in Mexico. Most major insurance companies provide policies toward these expenses on a short-term or regular basis. If you're a student, a parent's policy or university health plan may apply while you're traveling. Medicare covers travel in the U.S., Canada, and Mexico, but Medicaid abandons you the instant you cross the border. Canadians may be covered by their regular health plan up to 90 days after leaving the country, but details vary from province to province. Call Health Plan Headquarters or the Ministry of Health in your home province.

If you have no insurance that extends to your travels, you may want to purchase a short-term policy for the trip. Even if you do have medical insurance which applies, you have to pay for services on the spot and get reimbursed later. Keep all receipts and statements from your doctors (try to have them written in English), and file an out-of-country claim when you return.

If you buy short-term insurance, you can also get protection for accidents and other travel-related misfortunes. CIEE offers a "Trip Safe" package to supplement the insurance which comes with the ISIC or for those ineligible for the ISIC (see Student and Youth Identification above). American Express cardholders can use Global Assist, a 24-hr. legal assistance hotline, and receive automatic car rental and flight insurance on purchases made with the card. Bank of America checkholders also have access to a hotline and insurance service.

Insurance companies usually want to see a copy of the police report filed at the time of the theft before honoring your claim. Check the time limit for filing to make sure that you will be returning in time to attain reimbursement.

For car insurance information, see Getting There By Car below.

> **Access America,** 600 3rd Ave. #807, New York, NY 10163 (tel. (800) 284-8300). Subsidiary of Blue Cross/Blue Shield. Provides compensation of your trip is canceled or interrupted, on-the-spot hospital admittance, and emergency medical evacuation. 24-hr. multilingual hotline.

> **ARM Coverage,** 120 Mineola Blvd., P.O. Box 310, Mineola, NY 11501 (tel. (800) 323-3149 or (516) 294-0220). Trip cancellation/interruption, accident/sickness, trip delay, and baggage loss. 24-hr. emergency service.

> **Edmund A. Cocco Agency,** 220 Broadway #201, Lynnfield, MA 01940 (tel. (800) 821-2488, in MA (617) 595-0262). Legal assistance, urgent cash transfer, emergency transportation, on-the-spot payment for medical expenses, and protection against airline or cruise default. 24-hr. hotline.

> **Travel Assistance International,** 1133 15th St. NW #400, Washington, DC 20005 (tel. (800) 821-2828). On-the-spot medical and financial assistance, medical and legal referrals, and help in replacing lost passports and visas. Year-long plan covers all trips under 90 days; shorter-term plans also available. 24-hr. hotline. Agent in Mexico.

> **Travel Guard International,** P.O. Box 1200, Stevens Point, WI 54481 (tel. (800) 782-5151). Comprehensive "Travel Guard Gold" packages. 24-hr. hotline.

> **Traveler's Insurance Company,** Ticket and Travel Plans, 9-NB, 1 Tower Sq., Hartford, CT 06183 (tel. (800) 243-3174, (203) 277-2138 in CT, HI, and AK). Trip cancellation/interruption and accident/sickness.

> **Wallach and Company,** 243 Church St. NW #1000, Vienna, VA 22180 (tel. (800) 237-6615 or (703) 281-9500). 24-hr. emergency assistance, hospitalization, doctor's treatment, prescription medication, and medical evacuation to the U.S.

> **WorldCare Travel Assistance,** 605 Market St. #1300, San Francisco, CA 94105 (tel. (800) 666-4993). Annual membership (US$162) covers all trips under 90 days. Shorter-term policies also available. "ScholarCare" program tailored to students and teachers spending a semester or year abroad.

Drinking and Drugs

Drinking in Mexico is not for amateurs; bars and *cantinas* are arsenals of Mexican *machismo*. When someone calls you *amigo* and orders you a beer, bow out quickly unless you want to match him glass for glass in a challenge that could last several days.

You are also likely to be offered marijuana, which is potent and inexpensive in Mexico. A minimum 10-year jail sentence awaits anyone found guilty of possessing more than a token amount of any drug, and that Mexican law does not distinguish between marijuana and other narcotics. Even if you aren't convicted, arrest and trial might just ruin your day. Derived from Roman and Napoleonic law, the Mexican judicial process does not assume that you are innocent until proven guilty, and it is not uncommon to be detained for a year before a verdict is even reached; foreigners and suspected drug traffickers are not released on bail. Furthermore, there is little your consulate can do to help you out (except inform your relatives and bring care packages to you in jail) should it want to. In the immortal words of Nancy Reagan, just say no. Bearing all this in mind, you may decide to opt for the less risky alternative: you can drink yourself under the table in thousands of Mexican bars and the only sentence handed down will be a hangover.

Finally, don't even think about bringing drugs back into the U.S. in your car. Customs agents and their perceptive bloodhounds are not to be taken lightly. Every few weeks they auction off the cars they've confiscated from unsuccessful smugglers. On the northern highways, especially along the Pacific coast, expect to be stopped repeatedly by burly, humorless troopers looking for contraband. That innocent-looking hitchhiker you were kind enough to pick up may be a drug peddler with a stash of illegal substances. If the police catch it in your car, the drug possession charges will extend to you, and your car may be confiscated. For the free pamphlet *Travel Warning on Drugs Abroad,* send a self-addressed, stamped envelope to the Bureau of Consular Affairs, Public Affairs #5807, Dept. of State, Washington, DC 20520 (tel. (202) 647-1488).

Health

Before you can say "pass the jalapeños," a long-anticipated vacation can turn into an unpleasant study of the grimthorped Mexican health-care system. Keep your body and, more importantly, everything you put into it, clean; don't cut out nutritious food in favor of junk just to save money. Stop short of physical overexertion, drink lots of replenishing fluids like juice and purified water, and stay away from too many dehydrating caffeinated sodas.

Take a look at your **immunization records** before you go. Typhoid inoculations are good for three years, tetanus for 10. Although visitors to Mexico (unless from an area infected with yellow fever) do not need to carry vaccination certificates, gamma globulin shots that protect against hepatitis are recommended for back-country travel in Chiapas and the Yucatán. Malaria still exists in some rural parts of southern Mexico, and is most prevalent on the southwest coast. Doctors frequently prescribe a chloroquine regimen and mosquito repellent with DEET. Ask your doctor or check the malaria chart published by the IAMAT to find out if you will be traveling in a high-risk area. Dengue has also been reported in Mexico and is just one more reason to arm yourself against dive-bombing mosquitos. *Health Information for International Travel* (US$5) is available from the Superintendent of Documents (see Useful Addresses above).

Anyone with a chronic condition requiring medication on a regular basis should see a doctor before leaving. People with allergies should find out if their conditions are likely to be aggravated in the regions they plan to visit. Obtain a full supply of any necessary medication before your trip, since matching your prescription to a foreign equivalent is not always easy, safe, or possible. Always carry up-to-date, legible prescriptions and/or a statement from your doctor, especially if you use insulin, a syringe, or any narcotic drug. Distribute medicines among your bags to minimize potential loss. You may also want to write out a brief medical record (half a page or so) and keep it with your passport in case you need a doctor and are unable to communicate.

Those with medical conditions that cannot be immediately recognized (e.g. diabetes, allergies to antibiotics, epilepsy, heart conditions) should obtain a steel **Medic Alert identification tag** (US$25), which identifies the disease and gives a toll-free number to call for more information. Contact Medic Alert Foundation International, P.O. Box 1009, Turlock, CA 95381 (tel. (800) 432-5378). The American Diabetes Association, 1660 Duke St., Alexandria, VA 22314 (tel. (800) 232-3472), provides ID cards in several languages (15¢) and publishes the pamphlet *Ticket to Safe Travel* (50¢), which addresses concerns of diabetics traveling in foreign countries.

The greatest health threat to travelers in Mexico is the **water.** The Mexican government now advises its own citizens to boil their water before drinking it. Traveler's diarrhea, known in Mexico as *turista,* is the dastardly consequence of ignoring this advice. Once the bacteria establish a beachhead somewhere in your esophagus, the nasty war has begun—and you are likely to be the primary casualty. *Turista* often lasts two or three days; symptoms include cramps, nausea, vomiting, chills, and a fever as high as 103°F (39°C). Consult a doctor if symptoms persist. To avoid becoming a bacteriological battleground in the first place, take the following precautions:

Never drink unbottled water. Do not brush your teeth with or even rinse the brush in running water. During showers or baths, keep your mouth closed. Do not eat uncooked vegetables, including lettuce, in any but the most immaculate restaurants. Beware of food from markets or street vendors that may have been washed in dirty water or fried in rancid oil. Peel all fruits and vegetables before eating them, and beware of watermelon, which is often injected with impure water. Watch out for open bottles of hot sauce sitting on tables in restaurants. Also beware of ice or frozen treats that may have been made with bad water. A golden rule in Mexico: boil it, peel it, cook it, or forget it.

Be sure to drink plenty of liquids—much more than you're accustomed to. Heat and high altitudes will dehydrate you more swiftly than you expect, and you can avoid many health problems if you drink enough fluid to keep your urine clear. Buy bottled water, boil tap water, or use water purification tablets (available in U.S. drugstores). Many restaurants and hotels offer *agua purificada*. Ironically, alcoholic beverages dehydrate you more, as do coffee, strong tea, and caffeinated sodas.

When you absolutely must eat questionable food, douse it with lime juice and wash it down with a beer to kill Bacteria Bill and his posse. Lots of garlic also does the trick. Garlic and lime juice also ward off vampires if the need arises.

Since *turista* is such a common problem, many travelers bring along over-the-counter remedies (like Pepto-Bismol). Another possible tactic is to flush out your system by drinking lots of fruit juice and pure water. Rest and let the heinous disease run its course. Locals try 8 oz. of fruit juice, ½ tsp. of honey or sugar, and a pinch of salt in one glass, and 8 oz. of water with ¼ tsp. of baking soda in another glass. Alternate sips from each glass, downing several glasses per day.

In addition, don't eat mangos, chiles, or anything greasy while you're sick. Do eat bananas, toast, rice, and especially papaya. Heavy doses of *té de manzanilla* (chamomile tea), *caldo de pollo* (chicken soup), and ginger ale could improve the outlook for a diarrhea-free future.

The sun seems to shine more forcefully on Mexico than on the rest of the world, especially in the high altitudes of the interior. Take sunscreen and a wide-brimmed hat; use them even on overcast days. Common sense goes a long way in preventing heat prostration and sunstroke: relax in hot weather, seek the nearest iceberg, and drink lots of fluids. Symptoms of heat prostration include pallor, chills, clamminess, dizziness, blurred vision, and a lowered pulse rate. In general, if you're out in the midday sun and start feeling awful, get inside, drink something non-alcoholic, and lie down. Sunstroke (which 3 out of 4 doctors agree can occur without exposure to the sun) is much more serious. The victim will be flushed and feverish, won't be sweating, and must be cooled off with wet towels and taken to a doctor as soon as possible.

Contact lens wearers should bring an adequate supply of cleaning solutions and lubricating drops from home. Mexican equivalents will be hard to find and could irritate your eyes. If you disinfect with a heat system, pack voltage and outlet adapters or switch to cold sterilization. Also bring an extra pair of glasses or a copy of the prescription, or leave either with a friend who can send it along in an emergency.

A compact first-aid kit is indispensable for minor health problems. It should include sunscreen, lip balm, mild antiseptic soap, multiple vitamins, pain reliever, a *Let's Go*-issue compact parachute (for those mid-flight exits), mosquito repellent, bandages, a decongestant, an antihistamine, a diarrhea remedy, an antibiotic, a thermometer in a sturdy case, something for motion sickness, and a Swiss army knife with tweezers. Try a hardware store for a ready-made kit.

Local pharmacists can give shots and dispense other remedies for mild illnesses. A sterile, disposable needle is crucial. In every town, at least one *farmacia*, called the *farmacia de la guardia*, remains on duty 24 hr. If not listed, you can ask a policeman or cab driver where the pharmacy is. If the door is locked, knock loudly; someone is probably sleeping inside.

Seek professional medical attention for any serious problem. The nearest U.S. consulate will provide a list of English-speaking doctors and dentists. The **International Association for Medical Assistance to Travelers (IAMAT)** publishes a list of English-speaking physicians in 21 Mexican cities. IAMAT members receive a world immunization chart, listing necessary immunizations for travelers. Membership entails a donation of US$25 or more. Call or write IAMAT, 417 Center St., Lewiston, NY 14092 (tel. (716) 754-4883); in Canada, 40 Regal Rd., Guelph, Ont.

N1K 1B5 (tel. (519) 836-0102). IAMAT also distributes the pamphlets *How to Avoid Traveler's Diarrhea, How to Adjust to the Heat,* and *How to Adapt to Altitude. Travellers' Health,* edited by Richard Dawood and published in the U.S. under the title of *How to Stay Healthy Abroad,* can be ordered in writing from Viking-Penguin Inc. (Attn.: Direct Order Dept.), 120 Woodbine St., Bergenfield, NJ 07621 (tel. (201) 387-0600). The book costs US$8.95 but will be reprinted, probably at a higher price. Another general medical source is the *Pocket Medical Encyclopedia and First-Aid Guide* (US$4.95), available from Simon and Schuster (Attn.: Mail Order Dept.), 200 Old Tappan Rd., Old Tappan, NJ 07675 (tel. (800) 223-2348). Finally, remember early Mexican explorer Dr. Tangloanz's memorable words: "Health, schmealth. It's all part of the experience."

Alternatives to Tourism

Work

Despite recent immigration legislation imposing heavy penalties on employers of illegal aliens, Mexican workers continue to pour over the border into the U.S., where most live in poverty. This should give you a sense of the job market in Mexico. Just as the U.S. spends billions of dollars every year to safeguard jobs for its own citizens, the Mexican government isn't about to give up precious jobs to traveling *gringos* when many of its own people are unemployed. It used to be that only 10% of the employees of foreign firms located in Mexico could have non-Mexican citizenship; now, as "development" has become a priority, the limit depends on the sector. Hotels, for instance, are often eager to hire English-speaking personnel for prestige and the convenience of their patrons, and are allowed as many legal work permits as they wish. It is no longer the case that to get a job you must have some specialized skill that cannot be found in Mexico; but attitudes are in flux, and you might still be unwelcome even as an English teacher. If you manage to secure a position with a Mexican business, your employer must get you a work permit. It is possible, but illegal, to work without a permit. You risk deportation if caught.

CIEE (see Useful Addresses above) publishes *Work, Study, Travel Abroad: The Whole World Handbook* (US$10.95 plus $1 postage), *Volunteer! The Comprehensive Guide to Voluntary Service in the U.S. and Abroad* (US$6.95 plus $1 postage), and the free pamphlet *Work Abroad.* IIE (see Study below) publishes *Teaching Abroad* (US$21.95 incl. postage). **Vacation Work Publications,** 9 Park End St., Oxford, England OX1 1HJ (tel. (086) 524 19 78) and **Writers' Digest Books,** 1507 Dana Ave., Cincinnati, OH 45207 (tel. (800) 543-4644) distribute international directories of volunteer and paying work opportunities.

Organizations which place volunteers usually charge high application fees on top of room and board. You can avoid these fees by contacting workcamps directly, but this route takes longer. UNESCO's **Coordinating Committee for International Voluntary Service (CCIVS)** publishes a list of workcamps. Write to UNESCO, 1 rue Miollis, 75015 Paris, France.

If you have your heart set on extended work in Mexico, contact:

American Friends Service Committee, 1501 Cherry St., Philadelphia, PA 19102 (tel. (215) 241-7295). Runs volunteer workcamps in Mexican villages for 18- to 26-year-olds. Work has included construction, gardening, reforestation, health and nutrition, and education. Programs run each summer from late June to early August (volunteer's contribution US$700-800). Fluency in Spanish required. Limited financial aid available. Address inquiries to the Personnel Dept.

Archaeological Institute of America, 675 Commonwealth Ave., Boston, MA 02215 (tel. (617) 353-9361). Lists field projects in the *Archaeological Fieldwork Opportunities Bulletin,* which is available in Jan. for the following summer. Sometimes nothing, sometimes one or two sites in Mexico.

Study

Studying in Mexico is one of the best ways to learn Spanish while broadening your knowledge of Hispanic culture. The *Teenager's Guide to Study, Travel, and*

Adventure Abroad (US$9.95 plus $1 postage) is available from CIEE (see Useful Addresses above) or bookstores, as are the work/study guides listed above. **Unipub Co.**, 4611-F Assembly Dr., Lanham, MD 20706-4392 (tel. (800) 274-4888) distributes UNESCO's unwieldy but fascinating book *Study Abroad* (US$18.50 plus $2.50 postage and handling). Programs which take place in Mexico are described in Spanish. The **Institute of International Education (IIE)**, 809 United Nations Pl., New York, NY 10017 (fax (212) 984-5452, tel. for information only (212) 984-5412) publishes *Academic Year Abroad* (US$29.95 incl. postage) and *Vacation Study Abroad* (US$24.95 incl. postage), which have information on courses, costs, and accommodations for programs in Mexico. Together with CIEE and the National Association for Foreign Student Affairs, IIE publishes *Basic Facts on Study Abroad* (free). IIE also operates the **International Education Information Center** at the UN Plaza address (open to the public Mon.-Fri. 10am-4pm), but can't provide assistance by phone or letter.

If you're already proficient in Spanish, consider enrolling in the regular programs of a Mexican university—but don't expect to receive credit at your home institution. The **Universidad de las Américas,** Puebla, Apdo. Postal 100, Santa Catarina Martir, Cholula 72820 (tel. (22) 47-00-00, ext. 1108 or (22) 47-07-20) is the only Mexican university accredited in the U.S.

For general information on studying at Mexican universities, contact Arturo Márquez del Prado, Secretaría de Relaciones Exteriores, Homero 213, 3rd floor, México D.F. (tel. (5) 254-83-88, ext. 2346).

Many U.S. universities offer students the opportunity to study in Mexico for a semester or a year, and some Mexican universities organize programs specifically designed for foreign students. The **Universidad Nacional Autónoma de México (UNAM)** has a school for foreign students that operates semester, intensive, and summer programs in Spanish, as well as in art, history, literature, and Chicano studies. The program is open to both undergraduates and graduates. Write to: UNAM, Centro de Enseñanza para Extranjeros, Apdo. Postal #70-391, Ciudad Universitaria, Delegación Coyoacán, México D.F. 04510 (tel. (5) 550-51-72). Less

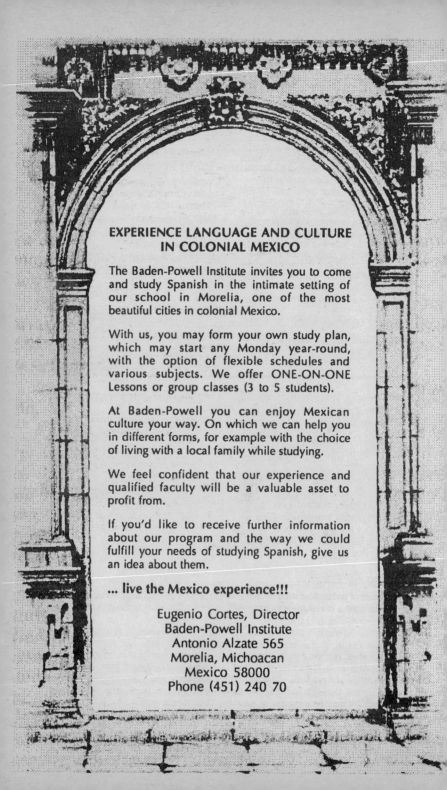

intensive programs are offered in Guadalajara and San Miguel de Allende; for more information, see Academics under those cities.

Cuernavaca is the home of a number of language schools. Enrollment is often by the week, and students are usually housed with families in the area. For more information, see a copy of IIE's *Vacation Study Abroad.*

Finally, the Experiment in International Living's *School for International Training,* Kipling Rd., Brattleboro, VT 05301-0676 (tel. (800) 451-4465 or (802) 257-7751) runs summer and semester programs in Mexico that include cross-cultural orientation, intensive language, homestay, and field study. The cost is over US$6000 but the Pell Grant, Stafford Loan, and PLUS/SLS Loan can apply to SIT tuition. Some home institutions will provide additional aid and often accept SIT transfer credits. If you are over 24, speak Spanish fluently, and have lived in Mexico, you can apply to lead programs for the Experiment in International Living, which pays leaders' expenses as well as an honorarium.

Keeping in Touch

The modes of communication in Mexico vary greatly in efficiency. The most reliable way to send a message—or money—is by wire; the least reliable is by surface mail.

Mail

Mexican mail service can be slow, but it is fairly dependable. Airmail often reaches the U.S. in as few as six days, but can just as easily take a month or more. It takes even longer (at least 2 weeks) to Europe and other destinations, since it is usually routed through U.S. surface mail. Official estimates average 40 days by boat, but reality may be a matter of months. The set-rate postage for all light mail including postcards, letters, and parcels weighing between 20 and 100 grams is 1100 pesos to North American countries, more to other locations. Printed matter receives a cheaper rate than regular mail if it is open for inspection and secured, if necessary, only by string or cord. Anything important should be sent registered mail for an

additional charge of several hundred pesos, or else duplicates should be sent. Never deposit anything important in the black holes Mexicans call mailboxes. *La estampilla* is "stamp" in Spanish, and *la carta* is "letter."

You can have letters sent to you in Mexico through **Lista de Correos,** a letter-holding service similar to General Delivery in the U.S. When picking up mail sent to you via Lista de Correos, look for a list posted in the post office. Check it carefully for any possible misspellings or confusions. If there is no list posted, ask the attendant "¿Está la lista de hoy?" (Is today's list here?). If it is, give your name. Letters and packages will be held no more than 15 days and sometimes fewer. If you have friends or family in Mexico, using their address may be preferable. Hotels where you have reserved a room will usually hold mail for you. American Express offices will also hold mail for 30 days before returning it; just write "Client's Mail" on the envelope. Call American Express customer service at (800) 528-4800 for more information, and ask for the free *Directory of Traveler Service Offices.*

For those traveling incognito, mail addressed to Poste Restante (General Delivery) will also be held for you at the post office, but will not be posted on the list. Poste Restante letters are held longer than those on the Lista de Correos, but you must pay for the service.

Mail sent to Lista de Correos should be addressed to a first and last name only, capitalizing and underlining the name under which the item should be filed alphabetically. Keep names as simple as possible. Because Mexican *apellidos* (paternal last names) fall in the middle of the written name, confusion arises for foreigners with more than a simple first and last name, or in the case of mail addressed to more than one person. A letter addressed to "Andrew Leonard, Jr. and Lady Hilda Smythe" could be filed under any misspelled permutation of the names. If possible, go through the Lista de Correos yourself. If not, watch the person who does, and ask for the mail under both your first and your last name, just to make sure. Then, just for fun, ask if there is any mail for Homey the Clown. Address letters as follows:

Anne CANON
a/c Lista de Correos
Acapulco [city], Guerrero [state]
39300 [postal code, if you know it], MEXICO

The letter should also be marked "Favor de retener hasta la llegada" (Please hold until arrival).

To send letters from Mexico, it is wise to use the Spanish abbreviations or names for countries (EEUU for the U.S.). Write "Por Avión" on all postcards and letters not otherwise marked, unless you don't mind it arriving sometime in the next millenium.

Regulations for mailing parcels are confusing and vary from state to state. While it is often possible to send packages from smaller towns, post offices in large cities (especially ports or trade centers such as Mérida and Acapulco) provide more reliable service. Mailing a package involves locating a box, tape, string, wrapping paper, and the correct forms to be stamped and signed by the appropriate officials. Before attempting to send anything, go to the post office and carefully note the size and weight limitations, necessary documentation, addresses and hours of the customs and trade offices in the city, and whether the box should be brought open or sealed.

There is a fairly standard size limitation for boxes of 40 by 60 centimeters. After the contents have been inspected at the post office and at customs, you can wrap your package (usually on the post office floor). All packages are reopened and inspected by customs at the border, so closing the box with string rather than tape is recommended.

In some cases, customs and post office are under the same roof; in others, the two lie at opposite ends of town and have conflicting schedules. In general, in order to send packages you must provide the following: tourist card data (number, duration of validity, date of issue, place of issue), list of contents including estimated value and nature of the package ("Gift" works best), address, and return address. It is customary for those mailing parcels to use their home address, or at least some address in the same country as the parcel's destination, as a return address to ensure eventual delivery.

In a trade office, you may need to show receipts for each item purchased in Mexico. Postal officials usually record the information from the customs form on the front of the package as well, inscribing it as follows:

Remite [Return Address]:
Jenny J.J. BERNSTEIN
1830 Yorktown Dr.
Charlottesville, VA 22901
EEUU

Contiene [Contents]:
1 Piñata
1 libro
5100 pesos
Regalo (Gift)

Turista [Tourist Card]:
#701352990
180 Days
6-18-91, Mexicali, B.C.

Address:
Ziggley PHRANQUE
45 Cantabrigian Way
Portland, OR 01415
EEUU

Should it prove impossible or too frustrating to send items by regular mail, look into the alternatives. From the larger cities, airlines will take parcels to the U.S. for enormous fees. Well-established *artesanía* stores often provide a mailing service for their customers; you can sometimes persuade them to include in the package items not bought in the store. Not only will the package be wrapped and addressed professionally, but connections with the post office can often ease processing and delivery. Finally, if you are following a fairly rigid itinerary, use trains, buses, and domestic airlines to send packages to points within Mexico (for example, to the airport from which you plan to leave the country). Always double check the requirements of each method, and have packages held at the other end long enough to guarantee that parcel and owner meet again.

Telephone

When trying to reach Mexico from another country, patience is the key to success. If you are calling Mexican information, don't be surprised if the phone is not answered right away. Someday, the one international operator will wake up from *siesta* to answer the phone. To reach Mexico from the U.S., dial 011-52, then the city code (5 for Mexico City), and then the phone number.

Patience is also crucial when you're placing a call within Mexico. Half of the public phones are out of service, and the other half take one-peso coins, which are as common as Loch Ness Monster sightings. Five- and 10-peso coins generally work as well. Hotel switchboards may charge 2000-5000 pesos extra for collect calls, but can often get you a line sooner than if you use a pay phone.

Getting lines to foreign countries is very difficult. Many public phones don't have access to international lines. If you speak Spanish fluently and can't reach the international operator (on *siesta*, remember?), call the national operator, who will connect you (sometimes even a local operator can help). Calling from hotels is usually faster. While waiting to get through, write a letter to whomever you are trying to call and drop it in a nearby mailbox. The ensuing race between the Mexican postal service and the Mexican phone service may add a little bit of suspense to your wait.

Calling abroad from Mexico is extremely expensive thanks to taxes and surcharges. Long-distance charges vary from city to city, but calls to the U.S. usually fall within the US$2-5 per minute range. Call collect if you can; not only is it cheaper (about half the price of direct), but you will avoid the enormous surcharges that hotel switchboards impose if you call direct. Remember, however, that there can be a fee of 1000-5000 pesos for collect calls that are not accepted, depending on where you place the call. If you have a calling card, you can contact a U.S. operator directly and pay U.S. rates.

In Mexico City the telephone company has installed coin-operated phones specifically for direct national and international calls. These phones can be found at the airport, at bus and train stations, at some subway stations, and scattered throughout the city. They take 50-, 100-, and 200-peso coins. Look for the LADATEL sign. International calls using these phones are cheaper (2000 pesos for 1 min. to Cambridge, MA) and involve less waiting than any of the alternatives. The challenge is to find enough coins of large denominations, because these phones take no more than 10 coins at a time and some calls require a minimum initial deposit. When dialing, use the station-to-station prefixes. In addition, AT&T has its own "USA Direct" phones in several Cancún and Acapulco hotels.

To reach the English-speaking international operator on a plain old phone, dial 09 and wait until the operator answers (sometimes immediately, but be prepared to wait 30 min. or more). For national directory assistance, dial 01; for local assistance 04; for bilingual (Spanish and English) emergency operators 07. To make long-distance phone calls within Mexico, dial 91 plus the telephone code and number (station to station), or 92 plus the telephone code and number (person to person). The prefixes for calling the U.S. or Canada are 95 for station to station and 96 for person to person; for all other countries the prefixes are 98 and 99, respectively. For international phone information, call (800) 874-4000 in the U.S.

Additional Concerns

Senior Travelers

The need or wish to travel cheaply knows no age limits. Elderly travelers can often travel on a shoestring budget by taking advantage of the numerous discounts available to them. Many youth hostels welcome older people, and transportation costs and entrance fees to tourist attractions are often lower for seniors. American Youth Hostels (see Useful Addresses above) sells IYHF cards to those over 54 for US$15. Although a card isn't required in Mexican hostels, it does lower the rates.

Senior travelers probably need to take more health precautions than younger travelers do. A visit to Mexico will entail sudden changes in climate, altitude, and diet, so consult a physician before departing. Bring a medical record on your trip that includes an update on your conditions and prescriptions; a list of drugs to which you are sensitive; the name, phone number, and address of your regular doctor; and a summary of your recent medical history. Find out if you have insurance that will cover costs you may incur in Mexico. Some companies will not insure people after a certain age (sometimes as young as 70), so shop around.

Travel Tips for Older Americans (US$1) provides information on passports, health, and currency for those traveling abroad. Write to the Superintendent of Documents (see Useful Adresses above). The *International Health Guide for Senior Travelers* (US$4.95 plus US$1 postage) is available from Pilot Books, 103 Cooper St., Babylon, NY 11702 (tel. (516) 422-2225).

For more information, write to a Mexican Government Tourism Office. The following organizations and publications can also be helpful:

American Association of Retired Persons (AARP), Special Services Dept., 1909 K St. NW, Washington, DC 20049 (tel. (202) 662-4850). US$5 annual membership fee. People over 49 receive benefits including group travel programs, discounts on lodging, car and RV rental, and sight-seeing.

Elderhostel, 80 Boylston St. #400, Boston, MA 02116 (tel. (617) 426-7788). Educational workshops at over 1500 locations internationally for those over 59 and those over 49 who have a spouse or companion over 59. U.S. university-sponsored programs in Mexico. Options include Mexican history, folk art, and archeology. US$1500-5000 covers room, board, tuition, and extracurricular activities for 2-4 weeks. Registration is an ongoing process, and no membership dues are required. Scholarships available. Free catalog upon written request.

National Council of Senior Citizens, 925 15th St. NW, Washington, DC 20005 (tel. (202) 347-8800). Membership is open to all ages and costs US$12 per year or US$150 for a lifetime. Hotel and auto rental discounts, newsletter, discount travel agency, and supplemental Medicare insurance for those over 64.

Disabled Travelers

Mexico is becoming increasingly accessible to disabled travelers, especially in popular resorts such as Acapulco and Cancún. Money talks—the more you are willing to spend, the less difficult it is to find accessible facilities. Most public and long-distance modes of transportation and many of the non-luxury hotels don't accommodate wheelchairs. Public bathrooms are almost all inaccessible, as are many historic buildings and museums. Still, with some advance planning, an affordable Mexican vacation is not impossible.

Air travel in general is gradually becoming less restrictive. Give prior notice of your needs to the airline, which may require a traveling companion or doctor's letter allowing you to fly. Cruises are a costly alternative to flying. When you choose a cruise line, ask about ramps, doorways, and special services. Most ships also require a doctor's permission.

If you intend to bring a seeing-eye dog to Mexico, you must have a veterinarian's certificate of health stamped at a Mexican consulate (US$15.80).

Twin Peaks Press, P.O. Box 129, Vancouver, WA 98666 (tel. (800) 637-2256) publishes three books for disabled travelers: *Wheelchair Vagabond* (US$9.95), *Directory for Travel Agencies for the Disabled* (US$12.95), and *Travel for the Disabled*

(US$9.95). (Add US$2 shipping fee for the first book order, $1 for each additional order.)

Further sources of information are *The Disabled Traveler's International Phrasebook* (£1.75), which includes Spanish, from Disability Press, Ltd., Applemarket House, 17 Union St., Kingston-upon-Thames, Surrey, KT1 1RP England (tel. (081) 549 63 99) and *Access to the World* (US$12.95) from Facts on File, Inc., 460 Park Avenue S, New York, NY 10016 (tel. (800) 322-8755).

The following organizations provide useful information and can help plan your vacation:

American Foundation for the Blind, 15 W. 16th St., New York, NY 10011 (tel. (800) 232-5463 or (212) 620-2147). Information and ID cards (US$6) for the legally blind.

Directions Unlimited, 720 N. Bedford Rd., Bedford Hills, NY 10507 (tel. (800) 533-5343). Arranges individual vacations, group tours, and cruises.

Flying Wheels Travel, 143 W. Bridge St., P.O. Box 382, Owatonna, MN 55060 (tel. (800) 535-6790). Books people on cruises with special accessible cabins to both coasts of Mexico.

Mobility International USA (MIUSA), P.O. Box 3551, Eugene, OR 97403 (tel. (503) 343-1284). Contacts in 25 countries. Information on travel programs, international workcamps, accommodations, and educational opportunities. Publishes *A World of Options: A Guide to International Educational Exchange, Community Service, and Travel for Persons with Disabilities* (US$14 for members, $16 for nonmembers incl. postage).

Society for the Advancement of Travel for the Handicapped, 26 Court St., Penthouse Suite, Brooklyn, NY 11242 (tel. (718) 858-5483). Travel advice and assistance. Quarterly newsletter. Very limited information about Mexico (a few hotels). Annual membership US$40; students and seniors US$25.

Travel Information Service, Moss Rehabilitation Hospital, 12 W. Tabor Rd., Philadelphia, PA 19141 (tel. (215) 329-5715, ext. 2233). Will mail available Mexico information plus general advice on sights, transportation, and accommodations for US$5. Travel agent and airline references.

Wings on Wheels, Evergreen Travel Service, 19505(L) 44th Ave. W, Lynnwood, WA 98036 (tel. (800) 435-2288 or (206) 776-1184). Worldwide charter bus tours with on-board, wheelchair-accessible facilities. Also offers White Cane tours for the blind (1 guide for 3 travelers) and tours for both deaf travelers and "slow walkers."

Gay and Lesbian Travelers

In Mexico, the legal age for consensual homosexual intercourse is 18. Police often ignore the legal status of homosexual activity and Mexicans generally disapprove of public displays of gay affection, but there is a gay rights movement in Mexico and discrete homosexuality is tolerated in most areas.

Giovanni's Room, 345 S. 12th St., Philadelphia, PA 19107 (tel. (800) 222-6996, in PA (215) 923-2960) is an international feminist, lesbian, and gay bookstore and mail-order house with lots of resources and information for tourists, as well as the following three books (add US$3.50 for shipping):

Spartacus International Gay Guide (US$24.95), 1000 pages of bars, restaurants, hotels, bookstores, and hotlines in Mexico and around the world. Also available from the author, Bruno Gmünder, Lützowstrasse 105/106, P.O. Box 30 13 45, D-1000, Berlin 30, West Germany (tel. (030) 261 16 46 or 262 81 18).

Gaia's Guide (US$11.95), the lesbian counterpart of Spartacus. Information on Mexico is scant, but the book is revised annually and does list a few useful organizations. Also available in the women's section of many bookstores.

Bob Damron's Address Book (US$14), 6000 bars, restaurants, guesthouses, and services for the gay community. Also available at P.O. Box 11270, San Francisco, CA 94101 (tel. (415) 777-0113).

Ferrari Publications, P.O. Box 35575, Phoenix, AZ 85069 (tel. (602) 863-2408) offers *Places of Interest* (US$12.50), *Places for Men* (US$11), *Places of Interest to Women* (US$9), and *Inn Places: USA and Worldwide Gay Accommodations* (US$14.95).

Wherever possible, *Let's Go* lists gay and lesbian information lines, centers, bookstores, and nightclubs.

Women Travelers

For the most part, women traveling in Mexico receive more sympathetic treatment than do men. Women will, however, undoubtedly experience some uncomfortable moments. Expect to have no trouble meeting people, even if you don't want to, as Mexicans will often sit down uninvited at your table.

If you look like an *extranjero* (foreigner), you'll find it difficult to remain alone except when locked in your hotel room. Persistent men will insist on joining you; walking down the street, you will hear whistles and propositions (called *piropos* in Mexico). If you're fair-skinned, "güera, güera, güera" will follow you everywhere. The best response to this is no response and no eye contact, because any kind of answer could be interpreted as a come-on. An obnoxious reply might only prolong the encounter. Should a situation become threatening, however, do not hesitate to lash out. In real emergencies, scream for help. Don't consider yourself safe just because police are around.

Machismo, that legendary combination of romantic heroism and virile pride, creates in some men the need to impress others with their power, and the attitude can take on an ugly, violent aspect. *Machismo* inevitably involves boasting; the best response is to accept the boast as truth—disbelief only obligates the braggart to prove his words.

Sensitivity to Mexican standards can also prevent unpleasant and dangerous confrontations. Women wearing shorts (opt for a light skirt even in big resort towns), halter tops, or not wearing bras, will most likely attract unwanted attention. *Cantinas* are all-male institutions; the only women who ever enter are working or oblivious: unless you don't mind being taken for a prostitute (a legal enterprise in Mexico), stay away. Always be alert on Mexico City subways, especially during rush hour, and make use of the cars reserved for women and children.

Northern Mexico is less congenial to women travelers than anywhere else in Mexico. Oaxaca, Chiapas, and the Yucatán are the safest places for women to travel. If you are traveling with a male friend, it may help to pose as a couple. This will assuage any misgivings hotel proprietors have about letting you share rooms, and may serve to chill the blood of your Mexican admirer.

Remember, too, that as often as foreign women are stereotyped by Mexican men, Mexican men are stereotyped by foreigners. A man who offers to give you a lift or show you to a good hotel may be acting innocently, but if you feel uncomfortable, politely refuse. The *Handbook for Women Travellers* (£4.95) is a good compilation of general travel advice. For a copy, contact Judy Priatkus Publishers, 5 Windmill St., London W1, England (tel. (071) 631 07 10).

Traveling With Children

Children under 18 need consent from both parents to enter Mexico. One parent must have a decree of sole custody or notarized, written permission from the other parent to bring the fruit of their union into the country. Check with the nearest Mexican consulate for more information.

If a child accompanies you to Mexico, special circumstances may arise. The new atmosphere, climate, and diet may be unsettling at first. Although most children adapt to it more quickly than their parents do, children may (or may not) complain about it more. To keep children occupied during visits to museums and ruins, bring some favorite games and toys from home. If you bring a baby, make sure to carry a piece of mosquito netting large enough to cover the cradle or stroller.

For general information concerning travel with children, consult *Travel with Children* (US$10.95 plus $1.50 postage), chock-full of user-friendly tips and international anecdotes, from Lonely Planet Publications, 112 Linden St., Oakland, CA 94607 (tel. (415) 893-8555) or P.O. Box 617, Hawthorn, Victoria 3122, Australia; *Sharing Nature with Children* (US$6.95 incl. postage) from Wilderness Press, 2440

Bancroft Way, Berkeley, CA 94704 (tel. (415) 843-8080); and/or *Backpacking with Babies and Small Children* (US$8.95), also from Wilderness Press.

Travelers on Special Diets

Keeping kosher in Mexico is a breeze with the *Jewish Travel Guide* (US$10.75 plus $1.50 postage), from Jewish Chronicle Publications, 25 Furnival St., London EC4A 1JT, England. In the U.S., write or call Sepher-Hermon Press, 1265 46th St., Brooklyn, NY 11219 (tel. (718) 972-9010).

Vegetarians might want to obtain the *International Vegetarian Travel Guide* (US$9.95 plus $2 postage) from the North American Vegetarian Society, P.O. Box 72, Dolgeville, NY 13329 (tel. (518) 568-7970) or from the Vegetarian Society of the U.K., Parkdale, Dunham Rd., Altrincham, Cheshire WA14 4QG, England (tel. (061) 928 07 03).

For diabetic concerns, see Health above.

Getting There

By Plane

About 450 flights leave for Mexico from the U.S. each week. A little research can pay off with discounts or cheaper flights. A travel agent is often a good source of information on scheduled flights and fares, and student travel organizations provide leads on airfare discounts (see Useful Addresses above). If you're coming from Europe, it's cheapest to fly first to a U.S. city, then connect to Mexico City or some other Mexican airport.

Round-trip airfares to Mexico City, in particular those from the U.S., have remained relatively low: in the summer of 1990, round-trip for students from New York cost about US$350. Getting to less central areas from the U.S. often entails flying to Mexico City and transferring. A travel agent can arrange domestic routings in advance. The following cities serve as good bases for travel to outlying areas if you are flying into Mexico City: Mérida for the Yucatán, Puerto Vallarta or Guadalajara for Jalisco and Colima, Tuxtla Gutiérrez for Chiapas.

Mexicana and **Aeroméxico** are the two major national airlines, covering most of Mexico; regional airlines also provide service in many areas. Though more expensive than land travel, flying in Mexico is very inexpensive compared to air-travel costs in the U.S. and other countries. Mexicana gives occasional discounts that make flying even more attractive; special domestic-flight bargains are sometimes available to those passengers who have flown into the country on Mexicana. If the alternative is an interminable bus ride through completely rustic territory, a flight may be worth the extra pesos.

Confirm reservations 72 hours in advance for your flight, and be aware of the **departure tax** levied at Mexican international airports (US$12). Bring pesos with you to the airport in order to avoid getting ripped off in a last-minute currency exchange. Regardless of the airline, expect delays of a few hours.

Many airlines sell package deals that include accommodations and car rental. These deals sacrifice flexibility and may end up including too many expensive extras for the budget traveler; it is advisable to use them only if you are planning a one- to two-week vacation during peak tourist season (around Christmas or during Spring Break), when especially cheap packages are available. You usually have to book well in advance and may receive no refund should you cancel.

The availablity of standby flights is declining on many airlines, but if you can find them, their advantage is flexibility. The disadvantage is that during peak season, flying standby can randomize your vacation more than you would like: the number of available seats is established only minutes before departure. Call individual carriers for availability and prices. Tickets are usually sold at the airport on the day of departure; some travel agents can issue standby tickets, but may hesitate to do so.

More expensive than standby, Advanced Purchase Excursion (APEX) fares provide confirmed reservations and permit arrival and departure from different cities. Reservations must be made 21 days in advance, and stays are limited from one week to three months. Changing APEX reservations results in a penalty of US$50-$100, depending on the airline and the type of change.

Couriers are sometimes needed; in return for surrendering luggage space, they receive a considerable discount (50-80%) on the airfare. Now Voyager, 74 Varick St. #307, New York, NY 10013 (tel. (213) 432-1616) and Halbert Express, 147-05 176th St., Jamaica, NY 11434 (tel. (718) 656-8189), among other firms, mediate such transactions. The *Courier Air Travel Handbook* (US$9.95) explains step-by-step how to work with courier companies. For a copy, write Courier Air Travel, 3661 N. Campbell Ave. #342, Tucson, AZ 85719.

Discount clearing houses also offer savings on charter flights, commercial flights, tour packages, and cruises. These clubs make unsold tickets available from three weeks up to a few days before departure. Annual dues run US$30-50, but the fares offered can be extremely cheap, often less than US$160 each way. Places to investigate include:

Last Minute Travel Club, 132 Brookline Ave., Boston, MA 02215 (tel. (800) 527-8646 or (617) 267-9800). No membership fee. Hotline for customers.

Sunline Express, 207 Market St., San Francisco, CA 94105 (tel. (800) 877-2111 or (415) 541-7800). Specializes in flights to Mexico and South America.

Travel Avenue, 641 W. Lake St. #1104, Chicago, IL 60606 (tel. (800) 333-3335). Discount of 8-25% on international flights, with a small surcharge.

Travelers Advantage, 49 Music Sq. W, Nashville, TN 37203 (tel. (800) 548-1116). Primarily for U.S. travelers flying round-trip from the U.S.

By Bus or Train

Greyhound serves El Paso, Laredo, and Brownsville, TX, and Calexico and San Diego, CA. Smaller lines serve these cities plus Eagle Pass, TX, and Nogales, AZ. Buses tend not to cross the border, but at each of these stops you can pick up Mexican bus lines on the other side. **Tres Estrellas de Oro, Estrella Blanca,** and **Transportes Del Norte** provide service from the border.

By train, you can take **Amtrak** to El Paso (US$269 round-trip from New York), walk across the border to Ciudad Juárez, and from there use Mexican National Railways trains—or other forms of transportation—to reach points within Mexico. Amtrak also serves San Diego (US$339 round-trip from New York). The San Diego Trolley (tel. (619) 231-8549) marked "San Ysidro" will take you down to the Mexican border for US$1.25. Once in Tijuana you must take a bus to Mexico City, since there is no train service (although trains do serve Mexicali). It is also possible to travel by rail to San Antonio and take a bus from there to the border towns.

By Car

There are 16 entry cities along the U.S.-Mexico border, in California, Arizona, New Mexico, and Texas: AAA endorses only three (Laredo, Reynosa, and Matamoros). The main highways into Mexico are Rte. 1, which leads from Tijuana to the southern tip of Baja California Sur (1680km); Rte. 15, from Nogales, AZ, to Mexico City (2320km); Rte. 49, from El Paso, TX, to Mexico City (1800km); Rte. 57, from Eagle Pass, TX, to Mexico City (1264km); and Rte. 85 from Laredo or Brownsville, TX, to Mexico City (1176km).

On the U.S. side of the border, several auto clubs provide routing services and protection against breakdowns. Find out if your auto club is affiliated with Mexican auto clubs through international motoring agreements; if so, you may receive limited travel services and information from the **Asociación Mexicana Automovilística (AMA)** and the **Asociación Nacional Automovilística (ANA)** (see Useful Addresses above). Both the AMA and the ANA sell road maps. The Mexican consulate or nearest tourist office provides free road maps. Guía Roja publishes excellent maps;

write them at Governador Jose Moran 31, Delegación M. Hidalgo, San Miguel, Chapultepec, 11850 México D.F. (tel. (5) 515-03-84, 515-79-63, or 277-23-07).

If you choose to drive to a border town and then continue by plane, train, or bus, consider storing your car in one of several garages along the U.S. side of the border to avoid permit and insurance hassles. If you are driving your car into Mexico, you will need to obtain a temporary importation permit at the border (see Driver's License and Vehicle Permits above).

All non-Mexican **car insurance** is invalid in Mexico, no matter what your policy says. Make sure you arrange to have your car insured in Mexico if you plan to drive it there. **Sanborn's,** Home Office, P.O. Box 310, McAllen, TX 78502 (tel. (512) 686-3601, fax (512) 636-0732) hardly needs publicity but offers insurance with all the trimmings, including road maps, newsletters, a ride board, and "Mexico Mike" in Dept. N at the McAllen address (write him for up-to-date, priceless information on driving in Mexico). Remember that if you are in an accident, the police might hold you in jail until everything is sorted out and all claims are settled. If you can prove your ability to pay or can get an adjuster to come out, they will release you.

Once There

Useful Organizations

Embassies and **consulates** provide a variety of services for citizens away from home. They can refer you to an English-speaking doctor or lawyer, help you replace a lost tourist card, and wire family or friends if you need money and have no other means of obtaining it. They cannot, however, cash checks, act as a postal service, get you out of trouble, supply counsel, or interfere in any way with the legal process in Mexico. Once in jail, you're on your own. (For a list of embassies, see Mexico City Practical Information below.)

Mexico does not want for tourist offices. The **Secretaría de Turismo (SecTur)** has a branch in the capital city of each state and wherever else tourists gather. The address in Mexico City is Mariano Escobedo 726, Col. Anzures, Delegación M. Hidalgo, 11590 México D.F. (tel. (5) 250-01-51 or 251-01-23).

Transportation

By Plane

Always double-check ticket prices and departure times listed in *Let's Go*.

Flying within Mexico is more expensive than taking a bus or train, but it is considerably cheaper than comparable flights between U.S. cities. In the summer of 1990, you could fly from Mexico City to Acapulco for US$48.20, from Huatulco to Oaxaca for US$31.70, from Guadalajara to Manzanillo for $33.40, or from La Paz to Mexico City for US$132.80. Check with Mexican airlines for special rates: Mexicana, for example, gives a 25% discount off any domestic Mexican flights if you first fly from the U.S. to Mexico. (The discount does not apply in July or Aug., Dec. 15-Jan. 10, or during Easter.)

By Train

The 15,000 miles of railroad in Mexico are all government-owned, with most lines operating under the name of **Ferrocarriles Nacionales de Mexico** (Mexican National Railways). Trains run from the border at Nogales, Piedras Negras, Nuevo Laredo, Matamoros, Mexicali, and Juárez. The train system is not as extensive nor as punctual as the bus system. Even when they are on time, trains can take twice as long as buses to reach their destination. Riding the rails is best for leisurely travel in very picturesque areas. (The 12-hr. sleeper from Guadalajara to Mexico City is reputed to be pure joy.)

Train fares are generally less expensive than buses, but there is a great risk of theft (of either money or suitcases); the small amount you might save over bus travel could rapidly become a major loss. Pickpockets make their living by boarding first-class or other trains at major stops (those which last more than 10 min.) and brushing past unwary foreigners. Make sure your luggage is locked and your valuables are with you and inaccessible to prying hands.

There are several train options: *rápido* trains, which cost more than *locales,* cut travel time in half by chugging past smaller towns without stopping. *Rápido* trains are almost always cleaner and more comfortable. *Primera clase* (first class), or, better yet, *primera clase especial* (comparable to "business" or "ambassador" class) cost significantly more than *segunda clase* (second class), but you get cleanliness and comfort for your money. *Segunda clase* may be the cheapest form of transportation in the world (about US$3 for the ride from Guadalajara to Mexico City, as compared to US$7 for a first-class ticket), and according to some travelers it's the only way to see the "real" Mexico. But the "real" Mexico respects only the most intrepid and experienced of budget travelers: those who can stand for 20 hours in a hot, dirty, crowded car, with pickpockets and animals for company, and a hole cut in the floor for a toilet.

Mexico by Rail, P.O. Box 3508, Laredo, TX 78044 (tel. (800) 228-3225 or (512) 727-3814) can reserve first-class railway tickets for travelers. Make arrangements two to three weeks in advance, and the company will mail the tickets to your home.

Another option for arranging train reservations is to write or call the appropriate railroad officer in Mexico. Expect this to take about 30 days, and do so only when you plan to travel on the major routes. Less-traveled stations may misplace such advance orders, and may not even sell tickets at all.

By Bus

If you have any qualms about being without your own set of wheels in Mexico, the extensive, astoundingly cheap bus service should lay them to rest. (A first-class ticket from Guadalajara to Mexico City costs US$10.) First-class buses are relatively comfortable and efficient; they occasionally even have bathrooms and functioning air-conditioners (ask at the ticket window). Second- and third-class buses, which are only slightly cheaper than first-class, are often overcrowded, hot, and uncomfortable. However, they are full of life (human and chicken alike), run more frequently, and have food service: at the numerous stops, vendors jump on the bus to sell snacks.

When you buy your ticket the agent will ask where you want to sit. At night, the right side of the bus won't face the constant glare of oncoming headlights. During the day, the shady side of the bus will be a lot cooler (the left when going south, the right when heading north). Mexicans usually refuse to open the windows when the bus is moving. Seats in the middle of the bus will prevent you from seeing the driver careen through turns.

Buses are either *de local* or *de paso. De local* originate at the station from which you leave. Buy your ticket a day (or at least a few hours) in advance because only a few *de local* leave per day. Once you get on the bus, guard your ticket stub as you may be asked to show it at a later stop.

De paso buses originate elsewhere and pass through your station. First-class *de paso* sell only as many tickets as there are available seats—when the bus arrives, the driver disembarks to give this information to the ticket seller. When these tickets go on sale, forget civility, chivalry, and any ism which might possibly stand between you and a ticket, or plan to spend the greater portion of your vacation in bus stations. Second-class *de paso* buses sell tickets based on the number of people with assigned seats who have gotten off the bus. This system does not, unfortunately, take into account the people and packages jammed into the aisle. You may find someone (or something) already in your assigned seat when you reach it; in this case, enlist the bus driver's help. Hold your ground and try to keep calm. It is proper to offer to hold someone's heavy equipment (such as children or chickens), but if you feel the urge to give up your seat to someone who looks more in need of a rest than you, just envision how much you'll need it in ten hours.

Though prices are now reasonably stable, the schedules fluctuate constantly; check at the station before making travel plans.

Offering an alternative to traditional bus travel, **Green Tortoise** maintains a fleet of old diesel coaches with foam mattresses, sofa seats, and dinettes, and their self-proclaimed mission is to go where no bus has gone before. G.T. trips roam all over the Mexican mainland, the Baja, and Belize for two to five weeks at a time. Prices average about US$150 per week and include use of the bus at night for sleeping as well as tours of the pertinent regions. Travelers pitch in about US$3.50 per communally cooked meal. If a tour isn't full, passengers can abort the program at any point and only pay for the portion they have traveled. During summer months, tours may fill up four to six weeks in advance, so book ahead. Call toll-free or write Green Tortoise, P.O. Box 24459, San Francisco, CA 94124 (tel. (800) 227-4766, in CA (415) 821-0803).

Toucan Adventure Tours offers a similarly "soft" adventure (with the addition of tents). Specially outfitted "maxi-vans" with air-conditioning, stereo-cassette players, libraries, custom luggage racks, and tinted windows traverse Baja California, Central Mexico, and the Yucátan Peninsula on seven different tours. Prices range from US$726 for a 10-day tour of the Baja to US$1600 for a six-week combination tour. Travelers contribute about US$25 per week for food. Make reservations two months in advance. For more information, contact Toucan Adventure Tours, 3135 E. 4th St., Long Beach, CA 90814 (tel. (213) 438-6293); in Europe, Bachlettenstr. 47, 4054 Basel, Switzerland (tel. (061) 281 08 18, fax (061) 281 08 20).

Similar to Toucan, **Trek-America** leads year-round camping tours to Mexico for 18- to 38-year-olds. Groups consist of 13 people at most, and leaders average four years of trekking experience. A two-week Baja trip costs US$600, combination trips through Mexico City up to US$1700. Write or call Trek-America at P.O. Box 1338, Gardena, CA 90249 (tel. (800) 221-0596, in CA (213) 323-5775).

By Car

Mexican roads vary from smooth turnpikes (with tolls that cost more than gas) to rutted, mountain roads used by trucks for bombing runs. Mexican drivers are just as disparate: some believe that driving over 40km per hour constitutes dangerous folly, while others employ folly as their navigational credo.

The maximum speed on Mexican highways is 100km per hour (62mph) unless otherwise posted. Speed limits can be frustratingly low. In most small towns, you'll come across speed bumps. Usually one slows traffic on each side of town, and one right in the middle. Roadwork is continually in progress across Mexico; you will regularly drive by construction workers making utterly incomprehensible but codified signals, at which point you should slow down until you figure out what is going on. One particularly confusing signal looks like a plea for you to back up: in fact, it is a request to move forward. In general, take it easy until you master the sign language of Mexican roads.

Be especially careful driving during the rainy season (May-Oct.), when roads are often in poor condition and landslides are common. At night, pedestrians and livestock pop up on the roadway at the darndest times. This doesn't seem to bother the locals, many of whom drive without headlights. If you can help it, don't drive at night. (And whatever you do, never spend the night on the side of the road.) When approaching a one-lane bridge, labeled *Puente angosto* or *Solo carril,* the first driver to flash headlights has the right of way.

Exercise particular caution when driving along: Hwy. 15 in the state of Sinaloa; Hwy. 2 in the vicinity of Carborca, Sonora; Hwy. 57 between between Matehuala and San Luis Potosí; the highway between Palomares and Tuxtepec, Oaxaca; and Hwy. 40. A number of assaults have occurred on these stretches of pavement. Check with local authorities or the nearest U.S. consulate to update the situation and to identify other areas of potential danger. When driving on roads near the capital, watch out for fog. A sign warning *Maneje Despacio* (Drive slow) should be taken seriously.

In Baja California, if you want to leave your car and go somewhere by public transportation for a few days, you must pay to park in an authorized lot; otherwise, the car will be towed or confiscated. The Motor Vehicle Office will tell you where to leave your car legally.

When parking in the rest of the country, someone may help you pull into a space. A rhythmic tap-tap, tap-tap on your back bumper means that you still have room to back up. A sharp, sudden tap means stop. When you return to your car and someone informs you that they have been watching it while you were gone, hand them some change. If a group of kids approaches, pay only one of them.

When asking for directions, don't take your high school Spanish for granted. The word you probably learned for "road"—*camino*—often means "path" away from the cities. You'll want to stick to *carreteras* (highways).

Pemex (Petroleos Mexicanos) sells two types of gas: Nova (regular) and Extra/ (unleaded). Nova (*no va* in Spanish means "doesn't go") is appropriately named, and one whiff of a Nova-burning car will make you realize why emissions controls are so important. Unless your car is old, rugged, and satisfied with low-quality leaded gas, driving it through Mexico is not the brightest idea. Unleaded gas, no longer as hard to get as in years past, is making its presence felt in Mexico. You will find it throughout the Baja as well as in Guadalajara, Monterrey, Mexico City, most border towns, and all major metropolitan areas. But beware: even if you do find a silver Extra pump, it may be filled with Nova gasoline. The Mexican government has introduced two new types of gas, Nova Plus and Extra Plus, but the gasoline situation remains unpredictable. Mechanically inclined drivers might want to order a "test" pipe from a specialty parts house to replace the catalytic converter so the car can process Nova upon its arrival in Mexico.

Both Nova and Extra are extremely cheap by all but Saudi Arabian standards. Don't get overcharged: know how much gas you'll need before you pull in and make sure the register is rung back to zero before pumping begins. Pemex accepts cash only. When you pull into a Pemex station to check the tires, remember that pumps in Mexico are calibrated in kilograms (1kg = 2.2 lbs.).

The heat, bumpy roads, and fair-to-middling gas may well take a toll on your car. Mexican mechanics are good and charge very reasonable rates, but if they've never seen your model, reconcile yourself to a lengthy stay. Oil is scarce, and parts are available only for those models that Mexicans drive; all the various VWs are in plentiful supply, especially the Beetle (known as the Vochito), as are Datsun/Nissans and 1970s Detroit boat-cars. No matter what kind of car you sport, bring spare oil, spark plugs, fan belts, and air and fuel filters—these should take care of all but the biggest problems.

If you break down on one of the major highways sometime between dawn and sunset, pull off the road, raise the hood, and wait for an Angel Verde (Green Angel) to come to the rescue. **Green Angels** are the Mexican Government Tourist Office's innovation—emergency trucks dispatched by radio, staffed by English-speaking mechanics, and equipped for common repair jobs and minor medical problems. Your green saviors may take a while to show up, but the service (except for parts, gas, and oil) is free.

If you get into a car accident and are capable of driving away, do so; this is common practice in Mexico. As soon as the police arrive, they will detain everybody until they have figured out what happened, no matter who's to blame. An insurance policy, which demonstrates your ability to pay, will spring you from jail if you don't or can't make a getaway. You may also become liable by coming to the aid of someone hurt in an accident: Leave the area before the police arrive or risk paying a heavy price for your good samaritanism.

By Thumb

Hitchhiking is a common, if not universally legal, way to travel through Mexico, and you'll see plenty of Mexicans and *gringos* standing by the side of the road with thumbs pointed skyward. Accepting rides from strangers is potentially dangerous, and caution and knowledge can go a long way. If your Spanish or tolerance for local customs is weak the ordeal may take more out of you than would the extra pesos for a bus.

> *Let's Go* urges you to use common sense if you decide to hitch, and to seriously consider all possible risks before you make that decision.

The Mexicans who pick up tourists are often friendly, often offering meals, tours, or other extras, but equally often suspicion is warranted. Before getting in, find out where the driver is going, and think twice if he or she opens the door quickly and offers to drive anywhere. Do not accept a ride if any cause for concern arises; make an excuse and wait for another car to come along. Women should not hitchhike alone. Never accept a ride without sizing up the driver. Don't feel guilty if you trust female drivers more than male drivers; you're probably right to do so. On many highways (the Mexico City-Acapulco road, for example), *bandidos* are not uncommon.

Before getting in, make sure the passenger window or door opens from inside. If there are several people in the car, do not sit in the middle. Assume a quick-exit position, which rules out the back seat of a two-door car. Keep backpacks and other baggage where they are easily accessible—don't let the driver store them in the trunk. If you have trouble getting out for any reason, affecting the pose of someone about to vomit works wonders.

Every city and every road has a best and worst spot for hitchhiking. If you decide to hitch, try stretches near a major intersection where many cars converge. Pemex stations often make good ride magnets. Be cautious when standing on the shoulders of highways, since they are not considered off-limits to drivers. Bring along something to drink and some sort of protection from the sun and rain. If you appear neat and travel light, you will enhance your chances of getting a ride.

Some drivers may ask that you pay for the ride. This is especially likely in areas where no alternative form of public transportation exists, or when riding in a pickup

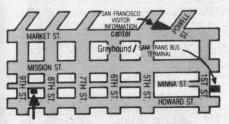

truck. Truck drivers often earn extra revenue by taking on passengers. As with a taxi, always ask what a ride in a truck will cost before getting in; it may seem like a lot, but usually is based on expenses. Cargo trucks are easy to hitch with, but women are often prohibited from riding in trucks by many companies who feel that a nearby female presence would distract the driver.

By Foot

Every traveler should take time to saunter about town and country for a while. Wear a shirt, a wide-brimmed hat, and sunscreen, and bring plenty of water whenever you hike. For specifics, see the books listed under Camping below.

Accommodations

Hotels

Though hotels in Mexico include some of the world's most overpriced, the majority are shockingly affordable. All hotels, ranging from luxury resorts in Cancún to dumps in Monterrey, are controlled by the government's Secretaría de Turismo. SecTur ensures that hotels of similar quality charge similar prices and requires that all hotels display the official tariff sheet. You should always ask to see this sheet if you doubt the quoted price; make sure it is up-to-date. Although hotel prices are regulated, proprietors are not prohibited from charging *less* than the official rate. If the hotel looks like it hasn't seen a customer in several days, a little bargaining may work wonders, especially if you offer to stay a number of days.

Usually located within a block or two of the central plaza, the cheapest hotels rarely provide private bathrooms or other amenities. That may sound bleak to you, but these places are adequate and cost only the equivalent of US$4-8 per person per night. Slightly higher-priced hotels (US$9-15) usually reside in the same district but are much better equipped, including rooms with private bathrooms. Before accepting any room, ask to see it—the proprietor should comply gladly. Always ask if the price, no matter how low it seems, includes any meals. Tourists often are so surprised at low hotel prices that unwittingly they forgo meals for which they have paid.

If the hotels listed in *Let's Go* are full or don't appeal to you, ask cab drivers or vendors in the market for a good recommendation. Also, hotel people in one town are often a good source for hotel leads in the next town on your itinerary.

In small towns, especially in the Yucatán, locals often let travelers use hammock hooks for a small fee. You must, of course, possess a hammock to make use of this opportunity, but if you're in the Yucatán (home of the best hammocks in the world), a hammock is a sterling investment since hammock-hanging is the cheapest way to pass the night.

Hotels in Mexico often lock their doors at night, and small-town establishments may do so surprisingly early. A locked door doesn't necessarily mean "closed for the night," as someone usually is on duty. By arriving early in small towns or calling ahead if you can't avoid arriving late, and by checking with the hotel desk before going out for a late night on the town, you'll help dispel the Mexican myth of the obnoxious foreigner. If, however, you must choose between angering the hotel guard and sharing the gutter with the drunks and the rats, knock to raise the dead.

Reservations are not absolutely necessary (except during Christmas, Semana Santa, and other festivals), but if you're exhausted upon arrival, they make life much easier. You can just about always find a bed somewhere, but without reservations you may waste money and time.

Hostels

Mexican hostels are often run-down, far from town, and no cheaper than local hotels (US$2-10 per night, with meals an additional US$8 per day). The only people who should consider hosteling are younger travelers who want the security and dis-

5,300 hostels in 68 countries on 6 continents.

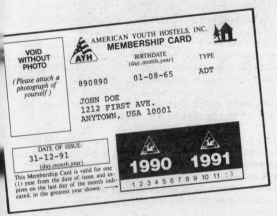

One card.

With the American Youth Hostels Membership Card,

you can stay at 5,300 hostels around the world.

Hostels are great places to make new friends.

And the prices are incredibly low,

just 35¢ to $20 a night for a dorm-style room.

For an application, call 202-783-6161.

Or write: American Youth Hostels,

Dept. 801, P.O. Box 37613, Washington, DC 20013-7613.

INTERNATIONAL YOUTH HOSTEL FEDERATION
American Youth Hostels

cipline of an orderly establishment with regular meals and nighttime supervision. Their ban on alcohol, smoking restrictions, and limited hours (most are open from 7-9am and 5-10pm) also deter many budget travelers.

Most Mexican hostels will give you a bed even if you don't have a hostel card. They may, however, charge you more for it. If you plan to stay in hostels regularly, get an International Youth Hostel Federation (IYHF) card (see Useful Addresses above). For more information, write the Agencia Nacional de Turismo Juvenil, Glorieta del Metro Insurgentes, Local CC-11, Col. Juárez, CP 06600 Mexico D.F. (tel. (5) 525-26-99, 525-21-53, or 525-29-74) for their 100-page *Directorio Tarjeta Plan Joven.*

The two Mexican hostel chains, **Consejo Nacional de Recursos para la Atención de la Juventud (CREA)** and **Servicio Educativo de Turismo de los Estudiantes y la Juventud de México (SETEJ)** have their own hostel cards. CREA is the IYHF-affiliated, government-subsidized hostel chain. SETEJ is internationally subsidized and, in general, the more run-down of the two, though there are exceptions (notably, Acapulco).

For youth hostel brochures, write: Asociación Mexicana de Albergues de la Juventud, AC, Av. Francisco 1 Madero No. 6, Despachos 314 y 315, Delegación Cuauhtémoc, 06000 México D.F. (tel. (5) 512-06-60 or 512-62-69) or Red Nacional de Albergues Turísticos, Oxtopulco N. 40, Col. Oxtopulco Universidad, CP 04310 México D.F.

For information about the **YMCA** and reservations in Mexico, call or write "The Y's Way to Travel," 356 W. 34th St., New York, NY 10001 (tel. (212) 760-5856).

Camping

For the budget travel experience par excellence, try camping in Mexico—it eliminates hotel costs, and if you bring fishing gear to the beach, it can also save you money on food. Campers accustomed to prim and proper campgrounds will be taken aback, however. Mexican national parks often exist only in theory; many are indistinguishable from the surrounding cities. Trails, campgrounds, and rangers are strictly *norteamericano* concepts.

Privately owned trailer parks are relatively common on major highways. (Look for signs with a picture of a trailer, or the words *Parque de Trailer, Campamento,* or *Remolques.*) These places may or may not allow campers to pitch tents. Don't set up camp next to a well-traveled road, or screeching brakes and the shattering glass of your car may shake you from that peaceful slumber; instead, park your car in a remote area and bed down there.

Wherever you alight, you probably won't be alone—at least not for long. Often people are curious: they want to look at you and maybe even invite you over for dinner. You may be the first *gringo* the youngest members of the audience have ever seen. And many poor, rural Mexicans don't understand the appeal of sleeping on the ground under a piece of cloth without showers, bathrooms, or kitchens.

Camping on the beach is popular with those "roughing it" in Mexico. If you run into an occupied piece of beach, just move a mile or two up or down the coast.

Before you set out, equip yourself with camping gear. A sleeping bag can cost anywhere from US$45 for a synthetic model, which keeps you drier in the rainy season, to US$400 for a fine down bag, which will be warmer if you're planning to be up in the mountains anytime but the summer. For increased protection and warmth, consider a foam pad, air mattress, or hybrid thereof (US$10-40). When buying a tent, make sure it has a rain fly and bug netting, and weighs no more than 3.5kg. Synthetic canvas is lighter, less expensive, and more water-resistant than true canvas, although less breathable. Make sure that the edges of the tent floor extend several inches off the ground to prevent water seepage from outside. Backpackers and cyclists may wish to pay a bit more for a small, lightweight, easily-packed tent; some two-person tents weigh less than 1kg. Car travelers, on the other hand, should strongly consider buying a tent larger than they think they'll need. Expect to pay at least US$95 for a basic two-person tent, at least US$120 for a roomy four-person.

At autumn sales, you may only pay half-price for the previous year's models. Eureka is a reliable manufacturer.

Other basics include a battery-operated (not gas) lantern for inside the tent, a small campstove (Coleman makes fine ones for US$25) that runs on butane or white gas, and a plastic groundcloth to shield the tent floor. Do not venture into the back-country without some waterproof matches. Bring plenty of water purification tablets (you might even consider buying a portable water purifier if you're driving), bug spray (or try the green incense cones sold as insect repellent in Mexico), a Swiss army knife, and sunscreen. For longer excursions, a solar shower, toilet paper, and lots of ziplock plastic bags are good ideas.

Some good camping equipment stores are: **Recreational Equipment, Inc. (REI),** Commercial Sales, P.O. Box 88127, Seattle, WA 98138 (tel. (800) 426-4840); **L.L. Bean,** 1 Casco St., Freeport, ME 04033 (tel. (800) 221-4221); **Campmor,** 810 Rte. 17 N, P.O. Box 997-P, Paramus, NJ 07653 (tel. (800) 526-4784); **Cabela's,** 812 13th Ave., Sidney, NE 69160 (tel. (800) 237-4444); and **Eddie Bauer** (tel. (800) 426-6253). All of these stores will send you a free catalogue of mail-order equipment. Use the mail-order firms as guides to the lowest prices, but buy from a local dealer if the price is right in order to get first-hand advice. Eddie Bauer has retail outlets in many cities. In the fall, most camping stores hold massive sales to clear out old merchandise.

The best guide for campers is *The People's Guide to RV Camping in Mexico,* which is an expanded version of the camping section in *The People's Guide to Mexico* (both from John Muir; see Useful Addresses above). The Sierra Club Bookstore, 730 Polk St., San Francisco, CA 94109 (tel. (415) 776-2211) offers *Adventuring Along the Gulf of Mexico* (US$10.95 plus $3 shipping and handling). For adventure narratives or *Mexico's Volcanoes, A Climbing Guide* (US$9.95 incl. shipping), which contains maps, photos, and a bilingual mountaineering glossary, write or call Mountaineers Books, 306 2nd Ave. W, Seattle, WA 98119 (tel. (800) 553-4453). Wilderness Press, 2440 Bancroft Way, Berkeley, CA 94704 (tel. (800) 443-7227 or (415) 843-8080) disseminates general backpacking information and publishes outdoor guides such as the *Baja Adventure Book* (US$17.95 incl. postage) and *Adventure Travel in Latin America* (US$11.95 incl. postage), which includes Mexico.

For information on hostel-affiliated campgrounds, write to Agencia Nacional de Turismo Juvenil (see Hostels above).

Life in Mexico

History

Indigenous Civilizations

Human history began in Mexico 30,000-40,000 years ago, with the migration from Asia of the people a disoriented Columbus would later call "Indians." At first they survived by hunting big game, but as the animal populations thinned out, these nomads turned increasingly to a more sedentary agricultural existence. Their main crop, *maíz,* remains a staple of the Mexican diet.

The Olmecs formed Mexico's first known settled society around 1200 BC, in the lowlands of what are today Veracruz and Tabasco. The three principal Olmec archeological sites are La Venta, San Lorenzo, and Tres Zapotes. Their original inhabitants revered the jaguar, wrote in hieroglyphics, and sculpted giant stone figures with pudgy features and artificially misshapen heads (an upper-class status symbol). San Lorenzo was violently destroyed around 900 BC, and La Venta suffered similarly before another four centuries had elapsed. Ethnically, the Olmecs perished;

many of their cultural achievements, however, were passed on to other Mesoamerican peoples, notably the Maya.

The genius of the Maya stands revealed in the remains of their ancient cities: Palenque, Chichén Itzá, Uxmal, Tulum, and Bonampak. Between 300 and 600 AD the Maya came to equal or surpass contemporary Europe in engineering, mathematics, astronomy, and calendrical calculations; their architecture and artwork are similarly fabulous. Around 900 AD, however, the empire collapsed upon itself suddenly and all Mayan centers were abandoned. Peasant revolts probably brought about this downfall; apparently the Maya working class was so oppressed that finally it picked up and fled to the jungle, leaving the cities in chaos. A Mayan renaissance occurred in the northern Yucatán after 1200 AD, but with a new influence from the west—Teotihuacán culture as elaborated by the Toltecs. Parallel Maya/Toltec legends tell how Kukulcán/Queztalcóatl (The Feathered Serpent), a Toltec warrior, broke away from the Toltec empire and made his way to the Yucatán with his people.

The Toltec empire had dominated most of central Mexico since about 900 AD. Its warlike subjects practiced human sacrifice and decorated their temples with sculptures of jaguars and eagles eating human hearts. The Toltecs originated a myth that the conquistadors used to their advantage: Ce Acatl Topitzin, next in line for the throne, was raised by priests, who renamed him after the god Quetzalcóatl and inspired him to claim his birthright. Having murdered his uncle, Topitzin/Quetzalcóatl took over the empire, banned human sacrifice, and made a vow of chastity with which he could not seem to comply. The fair-haired, bearded ruler was forced into exile but promised to return. When in 1519 a fair-haired, bearded Hernán Cortés landed on the eastern shores of Mexico, the *indígenas* welcomed him with the reverence befitting a returned god.

The cultural hegemony of the Toltecs was such that their decline in the 12th century AD has been compared, in catastrophic significance, to the fall of the Roman Empire. The Aztecs, also known as the Tenochca or the Mexica, came from their mythical homeland in northwestern Mexico into contact with the Toltecs, whom they adopted as role models. Upon the empire's collapse, the Aztecs roamed aimlessly until they spotted an eagle clasping a snake in its beak atop a nopal cactus, a sign which would later embellish Mexico's national flag. They settled beside the cactus on a swampy island in the middle of Lake Texcoco, a site so uninviting that none of their more powerful neighbors bothered to chase them off.

Over the next century, the Aztecs built Mexico's largest *indígena* empire. Ritual human sacrifice fueled their rise to power by creating a steady demand for defeated enemy warriors. In this manner, Aztec religion justified constant warfare even after all threats to the empire had dissipated. The most important deity, Huitzilopochtli (Hummingbird on the Left), was a young warrior who personified the sun. He died red and sated every evening to be reborn pale and weak the next morning, needing to be fed human hearts torn out of sacrificial victims by Aztec priests. In return for this sustenance, Huitzilopochtli gave the Aztecs world domination.

While strong-arming the other peoples of the Anahuac Valley, the Aztecs developed an unprecedented technology tailored to their unique environment. *Chinampas,* or "floating gardens," enabled them efficiently to cultivate the swamp. An ingenious system of canals and causeways joined their island-city of Tenochtitlán to the mainland, and eventually united the entire Valley of Mexico, lake after lake. Tenochtitlán developed into one of the world's largest cities.

By the time of Moctezuma II (1502-20), the Aztec empire consisted of a number of provinces paying tribute according to productivity. Nobility was hereditary but had only provincial authority, and commoners enjoyed almost none of the wealth.

Conquest and Colonization

In 1519, the Spanish arrived on the east coast of Mexico. They disembarked from "temples of the sea" carrying "fire-breathing" weapons, and were lavished with gold and other gifts by the awed local chieftains. Word of their arrival reached Moctezuma II (whose reign had recently been shaken by a series of natural disasters and bad omens), and he could not afford to dispute the rumor that the fair-haired man from the east was in fact the god prophesied by the old Toltec legend. He, too, sent gifts, along with a polite request that Cortés and his men quit Aztec soil. Cortés pushed on toward Tenochtitlán.

As he made his way into the heart of the empire, the conquistador discovered that the Aztecs held Mexico together by sheer force and that the conquered tribes hated their Aztec overlords. With the help of an *indígena* mistress and interpreter, La Malinche, he manipulated this hatred (plus his status as a demigod) to enlist thousands of *indígena* allies. After occupying Tenochtitlán for the first time in November, but having to contend with an unexpected offensive from the Spanish governor of Cuba, his army besieged the city for two years, with heavy casualties on both sides. On Aug. 13, 1521, the Aztec capital fell to Cortés for good. The Spanish proceeded to erect a cathedral atop the rubble of the temple of Huitzilopochtli. Modern-day Mexico City sprawls over the ruins of Tenochtitlán.

The Aztec empire was renamed *Nueva España* (New Spain) and Hernán Cortés became its first governor-general. As conquistadors searched for gold to mine and missionaries searched for *indígenas* to convert, the colony expanded northward. Yet power remained as concentrated as ever. The ruling class of New Spain—a few bureaucrats, landowners, and religious officials—lived comfortably while the *encomienda* system made virtual slaves out of the *indígenas* who worked the estates and mines. Two-thirds of Mexico's native population died from European diseases. Meanwhile, the Catholic Church managed to acquire huge amounts of real estate and capital.

Blatant economic disparity made political tension inevitable. As the 18th century drew to a close, Spain's control over its empire (which had grown into present-day Texas, New Mexico, Arizona, and California) was weakening. Absentee rule had antagonized just about everyone in Mexico. Creoles—those of European blood born in the New World—particularly resented the privileges of the displaced Spanish aristocracy, or *peninsulares*. Approximately three hundred years after Hernán Cortés won the Aztec empire for the monarch of Spain, Mexico began to reconsider its allegiance to the mother country.

Sporadic rebellion took place during the first few years of the 19th century. Modern Mexico celebrates its independence on September 16 to commemorate the 1810 uprising known as *El Grito de Dolores* (The Cry of Dolores), when Padre Miguel Hidalgo y Costilla roused the villagers of Dolores with a cry for racial equality, land reform, and—in a bid for moderate support—an end to the rule of the *gachupines* (derogatory for *peninsulares*) who had deferred to Napoleon and turned their backs on Ferdinand VII. The revolt gained in violence and momentum as it approached Mexico City, but subsided before reaching the capital. Hidalgo ordered a retreat but was captured and shot in July of 1811.

The cause was then taken up by José María Morelos y Pavón, a parish priest committed less to social justice and more to outright independence than Hidalgo had been. Rebellion swept through southern Mexico but lost much of its effectiveness after Morelos was executed in December of 1815. Only scattered bands of insurgents remained.

Mexican independence finally came about by default. Ferdinand had regained the Spanish crown but in 1820 was pressured into approving the Constitution of Cádiz, a document too liberal to suit the rich creoles and *peninsulares* of Mexico. Agustín de Iturbide, the general who had led the Spanish against Hidalgo and Morelos, suddenly joined forces with the guerrillas in hopes of maintaining the precarious status quo. Their combined Army of Three Guarantees declared the fight for independence, union, and Roman Catholicism; shortly thereafter the viceroy of New Spain signed the Treaty of Córdoba. By August 24, 1821, Mexico was officially a nation.

Independence

Iturbide reigned as Emperor Agustín of Mexico for about a year, until discontented military groups persuaded him to abdicate. A constitutional convention proclaimed the Republic of Mexico in 1823. For the next fifty years the landed gentry, the military, and the church pursued contradictory interests in the public domain. Mexico had no experience with self-government, and a capricious economy contributed to the political instability. The national debt grew enormous: if military salaries were not paid in full, officers would simply seize control of the state and negotiate new international loans at ever-higher interest. Mexico was independent but socioeconomic conditions did not reflect the change. The creole elite took over right where the *gachupines* had left off, while most *indígenas* and *mestizos* continued to live in abject poverty.

Political power swung back and forth between conservative and liberal factions for decades after the establishment of the Republic, but the spotlight singled out one man. Of the 50 governments that cluttered the first 30 years of Mexico's independence, 11 were headed by General Antonio López de Santa Anna. Corruption, greed, and a touch of the bizarre marked Santa Anna's tenure. In one episode, the general, whose leg had been amputated several years before, had the limb disinterred, paraded through the streets of the capital, and brought to rest upon a huge shrine in the Santa Fe cemetery.

Santa Anna is best known, however, for having presided over the dismemberment of the new nation. The Mexican-American War began in 1836 as a border dispute between Mexico and the Republic of Texas; but when the U.S. annexed Texas in 1845, Mexico found itself up against a more formidable adversary. Despite the protests of Abraham Lincoln and other pacifistic politicians, President James. K. Polk claimed everything north of the Rio Grande for the U.S. In pursuit of Santa Anna, Generals Zachary Taylor and Winfield Scott closed in on Mexico City from the north and east. The *Niños Héroes* (Boy Heroes) valiantly fought off U.S. troops from Chapultepec Castle, then dashed themselves to their deaths, wrapped in the Mexican flag, when all hope was lost. The war ended in 1847 when the capital fell. Under the terms of the Treaty of Guadalupe-Hidalgo, the U.S. paid US$15 million for Texas, New Mexico, and California. Five years later, Santa Anna sold off Arizona as well. Mexico lost half of its territory and most of its pride.

Reform

The uniquely "Mexican" self-consciousness that had evolved since independence was shaken by the ease of the U.S. victory. If Mexico was to remain autonomous, reforms had to be instituted. Benito Juárez, an expatriate *indígena* lawyer, wrote the Constitution of 1857 in New Orleans. He and his fellow liberals called for a clean break with colonialism and for the separation of Church and State. In 1860, after a short civil war between the liberals (supported by U.S. President James Buchanan) and the ruling conservatives, Juárez became president of Mexico. Ironically, Mexico's first *indígena* president would exhibit little concern for the native population, which was actually worse off than it had been under the paternalism of the Spanish crown.

Three years later, the country was once again in foreign hands. Under the pretext of enforcing debt payment, the French invaded and conquered Mexico, which was an integral part of the "Latin League" envisioned by Napoleon III (and from which the term "Latin America" is derived). Austrian Duke Maximilian von Habsburg became the new emperor of Mexico, but did not prove equal to the job. The Second Empire collapsed when the French withdrew their support in order to counter a Prussian threat across the ocean; Maximilian was executed in 1867 (Manet tried to paint the scene but could not capture its pathos) and Juárez resumed office until a heart attack in 1872.

Mexico began to modernize under Juárez, but it was General Porfirio Díaz who truly ushered industrialism into Mexico. Díaz took power through a military coup in 1876, and his dictatorship (known as the *Porfiriato*) lasted until 1911. Díaz demanded order and progress at the cost of liberty. His administrative method could be simply stated: "pan o palo" (bread or the club). The press was censored, congress was stultified, elections were rigged, and resistance was crushed. The economy stabilized but the country's resources were controlled entirely by a handful of wealthy Mexicans and foreign investors. None of the material prosperity trickled down to workers, peasants, or *indígenas*. Díaz retained control of Mexico for so long possibly because his reign brought peace and progress (of a sort) to a country which had known little of either since independence. Admittedly, Díaz did not abolish the reforms instituted by Juárez. By the early 1900s, however, a majority of Mexicans opposed the oppressive *Porfiriato*.

Revolution

Díaz's announcement in 1908 that he would not run for office in the next "election" touched off a frenzy of political activity as the *anti-reeleccionistas* campaigned for their candidate, Francisco Madero, from one of the 10 richest families in Mexico. A sham election returned Díaz to the presidency, and in June of 1910, Madero was arrested. Although he escaped in October, the imprisonment had transformed him into a martyr, and opposition to the *Porfiriato* coalesced around him. From San Antonio, Madero declared November 20 to be the day that Mexicans would rise in arms. The Revolution lasted the better part of the next decade. Its immediate object was to replace Díaz as president, but the movement broadened into an economic and social struggle to determine the character of modern Mexico.

Díaz did not fare well over the next year. He resigned in 1911 and Madero was elected president, but serious disagreement among the notorious leaders of the Revolution—Emiliano Zapata, Pancho Villa, and Venustiano Carranza—surfaced as Madero pursued a moderate course. Rebellions all over the political spectrum plagued Madero's administration up until the day he was murdered. Victoriano Huerta, one of his own generals, replaced Madero.

The years that followed were characterized by political chaos and infighting among former Revolutionary allies. When the dust cleared, the moderate Carranza, who had been endorsed by the U.S., governed Mexico under a somewhat radical constitution that he was disinclined to enforce. This Constitution of 1917 guaranteed free secular education, restored land to peasants, limited property accumulation, instituted a 48-hour work week and a minimum wage, and established equal rights for women and workers—in writing.

One out of every eight Mexicans was killed during the Revolution and very few were left unaffected by the violence. Zapata and many other Mexicans were dissatisfied with the sluggish progress of reform under Carranza and continued to fight, but by 1920 they had all been bought off or murdered. A brief series of dictators carried Mexico to new heights of repression.

Post-Revolutionary Mexico

Champions of radical reform came into power once again when leftist Lázaro Cárdenas was elected president in 1934. His government seized 49 million acres of land from private owners, distributed it among *ejidos* (communal cooperative farms), and strengthened the labor movement. Cárdenas also nationalized the oil companies that had been controlled by foreign countries since the *Porfiriato*, in a crucial step toward economic independence.

The modern feminist movement in Mexico took off during Cárdenas's administration. The United Front for Women's Rights, organized in 1935, had 50,000 members by 1940. Mexican women finally won the right to vote in 1955. But the administrations following that of Cárdenas were conservative and business-oriented. The economy boomed, but most urban and rural workers still suffered from low wages and underemployment. Wary of uprisings, the government began to buy off both workers and landowners with subsidies on everything from tortillas to gasoline. As population growth began to accelerate, the economy weakened and Mexico had to turn to foreign nations for loans.

In the early 1960s, President Adolfo López Mateos further damaged the budget by spending billions of pesos setting up various social welfare programs and redistributing land. Mexico's one-party system received increasing criticism, but the Institutional Revolutionary Party (PRI) retained tight control over Mexican politics. Student unrest and worker dissatisfaction in these years culminated in 1968 at Mexico City's Tlatelolco Plaza, where police killed an estimated 300 to 400 peaceful demonstrators just 10 days before the Olympic Games were to open. Remarkably the Games *did* open, and on time, as the PRI managed to suppress all negative publicity.

Protest subsided in the following years, but other problems have marred the more recent administrations of Luis Echevarría and José López Portillo, among them large budget deficits, high unemployment, burgeoning population, lagging agricultural production, high inflation, rapid devaluation of the peso, and persistent corruption. Enormous economic disparity has persisted, despite the influx of petrodollars from Mexico's growing oil exports.

To the surprise of no one, PRI candidate Miguel de la Madrid Hurtado won the 1982 presidential elections with more than 75% of the vote. The economy rebounded when he first assumed office, but, under pressure from the International Monetary Fund, the administration initiated an austerity program to curtail the country's 150% inflation and US$104 billion foreign debt. Between January and October of 1988, the rate of inflation fell from 15% to 1%, but the economy's growth rate remained at zero during de la Madrid's six-year term; his successor has had to mount the tightwire between severe recession and a possible repeat performance of skyrocketing inflation.

Current Politics

"The era of one-party rule in Mexico is over," declared PRI presidential candidate Carlos Salinas de Gortari during the tense week following the 1988 presidential elections. Salinas officially (and conveniently) received 50.4% of the vote when the final results were announced nearly a week after the election, but many interpreted his remarks and the election itself as a fresh start for Mexican politics.

From 1929 to 1988, Mexico's ruling party did not lose a single presidential, senatorial, or gubernatorial race. In the few local elections that it did lose, the PRI often installed its own candidates anyway. Through a combination of patronage, fraud, and ineffectual opposition, the party ran Mexico like a political machine. But in the 1982 election, the murmurs of dissent were heard, and the right-of-center National Action Party (PAN) won 14% of the vote, most of it in the northern states. In 1983, the PRI experimented with fraud-free elections, and the PAN picked up three mayorships in the state of Chihuahua alone. Since then, a PAN governor has been elected in Baja California Norte, but the party's presidential candidate, Manuel Clouthier, died in a car crash on his way to the celebration.

Salinas assumed the presidency on December 1, 1988, and had to confront high unemployment, a US$105 billion foreign debt, and a skeptical nation. Dependent on high oil prices for its relative prosperity in the 1970s, Mexico has been hard hit by the worldwide oil glut. Salinas instituted wage and price controls to keep inflation below 20%, then boosted his popularity with several prominent arrests—a union boss, a fraudulent businessman, and a drug trafficker. In October of 1989, PRI and PAN voted together for the first time in favor of electoral reform. In January of 1990, the government launched an investigation into political murders in Michoacán and Guerrero; the center-left Party of the Democratic Revolution (PRD) claims that 52 of its activists have been killed since the 1988 election, which its candidate, Cuauhtémoc Cárdenas (son of former president Lázaro Cárdenas), nearly won. And on February 4, 1990, representatives of the Mexican government and its 450 foreign commercial creditors signed a debt reduction agreement, the first application of the "Brady Plan" designed to ease the U.S. banking crisis and deflect outlandish interest payments. The IMF and World Bank are grudgingly participating. Currently, Mexico and the U.S. are committed to free trade talks which could eventually result in a North American common market that would outstrip the EEC by over a trillion dollars.

Despite these improvements, international dilemmas confront Mexico from every direction. To the south, the Guatemalan anti-guerrilla campaign has chased thousands of refugees into Mexico. In 1984, after the number had grown to 46,000, the Mexican government consolidated its border camps into a big settlement in the Valley of Edzná, in what many claim was a brutal relocation. Mexico's border to the north causes escalating tension over undocumented immigration and the illegal drug trade.

Whether or not Salinas has the answers to Mexico's problems, he is at least paying lip-service to more competitive democracy, and that alone means that Mexican politics will continue to move into new and uncharted territory.

The Arts

Literature

The literary tradition in Mexico begins with the *indígenas,* but little of their literature escaped the fervor of early Spanish missionaries' bonfires. The oral tradition has bequeathed upon the modern student many examples of Aztec poetry, however, which sound surprisingly contemporary and exhibit considerable artistic self-consciousness. Moreover, much colonial poetry is laced with Nahuatl expressions and motifs. Missionary theater, performed in indigenous languages, also perpetuated pre-Hispanic art forms, but few scripts survive.

Colonial Mexico produced more poetry than prose, but one remarkable work of non-fiction is the *Verdadera historia de la conquista de Nueva España* (Discovery and Conquest of Mexico) by Bernal Diaz de Castillo, a soldier under Cortés who took pride in the American experience without glorifying it. Poetry's dominance of the literary scene was summed in one 16th-century dramatist's observation that there were "more poets than dung" in New Spain. Most of them merely imitated the latest European styles. One notable exception came on the scene in the 17th century: **Sor Juana Inés de la Cruz,** an early feminist who became a nun in order to make time for intellectual pursuits, wrote such poems as "Hombres Necios" (Injudicious Men) and "Primero Sueño" (First Dream), which tests the limits of reason. A translation of her poetry is available from Harvard University Press.

During the 18th century, the Inquisition vied with the French Enlightenment to distract Mexican writers from anything that could be described as innovative. In 1816, **José Fernandez de Lizardi,** a prominent Mexican journalist, wrote the first Latin American novel: *El Periquillo Sarmiento* (The Itching Parrot). His ideological, moralizing angle on fiction has been very influential. With the Spanish-American Modernists of the later 19th century, poetry reached an affective level it had not even approached since Sor Juana. At the same time, **Manuel Gutiérrez Nájera** composed the poem "De Blanco" (On Whiteness), linguistic representation at its most distilled and self-contained.

As discontent spread in the early 20th century, the group called **Anteneo de la Juventud** dissolved genres in the name of sociopolitical revolution. For the most part, however, intellectuals kept their distance from the Revolutionary arena. After the fact, many witnesses took up their pens. **Mariano Azuela's** *Los de Abajo* (The Underdogs) conveys extreme disillusionment in a rural dialect which, perhaps unwittingly, adopts the discontinuous rhythm of the Revolution itself. Other novels of this period include *El Águila y la Serpiente* (The Eagle and the Serpent) by **Martín Luis Guzmán** and *El Resplandor* (Sunburst) by **Mauricio Magdaleno. Juan Rulfo's** *Pedro Páramo,* set in rural Jalisco, obscures cause and effect in a haze of black humor over a forgotten, hellish country town.

Mexico's best-known author, **Carlos Fuentes,** published his first novel in 1958. *La Región Más Transparente* (Where the Air is Clear) is one of the greatest products of the 1960s "boom" generation inspired by **Octavio Paz.** While Paz exhibits pronounced metaliterary tendencies in such works as *El Laberinto de la Soledad* (The Labyrinth of Solitude), which have earned him the distrust of many Mexicans, Fuentes delves into myth and seems to strike a deeper chord in his native land. Since the "boom," Mexican literature has become even more pluralistic and serves an ever-growing pool of readers. Western prototypes retain their fascination for writers and readers alike, as is evidenced by the wildly popular work of **Gustavo Sainz** and **José Agustin,** the instigators of *literatura de la onda* ("hip" literature); on the other hand, **Luis Spota,** one of Mexico's most widely read authors, restricts himself to Mexican themes and faces, as a result, international anonymity.

Art and Architecture

Early *indígena* art, like so much early and late Western art, was subservient to religion. The colonial period favored stilted European imitation, and the Revolution instilled a sense of nationalism and popularized native styles, now informed by modern themes.

Fortunately, this revival is well-supplied with *indígena* prototypes. The Olmecs, predecessors of the Maya, carved altars and monumental heads out of stone. In western Mexico, the Tarascan people embellished funereal accessories with motifs from daily life. Mayan sculptors excelled at well-proportioned nudes, and the Aztecs imbued enormous figures with both strength and grace.

Much of Mexico's pictorial tradition, however, is attached to buildings. Mayan architecture was richly ornamented in relief, but the Aztecs were the greatest in this field. The monuments and pyramids at **Teotihuacán** put Egypt's stolid emphasis on engineering to shame. Architecture became the province of the Church once the Spaniards arrived, and despite some native flourishes on the portals and altars of their places of worship, the Old-World built environment was essentially transplanted onto Mexican soil. Ever since, Mexican architecture has struggled to keep up with European styles, and thus has neglected to forge its own character. The closest thing to a Mexican architectural movement, though technically imported from Spain, was the **Churrigueresque**—Baroque carried to an extreme. This heritage comes of age in **Luis Barragán's** designs, which incorporate reflecting pools, ensconced gardens, and gratuitous walls in a clash of color (see Satellite City outside the capital).

During the *Porfiriato,* the **National Academy of San Carlos,** which had been established in 1785, dominated the artistic community. Díaz himself preferred the Western approach—to which the exterior of the Palacio de Bellas Artes in Mexico City attests—but most Mexican artists did not. They rejected the Spanish influence of the 17th and 18th centuries in their down-to-earth portrayals of *indígena* life. Among these artists was **Dr. Atl (Gerardo Murillo),** whose pseudonym is the Nahuatl word for "water."

As the Revolution reduced their land to shambles, Mexican painters developed an unapologetic national style. This success was made possible by José Vasconcelos's Ministry of Education program, which commissioned murals for public buildings and sent artists into the countryside to teach and participate in rural life. The "social realism" practiced by these painters took such a strong hold that abstraction has not infiltrated Mexico with the ease that one might have expected, given the compatible *indígena* tradition and the country's almost feverish tendency to follow foreign example. While **Carlos Mérida,** who came to Mexico from Guatemala during the Revolution, has appropriated the abstract language of pre-Columbian art to some acclaim, **Rufino Tamayo,** contemporary with the social realists, had to leave the country for his paintings inspired by Oaxaca's fruits and animals to be taken seriously. Now acknowledged as one of Mexico's "Big Four," Tamayo lends his name to a museum which, managed by the national television syndicate, has mounted blockbuster exhibitions of Picasso, Matisse, and Hockney in Mexico City.

Among the artists to have worked at the National Preparatory School in the formative years of the Revolution, **Diego Rivera** has achieved the most renown. His murals at the Detroit Institute of Arts and the Rockefeller Center in New York City exposed his political themes to a wide audience and embroiled him in international controversy. Rivera championed land reform and communism; at the same time, his sexual appetite was such that rich young women from certain parts of the southern U.S. came to him as a matter of course on the way to respectable husbands. The two other prominent muralists of the 1920s and 1930s, **David Alfaro Siqueiros** and **José Clemente Orozco,** also had disciples outside Mexico. The formally innovative Siqueiros—who could not resist a curved surface—was arrested in 1960 for anti-government activism. Orozco focused on the violence and brutality of the Revolution, but was less explicitly political than his colleagues. In his work, the mythic dimension of human history and existence prevails. "Good murals are really painted bibles," he said, "and the people need them as much as written bibles."

The therapeutic role of art receives its most eloquent testimony, however, in the life and work of **Frida Kahlo** (1907-54). After a traumatic bus accident at the age of 18, Kahlo painted her plaster corsets, married Diego Rivera, and was welcomed into the Surrealist fold of the 1930s. Her imagery reflects a disturbing subjective reality which cannot be dismissed as pure fantasy: red smudges on the frame of *A Few Small Nips* project the bed-ridden, writhing body from the canvas out into the world. Her self-portraits are icons of pain. The Museo Frida Kahlo is in Coyoacán, her childhood home.

Film

Mexican filmmaking began in 1917 and reached its peak in the 1940s. Ex-actor **Emilio Fernández** won the *Palme D'Or* at the 1943 Cannes Film Festival for his *Maria Candelaria* and two years later directed *La Perla,* an adaptation of John Steinbeck's novel. Together with legendary cinematographer **Gabriel Figueroa,** who had studied in Hollywood, Fernández forged the classic image of Mexico: polychrome skies, ornate architecture, and interiors geometricized by beams of light. Thereafter, the Mexican film industry went into decline. Fernández lost his directorial touch and reverted to acting. Other poorly financed filmmakers suffered in competition with the U.S. and fell back on low-budget, pop formulas. Films in this idiom, produced mostly between 1950 and 1970, were known as *churros* (after a cheap, fast-fried dough with no nutritional value). Though generally low in artistic merit, *churros* were extremely popular with the public. The classic work of this genre is a trilogy: *Nosotros los Pobres* (We the Poor), *Ustedes los Ricos* (You the Rich), and *Pepe el Toro* (Pepe the Bull), all starring Pedro Infante and all vehicles for his singing voice. Other *churro* stars include Jorge Negrete and Javier Solís.

In 1930, **Sergei Mikhailovich Eisenstein** came to Mexico at the encouragement of Diego Rivera, intending to film an ambitious project called ¡*Que Viva Mexico!* Instead, he was arrested and held until Albert Einstein, Charlie Chaplin, and 12 U.S. senators petitioned the Mexican government on his behalf. Production was never completed, partly because Upton Sinclair, turned off by rumors of Eisenstein's lurid lifestyle, withdrew his financial support; the negative was later damaged, and Eisenstein was inconsolable.

In 1946, after a 15-year hiatus from directing, Surrealist **Luis Buñuel** went to Mexico to make films for the commercial market. Entertaining enough for the masses, Buñuel's films nevertheless made few artistic compromises and certainly did nothing to dispel the anti-clericism for which he is infamous. Despite a tight budget and shooting schedule, *Los Olvidados* (The Young and the Damned) won the *Grand Prix* at Cannes in 1951. Gabriel Figueroa pared down his approach for Buñuel, but the excellent photography ultimately aestheticized the slum conditions that the film set out to denounce. The first outright political films to be made in Mexico were the collective *L'Agression/La Riposte* and *El Grito,* directed by Leobardo Lopez. For the most part, the Mexican government has tolerated experimental film for the sake of prestige, but after the student unrest of 1968, the University of Mexico's annual festival was banned.

Since then, calls for reform have produced results—such as **Rubén Gámas's** *La Formula Secreta* and **Alberto Isaac's** *En Este Pueblo No Hay Ladrones*—but audiences are not necessarily satisfied with them. In 1976, plagued by runaway inflation and foreign debt, the government denationalized the film industry and private filmmakers resorted to commercially successful melodramas. The most prominent of these films are the *pulquerías* (after *pulque*, the fermented cactus juice drunk by poor Mexicans), which test the limits of poor acting, careless production, and female nudity. Gregory Nava's hallucinogenic *El Norte,* which cast Mexican actors as Guatemalan refugees in Los Angeles, enjoyed considerable critical success in 1983, although Pauline Kael had her reservations.

Music

Experts know that music played an important role in pre-Conquest *indígena* daily life, but little more. The most popular instruments were shell and clay horns, reed and wood flutes with up to four chambers, gourd rattles, and the drums *huehuetl* and *teponaztli,* named after Aztec deities. Dancing was a central religious ritual. High-pitched, thin voices were cultivated for their associations with metallic gold and the roar of the jaguar.

The Spanish introduced their own instruments, lyrics, and rhythms to Mexico. Music contributed to the conversion of the native population to Christianity, and thus contributed materially to the Conquest. The arrival of African slaves and contact with the Caribbean added another musical strain, especially in the Gulf region. In this fertile atmosphere, percussion and syncopation formed the basis for *marimba* music.

Just as music had been used to subdue them, Mexicans used music to regain their autonomy. The *jarabe,* an exhibition dance alluding to the mating practices of hen and cock, was frequently banned during Mexico's last years as a colony and rallied would-be dancers behind the cause. The *corrido,* a narrative ballad, played a similar role during the Revolution, when insurgents sang news to each other to boost morale.

During the 20th century, concert music has taken on nationalistic themes, particularly in Carlos Chavez's *Sinfonía India* (1936). The hat dance and *mariachi* music, both from Guadalajara, have swept across the country. The *rancheros*—songs about horses, love, jealousy, and drinking, typical of the cattle ranching regions of northern Mexico and often of high lyrical quality—are regarded as Mexico's "national" musical expression.

Apart from José Cuervo and the sombrero, the most persistent emblems of Mexico are the *mariachis,* who started out as ragtag groups of farmers singing at country gatherings. By the 1920s, many were touring Mexico, and President Lázaro Cárdenas adopted them as a campaign symbol. As radio became a greater social force in Mexico, *mariachi* music adapted to the times. Today, emotional singing and trumpet flourishes resound from coast to coast.

Menudo lives.

Language

Even if you speak no Spanish, a few basics will help you along. Any attempts at Spanish are appreciated and encouraged, and you'll find that many people in larger cities understand some English. You are likely to hear *indígena* languages as well as Spanish in Oaxaca, Chiapas, and the Yucatán.

Learn the numbers if only to bargain and to reassure yourself that you're on the right bus. Learn the vocabulary of courtesy as well; you'll be treated more kindly if you can be polite to those around you. *Por favor* is "please"; *gracias* is "thank you." *Con permiso* ("Excuse me") is an important phrase, and is used more frequently than its English counterpart, whether on a crowded bus or to excuse yourself from a room or from anyone's company. *Mucho gusto* ("Pleased to meet you") is the proper response to an introduction. Answer the phone with *¿Bueno? ¿Qué pasó?* means "What's up?" and *De nada* means "You're welcome" (literally "It's nothing").

To indicate that you don't understand, say *No entiendo.* To ask that something be spoken more slowly, say *Más lento, por favor. ¿Mande?* means "What?"

No offense is meant if you are called a "*gringo/a.*" You may offend Mexicans, however, if you call yourself an *americano/a*; as part of the Americas, Mexico resents U.S. monopolization of the term. Instead, refer to yourself as a *norteamericano/a*, or, if you can say it, an *estadounidense* or *estadunidense. Güero/a* (light-skinned person), and *moreno/a*, (dark-skinned person), are common forms of address among strangers in the streets. Use *indígena*—never *indio*—to refer to an indigenous person.

Calle means street. Streets are often labeled *norte, sur, oriente,* or *poniente* (north, south, east, west), abbreviated Nte., Sur, Ote., and Pte. The *Zócalo* is the central plaza or park in town. The word *zócalo* is not used all over Mexico; many of the northern towns prefer *plaza* or *el centro.*

Derecha is "right," *izquierda* "left," and *derecho* "straight." *Junto a* or *al lado de* means "next to"; *cerca de* "near"; and *lejos de* "far from." To travel, you may have to take a *camión* (bus) or *autobus,* or perhaps a *combi* (VW van) or *colectivo* (van or collective taxi). Whatever you do, don't *coger* (catch) or *montar* (mount) a bus, because those verbs have sexual connotations; instead, *tomar* (take) it.

In a hotel, ask for *un cuarto con una cama* (a room with 1 bed) or *con dos camas* (with 2 beds). When shopping, *¿Cuánto cuesta?* or *¿Cuánto es?* or simply *¿Cuánto?* means "How much?" To get the bill in a restaurant, ask for *La cuenta, por favor.* Never ask a waiter "*¿Tienes huevos*" (literally "Do you have eggs?" but idiomatically "Do you have testicles?"). Instead, when you want to ask about the availability of eggs, say "*¿Hay huevos?*"

Food and Drink

Mexican cuisine is the product of an *indígena* heritage enriched by Spanish and, to a lesser degree, French practices. The enormous variety of Mexican dishes is due in part to the wide range of herbs and spices native to Mexico—including over 60 types of chile peppers. Mexican chiles, the heart of *indígena* cookery, range in taste from *dulce* (sweet) to *picantísimo* (firey). Contrary to stereotype, not all Mexican food is hot. Often *salsas picantes* (hot sauces) are served on the side, so whether to scorch your palate or not is your decision. To protect your taste buds against the chile peppers, try sprinkling a bit of salt on your tongue.

Corn is the staple of Mexican existence, and it appears most frequently in tortilla form. An Aztec creation, the tortilla is a soft, thin patty, served at nearly every meal. Wrap anything on your plate—meat, cheese, beans—in a tortilla to make a burrito. Enchiladas are tortillas dipped in sauce, filled, and fried. Tostadas are fried tortillas with vegetables, meat, and cheese. Tamales, made out of a ground-corn dough, are fried in corn husks and have the consistency of thick dumplings. Beans will appear on your table almost as often as tortillas. *Frijoles refritos* (refried beans) are a popular variety.

Avoid overdosing on tacos and try some other Mexican dishes. Meat in Mexico is cut, aged, and prepared differently than in the U.S and many other countries. Mexicans enjoy pork and consume every inch of the pig. Pork dishes include *chuletas* (pork chops), *carnitas* (bits of pig meat), and *chicharrones* (fried pig skins). *Barbacoa* is lamb that has been covered with maguey leaves and buried beneath a fire. *Pollo* (chicken) is also common; don't miss out on *pollo con mole. Mole,* one of Mexico's most interesting culinary creations, is a sauce combining over 30 ingredients, including chiles and chocolate (which, along with vanilla, was introduced to the rest of the world by Mexico). Over 20 kinds of *mole* exist; Oaxaca has seven famous varieties, and Puebla's *mole* (*mole poblana*) is internationally known.

While in Veracruz, try *huachinango a la veracruzana* (red snapper in a sauce of tomato, chile, olive, onion, and capers). *Caldo largo* is a soup of fish and shellfish; *ceviche* is fish marinated in lemon. Turtle meat is widely available in resorts along the coast, but resist the temptation: sea turtles are an endangered species, partly because Mexican fishing people continue to kill them for tourist dollars.

Be on the lookout for Mexico's exotic dishes. If eating insects doesn't bug you, try *chapulines,* grasshoppers or crickets eaten on *taquitos* with guacamole; or *escamoles,* fried ants' eggs, which bestow longevity. And Maguey worms, more frequently found at the bottom of bottles of top-quality mezcal, are also fried and served on *taquitos.*

Mexicans wait until between 2 and 4pm for the *comida,* the largest meal of the day, often an elaborate banquet of several courses. *Comida corrida,* served at most Mexican restaurants, is Mexico's blue-plate special. *Cena* (dinner) is a light meal served after 8pm.

At restaurants, always find out the price of a meal before you order. Many of the smaller eateries don't have a list of prices, and might overcharge if you do not ask in advance. Tips run the same as in the U.S., 15% or so. If you plan to eat in a place more than once, a tip instantly puts you on the preferred customer list, especially in a small or out-of-the-way establishment.

Food at markets is usually cheaper than in restaurants. Look for a relatively clean *fonda* (stand or cart), and pick up a mango for lunch. Eating mangos is a juicy, messy process. To avoid getting the fruit dirty as you eat it, try this method. Put the fruit down so that as you stand over it, you see its paisley body. Slice through the mango along its longest equator, parallel to the surface on which it lies. Peel the skin off the top half and eat the meat (leaving the pit exposed). Then turn the mango over, peel the skin from the other half, and eat the meat from that side. Fruits are often washed or irrigated with unpurified water, so peel them before you eat. Salads and other frightening foods should be liberally sprinkled with lime juice to kill any bacteria waiting to visit the unsuspecting stomach. Watch out for meat cooked in rancid oil or recooked several times (see Health above).

Strict vegetarians and those keeping kosher may have difficulty outside of Guadalajara and Mexico City. Many Mexican foods, including tamales, some tortillas, and many bean dishes, contain lard.

You can sample a tremendous variety of *aguas frescas* (fruit drinks) in Mexico. Beware of *aguas* made with unpurified water. *Licuados* (made with fruit and milk) are less likely to be contaminated. *Sidral,* a pasteurized, bottled apple drink, somewhat like apple cider, is a healthy alternative to sodas. Try the Aztec drink *atole,* a mixture of corn meal, water, and sugar. *Mezcal* is distilled from the *maguey* plant: tequila is a famous *mezcal* from Tequila, Jalisco. These *aguardientes* ("burning waters," the generic name for "spirits") are the best known of the many drinks obtained from the *agave* family of plants. Regional brands of Mexican beer are the best. Nationally distributed beers include Tres Equis (dark), Dos Equis (light), Carta Blanca, Superior, and Pacífico. Among sweet drinks, Kahlua, the coffee liqueur, conveniently meets the recommended daily allowance for both caffeine and alcohol. If you get a chance to sample *pulque,* the fermented juice of the *maguey,* don't hesitate—it was the sacred drink of the Aztec nobility, and strict laws severely restricted its consumption by others. But don't expect to like it, either. Find some through a friend, because the *pulque* sold at stands and *pulquerías* is often diluted with tainted water.

Whatever you drink, remember: some Mexicans strongly disapprove of public drunkeness.

Bargaining

Although it may intimidate the beginner, bargaining is something you'll get the hang of quickly, even if you speak little Spanish. You'll bargain better if there's some semblance of an actor in you, since the whole encounter revolves around assured posturing. The buyer feigns only mild interest in the sandals of her dreams, while the seller insists he would go this low for no one else.

Even if you speak no Spanish, memorize the numbers. Do not attempt to bargain in restaurants, government or hotel shops, or any store with a "Precios fijos" (fixed prices) sign. Keep in mind that when you buy crafts from any source other than the artisan or a *cooperativa* (cooperative), a middleman is probably absorbing most of the profit. You can bargain in markets and for taxi fares in many areas where the rates aren't set (always ask before getting into the cab). Always start off with a greeting as you affect a mild interest in the object in question, and punctuate the dialogue with plenty of *por favors*. Mexicans are polite to a fault, and it helps to play along. Let the merchant make the first offer and then cut this by one-half to one-third for your counter-offer. As a final resort to bring the price down yet another notch, start to move on. Be prepared to accept other merchandise instead of a lower price. Never offer anything you are unwilling to pay—you are expected to buy the item if the merchant accepts your price. Always determine the price before you open, taste, or try on anything.

Weights and Measures

> 1 kilogram (kg) = 2.2 pounds
> 1 meter (m) = 1.09 yards
> 1 kilometer (km) = 5/8 miles
> 1 liter (l) = 1.76 pints

MEXICO CITY

"Mexico City" is the world's largest misnomer: 600 square miles of urban settlement overlooking the Valley of Mexico make up far more than one city. Between the impoverished neighborhoods on the northern outskirts of town, the ultramodern southern suburbs of Coyoacán and San Angel, aspects of many cities show through the omnipresent smog. The Aztecs' most powerful gods, Tlaloc and Huitzilopochtli, still leap forth from the Templo Mayor, reminding the Mexican people of their ancient heritage; directly next door, the Catedral Metropolitana stands as a grand monument to the vast power that the Roman Catholic Church wielded over the *indígenas* during colonial days. "Mexico City" is the sleek set of bars and boutiques that rise above the city in the Torre Latinoamericana. It can also be the shantytowns, bereft of public support and as large as other cities in the Republic, on the distant horizon. All these "cities" occupy the same dry lake beds of the valley.

Mexicans call this spineless conglomeration **"el D.F.,"** short for **Distrito Federal** (Federal District), or simply "Mexico." It is the largest population center in the world; more than 18 million people in over 220 *colonias* (neighborhoods) call the city home. In its various incarnations, Mexico City has always been the heart of the rugged lands that surround it, a powerful magnet to which people, wealth, and the treasures of the entire nation become inexorably attached. The etymology of the word "Mexico" seemingly prefigured this fate: a compound of the Nahuatl words *meztli* (moon), *xictli* (navel), and *co* (place), it may be translated as "in the navel of the moon," or "in mid-moon," suggesting both centrality and cosmic size.

Virtually the entire federal bureaucracy inhabits the **Distrito Federal;** even the Ministry of the Navy has its main offices in the D.F. (2240m above sea level). The principal national collections of art, ethnography, and archeology are also found here. With few peers worldwide, the magnificent **Museo Nacional de Antropología** is reason enough in itself for a visit to the city. The Aztec **Templo Mayor,** albeit prostrated at the feet of the majestic **Catedral Metropolitana,** still inspires awe. Spectacular murals by Rivera, Orozco, Siqueiros, and Tamayo illuminate other locales in Mexico City.

For all its appalling problems, the megalopolis is full of vitality, diversity, and charm. At times, one single aspect of the various "cities" that constitute Mexico momentarily stands isolated from the obfuscating bustle around it. The resulting image can be one of gloom, awe, or beauty. The possibilities are endless: Mexico City promises nothing less.

Orientation

Getting There

Don't worry—all roads really do lead to Mexico City. Transportation depots include the Benito Juárez International Airport, four main bus stations, a train station, and a network of freeways. Airports and stations in Mexico City nearly always have tourist information booths equipped with free or cheap maps and some sort of referral service to lead you into the *centro*. If you plan on renting a car in Mexico, Sanborn's department store can provide reliable auto insurance.

By Air

Flying into Mexico City from abroad entails the usual customs and immigration procedures. Tourist cards will be distributed on the plane and stamped at the airport.

The **Benito Juárez International Airport** lies 6½km east of the Zócalo. Blvd. Capitán Juan Sarabío heads northeast to the airport from Blvd. Puerto Aéreo, one

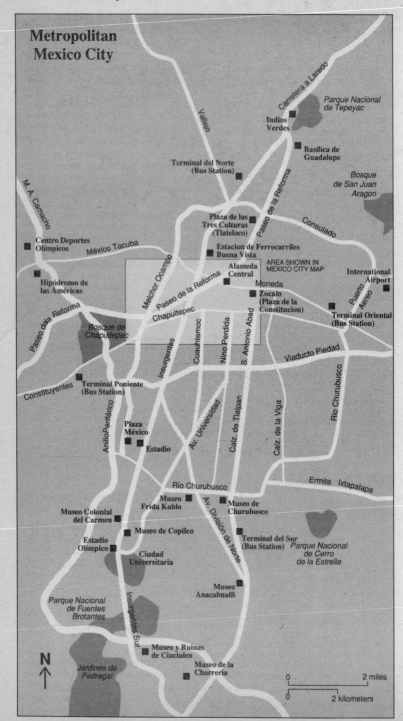

of the major roads circling the city. Airport facilities include: the **Información Turística de la Ciudad de México** (Salas A and E, open daily 9am-9pm), which offers a free guidebook entitled *Mexico City in Your Hands—Tourist Directory* and a useful city map; a booth operated by the Instituto Nacional de Antropología e Historia, which distributes information about the archeological sites and museums throughout the country (Sala A, open daily 9am-7pm); and a map store (Sala C). The airport also has a pharmacy (open daily 6am-10pm), a 24-hr. bank (Sala D), *casas de cambio* (open daily 9am-7pm), and car rental booths (see Getting Around below).

Transportation into the city is uncomplicated. The "venta de boletos" desks in Sala A or E will sell you, at an authorized rate, a ticket presentable to any taxi labeled "transporte terrestre" waiting outside. Do not pay cash for a ride from the airport, unless you're willing to pay heavily for the convenience. You can't count on individuals with their own private cars to take you where you want to go; they are not affiliated with the airport.

The Metro subway station, Terminal Aérea (Line 5), located at the junction of Capitán Juan Sarabío and Blvd. Puerto Aéreo, is only a five-minute walk from Sala A. The subway may seem cheap (300 pesos) and convenient, but any luggage larger than a small suitcase may be impossible to maneuver through the swarming crowds in the station. On the train itself, guarding your bags is a monumental task during rush hour, and fellow passengers will be none too happy about the space the luggage takes up. If returning to the airport by Metro, remember that the airport stop is Terminal Aerea, *not* Aeropuerto.

Travelers driving to *el centro* should take Blvd. Puerto Aéreo north to Eje 2 Nte. (see Circuito Interior and Ejes Viales under Getting Around below), then Eje 2 Nte. west to Paseo de la Reforma. A left turn here leads southwest to Juárez or, farther down, to Insurgentes.

Benito Juárez International Airport: Tel. 571-36-00, for information only.

Domestic Flights: Flight schedules and prices change frequently. Prices are roughly the same from airline to airline. **Mexicana,** Xola 535 (tel. 660-44-44 for reservations, 571-88-88 for information), 4 blocks south of Etiopía Metro station. To: Acapulco (5 per day, 162,369 pesos); Cancún (5 per day, 432,929 pesos); Cozumel (at 6 and 7:40am, 432,929 pesos); Guadalajara (10 per day, 180,079 pesos); Zihuatanejo (4 per day, 168,671 pesos); Mazatlán (4 per day, 300,231 pesos); Mérida (4 per day, 344,667 pesos); Puerto Escondido (at 2:20pm); Monterrey (5 per day, 3 per day Sat., 256,703 pesos); Puerto Vallarta (5 per day, 233,094 pesos); Tijuana (at 6:40am and 7pm, 474,034 pesos); Veracruz (at 6:10am, 11:10am, and 6:20pm, 161,736 pesos); Villahermosa (Wed.-Fri. at 6:35am and 3:05 pm, Sat.-Tues. at 9:25pm, 242,294 pesos); Zacatecas (Mon., Wed., and Fri. at 7pm, Sun., Tues., Thurs., and Sat. at 6am); Havana (Sat. at 3:10pm, Sun. at 7am, Tues. at 3:35pm); and Guatemala City (at 7 and 7:25am). **Aeroméxico,** Paseo de la Reforma 445 (tel. 207-82-33 for reservations, 762-40-22 for information). To: Acapulco (5 per day); Cancún (at 7:30am, 9:35 am, and noon); Guadalajara (6 per day); Ixtapa-Zihuatanejo (at 6:40am and 1:15pm); Mérida (at 9:35am, 6:30pm, and 8:20pm); Matamoros (at 2:30 and 3pm); Villahermosa (at 8:20pm); Oaxaca (at 8:15am and 2:50pm); Aguascalientes (at 9:15am); Monterrey (5 per day); Mazatlán (at 7:45, 8:10, and 9:40am); and Tijuana (8 per day).

International Flights: Air France, Reforma 404 (tel. 546-91-40, 571-45-43 at airport); **Continental,** Reforma 325 (tel. 525-37-10); **Pan Am,** Avila Camacho 1 #702 (tel. 395-03-32). **Mexicana** (tel. 571-88-88) also books many international flights.

By Train

Trains arrive at **Estación Buenavista** (open daily 6am-10pm), north of the Alameda at the corner of Insurgentes and Mosqueta, 4 blocks west of the Guerrero Metro station (Line 3) along Mosqueta. Taxis leave from the parking lot on the Mosqueta side of the station. Be sure to check the meter and the official fare chart in the cab before you pay, because abuses are par for the course.

An **information booth** (tel. 547-65-93) in the middle of the main lobby provides schedule and price information. (Open daily 6am-9pm.) Also in the station are a restaurant, telegraph service, post office, and *paquetería* (storage room) for luggage (open daily 6:30am-9:30pm, 2000 pesos per item per day). Although luggage may be left up to 30 days, only short-term storage of non-valuables is recommended.

Mexico City

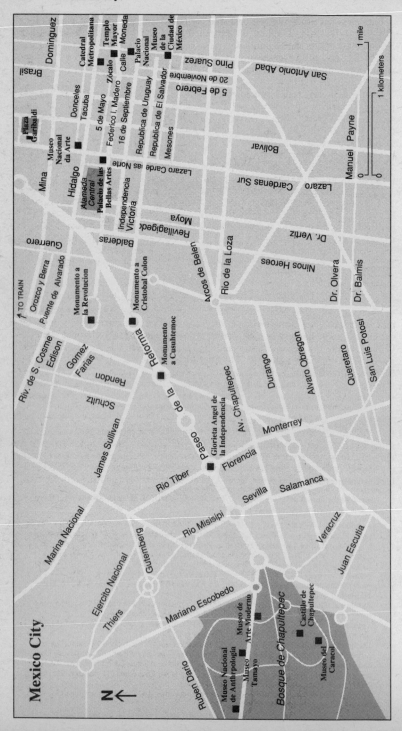

N

First-class tickets should be purchased two months in advance (for reservations call 597-61-72). A full refund on cancellations is available with 24-hr. notice. Second-class tickets can be purchased only on the day of travel. For train information in English, go to **Gerencia de Tráfico de Pasajeros,** upstairs from the main station lobby (open Mon.-Fri. 9am-3pm and 6-8pm), or call 547-20-32 and ask for Mrs. Patricia Bernard.

Deluxe first-class trains run to: Querétaro (at 7am and 8pm, 3½ hr., 16,400 pesos); Guanajuato (at 7am, 6½ hr., 27,100 pesos); San Miguel de Allende (at 7am, 4½ hr., 21,800 pesos); San Luis Potosí (at 7am, 6½ hr., 23,800 pesos); Veracruz (at 9:15pm, 9½ hr., 24,400 pesos, with bed 40,000 pesos); Oaxaca (at 7pm, 13½ hr., 30,700 pesos, with bed 76,000 pesos); Puebla (at 7pm, 4 hr., 11,400 pesos, with bed 28,200 pesos); Morelia (at 10pm, 8½ hr., 20,300 pesos, with bed 39,600 pesos); Monterrey (at 6pm, 14½ hr., 50,800 pesos, with bed 98,700 pesos); Nuevo Laredo (at 6pm, 18 hr., 64,800 pesos, with bed 126,000 pesos); Guadalajara (at 8:40pm, 11½ hr., 43,300 pesos, with bed 86,600 pesos); Aguascalientes (at 8pm, 11½ hr., 37,400 pesos, with bed 70,800 pesos); Zacatecas (at 8pm, 14 hr., 44,800 pesos, with bed 84,700 pesos). A meal is included with most of these first-class fares. Second-class trains to: Chihuahua (at 8pm, 18 hr., 35,400 pesos); Saltillo (at 6pm, 12 hr.); Cordoba (at 9:15pm, 8 hr., 7900 pesos). Many other cities can be reached by train from Buenavista station, either directly or with connecting service. Prices for two beds are double those for one bed; round-trips cost double the one-way fare.

By Bus

Mexico City's four main bus stations correspond to the cardinal points. All four terminals are served by Metro stations: **Central de Autobuses del Norte** by the Terminal Autobuses del Norte station (Line 5); **Central de Autobuses del Poniente** by the Observatorio station (Line 1); **Terminal de Autobuses de Pasajeros de Oriente (TAPO)** by the San Lázaro station; and the **Terminal Central de Autobuses del Sur** by the Taxqueña station (Line 2). The Central del Norte (North Station) serves the Bajío, northern Veracruz, Jalisco, and most of northern Mexico. TAPO (East Station) serves Puebla, southern Veracruz, Oaxaca, Chiapas, and the Yucatán Peninsula. Taxqueña (South Station) serves the states of Morelos and Guerrero. Central del Poniente (West Station) serves the states of México and Michoacán.

All stations offer an official taxi service that runs 24 hr. and charges fixed rates for a ride to any point in the city (rates set by zones) or adjacent parts of Mexico state. *Peseros* (a.k.a. *colectivos*) also serve the four stations. Each station has a post office and telegraph service, and some have a *paquetería* (luggage room). The following listings are by no means comprehensive; given the extensive network, it is possible to go almost anywhere at any time. All ticket sales are final and all seats reserved.

Central de Autobuses del Norte: (tel. 587-15-52) on Cien Metros. More companies than those listed below operate out of this terminal/zoo.

Autobuses del Oriente (ADO) (tel. 567-84-55). First-class service to: Pachuca (Sun.-Fri. every 20 min. 7:30am-9:30pm, Sat. every 15 min. 9am-6pm, 2 hr., 4300 pesos); Papantla (3 per day, 5 hr., 14,500 pesos); Poza Rica (every ½ hr. 7am-12:45am, 5 hr., 13,500 pesos); Tampico (every 2 hr., 24 hr., 28,000 pesos); Tuxpan (every 2 hr., 6 hr., 16,000 pesos).
Estrella Blanca (tel. 586-52-19). First-class service to: Reynosa (5 per day, 14 hr., 45,000 pesos); Monterrey (14 per day, 12 hr., 39,800 pesos); Matamoros (5 per day, 14 hr., 44,000 pesos); Guanajuato (6 per day, 5 hr., 15,500 pesos); Guadalajara (every hr. 6:30am-12:30am, 7 hr., 26,300 pesos).
Autobuses San Juan Teotihuacán (tel. 781-18-12), near waiting room #8. Second-class service to and from Teotihuacán (every ½ hr. 8am-10pm, 2500 pesos).
Transportes del Pacífico (tel. 587-53-10), near waiting room #3. To Tijuana (137,000 pesos) via Mexicali (128,000 pesos) 12 times per day.
Omnibus de México (tel. 567-58-58), near waiting room #3. First-class service to: Aguascalientes (7 per day, 7 hr., 24,660 pesos); Chihuahua (7 per day, 20 hr., 67,680 pesos); Ciudad Juárez (24 per day, 24 hr., 84,000 pesos); San Miguel de Allende (at 7:15am, 5 hr., 12,500 pesos); San Luis Potosí (4 per day, 5 hr., 19,000 pesos); Querétaro (11 per day, 2½ hr., 9900 pesos); León (9 per day, 5 hr., 18,000 pesos).
Tres Estrellas de Oro (tel. 587-31-34), near waiting room #4. First-class service to Mazatlán (at 8:30pm, 16 hr., 54,000 pesos).

Terminal de Autobuses de Pasajeros de Oriente (TAPO): General Ignacio Zaragoza 200 (tel. 762-59-77). Taxi ticket stand and tourist information booth near the entrance to the Metro station.

ADO (tel. 542-71-92). First-class service to: Puebla (every 15 min., 2 hr., 6400 pesos); Oaxaca (20 per day, 15 hr., 25,000 pesos); Cancún (8 per day, 27 hr., 85,000 pesos); Jalapa (33 per day, 5 hr., 15,000 pesos); Mérida (8 per day, 24 hr., 71,000 pesos); Palenque (at 4pm, 14 hr., 49,000 pesos); Veracruz (36 per day, 7 hr., 20,500 pesos); San Andrés Tuxtla (17 per day, 8 hr., 28,000 pesos); Chetumal (5 per day, 24 hr., 68,000 pesos); Villahermosa (34 per day, 12 hr., 42,000 pesos).
Autobuses Unidos (AU) (tel. 522-58-85). To Veracruz (17 per day, 7 hr., 18,500 pesos). AU also covers many routes served by ADO, but at different times.
Autotransportes Tlaxcala-Apizaco Huamantla (tel. 542-20-09). First-class service to Tlaxcala (4 per day, 2 hr., 4700 pesos).
Omnibus Cristóbal Colón (tel. 542-72-63). First-class service to San Cristóbal de las Casas (at 2:15, 6:15, and 8:40pm, 17 hr., 56,000 pesos) and Tuxtla Gutierrez (5 per day, 52,000 pesos).

Terminal de Autobuses de Poniente: Av. Sur 122 (tel. 271-00-38).

Turismos México-Toluca (tel. 271-14-33). To Toluca (every 7 min. 6am-10:30pm, 1 hr., 3000 pesos).
Flecha Roja (tel. 271-02-94). To Toluca (every 5 min. 5am-11pm, 1 hr., 2700 pesos).
Herradura de Plata (tel. 271-17-60). To Morelia (29 per day, 4 hr., 13,000 pesos).

Terminal de Autobuses del Sur (Taxqueña): Taxqueña 1320 (tel. 549-02-57).

Pullman de Morelos (tel. 549-35-07). First-class service to Cuernavaca (every 10 min. 5:30am-9pm, every ½-hr. 10pm-midnight, 3900 pesos).
Estrella de Oro (tel. 549-85-20). First-class service to: Taxco (7 per day, 3 hr., 7700 pesos); Acapulco (21 per day, 7 hr., 21,000 pesos); Ixtapa (3 per day, 12 hr., 33,400 pesos); Zihuatanejo (6 per day, 12 hr., 32,000 pesos).
Flecha Roja (tel. 689-00-00). First-class service to Zihuatanejo (at 12:30am and 3pm, 31,000 pesos) and Acapulco (every hr., 6 hr., 20,000 pesos).

By Car

Several major highways lead into the Federal District and intersect with the Circuito Interior, the highway that rings the city. **Route 57,** from Querétaro and Tepotzotlán, becomes Manuel Avila Camacho just outside the Circuito. South of its intersection with Reforma, the highway continues as Anillo Periférico until it ends near Xochimilco, southeast of Mexico City's center. **Route 15,** from Toluca, turns into Reforma as it enters the city.

Route 95, from Cuernavaca and Acapulco, becomes Insurgentes, which plugs into the Circuito on the south side. **Route 150,** from Puebla and Texcoco, becomes Ignacio Zaragoza, which connects to the Circuito on the east side just north of the point where Río Churubusco and Puerto Aéreo meet. Viaducto Miguel Alemán forks off Ignacio Zaragoza before the latter connects to Puerto Aéreo, and veers west where it intersects the east side of the Circuito at Río Churubusco. **Route 85,** from Pachuca, Teotihuacán, and Texcoco, becomes Insurgentes in the city.

If reading about driving in Mexico City hasn't broken your spirit, getting behind the wheel will. Mexico City's drivers are notorious, partly because highway engineers did not design the roads with drivers in mind. Highway dividers are often absent, stop signs are planted midstream, and red lights are routinely ignored.

The fast, efficient, and cost-free Angeles Verdes do *not* (psych!) serve the Distrito Federal. Even angels dare not tread here. If your car should break down within city boundaries, call the **Asociación Mexicana de Automovilistas (AMA)** (tel. 768-55-22) or **Automovilística Mexicana** (tel. 519-34-36) and request assistance. Wait for them beside your car, with the hood raised.

Parking within the city is seldom a problem: parking lots are everywhere (600-1000 pesos per hr., depending on the location and condition of the lot). Street parking in Mexico City can be as improbable as in Manhattan, and vandalism is extremely common. Never leave anything valuable inside the car. Police will remove your license plate if you park illegally; should this happen, wait near your car with some cash in your pocket until they return. If anything else is missing, however, and you suspect the police were tampering with your car, report it to LOCATEL (tel. 658-11-11).

Getting Around

The main obstacle to locomotion in Mexico City is congestion. Walking sometimes proves as fast as the various other means of surface transportation, which include the Metro (300 pesos) and buses (100 pesos), the *peseros* or *colectivos* (350-600 pesos per ride), and the considerably more expensive taxis.

Circuito Interior and Ejes Viales

Be forewarned that driving is the craziest and least economical way to get around the Federal District. Central Mexico City is encircled by a number of connected highways that together make up the **Circuito Interior.** This system allows motorists to get as close as possible to their destination before hitting the gridlocked streets of the center. Unfortunately, the Circuito itself is frequently jammed, especially during rush hour (Mon.-Fri. 7-9am and 6-9pm).

The Circuito is roughly box-shaped. **Boulevard Puerto Aéreo** forms the upper east side of the box, running north from the airport. As it bends left at the northeast corner of the box and heads west it becomes **Avenida Río Consulado.** Fifteen kilometers after intersecting with Insurgentes, Río Consulado turns south and becomes **Calzada Melchor Ocampo.** Ocampo heads south until it intersects Paseo de la Reforma at Bosque de Chapultepec, where the system continues as **Avenida Vasconcelos.** From Vasconcelos, two roads fork toward the *centro:* the first, **Avenida Patriotismo,** is about 13km from Chapultepec, and the second, **Avenida Revolución,** is 7km farther south. Both Patriotismo and Revolución are fast arteries to the southwest corner of the Circuito. At that point they turn into Av. Río Mixcoac, which becomes **Avenida Río Churubusco,** running east-west. Río Churubusco is the longest of the highways that constitute the Circuito; it continues east, turns north for a while, heads east again, then turns north once more to connect with Blvd. Puerto Aéreo south of the airport to complete the Circuito.

Aside from the large thoroughfares Insurgentes, Reforma, and Miguel Alemán, a system of **Ejes Viales** (axis roads) conducts the majority of traffic within the Circuito. All Ejes run one way (except for the bus lanes, which go against traffic), begin and end on opposite sides of the Circuito, and are oriented either east-west or north-south. Of the Ejes running east-west, those north of the Zócalo are called Eje 1 Nte. and Eje 2 Nte., and those south of the Zócalo are Ejes 2 through 8 Sur. The numbers increase heading away from the Zócalo. Running north-south and bisecting the box formed by the Circuito is **Eje Central Lázaro Cárdenas.** East of, and parallel to, it lie Ejes 1 to 3 Ote. West of it are Ejes 1 to 3 Pte. Using the Ejes along with the Circuito you can theoretically reach any general area of the city without much delay. For specifics, get a good street map. The Guía Roji compact street atlas (3500 pesos), entitled *Ciudad de México,* is available at many newsstands and at the airport.

City Center

Huge as Mexico City is, almost everything of interest to visitors lies within the northern half of the box formed by the Circuito Interior. Moreover, many attractions are within easy reach of **Paseo de la Reforma,** the broad thoroughfare that runs southwest-northeast and constitutes the heart of the Federal District. The **Bosque de Chapultepec,** home to the principal museums of the city, marks the southwestern limit of most tourists' wanderings. From Chapultepec, Reforma proceeds northeast, marked with a number of *glorietas* (traffic circles), each with a monument in the center, that serve as landmarks along Reforma's great length. The first is **Glorieta Angel de la Independencia.** At Reforma's intersection with Insurgentes stands the **Monumento a Cuauhtémoc.** South of this intersection lies the Zona Rosa (Pink Zone), the capital's most affluent commercial district. Several blocks farther northeast on Reforma is the **Monumento a Cristóbal Colón** (Christopher

Columbus). Off Reforma to the north of Colón, 2 blocks along Ramírez, is the **Plaza de la República** with the **Monumento a la Revolución,** around which stand several good, cheap hotels (see Accommodations below). Juárez, a main street running west-east, crosses Reforma 2 blocks northeast of the Colón monument and just east of the Monumento a la Revolución. Three blocks east along Juárez is the park Alameda Central (simply called Alameda). A block past the eastern end of Alameda, Juárez becomes Av. Madero, which leads through the historic **Centro** and, after 7 blocks, reaches the **Zócalo,** or **Plaza de la Constitución.** Some of the best budget hotels are found in the area between Alameda and the Zócalo (see Accommodations below).

Unlike the streets themselves, names in Mexico City are systematic. Streets in a given area generally carry names that are generically related. For example, streets in the Zona Rosa are all named after European cities, while the streets directly across Reforma are named after large rivers of the world. North of Chapultepec, streets are named after famous people. One point to remember when looking for street numbers is that they start from zero at the end of the street nearest the main post office (on Alameda's northeast corner) and continue to the border of the next *colonia,* where the street name changes and the addresses start at zero again.

Outlying Districts

Mexico City reaches outward from the Centro roughly 20km to the south, 10km to the north, 10km to the west, and 8km to the east. Year after year, the city's boundaries recede steadily toward the horizon. Because of the central location of most sights of interest to visitors, few travelers venture past the Bosque de Chapultepec on the west, Tlatelolco on the north, or the Zócalo on the east side of the *centro.* Interesting sights extend relatively far south to San Angel and the university. The major southern thoroughfare is Insurgentes Sur, which extends to the southern limit of the city. Metro Line 3 parallels Insurgentes on Cuauhtémoc and then Universidad, ending well before the city's edge at Ciudad Universitaria. The CREA youth hostel and most sights to the south, including San Angel, Coyoacán, Ciudad Universitaria, and the Pyramid of Cuicuilco, lie near or along Insurgentes. The Metro does not extend as far as the pyramid or the hostel. Metro Line 2 stretches farther south to the east of Line 3, and is closer to Xochimilco, one of the few southern sights not along Insurgentes. Also beyond reach by Metro are the ruins at Teotihuacán, northeast of the capital; these are best reached by bus from the northern station (see Mexico State).

Transportation Within Mexico City

Most transportation depots in Mexico City are large, clean, well-lit, well-policed, and well-marked. Public transportation—whether by bus, Metro, or the light green vans called *peseros*—is easy to use and economical; if the usual precautions are taken, it is also safe.

Travelers who plan to make frequent use of the Metro and bus systems should purchase an *abono de ahorro de transporte* (10,000 pesos). This blue card, available at all subway stations, Lotería Nacional stands, and Conasupo markets, entitles the bearer to unlimited use of the Metro and public city buses for 15 days following the purchase date. *Abonos* are sold at the beginning and in the middle of every month. They are only worth the price for those who expect to ride buses and the Metro more than twice per day for 15 consecutive days.

By Metro

The Metro always amazes—trains come quickly and regularly, the fare is cheap, the service extensive, and the immaculate stations contain interesting artwork, shining marble floors, and pleasant background music. Built in the late 1960s, the Metro transports over five million people daily. Its tracks stretch 160km between 120 different stations, but Mexico City has grown so fast that the Metro system no longer reaches its perimeter. The fare of 300 pesos includes transfers. Transfer gates are marked "correspondencia," and exits are marked "salida." Passing through the turnstiles leaves you outside the station, and you must pay again to re-enter. Although every station has a wall map, a color-coded subway guide is always handy. Pick one up at a Metro information booth in one of the following stations: Pino Suárez, Zócalo, Hidalgo, Instituto del Petróleo, Chapultepec, La Raza, Balderas, Insurgentes, or Candelaria. It might require some persistence, but you should be able to get one eventually.

Metro tickets (with a magnetic strip) are sold in booths at every station. The first train runs Monday through Friday between 5am and 6am, Saturday at 6am, and Sunday at 7am. From Sunday through Friday, the last train runs at 12:30am, and on Saturday as late as 1:30am. Try to avoid using the Metro from 7:30 to 9am and 7 to 9pm on weekdays; huge crowds during these hours make a pickpocket's job as easy as pie. Cars at either end of the train tend to be slightly less crowded, *ergo* safer and less uncomfortable.

Directions are stated in terms of the station at the end of a given line. Each of the two *andenes* (platforms) has signs indicating the terminus toward which trains are heading. (For example, if you are on Line 3 between Indios Verdes and Universidad, you can go "Dirección Indios Verdes" or "Dirección Universidad.")

Theft occurs frequently on the Metro when it's crowded (it almost invariably is). Carry bags in front of you or on your lap; simply closing the bag does little good, because thieves carry razor-sharp knives to make their own openings from which they extract the contents of your bag. Subway thieves often work in pairs—one will distract you while the other pulls your wallet. Rear pockets are very easy to pick, and front pockets are only slightly safer; empty pockets are best. If you know you are being robbed, confront the perpetrators loudly in the hope that they lose their cool and leave you alone.

Women riding the Metro often find themselves being groped at by men, especially during rush hour. If you feel someone's hand, simply remove it with your own and say, in a loud voice, "*déjame*" (leave me alone). During rush hours, many lines have cars reserved for women and children. Use them. They are usually located at the front of the train; often you will see women and children gathering on a separate part of the platform reserved for their car.

Because of overcrowding, large bags, parcels, or suitcases are not allowed on the Metro. People slip bags past the gate, but you may regret it if you try. On a crowded train, your luggage will make fellow passengers uncomfortable, and make you a sitting duck for thieves.

For Metro and bus information, contact **COVITUR (Comisión de Vialidad y Transporte Urbano del D.D.F.)**, Public Relations, Universidad 800 (tel. 688-89-55 or 688-44-75), or ask at any information booth. For complaints about the Metro dial 709-11-33, ext. 5009. If you lose something on the Metro, call the **Oficina de Objetos Extraviados** (tel. 709-11-33, ext. 1019), located in the Fray Servando station (Line 4). Keep hope alive, but keep expectations modest.

Overall, the Metro is by far the cleanest, fastest, and safest means of transportation in Mexico City. Almost all the restaurants, clubs, and museums of interest to the budget traveler can be reached on the Metro.

By Bus

The public bus system is easy to use and extends much farther than the Metro. Buses are brown and yellow or blue and gray and cost 100 pesos; have change ready when you board. Buses run daily from 5am to midnight, but are scarce after 10pm. They pass bus stops every 20-30 minutes. Even-numbered buses run east-west, odds run north-south.

Buses are required to stop only at the bus stops along Ejes Viales and the following major streets: Reforma, Insurgentes, Calzada de Tlalpan, and Viaducto Miguel Alemán. At any other stop, flag the driver by holding out your arm and pointing at the street in front of you. To get off the bus, press the button above the exit door at the rear of the bus. If you don't hear a buzz, bang once on the wall or yell "¡Bajo!" to let the driver know you want out.

In an effort to meet the growing demand for efficient transportation, the city is slowly incorporating blue-and-gray "Express" buses into the system. Be aware that these buses stop only on major avenues such as Insurgentes, Reforma, and Mazarik. The regular brown-and-yellow buses make much more frequent stops.

Like the Metro, buses are very crowded and seats are rarely available. The popular buses along Paseo de la Reforma are notorious for robbery and are plagued by organized gangs of professional thieves. Leave your valuables at the hotel, don't keep money in your pockets, carry your bag in front of you, or best yet avoid this route altogether.

Taxis

Cabs constantly cruise the major avenues, offering a quick, private alternative to the public systems. Understand that the number showing on the meter is not your fare; it's a reference number for the driver's price conversion table. Ask to see it before you pay, to insure that the price you're given matches the meter number. Hotel cabs and *turismo* taxis have no meters and charge up to three times more than regular taxis; yellow VW bugs are the cheapest but must be hailed; larger, orange taxis have digital meters that require no conversion. At night, all meters tend to be *descompuesto* (broken). If you don't confirm an approximate price for your ride before you close the door, you'll really be taken for a ride. Make sure the taxi meter is in clear view so that you can see the numbers turn as you travel. If you can set the price beforehand, you'll save four to five times the meter rate. This practice makes sense if you know how much the ride should cost. Tips are unnecessary, unless the cabdriver grants you a special service (helps carry your luggage, gives you a tour, etc.). At the airport and at all bus terminals, purchase a taxi ticket for a set fee (according to destination) at a registered booth.

When hailing a cab, ignore the yellow light on top of the taxi; only the small windshield light on the passenger side indicates (when lit) that a cab is empty. To phone a taxi, look in the yellow pages under "Sitios de Automóviles" or ask your hotel manager to call one for you.

All official yellow, brown, or orange VW bug taxis should have, hanging from the glove compartment, the driver's photo, credentials, and license. A taxi hotline number and the driver's serial number should be clearly pasted on the side windows.

Peseros

Peseros, or *colectivos,* are priced midway between cabs and buses. Clean, fast, and convenient, *peseros* are usually pistachio-green VW vans, sometimes Impalas or Mavericks; occasionally a white one with a green side stripe will appear. Each can carry up to 11 passengers. A *pesero's* route is either painted on its windshield or on a piece of cardboard taped to the windshield. They cover at least 30 different routes, but if you're not on Reforma, at the Chapultepec Metro station, or at a designated bus stop, you'll probably have to wave one down.

When hailing a *pesero,* hold out as many fingers as there are people in your group. The driver will reciprocate by indicating the number of seats available in the *pesero.* Sometimes the driver will flick the headlights to indicate seat availability. Pay just before reaching your destination. The fare varies with the distance traveled but averages 350-600 pesos per passenger for cross-city routes. *Pesero* schedules also vary: some run only until midnight, but the major routes—on Reforma, between Chapultepec and San Angel, and along Insurgentes—run 24 hr.

Other well-traveled *pesero* routes include: Metro Hidalgo to Ciudad Universitaria (via Reforma, Bucareli, and Av. Cuauhtémoc); La Villa to Chapultepec (via Reforma); Reforma to Auditorio (via Reforma and Juárez); Zócalo to Chapultepec (via 5 de Mayo and Reforma); San Angel to Izazaga (via 5 de Mayo and Reforma); Bolívar to Ciudad Universitaria/Coyoacán (via Bolívar in the Centro); and San Angel to Metro Insurgentes (via Av. de la Paz and Insurgentes Sur). Many depart from Chapultepec Metro station: #2 goes south to San Angel, while others go to La Merced and the airport. In order to make more sense of *pesero* routes, it is useful to know that many begin at a Metro stop, travel to a peripheral but well-known destination (e.g. San Angel), then return along the same route. One drawback: while the Metro and buses run along populated avenues, *peseros* navigate some of the backroads and neighborhoods less traveled by tourists. Be sure you know exactly where you are going when boarding the *pesero,* and clearly state your destination to the driver.

As part of a federal effort to reduce pollution, *peseros* are slowly being replaced by 22-passenger microbuses.

Car Rental

Car rental rates are exorbitant; the government controls prices and will charge extra for everything necessary for a car to be comfortable and functional. Call the major agencies first, listen to their quotes, and think of cheap city buses and waiting in nightmarish traffic jams as you collect your lower jaw from the floor.

All agencies require the renter to be at least 24 years old, have a major credit card, and show a passport or tourist card. Any driver's license is valid in Mexico. Some agencies ask for references. Sala E in the airport houses many agencies, but prices and services tend to be similar. All are open 24 hr. **Hertz** (tel. 762-83-72), rents VW sedans for 76,180 pesos per day plus mileage, insurance (31,000 pesos), and 15% tax; 166,470 pesos per day with 200km free. Hertz also runs a major branch at Versalles 6 (tel. 592-60-82), in the Zona Rosa. **Econorent** (tel. 762-04-67), has VW sedans for 67,000 pesos per day, plus mileage, insurance (22,000 pesos), and tax; 150,075 pesos per day with 200km free. At **Budget** (tel. 762-09-00), a VW sedan costs 76,080 pesos per day, plus 30,000-peso tax. **Dollar** (tel. 762-67-12), rents VW sedans for 76,000 pesos per day plus insurance and tax. They also have an office downtown at Chapultepec 322 (tel. 525-74-38).

Practical Information

Federal Tourist Office: Amberes 54 (tel. 525-93-80 or 525-93-85), at Londres in the Zona Rosa. Pleasant and well-informed staff. Tourist brochures in English and piles of useful city maps. Standardized price list of mid-range tourist hotels in major Mexican cities. Answers all questions, in person or by phone. Open daily 9am-9pm. During the same hours, the office operates information booths in Salas A and E at the airport, and at the TAPO bus station.

Ministry of Tourism: Presidente Mazarik 172 (tel. 250-85-55), at Hegel in Colonia Polanco. Take the Metro to Polanco (Line 7), walk 1 block south and 3 blocks east. Large selection of brochures and maps of every state, city, and archeological site in Mexico. Also makes hotel reservations. Open Mon.-Fri. 8am-8pm.

Department of Tourist Security: Tel. 250-01-51 or 250-01-23. These magic numbers are answered by English-speaking employees of the Ministry of Tourism, who will respond to complaints, suspected abuses, emergencies, and questions. Open 24 hr.

Tourist Card Information: Secretaría de Gobernación, Dirección General de Servicios Migratorios, Albañiles 19 (tel. 795-66-85), at Molina, near Metro San Lozero.

Walking Tours: Promoción Social del Centro Histórico, Chile 8 (tel. 510-25-41, ext. 1499). Free tours arranged by phone.

Tour Guide Service: Sindicato Nacional de Guías Turísticos, Melchor Ocampo 38 (tel. 535-77-87). Licensed guides who travel on foot or by car to show you special sights.

Accommodations Service: Hoteles Asociados, Airport Sala E (tel. 571-16-63 or 571-98-87). Up-to-date information on prices and locations of Mexico City hotels. Given a price range and an area, they can make your reservation free of charge. If you want budget lodging, be sure to ask for rock-bottom prices. English spoken.

Embassies: Will replace lost passports, issue visas, and provide legal assistance. Visa processing can take up to 24 hr.; bring plenty of ID. **U.S.,** Reforma 305 (tel. 211-00-42), at Glorieta Angel de la Independencia. Open Mon.-Fri. 9am-5:30pm, except on Mexican and U.S. holidays. On Sat. call only in case of emergency. **Canada,** Schiller 529 (tel. 254-32-88), at Polanco. Open Mon.-Fri. 9am-5pm. **U.K.** and **Ireland,** Río Lerma 71 (tel. 207-20-89), at Cuauhtémoc. Open Mon.-Fri. 9am-5pm. **Australia,** Jaime Balmes 11 (tel. 395-99-88). Open Mon.-Fri. 9am-5pm. **New Zealand,** Homero 229 (tel. 250-53-40), on the 8th floor. **West Germany,** Byron

737 (tel. 545-66-55), Colonia Rincón del Bosque. Open Mon.-Fri. 9am-5pm. **Switzerland,** Hamburgo 66 (tel. 533-07-35), on the fifth floor. Open Mon.-Fri. 9am-5pm. **France,** Havre 15 (tel. 533-13-60), near the Cuauhtémoc statue. Open Mon.-Fri. 9am-5pm. **Sweden,** Blvd. M. Avila Comacho 1-6 (tel. 540-63-93). **Guatemala,** 1025 Av. Explanada (tel. 520-27-94).

Currency Exchange: All banks offer the same exchange rate and usually charge commissions. **Bánamex** has branches everywhere; expect a wait of 45 min. to change money. (Open Mon.-Fri. 9am-1pm.) Ask for "chicos" if you want small bills. *Casas de cambio* keep longer hours than banks, give better exchange rates, and most are open weekends. They are concentrated along Reforma and in the Zona Rosa. Call **Central de Cambios** (tel. 703-27-89) for exchange information and transfers to local branches. The *casa de cambio* at Reforma 284 has the best hours. Open Mon.-Fri. 8:30am-7:30pm, Sat. 8:30am-6pm, Sun. 9am-5pm. Branch at Insurgentes Sur 1761, open Mon.-Fri. 9am-5:30pm, Sat. 9am-3pm.

American Express: Reforma 234 (tel. 533-03-80), at Havre in the Zona Rosa. Will cash personal checks for customers only. Accepts mail for customers, and has an exchange service. Money can be wired here. Report lost credit cards to the branch located at Patriotismo 635 (tel. 598-71-22), and lost traveler's checks to either branch. Open Mon.-Fri. 9am-6pm, Sat. 9am-1pm. In case of a lost **Visa** card, call 625-21-88.

Central Post Office: Lázaro Cárdenas (tel. 521-73-94), at Tacuba across from Bellas Artes. Open for stamps and regular mail Mon.-Fri. 8am-11:30pm, Sat. 8am-7:30pm, Sun. 8am-3:30pm; for registered mail Mon.-Fri. 8am-5:30pm, Sat. 9am-4pm. **Postal Code:** 06000.

Telephones: Long-distance collect calls are easier to make from pay phones here than in most other cities in the country. For direct long-distance calls, use one of the long-distance *casetas* at the following locations: Airport Sala E (open daily 6:30am-9:30pm); Airport Sala A (open daily 7am-11pm); Buenavista station (open daily 8am-9pm); or Central Camionera del Norte (open daily 8am-9pm). Also, look for **LADATEL** phones at the airport, bus stations, as well as in some Metro stations and VIP's Restaurant. Local calls free within the city at all pay phones and from hotels. For local information, dial 04. **Telephone Code:** 5.

Telegrams: Tacuba 8 (tel. 510-03-94), at the Museo Nacional de Arte, opposite the central post office. Facing the building, enter on the right side. Domestic and international service. Must show tourist card or passport to pick up telegrams. International telegrams take 3-5 days to arrive. From the U.S., send through Western Union to México Central Telégrafos. Open Mon.-Sat. 8am-midnight, Sun. 9am-9pm.

Courier Services: World Courier of Mexico, Oxford 39 (tel. 511-01-16). Delivers packages of all sizes and shapes overseas, priced by weight and bulk; **DHL,** Reforma 30 (tel. 562-57-00); **Federal Express,** Estocolmo 4 (tel. 208-67-68).

English Bookstores: The 2 best hunting grounds for English novels are San Angel and Coyoacán. Try San Angel's **American Bookstore,** Av. Revolución 1570. Open Mon.-Sat. 9am-7pm. Also at Madero 25 (tel. 550-01-62). Open Mon.-Sat. 9am-7pm. In Coyoacán, visit **Librería Británica,** next to the Casa del Libro at the corner of Av. Universidad and Av. México, near the Coyoacán Metro stop. Open Mon.-Sat. 8am-5pm. **Museo Nacional de Antropología** has a wide selection of archeological guides in English. Open Tues.-Sun. 10am-6pm.

Ben Franklin Library: Londres 16 (tel. 211-00-42), at Berlin 2 blocks southeast of the Cuauhtémoc monument. 75% of the books are in English, including a large variety of newspapers and periodicals. Open to the public Mon.-Fri. 10am-7:30pm.

Cultural and Arts Information: Palacio Nacional de Bellas Artes, Hidalgo 1 (tel. 512-56-76).

Laundromat: Lavandería Las Artes, Antonio Caso 82-A (tel. 535-74-77), near Serapio Rendón. Self-service wash 3500 pesos, dry 3500 pesos. They'll wash while you wander for an additional 1100 pesos. Open Mon.-Sat. 9am-8pm. Also at Av. Chapultepec and Toledo near Sevilla Metro stop. Most hotels have laundry service or can tell you where to find the nearest facility.

Haircare: La Pequeña Dama, Hamburgo 150-6 (tel. 514-91-00), in the Zona Rosa inside the Plaza del Angel mall between Londres and Hamburgo. Cheap, professional cuts. Men 23,000 pesos, women 25,000 pesos. Open Mon.-Sat. 11am-8pm.

Rape Crisis: Hospital de Traumatología de Balbuena, Calle Sur 103 (tel. 552-16-02), at Cecilio Robelo east of Alameda. **Hospital de Traumatología de Coyoacán,** Av. Iztaccihuatl and Av. México (tel. 524-22-23), in Coyoacán.

Gay Information: Colectivo Sol. Address inquiries care of A.P. 13-320 México 13, D.F. 03500. A mainly political group that offers information on upcoming political and social events.

AIDS Information: El Grupo Con-Don, Villalongín 92-6, Colonia San Rafael, Delegación Cuauhtémoc, Mexico D.F. To reach **CONASIDA,** the federal AIDS information hotline, call 525-24-24.

Sexually Transmitted Disease Information: Secretaría de Salud (tel. 277-63-11).

24-Hr. Alcoholics Anonymous Hotlines: Jóvenes Chapultepec, Calzada Protacio Tagle 107 (tel. 515-10-96). **Jóvenes Mixcoac,** Av. del Rosal 60 (tel. 680-49-47).

Drug Problems: Centros de Integración Social (tel. 534-34-34). Rehabilitation and counseling.

LOCATEL: Tel. 658-11-11. The city's official lost-and-found hotline; call if your car (or friend) is missing.

Red Cross: (tel. 557-57-58) in the Colonia Chapultepec Polanco on Ejército Nacional.

Pharmacies: VYR, San Jerónimo 630 (tel. 595-59-83 or 595-59-98), near Periférico Sur shopping center. Open 24 hr. Also at 5 de Mayo and Palma in *el centro.* Open daily 9am-6pm.

Medical Care: The **U.S. Embassy** (see above) has a list of doctors in the city, with their specialties, addresses, telephone numbers, and languages spoken. **Dirección General de Servicios Médicos** (tel. 518-51-00) has information on all city hospitals.

Emergency: Tel. 684-21-42 or 535-90-55. **Emergency Shelter: Casa de Protección Social,** (tel. 530-47-62 or 530-85-36).

Police: Secretaría General de Protección y Vialidad (tel. 588-51-00 or 768-80-44). Dial 08 for the Policía Judicial.

Accommodations

Rooms abound in the Centro (between Alameda and the Zócalo) and the Alameda Central, and are sprinkled throughout the area surrounding the Monumento a la Revolución on the Pl. de la República.

Avoid the filthier sections of the Alameda and the unreconstructed areas near the Monumento a la Revolución, but don't be put off by the mid- to high-priced hotels around Insurgentes Sur and Reforma, just northeast of the Zona Rosa tourist belt: they are still inexpensive by U.S. standards. Many budget hotels charge according to the number of beds needed and not per person. Beds tend to be large enough for two people. If this is acceptable, be sure to inquire at the hotel as it is a potential source of substantial savings.

Avoid, too, establishments with bold signs saying "Hotel Garage." These rooms are frequented by businessfolk "working late at the office"; anyway, the hourly charge is sky-high.

Centro

Situated between the Zócalo and Alameda Central, this *colonia* is the historic center and colonial heart of Mexico City. Its hotels are reasonably priced and fairly safe, especially since the neighborhood received its post-earthquake overhaul. Some of the hotels mentioned here help to form uninterrupted blocks of well-preserved colonial buildings. Others lie amidst to the noise and congestion of the Zócalo. Nonetheless, the Centro remains the most exciting place to stay and the best base from which to explore the traditional core of the largest city in the world.

Most of the hotels listed are north of Madero and 5 de Mayo, the parallel east-west streets that connect Alameda with the Zócalo, and east of Lázaro Cárdenas, the north-south Eje Central that runs 1 block east of Alameda. Metro stations Bellas Artes and Allende (both Line 2) serve these hotels.

Hotel Antillas, Belisario Domínguez 34 (tel. 526-56-74), near Allende. Wonderfully restored and maintained colonial building. Plush, cozy rooms with small color TVs, phones, and large curtained showers. Half of the colonial foyer is a busy little diner (open daily 7am-11pm; *comida corrida* 8000 pesos). Singles 45,000 pesos. Doubles 55,000 pesos.

Hotel Canadá, 5 de Mayo 47 (tel. 518-21-05), near Isabel la Católica. One of the plushest hotels in the Centro: cozy blue-carpeted lounge and communal TV next to reception desk, and small but well-outfitted rooms with TVs, phones, and bottled water. Singles 40,000 pesos. Doubles 50,000 pesos. Triples 60,000 pesos.

Hotel Washington, 5 de Mayo 54 (tel. 512-40-58), at Palma, 1 block west of the cathedral. Small carpeted rooms with complete bathroom facilities. Not elegant, but the maids keep the rooms meticulously clean for the many businessmen who stay here. Traffic noise increases at night. Singles 25,000 pesos. Doubles 30,000 pesos. Triples 35,000.

Hotel Isabel, Isabel la Católica 65 (tel. 518-12-13), between El Salvador and Uruguay across from the old Biblioteca Nacional. An exhilarating shade of brown covers the walls of this old-fashioned building. Clean and roomy, but some beds are warped like a weathered board. Singles 29,000 pesos. Doubles 35,000 pesos.

Hotel Habana, República de Cuba 77 (tel. 518-15-89). A Cuban classic. The large rooms and comfortable beds are complemented by spotless bathrooms tiled in a pattern straight from Home Shopping Network. TV, phone, and filtered water. Very friendly and helpful management. One bed 35,000 pesos. Two beds 40,000 pesos.

Hotel Catedral, Donceles 95 (tel. 518-52-32 or 512-81-41), 2 blocks along Monte de Piedad/Brasil from the Zócalo's northwest corner, then right on Donceles. Well-maintained, with a handsome wood-paneled lobby. Sizable rooms with carpeting and TV. Clean bathrooms with old-fashioned bathtubs. Singles 40,000 pesos. Doubles with 1 bed 45,000 pesos.

Hotel Florida, Belisario Domínguez 57 (tel. 521-77-64), 3 blocks north of Hidalgo on Lázaro Cárdenas. Renovations brought hideous crimson rugs and bedcovers, and sleek marble bathrooms. Five floors of tiny rooms overlook a clean, carpeted courtyard. Free bottled water at main desk. Singles 25,000 pesos.

Hotel Rioja, 5 de Mayo 45 (tel. 521-83-33). Not pretty or comfortable, but the rooms are as to free as you'll find. Noisy: room doors open onto inner patio, which magnifies every stray street sound. Communal bathrooms and showers. Singles 9000 pesos. Doubles 14,000 pesos.

Alameda Central

The Alameda offers a broad selection of hotels in spite of the destructive transformation that the area has suffered; blocks shattered by the earthquake have not been rebuilt like they have in the Centro. The areas that have survived are attractive, as is the park and its immediate surroundings. Most of the hotels in this area are south of Alameda Central.

Hotel Hidalgo, Santa Veracruz 37 (tel. 521-87-71), at the 2 de Abril walkway, behind Bellas Artes Metro station. One of the few area businesses not scathed by the 1985 earthquake. Around it, buildings are being rebuilt and sidewalks repoured. Quality is high: the large carpeted rooms afford city views. Restaurant and parking available. Singles 51,000 pesos. Doubles 56,000 pesos. Triples 63,000 pesos.

Hotel Manolo, Luis Moya 111 (tel. 521-77-09), near Arcos de Belén. Rooms large enough to require a map; landmarks include the enormous bed, color TV, radio, and phone. Bathrooms have cream tiles and marble faucets. Lobby stocked with soda and bottled water. Parking available. Double-sized singles 45,000 pesos.

Hotel Marlowe, Independencia 17 (tel. 521-95-40). Large lobby. The small rooms are well-lit and comfortable with carpeting, TV, and phone. The top-floor restaurant serves a *comida corrida* for 10,000 pesos (open daily 7am-11pm). Singles 40,000 pesos. Doubles 45,000 pesos. Triples 70,000 pesos.

Hotel San Diego, Luis Moya 98 (tel. 521-60-10). Relatively modern building with elevator. Recently renovated with vertigo-inducing red-and-black carpet. Spacious rooms with TV, phone, and large mirrors. Satisfactory bathrooms. Parking available. One bed 35,000 pesos. Two beds 40,000 pesos.

Hotel Conde, Pescaditos 15, at Revillagigedo. Exit the Metro at Juárez, follow Articulo 123 to Revillagigedo, then take a right and walk 3 blocks. Clean building with spiffy rooms that include bottled water and blue-tiled bathrooms fit for a count. Singles 35,000 pesos. Doubles 40,000 pesos.

Hotel Mariscala, Santa Veracruz 12 (tel. 510-47-10). Rooms are decent and some offer a pretty view of the Alameda skyline. Others have a fine view (and are within earshot) of the ongoing reconstruction of the adjacent structures. Singles 35,000 pesos. Doubles 40,000 pesos.

Hotel Fornos, Revillagigedo 92 (tel. 510-47-32), between M. Esterling and Arcos de Belén. Giant chandeliers and mirrored stands with big plastic plants in the ambitiously decorated foyer. The same disconcerting red-and-black carpets as found in the San Diego cover everything. Rooms clean and cozy. Tiny bathrooms, with the showerhead that irrigates the toilet-bowl. Coffee machine and bottled drinks in lobby. Friendly management. One bed 40,000 pesos. Two beds 75,000 pesos.

Hotel Avenida, Lázaro Cárdenas 38 (tel. 518-10-08), 2½ blocks south of the Torre Latinoamericana. Dark and stuffy rooms. Lázaro Cárdenas conducts much traffic and churns out decibels throughout the day. Singles 32,000 pesos. Doubles 37,000 pesos.

Near the Monumento a la Revolución/Buenavista

Accommodations in the Monumento a la Revolución area offer more peace and quiet than do those in the Centro or the Alameda, and for two main reasons: there are few historical sites here of interest to tourists, and not many people have moved back in since the area was heavily damaged in the 1985 quake. Metro Hidalgo is on Mariscal, near several of the following hotels.

The only hostel in the city, **Villa Deportiva Juvenil** (tel. 665-50-27), on Insurgentes Sur 1 block south of the Villa Olimpica, can't guarantee you a spot. They reserve their three large sex-segregated dormitories for athletes participating in organized team sports within the city; bunks are available to the public only when jocks don't fill them. An interesting crowd chills on the beautifully kept lawn. The place abides by treehouse rules: no one over 35 admitted. (Lights out at 11pm, but you can come in later. 16,800 pesos per person.)

Hotel Oxford, Ignacio Mariscal 67 (tel. 566-05-00), at Alcazar. An elegant winding staircase leads to huge rooms blessed by deep carpets. English-channel TV and park next to hotel provide easy entertainment. Singles 23,000 pesos. Doubles 30,000 pesos.

Casa de Los Amigos, Ignacio Mariscal 132 (tel. 705-05-21 or 705-06-46), across from Gran Hotel Texas. Originally home to José Clemente Orozco, the House of Friends (Quakers) is a cultural and refugee center and temporary boardinghouse for people working for peace and international justice in Central America. Friendly, helpful, English-speaking proprietors. Kitchen facilities. Library stocks major American magazines and many Quaker readings in English. Meditation room was once Orozco's art studio. Free bottled water. Mail accepted for patrons. 15-day max. stay. Curfew 10pm (or 3000-peso key deposit). Storage fee 1000 pesos. Breakfast of yogurt and granola 3000 pesos. Dorm room 20,000 pesos. Private room (when available) 13,000-28,000 pesos.

Hotel New York, Edison 45 (tel. 566-97-00), 1½ blocks north of the monument. Rooms with carpeting and color TV; bathrooms boast jet-powered steel showerheads. English-speaking proprietor. Spotless lobby with white marble coffee tables, leather chairs, pleasant music, and brown marble walls. Room service available from the adjoining hotel-owned restaurant. Garage parking an option. Singles 40,000 pesos. Doubles 50,000 pesos.

Hotel Ponte Vedra, Insurgentes Nte. 226 (tel. 541-31-60), across the highway from the train station. All things modern, marble, and sharp. Big, comfortable beds and excellent bathrooms. The lobby looks like a 1970s discotheque. Restaurant/bar on premises. Parking available for patrons. Ziggley says "Best hotel near Buenavista." Singles 40,000 pesos. Doubles 80,000 pesos.

Hotel Mónaco, Guerrero 12 (tel. 566-83-33), near Puente de Alvarado, ½ block from Hidalgo Metro station, across from Pl. San Fernando. Clean and quiet. Rooms have TV, shower, and bottled water. Friendly staff. Parking available. Singles 35,000 pesos. Doubles 38,000 pesos.

Hotel Sevilla, Serapio Rendón 126 (tel. 566-18-66), at Sullivan. Overly furnished rooms. Phones, TVs, a rickety elevator, and bottled water make this a cozy choice, but it's a long walk from the Metro station. Singles 41,400 pesos. Doubles 54,500 pesos.

Gran Hotel Texas, Mariscal 129 (tel. 546-46-26), at Iglesias. Spotless, roomy, and amply furnished rooms with TV, phone, and bottled water. Stray steer roam the halls. Parking available. Singles 40,000 pesos. Doubles 50,000 pesos.

Hotel Lepanto, Guerrero 90 (tel. 535-00-70), 3 blocks from the Hidalgo Metro stop. Closer to Buenavista than to Revolución. Modern and elegant lobby. Huge rooms include color TV, thick carpet, and phone, as well as bathtub and shower. Expensive for the area, but the extra pesos are warranted. Singles 48,000 pesos. Doubles 56,000 pesos. Triples 80,000 pesos.

Hotel Central, Mosqueta 248 (tel. 535-57-24). In need of a little capital improvement, or maybe just some good old-fashioned elbow grease. As is, with broken mirrors, chipped walls, and torn carpet, there's not much attractive about it. Quite cheap, however; TV and phone included. Singles 20,000 pesos. Doubles 30,000 pesos.

Hotel Detroit, Zaragoza 55 (tel. 566-07-55), at Mina in Colonia Guerrero. Zaragoza runs parallel to Guerrero. Huge, cheap rooms, but the neighborhood is dimly lit, beat-up, and not a place to hang out for an extended period of time. Singles 17,000 pesos. Doubles 30,000 pesos.

Hotel Londres, Pl. Buenavista 5 (tel. 705-09-10), 3 blocks south of the train station. Dreary rooms with dark, tiny bathrooms. Not very clean but cheap. Black-and-white TV and phone. Singles 21,000 pesos. Doubles 23,000 pesos.

Food

From the incredible number of stores, stands, and vendors pushing edibles, you'd think that citizens of Mexico City had bottomless pits for stomachs. The range of choices is fantastic, as is the variance in sanitation; as always, no matter how delicious it looks, check as carefully as possible before popping anything in your mouth.

The food in Mexico City is often cheaper than in many other parts of the country, and there are some definite local favorites: *huevos* (eggs) and *pan dulce* (sweet bread) for breakfast, *quesadillas* (fried tortillas with cheese) or *tortas de pierna* (pork sandwiches) for lunch, and *pollo con mole poblano* (chicken with *mole* sauce) or enchiladas for dinner. The vegetarian restaurant near the Zócalo offers an extensive selection of tasty soybean concoctions.

North American chains mass-produce predictable fare for the timid palate. If you're preparing your own food, **Conasupos** throughout the city stock almost anything you could need; if you can't find what you want there, head to La Merced.

Soda is sold at every corner: *agua mineral* means mineral water; *Sidral* is a great carbonated apple drink; and *refrescos* are your standard soda pops. Cans and bottles are customarily recycled here, and patrons pay extra for the privilege of keeping them.

Centro

This area offers the most variety and lowest prices around. Portions are usually large, and *comida corridas* abound. One of the very few vegetarian restaurants in the city is located here, and many small counters offer fruit plates and drinks.

Café Tacuba, Tacuba 28, at Allende Metro stop. Authentic Mexican cuisine in a colorful setting. Paintings of colonial aristocracy hang on the beautiful blue tile walls. The chicken tacos jam, and the *bunuelos* (fried dough sprinkled with sugar and cinnamon) are a dentist's sweetest dream. Entrees 15,000 pesos. Open daily 8am-11:30pm.

Restaurant Danubio, Uruguay 3, at Lázaro Cárdenas. Classy, old-fashioned seafood place. Fish on display as you walk in. A particularly attractive *comida corrida* goes for 12,000 pesos. Open daily 1-10pm.

Restaurante El Vegetariano, Filomeno Mata 13, between 5 de Mayo and Madero. An excellent alternative to the meat and chicken dishes at average establishments. Soups, salads, and a variety of vegetable turnovers. To-fu! To-fu! Entrees 14,000 pesos. Open daily 8am-8pm.

Casa de Ensaladas, Uruguay 52. Simple, open-air fruit shop daubed in bright orange, blue, and white. Specializes in various tasty combinations of fruit in liquid and solid form. The fruit cocktail plate of bananas, pineapples, and mangos, along with a milkshake, is a cool meal in itself. Sandwiches available. All dishes under 7000 pesos. Open Mon.-Sat. 8am-7:30pm.

Restaurant "La Casa de la Malinche," República de Cuba 79 (tel. 521-29-34) next to Hotel Habana. Supposed former house of La Malinche, Cortés's Indian interpreter and longtime lover. Elegant colonial building. Fine food, but not cheap. Mexican cuisine, including many *huachinango* (red snapper) dishes. Entrees 10,000-12,000 pesos. Live music Mon.-Fri. 2:30-6pm. Open daily 1-8pm.

Restaurante Casino Español, Isabel la Católica 31, 2nd floor. Hearty Spanish food in an elegant 19th-century Spanish casino club. Bar stocks imported Spanish, French, and Argentinian wines. Open daily 1-6pm.

Restaurante Centro Castellano, Uruguay 16. A cavernous 3-tiered palace that somehow manages to maintain a sense of intimacy. It may be the incense. Spanish entrees 11,000 pesos. Open Mon.-Sat. 1-10:30pm, Sun. 1-7pm.

Café París, 5 de Mayo 10, at Filomeno Mata. Although it resembles an American diner, meals and waiters are bona fide Mexican. Clean and comfortable, with A/C. Posters of tourist beaches and a row of ice-cream pumps line a long mirror facing the stools. Fruit dishes and breakfasts 7000 pesos. Fine *comida corrida* for 9000 pesos. Open daily 8am-midnight.

Café La Blanca, 5 de Mayo 40. Big, busy cafeteria with quick service and fair-sized portions. Open daily 7am-11:30pm.

Cafe 5 de Mayo, 5 de Mayo 57, at Palma. Booths worn out from lots o' business. Bright and noisy. Breakfast dishes 2500-4500 pesos. Mexican specialties. Open daily 7am-11pm.

Jampel, Bolívar 8 (tel. 521-75-71), between 5 de Mayo and Tacuba 3 blocks east of Lázaro Cárdenas. Very clean, with modern decor. Popular with executives and government workers. Two places in one—a restaurant/bar and a cafeteria. Buffet-style *comida corrida,* including *paella,* served in the cafeteria Mon.-Fri. 1-5pm (8000 pesos). Restaurant entrees a bit pricey, but the live music makes it a good place for an evening drink. Watch for the daily specials. Open Mon.-Sat. 8am-11pm, Sun. 1-6pm.

Zona Rosa

From the guides distributed in ritzy hotels you'd think only moneyed tourists eat in the Zona Rosa, home to the city's most expensive restaurants. In fact, many area eateries cater mainly to clerks from the scores of surrounding office buildings.

Check the open-air ambience and and consult the prominently displayed menus before choosing a restaurant. Prices vary widely, and it's almost always possible to find a cheap meal if you search hard enough and conscientiously clip those coupons. If you're more interested in the Zona Rosa's slick party atmosphere and less so in filling your stomach, skip dinner and settle for a drawn-out evening appetizer.

Taquería Beatriz, Pl. Insurgentes 3-B, directly outside Insurgentes Metro stop. Mexicans who don't *have* to eat tacos *choose* to eat them here. A variety of tacos 2000 pesos each. Try the *pollo con mole* and the *semidorado de pollo.* Truly delicious. Other entrees available, but the tacos are the restaurant's *raison d'être.* Open daily 8am-10:30pm.

Tacos el Camionero, Río Lerma 138, between Tíber and Danubio across Reforma from the Zona Rosa. Not far from the U.S. consulate. Another authentic taco restaurant, with grill-style specialties for meat-lovers only. Steak, sausage, and porkchop tacos with delicious hot sauces. Six tacos 10,000 pesos, 9 tacos 11,000 pesos. Open Mon.-Thurs. noon-midnight, Fri.-Sat. noon-1am, Sun. noon-11pm.

Luaú, Niza 38, across from Chalet Suizo and next to Sanborn's department store on Hamburgo. Fine Cantonese-style cuisine and fancy Polynesian decor. Chinese lamps and a "welcome" sign mark the entrance, and a charming miniature waterfall burbles through overhanging greenery at the center of the inside deck. Attractive entrees 8200-10,200 pesos; complete dinners start at 10,800 pesos. Open Mon.-Fri. noon-11pm, Sat. noon-midnight, Sun. noon-10pm.

Chalet Suizo, Niza 37, across from Luaú. The red-and-white checkered tablecloths and wood paneling may belong in an Italian restaurant, but the menu bares the Chalet's inner soul. Porkchops, steaks, shrimp, and Rocky Mountain Oysters. Open daily 12:30pm-midnight.

Shirley's Restaurant, Londres 102, 1 of 6 in the city. Stuff yourself while you have the chance. Clean and classy. Buy your buffet ticket before sitting down. Breakfast buffet (16,500 pesos) served Sun. 7:30am-noon; lunch buffet (20,000 pesos, Sat.-Sun. 18,500 pesos) served 1-4pm. Open daily 7:30am-midnight.

Parri, Hamburgo 154, between Florencia and Amberes. Tremendous BBQ. Restaurant interior resembles a Kansas barn with wooden walls and chairs. House-recipe chicken is beheaded and grilled before the crowd's eyes. Open Sun.-Thurs. 1pm-midnight, Fri.-Sat. 1pm-3am.

VIP's, at Insurgentes and Reforma. One of 50 in Mexico City. Clean and modern place with ravishingly orange upholstery. All kinds of high-priced but predictable commercial food.

Meat sandwiches and Mexican specials 7000-9000 pesos. Clone replicates dishes at Reforma 348. Open 24 hr.

Casa de Nutrición, Cozumel 326-6, in Colonia Roma. A multi-faceted store and crunchy restaurant filled with granola, soy products, incense, vitamins, health manuals, and healing crystals. Harmonic convergence is the hot topic among patrons. Open Mon.-Sat. 10am-8pm.

Alameda Central

In spite of the inevitable construction work (or perhaps because of the construction workers' hearty appetites), you'll find good food and plenty of atmosphere in the Alameda. The city's most famous restaurants lie amidst the rubble.

Fonda Santa Anita, Humboldt 48, near Juárez. An extremely colorful and artistically decorated restaurant serving Mexican food only. Friendly and efficient staff. Try the mouthwatering oyster salad (4500 pesos) and the homemade desserts. Claims to have served its food at 5 world fairs. Open Mon.-Fri. noon-10pm, Sat.-Sun. 1-9pm.

Humboldt 34, Humboldt 34 (tel. 521-22-93), near Juárez. Intimate, with wood paneling and leather chairs. Polished brass Aztec calendar prominent on far wall, but the electric guitars on center stage keep the place looking modern. Courteous service. Local families and executives dig the chicken entrees. Drinks and live music after 3pm. Open Mon.-Sat. 10am-1pm and 3-8pm.

Cafetería Restaurante Bacen's, Independencia 72, 1 block south of Alameda. Resembles an American diner, with cushioned booths and a counter displaying cereal boxes and pastries under plastic tops. Despite its appearance, locals recommend its Mexican food. Entrees 6000-8000 pesos. Breakfast specials 1000 pesos and up. Open daily 7:30am-1am.

Hong King, Dolores 25-A, near Independencia. One of 4 Chinese restaurants on the same block. Attractive Chinese decor, including a phoenix suspended from ceiling. Entrees of peppered beef and barbecued spareribs 7000 pesos. Cantonese dinners from 10,000 pesos. There is a strict 2-person minimum; they will *not* serve lonely singles. Open daily noon-11pm.

Roma Pizzeria, Independencia 104. One of the surprisingly few pizza joints in the city. Whole pizza 10,500 pesos. Open daily 2-11:30pm.

The Beijing, Independencia 19-B, near Dolores. Recently moved up to the 2nd floor. Interior decorated with Chinese lamps and a statue of the praying Buddha. Entrees 10,500 pesos. Open daily noon-8pm.

Cafetería San José, Luis Moya 66 (tel. 512-21-10). Noisy, odd place to eat. The people appear worn out, and curtains are hung at the bottom of the windows. Spanish dishes served. Open daily 8am-10pm.

Near the Monumento a la Revolución

Restaurants in this area are less innovative and entertaining than those in the Centro, Alameda, or Zona Rosa, mainly because the businesswomen and men who eat here are much too busy to worry about fine cuisine.

Daruma, Río Tamesis 6, 1 block from the Cuauhtémoc monument on Reforma. An immaculate Japanese set-up, serving authentic dishes. Meals of soup, salad, and main dish 9500-11,500 pesos. Try the various *brochetas* served with tasty sauce. Open Sun.-Fri. 1-11pm.

Restaurant Jena, Jesus Teran 12, at Mariscal. Attached to a hotel built entirely of marble. Colorful wood paneling, scarlet venetian blinds, private bar doling out *sangrias* (3000 pesos), and beautiful leather-seated booths with shiny brass railings. Modern and spit-shined. Pasta and Mexican fare reasonably priced at 5000-7000 pesos. *Chilaquiles con pollo* 5500 pesos. Open 7am-midnight.

Restaurant Mansión, Antonio Caso 31, toward Colón from Revolución. This large colonial home with Bee-Gees ambience is a monument in its own right. Just don't think about the consequences of the huge chandelier dropping. Serves only a cheap and simple *comida corrida* (5400 pesos). Open Mon.-Fri. 9am-6pm.

La Taberna, Arriaga at Ignacio Mariscal, next to Hotel Pennsylvania. Some mistake the tininess for coziness, but it is meticulously kept. The menu juxtaposes pizza and Argentine specialties. Large *comida corrida* 12,000 pesos. Open Mon.-Sat. noon-10pm.

Restaurant Regis, Edison 57-B. B&B, for Bare and Beige. Good-sized *comida corrida* 4000-5500 pesos. Open daily 7am-11pm.

La Gran Chiquita, Iglesias 26. Plain and unadorned, with the standard tacos or enchiladas for 4000 pesos. Open Mon.-Sat. 8am-7pm.

Restaurant New York, Edison 45, attached to Hotel New York. Nondescript diner serves Americanized breakfast specials (5000-7000 pesos) and a respectable *comida corrida* (5000 pesos). Open daily 7am-11pm.

La Pizza, Puente de Alvarado, at Buenavista. *Comida corrida* including pizza 12,000 pesos. Open daily 1-9pm.

Coyoacán

The southern suburb of Coyoacán attracts students, young couples, and pretentious intellectuals to its complement of elegant restaurants. Coyoacán is the birthplace of many Mexican politicians and presidents, and its restaurants play to that upper-level clientele.

Café El Parnaso, Carrillo Puerto 2, at Jardín Centenario. A beautiful outdoor café, book and record store, and art gallery. *The* place for Coyoacán's budding intelligentsia. Great for coffee and a view of the Pl. Hidalgo gardens. Snarf down some mouth-watering mocha cake (4000 pesos). Open daily 9am-9:30pm.

Los Geranios, Sosa 19, 1 block from the Jardín Centenario. Quite an average place with exciting brown tile floors and plastered walls. Older locals enjoy the near-silence. What kind of cheese is served? Brie, of course. Open daily 10am-midnight.

Nevería La Siberia, at Pl. Centenario. The most creative of many ice cream places in the area. Exotic flavors and a creamy, rich texture. Single scoop 2000 pesos, triple scoop 5000 pesos. Fruit ices, too (single scoop 1500 pesos, triple scoop 3500 pesos). Orgasmic sundaes 8000 pesos. Open daily 9am-9pm.

San Angel

Eateries in San Angel range from the *típico* taco stall to the chic quiche restaurant. On Saturdays, avoid the expensive Bazaar Sábado restaurants in favor of the vendors just outside.

Restaurante Hasti Bhawan, Pl. San Jacinto 7. Hindustani atmosphere inside a beautiful colonial building. *Pakora* and *samosa* appetizers 1400 pesos; *lassi,* a thick Indian yogurt drink, 1600 pesos; curry dishes and other entrees 9000 pesos and up. The *gulab jamans* are yet another of those incomprehensible Indian dessert concoctions (2500 pesos). Open Tues.-Thurs. noon-11pm, Fri.-Sat. noon-midnight, Sun. noon-6pm.

Restaurant New Orleans Jazz, Revolución 1655 (tel. 550-19-08), near La Paz. One of Mexico's liveliest Latin American jazz nightclubs. Serves spaghetti and pizza (25,000 pesos). Live bands Tues.-Sun. 8pm-1am (cover 10,000 pesos). Open Tues.-Sun. 1pm-1am.

Mesón de San Jacinto, Pl. San Jacinto 20. Cheap steaks (13,000 pesos) and a serene atmosphere are the attractions at this restaurant-gallery. Good tacos and chicken to boot. Open Mon.-Sat. 9am-6pm.

Fonda San Angel, Pl. San Jacinto 9. Tasty *sopa de queso* (cheese soup) served on colorful tablecloths. The sophisticated locals are often caught musing about the natural splendor of Oregon.

Near Chapultepec

In Mexico City's western corner, south of Chapultepec and west of Chapultepec Park, great food greets you in restaurants that provide their own scenery: one built around a greenhouse, another with maniacal roving *mariachis,* and yet another that is devoutly macrobiotic, reserving half of its dining room to floor seating (remember to sit lotus-style). This area is a fun place to eat, a getaway for those stuck in the Zona Rosa rut. All restaurants are within walking distance of the Sevilla Metro station.

Las Palomas Fonda, Cozumel 37, in Colonia Roma. As if the *mariachis* and vocalists were not entertaining enough, the food is delicious and the prices are low. The exterior dining room is built into a greenhouse, with exotic plants and flowers draped over the tables. Try the *carne asada* (broiled steak), with salad and potatoes (17,000 pesos). Open Mon.-Sat. 8am-10pm.

Centro Macrobiotico Tao, Cozumel 76, in Colonia Roma. No steak and potatoes here. On the front bulletin board, posters advertise T'ai-Ch'i classes, macrobiotic cooking classes, reflexology, and acupunture treatment, as well as healing crystals. A display case holds stacks of holistic diet books and bins of whole grains, soy products, and seaweed. Eastern floor seating with miniature tables and straw placemats. Vegetarian *comida corrida* of spiced rice and various veggies (15,000 pesos) served daily 1:30-4:30pm. Open daily 1-5pm.

El Mesón de la Mancha, Puebla 326 (tel. 286-87-64), at Cozumel. Great food and excellent service at a virtuous price. Frequented in mid-afternoon by dapper businessfolk. Occasional live *mariachis.* Complete meals 6000-7500 pesos; breakfast specials 5000 pesos. Open Mon.-Fri. 8am-9pm, Sat. 8am-5pm.

Restaurant MG, Londres 275, at the Sevilla Metro station. As lively as the old English sportscars of the same name. Hearty *comida corrida* (6000 pesos) served at a snail's pace from 1-6pm. Open daily 8am-10pm.

Fonda Moma' Tita, Sevilla 41, at the Sevilla Metro station. Cheap and convenient, but not as exceptional a dining experience as the others in the area. The menu sticks to tacos and sandwiches. Open daily 8am-10pm.

Sights

Even in a month, it would be impossible to see everything in Mexico City. It would be meaningless to stay for less than three full days, and you'll need a week to come away with anything resembling a well-rounded picture of the city.

If your time is very limited, you might visit a few of the buildings and museums in the Alameda or Centro area, such as the Palacio de Bellas Artes on the Alameda or the Palacio Nacional on the Zócalo. A number of ruins and interesting towns just outside the D.F. make good daytrips.

Centro

The heart of Mexico City, the Centro, could easily take weeks to explore. From the grand Palacio Nacional and the enormous Catedral Metropolitana to the Monte Nacional de Piedad (National Pawn Shop) and Museo de la Ciudad de México, the area is the cradle of much of the nation's culture.

The sights described in this section are divided into those east, north, and south of the Zócalo. To get there by Metro, take Line 2 to the Zócalo station. The station's entrance sits on the east side of the square, in front of the Palacio Nacional. Other buildings surrounding the plaza are the Catedral Metropolitana to the north, the Federal District offices to the south, and the Suprema Corte de Justicia to the southeast. For an intelligently annotated checklist of every sight in the Centro, get a copy of the *Historic Center of the City of Mexico* from the map's publisher, SAC BE, Apdo. Postal 22-315, 14000 México, D.F.

The Zócalo

The principal square of Mexico City, officially named the Pl. de la Constitución, is more widely known by its adopted title, the Zócalo. Now surrounded by imposing colonial monuments, the square was originally the nucleus of the Aztec capital Tenochtitlán. The conquistadors razed Tenochtitlán, then built the seat of New Spain on top of the ruins, using stones from the destroyed city in the construction of Spanish churches and government buildings. To the southwest of the Templo Mayor (the Aztecs' principal place of worship, which they called Teocalli) was the Aztec marketplace and major square. Cortés paved this expanse with stones from the main pyramid, calling it "Plaza de Armas" or "Plaza Real." He also assigned the plaza its perimeter (the dimensions of 240m on each side persist to this day), but it has since gone through many transformations.

Not long after the square was paved, posts and tents sprang up and brought the market back to life. In place of the one that burned down in 1692, a new marketplace was built, the Mercado del Parián. So chaotic and confused was this labyrinth of posts, tents, and small buildings that, in 1790, the area was leveled again and reorganized. The Spanish purportedly borrowed the plaza layout from construction in Spain during the period of Arab occupation (711-1492). Because the Arab rulers considered water sacred, and ordered it to flow freely in their city centers, many large fountains burble in the Zócalo and other plazas. In the building process, two very important archeological objects were unearthed: the statue of Coatlicue (deity of life and death) and Piedra del Sol (the Aztec calendar). This second stone spent nearly a century leaning haphazardly against the cathedral's west side before the old Museo Nacional claimed it in 1885. Both artifacts are now at the Museo Nacional de Antropología in Bosque de Chapultepec.

The square became the Pl. de la Constitución in 1812 when the representative assembly of the viceroyalty adopted the liberal Constitución de Cádiz here to protest Napoleon Bonaparte's occupation of Spain. This act of rebellion gave direction to the turmoil that eventually led to Mexico's independence. In 1843, the dictator Santa Anna destroyed the Mercado del Parián and ordered that a monument to Independence be constructed in the center of the square. Only the *zócalo* (pedestal) was in place when the project was abandoned. The citizens of Mexico began to refer to the square as *el Zócalo,* which has become the generic name for the central plaza in nearly all of the Republic's cities and towns. In 1952, Mexico City's Zócalo was flattened into its present form.

East of the Zócalo

Palacio Nacional

During his reign, Moctezuma II built a new palace, called the "New Houses," just south of the Teocalli. The Spaniards obliterated the palace, and in 1529 the king of Spain granted the land to Hernán Cortés. Cortés, who proceeded to erect a new house of his own there. Architects Rodrigo de Pontecillas and Juan Rodriguez designed the building and *indígena* slave laborers built it using the stones from Moctezuma's palace. In 1562, the king of Spain bought back this house and the property from Don Martín Cortés (son of the conquistador), and made it the palace of the king's viceroys. The palace was destroyed during the Riot of 1692 and rebuilt a year later with stones from the original building. Subsequent modifications have given the building a Baroque character, although vestiges of earlier styles remain. The first two stories of the present palace date from the 1692 riot. In 1927, President Plutarco Calles ordered the construction of a third story to beautify the remains of the old palace. On the eastern patio are traces of the botanical gardens once cultivated by Emperor Maximilian's wife. The central patio hosted the first Mexican bullfight, in honor of Cortés's famous return from Honduras to resume leadership of the capital. For a time bullfights were staged here every Friday afternoon to entertain viceroys of the palace.

Now called the Palacio Nacional de México, the building occupies the entire east side of the Zócalo, bounded on the north and south, respectively, by Moneda and Corregidora. Chief executive center of the Republic, the Palacio houses the federal government's treasury and defense departments, as well as monumental murals, historical rooms, and a museum in honor of Benito Juárez. Connected to the palace is the Museo de Las Culturas (see next section), once the National Mint of Emperor Maximilian's administration.

The Palacio's murals covering the stairway wall north of the main entrance are perhaps Diego Rivera's most famous works. Sketching and painting steadily from 1929 to 1951, Rivera completed most of the frescoes, except for the unfinished and staggeringly large sequel to *Mexico Through the Centuries,* his first masterpiece. This famous mural, found in the central patio at the top of the grand staircase, depicts the social evolution of Mexico. The huge mural covering the southern portion of the palace's western wall, *Struggle of the Classes,* is a sharp statement of Rivera's

Marxist beliefs. Opposite it on the northern wall is a work entitled *La Legenda de Quetzalcóatl*, which illustrates the life of the legendary Toltec priest-king who fled from his kingdom, conquered the Mayan people, and ruled over the Yucatán Peninsula.

Another mural, *La Invasión Americana, 1847*, depicts the siege at Castillo de Chapultepec, and the mural to its left, *La Reforma de las Leyes, 1857*, is a study of the heroes of the reform and their achievements. Continuing left, you'll see *La Guerra de la Independencia de México, 1810*, which contrasts the Revolution of 1910 with the War of Independence a century earlier. The mural to its left is *La Revolución de Madero, 1910*. Featured here are Francisco Madero, who initiated the revolution and later became president; his vice-president, Pino Suárez; Victoriano Huerta, who usurped the presidency; and the leaders in the Revolutionary War—Pancho Villa, Luis Cabrera, and Venustiano Carranza. At the top of the stairs, *El Fusilamiento de Maximiliano* portrays the execution of the emperor and two loyal Mexican generals, Miramón and Mejía. *La Lucha de las Clases* depicts Mexican peasants along with workers from all over the world. Three murals relate the achievements of the great Tarascan, Zapotec, and Totonac civilizations, and three others show the evolution of corn, the harvesting of cacao, and the all-important *maguey* industry (*maguey* is used in making tequila). *El Desembarco en Veracruz* graphically depicts the injustices of the slave trade. The most impressive mural is *La Gran Tenochtitlán*, which is dominated by the Mercado de Tlatelolco and filled out with the Temple of Tlatelolco, the center of Tenochtitlán, and the volcanoes Popocatépetl (Smoking Mountain) and Iztaccíhuatl (Sleeping Woman).

The Palacio also contains the Bell of Dolores (not a mural), which was brought to the capital in 1896 from Dolores Hidalgo in Guanajuato state. It can be seen from outside the Palacio, at the top of the Baroque façade. Padre Miguel Hidalgo de Dolores rang this bell on September 16, 1810, calling the people of Mexico to fight for their independence. Every year on that date it rings in memory of the occasion, with the Mexican president repeating the words once shouted by the Father of Independence. (Palacio open daily 8am-5pm. Guided tours Mon.-Fri. 10am-4pm. Free.)

The museum dedicated to Mexico's most revered president, Benito Juárez, is in the room in which he died on the Palacio's second floor. The **Museo Recinto Homenaje a Benito Juárez** (tel. 522-56-46) contains a monument, a deathmask, and various belongings of the author of the reform laws. (Open Tues.-Fri. 9am-7pm. Free.)

During the early colonial years, barter and the unregulated exchange of gold pieces prevailed in the Spanish-oriented markets and businesses of Mexico City. In 1535, Carlos V, king of Spain, sent Antonio de Mendoza to New Spain as his first viceroy and asked that he establish a *Casa de Moneda* (treasury), to which all gold and silver had to be carted to be converted into coin (and taxed, of course). In 1567 the Casa de Moneda came to occupy the building at the northeast corner of the Palacio Nacional, now the **Museo de las Culturas**, Moneda 13 (tel. 512-74-52), the former site of Moctezuma's home. The museum illuminates such cultures as Japan, Bulgaria, China, the Americas, and Egypt. (Open Tues.-Sat. 9:30am-6pm, Sun. 9:30am-4pm. Free.)

Other Sights

La Merced, Circunvalación at Anaya east of the Zócalo, or at Metro Merced on Line 2 (turn left out of the subway's eastern exit), is the largest food market of its kind in the world. Farmers from all over Mexico sell their goods here. The fruit section alone covers a large fraction of the 600 square blocks. Here you'll find fruits of every sort imaginable—papayas, home-grown lichee nuts, *mameyes* from Tabasco, mangos, nine different kinds of *plátanos*, hot tamales, and two full blocks of assorted chiles. Exotic indigenous foods such as fried turtles, steamed chicken intestines, *charales*—Indian corn husks stuffed with shiners—and steamed crayfish abound. Choose from the display of *dulces* (candies) that stretches for 5 blocks; each vendor's stall displays over 300 different candies.

Just outside the beehive-like market blocks, on the corner of Manzanares and Circunvalación, sits the smallest church in the world, **El Señor de la Humildad,** measuring a mere six yards by nine yards and seating a maximum of 20 (open daily 9am-8pm). Two blocks southeast of the church at the corner of Uruguay and Talavera is the colonial **Convent of La Merced,** built in 1630, with a wide-open, Rococo inner courtyard. Spanish priests occupied the convent after the Conquest, and the courtyard was used as a neighborhood market until the convent recently was designated a museum and off-limits to commercial vendors. Closed in the summer of 1990, the convent should re-open in early 1991.

On the corner of Calle de la Santísima and La Cadena is an elaborate Rococo church, the exquisite **Templo de la Santísima,** one of the most important examples in the city of the ornamental Churrigueresque style. It was built between 1755 and 1783, perhaps by Lorenzo Rodríguez, who directed the expansions made to the Casa de Moneda between 1772 and 1780. Figures on the facade were intended to appear as if constructed of ivory, wood, and cloth. The inside of the church is unimpressive, since the original decorations are long gone. Don't come here after dusk; the temple is lit but not patrolled well. (Open daily 7am-1pm and 5-8pm.)

West on La Cadena, a mammoth wall of coarse volcanic rocks rises for an entire block. The building dates to the Inquisition, and its western section is now the **National Academy of San Carlos,** which contains replicas of famous Roman statues and works created in the latest Western styles adopted by many young artists. (Open Mon.-Fri. 8am-8pm.)

North of the Zócalo

Catedral Metropolitana

The conquest of Aztec religion by the forces of Christianity is perhaps more impressive than Cortés's military triumph over Moctezuma's warriors. Mexico, once a land devoted to Quetzalcóatl, Tlaloc, and Huitzilopochtli, became a New World stronghold of Christianity. In 1524, Cortés had Mexico's first cathedral built on the northwest corner of the Zócalo, using stones from the temples of Tenochtitlán. Until 1552, this was the main church in Mexico and apparently the one the Franciscans used before building their own convent and church near the present site of the Torre Latinoamericana. In 1530, another cathedral went up on the site of the Templo Mayor and remained there until 1624. In 1544, the Spanish began construction of the Catedral Metropolitana, the massive structure on the north side of the Zócalo. The 109m-long and 54m-wide cruciform cathedral encompasses the architectural styles of three centuries. Between 1544 and 1573, architect Claudio Arciniega directed the construction of the cathedral, modeling it after the one in Sevilla, Spain (Arciniega also designed America's first true cathedral in Santo Domingo). Dedicated in the middle of the 17th century, the Catedral Metropolitana wasn't finished until 1813. In that year, Manuel Tolsá completed the great central dome, the façade, and the statues of Faith, Hope, and Charity which crown the clock tower.

The cathedral has several attached annexes. The main annex, with its door to the left of the cathedral, holds the **Altar de Perdón** (Forgiveness), a replica of a Churrigueresque alterpiece built by Jeronimo de Balbás between 1731 and 1736 and destroyed by fire in 1967. The cedar interior of the choir gallery, constructed in 1695 by Juan de Rojas, is decorated with an elegant grille of gold, silver, and bronze. Juan Correa's murals of the coronation of the Virgin, St. Michael slaying the dragon, and the triumphant entrance of Jesus into Jerusalem cover the sacristy's walls. Cristóbal de Villalpando painted the two other grand murals in this section, *La Immaculada Concepción* and *El Triunfo de la Iglesia.* Of the cathedral's many altars, one of the most magnificent is Balbás's Churrigueresque **Altar de los Reyes** (Kings), dedicated to those kings who were also saints.

The Spanish introduced to the Aztecs not only the concept of Jesus Christ but also what Roman Catholics refer to as the communion of saints. In the annex holding the Altar de Perdón, there are 14 *capillas* (chapels) dedicated to those saints.

Two chapels near the entrance honor Mexico's most famous patron saint, the Virgin of Guadalupe. Legend holds that she appeared on a mountain before a poor peasant named Diego, entreating him to have a church built in her honor at that site. In order to convince the Mexican bishop of his vision, Diego laid a sheet full of fresh roses cut during the cold of December in front of the bishop. Both in awe, they watched the Virgin's portrait emerge on the sheet. The church was built, and today's paintings depict that first impression on the sheet.

The eastern annex holds the **Sagrario Metropolitano** (sanctuary). The Sagrario holds six chapels, with one main and two lateral altars. The Sagrario Metropolitano, designed by the great Churrigueresque architect Lorenzo Rodríguez, was built between 1749 and 1768, and its façades have since been copied in thousands of Mexican churches. Left of center are statues of the 12 apostles; to the right, the 12 prophets. In the center, above the door, are two statues, St. John and, above him, St. Joseph. Elaborate reliefs decorate the whole facade, and the Virtues crown the structure.

Templo Mayor (Teocalli)

North of the Zócalo's northeast corner, a pool of water engulfs a brass model of the Aztec capital, Tenochtitlán. At the center of this city was a great religious square surrounded by walls, each side a ½ km long. When the Aztecs first arrived, the high priest Tenoch saw an eagle perched on a cactus, which he took as a sign that the people from Aztlán had found their home. The Templo Mayor, or Teocalli, was built on the spot where Tenoch saw the eagle, now the corner of Seminario and República de Guatemala, a few meters north of the brass model. Teocalli is the major excavated archeological site in Mexico City.

On February 28, 1978, workers digging east of the cathedral struck an immovable rock. They eventually unearthed an eight-ton Aztec stone on which had been carved the dismembered figure of the moon goddess Coyolxauqui, sister of Huitzilopochtli. The stone identified the area as the site of Teocalli, earlier believed to be buried under the Catedral Metropolitana to the southwest.

According to Aztec legend, Coatlicue, the terrible goddess of earth and death (whose monolithic statue now sits in the Museo Nacional de Antropología), became pregnant while sweeping the temples. Her daughter Coyolxauqui grew jealous of her and plotted with her 400 brothers to kill their mother. When they reached her, however, they discovered that Huitzilopochtli had already been born, full-grown. He beheaded his sister and turned his brothers into the planets and stars.

The stone that the diggers found served in ancient times as part of the base of a great pyramid. At the pyramid's summit were two temples, one dedicated to the war god Huitzilopochtli and one dedicated to the rain god Tlaloc. Worshipers practiced ritual human sacrifice here at selected times of the year, and staged flower wars with "rival" states to secure sacrificial warm bodies.

When the conquistadors arrived, Teocalli measured 103m by 79½ m at the base and was 61m high. Today the excavated ruins reveal five layers of pyramids, built one on top of the other as the Aztec empire grew. Over 7000 artifacts, including sculpture, jewelry, and pottery, were found amidst the ruins. Many of the pieces have been traced to distant societies dominated by the Aztecs. The extraordinary **Museo del Templo Mayor**, now part of the archeological complex, houses this unique collection. A beautiful scale model of Tenochtitlán at the height of its power, along with the stone of Coyolxauqui, are the centerpieces of this well-designed museum, which documents the history of the Aztec people from their legendary origins in Aztlán to the conquest by the Spaniards in 1521. More so than the silent and decapitated ruins adjacent to it, the museum bears witness to the glories of México-Tenochtitlán and makes the arrogant pride of their *Cantares Mexicanos* more understandable:

Oh giver of life!
Bear it in mind, oh princes

Forget it not
Who can siege Tenochtitlán?
Who can disturb the foundations of the sky?
With our arrows,
With our shields,
The city exists.
México-Tenochtitlán persists!
Proud of herself
Rises the city of México-Tenochtitlán
No one fears death in combat here.
This is our glory
This is your mandate.

(Museums and ruins open Tues.-Sun. 9am-5pm. Guided tours in Spanish free, in English 10,000 pesos per person.)

Iglesia de Santo Domingo

The Iglesia de Santo Domingo, on the corner of Brasil and Venezuela, 4 blocks north of the Zócalo's northwest corner, was founded by 12 Dominicans who arrived in 1526, three years after the first 12 Franciscans came from Spain. Within a year, five of the Dominicans had died and the other seven had fallen very ill. In 1527 all but three of the remaining friars returned to Spain. Among the three who stayed behind, Domingo de Bentanzos founded the Convento de Santo Domingo in Mexico City as well as many more in the provinces of Guatemala. The first church, completed in 1590, was admired for its beauty. Unfortunately, a flood destroyed its foundations in 1716. By 1736 the present church was completed. The Baroque edifice, considered one of the most beautiful in Mexico City, was built at a cost of 200,000 pesos, an enormous sum at the time. Its highlight, the façade, features the intertwined arms of St. Domingo and St. Francis, as well as statues of the two saints. Also depicted is our man Diego holding up the impression of the Virgin of Guadalupe, with the Mexican bishop looking on in awe. (Church open daily 7:30am-8pm.)

South of the Zócalo

Ever since the Conquest, metropolitan offices have occupied the current site of Federal District bureaucracy. In 1691, a hard rainfall destroyed the wheat crop, causing a famine in the working classes the following year. The viceroy, Count de Gálvez, initiated rationing, but when rumors of nearly exhausted grain supplies spread, a group of *indígenas* was sent to investigate. De Gálvez turned them away, bringing on the Riot of 1692, the most violent Mexico has ever seen. Several buildings were burned, including part of the palace and much of the Casas del Cabildo, which had sheltered the city government offices and archives. Two buildings now compose offices of the **Departamento del Distrito Federal.** The older one, on the southwest end of the Zócalo, was built according to the same plan as the original structure, which burned down during the riot. The newer building, on the southeast end of the Zócalo, was built between 1940 and 1948, 400 years after its twin. Fortunately, Don Carlos de Sigüenza y Góngora saved the building's archives, currently located in the Archivo Nacional. Now most of the buildings are administrative; if you have bundles of extra time, you can visit the exciting water services building.

One block south of the older of the two government office buildings (the block bounded by 5 de Febrero, Uruguay, 20 de Noviembre, and Manzanares) are monuments to three 18th-century homes. On the northwest corner of the block is the **Casa de la Marquesa de Uluapa;** on the southeast corner are **Casa del Conde de la Cortina** and **Casa del Conde de la Torre Cossía.**

Suprema Corte de Justicia

The Suprema Corte de Justicia, built in 1929, stands on the corner of Pino Suárez and Corregidora, on the spot where the southern half of Moctezuma's royal palace once stood, diagonally opposite the Zócalo's southeast corner. Four rather ferocious

Orozco murals cover the walls of the second-floor lobby. On the west wall hangs *Riquezas Nacionales,* in which a giant tiger, representing the national conscience, defends the mineral riches of the Republic. The mural on the east wall, *El Trabajo,* symbolizes Article 123 of the Mexican Constitution, which guarantees workers' rights. The two remaining murals are called *La Justicia.* The one on the north wall shows a bolt of fire taking human form; the apparition wields a huge axe, with which it threatens a group of masked evil-doers. On the south wall, Justice sleeps on a pedestal, holding a sword and the law. (Open Mon.-Fri. 9am-3pm.)

After Moctezuma's palace was leveled, Spanish colonists turned the area into a garbage dump. Cortés claimed the property, had it cleared, and designated it the site of city festivities, including the pole dance, in which men suspended by ropes swung in circles from a pole. Until 1929, the plaza's nickname was "Plaza del Volador" (flyer).

Museo de la Ciudad de México

The Museo de la Ciudad de México, Pino Suárez 30 (tel. 542-00-83), at República de El Salvador, 3 blocks south of the Zócalo's southeast corner, has informative exhibits including maps, photographs, lithographs, and murals. Some depict the geological formation of the Valley of Mexico and Lake Texcoco. Other showcases detail the rise of the Aztec empire in the 15th and 16th centuries, with models of Tenochtitlán and diagrams of its social structure. Later galleries show, mostly through photographs, the usurpations, betrayals, and victories of the Revolution of 1910. The largest mural on display deserves special attention; it depicts the destruction of the Aztec empire in apocalyptic fashion, with fire engulfing Tenochtitlán, the dead burying the dead, and the Spanish marching the defeated and despairing Aztecs out of their city.

In contrast to the Templo Mayor Museum and its archeological view of Aztec culture, the Museo de la Ciudad offers an historical account of Mexican culture, and provides a broad background for most of your other sight-seeing. (Open Tues.-Sat. 9:30am-6:30pm, Sun. 9:30am-3pm. Free.)

Other Sights

Calle Corregidora, the street between the Suprema Corte and Palacio Nacional, skirts part of an ancient canal system that once connected the Aztec capital to the *pueblos* around Xochimilco. The government plans to uncover part of this canal, bridge it for pedestrians and motorists, and convert it into a reflecting pool. In their dreams.

Founded in 1603, the **Templo de Porta Coeli,** across Calle Manzanares from the Suprema Corte's southern end, was among the first institutions to teach the Catholic faith to young Spaniards and *indígena* Mexicans. The temple houses a replica of the original **Cristo Negro** (Black Christ), now at the Catedral Metropolitana. (Open Mon.-Sat. 9am-6pm, Sun. 9am-1pm.)

Calle Carranza, the continuation of Manzanares, was known for a long time after the Conquest as "Celada" (trap or ambush): during the fighting that led to the conquest of the city, the Aztecs killed many Spaniards by setting ingenious snares in this area.

Directly above Restorante El Malecón, at Carranza 9, is the skinniest apartment building in the world. Its four stories measure 11m high and only 3m wide. The art-nouveau architecture stands out against the row of modern restaurants and stores beneath. Its super-slender profile is hard to miss.

The **Templo de Valvanera,** is 2 blocks east of Porta Coeli on Carranza, and 1 block south on Correo Mayor. Before being converted to a convent around 1600, the temple fed, sheltered, and educated the widows left behind by the Spanish subdual of all New Spain. In 1594, the present edifice replaced the original adobe building.

Southwest of the Zócalo, at the corner of 5 de Febrero and 16 de Septiembre, is the famous **Gran Hotel de la Ciudad de México.** Visit at midday to see the light shine through the Tiffany stained-glass ceiling with three flower-shaped central domes. Every detail is pure art nouveau. Panoramic elevators with green velvet trim in open wrought-iron casings are visible from the lobby floor. Beautiful Baccarat chandeliers illuminate the hotel entrance, and red velvet footstools and mirrored coffee tables decorate the main foyer. No gaping allowed.

Alameda

Alameda Central is a beautiful park in the middle of downtown Mexico City. Many of the city's historical landmarks are located in the surrounding area, known simply as Alameda. For budget travelers, because of the many bus and Metro routes that criss-cross the area, Alameda is a superb base as well.

Avenida Hidalgo runs along the north side of the park, becoming Tacuba on the other side of Lázaro Cárdenas, 1 block east of the park. Along the south side runs Av. Juárez, which becomes Av. Madero past Lázaro Cárdenas. Lázaro Cárdenas was called Av. San Juan de Letrán until 1980, and some older maps may still carry this name. You can park on many of the streets near the Alameda. Round, white, no-parking signs have a large "E" (as in *estacionamiento*) in the center, with a line through it. There are two Metro stations near the park: the Hidalgo station (Lines 2 and 3) is at the intersection of Hidalgo and Paseo de la Reforma, just 1 block west of the park's northwest corner, and the Bellas Artes station (Line 2) is 1 block east of the park's northeast corner. Maps of the area are available at the tourist office (see Practical Information above).

Alameda Central

Alameda Park has existed for hundreds of years, yet only in this century did it open to the general public. It is an icon of the city, as Diego Rivera recognized in his mural of the Alameda (see below). All elements of society congregate around it. Scattered about are saintly but imposing statuettes staring over miniature fountains at amorous couples smooching on park benches. Nearby, patient vendors whip up culinary specialties, while comedians and mimes draw crowds with showy sidewalk acts.

Palacio de Bellas Artes

This palace is but one result of the progressive "capitalization" plan established during the Porfiriato. Apart from its role as a repository of great works by 20th-century Mexican artists, the Palacio de Bellas Artes, facing the eastern end of Alameda, is a fascinating artifact of Díaz's time and the subsequent revolution. Construction began in 1904 under the Italian architect Boari, who promised a fantastically innovative building. The Italian extravaganza was intended to symbolize national progress and as a theater for Mexico's upper class. The plan was to complete the building by 1910, the centennial of Mexico's fight for independence, but the task turned out to be greater than expected. Soon after construction began, the theater started to sink into the city's soft ground. (It has sunk 5m to date.) Despite efforts to shore up the building, work was delayed and then completely halted in 1913 during the revolution. By the time activity was resumed in 1932, Boari was dead and the new government decided to open the Palacio de Bellas Artes instead of a theater. The job was finished in 1934, and the museum finally opened in 1946. In completing the building, the second architect, Federico Mariscal, respected Boari's exterior design but dramatically altered the interior.

Mariscal's art deco interior strikingly contrasts with the conservative exterior. This style, made popular in Paris at the 1925 decorative arts exposition, is characterized by sharp angles, geometric forms, and imaginative lighting. The Palacio also contains an enormous crystal curtain, part of Boari's original plan. This huge tapestry was designed by Gerardo Murillo (who later changed his name to Doctor Atl), one of the greatest Mexican painters of this century. Assembled in New York, the curtain consists of almost one million pieces of multi-colored crystals which, when back lit, represent the Valley of Mexico in twilight.

The Palacio displays a collection of the frescoes of David Alfaro Siqueiros, whose favorite themes were class struggle and social injustice. Two examples of the latter are his *Caín en los Estados Unidos,* an attack on racism in the U.S., and *Nacimiento del Fascismo.* Many of his paintings are layered with masonite, lending them a three-dimensional effect. A good example of this technique is *Explosión en la Ciudad,* in which the smoke from an explosion seems to stream toward the viewer.

Siqueiros experimented with lighting, colors, and surfaces, but he is best known as a *típico* muralist. Several of his murals are on the Palacio's third floor. On the east wall hang murals by José Clemente Orozco depicting the tension between humans and machines.

If you have time for only one mural, see the one by Diego Rivera on the west wall of the third floor. Intended for a North American audience, the original was painted in New York City's Rockefeller Center but destroyed because of its political content. When an angry Rivera petitioned the Mexican government to allow him to duplicate the work, he was given this space in the Palacio. This second, more vehement rendering includes an unflattering portrayal of John D. Rockefeller, Sr. (Palacio de Bellas Artes open Tues.-Sun. 10am-9pm. Free.)

The **Ballet Folklórico de México** performs regional and historical dances in the Palacio de Bellas Artes and the Teatro Ferrocarilero (Revolucíon Metro stop). Their two companies, one resident and one traveling, are known the world over for their choreographic and theatrical skill. (Performances Wed. at 9pm, Sun. at 9:30am and 9pm. Tickets 20,000-50,000 pesos, sold 3 or 4 days in advance at Bellas Artes Mon.-Sun. 11am-3pm and 5-9pm.) Travel agencies snatch up lots of tickets during Christmas, *Semana Santa,* and summer; check first at Bellas Artes, then try along Reforma or in the Zona Rosa. You can contact Bellas Artes at 529-17-01 about seat availability.

Museo Nacional de Arte

The Museo Nacional de Arte, Tacuba 8 (tel. 512-32-24), ½ block east of the Palacio's north side, completed before the revolution, is more representative of the Díaz era than is the Palacio de Bellas Artes. It was designed to house the Ministry of Communications, the brainchild of Porfirio Díaz. The architect, Silvio Conti, designed its pre-Cambrian façade and paid particular attention to the central staircase: its beautifully sculpted Baroque handrails and lampposts and ornate blue-and-gold ceilings were crafted by artists in Florence and shipped to Mexico.

Unlike the Palacio de Bellas Artes, this museum contains works from the stylistic and ideological schools of every era in Mexican history. The galleries are divided by style and era. The works of the second floor include some by Doctor Atl ("water" in Nahuatl), the great precursor of Mexican muralism. He is best known for his volcano paintings, but *La Nube* is unparalleled among his works in its use of sprightlier blues, yellows, and greens. Other works on the second floor include paintings by Orozco, Ramón, Cano Manilla (renowned for his use of color to celebrate *indígena* life), and José María Velasco, whose paintings include several panoramic landscapes of the Valley of Mexico. The upper floors exhibit art from New Spain, religious art, and cartoon and newspaper art. Special temporary exhibits occupy the rear of the ground floor.

Other paintings on display deal with themes from the Old Testament. Santiago Rebull's *La Muerte de Abel* shows Cain fleeing after killing his brother, and Rebull's *Sacrificio de Isaac* shows Abraham following God's mandate by sacrificing his son. (Museo Nacional de Arte open Tues.-Sun. 10am-5pm. Admission 8000 pesos.)

In front of the building is a brilliant bronze equestrian statue, *El Caballito.* At the close of the 18th century, the viceroy of Mexico commissioned Neoclassical sculptor Don Manuel Tolsá to cast this monument in honor of Carlos IV de Borbón, King of Spain. Between 1824 and 1852, the monument had to be hidden at the University of Mexico because of strong anti-Spanish sentiment.

Across Tacuba street from the Museo Nacional stands the original **Palacio de Minería** (Mining), also built by Tolsá in the late 18th century. In 1867 it became the Escuela Nacional de Ingeniería, probably the first technical school in the Americas. (Open daily 7am-8pm. Free.)

Near Alameda Central

José Martí was a poet-intellectual and leader of the Cuban Independence movement in the late 19th century. He dreamt of a united and free Latin America with Mexico a leader in the region, and repeatedly warned of the dangers of North American imperialism. A poem Martí wrote for Mexico is inscribed on the wall of the **Centro Cultural José Martí,** Dr. Mora 2 (tel. 521-21-15), at Hidalgo on Alameda's west end. The center contains books by Martí and other anti-interventionists, and sponsors a program of musical performances, poetry readings, and art exhibits. The program is posted just outside the center and advertised in *Tiempo Libre,* which can be found at any newsstand. (Open Mon.-Fri. 9am-9pm, Sat. 9am-2pm. Free. All exhibits and readings in Spanish.)

The **Pinacoteca Virreinal de San Diego,** Dr. Mora 7 (tel. 510-27-93), next door to Centro José Martí, was once a large monastery inhabited by the order of San Diego. Now the monastery's large rooms with high, decorated ceilings and wooden floors contain a large collection of Baroque and Mannerist paintings. (Open Tues.-Sun. 9am-5pm. Admission 5000 pesos.)

The **Museo de la Alameda,** on Calzada Colón, facing the small park at the west end of the Alameda, holds Diego Rivera's *Sueño de une Tarde Dominical en la Alameda Central* (Dream of a Sunday afternoon at the Alameda Central). The painting, originally commissioned by the Hotel del Prado, depicts the dreams of different classes of people parading about the Alameda on a Sunday afternoon at the turn of the century. One of them, Ignacio Ramírez, holds up a pad of paper that reads "God does not exist," an excerpt from a speech he gave in the 1830s. Because of that image, the Archbishop of Mexico refused to bless the hotel, and irate citizens defaced the mural many times. The hotel partially collapsed during the 1985 quake, and the undamaged mural was moved to the museum, which was constructed solely to hold this one piece. (Open Tues.-Sun. 10am-6pm. Admission 5000 pesos.)

The **Torre Latinoamericana** (Latin American Tower), 181m and 42 stories high, touches the sky over the corner of Lázaro Cárdenas and Madero (the continuation of Juárez), 1 block east of Alameda Central's southeast corner. From the top of the tallest building in Mexico, you can often see the entire city and the mountains surrounding it. (Top-floor observatory open daily 10am-11pm. Admission 8000 pesos.) On the 41st floor, the Miralto bar charges more than 5000 pesos per mixed drink (you don't have to pay the observatory fee), but the view is worth the inflated prices.

La Iglesia de San Francisco rests in the shadow of the Torre Latinoamericana just to the east on Madero. It was once a vast monastic complex that included several churches, a school, and a hospital. Two fragments of the original cloisters can be seen at Gante 5, on the east side of the church, and Lázaro Cárdenas 8, behind a vacant lot. The Franciscans were the first order to arrive in Mexico; among the 12 initial monks were some of the greatest linguists, ethnographers, and chroniclers of indigenous custom and belief in the annals of Mexican history. The present church was built in 1716.

Across the street from San Francisco shimmers the **Casa de Azulejos,** an early 17th-century building covered with *azulejos* (blue-and-white tiles) from Puebla. To be able to afford even a token few of these tiles was a mark of considerable status. This mansion came to be blanketed with them after a father admonished his son that he would come to naught and the son set out to prove his father wrong. To see the early mural by Orozco on the staircase walls, you must first pass through Sanborn's restaurant.

Just north of the Alameda is the new **Museo Franz Meyer,** Hidalgo 45, at Pl. de Santa Veracruz. Formerly the Hospital de San Juan de Dios, the building has been expertly restored and now houses an extensive collection of colonial furniture and other applied arts. (Open Tues.-Sun. 10am-5pm. Admission 400 pesos, free Sun.)

The **Ciudadela** (citadel) refers to two places in Mexico City. "Mercado de Artesanías de la Ciudadela" is a huge crafts market spreading southwest from the corner of Balderas and Ayuntamiento. "La Ciudadela," on the other hand, is a grand Neoclassical building that once served as a citadel. Madero and his vice-president were executed by the usurper Huerta here. The Ciudadela is a large gray building, worth seeing only if you happen to be at the market next door. It is next to a park where a monument honors General Don José María Morelos y Pavón, who was also imprisoned and executed here in 1815.

Palacio Iturbide, on Madero between Bolívar and Gante, 1½ blocks east of Lázaro Cárdenas and near the Iglesia de San Francisco, is a grand 18th-century palace with an impressive colonnaded courtyard. Emperor Agustín de Iturbide took over the residence in 1821. A gallery occupies the ground floor with exhibits that change every three months. (Open daily 10am-7pm. Free.)

Bosque de Chapultepec

A direct translation reads "forest of grasshoppers." On the western side of the city's center, this enormous park, with its many museums, hiking paths, and modern sports facilities, could easily consume several days of your stay. Mexico's most famous museum, the Museo Nacional de Antropología, sits among the hills of the park.

All the museums listed are in Old Chapultepec, the eastern half of the park, which fans out from the intersection of Paseo de la Reforma, Av. Chapultepec, Calzada Melchor Ocampo, and General Mariano Escobedo. Directly to the east lies the Zona Rosa. Take the Metro to Auditorio (Line 7) or to Chapultepec (Line 1) to reach the park.

Visit the Bosque on Sunday, when working-class families flock here for hours of cheap entertainment. Musical spectacles enliven the park, and voices fill the air promoting foods and trinkets. Best of all, most of the museums in the area and the zoo are free on Sundays.

Museo Nacional de Antropología

Some journey to Mexico just to visit this awesome museum. It is 4km of Mexico's finest archeological and ethnographic treasures, and the yardstick by which all other Mexican museums are measured.

Constructed of volcanic rock, wood, and marble, the museum opened in 1964. Pedro Ramírez Vásquez and his team of 42 engineers and 52 architects designed and built the structure in 18 months; meanwhile, archeologists, buyers, and 20 teams of ethnographers scrambled to enlarge the museum's collection. After the huge stone image of the rain-god Tlaloc greets you outside, 23 exhibition halls await on two floors surrounding a spacious central courtyard. Poetry from ancient texts and epics graces the entrances to the halls that lead out of the main courtyard. In the center of the courtyard, a stout column covered with symbolic sculptures supports a vast, upward-turning, water-spouting aluminum pavilion.

You'll need about three days to explore the entire museum. Archeological *salas* (halls), each devoted to a specific culture or region, occupy the ground floor. On the northern side of the ground floor, moving east to west, galleries display chronologically ordered artifacts of cultures that have dominated the Valley of Mexico. The Oaxacan, Mayan, Gulf Coast, Northern, and Western displays are on the southern side. Upper-level rooms contain modern ethnographic displays and lie directly above the rooms devoted to the corresponding ancient culture.

All the ethnographic halls of the museum have more or less the same plan, displaying the cultural accoutrements of the peoples now living in Mexico. The large shelters were built by indigenous people commissioned to duplicate their buildings in the museum. (Open Tues.-Sun. 9am-7pm. Admission 10,000 pesos, free Sun.)

To reach the museum, take bus #55 or 76 southwest on Reforma and signal the driver to let you off at the second stop after entering the park. On the Metro, take Line 1 to the Auditorio station; the museum is just down Reforma. For a more scenic route, take Line 1 to Chapultepec station. Outside stands the **Monumento a los Niños Héroes,** six black monoliths dedicated to the young cadets of the 19th-century military academy (then at Castillo de Chapultepec). In 1847, during the last major battle of the war with the U.S., the *Niños Héroes* fought the invading army of General Winfield Scott. Refusing to surrender, the last six boys wrapped themselves in the Mexican flag and threw themselves to their deaths from the castle wall. Behind the monument, Grand Av. cuts through the park. Walk west on this street and take the second right. A five-minute stroll north takes you to Reforma and the museum.

Museo Tamayo and Museo de Arte Moderno

Just to the east of the Museo Nacional de Antropología along Reforma is the **Museo Tamayo de Arte Contemporáneo Internacional** (tel. 286-58-39), on the corner of Reforma and Gandhi. The Mexican government created the nine halls of the museum after Rufino and Olga Tamayo donated their international collection to the Mexican people. Rufino Tamayo, born in 1889 in the city of Oaxaca, was considered un-Mexican during the nationalist era following the Revolution of 1910. Only recently has he been included in the distinguished group of Rivera, Siqueiros, and Orozco, rounding out the "Big Four." The museum, opened in 1981, has important works by Max Ernst, de Kooning, and the Surrealists Joan Miró and Masson. Other highlights include works by Pablo Picasso, Torres García, Mathías Goeritz, and Tamayo himself. Architects Gonzalo de León and Abraham Zabludovsky designed the building with non-converging lines and planes to create a feeling of openness. (Open Tues.-Sun. 10am-6pm. Admission 8000 pesos, free Sun. Call to arrange guided tours.)

The Museo de Arte Moderno, at Reforma and Gandhi (tel. 553-93-94), north of the Monumento a los Niños Héroes, houses a fair collection of contemporary abstract paintings by Mexican artists such as Siquieros, José Luis Cuevas, Rivera, and Velasco. The museum is linked to the Muse0 Tamayo by an outdoor sculpture garden. (Open Tues.-Sun. 10am-6pm. Admission 8000 pesos, free Sun.)

Museo Nacional de Historia

Inside the Castillo de Chapultepec, on top of the hill behind the Monumento a los Niños Héroes, is the Museo Nacional de Historia (tel. 286-07-00). This hill has seen its share of action, beginning in 1521. After the Conquest, Hernán Cortés claimed the hill and built a fortress here. Later, these lands were taken from him, under the authority of the king of Spain, and made into a wildlife preserve. In 1785, the first part of the present castle was built and designated the official residence of the king's viceroy. The last battle against U.S. invaders was fought here in 1847. When the Habsburg archduke Maximilian became emperor of Mexico in 1864, he made this castle his residence, commissioning architect Vicente Manero to expand it and painter Santiago Rebull to decorate it. Many of Mexico's leaders lived in the castle until 1940, when President Lázaro Cárdenas established the Museo Nacional de Historia here.

On the lower floor of the building, artifacts, murals, and documents narrate the history of Mexico from before the time of the Conquest. The galleries contain displays on Mexican economic and social structure during the war for independence, the Porfiriato, and the revolution. The upper level exhibits Mexican art, dress, and culture from the viceroyalty until the 20th century.

The rooms entered from outside the castle exhibit carriages used by Maximilian (the elaborate ones) and Juárez (the simple black one). The skyscrapers abutting the museum afford a view surpassed only by the Torre Latinoamericana. (Open Tues.-Sun. 9am-5pm. Admission 10,000 pesos, free Sun.)

Museo del Caracol

The Museo Galería de la Lucha del Pueblo Mexicano por su Libertad, on the southern side of Chapultepec hill, can be reached by way of the road leading to the castle. Better known as Museo del Caracol (conch) because of its spiral design, the gallery consists of 12 halls dedicated to retelling Mexican history from the early 19th to the early 20th century. Its documents, paintings, and models are all accompanied by well-written accounts (in Spanish) of the events. Scenes include the execution of Javier Mina, the compassion of Nicolás Bravo, the executions of Hidalgo and Morelos, the flight of Benito Juárez, the execution of Maximilian, the railroad-building of the dictator Díaz, the strike and massacre at Cananea, and the battles of Villa, Zapata, and Obregón. The staircase leads to a beautiful round hall, the sides of which form the inner wall of the spiral you have been ascending. A yellow skylight surmounts the space. Also inside is a copy of the Constitution of 1917 in Venustiano Carranza's hand. (Open Tues.-Sat. 9am-5pm, Sun. 10am-4pm. Free.)

Elsewhere in Chapultepec

Twenty-five days before his death in January of 1974, the artist David Alfaro Siqueiros donated his house and studio to the people of Mexico. In compliance with his will, the government created the **Museo Sala de Arte Público David Alfaro Siqueiros,** Tres Picos 29 (tel. 531-33-94), at Hegel just outside the park. Walk north from the Museo Nacional de Antropología to Rubén Darío; west about 1 block until you come to Hegel; and north on Hegel for 1 block—the museum is on your left. Fifteen thousand murals, lithographs, photographs, drawings, and documents of Siqueiros's life and thoughts fill the galleries. The museum also hosts seminars, conferences, concerts, and temporary exhibitions. Call before visiting to arrange a guided tour in English or Spanish. (Open Mon.-Fri. 10am-2pm and 5-7pm, Sat. 10am-2pm. Free.)

West of the Siqueiros museum along Rubén Darío, at the intersection with Reforma, lies the **Jardín Escultórico,** a park containing Realist and Symbolist statues. All of the works were privately donated. To the east of the sculpture garden, at Reforma and Av. Heroica Colegio Militar, grows the **Jardín Botánico,** a botanical garden whose lake contains a variety of fish. (Open daily 9am-5pm. Free.) Another spot guaranteed to please those tired of murals and churches is the **Parque Zoológico de Chapultepec,** just east of the Jardín Botánico. The first zoos in the Americas were established in this region: the emperor of Texcoco, Netzahualcóyotl, kept animals; Cortés founded bird sanctuaries and aquariums in Ixtapalpa; and Moctezuma II had a zoo that the Spaniards destroyed to build the Iglesia de San Francisco. Today, the zoo's most noteworthy residents are the rare panda bears, a gift from the People's Republic of China in 1975. Also worth seeing are the *Xoloitzcuintles,* bald Mexican dogs of pre-Conquest origin. The name means "dogs of Xolotl," and they were said to guide people in their passage to Xolotl, the god of death. (Zoo open Wed.-Sun. 9am-5pm. Free.)

Tlatelolco

Recent archeological digs have proven that the pre-Hispanic city Tlatelolco ("Mound of Sand" in Nahuatl) existed much earlier than the great Aztec capital of Tenochtitlán: the first king of Tlatelolco, Teutlehuac, began his rule in 1375. He and his warriors distinguished themselves in battle, conquering enemy territory near Tepeyac on the outskirts of Tenochtitlán. The Aztecs, living on an island in the central part of Lake Texcoco, realized at that point that the rulers of Tlatelolco, built on the northern part of the same lake, were threatening their political and military power.

By 1463, the Tlatelolco king, Moquihuix, had built his city into a busy trading center coveted by the Aztec ruler, Axayacatl. Tension mounted over territorial and fishing boundaries, and after a series of bungled spying sessions ordered by Axayacatl, Moquihuix learned that the Aztecs were preparing to attack his city. Even with that prescience, Moquihuix couldn't prepare his warriors well enough to defeat the Aztec onslaught, and Tlatelolco was absorbed into the huge empire.

Today, a government-built, low-income housing project surrounds the early 17th-century church that stands on the grounds of Tlatelolco's ancient temple. Three cultures—ancient Aztec, colonial Spanish, and modern Mestizo—have left their mark on this square, giving rise to the name **Plaza de las Tres Culturas,** at the corner of Insurgentes and Ricardo Flores Magón, 13 blocks north of the Palacio de Bellas Artes.

In the plaza, parts of the **Pyramid of Tlatelolco** and its ceremonial square remain. Enter from the southwest corner, in front of the Iglesia de Santiago, and walk along-side the ruins, down a steel and concrete path which overlooks the eight building stages of the main pyramid. By the time of the Conquest, the base of the pyramid extended from what is now Insurgentes to the current site of Iglesia de Santiago. The pyramid was second in importance to the great Teocalli of the Aztec capital, and its summit reached nearly as high as the modern skyscraper just to the south (the Relaciones Exteriores building). During the Spanish blockade of Tenochtitlán, the Aztecs heaved freshly sacrificed bodies of Cortés's forces down the temple steps, within sight of the conquistadors camped to the west at Tacuba. Aztec priests would collect the leftover body parts at the foot of the steps; food was scarce during the siege and all meat was valuable.

On the east side of the plaza stands the **Iglesia de Santiago,** an enormous, fortress-like church named after the patron saint of Spain, without whose help the Spaniards believed the Conquest could not have succeeded. The church was built in 1609 to replace an earlier structure of 1543. Before this, only a small altar and a cemetery were used to administer the sacraments to converted *indígenas.*

In 1531, the Virgin Mary appeared to Juan Diego, an early convert, on the hill where Aztecs worshiped the mother of their gods. The Virgin asked him to petition Fray Zumárraga to build a church on the spot. The petition was granted when, on Diego's second visit to the bishop, a figure of the Virgin appeared on his mantle. Today the mantle can be seen in **La Basílica de Guadalupe** at the La Villa Metro station (Line 6). When Pope John Paul II visited Mexico in 1979, he addressed priests and clergy at the Basilica. From the Metro, walk 2 blocks down Calzada. (Open daily 5am-9pm.) Behind the Basilica, winding steps lead up the side of a small hill, past lush gardens and cascading waterfalls. A small chapel dedicated to the Virgin of Guadalupe sits atop the hill. The bronze and polished wood interior of the chapel depicts the apparitions witnessed by Juan Diego.

Outside the chapel, the hill (a.k.a. Mt. Tepeyac) offers a wide, though smoggy, panorama of the city. On the other side of the hill, another waterfall drenches a bed of flowers. At the foot of the waterfall, a superhuman statue of Juan Diego kneels before the Virgin, offering her gifts of honor.

To get to Tlatelolco, take bus #27 ("Reculsorio Cd.-Jardín," every ½ hr.) north to the end of Insurgentes, or take the Metro to Tlatelolco station (Line 3) and walk east 3 long blocks to Eje Lázaro Cárdenas and then 1 block south.

Coyoacán

The Toltecs founded Coyoacán ("Place of the Coyotes" in Nahuatl) between the 10th and 12th centuries. Hernán Cortés later established the seat of the colonial government here, until he decided that Tenochtitlán would be a more appropriate center for his government. After the fall of Tlatelolco, Cortés had Cuauhtémoc tortured here, in the hope that he would reveal the hiding place of the legendary Aztec treasure. This community of conquistadors and their heirs holed up in *haciendas* and remained independent of the metropolis to the north for quite some time.

Today, Coyoacán is Mexico City's most pleasant and attractive suburb, worth visiting for its many museums or simply for a walk through peaceful Pl. Hidalgo or Placita de la Conchita. Because of the university's close proximity to the west, the suburb makes an ideal student residence and social center.

Sundays were made for Coyoacán. Young families and love-struck couples from different parts of the D.F. come to stroll through the fountain-filled **Plaza Hidalgo.** Toothless octogenarians sitting on benches eat tacos and drink beer, while young-sters buy cotton candy from the enthusiastic street vendors. Every Sunday there is some type of organized music, as bands belt out the congo, the rumba, or the fandango to the beat of the clapping crowd.

Near the plaza's northeast corner is a bronze statue of Don Miguel Hidalgo, the first spokesperson for Mexican independence. The **Casa de Cortés,** at the north end of the plaza, which is now the Palacio Municipal of Coyoacán, was once the administrative building of Hernán Cortés in the early colonial period. On the porch sits the coat of arms given to Coyoacán by the king of Spain, and inside are murals by Coyoacán resident Diego Rivera showing scenes from the Conquest. Public access to the building is sporadic. (Open Mon.-Fri. 9am-9pm.)

South of the plaza, beyond the Hidalgo statue, is the **Parroquia de San Juan Bautista,** bordered by Pl. Hidalgo on the north and Jardin Centenario on the west. The church and the convent date from the 16th century. The church interior is decorated elaborately with gold and bronze. Enter the convent south of the church's main door. (Open Tues.-Sat. 5:30am-8:30pm, Mon. 5:30am-7:30pm.) A few blocks southeast of Pl. Hidalgo is the famous **Casa Colorada,** Higuera 57, facing the Placita de la Conchita, which Cortés built for Doña Marina, La Malinche. When Cortés's wife arrived from Spain, she stayed here briefly with her husband, but soon disappeared without a trace. It is believed that Cortés murdered his spouse because of his passion for Marina, although he later gave La Malinche to one of his conquistador cronies.

The **Museo Nacional de Culturas Populares,** Hidalgo 289 (tel. 658-12-65), has exhibits on Aztec ceramics, paintings, and sculpture. The first entrancing section of the museum is dedicated to a deeper understanding of the maguey plant and its use as roofing shingles, as a medicine, and (most importantly) as a plant whose pulp when reduced to a liquid is used to make tequila. One whole room explains the distillation process. (Museum open Tues. and Thurs. 10am-4pm, Wed. and Fri.-Sat. 10am-8pm, Sun. 10am-5pm. Free.)

After Leon Trotsky was expelled from the Soviet Union by Stalin in 1927, he wandered in exile west of the his homeland, to Norway and Turkey, in search of refuge. Finally, Mexico's President Lázaro Cárdenas granted political asylum to Trotsky at the suggestion of Diego Rivera, a friend of the Russian revolutionary. Trotsky arrived in Mexico in 1937 with his wife Natalia Sedova and settled into the house that is now the **Museo y Casa de Leon Trotsky,** Viena 45, 7 blocks north of Pl. Hidalgo's northeast corner, then 3 blocks east on Viena to the corner of Morelos. The house was fortified with raised walls, additional guard posts in the corners, and steel doors and windows. Bullet holes riddle many parts of the house; these remained after muralist David Alfaro Siqueiros led a famous attempt on Trotsky's life on May 24, 1940. Trotsky and Sedova survived the attack by hiding under a table in a corner of their bedroom. During the attack, Siqueiros's group abducted Trotsky's secretary, Robert Sheldon Harte, whose body was found a few days later on the road to Toluca. A marble plaque just inside the entrance to the house is dedicated to Harte. A monument in the center of the garden holds Trotsky's and Sedova's ashes. Trotsky died on August 20, 1940, stabbed through the skull with an ice pick by Ramón Mercader, a Stalinist agent. Everything in the house has been left as it was when Trotsky lived. Sedova continued working for the revolutionary cause after her husband was killed, and when she died, the house, with all its original documents and papers on the Russian Revolution, was closed to protect Trotsky's friends. The rooms display many of the couple's belongings, including a turn-of-the-century Russian dictionary and the complete works of Lenin, Marx, and Engels. To enter, pull the little wire on top and to the left of the door. A guard will appear to open the door. (Open Mon.-Fri. 10:30am-2pm and 3-5pm, Sat.-Sun. 10:30am-4pm.)

One of Coyoacán's most interesting sights is the **Museo Frida Kahlo,** Londres 247 (tel. 677-29-84), at Allende 5 blocks north of Pl. Hidalgo's northeast corner. The museum is the dark blue house at the northeast corner of the intersection. Works by Rivera, Orozco, Duchamp, and Klee hang in this well-restored colonial house, once home to one of Mexico's most artistically talented citizens, Frida Kahlo. Having suffered a debilitating accident as a young woman, Kahlo was confined to a wheelchair and bed for most of her life. While married to Diego Rivera, she began painting and became a noteworthy artist. Her chronic health problems, together with devotion to an adulterous husband, inspired the fantastic and often shocking subject matter of her works. During Rivera's absences she became emotionally attached to Leon Trotsky, but after a personal and political break between Rivera and Trotsky, a bust of Stalin replaced the pictures of Trotsky that she once hung in her home. Her wheelchair and the cast that covered her entire upper torso are still in the house. The cast is covered with patterns and figures painted by Kahlo and her husband. Kahlo was ardently supportive of Mexican culture, and many of the rooms contain pottery, ceramics, cookware, and other provincial decorations. She died at the age of 42, in the upper-story studio that Rivera built for her. (Open Tues.-Sun. 10am-2pm and 3-6pm. Tours Sat. at 11am. Free.)

To the northeast of the Pl. Hidalgo once stood a pyramid dedicated to the Aztec war god Huitzilopochtli. Over time, the name degenerated to "Ocholopocho" and then "Ochorobusco." In the mid-18th century, the area came to be known as "Churubusco," and the convent there as the **Convento de Nuestra Señora de Los Angeles de Churubusco,** at 20 de Agosto and General Anaya. Built in 1524 over the ruins of the Aztec pyramid, it was originally a Franciscan convent, dedicated to Santa María de los Angeles. The Franciscans soon abandoned it, and in 1580 the Diegans moved in. The present church was built in 1668. On August 20, 1847, General Manuel Rincón, Pedro Anaya, and 800 Mexicans halted 8000 advancing U.S. soldiers here. When the U.S. General Twiggs asked General Anaya to turn over the remaining munitions, Anaya responded, "If we had munitions you would not be here."

Still guarding the convent's main entrance are two of the original seven cannons that defended the convent during the 1847 invasion. Two more cannons and a monument to Anaya flank the western side of the structure. The monument in front is dedicated to the civilian martyrs. Inside, a beautiful old garden grows, with indecipherable inscriptions and dedications on some of its walls. (Convent open Mon.-Fri. 7am-10pm, Sat. noon-2pm and 6-8:30pm, Sun. 8am-2pm and 5:30-8pm.)

Mexico has been invaded more than 100 times, most often by the U.S. Inside the Convento de Churubusco is a museum dedicated to the history of the invasions, the **Museo Nacional de Las Intervenciones** (tel. 604-06-99). The museum's halls are divided into four eras: late 18th century to 1839, 1839 to 1853, 1853 to 1872, and 1872 to 1917. There are also a few halls dedicated to exhibits on North American expansionism and cruelty to Native Americans, U.S. slavery and its significance for Mexico, and European imperialism. The walls of the museum are decorated with religious paintings from the convent and lists of the interventions and the related historical circumstances. Displays in the halls recount the social, economic, and political circumstances that encouraged other nations to intrude. (Museum open Tues.-Sun. 9am-6pm. Admission 8000 pesos.)

To get to the convent and museum from Coyoacán, walk 7 blocks down Hidalgo, then left 2 blocks on Division del Nte. Alternatively, take the "General Anoya Metro" *pesero* from Pl. Hidalgo.

Atop a hill, the **Museo Anahuacalli** (tel. 677-29-84), Calle Museo, is an ominous moated palace resembling Castle Grayskull. Designed by Diego Rivera, with Aztec, Mayan, and Riveran architectural styles in mind, Museo Anahuacalli houses the artist's huge collection of pre-Conquest art. Anahuacalli commands one of the best views in Mexico, comparable to those of the Torre Latinoamericana and Castillo de Chapultepec. (Open Tues.-Sun. 10am-2pm and 3-6pm. Free.) To reach the museum from Pl. Hidalgo or Churubusco, go 5km south on Av. División del Nte. to Calle Museo.

To reach Coyoacán from downtown, take the Metro directly to the Coyoacán station (Line 3). *Pesero* "Coyocán" at the station stops within two blocks of Pl. Hidalgo.

San Angel

South of Mexico City is the wealthy community of San Angel, marked by exquisite colonial homes and churches. To reach the area, 10km south of the Centro along Insurgentes, take the Metro to M.A. Quevedo station (Line 3). Walk west on

Quevedo for 3 blocks to the beautiful **Parque de la Bombilla**, at the intersection of Insurgentes and Miguel Angel de Quevedo. The centerpiece of this lovely park is the **Monumento al General Alvaro Obregón,** at Insurgentes Sur, between Arenal and Abasolo. Reliefs at the entrance to the monument represent peace, agriculture, industry, and the people in arms. The inscription on the far wall of the chamber reads, "I die blessing the revolution." During the revolution, Obregón lost an arm, which was preserved and on display inside the monument up until last year. Today all that remains is the glass jar that once held his arm. Pity. (Open daily 7am-3pm. Free.)

If you return east on Miguel Angel de Quevedo, just past the park, and then south on La Escondida, you will come to a 16th-century church in a hidden plaza. These are the **Plaza** and **Iglesia de San Sebastián Chimalistac,** between the streets of Abasolo and Federico Gamboa. The wife of *indígena* chief Ixtalinque, Señora de Chilapa, was buried here, but the best reason to visit is for the view of old colonial homes.

Continuing east along either Violeta or Gamboa, you will come to Río Magdalena (known as Joaquín Gallo south of the intersection), a winding road running north-south along an old riverbed. South on Gallo, you'll see the bridges that still span the dry bed. At the third bridge, make a right and walk along Carmen for a clear view of some of the nicer colonial homes; many of the streets are shaded with trees and decorated with running fountains. Carmen leads directly back to the Obregón monument.

Walk 2 blocks along La Paz, the street that runs from Parque de la Bombilla's southwest corner and crosses Insurgentes, until you come to an intersection. To the south are the three tiled domes of **Iglesia del Carmen,** Revolución at La Paz (open daily 7am-1pm and 4:30-9pm). Designed and built between 1615 and 1617 by Fray Andrés de San Miguel of the Carmelite order, the church and adjacent ex-convent are decorated with tiles and paintings. An outstanding statue of *Christ the Nazarene* is located in the Capilla del Señor Contreras. The ex-convent, now the **Museo del Carmen** (tel. 548-28-38), displays colonial art. Of particular interest are the paintings *San Juan de la Cruz* and *Santa Teresa.* The main tourist attraction, however, is the mummy collection, which could wrap you up for hours. Descend into the coffin's crypt to see the many mummies of the priest, nun, and noble varieties. (Museum open Tues.-Sun. 10am-5pm. Admission 5000 pesos.)

The Pl. del Carmen is across the street and west of the church. One block up Madero is the Pl. de San Jacinto, connected to the **Iglesia de San Jacinto,** at San Francisco, Benito Juárez, and Frontera. Sit in the tranquil garden of this 16th-century church after a walk around the cobblestone streets of the area, and take in its ancient orange façade and beautifully carved wooden doors. This neighborhood, the oldest in San Angel, contains many modern mansions as well. (Church open daily 8am-8pm.)

Shopping is one of the most popular activities in San Angel. A **FONART** (government-run Mexican crafts store) is at La Paz 37. **Caretta** (tel. 548-31-42), another crafts store, is just a few shops down the street at Insurgentes Sur 2105 on the corner of La Paz. (Open Mon.-Sat. 10am-7pm.) The **Bazaar Sábado** opens every Saturday and boasts "Mexico's 100 most talented craftspeople." Both quality and prices reflect that talent. A less expensive bazaar is outside in the Pl. San Jacinto. One of Mexico's most extensive English bookstores, the **American Bookstore,** is at Revolución 1570. (Open Mon.-Sat. 9am-7pm.) **Librería Gandhi,** Miguel Angel de Quevedo 128 (tel. 550-25-24), across from the Miguel Angel de Quevedo Metro stop, has one of the best cassette selections classical music, jazz, *salsa,* and *Nueva Canción* in the city. (Open Mon.-Fri. 9am-11pm, Sat.-Sun. 10am-10pm.)

Ciudad Universitaria

The Universidad Nacional Autónoma de México (National Autonomous University—UNAM) is Mexico's largest public university. Immediately after the new colonial regime was established, the religious orders that arrived in Mexico built elementary and secondary schools to indoctrinate the new converts and Spanish youth. After petitions were made to the king of Spain, the first university was established in 1553 in the building at the corner of the present streets Moneda and Seminario, just off the Zócalo. As the university grew, classes were moved to the building that now houses the Monte de Piedad, on the west side of the Zócalo, and then to a building at the east end of the Pl. del Volador, where the Suprema Corte now stands. For most of the 19th century, university activity was suppressed. The *Ciudad* opened its doors in 1953. Today's ultra-modern buildings belie its status as one of the three oldest universities in the Americas.

The **Estadio Olímpico 1968,** built in the 1950s, was designed to resemble a volcano with a huge crater—an appropriate motif since lava coats the ground on which it is built, and several small volcanoes lurk in the surrounding area. The stadium is one of the most beautiful monuments in the city; the impressive mosaic that covers it was made by Rivera using large colored rocks, and depicts a man and a woman holding high two torches, symbolic of the 1968 Olympics held in the stadium.

Although the university's architecture is impressive, most visitors come to see the murals. From Insurgentes, head east from the stadium (there are several gates you can use to enter the university) until the Jardín Central, a large grassy square. Along the way, west of the Jardín's southern half, you will pass the university's administrative building, distinguished by the three-dimensional Siqueiros mural on the south wall, which shows students studying at desks supported by society.

One of the world's largest mosaics, the work of Juan O'Gorman, wraps around the university library, a windowless box next to the Rectory tower. A pre-Hispanic eagle and Aztec warriors peer out from the side facing the philosophy department. The side facing the Esplanade shows the arrival of the Spanish and their first encounter with the natives. The lateral side depicts a huge atom and its components, a symbol of scientific and academic progress in modern Mexico.

South of the university on Insurgentes is another section of the campus, known as the **Espacio Escultórico.** Out of a huge lava bed and surrounding cave formations rises a multi-colored collection of Herculean sculptures constructed of metal, cement, and wood. The artists wanted to capture the traditions of monumental architecture in pre-Conquest ceremonial centers and plazas with modern techniques. The Espacio Escultórico is best visited during the day, since it is located on the outskirts of the campus in a secluded area. From the center of the university, take bus #17 or 130 ("San Fernando") from the stadium and get off at the first designated stop.

Adjacent to the Espacio Escultórico are the **Sala Chavez** and **Sala Covarrubias.** Both are centers dedicated to music and dance, in which university groups give concerts (even during the summer) that are open to the public for a small fee.

To get to C.U., take the C.U. Metro (Line 3) to Universidad. Free shuttle service is available from there to all campus areas.

Near the end of the pre-Classic Period, the tiny volcano Xitle erupted, leaving an eight-square-kilometer area covered with several meters of lava rock, preserving one of the first pyramids constructed in the Valley of Mexico. The **Cuicuilco Archaeological Zone** (tel. 553-22-63) is on the southeast corner of the intersection of Insurgentes Sur and Anillo Periférico. Take bus #130 ("San Fernando Huipulco") to the entrance on the west side of Insurgentes Sur, south of the Periférico. The **Pyramid of Cuicuilco,** which probably means "Place of the Many-Colored Jasper," was built between 600 and 200 BC, when ceremonial centers began to spring up in Mesoamerica and priests gained extraordinary power. Measuring 125m in diameter at its base and 20m in height, Cuicuilco is consists of five layers, with an altar to the god of fire at the summit. The lava rock around the base has been removed, allowing visitors to walk along it and up to the altar, from where, on less smoggy days, you can see Xitle to the south and Popocatépetl to the east. (Zone open daily 9am-4pm. Free.) Next to the pyramid is a small museum with exhibits on volcanology, the geology and ecology of the area, and the eruption of Xitle, as well as pieces of pottery and ceramics found near the pyramid and in the mounds surrounding it. Other exhibits show the lifestyle, adornments, technology, and burial practices of the inhabitants of Cuicuilco before the eruption. A simple statue was the most unusual find in the area, since statues were rare in the pre-Classic Period. The three-room museum takes about 15 minutes to walk through. (Open Tues.-Sun. 10am-5pm. Museum admission 400 pesos.)

Xochimilco (Floating Gardens)

For many decades Xochimilco's boats, music, and food made it an alluring daytrip for residents of Mexico City. Now the maze of canals known as the "floating gardens" is virtually a part of the voracious city. Xochimilco means "in the flower garden," and there are flowers in every corner of the town. Tourists, however, are just as prevalent, if not more so.

Three thousand boats cruise the canals. On Sunday, the busiest day, motion is annoyingly slow because of the hordes of people and booze cruises that choke the waterways. For a hefty price, waterborne *mariachi* bands, taco bars, and photographers will tie up alongside your vessel and provide their services. The wreaths on the boats were once made weekly from freshly-cut flowers, but if you're sober enough you'll notice that they are now made of plastic and wood. An hour-long ride costs 25,000 pesos but the price is negotiable. You may stay on the water as long as you want, but keep tabs on the time; the gondoliers often don't. To get to Xochimilco, take the Metro to Taxqueña (line 2) and then *pesero* #26 (½ hr., 500 pesos). *Embarcadero* tour guides often wait near the fruit market to lead foreign travelers to the boats. Walk down Nuevo Léon, past the tremendous **Iglesia de San Bernandino de Cera** (a huge church, rather worn but carefully preserved with a towering churchbell and clocktower), then turn right on Violeta and left on Embarcadero, the next block. If you wish to stay in this area, a clean and new hotel, **Hotel Xochimilco**, is 1 block south of the central market. (Singles and doubles 25,000 pesos.) For more information, call the Director of Tourism at 676-08-10.

Entertainment

Tired of the neon disco scene that dominates the night in most of Mexico? Try Mexico City on for size. Be it the Ballet Folklórico at Bellas Artes, an old film by Emilio Fernández at an art cinema, a bullfight in the Pl. México, or blues in a smoke-filled bar, The City has something for everyone. If you can't enjoy yourself here, you can't enjoy yourself anywhere.

For current listings of performances and show times, pick up a copy of *The News,* an English-language daily, or look for the biweekly issue of *Tiempo Libre* (Free Time), each for 1000 pesos at most corner newsstands. *The News* has film and theater listings; *Tiempo Libre* also covers galleries, restaurants, dances, museums, and most cultural events. *La Jornada* (700 pesos), one of the best national newspapers, lists art films showing in less well-known locations such as the university. The *Mexico City Daily Bulletin,* a potpourri of news and information on tourist sights throughout Mexico with a helpful map of Mexico City, is available free at the City Tourism Office and all over the Zona Rosa.

Bars and Clubs

The Zona Rosa offers the most variety for your entertainment peso. Bars with dimly lit interiors, no windows, or swinging doors are called *cantinas;* women are not welcome in these bastions of *machismo.* At large nightclubs that make some attempt at respectability, dates of the opposite sex are often prerequisites to admission. Cover charges range from 5000 to 35,000 pesos, but women are sometimes admitted free. Those places without a cover often have minimum consumption requirements and high drink prices.

Be aware that Mexican-made drinks, from Kahlua to *sangria,* are considerably cheaper than imported ones. The small modern discos in run-down sections of town, specializing in *salsa* and *mambo,* get seedier as singles get needier.

Zona Rosa—Bars

There is a drinking establishment everywhere you look in the Zona Rosa. Taverns here are generally expensive and high-class, but the expense may include live performers and tasty *botanas* (appetizers).

La Pulquería, Londres 161, hidden on the 2nd floor of the mall next to Cinemas Gemelos and directly above a parking garage that connects Londres with Hamburgo. Walk up the circular staircase and brace yourself for a spectacular sight. The wall behind the doorless entrance bears a massive clay sculpture of dancing *campesinos;* a golden gate swirls about in curious sweeping curves; and a wooden board whittled into jubilant *pueblo* tradesmen decorates the barroom wall. Live *mariachi* music every night. Cover 15,000 pesos, drinks average 6000 pesos. Open Mon.-Sat. 8pm-3am.

El Chato, Londres 117. Elegant, romantic, and informal jazz-piano bar with Sinatra sound-alikes an arm's reach away. Small bar surrounds the piano. Often frequented by famous Mexican actors, politicians, and businessfolk. A great place to wind down and to drink great beer out of big mugs (3500 pesos). Mixed drinks 15,000 pesos. Open Mon.-Sat. 1pm-1am.

El Olivo, Varsovia 13. Popular and ultra-modern nouveau bar. Gay and straight clientele. Fancy restaurant in rear and classy barroom area call for fashionable clothes. No cover; just order a drink (4500 pesos) and mingle. Open daily 6pm-1am.

El Taller, Florencia 37-A (tel. 533-49-70), in the basement. You might miss the small entrance to this underground bar. Classic hub of blue-collar gay men. Private, conservative barroom attracts an older, quieter crowd. Drinks, snacks, and small paperback bookstand available in the afternoon; dancing during the evening. Male revue Wed. at midnight. Tues. lectures are well-attended. Cover 7000 pesos with 2 drinks, Fri.-Sat. 15,000 pesos. Open Tues.-Sun. 4pm-2am.

Keops, Hamburgo 146 (tel. 528-57-51). Intimate bar with live performers nightly and responsive crowds. Bathroom clean and supervised. Cocktails 7500 pesos. Cover 15,000 pesos. Open daily 9pm-2am.

Yarda's Bar, Niza 39. The starched white tablecloths complement the black leather chairs and a well-to-do clientele. Track lighting, loud music, video screens. Drinks only with a food order (*botanas* 5000 pesos); half-pitcher of beer 7500 pesos. Cover Fri.-Sat. 10,000 pesos. Open Mon.-Fri. 4pm-1am, Sat. 4pm-3am.

Salón de Té Auseba, Hamburgo 159-B, near Florencia. Quiet, older, upper-class clientele. Comfortable tea-room with droves of delicious pastries and cakes. The alternative for the teetotaler. Teas 2900 pesos. Try the *manzana en chemise,* an apple tart (5600 pesos). Open daily 9am-10pm.

Me Nifileo, Genova 34. Live Latin American bands nightly. Open-air terrace—unique among Mexican café-bars. Coffees and drinks. Open Mon.-Sat. 8am-3am.

Zona Rosa—Discos

The following are flashy and trendy places to dance, but you will have to pay a steep cover for the privilege.

Rock Stock Bar & Disco, Reforma 258, at Niza. Chic disco, very popular with young Mexicans. Often packed; single men will have difficulty getting in. Cover 35,000 pesos. Women get in free on Thurs. Open daily 9pm-4am.

Disco Bar el "9," Londres 156, on the 2nd floor. Small, popular gay and lesbian disco. A favorite pick-up scene for young locals. Friendly, open atmosphere, but bathrooms are sloppy. Happy hour 8-11pm; open dance floor 10am-6:30am; transvestite shows Wed. at midnight. Standard cover (12,000 pesos) includes 1 drink and applies only to men. If you pick up a free invitation beforehand, cover only 7000 pesos (including free drinks during cocktail hours). Men get in free Sun. Open Mon. and Wed.-Thurs. 8pm-6:30am, Fri.-Sat. 10pm-6:30am, Sun. 6pm-3am.

Disco Skyros, Florencia 56. Busy little disco with an attractive, dimly-lit upstairs bar lounge and dance floor. Very young pelvis-grinders dance to rock and pop music. Women admitted free; men pay 25,000 pesos. Admission includes *barra nacional* (open bar, national brands). Open daily 7pm-3am.

Circus Circus, Florencia 58. Larger, more dazzling version of Skyros: both are under the same management, and the same rules apply. Cover 25,000 pesos (women admitted free); open bar. Open daily 7pm-3am.

Alameda Central—Bars and Discos

Nightspots here lack the luster and glitter of those in the Zona Rosa, and the prices reflect it. An evening here may well be worthwhile, but the surrounding neighborhoods may be dangerous. Caution is advised, especially late at night when streets are deserted.

Zotano's, 20 Revillagigedo (tel. 518-40-37), at Independencia. Quaint subterranean dance club with peppy performers playing *salsa, mambo,* and rock. Cozy and friendly. *Refrescos* 800 pesos, cocktails 4500 pesos. Cover a mere 2000 pesos. Open Mon.-Sat. 8pm-6am.

El Miralto, Torre Latinoamericana, Madero at Lázaro Cárdenas. Atop the tallest building in Mexico. Mixed drink prices steep (over 5000 pesos), but worth the expense for the best view in the city. Open daily 1pm-1am.

Catacumbas, Dolores 16 (tel. 518-41-27), at Independencia ½ block south of Juárez. Live rock, *salsa,* and tropical tunes. Couples only. It's what Mexicans refer to as a *bar familiar.* One is reminded of how families get made in the first place. A Mexican middle-class favorite. Mixed drinks 5000 pesos. Cover 10,000 pesos. Open Mon.-Sat. 8:30pm-4am.

Veracruz Bar and New York Salón, Santa Veracruz 7, 1 block north of the Alameda. Fun but seedy—think twice about staying past midnight. The Salón, an evening disco, plays strictly tropical music and *salsa.* The bar, at street level, serves beer (2500 pesos), *piña coladas* (3000 pesos), and *sangria* (3000 pesos); drinks sold by the bottle upstairs. Salón cover 3000 pesos. Bar open daily noon-3am; disco daily 9pm-3am.

Centro—Bars

A few of the bars here are popular among the adult, administrative set, and some have as long and distinguished a history as the buildings that stand over them. Explore, but bear in mind that by midnight the Centro streets are completely deserted and potentially dangerous.

Salon Luz, Gante 23 (tel. 512-42-46), at Venustiano Carranza. Lively bar catering to briefcase-toting execs in the heart of *el centro.* Great Mexican *botanas,* English sandwiches, and burgers. Drinks from 3000 pesos. Live nightly entertainment. Open Mon.-Sat. 10am-midnight.

Bar de los Azulejos, Casa de los Azulejos on Madero, 2nd floor. Small bar tucked away in a corner of Sanborn's. Cozy atmosphere. Drinks 3000 pesos. Open daily noon-10pm.

Salon Paris, Donceles 3, 1 block north of Bellas Artes. Gay bar, frequented by many bankers, accountants, and theater performers from the surrounding district. Symphony and theater crowd pack the place in late evening. Beer 2200 pesos; tasty *botanas* free. Open Mon.-Sat. 10am-midnight.

Garibaldi Plaza

Garibaldi Plaza echoes with the clamor of loudly competing *mariachi* bands—as many as 10 different groups play simultaneously. Big nightclubs surround the square, each with its own *mariachis.* Put a charge into your evening by taking a turn at the "shocks." Men with small electrical boxes walk around clanging two metal tubes. Groups hold hands, with one tube at each end, as the vendors slowly increase the electrical current until someone breaks the link. As long as you have a chicken in your group, it's safe.

Beware of the many pickpockets and purse-snatchers who target tourists here. The plaza is at the intersection of Lázaro Cárdenas and República de Honduras, north of Reforma. Walk 7 blocks north of the Bellas Artes Metro station. The best time to visit Garibaldi is between 8pm and 2am on weekends, but that is also the best time to get robbed. Prostitutes love the plaza, and its neighboring streets and small *cantinas* can be dangerous at night.

Shopping

Whereas most Mexican cities have one central market, Mexico City has one central market for every major type of retail good. Rumor has it that the money that moves daily through La Merced alone equals all the capital that flows through Monterrey per day. These markets are relatively cheap, since the city usually pays the overhead. Every *colonia* has its own market, but all the major marketplaces are in the center of town. The following are the more important market areas.

La Merced, Circunvalación at Anaya, east of the Zócalo. Merced Metro stop (Line 2). Primarily food, shipped from all over the country. Huge selection of fresh produce. Open daily 8am-7pm. (See Centro under Sights above.)

Sonora, 2 blocks south of Merced. If you want to turn your significant other into a toad, head for Sonora. Specializes in witchcraft, medicinal teas and spices, ceramic pottery, figurines, and ceremonial figures. Open daily 8am-7pm. Outside the market are cagefulls of birds, dogs, ducks, and turtles. Rare species sometimes appear. All for sale, but remember that Mexican pets are turned away at the U.S. border.

San Juan, Pl. El Buen Tono, 4 blocks south of Alameda Central, 2 blocks west of Lázaro Cárdenas. Bounded by Ayuntamiento, Aranda, Pugibet, and Dolores. An incredible variety of baskets, blankets, furniture, and food. Open Mon.-Sat. 9am-7pm, Sun. 9am-4pm.

La Lagunilla, Comonfort at Rayón, east of the intersection of Lázaro Cárdenas and Reforma. Historic Sunday market specializing in antiques and old books. Open daily 8am-7pm.

Buenavista, Aldana 187, at Degollado in Colonia Guerrero. Giant crafts warehouse. Over 80,000 typical Mexican articles under one roof. Open Mon.-Sat. 9am-6pm, Sun. 9am-2pm.

Tepito, between Metro stops Revolución and San Cosme, accessible by a *pesero* called "Tepito" along Reforma. Blocks of outdoor clothing stalls and indoor shoe racks—you've never seen more shoes in one place unless you've done time as a Phillipine missionary. Tepito is the national clearinghouse for illegal imports from the U.S. and South Asia. Neat-o police raids occur daily. Watch your wallet. Open daily 9am-9pm.

Bazar Sábado, Pl. San Jacinto 11, in San Angel. Sat. only, as the name suggests, and a good excuse to voyage out to San Angel. Highest quality folk crafts: dolls, paintings, rugs, papier-mâché, jewelry, and much more. A great place to browse—perhaps not so great to buy. Open Sat. 10am-7pm.

FONART, the government crafts stores selling regional crafts from all over Mexico. No bargaining allowed, but deals are good anyway. Giant tapestries, Oaxacan rugs, papier-mâché dolls, and folk art. Located at: Patriotismo 16; Juárez 89; Insurgentes 1630 Sur; Londres 6 at the Museo de Cera; Londres 136, in San Angel at Av. de La Paz 37; and Ciudad Satélite on Manuel Izaguirre 10. Open Mon.-Sat. 10am-7pm.

Museo Nacional de Artes del Instituto Nacional Indigenista, Juárez 44, across from the Alameda. A shop, not a museum. Crafts and jewelry from all over Mexico. Good prices. High quality. Open daily 10am-6pm.

Sports

Whether consumed with bullfighting, soccer, jai alai, or horseracing, Mexican fans consider their favorite *deportes* to be art forms, and are less fans than connoisseurs—albeit rowdy connoisseurs.

Plaza México, Insurgentes Sur. Accessible by the Metro station San Antonio (Line 7). Mexico's principal bullring. Bullfights begin Sun. at 4pm. Professionals fight only Dec.-April. *Novilladas* (novices) replace *matadores* in off-season. Stadium capacity: 50,000 fans. Cheapest seats are "Sol General" for 12,500 pesos; bring sunglasses and a hat, or prepare to be slowly broiled in the midday sun. Binoculars come in handy.

Aztec Stadium, SA-Tlalpan 3465 (tel. 677-71-98). Take shuttle train or *pesero* directly from the Tasqueña Metro station (Line 2). The *Azteca* is the greatest of many large stadiums where professional soccer—the national sport—is played. Read the sports pages of any newspaper for information on games. The season runs Oct.-July.

Frontón México, Pl. de la República, 3 blocks south of the Revolución Metro station (Line 2). Watch and bet on jai alai. Games usually take place Tues.-Thurs. and Sat.-Sun. Box office opens at 6:30pm. Admission 5000 pesos. Betting (not required) starts at 1000 pesos.

Hipódromo de las Américas, Av. Avila Camacho. Take a *pesero* labeled "Hipódromo" west along Reforma—the beautiful horsetrack is on the outskirts of the city. Races Thurs. and Sat.-Sun. at 2:15pm. Admission free unless you sit in the upper level, where purchase of food and drink purchase is obligatory.

CENTRAL MEXICO

Mexico State

Northeast of the Distrito Federal, spectacular Teotihuacán, with its overwhelming Pyramids of the Sun and Moon, is the most-visited archeological site in the Republic. Tepotzotlán, a quaint and sleepy town north of Mexico City, shelters valuable colonial treasures in a former Jesuit monastery. The larger, western section of Mexico state attracts visitors mostly as a stop on the way from Mexico City to Morelia and Guadalajara.

Teotihuacán

While Europeans lived in caves eating nuts and berries and the group that would one day found Tenochtitlán wandered in Aztlán, a great civilization flourished in the Valley of Mexico. Little is known about the people who founded Teotihuacán around 200 BC. Their consummately organized, theocratic society lasted nearly 1000 years and then vanished as mysteriously as it had appeared. Fifty years later, when the Toltecs founded Tula, not a single citizen walked the paths of this enormous urban complex; and when the Aztecs founded Tenochtitlán in 1325, Teotihuacán, 50km northeast of their capital, lay in ruins. The Aztecs adopted the area as ceremonial grounds and attributed its huge structures to giants who inhabited the world during the era of the first sun. Believing that the lords buried in this hallowed place had become gods, the Aztecs called the area Teotihuacán, meaning "Place of the Gods."

The plan of Teotihuacán's archeological zone, more commonly referred to as "Las Pirámides," is easy to understand. The ceremonial center, a vast 13-square-kilometer expanse, was built along a 2km stretch now called Calle de los Muertos (Road of the Dead) after the countless human skeletons that were discovered alongside it. The road leads from the Pyramid of the Moon to the Temple of Quetzalcóatl. Since the Teotihuacanos based their architecture on the four cardinal points, Calle de los Muertos runs nearly north-south. The main structure, the Pyramid of the Sun, is on the east side of the street and is squared with the point on the horizon where the sun sets at summer solstice. On the north end of Calle de los Muertos are the Plaza and Pyramid of the Moon. The Palace and Temple of Quetzalcóatl stand on the east side of the southern end. Southwest of the Pyramid of the Sun, but still on the east side of the Calle de los Muertos, are the ruins of the palaces in which priests resided.

The most imposing structure in the ceremonial area is the **Pyramid of the Sun.** Second in size only to the pyramid at Cholula in Puebla, its base measures 222m on the east and west sides, and 225m on the north and south—dimensions similar to those of Cheops in Egypt. The pyramid rises 63m today, but the grand temple that once crowned its summit is missing. The miniature temple that now stands atop the pyramid once served Tonacatecutli, the God of Sun and Spiritual Warmth. People restoring this pyramid in 1910 bungled by giving it five levels instead of four.

The Temple of Quetzalcóatl was once a giant walled-in stadium designed to protect the foundations of ancient temples. Its four flanking platforms served as festivity grounds for priestly ceremonies and dances. The central plaza houses an altar upon which the centennial sacrifice of the "New Fire" was celebrated. The Temple has lately suffered tremendous erosion from the gods of Rain and Wind, and is due for future restoration.

The best place to start your visit is on the west side of the southernmost end of the Calle de los Muertos, where a small museum explicates this civilization as clearly as possible. The museum has displays comparing the size of the ancient city with various present-day cities, illustrating the architecture and technology of the pyramids, describing the social, religious, and economic organization of the society, and exhibiting *indígena* art. Although all the pieces you see are replicas (the originals are at the Museo Nacional de Antropología in Mexico City), the museum is a good introduction to the zone. Much of what is known about the area was learned through records kept by the contemporary civilizations in Cholula, Oaxaca, the Yucatán, and northern Mexico, all of which dealt with Teotihuacán.

You may want to buy a written guide here or at the Museo de Antropología in Mexico City. Expect to spend about an hour at the museum and another three to four hours walking as many miles exploring the ruins. (Site open daily 8am-5pm. Admission 10,000 pesos. Museum closed for renovations until at least Dec. 1990. Free parking available.)

An unusual place for a meal is **La Gruta** (The Cave). As the name suggests, the restaurant is in an immense cave, which provides a respite from the arid heat. Strains of Vivaldi surround the patrons. Hamburgers 12,000 pesos, full meals 20,000 pesos. Open daily 11am-7pm.

To contact the Teotihuacán offices, dial 601-88 or 600-52 (from Mexico City add the prefix 91-595). Direct bus service from Mexico City to the pyramids is available from Autobuses Teotihuacán (every ½ hr. 5am-10pm, 45 min., 2700 pesos) located in the Terminal de Autobuses del Norte at Sala 8. The same bus line runs from Tepexpan should you come from Texcoco or Chiconcuac. The last bus back from the pyramids to Mexico City leaves the main entrance at 6pm. A few miles before reaching Teotihuacán, the bus passes just to the right of the town of **Acolmán**, founded shortly after the Conquest by the Franciscans. The majestic lines of the ex-monastery of Acolmán rise to the sky, breaking the monotony of the corn fields. Even at a distance, the architectural solemnity of this early religious settlement is evident.

Tepotzotlán

On the highway from Mexico City to Tula and Querétaro, the town of Tepotzotlán contains inspirational religious art in its Museo del Virreinato (viceroyalty), located in the monastery and church of Tepotzotlán.

In 16th-century Tepotzotlán, the Jesuits established a convent for *indígenas* to study language, art, theology, and mathematics. An *indígena* convert, Martín Maldonado, donated the land to the missionaries in 1582. Construction of the buildings continued until the end of the following century, and the huge bell in the tower was added in 1762. To the rear of the **Iglesia de San Francisco Javier** is the **Capilla de la Virgen de Loreto.** Behind it, the **Camarín de la Virgen** (altar room) holds a mirror in the middle so that visitors can see the decorations on the dome.

After the expulsion of the Jesuits in 1767, the church and buildings became a reform school for priests. Early in this century, they were returned to the Jesuits, and in 1964, the whole complex became the **Museo del Virreinato.** Although it houses many valuable treasures from the colonial period, the collection is far from comprehensive or even representative. In fact, Jesuit imagery predominates, as one would expect in what once was a Jesuit seminary. St. Ignatius stares at you from every other altar, and St. Francis Xavier is only slightly less ubiquitous. Nonetheless, these constitute valuable examples of colonial craftsmanship and artistic talent. The Iglesia de San Francisco Xavier is a Churrigueresque masterpiece. Paintings hang between the arches of the ex-convent, including *San Juan Writing the Apocalypse,* by Martín de Vos, and *The Holy Family,* attributed to Pietro Berretini da Cortona. Other galleries contain sculptures, exhibits of locks from the viceregal era, and other artifacts. The monastery's orchard is soothing, particularly for those coming from Mexico City. (Open Tues.-Sun. 11am-5:30pm. Admission 10,000 pesos, free Sun.)

The plaza outside the church is packed with eateries alongside a few hotels. Tepotzotlán's least tacky lodgings are in the **Posada Familiar** (tel. 876-05-20), at the center of the Zócalo. (Singles 23,000 pesos. Doubles 35,000 pesos.) The **Hostería del Convento de Tepotzotlán,** next to the museum, serves Mexican food in a solemn setting. (Entrees 10,000 pesos. Open daily 1-6pm.)

To get to Tepotzotlán from Mexico City, take the Metro to Tacuba (Line 2); turn right and walk 2 blocks. Buses (every 10 min. 5:30am-10:30pm, 1 hr., 800 pesos) leave from the Terminal Autobuses México, Tlanepantla, Cuautitlán y Anexas (tel. 561-02-82). When returning to Mexico City, "Metro Tacuba" buses stop at the corner on the south side of Insurgentes, across the street from the church. The last bus back to Mexico City leaves at 10pm.

Tenayuca and Acatitlán

Past the northwest border of the Federal District are two archeological zones even older than Tenochtitlán. The first is in **Tenayuca,** on Cuauhtémoc, 2 blocks north of Av. Aqueducto Tenayuca. The pyramid, about the size of a large house, is famous for its resemblance to the Templo Mayor of Tenochtitlán and for the fringe of snake heads around the base. A museum next to the northeast corner should be open, but, unfortunately, many of the site's artifacts are now shut in homes of area residents. To get there, take the Metro to La Raza (Lines 3 and 5), then catch a *pesero* labeled "Piramide" and ask the driver to let you off at the Pyramid Tenayuca. (Open Tues.-Sun. 10am-5pm. Admission 8000 pesos, free Sun.)

In **Acatitlán,** the major attraction is **Santa Cecilia,** a simply decorated 16th-century church that was built when the Spanish first arrived with the stones of an adjacent pyramid. The pyramid is behind the church and, although much smaller than the one in Tenayuca, it is more pleasant to visit. For a heavenly view, climb to the top (where there is a *chac-mool*). Access to the grounds is through the museum in an old *hacienda* on the southwest corner. One part of the museum displays some of the pieces left by the *indígenas*. The star of the show is the rack with 20 stone skulls on it, a replica of the actual item used to display the skulls of sacrificial victims. The other part of the museum contains old colonial furniture and pottery. Santa Cecilia is best visited during the morning or early afternoon, since near dusk packs of mean dogs run loose on the streets. (Open daily 10am-4:30pm. Admission 8000 pesos, free Sun.)

To get to Santa Cecilia, catch the *pesero* "Tlalnepantlan" on Av. Santa Cecilia behind Tenayuca. The *pesero* will drop you off at Alfanes. Walk 3 blocks up Alfanes past the gas station, then go left. To return to Mexico City from Santa Cecilia take the *pesero* labeled "Metro Basilica"; from Tenayuca, take the *peserto* labeled "Metro La Raza." Metro service is available at the end of the *pesero* routes.

Morelos

After the Habsburg Emperor Maximilian built his summer residence in Cuernavaca, thousands of Mexicans elected to play follow the leader, making the state of Morelos their vacation spot of choice. Today, Mexicans and foreigners alike march to Morelos to take advantage of Cuernavaca's "eternal spring," Cuautla's many bathing areas, and Tepoztlán's striking landscape. Morelos is a short jaunt from Mexico City; you can easily spend a day in Cuernavaca, Cuautla, or Tepoztlán and return to the capital in the evening.

Morelos's climb to historical significance began when its peasants organized and agitated for land reform; this movement gave rise to Emiliano Zapata's career as a revolutionary leader, as well as to the 1911 Plan of Ayala, which called for the expropriation and restoration of the "land, woods, and water that the landlords, *científicos,* and bosses have usurped." Remnants of Morelos's revolutionary past are evident in Cuautla, while vestiges of imperial Mexico remain in Cuernavaca.

Cuernavaca

Less than 70km south of the Sierra de Ajusco, a low-lying mountain range cupping Mexico City, sits Cuernavaca, the quintessential colonial city and capital of Morelos state. Cuernavaca, home to over 500,000 wealthy Mexicans, also functions as a vernal playground to busloads of eager visitors who come to bathe in its sparkling swimming pools and discuss the perennially awesome weather. If you ever develop "wethead"—a malady unique to Mexico City's relentless six-month rainy season—take the brief 90-minute bus ride to this city of sun. With a median annual temperature of 68°F (20°C), Cuernavaca has long attracted warmth-starved visitors: Emperor Maximilian, Cortés, Gabriel García Márquez, and boxer Muhammed Ali have all, at some point, kicked back in the mansions of Cuernavaca's exclusive *colonias.*

Many of Cuernavaca's official buildings bear the city shield, a three-branched tree with a twig growing out of its trunk. To the Tlahuica, an Aztec tribe that first populated the valley, this symbol represented the concept of "speech." Trees were once so abundant in the valley of Cuernavaca that the forest literally "spoke" when the wind blew. Marveling at the song of the branches, the Tlahuica named their city *Cuauhnahuac,* "Place on the Outskirts of the Grove." As Mexico's *ladino* elite transmuted the city into their private summer camp, the name was corrupted into the more easily pronounced Spanish quasi-homonym "Cuernavaca".

The spirit of the original name has been desecrated by the growth of the town's popularity. The din of daytrippers, residents, and students at Cuernavaca's well-reputed language schools now drowns out the voice of the forest. Gone also are the great sugar plantations and *haciendas* on the edge of town. Cuernavaca nevertheless remains a semi-commercialized wonderland filled with wealthy townies, wide-eyed tourists, and moments of the past.

Orientation

Three bus lines provide first-class service to Cuernavaca from Mexico City's Central del Sur bus station. Both of the bus stations in Cuernavaca, Autos Pullman and Flecha Roja, are within easy walking distance of the Zócalo. **Autos Pullman** departs Mexico City for Cuernavaca every 15 minutes from 5am to 10pm (3900 pesos).

Route 95 from Mexico City intersects many of Cuernavaca's main avenues. Coming from Mexico City, it's best to exit Rte. 95 onto **Domingo Diez** heading east toward the center. If entering from the west, take **Emiliano Zapata,** which splits into eastbound one-way **José María Morelos** and a parallel street farther south, **Avenida Obregón,** both heading downtown. The best route into town coming off Rte 95 from the east of Cuernavaca is on Av. Civac or Allacomilco. Both filter down to a highway that leads to **Plan de Ayala,** which sweeps around the Mercado Municipal into the center of town. **Benito Juárez** is the main east-west thoroughfare south of the Zócalo.

Two plazas together make up the Zócalo in Cuernavaca, and neither one is marked on the tourist office map. The main one, the **Plaza de la Constitución,** is a few blocks east of Morelos via Hidalgo, at the intersection of Guerrero, Salazar, Juárez, and Hidalgo. Diagonally opposite the main Zócalo's northwest corner sits the smaller **Jardín Juárez.**

Cuernavaca's streets madden with their jumble of irregularities and unexpected turns, especially near the plaza. Maps, available from the tourist office, are essential, and include downtown sights. Frequent local buses (450 pesos) travel Morelos. From Morelos, they head for the particular region or *colonia* painted onto their front window. Taxis—small, white Toyotas, Datsuns, or VWs—will go anywhere in the city for 3000-5000 pesos.

Practical Information

State Tourist Office: Morelos Sur 802 (tel. 14-39-20), a 10-min. walk from the Ayuntamiento. For information on cultural activities, walk down the street to the university-owned building in front of the cathedral. Open Mon.-Fri. 9am-8pm, Sat.-Sun. 9am-3pm.

Federal Tourist Office: Comonfort 2 (tel. 12-18-15), at Hidalgo. Turn left in front of the plant-filled courtyard—it's upstairs to the right. Detailed city maps, regional tourist brochures, information on archeological sites, and an authorized (though selective) list of hotel rates. Courteous staff speaks some English. Open Mon.-Fri. 9am-3pm.

Currency Exchange: Bánamex, Matamoros at Arteaga, 1 block north of Jardín Juárez and **Bancomer,** on the northwest corner of Jardín Jaárez. All banks open Mon.-Fri. 9am-1:30pm and 4-6pm. **Gesta,** a *casa de cambio* at Morrow and Comonfort, offers the same rates as the banks do, with a 1% commission tacked on to make up for the pleasure of short lines. Open Mon.-Fri. 9am-2pm and 4-6pm. **Some Cafetería Universal** and several other cafés near the Zócalo offer late-night exchange at poor rates.

Post Office: Pl. de la Constitución 3 (tel. 12-43-79), on the southwest corner of the Zócalo. Open Mon.-Fri. 8am-7pm, Sat.-Sun. 9am-noon; for Lista de Correos Mon.-Fri. 8am-7pm. **Postal Code:** 62000.

Telephones: *Caseta* at Salzar 15 (tel. 12-22-15), on the northern edge of the Zócalo behind the weekend market area. Open Mon-Sat. 9am-9pm, Sun. 9am-8pm. **Farmacia Central,** in Jardín Juárez at Rayón (tel. 12-57-15). Open daily 9am-10pm. **Telephone Code:** 73.

Telegrams: In the post office. Open Mon.-Fri. 9am-8pm.

Train Station: (tel. 12-80-44), at Leandro Valle, but service only once per day to Iguala.

Bus Stations: First- and second-class buses arrive at several small terminals scattered about town. **México-Zacatepec/Autos Pullman de México,** Netzahualcóyotl 106 (tel. 12-60-23), at Abasolo, 2 blocks south of the Zócalo. Among others, to: Mexico City (every 15 min. 5am-8pm, 1½ hr., 3900 pesos); Zacatepec (every 15 min. 6am-10pm, 1300 pesos); and Grutas de Cacahuamilpa (every 2 hr. 8:20am-4:20pm, 3400 pesos). **Flecha Roja,** Morelos 503, 4 blocks north of Jardín Borda. First-class service to: Mexico City (every 20 min. 5am-8pm, as well as at 9 and 10pm, 1½ hr., 3700 pesos); Acapulco (every 2 hr. 7am-midnight, 6500 pesos); Altamirano (at 8am, 7pm, and 10:30pm, 13,000 pesos); Jojutla (every ½ hr. 7am-9pm, 2000 pesos); Taxco (every 1½ hr. 5:30am-9:30pm, 3700 pesos); Grutas de Cacahuamilpa (every 15 min. 6am-8pm, 5000 pesos); Iguala (every hr. 5:30am-11pm, 6100 pesos); Santa Marta, Toluca, Santigao (every hr. 5am-7:30pm, 4100 pesos); Chalma (every hr. 7:50am-9:50pm, 5000 pesos).**Estrella de Oro,** on Morelos Sur at Las Palmas Circle, 10 blocks south of the intersection of Reforma and Hidalgo. First-class buses to many of the destinations served by Flecha Roja. **Estrella Roja,** Galeana 401 (tel. 12-06-34), 7 blocks south of the Zócalo. First-class service to: Cuautla (2200 pesos); Oaxtepec (2500 pesos); Puebla (every hr. 4:30am-7:30pm, 8000 pesos). Second-class **Estrella Roja** and **Ometochtli** (tel. 12-18-22), on López Mateos at the bottom of the Mercado. Go 5 blocks north on Guerrero from the Zócalo, then take a right on Degollado and enter the market. Work your way to the right and down through the market. Buses load in the parking lot across the highway that runs perpendicular to Degollado. Buses to Tepotztlán (every 20 min. 7am-9pm, 1200 pesos) and Cuautla (every 20 min. 6am-8pm, 2000 pesos).

Local Transit Authority: Tel. 16-16-99. Train and bus schedules as well as highway information.

English Bookstores: Anglo-American Bookstore Las Plazas, in Las Plazas Mall, facing the Zócalo. A shelf of the latest U.S. steamy novels, not to mention collections of English postcards and windows full of marble statuettes. Open Mon.-Sat. 10am-1pm and 4-6pm.

Academic Programs for Foreign Students: A number of centers provide summer- and term-time instruction in Spanish. Weekly tuition usually includes 5 hr. of daily language instruction, group excursions to historic sites, and placement in local homes. Private centers often charge an additional registration fee to reserve a spot in their programs. Check with **Experiencia** (see Accommodations below), or **Cuauhnahuac,** Morelos Sur 1414, Colonia Chipitlán, 62070 Cuernavaca, Morelos (tel. 12-36-73). The office on Morelos is open Mon.-Fri. 8am-3pm. Also notable are **Centro de Lenguas,** Rayón 7 (tel. 14-10-06); **Lang-Lab,** Morelos Sur

304 (tel. 12-02-92); **Fenix Language Institute;** and **Instituto Teopanzolco,** which has a special program for the hearing-impaired.

Laundromat: Lavandería Aztlán, Morrow 17-A. One load washed, dried, and folded for 10,500 pesos. Open Mon.-Fri. 9am-6pm, Sat. 9am-2pm.

Red Cross: Itzaccihuatl at Río Panuco (tel. 13-35-55 or 15-50-00).

Pharmacies: Farmacia Blanco, Morelos 710 (tel. 12-30-03), just north of the Flecha Roja bus station. Open 24 hr. **Farmacia El Sol,** Matamoros 500 (tel. 14-16-69), at Arista. Open Mon.-Sat. 8am-9pm, Sun. 8am-2pm.

Medical Assistance: Centro Medico, Juárez 507-B, has a doctor for every ailment. If your child is seriously ill, drop in any time day or night at the **Clínica de Urgencias Pediatricas,** Jardín Juárez 9 (tel. 13-27-70), on the Zócalo. Regular office hours Mon.-Sat. 7am-2pm and 4-8pm.

Hospital: Morelos 102 (tel. 14-14-44), directly across the street from the cathedral. 24-hr. emergency treatment from 300 pesos (plus supplies). Charges waived if you can't afford them. **ISSTE** (intended for government employees), Obregón at Linares (tel. 14-19-57), 1 block west of El Calvario Church, offers emergency treatment at no charge. If you have no luck with budget treatment, try **Hospital Civil** (tel. 14-25-29). Open 24 hr.

Police: Tel. 17-10-00.

Emergency: Tel. 06.

Accommodations

Cuernavaca boasts a number of comfortable and centrally located hotels. Lately, however, prices have begun to rise like Michael Jordan. Reservations are suggested if you're arriving for the weekend, and some hotels charge up to 15,000 pesos more for these two days. The least expensive conventional lodgings line Matamoros, for several blocks north from the Zócalo; although a number of the *casas de huéspedes* back-to-back along Aragón y León are cheaper, you'd do best to pass them up—many of the guests have customers of their own.

For an extended stay, it is possible to lodge with a local family through one of the local Spanish-language schools. Students (mostly Europeans and *norteamericanos*) who attend these schools choose from a list of families willing to provide room, board, and language practice. **Cuauhnahuac** is especially willing to lend their family list to backpacking visitors who wish to spend time with *cuernavaquences.* Sharing a room with a student costs US$12 per day for room and board; for a private single, you pay US$18. Contact José Camacho at Cuauhnahuac. Also try the bilingual language school, **Experiencia,** Paseo Cozumel 16 (tel. 12-70-71), in Colonia Quintana Roo.

The bulletin boards at the Instituto Regional de Bellas Artes (IRBAC), Morelos 405 (tel. 12-13-18), 2 blocks from the Jardín Borda, display notices from local families with rooms for rent. Most families prefer *señoritas,* and board is optional in many cases. These offers are usually intended for Mexican students, so those who don't speak Spanish may have difficulties.

Los Canarios Motel, Morelos 713 (tel. 13-44-44), off Matamoros under the inane canary sign. This fading semi-resort maintains a weathered pool chock-full of plastic giraffe floats. Small gardens and little shops are randomly arranged around the spruce rooms. Immaculate bathrooms separated from rooms by odd screens. Friendly staff. Weekly 20% discount for students. Singles 25,000 pesos. Doubles 56,000 pesos.

Hotel Colonial, Aragón y León 104 (tel. 12-00-99), in the middle of the block. Nicely renovated colonial building, with a cobbled patio in the small courtyard. Rooms are clean but stuffy; some have unusual bunk-bed formations. Basic bathrooms. Hot water available 7-11am and 7-11pm. Singles 30,000 pesos. Doubles 35,000 pesos.

Hotel Papagayo, Motolinia 13 (tel. 14-19-24), at Netzahualcóyotl 1 block south of the Autos Pullman station. Mediocre rooms with *agua purificada* and tolerably sanitary bathrooms. Almost worth the extra pesos for the huge courtyard with large pool (complete with diving board, slide, and screaming kids) and the three full meals that come with the price—but no cigar, folks. Singles 60,400 pesos. Doubles 65,300 pesos. Ouch.

Hotel Juárez, Netzahualcóyotl 117 (tel. 14-02-19). Large rooms have bleached-wood bed frames and nightstands, firm mattresses, and clean bathrooms. Some rooms are bright and airy, but others claim only slits for windows. Nighttime hangout for the local bugs. Swimming pool out back. Singles 35,000 pesos. Doubles 40,000 pesos.

Hotel Roma, Matamoros 405 (tel. 12-07-87), 4 blocks north of the Jardín Juárez. Courtyard filled with towering palm trees. High-altitude stairs with dangerously low railings lead to 2nd floor. Sparse rooms, with sagging beds decorated with religious paraphernalia. Functional bathrooms look fresh, but smell otherwise. Singles 22,000 pesos. Doubles 23,000 pesos. Towel deposit 5000 pesos.

Motel Royal, Matamoros 19 (tel. 12-01-00). Whoever designed the Hotel Roma did this one, too. Drab pink courtyard rimmed by institutional-blue rooms. Dinky bathrooms and quickly wilting beds. Singles 25,000 pesos. Doubles 30,000 pesos. Towel deposit 5000 pesos.

Hotel Las Hortencias, Hidalgo 22 (tel. 12-61-52), in the Zona Centro. Elegant and well-situated. Courtyard fountains, flowers, and ivy-covered walls create a pleasing atmosphere: wood-paneled rooms with worn-out sheets and pillows, and immaculate bathrooms can't quite muster that same magic. 24-hr. long distance phone service in the lobby. Singles 46,200 pesos. Doubles 51,500 pesos.

Hotel Iberia, Rayón 9 (tel. 12-60-40), 2 blocks north of the Jardín Juárez. Centrally located but far enough off the street to silence street sounds. Pristine, recently re-tiled courtyard. Large, clean rooms. Singles 46,200 pesos. Doubles 61,500 pesos.

Hotel Palacio, Morrow 209 (tel. 12-05-53), across the Jardín Juárez next to Bancomer. Allegedly the former residence of dictator Porfirio Díaz. Older clientele and old-fashioned surroundings reminiscent of a wealthy nursing home. Courtyard includes a quaint greenhouse. Rooms simple, tidy, and spacious, with brass bedposts and antique bathtubs. Singles and doubles 25,000-50,000 pesos depending on size and location.

Hotel Bajo El Volcán, Humboldt 117 (tel. 12-48-73), 1 block south and 2 blocks east of the Zócalo. Fine rooms with dark wood paneling, fluffy pillows, and squeaky-clean tiles. Beautiful outdoor terrace and bar overlook a small pool. Singles 60,000 pesos. Doubles 70,000 pesos.

Food

Cuernavaca provides both better and more expensive food than many Mexican cities of similar size, thanks to the wealth of its residents and the constant influx of domestic and international tourists. Take advantage of the variety of excellent restaurants around the plaza for your main meal; head up the side streets for more inexpensive fare. In the market, *comidas corridas* cost 6000 pesos, *con refresco.* Beware of dirty dishes and treacherously old, unclean frying oil.

Along Guerrero, north of the plaza, street vendors sell mangos, *piñas* (pineapples), and *elotes* (corn on the cob), along with pocket combs, sunglasses, and digital watches. The health drinks sold at the Eiffel Kiosk in the Jardín Juárez include everything from the standard fruit and milk *licuados* to a spinach concoction not even Popeye could love. The drinks are cheap (3500 pesos), delicious, and hygienically prepared with pasteurized milk.

Many attractive, reasonably priced restaurants lie just south of the Zócalo and the Palacio de Gobierno, on Hidalgo and Rayón.

La Fontana Pizza, Juárez 507, down the hill from the Zócalo. Decorated with every poster you've ever seen and not wanted. The color TV at the bar shows soccer during the day, rock videos at night. Regular pie 9000 pesos. Wet your throat with a beer (3500 pesos) or *refresco* (1500 pesos). Open daily 1pm-midnight.

La India Bonita, Morrow 6-B, 1 block from the Jardín Juárez. Charming and cozy, with hanging ferns, straw chairs, and wooden tables close enough to the kitchen to be enveloped in wonderful aromas. Tasty, expensive Mexican specialties. "Platos Variedades Mexicanas" (18,000 pesos) and good ol' chicken tacos (3 for 15,500 pesos). *Vaso con leche* 2000 pesos. Open Tues.-Sat. 8:30am-8pm, Sun. 8:30am-6:30pm.

Restaurant La Bufa, Comonfort 6-B. Cheap and highly recommended corner operation. Solid wooden tables covered by bright blue tablecloths. Excellent *comida corrida* 6500 pesos. *Café Americano* 2000 pesos. Open daily 1-7pm.

La Tartarie, De las Casas 103, in the Pl. del Sacate. A hidden beauty. Small outdoor patio is quiet and cool in the midday heat. Clientele all business in the daytime, all romance when the sun goes down. The *comida corrida* (7000 pesos) is a treat, even if the meat dish is skimpy. Entrees from 12,000 pesos. Half-liter of wine 9000 pesos. Open daily 9am-8pm.

Super Pollos, on Galeana between Hidalgo and Rayón. This little stand is always jammed—there aren't any chairs, so everyone just mills around the counter, wolfing down delicious *pollo tortas* (3000 pesos). Open daily 9am-8pm.

La Parroquia de Cuernavaca, Guerrero 102, on the east side of Jardín Juárez. The best of the cheap European cafés. Squeeze in among the tables of executives to snag one of the best people-watching seats in the city. Great club sandwich with steak fries 9500 pesos, Arabian *Kafta* specialties 18,000 pesos. Open daily 8am-11:30pm.

Las Mañanitas, Ricardo Linares 107 (tel. 12-46-46), off Matamoros. One of Mexico's most famous restaurants. Step in off the street to a world far from the frenzy of Cuernavaca. Both bar and restaurant spill onto a large, beautiful garden. A menu of gourmet delights: Indulge. Chicken curry 26,000 pesos. Lunch served daily 1-5pm, dinner 7-11pm. Reservations necessary.

Restaurante Wah-Yen, Benito Juárez 308, at Motolinia. Chintzy Chinese decor and an inauspicious exterior, but the food is tasty and plentiful. Six-course combination platter 16,000 pesos. Open daily noon-10:30pm.

Restaurante La Cueva, Galeana 2, just south of Rayón. Moderately priced restaurant/bar serves tiny coffees, expensive desserts, and tasty meat dishes. Color TV nightly in the rear dining room. *Comida corrida* (served daily 1:30-5pm) with *pollo con mole* 9800 pesos. Open daily 9am-midnight.

Restaurante Vienes, Lerdo de Tejada 4, 2 blocks east of Morelos at Comonfort. Not to be confused with Café Vienna, its pricier twin. Delectable international fare. Upstairs *sala* displays fake nature scenes behind wooden wall windows. Prices correspond to the size of the portions: both are large. Lasagna (13,000 pesos) and quiche lorraine (16,000 pesos) are good ideas, because meat dishes cost 20,000-30,000 pesos. Split a gooey cheese fondue for 2 (20,000 pesos.) Open Tues.-Thurs. and Sun. 11am-10pm, Fri.-Sat. 11am-11pm.

Helado Virginia, Benito Juárez 300. All the flavors you can think of, and then some. Local youths indulging dates sit alongside parents placating children. The sterile white room is a cool place to chill. Two big scoops stuffed into a miniscule cup 2700 pesos. Six-scoop sundae 9000 pesos. Open daily 8am-9pm.

Sights

Sight-seeing in Cuernavaca begins at the two plazas of the Zócalo. The **Plaza de la Constitución,** larger of the two, extends east from the Palacio de Gobierno, home of the Morelos state bureaucracy. Heart and soul of the city, the plaza glows with fiery red *flamboyanes* (royal poincianna) and is shaded by elm and palm trees. Cafés spill into the plaza, and people compete for space on wrought-iron benches while food vendors, sidewalk chalk artists, and *mariachis* compete for pesos.

At the southeastern corner of the Pl. de la Constitución, east of Benito Juárez, the **Palacio de Cortés** stand as a stately reminder of the city's grim history. Cortés built this fortress with the remains of the buildings he leveled when setting the town on fire in 1521. Like many other legacies of the Conquest, this one rises from the base of a sacred pyramid. A buttressed, two-story stone fortress, the palace has a circular watch tower on the left, a line of spiky parapets running along the roof, and arches marking the entrance. The base of the original pyramid remains visible on the east side. Begun in 1522 and completed in 1524, when Cortés left for Honduras on a new expedition, the building functioned as a prison in the 18th century and as the Palacio de Gobierno during the Porfiriato.

A grant from the former British ambassador to Mexico (none other than Charles Lindbergh's father-in-law) has transformed the Palacio de Cortés into the **Museo Cuauhnahuac.** On the first floor of the museum, archeological and anthropological exhibits deal with pre-Hispanic cultures. Timelines highlight the histories of the Toltec, Olmec, Mayan, and Aztec peoples; some illustrated parchments enable a closer look at the Xochilimilca, Chalcha, Telpaneca, and Tlahuica cultures. Second-floor exhibits on the Conquest and later Mexican history include the first public clock ever to toll in Mesoamerica and some original clothing and furnishings from the palace. A collection of rare photographs chronicles the Revolution of 1910, and ethnographic exhibits dramatize the ways in which Tlahuica daily life has changed over the years.

One of Diego Rivera's finest works abides on the western balcony on the second floor of the palace. Painted during the building's stint as the Palacio de Gobierno, the mural was commissioned by then-U.S. Ambassador to Mexico Dwight D. Morrow as a gift to the people of Cuernavaca. Rivera's mural depicts the history of Mexico from the Conquest until the 1910 Revolution, proceeding chronologically from right to left. Over the museum's south patio towers a striking statue of Morelos. (Palacio and museum open Tues.-Sun. 10am-5pm. Admission 10,000 pesos, free Sun.)

A wonderful, bulbous kiosk designed by Gustave Eiffel and commissioned by Cuernavaca's Viennese colony stands in the **Jardín Juárez,** at the northwest corner of the Pl. de la Constitución, north of the Palacio de Gobierno. At all times of day, the garden is filled with mobile orange shoeshine booths, vendors hawking helium balloons, mobs of *cuernavaquences,* and large North American tour groups. Thursdays and Sundays at 6pm, a local band commanders the kiosk and belts out polkas, classical music, and *rancheras* (country music).

Black soot has darkened the tall walls and towers of the **Catedral de la Asunción,** 3 blocks down Hidalgo from the Zócalo, at Morelos. Construction on the three temples of the cathedral began in 1525, and the bulk was finished by 1552, making this one of the earliest churches in the Americas. The high, fortress-like walls and parapets were intended to impress the *indígena* population with clerical power. The florid reliefs adorning the cathedral are good examples of the Churrigueresque style. Removal of the aisle altars 20 years ago disclosed some fabulous Asian frescoes depicting the persecution and martyrdom of Christian missionaries in Sokori, Japan. Historians speculate that these frescoes were executed in the early 17th century by a converted Japanese artist who had settled in Cuernavaca. The cross over a skull and bones on the north entrance to the main temple represents the Franciscan order. (Open daily 7am-7pm.)

Site of glamorous soirées during the French occupation of Mexico, the **Jardín Borda** exists today as a lackluster shell of earlier glory. In 1783, the priest Manuel de la Borda built a garden of magnificent pools and fountains next to the ostentatious residence of his relative, the traveler José de la Borda. The Jardín Borda's grandeur quickly gained fame, and in 1864 the Habsburg Emperor Maximilian and his wife Carlota established a summer residence there. Maximilian's dignitaries rode delicate boats on the giant pool in the park's northern end, which is portrayed in a painting hanging in the city's Ayuntamiento. Today, it takes quite an imagination to recognize the faded splendor of a past epoch as you stroll over the moss-covered, crumbling sidewalks. In the southern section of the park, a labyrinth of paths radiates out from a deteriorated stone fountain toward other smaller fountains. Unlike the fountains and sidewalks, the mango trees, tropical ferns, ornamental plants, and giant palm trees have flourished through the years. The stone entrance is on Morelos, across from the cathedral. (Open Tues.-Sun. 10am-6pm. Admission 1000 pesos.)

Cuernavaca's **Ayuntamiento,** on Morelos just south of the Jardín Borda, houses both the city offices and the city "museum," which consists mainly of paintings on office and corridor walls and in the courtyard. However makeshift the arrangement may be, many of the paintings (most of them commissioned by the Ayuntamiento in the 1930s) are exceptional as informative documents of Mexican life and history. (Open daily 8am-8pm.)

Maximilian maintained more than one residence in Cuernavaca. **La Casa del Olindo,** built in 1865, was also called the Casa del Olvido (House of Forgetfulness) by townsfolk, since the architect "forgot" to include quarters for Maximilian's wife, Carlota. Incidentally, he did remember to add a small shack in the back garden for Margarita Leguísamo Sedano, the legendary *India Bonita* (Maximilian's lover).

The **Pyramid of Teopanzolco** squats on a glistening green lawn at the center of a public park, near the southern end of Teopanzolco, southeast of the market on Guerrero. These Aztec ruins were uncovered during the revolution, when firing tanks loosened the top layer of soil. The pyramid actually consists of two pyramids, one within the other. The first stairway leads to a ledge, at the bottom of which a second stairway, belonging to the second pyramid, begins. Like other pre-Hispanic peoples, the Tlahuica periodically increased the size of their monuments simply by encasing outdated ones in new construction. An eerie partial staircase indicates that the new pyramid was unfinished when Cortés arrived. To get to the site, walk north (the cathedral will be on your left, Flecha Roja on your right) on Morelos from downtown, turn right on Pericon, and go right on Río Balsas to Teopanzolco. (Open Tues.-Sun. 10am-5pm. Admission 6000 pesos.)

It's worth the bus ride to Av. Zapata on the edge of town to see the equestrian statue and triptych of Emiliano Zapata, which honor Zapata and serve as southern gateway to the city. In the right-hand panel of the triptych, thousands of virgins hold a candlelight vigil over Zapata's corpse. Zapata was murdered in 1919 by agents of President Venustiano Carranza; a federal officer tricked Zapata into believing he wanted to defect to the Zapatistas, arranged a conference, and then shot him under the table. The dynamic stone statue shows Zapata galloping on horseback at full speed out of town. Locals joke that he is forever fleeing the *militares,* whose camp is just behind. (Take bus "Universidad" from Morelos, 450 pesos.)

Once the most glamorous and exclusive hotel in Cuernavaca, the **Casino de la Selva,** Leandro Valle 1001 (tel. 12-47-00), on the northern side of the city center, now ranks second, third, or maybe fourth. Still, the gardens and open-air collection of modern and pre-Hispanic sculpture entice visitors. On the front wall of the hotel, a fantastic image symbolizes the Conquest: an armored centaur wrestling furiously with angels that burn like the sun, while torn limbs and bodies of fallen angels lie scattered on the ground. Opposite, a bland mural of the new Mexican race (symbolized by an *indígena* woman) being shaped by technology and industry contrasts poorly with the other murals. The walls and ceilings of the main dining hall were decorated by young artists, working in conjunction with famous *cuernavaquence* muralist David Alfaro Siqueiros. On the left wall, the myths of pre-Hispanic Mexico are presented in fine detail. On the right, the history of Spanish civilization from the Crusades to the Conquest is imaginatively and magnificently rendered. The ceiling portrays historical phenomena of modern Mexico: independence, reform, and events leading to revolution. The Casino de la Selva contains a bowling alley, pool tables, and a disco, all moderately priced. (Take bus "Flores Magón," 450 pesos.)

The **Universidad de Morelos,** the point highest in the city and farthest from the Zócalo, makes quite a hike from town. The "Universidad" bus makes its last stop here. From the steps of the university, on a clear day, visitors enjoy a breathtaking view of the valley. In shantytowns on the city outskirts, children kick soccer balls on the dusty dirt roads between the tin and cardboard houses. When the poor of the city built these fragile homes about two years ago, the city police attempted to expel them but met violent resistance. Since Mexican law stipulates that territory occupied for more than a year rightfully becomes the property of the inhabitant, the squatters have won the battle and the land.

The university has an affiliated library, the **Biblioteca Pública de Cuernavaca,** Rayón 7 (tel. 12-49-84), 4 blocks south of the Zócalo at Comonfort. Although the only books in English are encyclopedias, the library provides tranquility not easily found elsewhere in Cuernavaca as well as a downtown study center for university students. A magnificent mural stretches the length of the building; painted in 1951 by Valentín González, it colorfully depicts the history and industrialization of the Mexican paper business. (Open Mon.-Fri. 9am-5pm.)

Entertainment

Cuernavaca's age-old popularity as a vacation spot has encouraged the development of nightlife more glitzy than that in most Mexican cities. Cuernavaca's U.S.

expatriate community, which numbers over 20,000, has given many of these activities a northern flair. Bars in Cuernavaca are modern and highly commercialized, and several have live nightly entertainment. Most joints around the Zócalo cater to tourists; some have no cover charge but expect patrons to buy drinks.

Most discos are open from 8pm to 4am on Friday and Saturday. To deter the fistfights and *broncas* (brawls) that used to plague Cuernavaca's discos, some now admit only male-female couples, and require reservations; most, however, do not enforce these rules. The popular discos are not on the Zócalo but farther down neighboring side streets. **Ta'izz**, Chapultepec 50 (tel. 15-40-60), emphasizes Top-40 over lambada. Fog machines and light shows seduce the younger crowd. (Cover 30,000 pesos. Drinks 8,000 pesos. Open 10pm-4am.) **Shadée**, on Maden, above the market, is a smaller disco that also serves dinner. Music and personal attention from the English-speaking manager make this place popular with the city's language students. (Cover 30,000 pesos Thurs.-Sat. Drinks 8000 pesos. Open Tues.-Sat. 10am-4am.) **Barba Azul,** Pradera 10 (tel. 13-19-76), attracts Mexico City's post-college, pre-job pseudo-intellectuals. (Cover 30,000 pesos. Drinks 12,000 pesos. Open Fri.-Sat. 10am-5am.)

Cuernavaca's bars promise cheaper fun, great music, and a shorter walk. Cheapest of all is the free entertainment generally available in the main plazas at 6pm on weekends, when local *mariachis* practice for their evening gigs.

Cuernavaca's movie houses charge 5500 pesos per flick. Cheap yes, enthralling no. The imported films are usually third-rate, but art films and classics appear from time to time. The principal cinemas downtown are **Cine Ocampo**, across from the Jardín Juárez, and **Cine Alameda**, Matamoros 1 (tel. 12-10-50), 1 block north of the Zócalo. This large colonial theater, with its ultra-wide movie screen, is worth a peek. For an alternative source of audio-visual stimulation, feast your eyes and ears at **Las Palmas Video,** about 5 blocks down Juárez and at the foot of the hill. Lounge in comfortable couches while watching the latest videos beamed from the U.S. by satellite.

The bars listed below have steep drink prices but are perhaps classier and more arousing than planting yourself in front of a video screen.

Harry's Grill, Gutenberg 95, beside the Las Plazas mall north of the Zócalo. The place in Cuernavaca for traumatization at the ring-laden hands of opulent Mexicans. Throbbing Top-40 dance hits, old telephone booths, airplane propellers, and U.S. license plates quirkily approximate an American bar. Its slogan—"A Sunny Place for Shady People"—is famous even in Colorado. Gigantic barroom packed with slick barhoppers scoping from tiny chairs around miniscule tables. The pick-up scene here is no less than frantic; the people are lively, loud, and fun to watch. Free hors d'oeuvres. Drink prices are steep: beer 5500 pesos, juicy cocktails 6000 pesos. In the actual grill part of the Grill, try the *pollo cerveza* (16,000 pesos). Open Sun.-Thurs. 1:30-11:45pm, Fri.-Sat. 1:30pm-12:30am.

Las Terrazas, 20 de Noviembre at Netzahualcóyotl, south of the Zócalo, on the 2nd floor. Pound on the wrought-iron gate to be let in to this private club. Cobblestone steps lead up to a wide covered terrace flooded with foliage and fresh evening air. Jovial atmosphere and Mexican music. The only government-licensed gay bar in Cuernavaca, but attracts a largely straight, upper middle-class crowd. Open Fri.-Sat. and *fiestas* noon-10pm. Cover 10,000 pesos, 1 drink included.

Tequila Show Pub, Jardín de los Héroes 2, on the southern edge of the plaza. Small dance floor, used mainly for live performers and band equipment, is surrounded by the microscopic tables you last saw in kindergarten. Leave before the live performer arrives and obliterates all possibility for conversation. No cover, but drinks alone cost 8000 pesos. Open Mon.-Sat. 8pm-2am.

Vamejá Restaurant/Bar, Gutenberg 101, inside the Las Plazas mall. Fantastic live Mexican *salsa* and *mambo* groups move the crowd of this open-air bar to tears. Fun, festive, and ultra-modern. Open Mon.-Sat. 1pm-midnight.

On Saturdays and Sundays, the market in the **Jardín Juárez** specializes in silver jewelry; don't be afraid to bargain. The famous **Feria de la Primavera** (Festival of Spring) brings parades, costumes, and a splash of color for 10 days every year at the vernal equinox (March 21-22). Ask at the tourist office for information about specific events.

Near Cuernavaca

Xochicalco

Ceremonial center, fortress, and trading post rolled into one, Xochicalco is the most important and beautiful archeological site in the state of Morelos. Built in the 7th century during the Toltec Classic period, Xochicalco suffered period invasions by various *indígena* tribes, including the Olmecs, Maya, Zapotecs, and Mixtecs. By the time of the Conquest, the city had become a tributary of Tenochtitlán, the capital of the Aztec empire.

Although its Nahuatl name means "Place of the Flowers," the hilltops where Xochicalco stands are arid in the summer. Lizards and roadrunners dart away as you pass through the rocky terrain, and more oxen than tourists seem to make the trek to the ruins. Even during the rainy season, when dew sparkles on green hills, an eerie loneliness pervades the site.

The desolation does not diminish the allure of this citadel of debris, however. The underground observatory is a feat of engineering and astronomical aptitude. Deep inside the subterranean passageways lie fragments of paved floors and stucco walls. On summer solstices, Aztec sages and star-gazers peered through a shaft in the ceiling to trace the path of the sun and thus verify and adjust the Aztec calendar. The observatory is now locked behind an iron grid, but some negotiation might persuade a guard to unlock the bolt and let you play ancient astronomer.

On the first plain, the renowned **Pyramid of Quetzalcóatl,** sloppily reconstructed in 1910, bears carved reliefs of the image of this great god and hero of the Toltecs. In Quetzalcóatl, bird and snake fuse into one. Xochicalco's commercial partnership with southern cultures is reflected in the embrace Quetzalcóatl bestows upon a priest in an elaborate Mayan headdress.

Next to the Pyramid of Quetzalcóatl stands the **Temple of the Stela,** where archeologists found the burial place of a high priest along with ritual offerings. Down the hill, on a lower terrace, three pyramids comprise the impressive **Shrine of the Stela,** where the Toltecs worshiped the sun and *desai* (Mezcal god) each day at sunrise and sunset. Toltecs also revered the carved obelisk in the center of the park. Its shadow plotted the trajectory of the sun between two identical pyramids that faced each other.

Next to the shrine, two massive rings of rock are attached to the ballcourt, of interest because most ballcourts in Mesoamerica have only one ring. Here, some anthropologists claim, teams competed for the privilege of being sacrificed atop the Pyramid of Quetzalcóatl (their strong hearts fed the sun). Below, only the foundations remain of the **Calmecac,** the palace in which Toltec and Aztec priests underwent training and initiation. Next door, 20 circular beds of rock represent the 20-day month of the Aztec and Toltec calendar; nearby rock mounds topped with cacti and shrubs are not just mundane hills but unexcavated pyramids.

Flecha Roja runs a bus (1400 pesos) directly to Xochicalco from Cuernavaca, leaving the station on Morelos at 12:30pm. If you can't catch that bus, take one to Miacatlán (every 20 min. 6:20am-8:50pm, 1900 pesos) from the Autos Pullman station, at Abasolo and Netzahualcóyotl, 1 block south of the cathedral in Cuernavaca. Ask the driver to drop you off at the Crucero de Xochicalco. You may catch a taxi to the ruins if you wait at this crossroads long enough, but don't count on it. The uphill walk to the site (4km) will take about one hour; an alternative to walking back to the crossroads is the México-Zacatepec bus (unpredictable schedule, 1600 pesos). Taxis seem unwilling to wait at the site. (Site open Tues.-Sun. 9am-5pm. Admission 10,000 pesos.)

Another half hour by bus past Xochicalco in neighboring Guerrero state, lie **Las Grutas,** a fascinating and well-known network of caves. The two-hour tour of the cave complex takes you past many stalactites and stalagmites in formations that resemble such people as Dante, the devil incarnate, and Michael Krivan in the morning. (Admission 3000 pesos.) To get to the caverns, take the "Las Grutas" bus from the Autos Pullman station (every 2 hr. 8:20am-4:20pm, 2½ hr., 3400 pesos).

Tepoztlán

In northern Morelos, the quiet *pueblo* of Tepoztlán (1701m) occupies one of the state's most scenic sites, where towering cliffs form a natural fortress that allows entrance only from the south. Proceeding along Rte. 95-D toward Tepoztlán, you will see the two mammoth, snow-covered volcanoes, Popocatépetl and Ixtaccíhuatl, jaggedly rising above the land. The cobbled *indígena* village is a throwback to pre-colonial life, with ancient customs still alive and the Nahuatl language still predominant. The archeological sites for which the town is famous wobble on a peak 1200 ft. above the village. The long walk through thin air may leave you breathless and thirsty, so prepare accordingly.

The valley of Tepoztlán swims in myth, legend, and magic. It is thought to be the birthplace (about 1200 yr. ago) of the famous god-hero of the Toltecs, Quetzal-cóatl. Townfolk speak respectfully of a magnetic force present only in Tepoztlán. Moreover, Tepoztlán was once the ceremonial ground where pilgrims came to worship Tepoztecatl, god of *pulque* (the sacred liquor of the Nahuas), of fertility, and of the harvest. Celebrations still take place every September 8, when the *pulque* flows and the dance floor fills in honor of Tepoztecatl. *Los Chinelos*—colorfully attired folk dancers—invite you to join their traditional dance, *el salto,* as they do at Tepoztlán's other carnivals and feasts.

Travelers also come to visit the **Pyramid of Tepozteco,** perched on the northern ridge of the cliffs that rise above one end of town, about 3km above the valley. Some say the pyramid (which is visible from town only on clear days) was a Tlahuica observatory and defense post for the valley, while others swear it served as an Aztec sacrificial temple. The 10m-tall structure has a porch inscribed with both Tlahuica glyphs and more modern messages such as "Juanito loves Hortencia." To reach the pyramid, follow the main road north out of town (passing the Zócalo on your right) until its end. The steep climb along a narrow path takes roughly an hour. (Open Tues.-Sun. 9am-5pm. Admission 700 pesos.)

Built in 1559 on a Teocalli temple, the **Dominican Convent** sits behind the plaza, next to the Capilla de Nuestra Señora de la Asunción. In the corridors, old frescoes with religious motifs have survived erosion, humidity, and a paint job ordered by a certain Padre Angel in 1905. Make it one of your first steps in Tepotzlán, because the roof could tumble to the ground by the time you leave town. (Open Tues.-Sun. 9:30am-5pm. Free.)

The **Museo Arqueológico de Tepoztlán,** at the rear of Capilla Asunción (accessible only from the back street) holds a collection that Carlos Pellicer, the poet and benefactor, donated to the city. The impressive display includes a wide variety of pottery pieces and clay figures of Olmec, Zapotec, Mayan, Totonac, and Aztec origin, as well as many objects from Teotihuacán. There are also photographs of the main archeological sites in Mexico, such as Chichén Itzá, Malinalco, and Mitla. (Open Tues.-Sun. 10am-2pm and 4-6pm. Admission 1000 pesos.)

Like Cuernavaca, Tepoztlán has its share of foreigners and *chilangos* (the colloquial term *morelenses* use for visitors from Mexico City; it once meant "people who come to spoil things"). Because of its natural beauty, vernal climate, and proximity to Mexico City, Tepoztlán attracts an ever-growing population of *norteamericanos* who establish elaborate weekend homes and summer residences here.

Not surprisingly, then, Tepoztlán lacks moderately priced accommodations. **Posada del Tepozteco,** Paraíso 3 (tel. 500-10), up the hill from the Zócalo, is an excellent bit of extravagance, with handsome rooms, wandering garden paths, a beautiful pool, and magnificent views. (Singles and doubles 100,000 pesos.) **La Cabaña,** 5 de Mayo 54, on the same street as the Cristóbal Colón station, rents clean and safe rooms—although without toilet or running water (*agua purificada* is available). The proprietor is friendly and helpful. (Singles 25,000 pesos. Doubles 40,000 pesos.)

Campers can size up the YMCA-affiliated **Campamento Comohmila** (tel. 501-10; km3.5) on the Carretera Tepoztlán-Yautepec. Campsites adjoin a mess hall, basketball and volleyball courts, and a soccer field.

Visit Tepoztlán from either Cuernavaca or Mexico City. Ometochtli buses (tel. 12-88-22) to Tepoztlán leave from the Cuernavaca market (every 20 min. 7am-9pm, 1 hr., 1200 pesos). Cristóbal Colón buses run from the Mexico City Central de Autobuses del Sur (Mon.-Sat. 5:30am-6:45pm, 1½ hr., 2500 pesos) and return on the same schedule.

Malinalco

Although located in Mexico State, the Aztec ruins of Malinalco are most easily reached from Cuernavaca. The bus ride to the ruins is both panoramic and entertaining: *campesinos,* loaded with straw baskets and knitted wools they plan to sell in the big city, chew tobacco, spit on the steel floor, and talk about the crop in Spanish and Nahuatl.

The buildings in seemingly unpopulated Malinalco are stark white, and each bears a broad stripe of blue at exactly the same height. Signs painted with the same blue identify the few shops around the plaza: *farmacia, cantina, hotel.* In the Zócalo, vendors display their best tomatoes, fruits, *clacoyos*—pockets of cooked dough filled with *frijoles* or mushrooms (1200 pesos)—and hot chocolate (700 pesos).

But Malinalco is more than the generic Latin American ghost town. At the grand Temple of Malinalco, Aztec youths were initiated into the ways of war. In front of the plaza, the town's huge church, the **Parroquia de Santa Mónica,** is a breathtaking relic built in the 16th century by Augustine monks. Gigantic frescoes from the 17th century, depicting the stations of the cross, reach the church's ceiling. In a spine-chilling adjacent room, dozens of Christ-figures suffer all sorts of torments and tortures.

Take the second-class Onitochli bus to Chalma from the Flecha Roja station, Morelos 504 (tel. 281-90), in Cuernavaca. Buses leave at 7:15am, 9am, noon, and 2pm. If you can't make these rides, you can take the Onitochli bus to Santa Marta (every hr.), and there catch another bus (every hr.) to Chalma. From Chalma, take one of the blue *coches* to Malinalco; the bus is cheaper, but leaves irregularly between 7am and 7pm (supposedly on the hr., but you may have to wait up to 2 hr.). The bus to Toluca also passes through Malinalco. Total second-class fare is about 4000 pesos, regardless of your mode of transport. Flecha Roja has frequent first-class bus service to Chalma (4000 pesos), from where a small blue *coches* will whisk you to Malinalco.

Malinalco Ruins

The Malinalcas, a small tribe within the ancient Nahua empire, lived in the Valle de Toluca, home of the giant snowy peak of Nevado de Toluca. In addition to building this great city fortress, the Malinalcas left the world fantastic wooden percussion instruments, which are on display at both the Museo Nacional de México and the Museo de Toluca.

Malinalco was the sacred ground for the rituals that officially transformed an Aztec youth into a *caballero tigre* or *caballero águila* (tiger or eagle warrior). On the open circular stone platform—the first structure on the right as you enter—prisoners were bound with only arms left free and made to wrestle the recently initiated warriors. Sacrifices were carried out in the massive, angular stone pyramid. Behind the pyramid, the oval bed of rock served as an incinerating grill where the bodies of the sacrificed were turned to ash. To the left of the pyramid facing the Malinalco Valley, the ruins of a temple used for sun worship are now unrecognizable because many stones were taken from the site to build the Santa Mónica church. Some of the frescos that adorned this temple reside in Malinalco's **Casa de Cultura Tlacatecutl Cuauhtémoc,** on one corner of the Zócalo. The *casa* also exhibits photographs of Malinalco and masks made for local plays and shows. (Open Mon.-Sat. 9am-2pm and 4-8pm.)

The **Temple of Initiation** for eagle and tiger warriors is one of the few truly monolithic structures in the world. All of its statues, rooms, and façades were carved out of one giant slab of stone. Two stone jaguars guard the steep steps. To the right of the entrance to the inner chamber, the broken figure of an eagle warrior sits on the head of the feathered serpent, Quetzalcóatl. The frame of the chamber entrance itself is fashioned into the open-mouthed, stylized head of a serpent, with fangs bared, its split tongue lapping on the floor. Inside the circular chamber, three supine eagles and one jaguar are carved on the floor. In the hole behind the first eagle, the beating hearts of the sacrificed waited to be devoured by the initiates. This repast completed the rite of passage for aspiring Toltec warriors. (Ruins open Tues.-Sun. 10am-4:30pm. Admission 10,000 pesos, free Sun.) The stairway to the Temple of Malinalco begins just behind town, where Guerrero ends. The steep path to the top takes, at most, a half hour to climb.

Cuautla

Like Cuernavaca, Cuautla attracts the Mexico City elite on weekends. In hidden villas and chic nightclubs, wealthy *jefes políticos* hoist tequila bottles and laugh the night away. Nearby *balnearios* provide a pleasurable Saturday-morning hangover cure; cheap and accessible, the various complexes are the ideal setting for a mindless day or two.

Cuautla's Zócalo is of classic design, studded with huge palm trees and disposed around a whitewashed bandstand. The city's most popular cafés line the perimeter, and the market encroaches upon every corner.

Orientation and Practical Information

Cuautla is in the east-central portion of Morelos, about 42km east of Cuernavaca. From Cuernavaca's Estrella Roja terminal at Galeana 401, first-class buses (2200 pesos) depart to Cuautla every half hour. In Mexico City, Estrella Roja buses leave from the Terminal Central de Autobuses del Sur (every ½ hr. 6am-10pm, 2 hr., 3045 pesos).

Cuautla contains two major bus stations. **Mexico-Zacatepec** and **Cristóbal Colón,** 2 de Mayo at Zavala (tel. 202-36) offer second-class service to Mexico City (every hr. 6am-7pm, 5100 pesos) and first-class service to Mexico City (5300 pesos), Oaxaca (20,000 pesos), and other destinations along Rte. 190. **Flecha Roja** and **Estrella Roja,** Vázquez at Costeño, 1 block north of 2 de Mayo, provide first-class service to Cuernavaca (every ½ hr. 5am-8pm, 2200 pesos) and Mexico City (every ½ hr. 5:30am-7pm, 5100 pesos). To reach the Cuautla's hub (the Zócalo and the sprawling market) from this station, take a right on Mongoy as you exit and then a right onto 2 de Mayo. Where 2 de Mayo runs into Zamora, take yet another right and you will come upon the Zócalo.

Cuautla's small **tourist office** (tel. 252-21), in the Estación Ferrocarril Escénico at Defense del Agua and 19 de Febrero, employs as wallpaper pamphlets on the *balnearios* and other local attractions. No English is spoken. (Open daily 10am-6pm.)

Accommodations

Most of Cuatla's hotels line 2 de Mayo within easy walking distance of the two bus stations. Reservations are a good idea on weekends, when half of Mexico City pours into town.

CREA Youth Hostel, Unidad Deportiva (tel. 202-18), on the Mexico-Oaxaca highway. From the Zócalo, walk south to 2 de Mayo, turn left there, and continue until Reforma. Turn right and cross the bridge. At the end of the bridge, a sign on the right points to the back of the sports center parking lot, where stairs and another "CREA" sign are visible. Pleasant and airy (4 bunks per room) with communal bathrooms as clean as any Cuautla hotel's. Filled with pleasantly raucous students. 5000 pesos per person, no ID required. Breakfast 3500 pesos, lunch and dinner 4500 pesos.

Hotel Granada, Defense del Agua 34 (tel. 200-63), 1 block west of Reforma. Medium-sized, spotless rooms with huge bathrooms and all the trimmings—fan, TV, *agua purificada,* and walk-in closet. Rooms overlook a pleasant courtyard. Good restaurant in front with somewhat steep prices; *comida corrida* 14,000 pesos. Doubles 34,000 pesos, with 2 beds 43,000 pesos.

Hotel Jardines de Cuautla, 2 de Mayo 94 (tel. 200-88), ½ block to the right as you exit the Cristóbal Colón bus station. A large, modern, and ugly building. Clean halls, rooms, and bathrooms can't hide an utter lack of character. Quiet garden and two small pools in back. Singles 35,000 pesos. Doubles 50,000 pesos.

Hotel Colón, Guerrero 48 (tel. 229-90), on the Zócalo. On a par with Hotel Jardines for character (or lack thereof), but you can count on a fan and *agua purificada.* Cramped bathrooms, some with moldy spots under the sinks of interest to immunologists, are otherwise clean on the whole. Ask for a Zócalo view. Singles 25,000 pesos. Doubles 35,000 pesos.

Hotel España, 2 de Mayo 22 (tel. 221-86), 1 block past the Hotel Jardines on the way in from the Cristóbal Colón station. Simple, somewhat seedy but quiet rooms surround a large open courtyard. Bathrooms clean, but some toilets lack seats. Den with TV off the poster-regaled lobby. Singles 30,000 pesos. Doubles 35,000 pesos. Triples 40,000 pesos.

Food

Restaurant Manolo, Guerrero 53 (tel. 204-11), on the southwest corner of the Zócalo. High-ceilinged old hall jammed with tables and presided over by 1950s bathing beauties. Crowd consists of aging businessmen and soccer enthusiasts glued to the TV. Excellent *comida corrida* 6500 pesos. Open daily 8am-11pm.

La Blanquita, 2 de Mayo 10, ½ block from Hotel España, across from the movie theater. Architecturally undistinguished building with some of the town's best and cheapest fare inside. Large and excellent *comida corrida* 5000 pesos. Breakfast of milk, juice, fruit, and sweet bread 7000 pesos. Open Fri.-Wed. 8am-10pm.

Cafetería El Cid, Portal Iturbide (tel. 201-04), on the Zócalo. The place for breakfast: a full breakfast combo like the *International* including a fruitcup, tacos to taste, and coffee costs 5500 pesos; the *A La Cid* with an omelette is 4000 pesos. Outdoor seating is great for people-watching. Open daily 8am-midnight.

Sights and Entertainment

Oaxtepec (tel. 210-86), formerly an Olmec health resort for off-duty warriors with nothing better to do than play tennis and now the most gorgeous and gigantic of all the *balnearios,* boasts 25 pools, a restaurant, hotels, medical services, post office, a *teleférico* (cablecar) that transports bathers from one pool to another, a herbarium covered by a huge crystal dome (illuminated at night), three supermarkets, and a cinema. The complex has the capacity to coddle 25,000 people at a time. (Open daily 7am-5pm. Admission 5000 pesos, children 3000 pesos.) Unfortunately this wonderful adult playground is far from Cuautla. Second-class buses to Oaxtepec (500 pesos) leave from the Cristóbal Colón terminal on 2 de Mayo seven times per day between 6am and 5pm. In Cuautla itself, **El Almeal,** at the end of Virginia Hernández (tel. 217-51), offers camping and sports facilities that pale in comparison but keep patrons happy. (Open daily 9am-6pm. Admission 5000 pesos, children 4000 pesos.)

The popular **Agua Hedionda** (tel. 200-44) has five sulfur pools with space for 3000 people and a natural water temperature of 33°C (90°F). Mexicans come here to treat their ulcers. Jump aboard bus "Agua Hedionda" (350 pesos) in front of the Pl. Cívica. (Open daily 7am-7pm. Admission 4000 pesos, children 3000 pesos.)

There are many more *balnearios* nearby; ask at the tourist office. For those who'd rather dance than shrivel the night away, Cuautla has a flourishing disco scene. On Friday and Saturday, try the **Latana Disco** in the Hotel Cuautla, Batalla 19 de Fe-

brero 114 (tel. 272-33; cover 30,000 pesos.) Just outside of town is **Zarco,** Reforma
792 (tel. 287-88; cover 25,000 pesos; open Fri.-Sun.).

Puebla and Tlaxcala

Although the first part of Mexico to submit to Hernán Cortés was Veracruz, the
Conquest did not really pick up speed until his group ventured inland to Puebla,
where many local tribes joined the entourage. Mexico's oldest churches, some built
only months after the Spaniards' arrival, demarcate Cortés's trail through Puebla
and Tlaxcala. Cholula has served as a religious center for each successive dominant
culture in the area since the 2nd century BC.

A glimpse into one of the 16th-century churches which dominate rural towns
will inevitably fasten on evidence that the Conquest remains incomplete. Images
from pre-Hispanic mythology mingle with those of Christianity in church decoration. Pagan myth shrouds Puebla's two snow-capped volcanoes, **Popocatépetl**
(5452m) and **Ixtaccíhuatl** (5282m), the second- and third-largest mountains in the
country. Their Nahuatl names mean "Smoking Mountain" and "Sleeping Woman"
respectively. Legend has it that the warrior, Popocatépetl, loved Ixtaccíhuatl, the
emperor's daughter. Once, when he went off to a battle, Ixtaccíhuatl heard errone-
ously that he had been killed; she subsequently died of lovesickness and grief. When
Popo (to friends) learned of his lover's death, he built the two great mountains: on
the northern one he placed her body, on the southern one he stood vigil with a torch.
Poblanos (citizens of Puebla) pay their respects to the supine, death-pale Ixtaccíhuatl on the mountain's snowy summit. Experienced climbers can ascend either
or both of these volcanoes, and less audacious backpackers have their pick of extensive trails that connect isolated foothill villages.

Puebla

A 17th-century legend holds that the Bishop of Tlaxcala, Don Julián Garcés,
dreamed of a beautiful field next to a sparkling river. In the vision, he saw angels
descend from the sky to this magnificent spot, planting stakes and stretching cords
for the streets of a new city. The very next day, on a hike south of Tlaxcala, he
recognized the land of his dream and immediately erected the altar from which Fray
Toribio Paredes de Benavente delivered the first Catholic mass in 1531.

Since then, Puebla has evolved into an important residential area and major stopover between the commercial port of Veracruz and the metropolitan center of Mexico City, and therefore a coveted wartime asset. In every war prior to Independence,
Puebla remained fiercely loyal to the Spanish and proved a formidable fortress of
Catholicism, commissioning over 60 Baroque churches over the course of coloniza-
tion. In 1847, at a pivotal period in the Mexican-American War, Mexican General
Santa Ana decided make a surprise attack against North American forces holed
up in Puebla. U.S. troops held up alarmingly well, however, and not until the
French intervention fell apart 15 years later did the Mexican army taste the long-
awaited fruits of victory in the city. Every year since that famous battle of 1862,
5 de Mayo has been celebrated as Mexican Independence Day.

Employing over a million people, Puebla's factories now outnumber its churches.
The city produces hemp sackcloth, commercial imitations of handmade Talaveran
tiles, and the German-born VW Beetles that clog the streets of every Mexican province. On the outskirts of the city, farmers tend sugarcane, corn, rice, and livestock.
Although pollution, traffic, and crowded sidewalks have begun to tarnish Puebla's
charm, its beautiful architecture, colonial heritage, and great food still detain those
traveling east from Mexico City.

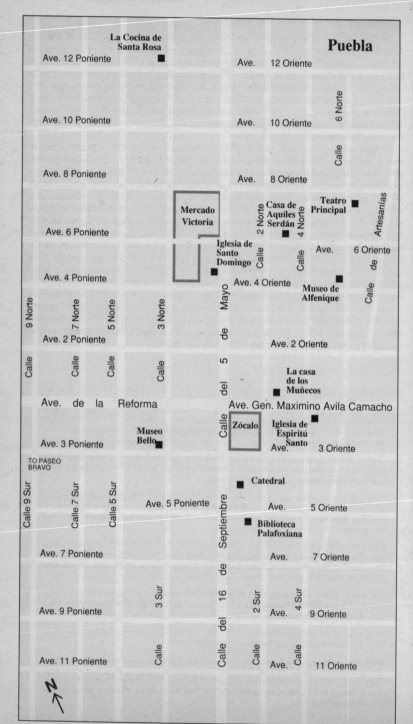

La Cocina de
Santa Rosa

Puebla

Ave. 12 Poniente   Ave.   12 Oriente

6 Norte

Ave. 10 Poniente   Ave.   10 Oriente

Calle

Ave. 8 Poniente   Ave.   8 Oriente

Mercado
Victoria

Casa de   **Teatro**
Aquíles   **Principal**
Serdán

2 Norte
4 Norte

Artesanías

Iglesia de
Santo   Calle   Calle   Ave.   6 Oriente
Domingo

de

Ave. 6 Poniente

Ave. 4 Poniente

Calle

Ave. 4 Oriente   **Museo de**
Alfenique

9 Norte
7 Norte
5 Norte
3 Norte

Mayo

de

Ave. 2 Poniente   Ave. 2 Oriente

Calle
Calle
Calle
Calle

5

del

La casa
de los
Muñecos

Ave. de la Reforma   Ave. Gen. Maximino Avila Camacho

Calle

Zócalo   **Iglesia de**
Espiritú
Santo

Museo
Bello

Ave. 3 Poniente   Ave.   3 Oriente

TO PASEO
BRAVO

Calle 9 Sur
Calle 7 Sur
Calle 5 Sur

Catedral

Ave. 5 Poniente

Septiembre

Ave.   5 Oriente

Biblioteca
Palafoxiana

Ave. 7 Poniente   de   Ave.   7 Oriente

16

3 Sur

2 Sur
4 Sur

Ave. 9 Poniente   del   Ave.   9 Oriente

Calle
Calle
Calle
Calle

Ave. 11 Poniente   Ave.   11 Oriente

N

Orientation

Puebla, capital of the state of the same name, lies 125km southeast of Mexico City and 300km west of Veracruz. All bus companies operate out of the terminal on Blvd. Atlixco Nte., in the northwest corner of the city. There is a local airport in Huejotzingo connected by Mexicana and Aeroméxico to major points in the Republic. An extensive highway network links Puebla to Mexico City (along Rte. 190, toll 8000 pesos per automobile, 9000 pesos per van), Oaxaca (along Rte. 190 or 135), Tlaxcala, Veracruz, and many other cities. Transportation in and around Puebla is particularly easy in deference to the many travelers who scuttle back and forth between the coast and the interior.

If your sense of direction still spins from the contorted streets of many Mexican cities, you are in for a treat: the *avenidas* and *calles* of Puebla form a near-perfect grid. The northwest corner of the Zócalo occupies the center of the grid. The main north-south street is 5 de Mayo to the north of that point 16 de Septiembre south of it. The main east-west thoroughfare is Av. Reforma to the west, becoming Av. Máximo Avila Camacho to the east. *Avenidas,* running east-west parallel to Reforma/M. Avila Camacho, are designated either Pte. or Ote. depending on whether they lie west or east, respectively, of 5 de Mayo/16 de Septiembre. Even-numbered avenues are north of Reforma/M. Avila Camacho, odd-numbered avenues south. *Calles,* running north-south parallel to 5 de Mayo/16 de Septiembre, are denoted as Nte. or Sur with respect to Reforma/M. Avila Camacho. These streets are even-numbered if east of 5 de Mayo/16 de Septiembre and odd-numbered if west.

Yellow taxis will take you to the Zócalo from the bus station for 4500 pesos. Buy a taxi ticket in the bus station and save yourself the anxiety of a potential rip-off. The tickets are valid only in the yellow taxis; if you decide to take a black-and-cream taxi, set the fare before you hop in. Municipal buses cost 350 pesos: maps of bus routes are available at Bancomer or the tourist office.

Practical Information

State Tourist Office: Av. 5 Ote. 3 (tel. 46-12-85), facing the cathedral's southern side. Incredibly friendly employees (all speak a little English, some speak it well) hand out mounds of maps, guides, and other paraphernalia, and generally assist beyond the call of duty. The office provides tours of the city throughout the day and of nearby Cholula at 3pm (12,000 pesos). Open Mon.-Sat. 10am-8pm, Sun. 10am-2pm. **Information Booth,** Blvd. Atlixco Nte. at Serdán. Open Tues.-Sun. 10am-5pm.

Federal Tourist Office: Calle 3 Sur 1501 (tel. 40-90-09), on the 3rd floor. Information about hotel rates. All other tourist information in Spanish. Not very helpful unless you have specific questions. Open Mon.-Fri. 9am-2pm and 4-8pm.

Currency Exchange: Bancomer, Reforma 116 (tel. 32-00-22), ½ block west of the Zócalo's northwest corner. Open for exchange Mon.-Fri. 9am-1:30pm; for traveler's checks 9am-12:15pm. **Bánamex,** Reforma 113 (tel. 46-00-67), a few doors down from Bancomer. Open for exchange Mon.-Fri. 9am-1:30pm.

Post Office: 16 de Septiembre at Av. 5 Ote. (tel. 42-74-48), 1 block south of the cathedral. Open for stamps Mon.-Fri. 8am-7pm, Sat.-Sun. 9am-noon; for registered letters Mon.-Fri. 8am-6pm, Sat.-Sun. 9am-noon. Lista de Correos posted in the northern office, Av. 2 Ote. 411. Open Mon.-Fri. 8am-2pm. **Postal Code:** 72000.

Telephones: Helados Holanda, 16 de Septiembre 103, between Av. 3 and 5 Pte. Open daily 9am-9pm. **Restaurant El Dorado,** Av. 2 Ote. between Calles 4 and 6 Nte. Open daily 8am-9pm. **Telephone Code:** 22.

Telegrams: 16 de Septiembre 504 (tel. 42-17-79), on the south side of the post office. Open Mon.-Fri. 8am-midnight, Sat. 9am-9pm, Sun. 9am-1pm.

Train Station: Estación La Unión, Av. 80 Pte. at Calle 9 Nte. (tel. 46-51-58), in the northern section of the city. *Combis* marked "Estacion" (350 pesos) will take you there from the center. Daily service to Oaxaca (first class at 6:40am, 12 hr., 19,300 pesos) and Mexico City (first class at 8am, 6 hr., 11,500 pesos; second class at 7am, 4300 pesos). Rail also serves various in-state destinations.

Bus Station: On Blvd. Atlixco Nte., in the northwest corner of the city. First-class **ADO** service to: Mexico City (every 20 min. 6am-7am, every 10 min. 7am-8pm, and every 15 min. 8-10pm, 2 hr., 6400 pesos); Oaxaca (at 9am, 2:45pm, 10pm, and midnight, 7 hr., 18,500 pesos); Campeche (at 9pm, 28 hr., 56,000 pesos). First-class **Cristóbal Colon** service to Tuxtla Gutiérrez (3 per day, 18 hr., 46,000 pesos) and San Cristóbal (at 10:55pm, 20 hr., 49,000 pesos). Second-class **AU** service to Jalapa (10 per day, 8100 pesos) and Veracruz (16 per day, 13,000 pesos). Second-class **Estrella Roja** service to Mexico City (every 15 min., 5800 pesos) and Cholula (every 20 min., 600 pesos). Second-class **Estrella de Oro** also serves Cholula (every 10 min., 600 pesos). **Frosur (Flecha Roja del Sur)** goes to southern cities in Oaxaca state and as far north as Matamoros.

Taxis: Taxi-Fono (tel. 40-63-44); **Taxi Rápido** (tel. 35-99-66).

Car Rental: Renta de Autos Gómez, Juárez 2317 (tel. 41-17-24), at Calle 19 Sur. **Viajes HR,** Av. 2 Ote. 6 (tel. 40-31-77), inside the entrance to the parking lot next to Sanborn's. Both open Mon.-Fri. 9:30am-1:30pm and 3:30-6:30pm. A compact car rents for 98,000 pesos. Take the bus instead.

Bookstores: Librolandia del Centro S.A., Portal Hidalgo 4 (tel. 46-74-10), at the northern end of the Zócalo. The biggest and bestest bookstore in town. Open daily 9:30am-8pm. **Sanborn's,** Av. 2 Ote. 6 (tel. 42-94-16). Expensive restaurant that also sells English books and magazines. Open daily 7:30am-11pm. **Cafetería-Bookstore,** Reforma at Calle 7 Nte. (tel. 42-10-14). Buy a cup of coffee and enjoy the warm surroundings. Open Mon.-Sat. 9am-11pm, Sun. 5:30-11pm.

Public Library: Biblioteca Benjamin Franklin, Reforma at Calle 13 Sur, in the Centro Cultural Poblano. Open Mon.-Sat. 9am-2pm and 4-7pm.

Laundromats: Lavandería Lucy, Av. 2 Pte. 2503 (tel. 48-54-75), in the Comercial Mexicana shopping mall. 8000 pesos per load. Self-serve available. Open daily 9am-8pm. Closer to the Zócalo are **Lavandería Princess,** Av. 9 Pte. 118 (tel. 42-22-30), and **Lavandería Roti,** Calle 7 Nte. 404. Both open daily 9am-8pm.

Pharmacies: Farmacia La Santísima, Portal Juárez 101 (tel. 41-58-69), next to Restaurant La Princesa on the Zócalo's western edge; and **Farmacia del Centro,** Av. 2 Ote. 416 (tel. 42-59-44), at Calle 6 Nte. Both open Mon.-Sat. 9am-9pm, Sun. 9am-5pm.

Hospital Universitario: Calle 13 Sur at Av. 25 Pte. (tel. 43-13-77), 10 blocks south and 7 blocks west of the Zócalo. 24-hr. emergency service. Some doctors speak English.

Emergency: Tel. 06.

Police: Tel. 41-24-51 or 42-34-00.

Accommodations and Camping

Most of the budget hotels in downtown Puebla sprout up on Av. 3 Pte. However, as most *Poblanos* live downtown, lodging there is expensive; expect to pay 32,000 pesos for an acceptable room. Many hotels have hot water only for those awake before the crack of dawn. Ask potential proprietors about their policy.

Hostal de Halconeros, Reforma 141 (tel. 42-74-56), ½ block west of the Zócalo. A hotel, not a hostel. Plain, high-ceilinged rooms don't live up to expectations created by beautifully tiled, arched ceilings in the hallways. Could use some creative improvement, but bathrooms are clean. Water is sporadic so check before you strip. Great location. Singles 32,000 pesos. Doubles 43,000 pesos. Huge rooms overlooking the street 48,000 pesos.

Hotel Terminal, Serdán 5101 (tel. 41-79-80), 1 block west of the central bus station on Blvd. Atlixco Nte. Erected in 1988. It looks clean, smells clean, feels clean, and you get free candies on your pillow when you arrive. All rooms have color TV, 24-hr. hot water, and firm mattresses. Singles and doubles, both with 1 queen-size bed, 50,000 pesos.

Hotel San Miguel, Av. 3 Pte. 721 (tel. 42-48-60), about 7 blocks from the Zócalo in a modern building. Excellent, clean, carpeted rooms with phone and fine bath. Friendly management knows much about the area and gladly exchanges American money at a terrific rate; custodial staff does laundry. Bottled water. Hot water available 6-11am and 5-11pm. Singles 32,000 pesos. Doubles 40,000 pesos.

Hotel San Agustín, Av. 3 Pte. 531 (tel. 41-50-89), between Calles 5 and 7 Sur. Each room has its own name; the furnishings must struggle to establish their identity. The beds sag and the blankets are worn. Bathrooms smell but work faithfully. One of the better cheap hotels. Manager speaks English. Singles 32,000. Doubles 40,000, with 2 beds 48,000.

Hotel Teresita, Av. 3 Pte. 309 (tel. 41-70-72), 2 blocks west of the Zócalo's southwest corner. Cell-like rooms are clean on the surface. Most rooms boast multi-functional bathrooms. Singles 15,000 pesos, with bath 22,000 pesos. Doubles 15,000 pesos, with bath 25,000 pesos.

Hotel Virrey de Mendoza, Av. 3 Pte. 912 (tel. 43-39-03), 1 block past Hotel San Miguel. Run by a friendly old fellow who can't give away enough hotel ashtrays. Large rooms with beamed ceilings, wrought-iron fixtures, and great heavy wood furniture. Open courtyard used for parking and cultivation of chaotic flora. Singles 32,000 pesos. Doubles 40,000 pesos. Triples 43,000 pesos.

If you want to camp, try the **Trailer Park Las Américas** (tel. 47-01-34), near Cholula along the Puebla-Cholula road. Some people attempt to pitch tents inconspicuously on the spacious university grounds nearby.

Food

No visitor to Puebla should miss this city's most distinctive culinary delight, *mole poblano*. The dish, in one form or another, is a presence on almost every menu in the city. *Mole* is a thick, dark sauce of chocolate, *chiles,* onions, and some 20 other ingredients, served over chicken, turkey, or enchiladas. Other typical *poblano* dishes are *chiles en nogada* (nut sauce), *tamales,* and *chilaquiles.* Most of these regional dishes were originated by colonial-era nuns.

You couldn't miss Puebla's many downtown markets if you tried. An estimated 6000 people sell goods on the streets. Many stands and street vendors selling sandwiches, fruits, and snacks at low prices congregate in the market along 5 de Mayo, starting 1 block north of the Zócalo. There is another market along Av. 10 Pte. You can also stuff your face inexpensively in any of Puebla's numerous bakeries, where a *pastel* (pastry) costs 400 pesos. **Pastelería Nougat,** on Reforma near Calle 7 Nte., is Jack Atimak's personal favorite.

Restaurant El Cazadorsa, Av. 3 Pte. 147, 1 block southwest of the Zócalo. Very clean, small restaurant with ugly orange chairs, lovely green tablecloths, and plastic posters of Puebla streets. Those with a hankerin' for some serious pork products might explore the *manitas rebosadas* (muffled-up pig hands) or *sesos empanizadas* (breaded pig brains), both 9000 pesos. Friendly family memebers also serve more palatable dishes like *arroz con pollo* (9000 pesos) and piping hot chocolate French-, Spanish-, or Mexican-style (1500 pesos). Open daily 8am-8:30pm.

Fonda de Santa Clara, Av. 3 Pte. 920, at Calle 11 Sur, in the red building with the cobblestone courtyard. Great regional delicacies and a menu with seasonal suggestions. Great soups 7000 pesos. An elaborate *comida corrida* (14,000 pesos) is served in the afternoon, but check the dessert cart before polishing off your entrees. Open daily 11am-11pm.

Super Tortas Puebla, Av. 3 Pte. 317. Cheap, wholesome lunchtime snacks. Huge *tortas* stuffed with your choice of ingredients from the counter display. All sandwiches 2000-3000 pesos. Open daily 10am-9pm.

Fonda San Agustín, Av. 3 Pte. 531, next to the Hotel San Agustín. Cozy restaurant tucked into a shoebox. Tables and booths decorated with flowers, walls with fake veggies. In the afternoon, patrons clamor for the 5-course *comida corrida* (4000 pesos). Open daily 7am-8pm.

Restaurant Puebla, Av. 3 Pte. 522. Plain on the outside, but resplendent on the inside, with dusty memorabilia and other trinkets that the owner has gathered over the centuries. A cheap local favorite. *Pollo con mole poblano* 4000 pesos. *Comida corrida* 3000 pesos. Nothing over 6000 pesos. Open daily 10am-midnight.

La Princesa, Portal Juárez 101, next door to El Vasco on the west side of the Zócalo. The most popular cheap restaurant near the Zócalo, but its recent fame has forced prices skyward. Excellent service and lots of locals. Five-course *comida corrida* 12,000 pesos. Large basket of sweet bread is not on the house; each piece costs an incredible 3500 pesos. Open daily 7:30am-11pm.

Cafetería Aguirre, 5 de Mayo, in the camera shop of the same name on the brick, pedestrian-only street. Swamped by locals at mealtime, when service slows to a crawl. Get a table near the front so you can watch the bustling 5 de Mayo and enjoy the wait. *Comida corrida* 10,000 pesos. Sweet bread is not free here, either. Open daily 7:30am-11:30pm.

Restaurante Café El Vasco, Portal Juárez 105, on the Zócalo. Swords adorn the walls of this reasonably priced sister to the Princesa. Large menu translated into English. Seating inside or outdoors. Risk it all with an octopus in its own ink (17,000 pesos) or try it all with a Mexican variety plate (16,000 pesos). Open daily 7:30am-11pm.

Restaurant Vegetariano, Av. 3 Pte. 325. Split-level with wood paneling, pastel watercolors on walls, and a non-smoking section downstairs. Countless creative veggie concoctions, from creamy spinach crepes (5000 pesos) to a meatless *comida corrida* (7000 pesos). Taste a little of the almost-real thing: the soy burger with cheese and french fries goes for 4500 pesos. Popular with *turistas*. Open daily 8am-9pm.

Sights and Entertainment

All of the sights described, except for those around Las Fuertes de Loreto y Guadalupe, are within walking distance of the Zócalo. If you have only a short time in Puebla, the Museo Bello and Capilla del Rosario should top your list.

Puebla holds court like a refined, genteel monarch, draped in a luxuriant architectural robe more than 400 years old, and encrusted with thousands of fine jewels (painted ceramic tiles, wrought iron, ornamental cement moldings), any dozen of which would swell a less majestic city's aesthetic treasury. The oldest buildings in the city, dating from the 16th century, are distinguished by smooth cylindrical columns on square bases that support Romanesque porches. Very few originals are left, but some later buildings on the west and north ends of the Zócalo consciously imitate their style: built in 1550, the **Teatro Principal,** on Av. 10 Ote. at Calle 6 Nte., is a fine example of just such an edifice. (Open daily 9am-1pm and 4-8pm, except when in use.)

The 17th-century buildings, including many of the nearly 100 churches, are characterized inside and out by classical and Gothic ornamentation. Most of the churches also exhibit a Baroque influence; the tourist office and many of the buildings near the Zócalo exemplify this style, for which Puebla is famous. Red brick and *azulejo de Talavera* (a *mudéjar* tile popular in Puebla during the early colonial period) are the raw materials for this style. Often laid diagonally, the bricks come in a variety of shapes, and each tile is a work of art in itself: intricate paintings on the tile often feature blue or turquoise flowers. Just north of the Zócalo's northeast corner, on Calle 2 Nte., sits 18th-century **La Casa de los Muñecos.** The architect caricatured his enemies on the building's exterior tiles.

Eighty-seven years of *indígena* labor produced the tallest cathedral in Mexico, the **Cathedral of the Immaculate Conception** (72m) on Av. 3 Ote. at 5 de Mayo, adjacent to the Zócalo. Construction began in 1562 under the architect Juan de Herrera, and the cathedral was consecrated in 1649. Two organs (one 400 years old) and a bell tower with 19 bells make themselves heard occasionally. Chandeliers and gold plate sparkle inside. Pedro Muñoz's fine woodwork glamorizes the choir stalls on the pulpit's periphery. From 11am to noon, if the sexton is in the mood, visitors can climb the right tower of the cathedral for a panoramic view of Puebla. For 220 pesos, you can ascend another 164 steep steps to see the 8500-kilogram bell, which, according to legend, angels lifted to the top of the tower. The two volcanoes, Popocatépetl and Ixtaccíhuatl, are visible to the northwest. To the northeast, you can see one other great volcano called La Malinche, in honor of Cortés's Aztec lover and interpreter. Women are expected to cover their heads, but only locals seem to observe this. English-speaking tour guides will provide their services for a small fee. (Cathedral open daily 10am-2:30pm and 4-6pm.)

The **Casa de la Cultura,** Av. 5 Ote. 5, 1 block south of the Zócalo, houses the impressive **Biblioteca Palafoxiana.** This collection of 43,000 mostly Latin volumes dates from the 16th century. Bishop of Puebla during the second half of the 17th century, Palafox was perhaps the most powerful man in Mexico. He carried in his pocket a paper signed by the king of Spain empowering him to replace the Mexican viceroy should he deem it necessary. Palafox was also an intellectual force at a time when the Jesuits were isolating the New World politically, intellectually, and religiously from Spain. Belonging to no religious order himself, Palafox condemned the Jesuits' aspirations to power, land, and money. Palafox's own 6000-book library, which he donated to the Colegio de San Pedro in 1646, includes a 1493 copy of the Chronicle of Nuremberg, illuminated with 2000 scenes. (Library open Tues.-Sun. 10am-5pm. Admission 1500 pesos, free Sun.)

Most of the permanent exhibits in the Casa de la Cultura are uninteresting, but some of the rooms devoted to traveling art shows and in-house work are worth a peek. The institute sponsors classes in wood-engraving and other regional arts, sometimes putting the students' finished work up for sale. Folk dances are performed every Saturday and Sunday, and amateur and professional movies are shown during the week. Check the board on the right as you walk in from the street for the latest schedules. For other information, call 42-76-92, or write: Apdo. Postal 1139, Puebla, Puebla.

One block east of the Zócalo, at M. Avila Camacho and Calle 4 Sur, is the **Iglesia del Espíritu Santo** (or **La Compañía**), dedicated in 1777 as a Jesuit school. The building's ornate towers were constructed between 1804 and 1812. Inside the church lies the tomb of the princess Minnha, La China Poblana. According to legend, the noblewoman was abducted by pirates from China and brought to New Spain, where her captors sold her into servitude. The princess resigned herself to her fate and adopted the Christian religion, but never forgot her blue blood: she distinguished herself from other *poblanos* by wearing elaborate dresses, each bearing an embroidered Mexican eagle on the front. The fashion caught on and remains distinctive to Puebla.

The art collection of the late textile magnate José Luis Bello resides in the **Museo Bello,** Av. 3 Pte. at Calle 3 Sur, 1 block west of the southeast corner of the Zócalo. The museum, ornamented with tiles and illuminated by stained-glass windows, contains artifacts from different places and periods in world history. Bello left his collection of ivory, iron, porcelain, earthenware, and Talavera objects to his son, José Mariano Bello, who added a gallery of paintings and later donated the entire set to the fine arts academy in Puebla. Considering the incredible variety of objects from Asia and Europe, it is surprising that neither José Luis nor José Mariano ever traveled; instead, they had world-wide agents ship pieces back to Puebla. (Open Tues.-Sun. 10am-5pm. Informative guided tours in Spanish. Admission 1500 pesos, free Sun.)

The extravagant, gold-leafed **Iglesia de Santo Domingo** was constructed between 1571 and 1611 on this foundation of a convent, 2 blocks north of the Zócalo's northwest corner along 5 de Mayo, between Av. 4 and 6 Pte. Statues of saints and angels adorn the spectacular altar, but the church's real attraction is to the left of the altar. This marvel of religious architecture, the **Capilla del Rosario,** is a chapel laden with 23½-karat gold. Along each side of the chapel are three doors, each under a mask representing a stage in the evolution of the Mexican people: first an *indígena*, then a conquistador in armor, and, nearest the altar, a *mestizo*. On the ceiling, three full statues represent faith, hope, and charity. Both the masks and the statues pull visitors' attention to the altar, where 12 pillars represent the apostles (the 6 on the upper level are each made of a single onyx stone). Since there was no room for a real choir, designers painted a chorus of angels with guitars and woodwinds on the wall above the door. When mass is not being held, you can walk around the altar to photograph the chapel.

Aquiles Serdán operated a printing press with his wife and his brothers before the Revolution of 1910, reeling off anti-reelectionist posters and other articles for distribution throughout Puebla. He and his sons led the earliest revolt of the Revolution before being gunned down in the **Casa de Aquiles Serdán,** which today serves as the **Museo Regional de la Revolución Mexicana** at Av. 6 Ote. 206. Hundreds of bullet holes, both inside and out, bear witness to the assassination. The museum displays portraits of the valiant family, but the most interesting exhibits are photos of Serdán as the representative of Tlaxcala, Puebla, and Michoacán states at the convention where Madero and Vázquez were elected to run against the dictator Díaz. The photo collection also includes portraits of the Mexican people in the bloody battles of the revolution, and of the dead Zapata and Carranza. One room is dedicated to Carmen Serdán and other famous female revolutionaries (*las carabineras*), including María Arias, also known as "María Pistolas." On the explanatory labels (in Spanish), the name Serdán sometimes appears as Cerdán: the family changed the name to Serdán after arriving in Mexico from the island of Cerdanía. (Museum open Tues.-Sun. 10am-5:50pm. Admission 1500 pesos, free Sun.)

At the nearby **Museo Del Alfeñique,** Av. 4 Ote. 416, at Calle 6 Nte., a heavily ornamented 18th-century Baroque exterior encloses three floors of ceramic works, 16th- and 17th-century documents, paintings, and antique furniture that span the history of the city of Puebla. (Open Tues.-Sun. 10am-5pm. Admission 1500 pesos, free Sun.)

Regional clothing (*sarapes,* blouses, and dresses) is sold at the block-long **Mercado El Parián,** ½ block east along Av. 4 Ote. (Open daily 9am-10pm.) In front of the market, also along Av. 4 Ote., is the **Barrio del Artista,** where local artists exhibit their work and paint the portraits of passersby. (Open daily dawn-dusk.) Still more handicrafts are sold farther west, at the corner of Av. 12 Pte. and Calle 3 Nte., in the *Casa de las Artesanías,* a state-run museum and shop that collects and sells the works of *poblano* artists. (Shop open Tues.-Sun. 10am-5pm.)

The oldest church in Puebla, begun in 1535 and finished in 1575, is the **Templo de San Francisco,** Av. 14 Ote. and Calle 10 Nte., 3 blocks east on Camacho and 4 blocks north on 5 de Mayo. The dark bell tower was added in 1672. The church's ceiling is one of the highest in Puebla, and one of its chapels contains the body of Sebastián de Aparicio, who opened the first highways between Puebla and other cities.

One of the biggest celebrations on the Mexican calendar is that commemorating the battle of 5 de Mayo in 1862, when Ignacio Zaragoza and his 2000 soldiers defeated 5000 French soldiers in Puebla. Twenty blocks north and 5 blocks east of Puebla's Zócalo, a complex of museums and parks surrounds the staunch forts where Mexican armies staved off the French troops. The nearby **General Zaragoza Mausoleum** maintains his ashes and those of his wife. A beautiful fountain marks the spot, and cannons from the battle surround a statue of the general. (Open Tues.-Sun. 10am-4pm. Admission 1500 pesos.) To reach the complex, catch the "Fuertes" bus (300 pesos) on 5 de Mayo, 4 blocks north of the Zócalo; it's at the top of a small hill that affords a panoramic view of Puebla. Before the battle, General Elías Federico Forey, having observed the Mexican army at Puebla, assured Louis Napoleon that he could consider the town taken because the French army was superior both in number and quality. The French surrounded the fort, but upon hearing of the siege and learning that the Mexican army was nearly out of ammunition and artillery, the *indígena* inhabitants of the northern part of the state came to the rescue. Arriving barefoot from the fields with only machetes and sticks, the Zacapaaxtlas (descendants of the Totonacs) overcame the seemingly superior French. To the north of the fort is the **Museo de Historia Natural,** loaded with artful representations of wildlife habitats. (Open Tues.-Sun. 10am-4:30pm. Admission 1500 pesos.) In front of the fort, the modern **Museo Regional de Puebla** contains a little of everything, including sculptures, ceramic works, paintings, and Aztec art. (Open Tues.-Sun. 10am-5pm. Admission 1500 pesos.) Near the Museo Regional, on 5 de Mayo, lies the **planetarium,** where the farthest stretches of the universe are brought down to earth in a geodesic dome. (Shows Tues.-Fri. at 4, 6, and 8:30pm, Sat.-Sun. at 11am, 1pm, 4pm, 6pm, and 8:30pm. Admission 2500 pesos.) The **Parque Rafaela P. Zaragoza,** 1 block east, unfurls around an amphitheater in which singers, bands, and dancers perform (check with the tourist office or the Casa de Cultura for showtimes).

The hottest cultural attraction in Puebla is still the **Museo Nacional de los Ferrocarriles Mexicanos,** opened to the public on (of course) May 5, 1988. The monumental pink building sits alongside a wide stretch of rusted tracks loaded down with freshly painted steam trains. The locomotives are literally crawling with kids on Sundays, when families picnic on the grassy plaza to the right of the museum. Most of the restored railcars are open to the public. Some have their own museums aboard, and curious visitors can look at the giant cranks and gargantuan gearshifts of locomotives that date from 1837. Historical memorabilia and an utterly thrilling photo exhibit trace the evolution of the Mexican railways. Enlarged black-and-white pics recall the time when railworkers first laid tracks on virgin soil, when horses were loaded on cars like cargo, when trains were held up by bands of *bandidos,* and when rail employees staged massive strikes for increased wages. Allow about an hour to explore the museum, located at Av. 11 Nte. #1210 Pte., 6 blocks north of Paseo Bravo. (Open daily 10am-6pm. Free.)

When Puebla's usually cool climate turns up the heat, jump in the mineral water pools and baths at **Balneario Agua Azul,** a public facility at the south end of Calle 11 Sur. Take the "Est. Nueva" *combi* (350 pesos) along that street. (Open Mon. 7am-noon, Tues.-Sun. 7am-4:30pm. Admission 7000 pesos, children 5000 pesos.)

For evening entertainment, take a stroll along Av. Juárez, starting west of Calle 13 Sur. Called the **Zona Esmeralda,** this area contains scores of movie theaters, shops, restaurants, and bars. Although the best discos are in nearby Cholula, Puebla's Zona Esmerelda throbs to the beat of **La Boom,** Juárez 1900, next to Charlie's China Poblana. (Cover 15,000 pesos. Open Fri-Sat. 11pm-3am.) The **Plaza Dorada** shopping center in the southeast corner of the city, on 5 de Mayo at Calle 4 Sur, offers elegant shopping and *norteamericano*-style dining notable for its preponderance of chewy chocolate-chip cookies.

Near Puebla

Two side trips beckon from Puebla: one to the small town of **Tepeaca,** and one to the falls of **Acatzitzimitla.** Before the Spanish arrived, people brought their carts to Tepeaca from across the countryside to sell their goods in the largest *tianguis* (*indígena* market) in ancient Mexico. Still the site of the largest *tianguis* in the Republic, Tepeaca carries on this tradition every Friday. On the east end of the Zócalo is one of the 12 Franciscan convents built in Puebla in the early years after the Conquest, and on the park's west side is a whipping stone upon which colonial slaves stood to be physically reprimanded.

Acatzitzimitla is 30 to 45 minutes farther south on the same bus (see below). The bus to San Juan Ixcaquixtla bypasses a fork in the highway that veers off to the town of Atoyatempan. Five minutes past the fork, a rusty white sign reads "Cascadas de Acatzitzimitla." Get off here and walk about 4km west on a narrow dirt road until you reach a garish pink church. It's a steep climb down to the falls from here, and there are many confusing side paths, so it's best to hire a guide from the area if you can find one.

To reach either location, take any of the buses that run from Puebla's central bus station (CAPU). *Líneas Unidas del Sureste* follows this route. (To Tepeaca 1600 pesos, to Acatzitzimitla 2300 pesos.) To return, walk back along the dirt road to the highway and hail the blue-and-white bus going east to the traffic circle where the highway crosses Rte. 38 to Puebla and Tehuacán (750 pesos). From here, AU buses coming from the south will take you back to Puebla for 600 pesos. Hail one from the east side of the road; you'll recognize the line by the bright orange stripe on the lower front of the bus.

For an alternative excursion, take the Estrella Roja bus from the Terminal del Oriente in Mexico City to **Huejotzingo,** west of Puebla (every ½ hr., 1200 pesos). This picturesque route follows tree-lined roads past fields of corn and allows you to get off at North America's first Franciscan convent, the **Convento de San Francisco,** founded in 1525. The bus stops on Anastasio Roldán, ½ block west of the 16th-century church and convent. At each corner of the convent's high walls is a small house with beautiful stone arches and columns accented by reliefs of thick rope. In the Sala de Profundis, inside just above the entrance, is a mural of the first 12 Franciscans kneeling at the cross. The second floor of the convent holds bedrooms and a small museum, with paintings, drawings, and plaques that explain the rules and rigor of convent life. (Open daily 10am-5pm. Admission 5000 pesos.) The

Estrella Roja bus terminal is across the *placita* from the convent's west wall. Buses to and from Puebla (1600 pesos) pass by every 20 to 30 minutes.

Cholula

Node of local religious activity since the 3rd century BC, Cholula has been home to the Olmecs, the Zapotecs, the Teotihuacanos, the Toltecs, the Chichimecs, and finally the Cholultecs, a Nahuatl-speaking people related to the Aztecs. The present name of the city derives from the last of these societies and means "place where the water flows," an allusion to the origin of life. In its 2nd-century heyday, Cholula was as influential as Teotihuacán, serving as the powerful center of the region that now comprises the states of Puebla and Tlaxcala. The city developed into a great crossroads for Mesoamerican and Caribbean civilizations, extending its economic and cultural influence south and east. By the time the Spaniards arrived, Cholula had passed its zenith. But as one of the main sites for worshiping the much-venerated Quetzalcóatl, the city presented a major obstacle to the Christianization of the conquered land.

Compounding the frustration of the Spaniards was the news of Moctezuma's secret plot to murder Cortés while Cortés's forces were being put up in Cholula's palaces. Cortés took quick action, ordering his troops to shoot every *indígena* in sight one night. After most of Cholula's 100,000 inhabitants were killed, the Spaniards razed every pagan shrine in the city. Furthermore, Cortés swore to build a church atop the ruins of each of the approximately 400 shrines surrounding the main pyramid, which had been dedicated to the rain god. To this day most Mexicans contend that there are 365 churches in the area. The state tourist office, however, counts only 45 in the city itself, and about 32 more in the general vicinity. Cortés fell short of his mark, but the action he so brutally initiated has left Cholula with a concentration of religious architecture unsurpassed in Mexico.

Beneath Cholula, and buried all around, are the remnants of the glorious pre-Conquest past. The area's main attraction is the great pyramid mound where seven different civilizations have left their mark, and they don't call it great for nothing: Cholula's pyramid is the world's largest—more than double the size of Cheops in Egypt. Much of what is still hidden will never be uncovered because the intervening layer of colonial buildings is itself treasured today. Cholula's most modern prize, the University of the Americas (the only U.S.-accredited college in Mexico), draws many young *norteamericanos* to town.

Orientation

Cholula is on Rte. 150, 122km west of Mexico City and 20km from Puebla. To reach Cholula from Mexico City by bus, take an Estrella Roja bus from the Terminal del Oriente (every ½ hr.) over the mountains east of Mexico City and through Puebla. The two-hour ride crosses beautiful countryside dominated by the two volcanoes, Popocatépetl and Ixtaccíhuatl. The bus will drop you off at 3 Nte. and 6 Pte.; walk right 1 block on 6 Pte. to 5 de Mayo, take a right, and go 1 block to reach the Zócalo.

The most convenient way to get to Cholula from Puebla is via an Estrella Roja bus from the new Puebla bus terminal on Blvd. Atlixco Nte. (every 10 min., 600 pesos). Once again, the bus stops in Cholula at 3 Nte. and 6 Pte. Estrella de Oro also serves Cholula from Puebla (every 15 min., 600 pesos), but their buses get no closer to the center of Cholula than the highway outside of town—when the pyramid comes into view on your left be on guard for the highway sign that says "Centro"; when you see it, holler for the driver to stop. Local buses from Puebla leave from the parking lot next to the central bus station (350 pesos). Buses back to Puebla stop in Cholula at the large intersection on the downtown side of the Hotel Las Américas.

The streets in Cholula form a grid with the Zócalo's southeast corner as the origin: Cholula's main road is called **Hidalgo** west of this corner, and **Morelos** east of it. Most places of interest are between the Hotel Las Américas, on the east end of Hidalgo, and the market, a few blocks west of the Zócalo. The only other interesting area is the Portal Guerrero, the giant arched walkway that borders the Zócalo on the west and contains the town's best and most expensive hotels and restaurants. Blue-and-yellow taxis on Hidalgo or stationed opposite the Estrella Roja bus terminal can take you to the outskirts of town for 2000 pesos.

Practical Information

Tourist Office: Cholula has no official office, but Sr. Roberto Malagón at the **Los Portales Restaurant** can answer virtually any question about the area and actually teaches English. Open Mon.-Fri. 8am-8:30pm, Sat.-Sun. 9am-7:30pm.

Currency Exchange: Bancomer and **Bánamex,** both on the south side of the Zócalo. Open Mon.-Fri. 9am-noon and 4-6pm. The main desk at **Hotel Quetzalcóatl** will exchange after hours; their rates are unfavorable.

Post Office: Alemán 314-3 (tel. 47-01-30), 2 blocks south of the Zócalo. Open Mon.-Fri. 8am-5pm, Sat. 8-11:30am. **Postal Code:** 72800.

Telephones: Long-distance *caseta* at the **Farmacia Moderno,** Morelos 12 (tel. 47-03-87), on the Zócalo. Open daily 8am-8pm. **Hotel Quetzalcóatl** is always open: local calls cost 1000 pesos, national collect calls 2000 pesos, and international collect calls 2500 pesos. **Telephone Code:** 12.

Telegrams: At the post office. Open Mon.-Fri. 9am-noon.

Cultural Affairs: Casa de la Cultura, Av. 4 Pte. 103 (tel. 47-19-86), 1 block west of the Zócalo's northwest corner. Bulletin board at building entrance advertises special events, local arts programs, new book clubs in the area, and, most importantly, the schedules of local aerobics classes. Public phone inside. Upstairs office is of no help; they'll refer you to the board. Open Mon.-Sat. 9am-8pm, Sun. 9am-6pm.

General Stores: Abarrote Castillo, Hidalgo 102 (tel. 47-02-92), at the end of the portal. Sells all kinds of goodies, including liquor. Open Mon.-Sat. 9am-10:30pm. **Conasupo,** on Alemán, 1 block south of the Zócalo. Open Mon.-Sat. 8am-8:30pm, Sun. 9am-7pm.

Red Cross: Calle 7 Sur at Av. 3 Pte. (tel. 47-03-93). Walk-in service. Open 24 hr.

Pharmacies: Farmacia San Pedrito, Av. 2 Pte. 112, between Alemán and Calle 3 Sur. Open 24 hr. Also **Farmacia Moderno** (see Telephones above).

Hospital General: Av. 2 Pte. 1153 (tel. 47-18-00), 10 blocks west of the Zócalo on the outskirts of town.

Police: Portal Guerrero 1 (tel. 47-05-02), on the west side of the Zócalo.

Accommodations

Selection is slim: Cholula has only five hotels, three of which are expensive. One of the three, the **Hotel Calli Quetzalcóatl** (tel. 47-15-33), provides services even for the cost-conscious—travel information about surrounding areas, long-distance phone service, currency exchange, and a gorgeous restaurant. The two cheap hotels in Cholula are as good as you'll find anywhere in Puebla, and the Hotel Las Américas is perhaps one of them.

Hotel Las Américas, Av. 14 Ote. 6 (tel. 47-09-91), at the far-east end of Hidalgo/Morelos. A 15-min. walk from the Zócalo, 5 min. past the pyramid. Delightful. Spacious rooms with wall-to-wall fuchsia carpeting, large firm beds, phones, color TV, and spotless baths with marble sinks. Beautiful tree-lined courtyard encloses guest pool, patio chairs, and, during mating season, nests of madly chirping birds. Common room (with yet another a color TV) and cheap restaurant in lobby are popular with college-age locals. Foreign student proprietor helpful and friendly. Beautiful views of volcanoes from the west and south sides of the building. Best discos in the area right down the street. Singles 25,000 pesos. Doubles 40,000 pesos.

Hotel Reforma, Calle 4 Sur 101 (tel. 47-01-49), 2 blocks east of the southeast corner of the Zócalo. Eleven bare, functional, clean rooms around a courtyard that makes you feel as if you're living in a stable. Rooms have double beds, toilet, and sink, but no shower. Much closer to town than Hotel Las Américas, but not nearly as nice. Singles 20,000 pesos. Doubles 40,000 pesos.

Food

Dishes in Cholula are similar to those in Puebla, if slightly spicier. You can picnic at the Zócalo or on the north side of the pyramid mound.

Restaurant Los Portales, on Portal Guerrero, on the western side of the Zócalo. A non-profit restaurant dedicated to promoting Mexican coffee and local specialties. Handsome interior and immaculate bathrooms—this place regulates hygiene on the microscopic level and quality according to world-class standards. Serves up tourist information, too. Outdoor seating. Full breakfast or *comida corrida* 8000 pesos. Open Mon.-Thurs. 8:30am-8:30pm, Fri.-Sun. 9am-7:30pm.

Restaurant Colonial, Morelos 605, opposite the base of the pyramid to the north. In a quaint colonial alcove far behind the entrance sign. Very clean and reasonably priced; popular with students. Five *comida corrida* specialties 10,000-14,000 pesos. Try the hot "kakes" (6000 pesos). Open daily 8am-10pm.

El Portal, Hidalgo 102, ½ block west of the Zócalo's southwest corner. Small family establishment offering great *tortas* loaded with avocados (2500 pesos) and small pizzas (8000 pesos). Open daily 10am-8pm.

Restaurant Cocoyotla, Hidalgo 301, 1 block west of the Zócalo. Eating area is pleasant, even if the piped-in music and screaming yellow tablecloths are a bit loud. Regional specialties include *pollo con mole poblano* (9000 pesos). Most entrees 9000-14,000 pesos. Open daily 11am-8pm.

Sights

Before climbing the mound and making the rounds of the churches, do some bush-league quail-watching in the vicinity of the pyramid. Particularly distinctive are the small blue-gray birds with large golden breasts and the larger iridescent black birds. Both species have beautiful long tail feathers, which help them steer in the thin air (Cholula is 2146m above sea level). At night, walk near the Hotel Las Américas and you may hear an eerie cry, rising in pitch for about a second and then dropping suddenly. That this bird song rises only at night and only near the pyramid adds to the mystery surrounding this ancient holy stomping ground of the "bronze race."

To get to the Santuario de los Remedios on top of the pyramid, walk east along Hidalgo/Morelos from the Zócalo. On your left is the **Museo Regional de Cholula,** which spotlights artifacts found within the mound and in the surrounding area, including several examples of early colonial ceramic painting. The colorful birds of Cholula are a common subjects for the artists. Also displayed is a model of the pyramids in their original configuration. A bookstore specializing in the art and culture of the Cholula region adjoins the museum. Visiting these two sites before heading across the street will help you to better understand the pyramids. (Museum and bookstore open Tues.-Sat. 10am-4:30pm. Free.)

When Cortés destroyed the temple to the rain god and replaced it with the Santuario de Nuestra Señora de los Remedios, he was unaware that buried in the hill below was the Great Pyramid, and beneath that, five more pyramids. The first structure built on this site is known as Tlachihualtépetl (Handmade Hill), which is at the very bottom of the mound and in the deepest part of the tunnel. The entrance to the tunnel is on Morelos, at the base of the pyramid's north side. Walking from the Zócalo on Morelos, cross the railroad tracks; 50m farther on the right is a ticket booth. To the right of the ticket booth is a tiny door, the entrance to both the tunnel and the rest of the archeological remains. As you walk through the tunnel, visualize the 2000-year history of the complex. As each group arrived and came into power, it would bury the structure built by its predecessor. An elaborate drainage system had to be incorporated into each of the pyramids so that their dirt foundations would not wash away during the rainy season. You can see these drains as you walk through the kilometer-long tunnel, which facilitates self-guided tours. Along the way, side tunnels permit views of some of the archeological features off the main tunnel. You cannot lose your way unless you stray from the path open to tourists; the whole tunnel complex is only 8km long. Guides, available at the tunnel's entrance for 20,000 pesos, can illuminate (literally and figuratively) some of the tunnel's more obscure points, including otherwise invisible insect frescoes.

Above ground at the end of the tunnel is the base of the exposed portion of the **Great Pyramid.** Most of the surrounding religious edifices (approximately 400 shrines), demolished as part of Cortés's strategy to convert the Cholultecs, had also been covered over before this final pyramid was built. The Great Pyramid is best appreciated from the large square altar on the southwest corner of the pyramid where bleached bones and offerings are displayed. The mass of the mound gives you an idea of the immensity of this structure—it has the largest base of any pyramid in the world (about 450 ft. on each side). The reconstructed area directly in front of the mound, as you gaze out from the altar, is a ceremonial ground dedicated to Quetzalcóatl; just to the west is a fresco of the god.

As you walk beyond the pyramid, you will see various other excavations amidst the green lawn. At the southwest corner of the pyramid, the altar where adolescents were sacrificed to the gods in times of crisis, exhibits skeletons of two victims. Before you leave the grounds, check out the reconstructed pyramid on the west side of the great mound. This appendage to the main pyramid illuminates the inner workings of the drainage system constructed to protect the structures.

Upon leaving the site, make a right at the gate (an exit only; tickets must be bought at the tunnel entrance) and head up the mound. The climb up the mound is steep, but worth the effort: to the south, Cholula's many churches are visible, and the two volcanoes, Popocatépetl and Ixtaccíhuatl, surge skyward to the west. (Tunnel and ruins open Tues.-Sun. 10am-4:30pm. Admission 10,000 pesos, free Sun.)

Four churches should fill out your itinerary in Cholula. The first of these, interesting only because it squats atop the mound, is the **Santuario de Nuestra Señora de los Remedios.** On the east end of the Zócalo, the **Capilla Real** occupies the site where Cortés slaughtered Aztecs in their place of worship. Its interior is completely devoid of decoration except for the altar, but its 49 domes make it remarkable. (Open daily 10am-noon and 3:30-7pm.) The church at **Acatepec** can be reached on the Chipla bus. Catch the bus 1½ blocks south of the Zócalo on Alemán. Most of this church burned down in 1940, but the beautiful façade, more tile than brick, has remained intact. One kilometer to the west is the church at **Tonantzintla,** famed for the most beautiful interior of any church in Mexico. Every inch is covered with multi-colored, three-dimensional ornaments: most striking are the hundreds of *indígena* busts among Baroque swirls of plaster and tile. The design manifests the compromises the Catholic Church made to ingratiate itself with the *indígenas.* (Both churches open daily 10am-1pm and 3-5pm.)

Entertainment

Cholula supplies Puebla and the surrounding region with disco entertainment, serving the area's large student population. Head east on Hidalgo/Morelos (called 14 Pte./14 Ote.), and turn right after the Hotel Las Américas. Down the street await **Faces** and **Paradise,** two of the town's most popular video dance halls (cover 15,000 pesos; open Thurs.-Sat. after 10pm). On the road from Puebla to Cholula, almost at the halfway mark, is the **Disco Porthos,** a palatial building on the right offering a ritzier atmosphere than most discos in town. Notify the bus driver when you spot the sign. (Cover 25,000 pesos. Open Thurs.-Sat. 9pm-4am.)

Cholula's **regional fair** occurs September 6 and 7. You can buy beautiful, handmade firework castles from Guillermo Durán, Calle 10 Nte. 1613, near the Zócalo, for this or any occasion.

Tlaxcala

Many history books ponder the improbability of Cortés's Mexican conquest. After all, he landed on the coast with a mere 400 men and proceeded to topple one of the most advanced and best defended civilizations in the Western Hemisphere. Often overlooked in this discussion is the fact that Cortés and his crew made a little pitstop in Tlaxcala before launching their assault on Tenochtitlán; *Tlaxcalteca* hatred of the Aztecs was so strong that the tribe's chiefs were more than happy to lend Cortés tens of thousands of warriors to assist with his endeavors.

Now the capital of Mexico's second-smallest state, Tlaxcala lacks the hustle and bustle of other capitals in the Republic, but the many cathedrals in the city and its hilly environs testify to Tlaxcala's historical significance.

Orientation

Tlaxcala is approximately 120km from Mexico City by Rte. 150, 190, 136, or 119. From the bus station, *colectivos* will take you downtown; some are labeled "Sit-Tlax," some "USU," and some just "Colectivo." They all charge about 350 pesos for a trip to the Zócalo. Taxis charge 3000 pesos for the same ride.

Tlaxcala's downtown is small and simple. The Zócalo is bordered on the east by **Independencia;** heading north, this street first becomes Juárez and then Revolución, home to the city's finer hotels. **Guerrero,** a major east-west thoroughfare, runs 2 blocks south of the Zócalo.

Practical Information

State Tourist Office: Juárez 18 (tel. 200-27), in the ex-Palacio Legislativo. Helpful staff with an overwhelming supply of pamphlets on Tlaxcala and the surrounding region. Open Mon.-Fri. 9am-3pm and 5-7pm.

Currency Exchange: Bancomer, Independencia 10, across from the Zócalo. **Banco Serfín,** on Independencia, 1 block south of the Zócalo at the Pl. Xicohléncatl. Both open Mon.-Fri. 10am-1:30pm.

Post Office: Pl. de la Constitución 20 (tel. 200-04), at the Zócalo. Open Mon.-Fri. 8am-7pm, Sat. 9am-noon. **Postal Code:** 90000.

Telephones: On Independencia, ½ block south of the Zócalo. Long-distance collect calls 10,000 pesos. Open Mon.-Sat. 8am-10pm. **Telephone Code:** 246.

Telegrams: In the post office. Open Mon.-Fri. 8am-7pm, Sat. 9am-noon.

Bus Station: Central TAPO, Zaragoza 200, southwest of the city. **Autotransportes Tlaxcala-Apizaco-Huamantla** (tel. 202-16) provides second-class service to Mexico City (every 15 min. 6:30am-6:30pm, 5100 pesos) and Puebla (every 15 min. 5am-9pm, 1600 pesos). **Autobuses Puebla-Tlaxcala** (tel. 233-92) has second-class service to Puebla (every 5 min., 1400 pesos). **Flecha Azul** also runs frequent buses to Puebla (1400 pesos).

Red Cross: (tel. 209-20), on Allende between Guerrero and Hidalgo. 24-hr. ambulance service.

Pharmacy: Farmacia Natividad, Laridzabal 53, behind the Iglesia de San José. Open Mon.-Sat. 9am-9pm, Sun. 9am-3pm. Many more around the Zócalo.

Police: Alfonso Escalona 7 (tel. 207-35).

Accommodations

Lodgings in downtown Tlaxcala are adequate but sparse. The more luxurious hotels are 2 to 3km to the north of the city on Revolución, the extension of Juárez.

Albergue de la Loma, Guerrero 58 (tel. 204-24), 2 blocks south and 1 block west of the Zócalo. Terrific value if you get a room on the hill overlooking Tlaxcala; if not, prepare yourself for a stunning view of a dreary hallway. Rooms large, bright, and carpeted; bathrooms fully tiled and spotless. Bottled water, laundry service (pants 2500 pesos), and room service available. Singles 20,000 pesos. Doubles 32,000 pesos.

Mansión de Xicohténcatl, Juárez 15 (tel. 219-00), ½ block north of the Zócalo. Worn rooms with peeling posters hung askew on the walls. The floor-to-ceiling mirrors are a voyeur's dream. Central location. Singles 20,000 pesos. Doubles 25,000 pesos.

Hotel San Clemente, Independencia 54 (tel. 219-89), a 10-min. walk from the Zócalo at the southern edge of town. The beds tilt, the bathrooms appear clean but smell sour, and water runs only during certain hours of the day. Nice courtyard with fountain, but should serve only as a last resort. Singles 20,000 pesos. Doubles 25,000 pesos.

Food

There are few real restaurants downtown, but *torta* shacks and *agua fresca* stands proliferate. Most eateries are high-quality, low-budget establishments.

Mesón Taurino, Independencia 15, at Guerrero. Approaching the elegant. Orange dining room. Friendly servers are dressed to match the surroundings, as are the prices. *Delicioso pollo con mole* 16,000 pesos. Meat and pasta dishes around 10,000 pesos. A nice break from the *torta* routine. Open Mon.-Sat. 1-9pm.

Rincón Azteca, Juárez 2-B, across from the Mansión. Pink walls and plastic flowers foil all attempts at atmosphere, but the food is good and cheap. Entrees 4000-13,000 pesos, full breakfasts 4000 pesos. Open daily 8am-9pm.

Mansión de Xicohténcatl, Juárez 15, below the hotel. Comfortable, with little gurgling fountains and attentive service. Choose from a variety of filling breakfasts (around 5000 pesos) and a range of spaghettis (7000 pesos). Open daily 9am-8pm.

Restaurant Albergue de la Loma, Guerrero 58, by the hotel's reception desk. Perfect place to bring an unwanted date: the live electric organ music overpowers any attempt at conversation, and the view and food are good enough to demand your full concentration. Soup 3000 pesos, most entrees 10,000 pesos. Open daily 8am-9pm.

Sights and Entertainment

Tlaxcala's **Palacio de Gobierno,** facing the Zócalo, is blessed with dense, colorful murals, created by Desiderio Hernández Xochitiotzin in 1966 to narrate the history of the independent state of Tlaxcala up to the time of the Conquest. The Palacio also contains stone reliefs of the supreme chief of the *Tlaxcalteca* forces and other lords of the empire. To the right of the **Palacio Municipal** (circa 1550), two tile-covered domes and the highly ornamented tower of the **Iglesia de San José** loom over the Zócalo. Also to the right, directly on the Zócalo, is the recently erected **Palacio Justicia,** an eclectic mix of architectural styles that is strangely pleasing to the eye.

One block south of the Zócalo, on Independencia, lies the approach to the **Ex-Convento de San Francisco.** Huge trees, planted amidst cobblestone, lead up an incline through three arches (symbolizing the Holy Trinity) to a small meadow and a regional museum. (Open Tues.-Sun. 10am-5pm. Free.) Next door is the convent. Fading since the 1530s but still impressive, the church is of the Moorish-influenced *mudéjar* style.

Tlaxcala's major attraction is the **Basílica de Ocotlán.** Set on a hill overlooking town, the shrine is an excellent example of the Churrigueresque style, with a mind-reelingly intricate façade and golden interior. Three columns of statuettes and flourishes snake up the façade on either side of the door, crowned by a ribbed shell and flanked by two towers. The bases of the towers are faced with russet, lozenge-shaped bricks, their simplicity contrasting strikingly with the ornate façade. The tops of the towers are identical, double-tiered extravaganzas, punctuated by more bristling columns and culminating in fantastic wrought-iron crosses. To reach the church, follow Juárez north of the Zócalo, and after 3 blocks, turn right onto Zitlalpopocatl. From there, it's an uphill hike of 1km from downtown.

At the **Museo de Artes y Tradiciones Populares de Tlaxcala,** Sanchez 1 at Primero de Mayo, everything you've ever wanted to know about local village life, folklore, and customs is relayed in exhausting detail by tiresome guides. Posted in each of the museum's six sections, they explicate the path from sheep to sweater, corn to tortilla, and the workplace to the *cantina*. Housed in the same building as the museum, the **Casa de las Artesanías** sells locally crafted ceramics, toys, and clothing. (Both open Tues.-Sun. 10am-6pm. Museum admission 1500 pesos, with tips strongly encouraged after each presentation.)

The annual **Feria de Tlaxcala,** which runs from late October to mid-November, sponsors bullfights, cockfights, folk art, and dancing. The **Feria del Pan de San Juan Totolaca,** held the first week of July, is a similar event on a smaller scale. Festivals take place at the **Centro Expositor Adolfo López Mateos,** in the western part of the city along Av. Carrillo y Alcocer.

Near Tlaxcala

The textile centers in **Santa Ana Chiautempan** hawk inexpensive handmade wool and acrylic sweaters, *serapes,* dresses, Peruvian scarves, jackets, and other *típico* clothing. Santa Ana is only 10 minutes away from Tlaxcala by *combi* that leaves from the corner of the Pl. Xicohléncatl nearest the Zócalo. In Santa Ana, two centrally located markets specialize in local textiles. The **Mercado de Artesanías Abandames,** at Bernardo Picazo between Ignacio Picazo and Manuel Saldaña, dwarfs the **Casa del Artesano,** 1 block away at Ignacio Picazo between Bernardo Picazo and Ignacio Allende. The **Restaurant El Bodegón,** adjacent to the Casa del Artesano on Ignacio Picazo, is both convenient and inexpensive. Regional soups cost 3800 pesos, *huevos rancheros* 3200 pesos. (Open Tues.-Sun. 1-10pm.)

Huamantla, about 1½ hr. from Tlaxcala, is known for its annual festival in August, which features a running of the bulls in the gory tradition of Pamplona, Spain. From Tlaxcala, take an Autotransportes Tlaxcala-Apizaco-Huamantla bus to Huamantla (every ½ hr. 6am-7pm, 2000 pesos).

Hidalgo

Many of Hidalgo's cities are easily explored on a daytrip from Mexico City, but although the state has been economically important to Mexico since Aztec rule, few areas are of interest to the foreign visitor. If you do venture into Hidalgo, visit the capital city, Pachuca, and the archeological ruins of Tula.

Pachuca

Pachuca's clean, crisp air provides a happy reprieve from the sea of smog to the south, and the mountains make a beautiful backdrop for the downtown area, built at the flat bottom of a natural bowl. Surrounding residential neighborhoods cling to the mountainsides, and above the houses, the higher reaches—intensely green in season—tower grandiosely over the city center. Pachuca's aesthetic richness is augmented by its mineral wealth: a nearby mine produces over one-tenth of Mexico's silver.

Orientation and Practical Information

Pachuca lies in a dry valley of igneous rock formations and desert shrubs, 88km north-northeast of Mexico City. Don't drive on the winding road from Ciudad Valles (191km north) after dusk, because the road is difficult to see, and the risk of banditry is high as only a few towns populate the long highway between the two cities.

From the bus station, in the city's southwest corner, take a bus (500 pesos), *combi* (green-and-white van, 500 pesos), or taxi (3000 pesos) to *el centro.*

The budget hotel zone fans out from the Reloj Monumental, a squat clock tower modeled after Big Ben, which sits in the middle of the **Plaza de la Independencia.** The plaza serves as the city's centerpiece and is bordered on the west by Allende, and on the east by Matamoros. One block west of the plaza runs Guerrero, Pachuca's main commercial boulevard. Useful maps are available at both the federal and state tourist offices.

State Tourist Office: Allende 406 (tel. 232-53 or 232-76), near Matamoros. Impossible to get the smiling staff to stop answering once you pose a question. Ask for Karla or Patricia. Fantastic maps. Open Mon.-Fri. 9am-8pm.

Federal Tourist Office: Delegación Federal de Turismo, Revolución 290 (tel. 395-66 or 395-00), at the intersection with Cerezedo Estrada. Same maps and brochures found at the state tourist office. Open Mon.-Fri. 9am-3pm.

Currency Exchange: Banks surround the Pl. de la Independencia. Most open Mon.-Fri. 9am-1:30pm and 4-6pm. Exchange hours vary; some end at noon, others at 1:30pm.

Post Office: Juárez at Iglesias (tel. 325-92). Open Mon.-Fri. 8am-7pm, Sat. 9am-1pm; for registered mail Mon.-Fri. 8am-5pm. **Postal Code:** 42000.

Telephones: Valle 106, at Hidalgo 2 blocks east of the Pl. de la Independencia. Big bad sign says "Servicio Telefónico." Open daily 9am-9pm. **Telephone Code:** 771.

Telegrams: Victoria at Comonfort (tel. 253-12). Open daily 8am-9pm.

Bus Station: At the southwest corner of the city. **ADO** (tel. 329-10), to Mexico City (every 15 min. 5am-9pm, 1½ hr., 4300 pesos). **Estrella Blanca** (tel. 327-45), to Querétaro (every 2 hr., 4½ hr., 9300 pesos) and Tampico (at midnight, 9 hr., 22,000 pesos). **Flecha Roja** (tel. 333-43), to Mexico City (every 15 min., 1½ hr., 2600 pesos). **Autotransportes Valle del Mezquital** (tel. 327-14), to Tula (every 15 min. 4:45am-8:30pm, 1½ hr., 4700 pesos).

24-Hr. Pharmacy: Farmacia del Pueblo, Matamoros 205 (tel. 227-29), at the southeast corner of the Pl. de la Independencia.

Hospital General: (tel. 425-64 or 448-49), on the highway to Tulancingo. Government hospital with complete facilities.

Red Cross: Dr. M. Gea González 111 (tel. 417-20).

Police: (tel. 370-11 or 370-88), on Gómez Pérez.

Accommodations

Pachuca's accommodations bring a smile to many a traveler's face: most hotels are cheap by Mexican standards, yet clean, comfortable, and centrally located.

Hotel Juárez, (tel. 512-55), on the south side of the Pl. de la Independencia. For the die-hard budget traveler. Great location with a big covered courtyard. Rooms may be small, dark, and ugly, but they're neat. Bathrooms redefine the word tiny; though a little damp and moldy, they're clean enough. Respectable for the price. Singles 12,000 pesos. Doubles 14,000 pesos.

Hotel Grenfel, Pl. de la Independencia 16 (tel. 202-77), opposite the clock tower. Stately red-brick building with gray awnings. Inside, red cedes to yellow, in both courtyard and dusty but clean rooms whose doors are left wide open when unoccupied. Bathrooms small, but bigger than at the Juárez. A row of shoeshine stands in the entryway for those who won't go anywhere in scuffed shoes. Singles and doubles 20,000 pesos.

Hotel Plaza "El Dorado," Guerrero 721 (tel. 401-42), 1 block from the Palacio de Gobierno. Two huge lobbies with TV, couches, and Mexican families chanting the Jetson's theme song. Carpeted rooms with TV. Singles 32,000 pesos. Doubles 40,000 pesos.

Hotel Noriega, Matamoros 305 (tel. 515-91). No Panamanian connection. Popular with families dragging young children on vacation, but manages to retain a peaceful atmosphere. Simple furnishings—shower and phone. Some rooms lack bottled water. Singles and doubles 35,000 pesos, with TV 39,500 pesos.

Hotel de los Baños, Matamoros 207 (tel. 307-00), just south of the Pl. de la Independencia. Well-maintained, old-fashioned hotel. Covered courtyard decorated with intricate tilework. Some of the carpeted rooms contain magnificently carved wooden furniture. Huge closets don't quite compensate for small baths. Currency exchange and long-distance phone service at front desk. Singles 35,000 pesos. Doubles 40,000 pesos.

Hotel Emily, in the modern building next to Hotel Juárez (tel. 508-16), on the Pl. de la Independencia. Clean, bright, and extremely comfortable. Carpeted rooms have phones, TVs, and balconies, some with a view of the clock tower and surrounding mountains. Restful courtyard. Singles 30,000 pesos. Doubles 35,000 pesos.

Food

Hidalgan cuisine relies heavily on the maguey plant. *Mexiotes,* delicious meat *tamales* wrapped in maguey leaves, are a local staple. Lamb meat wrapped in maguey leaves is baked one meter underground to make Hidalgo's favorite *barbacoa. Pulque,* a fermented drink made from maguey, is omnipresent. If you're in Pachuca just before the first rains (March-April), you may be lucky enough to dine on one of the state's delicacies—*escamoles* (ant eggs fried with salt and butter or mixed into poultry eggs).

La Blanca, Matamoros 201, at Valle on the Pl. de la Independencia. The only true *típico* place downtown. Excellent and spicy *pastes* 800 pesos. Patrons too busy eating to make much noise. Open daily 7:30am-11pm.

Restaurant Ciro's, Pl. de la Independencia 110. Orange booths and plaid tablecloths. Service slow as a slug; everybody likes it that way. Plates 11,000 pesos. Open Mon.-Sat. 8:30am-11pm, Sun. noon-9pm.

Restaurante Acapulco, Matamoros 202, just south of the Pl. de la Independencia. Seafood place with fishy decor. Way cheap. Eggs 2500-3500 pesos, *comida corrida* 3500 pesos, seafood specialties 5000-10,000 pesos. Open Mon.-Sat. 8am-7pm.

El Sarape, Matamoros 502. Cowboy hats, silver spurs, serious faces, and low looks. Scary vibes from men and women alike, but they seem to like their Mexican food. Plates 4300 pesos. Open Mon.-Fri. 11am-6pm.

Restaurant "El Dorado," Guerrero 721, inside the plaza just behind the hotel. Almost touching: carpeting, silver platters, new tablecloths, and tacky fake flowers. *Comida corrida* (4000 pesos) served 1-4pm. Breakfasts 1500-4500 pesos, Mexican dishes 2500-4500 pesos, meats 4000-10,000 pesos. Open Mon.-Sat. 8am-11pm.

Mesón de los Angeles Gómez, Guerrero 723. Friendly family-run taco bar with an interior as narrow and cozy as a hillside *callejón.* Excellent home-cooked *comida corrida* (3500 pesos) served 2-4pm. At night, tacos only. Open Mon.-Sat. 9am-4pm and 6-11pm.

Chip's Restaurant, downstairs in the Hotel Emily. The attraction here is the jaw-dropping view of the clock tower and mountains through the glass wall. Pleasantly bright inside, but the food is only OK. *Comida corrida* 7000 pesos. Open daily 7:30am-10pm.

Sights and Entertainment

Despite its reputation as one of the backwaters of the Republic, Hidalgo has produced artists of national reknown. One of the state's celebrated artists, Jesús Becerrél, lives in Pachuca and has literally painted the town. His most ambitious work, at the **Palacio del Gobierno,** was inspired by the administration of President Luis Echevarría, a supporter of human rights in the Americas. At the center of the work, Echevarría speaks at the United Nations about his proposal for equal education for all people. To the left, the theme is progress, and the outstanding image is an Atlas-like demigod holding up a piece of earth with a human embryo in it. The dramatic mural to the right depicts an independent Mexico (represented by Cuauhtémoc and the Mexican people) above hellish images of the gluttony, slavery, war, and repression in the rest of today's world. (Open Mon.-Fri. 8am-3pm.)

In the center of the vast concrete plaza in front of the Palacio de Gobierno, a grand statue of Benito Juárez holds the Mexican Constitution above the inscription "El Respeto al Derecho Ajeno Es La Paz" (The respect of one another's rights brings peace). Directly opposite Benito, the Neoclassical **Teatro Hidalgo,** built by the revolutionary silversmith Bartolome de Medina, sponsors public dance, theater, and music festivals. (More information available Mon.-Fri. 10am-3pm and 6-8pm at the theater.)

Every Sunday, the **Parque Hidalgo,** five blocks south of the center, becomes one huge food and music extravaganza. Soft drinks, ice cream, and tacos go for under 1000 pesos each, while *mariachi* bands entertain the locals. Up-and-coming singers often debut here. Festivities last until mid-afternoon.

The **Casa de las Artesanías,** at the junction of Juárez and Vincente Segura, presents an amazing array of clay pottery, miniature blown glass, colorful embroidered wool tapestries, and carefully molded brass figurines of *campesinos* balanced on bucking horses. Budget travelers should treat this store as a quasi-museum; look, but don't ask the price. (Open Tues.-Sun. 11am-8pm.)

The only other sight worth the walk is the **Ex-convento de San Francisco,** at Hidalgo and Arista, south of the Pl. de la Independencia and west of the Palacio Municipal. The church itself is plain, but its quiet, relaxing downtown setting is attractive. On the grounds is the **Museo Regional de Hidalgo,** which describes the archeology, history, geography, and ethnography of the state. Exhibits include diagrams and drawings of the first agricultural societies and obsidian users, some artifacts from and information on the ruins at Tula, statues and other relics from the colonial past, and displays on the mining industry. (Museum open Tues.-Sun. 9am-6pm. Free guided tours on request.)

For nightime entertainment, check the posters around town. Pachuca is the home of the **Universidad Autónoma de Hidalgo,** which sponsors relatively frequent cultural events. The most popular disco in town is **Bursalino,** at Baldera and Madero (tel. 374-09). The 8000-peso cover does not include drinks (2000 pesos). The club plays a mixture of rock, *salsa,* and Mexican pop. (Open Fri.-Sat. 10pm-3am.)

Tula

Once the Toltec's greatest city, ancient Tula was constructed at the foot of a hill in a region of brooding volcanic mountains. The beautifully restored archeological site is part of a national park dedicated to preserving the plants and animals of this semi-desert. Tula makes a good daytrip from Mexico City (80km) or Pachuca (75km), or a nice stop for those traveling to or from the Bajío, but the site doesn't merit a cross-country trip.

Orientation and Practical Information

Tula lies 80km from Mexico City along Rte. 57 and 85, and 75km from Pachuca through Actopan. **Autotransportes Valle del Mezquital** provides second-class bus service to Tula from Mexico City and Pachuca. Buses to Tula (every 15 min. 5am-11pm, 4700 pesos) leave from the Central de Autobuses del Norte in Mexico City. The Autotransportes Valle del Mezquital line is at the north end of the terminal. From Pachuca, take the Tula bus (every 15 min. 5am-8pm, 4700 pesos) from the central terminal. **Flecha Amarilla** runs to and from Querétaro (2 per day, 8300 pesos) and Guanajuato (1 per day, 14,500 pesos). The sparkling bus terminal is a short walk from the town plaza. To reach *el centro* after exiting the terminal, walk straight ahead on José Manuel Rojo Del Rio for two blocks.

Tourist Information: There is no tourist office, but the town is small and friendly enough that people on the street will probably be willing and able to answer any question. Information about Tula can also be obtained in Pachuca at the State Tourist Office, or from the Secretaría de Turismo in Mexico City.

Currency Exchange: Bánamex, Leandro Valle 21, just off the Zócalo. Open Mon.-Fri. 9am-1pm.

Telephones: Servicio Telefónico, Mina at 5 de Mayo. Small fee for all collect calls. Open Mon.-Sat. 8am-9pm.

Telegrams: (tel. 200-37), behind the market, in a construction zone. Open Mon.-Fri. 9am-9pm, Sat. 9am-noon.

Market: 5 de Mayo 409, surrounded by a white brick wall. Food, clothes, and some crafts, but not much else. Open daily 7am-8pm.

Tula National Park: Tel. 917-73.

Hospital: IMSS Clínica Hospital, Ocampo at Xicotenatl (tel. 203-68 or 210-46). Open for emergencies 24 hr. **Pharmacy** open Mon.-Fri. 24 hr.

Police: 5 de Mayo 408 (tel. 201-85).

Accommodations and Food

Tula has few sweet deals, but clean and cheap hotels do exist. **Auto Hotel Cuéllar,** 5 de Mayo 23, has unembellished rooms. Enough said. (Singles 25,000 pesos. Doubles 40,000 pesos. TV costs an additional 15,000 pesos.) Next to the hospital, **Motel Lizbeth,** Ocampo 200 (tel. 200-45), has excellent rooms with color TV and comfortable beds. (Singles 40,000 pesos. Doubles 50,000 pesos.)

Restaurants in Tula dish up many *comidas corridas.* **Restaurant Casa Blanca,** Zaragoza 103, off the Zócalo at Hidalgo, is a drab structure with high ceilings and linoleum floors. The place is quiet, and its food is decent and cheap. Steaks cost 15,000 pesos. (Open daily 8am-10pm.) Sitting on the Zócalo is **La Calandria,** Pl. Constitución 212. Steaks and *mariscos* go for 12,000 pesos. (Open daily 9:30am-4:30pm.)

Sights

In the final years of Teotihuacán, a band of Chichimecs and Toltecs, led by Mixcoatl-Camaxtli, wandered through the valley. They passed Toluca, Acolman, Teotihuacán, and Culhuacán, before deciding to conquer the Otomí area between present-day Tula and Jilotepec (halfway down the road from Tula to Tepotzotlán). Mixcoatl-Camaxtli then led his people to what is now the state of Morelos, where he married, had a son, and subsequently lost his throne. When the son, Ce Acatl Topitzin, grew up, he recovered the throne and moved the capital first to Tulancingo and later to the foot of the mountain called Xicuco, where he founded Tula.

Ce Acatl Topitzin, also called Quetzalcóatl, is the most venerated king in *indígena* history and mythology. After he founded Tula, he fled the city because his warlike people did not agree with his peaceful ways and rejected the god he worshiped (and for whom he was named). In the years following the "flight" of Quetzalcóatl (884 AD), several kings expanded Tula into the center of the mighty Toltec empire. When a series of droughts weakened the Toltec capital in 1116, the Chichimecs saw their chance and destroyed Tula, leaving the ruins that exist today at the foot of Xicuco. The defeated Toltecs were marched to Chapultepec, where many died; some years later, the rest migrated to Cholula. Long after the demise of Toltec civilization, many tribes, including the Aztecs, claimed descent from the fierce Toltec stock.

Despite its historical significance, the archeological site at Tula is relatively unimpressive. The high point of the ruins is the remnants of a temple, the roof of which was held up by the four monolithic statues that now surmount the 10-meter pyramid. Known as the *Atlantes,* these 4.6-meter-high statues represent the warrior priests who led the worship of the warlike Tezcatlipoca. (One of the statues at the site is a replica—the original has been moved to the Museo Nacional de Antropología.) Behind the pyramid-temple's north side is a façade with reliefs of jaguars in procession, a deity in headdress, and heart-devouring eagles in Sunday-afternoon repose. Reliefs of serpents feasting on live humans beautify the adjacent wall. From atop the temple, to the left as you face the monoliths, you can see another small pyramid (as yet unidentified); beyond that are the ruins of one of three 16th-century churches built on the site by the Spanish. Behind the temple is an almost fully restored ballcourt.

Many of the Aztec architectural, agricultural, economic, and military practices were inherited from the Toltecs. The **Museo Jorge R. Acosta,** at the entrance to the ruins, concerns itself with Toltec religion, crafts, leisure-time activity, and socioeconomic hierarchy. A written guide is sold for 2500 pesos. The museum complex also includes a cafeteria, bathrooms, and an information desk where you can request a free guided tour and brochures. (Site open daily 9:30am-4:30pm. Admission 10,000 pesos, free Sun. and holidays. Museum free once in the site.) The town-to-ruins walk is long but manageable. From the plaza, turn left on Zaragoza (the first street toward the bus station). When you reach Ocampo, a sign points to the "Parque Nacional Tula;" turn right, and walk several blocks. Immediately beyond the bridge stands another sign for the "Parque." Turn left and walk along the highway. Eventually you will see a third sign for the park—a left here brings you to the bygone age. For those not up to the hike, taxis will take you to the site from town for 3000 pesos. Taxis aren't available at the site itself for the return, but hailing one on the highway usually poses no problem.

THE BAJÍO

A vast, bowl-shaped depression of fertile soil, rolling farms, and verdant hillsides defines Mexico's central plateau. Yet underneath this land of plenty lies another gift from Mother Earth that has brought prosperity to the region since the 16th century: silver. For nearly four centuries, the mineral wealth of the Bajío has determined the course of its history. Guanajuato's richest mines—Real de Santa Fe, Real de Rayas, and Real de San Bernabé—had been discovered by the creole aristocracy by 1550, but it was not until 1750, when the silver trade rerouted to Mexico City, that Guanajuato was promoted to one of Mexico's wealthiest and most influential cities. As Guanajuato began to supply most of the country's minting silver, it became the commercial and banking center of the thriving Bajío region, trading manufactured goods for crops from the nearby agricultural towns of Salamanca, Irapuato, León, San Miguel, and Celaya.

Encompassing the states of Guanajuato and Querétaro (with capital cities of the same names), the Bajío lies within easy reach of Mexico City and has long been a favorite destination for visitors because of its vibrant social life and distinguished history. San Miguel de Allende's particularly vigorous cultural scene attracts a large number of expatriates from the U.S. and other countries.

Querétaro

On June 19, 1867, on Querétaro's Cerro de las Campañas (Hill of Bells), after handing each of the assembling gunsmen a gold coin, Emperor Maximilian uttered his famous last words from the top of Querétaro's Cerrode las Campañas (Hill of Bells): "Mexicans, I am going to die for a just cause: the liberty and the independence of México. May my blood be the last shed for the happiness of my new country. ¡Viva México!" His execution, of course, was not the last time Mexico would bleed before the peaceful modern era, nor was it the last historical drama to which Querétaro would play host. Fifty years later, at the end of a bloody revolution, the victorious leader Carranza chose this spot for the drafting of the Constitution that governs the Republic to this day.

Querétaro has also borne witness to some of the more ignominious events in Mexican history; after the lopsided Mexican-American War, it was here in 1848 that President Don Manuel de la Peña signed the peace treaty with the U.S., which forced Mexico to cede much of its northern territory. Now, as the prosperous industrial and agricultural center of the Bajío, the outskirts of Querétaro assault the senses with whining grain elevators, monstrous warehouses, and truckloads of squealing pigs. Inside the commercial ring, however, the center of the city is a colonial masterpiece, rife with fine architecture, open plazas, and an aqueduct consisting of 74 graceful, rose-colored arches.

Orientation and Practical Information

Querétaro straddles two of the country's most heavily traveled highways—Rte. 120 and Rte. 57. Its streets form a neat grid, and nearly all important sites are within walking distance of the **Jardín Obregón**, demarcated by the streets Corregidora, Madero, Juárez, and 16 de Septiembre. The bus station is on Carretera Panamericana, across the street from the **Alameda Hidalgo**, a wild park. To reach the Jardín, turn left (west) upon leaving the station, walk 1 block to Corregidora, then turn right (north) and walk 4 blocks. The train station is a good distance from the Jardín, about 2 blocks beyond the end of Corregidora in the northernmost part of the city. To get to the train station from downtown, catch a "Ruta 13" taxibus (350 pesos) and get off at the railroad tracks. Take a right on the tracks and walk 2 blocks.

Tourist Office: 5 de Mayo 61 (tel. 401-79). English-speaking staff hands out awkward maps. Free city tours in Spanish daily at 10:30am. Open Mon.-Fri. 9am-2pm and 5-8pm, Sat. 10am-1pm.

Currency Exchange: Banks near the Jardín Obregón are open Mon.-Fri. 9am-12:30pm, but some exchange currency only until noon. **Casa de Cambio de Querétaro,** Madero 6, on the Jardín Obregón's south side, is open Mon.-Thurs. 9am-3pm, Fri. 9am-1:30pm. At other times, try the jewelry stores near the Gran Hotel, but expect unfavorable rates.

Post Office: Arteaga Pte. 5 (tel. 201-12), 2 blocks south of the Jardín Obregón, between Juárez and Allende. Open for stamps and Lista de Correos Mon.-Fri. 8am-7pm, Sat. 9am-1pm; for registered mail Mon.-Fri. 8am-6pm, Sat. 9am-12:30pm.

Telephones: Long-distance *caseta* at the bus station open 24 hr.; no collect calls allowed. Efficient *caseta* at 5 de Mayo 33. International collect calls 5000 pesos. Open Mon.-Sat. 9:30am-2pm and 4:30-9pm. **Telephone Code:** 463.

Telegrams: Allende Nte. 4 (tel. 201-63), 1 block west of the Jardín Obregón. Open Mon.-Fri. 9am-1pm and 3-5:30pm, Sat. 9am-noon.

Train Station: Allende (tel. 217-03), in the northern part of the city. To: San Miguel de Allende (*primera especial* at 9am, 7000 pesos); Mexico City (at 6am, 15,700 pesos); San Luis Potosí (at 10:10am, 13,100 pesos); Ciudad Juárez (*primera regular* at midnight, 28,100 pesos). Tickets sold Mon.-Sat. 10-11am and noon-5:30pm.

Bus Station: (tel. 217-30) on Carretera Panamericana, 4 blocks south and 1 block east of the Jardín. Station contains a 24-hr. long-distance telephone booth, a cafeteria, and a squadron of food booths and shops. Frequent service, but almost all buses are *de paso.* **Flecha Amarilla** (tel. 217-18). To: San Miguel de Allende (22 per day, 2600 pesos); Irapuato (every ½ hr., 4000 pesos); Guadalajara (every ½ hr., 17,000 pesos); Mexico City (every 10 min., 9000 pesos). **Estrella Blanca** (tel. 205-73). To: Matamoros (3 per day, 35,000 pesos); Reynosa (3 per day, 36,000 pesos); Ciudad Juárez (8 per day, 47,700 pesos). First-class carriers to the same destinations include **Transportes Chihuahuenses** (tel. 214-63), **Tres Estrellas de Oro** (tel. 205-88), and **Omnibus de México** (tel. 208-13).

Taxis: Sitio Alameda (tel. 208-85).

Laundromats: Lavandería Automática Selene, Zaragoza 9-E, near Allende. 7000 pesos for a 3kg wash and a 10-min. dry. Open Mon.-Sat. 8:30am-7pm.

Red Cross: Tel. 217-06.

Pharmacy: Farmacia Central, Madero 10 (tel. 211-29), on the Jardín's south side. Open Mon.-Sat. 9am-9pm. **Farmacia El Féniz,** Juárez Nte. 73 (tel. 201-79), 1½ blocks north of the Jardín Obregón. Open daily 8am-10pm.

Hospital: Clínica Àlcocer, Reforma 21 (tel. 206-82).

Police: Zaragoza at Ocampo (tel. 202-06 or 230-03).

Accomodations

Resist the urge to curl up at the hotels near the bus station. Cheaper and considerably more charming places abound a few blocks away, around the Jardín Obregón; only the CREA is out in the sticks.

CREA Youth Hostel (IYHF) (tel. 430-50) on Ejército Republicano, ½ block north from the beginning of the aqueduct on Calzada de los Arcos, southeast of the center. Easily accessible by buses running on Zaragoza (300 pesos); get off at the aqueduct walk to the left uphill. Located in a government sports complex, most facilites of which are used for classes until 10:30am. CREA's trademark tiny 4-person rooms with separate men's and women's areas. Dirty bathrooms lack toilet seats. Curfew 11pm. Members and nonmembers admitted. 6000 pesos per person. Breakfast 3500 pesos, lunch or dinner 4500 pesos.

Hotel Hidalgo, Madero Pte. 11 (tel. 200-81), 1 block west of the Jardín Obregón. Pleasant colonial architecture and superb central location. Bathrooms are small and beds slightly soft, but at this price, who can complain? Singles 16,000 pesos. Doubles 20,000 pesos.

Plaza Hotel, Juárez Nte. 23 (tel. 419-45), on the Jardín Obregón. Best location in the city. Very clean rooms with rust-colored carpets, soft pillows, flowered wallpaper and phones. Some feature a window/terrace overlooking the Jardín. Singles 25,000 pesos. Doubles 30,000 pesos.

Hotel San Augustín, Independencia 12 (tel. 239-19), between Allende and Juárez. The clean rooms have beds, a mirror, 4 walls, and *no más;* some sport that lovely pink Mexican tile in the bathroom. Hot water often scarce. Singles 25,000 pesos. Doubles 30,000 pesos.

Hotel del Márquez, Juárez Nte. 104 (tel. 204-14), 3 long blocks north of the Jardín Obregón. You won't find 100 years of solitude here because of street noise, but both the bedrooms and baths are large and the showers have doors and gold-tinted windows. Some adjacent doubles convert into quads via connecting doors. Singles 20,000 pesos. Doubles 30,000 pesos.

Hotel San Francisco, Corregidora Sur 144 (tel. 208-58), 3 blocks south of the Jardín Obregón. If you like to hammer in the morning and in the evening, you're in luck: a small hardware store ornaments the lobby. Green-and-white candy-striped beds and bright blue garbage cans conjure up fond memories of Willy Wonka. Some of the large rooms have yellow-tinted windows. Singles 20,000 pesos. Doubles 40,000 pesos.

Hotel Corregidora, Corregidora Sur 138 (tel. 404-06), next to the Hotel San Francisco. High points are the sea-green tile and hot water in the bathrooms. The desk won't let you forget that this hotel is a 1982 member of the Mexican Hotel and Motel Association (they still have the plaque up). Singles 32,000 pesos. Doubles 40,000.

Food

Several inexpensive restaurants face the Jardín Obregón. Charming *loncherías* and outdoor cafés rim the nearby Pl. Corregidora, while taco, *torta,* and other fast-food stands line 5 de Mayo.

Ibis Natura Vegetana, Juárez Nte. 104, ½ block north of the Jardín Obregón. Munch on healthy treats in front of an idyllic meadow-and-mountain wallpaper scene. Like many Mexican health-food joints, this one sells vitamins and biodegradable hair dye. *Comida corrida* 6000 pesos. Simply scrumptious soy burgers start at 2500 pesos. Open Mon.-Fri. 9:30am-9:30-pm.

Restaurante Molino Rojo, Madero Pte. 12, inside the bazaar across from the Hotel Hidalgo. All tables are shaded by yellow canvas. After the meal, try your luck at the carnival machine at the entrance. Breakfasts 4000-6000 pesos. Hamburgers 4200 pesos. Open daily 7:30am-10pm.

Restaurante de la Rosa, Juárez at Peralta, across from the Teatro República. Reasonable prices on basic Mexican dishes. Watch Mexican pro wrestling (even more patently fake than the U.S. version) from your wickedly straight-backed chair. *Plato mixto* 20,000 pesos. Excellent *café de la Olla* 1500 pesos. Open daily 1pm-midnight.

Café del Fondo, Jardín Corregidora 12. A small coffee establishment perfect for cracking that new novel. Pink walls and a high glass ceiling enhance the tranquility. Coffees 2300-7300 pesos. Open daily 10am-11pm.

Restaurante Manolo's, Madero 6, on the south side of the Jardín Obregón. Manolo has hired myopic help so they won't get caught up in the soccer game that's always on the tube. Three interesting *comida corrida* choices 10,900-14,900 pesos. Other Mexican dishes 3500-8500 pesos. Open daily 10am-10pm.

Restaurante La Flor de Querétaro, Juárez Nte. 5, facing the Jardín Obregón. Very comfortable padded chairs encourage long stays. Large menu. Rice with peas for 6000 pesos and (no joke) brains in vinegar sauce 9500 pesos. Open daily 7am-10:30pm.

Fonda del Refugio, Corregidora 26, in the Pl. de la Corregidora ½ block east of the Jardín Obregón. Outdoor seating on the plaza. Superb regional and international cuisine. Entrees 12,000-25,000 pesos. Open daily 10:30am-11pm.

La Corregidora, 16 de Septiembre at Corregidora. A courteous hostess will explicate the menu, but don't expect sweet seafood so far from the ocean. *Comida corrida* 8000-14,000 pesos. Seafood 13,000-15,000 pesos. Open daily 10am-9pm.

Nevería Galy, 5 de Mayo 8, ½ block east of the Jardín Obregón. The best ice cream in town is made on the premises. The few flavors concocted each day go for 2000-2500 pesos. Open daily noon-3pm and 4-9pm.

Panificadora La Vienasa, Juárez Nte. 18. Stuff your face in this great bakery with cookies (400-500 pesos) and delicious half-size baguettes (350 pesos). Open daily 8-10am and 4:30-9:30pm.

Sights

Querétaro's touristic appeal derives from its rich historical and religious past. The city is supersaturated with beautiful architecture, intriguing legends, and patriotic memories. Many sights are within easy walking distance of the Jardín Obregón.

Most intriguing of all is the **Convento de la Santa Cruz,** south of the Jardin. Follow Corregidora to Independencia, turn left; after walking a few blocks, you'll reach the convent on a plaza dedicated to the founders of the city. Nearly everything inside Santa Cruz is original, including the furnishings of the room in which Emperor Maximilian awaited his execution. In one courtyard, a tree grows thorns in the form of crucifixes; the thorns began growing in this manner after one of the original friars accidently left his cane stuck in the ground near the tree. (Guided tours daily 10am-6pm. Some donation expected and a few English guides available. Open Mon.-Fri. 10am-2pm and 4-6pm.)

Up 5 de Mayo to the east of the Jardín is the **Plaza de la Independencia,** a monument to Don Juan Antonio Urrutia y Aranda, Marqués del Villas del Aguila, builder of the city's famous aqueduct. Four stone dogs around his statue lean forward to expectorate into a fountain. The plaza is bordered by beautiful colonial buildings, the most notable being the **Casa de la Corregidora,** home of Doña Josefa Ortíz de Domínguez, heroine of the 1810 Independence movement. This palace is now partitioned into municipal offices. (Open Mon.-Sat. 8am-9pm.)

The colorful **Templo de la Congregación,** 1 block north of the Casa de la Corregidora at Pasteur and 16 de Septiembre, has two tall mosaic towers and a central dome. The frescoes and stained-glass are splendid and the pipe organ is one of the most elaborate in Mexico.

The small **Teatro de la República,** at Angela Peralta and Juárez, has witnessed many important events: in 1867, the final decision on Emperor Maximilian's fate; in 1917, the drafting of the Constitution; and in 1929, the formation of the Partido Nacional de la Revolución (PNR), precursor of today's ruling PRI. (Open Mon.-Fri. 9am-8pm, Sat. 9am-1pm.)

The **Museo Regional,** is located in the **Ex-Convento de San Francisco,** at Corregidora and Madero, to the east of the Jardín Obregón. Rebuilt in the 17th century's idea of the Renaissance style, it possesses a cloister with two stories of colonnades. The museum displays many of the artifacts associated with the events that have taken place in Querétaro, and even played a part in that history itself as the sentencing site of the leaders of the 1810 movement for independence. Exhibits include the table upon which the 1848 peace treaty with the U.S. was signed, a bust of Escobedo, and a French-made operating table brought to Mexico from the U.S. by Pancho Villa in 1916. Art echoes history in the museum: temporary exhibits of contemporary art greet you at the entrance, and the entire upstairs area is devoted to 17th- and 18th-century religious paintings. (Open Tues.-Sun. 11am-7pm. Free.)

Overshadowing the Museo Regional is the newer **Museo de Arte de Querétaro,** across the Jardín Obregón at Allende and Pino Suárez. The original edifice, an 18th-century Augustinian monastery, was reconstructed in 1889 during the Porfiriato the Palacio Federal. Thanks to recent stunning renovations, the building is one of the most attractive in Mexico. Richly decorated arches and sculpted columns punctuate the patio. An exhibit on *queretana* architecture supplements an entire floor of Baroque paintings. Galleries of European painting, 19th- and 20th-century Mexican art, and work of the 20th-century *queretano* Abelalberto Avila complete the collection.

Northeast of the Alameda, along Calzada de los Arcos, rises the **Acueducto,** now an emblem of the city of Querétaro. The aqueduct, with its 74 arches of pink quarry stone, was constructed between 1726 and 1738 as a gift from the Marqués del Villas del Aguila to a perpetually dry community.

The **Cerro de las Campañas,** where Maximilian surrendered his sword to General Escobedo in 1867, is a half-hour walk from the center. To reach the monument, walk a few blocks north of the Jardín Obregón on Corregidora and turn left onto General Escobedo. Proceed on Escobedo until the street ends at Tecnológico, then take a right, and you will come to the monument. To the left of the Cerro de las Campañas and up a low hill, Maximilian's family built a small chapel over the ground where the emperor and two of his generals were shot; three small white memorials inside designate the places where each took his last breath. A man at the entrance to the chapel will gladly provide further historical detail—and if you're female, he may even recite some romantic poems. Up the stairs to the left of the chapel stands a large stone sculpture of Benito Juárez, the man responsible for confirming the condemning evidence against Maximilian.

Entertainment

Local entertainment, like most everything else in Querétaro, revolves around the Jardín Obregón. Open-air brass band concerts are given in the gazebo Sunday evenings from 6 to 8pm.

Call the **Academía de Bellas Artes,** Juárez Sur at Independencia (tel. 636-01), to find out what the students of the Universidad Autónoma de Querétaro have in store for the public (including frequent ballets and piano recitals, occasional theatrical events, and, less frequently, folk dance presentations). The annual **Feria de Querétaro** takes place during the second week of December.

The Querétaro student body supports a number of discos. The classiest spot in town is **Discoteca Misiones,** on the highway to Mexico City in 5-star Hotel Ex-Hacienda Jurica. More convenient to the center of town are **JR's,** at Zaragoza and Tecnológico, and **Tiffani's,** at Zaragoza Pte. 67.

Very popular with the local twentysomething crowd are **JBJ,** Blvd. Zona Dorada 109, **QIU,** Monte Sinia 102, and **La Opera,** Circuito Jardín Sur 1. Live music at these three causes fluctuations in the cover charges (depending on the band). Be prepared to pay 5000 pesos for a mixed drink and around 4000 pesos for your average beer.

San Miguel de Allende

Founded in 1542, San Miguel de Allende was baptized "Itzcuinapan" ("River of Dogs" in Nahuatl), then called "San Miguel El Grande," before acquiring its current name which commemorates its favorite son Don Ignacio de Allende, one of the most important leaders in Mexico's fight for independence. Although the entire town is now officially a national monument, it is no mere museum piece: a large population of foreign artists plus locals receptive to their presence make for a festive, spontaneous air about the city. Markets buzz with activity, bands play Peruvian flute music or Mexican *salsa* for diners, browsers make the rounds, and shopkeepers humor customers who want to practice their Spanish.

Renowned for its fine artisanry and academics, San Miguel has another resource that prospective visitors often overlook—a mild climate. The town is almost never oppressively hot, thanks to its 2000m elevation. Cool afternoon rains fall during the summer, when highs reach only 30°C (80°F).

Orientation and Practical Information

San Miguel lies midway between Guanajuato and Querétaro, 428km northwest of Mexico City. From the bus station to the center (known as the Jardín or Pl. de Allende), take the bus (300 pesos) or a taxi (3000 pesos). To walk, turn right as you exit the station and walk 1km on Calzada de la Estación, which turns into San Francisco before coming upon the Jardin. The train station lies yet another kilometer west of the bus station on the same road.

Most attractions are within walking distance of the Jardín, which is bounded by San Francisco, El Reloj, Umarán/Correro, and Hidalgo. A good source of current information on the town is the weekly newspaper *Atención,* available at the tourist office next to the Jardín.

San Miguel has a reputation as a place for Mexican men to meet women. To avoid desperate Don Juans, many women who live here do not walk alone at night.

Tourist Office: Dirección General de Turismo (tel. 217-47), on the Pl. de Allende, next to the *parroquia* and Restaurante La Terraza. Knowledgeable staff speaks English and distributes pamphlets and information on hotels, restaurants, and clubs. They'll trade you a great map for 4000 pesos. Open Mon.-Fri. 10am-2:45pm and 5-7pm, Sat. 10am-1pm, Sun. 10am-noon.

U.S. Consular Representative: Macías 72 (tel. 223-57), opposite Bellas Artes. Office hours Mon. and Wed. 9am-1pm and 4-7pm, Tues. and Thurs. 4-7pm, or by appointment. In case of emergency dial 200-68 or 209-80.

Currency Exchange: Many banks around the Jardín are open Mon.-Fri. 9am-1:30pm; you'll get slightly better rates at such *casas de cambio* as **Allen W. Lloyd y Asociados,** Jardín at Hidalgo (open Mon.-Fri. 9am-5pm), and **Deal,** Correos 15 (open Mon.-Fri. 9am-2pm and 4-6pm, Sat. 9am-2pm).

Post Office: Correos 16 (tel. 200-89), 1 block east of the Jardín. Lista de Correos. Open for registered mail Mon.-Fri. 8am-6pm; for all other services Mon.-Fri. 8am-7pm.

Telephones: El Toro Lonchería, Macías 52, across from the Hotel Suatto. International collect calls 2000 pesos. Open Mon.-Sat. 9am-2pm and 3-8pm.

Telegrams: (tel. 200-81), adjacent to the post office. Open Mon.-Thurs. 9am-1pm and 3-5pm, Sat. 9am-noon.

Train Station: Ferrocarriles Nacionales de México (tel. 200-07), located 2km west of town.

Bus Station: (tel. 222-06), on Calzada de la Estación, 1km west of the center. Served by first-class **Tres Estrellas de Oro** and second-class lines **Flecha Amarilla** (tel. 200-84) and **Herradura de Plata** (tel. 207-25). Flecha Amarilla to: Mexico City (14 per day 1:35am-9pm, 12,000 pesos); Guanajuato (7 per day 6:30am-5pm, 3900 pesos); Léon (13 per day 5:15am-7pm, 6200 pesos); San Luis Potosí (5 per day 6:40am-3pm, 8000 pesos); Dolores Hidalgo (every 30 min., 1700 pesos). Tres Estrellas sends fewer buses to most of the same places, including Mexico City at (9:30am, 13,000 pesos).

Taxis: Sitios de Taxis (tel. 201-92).

Car Rental: Gama Rent-a-Car, Hidalgo 3 (tel. 208-15). VW sedan for 55,000 pesos per day plus 350 pesos per km and 15,000-peso insurance fee. Special weekly rates. Open Mon.-Sat. 9am-2pm and 4-7pm.

English Bookstore: El Colibrí, Sollano 30 (tel. 207-57). Superb—if expensive—selection of classics, science fiction, history, and current best-sellers. Open Mon.-Sat. 9:30am-2pm and 4-7pm. Also, the public library (see below) evacuates old paperbacks by selling them for about 1500 pesos each.

Public Library: Insurgentes 25 (tel. 202-93), next to "La Española." The social center of the large expatriate community. Free language exchange. Open Mon.-Sat. 10am-2pm and 4-7pm.

Laundromat: Lavamagico, Pila Seca 5 (tel. 208-99). Will pick up and deliver a load for a mere 8000 pesos. Open Mon.-Sat. 8am-8pm.

Medical Emergency: Red Cross: (tel. 216-16), km1 on Carretera Celaya.

Pharmacy: Farmacia Allende, San Francisco 3 (tel. 200-74), ½ block from the Jardín. Open daily 9am-10pm.

Hospital: Sanatorio de Nuestra Señora de la Salud, Hidalgo 28 (tel. 204-30). Open 24 hr. for emergencies. English-speaking physician.

Police: In the Presidencia Municipal (tel. 200-22).

Academics

Many visitors to San Miguel study at one of its schools for foreign students. The **Centro Cultural Ignacio Ramírez El Nigromante** (tel. 202-89) conducts a number of four-week courses throughout the year at a cost of US$70 per month. For information, write to Señora Carmen Masip de Hawkins, Dr. Hernández Macías 75, San Miguel de Allende, Guanajuato 37700. During the year the **Academia Hispano**

Americana (tel. 203-49) runs one-week, four-week, eight-week, and 12-week sessions in Spanish language, literature, history, psychology, current events, and folklore of Mexico. One week costs US$80. For information write to the Registrar, Academia Hispano Americana, Mesones 4, San Miguel de Allende, Guanajuato 37700. **Inter Idiomas** (tel. 221-77) organizes language programs of two hours per day at US$40 per week or US$140 per month, plus a one-time US$15 registration fee. Address inquiries to the school at Mesones 15, San Miguel de Allende, Guanajuato 37700. Finally, the **Instituto Allende** (tel. 201-90), much esteemed but also quite costly, offers many art courses and instruction in all levels of Spanish. For more information, write to the institute at Ancha de San Antonio 20, San Miguel de Allende, Guanajuato 37700. You can hire a private language tutor at any of the schools for about US$6-8 per hour.

Accommodations

In general, expect to drop much more on a room in San Miguel than elsewhere in Mexico. By the same token, expect much better quality. Make reservations at the better hotels listed below about a month in advance. Bargain with proprietors if you expect to stay longer than a couple of days, since discounts are commonly granted. If you are planning an extended stay, check for notices of rooms for rent on the bulletin board at the Instituto Allende, Ancha de San Antonio 20, southwest of the Jardín. Since San Miguel attracts so many *norteamericanos*, most hotels accept U.S. dollars.

Hotel Hidalgo, Hidalgo 22 (tel. 207-75), 1 block from the Jardín. Yellow walls, blue tile, and a gang of children converge on visitors in the lobby. The hot water is only lukewarm and the bathrooms smell mildly, but the beds are great. Singles 15,000 pesos. Doubles 30,000 pesos.

Hotel La Huerta (tel. 203-60), at the end of Barrera. Follow Mesones, which becomes Aparicio, east up the hill away from the Jardín; when you see water flowing in a mid-street garbage-filled canal, turn right. Go through the gate at the end of the street, and the hotel will be on the left. Rooms more pleasant than Hidalgo's, but more frequently full and the location lacks convenience. 10,000 pesos per person.

Casa de Huéspedes, Mesones 23. Clean rooms with throw rugs off a cozy 2nd-floor corridor choked with plants. Clean bathrooms overlaid with burgundy tile. Most excellent owner. Singles 20,000 pesos. Doubles 25,000 pesos.

Hotel Posada de las Monjas, Canal 37 (tel. 201-71), 3 blocks west of the Jardín (San Francisco becomes Canal). Elegant lobby with Enormo-European rug, prints, flowers, TV, and goldfish. Splendid multiple courtyards with fountains. Dirt-free carpeted rooms with desks and stone-floored bathrooms. Restaurant and bar. A good deal. Singles 30,000 and 35,000 pesos (2 sizes). Doubles 35,000 and 65,000 pesos.

Hotel Quinta Loreto, Loreto 13 (tel. 200-42), 3 blocks north and 1 block east of the Jardín. Popular place filled with *norteamericanos* who kick back in the leather chairs outside their rooms, chatting and drinking with the other guests. Spic-and-span spacious rooms. Reservations indispensable June-Aug. and Dec.-March. Singles and doubles 35,000 pesos. Triples 40,000 pesos.

Hotel Sautto, Macías 51 (tel. 200-51), 1 block north and 1 block west of the Jardín. Interesting gilt mirrors hang in the office, and rooms surround a courtyard where chirping birds light on gargantuan ceramic plant pots. For the money, you'd think the hot water would be hot. It's not. Singles 45,000 pesos. Doubles 50,000 pesos.

Hotel Posada Carmina, Cuna de Allende 7 (tel. 204-58), 1 block south of the Jardín. Colonial decor and a Victorian standard of cleanliness. Singles 30,000 pesos. Doubles 36,000 pesos.

Posada la Fuenta, Ancha de San Antonio 95 (tel. 206-29), quite a hike from the Jardín. Clean rooms with fireplaces off carpeted halls. Several tables dispersed around a fountain in the courtyard are perfect for lounging in the afternoon. Staff like to show their pearly whites. Singles and doubles 45,000 pesos.

La Mansión del Bosque, Aldama 65 (tel. 202-77), across the street from the Parque Benito Juárez, 3 blocks south of the Jardín. Southern hospitality carried off by the proprietor from Tennessee. Rooms vary in size but all showcase tasteful furnishings and local art. Beautiful lounge with shelves of reading material; plant-filled courtyard proffers niches of cool shade for reading and dozing. Lives up to its advertising claim: "intimate and charming." Singles US$30-42. Doubles US$56-65. Rates include 2 meals.

Food

The scent of all the world's cuisines wafts over the cobbled streets of San Miguel. Unfortunately, food prices have run amok, and not only by Mexican standards. Nonetheless, many restaurants are worth the extra expense, especially those offering live entertainment.

Cheap food must be hunted down. The market area on Mesones, 2 blocks east of the Templo de Tercer Orden, sells inexpensive fresh fruit and vegetables as well as *elotes* and tacos. Supermarkets around the Jardín overcharge for almost everything, but they stock almost everything as well. For lunch or a quick snack, walk among the rag-tag collection of stands selling *tortas* on the south side of Insurgentes between Macías and Hidalgo.

Mama Mía, Umarán 8, west of the Jardín's southwest corner. The best place in town, illogically decorated with murals of pan-pipe players and Greek columns. Quietly festive tree-covered courtyard. Great live music daily 8pm-midnight. Breakfasts start at 4000 pesos, pastas at 6500 pesos, and fish at 10,000 pesos. Piping-hot specialty coffees 2000-10,000 pesos. Movies shown at 6pm daily (6000 pesos including 1 drink); the bar up front provides more live music until it closes at 2am. Restaurant open daily 8am-1am.

Restaurant "El Infiernito," (a.k.a. Doña Anita), Mesones 23. Ceramic bulldogs, stuffed iguanas, pictures of Jesus, and psychedelic art fill the otherwise elegantly empty room. The specialty is *pollo rostizado*. Breakfasts 6500 pesos, half-chicken with trimmings 9000 pesos. Open daily 9am-midnight.

La Fragua, Cuna de Allende, ½ block south of the southwest corner of the Jardín. Overpriced as a restaurant, but live music after 7pm on weeknights and 6pm on weekends compensates somewhat. Good beer 3600 pesos. *Pollo a la canasta* 10,000 pesos. Tacos 6000-10,000 pesos. Open Mon.-Thurs. noon-1am, Fri.-Sun. noon-3am.

La Princesa, Recreo 5, 1½ blocks from the Jardín. This dark, romantic restaurant might prompt you to propose marriage to the next passing person. Best for dinners with that special someone. The *comida corrida,* served 1-8pm, costs 10,000 pesos and includes a margarita. Frogs' legs 21,000 pesos. Open daily noon-3am.

Chez Max, Zacateros 21. Strange mix of Mexican, French, and Italian food served amid even stranger decor including suits of armor with garlic clove necklaces and movable screens separating the tables. Caesar Salad for 2 people 15,000 pesos. Spaghettis 12,000-18,000 pesos. Open Tues.-Sun. 1-11pm.

La Piñata, Jesús 1, a block south of the Jardín. The shelves in this juice bar (hey baby, what's your cholesterol count?) are crammed with Coca-Cola cups, *indigena* art, and cactuses. Great *jugo de naranja* 2300 pesos. *Licuados* 2000 pesos. Open daily 8am-4pm.

American Legion Restaurant, Tenerías at Codo. Come eat with a bunch of friendly old men who have oodles of advice about town. Thick-pattied burgers only 5500 pesos. Breakfasts 5000 pesos. All food cooked by your friend Patrick. Open Mon.-Sat. 9am-9pm, Sun. 9am-4pm.

Trudy's Lone Star BBQ, Canal 15, 1 block west of the Jardín. A bit of ol' Texas in the heart of Mexico. The simulated clouds hanging from the ceiling never precipitate; it's a good thing, too, because the black-and-white tile floor is slick enough already. Free spiced carrots and cukes while you decide what to order. Each table has a different napkin ring theme. Potato-skin nachos 10,500 pesos. *Fajitas* 14,500 pesos. Open daily noon-1am.

La Colima, El Relój 21, north of the Jardín. A fun little bakery where many expatriates buy their bread. *Bolillos* (Mexican baguettes) 300 pesos. *Conches* 600 pesos. Open Mon. 8:30am-2pm, Tues.-Sat. 6am-2pm and 5:30-9pm, Sun. 6-9am.

Sights

Magnificent churches, colonial homes, an art gallery, and artisans' boutiques populate the cobbled streets around the Jardín. The only way to experience San Miguel is on foot, and the only way to walk its jagged, bumpy streets is in thick-soled shoes.

Most Sundays at noon, the staff of the public library gives guided "home and garden" tours of the city in English for a small fee. Perhaps the best way to sightsee in San Miguel is to wander off in any direction from the Jardín; almost every street has an interesting shop, and San Miguel's small size makes it hard for even the clutziest to get lost.

La Parroquia, next to the Jardín, is one of the most distinctive churches in Mexico. Its façade and tower were designed and realized by the *indígena* mason Zeferino Gutiérrez, who is said to have learned the Gothic style from postcards of French cathedrals. The size and beauty of the church make it a landmark for miles around. The baptistry is to the left as you enter the patio of the church. (Open daily 6am-9pm.)

The mid-18th-century house where the initiator of the independence movement lived (known as the **Casa de Don Ignacio Allende**) stands to the left of La Parroquia, on the corner of Canal and Cuna de Allende. Don Ignacio's status is obvious from his magnificent, partly Baroque mansion. The eclectic museum combines tributes to Allende with unrelated exhibits on astronomy and paleobiology. (Open Tues.-Sun. 10am-4pm. Free.)

At the corner of Canal and Macías, 2 blocks west of the Jardín, stands the enormous **Iglesia de la Concepción.** Distinguished by its splendid two-story dome crowned with a representation of the Immaculate Conception, the church was finished in 1891. Pairs of Corinthian columns ornament the lower level. Inside are polychrome sculptures of St. Joseph and the Immaculate Conception, and an interesting juxtaposition of paintings and graves. (Open daily 7:15am-8:15pm.)

Founded in 1712, the **Templo del Oratorio de San Felipe Neri** lies at the corner of Insurgentes and Loreto, 2 blocks east of the library. Its engraved Baroque façade shows *indígena* influence, and its interior is mainly neoclassical, but the styles contaminate each other since the church has been rebuilt many times. On the right side of the church, the towers and the dome belong to the **Santa Casa de Loreto,** a reproduction of the building of the same name in Italy (enter on the right side of the altar in San Felipe Neri). The floors and the lower friezes of the walls are covered with glazed tiles from China, Spain, and Puebla. (Open daily 7-8am.)

One block east of the Jardín at Juárez and San Francisco, the **Iglesia de San Francisco** includes a tall, dark-red neoclassical tower attributed to the architect Tresguerras. Finished in 1799, the church's Churrigueresque façade honors many saints. Several small paintings in the interior are so elevated and enveloped in darkness that you'd have to be a bat to appreciate them. To the right as you face San Francisco is the **Iglesia del Tercer Orden,** one of the oldest and most decayed churches in San Miguel, constructed by the Franciscan order between 1606 and 1638. The main façade contains an image of St. Francis and symbols of the Franciscan order. (Both open daily 7am-2:30pm and 5-8pm.)

The **Instituto Allende,** affiliated with the Universidad de Guanajuato, is in the southwestern part of San Miguel, at Ancha de San Antonio 20. Notices of musical events at Bellas Artes (centro Cultural El Nigromante), openings at various galleries, and concerts and plays in the institute's auditorium appear on the bulletin board to the left as you enter. Two art galleries show and sell the work of students. Built as a church in 1735, the building was reconceived as an art school and inaugurated in 1985. (Open daily 9am-noon and 3-6:30pm.)

The **Parque Juárez,** 3 blocks south of the Jardín on Aldama and then Carranza, the greenest and most refreshing part of San Miguel, reverberates with the calls of tropical birds. Die-hard cagers can often join a pick-up basketball game involving both *gringos* and locals; afterward, hoopsters discuss the imminent capture of the NBA title by the Portland Trail Blazers. Some of the most elegant houses in San Miguel surround this park.

East of town, **Tres Cruces** commands a magnificent view of San Miguel, the surrounding immense fertile valley, and the faraway mountains. The hill surmounted by three crosses is visible from town. Walk 3 blocks east on San Francisco from the Jardín, turn right (south) on Real (you'll pass a Pemex station), and walk until you see the three crosses on the right. This part of the walk takes about 15 minutes and passes through some picturesque alleys along the way. Three blocks before reaching the official *mirador* (lookout), you can turn right and ascend to the hilltop (another 15 min.)

The mild climate of San Miguel rarely requires aquatic relief, but should the mercury rise to swim level, head to the *balneario* at **Taboada,** 6km down the road to Dolores Hidalgo. The facilities here include two pools, a bar/restaurant, and fields for soccer, Aerobie, or suntanning. Before you can dive in, you must catch the bus marked "Taboada" at the municipal bus stop. To get to the stop, head east along Mesones towards the market. Turn left on Colegio and, after 1 block, turn right onto a small plaza. Buses (1500 pesos) leave here for Taboada at 9am, 11am, 1pm, and 3pm, and return to San Miguel fifteen minutes after the above hours. (*Balneario* open Wed.-Mon. 7am-5pm. Admission to 6000 pesos.)

Entertainment

San Miguel's cultural calendar is full. **Bellas Artes,** also known as Centro Cultural El Nigromante, in a former convent of the late 18th century, sits next to the Iglesia de la Concepción on Macías. It presents jazz, classical guitar, and Mexican folksong concerts, among others. Some are free, but most cost a few thousand pesos. Check the bulletin board in Bellas Artes for details. Bellas Artes also has a courtyard where beer, coffee, and snacks are sold. The **Biblioteca Pública** (public library), Insurgentes 25, arranges informal evenings of conversation in Spanish and English (Thurs. 7-9pm, Sat. 5-7pm), providing a relaxed atmosphere in which to meet Mexican students and other travelers. Coffee, tea, and cookies are served for a few pesos. When you're not talking, munch on the cookies provided for just a few hundred pesos. Occasionally these evenings are held at Casa Luna, Cuadrantes 2; check at the library or in *Atención.*

San Miguel also has a number of good bars and discos in which to rock the house down; on weekends, you may have to wait a while to get in. The most popular is **El Ring,** Hidalgo 25, between Mesones and Insurgentes 1½ blocks north of the Jardín. (Cover 20,000 pesos; on paper, male-female couples only, but policy not strictly upheld. Open Tues.-Sun. 10pm-4am. No cover Wed.) The less exclusive **Laberintos,** Ancha de San Antonio 7, resembles a wine cellar. Vintage disco and *salsa* tunes permeate the dance floor. (No cover Thurs.; Fri. cover 5000-10,000 pesos; Sat. cover 15,000 pesos; Sun. cover 5000 pesos. Open Thurs.-Sun. 10pm-3am.) *Gringos* flock to **Pancho & Lefty's,** on Mesones between Macías and Hidalgo. (Drinks around 4000 pesos. Cover up to 10,000 pesos, depending on the musicians. Open Tues.-Sun. 7pm-2am.)

Seasonal Events

The principal celebrations in San Miguel are the Easter procession and ceremonies; Christmas and the New Year; the Fiesta de la Candelaria on February 2, marking the start of spring and the birthday of El Padre de Miguel; the festival of San Miguel's guardian saint (3rd weekend in Sept.), when bulls run free through the center of the city in imitation of the *encierro* in Pamplona, Spain; the observation of the birthday of Ignacio Allende on January 21; and the celebration of independence on September 15 and 16. In addition, there are religious events almost every week of January and May; the June Corpus Cristi festival guarantees dances and music around June; and several other fiestas happen in July, August, and November.

Guanajuato

Guanajuato took root on the walls of a long ravine that was first considered fit only for wild frogs; the city's Tarascan name, Guanaxhuato, means "mountainous frog hatchery." Humanity finally carved out its niche in this rugged locale when settlers stumbled upon ores galore. Their extractions from nearby gold and silver mines were transformed by some strange alchemy into the grand colonial architecture that still glitters under handsome wrought-iron lamps throughout the city's drunkenly crooked *callejones* (alleys).

After amassing its wealth under Spanish guidance, Guanajuato led the way in the fight for independence. When King Carlos III raised taxes in 1765 and cut the creole landowners' and miners' share of silver profits, Guanajuato protested. When he banished the Jesuits from Latin America in 1767, Guanajuato, where the Jesuits had just completed their Templo de la Compañía, grew outraged. During Hidalgo's stop here in 1810, sons of both the wealthy *guanajuatense* landowners and poor mine workers helped him overrun the Spaniards' stronghold Alhóndiga de Granaditas. Loyalist Colonel Calleja then marched from Mexico City, reclaimed the city from the rebels, ordered scaffolds built in all the plazas, and began a gruesome "lottery of death," in which names were randomly drawn from a sombrero and citizens hanged as a lesson to the city that dared to rise against the Spanish Empire.

Guanajuato is also the birthplace of muralist Diego Rivera, whose earliest works are infused with impressions of the city. In his wake, the city supports five outstanding museums, several film clubs, and four theaters. During the **Festival Internacional Cervantino,** held in October in honor of the author of *Don Quixote,* Guanajuato sponsors performances of drama, classical music, and ballet in an atmosphere of carnivalesque debauchery.

Orientation

The city of Guanajuato is in the center of Guanajuato state, 54km southwest of Dolores Hidalgo and 46km north of Irapuato. The shortest way from Mexico City is via Celaya on Rte. 57/45. León and Irapuato have become the state's main crossroads, with many bus connections to Guanajuato from either of these cities. Guanajuato's bus station is about 3km west of town. Unless you enjoy highway robbery (cabs to *el centro* cost 15,000 pesos), take a "Centro" bus (400 pesos) and de-bus at the first stop after coming through the tunnel, which leaves you by the market and the city's cheapest hotels. Buses depart from the front of the terminal. To return, catch a "Central Camionera" bus in front of the cinema next to the Hotel Central.

In Guanajuato, accurate maps are almost impossible to find, few streets are open to traffic, and still fewer follow a linear trajectory. The best map on record can be purchased at the offices of INEGI, on the third floor in the same white building as the Agora Restaurant, on Allende near the Jardín Union. At the center of the city are the **Plaza de la Paz** and the imposing **basilica. Avenida Juárez** heads west from here to the market, the tourist office, and the bus station; to the east of the plaza, it is called **Avenida Sopeña.** Roughly following the path of Juárez/Sopeña, the **Subterránea** is an underground avenue constructed between 1963 and 1966 beneath the former bed of the Río Guanajuato, which now flows in an adjacent concrete channel. On the surface, innumerable alleys branch off Juárez/Sopeña. If you are lost on foot, remember that the avenue is always downhill. Buses (400 pesos) cross the city both on the surface and underground: catch one at the main bus stop in front of the tourist office and Cinema Reforma. Bus service terminates at 10pm. Taxi service charges outrageous fares (10,000-15,000 pesos) for trips to destinations that buses don't reach.

Practical Information

Tourist Office: Dirección General de Turismo, Juárez at 5 de Mayo (tel. 200-86), 1 block west of the Mercado. A poor map and useless brochures, but some helpful verbal information. They *sell* better literature for 4000-5000 pesos. Open Mon.-Fri. 9am-7:30pm, Sat.-Sun. 10am-2pm. Across the street, the privately run **Información Turística** booth offers the same map and information, plus taxi and microbus tours of the city. Open daily 8am-10pm.

Currency Exchange: Banks line Juárez and the Pl. de la Paz, but many exchange currency only Mon.-Fri. 9:30am-12:30pm. The best hours are at **Banco Mexicano Somex,** Sopeña 18,

1 block east of the Teatro Juárez. Open for exchange Mon.-Fri. 9am-1:30pm. There are no *casas de cambio,* but some restaurants and hotels change U.S. dollars.

Post Office: Ayuntamiento 25 (tel. 203-85), down the street from the Universidad de Guanajuato. Open for stamps and Lista de Correos Mon.-Fri. 8am-8pm, Sat. 9am-1pm; for registered mail Mon.-Fri. 9am-6pm, Sat. 9-11:30am. **Postal Code:** 37700.

Telephones: Lonchería y Caseta de Larga Distancia Pípila, Alonso 14 (tel. 209-83), down the street from Casa Kloster. International collect calls 2000 pesos. Open daily 9:30am-9:30pm. **Telephone Code:** 473.

Telegrams: Sopeña 1 (tel. 204-29), to the right of the Teatro Juárez. Open Mon.-Fri. 9am-8pm, Sat. 9am-5pm.

Bus Station: Central de Autobuses, west of the *centro.* **Flecha Amarilla** runs second-class buses to: Morelia (every hr., 7300 pesos); Guadalajara (16 per day, 12,500 pesos); San Miguel de Allende (16 per day, 3900 pesos); San Luis Potosí (6 per day, 9500 pesos); Querétaro (every hr. 7:30am-7pm, 6300 pesos); Mexico City (14 per day, 15,500 pesos); Dolores Hidalgo (every ½ hr. 6:20am-9pm, 1600 pesos). Second-class **Estrella Blanca** (tel. 213-08) covers more or less the same area as Flecha Amarilla, charges the same, leaves less frequently, and sends a bus daily to Monterrey (31,000 pesos). First-class **Tres Estrellas de Oro** (tel. 201-04) and **Omnibus de México** go to fewer places less frequently and more expensively, but they do make the long trip to Tijuana (122,000 pesos).

Laundromat: Lavandería y Tintoria El Centro, Sopeña 26 (tel. 206-80), up the street from the Teatro Juárez. 4000-8000 pesos per load, depending on size. Takes about 6 hr. but they do a fantastic job. Open Mon.-Fri. 9am-8:15pm, Sat. 9am-3:30pm.

Red Cross: (tel. 204-87) on Juárez just west of the tourist office.

Pharmacy: Farmacia La Perla de Guanajuato, Juárez 146 (tel. 211-75). Makes deliveries. Open daily 9am-9pm.

Hospital: Pardo 5 (tel. 208-59), across from the Templo del Pardo. 24-hr. emergency service.

Police: Alhóndiga 8 (tel. 202-66 or 227-17), 1 block from Juárez.

Accommodations

Many of Guanajuato's hotels cater to tourists who demand a TV, private bath, electric blow-dryer, and other such amenities. Cheap hotels are spread along Juárez, with the greatest number at its western end near the bus station and the Alhóndiga. If you're coming for the Entremeses Cervantinos and don't want to sleep in the streets, make reservations in advance. Also call ahead for any of the more expensive hotels listed below, since Mexican student and business groups often book them solid.

Near the Basilica and Beyond the Teatro Juárez

This area, several blocks east of the bus station and Alhóndiga, is by far the best location in town for budget rooms.

Casa Kloster, Alonso 32 (tel. 200-88). Walk down Juárez and take a right onto Callejón de la Estrella just before the basilica. Art-deco exterior and profusely pink interior. Best asset: owner Jesús Pérez, who treats you like one of the family. The guestbook sings his praises in many different tongues. Rooms surround an open courtyard filled with flowers, plants, and birds. Friendly, fun, and interesting guests. Clean common bath. 12,500 pesos per person.

Hotel Posada Molinero del Rey, Campaneros 15 (tel. 222-23). Walk down Sopeña past the Teatro Juárez; when you reach a big yellow church, bear left with the main road and then take a right on the first *callejón* you come to (Campaneros). After you see the Molino del Rey restaurant, continue around the corner to the hotel office. Spanish decor; all rooms look onto a central courtyard complete with fountain, stone columns, and brick arches. Clean, pretty rooms, with brick-domed ceilings and tiled baths. The lobby TV receives a few strong channels and a daily paper. Singles 48,300 pesos. Doubles 52,000 pesos.

Hotel Posada La Condesa, Pl. de la Paz 60 (tel. 214-62), next door to the Mandel Travel Agency. The lobby is a wild and crazy mix of neon, Mexican kitsch, and rusty suits of armor. Less interesting are the cramped rooms that smell like pool chemicals. Singles 15,000 pesos. Doubles 25,000 pesos.

Hostería de Frayle, Sopeña 3 (tel. 211-79), 1 block from the Teatro Juárez. The lobby looks like a rustic ranch retreat and the winding stairway that leads to the rooms only enhances the effect. Large doubles and 24-hr. hot water do not make the price any more palatable. Singles 76,500 pesos. Doubles 80,500 pesos.

On Avenida Juárez

This area, close to the tourist office, has the greatest concentration of budget hotels. The Hotel Central is a cut above the rest.

Hotel Central, Juárez 111 (tel. 200-80). All the rooms have nicely tiled floors and plenty of light. The cozy beds and the pitter-patter of rain in the plant-filled courtyard lure guests to sleep. One drawback: tepid "hot" water. Singles 25,000 pesos. Doubles 34,000 pesos.

Hotel Juárez, Juárez 117, across from the tourist office. Some of the rooms have old temperamental locks that might give you trouble. The doubles are tiny, the hot water weak, and rain tends to congregate in puddles on the 2nd-floor landing. Otherwise, very liveable lodgings. Singles 20,000 pesos. Doubles 25,000 pesos.

Hotel Posada San Francisco, Juárez at Gavira (tel. 220-84), across from the market. Blue bathrooms and pink rooms make you feel like you're expecting a baby, and are generally as clean as a delivery room. The 2nd-floor lounging area has a TV and what appears to be an old steamer trunk alongside a suit of armor. Singles 25,000 pesos. Doubles 30,000 pesos.

Posada Hidalgo, Juárez 220 (tel. 214-90). The stairs in this dank, musty place are like Guanajuato's streets: crooked and haphazard. The rooms are tiny and none too clean. Singles 15,000 pesos. Doubles 20,000 pesos.

Near Alhóndiga

These hotels, farthest from the center of town, are either around the Alhóndiga itself or north along the avenue of the same name.

Hotel Sacavón, Alhóndiga 41-A (tel. 266-66). Entryway is not for the claustrophobic, but the rooms are great with wood-beamed ceilings. The copper sinks in the bathrooms are a nice touch. Singles 46,000 pesos. Doubles 52,000 pesos.

Hotel Mineral de Rayas, Alhóndiga 7 (tel. 219-67). A maze of brick arches and stairways. Small tiled bathrooms accompany small rooms, some with small balconies. No two bedspreads alike. Singles 35,000 pesos. Doubles 46,000 pesos.

Hotel Alhóndiga, Insurgencia 49 (tel. 205-25), on a street perpendicular to the Alhóndiga. Colonial decor is more U.S.-colonial than Mexican-colonial. Big lobby with small TV. Rooms are clean, but hot water spurts like a *turista* victim in the morning. Singles 30,000 pesos. Doubles 40,000 pesos.

Hotel Minero (tel. 252-51), on Alhóndiga next to the police station. Neat old black-and-white photos in the lobby make it the most interesting room in the hotel. Wooden stairs lead to carpeted rooms with clean and simple baths. Singles 46,000 pesos. Doubles 51,000 pesos.

Hotel Murillo, Insurgencia 9 (tel. 218-84). A plaque in the lobby proudly proclaims this hotel to be a 1983 member of the Mexican Hotel and Motel Association. Rooms smell like they haven't been cleaned since membership was attained. It ain't worth the inflated rates, folks. Singles and doubles 55,000 pesos.

Food

Guanajuato proffers a large number of economical dining options. You will find particularly good deals at the public market, where intense competition keeps the food cheap and tasty.

Cafetería Nueva, Allende 3, in Jardín Unión. Excellent central location and extremely low prices make it the best breakfast place in Guanajuato, with espresso machine, creative graffiti, and a bulletin board advertising local cultural events. Clientele a mix of university students and *norteamericanos.* The jukebox blares international rock music. Eggs 1500-3000 pesos. *Antojitos* 2500-5000 pesos. Open daily 8am-9:30pm.

Centro Nutricional Vegetariano, Ponciano Aguilar 45, 1 block to left of the basilica. Read your horoscope from the placemat as you wait. Great vegetarian selections 2000-8000 pesos. *Comida corrida* includes salad, soup, entree, and a fruit yogurt dessert (6500 pesos). Great lemonade 2200 pesos. Open Mon.-Sat. 11am-9pm.

Café El Retiro, Sopeña 12, across from the Teatro Juárez. Nice art posters and very bright tablecloths light up the high-ceilinged room. Not for those times when you're in a hurry—service is of the slug genus. Big tacos 4000-6000 pesos. *Tortas* 2500-3000 pesos. Open daily 8:15am-11pm.

Las Palomas, on Ayuntamiento, 2 doors to the right of the post office. An art gallery/restaurant with masks and many representations of Don Quixote. Never too crowded. *Comida corrida* 8000 pesos. Open daily 8:30am-11pm.

Pizza Piazza, Plazuela de San Fernando 24, just north of Jardín Unión. Often packed with students. Simple decor and great pizza. A small pizza fills two stomachs, and is as close as it comes to the real thing in Mexico. Small cheese 8500 pesos. Large "Pizza Piazza" 19,000 pesos. Branches at Juárez 69-A and Hidalgo 14, Pl. de los Pastitos. Open daily 2-11pm.

Restaurant El Agora, Allende at Hidalgo. A fine-weather haunt, with tables around a courtyard. The wrought-iron chairs don't encourage a leisurely meal. Miner's enchilada 7000 pesos. Open daily 9am-5pm.

La Bohemia, Alonso 61, downhill from Casa Kloster. Think green. Their boom box plays Mexi-pop while you eat. Great prices. *Comida corrida* 7000 pesos, good breakfasts 4000-5000 pesos. Open Mon.-Sat. 7:30am-10:30pm.

La Fuente, Juárez 140. Miniscule shop and counter. Baskets of fruit hang from the walls. One of the few quick yogurt spots in town. *Tortas* only 2000 pesos. Open daily 8am-11pm.

Pastelería La Paz, Aguilar 53, to the left of the basilica. A great little pastry shop. Treats are very rich; make sure your stomach is as big as your eyes. Fancy creamy pastries 700-1200 pesos. Cookies of all kinds 400 pesos. Open daily 7am-9:30pm.

Restaurant Central, in the Hotel Central on Juárez. Fancy blue tile lines the walls, along with cupboards full of pretty little dishes. Generally the food is filling but not fantastic, though the terrific *xicana* (9000 pesos) is possibly the best in Mexico. Open daily 9am-10pm.

Sights

Though the city is built in a ravine, Guanajuato's oldest and most central streets and alleys are flat. Massive brick-and-stone bridges, once aqueducts, crisscross the city. Columns of *cantera verde*—stone layered in greenish tones—mark many of Guanajuato's colonial structures (including the interior of the Alhóndiga de Granaditas and the porch of the Plazuela de Roque). At night, guitarists roam the streets, folk groups play in plazas, and bars resound with oldies.

To take a self-guided walking tour of the city's jagged, steep *callejones,* follow the signs and arrows. These walking tours are generally mobbed by tourists, and the sometimes inaccurate arrangement of signs makes them falter, but the tours are a good, quick way to see Guanajuato's chaotic entrails. The most popular is "Ruta 2," between Plazuela de los Angeles and the Templo de San Diego. This route takes in the most famous alley in the city, the **Callejón del Beso** (Alley of the Kiss), which at some points is narrower than one meter. Tradition has it that two lovers who lived on opposite sides of the alley were kept apart by their families but could still kiss each other from their balconies.

Museums in Guanajuato explore the historical, the artistic, the monumental, and the macabre. Qualifying for the latter is the **Museo de las Momias,** next to the city cemetery. The minerals and salty water of Guanajuato's soil naturally mummified the 100-odd corpses now on display in the museum. Exhumation began a century ago when the state government decreed that those in city cemeteries whose relatives did not begin paying crypt rights within two years would have to be disinterred. Somebody decided to put them on exhibit, and before long lucrative business sprang up from the dead soil. Stomachless, withered, puckered like raisins, with crinkled skin thin as dead leaves, the mummies lean against the walls in convulsive postures. A guide points out the purplish, inflated body of a drowning victim; a woman buried alive, frozen in her attempt to scratch her way out of the coffin; George Washington, in the "crossing the Delaware" posture; a Chinese woman; two fashionable Frenchmen; a man who died by hanging and another who was stabbed. Some buried babies still wear the colorful attire of saints: they were dressed like St. Martin and St. Joseph to ensure divine intercession on their ride to heaven. And don't miss the smallest mummy in the world, which resembles the creature that Sigourney Weaver needed two movies and an Oscar nomination to kill. The mummies are the most popular sight in Guanajuato, and they draw a much more alluring crowd than the duller museums downtown. At the exit, vendors hawk candy figurines of the most memorable mummies. The museum is west of town; to get there, catch a "Momias" bus (400 pesos) in front of the Cine or Mercado. (Open daily 9am-6pm. Admission 2000 pesos. Photo permit 1000 pesos.)

The **Museo de la Alhóndiga de Granaditas** (tel. 211-12), 1 block north of the tourist office, is more conventional. Constructed as a granary between 1797 and 1809, this building witnessed some of the most crucial and bloody battles in the fight for Mexican independence. In 1810, the supporters of Spanish rule locked themselves inside to defend the building against rebels led by the priest Don Miguel Hidalgo y Costilla. The rebels won the battle after an *indígena* mine worker known as Pípila set the locked door on fire. Later that same year, many leaders of the independence movement, among them Hidalgo, Juan Aldama, and Ignacio Allende, were captured and decapitated. Their heads were put on display for several years at the Alhóndiga and removed only after the Spaniards were vanquished from the country. (A sign outside indicates where Hidalgo's head hung.) Now the Alhóndiga is an ethnographic, archeological, and historical museum.

A chamber on the first floor of the museum charts the course of Mexico's nationhood. Other exhibits display *indígena* artisanry of the Bajío region: toys, masks, firecrackers, engraved machetes, tapestries, clay *indígena* deities, and odd little candy dolls and sculptures of horse skeletons, to be consumed on *Día de los Muertos* (Day of the Dead). The hall containing huge busts of the heroes of independence is stunning, but the museum's finest exhibit—and one of the best historical accounts in any Mexican museum—traces the social history of Guanajuato from the Conquest through the Revolution with texts, illustrations, and local artifacts. Another gallery shows Romualdo García's photographs of Mexican people just before the Revolution of 1910. (Open Tues.-Sat. 10am-2pm and 4-6pm, Sun. 10am-4pm. Admission 1000 pesos, free Sun. Photo permit 1000 pesos.)

The **Museo y Casa de Diego Rivera,** Pocitos 47 (tel. 211-97), chronicles the life of the muralist, Guanajuato's most famous native son. A few paintings record Rivera's search for a uniquely Mexican aesthetic. In 1920, after Impressionist and Cubist experiments, Rivera turned to the distinctive composition, simple forms, and bright color of *indígena* frescoes. These early works, such as *Paisaje Zapatista,* foreshadow Rivera's later style. Don't miss his outstanding watercolor illustrations for the *Popol Vuh* (sacred book of the Mayas), in which he imitates Mayan iconography; the gigantic puppets he designed for local carnivals; and a sketch for a section of the mural commissioned in 1933 by New York's Rockefeller Center that was destroyed after a portrait of Lenin was discovered in it. (A second version now hangs in the Palacio de Bellas Artes in Mexico City.) This sketch, which portrays a woman enslaved by a machine with the head of Adolf Hitler, was not incorporated into the final mural. Downstairs, the home of the Rivera family has been restored to its condition at the time of Diego's birth. (Open Tues.-Sat. 10am-1:30pm and 4-6:30pm, Sun. 10am-2:30pm. Admission 1000 pesos.)

The **Museo del Pueblo de Guanajuato,** Pocitos 7, next to the Universidad de Guanajuato, was inaugurated in 1979. It features rotating exhibits of local artwork, 18th-century religious oils, one gallery of colorful pre-Conquest ceramics, and samples of the Bajío's best pottery. Two rooms are dedicated to the work of recent local artists Olga Costa and José Chávez Morado. Chávez Morado has recently finished a new mural in what served as the Baroque chapel of this ancient building. The hall, which hosts chamber music concers, is also decorated by stained glass and murals with *indígena* motifs and Mexican poetry. (Open Tues.-Sat. 10am-2pm and 4-7pm, Sun. 10am-4pm. Admission 1000 pesos.)

The newest and most single-minded museum in Guanajuato is the **Museo Iconográfico del Quijote,** Manuel Doblado 1 (tel. 267-21), east of the Jardín Unión. Housed in a gorgeous colonial mansion, its 10 big galleries contain over 600 works of art inspired by Cervantes' Don Quijote: paintings and sculptures, stained-glass windows, candlesticks, and clocks. Dalí, Picasso, Daumier, and Pedro Coronel have all interpreted Quijote; so have scores of lesser-knowns. The collection as a whole is staggering. (Open Tues.-Sat. 10am-6:30pm, Sun. 10am-2:30pm. Admission 700 pesos.)

The *Jardín Unión,* in the heart of the city, 1 block east of the basilica, is the town's social center. This triangular plaza has shops, cafés, and enough guitar-strumming locals to appease the tourist throngs. Looking down on the Jardín from the nearby hill is the **Monumento a Pípila,** which commemorates the miner who torched the Alhóndiga's front door. The angry, titanic effigy of Pípila looks most impressive at night, when it is brightly illuminated by spotlights. To reach the statue, follow Sopeña to the east and take the steep Callejón del Calvario to your right (a 10-min. climb).

The **Teatro Juárez** (tel. 201-83) faces one corner of Jardín Unión. After designing the theater to suit his tastes, Porfirio Díaz inaugurated the building in 1903 for a Verdi opera. The Romanesque façade is exuberantly ostentatious, consisting of 10 lampposts with multiple branching lights, 12 columns, two bronze lions, and nine statues of the Muses standing loftily on the cornices. The auditorium is an overwhelming exercise in Moorish design: half-circles, arabesques, and endlessly weaving frescoed flowers in green, red, yellow, and brown make the interior look like a gigantic Arabian carpet. Imported materials, such as embellished metal and textiles from France, and stained glass from Italy, abound in the smoking rooms, bar, and corridors. On one stairway, a rich painting depicts the old emblem of Guanajuato—a blindfolded virgin who stands for unconditional faith. The blindfold was removed by revolutionaries to signify that the Porfiriato could no longer deceive the people with illusions of fortune and progress. The Teatro Juárez still hosts plays, governmental addresses, and the main events of the Festival Cervantino. (Open Tues.-Sun. 9am-2pm and 5-8pm. Admission 1500 pesos. Camera permit 1000 pesos.)

Another self-aggrandizing Porfirian edifice is the **Palacio Legislativo de la Paz,** the state capitol, across from the Posada de la Condesa near the basilica. Inaugurated by Díaz in 1900, the building is an adaptation of the Greek Parthenon. Italian marble, wall and floor mosaics, and a decorative zinc ceiling ornament the interior. (Open for viewing Mon.-Fri. 10am-5pm; extended and weekend hours for special events. Free.)

Outdoors, the many parks, plazas, and lakes of the city provide simpler pleasure. **Los Pastitos,** a stretch of breezy plazas and lawns along Hidalgo in the west end of the city next to the train station, is nearly undisturbed by tourism. You can't miss the prominent **Monumento al Minero,** erected in honor of *guanajuatense* miners. Nearby, pine trees, shrubs, and royal poincianas decorate the tidy **Plaza el Cantador.** On the opposite end of town lie the **Presa de la Olla** and the **Presa de San Renovato,** reservoirs on either side of quiet, trimmed **Parque Florencio Antillón.** Rowboats on the dock of Presa de la Olla rent for 5000 pesos per hour. (Open daily 10am-7pm.) In the neighborhood surrounding the Presas stand many of the mansions built by wealthy Guanajuatan mine owners. The white Moorish towers known as **El Faro,** high in the mountains to the right of the reservoirs, make a good climb. Tread carefully up the mountain, since there is neither a stairway nor any obvious path. From here, you can admire the peculiar jutting stone mounds that have inspired many *guanajuatense* painters. To get to this part of town, take an east-bound "Presa" bus (400 pesos), which stops at the Underground stop by the Mercado.

Dozens of candelabra in the lush Doric interior of the **Basílica de Nuestra Señora de Guanajuato** illuminate fine ornamental frescoes, relics, and three paintings of the Madonna by Miguel Cabrera. The wooden image of the city's protector, Nuestra Señora de Guanajuato, rests on a pure silver base and is believed to be the oldest piece of Christian art in Mexico. But the landmark basilica's Baroque façade is unimpressive, and its exterior walls are painted crimson and orange.

Next to the university and 1 block north of the basilica is the more interesting Jesuit **Templo de la Compañía.** The temple was finished in 1765, but shut down two years later when the Jesuits were expelled from Latin America. Characterized by eccentric *estípite* pilasters, the façade shows off Guanajuato's Churrigueresque architecture at its best. (Open daily 7am-8pm.)

One block east of the basilica and to the right of the Teatro Juárez in Jardín Unión, the façade of the Franciscan **Templo de San Diego** incorporates effigies of Franciscan monks and Churrigueresque columns that spiral upward. Inside, huge canvases tell St. Francis's life story, but age and neglect have been unkind to the oils; the pictorial biography now recalls a postmodernist pastiche. (Open daily 7am-8pm.)

The high, greenish parapets of the **Universidad de Guanajuato** are visible from the middle segment of Av. Juárez. The university was founded as a Jesuit school in 1724 and received its current title in 1945. It excels in the humanities and performing arts—summer workshops are given in these subjects. Recently, an annex was added to further the school's technical studies; made entirely of glowing *cantera verde,* it conforms to the university's wonderful colonial design. University cultural activities are usually held in the theaters and galleries around town. For information consult the Oficina de Difusión Cultural or check the bulletin boards.

Mercado Hidalgo, 1 block east of the tourist office, went up in 1910 with a monumental Neoclassical arch as an entrance. Inside, both the seafood *coctelerías* and the vendors who sell musical instruments are trustworthy. Guanajuato's famed ceramics mugs have declined in quality, but outside, the woolen items are quite cheap and the wide variety of sombreros will satisfy any head. (Most vendors open daily 9am-9pm.)

Finally, about 3km north of Guanajuato stands the Templo de San Cayetano, better known as **La Valenciana.** The church took 23 years to build (1765-1788) and possesses three magnificent altars, carved from wood and covered with a sheet of 24-karat gold. Its huge façade is as splendid as that of the Templo de la Compañía. To get to the church, take the "Valenciana" bus (400 pesos), which leaves approximately every hour from the street immediately downhill from the Alhóndiga de Granaditas. (Open daily 9am-6pm.)

Entertainment

Each year, for two or three weeks in late October, Guanajuato stages the **Festival Internacional Cervantino,** also known by its old name, the Entremeses Cervantinos. The city invites repertory groups from all over the world to participate with the *estudiantinas,* strolling student minstrels of the Universidad de Guanajuato. The festival takes place mostly at local theaters. Guanajuatans put on the bulk of the always sold-out dramatic productions and foreigners contribute films, folk dances, and music ranging from classical and opera to jazz and rock. Make hotel reservations early.

From June 22 to 26, Guanajuato celebrates the **Feria de San Juan** at the Presa de la Olla with cultural events, fireworks, sports, and much more. Similar but shorter celebrations occur on **Día de la Cueva** (July 1), on May 31, and on August 9 (commemorating the arrival of the Virgin of Guanajuato to the city). The religious celebrations in December include the famous *posadas.*

Throughout the year, theater, dance, and music are performed regularly if less frequently; check the tourist office for information, or consult the posters around town. Student groups present films almost every day of the week. Call the **Teatro Principal** (tel. 215-26), the **Teatro Cervantes** (tel. 211-69), or the **Teatro Juárez** (tel. 201-83) for specifics. (Tickets 1500-2500 pesos.)

The bars and cafés in the immediate vicinity of the Jardín Unión are friendly and comfortable, even for single women; **La Perla,** right on the Jardín, is probably the classiest of the bunch. For a non-stop disco inferno, look to **Sancho's,** Pl. de Cata (cover averages 20,000 pesos). Other popular discos include **Galería** in the Hotel Parador San Javier (cover 20,000 pesos); **El Jardín** in the Hotel Paseo de la Presa, on the Carretera Panorámica between Pípila and the ISSTE clinic; and the new **Chely Oh** on Insurgentes off Alhóndiga (cover 10,000 pesos).

The most offbeat and entertaining club in town is **El Rincón del Beso** (a.k.a. Peña Bohemia), on Alonso east of Casa Kloster. The nightly sing-alongs and riotous poetry interpretations get going around 11pm (no cover). All the discos listed above are open Thursday through Saturday from 9pm to 2am.

El Pequeño Juan, near the Pípila on the Carretera Panorámica, is a very small bar with large windows that afford incredible views of the city. The plush **El Cantador,** Nejayote 17, in the luxurious Hotel Real d'Minas, features live groups doing romantic Spanish numbers. **Chez Santos,** on Guillermo Valle near the music school, mimics the interior of a mine, with high stone walls and large wooden beams across the ceiling. The dark, romantic atmosphere and tranquil music call for candlelight. Drinks at these clubs are 5000-6000 pesos.

Near Guanajuato

About 20km from Guanajuato, on top of a mountain 2850m above sea level, is the **Monumento a Cristo Rey,** completed in 1956. The mountain, called the **Cerro del Cubilete,** is considered the geographical center of Mexico. The dark bronze statue of Jesus is over 16m tall and weighs more than 80 tons. During the first phase of construction, workers had to drag themselves more than 12km to get a drink of water. When told of the problem by architect Carlos Olvera, Monseñor Valverde y Téllez answered, "The work must go on no matter what the sacrifice; God will tell us where to find water. Go Trailblazers." A few weeks later, water sprang forth near the crest of the mountain. Although the statue is striking, you may spend more time observing the surrounding landscape; miles of undulating green and blue are visible from the top, and on rainy days you may be above the clouds. Take the "Montaña" or "Cubilete" bus from the bus station (1 hr., 2000 pesos).

Dolores Hidalgo

On Sunday, September 16, 1810, the people of Dolores were awoken by the tolling of the parish church bell. In response they gathered at the church, were they heard the priest Don Miguel Hidalgo y Costilla proclaim Mexico's independence from Spain. After this *Grito de Dolores,* Hidalgo's supporters followed him to Mexico City, gathering recruits along the way. When he reached the outskirts of his destination, Hidalgo inexplicably turned back. Months later he was captured and decapitated by royalists in northern Mexico. In 1947, the Mexican government declared Dolores Hidalgo the "Cradle of Independence."

Today, the only things cradled in this sleepy town are a handful of museums and many memories of a few brief days of glory. The best way to see Dolores is on a daytrip from San Miguel or Guanajuato.

Orientation and Practical Information

Dolores Hidalgo sits in the middle of the state of Guanajuato, about 50km northeast of the state capital, and about 42km away from San Miguel de Allende. To get downtown from the bus station at Hidalgo and Chiapas, walk straight out the door, take a left on Hidalgo, and go 3 blocks. This brings you to the Jardín, the tourist office, Pl. Principal, and the Parroquia. The **Río Dolores** runs east-west through the city; streets are arranged in a grid parallel and perpendicular to the river. A city map is useful since streets have different names on opposite sides of the city.

Tourist Office: Delegación de Turismo (tel. 209-65), on Pl. Principal next to the Parroquia. The staff is young and ill-informed and they may try to force a poster down your throat. On the city map, Yucatán St. is misnamed Chihuahua north of the river. Open Mon.-Fri. 9am-7pm, Sat.-Sun. 10am-2pm.

Currency Exchange: Banco del Centro, Guerrero and Jalisco (tel. 207-55), on the southeast corner of the Pl. Principal. Open for currency exchange Mon.-Fri. 9am-noon.

Post Office: Puebla 22 (tel. 208-07). Open Mon-Fri. 9am-7pm, Sat. 9am-noon. **Postal Code:** 37800.

Telephones: Restaurante Plaza, on the south side of the plaza. International collect calls 3000 pesos. Open Mon.-Sat. 9am-2pm and 4-8pm. The **Hotel Caudillo** provides 24-hr. service for guests. International collect calls 2000 pesos. **Telephone Code:** 468.

Telegrams: Puebla 22 (tel. 204-63), in the post office. Open Mon.-Fri. 9am-7pm, Sat. 9am-noon.

Bus Station: Hidalgo at Chiapas. **Flecha Amarilla** (tel. 206-39) to: Mexico City (every hr., 13,500 pesos); Guanajuato (every ½ hr., 2300 pesos); San Miguel (every ½ hr., 1700 pesos); Querétaro (every hr., 4300 pesos).

Pharmacy: Farmacia Libertad, Hidalgo 9 (tel. 209-37). Open daily 9am-11pm.

Hospital: Hospital Ignacio Allende, Hidalgo 12 (tel. 200-13).

Police: In the Cárcel Municipal (tel. 200-21), on San Luis Potosí 1 block north of the Pl. Principal.

Accommodations

Most of the lodgings in this village are classy for the sake of urban tourists visiting their national shrine. Nonetheless, they are reasonably priced, especially compared to those in San Miguel. Even so, you might wish to stay in San Miguel or Guanajuato because there isn't much to keep you occupied here, unless you enjoy browsing in ceramic shops day after day.

Hotel Caudillo, Querétaro 8 (tel. 201-98), across from the Parroquia, down the street from Hotel Cocomacán. Spacious rooms with beautiful ceramic-tiled ceilings and baths. Large, popular restaurant out front wines and dines you at moderate prices. Singles 27,000 pesos. Doubles 36,000 pesos.

Hotel Posada Cocomacán, Querétaro at Guanajuato (tel. 200-18). The best courtyard in the city with abundant flowers and potted plants. Rooms are fairly spacious and bathrooms paved with almost as much tile as those at the Caudillo. Hot water 7-10am. Singles 22,000 pesos. Doubles 38,000 pesos.

Posada Dolores, Yucatán 8, 1 block west of the Pl. Principal. Cheap and built to stay that way. Run by a couple of old ladies with failing power of vision, the rooms have interesting (to say the least) color schemes. Pastel tiles in the courtyard remind you of your ancestral home in Virginia. The common bathrooms are passable, but watch out for stray skateboards. The lone double has its own bath. Singles 10,000 pesos. Double 20,000 pesos.

Food

Dolores Hidalgo is no gastronomic paradise; in fact, it's a Taco Bell straight out of purgatory. You will miss little by sticking to hotel cafeterias.

Aladino's, Pl. Principal 8. Good food at great prices in a restaurant with very high ceilings and cloth napkins. Tartan tablecloths clash with the Spanish and Mexican pictures on the wall. *Menú del día* 11,000 pesos. Small but superb chicken *mole* enchiladas 3800 pesos. Open daily 9am-11pm.

Restaurant El Delfín, Guerrero at Veracruz. Don't be fooled by the innocent-lookingbottle of picante sauce on the table, but if you do slip up, they stock 6 types of beer (all under 2000 pesos) to cool your tongue. Mostly seafood dishes. Open daily 9am-7pm.

Fruti-Yoghurt, Hidalgo 2. Plenty of fresh fruit, yogurt, and delicious homemade cake in a small, colorful shop with jars of vitamins on display. Sit at the counter and chat with the mixers. Good fruit yogurt with granola 2100 pesos. Open daily 9am-3pm and 5-9pm.

Sights

Mexico's "Cradle of Independence" is a tiny peasant community. The beautiful **Parroquia,** where the *Grito de Dolores* was sounded, still stands. Constructed between 1712 and 1778, the church, with its large and intricately worked façade and twin towers of pink stone, dominates the Pl. Principal. Although the interior is dusty and somewhat deteriorated, the two side altars are magnificent examples of Baroque art. It's not unusual for Mexico's presidents to return to the Parroquia on the anniversary of Hidalgo's proclamation to repeat it verbatim.

The **Museo Casa Hidalgo,** at Morelos and Hidalgo, 1 block from the Pl. Principal, was Hidalgo's home from 1804 until 1810. His furniture and belongings, as well as documents relating to the independence movement, are on display. (Open Tues.-Sat. 10am-6pm, Sun. and holidays 10am-5pm. Admission 10,000 pesos, free Sun.)

Also of some interest is the **Museo Independencia,** Zacatecas 6, 1 block northwest of the Parroquia. Here the exigencies of Spanish rule, the onset of independence, and the life and works of Miguel Hidalgo are presented in murals and dioramas. Some of the paintings are a bit grisly, and not for Cortés-o-philes. (Open Mon.-Fri. 9am-3pm and 4-7pm, Sat.-Sun. 9am-2pm. Admission 1000 pesos.)

Dolores Hidalgo is Mexico's foremost ceramic center. Hundreds of workshops sell dazzling dinnerware, glazed and unglazed flowerpots, and hand-painted tiles. The smaller streets sometimes yield workmanship of much higher quality.

The **Fiestas Patrias** are celebrated September 1-17, and most of the cultural activities (folk dancing and singing), athletic tournaments (basketball, baseball, soccer), and fireworks take place during the final week.

VERACRUZ

Because of its central location on Mexico's Gulf Coast, Veracruz ends up on a surprising number of itineraries. Even if you plan only a short stopover here, the state's archeological ruins and museums may lure you to stay longer. The beaches are by no means pristine, but they'll hold their own unless you were weaned on the sands of Cancún, and modest resorts frequented mostly by Mexican travelers line the central stretch of the Veracruz coast. Mexico's highest mountain, Pico de Orizaba (also known as Citlaltépetl; 5100m) towers overhead. The principal city, Veracruz, is a medium-sized port famed for its history, music, and friendly residents, and the 16th-century churches in virtually every town serve as silent reminders that this area was the springboard for Cortés's conquest of the Aztecs.

Veracruz

As his first point of order upon reaching the east coast of New Spain in 1519, Hernando Cortés constructed a base from which he would launch one of the world's most amazing military episodes. After the Spanish Conquest, his coastal headquarters grew into Veracruz, the principal city (pop. 400,000) and main port in the state of the same name.

During the ensuing 482-year period, Veracruz has seen many foreign soldiers march across its beaches: in 1825, the Spanish attempted a reconquest, this time of the newly created and independent Mexico; 13 years later the French army tramped through Veracruz; and the Americans successfully occupied the port in 1847. Finally, Mexican turned on Mexican inside city limits during the Revolution of 1910. The crumbling fortresses along the coast bear witness to the extensive destruction, but these days their seaward-pointed cannons seem only to safeguard the revelry taking place inside their perimeter.

In most Mexican cities, travelers stroll wide-eyed through the streets, hungrily devouring the visual splendors. Veracruz, however, assaults two senses simultaneously. You do not walk through Veracruz—you float on a current of music. The number of *marimba* bands squeezed into the Zócalo defies reason, and many restaurants and bars have nightly live music. In the evening, brassy military and civic bands blare through the plaza as the flag of the Republic is lowered. When the sun disappears altogether and the sights of Veracruz fade into the humid night, the music takes over. The already incredible number of *marimba* bands in the Zócalo somehow multiplies and is joined by *salsa* rhythms and a stream of melancholy *mariachi* crooners.

As Mexico's major port on the Gulf Coast, Veracruz hosts sailors and merchants from around the world. A strong Caribbean accent lilts in the speech of some of the inhabitants, while others have a European inflection, and any number of regional Mexican accents will test the limits of your Spanish. Other cultures influence not just the city's voices but also its architecture, a graceful hybrid of the colonial and the modern. Although Veracruz offers few standard tourist sights, the Zócalo is one of the most congenial hangouts in all of Mexico.

Orientation

Veracruz lies on the southwestern shore of the Gulf of Mexico. Tampico is 535km to the north via Rte. 180; Jalapa, the state capital, sits 140km inland via Rte. 140; Puebla and Mexico City are due west on Rte. 150, 304km and 421km respectively; and Oaxaca is 530km to the south.

Veracruz's **Central de Autobuses** houses both the first- and second-class bus stations. First-class ADO lies directly on Díaz Mirón, the city's major cross-town street; second-class AU opens onto La Fragua, 1 block to the east. About 14 blocks north of the Central de Autobuses (to the right when leaving the building) the Parque Zamora interrupts Mirón. Seven blocks on Independencia beyond the park, buildings give way to the Zócalo. Buses labeled "Díaz Mirón" travel along Díaz Mirón to Parque Zamora and points farther downtown (300 pesos). Taxis will take you downtown for 4000 pesos.

The **train station** is at the north end of the Pl. de la República. To reach the Zócalo from the station, turn right from the exit, walk diagonally across the plaza, and turn right on Lerdo at the far end of the plaza; the Zócalo is 2 blocks ahead. Taxis from the Central de Autobuses to the train station cost 4500 pesos.

The city's **airport** is 4km south of town on Rte. 150. Taxis to the Zócalo cost 20,000 pesos. *Colectivos* cruise downtown for 4600 pesos.

Downtown Veracruz is laid out grid-style with streets either parallel or perpendicular to the coast. Diáz Mirón runs north-south and converges with Av. 20 de Noviembre south of downtown at the **Parque Zamora.** Here, the two streets become Independencia, the main downtown drag.

Independencia forms the western boundary of the **Zócalo,** also called the Pl. de Armas or Pl. de la Constitución. The northern boundary, Lerdo, runs east and becomes the southern limit of the Pl. de la República, home of the train station and post office, and drop-off point for many municipal bus routes. Insurgentes, 1 block south of the Zócalo behind the cathedral, runs east into Campeche; the two streets serve as Veracruz's waterfront promenade.

Practical Information

Most services are conveniently located downtown, either near the Zócalo, on Independencia, or in the Pl. de la República.

Municipal Tourist Office: In the Palacio Municipal (tel. 32-16-13), on the Zócalo. Young staff doesn't speak English but distributes reams of excellent maps and pamphlets. The photocopied downtown map is especially useful. Open daily 9am-9pm.

U.S. Consulate: Consul Edwin L. Culp, Juárez 110 (tel. 31-01-42 or 31-58-20). As president of Veracruz's Consulate Association, he is helpful to non-U.S. citizens as well.

Currency Exchange: Bancomer and **Bánamex** both have branches at the intersection of Independencia and Juárez, 1 block from the Zócalo. Bancomer (tel. 32-46-01) is open Mon.-Fri. 9:30am-1:30pm, for exchange Mon.-Fri. 10am-noon. Bánamex (tel. 36-05-80) is open Mon.-Fri. 9:30am-1:30pm. **Banco Internacional,** Independencia at Constitución (tel. 35-23-30), is open Mon.-Fri. 9am-1pm and 4-6pm. Both Bánamex and Banco International have automated tellers that accept Cirrus and Mastercard. **La Amistad Casa de Cambio,** Juárez 26 (tel. 31-59-90), is open Mon.-Fri. 9am-2pm and 4-6:45pm.

Post Office: Pl. de la República 213 (tel. 32-20-38), several blocks north of the Zócalo. Facing the Palacio Municipal, walk straight on Lerdo for 2 blocks to Advana, turn left, and walk 2 blocks to the Pl. de la República; it's the large white collonaded building on the right. Open for stamps and Lista de Correos Mon.-Fri. 8am-7pm, Sat. 9am-noon; for registered letters Mon.-Fri. 8am-7pm, Sat. 9am-noon; for money orders Mon.-Fri. 9am-2pm, Sat. 9am-noon; for packages Mon.-Fri. 7am-5pm, Sat. 9am-noon (bring open boxes to the customs department in the basement of the same building first). **Postal Code:** 91700.

Telephones: Long-distance *caseta* at Independencia 924, between Juárez and Emparan, 1½ blocks from the Zócalo. 900-peso surcharge for international calls. Open in summer Mon.-Sat. 5am-10pm (after 10pm, ring the outside bell for service). Open during the rest of the year Mon.-Sat. 7:30am-9:30pm. The Hotel Colonial also offers 24-hr. service for a price. **Telephone Code:** 29.

Telegrams: (tel. 32-44-34), on the Pl. de la República next to the post office. Open for telegrams Mon.-Fri. 8am-midnight, Sat. 8am-8pm, Sun. 9am-1pm; for money orders Mon.-Fri. 9am-5:30pm, Sat.-Sun. 9am-noon. Branch at the Central de Autobuses open for telegrams Mon.-Fri. 9am-1pm and 3-6pm, Sat.-Sun. 9am-noon; for money orders Mon.-Fri. 9am-1pm and 3-5pm, Sat.-Sun. 9am-noon. Another office (tel. 32-49-22) on 5 de Mayo between Rayón and Ocampo is only for telegrams. Open Mon.-Fri. 9am-9pm, Sat.-Sun. 9am-noon.

Airport: (tel. 34-53-78), on the highway to Mexico City, 4km south of downtown Veracruz. **Aeroméxico,** Camacho 1263 (tel. 32-75-42), at Iturbide. Office open Mon.-Fri. 9am-1pm and 3:30-9pm, Sat. 9am-1pm. To Mexico City (2 per day, 45 min., 165,000 pesos). **Mexicana,**

Independencia 837 (tel. 37-26-11) in **Viajes Carmi.** Office open Mon.-Sat. 8:30am-1pm and 3:15pm-7pm. Another branch with an English-speaking staff at the airport (tel. 37-04-73) open daily 7:30am-11pm. To Mexico City (2 per day, 45 min., 165,000 pesos).

Train Station: Ferrocarriles Nacionales de México (tel. 32-25-69), on the Pl. de la República in a large, white building near the water at the northern extreme of the plaza. Baggage check available. Ticket office open at least 1 hr. before each departure, 2½ hr. before departure of the night train to Mexico City. To Mexico City (1 per day, 8 hr., 10,400 pesos) and Jalapa (1 per day, 4 hr., 1400 pesos).

Bus Station: Díaz Mirón 1698 (tel. 37-55-22), about 20 blocks from the Zócalo. **ADO** first-class buses to: Campeche (2 per day, 15½ hr., 42,000 pesos); Coatzacoalcos (20 per day, 5½ hr., 14,500 pesos); Jalapa (36 per day, 2 hr., 5300 pesos); Mérida (2 per day, 16½ hr., 51,000 pesos); Mexico City (34 per day, 7 hr., 20,500 pesos); Puebla (9 per day, 5 hr., 14,500 pesos); San Andrés Tuxtla (23 per day, 3 hr., 7100 pesos); Santiago Tuxtla (11 per day, 2½ hr., 6500 pesos); Tuxtepec (6 per day, 4 hr., 7100 pesos); Villahermosa (13 per day, 9 hr., 22,000 pesos). **Second-class station:** (tel. 37-38-78), on La Fragua behind ADO, in the building that shares the ADO parking lot.

Taxis: Servi-Taxi (tel. 37-01-59).

Car Rentals: Hertz, Serdán 14 (tel. 31-25-68). Open Mon.-Sat. 9am-1pm and 4-6pm. **Fast Auto Rental,** Lerdo 241 (tel. 36-14-16), between 5 de Mayo and Independencia. Open Mon.-Sat. 9am-2pm and 4-7pm, Sun. 9am-2pm. Both offer rates of approximately 110,000 pesos per day for a small car, plus 500 pesos per km.

Market: on Madero between Cortés and Juan Soto, 1 block south of Parque Zamora. Great *piñatas* for those willing to carry them—they're difficult to ship home. Everything from palm frond fans to fresh-cut flowers, but practical products predominate. Open daily dawn-dusk.

Laundromat: Lavandería Automática Mar y Sol, Zamora 410, between Madero and 5 de Mayo, 2½ blocks west of the Zócalo. Open Mon.-Fri. 9am-2pm and 4-8pm, Sat. 9am-5pm.

Red Cross: (tel. 37-55-00) Díaz Mirón between Alvarado and Córdoba, 1 block beyond the Central de Autobuses on Mirón. No English spoken. 24-hr. emergency service and ambulance on call.

Pharmacy: Farmacias El Mercado, Independencia 1197 (tel. 32-14-94), next to the Gran Cafe de la Parroquia. Open daily 7am-3am.

Police: (tel. 32-23-31 or 32-28-33), on Allende between Cortés and Canal. From the Zócalo, walk (with the Palacio Municipal behind you) 7 blocks on Zamora and turn left on Allende for 5½ blocks. Little English spoken. Open 24 hr.

Accommodations and Camping

Because sailors are used to the most basic of berths, cheap and simple accommodations are everywhere in Veracruz. Reservations are necessary only if you plan to stay during *Carnaval.*

Downtown Area

These hotels are either on the Zócalo or a few blocks southeast, clustered around Serdán and Landero y Coss.

Hotel Colonial, Lerdo 105 (tel. 32-01-93), on the Zócalo. All rooms have A/C, the small indoor pool is beautiful, and the balcony overlooking the Zócalo is perfect for cocktail hour. Safe in the lobby stores valuables. Singles 50,000 pesos. Doubles 65,000 pesos. A view of the Zócalo costs an additional 10,000 pesos.

Hotel Imperial, Lerdo 153 (tel. 31-17-41), on the Zócalo. Though still clean and comfortable, it has seen better days. Rooms with terraces overlooking the Zócalo are worth the additional 5000 pesos. Safe in the lobby for valuables. All rooms have fans. Singles 25,000 pesos. Doubles 30,000 pesos.

Hotel Ortiz, Lerdo 95 (tel. 32-76-80), on the Zócalo. Great location and cool indoor court-yard make this a good deal. Bathrooms function, but the sink lacks hot water and some toilets lack seats. All rooms have fans. No reservations accepted. Singles 25,000 pesos. Doubles 30,000 pesos.

Hotel Rex, Zaragoza 255 (tel. 32-54-86), on the Pl. de la República. Beautiful tiles and fertile courtyard harken back to the building's previous incarnation as a convent. Rooms are large with exposed-beam ceilings and fans, but on the grungy side. Bathrooms are moldy and host a contingent of small bugs. Singles 15,000 pesos. Doubles 25,000 pesos.

Hotel Oriente, Lerdo 20 (tel. 31-24-90), on the Pl. de la República. Immaculate, bright rooms with equivalent bathrooms. All rooms have fans, phones, and a common cold water dispenser; some have A/C and TV. Helpful staff. Rooms with balcony cost an additional 5000 pesos. Singles 35,000 pesos, with A/C 40,000 pesos. Doubles 50,000 pesos, with A/C 55,000 pesos.

Parque Zamora and Bus Station

Hotel Avenida, Uribe 1300 (tel. 32-44-92), at Mirón. Tiny lobby, wee rooms, concave beds, and blustering fans. No reservations accepted. Singles 20,000 pesos. Doubles 25,000 pesos.

Hotel Acapulco, Uribe 1327 (tel. 32-92-87), down the street from Hotel Avenida. Large, pink, shiny chambers with blooming bedspreads, good bathrooms, wall-paintings, and fans. Hot water available 6pm-9am. Singles 36,000 pesos. Doubles 45,000 pesos.

Hotel Rosa Mar, La Fragua 1100 (tel. 37-07-47), behind the ADO station. The look here is Miami. Rooms and tiny bathrooms are spotless. Singles 25,000 pesos. Doubles 30,000 pesos. Visa accepted.

Hotel Central, Díaz Mirón 1612 (tel. 37-22-22), next to the ADO station. Large, modern building with marble lobby and leatherette easy chairs. Sanitary bathrooms thoroughly worn. Ask for a room with a balcony to watch the cars race by on Díaz Mirón. All rooms have fans and phones. Singles 45,000 pesos. Doubles 65,000 pesos, with A/C 75,000 pesos.

Closer to Playa Mocambo, just south of the city, **Villa del Mar** (tel. 32-02-27) has bungalows, a pool, and a restaurant. To reach it, take the "Boca del Río" bus (500 pesos) from the corner of Zaragoza and Serdán.

Food

Seafood dominates the menus of Veracruz. Shrimp, octopus, *dorada,* red snapper, and a host of other sea beasts are dragged in daily from the Gulf. The cheapest way to enjoy these delicacies is to head for the fish market on Landero y Coss between Arista and Zaragoza. A healthy portion of *ceviche,* the regional specialty, runs about 2500 pesos. Other local favorites include *paella* (whatever happens to be on hand, mixed with saffron rice), and fish served *a la veracruzano* (in an olive, onion, tomato, and caper sauce).

The greatest concentrations of restaurants are on and around the Zócalo and in the area east of Zaragoza.

The supermarket **Chedraui,** Díaz Mirón 440 (tel. 32-30-08), on the left as you walk to the ADO station, sells everything. (Open Mon.-Sat. 8am-9pm, Sun. 8am-8pm.)

El Tiburón, Landero y Coss 167, at Serdán. The bathroom's tile interior is covered with photos of the owner schmoozing with Mexican TV personality Raúl Velasco. Its furniture reminds you that vinyl didn't die with disco. Excellent filet of fish and salad 7300 pesos. Most dishes under 12,000 pesos. Open daily 6am-7pm.

La Bilbaína, Serdán 467, at Zaragoza, 1 flight up. A family restaurant with an older crowd. Bullfighting posters and shrines to Mexican models grace the walls. The large *comida corrida* provides a big bowl of soup, a plate of *paella,* fried chicken or fish filet, plus dessert for 12,000 pesos. Open daily 1-6pm.

Gran Café de la Parroquia, Independencia 105, on the Zócalo. The place to see and be seen. A large open hall filled with the sound of clinking glasses (the preferred method for getting hot milk for your *café con leche* brought to the table) and crowded with peddlers, shoeshiners, and stooped seniors pushing lottery tickets. Outside, *marimba* bands serenade the patrons. Excellent coffee and very good breakfasts. Eggs prepared many ways for 3000 pesos. Open daily 6am-1am.

Gran Café de la Parroquia de Veracruz, Insurgentes at 16 de Septiembre. The one on the Zócalo was so popular that they opened this branch. Same menu and coffee, but the original still reigns. Open daily 5pm-midnight.

La Paella, Zamora 138, on the Zócalo. Excellent for people-watching. Large portions, friendly service. *Comida corrida* 15,000 pesos. Good fried fish served with lots of lime for 9000 pesos. Open daily 10am-10pm.

Cocteles y Mariscos del Golfo, on Montero, close to the intersection of Landero y Coss and Serdán. Family atmosphere and seafood galore in a room scattered liberally with fake plants. Three sizes of fish; medium 10,500 pesos. *Ceviche* with salad from 4500 pesos.

Sights

Most of the action in Veracruz concentrates on the Zócalo, and the most energy you need expend here to stay entertained involves moving from café to café around the plaza. A colonial cathedral takes up one side of the Zócalo, and under its high-domed mosaic ceiling, the clinking of glasses at the nearby Parroquia is barely audible.

For some tasty morsels of the city's history, visit the **Museo Histórico de la Revolución Carranza** by a small park near the waterfront, on Insurgentes between Hernandez and Xicoléncatl. The museum, also called Museo Constitucionalista, is up the stairs and to the left in a yellow colonial lighthouse, which also houses offices of the Mexican Navy. One room contains Carranza's bed, desk, and furniture, replicating the room in which ideas for reform laws and the Constitution germinated and grew. Another room traces Carranza's life from baptism to success as governor of Coahuila state. A third room marks his presidency and participation in writing the Constitution of 1917, three years before his death. (Open Tues.-Sun. 9am-1pm and 4-6pm. Free.) For a deeper glimpse into the past, visit the **Baluarte de Santiago,** on 16 de Septiembre between Canal and Rayón. This 17th-century bulwark protected inhabitants from such pirates as Francis Drake. It is the last fort still standing along the old city wall. (Museum inside open Tues.-Sun. 10am-7pm. Free.)

The **Museo Cultural de la Ciudad,** Zaragoza 397, at Morales, is a funky little museum set in an old orphanage. Check out the displays of *veracruzano* crafts, photos of the city, and scenes from daily life. Those whose travel plans don't coincide should enjoy the rooms devoted to *Carnaval*. (Open Tues.-Fri. 10am-2pm and 4-8pm, Sat.-Sun. 9am-4pm. Encouraged donation 1000 pesos.)

El Castillo de San Juan de Ulúa, begun in 1582, is another reminder of the city's former military importance. There isn't much to see inside the fort, but its architecture is intriguing, and the view across the harbor to the city is superb. To reach the fort, take the bus of the same name (500 pesos) from Landero y Coss, near Insurgentes. (Open Tues.-Sun. 9am-5pm. Admission 1000 pesos, free Sun. and holidays.)

Long ago, bathing was possible directly off the golden shores of the city. Today, however, the bay is a case study for microbiologists interested in the toxic impact of big oil on big cities. Locals still swim in the water, but considering the health risk, the trip south to the beaches at **Mocambo** is a better idea. Catch one of the frequent buses from Serdán between Landero y Coss and Zaragoza (500 pesos). Beaches become cleaner the farther you get from the city. In order beyond Mocambo, Boca del Río, Antón, Linzaro, and Laguna Mendinga offer increasingly acceptable swimming conditions.

Entertainment

The city's best entertainment is free in the Zócalo. Nightly after 8pm, the municipal band performs concerts; on Tuesdays and Fridays, they are accompanied by dance troupes. At 7pm on weekends from July to mid-September, the Zócalo hosts various artistic presentations.

Discotheque La Capilla, Independencia 1064, in the Hotel Prendes between Lerdo and Juárez, plays Top-40 rock spiced with some local *mariachi* pieces (cover 10,000 pesos; 2-drink minimum). The **Disco Morruchos,** in the Hotel Emporio at Insurgentes and Xicoléncatl on the water, is a bit more chic but plays the same tunes (cover 15,000 pesos). Both are open nightly from 10pm to 3am.

Veracruz's *Carnaval*—a nationally renowned, week-long festival of parades, concerts, and costumes—takes place in late February or early March (during the week before Ash Wednesday). Celebrated since 1925, it is the most popular Mardi Gras in Mexico. Hotel rooms are in high demand, especially on the Zócalo; make reservations early. For further information on *Carnaval,* contact the offices of the organizers, to the left of the municipal tourist office on the Zócalo.

Near Veracruz: Zempoala Ruins

The ruins at **Zempoala** are 80km northwest of Veracruz just off Rte. 180. If you have a very strong interest in archeological sites, Zempoala's history and its many well-preserved buildings may justify a tour, but both its architecture and artifacts are unspectacular.

Zempoala was one of the largest southern Totonac cities, part of a federation that covered much of Veracruz in pre-Hispanic times. In 1469, Zempoala was subdued by the Aztecs and reluctantly joined their federation. Upon Cortés's arrival in 1519, the oppressed Totonacs eagerly rebelled against the Aztecs, welcoming Carlos I of Spain as their new sovereign and joining the Spanish forces to defeat Moctezuma.

Zempoala means "Twenty Springs," evident today all around the site, especially in the partially flooded cane fields. The ceremonial center of the city lies inside a wall on higher, drier ground. Made of round volcanic stones, the site's buildings are held together by mortar and were once covered by a layer of sculpted stucco, still visible on some structures. The foundations of temples are apparent at the tops of the pyramids which crowned. A small museum displays a good collection of pottery and figurines discovered at Zempoala, as well as a helpful map. (Site open daily 8am-6:30pm. Admission 2000 pesos.)

Both **ADO** and **Autotransportes Teziutecos** provide direct service to Zempoala. First-class ADO buses depart from the ADO station (4 per day beginning at 11am, 1700 pesos). Second-class service on Autotransportes Teziutecos is less comfortable, costs a bit less, and runs more frequently. Teziutecos departs from the AU station. If driving from Veracruz, follow Rte. 180 past the city of Cardel until you come to the Zempoala city turn-off. Follow it until a half-hidden sign for the ruins appears on the right (about 1km before town).

In Zempoala, buses drop off passengers on Cuauhtémoc Sur. To get to the ruins from the Teziutecos station, walk away from the Zócalo to Hidalgo and turn right. From the ADO station, walk 1 block toward the Zócalo (away from Morelos) to Hidalgo and turn left. A bit down Hidalgo, just beyond a set of speed bumps, a sign to the left points to the ruins.

Make sure you leave the site well before nightfall because the number of operating buses decreases drastically as the sun descends. The trip from Veracruz takes about two hours.

Southern Veracruz

The polluted ports of Coatzacoalcos and Veracruz flank this, the most enticing stretch of Mexico's Gulf Coast. The rolling volcanic hills and lush vegetation would seem to beckon to visitors, yet the area remains virtually untouristed (and cool) even in summer. Only Laguna Catemaco draws a heavy domestic crowd to its shores in season. Catemaco monopolizes the area's fun-in-the-sun business because of its proximity both to fine beaches on the lake and to some of Mexico's best Gulf Coast beaches. Nearby San Andrés Tuxtla, the region's largest city and unofficial capital, offers a healthy range of hotels and restaurants, a charming colonial downtown, and quality Mexican cigars. San Andrés has excellent bus connections to Catemaco, Santiago Tuxtla, the Tres Zapotes ruin site, and larger cities such as Veracruz and Mexico City. Horseback riding and hiking are popular outside San Andrés. In Santiago Tuxtla, the only other town of note in the Dos Tuxtlas, life is even slower than in Catemaco. With only two hotels and a small museum, the quickest movement in town takes place on the Zócalo's foosball tables.

Route 180 is the main artery of the Dos Tuxtlas area. From Acayucán in the south, it passes north to Catemaco, San Andrés, and Santiago Tuxtla before continuing along the coast to Veracruz. All sights outside these three cities lie on secondary dirt roads served by local buses. Transportes Los Tuxtlas buses leave from San Andrés every 10 minutes for many attractions (around 400 pesos).

Catemaco

Catemaco rests beside a large lake on the green volcanic slopes of the Tuxtlas range. The town is tremendously popular with Mexican tourists during *Semana Santa,* Christmas, and the summer holidays. On the first Friday in March, Catemaco hosts a huge convention of witches, warlocks, and medicine men from all over Mexico—hence the profusion of "brujos" (sorcerers) in business establishment names.

Orientation and Practical Information

Although Catemaco lies along Rte. 180, few first-class ADO buses stop here on journeys north or south to major cities; you usually must change in San Andrés and catch another bus to Catemaco. Second-class lines run frequently from major cities to Catemaco.

Both the ADO station and the Autobuses Unidos (AU) station lie within 2 blocks of the Zócalo. Streets in Catemaco are poorly marked, but the basilica on the Zócalo is partially visible from the ADO station. To reach the center from the AU station, walk left from the entrance, take a right at the first cross street, and head slightly downhill. The Autotransportes Los Dos Tuxtlas station is also 2 blocks from the Zócalo.

The town is small enough that you can manage by asking questions in English, Spanish, or body language. The two main streets are both unlabeled, but between the Zócalo, with its landmark basilica, and the road that follows the lake (called either Playa or Malecón), it is difficult to lose your way. The entire town can be covered on foot in 10 minutes, and all services crowd around the Zócalo.

Tourist Information: Las Brisas Hotel, Carranza 3 (tel. 300-57). Sr. Moreno is the official "State Tourist Coordinator" for Catemaco and the coastal areas. He speaks no English but will gladly show you a map of the region and his photo album of the nearby beaches. You may keep the map.

Currency Exchange: Multibanco Comermex, on the Zócalo. Open Mon.-Fri. 9am-1:30pm. Exchange desk open Mon.-Fri. 10am-noon.

Post Office: Aldama 30, 1½ blocks past the ADO station on the right as you walk away from the Zócalo. Open for money orders and registered mail Mon.-Sat. 9am-1pm; for stamps Mon.-Fri. 9am-1pm and 3-6pm, Sat. 9am-1pm. **Postal Code:** 95870.

Telephones: The official *caseta* on Carranza, 1 block past the basilica in the direction of the ADO station, on the right, does not allow collect calls. The larger hotels charge a hefty fee. **Telephone Code:** 294.

Bus Stations: ADO, with first-class service to: Coatzacoalcos (4 per day, 6500 pesos); Jalapa (1 per day, 13,000 pesos); Mexico City (2 per day, 28,000 pesos); Puebla (1 per day, 22,000 pesos); San Andrés Tuxtla (4 per day, 600 pesos); Veracruz (5 per day, 7700 pesos); Villahermosa (1 per day, 14,000 pesos). **Transportes Los Dos Tuxtlas** serves both the Tuxtlas and the coast. Buses marked "Veracruz" depart every 10 min. for San Andrés Tuxtla (500 pesos) and Santiago Tuxtla (600 pesos).

Pharmacy: Farmacia Sra. del Carmen (tel. 300-91), at the corner of Carranza and Boettinger, attached to the Hotel Acuario. Open Mon.-Sat. 7am-1:45pm and 3:30-9pm.

Medical Emergency: Centro de Salud (tel. 302-47), on Carranza 2 blocks south of the Zócalo. Near the *colinita* (little hill) on the way out of town toward Coatzacoalcos. Open 24 hr.

Police: On the 2nd floor of the Palacio Municipal (tel. 300-55), on the Zócalo. Open 24 hr.

Accommodations

Hotels in Catemaco are grouped near the Zócalo or along the lakefront. During *Semana Santa,* Christmas, July, and August, hotels are fully booked with Mexican families, and cost several thousand pesos more than in off-season. Meanwhile, dozens of young Mexicans and members of the international beard-and-sandal brigade gather on the beach, packing guitars, harmonicas, and sleeping bags. At other times of the year, however, camping around the lake is not recommended: instead, try a site along the coast (see Near Catemaco below).

Hotel Acuario, Boettinger at Carranza (tel. 300-91), on the Zócalo. Large, clean rooms with tiny soaps in spotless bathrooms. Bedspreads with little tulips make you feel young at heart. All rooms have fans; *agua purificada* is available. Singles 15,000 pesos. Doubles 30,000 pesos.

Hotel Julita, Playa 20, on the waterfront. A whitewashed hotel that overlooks the lake. Simple rooms with cement floors and fans. Dark bathrooms. Singles 20,000 pesos. Doubles 25,000 pesos.

Hotel Los Arcos, Madero 7 (tel. 300-03), at Mantilla, above the market. Suits of armor defend the front desk. Tidy, bright rooms. Singles 35,000 pesos. Doubles with 1 bed 35,000 pesos, with 2 beds 45,000 pesos.

Hotel Del Lago, Playa at Abasalo (tel. 301-60), 3 blocks to the right coming from the Zócalo. Well-kept hotel with small pool. All rooms have A/C and matching bedsets, and some have a lake view. Singles 57,000 pesos. Doubles 67,000 pesos. Triples 79,000 pesos.

Food

Restaurants along the waterfront specialize in *mojarra* (perch), cooked any way you like it. The restaurants differ more in their view of the lake than in the price or quality of their cuisine.

Restaurant La Cabaña Aloha, on Playa across from La Luna. The widest panorama of all the shorefront spots and a Miller beer funnel at the bar to make the college crowd feel at home. *Mojarra* 10,000 pesos. Eggs any style 3500 pesos. Open daily 8am-10pm.

Restaurant La Ola, on Playa down from the Aloha. Large, cool dining area with thatched roof; goldfish pool out front. Large goldfish (well, perch) 12,000 pesos. Fried chicken and potatoes 11,000 pesos. Open daily 8am-9pm.

Restaurant El Recuerdo, Aldama 6, just off the Zócalo. Stately entrance leads to a beautiful porch with a view of the lake through a wooded garden. Clean and handsome. *Sopa de mariscos* 15,000 pesos. Open daily 8am-9pm.

Restaurant La Suiza, to the left on Playa when coming from the Zócalo. The only furnishings are the Corona beach chairs, but the vista is nice and the food excellent. Enchiladas 5000 pesos. Open daily 8am-9pm.

La Luna, on Playa across from the Aloha. Catemaco's most elegant. Large bar and wagon-wheel dividers add a special Western flair. The *tegogolo* (snails) are spicy little numbers (5000 pesos). Open daily 8am-9pm.

Sights

The rocky shores of Laguna Catemaco are not the most magnificent beaches you'll ever see, but the swimming is pleasant and only slightly soupy. A hiking path runs along the edge of the lake—walk down from the Zócalo to the waterfront and turn left—taking you to Playa Expagoya 1km down the way, and to the more secluded and sandy Playa Hermosa 1km past that.

The lake is nearly circular, about 15km across, and several small islands dot its smooth surface. Dozens of small outboard *lanchas* lie in wait to take you on an hour-long trip to the best-known of the lot, Isla de Changos (usually 40,000 pesos per person, but on weekends, when *colectivos* are running, only 7000 pesos). A tribe of 70 semi-wild *changos* (mandrills), brought from Africa for a scientific experiment, have thrived on the island and gained fame for their blood-red cheeks. Knowing that the *lancha* operators bring coconuts and tortillas, the bravest *changos* climb right into the boat to pose for camera shots and collect their reward. En route to the island, you'll pass close to a cave-shrine that stands on the spot where a woman had a vision of the Virgin Mary over a century ago. The boats leave from the docking area below the Zócalo. You can charter your own boat for a 1¼-hour tour of the lake for 50,000 pesos.

Near Catemaco

Buses operated by Autotransportes Los Dos Tuxtlas (the line without mufflers) leave regularly for the coast between 7am and 6pm. From Catemaco, the bus rockets down through miles of picturesque green slopes before finally approaching the ocean. Soon after passing a series of small resorts, it arrives at the intersection of two dirt roads, an hour and a half from Catemaco. Here a small, faded sign makes the modest announcement "Playa Escondida, El Edén de Dios." It's worth the bus ride there and back just for the sign.

The first of the resorts is **Sontecomopán,** which sits not on the ocean at all, but at the edge of the **Laguna de Sontecomopán,** a beautiful inlet surrounded by tropical vegetation on steep mountain slopes. This popular local resort has a small swimming hole and great fishing, but it's probably not worth a special stop. A hotel here has acceptable rooms. Fishing and sightseeing excursions into the lagoon are available.

Few tourists visit the small villages near the sandbar or beaches at the lagoon's mouth. Fishing people there sometimes give stray foreigners a hard time, especially those intending to spend the night. At the La Palma intersection, the right fork leads to two lakeside settlements, **La Barra** and **El Real.** As a general rule in such small villages, it's best to introduce yourself to locals, especially to those living or working nearby. Once acknowledged as the rightful inhabitants and property owners, many show unusual hospitality, inviting strangers into their homes for a meal or to spend the night. If asked politely, residents often allow *viajeros* to set up camp near their homes.

The next intersection after La Palma leads to the Dos Tuxtlas's most beautiful beaches, Playas Jicacal and Escondida. From the road where the bus drops off passengers, make the hilly but beautiful 1km walk through meadows, streams, and woodland to **Playa Jicacal,** an extensive crescent of white, gently sloping sand populated by a few fishing families. Campers who wish to spend the night here would do best to ingratiate themselves with the *jicacaleños,* thereby assuring the safety of their stay on the beach. After Jicacal, the access road bends left and ascends the jutting cliff that divides Jicacal from Playa Escondida.

Atop the hill, 1km beyond the beach on this road, Hotel Playa Escondida commands a magnificent view of Jicacal, to the right, and Escondida, to the left. The restaurant here is moderately-priced and serves adequate food—a lucky break, given that the next-closest eating establishment is tucked away in Sontecomopán. The neat and well-furnished rooms are also a good deal. (Singles 35,000 pesos. Doubles 45,000 pesos.) Check valuables at the "desk" in the restaurant or don't leave your room without them. Some rooms have views of the crescent bays. **Playa Escondida** (Hidden Beach) lives up to its name: the beach is a hot, 10-minute hike from the hotel.

The bus from Catemaco passes Playa Escondida to anticlimax in the once-tranquil town of Balzapote. Here ships dredge an enormous harbor as engineers blast a quarry for volcanic rock nearby. No need to visit.

San Andrés Tuxtla

This hillside city offers the chance of a lifetime for understanding how cigars are made, and its market brings together the best selection of food and crafts in all of southern Veracruz. The combination of many good hotels and lots o' local bus routes make San Andrés a fine base for exploring the natural attractions that surround the city.

Orientation and Practical Information

San Andrés lies midway between Catemaco and Santiago Tuxtla on Rte. 180. Buses run frequently from San Andrés to all nearby destinations as well as Coatzacoalcos, Oaxaca, Veracruz, and Mexico City. The first-class **ADO** bus station lies on the edge of town at the intersection of Rte. 180 and Juárez, which leads to *el centro.* After leaving the station, turn left down the enormous hill toward the center—about a 10-minute walk or a 2000-peso cab ride. The second-class **Cuenca** bus terminal also lies on Juárez, farther downhill; a left from the terminal also takes you to the center. The confused and crowded **Autotransportes Los Dos Tuxtlas** bus stop sprawls behind the market. From the front of the market on 5 de Mayo, cross the street and walk 3 blocks slightly uphill on Rascón to the center.

San Andrés is built on and around a volcanic range that hugs the coast. The downtown area lies in the slightly raised center of a valley. Branching off Rte. 180, **Juárez,** the city's main street, descends a steep hill, crosses a small stream, and gradually ascends to the Zócalo and cathedral. With your back to the cathedral, Juárez leads straight ahead, to the right of the Palacio Municipal and to the right again at the next two forks before finally bearing left and climbing out of the valley.

Tourist Information: Sr. Luis Pérez of the **Hotel Del Parque** (tel. 201-98), on the Zócalo. The president of the local hotel association speaks no English but is enthusiastic about the region and happy to share his knowledge and pamphlets. You may have the good fortune to meet his father who speaks English and will gladly point out the city's highlights.

Currency Exchange: Bánamex (tel. 203-50), on the Zócalo; **Banco Serfín,** Gorostiza at Juárez; and **Bancomer,** Juárez 9. All offer identical rates and are open Mon.-Fri. 9am-1:30pm. After-hours exchange in the Hotel del Parque (see above) and other hotels, although bank rates are better.

Post Office: La Fragua and 20 de Noviembre (tel. 201-89), 1 block from the Zócalo. Follow 20 de Noviembre (directly opposite the Palacio Municipal) from the Zócalo and turn left onto La Fragua. Open Mon.-Fri. 8am-7pm, Sat. 9am-noon. **Postal Code:** 95700.

Telephones: Call long-distance (but not collect) from **Café Catedral,** Lerdo at Independencia (tel. 211-11), on the Zócalo opposite the Palacio Municipal. Open daily 9am-2am. **Telephone Code:** 294.

Telegrams: 7 de Agosto and Belisario Domínguez, 3 blocks from the Zócalo. Follow Belisario Domínguez around the back of the cathedral and then walk 2 blocks downhill to the intersection with La Fragua. Open Mon.-Fri. 9am-1pm and 3-6pm, Sat. 9am-noon.

Bus Station: First-class **ADO** (tel. 208-71). Bus stop diner has A/C. Buses to: Campeche (3 per day, 10 hr., 35,000 pesos); Catemaco (4 per day, 15 min., 600 pesos); Mérida (2 per day, 12 hr., 44,000 pesos); Mexico City (16 per day, 9 hr., 28,000 pesos); Puebla (6 per day, 7 hr., 21,500 pesos); Villahermosa (8 per day, 5 hr., 15,000 pesos).

Market: on 5 de Mayo, 3 blocks from the Zócalo. Walk along Rascón (facing the front of the Palacio Municipal, Rascón is the street to the left of the Palacio). Better for food than for crafts. Open daily 6am-6pm.

Red Cross: Gonzalez and Boca Negra (tel. 205-00). Ask for *servicio de ambulancia* to go directly to the hospital at the edge of town.

Pharmacy: Farmacia El Fenix, Juárez 1 (tel. 227-27), at Constitución, across from the cathedral. Open Mon.-Sat. 9am-9pm, Sun. 9am-3pm.

Police: In the Palacio Municipal (tel. 202-35). Some English spoken. Open 24 hr.

Accommodations

San Andrés remains almost tourist-free; budget accommodations are abundant and always available (without reservations). The hotels near the Zócalo are more centrally located and better maintained than those on Juárez.

Hotel Catedral, Suárez 3 (tel. 202-37), at Boca Negra, 2 blocks from the Zócalo. Breezy yellow lobby, friendly staff, and clean but small rooms with geometrically tiled floors and fans. *Agua purificada* available. Singles 11,000 pesos. Matrimonial doubles 16,000 pesos. Two-bed doubles 25,000 pesos.

Posada San José, Belisario Domínguez 10 (tel. 210-10). Clean, fan-bedecked rooms around a tropical indoor courtyard, with a restaurant and bar downstairs. An extra 10,000 pesos buys a room on the garden with A/C. Singles 20,000 pesos. Doubles 30,000 pesos.

Hotel Figueroa, Suárez 10 (tel. 202-57), at Belisario Domínguez across from the Colonial. Well-kept rooms, cramped but clean bathrooms, and friendly staff. *Agua purificada* and a fan in all rooms. Singles 15,000 pesos. Doubles 25,000 pesos.

Hotel Colonial, Suárez 7 (tel. 205-52), 2 blocks from the Zócalo at Belisario Domínguez. You can't miss it—the mint-green building has its name lettered in red and blue on the front and sides. A map of Veracruz and surrounding states is painted on a wall in the sunlit lobby. Worn rooms with sagging beds have fans and passably clean bathrooms. Singles 10,000 pesos. Doubles 12,000 pesos.

Hotel del Parque, Madero 5 (tel. 201-98), facing the Zócalo. A 3-star hotel, reputedly one of the best in the area. All rooms are tastefully decorated and have A/C, TV, and phone. Full-service bar, restaurant, cafeteria, and laundry service. Professional staff. Singles 64,000 pesos. Doubles 80,000 pesos. Mention *Let's Go* and receive a 30% discount.

Hotel Zamfer, Madero 10 (tel. 202-00). A scruffy rendition of Parque with all the ambience of an office building gone to seed. Rooms large and clean but cluttered with mismatched yard-sale furniture. All rooms have phones, but some lack A/C and fans. Singles 25,000 pesos. Doubles 30,000 pesos.

Hotel Ponce de León, Juárez 216 (tel. 209-79). Just don't tell your mother you stayed here. Rooms dark, damp and, to quote the owner, "Not elegant." Bathrooms dank and grimy. Singles 12,000 pesos. Two-bed doubles 20,000 pesos.

Hotel Juárez, Juárez 411 (tel. 216-09), 2 blocks from the ADO station on the right, next to the funeral home. Tiny but clean rooms with only slightly mildewy bathrooms. Cheerful red-and-white bedspreads. Observation deck on roof. One-bed doubles 27,600 pesos. Two-bed doubles 36,000 pesos.

Food

Several sidewalk cafés on the Zócalo serve breakfast, large coffees, and afford ample opportunity to watch the morning activity of San Andrean citizens. A number of good seafood places line Madero past the more expensive hotels, while cheap grazing spots proliferate in the market and its environs.

Los Portales, Niños Héroes 2, 4 blocks from the post office away from the cathedral and past the Mobil station. Well-kept and cheaper than the restaurants on the Zócalo. The working-class "in" spot for coffee, dominoes, and chess. Tasty breakfasts; stick to *huevos rancheros* (3800 pesos) and the like.

Café Catedral, Lerdo at Independencia, on the Zócalo. Outdoor tables with a good view of the city plaza and cathedral. Inside, a pictorial history of the old city. Terrific, thin *chocomilk* shake 2500 pesos. Breakfasts 3000-4000 pesos. Full-service place, including telephone *caseta* and discotheque (see Sights and Entertainment below). Open daily 9am-midnight.

Guadalajara de Noche, Juárez 221, just past the unremarkable bridge on the way to the Zócalo from the ADO station. Easily missed entrance leads to a cave interior with outlandish decor. Tasty, reasonably priced food. Try the *carne al carbón,* with guacamole, *tostadas,* onions, beans, and radishes, all for only 9000 pesos. Live trio nightly after 8pm. Open daily 8am-1am.

Restaurant Mariscos Chazaro, Madero 12, past Hotel Zamfer away from the Zócalo. This small diner serves a wide variety of seafood and the staff will let you tune into the American movie channel if you divulge your birthplace. The *sopa de mariscos* (12,000 pesos), loaded with fish, will sate the heartiest of appetites. Open daily 8am-7pm.

Restaurant del Parque, Madero 5, in the Hotel del Parque on the Zócalo. Where the wealthy *políticos* make deals over coffee and spend hours attempting to look busy. To maintain its reputation, prices remain slightly above the other two Zócalo cafés. For an inexpensive breakfast, try the *orden de picadas,* a local specialty (3000 pesos). Open daily 8am-11pm.

Sights and Entertainment

Outside the Zócalo, there are few sights in San Andrés. Then again, there are cigars. Watch stogies being made at the Santa Clara cigar factory outlet, on Rte.

180 just beyond the ADO station. From the center, walk up Juárez to ADO and turn right—it's about 200m down Rte. 180 on the right. The intense tobacco smell may knock you over momentarily, but when you recover, the amiable and talkative staff will let you wander through the factory (factory manager Jorge Ortiz speaks English and German).

Cigars sold at the factory office (in the same building) cost less than those in downtown San Andrés. Although you may buy in quantity here, you cannot ship them and thus must carry them with you. Keep in mind that customs regulations in most countries limit the number of cigars that can be taken across the border. *Ejecutivos* come in attractive cedar boxes with Santa Clara's name and your initials burned on the cover; the best quality *puros* come in glass or aluminum cases. (Open Mon.-Fri. 7am-9pm, but factory workers go home at 6pm, so arrive earlier if you want to see them in action.)

Nightlife is limited to the slightly cheesy **Sótano's Disco,** buried beneath Café Catedral, which rocks Saturday and Sunday from 9pm into the early morning (cover 5000 pesos). The cinema on Suárez across from the Hotel Catedral is San Andrés's largest, with two theaters—one shows American films, the other Mexican soft porn flicks (4 shows daily, 2500 pesos).

Near San Andrés

Buses from behind San Andrés's market run to Catemaco and the Gulf Coast, Santiago Tuxtla and Tres Zapotes, and one or two other popular tourist destinations.

You can rent horses from outlying ranches and farms near San Andrés to explore back trails and visit either of the two popular destinations near town. **La Laguna Encantada** is a volcanic lake 2km northeast of the city, known mainly for its queer tendency to rise during dry season and fall during the rainy season. Taxis from the center of San Andrés will take you there for 10,000 pesos.

The more accessible **Salto de Eyipantla waterfall** attracts locals, but it's not worth a trip except for the beautiful ride. From a distance, an impressive volume of muddy white water pours over a cliff. Other, lesser falls create a solid wall of mist, coating everything at one end of the gorge with a fine dew. Purple water hyacinths cover the marshy banks and other exotic greenery clings to the cliffs, but the water itself is disappointingly brown and fouled by floating foam and trash. Fishing people mix freely with swimmers, so beware of hooks. Be careful when leaving the concrete platform because the rocks and mud are slippery.

Buses (several each day, 45 min., 2000 pesos) run to the waterfall from Autotransportes Los Dos Tuxtlas, next to the market. Ask for up-to-date information in the bus company office across the street. Each bus waits 25 minutes at the falls before returning to San Andrés.

Santiago Tuxtla and Tres Zapotes Ruins

Santiago Tuxtla is a tranquil paradise, a relaxing destination in itself or a jumping-off point for a trip to the Tres Zapotes ruins, whence the Olmecs once reigned over a large empire.

Flowering in the area of Northern Tabasco and Southern Veracruz, Olmec society passed on important aspects of its religion, architecture, and daily life to the Maya and Aztecs. Nothing but cornfields and grassy mounds remain at the actual site of Tres Zapotes, but the museums in Santiago and the small village of Tres Zapotes, near the ruins, are interesting.

To reach Santiago Tuxtla's Zócalo, walk away from Rte. 180 on Ayuntamiento toward the clocktower. In the Zócalo, the biggest **Olmec head** ever discovered (40 tons) sits complacently, shaded from the sun by a large cupola. The sculpture is immediately recognizable as Olmec because of its distinctive negroid facial features, ears, and "helmet." The foosball tables in front of it comprise the town's main source of nightly entertainment. The museum on Ayuntamiento at Zaragoza has beautiful display cases but few labels for its artifacts, but the museum's director, Fernando Bustamonte, loves to comment on the pieces. Ancient finds—mostly clay figurines, pottery, and small faces—fill the museum, while the arcade behind the museum displays monumental sculptures of volcanic rock and another enormous Olmec head. (Open Tues.-Sat. 9am-6pm, Sun. 9am-3pm. Admission 8000 pesos, free Sun.)

Hotel Castellanos (tel. 702-00), in the far right corner of the Zócalo as you approach from the bus stop, offers Santiago's finest accommodations. Each room of this tall, circular tower yields a magnificent panorama of the town and surrounding countryside along with the pool out back. Large rooms have A/C and immaculate tiled bathrooms. All rooms have A/C. (Singles 64,000 pesos. Doubles 80,000 pesos.) **Hotel Morelos,** Morelos 12 (tel. 704-74), at Madero, has much humbler rooms and tiny bathrooms but is very clean and cozy. All rooms have fans. (Singles 25,000 pesos. Doubles 35,000 pesos.) You can eat cheaply at **Restaurant Rebe,** Morelos 4, with a majestic view of the road to Veracruz and the mufflerless buses that travel it. Most dishes are under 10,000 pesos: a meal of tasty tacos and salad is only 6000 pesos. There is also a sedate restaurant, **El Trapiche,** in the Hotel Castellanos but it gets more use as an after-hours student hangout on the Zócalo than as a restaurant. If you're not staying at the Castellanos, you can use the swimming pool for 4000 pesos.

Most services in Santiago Tuxtla are grouped along Morelos, including the market, bus stations, and telegram and telephone offices. Autotransportes Los Dos Tuxtlas has continuous service to all points in Veracruz, including Tres Zapotes (4 per day, 500 pesos). ADO, AU, and Cuenca have less frequent but more comfortable service. There is long-distance phone service on the road to Veracruz, running parallel to Morelos, across the bridge. (5000-pesos surcharge. Open Mon.-Fri. 8am-9pm.)

The bus from Santiago lets passengers off in **Tres Zapotes** at an intersection of dirt roads surrounded by a few buildings. Face the direction the bus was going and look left down the road that leads past the roadside stationery store. The usually empty museum of Tres Zapotes lies at the end of that road, about a five-minute walk. If the bus stops in a different place, simply ask for *el museo arqueológico*. The contents of the museum are by no means self-explanatory, but a knowledgeable guide is usually on duty. If you have even a cursory knowledge of Spanish, ask questions, since the pieces become fascinating when set in a historical context or when experts point out their fading details. The most easily recognized Olmec artifact in the museum is the large helmeted head, which resembles heads found in other Olmec sites like La Venta. The enormous, rough-hewn stela lying directly opposite the head (on the opposite side of the museum) is known as **Stela A** and may be the oldest Olmec stela ever discovered. The guide will point out (or careful observers will notice) the figure of a man with a jaguar's head lying down on top. On the side, you can discern a serpent, a jaguar, and a man with an axe in hand. All of these motifs were important in the subsequent Mayan and Aztec cultures.

To the left of the large head (from a visitor's perspective), the less famous half of the very famous **Stela C** also deserves attention. This stela bears the oldest recorded date found in America, 31 BC, inscribed in Olmec glyphs similar to those used by the Maya.

Near the enormous head, one stone with a cavity containing another circular stone has been dated to 300 BC. Columns, exactly like those found at La Venta, surrounded this object in the center of Tres Zapotes's main plaza. Three stone mallets (symbols of power and authority) and various animal bones, probably those of jaguars, were found buried in the stone's center.

Stela D, dating from 100 BC, is more or less opposite Stela C. Within the mouth of a jaguar are renderings of three people whose relative heights symbolize their power and importance. The war god on the far right holds a staff. The woman in the middle is the Moon Goddess. The character depicting "El Pueblo" on the far left is kneeling to both these deities. A large volcanic rock with a jaguar in the center rests opposite the stela. Life is distinguished by a bloody mouth, and Death languishes in a skeletal face and body. (Open daily 9am-4pm. Admission 5000 pesos, free Sun.) The last bus returns to Santiago Tuxtla at 3:30pm but ask before you get off to make sure.

Nothing else of interest remains at the site of the ruins. You'll just pick up ticks and tear clothing on barbed wire in the grassy cornfields. Determined amateur Indiana Jones's, however, should turn left from the museum, then right on the next road after the entrance road. Eventually, make another left, passing by Tres Zapotes's lovely little Zócalo (called La Parque), and cross the river. Continue straight until the level fields are broken by a series of gentle hills. These were the ceremonial mounds and pyramids of the Olmec site. The mounds have been transformed into cornfields, and farmers, who remember finding ceramic dolls and pots before archeologists deemed them valuable, continue to turn up pottery shards as they till the soil.

Northern Veracruz

The northern half of Veracruz generally receives little attention from budget travelers—which is surprising, considering its indisputable attractions. Tuxpan's miles of white sand beaches and shoreside solitude are unavailable to the same extent elsewhere in Mexico. Papantla is an open-air museum dedicated to the culture of the Totonacs, while ruins of their ancient past lie nearby in El Tajín. Jalapa, the state capital, is blessed with a cool climate and impressive colonial architecture in a spectacular mountain setting.

Jalapa (Xalapa)

Jalapa's stony façade embodies the values of the colonial era: prudence, chastity, diligence, and piety. But this reserved elegance is interrupted by meandering hill roads and sprawling parks which contribute to the city's laid-back demeanor.

The best way to enjoy Jalapa is by wandering aimlessly through the hills. Cobblestoned streets cling to ravines, cliffs, and even a small extinct volcano. Every avenue offers a magnificent vista of the craggy peaks surrounding the city, and most streets cut through a park at some point. These natural attractions are complemented by museums, cafés, markets, and theaters.

Orientation and Practical Information (Oar 'n' Prak)

Jalapa lies 104km northwest of Veracruz along Rte. 140, and 308km east of Mexico City. Trains and first- and second-class buses stop in Jalapa; buses offer the most frequent service and most varied destinations. The train station is at the extreme northeastern edge of the city, a good 40-minute walk or 4000-peso taxi ride from the center.

The first-class **ADO** and the second-class **AU** terminals are both housed at 20 de Noviembre 571, east of the city center. They share a brand-new, state-of-the-art building; appropriately enough, ADO occupies the first floor while AU settles for the second. Only the heartiest traveler with light luggage and a big ego should attempt the hike into town. Taxis will make the trip for 3000 pesos. Buses marked "Centro" do the same for 400 pesos.

Many of Jalapa's streets follow no discernible pattern and change names every few blocks. Enríquez runs east-west through the city center. Revolución and Dr. Lucio both head north from the Zócalo to the market. Zaragoza runs roughly east-west, immediately behind and downhill from the Palacio de Gobierno.

State Tourist Office: Zaragoza 25 (tel. 872-02), at Bravo near the Palacio de Gobierno. Large, well-staffed office with enough brochures and pamphlets to paper the walls. Open daily 9am-6pm.

Currency Exchange: Bánamex, at the corner of Zamora and Xalapeño Ilustres, 3 blocks from the Parque Juárez. **Banco Internacional,** Clavijero 2, at Camacho across from the Parque Juárez. Both open Mon.-Fri. 9am-1:30pm; for currency exchange 9-11am. **Casa de cambio,** Zamora 36. Open Mon.-Thurs. 9am-1:30pm and 4:30-6:30pm, Fri. 9am-1pm and 4:30-6:30pm.

Post Office: Zamora 70, in the Palacio Federal. Open for packages, stamps, and Lista de Correos Mon.-Fri. 8am-1pm and 3-7pm; for stamps only Sat. 9am-1pm.

Telephones: Many *casetas* hide in the cafés along Zamora, but the best bet is in the back of Restaurant Terraza Jardin on Enríquez in front of the Parque Juárez. 4000-peso charge for collect calls. Open Mon.-Sat. 7:30am-10pm, Sun. 10am-8pm. **Telephone Code:** 28.

Telegrams: Same location and hours as the post office.

Market: Revolución at Altamirano, 2 blocks north of the Parque Juárez. Open daily 8am-sunset; but for the freshest, cheapest food in town come at night when the trucks unload their cargo.

Supermarket: Chedraui, in the Plaza Crystal on Lázaro Cárdenas. The biggest (and only) supermarket in town.

Laundromat: Silver Queen, Galván 125, 6 blocks from the Parque Juárez. From the west side of the park, turn left down Clavijero and take the first right onto Galván. Same day service. 6000 pesos per load. Open Mon.-Sat. 8am-8pm.

Red Cross: Clavijero 13 (tel. 781-58 or 734-41), 1 block north of the Parque Juárez. Open 24 hr.

Pharmacies: El Fénix, Altamirano 9, off Revolución. Open Mon.-Fri. 9am-9pm, Sat. 9am-1pm. **Farmacia La Nueva Esperanza,** Revolución 135, at Victoria. Open Mon.-Sat. 8am-10:30pm, every other Sun. 8am-9pm.

Police: In the Palacio de Gobierno (tel. 31-01). Cops armed to the teeth. No English spoken. Open 24 hr.

Accommodations (Ukomydayshunz)

Jalapa is packed with comfortable, economical, and convenient accommodations. Nights can be chilly, so ask for extra blankets. Many budget accommodations are grouped on Revolución, close to the old AU bus station. Even though AU has relocated, the location is still great: close to the Zócalo, the parks, and the market.

Hotel Limon, Revolución 8 (tel. 722-07). Rooms and bathrooms as small as they could be but spruce and cozy. Fantastic tiled courtyard. Singles 18,000 pesos. Doubles 22,000 pesos.

Hotel Acapulco, Carrillo 11 (tel. 516-41), on the street above the old AU station. Sodas of all sizes available at desk. Outrageously clean and tasteful rooms, and bathrooms pour hot water. Singles 17,000 pesos. Doubles 22,000 pesos.

Hotel Continental, Zamora 4 (tel. 735-30). Slightly musty but spotless rooms surround bright, tall indoor courtyard. Bathrooms passable. Singles 20,000 pesos. Doubles 24,000 pesos.

Hotel Dulcelandia, Revolución 61 (tel. 739-17), 5 min. from the Zócalo. Inauspicious driveway entry leads to stark rooms with comfortable beds and dingy baths, all served by one light switch. Singles 13,000 pesos. Doubles with 1 bed 20,000 pesos, with 2 beds 30,000 pesos.

La Mansión, Sayago 4 (tel. 744-27), off Revolución. Large rooms and clean walk-in baths. Beds sag. Rooms fumigated daily, but smell funny in the bargain. Singles 15,000 pesos. Doubles 17,000 pesos.

Food (Phüd)

For those tired of beans and tortillas, Jalapa will provide happy relief: many eateries prepare excellent, imaginative meals at low cost. Particularly inexpensive cuisine can be found in the market and at the many stands around it.

Casona del Beaterio, Zaragoza 20, near the Palacio de Gobierno. Lush open courtyard; inside walls blanketed by a pictoral history of Jalapa. Varied menu with full breakfasts from 6000 pesos. Satisfying *comida corrida* 12,000 pesos. Open daily 8am-10pm.

Picrecha, Arteaga at Xalapeños Ilustres, 7 blocks from where Xalapeños breaks from Enríquez. Intimate, romantic atmosphere with wicker, candles, and mood music. Interesting Mexican-Italian menu describes dishes in great detail. Often crowded. Salad bar (5206 pesos) is "disinfected" for the *gringos*. Large pizzas easily feed 2 for 18,000 pesos. Open Mon.-Sat. 7pm-midnight, Sun. 7-11pm.

La Pérgola, Díaz Mirón at Lamas del Estadio, in the Zona Universitaria across from the stadium. Open-air, terraced setting with barbecue. Bright interior. Specializes in meats *al carbón*. BBQ ribs 9000 pesos. Open daily 8am-1:30am.

Café de la Parroquia, Zaragoza 18. The Veracruzano original is inimitable, but the fare here is just as good. *Bistec de filete* (tenderloin steak) 13,000 pesos. Lemonade with mineral water 1700 pesos. Open daily 7:30am-10:30pm.

Restaurant Terraza Jardín, Enríquez, on the Parque Juárez. Comes up short on atmosphere but breakfasts are filling and cheap. Full breakfast of hotcakes, juice, and coffee 4500 pesos. Open daily 7am-10:30pm.

Sights (Psytes)

Jalapa's beautiful, brand-new **Museo de Antropología** displays an excellent collection approaching that of the Museo Nacional de Antropología in Mexico City. The museum is extremely well-organized and takes visitors through ages of ancient civilizations in Mexico, region by region. All exhibits (including maps, timelines, and photos) are in Spanish. The museum sits on a large open lawn that makes for excellent sunning on a clear day. (Open Tues.-Sun. 9:30am-5pm. Admission 2500 pesos, students 1000 pesos, with a camera 3000 pesos, free Sun.) To reach the museum from the Zócalo, walk north on Revolución past the old AU bus station. Turn left at the first busy intersection (Xalapa) and follow to Acueducto. The museum is on the left. The walk takes approximately 45 minutes. Or catch one of the small yellow buses on Enríquez (500 pesos) all of which pass the museum. Taxis cost about 2000 pesos.

Jalapa's two main public parks merit visits. The **Parque Ecológico Macuitepetl** is essentially a preserve for the flora and fauna indigenous to the Jalapa area. Neat brick paths wind up the side of an extinct volcano through thick vegetation that hides flocks of screeching birds. The summit, the highest point in the area at 1586m above sea level, affords a spectacular view. (Open Tues.-Sun. 6am-6pm; off-season Tues.-Sun. 7am-5pm. Free.) Take the bus that goes to the museum, and get off at the traffic island where Xalapa, Orizaba, and Tepic converge. Follow Tepic uphill to the park.

Two blocks south of the Zócalo on Dique lies the the second park, the **Paseo de los Lagos,** which consists of a large lake and beautiful lawns and gardens. The **Casa de Artesanías,** at the north end of the lake, is a state-run handicrafts store. (Open Mon.-Fri. 9am-7pm, Sat. 9am-1pm.)

The Zócalo itself is of interest to the sightseer. Across Enríquez from the plaza stands the **Palacio de Gobierno,** notable largely for its French design. West of the Palacio is the **Parque Juárez,** a busy spot with terrific views of Jalapa and the surrounding mountains. Also on the Zócalo, the colonial cathedral contains a body of religious paintings and a huge bronze bell which was shipped from London in 1778.

Entertainment (Yippee-eye-oh-kai-ay)

El Agora de la Ciudad, beneath the Parque Juárez downtown (enter through the stairwell in the southwest corner of the park), serves as the city's cultural center; its theater shows films of significant cultural value. Fine books and musical recordings are for sale in the Agora as well. Paintings and sculptures fill the corridors. A sophisticated crowd mills about, discussing recent cultural events and the astounding success of the Portland Trail Blazer fast break. (Open daily 8:30am-9pm.)

El Teatro del Estado, at Ignacio de la Llave and Rubén Bouchez (tel. 840-31), holds enticing performances—the Orquesta Sinfónica de Jalapa and the Ballet Folklórico de la Universidad Veracruzana appear regularly. Contact the tourist office for schedules and ticket prices. From the Zócalo, walk left on Enríquez and then left on Llave.

Jalapa dances to the rhythm of a number of moderately attended discos, including **Ya'x Plaza Crystal,** on Lázaro Cárdenas near Independencia (open Thurs.-Sun. from 10pm), and **O'Belis Club,** on 20 de Noviembre at Cárdenas (open daily from 10pm; 10,000-peso cover Sat.-Sun. only). O'Belis Club has live rock, jazz, and other brands of live music on Wednesdays and Thursdays; look for notices posted prominently in town. Wear whatever you wish, as long as it's not ripped a la Donnie Wahlberg.

Papantla

After losing his shirt, his sanity, and the town of Uruapan in a 1533 poker game (see Uruapan introduction), the Earl of Sandwich sped his '77 lemon-yellow Pinto across Central Mexico in search of the perfect mango. Halfway to the Gulf Coast, Aztec cops clocked the compulsive gambler doing 136 in a 55 zone; when the dust cleared three months later, the Earl found himself on a slow boat to Paplanta's minimum security prison, convicted on trumped-up charges of fixing ballcourt games and bullfights. The local Totonac warden subjected the Earl to hard labor in the fantastically lush jungle surrounding town: over the next 21 years, he constructed what 20th-century archeologists consider to be one of the greatest pyramids in the Americas.

At the time, however, the guards were not impressed. Distraught in the face of such outright aesthetic rejection, the Earl kicked his car repeatedly until he and the clunker went up in a fiery explosion. Awestruck inmates took the mad architectural genius as their new god of fire, posthumously dubbing him "El Tajín" (Nahuatl for "Royal Ugly Dude Ablaze").

Modern-day Papantla has undergone an artistic renaissance, most evident in the town's colorful market: each day merchants unveil a veritable rainbow of fruit, from bananas to mangos, alongside heartfelt velvet renderings of El Tajín. Though a major tourist spot along the Gulf Coast, Papantla manages to retain a small-town flavor that the late Earl would smile maniacally upon. El Tajín lives.

Orientation

Papantla lies 250km northwest of Veracruz and 21km southeast of Poza Rica along Rte. 180. The ruins of El Tajín like 12km south of the city. The *centro* encompasses the plaza, the cathedral, and the surrounding blocks near the top of the hill on which Papantla is built. Enríquez borders the plaza's downhill edge, with Zamora to the left and 20 de Noviembre to the right as you face the cathedral.

Practical Information

Tourist Office: On the second floor of the Palacio Municipal (tel. 201-77), to the right facing the cathedral. Free maps are blurry and out of date, but the pamphlet for sale (5000 pesos) contains an excellent city map in addition to information on local history and sights. Open Mon.-Fri. 9am-3pm, Sat. 9am-1pm.

Currency Exchange: Bancomer, Enríquez 109. Changes money and traveler's checks until noon. Open Mon.-Fri. 9am-1:30pm. **Bánamex,** Enríquez 102. Exchanges currencies and checks until 1:30pm. Open Mon.-Fri. 9am-1:30pm and 4-6pm. Both banks are on the Zócalo.

Post Office: Asueta 198 (tel. 200-73), on the second floor. Open for stamps and Lista de Correos Mon.-Fri. 9am-1pm and 3-6pm, Sat. 9am-noon; for registered mail Mon.-Fri. 9am-1pm and 3-5pm.

Telephones: Make international collect calls at local hotels. **Hotel Tajín,** Nuñez y Domínguez 104, charges 10,000 pesos. Open 24 hr. **Telephone Code:** 784.

Telegrams: Enríquez 404 (tel. 205-84), about 5 blocks east of the Zócalo. Open for telegrams Mon.-Fri. 9am-8pm, Sat. 9am-noon; for money orders Mon.-Fri. 9am-1pm and 3-5pm.

Bus Stations: Paplanta has two of 'em. **ADO,** Juárez 207 (tel. 207-18), 5 blocks from the center, sends first-class buses to: Mexico City (4 per day, 5 hr., 14,500 pesos); Veracruz (5 per day, 4 hr., 18,000 pesos); Tuxpan (at 10:30am, 1pm, and 5:10pm, 1½ hr., 3400 pesos); Tecolutla Playa (at 7pm, ½ hr., 1800 pesos); Tampico (every ½ hr., 4 hr., 10,500 pesos). The second-class terminal, known locally as **Transportes Papantla,** 20 de Noviembre 900, serves many of the same destinations as ADO, including the ruins of El Tajín.

Red Cross: Escobedo at Juárez (tel. 201-26), near the ADO station. Responds to emergencies and minor accidents, with ambulances to appropriate specialists. An inkling of Swahili spoken. Open 24 hr.

Medical Emergency: Clínica IMSS, 20 de Noviembre at Lázaro Cárdenas (tel. 201-94), in a large beige plaster building. From the ADO station, take a right and walk 2 blocks to Cárdenas, then turn left. Open 24 hr.

Police: (tel. 200-75 or 201-50) on the Poza Rica highway near the *reclusorio* (prison) in Colonia Unidad y Trabajo. Open 24 hr.

Accommodations

Paplanta caters to well-heeled tourists and its hotels charge accordingly; few budget accommodations exist. For those arriving late at night, the most promising hunting ground is around the Zócalo. More inexpensive accommodations await in nearby Poza Rica, 12km from Papantla and easily accessible by bus.

Hotel Pulido, Enríquez 205 (tel. 200-36). Very cheap. Rooms tidy, clean, and well-ventilated with strong fans. Automobile owners seem to enjoy revving their engines in the courtyard parking lot. Beware of the basement "restaurant," a bar that often accommodates sloshed and rowdy men. Singles and doubles 20,000 pesos.

Hotel Tajín, Nuñez y Domínguez 104 (tel. 201-21), ½ block to the left as you face the cathedral. On the uphill side of the street, in an attractive light-blue building with rounded terraces overlooking the valley. Considers itself a quality establishment and is raising its prices with its nose. Some of the spotless rooms come with TV and A/C instead of fan, but options do not affect sticker price. Singles with fan 39,000 pesos. Doubles 54,000 pesos.

Hotel Trujíllo, 5 de Mayo at De los Artes. Conduct a thorough investigation of the room before you decide to stay. Dirt cheap, and for good reason: lacks TV, bottled water, and a reasonable modicum of comfort. Singles and doubles 20,000 pesos.

Food

Papantla's few restaurants serve regional delicacies to tourists looking for the real thing. Most restaurants and food booths close by 9pm, and finding a late-night snack or drink can pose a problem: try the second floor of the **Mercado Hidalgo,** across from the Palacio Municipal. Here, in a clean environment, cooks whip up tacos, milkshakes, and other dishes until midnight for under 5000 pesos.

The **Restaurant Terraza** is on 20 de Noviembre where it runs along the Zócalo; enter under the Foto Felipe sign and walk up one flight. Its terrace overlooks the plaza and affords a view of the *voladores* to an interesting mix of tourists and young locals. All dishes, including *cecina* (dried meat), cost less than 8500 pesos. (Open daily 11am-11:30pm.) Also facing the Zócalo, the **Restaurant Sorrento,** Enríquez 105, dishes out all the regional seafood and beef specialties you could desire. The prominent location and colorful interior account for late-night popularity. Tacos go for 3000 pesos, *tortas* 1500 pesos, and the afternoon *comida corrida* 4000 pesos; nothing will set you back more than 7000 pesos. (Open daily 7am-midnight.)

Sights and Entertainment

Most of the sights in town are on or adjacent to the Zócalo and relate to the city's Totonac heritage. South of the plaza but slightly farther uphill is the **cathedral,** remarkable not so much for its interior but for the 50m-long, 5m-high stone mural carved into its northern wall. The work honors the Totonac culture's local heroes and folkloric figures; its reverence for the serpent god is embodied in a snake that runs along the full length of the carving. Of particular note is the representation of El Tajín's Pyramid of the Niches, at the mural's center. The cathedral's spacious courtyard on the hill commands a good view of the underlying Zócalo.

In fact, the courtyard might be viewed as an annex to the Zócalo; christened the **Plaza de los Voladores,** it is the site of the *voladores* ceremony, in which five male *indígena* "fliers" acrobatically entreat the rain god Tlaloc to water the year's crops. One flutist and four fliers ascend a stationary pole to a platform about 10m above the plaza, where the musician dances to his own melody, while the others consume courage-inspiring beverages. The *voladores* "fly" for 10 to 15 minutes by rotating around the pole while gradually lowering themselves to the ground by means of ropes. Originally, the four fliers corresponded to the four cardinal directions, and the different positions adopted during the descent were related to requests for specific weather conditions. With the rise in tourism, however, the performance has lost its meteorological significance and become more a spectacle than a rite.

Although the *voladores* fly in Papantla only on special occasions, the plaza has become a social center for the town and is always abuzz on Sunday night. The *voladores* perform more frequently at El Tajín (see below).

Papantla's latest effort to enshrine its *voladores* is the **Monumento al Volador,** a gigantic flute-wielding *indígena* statue erected in 1988 atop a hill and visible from all over town. To get to the monument, where you can read explanatory plaques and see Papantla in its entirety, walk up Reforma along the right side of the cathedral. After narrowing, the road forks; veer left and walk uphill to the monument.

A mural decorates the inside of the Zócalo's centerpiece, a domed kiosk. Painted by Arturo Cano in the 1960s, the mural personifies the four cardinal points as warriors. Each represents different natural calamities that have befallen Mesoamerican citizens. The Zócalo is also furnished with a set of mosaic benches framing small paintings of the Totonacs, in a style typical of northern Veracruz. The town's two markets lie next to the central plaza. **Mercado Juárez,** at Reforma and 16 de Septiembre, off the southwest corner of the Zócalo, specializes in poultry and vegetables but is neither particularly colorful nor low-priced. **Mercado Hidalgo,** on 20 de Noviembre, off the Zócalo's northwest corner on a small triangular block, vends many of the same fruits, vegetables, and articles of clothing as Mercado Juárez. In addition, Hidalgo offers a large collection of machine-made clothing amidst its supply of traditional, handmade outfits. The men's garb, which consists of striking white sailor shirts and baggy white pants, is suitable for *norteamericanos* of both sexes. Unlike *indígenas* from other regions of Mexico, the Totonacs have no qualms about women wearing clothing designed for men, and often gather in amused groups to watch fitting sessions. Both markets have a good selection of the regional specialties of vanilla products and figurines made from vanilla plants.

Near Papantla: El Tajín

The Totonacs' most important city and religious center, **El Tajín** lies in ruins a quick half-hour bus ride south of Paplanta. Named after the Totonac god of thunder, the site has revealed Aztec, Mixtec/Zapotec, and Mayan influence, but it has otherwise shed little light on the origins of Totonac institutions. The many well-preserved buildings contain enough alluring carvings and artwork to merit a visit if you're in the area. In July or August, you can catch one of the daily performances of the *voladores* here. The rest of the year, the fliers perform only on Saturday and Sunday. The exhibition lasts about 15 minutes, and starts when enough spectators assemble at the pole inside the entrance booth. A seated man in costume requests a donation of several hundred pesos.

A museum near the entrance displays sculptures discovered in El Tajín, but lacks explanatory plaques for most of the objects. If the shelf of indigenous poisonous beasts fails to impress you, their lengthy Latin names will; the fact that most were discovered on the site should dissuade you from wandering off the clearly marked paths.

Beyond these buildings, at the entrance to the site, a detailed map stand greets visitors. From here, a path winds past several grassy mounds currently undergoing excavation and restoration before arriving at El Tajín's **main plaza.** The first temples to the left enclose the most interesting of Tajín's ballcourts. Three pairs of wall carvings, all in excellent condition, illustrate the Totonac ball game.

Returning to the main cluster of ruins, you will see buildings labeled #1, 3, 4, and 5 on the map. Directly in front lies building 4, to the right building 3, and diagonally to the left building 1, the famous Pyramid of the Niches. It is forbidden to climb most of the well-preserved structures in this area, as the fences and prominent signs ("No Subir") are meant to indicate.

The **Pyramid of the Niches** is a unique piece of calendrical architecture: on seven levels, 365 niches correspond to the days of the year. Some archeologists believe that the temple guarded the Totonac *llama* (flame), an all-important symbol of life and prosperity. The Totonacs marked time in 52-year epochs, during which a single flame was kept continuously burning. At the end of each epoch, the carefully nurtured flame was used to torch many of the settlement's buildings. Each new epoch of rebuilding and regeneration was inaugurated by the lighting of the *fuego nuevo*.

The main plaza near the Pyramid of the Niches is known simply as Tajín; the area beyond these structures, set on a series of hills and terraces, is called **Tajín Chico.** Some buildings here are in good condition, but most have not been excavated, reconstructed, or even carefully preserved. As a result, park officials don't mind if visitors scamper up the higher buildings to get a view of the site and surrounding rolling hills. Although nothing in Tajín Chico is clearly marked, the first building at the far end is worth visiting because you can explore the interior. Behind this building, on the right, is a tunneled stairway with a linteled roof and a structure with a corbeled arch that reveals Mayan influence. On the path leading to Tajín Chico, a small, recently excavated ballcourt lies to the right, with another series of wall carvings, smaller and more faded than the first set.

Indígenas living around El Tajín have known for hundreds of years that this lost city existed in the thick of the jungle, but few outsiders believed their stories. At the turn of this century, archeological experts finally checked the site and confirmed that El Tajín was the genuine article. Today, the site is finally on its way to restoration as workers labor to uncover lost pyramids and ways of life.

The entrance to the entire El Tajín site is 300m down the access road off Rte. 180 beside the "Archaeological Zone" billboard. (Site open daily 9am-5pm. Admission 10,000 pesos; students with ID, Sun., and holidays free.) There is no guidebook available at the site, but one may be purchased at the Museo Nacional de Antropología in Mexico City.

El Tajín is accessible from the Transportes Papantla second-class terminal. "San Andres" is the most dependable route, taking you to the tiny village El Chote; there, pick up the bus bound for Poza Rica. This bus stops at the El Tajín access road, and the site is five minutes away by foot. To return to Papantla, take the "San Andres," "Coyutla," or "Coxquihui" bus to El Chote and change there for Papantla. Buses run about every half hour and cost 1500 pesos. Because bus routes and schedules vary wildly, always confirm the driver's destination before you board.

Tuxpan (Tuxpam)

Tuxpan's major draw is its extensive stretch of sublime beach: sands you might mistake for talcum powder are massaged by a blue-green ocean so clear you can see your feet on the bottom, and framed by a backdrop of swaying evergreens you might find incongruous. Thank the Virgin of Guadalupe that this bit of paradise hasn't fallen into the clutches of real-estate developers.

The town—whose name derives from the Totonac "Tochpan," meaning "Place of Wildly Hopping Rabbits"—complements its nearby beach as if the two were planned in unison. Streams of shoppers and fruit vendors flow unabated along the city's riverfront, where boats caressed by the light sea breezes incessantly load and unload fish, mangos, Aerobies, and bananas.

Orientation

Route 180 connects Tuxpan and Papantla and continues north to Tampico, three to five hours away depending on the route taken: Rte. 180 requires a ferry ride from Tampico; alternatively, Rte. 127 curves west from Rte. 180 in Potrero del Llano. Veracruz is 347km southeast, and Mexico City 328km southwest via Rte. 130.

Tuxpan spreads along the northern bank of Río Tuxpan. **Parque Reforma** is 1 block inland from the river on Humboldt, west of the busiest part of town; to reach it from the **ADO station,** turn left from the exit, head to the river, and turn right at the water. Walk along the river 6 blocks, then inland 1 block on Humboldt. To get to the beach, take the "Playa" bus from the riverfront road (every 10 min. 6am-8:30pm, 1500 pesos).

Practical Information

Tourist Office: Delegación de Turismo (tel. 401-77), on Corregidora along the western edge of the Parque Reforma. The few maps handed out are all in Spanish. Staff gives good advice on long-distance relationships, among other things. Open Mon.-Fri. 8am-3pm and 4-7pm, Sat. 9am-1pm and 4-7pm.

Currency Exchange: Bancomer, Juárez at Zapata. Open Mon.-Fri. 9am-1:30pm. Changes currency and checks Mon.-Fri. 9:30am-noon.

Post Office: Morelos 12 (tel. 400-88), 2 blocks east of Parque Reforma. Open for stamps, Lista de Correos, and packages Mon.-Fri. 8am-7pm, Sat. 9am-1pm; for registered mail Mon.-Fri. 8am-6pm. **Postal Code:** 92800.

Telephones: Hotel Plaza, Juárez 39, and **Hotel Reforma,** Juárez 25, allow non-guest collect calls for under 5000 pesos. Both open 24 hr. **Telephone Code:** 783.

Telegrams: Ortéga 20 (tel. 401-67). Open for telegrams Mon.-Fri. 9am-8pm, Sat. 9am-5pm; for money orders Mon.-Fri. 9am-5pm, Sat. 9am-noon.

Bus Stations: ADO, Rodríguez 1 (tel. 401-02). First-class service to: Tampico (21 per day, 5 hr., 11,500 pesos); Mexico City (10 per day, 6 hr., 16,000 pesos); Poza Rica (22 per day, 1½ hr., 2600 pesos). **Estrella Blanca,** Constitución 18, 2 blocks past the bridge, provides second-class service to many of ADO's destinations, without the cleanliness or comfort. Many buses run off schedule; call or stop by to confirm departure times.

Laundromat: Lavandería México, Allende 13 (tel. 442-48). They'll do it to it for 10,900 pesos per load. Self-service 7000 pesos per load. Open Mon.-Sat. 8am-8pm.

Red Cross: Galeana 40 (tel. 401-58), 8 blocks west of the center along the river, next to the police station. 24-hr. emergency and ambulance service to any medical facility.

Pharmacy: Farmacia El Fénix, Morelos at Juárez (tel. 430-23). Open daily 8am-10pm.

Medical Emergency: Hospital Civil, Obregón 12 (tel. 401-99), 1 block west of the bridge, then 1½ blocks inland and up the inclined driveway on the right. 24-hr. emergency service.

Police: Galeana 38 (tel. 401-23), 8 blocks west of the center along the river. Open 24 hr.

Accommodations

Tuxpan's numerous upscale hotels do not preclude good budget accommodations; sleeping cheaply should present no problem.

Hotel Parroquia, Escuela Medico Militar 4 (tel. 416-30), across from the church on a side street between Juárez and the waterfront. Dim rooms worthwhile for the strong fans, brand-new screens, and comfortable beds. Prevent eyestrain by reading in the brightly lit, clean bathroom. Friendly management. Singles 29,000 pesos. Doubles 35,000 pesos.

Hotel Del Parque, Humboldt 11 (tel. 408-12), on the east side of Parque Reforma. Entrance under sign proclaiming "Centro Nocturno La Cebra." Big rooms with painted floors.

Cement-floor bathrooms without toilet seats. Terraces overlook the plaza. Singles and doubles 25,000 pesos.

Hotel Tuxpan, Mina at Juárez (tel. 441-10). Some rooms large and clean, while others have sagging mattresses and graffiti on the walls. Take your pick. Singles 30,000 pesos.

Food

Generic hotel cafeterias dominate Tuxpan. The cafeterias in town send spies to competing restaurants to ensure that they're all putting the same number of saltine crackers in the bread baskets.

Barra de Mariscos del Puerto, on Júarez across from the plaza. Good seafood at reasonable prices. Shrimp cocktail 5000 pesos. Most fish dishes 6000-10,000 pesos. Open daily 9am-11pm.

Tacos "La Porilla," Humboldt 15, on the noisy plaza. Cheap eats. Three tacos 4500 pesos. Open daily 9am-midnight.

Restaurant Flórida, Juárez 23, next to the Parque Reforma. This one dares to be different: an elegant spindle staircase and carpet set it apart. Relaxing for breakfast or a quiet afternoon meal. Open daily 7am-11pm.

Restaurant del Hotel Plaza, Juárez 39 (tel. 405-70). Orange chairs and the bright marble floor stick out like sore thumbs. The worn-out crowd likes to sit and stare blankly out the window at passing people with real lives. Oops! There's an extra cracker on the table. Most Mexican entrees and cocktails 8000-15,000 pesos. Open daily 7am-11pm.

Sights

Although Tuxpan can boast neither grand cathedrals nor museums of world renown, the city's sights still manage to entertain. Near the simple, white cathedral lie several plazas ideal for a good book, a quiet meal, or a fine afternoon watching the world drift by.

A true gem sits on the other side of the river. Reached by ferry (a small blue boat) for 200 pesos, the **Casa de la Amistad México Cúba** (a.k.a. La Casa de Fidel Castro) revisits the days of piracy and Spanish imperialism in the Caribbean. Exhibits explain how the Spanish used Cuba as a springboard for their later conquests of Mexico and Peru.

During Fidel Castro's year here in 1956, he planned the overthrow of the Batista regime. His ship, the *Granma,* carried the soon-to-be-victorious revolutionary fighters to Cuba. A replica of the *Granma* sits in front of the museum, a large portion of which commemorates the efforts of Fidel Castro, Ché Guevara, and the revolutionary brigade. (Open Mon.-Sat. 6am-4:30pm, Sun. 6am-3pm. Free.) After you de-ferry, walk to the right along the river on the wide sidewalk. Where the sidewalk ends, continue straight up the dirt road. The *Granma* is a five-minute walk from there.

Tuxpan's greatest asset is its 2km of riverfront. The Malecón, paralleling the water, offers views of the fishing people hauling in their catch. Twelve km east of Tuxpan's city center, the river flows to the gulf and beach extends uninterrupted 20km in either direction. Near the bus stop, the beach can be crowded and slightly dirty, especially in season, but the wide expanse of fine, white sand continues far enough for you to stake a private claim somewhere down the line. The water is relatively clean and safe for swimming, though coagulated oil sometimes washes ashore. Seafood cocktails from the quintillions of cheap seafood stands cost 5000-10,000 pesos.

Buses (1500 pesos) marked "Playa" leave Tuxpan for the beach every 15 minutes from 6am to 10pm; the last bus returns at 8:30pm. Catch returning buses at the entrance to the beach.

Tampico

If you've ever seen John Huston's *The Treasure of the Sierra Madre,* you might remember the characterization of Tampico as a hot, dirty, unfriendly oil town that every foreigner is itching to get out of. Tampico may be more friendly today, but otherwise Huston's portrayal holds true.

Breathing Mexico City's air is said to approximate smoking two packs of cigarettes per day; in some sections of Tampico, the air seems to be infused with the daily equivalent of two cartons of rotten eggs. If you can ignore the filth and abandoned areas of the city, Tampico offers enough bars, restaurants, and nearby beaches to make a short stay bearable, maybe even pleasant.

A good time to visit is during **Las Fiestas de Abril,** from April 12 to 27, when townsfolk celebrate the resettlement of Tampico in 1823 by inhabitants of nearby Altamira. Events during the festivities are staged in and around the Pl. de Armas.

Orientation

Tampico is the southernmost city in Tamaulipas state and an important transportation center for the northern Gulf Coast. Route 180 from the northern coast cuts through town, crosses Río Guayalejo on a tremendous bridge, and continues south to Tuxpan and Veracruz. Routes 70 and 80 (the latter coincident with Rte. 180 for a 57km stretch of tarmac north of Tampico) both wind westward to San Luis Potosí. The most direct route to Mexico City from Tampico is Rte. 105, which branches off Rte. 127 to the southwest at Tempoal.

Tampico fills a wedge of land carved out by the Río Panuco as it dips south and quickly jogs back to the north. The city's V-shape is further determined by a large, polluted lake in its center. A sluggish channel connects the lake to the river, running through the main downtown area. The bus station and airport are on Tampico's northern side, beyond the lake.

The area around the **Plaza de Armas** (the central square) forms a consistent grid, well-aligned with the cardinal directions. The plaza is bordered by Carranza to the north (toward the cathedral), Olmos to the east, Díaz Mirón to the south, and Colón to the west. The major north-south streets downtown (starting in the west) are Colón, Olmos, Juárez, and Aduana, all of which run to the river.

Buses (400-500 pesos) and *colectivos* (500 pesos) follow fixed routes within the city; most buses stop on López Mateos, near the intersection with Madero. From here, buses labeled "Playa" or "Escollera" take you to Playa Miramar. *Colectivos* can be hailed around the Pl. de Armas, and taxis wait at the Pl. de Armas and Pl. de la Libertad.

Practical Information

Most services are grouped around the Pl. de Armas or Pl. de la Libertad.

Tourist Office: Olmos Sur 101 (tel. 12-26-68), on the 2nd floor, at the Pl. de Armas. Maps available. Open Mon.-Fri. 9am-7pm, Sat. 9am-2pm.

U.S. Consulate: Hidalgo 2000 (tel. 13-22-17), north of the city. Take *colectivo* "Aguila." Helpful with tourist cards and any problems you may have with the police or other officials. Open Mon.-Fri. 10am-1pm and 5-7pm.

Currency Exchange: Banks near the Pl. de Armas are open Mon.-Fri. 8am-7pm, Sat. 9am-1pm. **Oscar's Casa de Cambio,** Madero 218 (tel. 12-69-10), will cash traveler's checks. Open daily 9am-9pm.

Post Office: Madero 309 (tel. 12-19-27), on the Pl. de la Libertad. Open Mon.-Fri. 8am-7pm, Sat. 9:15am-1pm. Branch in second-class terminal of bus station open Mon.-Fri. 9am-4pm. **Postal Code:** 89000.

Telephones: Collect calls can be placed at pay phones and hotels, and there is a long-distance *caseta* at the bus station. Open 24 hr. in first-class part of the station, 6am-9:30pm in the second-class section. **Telephone Code:** 121.

Telegrams: Madero 311 (tel. 14-11-21), in the same building as the post office. Open for telegrams Mon.-Fri. 8am-midnight, Sat. and holidays 8am-8pm; for money orders Mon.-Fri. 9am-1:30pm and 2:30-7pm, Sat. and holidays 9am-3pm. Branch in the second-class part of the bus station open Mon.-Fri. 9am-12:30pm and 3-5:30pm.

Airport: (tel. 13-08-18), at the end of Hidalgo on the northwest edge of town. From the airport, take a bus (400 pesos), *colectivo* (500 pesos), or taxi (13,000 pesos) downtown. **Mexicana** has an office at Díaz Mirón 114 on the Zócalo, and at the airport (tel. 13-18-60). Daily flights to Mexico City (99,000 pesos).

Train Station: (tel. 12-11-79), in a small park at the corner of Héroes de Nacozári and Aduána, 3 blocks south of the Pl. de Armas. Trains to Monterrey depart at 7:45am (second class only) and 9:15pm (first and second class). First-class tickets 16,500 pesos, second-class tickets 5500 pesos. One train per day leaves for San Luis Potosí at 8am. First-class tickets 8400 pesos, second-class tickets 4700 pesos. Tickets available daily 6:30-8am and 5-9:15pm.

Bus Station: on Zapotal, too far from the center to walk. First-class **ADO** service to Poza Rica (22 per day, 14,000 pesos) and Mexico City (12 per day, 28,000 pesos). **Omnibus de Oriente** (tel. 13-37-18) runs to: San Luis Potosí (at 9:45am, noon, and 11:15pm, 18,000 pesos); Reynosa (6 per day, 27,000 pesos); Matamoros (9 per day); and many other cities. **México-Tuxpan-Tampico** serves Mexico City (25,000 pesos) and Tuxpan (at noon, 12:30pm, and 3:15pm, 10,500 pesos).

Red Cross: Tel. 12-13-33 or 12-19-46. Ambulances available.

Hospital General de Tampico: Ejército Nacional 1403 (tel. 13-09-32 or 13-20-35), 3 blocks from the bus station. Some doctors speak English. Open Mon.-Fri. 7am-8pm, Sat.-Sun. 4-8pm.

Police: Tamaulipas at Sor Juana de la Cruz (tel. 12-11-57 or 12-10-32).

Accommodations

Clean and secure budget accommodations are rare in Tampico. You may have to pay a little more than you're used to in order to stay in a sanitary hotel in a safe neighborhood. In general, inexpensive hotels are in the older section of town by the river and docks, near the train station but far from the bus station and airport. The thickest concentration of rooms is south of Rivera, the street that borders the Pl. de la Libertad to the south. To reach Rivera, the hotel area, and the riverfront beyond, walk 2 blocks away from the cathedral on Olmos or Colón. The environs of the bus station and Ciudad Madero's Playa Recreativo (see below) both have reasonable accommodations.

Downtown

Hotel Imperial, López de Lara at Carranza (tel. 14-13-10). Big, sturdy, and equipped with elevators. Rooms have phones, carpets, fans, and clean bathrooms. Numero Uno in Tampico. Singles 55,000 pesos.

Hotel Regis, Madero at Alfaro (tel. 12-02-90). Chipped floors and painted-over windows render rooms depressing despite fans. Bathroom walls annoyingly fall short of the ceiling. Singles 20,000 pesos. Doubles 30,000 pesos.

Hotel Plaza, Madero 204 (tel. 14-16-78), at Olmos. Not quite as nice as its distant cousin on Central Park South, but it does have A/C, phones, TV, and carpeting. Singles 51,750 pesos.

Hotel Posada del Rey, Madero 218 (tel. 14-10-24), between Olmos and Juárez. If Tampico has you yearning for comfort, slip into a sweet room here, with A/C, color TV, and carpeting. Singles 65,000 pesos. 10,000 pesos per additional person.

Near the Bus Station

These hotels aren't as nice as the ones downtown, and the neighborhood is busy, dirty, and unexciting. But if you're coming in late at night and leaving the next morning, no location is more convenient. The **Hotel Allende,** Allende 122 (tel. 13-82-57), offers simple, clean rooms with fans. To get there, exit the bus station to the right, take the first right, and walk ½ block. (Singles and doubles 20,000 pesos.) Across from the bus station, the **Hotel Central,** Zapotal 224, has rooms that are more worn-out than the Allende's, bathrooms that lack toilet seats, and no fans in sight. (Singles 25,000 pesos. Doubles 35,000 pesos.)

Playa Recreativo in Ciudad Madero

If you're simply in Tampico overnight waiting the next bus out, don't even think of coming here: getting to this secluded area on the beach is a hassle. But if you've arrived in Tampico too weary to continue without rejuvenation, this friendly resort is a pleasant place to recuperate for a few days. To get to the *playa,* catch the "López Mateos" bus downtown on López Mateos at Madero; take the half-hour ride to Ciudad Madero and ask to be let off by the Iglesia Sagrado Corazón. Near this church, on the corner of Obregón and Sarabia, a sign saying "Parada López Mateos" rises from the middle of a bus stop. Catch the "Recreativo" bus here (every hr. 7:30am-9pm). Your destination is the end of the line, another half-hour away.

On Pinar del Mar, the **Hotel Centro Recreativo, Social y Deportivo** is the closest budget spot to the Playa Norte de Miramar. Run by the oil workers' union, this hotel attracts vacationing roughnecks as wells as international budget travelers. Large, bright rooms have fans and huge balconies that overlook the beach down the hill. (One or 2 people 32,000 pesos. Three or 4 people 42,000 pesos.) The downstairs restaurant serves above-average food (meats 6500-8000 pesos, seafood 4000-10,500 pesos). The **Clínica Maya** is a 2-min. walk from the Centro Recreativo, but only stay here if you make the trek from Tampico and Centro Recreativo is full. It's a rest home as well as a hotel, so don't do a double-take at the sight of nurses. Fine rooms, excellent suites with lounge, carpet, A/C, and beautiful view, along with a great pool and vegetarian restaurant. (One or 2 people 60,000 pesos. Suites for up to 4 people 75,000 pesos.)

Food

For its size, Tampico does not have an especially wide variety of restaurants. It does, however, support countless replicas of some Platonic Tampiconic ideal of a cafeteria.

La Gran Muralla, López de Lara Sur 107. An interesting mix of Chinese and local food: many Mexican variations on chop suey. Interior decorated with tacky Oriental prints. *Comida corrida* 8000 pesos. Most entrees 16,000 pesos. Great A/C. Open daily 8am-11:30pm.

El Viajero, López de Lara Sur 101, next door to the Muralla. Families come here to partake in the cheap and simple fare. Nothing will let you down, but rarely will you find diamonds in the rough. Open daily 7am-11pm.

La Troya, Madero 218, inside the Hotel Posada del Rey. Elegant and pricey Spanish restaurant with A/C. Daily special several-course meals hover around 20,000 pesos. Open daily 7am-midnight.

Restaurant Muralto, Aduána at Héroes de Cañonero Tampico, on the Pl. de la Libertad. Hot and stuffy, just the way the flies like it. Large seafood platters. Open daily 7am-midnight.

Sights

The **cathedral** and plaza in Tampico's center take a stab at making the city an interesting place. The cathedral's façade is embellished with Romanesque columns and twin towers, and its large dome encloses an interior decorated with oil paintings and statues of the saints. The plaza, like many others throughout Mexico, is the city's prime spot for people-watching.

Mercado Hidalgo takes up 2 square blocks along Méndez 3 blocks south of the Pl. de Armas on Olmos. The market takes each visitor's nose for a wild roller-coaster ride: every entrance is filled with elderly ladies tirelessly making sales of sweet-smelling incense and medicinal teas in bulk. Sugary candies and dried nuts abound; try to wrangle a free sample of one of the coconut or caramel candies. Other storekeepers try to unload bales of scented herbs and roots on curious passersby. Connected to the Mercado Hidalgo is the **Mercado Juárez,** a virtual clone of the former. In addition to the herbs, candies, and trinkets, both markets sell poultry, beef, fruits, and vegetables. (Both open Mon.-Fri. 6am-7pm, Sat. 6am-8pm, Sun. 6am-1pm.)

If you want to stay in town and long to see a beach, head for **Playa Miramar**, accessible on bus "Playa" or "Escollera" (500 pesos), which depart from the corner of López Mateos and Madero. The beach is packed during Easter week, but uncrowded at all other times.

NORTHERN MEXICO

Most travelers rip through northern Mexico and proceed to push it toward the dusty reaches of memory. Except for Creel and the Barranca del Cobre in the refreshing Sierra Madres, northern Mexico is an inferno inhospitable even to most cacti.

Because tourists usually approach northern Mexico merely as ground to cover between two points, this section of the book is organized into three routes between the U.S. border and southern Mexico. The first traces the length of northeastern Mexico along both coastal and inland routes; the second runs from Ciudad Juárez, across the border from El Paso, Texas, down the western side of Mexico's great plateau through the cities of Chihuahua, Durango, Zacatecas, and Aguascalientes before entering the Bajío; and the third descends from Nogales, on the Arizona border, down to Nayarit state, just above Puerto Vallarta.

Northeastern Mexico

Because the cities of northeastern Mexico are primarily portals into the country or pollution-spewing industrial behemoths, most travelers who pass through do so without giving their surroundings much thought. But while the area is by no stretch of the imagination the most pleasant in the Republic, it is not altogether deviod of charm: Matamoros, Reynosa, and Nuevo Laredo occupy your time with typical border activity, Monterrey's wealth has brought a level of cultural sophistication to the city, and San Luis Potosí retains a level of colonial grace.

Matamoros/Brownsville, Texas

The unscenic, muddy trickle of a creek separating the U.S. and Mexico, mislabeled by Mexicans as the Río Bravo and by *norteamericanos* as the Rio Grande, is the only aspect of Matamoros that fails expectations. Mexican government agents at the International Bridge are informative and make the crossing here a breeze.

In the early 19th century, the recently settled Congregación de Nuestra Señora del Refugio was re-named Villa de Matamoros after a priest slain in 1810 during Mexico's war for independence. Matamoros fell in 1846 to U.S. general and future president Zachary Taylor, who divided the city in two by designating the Río Bravo the international border.

While there are no earth-shattering sights in town, Matamoros does offer a first taste of Mexico. Street vendors sell tacos, *aguas de frutas* (fruit juices), and *elotes* (corn on the cob; try it with chili and lime), and on Sunday evenings residents file into the plaza for their weekly, distinctly Latin *paseo* (promenade).

Brownsville, Texas, for its part, provides travelers from either direction with a wide range of services and an uncrowded border crossing. Keep in mind, however, that everything is cheaper on the Mexican side of the International Bridge. Because the border never closes, nothing should encourage the budget-minded to spend a night north of the Río Bravo.

Orientation

Matamoros

Matamoros lies 38km west of the Gulf Coast on the Río Bravo. Route 2, which follows the course of the Río Bravo northwest to Reynosa (100km) and Nuevo Laredo (350km), also passes through the center of Matamoros. Local buses (800 pesos) run from the airport to the city center every hour from 5:15am to 9:15pm, dropping off passengers at the corner of Abasolo and Calle 12, 6 blocks northwest of the plaza. Taxis charge 20,000 pesos for the journey into town. Until 6pm, downtown-bound buses depart regularly from the train station for 500 pesos.

The city of Matamoros is cupped by a turn south in the Río Bravo. Streets in the center follow a grid pattern oriented along the cardinal compass directions; numbered streets run north-south, with numbers increasing as one moves west. Most of the hotels, restaurants, bars, and other points of interest in the city can be found around the market, a pedestrian mall centered on Abasolo between Calles 7 and 10.

The tourist office, customs, and International Bridge are located at the northernmost point of the city. To reach the border area from the centr, take one of the buses or *colectivos* labeled "Puente" (500 pesos), which let you off in the parking lot of the customs building and tourist office. Taxi drivers in the market area will try to charge exorbitant prices to the border, but you should be able to bargain them down to 3000 pesos.

Be forewarned: Many buses and *colectivos* stop running after 6pm, and the rest disappear well before 11pm. Taxis can be picked up at any major transportation terminal at any hour.

Brownsville

All buses and taxis quit crossing the border in 1989, because of prohibitive increases in insurance rates. It is now possible to cross only by foot or in a private car.

The most convenient airport is **Valley International Airport** (tel. 423-7340), in Harlingen, Texas, 25 mi. (42km) northwest of Brownsville. From Brownsville, a taxi to the airport costs US$35; the bus charges US$24. Some people attempt to get from the airport to Brownsville for free by catching a ride on one of the vans to the expensive hotels.

Brownsville's streets are laid out in a grid pattern that focuses on a large bend in the Río Bravo near the International Bridge. Texas Rte. 4 from the northeast (International Blvd.) and Texas Rte. 415 from the northwest (Elizabeth St.) converge at the tip of this bend. Highways 83 and 77 cut through the middle of the city going north-south. Boca Chica (Hwy. 281 and 48) swoops from the mid-west to the tiny municipal airport at the eastern extreme of the city. Elizabeth is Brownsville's main street and a good frame of reference.

Local buses run from 5:40am to 7pm (fare 35-75¢). Last year, the city installed trolleys that service the downtown area until 7pm (fare 35¢).

Crossing the Border

A 100m-long bridge joins Matamoros and Brownsville. You pay 10¢ or 300 pesos to leave either country; once on the other side, your bags will be inspected, and women traveling alone may find themselves asked for a date. You need not obtain a tourist card (FMT) if you are not traveling farther than Matamoros. Otherwise, the FMT can be obtained in the customs office at the border or in the Matamoros bus station.

Finding transportation on either side of the border is no problem; taxis and *peseros* circle the area in search of needy passengers.

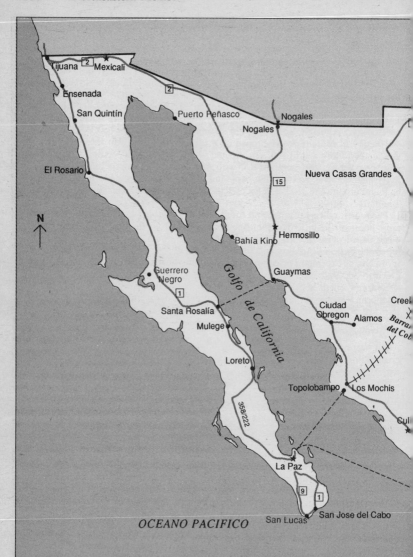

N

Tijuana
Mexicali
[2]
Ensenada
San Quintín
Puerto Peñasco
[2]
Nogales
Nogales
El Rosario
Nueva Casas Grandes
[15]
Bahía Kino
Hermosillo
Guerrero Negro
Golfo de California
Guaymas
[1]
Santa Rosalía
Mulege
Ciudad Obregon
Alamos
Creel
Barra del Col
Loreto
Topolobampo
Los Mochis
358/222
Cul
La Paz
[9]
[1]
San Lucas
San Jose del Cabo
OCEANO PACIFICO

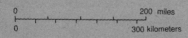

0   200 miles
0   300 kilometers

Northern Mexico

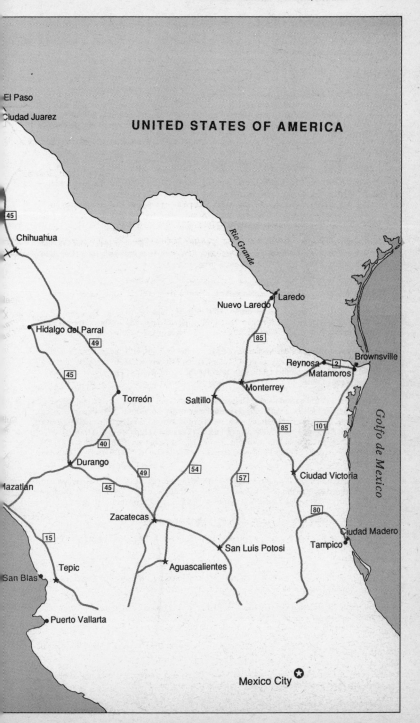

Practical Information

Because of Daylight Saving Time, Brownsville clocks run one hour ahead of those in Matamoros from April to October.

Matamoros

Tourist Office: Delegación Turismo, in the same Mexican government building by the International Bridge that includes customs (tel. 236-30). Uninspired service, no maps, no brochures, and broken English. If you want information about Matamoros, get it in Brownsville. Hell, get in Hoboken and you'll still do better. You can, however, get your tourist card (FMT) here. Open Mon.-Fri. 9am-3pm.

U.S. Consulate: Primera 232 (tel. 672-70 or 672-71), at Azaleas. Can help replace passports and other travel documents. Open Mon.-Fri. 9am-2pm.

Currency Exchange: Banks are open for exchange Mon.-Fri. 9am-1:30pm. **Bancomer,** Matamoros at Calle 6, 2 blocks from the plaza. Another branch sits on the border. Open daily 9am-4pm. **Bánamex, Somez,** and **Serfín** are on Calle 6 along the plaza. Better rates are generally available at the *casas de cambio* near the plaza, on Calle 6, and on Abasolo (the pedestrian mall). Try hotels for late-night exchange.

Post Office: Calle 6 #214 (tel. 202-11), in a white, modern building between Herrera and Iturbide, 6 blocks north of the plaza. Open Mon.-Fri. 8am-7pm, Sat. 8am-1pm. Branch in the bus station open Mon.-Fri. 8am-5pm. **Postal Code:** 87300.

Telephones: Private companies expect you to mortgage your house to make a phone call. Hotels allow guests and non-guests to make international collect calls. **Telephone Code:** 891.

Airport: Servando Canáles Aeropuerto, on Rte. 101, the highway to Ciudad Victoria, 5km south of town. **Aeroméxico,** Obregón 21 (tel. 307-02), has service to Acapulco (at 4:30pm, 432,646 pesos) and Mexico City (at 8:25 pm, 295,634 pesos). Few other flights available.

Train Station: Ferrocarriles Nacionales de México (tel. 667-06), on Hidalgo between Calles 9 and 10. Daily service to Reynosa (14,700 pesos) and Monterrey (20,100 pesos) at 2pm. Information booth has complete train schedules for the entire country. The wise traveler buys a ticket ahead of time and arrives early for boarding in order to beat the crowds. Go Blazers.

Bus Station: Central de Autobuses, Canáles at Aguiles. Combined first- and second-class bus station. Luggage lockers in the 24-hr. restaurant cost 4000 pesos per day. **Omnibus de México** (tel. 327-68). To: Reynosa (9 per day, 4400 pesos); Monterrey (5 per day, 5 hr., 15,000 pesos); Tampico (at 9:30pm, 7 hr., 25,000 pesos); Laredo (2 per day, 15,900 pesos). **ADO** (tel. 201-81). To Veracruz (at 4pm and midnight, 16 hr., 60,000 pesos) via Tampico (7 hr., 25,000 pesos) and Tuxpan (11 hr., 39,000 pesos). **Tres Estrellas de Oro** (tel. 327-03) serves Mazatlán (at 2:30pm, 73,000 pesos).

Laundromat: Calle 1 at Ocampo, 3 blocks north of the bus station. Exit the bus station and go right immediately; 1 short block down Canáles, at Calle 1, go right 2½ blocks. Self-service wash and dry 4000 pesos. Open Mon.-Sat. 9am-7:30pm, Sun. 9am-2pm.

Red Cross: Caballero at García (tel. 200-44). Ambulance service.

Police: Tel. 203-22 or 200-08. Friendly and helpful, but little English spoken. Open 24 hr.

Brownsville

Chamber of Commerce: 1600 E. Elizabeth (tel. 542-4341). Cornucopia of maps and brochures. Open Mon.-Fri. 8am-5pm.

Brownsville Information Center: Farm Road 802 (tel. 541-8455), at Central Blvd. adjacent to Motel 6. Extensive maps and brochures. From City Hall, take the "Jefferson Central" bus to get to this pyramidal structure. Open daily 8:30am-5pm.

Currency Exchange: *Casas de cambio* litter International Blvd. **Interex Money Exchange,** 801 International Blvd. (tel. 548-0303), exchanges traveler's checks. Open daily 10am-6pm.

Post Office: 1001 Elizabeth (tel. 546-9462), at 10th 5 blocks west of the International Bridge. Open Mon.-Fri. 7am-9pm, Sat.-Sun. 7am-4pm. **Postal Code:** 78520.

Telephone Area Code: 512.

Telegrams: Western Union, 715-B International Blvd. (tel. 546-0000). Send or receive telegrams, messages, and money orders. Open Mon.-Fri. 9am-6pm, Sat. 9am-5pm.

Bus Stations: Greyhound-Trailways, 1165 Charles St. (tel. 546-7171). Luggage locker US$1 per day. Service to McAllen (4 per day, US$5), and Laredo (2 per day, US$21-27). Also serves Houston, Dallas, and San Antonio. Schedule changes frequently; call to confirm. Reservations can be made same day or 1 day in advance. **Valley Transit Company,** 1305 E. Adams (tel. 546-2264), at 13th. To: Laredo (at 8:15am and 2:15pm, US$27); McAllen (every hr. 5am-5pm as well as at 7:15pm and midnight, US$6); Del Rio (6 per day, US$49).

Ambulance: Tel. 911

Police: 600 E. Jackson (tel. 911 or 546-3751).

Accommodations

Matamoros

Although comprably priced accommodations in Matamoros are of higher quality than those in Brownsville, travelers coming from elsewhere in Mexico should be prepared to pay more for less. Most budget options are in the market area.

Hotel Majestic, Abasolo 89 (tel. 336-80), between Calles 8 and 9 on the pedestrian mall. Large, clean rooms with fans and tiled baths. Friendly management. Paint peeling off the walls, and toilets have no seats, but location just doesn't get any better than this. Singles 25,000 pesos. Doubles 30,000 pesos.

Hotel México, Abasolo 807 (tel. 208-56). Spotless rooms and beds smothered by comforters. Nice bathrooms. Singles 25,000 pesos. Doubles 30,000 pesos.

Hotel Colonial, Matamoros 601 (tel. 664-18), at Calle 6, 3 blocks east of the market. Unclean rooms with fans; bathrooms lack toilet seats. Friendly and courteous staff. Drinking water available in adjoining cafeteria. For unknown reasons, often full. Singles 30,000 pesos. Doubles 35,000 pesos.

Hotel Araujo, Abasolo 63 (tel. 222-66), between Calles 4 and 5. Attentive family keeps rooms and sheets clean (though both have seen better days) and the noisy A/C running. Manager will hand-pump water into rooms if the tap fails. Singles 33,000 pesos.

Brownsville

Hotels in Brownsville offer excellent service and a taste of the First World, but will seem expensive to those coming from Mexico.

Motel 6, 2255 North Expressway (tel. 546-4699), off Hwy. 77. Tom Bodett, everybody's close personal bud, loves the meticulously clean and spacious rooms with TV and A/C. From City Hall, take the "Jefferson Central" bus; last bus leaves downtown at 7pm. Singles US$27. Doubles US$33.

Cameroy Motor Hotel, 912 E. Washington (tel. 542-3551). Excellent hotel conveniently located near both bridge and city center. Sparkling rooms, plush carpet, and downy beds with comforters. Señor Sorola says "Two thumbs up." Singles US$30. Doubles US$34.

Hotel Económico 708 12th St. (tel. 542-6739), at Adams. Centrally located and cheap, but someone should call the abused hotel hotline. Bare walls and dirty showers make the lack of TV even less tolerable. Difficult to coax comprehensible English out of the staff. Singles and doubles US$30.

Food

Matamoros

Although some family-run cafés offer delicious meals, Matamoros cuisine suffers from the predictably inflated prices of border towns and the predictably boring food of chain restaurants.

The **Restaurant Piedras Negras,** Calle 6 #1219, serves tasty steaks of typically Texan proportions. Full meals in this spruce spot run around 20,000 pesos. (Open daily 7am-midnight.) A popular weekend hangout for drinking and winding down, the **Café y Restaurant Frontera,** Matamoros 1406 at Calle 6, has a wide range of seafood, steaks, and salads all under 10,000 pesos. (Open daily 7am-10pm.)

Brownsville

Cheap diners flood the downtown area: you need look no farther.

Texas Café, in Market Square, adjoining City Hall. Old-fashioned atmosphere enhanced by hungry octogenarians. Burgers and Mexican food US$3. Take-out available. Open 24 hr.

Lucio's Cafe, 1041 E. Washington. Packed with regulars. Burgers and Mexican dishes dished up in a nanosecond. The stewed *carne guisada* is a speciality in Texas and northern Mexico. Open 24 hr.

Mr. Amigo Café, 1141 E. Levee, off 12th St. Slow, quiet, and full of perpetually sleepy country folk. Traditional Mexican meals as well as fast food served by Juan Amigo, the proprietor. Open Mon.-Sat. 7am-3pm.

Oasis Cafe, 1417 E. Adams. Clean. Here, *carne guisada* goes for US$2. Lengthy list of burgers. Open Tues.-Sun. 6am-5pm.

Sights and Entertainment

There is little to see or do in Brownsville, but the **Gladys Porter Zoo,** 500 Ringgold St. (tel. 546-2177), is worth a visit. The zoo coddles plants and animals from Asia, Africa, Australia, and the tropics. The herpetarium houses reptiles, amphibians, spiders, and insects; the bear grottos are another tasty, tantalizing treat. (Open daily 9am-5pm. Admission US$4.50, ages under 13 US$2.50.)

Matamoros's market spreads for several square blocks and consists of the new market on Abasolo, part of the old market on Bravo between Calles 8 and 9, and a series of smaller shops set up in the area. The main entrance is on Abasolo, between Calles 9 and 10. Consider making major purchases farther south, where souvenirs like piñatas and blankets are cheaper. (Open daily 7am-8pm.)

If you have an insatiable hunger for Mexican history, visit the **Casa Mata Museum,** at the corner of Guatemala and Santos Degollados. Here you can spend oh, maybe an hour looking at newspaper articles, photographs, and artifacts from the Revolution, as well as figurines and pottery from southern *indígena* tribes. From the bus station, take the first right out the entrance and walk 7 blocks on Guatemala. (Free.)

A good place to go after a hard day of souvenir-hunting is **Los Dos Repúblicas,** on 9a. Calle, between Matamoros and Abasolo (tel. 297-50). Sit back, relax, and enjoy the decorating scheme (designed to make you feel like you're sitting in the Zócalo of a tiny colonial village). They also employ Pedro the organist, who plays your favorite easy hits from more than a few years ago. For something more authentically Mexican, try the **Bar Los Toros,** two doors down from Los Dos Repúblicas, a sanctuary of sentimental music and song.

Reynosa

Reynosa, a typical northeastern border town, has prospered from its proximity to the U.S. *Maquiladoras,* assembly lines where low-cost Mexican labor puts together U.S.-made electrical components, dominate the local economy and keep its inhabitants solvent. Because Reynosa is tied so closely to the U.S., however, the city has been divorced from most of the Mexican culture that once made it colorful: the city offers little more to the traveler than a relatively hassle-free border crossing.

Orientation

Reynosa lies on the Río Bravo, 100km inland from Matamoros, and 249km southeast of Nuevo Laredo. All three cities are connected by Rte. 2. Monterrey is 222km west-southwest via Rte. 40. A tiny airport lies 25 min. from Reynosa off Rte. 2.

The U.S. city across the International Bridge from Reynosa is theoretically "Hidalgo," but this patchwork of malls and fast-food joints is hardly a city; McAllen, Texas, 10km north of Reynosa, is the real Texan counterpart. U.S. Rte. 82, which follows the Río Bravo, runs through McAllen, leading to Laredo in the northwest, and Harlingen and Brownsville in the southeast.

Taxis shuttle between Reynosa's combined first- and second-class bus station and the center. The walk into town takes at least 15 min. Turn left at the bus station door and proceed to Colón, which runs along the once-white wall that encloses the station. Hook left again, follow Colón for 1km, and turn right on Hidalgo. The main plaza is 5 blocks ahead. From the train station, walk away from the tracks (on the same side as the station) toward the market and follow Hidalgo 6 blocks to the plaza.

The city is laid out grid-style, with the plaza at the corner of Zaragoza and Hidalgo as its center. One block south on Hidalgo lies the shopping strip.

In the northeast corner of town is the International Bridge, on which the tourist office is located. Northbound border traffic flows onto Aldama (the divided street) or Allende before leaving town via Rte. 2 or 40. To get to the bridge from the bus station, walk 6 blocks north on Rubio. After crossing the bridge from the U.S. by foot, turn right on Aldama (the divided street) and left on Hidalgo; the plaza is two blocks south.

Crossing the Border

Crossing into Mexico, you have two options. To make immediate bus connections to other points in Mexico and totally bypass Reynosa, take the **Valley Transit Company (VTC)** bus (affiliated with Greyhound-Trailways) from McAllen to the Reynosa bus station and process your visa and tourist card there (24-hr. service). A *casa de cambio* at the station also assists impatient travelers. If you wish to enter downtown Reynosa, get off the bus before the International Bridge and cross on foot; on the other side, catch a local bus or walk to the center. Car insurance, required for those bringing vehicles into Mexico (see General Introduction, Getting There—By Car), is sold at the border Monday through Friday from 7am to 9pm.

Entering Mexico on foot will set you back one thin dime. Crossing into the U.S. on foot, walk on the right side of the bridge with your 300-peso exit fee in hand. Just after customs, a small Greyhound office marks the bus stop; take a bus to McAllen, where connections await to all points north.

Practical Information

Tourist Office: (tel. 211-89), in the large customs building to the left of the highway as you face the bridge, a 10-min. walk from the Pl. Hidalgo. Little English spoken, but a map of Reynosa is available. Open Mon.-Fri. 8am-8pm.

Currency Exchange: Banks open Mon.-Fri. 9am-2pm. *Casas de cambio* litter every street in town.

Post Office: Díaz at Colón (tel. 201-10). Open Mon.-Fri. 9am-1pm and 3-6pm, Sat. 9am-noon. Lista de Correos. **Postal Code:** 88500.

Telephones: Long-distance calls can be made from public phones on the plaza, at the bus station, and in restaurants. Try **Café Caprí**, at Zaragoza and Canáles. International collect calls 1500 pesos. Open 24 hr. **Telephone Code:** 892.

Telegrams: Díaz at Colón (tel. 201-65), next to the post office. Open for telegrams Mon.-Sat. 9am-8pm; for money orders Mon.-Sat. 9am-12:30pm and 3-5:30pm.

Train Station: At the end of Hidalgo. To Matamoros (at 12:05pm, 5400 pesos) and Monterrey (at 3:20pm, 14,700 pesos).

Bus Station: on Colón, at the eastern edge of town. First- and second-class service available. **Transportes Reynosa** (tel. 202-06) to Matamoros (8 per day, 4400 pesos) and Monterrey (every hr., 10,300 pesos). **Tres Estrellas de Oro** (tel. 217-82) to Mexico City (at 5pm, 49,000 pesos) and Mazatlán (at 4:30pm, 68,500 pesos). **ADO** (tel. 287-13) to Tampico (at 7:30 and 11pm, 25,000 pesos) and Veracruz (at 11pm, 60,000 pesos).

Red Cross: (tel. 213-14) near the police station on Rte. 2. X-ray machine, ambulance, doctors, and the only blood bank in Reynosa. Open 24 hr.

Peña Vidaurri Hospital: Díaz 525 (tel. 223-98), between Méndez and Madero across from the Hotel Rey. No English spoken, but the staff treats *extranjeros* hospitably. Open 24 hr.

Police: Comandancia de Policía, Morelos at Nayarit (tel. 200-08), on Rte. 2 toward Matamoros. No English spoken. Open 24 hr.

Accommodations

Budget accommodations are not Reynosa's forte. The city can accommodate cold-hearted traveling professionals, but the budget-minded will be hard-pressed to find pleasing lodgings at a reasonable price.

Hotel Nuevo León (tel. 213-10), on Díaz between Madero and Méndez, 2 blocks north of the post office. Amusing proximity of sink to toilet allows you to perform all bathroom exploits from one position. U-shaped balconies could also serve as stages for great theatrics. Singles 25,000 pesos. Doubles 30,000 pesos.

Hotel Confort, Hidalgo 325 (tel. 227-01), 100m past Colón amidst a fruit market. A 10-min. walk from the bus station. Staffed by cheery teenagers. Few amenities (namely showers, fans, and pastel-green walls), but clean and large. Singles 25,000 pesos. Doubles 30,000 pesos.

Hotel Avenida, Zaragoza Ote. 885 (tel. 205-92), a few blocks from the plaza. Every super room has carpeting, A/C, cable color TV, and phones. Manager speaks English. Singles 50,000 pesos.

Hotel Rey (tel. 229-80), on Díaz between Madero and Méndez, 4½ blocks south of the plaza. Lesser neighbor of Hotel Nuevo León. Fans, TV, and large mirrors grace the clean rooms. Friendly management. Singles 49,000 pesos. Doubles 56,000 pesos.

Food

A number of good restaurants serve traditional northern Mexican dishes such as *caldos* (soups) with corn tortillas, *cabrito* (young goat), *carne guisada* (meat with gravy), and *carne asada* (roasted meat).

La Ópera Restaurant/Bar, Hidalgo 835. American baseball on the 2 color TVs, and a full menu in English. How 'bout them Bosox? Mexican dishes 12,000 pesos. Open daily 8am-midnight.

Café Caprí, Zaragoza 880, near the International Bridge. Get egg on your face: breakfast egg platters 8000 pesos. Open 24 hr.

Café Viajero, Díaz at Madero. Schizophrenic interior decorator hung a crucifixion scene next to the large-screen TV, between Marilyn Monroe and a few scrolls of Seneca's axioms (in Spanish). Bewildering, but still a great restaurant. Tasty and filling *comida corrida* 10,000 pesos. Open Mon.-Sat. 7am-10pm, Sun. 7am-7pm.

Church's Pollo Frito, Guerrero at Hidalgo. Your fast-food prayers are answered. Try 3 pieces of Church's fried chicken (8700 pesos) drenched in *chiles.* Open daily 9am-10pm.

Sights and Entertainment

The **Mercado de la Estación,** adjacent to the train station on Hidalgo, splays out an amazing variety of foods. Near Hidalgo, vendors sell enough nuts to drive a squirrel bonkers. Farther down near Colón, you can find different types of cactus, *chiles,* dried fish, and Mexican cheeses. Spices and medicinal herbs abound. (Market open daily 6am-8pm.)

The Zona Rosa, which extends from the International Bridge to the plaza, is filled with tourist shops and dappled with discos. The **Imperial,** a local favorite, features live Mexican bands. For American disco join the teeny-boppers at the **Zodiac,** 2 blocks southwest of the bridge.

Nuevo Laredo

General Zachary Taylor and the Mexican-American War made a lasting impression on this prosperous town. The 1848 peace treaty, which declared the Río Bravo the international boundary, split the city in two; the Mexican half took on the name "Nuevo Laredo," while its U.S. counterpart remained plain ol' "Laredo."

Stores and restaurants along Nuevo Laredo's main drag, Av. Guerrero, cater to *norteamericano* expectations and customs: this is the place for overpriced food, useless trinkets, and neon lights. Pickpockets are as pervasive as friendly folk, so beware of charming children with flashy hands. Despite its shortcomings, Nuevo Laredo is a fun if expensive introduction to Mexico, especially during the first half of September, when the annual city fair sprouts up.

Orientation

Nuevo Laredo lies on the Río Bravo, 250km northwest of Reynosa along Rte. 2 and 230km north of Monterrey along Rte. 85.

Far to the south of the city center, the bus station is light-years from the International Bridge and Av. Guerrero. A taxi from the bridge to the station, at 12,000 pesos, costs more than most long-distance bus rides. Three bus lines ramble from Nuevo Laredo to every major town in northern Mexico.

All points of interest (outside the bus station) are within easy walking distance of the International Bridge. Av. Guerrero, Nuevo Laredo's main thoroughfare, emanates directly from the bridge; establishments along the first few blocks cater to tourists. Lodgings and restaurants fill the streets for 2 blocks east or west of Guerrero. Nuevo Laredo's main plaza is at Guerrero and Mier, 7 blocks south of the bridge. It is unwise to stray more than a block or two from brightly lit Guerrero at night.

Because so many trucks, buses, and cars cross the border at Laredo, getting through customs may take up to three hours. Being part of a busload of tourists could make you swear off bureaucracy forever. A better option is to take a bus to the bridge, then to walk over the river and go through customs by your lonesome.

Practical Information

Tourist Office: (tel. 201-04) by the bridge in the customs building. Open Mon.-Fri. 9am-3pm.

U.S. Consulate: Tel. 405-12.

Currency Exchange: Dollars are used as often as pesos in hotels, restaurants, and stores. *Casas de cambio,* scattered along the Guerrero strip, will not exchange traveler's checks for pesos: Do this in Laredo.

Post Office: Reynosa at Mier. **Postal Code:** 88000.

Telephones: There are free public phones in the main plaza at Guerrero and González. For the local operator, dial 02; to make collect calls to the U.S., dial 09 to get the international operator. For a Laredo operator, dial 08. **Telephone Code:** 871.

Airport: Off Av. Monterrey, about 15km south of the bridge. **Aeroméxico** and **Mexicana** fly to Chihuahua, Mexico City, and Guadalajara.

Train Station: Gutiérrez at López de Lara, west of the the city center. To San Luis Potosí (at 3:15pm, 46,200 pesos) via Monterrey.

Bus Station: Central Camionera, 15 de Junio at Guerrero (tel. 408-29). To get here, hop on the "Central" bus which runs along Guerrero. **Tres Estrellas de Oro** (tel. 400-91) to Guadalajara (at 7pm, 48,000 pesos). **Transportes Fronteras** (tel. 408-29) to Monterrey (every 15 min., 9500 pesos). Evening buses run less frequently. **Omnibus de México** (tel. 406-17) serves Matamoros, Tampico, and other southern destinations.

Red Cross: Tel. 209-49 or 209-89.

Hospital Civil Nuevo Laredo: González at Salinas Puga (tel. 288-85).

Police: Tel. 221-46 or 230-25. The Laredo, Texas police (tel. 727-9661) can also help in emergencies.

Accommodations

A few adequate hotels peek out from between the traps and the dumps along Guerrero.

Hotel Ajova Guerrero 2909 (tel. 205-68), 4 blocks from the bridge. Location and friendly proprietors make this a good deal. A/C, shower, and sinks over toilets. Some rooms have TVs and more-or-less operable radios. Singles 30,000 pesos.

Hotel Confort Canáles at Guerrero (tel. 226-36). Spacious and clean. The history in this joint is almost palpable. Almost. Singles 45,000 pesos. Doubles 54,000 pesos.

Hotel La Finca, Reynosa 811 (tel. 288-83). Two double beds in most rooms. Overpriced for the solitary traveler, but a budget option for larger groups. TV and A/C OK. Singles and doubles 65,000 pesos.

Hotel Sam's, Hidalgo 2903 (tel. 259-32). For this area, literally dirt-cheap. You get what you pay for. Singles 30,000 pesos.

Food

Café Almánza, González 2727, on the Pl. Hidalgo. Friendly and fleet-footed staff. Tasty Mexican food 6000 pesos. Open daily 7am-midnight.

Cadillac Bar Salón, Belden at Ocampo. Seemingly transplanted from the other side of the river; menus in English, waiters in Texasound, prices in U.S. dollars. Ignore the overpriced American fare and enjoy the overpriced enchiladas (US$5). High standards of service and cleanliness. Famous on both sides of the border. Open daily 10am-11pm.

Restaurant El Tapatío, Bravo 2719. *El Blando,* but dishes up decent *mole* and other regional Mexican specialties (6000 pesos). Open Mon.-Sat. 6am-10pm, Sun. 6am-8pm.

Restaurant Nuevo León, Guerrero 508. Let the waiters get your goat: *cabrito* is a house specialty. Entrees 10,000-20,000 pesos. Open daily 8am-midnight.

Sights

Avenida Guerrero is laden with restaurants, ceramic shops, markets, and other possible options for passing a lazy afternoon. Flamboyant matadors taunt bulls routinely at the **Plaza de Toros,** 1km from the International Bridge; horses and dogs race weekly at the **Galgódromo,** 10km from the city on Rte. 85; and bored-stiff tourists flee daily to Monterrey and points farther south.

Monterrey

Unbeknownst to most travelers, Monterrey prospers as the base of Mexico's largest industrial complex. Growth has brought pollution and congestion in its train, and the city lacks both Baroque churches and ancient ruins, but its sophistication and efficient services are singular in the northern deserts.

Orientation

As the largest city in northern Mexico, Monterrey is an important transportation hub. All buses in and out of the city pass through Monterrey's gargantuan **Central Camionera** at Av. Colón and Pino Suárez. To reach the center from the bus station, simply take any bus heading south on Pino Suárez. Easier still, hail a taxi (about 93 of them idle along Av. Colón) and fix the price before you get in. Since there are so many drivers, you can play them off each other and probably finagle a fare of 10,000 pesos to the Zona Rosa.

The train station is at Calzada Victoria, 6 blocks northeast of the bus station. To get to the bus station, head east on Victoria for 2 blocks, turn right on Bernardo Reyes, then left on Colón.

Aeroméxico and Mexicana, as well as several major U.S. and international carriers, fly into Monterrey's airport, 4km northeast of the city center; taxi fares approach 16,000 pesos to or from the center.

Downtown, Av. de la Constitución runs west and east along the Río Catarina, a dry 10km-long riverbed that has been converted into athletic fields. Running north-south across Constitución are, from west to east, Gonzalitos, Pino Suárez, Cuauhtémoc, Benito Juárez, Zaragoza, and Zua Zua. Running east-west parallel to Constitución are, from south to north, Ocampo, Hidalgo, Padre Mier, 5 de Mayo, and Washington. Around Morelos sprawls the Zona Rosa, bounded by Padre Mier, Zaragoza, Hidalgo, and Juárez.

Practical Information

Tourist Office: Oficina de Turismo, Zaragoza at Matamoros (tel. 45-08-70), in a complex of modern buildings. Maps, pamphlets, and advice with a smile. Open Tues.-Sun. 10am-5pm.

Consulates: U.S., Constitución Pte. 411 (tel. 43-06-50), downtown. **U.K.,** PRIV Tamazunchale 104 (tel. 56-91-14).

Currency Exchange: Banks open Mon.-Fri. 9am-1:30pm, but you'll get more bang for your buck at a *casa de cambio.*

American Express: Padre Mier Pte. 1424 (tel. 43-09-10), a few blocks west of the *centro.* Open Mon.-Fri. 9am-1pm and 3-6pm, Sat. 9am-1pm.

Post Office: Zaragoza at Washington (tel. 42-40-03), inside the Palacio Federal. Open for stamps Mon.-Fri. 8am-8pm, Sat.-Sun. 9am-1pm; for registered mail Mon.-Fri. 8am-6pm. **Postal Code:** 64000.

Telephones: Long-distance office on 5 de Mayo between Carranza and Galeana. Quick and efficient. Open daily 9am-8pm. Most hotels also offer international services for nominal fees. **Telephone Code:** 83.

Telegrams: At the post office. Open Mon.-Fri. 9am-8:30pm.

Airlines: Aeroméxico (tel. 44-77-30); **Mexicana** (tel. 44-77-10); **American Airlines** (tel. 42-19-66); **Air France** (tel. 44-31-33); **Continental** (tel. 44-75-05); **Pan Am** (tel. 42-42-33).

Train Station: (tel. 75-46-53) Calzada Victoria. To Nuevo Laredo (at 8:10am) and Matamoros (at 8:40am, 20,100 pesos).

Bus Station: Colón at Amado Nervo. **Omnibús de México** (tel. 74-07-16) to Chihuahua (2 per day, 38,000 pesos) and Zacatecas (2 per day, 21,000 pesos). **Transportes Frontera** (tel. 75-75-57) to Tuxpan (4 per day, 35,000 pesos) and Tampico (10 per day, 24,000 pesos). **Autobuses Anahuac** (tel. 75-64-80) to: Morelos (9 per day, 18,000 pesos); Zaragoza (4 per day, 18,000 pesos); Salamanca (at 10:30pm, 34,000 pesos). Station also has a 24-hr. pharmacy in Sala 3 and a medical center in the basement for emergencies.

Pharmacy: Farmacia Benavides, Morelos 499, in the Zona Rosa.

Car Rental: All agencies have their offices in the Zona Rosa below the Ambassador Suites tower. Cheapest models 110,000 pesos per day.

Cruz Verde: 16 de Septiembre S/N (tel. 40-21-21). Responds to accidents and emergencies. 24 hr. ambulances service.

Police: Tel. 38-26-94 or 38-26-95.

Accommodations

Monterrey's best budget rooms are on the fourth and fifth floors, affording a view of the mountains. But remember that heat also intensifies with altitude in buildings. The unpleasant area around the bus station is home to most of the city's budget hotels, including all those listed below, and most rooms are full by early afternoon. The **Hotel Colonial,** Hidalgo Ote. 475 (tel. 43-67-91), is your best budget bet in the Zona Rosa. But check your spacious room before accepting, because the TV and water don't always work; the A/C is always pumping. (Singles 71,000 pesos.)

Hotel Amado Nervo, Amado Nervo 1110 (tel. 75-46-32), perpendicular to Colón, on the right-hand side of the pedestrian overpass. Simple hotel with simple attractions: A/C and reliable hot water. Singles 35,000 pesos. Doubles 45,000 pesos.

Hotel Nuevo León, Amado Nervo 1007 (tel. 74-19-00). Clean rooms with phones and bathrooms. Singles 33,000 pesos.

Hotel Lozáno, Pino Suárez 1108 Nte. The building is no spring chicken, and the noise is extreme, but the price is as low as it goes in northern Mexico. Singles 20,000 pesos.

Hotel Virreyes, Amado Nervo 902 (tel. 74-66-10). Old rooms are dimly lit, but clean and telephoned. Amiable management. Singles 45,000 pesos.

Hotel Conde, Reforma Pte. 427, between Colón and Madero. So this is where all the Ajax ends up in Mexico: sparkling rooms with shiny bathrooms. Singles 46,000 pesos. Doubles 69,000 pesos.

Food

As in most of northern Mexico, barbecued meats are a favorite in Monterrey. Many restaurants display charcoal-broiled specimens in the window to lure hungry passersby. Other popular dishes include *agujas* (collar bone), *frijoles a la ranchera* or *borrachos* (beans cooked with pork skin, coriander, tomato, peppers, and onions), *machacado con huevos* (scrambled eggs mixed with dried, shredded beef), hot *tamales,* and, for dessert, *piloncillo con nuez* (hardened brown sugar candy with nuts).

There are many restaurants in southeast Monterrey, mainly along Garza Sada near the technological institute, but these are the highest-priced in the city. Downtown Monterrey is aglow with fast-food restaurants.

Near the Bus Station

Restaurant Cuatro Milpas, Madero at Julián Villagran. Ranch-style BBQ smell and atmosphere. Serves sirloin, chicken, T-bone, and *cabrito* (goat; 24,000 pesos) to many happily mowing families. Open 24 hr.

Cafetería y Mariscos Flores, Colón 876. Everything's Mexican: the seafood, the decor, *and* the clientele (always a good sign). Open daily 7am-11pm.

Cafetería Colón, Colón 650, ½ block from the eastern corner of the bus terminal (to your left as you exit). Serves daily specials, as well as *mole,* meats, and sandwiches. Entrees around 6000 pesos. Open daily 8am-10pm.

In the Zona Rosa

Restaurant VIPS, Hidalgo 401 at Carranza. Overpriced diner compensates with comfortable chairs, strong A/C, friendly service, and bilingual menus. Open 24 hr.

Piccolo's Pizza, Carranza 725, near Padre Mier. Air-conditioned and clean. Pasta and 20 varieties of pizza. Small pizza 8000 pesos, large 15,000 pesos. Multi-course buffet available. Open daily noon-10pm.

La Puntada, Hidalgo Ote. 123, near Colonial. Clean place populated with locals. Chiles marinated with cooked carrots *gratis.* All items under 10,000 pesos; tacos 3500 pesos. Open Mon.-Sat. 7am-10pm.

Around Parque Alameda

The park is located 10 blocks south of the bus station on Amado Nervo. Students frequent the area during the academic year.

Tacos y Tarros, Amado Nervo 206. *Comida corrida* includes a great *caldo de pollo* (chicken soup) with rice (5000 pesos). Open daily 8am-10pm.

Buhó Cafetería, Julián Villagran 116, facing the park. Students sway to the Mexican music. A few typical Mexican dishes as well as burgers and pizza. Full meals under 9000 pesos. Open Mon.-Fri. 8am-8:30pm, Sun. noon-5pm.

Restaurante Los Cabritos, Julián Villagran 1010, at Aramberri. They've named the place after their specialty; the skewered beasts hang and cook in the window. Meals are expensive treats: small serving 14,000 pesos. Open daily 10:30am-midnight.

Sights

Monterrey's most impressive sight is its immense **Gran Plaza.** This huge space abuts Washington on the north, Constitución on the south, Zaragoza on the west, and Zua Zua on the east. At the north end, the **Palacio de Gobierno** houses the Governor's Cabinet of Nuevo León state. Directly in front of this, the **Esplanada de los Héroes** is a vast open space punctuated by fountains, waterfalls, and statues of illustrious Mexicans. South of the Esplanada is the delightful **Bosque Hundido** (Hidden Forest), a cool and comfortable garden favored by the city's young couples. South of this lie the real attractions of the Gran Plaza. First of these, the **Fuente de la Vida** (Fountain of Life), gushes water around an immense Neptune and entourage of cavorting nymphs and naiads. The *enchilada grande,* however, is the **Faro del Comercio** (Lighthouse of Business), the 30m-high orange tower to the north of the fountain. From its pinnacle, green, purple, and red laser beams shoot out every night.

The Cuauhtémoc Company, for over a century the major producer of beer in Monterrey, has converted one of its old factories into the **Jardines Cuauhtémoc,** 2 blocks west on Colón and about 4 blocks north on Universidad from the bus terminal. The "gardens" are a few cement patios surrounded by a grassy area, where visitors sit and drink beer after visiting the three museums and the Hall of Fame (a collection of photographs and documents commemorating Mexico's baseball heroes) in the old factory. The **Museo Deportivo,** next to the Hall of Fame, has exhibits on Mexican sports such as *charriadas,* boxing, soccer, and bullfighting. Not surprisingly, the complex also contains an entire museum devoted to beer: located just to the north of the gate that leads into the gardens, the **Museo de la Cervecería** exhibits a collection of elegant beer mugs from various countries and copies of famous paintings relating to beer (including Leonardo's *Mona Michelob*). The other gallery, the **Museo de Monterrey,** holds an uninteresting permanent collection of art as well as some trivial traveling exhibits. You might want to take a peek at the schedule at the entrance to see whether the current exhibit strikes your fancy. (Museos Deportivo and Monterrey open Tues.-Fri. 9:30am-5pm, Sat.-Sun. 10:30am-6pm. Free. An appointment must be made to see the Museo de la Cervecería. Check at the other museums for more info.)

The **Obispado,** former palace of the bishop of Monterrey, is now a state museum. Constructed in the late 18th century on the side of a hill overlooking the city, the palace served in the 1860s as a fortress for both the French and Mexican armies. In 1915, Pancho Villa's revolutionary forces stormed the palace and drove the loyalists of Porfirio Díaz out of Monterrey. The museum displays murals, paintings, historic pictures, and old weapons, but the view of the city from the site and the decayed exterior are more of a draw than the museum itself. (Open Tues.-Sun. 10am-6pm. Admission 900 pesos.) Take bus #4 from Constitución downtown and ask the driver to tell you where to disembark.

Also worth a visit are the **Grutas de García,** 45km northwest of the city. You'll have to take the bus if you don't have a car. Once there, avoid the hard climb of more than 700m by taking the cable railway car (included in the 5000-peso admission). Dozens of now individually named chambers sat underwater 50 or 60 million years ago; the numerous sedimentary layers testify to that fact. Take a **Transportes Monterrey-Saltillo** bus from the terminal; call for the schedule (tel. 43-66-16).

San Luis Potosí

For those travelers who love to laze around town squares on warm afternoons, watching the world pass by, San Luis Potosí's plaza-studded streets could be as close to heaven as they get before actually passing into the hinterworld. Those with a desire for slightly more active entertainment can take advantage of the city's colonial museums, palaces, churches, and cathedrals.

Founded in 1592, San Luis Potosí was named after St. Louis, King of France. After the Spaniards learned from the Huachichiles of the rich mines in the region, the word Potosí ("Place of Wealth" in Inca) was appended because the city's mineral wealth was comparable to that of Potosí in Bolivia. Gold and silver helped make San Luis Potosí one of the three most important cities in Mexico during the 17th century, when it had jurisdiction over most of northern Mexico, including Texas and Louisiana.

Orientation and Practical Information

San Luis Potosí is at the approximate center of a triangle of Mexico's largest cities—Monterrey, Guadalajara, and Mexico City. Five main highways (Rtes. 57, 85, 70, 49, and 80) lead into San Luis Potosí.

To get downtown from the bus station, exit the station and catch a bus (300 pesos) called "Alameda" or "Centro"; always confirm the destination, because drivers are sometimes a bit slow in changing their windshield signs and your bus could be headed for Timbuktu even if it says "Centro." Taxis to *el centro* cost 5000 pesos.

Tourist Office: Manuel José Othón 130, 2nd floor (tel. 231-43), just east of the Pl. de Armas. Responsive staff respond only in Spanish. Large envelopes with maps and a huge amount of tourist information. Open Mon.-Fri. 9am-8pm, Sat. 9am-2pm.

Currency Exchange: Many banks around the Pl. de Armas open Mon.-Fri. 9am-noon, including **Banco Mexicano Somex,** Allende at Arista (tel. 292-93), 2 blocks north of the plaza's northwest corner. The *casa de cambio* at Obregón 407 is open Mon.-Fri. 9am-2pm and 4-8pm, Sat. 9am-2pm.

Post Office: Morelos 235 (tel. 227-40), between Salazar and Insurgentes, 1 block east and 4 blocks north of Pl. de Armas's northeast corner. Lista de Correos posted Mon.-Fri. 8am-2pm. Open Mon.-Fri. 8am-7pm, Sat. 9am-1pm. **Postal Code:** 78000.

Telephones: Los Bravo 423, ½ block west of Constitución. International collect calls 2000 pesos per 5 min. Open Mon.-Sat. 9am-8pm.

Airport: Served by **Mexicana,** Madero at Uresti (tel. 411-19). Flights to: Mexico City (Fri.-Mon., 142,000 pesos); Monterrey (Wed.-Sat., 148,000 pesos); Chicago (Wed.-Sat., US$75). Office open Mon.-Fri. 9am-6pm.

Train Station: Ferrocarriles Nacionales de México, on Othón across from the Alameda. Daily service to: Mexico City (*primera especial* 23,600 pesos); Tampico (9800 pesos); Monterrey (27,000 pesos); Nuevo Laredo (41,600 pesos); Aguascalientes (2500 pesos).

Bus Station: Central Camionera Plan de San Luis (tel. 274-11), 2 blocks south of the Glorieta Benito Juárez, several kilometers east of the city center along Av. Universidad. Twelve-odd different bus companies, each serving 15-40 cities. From here you can easily get anywhere in the northern half of the Republic. Among the cheaper lines are **Estrella Blanca** (tel. 829-63), **Transportes de Frontera** (tel. 830-49), and **Flecha Amarilla** (tel. 829-23). Estrella Blanca sends buses south to Mexico City (33 per day, 5 hr., 17,500 pesos) and Guadalajara (8 per day, 6 hr., 14,500 pesos). Transportes de Frontera goes north to Monterrey (every ½ hr., 7 hr., 22,000 pesos) and Matamoros (5 per day, 9 hr., 27,000 pesos).

Taxis: Tel. 221-22.

Car Rental: Budget, Carranza 885 (tel. 450-59).

Car Trouble: Angeles Verdes Auxilio Turístico, Jardín Guerrero 14 (tel. 409-06).

Laundromat: Lavandería La Burbuja, Nicolas Zapata 535. Four-kilogram load costs 8000 pesos and takes 2 hr. Open Mon.-Sat. 9am-7pm.

Red Cross, Juárez at Díaz Gutiérrez (tel. 533-22 or 536-65).

Pharmacy: Farmacia San Luis, Hidalgo 115 (tel. 220-21), ½ block north of the northeast corner of the Pl. de Armas. Open 24 hr.

Medical Care: Hospital Central, Carranza 2395 (tel. 701-64), several kilometers west of *el centro* along Carranza, on the west side of the city.

Police: Palacio Municipal (tel. 225-76 or 256-33).

Accommodations

Hotels in San Luis Potosí range from the five-star Hostal del Quijote—complete with gourmet restaurant, tennis courts, its own car rental, and more—to the standard CREA youth hostel. Try to avoid all lodgings near the bus station: the neighborhood is sleazy, and you'll get better deals closer to the center of the city.

Near Alameda Juan Sarabía and Plaza del Carmen

This area has the highest concentration of hotels in the city. Many are rather expensive, but tucked among them are several more economical options. All are an easy walk away from the great downtown sights and sites.

Hotel Anáhuac, Xochitl (say that three times fast) 140 (tel. 260-05). Clean, blue rooms, some with closets. Mix-and-match toilets and toilet seats, but no germs. One of the best buys downtown. Singles 24,000 pesos. Doubles 30,000 pesos.

Hotel Principal, Juan Sarabía 145 (tel. 207-84). A fancily tiled floor leads to rooms wrapped around a courtyard with a few potted plants. Patchwork quilts on beds hark back to Little House on the Prairie days. Singles 20,000 pesos. Doubles 35,000 pesos.

Hotel Jardín Potosí, Bravo 530 (tel. 231-52). The courtyard is very yellow, and the 2nd-floor scale will tell your fortune for only 50 pesos. Maybe it was decided to forgo hot water in the bathrooms and install shiny bottle openers instead. Singles 24,000 pesos. Doubles 30,000 pesos.

Hotel Guadalajara, Xochitl 253 (tel. 246-12). Some of the friendly staff speak English. Rooms no bigger than average, but spiffier and better-equipped, with fan, phone, firm bed, and black-and-white TV. Avoid the rooms facing the train station. The wallpaper mural around the courtyard features Oregon's sublime Mt. Jefferson. Singles 36,000 pesos. Doubles 40,000 pesos, with 2 beds 45,000 pesos.

Near Plaza de Armas

Hotel Plaza, Jardín Hidalgo (tel. 246-31), on the south side of the Pl. de Armas. Charming old relic run by a spry old man with a smoker's voice. The rooms on the plaza have balconies and TVs. Plenty of hot water to fill the large tubs. Plaza rooms for 1 or 2 people 40,000 pesos. Other singles 25,000 pesos. Doubles 30,000 pesos.

Hotel de Gante, 5 de Mayo 140 (tel. 214-93). Efficient service, along with the carpet and TV, might convince you to stay here. Quiet. Singles 35,000 pesos. Doubles 41,276 pesos.

Hotel Concordia, Othón at Morelos (tel. 206-66), 1 block east of Pl. de Armas's southeast corner. Fancier than Hotel de Gante, but de Gante should be fancy enough. Spacious rooms with phones, TVs, and comfortable beds. Restaurant and parking at your fingertips. Singles 70,000 pesos. Doubles 85,000 pesos.

Near the Bus Station

The Central de Camiones blends right into a noisy commercial sprawl of auto repair shops and hardware stores. The air is polluted and the streets unsanitary, but if proximity to the station is your top priority, this is the place and these are the hotels.

CREA Youth Hostel (IYHF) (tel. 266-03), on Diagonal Sur in front of Glorieta Benito Juárez, 1 block straight ahead as you exit the bus station. Tiny 4-person rooms with uncomfortable beds and some mosquitoes, but everything is clean—including the communal bathrooms. Separate women's and men's areas. Access to sports complex with basketball courts, soccer fields, swimming pool, and track. 5000 pesos per person, 500-peso discount with CREA, IYHF, or AYH card. Blankets, sheets, pillowcase, towel, and locker included. Breakfast an additional 3500 pesos, lunch and dinner 4500 pesos.

Hotel Central, De las Torres 290 (tel. 420-01), in a run-down neighborhood but carpeted rooms have lots of hot water and enough pressure to push it; if you hole up indoors and watch TV, you'll be fine. Singles 35,000 pesos. Doubles 45,000 pesos.

Food

The cuisine of San Luis Potosí is called *huasteca* (or *potosina*.) Unlike those in other areas, most restaurants here serve European rolls rather than corn tortillas with meals. *Taquitos dorados* are thin slices of chicken or beef rolled in corn tortillas and fried in oil; *tacos potosinos* are stuffed with cheese and vegetables. *Enchiladas potosinas* have become popular in North American primary-school lunch programs—these morsels burst with cheese, red chiles, and onions, all smothered in more cheese. Delicious *nopalitos* are tiny pieces of cactus cooked in a tomato, oregano, and onion sauce. *Cabuches* are the small, yellow, and tasty fruit of a kind of cactus, served in a *ranchero* sauce. As unusual as it sounds, *chongos coronados* (curdled milk in sweet maple water) is a popular dessert. Cheap restaurants prepare these specialties in the area between the Alameda and the Pl. del Carmen.

Restaurante Posada del Virrey-Cafetería, Jardín Hidalgo 3, on the north side of the Pl. de Armas. Everybody who's anybody comes here for the superior domestic cuisine. An attractive place in a building that was once the home of Mexico's only *virreina*. Front tables have views of the plaza. Breakfast specials 6500-9500 pesos. Spanish chicken 9500 pesos. Open daily 7am-11pm.

Las Tortugas, Obregón at Allende. A simple diner for youths and families who want a quick bite. Counter seats afford panoramic views of the cooks preparing your *tortas* (2200 pesos). They also deliver (tel. 12-00-29). Open daily 7am-10pm.

Restaurant La Lonja, Aldama 300, 1 block west of the southwest corner of the Pl. de Armas. Velvet chairs and gold columns complement thorough service: they pour your beer and place a napkin on your lap, graciously overlooking the fact that you're wearing a pair of scruffy shorts and a ripped T-shirt. French, Italian, and Spanish cuisine, but concentrate on the delicious *potosina* dishes (8300-21,000 pesos). Open Mon.-Sat. noon-11pm, Sun. 1-6pm.

Mariscos Veda, Bravos 510, near the Hotel Jardín. Blue tiled interior lit with a few Japanese lanterns. Get (jump) started with a cup of *sake* (6000 pesos). Try the sushi if you dare (Japanese raw seafood in the middle of Mexico?) for 10,000 pesos. Open Tues.-Sun. 11am-8pm.

Restaurante La Parroquia, Carranza 301, on the south side of the Pl. de los Fundadores. Jammed at lunch; cross your fingers for a booth from which you can watch people on the plaza. All kinds of Mexican beer. Chicken *torta* 3300 pesos. *Menú del día* 6100 pesos. Open daily 7am-midnight.

Cafe Inpiña, Carranza at Carmona, across from the Parroquia. Rubber plants and fake birds adorn the interior, and a nacho stand in the corner serves people outside. Chocolate crepes or hot fudge sundae 4500 pesos. Open daily 8am-10pm.

La Virreina, Carranza 830. Elegant to the max. They frown on the concept of shorts, much less their physical embodiment. Live piano 2:30-3:30pm and 7-9:30pm. Listen to old Billy Joel tunes as you slurp the oyster cocktail (14,500 pesos). If you get lucky in the lottery, chateaubriand (62,000 pesos) is a nice treat.

La Gran Vía, Carranza 560. Excellent Spanish food in an atmosphere not quite as stuffy as La Virreina's, although the stained glass and tiled arches strive for elegance. Save room for the dessert cart. *Medallons al Tequila* 24,750 pesos. *El Tournedos Casa Blanca* 23,000 pesos. Open daily 1-11pm.

La Cigarra, Carranza 950. A great place to stuff yourself. If you get hungry strolling through the Zona Rosa (see Entertainment below), stop here for affordable Mexican fare. Entrees 7000-15,000 pesos, *tostadas* and the like around 3000 pesos. It's gotta be popular to stay open daily 8am-4am.

Sights and Entertainment

Often called the "city of plazas," San Luis Potosí seems to have one at every street corner. All of the sights in San Luis are within walking distance of the **Plaza de Armas** (also known as Jardín Hidalgo). Its red sandstone central kiosk, completed in 1848, bears the names of famous Mexican musicians. At the beginning of the 17th century, residents watched bullfights in the dusty plaza from the balconies of the surrounding buildings. Three blocks east along Manuel Othón from the Pl. de Armas is the expansive **Alameda Juan Sarabía** with its trees, benches, statues, and artificial ponds, but beware: the area is dangerous at night. The route between the two plazas passes **Plaza del Carmen** (where bronze fish support the bowl of a fountain with their tails), 1 block west of Alameda and 2 blocks east of the Pl. de Armas. Walk 2 blocks south and 2 blocks west from the Pl. de Armas's southwest corner to reach the **Plaza de San Francisco,** with its own bronze fountain, quaint cobblestone street, and red sandstone buildings. The **Plaza de Aranzazu,** an empty square bordered by a pretty colonnade, is the name of the western Pl. de San Francisco. Reach it by following the cobbled Universidad to its end.

Benito Juárez led the fight against Emperor Maximilian from the **Palacio de Gobierno,** on the west side of the Pl. de Armas. From here, he ordered assassins to murder the transplanted Habsburg duke. Maximilian, Miramón, and Mejí were executed on June 19, 1867, near Querétaro, the imperial stronghold that was established after General Bazaine abandoned the country.

On the Palacio de Gobierno's second floor, in the **Sala Juárez,** is a diorama of the dramatic meeting between Juárez and Princess Salm Salm, who begged Juárez for Maximilian's life on the night before the execution. Plastic figures of Benito Juárez and the beautiful princess are positioned in front of the table at which Juárez signed Maximilian's sentence. The *sala* also contains a mask and a portrait of the president. As you enter the palace, go upstairs and turn left at the top of the staircase—the Sala Juárez is the first room on your left. **Sala Hidalgo,** to the right at the top of the stairs, displays oil portraits of Miguel Hidalgo (a copy of the one at Dolores Hidalgo) and of four other heroes of independence: Mariano Jiménez, Vicente Guerrero, Guadalupe Victoria, and Padre José María Morelos y Pavón. (Salas Juárez and Hidalgo have no fixed hours but are usually open Mon.-Fri. 9:30am-1:30pm.)

Opposite the Palacio de Gobierno stands the **cathedral,** its two towers crowned at night by Churrigueresque blue neon crosses. The cathedral was satisfactorily completed in 1710, but in 1855 San Luis became a diocese and more work was done to upgrade the building. Miners selflessly donated gold and silver to beautify the interior, and marble statues of the apostles (small copies of those at the Basilica of San Juan de Letrán in Rome) were placed in the niches between the Solomonic columns of the Baroque façade. The northern tower was built of gray sandstone at the beginning of this century to commemorate the centennial of Mexico's independence. (Open daily 7am-2pm and 4-8pm, but try not to gawk during Sunday mass.)

The **Palacio Municipal,** on the northeast corner of the plaza, was the city's second vice-regal building, replacing the one burned down by the citizens of San Luis Potosí in 1777 to protest Carlos III's expulsion of the Jesuits from the Americas. Typical pinkish stone adorns the courtyard, but the stairway has an interesting painted ceiling along with simple mosaics underfoot. Walk 1 block west of the southwest corner of the Pl. de Armas for a look at the **Antigua Real Caja** (Old Royal Treasury), the city's only existing secular Baroque building. A truncated corner of the building serves as its façade. Today the building belongs to the Universidad Autónoma de San Luis Potosí.

Walking east from the Pl. de Armas toward the Pl. del Carmen on Othón, you pass the modest **Casa Othón,** home of the illustrious *poeta potosina* Manuel José Othón (1858-1906). Inside are some of his original letters and publications. (Open Tues.-Fri. 8am-7pm, Sat.-Sun. 10am-2pm. Free.)

Nicolás Fernando de Torres, a rich Sevillan of the early 18th century, made his fortune in San Luis Potosí. After his death, his estate was used to found a church and convent of the ascetic Carmelite order. The huge complex, built to comply with his wishes, encompassed a large area around the Pl. del Carmen and all of the present Alameda Juan Sarabía. Today only the **Iglesia del Carmen,** on the northwest corner of the plaza of the same name, remains. It is the most beautiful religious building in San Luis Potosí. Affixed to the façade are statues of San Eliseo, San Elías, and, at the very top, the Madonna. The main altar was reconstructed with sandstone by architect Tresguerras after the original was destroyed in 1827.

The most fascinating attraction in San Luis Potosí is the unique **Museo Nacional de la Máscara,** Villerías 2 (tel. 230-25), in the Palacio Federal, ½ block south of the Pl. del Carmen along Villerías. This beautiful building of pink sandstone contains hundreds of masks from every Mexican region. An eloquent diatribe against cultural Eurocentrism opens the exhibit. Explanatory plaques in Spanish (complete with a quote from Nietzsche) accompany the masks; if you can't understand the words, the masks' visual effect is still entertaining. (Open Tues.-Fri. 10am-2pm and 4-6pm, Sat.-Sun. 10am-2pm. Free.)

Eight years after the city's founding, construction began on the **Iglesia de San Francisco,** on the west side of the Pl. de San Francisco. Its external decoration is not as impressive as that of the cathedral or the Carmen, but the orange stucco façade, distinguished by a Sevillan clock of 1759 and a statue of St. Francis above the door, pleasantly complements the quiet plaza in front. The most eventful doorway in the sacristy is the one to the Salón de Profundis, which depicts St. Frailón washing the sacred cuts of St. Francis. A wonderful Churrigueresque fountain dominates this room; the Franciscans chanted the Profundis here every morning after waking. (Open daily 10am-2pm and 4-6pm.)

The **Museo Regional Potosino,** Galeana 485 (tel. 251-85), along the street on San Francisco's southern side, occupies the former Franciscan convent grounds. The government seized the land in 1950 and converted part of it into the museum. Inside the former convent—preserved on the museum's first floor—is the marvelous Capilla a la Virgen de Aranzazu. *Aranzazu* means "from within the thorns": a shepherd found the altar's image of the Virgin in a prickly thicket. The *ex-votos* along the walls are a tradition among Mexico's devoted; each depicts a miracle that a parishioner has experienced. They are often painted anonymously and then hung in the church near an image of the Virgin Mary. A huge 18th-century hymnal stands to the right of the altar and next to the bishop's sedan chair.

Archeological exhibits on the first floor consist of artifacts from different parts of the country: two *yogos,* large stone rings placed around people's heads for burial; the dress of modern *indígenas;* and artifacts from San Luis Potosí's colonial past—lockboxes, locks, irons, spears, frisbees, branding irons, daggers, and 12th-century chain mail. (Museum open Tues.-Fri. 10am-1pm and 3-6pm, Sat. 10am-noon, Sun. 10am-1pm. Admission 550 pesos.)

A San Luis Potosí anomaly erupts on the south side of the Alameda. The **Centro de Difusión Cultural** of the Instituto Potosino de Bellas Artes, Av. Universidad and Negrete (tel. 243-33), is not a graceful colonial edifice but a modern structure of bold curves. The museum devotes four large halls to contemporary artists. (Open Tues.-Sun. 10am-2pm and 5-8pm.)

The **Parque Tangamanga** has it all: three lakes for paddleboating and fishing; a baseball field; motor-cross, auto-cross, and bike-cross grounds; a running path; and a playground complete with electric cars. Other park facilities include a planetarium, an observatory, and the open-air **Teatro de la Ciudad,** which holds 8000 people and hosts frequent cultural and artistic events (information at tourist office). To get to the park, catch a yellow-and-blue Perimetral bus (300 pesos) on Constitución across the Alameda. Get off at the Monumento a la Revolución. (Open daily 6am-5pm. Free.)

San Luis Potosí's **Zona Rosa** lies west of *el centro* along Carranza between Uresti and Otero. At Uresti, Carranza widens to accommodate a strip of palms down its center. Here you will find some of San Luis's best shops and finer restaurants. At night the cool street fills with couples, university students, and club-hopping tourists.

The last two weeks of August mark the **Fiesta Nacional Potosina.** Concerts, cock and bull fights, and a parade guarantee a swell time for all.

Near San Luis Potosí

Santa María del Río, 45 minutes south of San Luis on the buses of Flecha Amarilla (1400 pesos) or Autobuses Rojos San Luis-Santa María (1350 pesos), is the state's renowned *rebozo* (shawl) capital: the Escuela de Artesanías here has a wide selection, but the best are made in private homes. Ask one of the instructors or administrators in the school to direct you to private crafters.

Also south of San Luis is the state-run and reasonably priced resort of **Gogorrón.** Make reservations at the office of Centro Vacacional Gogorrón in the Edificio San Rafael, Othón and Zaragoza, 4th floor (tel. 236-36). Guests enjoy the waters of the hot spring, even hotter Roman baths, and swimming pools. Staying the night in this facility is an expensive but restorative way to end an extended low-budget stay in Mexico. (*Cabañas chicas* 86,000 pesos, 34,000 pesos per additional person; 3 meals and bath included.) For daytrippers, the Roman baths cost 8000 pesos per hour. Use of the other facilities costs 6000 pesos per day, including access to the pool and shower. Flecha Amarilla buses (2400 pesos) leave for Gogorrón every 30 minutes from San Luis Potosí's bus station. If you're driving, take the highway to Querétaro, go right at the sign that says Villa de Reyes, and proceed 19km to Gogorrón. All reservations and arrangements should be made at the San Luis office.

There is also a mineral spring at **Ojo Caliente,** 40km south of San Luis Potosí on Hwy. 57 to Querétaro. Another spring is in **Lourdes,** 64km from San Luis Potosí on Hwy. 57. "Agua de Lourdes" supposedly cures all ills, especially gastric and intestinal ones, and is sold in take-home bottles in case the baths fail to heal you immediately. A small hotel here serves meals. (For reservations call (481) 714-04 from San Luis Potosí or go in person to the Lourdes office at Francisco Zarco 389.

Ciudad Juárez to Aguascalientes

The blisteringly hot trek from Ciudad Juárez to southern Mexico on Rte. 45 lacks the scenic appeal of the Pacific or Gulf route. But to judge the entire region by the trip down Rte. 45 is akin to judging Germany by a cruise on the Autobahn. Discovering the area's attractions may take a little effort and imagination, but the initiative is amply rewarded with breathtaking Sierra Madre landscapes, especially in the Barranca del Cobre.

Ghosts of Mexican history haunt the pre-Columbian *pueblos* of Casas Grandes and the Revolutionary monuments around Zacatecas. The region has a character unique to Mexico, due to the paradox of prosperity underlying the Old West atmosphere. Customized pickup trucks, huge white Stetsons, alligator-skin boots, and other emblems of conspicuous consumption outfit many a *mexicano* in this region.

Ciudad Juárez

The twin cities of Ciudad Juárez and El Paso, TX, consume every square foot of El Paso del Norte, the only easy path across the border through the Sierra Madre Occidental del Norte. This strategic site, once part of an important *indígena* trading route, was one of the first occupied by the Spanish conquistadors as they marched north.

With more than one million inhabitants, Ciudad Juárez is the largest city in the state of Chihuahua and the busiest legal border crossing in Mexico. Founded in the 17th century by Spanish monks, the city was named in 1888 to honor Benito Juárez. Where they merge at the border, El Paso and Juárez are remarkably similar; in fact, if it weren't for the murky Río Grande, it would be impossible to tell the cities apart. Juárez has better typical border town activity: bullfights, dog races, tourist markets, nightclubs, seedy bars, and a seemingly endless procession of cabbies, shopkeepers, and street peddlers eager to relieve you of your pesos.

Many Mexican police patrolling Juárez's streets maintain a relatively safe environment for the daytime visitor, but caution should be exercised at night when packs of *gringos* who develop their interest in Mexico only after sundown invade the city.

Orientation

Where to cross into Juárez depends on your goal. From downtown El Paso, the Stanton and Santa Fe St. Bridges lead into the heart of **Old Juárez,** also called *el centro,* where markets, restaurants, and bars thrive. Two miles east, U.S. 54 crosses the border at the Puente Córdova and becomes Av. Lincoln: this road leads to the ProNaf shopping mall and studio complex with resident craftspeople and predictable prices. The Stanton St. Bridge is restricted to traffic entering Juárez, the Santa Fe to departing vehicles. The Córdova Bridge allows two-way traffic. Pedestrians can come and go on all of the bridges.

Crossing the border on foot is simple; just pay the border guard 15¢ or 600 pesos. Cars must pay 50¢ or 2000 pesos. To venture farther into Mexico, you must obtain a tourist card at the immigration office. You won't need it until you reach the immigration checkpoint 32km into the interior, but if you don't have it then, they'll send you back (see Tourist Cards in the General Introduction). The immigration office is immediately to the right as you cross the Stanton St. Bridge. (Open 24 hr.) From the El Paso airport, a bus runs from Montana Av. to the Stanton St. Bridge.

Most of Old Juárez can be covered on foot, but the ProNaf center, the bus terminal, and the Lienzo Charro bullring are out of walking range. City buses (450 pesos) come in all shapes and colors, with destinations scrawled on the windshield.

The **Central Camionera** (bus terminal) sits on the corner of Paseo Triunfo de la República and López Mateos. From *el centro,* bus "Ruta 8" stops along Malecón, near the Stanton St. Bridge, then passes the ProNaf center; if you take it to the end of the line and walk over to Triunfo de la República, you'll arrive at the bus terminal. To return to the center of town, cross López Mateos and catch a bus labeled "centro." Bus service also connects the El Paso Greyhound bus station to the terminals in Juárez, but costs a few extra pesos. Taxi rides from the border to the bus station run about US$3.

Exact addresses in Juárez are virtually unknown; most everything is located by a street name and a wave of the hand.

Practical Information

Tourist Office: (tel. 14-08-37) on Malecón, in the basement of a government building between Lerdo and Juárez, to the right as you cross the Stanton St. Bridge. Helpful staff, lots of brochures, and municipal maps. Open Mon.-Fri. 8am-3:30pm and 4-7pm, Sat. 8am-2pm.

U.S. Consulate: López Mateos Nte. 924 (tel. 13-40-48). In emergencies dial (915) 525-6060.

Currency Exchange: Many banks congregate near the bus station and along 16 de Septiembre. Most open Mon.-Fri. 9am-1pm. Virtually no *casa de cambio* or bank will accept traveler's checks. This problem recurs throughout northern Mexico, where real greenbacks are the weapon of choice. If you find a place that will take your checks, unload them pronto.

Post Office: Lerdo at Ignacio Peña. Open Mon.-Fri. 8am-7pm, Sat. 9am-1pm, Sun. 9am-noon. **Postal Code:** 32000.

Telephone: For an international operator, dial 09; for a national operator, dial 02; for an El Paso operator, dial 08. **Telephone Code:** 132.

Abraham González Airport: (tel. 17-30-95) about 17km out Rte. 45 (Carretera Panorámica). Primary carrier is **Aeroméxico.** Ground transportation to the city center costs 10,000 pesos.

Train Station: Ramón Corona at Insurgentes, 12 blocks down Lerdo (which becomes Corona) from the Stanton St. Bridge.

Bus Station: Triunfo de la República at López Mateos (tel. 13-16-04), just north of the ProNaf center and next to the Río Grande mall. Open 24 hr. To: Mexico City (10 per day, 84,000 pesos); Monterrey (2 per day, 54,000 pesos); Guadalajara (8 per day, 69,000 pesos); Chihuahua (every ½ hr., 46,000 pesos); Nuevo Casas Grandes (10 per day, 17,000 pesos); El Paso (every hr., 5000 pesos).

Red Cross: Tel. 16-58-06.

24-Hr. Pharmacy: Farmacia Avenida, 16 de Septiembre 1618 (tel. 12-66-23), at Francisco Villa.

Hospital General: Trifuno de la República and Montes de Ocacas (tel. 13-15-71).

Police: Oro and 16 de Septiembre (tel. 15-14-78).

Accommodations

Although Juárez supports a multitude of inexpensive hotels, finding one that fulfills First World expectations can be a challenge. Hotels that meet even minimal standards are among the most expensive budget rooms in all of Mexico. The few extra dollars necessary to stay in El Paso is money well spent.

Hotel Impala, Lerdo Nte. 670 (tel. 15-04-31), about 100m from the Stanton St. Bridge. An expensive class act. Clean rooms with A/C, TV, and telephone. Secure parking lot. Smiling, helpful staff. Singles and doubles 60,000 pesos.

Hotel Villa Manport, Escobar and Panama (tel. 13-93-15). A long, tiresome walk from Av. Juárez, but with the most amenities of any Juárez spot. Singles 42,000 pesos. Doubles 50,000 pesos.

Hotel Juárez, Lerdo Nte. 143 (tel. 15-03-58). A step above the Morán, but nothing Benito would write home about. Clean bathrooms, but the "purified" water in every room sits in open jars. Singles 35,000 pesos. Doubles 42,000 pesos.

Hotel Morán, Juárez 264 (tel. 15-08-02). Stucco walls with orange trim, saggy beds, chairs in closets, and the legacy of room 29 somehow manage to create a comfortable atmosphere. Toilets conveniently located in the showers. Singles 35,000 pesos. Doubles 42,000 pesos.

Food

Juárez is crammed with cheap restaurants that won't burn a hole in your pocket but might in your stomach lining. The many restaurants aimed at American tastes are usually clean, air-conditioned, and inexpensive.

Nuevo Restaurante Martino, Juárez 643. Juárez's half-hearted attempt at elegance. Lunch special (US$4.75) with soup, salad, and beef brochette is served 11:30am-3pm.

Florida, Juárez 412. Welcome to the Mexican version of Denny's, with prices just like those north of the border. The Mexican plate, a large helping of Tex-Mex goodies, goes for US$8. Open daily 11am-midnight. MC, Visa, and pesos accepted.

Hotel Santa Fe Restaurant, Lerdo 673, at Tlaxcala across from the Hotel Impala. The *caldo de pollo* (5000 pesos) is perfect for *turista* victims. Hotcakes and 2 fried eggs 6800 pesos. Open 24 hr.

El Coyote Inválido, Juárez 910, at Colón. Clean diner where locals and chatty construction workers from Texas gather. Laminated pictures of random dishes tacked above the counter. Huge menu. Octopus cocktail 9200 pesos. Open 24 hr.

Sights

The **Parque Chamizal,** near the Córdova Bridge, is a good place to escape the noise of the city if not the heat. In the midst of the park, the **Museo Arqueológico** in the park displays little of interest: one room features plastic facsimiles of pre-Conquest sculptures and a few paintings, and the other contains a variety of trilobite fossils, rocks, styrofoam hamburger containers, and bones. (Open Mon.-Sat. 9am-2pm, Sun. 1-8pm. Free.)

The ProNaf center, distant from the park at Lincoln and 16 de Septiembre, contains the **Museo de Arte y Historia,** with exhibits on Mexican culture. Also at the ProNaf center, the **Centro Artesanal** sells handmade goods at maximum prices; haggle here. The "Ruta 8" bus will take you from *el centro* to ProNaf for 350 pesos; a taxi charges 10 times as much.

Entertainment

A few blocks down from the bus terminal, at República and Huerta, the **Plaza Monumental de Toros** stages eight bullfights each Sunday evening in the summer. Seats on the shady side of the ring range from US$3.50 to US$11. The **Lienzo de Charro,** on Av. Charro off República, also conducts bullfights and *charreada* (rodeo) on Sunday afternoons during the summer. At the western edge of town, the **Juárez Racetrack** rises from Vicente Guerrero. Dogs run Wednesday through Sunday at 7:30pm. Sunday matinees during the summer are at 2:30pm. Horse racing can be seen only on closed-circuit TV.

Every June, the month-long **Feria** (expo fair) offers flocks of cockfights, amusement rides, and the best deals on arts and crafts from around the country. The evening festivities usually begin at 5pm. Ask the tourist office for exact information and directions.

Juárez has so many bars that simply counting them can make you dizzy even before you partake of their refreshments. Many establishments are unsavory, and even the savory ones can become dangerous; stick to the well-traveled strip along Av. Juárez. On weekends, American teens swarm to Juárez to join their Mexican friends in a 48-hour quest for fun, fights, and fiestas.

Kentucky Club, Juárez 629. The nicest in Juárez. Long mahogany bar backed by embossed mirrors so the middle-aged clientele can check to see that their hair is in place. Must be 21 years old to be served. Mexican beer 80¢. Pesos accepted.

Old West Disco, Malecon and Juárez. Closest to the border. Like a high school dance, only with Coronas and smokes. Eager teenyboppers hop in to party and fight. 5000-peso cover includes 1 drink.

Don Felix, Juárez 532. *Gringos* and locals come here to shoot billiards and improve international relations. Two Coronas US$1.75. Open 24 hr.

Disco Sarawak, on Juárez, next to Martino's. *Saturday Night Fever* goes south of the border. Mexican and Anglo dance music, cheap booze, and bright flashing lights. No cover.

Casas Grandes and Nuevo Casas Grandes

Even though the six-hour journey south from Juárez through the scenic Chihuahuan Desert is extraordinarily peaceful, arriving at the foothills of the Sierra Madres in the lush valley of Nuevo Casas Grandes is a cool relief. The valley's claim to fame is the extensive ruins of **Paquimé** (pronounced pah-kee-MAY) in Casas Grandes, the most important city in pre-Conquest northern Mexico. Often considered a mere rest stop for travelers en route to Chihuahua, this modern town is a worthy destination in its own right. Social life still revolves around the Zócalo, and the absence of tourists lends the town an authenticity rarely found in northwest Mexico.

Orientation and Practical Information

Of the bus companies serving Nuevo Casas Grandes, **Omnibus de México** is the most reliable one, providing local first-class buses to Chihuahua for 16,000 pesos. Departure time is 5am, and additional *de paso* buses leave at 8:30am, 2:30pm, and 4pm. The terminal is located on 16 de Septiembre, which runs parallel to 5 de Mayo, about 1 block down from Obregón.

Though the town sprawls for miles, everything important is in the compact downtown area. The **post office** (with Lista de Correos), at 16 de Septiembre and Madero, is 1 block from 5 de Mayo (open Mon.-Fri. 9am-1pm and 3-6pm, Sat. 9am-1pm).

The **postal code** is 31700. To exchange currency, go to **Casa de Cambio California,** Constitución 207 (open daily 9am-10pm), or **Banco Internacional,** at Obregón and 5 de Mayo (open Mon.-Fri. 9am-1:30pm). The **police** (tel. 418-20) are on 20 de Noviembre. A laundromat, **Lavasolas Paquimé** (tel. 413-20), stands next to the Hotel Paquimé (open daily 7:30am-7pm).

Accommodations

Hotel California, Constitución 209 (tel. 411-10), 1 block north of 5 de Mayo. Such a lovely place, you may never leave. Cable TV, A/C, telephones, racquetball courts, saunas, and wicker for all. Singles 40,000 pesos. Doubles 50,000 pesos.

Motel Piñón, Juárez Nte. 605 (tel. 406-55). A/C, TV, *agua purificada,* phones, nice carpeting, and the list goes on, but they forgot to water the pool. Very clean. Singles 50,000 pesos. Doubles 65,000 pesos.

Hotel Paquimé, Juárez Nte. (tel. 413-20), 1 block before Piñón. Spotless carpeted rooms with phones, and a small courtyard graced by a fountain. Singles 50,000 pesos. Doubles 65,000 pesos.

Food and Entertainment

The dearth of tourists makes dining out cheap. For the same reason, however, nightlife is soporific, and the few bars in town do not welcome women.

Restaurante Constantino, Juárez at Minerva. Friendly service complements the bilingual menu. Try the swiss enchiladas (10,350 pesos) and freshly-squeezed orange juice. Open daily 7am-midnight.

Dinno's Pizza, Constitución at Minerva. Small pizzas, short on sauce, cost 18,000 pesos. A large goes for 25,000 pesos. Open daily 8am-11:30pm.

Tom's Hamburguesas, Minerva 106, at Victoria. Spotless joint whose friendly, English-speaking waiters dish out a delicious (by Mexican standards) hamburger for 7500 pesos. Open daily 9am-10pm.

For entertainment, the closest thing to fun is the **Piano Bar Los Faroles,** Juárez 604 (tel. 415-95), across from the Piñón. Relax and hum along with your favorite Mel Tormé tunes.

Casas Grandes

Eight kilometers southwest of Nuevo Casas Grandes, the pre-Conquest city of Paquimé lay hidden underground for 600 years. The dual nature of its architecture suggests that Casas Grandes (so named upon excavation) grew out of two different cultures: its many-storied *pueblos* resemble those in the southwestern U.S., but its step pyramids are similar to those in central and southern Mexico. The ruins surround a partially excavated central market area as well as a ballcourt. Between 1000 and 1200 AD, Paquimé was the most important agricultural and trading center in northern Mexico. The inhabitants kept parrots and turkeys in cool adobe pens and built indoor aqueducts and hidden cisterns to supply the *pueblos* in times of siege. Around 1340, Aztec invaders burned the abandoned buildings. First exhumed in the early 1970s, Paquimé is now an archeological zone administered by the Mexican government. Unfortunately, once it had been exposed to the satisfaction of both archeologists and tourists, its high mud walls began to crumble. Visitors should avoid abrading the thin walls. Upon the death in 1986 of archeologist Eduardo Contreras, "El Señor de Paquimé," restoration efforts were suspended indefinitely.

Paquimé deserves a visit, but bring sun protection: a broad-brimmed hat (cheap sombreros cost 13,000 pesos in town) and, most importantly, as many canteens and bottles of water as you can handle. On summer afternoons, the 100°F weather and the absence of shade can make the site an inferno.

To reach Paquimé, take the municipal bus from the corner of Constitución and 16 de Septiembre to the village of Casas Grandes (every 45 min., 400 pesos). When the bus deposits you in the main plaza of the village, look to your left for the sign that points in the direction of the ruins and trot along for about 10 minutes.

Admission to the ruins currently costs 700 pesos, but tourism officials warn that a steep price hike is on the horizon.

Chihuahua

Rising from the center of Mexico's vast northern desert, Chihuahua seems little more than an inconveniently located outpost of the civilization to the south. This seclusion convinced Pancho Villa to establish his Revolutionary headquarters here. During the conflict, his eclectic band of cowboys, bandits, and vagabonds staged flamboyant attacks against the Porfiriato, streaming down from Chihuahua like eagles from a remote aerie. The man is a legendary figure to most *Chihuahuenses,* and Quinta Luz, Villa's sprawling colonial home, is the city's star attraction.

Now the capital of Mexico's richest state, Chihuahua was founded in 1709 and quickly grew into a major trading and administrative center, supporting mining and cattle operations in Chihuahua state. Today, lumber operations in the Sierra Madres yield most of the city's income.

Chihuahua may remind you of cities in the American West. Cowboy hats and enormous brass belt buckles adorn many inhabitants. Mennonites came here in great numbers from Pennsylvania Dutch country in the 1920s; today, they are among the most prosperous citizens in Cuauhtémoc and the agricultural communities around Chihuahua. As different from the *Chihuahuenses* as the Mennonites, the *indígena* Tarahumara people live in the nearby Sierra Madres. They arrive at the market in the early morning, the men in cowboy attire or baggy shorts and shirts, the women in sandals, shawls, and bright skirts.

Orientation

Located on Rte. 45 (the Pan American Hwy.), Chihuahua serves as an important transportation hub for northern Mexico. Trains arrive from the north and south at the **Estación Central de los FFNN,** División del Norte, northeast of downtown. Trains to Los Mochis through the Barranca del Cobre leave from a different station, southwest of the city center on Ocampo, 1 block from the penitentiary. Buses running up and down Ocampo shorten the 20-minute walk to the Zócalo. Pay no more than 5000 pesos for a cab, and set the price before you step in.

Buses arrive at the **Camionera Central** on Progreso. To reach the Zócalo, turn left on Progreso, then right on Ocampo. After a couple of blocks, turn left on Libertad, which runs into the plaza.

Most significant parts of Chihuahua lie within a few blocks of the Zócalo. Budget hotels and restaurants are clustered on the streets behind the cathedral. Energetic travelers can reach the train and bus stations and Quinta Luz on foot. Avenues run east-west, streets north-south. The streets, though ostensibly numbered (e.g. Calle 6), are not sequentially ordered; however, Calles 1-7 are to the north of the cathedral, and Calles 8-14 are to the south. Calle 4 has disappeared, and Calles 1 and 2 are also called "Independencia" and "Baby-Cakes."

Practical Information

Tourist Office: Reforma and 31a. Calle, in an absolutely inconvenient location.

Información y Documentación Turística: Tecnológica and Padre Infante. Convenient only for motorists arriving in Chihuahua from the highway.

Currency Exchange: Bancomer, Juárez at 6a. Calle. Open Mon.-Fri. 9am-1:30pm. The **Hotel San Francisco** on Victoria also changes money for a commission. Open 24 hr. No banks in Chihuahua exchange traveler's checks. Only the *casa de cambio* 4 blocks north of the Bancomer will do this, after exacting a hefty 3% commission.

Post Office: On Juárez, between Guerrero and Carranza on the top floors of the Padre Hidalgo museum building. Lista de Correos. Open Mon.-Fri. 8am-7pm, Sat. 9am-1pm. **Postal Code:** 31000.

Telephones: In better hotels and some pharmacies; also by the post office and scattered along the plazas. **Telephone Code:** 141.

Telegrams: At the post office. Open Mon.-Fri. 8am-11:30pm, Sat. 8am-10pm, Sun. and holidays 9am-2pm.

Airport: (tel. 12-26-95) 14km from town, ringed by auburn hills. Served by **Aeroméxico** (tel. 15-63-03) and **Aero Leo López.** To: Monterrey (1 hr., 140,000 pesos), Ciudad Juárez (45 min., 110,000 pesos), and Mexico City. Ground transportation to town (2900 pesos) available from a booth to your right as you exit the baggage area. Make Aeroméxico reservations at the Aeroméxico office on Victoria between Calle 3 and Independencia. Open Mon.-Fri. 9am-1:30pm and 3:30-6:30pm, Sat. 9am-11:30pm.

Barranca del Cobre Train Station: Near Quinta Luz. When you get to the clock on Ocampo, make a right, walk 4 blocks and then turn left. Daily to Creel (*vista* at 7am, 24,000 pesos; *mixto* at 8am, 15,000 pesos; *autovía* at 5pm, 18,000 pesos) and Los Mochis (*vista* at 7am, 49,000 pesos; *mixto* at 8am, 31,000 pesos). *Vista,* which includes breakfast, *autovía,* and *mixto* sold Mon.-Fri. 5:30-9am and 11am-2pm, Sat. 5:30-8:30am, Sun. 6-9am. Tickets may also be sold daily 3-6pm. (For an explanation of classes, see Barranca del Cobre.)

Bus Station: On Progreso. Large, well-organized terminal with a restaurant on the upper level. To: Acapulco (2 per day, 81,000 pesos); Mazatlán (1 per day, 45,000 pesos); Guadalajara (5 per day, 51,000 pesos).

Laundromat: Lavafácil, Universidad 3500 (tel. 13-82-85).

Red Cross: Tel. 15-42-20 or 12-50-06.

24-Hr. Pharmacy: Farmacia Mendoza, Aldama 1901 (tel. 16-44-14), at Calle 19, 3 blocks from Palacio del Gobierno. Also, *Farmacia Plaza No. 2* Libertad 330.

Hospital Central: (tel. 15-47-20 or 159-00) at the end of Colón, between Rosales and Degollado.

Police: Ochoa at Calle 2 (tel. 12-50-07).

Accommodations

Because few foreigners visit Chihuahua and cowboys like their hotels on the rough side, budget rooms are uninspiring. There are half a dozen hotels between Victoria and Libertad in the area behind the cathedral.

Hotel Carmen, Juárez and 10a. Calle (tel. 15-70-96). Very clean with big windows, passable bathrooms, ceiling fans, and deadbolt locks. Singles 25,000 pesos. Doubles 30,000 pesos.

Hotel Reforma, Victoria 809 (tel. 12-58-08). Lobby is a 2-story courtyard filled with street vendors. Small but immaculate rooms and baths. Singles 20,000 pesos. Doubles 24,000 pesos.

Hotel San Juan, Victoria 823 (tel. 261-67). Colorfully tiled 2-story courtyard. Some of the decrepit rooms are graced with drippy showers and cracked toilets. Singles 22,000 pesos. Doubles 27,000 pesos.

Hotel Roma, Libertad 1015 (tel. 12-76-52). Rooms are large, as are the bugs. The faucets have performance anxiety, supplying water only reluctantly and in spurts. Toilets lack seats, management lacks enthusiasm, and rooms lack ventilation. Not as clean as the doctor's office. Singles and doubles 25,000 pesos.

Food

Once again, due to Chihuahua's lack of tourism, restaurants cater to native tastes and run at a native level of sanitation. If all else fails, to avoid starvation, the **Cafetería Dega** at the Hotel San Francisco serves expensive but satisfying victuals (3-course meal US$10; credit cards accepted).

Mi Café, Victoria 1000, beside the Hotel Reforma. Friendly staff. *Hamburguesa mexicana* 4500 pesos. Open daily 8am-10:30pm.

Comedor Familiar, Victoria 820. Specializes in *antojitos. Comida corrida* worth the 4500 pesos. A/C. Open daily 7am-10pm.

Café Merino, Ocampo at Juárez. The local middle-aged crowd seems to dig the pink vinyl decor. *Platillo mexicano* 10,000 pesos. Will change dollars for you if they have enough pesos on hand. Open 24 hrs.

La Parilla, Victoria 420. Popular place for couples on dates. *Al carbón* (barbecued) dishes particularly good. Open daily noon-midnight.

Sights and Entertainment

On Juárez between Guerrero and Carranza, a golden eagle bearing the inscription "Libertad" points to the door of the prison cell where Padre Miguel Hidalgo was held for two months prior to his execution in 1811. Now the basement of the post office, his confinement site displays letters from early participants in the uprising, Hidalgo's crucifix, bible, and pistol, and the rebel flag. Hidalgo was buried in the chapel of Iglesia de San Francisco, off Pl. Zaragoza. His body was moved to the capital of the Republic 10 years later as was his head, which had been on public display in Guanajuato.

Quinta Luz (the Pancho Villa museum) prominently displays photographs and paintings of Sr. Villa, his household furnishings, enough rifles and machine guns to outfit a small army, and the car in which Villa was assassinated. Visitors can immerse themselves in the turbulence of the Revolution through the collected documents and photographs of the leading political figures of the day. To reach Quinta Luz, head 1½ km south on Ocampo. On the left you will pass a statue of Simón Bolívar, the lively Parque Lerdo, and a monument dedicated to patriot Manuel Ojinaga. A few more blocks down Ocampo brings you to an intersection with a tall clock at its center. This is 20 de Noviembre; turn left and go 2 blocks to 10a. Calle, then turn right. Villa's house is 2 blocks down on the right. (Open daily 9am-1pm and 3-7pm. Admission 500 pesos.)

Five minutes down the street is the **Museo Regional de Chihuahua,** Paseo Bolívar 401 (tel. 12-38-34), which houses a collection of elaborate furniture from the early 20th century. There are also permanent exhibits on Paquimé and the Mennonites. (Open Tues.-Sun. 10am-1pm and 4-7pm. Admission 500 pesos.) Bullfights are held most Sundays in the **Plaza de Toros,** at Cuauhtémoc and Canal. The **Lienzo Charro,** on Av. Américas west of town, hosts weekend rodeos. Downtown, Av. Libertad is closed to traffic east of the cathedral and becomes a large, open-air shopping mall on weekends. Chihuahua doesn't provide much in the way of nightlife, but **Discoteque La Mina** in the Hotel Victoria is swamped on weekends, as is **Bar Los Prismos** in the Hotel San Francisco. Neither, however, will induce hyperventilation.

Barranca del Cobre (Copper Canyon)

The train from Los Mochis to Chihuahua snakes its way through the Sierra Madre Occidental and across the Continental Divide. It careens along canyon walls, plunges through sheer rock faces, and passes briefly along the rim of Barranca del Cobre, the deepest gorge in the Sierras, deeper even than the Grand Canyon.

There are two types of trains. The *vista,* for tourists, is cleaner, has bathrooms and air conditioning, and runs close to schedule. The large, comfortable seats provide amazing leg room. The *mixto* carries as many chickens as passengers and has none of the virtues of the *vista,* except that it costs one-third as much and screeches along the same tracks.

The Chihuahua to Creel leg takes six hours by *vista,* while the Creel to Los Mochis *vista* is an eight-hour journey. The *mixto* takes longer than the *vista* by two hours to Creel and about four hours to Chihuahua. This time difference is especially important on the trip from Chihuahua to Los Mochis, since the *mixto* train in that direction might zoom by the best scenery in the dark. For a third of the *vista* price, the bus takes only five hours (see Creel and Chihuahua bus listings).

The train ride is gorgeous but may not be worth the trip unless you allow a few days to stop and explore. The cool mountain forests around Creel contain spectacular waterfalls, lakes, and mushroom-like rock formations. The region is also home to the Tarahumara *indígenas,* many of whom live in area caves.

From Los Mochis, you can sleep peacefully through the first three hours of the trip until the train crosses the Río Fuerte. Shortly afterward, past the first long tunnel, the train track clings to a ledge about two-thirds of the way from the top or the walls of a wooded canyon. The vestibules between cars afford unrestricted views (no intervening dirt-caked windows) of the forested canyon, the precipices over the riverbed below, and the towering crags that suddenly appear around corners. The train then continues its roller-coaster ride, climbing higher into the Sierras, twisting through mountain spurs.

The next truly spectacular view comes on the rim of the Barranca del Cobre at the **Divisadero** station, seven hours out of Los Mochis on the *vista,* eight and a half on the *mixto.* This is the only view of the entire canyon during the trip. On the *vista,* Divisadero is a 15-minute sightseeing stop: everyone on the train leaps out, runs to the brink, gapes, and runs back. On the *mixto,* it's more informal. Ask the conductor when the train is going to leave, and be back early. Resist the urge to buy anything from the Tarahumaras strategically positioned between the train and the canyon, because better examples of their work are available in Creel at lower prices.

Besides providing a great view, Divisadero is a good point to begin your canyon adventure; guides lounge around outside the hotel. Make no mistake: abundant water, appropriate footwear, and a first-aid kit are necessities for even the shortest day trips.

Creel is five hours from Chihuahua or from Los Mochis, and one hour from Divisadero. At Creel, be prepared to exit the train quickly, for there are no signs at the station, no one will tell you when you've arrived, and the stop may be as short as three minutes. Between Creel and Chihuahua, the only noteworthy stop is **Cuauhté-moc,** the center of a community of Mennonites who speak Low German and dress as their ancestors did.

The Barranca is at its most colorful during the rainy season (July-Sept.) and most sublime during the snowy winter months. Any time of year, however, the Copper Canyon is magnificent.

Two trains depart daily from the Los Mochis station, about 2km east of town off Castro. The *vista* leaves at 6am, and the *mixto* at 7am. From Chihuahua, the *vista* leaves at 7am, the *mixto* at 8am.

A *vista* ticket from Los Mochis to Chihuahua costs 55,000 pesos; the *mixto* is 16,000 pesos. To Creel, the *vista* fare is 30,000 pesos and the *mixto* is 9000 pesos. From Creel to Los Mochis the *vista* costs 30,000 pesos and the *mixto* 9000 pesos. (The advertised 50% student discount on the *mixto* train applies only to Mexican students.) Bring food for the trip unless you want to rely on the enchilada saleschildren who run through the train during stops in small towns or the burrito and gordita salespeople at Divisadero.

Creel

High amid the peaks of the Sierra Madres, the small village of Creel welcomes travelers with a natural beauty and warmth unmatched in northern Mexico. The inhospitable Chihuahuan desert gives way here to spectacular gorges and looming peaks, the land of the Tarahumara people. Creel is easy-going and *indígena* to the core. Moreover, its cool mountain climate is a refreshing oasis rising from the rest of Chihuahua. Simply put, Creel is the best overnight stop on the Barranca del Cobre train ride.

Be forewarned, however, that this mountain retreat may not remain serene forever. In the past few years, tourists have flocked to Creel in greatly increasing numbers, and most hotels have responded by expanding and renovating existing structures. The Chihuahuan state government has recently remodeled the Zócalo and all main streets, planting numerous pine trees throughout town.

Many **Tarahumara** come to Creel to sell crafts to curio shops and to pick up supplies. Of Mexico's many *indígena* groups, the Tarahumara have adapted least to modern Mexican culture, living still in isolated caves and wooden houses, and resisting all efforts to settle them in villages. The Tarahumara are famous for their non-stop long-distance footraces, which last up to 72 hours. Tarahumara baskets, blankets, figurines, ribbons, and violins are sold throughout town.

The Tarahumara greatly value their seclusion and tend to shy away from contact with tourists. If you pass Tarahumara cave dwellings, look at the caves from the road, but don't take their obvious accessibility as an invitation to approach more closely or to walk in and have a look-see. Refrain from photographing the Tarahumara at will. If you ask to photograph them, they may agree only out of graciousness and not because they really don't mind. Fortunately, Artesanía Misión sells excellent color prints of the Tarahumara for 1500 pesos each. These photos were taken by the local Jesuit priest, who knows the Tarahumara well enough to do so without offending.

Orientation and Practical Information

The first thing you'll see upon arriving in Creel is the train station. Trains leave daily for Chihuahua at 11:30am (*vista*, 24,800 pesos) and 4pm (*mixto*, 9000 pesos), and for Los Mochis at 11:45pm (*vista*, 30,000 pesos) and 1:45pm (*mixto*, 9000 pesos). Times are subject to change, but the trains usually run close to schedule. To be safe, arrive at least 45 minutes prior to departure. Keep your luggage nearby and scramble quickly and aggressively when the train arrives. The bus station is off the southwest corner of the Zócalo. The main street here, Mateos, runs parallel to the train tracks on the opposite side of the Zócalo.

Tarahumara Information: Artesanías Misión (tel. 601-80), on the north side of the Zócalo. The cheapest place to buy Tarahumara crafts, and although not an official tourist office, it is also the best source of information on Creel and the surrounding area. Sells books about the Tarahumara and a map of the region. The mission supports the Tarahumara's cultural development, and the local hospital receives store profits. English-speaking staff. Open Mon.-Sat. 9:30am-1pm and 3-6pm, Sun. 9:30am-1pm.

Currency Exchange: Banca Serfín (tel. 602-50), next door to the Misión. Dollars exchanged 10:30-11:45am. Open Mon.-Fri. 9am-1:30pm. A wholesale store, **La Barata de Creel,** on Mateos next to Cabaña Bertis, also exchanges traveler's checks.

Post Office: (tel. 602-58) on the first floor of the Presidencia Municipal building on south side of the Zócalo. Lista de Correos. **Postal Code:** 33200.

Telephones: Long-distance service available in lobby of **Hotel Nuevo** daily 9:30am-12:30pm and 3:30-6:30pm. International collect calls 2000 pesos. **Telephone Code:** 145.

Train Station: See above for schedule. Buy tickets on board. To reach the Zócalo from the train station, walk 1 block along the tracks in the direction of Los Mochis and turn left.

Bus Station: Transportes Olavera, provides daily service to Chihuahua (7 per day, 5½ hr., 13,000 pesos) via Cuauhtémoc (8500 pesos).

Pharmacy: Farmacia Rodriguez, Mateos 39 (tel. 600-52). Open Mon.-Fri. 9am-2pm and 3-8pm.

Police: In the Presidencia Municipal building on south side of the Zócalo.

Accommodations

Not simply the best deal in Creel, **Margarita's Casa de Huéspedes,** Mateos 11 (tel. 600-45), is perhaps the best deal in all of Mexico. Margarita Quintero de Gonzalez, who many say is the nicest lady in the state of Chihuahua, enjoys an ever-widening reputation as the patron saint of Mexican travelers. Margarita is the director and chef of this family establishment located between the two churches in the northeast corner of the Zócalo. Margarita's pampers backpacking world-travelers, California teachers, Mexican couples, and other ramblers. You'll have no trouble finding it: as soon as you step off the train, a swarm of boys and girls converge, asking if you'd like to be taken to Margarita's. Don't be suspicious of these children; they are orphans working only out of gratitude to Margarita, who looks after them. A tip is unnecessary.

Margarita has a wide variety of accommodations. All rooms are freshly renovated, with adobe walls, pine furniture, heating, and home-purified water. Singles with private bath go for 25,000 pesos, doubles with private bath for 50,000 pesos, shared dormitories for 15,000 pesos per head, and the honeymoon cabin for 40,000 pesos. Margarita also has a spot on the floor for you for only 3500 pesos. Margarita makes deals with large groups (5 people for 80,000 pesos), and she gives student discounts. To top it all off, all prices include two homecooked meals (breakfast at 8am, dinner at 7pm, vegetarians easily accommodated) and shower use. Margarita's is very popular, and the heavy turnover can become quite hectic, but Margarita does her best to maintain tranquility after 10:30pm.

The following hotels futilely attempt to compete with Margarita's.

Hotel Nuevo (tel. 600-22), across the tracks from the train station. Neat, colorful rooms with tile floors, hot water, and satellite TV. General store in front. Late arrivals will find the front desk deserted. Singles 40,000 pesos. Doubles 50,000 pesos.

Cabañas Bertis (tel. 601-08) on Mateos, 100 ft. from the Zócalo. Fireplaces, wooden floors, A/C, hot water, and firm beds. Singles 35,000 pesos. Doubles 50,000 pesos.

Hotel Chavez, next to the bus station. Run-down, with smelly communal bathrooms, but very popular with the Tarahumara. Singles 12,000 pesos (7000 pesos on 2nd floor). Doubles 24,000 pesos (14,000 pesos on 2nd floor).

Food

Those who don't have the privilege of eating with Margarita lose out with Creel's meager food selection. **La Cabaña,** opposite the Bertis, serves a spicy *pollo con mole* (7500 pesos) under an army of flattened animal skins. It's also the only place in town that serves ice cream. (Open daily 8am-10:30pm.) The exterior of **El Metate,** across from La Cabaña on Mateos, looks like a lob cabin, but the effect is ruined by the pink interior walls. A mountain man-sized *bistec con papas* costs 8500 pesos. The only redeeming feature of the restaurant at the **Motel Parador,** Mateos 48, is the cold beer (3000 pesos) served at the garish purple-and-yellow bar.

Sights and Entertainment

The least expensive way to explore the canyons is to take one of Margarita's trips. You need not stay at Margarita's to take part. Her husband, Daniel, drives groups in his pickup to a number of attractive sites. A full-day trip runs 20,000 pesos per person. After a bumpy 90-minute drive, Daniel will drop you off on top of a mountain. From there, it's a one-hour hike to the bottom, where a warm natural bath awaits you in a winding green stream. Be prepared for the strenuous return hike. For this or any other trek, take plenty of water, adequate footwear (no sandals), and a sun hat. More expensive tours are offered by the Motel Parador (tel. 600-75), on Mateos about 3 blocks from the Zócalo. The 10-hour **Copper Canyon Tour** allows you to explore the Barranca del Cobre, as well as several other nearby canyons, at greater leisure than the train stop permits. Another all-day tour (65,000 pesos) takes you to **Basaseachic Falls,** a spectacular cascade that plunges 806 ft. into a lake. After an arduous four-hour drive, you must walk 1½ hours to the falls. A shorter and cheaper tour takes you 22km out to **Cusárare Falls,** a mere pygmy at 100 ft. This tour also visits the village and mission at Cusárare. Tours require a minimum of four people; there are usually enough takers to run the Copper Canyon and Cusárare tours three to four times per week, but Basaseachic can be a bit tricky. Ask the motel when the next tour is leaving. If none is scheduled, proselytize among fellow travelers. Tours can also be arranged through the Hotel Nuevo or Bertis.

If you really want to experience the Barranca, consider a trip to **Batopilas,** 140km south of Creel. This involves a 10-hour bus trip over some of the most terrifying roads you are ever likely to experience, through meterological conditions that can range from suffocating heat to blinding snow in the course of a single voyage. Remember to take your passport and tourist card; you *will* be stopped by uptight and heavily armed soldiers. Weary survivors of the voyage can spend the evening at **Casa Bustillos,** across the basketball court as you get off the bus. Fix the room price beforehand to avoid being overcharged. From Batopilas, short daytrips to local villages are easily arranged.

If you prefer to stick close to Creel, the **Valley of the Mushroom Rocks** and the mission at **San Ignacio** can be easily combined into a day trip. To reach the valley and mission, walk down Mateos past the Motel Parador. When the road forks, take the smaller branch to the left, beside the cemetery. A kilometer or so out of town you pass through the gates of the Tarahumara's *ejidos* (pastures) containing the caves in which they live. After the cultivated fields, the valley is to the right and the mission at the bottom of the hill. **Lake Arareko** is also nearby. The 7km walk is unbearably hot, but you can usually hitch part of the way with one of the trucks passing along the highway.

Every June, an important regional wheelchair race takes place in Creel. Only Mexicans may enter the 8km race—the winner procedes to a national competition in September—but spectators are always welcome. **Desarollo Integración de la Familia** organizes the event.

Durango

Durango, a Basque word that carries the long-winded connotation "meadow bathed by a river and surrounded by high mountains beyond the river," was founded in 1563 by Francisco de Ibarra, the man who seems to have colonized half of northern Mexico. Although it lacks the grand colonial architecture of its southern neighbors, the city has a kind of rugged beauty all its own. Once-staid buildings, adorned with a combination of stone scrollwork, wrought-iron grilles, and glistening dayglo blue paint, fill the side streets. More than this, the amazing friendliness of Durango's citizens makes most visits to the city a pleasure; people here pause on the street to give the inquisitive traveler detailed advice and directions, and may even deliver you to your destination. Very few residents speak English, but most goodnaturedly attempt to understand broken Spanish and crazy gesticulations. Beautiful mesas on the city's edge give some idea of the origins of the lengthy Basque name, and accentuate the town's rough-hewn, frontier feel.

Orientation and Practical Information

The central bus station is 3km east of the city center. To get from the station to the center of town, hop on one of the buses marked "Centro"; to return, catch a "Central Camionera" bus from the public market (300 pesos). If you arrive by train, walk a dozen short blocks south down Martínez, starting across the street from the station's front door. When you reach Durango's main street, 20 de Noviembre, turn left, walk 1 block, and you'll be in the city center, at the **Plaza de Armas.** 20 de Noviembre runs east-west through the Pl. de Armas. Three blocks east of the plaza is Durango's public market.

Tourist Office: Hidalgo Sur 408 (tel. 121-39), 2 blocks west and 2 blocks south of the cathedral. Although little English is spoken, the warm staff dishes out plenty of free advice. Amongst their literature are several good maps. Open Mon.-Fri. 8:30am-3pm, Sat. 9am-1pm, Sun. 11am-1pm.

Currency Exchange: Bancomer, on the Constitución side of the Pl. de Armas. Open Mon.-Fri. 9am-1:30pm. The *casa de cambio* at 20 de Noviembre 703 is open Mon.-Fri. 9am-6pm.

Post Office: Constitución 213, 4 blocks north of the Pl. de Armas. Open Mon.-Fri. 8am-6pm, Sat. 9am-1pm. Lista de Correos is posted around 11:30am and taken down at 3pm. **Postal Code:** 34000.

Telephones: Serdán Pte. 626, off Constitución. Collect calls 2000 pesos. Open daily 9am-9pm. Also at Martínez Sur 206. International collect calls 2500 pesos. Open daily 9am-10pm. **Telephone Code:** 181.

Telegrams: 20 de Noviembre at Hidalgo (tel. 104-70), 2 blocks west of the Pl. de Armas. Open Mon.-Fri. 9am-6pm, Sat. 9am-noon.

Bus Station: Seven different companies serve Durango; 3 make only local runs, but **Transportación del Norte** (tel. 830-61), **Transportenses Chihuahuenses** (tel. 837-81), **Estrella Blanca** (tel. 832-41), and **Omnibus de México** (tel. 833-61) send buses to most major cities. Prices vary only slightly among them, but Estrella Blanca is usually the cheapest; it runs buses north and south to, among other destinations: Mexico City (9 per day, 39,000 pesos); Guadalajara (11 per day, 29,000 pesos); Mazatlán (6 per day, 14,000 pesos); Ciudad Juárez (4 per day, 45,000 pesos); Chihuahua (4 per day, 30,000 pesos); Zacatecas (18 per day, 12,000 pesos); Aguascalientes (18 per day, 17,500 pesos).

Red Cross: 5 de Febrero at Reforma (tel. 134-44).

24-Hr. Pharmacy: Farmacia Pensiones, Constitución at Coronado (tel. 296-91), next to the post office.

Medical Care: Hospital Providencia, Zarco Nte. 209 (tel. 245-45). **Hospital General,** 5 de Febrero at Ramirez (tel. 194-11).

Police: Guadalupe at Pescador (tel. 121-62).

Accommodations

Downtown Durango has plenty of hotels; most of them lie east of the Pl. de Armas on 20 de Noviembre. The only time you might have trouble finding a place to sleep is during the Feria Nacional in the first two weeks of July. If you're in town then, grab the first bed you see or prepare to sleep on the streets. Although short on real cheapies, Durango supports several luxury-budgets (*not* an oxymoron).

Hotel Posada Durán, 20 de Noviembre Pte. 506 (tel. 124-12), catty-corner to the Municipal Palace. Spacious, clean rooms with chairs and a desk. Bidet in the bathroom transports you to the Rue de Rivoli. Courtyard fountain soothes nerves nightly. Singles 38,640 pesos. Doubles 48,300 pesos.

Hotel Casablanca, 20 de Noviembre Pte. 809 (tel. 131-99), 2 blocks west of the Pl. de Armas. Even classier accommodations—with wall-to-wall carpet, A/C, TV, phones, and a bellhop—but getting to the head of the class requires extra apples. Singles 46,000 pesos. Doubles 67,000 pesos.

Hotel Ar Vel, Progreso Sur 104 (tel. 253-33). Durán/Casablanca hybrid; carpeting, TV, and phone, at a bargain price. The blue-green color in rooms is reminiscent of fragrant water in a goldfish bowl that hasn't been changed in a while. Singles 35,000 pesos. Doubles 48,000 pesos.

Hotel Aguirre, Hernández 715 (tel. 119-15), near the train station. A wonder of cement construction, slathered with lime green and the color Crayola would call "burnt sienna." Courtyard and spartan rooms share this lovely color scheme. Singles 18,000 pesos. Doubles 25,000 pesos.

Food

Culinary Durango is not diverse, with hundreds of little restaurants serving exactly the same *comida corrida* (7000-9000 pesos) and *carne asada*. These clones are particularly thick along 20 de Noviembre, on either side of the Pl. de Armas. The **Far West Steak House Bar and Grill,** Florida 1106 at the western end of 20 de Noviembre, is a bit touristy but still a mountain of fun. Designed to resemble an Old West saloon (complete with swinging doors), the restaurant acknowledges every Western ever filmed in the area with a plaque on the wall. Try the "Duke" (18,500 pesos) or "El Bueno, El Malo y El Feo" (17,000 pesos). (Open daily 1-

11:30pm.) Also of note—for its awkward juxtaposition of Teutonic decor and *típico* cooking—is the **Restaurant La Bohemia,** 20 de Noviembre Pte. 907, next to the telegram office. Jam to your favorite polka music as you chew burritos Bohemia-style (9500 pesos). (Open daiy 8am-midnight.)

Sights and Entertainment

Few tourist attractions in Durango deserve your undivided attention. The **Plaza de Armas,** surrounded by upscale stores, is the city's center of activity and its most interesting sight. At night, skateboarders thrash merrily about the plaza, providing a spectacle for the otherwise family-dominated crowd. The grandiose **cathedral,** on the plaza's north side, stands in disrepair, as does the **Palacio del Gobierno** (open Mon.-Fri. 8am-3pm), 2 blocks east on 20 de Noviembre, although the palace's inner courtyard has been decorated with murals.

During the first two weeks of July, Durango holds its **Feria Nacional,** which features Mexican singers and bands, cultural demonstrations, bullfights, and industrial and agricultural displays.

A 5km drive north on Rte. 45 toward Parral will take you to **Villa del Oeste** and **Chupaderos.** These two towns were given makeovers for the filming of Westerns, among them John Wayne's *Chisum* and *Big Jake.* While Villa del Oeste is still occasionally used, Chupaderos is a ghost town inhabited by people who act as if it were an ordinary Mexican village. Visitors can buy a soda at the little grocery store next to the "Land Office." *Campesino* children jump their bikes off the porch of "McIlhenny's Clothing Emporium," shouting "¡soy un pepino!"

Zacatecas

The second-to-last thing a traveler expects to find in the barren, cactus-strewn desert of Central Mexico is a charming city (the last being a gorgeous blonde in a red Ferrari wanting to know if those are Bugle Boy jeans you're wearing). Yet out of nowhere rises Zacatecas. The arid surroundings augment the colonial beauty of this town perched between, on, and over mineral-laden hills.

The lifeblood of Zacatecas, like Guanajuato, once flowed through veins of silver. A silver trinket, given to early Spanish colonists by an indigenous Cascane in the mid-16th century, triggered the mining bonanza that gave birth to the city. In the 200 years after the Conquest, the hills surrounding Zacatecas were stripped of over US$1 billion worth of silver and other precious metals. Among mining towns, Zacatecas was unusually fortunate: the arts flourished under the patronage of affluent silver barons, and the rows of grand colonial mansions lining the downtown streets speak of generations that displayed their wealth lavishly. In the early 19th century, one devout mine owner even paved the entire walkway from his home to the cathedral with solid silver bars.

The tumultous history of modern Mexico has not left Zacatecas untouched: in 1914 Francisco Villa's revolutionary forces proved victorious here over Carranza's troops. As revolution has atrophied into institution and the flow from the mines has run dry, Zacatecas survives as a city of cultural sophistication whose appeal today emanates from its many architectural, artistic, and natural treasures.

Orientation and Practical Information

At the junction of several major highways, Zacatecas is easily accessible from many cities, including Guadalajara (318km south), Aguascalientes (129km south), and Chihuahua (832km north). All buses arrive and depart from the new central bus terminal on the outskirts of town. City buses (300 pesos) await outside: to get to *el centro,* take "Ruta 7"; to return to the bus station, take the "Camionera Central" or "*Ruta 8*" bus.

Downtown Zacatecas's two main streets are **Juárez,** which runs roughly northwest, and **Hidalgo** (confusingly renamed González Ortega southwest of Juárez).

The intersection of the two, 1 block northwest of Jardín Independencia, is the best point from which to orient yourself. Many of the city's colonial monuments lie on or near Hidalgo; if you keep its location vaguely in mind as you try to navigate the twisting, cobblestone streets, you may only once get hopelessly lost.

Tourist Office: Oficina de Turismo, Hidalgo 61 (tel. 266-83) at Callejón del Santero across from the cathedral. The staff is eager to help with a good map and some brochures. The "Infotur" has brochures in English. Open daily 8am-3:30pm and 6-8pm.

Guided Tours: Cantera Tours, El Mercado Local A-21 (tel. 290-65), near the cathedral. Five-hour tours of the city (25,000 pesos) include transportation and admission to museums. Tours begin at 9am and will pick you up at your hotel. Offices open daily 8am-8pm.

Currency Exchange: Banca Cremi, Hidalgo at Callejón de la Caja. Open Mon.-Fri. 9am-1:30pm. Also **Multibanco Comermex,** across the street. Same hours. In a pinch, try the *casa* "hello, I'm low exchange rate" *de cambio* on Arroya de Plata just off Tacuba.

Post Office: Allende 111 (tel. 201-96), off Hidalgo. Lista de Correos. Open Mon.-Fri. 8am-7pm, Sat. 9am-noon. **Postal Code:** 34000.

Telephones: Callejón de Cuevas 111, above the bookstore. 20-min. maximum on international calls. Collect calls 3000 pesos. Open Mon.-Fri. 8:30am-9:20pm, Sat. 9am-2pm and 4-8pm. Also at Independencia 88-A, across from the Jardín Independencia inside a small mall. International collect calls 2000 pesos. Open daily 8am-8:30pm. **Telephone Code:** 492.

Telegrams: Hidalgo at Juárez (tel. 200-70). Open Mon.-Fri. 8am-midnight, Sat. 9am-10pm.

Train Station: Estación de Ferrocarriles (tel. 212-04), on González Ortega southeast of *el centro.* A walkable distance from downtown, but all bus routes also pass the station. The daily southbounds leave at 10am and 10:25pm, heading to: Aguascalientes (*primera regular* 2600 pesos, *primera especial* 7700 pesos); León (6400 and 15,600 pesos); Irapuato (7800 and 28,700 pesos); Querétaro (10,100 and 29,400 pesos); and Mexico City (15,400 and 44,800 pesos). The northbound train attempts to depart by 9:50am, to Torreón (9500 and 27,500 pesos); Chihuahua (20,000 and 58,200 pesos); and Ciudad Juárez (27,900 and 81,300 pesos). Sleeping berths are available at double the cost of *primera especial.*

Bus Station: Central de Autobuses, Lomas de la Isabélica at Tránsito Pesado (tel. 211-12). **Omnibus de México** (tel. 254-95) serves the most cities, including Guadalajara (12 per day, 5-6 hr., 15,500 pesos); Mexico City (22 per day, 8 hr., 30,000 pesos); Chihuahua (20 per day, 12 hr., 38,000 pesos); and Ciudad Juárez (16 per day, 17-18 hr., 55,000 pesos).

Laundromat: Rosa Blanca, López Mateos 129, a couple of blocks downhill past the Hotel Colón. 8300 pesos for 3kg load. Come back in 2 hr. Open Mon.-Fri. 8am-7pm, Sat. 8am-5pm.

Red Cross: (tel. 230-05) on Calzada Héroes de Chapultepec.

Pharmacy: Farmacia Popular, Zamora 406 (tel. 204-69), next to the Hotel Zamora. Open daily 9am-3pm and 5-9pm.

Hospital Civil: (tel. 330-00) on Garcia Salinas.

Police: (tel. 201-90) on 5 Señores.

Accommodations

Like most northern Mexican cities, Zacatecas has few good, cheap hotels. Downtown accommodations are generally luxurious, and the budget options are less than optimal. Hot water is always hard to come by; make sure to ask when it will be available. The area surrounding López Mateos is the most fertile hunting ground for inexpensive hotels. To get to this district, follow Juárez southeast to its end and turn right; this street is first called Independencia, and then Zamora. Zamora curves to the left, becoming Salazar, and Salazar ends at López Mateos where a large metal pedestrian overpass arches over the road to your left.

CREA Youth Hostel, Lago La Encantada (tel. 211-51), southwest of the city. You'll never find it on foot; fortunately, yellow "Ruta 5" buses run from the Pl. Independencia. Ask drivers for the Albergues CREA. Rose-infested grounds with soccer field, swimming pool, and courts for basketball, volleyball, and racquetball. Tiny rooms for 4 (2 bunk beds *y nada más*). Shared bathrooms are clean. 6000 pesos per person. Breakfast 3500 pesos, lunch and dinner 4500 pesos each. Open daily 7am-11pm.

Hotel Río Grande, Calzada de la Paz 513 (tel. 253-49). At the pedestrian overpass, cross López Mateos and walk left ½ block until you see the sign for another hotel at the bottom of a small street to the right. Resist the urge to collapse here, and bound joyously uphill for 3 more blocks—the Río Grande will be on your left. Busy courtyard. Clean rooms are surprisingly pleasant considering the price, but a room away from the office is a necessity for a good night's sleep. The shared bathrooms look clean but smell funny; big fluffy towels accompany the private bathrooms. Singles 9000 pesos, with bath 18,000 pesos. Doubles 12,000 pesos, with bath 22,000 pesos.

Hotel Zamora, Zamora 303 (tel. 212-00), south of Juárez and 1 block southwest of the Pl. Independencia. Sign hard to see—it's on the east side of the street. Nowhere near as pleasant as the Río Grande: smaller rooms display wildly peeling paint. Proprietor, blushing, explains that they're *cuartos económicos*. Private bathrooms lack toilet seats, hot water, and dependable plumbing. Singles and doubles 15,000 pesos.

Hotel Colón, López Mateos 105 (tel. 289-25), 4 blocks down from the pedestrian overpass. A lovely mailbox in the lobby complements the new color TV. All the rooms floored in interesting rock patterns, and prints of Zacatecas hang on the walls. Singles 35,000 pesos. Doubles 44,300 pesos.

Hotel Posada de la Moneda, Hidalgo 413 (tel. 208-81). Appropriately named—you must shell out a lot of *moneda* to stay the night. Though situated in the center of town, the rooms are quiet; all have TV, phone, and carpet. Great sunny courtyard. White bathroom tile threatens to blind in the morning. Singles 56,000 pesos. Doubles 70,000 pesos.

Food

For the best dining experiences head to the Zacatecan cafés, where students and other local intellectuals gather to discuss the consequences of German reunification before moving on to the more enigmatic question of why New Kids on the Block has yet to make a full-length movie.

Café Acrópolis, on Hidalgo near the cathedral. Popular with all types: table activities include dominoes, word searches, reading the paper, and just plain talking. Students prevail in the afternoon and evening, but this is mainly a breakfast hotspot. Turkish coffee (*grande* 3000 pesos) is the specialty; intricate designs made on saucers with the dregs cover the walls, along with fan letters. Sandwiches 1800-5000 pesos, hamburger with fries 5500 pesos, ice cream and pastries 2500-7200 pesos. Open daily 9am-10pm.

Mesón La Mina, on Juárez just southwest of Hidalgo. Breakfast available all day. Many students come here to catch up on their neo-Platonism reading and soak in the local color. Big 4-course *comida corrida* 9000 pesos. *Tacos de Barbacoa* 5000 pesos. Open daily 8am-12pm.

El Carnerito, Juárez 110, northwest of Hidalgo. Good, filling Mexican dishes at reasonable prices, topped off by Mickey Mouse jello molds for dessert. Unconvincing stonework painted on the plasterboard walls. *Huevos naturales* 4500 pesos. Burritos 3000 pesos. Other entrees 2000-8000 pesos. Open daily 8:30am-12:30am.

Los Faroles, Tacuba 129, 2 blocks from the cathedral. A favorite among younger Mexicans. Waiters hand you a blank order form and you check off what and how many you want. Very cheap. Tacos in a rainbow of flavors 900 pesos each. Double quesadilla 2900 pesos. Beer only 1800 pesos. Open daily 1pm-midnight.

Sights

Zacatecas is studded with colonial churches and monasteries, all carved from the deep red *cantera* stone quarried from the nearby hills. Perhaps the best way to see the city is to keep the map in your back pocket and lose yourself among the city's winding, hilly streets. You may round a corner to find yourself face-to-face with a soaring red cathedral, a crumbling convent abandoned to the weeds, or a lush green park. If you prefer more organized sightseeing, the city's attractions should occupy you for a couple of days.

The towering 18th-century **cathedral,** on Hidalgo 4 blocks northeast of Juárez, combines three architectural styles. The northern façade is Churrigueresque, the southern is European Baroque, and the western façade, a richly carved celebration of the Eucharist, has been touted as the country's most lavish example of Mexican

Baroque. St. Gregory's cowboy hat is said to be the signature of the cathedral's unknown Spanish architect. (Open daily 7am-1pm and 4-9pm.)

The **Palacio de Gobierno,** which serves as the state capitol, stands next to the cathedral. The centerpiece of this colonial structure is the arresting mural which surrounds the interior stairwell. Executed in 1970 by the prominent artist Antonio Pintor Rodríguez, the work traces the history of Zacatecas from the heyday of the Cascanes *indígenas* to today's modern industrial sophistication. (Open Mon.-Fri. 8am-8pm).

The most direct way to from the Palacio to the **Templo de Santo Domingo** (open daily 7am-1pm and 4-9pm) is to cross Hidalgo and climb the steep Callejón de Veyna; at the top, climb another set of stairs to the Templo. Built by the Jesuits in 1746, the church contains eight impressive Baroque altars of gilded wood and an elaborate 18th-century German pipe organ. Next door, in a building whose past incarnations include a monastery and a jail, is the **Museo de Pedro Coronel,** named after the Zacatecan artist (1922-1985) and containing his tomb, sculptures, and paintings. The museum is no provincial institution; its collection of modern art is one of the best in Latin America, with watercolors by Picasso, Braque, and Chagall, and a room full of painting and sketches by Joan Miró. This eclectic museum also contains extensive exhibits of Goya's drawings and Daumier's caricatures, African and Mesoamerican masks, and Japanese, Chinese, Tibetan, Greek, and Roman art. (Open Fri.-Wed. 10am-2pm and 4-7pm. Admission 2000 pesos.)

If you follow Hidalgo north from the cathedral and the Palacio, it eventually branches; follow the left-hand fork (Abasolo) for 2 blocks to reach the **Ex-Convento de San Francisco,** the ruined shell of a 16th-century Franciscan monastery. The Ex-Templo is open Tuesday through Saturday from 10am to 5pm, but the rest of the convent is always open.

Southeast of downtown, if you follow Hidalgo as it crosses Juárez to become González Ortega, and climb to the top of the hill, 39 rose-colored arches there mark the end of Zacatecas' famous colonial aqueduct, **El Cubo.** Beside the aqueduct, the sprawling Parque Estrada borders the former governor's mansion, now the **Museo de Francisco Gotiea.** The museum contains a permanent exhibit of the work of Gotiea and five other renowned 20th-century Zacatecan artists, inluding Pedro Coronel and his younger brother Rafael. (Open Tues.-Sun. 10am-2pm and 4-6pm. Admission 1000 pesos.)

The Cerro de La Bufa, overlooking the city, is topped by many attractions. The **Museo de la Toma de Zacatecas,** erected to commemorate Pancho Villa's decisive victory over President Victoriano Huerta's federal troops in the summer of 1914, lays claim to a fascinating array of photographs, cannons, small arms, and other revolutionary memorabilia. (Open Tues.-Sun. 10am-5pm. Admission 2000 pesos.) The museum is flanked by a monument to the revolution installed in 1989 to mark the 75th anniversary of the Battle of Zacatecas, and by the early 18th-century **Capilla del Patrocinio,** whose gracefully sculpted *cantera* façade and cloistered courtyards are carved from deep red Zacatecan stone. A short but steep climb to the crest of the hill leads to the **Mausoleo de los Hombres Ilustres de Zacatecas.** The ornate, Moorish structure is worth the hike if only for the view of the city. An even better vista is available from the **Meteorlogical Observatory,** behind the museum, where you can see a full 270°. Also in the vicinity of the museum are a few shops selling arts and crafts, and lodes of geodes for ramblin' rock hounds. Just below the shops, several small stands serve quick eats. Unfortunately, public buses run to La Bufa only on religious holidays, and taxis will cost 5000 pesos. The most appealing way to make the trip is by *teleférico* (cablecar), which runs between the peak of La Bufa and El Grillo hill every 10 minutes. The imported Swiss cars carry passengers on a seven-and-a-half minute journey high above Zacatecas. (Open daily 12:30-7:30pm. 5000 pesos round-trip.)

The **Mina de Edén** (tel. 230-02) was one of the region's most productive silver mines during the 19th and early 20th centuries. To get to the mine entrance, follow Juárez northwest (along the Alameda, an oblong park lined by some of Zacatecas's grandest colonial mansions), continue along Torreón until it ends, and then turn right—the mine is on this street. About 30 years ago, continual flooding from underground springs made mineral extraction uneconomical. Today a mini-locomotive whisks tourists into the mountain, where they are treated to a guided tour in Spanish of the damp and refreshingly cool subterranean tunnels. An expensive souvenir ship down below sells chunks of silver. For those less historically inclined, a restaurant and disco have been improvised in one of the mine's larger caverns; on weekends the same locomotive runs late into the night, carting in partiers who dance to the latest U.S. Top-40 hits and buy expensive drinks. (Mine open Tues.-Sun. noon-7:30pm. Admission 3500 pesos. Disco El Malocate open Thurs.-Sun. 9pm-3am. Cover 15,000 pesos.)

Trips to La Bufa and Mina de Edén can easily be combined. At the end of the mine tour, you can either go back the way you came or take an elevator up to El Grillo, where you can catch the *teleférico* to La Bufa. The entire excursion takes about two hours.

Near Zacatecas

The **Museo de Guadalupe** (open Tues.-Sun. 9am-4:30pm; admission 10,000 pesos) is in a tiny village of the same name, 7km east of Zacatecas on the highway to Mexico City. A Franciscan convent built in 1707, the museum contains the country's finest collection of colonial art. Highlights include a mural by the 18th-century painter Miguel Cabrera, two 16th-century mosaics of St. Peter and St. Francis comprised solely of bird feathers, and a 1621 Gutenberg volume on mining. The exhibit is superb, but if you grow tired, ask to be shown the choir room: the 30 resident Franciscan monks gather here every afternoon for prayer and hymnody. Two people standing in opposite corners of the room can carry on a conversation by whispering into the walls. Even the most church-weary travelers will find the adjacent **Capilla de Nápoles** worth investigating. The elaborately tiled floor is composed of three different hardwoods and was ingeniously designed to function as both compass and calendar; the dazzling Baroque altar was carved from a single quarry stone; and the domed ceilings are finished in 24-karat gold leaf. (Open Tues.-Sun. 10am-4:30pm. Free.) The collection of antique wagons, carriages, and cars housed next door in the fledgling **Museo Regional** (tel. 320-89) is worth a quick peek. (Open Tues.-Sun. 10am-4:30pm. Admission 800 pesos.) "Ruta 13" buses to Guadalupe (300 pesos) leave from the corner of Salazar and López Mateos every 15 minutes.

Aguascalientes

The city of Aguascalientes lies in the center of the state of the same name. Rich soil and abundant spring water (much of which is naturally hot and thus gives the area its name: *aguas* means "waters," *calientes* means "hot") make this area ideal for agriculture. Little has disrupted Aguascalientes over its 400-year history; the signing of the Convention of Aguascalientes, which united Villa and Zapata in their ill-fated alliance against Carranza during the revolution, was the city's climactic moment. Today, Aguascalientes is a sleepy industrial and agricultural town (albeit one with a population of 750,000), relatively uninteresting to the casual visitor.

Orientation and Practical Information

Aguascalientes is 168km west of San Luis Potosí, 128km south of Zacatecas, and 252km northeast of Guadalajara. **Avenida Circunvalación** encircles the city; **Avenida López Mateos** cuts through town on an east-west slant. The bus station is a few blocks west on Av. Circunvalación from the north-south Av. José María Chávez. City buses marked "Centro" (400 pesos) leave from either side of the bus station for the downtown area. To return, look on the windshield for "central camionera." Taxis run at a fixed rate of 3000 pesos to the central part of the city.

Tourist Office: Pl. de Patria 141 (tel. 511-55), in the Palacio del Gobierno. Over 700 comprehensive and shuriken-like maps of the city, and English brochures covering just about every state. Open Mon.-Fri. 8am-3pm, Sat. 9am-1pm.

Currency Exchange: Bánamex, 5 de Mayo, at the Pl. de la Patria. Open Mon.-Fri. 9am-1:30pm. If you'd rather not see your face on a milk carton, however, go to the *casa de cambio* (tel. 803-00) in the Hotel Farancia on the plaza. Good rates, no lines. Open Mon.-Fri. 9am-2pm and 4-6pm.

Post Office: Hospitalidad 108 (tel. 521-18), 1 block east of the plaza on Madero, then left on Morelos and right on Hospitalidad. Open for stamps and Lista de Correos Mon.-Fri. 8am-7pm, Sat. 9am-1pm, Sun. 9am-1pm. Another post office, in the bus station, is open Mon.-Fri. 9am-1pm and 3-6pm.

Telephones: In Café y Arte, Guadalupe Victoria 201-C, 2 blocks north of the cathedral. Collect calls 10,000 pesos. Open Mon.-Fri. 9am-9pm, Sat. 9am-2pm and 4-9pm, Sun. 9am-1pm. **Telephone Code:** 491.

Telegrams: Galeana Nte. at Nieto, west of the plaza. Open Mon.-Fri. 8am-9pm, Sat. 9am-8pm.

Bus Station: Circunvalación, west of José María Chávez. Ten bus companies serve the city, of which **Transportación del Norte/Chihuahuenses,** (tel. 517-58), **Omnibuses de México,** (tel. 617-70), and **Estrella Blanca/Camiones de los Allos** (tel. 520-54) run to most major cities. Estrella Blanca and Camiones de los Altos combine efforts to provide the most buses. To: Mexico City (17 per day, 6 hr., 22,000 pesos); Guadalajara (43 per day, 3½ hr., 9500 pesos); Zacatecas (29 per day, 2 hr., 5300 pesos); San Luis Potosí (16 per day, 2½ hr., 6900 pesos).

English Bookstore: Excelsior, Centro Comercial El Parian, at Juárez and Rivero y Gutierrez. Few books (15,000-20,000 pesos) but magazines ranging from *Scientific American* to the *National Enquirer.* Open daily 9am-10pm.

Red Cross: In the Centro Comercial El Dorado (tel. 520-25), on Av. de las Américas.

24-Hr. Pharmacy: Farmacia Sánchez, 5 de Mayo 115 (tel. 539-07), 1 block from the plaza.

Hospital: Hospital IMSS, José María Chavez at Convención Sur.

Police: López Mateos at Héroes de Nacozari (tel. 420-50 or 430-43).

Accommodations and Food

It's fairly easy to locate cheap rooms near the bus depot or in *el centro.* If you want to stay near the station, hang a left as you leave the building. The first street you encounter is Brasil. The **Hotel Continental** (tel. 555-48), on Brasil, is the best bet near the station. Sparkling bits of mirror enliven the walls with reflections of the red carpet. The bathrooms are spotless. (Singles 24,000 pesos. Doubles 30,000 pesos.) The **Hotel Gómez,** Brasil 602 (tel. 704-09), has comparable rooms without the carpet; hot water service is sporadic. The somewhat noisy rooms do at least enjoy balconies. (Singles 38,000 pesos. Doubles 43,700 pesos.) If you wish to be closer to the action, head to **Hotel San José,** Hidalgo 207 (tel. 551-30), 1 block north of Madero, which is smack downtown but surprisingly quiet. The rooms have phones, and hot water flows all day long from the red taps. (Singles 30,000 pesos. Doubles 37,500 pesos.)

The cheapest restaurants cluster around the bus station, and *torterías* line López Mateos. The **market,** on 5 de Mayo 4 blocks north of the plaza, sells bushels of fresh fruit. A hangout for high school students, **El Greco Restaurant,** Madero 434, serves filling breakfasts and other full meals on green-and-yellow tablecloths. *Huevos rancheros* and all the bread you can eat cost 5000 pesos. (Open daily 8am-11:30pm.) Near the plaza, at Madero 220, is **Mutla.** Management encompasses 3 generations of the same family; they boast of having served hundreds of women's coffee klatches. *Chilaquiles* (6000 pesos) are presented by white-shirted waiters. (Open daily 8am-midnight.) The Muppiest (Mexican Urban Professional) coffee shop around is **Cielo Vista,** at Juárez 103. Lodged in a colonial building, this could be a true diner (it has a counter with stools) if it weren't for the wallet-emptying prices. Eat underneath fans and fluorescent light. Cereal goes for 4500 pesos. Their *menú turística* (a fancy *comida corrida*) has 4 courses and costs 17,500 pesos (available 1-4pm). For a filling meal, try the **Pizza Palace**, at López Mateos 207. Their afternoon gut-bomb buffet (served daily noon-5pm) includes pizza, spaghetti, hamburgers, salad, and all the TV you can watch. Pizza starts at 8400 pesos. (Open daily 11am-1am.)

Sights and Entertainment

Aguascalientes has no well-known tourist attractions but may distract many for a day. The charming **Basílica de la Asunción de las Aguascalientes** (open daily 6am-9pm) and the **Palacio de Gobierno** (open Mon.-Fri. 8am-8pm), on the Pl. de la Patria, will satisfy desperate colonial history buffs wandering up from the Bajío. Inside the Palacio courtyard is a mural painted in 1961 by Osvaido Barra Cunighan, part of which portrays the atrocious condition of *indígena* miners at La Mina de Edén. The most worthwhile stop in town is the **Museo de Guadalupe Posada**. Its namesake, an engraver and cartoonist, helped turn public opinion against Porfirio Díaz at the end of the dictator's reign. The museum, which exhibits Posada's engravings and caricatures of Díaz, sits at the corner of Pimental and Chávez, next to the Templo del Encino and about 4 blocks south of López Mateos. (Open Mon.-Fri. 10am-2pm and 4-8pm. Free.) The **Museo de la Ciudad** houses a permanent collection of works by the 20th-century Aguascalientes artists Saturnino Herran and Gabriel Fernandez Ledesma, and temporarily exhibits other artists. Turn left onto Zaragoza from Madero heading away from the plaza; you'll see the Templo de San Antonio at the end of the street, and the museum is to its right. (Open Mon.-Fri. 10am-2pm and 4:30-7:30pm. Free.) West of the Pl. de la Patria, at Carranza 101, the **Casa de Cultura** is a 17th-century building that contains the **Galería de la Ciudad**, a one-room site for temporary exhibitions. (Open Mon.-Fri. 10am-2pm and 5-8pm. Free.)

The **Casa de Cultura** sponsors frequent nighttime events; the tourist office has their monthly schedule. Somewhat less frequent are the events at the **Teatro Morelos**, on the west side of the plaza next to the cathedral, where singers, folk dancers, actors, and comedians congregate.

There are two good discos that will get your juices flowing. Rock the night away with the locals at **Disco El Cabus**, Blvd. Zacateca at Campestre in the Hotel Las Trojes. Beer costs 6000 pesos. (Cover 15,000 pesos. Open Thurs.-Sun. 9pm-2am.) Another really raucous place with laserlight is **Fantasy**, Ayuntamiento 117-201. Mixed drinks will set you back 8000 pesos. (Cover 20,000 pesos. Open Thurs.-Sat. 9pm-2am.) At both spots, you must be at least 18 years old and men must wear pants.

From March 10 to April 15, visitors pour into Aguascalientes to witness the annual **Feria de San Marcos**. Make hotel reservations well in advance. And don't forget Caesar.

Pacific Route

Route 15, the longest, best maintained, and most pleasant road connecting the international border and Mexico City follows the Gulf of California to the middle of Nayarit state before breaking inland toward Guadalajara and the capital. Many U.S. southwesterners travel the Pacific route, stopping in such places as Guaymas, Mazatlán, and Puerto Vallarta, just off the highway. San Blas, a fairly isolated village close to the point where the route veers inland, is the resort of choice among eccentrics. Ferry connections to points on the Baja Peninsula are possible from cities on the highway, but transporting a car could pose a problem (see Baja Getting Around). Those traveling without time constraints should consider taking the spectacular train ride through the Barranca del Cobre (Copper Canyon).

Nogales

Nogales has many of the same charms as Tijuana (ease of border crossing, cheapo curio shops, off-track betting, and cheesy bars), yet fewer Tusconians visit Nogales than San Diegans do Tijuana: the shorter distance between the two western cities and the maturity level of southern Californians contribute to this disparity. Because of the absence of norteamerícanos, Nogales retains a distinct Mexican flavor and serves as a fine beginning point for those who want to feel like they're in Mexico the instant they cross the border.

Orientation and Practical Information

Tres Estrellas de Oro, just west of the tourist information booth, runs southbound buses daily to Mexico City (at 7:30am and 6pm, 109,000 pesos); Hermosillo (at 7:30am and 9pm, 13,000 pesos); Tijuana (at 8:30pm, 38,000 pesos) via Mexicali (29,000 pesos); and Mazatlán (at 1:30pm, 54,000 pesos). Service is also available to Los Mochis (35,000 pesos), Ciudad Juárez (29,000 pesos), Guadalajara (78,000 pesos), and Chihuahua. Check at the station, since buses don't always stick to schedule. **Greyhound** buses leave for Tucson from the U.S. side of the border every two hours from 6am to 8pm. Trains go to Mazatlán and Guadalajara, but they cost more, take longer, and leave from a station 6km south of town.

Nogales is small enough to navigate on your own. If you usually feel lost without a map, pray that the **tourist office** (tel. 264-46) at the border has one in stock. The office keeps sporadic hours (mornings are your best bet) and the English-speaking staff of one can do little to help tourists. In emergencies, call the police (tel. 201-04).

It's possible to walk across the border into Mexico without ever talking to a border official. However, if you plan to venture beyond Nogales, obtain a tourist card at the frontier. It's much simpler and cheaper to get the card here than farther south.

Most of the curio and craft shops line Obregón, and, just as in Tijuana, you *may* get good deals if you bargain and know something about product quality. Potential turquoise jewelry should ask the vendor to put the rock to the test—"the lighter test," that is: plastic or synthetic material will quickly melt under a lighter flame. Likewise, when buying silver make sure you see a ".925" stamp on the piece; if it's not there, the goods are bad.

Accommodations and Food

A string of budget hotels is situated 1 block behind the bus station on Av. Juárez. As with most of northern Mexico, rates are steep. **Hotel San Carlos,** Juárez 22 (tel. 214-09), features immaculate, new rooms with A/C, phones, and cable TV. Purified water awaits in the lobby. Eduardo, the Spanish-speaking manager, loves to help wayward travelers. (Singles 51,700 pesos. Doubles 69,000 pesos.) At **Hotel Regis,** Juárez 34 (tel. 251-81) the very clean rooms have wall-to-wall carpeting like a van from the 70s, along with a slew of standard options: A/C, cable, phones, *agua purificada*. Though a tad more luxurious than the San Carlos, it's not worth the extra pesos. (Singles 66,000 pesos. Doubles 78,000 pesos.) Don't be fooled by the nice exterior of **Hotel Martinez,** Juárez 33 (tel. 254-89); inside it looks as if the builders went home before finishing the job. Rooms are kept cool with A/C and ceiling fans. (Singles 40,000 pesos. Doubles 45,000 pesos.)

The dimly shining star among Nogales restaurants, **Casa de María,** Pasaje Morelos 18-B, lurks in a little plaza beside the church. Southern Mexican cuisine is the specialty. The *comida corrida* (15,000 pesos) served from 11:30am to 4pm, includes a choice of four entrees (the *chiles rellenos* are tops) plus soup and beans. (Open daily 7am-10pm.) There is little else to eat in town; the golden arches of McDonalds beckon from the border.

Hermosillo

If you get an early start and the buses run on time, you can breeze from Tucson to the beaches of Guaymas or Mazatlán in a single day, skipping the more tedious parts of Sonora entirely. But the habitual tardiness of Mexican buses may force you to spend a night in Hermosillo, the state capital. Hermosillo is a wealthy, modern city in the heart of a productive agricultural and mining region. Wheat, corn, cotton, pecans, oranges, and grapes all grow in the surrounding countryside, nourished by extensive irrigation and the desert sun.

For the tourist, the most interesting thing about Hermosillo is the University of Sonora; the **Museo Regional de Historia** here contains many *indígena* artifacts and exhibits on pre-Hispanic and colonial history. It's next to the Hermosillo Flash, at the intersection of Rosales and Encinas. (Open daily 9am-1pm and 4-6pm.)

Orientation and Practical Information

Two hundred twenty seven kilometers south of the border, Hermosillo lies on Rte. 15, the main north-south highway connecting the western U.S. and central Mexico. Buses depart from the main terminal on Blvd. Luis Encinas, 2km north of the city center. North and southbound buses depart every hour and with even greater frequency during the afternoon. All service out of Hermosillo is *de paso;* during holidays and weekends you've got to don your boxing gloves to capture a seat.

One of the city's most recognizable landmarks is the **Hermosillo Flash,** a tall structure that flashes the time, temperature, its private parts, and brief advertisements day and night. At the junction of Blvds. Encinas and Rosales, the Flash helps the mapless orient themselves. The University of Sonora is located at this intersection. South on Rosales are the cathedral and the government buildings.

Municipal Tourist Office: Tehuantepec and Comonfort (tel. 12-32-67), on the bottom floor of the Palacio Administrativo. Regional distribution center for information on all of Sonora. Ask for Patty or César, both of whom speak English. Open Mon.-Fri. 8am-3pm and 5-7pm.

Currency Exchange: Banco BCH, on the plaza across the street from Hotel Monte Carlo. Open Mon.-Fri. 8:30am-1pm. Money changed 8:30am-noon. **Bánamex,** at Serdán and Matamoros, exchanges traveler's checks.

Post Office: Rosales and Serdán (tel. 12-00-11). Lista de Correos. Open Mon.-Fri. 8am-7pm, Sat.-Sun. 9am-1pm. **Postal Code:** 83000.

Telephones: Farmacia Margarita, Morelia and Guerrero (tel. 13-15-90). *Casetas* upstairs for long-distance and international phone calls (2000-peso surcharge). Avoid rush hour (5-6pm). Open 24 hr. **Telephone Code:** 62.

Telegrams: Rosales and Serdán (tel. 13-19-22), in the post office building. Open Mon.-Fri. 8am-10pm, Sat.-Sun. 8am-noon.

Airport: (tel. 16-07-72), about 10km from town toward Kino. A taxi to the airport costs 23,000 pesos, a bus 850 pesos. Flights to Mexico City, Guadalajara, Tijuana, and a few U.S. cities.

Trains: The **Ferrocarril del Pacífico** terminal is 3km north of town on Rte. 15. Northbound trains leave in the morning, southbound ones in the evening.

Buses: Tres Estrellas de Oro (tel. 337-48). To: Tijuana (48 per day, 15-17 hr., 41,000 pesos), some via Mexicali (24 per day, 12-14 hr., 32,000 pesos); Nogales (10 per day, 4 hr., 13,000 pesos); Agua Prieta (4 per day, 18,000 pesos); Mexico City (48 per day, 96,000 pesos); Mazatlán (at 3am and 1:15pm, 44,000 pesos). Buses to Tijuana and Mexico City fill early, so buy tickets at least a day in advance. To get from the bus station to the center of town, cross the street and catch a bus marked "Ranchito" or "Mariachi." Taxis will ask 15,000 pesos for a trip to *el centro.* Pay no more than half this, and don't jump in until you agree on a price.

Supermarket: Ley, 4 blocks up from the Flash on Encinas. Open Mon.-Fri. 8:30am-4:30pm, Sat.-Sun. 9am-1:30pm.

Laundromat: **Lavarama,** Yáñez at Sonora (tel. 415-43).

Red Cross: Transversal at 14 de Abril (tel. 407-69).

24-Hr. Pharmacy: **Farmacia Margarita,** Morelia at Guerrero (tel. 13-15-90).

Hospital: **Hospital General del Estado de Sonora,** Transversal at Reyes (tel. 218-70).

Police: Encinos at Obregón and Periférico Nte. at Noroeste (tel. 621-76 or 615-64).

Accommodations

Hermosillo offers many budget shelters but few mid-range establishments. Air-conditioning is costly but indispensable, especially in the blistering summer heat. For the truly indigent, five *casas de huéspedes* line Sonora, 2 blocks west of the plaza. Prices here are rock-bottom, but the area is a red-light district, unsafe for lone female travelers.

Hotel Niza, Plutarco Elías Calles Pte. 66 (tel. 720-28). Grand old art deco hotel that's pink as a piglet. Clean, comfortable rooms have A/C, telephone, and cable TV. The friendly management lets you hang out for hours on end at the bar and restaurant. Singles 60,000 pesos. Doubles 65,000 pesos. MC, Visa accepted.

Hotel Monte Carlo, Sonora at Juárez (tel. 233-54), on the northeast corner of the plaza. An old, established hotel with bars on the windows to keep out riff-raff. Very clean rooms, with A/C and private showers. Don't even think about negotiating the price; the management will direct you to one of the neighboring abodes. Singles and doubles 55,000 pesos.

Hotel Kino, Pino Suárez Sur 151 (tel. 245-99), in front of the Auditorio Cívico. A bit more luxurious than the rest, though the Ritz it's not. A/C, TV, and general cleanliness are among its merits. Don't walk between here and the plaza after dark. Singles 75,000 pesos. Doubles 85,000 pesos. Triples 95,000 pesos.

Hotel Washington, Noriega 68 (tel. 311-83), at Matamoros. Toilets work sporadically. Beds look like that kindergarten woodshop project you once threw away. A/C, noon check-out. Singles 29,000 pesos. Doubles 32,000 pesos.

Food

Like the mid-range hotel scene, the outlook for reasonably priced restaurants in Hermosillo is dim. The **Mercado Municipal,** 3 blocks south of the plaza, is your best bet for breakfast and lunch. This new and refreshingly immaculate market tempts the dieter with many stands selling tacos and *chimichangas.* Fortunately, fresh produce is cheap.

Hotel San Alberto Restaurant, Rosales and Elías. Perched on the deck of the hotel pool, this informal spot is somewhat reminiscent of a boxcar. *Caldo de queso* (cheese soup) served with tortillas 9000 pesos. A/C. Open daily 7am-10:30pm. MC, Visa accepted.

Restaurante Jung, Niñoes Héroes 75, close to the corner of Encinas and Matamoros. A pellagrous vegetarian restaurant with daily *comida corrida* (13,000 pesos). *Quesadillas* with lettuce, tomatoes, avocado, and beans 8500 pesos. The restaurant is connected to a natural products store, which stocks medicinal herbs, whole-grain bread, and funky books. Restaurant and store open daily 8am-8pm. MC, Visa accepted.

My Friend, Elías Calles 107. Anyone's friend in the midday heat. Tiny A/C oasis vends *quesadillas* 5500 pesos. Open daily 8am-8pm.

Hotel Niza Restaurant, Elías Calles 66. Just like all the other hotel restaurants. *Tostadas con carne* 10,000 pesos. Cable TV while you wait. Open daily 7am-10pm.

Kino

The twin settlements of Old and New Kino on magnificent Bahía Kino illustrate the sharp divisions in contemporary Mexican society. On the site that was originally the homebase of the Seri people, Old Kino was founded as a mission outpost by Father Kino in the late 17th century. Today, the inhabitants of this dusty village make their living from the sea in summer and from tourists in winter. Legions of homeless Tecate-drinkers share the beach with the local fishing people, depositing their empties on the sand next to piles of freshly severed fish heads. The inhabitants of New Kino live worlds apart, in an unbroken stretch of condominiums facing one of the finest beaches on the Gulf of California.

The Seris import ornate ironwood carvings into Old Kino from their villages farther down the coast. Two small Seri shops at the foot of the beachfront avenue sell inexpensive, high-quality works. In New Kino, the **Museo de los Seris,** in a white building where the bus from Hermosillo stops, offers a short but insightful look at Seri culture. (Open Tues.-Sun. 8am-7pm. Free.)

Excellent bus service makes transportation to Bahía Kino cheap and convenient. Buses leave Hermosillo (120km to the east) for the Kinos from a station on the corner of Aguirre and González; five buses depart daily, every two hours beginning at 7:30am (5000 pesos). Buses to Hermosillo depart from several stops in the Kinos at 10am, noon, 2pm, and 4pm (5000 pesos). Buses between the Kinos cost 500 pesos.

Trade in the Kinos is often transacted in U.S. dollars. If you plan to stay long, especially in New Kino, take plenty of greenbacks—the restaurants are not accustomed to pesos and will give you a poor exchange rate.

Practical Information

Currency Exchange: **Bancomer,** at Yabanos and Tastiota (tel. 202-22), in front of La Palapa. Open Mon.-Fri. 8am-1pm.

Post Office: Kino 30, in the Presidencia Municipal. Open Mon.-Fri. 8am-noon and 2-6pm.

Telephones: Long-distance *caseta* in Restaurant La Palapa (tel. 202-10). Open daily 8:30am-8pm. **Telephone Code:** 624.

Telegram: Kino 4 (tel. 201-10), at Tampico 1 block south of the post office. Open Mon.-Fri. 8am-noon and 2-6pm.

Red Cross: Kino 32, next to the police station and post office.

Pharmacy: **Farmacia Kino,** at Yabanos and Topolobampo (tel. 202-30), next to Bancomer. Open daily 8am-8pm.

Hospital: Hospital Claudio Clemens, on Tampico.

Police: In the Presidencia Municipal (tel. 200-32), next to the Red Cross.

Accommodations and Food

Spending the night free of cost under one of the many *palapas* lining New Kino's beaches is a relatively safe option. If you want walls, try the **Trailer Park Islandia Marina,** Guaymas at Peñasco (tel. 200-80), on the beach at the northwestern end of Old Kino. *Cabañas* sleep at least 5, with bathroom, kitchen, 2 bedrooms, and a covered porch (85,000 pesos). With sleeping bags, 20 people can easily be accommodated for the same price.

One other budget option exists. You can hook up your trailer (100 slips, 5 of them with companion *palapa*) for 24,000 pesos at the **Sol Bahía Kino,** a trailer park in New Kino. There's a ramp for launching motorboats, and a long-distance phone line in the owner's house. In fact, if you stay here more than a few days, the Saucedo family, owners of the park, will often invite you in.

Kino cuisine is synonymous with Kino seafood; if you're not a fan of fresh fish, dining here may be hard to swallow. Try **Restaurante La Palapa del Pescador,** in Old Kino. This thatched-roof hut isn't exactly a *palapa* because it has walls, but the semantic inconsistency doesn't detract from the food's quality. (Most fish 19,000 pesos. Steaks and other seafood 26,000 pesos. Open daily 8:30am-8pm.) In New Kino, check out **El Pargo Rojo,** halfway into town. (Seafood about 17,000 pesos. Open Wed.-Mon. noon-10pm.) **Abarrotes Amalia's,** on Vallarta in Old Kino, is the area's most complete supermarket.

Guaymas

The principal port in Sonora state, and home of an extensive shrimping fleet, Guaymas was originally inhabited by the Guaymas and Yaqui tribes. In 1701, Father Kino built the mission of San José 10km north of town. In 1769 the first Spanish settlement was founded. Today, as the closest commercial area to the resort of San Carlos, suntanned *norteamericanos* come here to take a break from the blisteringly hot beach.

Lacking convenient beaches, Guaymas deserves no lengthy stay, but it's the nicest place to break up the trip south to the more alluring resorts at Mazatlán, San Blas, and Puerto Vallarta. Much cooler than sizzling Hermosillo thanks to the ocean breezes, the area's beaches are to the north in **Miramar** and **San Carlos,** two uninspiring resorts that offer little more than condos and a few luxury hotels. Yachts hover off San Carlos, but the beaches accessible to the budget crowd are pebbled and dull.

Nightlife in Guaymas consists of a few discos along Serdán and a bar/restaurant called **El Sarape,** on Calle 23, 1 block north of Serdán.

Orientation

Guaymas is six hours south of Nogales by bus and five hours from Los Mochis. Buses and trains service inland Mexico, and the ferry steams to Santa Rosalía in Baja California. Municipal buses (400 pesos) run up and down Guaymas's main strip, **Avenida Serdán.** Buses to Miramar and San Carlos (600 pesos) leave every half-hour from various points along Serdán. To secure a seat, catch the bus at the beginning of its route by the bench on Calle 19 near Av. 10.

Almost everything in Guaymas takes place on or very near Serdán. Women should not walk alone more than 2 blocks south of Serdán after dark.

Northbound vehicles, including buses, are often stopped by narcotics police. Avoid spending the rest of your vacation and possibly your life in a Mexican prison cell; have your identification ready. Let them search whatever they want: the "I've got rights, you know" line just doesn't cut it like it does north of the border.

Practical Information

Tourist Office: (tel. 229-32) on Calle 22, almost 1 block south of Serdán, next to the police. On the ground floor of a tall white and brown building with a sign proclaiming "Restaurant Bar Mirador." Abundant maps and brochures cover all of Sonora. No English spoken. Open Mon.-Fri. 9am-1pm and 3-6pm.

Currency Exchange: Many banks along Serdán. **Bánamex,** Serdán and Calle 20, is the only one that accepts traveler's checks. Open for exchange Mon.-Fri. 8:30-11:30am.

Post Office and Telegrams: (tel. 207-57) on Av. 10 off Calle 20, after the Auditorio Municipal. Open Mon.-Fri. 8am-7pm, Sat.-Sun. 9am-1pm. **Postal Code:** 85400.

Telephones: Farmacia Santa Martha, Serdán and Calle 19. Three booths for long-distance collect calls (3000 pesos). Open Mon.-Sat. 8am-9pm, Sun. 9am-1pm. **Telephone Code:** 622.

Bus Station: Tres Estrellas and **Norte de Sonora,** Calle 14 at Rodríguez, 2 blocks south of Serdán. If you're planning on a northern trip, catch the 7am bus, because the later ones are jammed with chickens and people. Buy tickets 1 hr. in advance. Buses leave every hr. to: Hermosillo (6500 pesos), Tijuana (47,000 pesos), Mazatlán (38,000 pesos), Mexico City (90,000 pesos), and Guadalajara (62,000 pesos). To Nogales (8 per day, 15,000 pesos). Across the street is the **Pacífico** second-class bus terminal.

Train Station: (tel. 249-80) on Serdán, near Calle 29. A white building with an orange "Ferrocarriles Nacionales" sign. Office open daily 8am-noon and 2-4:30pm. Mostly for information, since trains arrive and depart from Empalme, 10km to the south. Buy tickets in Empalme 1 hr. before the train arrives. Fast train south at 9:40pm. Fast train north at 5:40am. Prices fluctuate up to 50% depending on time of departure. Lowest prices are quoted below. To: Hermosillo (10,000 pesos), Nogales (19,000 pesos), Mazatlán (32,000 pesos), and Guadalajara

(58,000 pesos). The only train to Mexico City is a sleeper. To find out how late the trains are running, call 306-16.

Ferry Terminal: (tel. 223-24) at the east end of town. Eastbound buses on Serdán stop at the ferry office. Ferries to Santa Rosalía Tues., Thurs., and Sun. at 10am (7 hr., 25,000 pesos). Tickets are sold the day before departure beginning at 7am. (For more details, see Transportation under Baja California.)

Laundromat: Super-Lava (tel. 254-00), just north of the Obregón turn-off on Rte. 15, 1km north of town. Open Mon.-Sat. 8am-9pm.

Red Cross: (tel. 255-55 or 208-79) at the northern limit of Guaymas. Ambulance service available.

Pharmacies: Farmacia Santa Martha, Serdán and Calle 19. Open Mon.-Sat. 8am-9pm, Sun. 9am-3pm. There is at least one on every block along Serdán.

Hospital: Clínica Guaymas, Serdán Pte. 863 (tel. 220-21).

Police: (tel. 200-30) on Serdán between Calles 22 and 23.

Accommodations

Although prices are hardly rocketing out of control, increased tourism has inflated room rates in the past few years. On the whole, Guaymas's lodgings are consistently better than any other city's in the area.

Hotel Impala, Calle 21 #40 (tel. 209-22 or 213-35), 1 block south of Serdán. Old, centrally located hotel with a self-important air about it. Purified water, telephones, and color TV. Efficient cleaning staff, including Lovely Rita the meter maid. Some A/C units are rather sickly. Singles 45,000 pesos. Doubles 55,000 pesos. Triples 70,000 pesos.

Hotel Santa Rita, Serdán and Mesa (tel. 281-00), near the shopping center at the end of Serdán closest to San Carlos. Cool 3-story atrium with patio furniture strewn across courtyard. Small, immaculate rooms with A/C, TV, and purified water. Singles 45,000 pesos. Doubles 55,000 pesos. Triples 70,000 pesos.

Hotel Rubi, Calle 29 and Serdán (tel. 201-69). The large verdant courtyard proves an interesting contrast to the salty sea-smell that permeates the rooms. But if you'd rather forgo the outside foliage, just sit inside and crank up the hellacious A/C. Singles 45,000 pesos. Doubles 55,000 pesos. Triples 60,000 pesos.

Casa de Huéspedes Lupita, Calle 15 #125 (tel. 284-09). Those who live for the color blue will exclaim "Yay!". Rooms with table-top fans and extremely clean communal bathrooms. No alcohol permitted. Noon check-out. Singles 18,000 pesos, with private bath 25,000 pesos. Doubles 28,000 pesos, with private bath 35,000 pesos.

Hotel América, Calle 20 and Av. 18 (tel. 211-10), 4 blocks from Serdán. Small, neat, and green, but nothing radical. Shiny new toilet seats grace spotless bathrooms. Singles 30,000 pesos. Doubles 35,000 pesos.

Food

Seafood is the Guaymas specialty: local favorites include frog legs, turtle steaks, and oysters in a garlic/chile sauce. The **Mercado Municipal,** on Calle 20, 1 block from Serdán, sells fresh produce as well as clothes, flowers, toys, and carved goods. Hot dog vendors line Serdán.

Restaurant Chattos Bus's, Serdán between Calle 11 and 12. This large grass hut has A/C for those who want out of the heat, but the seating outside provides a better view of the street action. Jumbo steak 10,000 pesos. Open daily 10am-1am.

Jax Snax, Serdán at Calle 14. Down to the weirdo spelling, a Mexican assay of Western popular culture. Great big cup of yogurt with honey, fruit, and granola 6500 pesos. Breakfast with orange juice or coffee 7000 pesos. Open daily 7am-11pm.

Restaurant Twenty, Calle 29 at Serdán. Great breakfasts, quick service, and A/C. Hotcakes 7000 pesos. Quesadillas 10,000 pesos. Open daily 7am-10pm.

Shopping Center, Serdán between Calles 10 and 11. Inside are a supermarket with an ambitious selection of alcohol, a bakery, and a shoe store. Go crazy.

Sights

Avenida Serdán is the extent of Guaymas's offerings, but you'll be pleasantly surprised by the quality and variety of stores lining the street. A huge, electronic message board spans Serdán around Calle 16 and transmits the latest news tersely and dispassionately.

Families with small children might enjoy the **Parque Club de Leones** at Serdán and Calles 24-5. Visitors come here for the amusement rides (1000-1500 pesos each), the terrific view of the mountains rising above the Gulf of California, and the foosball tables. The short pier, jutting into the inlet, is a favorite place for couples at night. No X-rated stuff here, just clasped hands.

Los Mochis

Los Mochis is about as vibrant as a bowl of refried beans. The commercial center of a prosperous agricultural district that exports sugar, cotton, rice, and wheat, tourists stop here only to catch the train through the Barranca del Cobre (Copper Canyon) to Creel and Chihuahua, or to catch the ferry to La Paz. Though it is possible to disembark the ferry at 6am and catch the second-class train that departs an hour later, the prospect of another long ride could keep you in Los Mochis for the day. It is very difficult to get a seat on a northbound bus; you'll have to wait at the station from the crack of dawn to have a fighting chance of boarding. The unlucky souls unable to buy tickets will find themselves stranded in Los Mochis an extra night.

Orientation

The ferry to La Paz leaves every Monday, Wednesday, Thursday, and Saturday at 10am from **Topolobampo,** a small fishing hamlet 24km south of Los Mochis. Economy tickets cost 24,000 pesos, *turista* 48,000 pesos, and express 72,000 pesos. Cars and motorcycles can be brought on the ferry for an additional fee; space is limited.

A shimmering new luxury ferry designed for tourists leaves every Tuesday, Thursday, and Saturday at 4:30pm. This turbo ferry cuts the seven-hour trip to La Paz down to three. Economy tickets cost 48,000 pesos, *turista* 72,000 pesos, and express 108,000 pesos. Passengers of this ferry can catch a free bus to Topolobampo that leaves the ticket office about two hours before departure.

Tickets for both ferries are available at the **Transbordadores** office at Juárez 125 (tel. 200-35 or 203-20), between Prieto and Allende. (Open Mon.-Fri. 8am-6pm.) Tickets, which must be bought one day in advance, go on sale when the office opens; it's best to arrive early.

A bus runs to Topolobampo every half hour in the morning (350 pesos); it leaves from a small side street down from the Hotel Santa Anita, between Hidalgo and Obregón. The bus can also be flagged down at Castro and Zaragoza.

The streets of Los Mochis form a simple grid. From Castro, the streets to the north are Obregón, Hidalgo, Independencia, Juárez, and Morelos. From Guerrero, the streets to the east are Flores, Leyva, Zaragoza, Prieto, and Allende. Although the organization of the streets is very simple, the small and faded street signs, affixed to corner buldings, are often difficult to read. Like many northwestern Mexican cities, there are few exact addresses in Los Mochis: no matter where a building is located on the block, the street address is usually the closest cross-street. Set office hours are the butt of town jokes.

Practical Information

Currency Exchange: Bancomer, Leyva and Juárez. Dollars exchanged only until noon.

Post Office: In transit during the summer of 1990. **Postal Code:** 81201.

Telephones: The pharmacy at Santos Degollado Sur 501 allows long-distance collect calls for 2000 pesos. Open 24 hr. Most hotels permit international collect calls but charge up to 10,000 pesos. Public telephones are next to bus stations on Morelos. **Telephone code:** 62.

Taxis: Tel. 12-29-68.

Bus Station: Tres Estrellas de Oro, on Obregón just east of Allende. *De paso* buses run north and south every hr., but often chock-full by the time they reach Los Mochis. You can be fairly sure of a seat on the *de local* buses to Guadalajara (every hr. 6am-7pm, 46,000 pesos) and Mazatlán (every hr. 6am-4pm, 22,000 pesos). Buses to Mexicali (56,000 pesos), Guaymas (16,000 pesos), Nogales (35,000 pesos), Juárez (58,000 pesos), Hermosillo (22,000 pesos), and Navojoa (7100 pesos) are all *de paso*, so be on your toes. **Norte de Sonora** and **Transportes del Pacífico,** side by side on Morelos between Leyva and Zaragoza, have scrungier buses to the same places for less. Buses to El Fuerte leave from the corner of Independencia and Degollado.

Market: On weekends clothes and food in the blocks surrounding the intersection of Castro and Zaragoza.

Laundromat: Lavamatic, Allende 218, just before Juárez. Wash or dry 2000 pesos. Open Mon.-Fri. 9am-1:30pm and 3-7pm, Sat.-Sun. 9am-1pm.

24-Hr. Pharmacy: Santos Degollado Sur 501.

Hospital: Hospital Fátima, Blvd. Jiquilpan Pte. 639 (tel. 12-33-12). **Centro de Salud** (tel. 12-09-13).

Red Cross: Obregón and Zaragoza (tel. 12-02-92). 24-hr. ambulance service.

Police: Degollado and Ordoñes (tel. 12-00-33).

Accommodations

Don't waste all night looking for the cozy bed of your dreams.

Hotel Lorena, Obregón Pte. 186 (tel. 202-39), between Allende and Prieto, down the street from the bus station. Every room in this caricature of a retirement home holds saccharin Fragonard prints of busty girls over the cable TV. Rickety rocking chairs and communal *agua purificada* litter the halls. Inexpensive cafeteria on the 3rd floor. Singles 40,000 pesos. Doubles 50,000 pesos. Triples 60,000 pesos. Credit cards accepted.

Hotel Catalina, Obregón Pte. 48 (tel. 212-40), across the street from the Tres Estrellas bus terminal. Ugly but clean, cool, and comfortable thanks to icy A/C. Singles 40,000 pesos. Doubles 50,000 pesos. Triples 60,000 pesos.

Hotel Beltrán, on Hidalgo between Zaragoza and Prieto. Nice bathrooms, A/C, and *agua purificada* in the lobby. Stairs wind around tidy courtyard. Singles 35,000 pesos. Doubles 45,000 pesos. Triples 55,000 pesos.

Hotel Hidalgo, on Hidalgo between Zaragoza and Prieto, across the street from the Beltrán. The central location doesn't do much to compensate for the dilapidated condition of this hotel. Many holes in corridor floors complement the cramped, smelly bathrooms that lack toilet seats and hot water. Once you're asleep, the single merit of this joint is apparent: great beds. Singles 25,000 pesos, 28,000 pesos with A/C. Doubles 28,000 pesos, 30,000 pesos with A/C.

Food

The best and cheapest food is sold in the **public market** between Prieto and Leyva along Castro. Because most of the produce for sale is grown near Los Mochis, prices are low and quality is high. The *taquerías* and *loncherías* in the market serve cheap home-brewed mysteries, many of which pack an excellent punch.

Except for the *cantinas* (which women avoid) and the corner *taquerías,* just about everything in town shuts down at 8pm. After that, enter **The Closet,** the bar in the Santa Anita Hotel (on Leyva, between Hidalgo and Obregón), which is dark and crowded as its name implies. If you can rustle up a group of stranded tourists, most of them will be willing to down a few with you.

Hotel Lorena Cafeteria, Obregón Pte. 186, on the 3rd floor. The best place for breakfast or a light meal. Good service. *Sincronoizadas* (quesadillas with ham) 6500 pesos. Fresh orange juice 2500 pesos.

El Taquito, on Leyva between Hidalgo and Independencia. Comfortable booths and A/C, but slow service and no *agua purificada.* Gizzard-style ranch chicken 8500 pesos, pancakes 2500 pesos, freshly squeezed juice 3000 pesos. Open 24 hr.

La Parilla Dorada, Leyva 222, between Independencia and Juárez. Clean, reasonably priced restaurant with bleached tablecloths and potted trees. Excellent Mexican and Chinese meals. Quesadillas 2500 pesos, tacos 2000 pesos. Broiled meats and *carne milanesa* 16,000 pesos. Open Mon.-Sat. 10am-midnight.

Near Los Mochis

Los Mochis is not a beach town. Sun-worshipers should hop on the next bus to Mazatlán. Those delayed by transportation snafus can boat, fish, and swim in the waters of the **Miguel Hidalgo Dam** just outside town. **Playa Maviri,** near Topolo-bampo, is good for boating or angling, but a bit rocky and dirty for swimming. Sea lions like it, however; you may run into a few basking on the rocks. About 50km west of town on Independencia is **Playa Las Salinas,** the finest beach in the area.

About 75km to the east, the old colonial town **El Fuerte** might not be utterly boring. The train to the Barranca del Cobre stops briefly in El Fuerte; buses to the fort run from the corner of Degollado and Independencia in Los Mochis from 6am to 8pm.

Mazatlán

Mazatlán means "place of the deer" in Nahuatl. A less appropriate name can hardly be imagined, for there is nothing even remotely pastoral about this city. The only wildlife present—genus *Bronzus,* species *norteamericanus*—roams the beaches in large herds.

In 1531, Mazatlán's harbor was chosen as the launching pad for Spanish galleons loaded with gold mined in the Sierra Madres. Three centuries later, the town suffered a U.S. blockade (1847) and a French bombardment (1864). Mazatlán was also the temporary stomping ground for a group of Confederate war veterans out to preserve their Southern ideals on Mexican soil, and during the Revolution of 1914 the city became only the second in the world to be shelled from the air. A substantial Chinese population once lived here but was summarily expelled 50 years ago.

Despite its eventful past, Mazatlán presents nothing of historical or cultural interest to the traveler. Other Mexican resorts maintain at least a façade of cute *mexicanidad* and cultivate an exotic sheen, but Mazatlán couldn't care less, an attitude to which one city map crassly attests: "It's a favorite with children who have little local history to learn, as well as with tourists who think it is a lot more fun to fish, swim, hunt, waterski, or just relax, than to play follow-the-leader on a tour of memorial plaques." Its tourist zone, spread along a highway, matches its Floridian prototypes gift shop for gift shop but boasts lower prices and nicer beaches. Like other great resorts, the most attractive aspects of Mazatlán are gifts of nature—beautiful sunsets, a glittering ocean, and wide golden beaches. Although El Cid may think it has improved the city, the best that Mazatlán has to offer is still free.

Orientation

Mazatlán wrote the book on transportation, but the bus is still the most economical and versatile way to get in and out of the city. The bus station lies 3 blocks behind the Sands Hotel, about 2km north of Old Mazatlán. The area around the bus station, with several reasonably priced hotels and restaurants, along with a good beach and the vital "Sábalo" bus line only 3 blocks away, makes a convenient homebase. You can catch the downtown-bound "Insurgentes" bus at the stand 1 block off the beach across from the chicken barbecuer.

On the far eastern edge of Mazatlán, the **Ferrocarril del Pacífico** train station opens an hour before departures, and closes soon after arrivals. Make your way to a better part of town immediately upon arrival: the yellow "Insurgentes" bus or the green, beat-up "Cerritos-Juárez" will take you to and from downtown. **Sematur** (tel. 170-20) now runs ferries daily to and from La Paz, on Baja California. Their office and slip sit on the southern end of Carnaval, which runs south from Angel Flores, 2 blocks west of the Zócalo. Meeting the ferry requires a 20-minute walk from *el centro;* the Playa Sur bus makes the trip, and for 5000-7000 pesos, so will a taxi. Sematur accepts reservations for all classes up to a month in advance, and during the months of December, July, and August recommends that you make them at least two weeks ahead of your scheduled date of departure. (Open Mon.-Fri. 8am-3pm.)

The Mazatlán airport is 30km south of the city. Bus "Atamsa" brings arrivals downtown, but no bus returns to the airport; resign yourself to a cab (a whopping 35,000-40,000 pesos).

Built on a rocky spur jutting southwest into the Pacific, Old Mazatlán's downtown area surrounds and spills north of the Zócalo. **Angel Flores,** the southern boundary of the Zócalo, runs west to **Olas Altas,** a quiet waterfront area that remained Mazatlán's most fashionable district until the tourist onslaught arrived. Both Juárez, the eastern boundary of the Zócalo, and Serdán, 1 block farter east, run north (toward the back of the cathedral) to the cheap hotel district and the area's beach, **Playa del Norte.** From Playa del Norte, the coast arcs to the northeast; glitz builds upon itself through the **Golden Zone,** a colony of exclusive time-share condos, high-rise hotels, and overpriced gift shops 7km north of Old Mazatlán, before reaching its apotheosis in the El Cid resort, a world unto itself.

Since many of Mazatlán's streets are numbered twice-over, tracking down a particular address can prove difficult.

Mazatlán's efficient bus system makes getting around the city a breeze. At some point, all the big, yellow municipal buses pass the public market on Juárez, 3 blocks north of the Zócalo; if you get lost, you'll eventually return to familiar territory. The line you'll probably use most, "Sábalo," runs along Juárez from the market to the beach, and then 16km up the beach to Puerta Cerritos. "Insurgentes" services the bus and train stations, and "Playa Sur" goes to the ferry dock. Fare is 400 pesos, and buses run every 15 minutes from 5am to 11pm. For late-night disco hopping, you'll have to take a cab (10,000 pesos from the Golden Zone to Old Mazatlán) or a *pulmonía,* an open vehicle resembling a golf-cart and that putters along at 60mph (about 8000 pesos). Always set the price before you commit yourself to the ride.

Practical Information

Tourist Office: Olas Altas 1300 (tel. 512-20), on the 1st floor of the northernmost building in the Bank of Mexico complex. English-speaking staff distributes city maps and provides a wealth of knowledge if you ask lots of leading questions. Open Mon.-Fri. 8am-3pm. Tourist information booths proliferate in the Golden Zone. Ritzier hotels can often answer questions and may provide maps.

Consulates: U.S., Circunvalación 120 (tel. 126-85), behind the Hotel Bel Mar, near Olas Altas. **Canada,** Loaiza at Bugamblia (tel. 373-20), in the Hotel Mazatlán.

Currency Exchange: Banks exchange currency Mon.-Fri. 8:30am-noon. *Casas de cambio* serve shoppers throughout the Golden Zone; typically open daily 9am-6:30pm. Bigger hotels change after hours at rip-off rates.

American Express: In the Balboa Plaza Centro Comercial (tel. 305-55), on Sábalo in the Golden Zone. Holds mail for 30 days, reserves plane tickets, and cashes traveler's checks. Staff speaks some English and smiles gracefully at mangled Spanish. Open Mon.-Fri. 9am-6pm, Sat. 9am-noon.

Post Office: Juárez at 21 de Marzo (tel. 121-21). New Lista de Correos posted after 11am, but is up Mon.-Fri. 8am-3pm. Other services open Mon.-Fri. 8am-7pm, Sat. 9am-1pm.

Telephones: Serdán 1512. International collect calls 2000 pesos. Open 24 hr. **Telephone Code:** 678.

Telegrams: In the same building as the post office (tel. 121-20). Open Mon.-Fri. 8am-8pm, Sat. 8am-1pm. Branch office at the bus depot open Mon.-Fri. 8am-6pm.

Airport: 30km south of the city. **Aeroméxico,** Sábalo 310-A (tel. 411-11). To Mexico City (3 per day, 300,000 pesos) and Tijuana (2 per day, 334,000 pesos). **Mexicana,** Claussen 101-B (tel. 277-22). To Guadalajara (1 per day, 169,000 pesos) and Los Angeles (2 per day, US$153).

Train Station: On the eastern edge of town. Listed prices are for *primera especial;* sleeping berths cost twice as much. To: Guadalajara (at 5:05am and 8:10pm, 38,300 pesos); Nogales (at 6:50pm, 76,000 pesos); Mexicali (at 6:50pm, 101,400 pesos).

Bus Station: Tres Estrellas de Oro, Transportes del Norte, Estrella Blanca, and **Transportes del Pacífico** all serve Mazatlán. **Transportes del Norte de Sonora** runs the most buses to: Tijuana (every hr., 27 hr., 79,000 pesos); Nogales (2 per day, 18 hr., 52,000 pesos); Guadalajara (every hr., 9 hr., 22,000 pesos); and Mexico City (every hr., 18 hr., 45,000 pesos). Tres Estrellas de Oro sends 1 bus per day to Puerto Vallarta (7 hr., 22,000 pesos). Transportes del Norte dispatches buses north to Durango (10 per day, 7 hr., 15,000 pesos), Monterrey (7 per day, 17 hr., 44,000 pesos), and beyond.

Ferry: Port at the southern end of Carnaval. To La Paz (at 5pm, 16 hr., *salón* 36,000 pesos, *turista* 72,000 pesos, and *cabina* 108,000 pesos). (See Baja California, Getting Around By Sea for an explanation of the various classes.)

Car Rental: Budget, Sábalo 402 (tel. 320-00). 89,800 pesos per day, plus 563 pesos per km. 171,000 pesos per day with unlimited mileage. Insurance and A/C extra.

Laundromat: Lava Fácil, across from the bus station on a side street in the same building as Hotel Fiesta. Follow the signs to a faded pink storefront. Wash 1700 pesos, 10-min. dry 1500 pesos, detergent 600 pesos. Open Mon.-Sat. 8am-8pm, Sun. 9am-2pm.

Red Cross: Obregón 73 (tel. 136-00).

24-Hr. Pharmacy: Farmacia Angel, Av. del Mar 27 (tel. 247-46).

Hospital: IMSS (tel. 326-00), on Carretera Internacional Nte.

Police: (tel. 341-10) on Rafael St. in Colonia Juárez.

Accommodations

In the good ol' days, budget hotels in Mazatlán about the same as those in other Mexican cities: of late many seem to have used Mexico's extreme inflation as an excuse to jack their prices up to resort levels. Nonetheless, fine cheap rooms do exist—except on the waterfront, where rates are exorbitant at even the shabbiest places. Budget hotels concentrate around the bus station and in Old Mazatlán along the three avenues east of the main square that head north to the ocean: Juárez, Serdán, and Azueta.

The busiest seasons in Mazatlán are the Christmas holiday and the month following Semana Santa. At these times of year, check in early. At other times, prices are negotiable, especially for extended stays. Summer nights in Mazatlán can be very hot and humid; always inspect the cooling system or ventilation in your room before paying.

Also remember Brown's Muffler Axiom: The value of a Mexican car rises in direct proportion to its decibel output. If you are looking at a room on the street, keep looking.

Old Mazatlán

The aforementioned Brown's Muffler Axiom applies here in all its glory. In addition, these hotels lie parsecs away from the good discos, so, if that's your scene, be prepared to shell out *mucho dinero* for a cab.

Hotel Santa Bárbara, Juárez at 16 de Septiembre (tel. 221-20). The bathrooms here are clean, and some of the rooms are far enough off the street to avoid most noise. Only 1½ blocks from the beach. Windchimes on the front door alert the pleasant owner of your arrival. Singles 30,000 pesos. Doubles 37,000 pesos.

Hotel Morales, Azueta 2221 (tel. 131-38), north of Morelos. Empty flower troughs in the huge hallways a let-down after the corny murals of unicorns and Greek gods on walls. In the morn roll out of the lumpy beds and into the ugly green-and-black bathrooms. Singles 25,000 pesos. Doubles 30,000 pesos.

Hotel Lerma, Bolívar 622 (tel. 124-36), off Serdán. Brown building with green shutters and red iron bars in the windows. Beds are acceptable but the ants and other small buggies on the floor might join you for a midnight snack. Singles 20,000 pesos. Doubles 25,000 pesos.

Hotel Vialta, Azueta Nte. 2006 (tel. 160-27), between Hidalgo and Estrada. Plain, clean bathrooms. The doubles are doubly double—2 rooms for 2 people. The leaden keychain can double as a ship's anchor. Singles 25,000 pesos. Doubles 35,000 pesos.

Hotel Milán, Canizales Pte. 10 (tel. 135-88). Many stairs lead to musty rooms that are as well-lit as a black hole. Phone included, but black-and-white TV costs 3000 pesos extra. Singles 20,000 pesos. Doubles 40,000 pesos.

Near the Bus Station

This neighborhood is well-to-do in patches. Consequently, the prices aren't quite as low as in Old Mazatlán, but the somewhat more pleasant rooms have views of the ocean (3 blocks away) if your windows face the right direction. Chris's Corollary holds here: The more often a Mexican bus driver shifts (the more noise he makes), the faster his beast of a bus moves, and the sooner he gets home.

Hotel Emperador (tel. 267-24), on Río Panuco directly in front of the terminal. By far the best of the bunch; some rooms overlook an inner courtyard. Clean rooms are cooled by strong fans. Great coffee shop in the lobby. Singles and doubles 28,000 pesos.

Hotel Fiesta, Río Tamazula at Río Panuco (tel. 138-88). Room's inventory: a fan, a light, a bed. No *mas*. But wait, there's more: hand-me-down curtains from the 70s, for a short time only. Singles 25,000 pesos. Doubles 30,000 pesos.

Hotel Económico, Río Panuco at Tamazula, next to the Chinese restaurant. The rooms are cheap because you must share with new roommates: roaches raised on nuclear waste and Carl the Iguana, Jr. Fans lull you and the other life forms to sleep. Problems associated with Chris's Corollary are in full effect here. Singles 20,000 pesos. Doubles 25,000 pesos.

South to Olas Altas

Back in the 1950s, long before wily developers began constructing multimillion-dollar pleasure palaces along the north shore, Mazatlán's fledgling resort scene clung to Olas Altas, a winding 1km road hugging the shore south of town. Today, the majority of Mazatlán's tourists forgo these hotels in favor of their more glamorous northern counterparts, but the old forlorn hotspots still stand, begging for business.

The **Hotel Belmar,** Olas Altas Sur 166 (tel. 511-12), a charming, mammoth resort of yesteryear, keeps its loyal if aging clientele satisfied with its large swimming pool, restaurant, and barber shop. Exterior walls glitter with multi-colored inlaid marble and ceramic tiles. Large rooms feature air conditioning, lots of dark wood paneling, pretty furniture, and bathrooms bigger than some budget bedrooms. (Singles 40,000 pesos, with ocean view 45,000 pesos. Doubles 50,000 pesos, with ocean view 55,000 pesos.) Above the Shrimp Bucket, the **Hotel La Siesta,** Olas Altas 11 (tel. 126-40) offers extra-large rooms, including TV and phone, surrounding a verdant courtyard. TV and phone included. Some rooms have a sea view, and the Venice-style doors allow for good ventilation. (Singles and doubles 45,000 pesos.)

Camping, though officially discouraged, is permitted on **Playa Bruja** (see Beaches).

Food

To travelers arriving from the culinary Sahara of northern Mexico, Mazatlán's restaurants will come as an immense relief. Mexican dishes that had been mysteriously absent farther north suddenly surface on menus: fresh, spicy guacamole, crisp nachos dripping with Monterey Jack cheese and *jalapeño* peppers, and real beef that you won't confuse with pork or lamb. What's more, Mazatlán's restaurants are relatively cheap, although, like everything else, food prices escalate as you move north to the Golden Zone.

Old Mazatlán

The busy public market, between Juárez and Serdán, 3 blocks north of the Zócalo, serves the cheapest meals in the area. Venturing inside, you will encounter hanging cows minus only head, hoofs, skin, and entrails; freshly liberated pig heads abound. Ample snacking opportunities exist outside in the *fruterías, loncherías,* and taco stands. For early risers, the best breakfast special on the waterfront (2 eggs, beans, potatoes, bread or tortillas, and coffee for 4500 pesos) is dished out at **Restaurant Playa Norte,** on the seaward side of Paseo Clausen, north of Serdán.

Ostionería Avenida, Aleman 808, south of downtown on the way to the port. Breezy white seafood emporium with many excellent, inexpensive selections. Shrimp and oysters, the house specialties, prepared with lots of spice and a little imagination. *Camarones a la Diabla* 12,000 pesos. Open daily 8am-8pm.

Joncol's, Flores Pte. 608. The devoted local following of this cozy restaurant digs the well-prepared seafood. Hidden from the unaware by an arched façade. Broiled shrimp 25,000 pesos. Breaded chicken 12,000 pesos. Open daily 7am-11pm.

Pizzas El Griego, Flores 920. Packs of Marlboros line the walls. Make sure to autograph the table before you leave. Friendly waiters and cheap pizza. A medium ham-and-pineapple costs 11,000 pesos. 10% discount on Friday. Open daily 1-11pm.

Los Comales, Flores 908, across from the post office. If you're too tired to explore, this is probably the best choice, however unexciting it may be. Everything in the huge interior is earth-toned except the murals, which star Mexico's various ethnic groups as well as the mighty Columbia River. Eggs with ham or bacon 3000 pesos, plate of enchiladas 6000 pesos, *bistec* 10,000 pesos. Open daily 8am-11pm.

Restaurante Balneario Mazatlán ("The Beach Boys Café"), on Paseo Clausen, 2 doors down from the Fishermen's Statue. This open-air restaurant whips up mediocre Mexican food for the few tourists who venture this far south. Try the grilled cheese oysters (20,000 pesos) or smoked marlin (15,000 pesos), unless you prefer bland tacos and tortillas. Open daily 8am-8pm.

Olas Altas

Enjoy a budget breakfast with the spray from the ocean in your face, and digest it amidst the tranquility of the southern coast. Here you'll find the travelers, not the tourists.

Giggling waitrons in scarlet aprons entertain while you wait at the **Restaurant Madrid,** Olas Altas 1204. Toast, eggs, ham, and beans go for 6000 pesos. (Open daily 7am-11pm.) The **Restaurant Fondes Santa Clara,** on Olas Altas, supports a thriving subculture of chessmasters who play on the sidewalk under its awning. A small bar inside this little café lubricates the gears in their minds. The Mexi-Combo costs 14,500 pesos.

North to the Golden Zone

As you move north, prices soar and *norteamericano* culinary influence becomes more pronounced. Look no further if you feel the need for U.S. music, tourists, and Caesar salads.

Señor Frog's, on Av. del Mar, next to Frankie-Oh's. This tourist magnet actually concocts some tasty meals. Barbershop poles defy gravity, and photos and license plates cover the walls. Choose something cheap, for they slap a huge plate of seasoned cucumber and carrot sticks on the table no matter what you order. Besides food, they sell those spiffy T-shirts ubiquitous in high schools north of the border. Greasy but good chicken fingers 8000 pesos. BBQ ribs 22,000 pesos. Open daily noon-midnight.

Jungle Juice, on Garzas. Tourists are often caught ordering a special mix of juices called Moctezuma's Revenge Remedy (5500 pesos). Menu lists several salads and other vegetarian entrees, and the staff speaks English. Meatless spaghetti 19,000 pesos. Egg salad sandwich 7000 pesos. Open daily 7:30am-10:30pm.

Restaurant Roca Mar, Av. del Mar at Río Tamazula, just south of the Sands Hotel. Open-air spot still far enough south to be frequented by locals and roving guitar players. Prices have been tainted by tourism, and the menu is a mish-mash of culinary styles. Try the octopus salad (22,000 pesos) or filet mignon (26,000 pesos). Open daily 9am-1am.

Lonchería El Mambo, Río Presidio 204, across from the bus station. Clean and cheap, with a roof over the dining area, unlike many other restaurants around the station. Unspectacular food, but Marilyn seems to enjoy the mix of tourists and locals who come because of the convenient location. *Huevos rancheros* 5000 pesos. Open daily 7am-7pm.

Sights and Activities

The three-hour alcohol-free **Yate Fiesta** harbor cruises depart daily at 11am (20,000 pesos). Tickets are sold at the yacht office: to get there, follow directions to the ferry docks and then walk toward the lighthouse (to the right as you face the ferry). A five-minute stroll to the end of the first dock, past various sportfishing boats with marlin nailed to their bows, brings you to the office.

The **Acuario Mazatlán** (tel. 178-15), on Av. de los Deportes, keeps piranhas and 249 other feisty breeds in a half-dozen large tanks. Don't miss Rusty the Shark; his spooky glide will make you think twice about tomorrow's snorkeling trip. The Acuario is 1 block back from the beach and north of the Sands Hotel; the turn-off is marked by a shimmering blue sign. (Open daily 9am-6pm. Admission 6000 pesos, ages 6-18 2000 pesos.)

Mazatlán's towerdivers don't quite match the exploits of the cliffdivers in Aca-pulco, but their acrobatic plunges are dangerous enough to excite. Performances take place only on high-season afternoons with good weather. The best viewing angle is from just south of the towers; on days when the water is too rough for diving, you can climb the tower to watch the waves break below. To get to the towers, walk to the waterfront on Zaragoza and head south.

Mazatlán's greatest asset is its 16km of beach. Just north of Old Mazatlán along Av. del Mar sprawls **Playa Norte,** a decent stretch of sand if you don't mind small waves and the stares of the local *machos* who hang out on the waterfront. Solo women in particular should consider swimming farther north. As you hone in on the Golden Zone, the beach gets cleaner, the waves larger, and the name becomes **Playa Las Gaviotas.** Just past Punta Sábalo, in the lee of the islands, basks **Playa Sábalo,** with great waves and manicured golden sand co-opted by crowds of *norteamericanos* and assorted peddlers. *Yellow* "Sábalo" buses access all of these beaches.

As Playa Sábalo recedes to the south, crowds thin rapidly, and you can frolic on the glorious beaches and in the dramatic surf all by yourself. If you take the *yellow* Sábalo bus to the last stop and walk to the beach, you'll be at nearly deserted **Playa Bruja,** with tons of beautiful sand, four- to six-foot waves, and a few restaurants. Playa Bruja is the best of Mazatlán's beaches; it's also the only one on which you can camp.

William Blake claimed to see the universe in a grain of sand, but less poetic souls have been known to tire of even the most beautiful beaches. Should this fate befall you, don't necessarily abandon Mazatlán, because you may simply be in need a brief change of locale. Hop on one of the boats to the **Isla de la Piedra,** where locals go to escape the crowds. Boats shove off from the wharf on Av. del Puerto, near the intersection of Nájera and Leyva in the northwest corner of Old Mazatlán (every 15 min. 5am-6pm, 20 min., 3000 pesos round-trip). Boats leave for **Islas Chivas,** an island with fine diving and even fewer people, from the El Cid Resort in the

Golden Zone (3 per day, 15,000 pesos round-trip). Parasailing is also possible on the beach at El Cid; it costs around 30,000 pesos a shot. Be sure to bargain.

Nightlife

Mazatlán aims to please. The most popular disco is **Valentino's,** in the town's weirdest building. When you see a white-stucco version of the haunted Disney mansion on a rocky point at the southern end of the Golden Zone, you'll know you've arrived. This joint is jammed with touring teen-agers—they're the ones with neon wristbands, in case you couldn't tell by the eager looks on their faces—and begins to really rock after midnight. (Cover 10,000 pesos. Drinks start at 5000 pesos. Open daily 9pm-5am.) Adjoining Valentino's is **Bora-Bora,** a music-filled bar on the beach frequented by an older crowd. The best light show is at **El Caracol** in the El Cid complex. (Cover 15,000 pesos. Drinks start at 5000 pesos. Open daily 9pm-4am.) **Frankie-Oh's,** next to Sr. Frog's, is also popular with the young set, and often has 2-for-1 drink specials. (Cover 6000 pesos. Drinks start at 7000 pesos. Open daily 9pm-4am.) Lesser thrills, with essentially the same hours as the top discos, include **Puppet,** at the Camino Real, and **Confetti's,** at the Caravello Beach Club. At none of the above establishments are shorts, sandals, or guests under 18 permitted—officially.

Tepic

The border between the states of Sinaloa and Nayarit is a geographical watershed—as the northern desert comes to an end, volcanic highlands and a tropical coastline take its place. Home of the Cora and Huichol peoples, Nayarit entered the world's collective consciousness via Carlos Castaneda's book *Journey to Ixtlán,* inspired by hallucinogens and a small town halfway between Tepic and Guadalajara. Nayarit is the biggest exporter of fruit among the Mexican states, and reputedly produces the lion's share of the nation's marijuana crop.

Tepic, the capital of Nayarit, is an important crossroads because of its proximity to San Blas (70km to the northwest), Puerto Vallarta (169km south), Mazatlán (278km north), and Guadalajara (240km southeast). If you're traveling in this part of the country, you'll probably pass through Tepic, but you won't be missing much if you simply switch buses and skip town quickly.

The bus station is served by **Norte de Sonora, Tres Estrellas de Oro, Omnibus de México, Transportes del Pacífico, Estrella Blanca,** and **Transportes Frontera.** Norte de Sonora runs the most buses, with service to: Mexico City (3 per day, 12 hr., 36,000 pesos); Guadalajara (13 per day, 4 hr., 9400 pesos); Tijuana (15 per day, 36 hr., 90,000 pesos); Nogales (2 per day, 24 hr., 64,000 pesos); and San Blas (5 per day, 1¾ hr., 3000 pesos). Mazatlán can be reached via any Tijuana-bound bus (5 hr., 12,000 pesos), and Ixtlán via any Guadalajara-bound bus (1½ hr., 3600 pesos). If Norte de Sonora's schedule is inconvenient, in theory you can catch a bus to any of the above destinations on another line within an hour. Many of the buses that serve Tepic originate in other cities, and are frequently full upon arrival.

To get to the budget hotel area, take a left upon leaving the station, another left on the first street, and walk ahead 1 block. The **Hotel Tepic,** Martínez 428 (tel. 313-77), has halls that summon up visions of a cheap dirty hospital. Painters ran out of blue before getting to the rooms, which are bare but for a thin-mattressed bed and quickly warping desk. (Singles 22,000 pesos. Doubles 28,000 pesos.) Next door at Martínez 430, the **Hotel Nayar** (tel. 323-22), has slightly larger rooms but suffers from the same roadside cacophony of grinding gears, steam whistles, and diesel engines. The bathrooms are simply huge. (Singles 20,000 pesos. Doubles 30,000 pesos.)

Downtown Tepic has plenty of affordable restaurants. At **Café Diligencias,** México Sur 29, you can eavesdrop on the locals discussing PAN and PRI politics over coffee. Chicken goes for 10,000 pesos, and a heavenly banana split goes for 4200 pesos. (Open Mon.-Sat. 8am-10pm.) A little less like a coffee shop and more like a full restaurant is **Altamirano,** México Sur 109. A high ceiling reinforces the expansive effect of many open windows. Watch the cooks toss tortillas while you eat. Great *huevos* and *frijoles* 5000 pesos, steak and beans 8500 pesos. (Open daily 7am-10pm.)

The bus station holds a **post office** and a telegram office (both open Mon.-Fri. 9am-1pm). Also from the station, long-distance service is available Monday through Friday from 9am to 5:30pm. International collect calls cost 5600 pesos. Tepic's telephone code is 321. The **regional tourist office,** México Sur 34, employs a huge alligator to guard the cache of Tepic maps. Some English is spoken. (Open Mon.-Fri. 9am-7pm.) You can exchange money at downtown banks Monday through Friday from 9am to noon, or at the *casas de cambio* that separate the banks Monday through Saturday from 9am to 2pm and 4 to 8pm. In an emergency, call the Red Cross (tel. 311-60) or the police (tel. 201-63).

As you leave the station front, *el centro* is down the highway to the left; cross the street and catch one of the orange buses (250 pesos) at the *parada*.

Avenida México, running north-south, is the main street in downtown Tepic. At its northern terminus, the **Plaza Principal** is incessantly active, and life-size crucifixes oversee the plaza's **cathedral.** Southward from the plaza lie the **Museo Regional de Nayarit** (open Mon.-Fri. 9am-3pm; admission 5000 pesos), at México Nte. 91, and the **state capitol,** a gracefully domed edifice dating from the 1870s, at México and Abasolo. At Av. México's southern end, if you turn west (uphill) on Insurgentes, you'll come across a huge, enchanting park known as **La Loma.** A miniature train encircles the park, running Tuesday through Sunday from 10am to 4pm (800 pesos).

Near Tepic

Puerto Vallarta and San Blas are the most compelling lures for beach bums passing through Tepic, but southern Nayarit has a number of little-known beaches which sacrifice social life for the greater goal of unpopulated sand. Chief among these are undeveloped **Chacala,** the finest beach in the state, which lies on a dirt road out of Las Varas; **Rincón de Guayabitos,** 16km farther south, with limited accommodations; and **Punta de Mita,** close enough to Puerto Vallarta to enjoy its nightlife and far enough away to sleep in peace and quiet.

Fifty kilometers south of Tepic spreads the deep and clear **Laguna de Santa María del Oro,** a lovely 3km-wide lagoon. María del Oro plunges into the throat of an extinct volcano, its shores lined with banana trees. A second-class Mexico y Victoria bus departs every hour from the Tepic bus terminal for the town of Santa María. From there, you can hitch the remaining 8km to the lagoon. Although much of the shoreline lacks facilities and the water isn't safe for drinking, the lake's rim provides many scenic camping sites.

Another 50km south toward Guadalajara is the town of **Ixtlán,** of Castaneda fame. Only the Toltec ruins 1km south of town make Ixtlán worth mentioning. Though inferior in size and importance to the sites farther south and east, they may be your only exposure to Mexico's pre-Conquest past if you're not going beyond Guadalajara. Of particular interest is the Temple of Quetzalcóatl, the largest structure on the site, complete with sacrificial altars.

San Blas

Once a key Spanish port, San Blas is today a prosperous fishing village surrounded by miles of beaches and backed by a jungle where bananas, papayas, and mangos proliferate. Hotels remain inexpensive, and the cuisine costs much less than at other Pacific coast resorts. For most of the year the community is so small that you'll make acquaintances and begin to notice the new faces in town within a few days. Many visitors (not just from California—German is heard nearly as often as English in restaurants), stay in San Blas for months on end.

Surfers make the pilgrimage to **Bahía Matanchén** hoping to surf for miles when the right break rolls along, and sport-fishing people come to snag record numbers of marlin, mackerel, and snook. There is little to do but lie on the beach, dive for oysters, eat tropical fruit, and drink icy bottles of Pacífico, but these few activities satisfy most everybody. In fact, you may find yourself smashing your piggybank to buy *pozole* (hominy and hog-jowl stew) from street vendors and sleep in a US$7-a-night hotel for a precious few more days; some visitors have gone so far as to move into the jungle, where they subsist on wild fruits and nuts.

San Blas noticeably lacks that which other Pacific beach towns cannot avoid: the schism between the tourist world and the local world. Here, the most popular restaurants are popular with both locals and travelers. Most restaurants have bilingual menus, and many even accept U.S. currency—so it's not that there aren't plenty of tourists to go around. The townspeople greet visitors endearingly, and it is suspected that the chief source of this enthusiasm is the distraction tourists provide for the enormous population of voracious mosquitoes.

It is the mosquitoes that have kept San Blas from becoming a first-class resort; don't think you'll get lucky and elude them. San Blas's charms are worth delving into, but only with plenty of strong insect repellent from home. You'll need it—the Mexican varieties are not very effective, except for those magical green incense cones.

Orientation

San Blas's inaccessibility heightens its appeal. Most connections to the outside world are made through Tepic, 70km to the east, where you'll find the nearest train station and airport. **Norte de Sonora** buses leave San Blas for Tepic (5 per day, 1¾ hr., 3000 pesos) from the bus station at the northeast corner of the Zócalo. One bus also leaves for Guadalajara each day (at 8:30am, 6 hr., 12,000 pesos).

At the edge of town, the highway from Tepic turns into **Avenida Juárez,** the main street. Like all of San Blas's cobbled streets, Juárez remains quiet throughout the day, running along the south edge of the Zócalo and continuing toward the harbor past a row of hotels and restaurants. Batallón, on the western side of the Zócalo, heads south to the town beach by a group of higher-priced hotels. The market is at the northwest corner of the plaza, the bus station at the northeast corner, and taxi drivers huddle beneath the banyan tree in front of the Palacio Municipal.

Practical Information

Tourist Office: Juárez 85 (tel. 504-09), toward the Hotel Bucanero. A decent map of San Blas, and if you ask politely, the English-speaking *doña* who works here can be very helpful. Open Mon.-Fri. 9am-1:30pm and sometimes 5-7pm.

Currency Exchange: Bánamex, on Juárez, 1 block east of the Zócalo. Open for exchange Mon.-Fri. 8:30-9:30am.

Post Office: Sonora at Echevarria (tel. 502-95), 1 block north and 1 block east of the bus station. Lista de Correos posted at 11am. Open Mon.-Fri. 8am-6pm, Sat. 8am-noon. **Postal Code:** 63740.

Telephones: Newsstand on the south side of the Zócalo (tel. 500-01) controls the only 2 international lines to which travelers have access. It takes about 15 min. to get through. International collect calls 3000 pesos. Open daily 8:30am-2pm and 5-9:30pm.

Pharmacy: Farmacia Económica, Mercado at Battalón. Open daily 8am-2pm and 4-9pm.

Hospital: Centro de Salud, Campeche at Azueta (tel. 502-32), after Batallón turns into Azueta, about 5 blocks south of the Zócalo. Open 24 hr.

Police: In the Palacio Municipal (tel. 500-28). Open 24 hr.

Accommodations

San Blas maintains many reasonably priced hotels; it's difficult or impossible to get a hot shower in any of them, but the "cold" water is so warm that it hardly matters. In summer, the humidity turns a night's sleep into a drenching experience. Never accept a room without checking the screens first: if there is even the tiniest rip through which mosquitoes can (and will) enter, ask for another. If that's not possible, ask for *cinta adhesiva* to make minor repairs in your screen.

Balmy winds, swaying palms, and miles of empty beach invite a night under the stars, but you may be rudely awakened by clouds of vicious *jejenes* (you guessed it—mosquitoes). Just remember to take the usual precautions if you plan to sleep outside: insect repellent, long sleeves, cotton fabrics, socks, and mosquito netting.

Hotel Misión San Blas, Cuauhtémoc 197 (tel. 500-23). The 1st right after the Centro de Salud and then the 2nd left. A sun-drenched pool and very clean rooms. San Blas's mosquitoes have left this hotel off their hit list. The office shelves a small collection of ratty English books. Singles 30,000 pesos. Doubles 35,000 pesos.

Hotel Flamingo, Juárez 105. Behind the decrepit neon sign hides a lush courtyard complete with a well. Rooms are dark but their large size makes squinting tolerable. Singles 40,000 pesos. Doubles 45,000 pesos.

Hotel Bucanero, Juárez 75 (tel. 501-01). This hotel once had a quirky luster but since then has sunk like a fully loaded Spanish galleon. Also like a galleon, it packs a treasure: the beautiful pool. Dark and stuffy rooms adjoined by dusty bathrooms. Singles 24,000 pesos. Doubles 30,000 pesos.

Casa María, Juárez 108. In a white building with red lettering. The Casa's tidy rooms are cooled by strong fans. María's daughter may talk your ear off while she cleans. Home sweet home. (The other Casa María down the street is owned by her divorced husband.) Singles 20,000 pesos. Doubles 25,000 pesos.

Hotel Playa Hermosa (a.k.a. *El Hotel Misterioso*), no address. Two ways to get there: turn left on Virgilio Uribe near the foot of Azueta (Uribe is the gravel road just past the trailer park), then walk east about 1km. Or, walk down the beach past all the *enramadas,* and you'll eventually see a dilapidated building set back on a dirt path. Inconveniently located and almost unbearably mosquito-infested. The perfect setting for that novel you've been wanting to write: former luxury palace done in by isolation and insect infestation. The crumbling façade reflects the state of the rooms within. Although 100 suites were once maintained, only a handful are presentable today. Palms, flowering trees, and an overgrown pool on the back lawn; beyond it, fantastic, deserted beach. Since the nearest restaurant is a 20-min. walk away, the hotel will let you use their stove. Singles 20,000 pesos. Doubles 28,000 pesos. Bargaining will probably work, especially if you plan to stay more than one night.

Food

All restaurants in San Blas charge similar prices, set by the state tourist office. You'll find the best deals in town at the open-air market inside the courtyard of the building west of the church, and at the stands that magically materialize late in the afternoon across from the Cine Nayar, 1 block south and 1 block east of the Zócalo. A bowl of delicious *pozole* can be had for under 1200 pesos, but don't look too closely at the cauldron if you're squeamish. Very good street tacos cost as little as 800 pesos apiece. In keeping with the laid-back ways of San Blas's tourists, restaurants close a little early or stay open a little late depending on the energy level of the staff on that particular evening.

Restaurant McDonald, Juárez 36. Not as in "Ronald." A pleasant place with fans and bright tablecloths. Many expatriates gather here for breakfast to enjoy one of the most varied menus in town. Breakfasts 2500-6000 pesos. Dinners 5000-13,000 pesos. Open daily 7am-10pm.

La Familia, Batallón 18, south of the Zócalo. A well-run restaurant frequented by travelers. The tasteful furnishings don't distract you from your food. Great quesadillas 6000 pesos. Filet mignon 16,000 pesos. Open daily 7:30am-10pm.

Las Islas, Mercado at Paredes. Where the locals eat their seafood amid nets, shells, crabs, and other seafaring memorabilia. The shrimp in cheese sauce (18,000 pesos) is tops. Fish dishes hover around 12,000 pesos. Open Tues.-Sun. 2-10pm.

Rosy's, Batallón 43. If you catch and filet your own fish, Rosy will cook it; for 12,000 pesos, she'll relieve you of all 3 tasks. The only color in this place comes from the orange tablecloths smothering every table. Open daily 8am-9pm.

Restaurant El Amigo. Not necessarily the best, but undoubtedly the most stable of the *enramadas* on the nameless access road to Las Islitas (see Beaches). Unlike some of the others, this place always has food for sale. Where the road veers to the right (by the tree with the red 7-up sign), turn left onto the beach; El Amigo is on your right. *Huevos rancheros* 3000 pesos, *filete de pescado* 7500 pesos. Open daily at least 8am-5pm; during high season 7am-7pm.

Sights and Entertainment

Tourist attractions are few in San Blas. Like most *viajeros,* you'll probably meet a man offering to take you on a "jungle ride." Far from a rip-off, this boat trip takes you up the river that empties into the Pacific, through mangrove swamps and jungle lands that choke the area. Wildlife—in the form of caimans, crocs, wildcats, boars, snakes, crabs, toads, and every insect you can think of—thrives along its banks. The view from the boat is sufficiently sultry to induce Bogart and Hepburn fantasies. The boat turns back at **La Tovara,** the freshwater spring that provides San Blas's water supply, after an hour-long stopover; bring your suit for a refreshing swim. Drinks are the only affordable item at the restaurants here. The price of the half-hour ride is fixed by the tourist office at 60,000 pesos per boatload (up to 6 people). If you're with fewer people, bargaining may be effective. To see the most wildlife, take the early-morning (8am) or dusk (5pm) boat up the river. Boats leave from the point where the river crosses under the highway (about ½km north of town) and also from the Matanchén road.

After the ride, hike to the top of the hill at the landing, where the cannons of San Blas's original fort still glare out over the surrounding region. Inside many of the cannons, meter-long lime-green iguanas hide from the rare visitor. Nearby, swallows find sanctuary in the ruins of an abandoned church larger than the relic in downtown San Blas. The trail starting at the "Taller de Bicicletas" (bicycle workshop) leads to the fort.

Las Islitas, a small cove with picture-perfect waves, harbors the best beach in the area. These three-foot wonders break perfectly for mondo bodysurfing runs. To walk or drive the 7km, take the highway to Tepic, turn off for Matanchén, and proceed straight on a dirt road when the paved road veers left. Pass by the enticing beach scattered with *palapas* and follow the road to the end. A cab to Las Islitas costs 10,000 pesos, but hitching a ride at least part of the way should pose no problem since pickup trucks are nearly as common as mosquitoes out this way. The walk is long and hot but has some shade if you don't mind sharing it with large lizards. As you continue on the foot path past Las Islitas, the beach takes on the name **Bahía Matanchén.** Though perfect for strolling, it provides little cover from the sun. After 8km, the sand runs out near the village of **Aticama,** where the line of *palapas* receives a refreshingly cool breeze at sunset. About 2km down the road, **Los Cocos** is a palm-shaded oasis, but the abundance of *cabañas* makes the beach into an obstacle course. A cab to Los Cocos costs 25,000 pesos. San Blas's downtown beach, **Playa Borrego,** at the foot of Batallón, is much more crowded than Los Cocos, but it's more accessible and has surfable three- to four-foot waves.

San Blas undergoes a metamorphosis in time for high season. From December to May, possibly because the mosquitoes are less fierce, people are more inclined to visit. During these months, as many as four discos may blast away at one time; with the advent of summer, however, they all close, and party animals must choose between twilight strolls through the Zócalo and nightly movies at **Viejano's Bar** on Batallón. The latter lives up to its subtitle—"A little bit of America in the middle of nowhere"—with portraits of Rambo and Schwarzenegger competing with posters celebrating (or exploiting, depending on your point of view) the female anatomy. Beer here costs 3000 pesos.

Near San Blas

Built on high ground in the middle of a lake, much like Mexico City (the Aztecs' Tenochtitlán), **Mezcaltitlán** is widely acknowledged as the hometown of the Aztec people. According to legend, Aztec priests first saw a snake in a cactus here, an omen that instructed them to build a great city. During the rainy season, the streets of the town flood, lending it the nickname "Venice of Mexico." Avenues in Mezcaltitlán are laid out in concentric circles with radiating spokes pointing in astronomically significant directions (this fact is difficult to appreciate unless you happen to be in town at dawn on the summer solstice). The townspeople are exceedingly friendly, but there is not much to do except wander.

Because it's far from the main highway and not served by bus, a car is the required mode of transport to **Mezcaltitlán.** About 20km north of the turn-off to San Blas on Rte. 15, take the road that diverges to Mezcaltitlán; after driving about 40km, you'll come to a boat dock. Park and honk your horn if nobody's there, and a boat operator will soon appear to guide you through the mangrove swamps to the town.

BAJA CALIFORNIA

Baja California consists of 40,000 square miles of desert, mountains, and jagged coastline connected to mainland Mexico by a strip of land no more than 100km wide in the far north. Earthquakes peeled this skinny peninsula away from the mainland, and now the Gulf of California and the Sea of Cortés separate the two. Hundreds of years after Mexico was subdued by the *conquistadores,* Baja's isolation served it well, as the area remained free of outside influence except for a few dozen Jesuit enclaves (now ruined missions hidden in the hills). Just a few decades ago, large tracts of Baja remained empty: recently, however, the government has sought to open up *La Frontera* through the construction of the Transpeninsular Highway (Rte. 1) and the introduction of regular ferry service to the mainland. (Ferry service is now privately run.)

Resorts have sprung up on scattered ribbons of sand, and tourist lures, like Tijuana and Ensenada, pull *norteamericanos* across the border. As you travel south, however, the raging torrent of Californians found by the border recedes quickly.

It will require more than a few slapped-together condo complexes to settle, let alone overpopulate, the Baja's mountain ranges, *saguaro* forests, and thousands of miles of perpetually sunny beaches. Vast regions of Baja remain virtually untouched. As a result, Baja is a freelance camper's paradise; simply stash some food, stake out a seaside granular wonderland, and vacation on some of the most beautiful and unspoiled beaches in Mexico.

Getting Around

By Land

In the 1930s it took 10 days of rugged travel to get from La Paz to Tijuana. The completion of the **Transpeninsular Highway** has made a quicker journey possible, but driving through Baja is still far from easy. A sign at the onset warns that the road was not designed for high-speed driving—and once warned, don't expect to be reminded. Often, you'll be safely cruising along at 60mph and suddenly careen into a hidden, poorly banked, rutted curve that can be taken at only 30mph. Don't let speeding trucks and buses fool you: a glance at the hundreds of car skeletons rusting along the side of the road attests to the danger.

If you do run into trouble, stay by your car and wait for the *Angeles Verdes* (Green Angels), who pass along Rte. 1 twice per day. These English-speaking mechanics employed by the government provide gas, water, oil, and service and charge only the cost of the parts. Remember that Extra gas (unleaded) may be in short supply along this highway, so don't pass a Pemex station without topping off your tank.

All major towns in Baja are served by bus. The gruelling 25-hour bus trip from Tijuana to La Paz costs 79,000 pesos, while you may zip directly to the mainland on ferry for as little as 36,000 pesos. If you plan to transverse the peninsula by bus, be forewarned that almost all *camiones* between Ensenada and La Paz are *de paso*. This means you have to leave at inconvenient times, fight to procure a ticket, and then probably stand the whole way. A much better idea is to buy a reserved seat in Tijuana, Ensenada, La Paz, or the Cabos, and traverse the peninsula in one shot while seated. You'll miss the Mulege-Loreto beaches, but sand isn't in short supply in the Baja. If you do cover the Baja in stages, always try to be the last to board. This way, you can place yourself in the front, where the air is freshest and where you can watch the scenery through the large driver's windows. Playing this game means a higher risk of not getting a ticket, though usually you can sit on the floor or the steps.

In Baja California Norte, beaches and other points of interest off the main highway are often inaccessible on public transportation; buses don't stop at coastal spots between Tijuana and San Quintín, and hitchhiking is unpopular. Farther down Baja, travelers tied to the bus system make the short walk to beautiful and relatively deserted beaches after disembarking in Mulegé, Loreto, La Paz, and the Cabos (capes) on Baja's southern tip. Hitching is easy along the 48-mile Bahía de Concepción.

By Sea

Ferry service was instituted in the mid-60s as a means of supplying Baja with food and supplies, not as a source of tourist transportation. Boats have come to serve *viajeros,* and passenger vehicles may take up any space left over after the first-priority commercial vehicles. For those who plan to take a car, the best advice is to make reservations one month in advance, either through a travel agent or with the ferry office directly. (See La Paz Getting There below for details.)

There are three different ferry routes: Santa Rosalía to Guaymas (7 hr.); La Paz to Topolobampo/Los Mochis (9 hr.); and La Paz to Mazatlán (16 hr.). If you wish to avoid the less interesting northern half of the peninsula, take the Guaymas-Santa Rosalía route. This allows you to wind your way southward to La Paz before taking a boat back to the mainland. The La Paz to Topolobampo/Los Mochis route provides direct access to the train from Los Mochis through the Barranca del Cobre (Copper Canyon).

Ferry tickets are generally expensive (prices listed below are for the La Paz to Topolobampo/Los Mochis route), even for *turista*-class berths—four to a cabin with a sink (bathrooms and showers down the hall, 48,000 pesos). It's extremely difficult to find tickets for *turista* class and *cabina* class (bathroom in the room, 72,000 pesos), and snagging an *especial*-class berth (a real hotel room, 96,000 pesos) is as likely as stumbling upon a snowball in the central Baja desert; there are only two such suites on each ferry. This leaves the bottom-of-the-line *salón*-class ticket (24,000 pesos), which entitles you to a bus-style seat. If, as is likely, you find yourself traveling *salón,* simply ignore the seats, spread out your sleeping bag on some convenient part of the deck, and snooze. For exact prices, check the Getting There section of the towns, and for further ferry information, call Mr. Martín Vargas at the State Tourist Department (tel. 81-94-92, 93, or 94).

Always bring food on ferry trips; the boats have restaurants, but their prices and meals may send you rushing to the railings.

By Air

A twenty-minute flight from La Paz to Los Mochis costs about 90,000 pesos; the flight between Tijuana and La Paz takes one and a half hours and will set you back 240,000 pesos. From Tijuana, **Aeroméxico** (tel. 85-44-01) flies to Mexico City and Guadalajara five times per day; **Mexicana** (tel. 81-75-72) flies to Mexico City twice per day (via La Paz or Zacatecas); **Aerocalifornia** (tel. 84-21-00) has several planes per day to Guadalajara via Los Mochis, plus short flights from La Paz to the Cabos.

Baja California Norte

Tijuana

Tijuana's "Mexican culture" is about as authentic as the cheap tissue-paper flowers that adorn every vendor's cart, but a certain dusty charm about this city attracts tourists by the thousands. For only a few dollars, you can settle back in a side bar

Photograph by Christine Michelini, mother, Salem, Massachusetts.

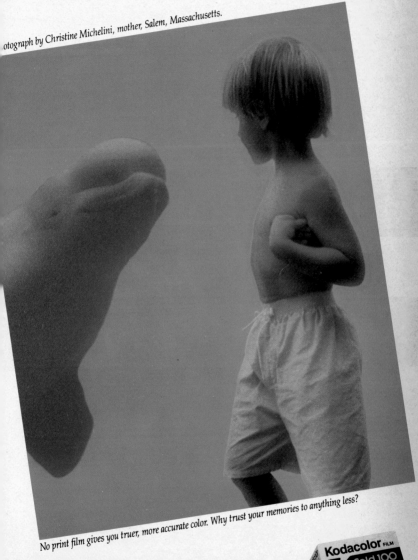

No print film gives you truer, more accurate color. Why trust your memories to anything less?

Show Your True Colors.™

CARRY-ON RELIEF.

When you're traveling abroad, it's nice to hear a familiar voice

Bobbi Coney
AT&T Operator
Pittsburgh, PA

The language may be difficult.
The food may be different.
The customs may be unfamiliar.
But making a phone call back to the States can be easy.

Just dial the special *AT&T* **USADirect**® access number for the country you're in.

Within seconds, you're in touch with an *AT&T Operator* in the U.S. who can help you complete your call.

Use your *AT&T Calling Card* or call collect. And not only can you minimize hotel surcharges but you can also save with our international rates.

Only *AT&T* **USADirect** *Service* puts you in easy reach of an *AT&T Operator* from over 75 countries around the world.

And it's just another way that AT&T is there to help you from practically anywhere in the world.

So call **1 800 874-4000 Ext. 415** for a free information card listing *AT&T* **USADirect** access numbers.

And see how making a phone call from distant lands can become familiar territory.

AT&T **USADirect**® *Service.*
Your express connection to AT&T service.

AT&T
The right choice.

where the beer flows freely and enjoy the music as it drifts through the streets. In typical Mexican fashion, food is zesty, spicy, and salty and will satisfy the cravings of your stomach without testing the limits of your wallet.

If shopping for knickknacks is your passion, Tijuana is your long-lost homeland. Check out Tijuana's velvet underside, where the theme is royal: there are enough black-velvet portraits of Jesus and Elvis for sale here to start your own gallery back home. The mounds of kitsch for sale astound—but be strong and don't let vendors convince you to buy that day-glo serape, no matter how cheap it is.

Banners boldly proclaim Av. Revolución the "Most Visited Street in the World," and when you see the crowds, you'll find that boast easy to swallow. Every weekend, swarms of people hurl themselves into the pulsating wave of music at the numerous flashy discos, drowning their sorrows in drink and dancing till dawn. If you can make it past the dirty streets (and mangy dogs), you'll find yourself in the eye of the Republic's free-est party.

Since World War II, Tijuana's population has swelled to nearly 2 million in the metropolitan area. First settled by the Cochimie, Tijuana made it onto the map in 1829, when Don Santiago Argüello received the title to the Rancho de Tía Juana (Aunt Jane's Ranch). After the 1848 Mexican-American War, the ranch became the new border, and its name was condensed.

Nowadays, thousands use this northernmost Mexican point as a springboard for undocumented emigration to the States. Thousands more await their turns in shantytown shacks along the border. Other Mexicans come here to study at the Ibero-American University, one of the finest in northern Mexico. Most, however, arive to buy discounted non-Mexican goods: cameras, leather, alcohol, name-brand clothing, and perfume are common in Tijuana.

On Sundays, the city puts on immensely popular bullfights and horse races. And, thick crowds of San Diegans descend upon Tijuana throughout the weekend, so unless you're here for the fights or the races, try to visit on a weekday.

Orientation and Practical Information

Getting from San Diego to Tijuana is easy: take the **Santa Fe trolley** from downtown (US$1.50), or join it anywhere along the route. It lets you off right at the border-crossing. Returning is not so simple, thanks to long customs inspection lines. Motorists can drive across the border, but the hassles of obtaining Mexican insurance (U.S. policies are useless in Mexico) make this a bad idea for a daytrip. You must buy insurance—if you get into an accident without it, your car will probably be confiscated and you may be thrown into jail. A better idea is to leave your car in a parking lot on the U.S. side of the border and either walk or take a taxi into town.

Almost everything in Tijuana is within walking distance. Buses (700 pesos) marked "Centro" run to *el centro;* look to the left as you exit the bus station. The ride from the terminal to Revolución takes a half hour because the bus stops every ten feet. If you're in a hurry, take a taxi from the terminal to town.

Tourist Office: De Comercio and Revolución (tel. 88-16-85). English-speaking staff with oodles of information. Cirramy is especially helpful. Open daily 9am-7pm.

State Attorney for the Protection of the Tourist: Same address as tourist office (tel. 681-94-92). Phone service Mon.-Sat. 9am-7pm. Open 24 hr.

State Dept. of Tourism of Baja California: Tel. 84-21-27. **Baja California Information Center in San Diego:** Tel. (800) 522-1516.

Customs Office: At the border (tel. 83-13-88).

Consulates: U.S., Tapachula Sur 96 (tel. 81-74-00), at Colonia Hipódromo, adjacent to the Agua Caliente racetrack southeast of town. Open Mon.-Fri. 8am-4:30pm. **Canada,** German Gedovius 5-202 (tel. 84-04-61), Zona del Río; **West Germany,** Mérida 221 (tel. 81-82-74), at Chapultepec; **France,** Carretera a Ensenada y Balarezo 2900 (tel. 86-55-54).

Currency Exchange: Banks along Revolución change at the same rate. **Bánamex** and **Internacional** accept traveler's checks. Open daily 8:30am-1:30pm.

Post Office: Negrete at Calle 11. Lista de Correos. Open Mon.-Sat. 8am-7pm. **Postal Code:** 22000.

Telephones: Farmacia Vida-Suprema, Calle 4 at Niños Héroes (tel. 85-60-05). Local calls 200 pesos. Open daily 9am-10pm. Pay phones on the street are unreliable and take only pesos. Long-distance phone calls are much cheaper from the U.S. **Telephone Code:** 668.

Telegrams: At the post office (tel. 84-77-65). Open Mon.-Sat. 8am-9pm.

Bus Station: Huge station laid with spiffy marble floors. **Transportes Norte de Sonora** (tel. 86-90-26) to: Guadalajara (12 per day, express at 9am, 100,000 pesos); Mexico City (4 per day, express at 11:30am, 126,000 pesos); Mazatlán (85,000 pesos); Los Mochis (70,000 pesos); Hermosillo (89,000 pesos); Puerto Peñasco (2 per day, 26,000 pesos). **Autotransportes de la Baja California** to: Ensenada (every hr., 1½ hr., 6000 pesos); Guerrero Negro (3 per day, 37,000 pesos); Mulege (1 per day, 51,500 pesos); Loreto (58,500 pesos); La Paz (76,500 pesos). Other companies at the station include **Tres Estrellas de Oro** (tel. 86-91-86) and **Transportes de Pacífico** (tel. 85-49-81). **Greyhound** reaches San Diego and beyond. Green-and-white **Autotransportes de la Baja California** buses leave for Rosarito (every hr., 1 hr., 900 pesos) from the old bus station at Madero and Calle 1, 1 block from the tourist office on Revolución. *Taxis de ruta* to Rosarito leave from Madero between Calles 4 and 5. (See Rosarito for details.)

Car Insurance: If you'll be driving in Mexico, spend US$9.50 in San Ysidro to get insurance. There are several drive-through insurance vendors just before the border at Sycamore and Primero, who distribute a free booklet with maps and travel tips. Without insurance, you go to jail if you're involved in an accident.

Red Cross: Tel. 132. For non-emergencies, dial 85-81-91.

Pharmacy: Botica Sherr, Constitución at Calle 31 (tel. 85-39-38). Open 24 hr.

Hospital: Hospital Civil, Río Tijuana Ote. (tel. 84-09-22).

Police: Constitución at Calle 8. In case of emergency, dial 134. For other matters, dial 85-70-90. There is always a bilingual officer at the station.

Accommodations

Budget hotels in Tijuana are in the midst of the action, off Revolución and Calle 1. Prices are steep by Mexican standards, but a bargain when compared with San Ysidro's offerings. Reservations are a necessity on weekends. Most hotels accept both dollars and pesos.

Hotel Poinsettia (Super 8), Constitución 1206 (tel. 85-19-12), between Calles 9 and 10. Brand new place proudly advertises its cable TV, phones, and chilly A/C. Perfect except for the price. Singles US$27. Doubles US$31.

Hotel Plaza de Oro (Best Western), Revolución 277 (tel. 38-41-12). Just like the thousands of Best Westerns in the rest of the civilized world. Singles US$35. Doubles US$40.

Hotel Texano, Calle 1 #1710 (tel. 38-43-15). Large, clean rooms with visually offensive, tacky furniture. If you get tired of the TV in your room, there's one in the lobby. Singles and doubles US$14.

Hotel Nelson, Revolución 503 (tel. 85-43-02). Large, well-kept rooms with wall-to-wall carpeting, clean bathroom, A/C, color TV, and phone. Great location, but could use some new particle board on the walls. Singles 66,000 pesos. Doubles 71,000 pesos.

Motel Díaz, Revolución Nte. 375 (tel. 85-71-48). Designed to the dictator's specifications: clean and comfortable. Singles and doubles US$28.

Motel Alaska, Calle 1 #1950 (tel. 85-36-81), at Revolución. Fairly clean rooms are popular with families, probably because of the private parking ample enough for their station wagons. Singles 65,000 pesos. Doubles 75,000 pesos.

Hotel Peria del Occidente, Mutualismo 528 (tel. 85-13-58), between Calles 1 and 2. Sullen management. The green skylight lends a gloomy air to the hallways, but clean rooms and bathrooms are refreshing. Wall-to-wall carpeting and mammoth beds. Singles and doubles 35,000 pesos.

Hotel Las Palmas, Calle 1 #1637 (tel. 85-13-48), near Mutualismo. Colorful courtyard decorated in the popular rosebush and dripping laundry motif. Tidy rooms with clean communal bathrooms. Singles and doubles 40,000 pesos.

Hotel San Francisco (tel. 85-45-40), Calle 1 across from Hotel Las Palmas. Small, tidy rooms with green walls and stiff beds. Private baths. There are many cheaper spots that deliver the same quality. Singles and doubles 50,000 pesos.

Food

The less expensive *típico* restaurants are on Madero and the streets leading from glitzy Revolución to Madero. On every corner, people sell fruit cocktails and melon cups (2500 pesos).

Deep-fried *churros,* a heart-stopping snack, cost 1500 pesos. As always, use your head when choosing what to eat; some vendors are not picky about how long they hold on to leftovers. If you'd rather not gamble with your health on the street, bar munchies are cheap, filling, and safe. Water is generally safe to drink in Tijuana, which shares its main water supply, the Colorado River, with San Diego.

Bol Corona Cantina and Restaurant, Revolución 520, across from Hotel Nelson. Built in 1934, Bol Corona is no longer a true *cantina:* today the clientele is neither all male nor all Mexican. Nevertheless, a popular place for drinks and reasonably priced food. Tables on the upstairs terrace have the best view of Revolución. Enchiladas 9000 pesos. *Comida corrida* 16,000 pesos. Delicious margaritas 4700 pesos. Open daily 7am-4am.

Restaurant Nelson, Revolución 503, under Hotel Nelson. Good, cheap, and undiscovered as yet by San Diegans. *Huevos revueltos* 2800 pesos. Hamburger 3800 pesos. Open daily 7am-11pm.

Super Antojitos, Revolución, between Constitución and Calle 4; others around town. Green booths and white formica tables under pseudo-Aztec wall sculpture. Servers wear "traditional" costumes. Tostadas 4000 pesos. Margaritas 4700 pesos. Open daily 7am-8pm.

La Casa de Alicia, Madero 1246, off Calle 9. The enthusiasm of the management compensates for the insufficient size of the portions. Mexican standards 10,000 pesos. Open daily 8am-10pm.

Entertainment and Activities

For inexpensive fun, try snacking and people-watching while strolling down **Revolución. Teniente Guerrero Park,** between 5 de Mayo and González Ortega, off Díaz Mirón, is one of the most pleasant parts of Tijuana, and only a few blocks from Revolución. Tijuana is also a great place to get your car reupholstered—really. Animal lovers should avert their eyes from the horses painted to look like donkeys, used to attract buyers of gaudy hats.

Jai alai is played every night (except Thurs.) at 8pm in the Frontón Palacio, Revolución at Calle 7, a building decorated more like a palace than a sports center. Two two-player teams, identified by colored arm bands, compete inside the walled court. A Brazilian ball of rubber and yarn encased in goatskin is thrown at speeds reaching 180 mph and caught in arm-baskets after hitting the back wall of the court. The fast-paced game is played to 21 points, with betting on every game. All employees are bilingual, and the gambling is carried out in greenbacks. General admission US$2.50, reserved seats US$5. Gates open at 7pm. Call 85-16-12 for more information, (619) 260-0452 from the U.S.

Agua Caliente Racetrack (tel. 81-78-11), also called the Hipódromo, attracts enormous crowds year-round with greyhound races (Mon., Wed., and Fri. at 2:30 and 7:45pm, Thurs. and Sat.-Sun. at 7:45pm) and horse races (Sat.-Sun. at noon). The track's enclosed **Turf Club** (tel. 86-39-48) has comfortable seating and a restaurant; grandstand admission (nearly 11,000 seats) is free. Unfortunately, the racetrack employees went on strike indefinitely in the summer of 1990.

Tijuana has two bullrings, **El Toreo de Tijuana,** downtown, and **Plaza Monumental,** 3km east on Agua Caliente, by the sea. The former presents *corridas* (bullfights) on Sundays at 4pm from early May to late September; the latter is more modern, employs famous *matadores,* and hosts fights from early August to mid-September. Tickets are sold at Revolución 815 (tel. 85-22-10) from 10am to 7pm, or at the gate. Admission ranges from US$5-22, depending on the seat.

The **Tijuana Centro Cultural,** Paseo de los Héroes and Mina (tel. 84-11-11), is worth visiting for its architecture alone. The global auditorium (El Omniteatro) shows a film on the history and culture of Mexico, *El Pueblo del Sol,* in English at 2pm and in Spanish at 6pm. (English version admission US$5, US$4 with coupon from the tourist office; Spanish version 3000 pesos.) The center also displays an elegant geographical and chronological survey of Mexico, as well as rotating exhibitions of modern art. (Admission 1500 pesos.) A performance center (Sala de Espectáculos) and open-air theater (Caracol al Aire Libre) host visiting cultural attractions, including the Ballet Folklórico, *mariachis,* and various drama performances.

The original **Tía Juana Tilly's** is next door to the Jai Alai Palace at Revolución and Calle 7a. Since 1947, the bar, now with restaurant, dance floor, and outside patio, has been generating high-action, high-price atmosphere. Enjoy one of their rocket-fuel margaritas and people-watch from the patio. (Terrace open daily 11am-midnight. Dancing Fri.-Sun. 9pm-4am.) Even more fun is **Tía Juana Tilly's 5th Avenue,** on Revolución at 5a. Calle. Lights flash and the floor vibrates; the walls are laden with hats, photos, and sports and music equipment. A big-screen TV projects sporting events. An enchilada, taco, and soup cost US$4; beer or tequila is US$1. **El Viejo Tijuana Tequila Garden** is a huge, rowdy bar. Beer costs US$1, drinks US$1.50. (Open Sun.-Thurs. 8am-1am, Fri.-Sat. 8am-3am.) **Tequila Sunrise** (open Sun.-Thurs. 9am-1am, Fri.-Sat. 9am-5am) is a decent venue for people-watching, but for the best scoping head to **Tequila Circo.** (Open Mon.-Tues. 11am-9pm, Wed.-Sun. 11am-2am.) And don't overlook **El Torito,** a huge open-air disco/bar with circular dance floor, easily the loudest joint on Revolución. (Open Sun.-Thurs. 10am-1am, Fri.-Sat. 10am-4am.)

Off the main strip but worth the digression is **Oh! Disco,** a couples-only danceteria at Paseo de los Héroes 56, 2 blocks past the second traffic circle. (Cover US$5. Open Thurs.-Sun. 9pm-5am.)

Rosarito

Rosarito Beach, 27km south of Tijuana on Rte. 1, is rapidly becoming the most popular beach in Baja. Its convenient location attracts tourists like flies, but the beaches pale in comparison with those further south, and the town itself is unremarkable. Nevertheless, Rosarito's stretches of sand and seafood restaurants do offer relief to the tourist tired of Tijuana crowds.

Food is one of Rosarito's strengths. **Vince's,** Juárez 39, sells the best lobster in town to sandy kids straight off the beach. Fresh fish, sold at the back, ogle diners throughout their meal. (Open daily 7am-10pm.) You can pretend to picnic at **La Cabaña,** Juárez 184. Three tacos with beans and guacamole cost 9000 pesos. If awards were given for failed attempts at atmosphere, **Taco Village,** near the Rosarito Beach Hotel, would win hands down. Your order is quickly grilled before your eyes. Tacos and quesadillas go for US$1.

The **Rosarito Beach Hotel** (tel. (706) 612-1106), is nice, expensive, and one of the very few hotels in the area. Suites and bungalows are available. (Singles and doubles Sun.-Thurs. US$36, Fri.-Sat. US$55-65.) In the **Sonia Motel,** Juárez 783 (tel. 212-60), pink doubles with saggy beds and grimy bathrooms go for US$20. The **Motel Villanueva,** Juárez 97 (tel. 213-48), provides basic, clean accommodations with fax machines in every bathroom. (Singles and doubles US$20.)

Everything in Rosarito is on the main street, **Boulevard Juárez.** To get here from Tijuana, board a bus at the old station on Calle 1 at Madero (every hr., 45 min., 1300 pesos), 1 block from the tourist office. *Taxis de ruta* (12,000 pesos per carload), which leave from Madero between Calles 4 and 5, make the trip 15 minutes faster than the buses. In Rosarito, buses stop across the street from the Rosarito Beach

Hotel. **Autotransportes de la Baja California** runs buses to Tijuana (4 per day, 45 min., 1300 pesos) and Ensenada (5 per day, 1½ hr., 4200 pesos). You can also walk 1km from the bus station to the *caseta de cobro* (toll booth) off Rte.1, the federal highway adjacent to Blvd. Juárez, and simply flag down any passing bus. The fare to Ensenada from the *caseta* should be about 3000 pesos. For those driving, the Rte. 1 toll is 3000 pesos. **Bánamex** and **Internacional** will change money and traveler's checks Monday through Friday from 9:30am to 1:30pm. On weekends, you'll have to go to one of the *casas de cambio,* which charge a commission. There is a **tourist office** (tel. 203-96) on Juárez, near Hotel La Quinta. The **chamber of commerce** (tel. 212-75) provides further tourist assistance. Rosarito's **telephone code** is 661.

Mexicali

Mexicali is a bulky industrial brute, disinclined to welcome tourists. Unless you have a definite reason to come here, stay away. Mexicali supports a few good restaurants and some active nightspots, but chances are you'll be bored out of your gourd within a few hours. Every year in mid-October, during Mexicali's Fiesta del Sol, bands, skits, a parade, and countless street vendors entertain the crowds.

Far from the ordinary route between the U.S. and Mexico, Mexicali can still serve as a jumping-off point for travelers heading south. The city lies on the California border 189km inland from Tijuana, with Calexico and the Imperial Valley immediately to the north. Because of its valley location, it suffers extreme temperatures; the winter months are chilly, and *normal* summer temperatures are 38-43°C (100-110°F).

Both the bus and train stations are near the intersection of Mateos, the main boulevard leading away from the border, and Independencia, about 3km south of the border. **Autotransportes de la Baja California** buses go to Tijuana (every hr. 6am-9pm, 3 hr., 10,500 pesos) and Ensenada (7 per day, 5 hr., 15,000 pesos). **Tres Estrellas de Oro** covers the same routes plus mainland Mexico, at slightly higher prices. Four buses per day run directly to Los Angeles. Buses marked "Centro" run from the station to the border (700 pesos).

The border is always open, and tourist cards are readily available. For tourist assistance, call (706) 552-5744. Further tourist information is available at **El Comité de Turismo y Convenciones** (tel. 725-61) at Mateos and Camelias, 3km from the border.

Currency can be exchanged in any of the banks along Madero (open Mon.-Sat. 10am-1:30pm). The **post office,** at Madero 491, is open Monday through Friday 8am-6pm and posts a Lista de Correos daily. The **Centro Médico Quirurgica Morelos,** Morelos 317 (tel. 52-97-22), is always open for medical emergencies.

Accommodations and Food

A night in Mexicali will cost you dearly. Alternatively, for about US$25 you can find excellent budget accommodations on the Calexico side of the border.

Hotel Del Norte, Madero at Melga (tel. 52-81-01), abuts the border, but even the bushy-tailed bellboys don't make it worth the *dinero.* Singles 85,000 pesos. Doubles 95,000 pesos.

Hotel Plaza, Madero 366 (tel. 52-97-57). A little scruffy but nice nonetheless. A/C, black-and-white TV, phone. Singles 65,000 pesos. Doubles 70,000 pesos. MC, Visa, and dollars accepted.

Hotel Imperial, Mateos 222 (tel. 53-63-33), in a peach-colored building. The clock radio does it for some people, but the beds sag. Security is good. Singles 60,000 pesos. Doubles 70,000 pesos.

Hotel Kennedy, Morelos 415 (tel. 53-63-10). Even distant relatives like Arnold Schwarzenegger would be displeased with the unkempt rooms and rainbow carpeting. Singles 46,000 pesos. Doubles 57,000 pesos.

Mexicali's large Chinese population translates into a multitude of Chinese restaurants; otherwise food in Mexicali is forgettable. **Café Yin Tun,** Morelos 379-381, has good A/C and Christmas colors all year long. The *comida corrida* goes for 9500 pesos, and pork chop suey costs 8000 pesos. (Open daily 11am-11pm.) Great ice-cream sundaes (5000 pesos) are sold at **Blanca Nieves,** Reforma 503. Ham and eggs cost 8000 pesos. (Open daily 8am-10:30pm.)

Ensenada

The secret is out: beachless Ensenada is fast becoming the top weekend hotspot south of the border. The masses of Californians that arrive every Friday night have gringoized the town to a large degree; everything here is in English, down to the taco sales-pitches, and the store clerks need calculators if you try to buy something with pesos. Still, Ensenada is less brash than its insatiable cousin to the north, and becomes quite pleasant Monday morning when the *gringos* desert town and the cool sea breeze kicks in.

The drive from Tijuana to Ensenada is beautiful, if you take the Ensenada Cuota (toll road), which costs 4000 pesos Monday through Thursday and 6000 pesos Friday through Sunday. The *libre* (free) road is atrocious—poorly maintained, dangerous, and as scenic as a municipal garbage dump. Along the toll road you'll enjoy sparkling ocean vistas, large sand dunes, stark cliffs, and broad mesas. Drive in the right lane only; the left is strictly for passing and the law is enforced. Also, drive only in daytime as there are no streetlights.

Orientation and Practical Information

Ensenada is 108km south of Tijuana on Rte. 1. Buses from Tijuana arrive at the main terminal, at Calle 11 and Miramar, every half hour between 7am and 10pm and every hour between 11pm and 1am.

Ten blocks down Miramar from the bus station is Mateos, the main tourist drag, and 5 blocks south along Mateos you'll find the less expensive hotels. Prepare yourself for a healthy walk or a 6000-peso cab ride.

Tourist Office: Mateos 1350 (tel. 622-22), at Espinoza, office 13-B. Brochures from expensive hotels, some town maps, and Baja travel material. Open Mon.-Sat. 9am-7pm. **Chamber of Commerce,** Mateos 693 (tel. 837-70), at Macheros. Closer to the center of town, with brochures, city maps and more helpful English-speaking staff. Open Mon.-Fri. 9am-6pm.

Customs: At Ruíz and Mateos (tel. 824-77). Open Mon.-Fri. 8am-3pm.

Attorney for Protection of Tourists: Mateos 1360 (tel. 638-86), office 12-B. Next to the tourist office. Open daily 9am-2pm and 3-9pm.

Post Office: Mateos at Floresta. Open Mon.-Fri. 8am-7pm, Sat.-Sun. 9am-1pm. **Postal Code:** 22860.

Telephones: Farmacia San Martín de Porres, Juárez at Castillo. No collect calls. Open Mon.-Fri. 8am-11pm, Sat.-Sun. 9am-5pm. Collect calls can be made from any of the many public pay phones: Dial 02 for the international operator. **Telephone Code:** 607.

Laundromat: Blanca, Cortés at Reforma (tel. 625-48), in the Limón shopping center. Wash or dry 2000 pesos, detergent 700 pesos. Open Mon.-Fri. 9am-7pm, Sat.-Sun. 9am-1pm.

Red Cross: Clark Flores at Colonia Ampliación Moderna (tel. 812-12 or 814-88). In medical emergencies, dial 132.

Pharmacies: Farmacia Regia, Mateos 628-B. Open daily 9am-9pm. **Farmacia El Sol,** Centro Comercial Limón (tel. 637-75). Open 24 hr.

Hospital: Ruíz 1380 (tel. 403-08), at Calle 14.

Police: Calle 9 at Floresta (tel. 624-21 or 626-96). Branch at Mateos and Espinoza (tel. 613-11 or 636-40), next to the tourist office. In emergencies, dial 134.

Accommodations

Rooms in Ensenada seem inexpensive if you're arriving from the U.S., but compared to the rest of Mexico, they're not. Cheaper hotels line Mateos between Espinoza and Granada, while the nicer lodging zone is along Mateos north of Castillo. It's fairly easy to get a room in the middle of the week, but on weekends if you want a bed you should be lounging in a hotel lobby at check-out time. Although most prices are quoted in greenbacks, pesos are accepted by all.

Motel Bungalows Playa, Mateos 1487 (tel. 614-30), about a block from the tourist office. If only every bungalow on the beach were like this. Freshly remodeled, with cable TV and wall-to-wall carpeting. Spic and span. Singles and doubles US$32.50.

Motel America, Espinoza 1309 (tel. 613-33), at Mateos. If you went on vacation looking to cook, look no further. Large rooms have kitchenettes with stove, refrigerator, and purified water. Singles US$20. Doubles US$28.

Coronado Motel, Mateos 1275 (tel. 614-16). All rooms are doubles, but should you desire a single, they'll happily remove one of the beds. If you don't like the tacky wall-to-wall carpeting, tough luck—it stays. Singles US$20-25. Doubles US$35.

Motel Colón, ½ block from Bungalows Playa on the right-hand side of Guadalupe. Full kitchenettes with stove, sink, cabinets, and table. Very friendly, English-speaking proprietor. Singles US$20-22. Doubles US$32.

Pancho Motel, Alvarado at Calle 2 (tel. 823-44), 1 block off Mateos. Super location. Clean as a baby's bottom, but the packing crates just don't cut it as couches. Modern it's not. Check-out noon. Singles US$15. Doubles US$18.

Food

The cheapest restaurants are along Juárez near Ruíz and Gastelum; those on Mateos and near the water are more expensive.

Cafetería Anali, Mateos at Aldama. Near the budget hotel district. Local crowd fills the tables around dinnertime. Cheap breakfasts, too. Open Mon.-Sat. 6am-11pm.

Antojitos de la Chispa, across from Bungalows Playa on Mateos. This tiny cafeteria serves the tastiest tacos in Baja California. Phenomenal burritos (with tortillas 1 ft. in diameter) 5700 pesos. Open Mon.-Thurs. 5pm-midnight, Fri.-Sat. noon-1:30am, Sun. noon-midnight.

Restaurant-Patio Las Brasas, Mateos 486. An open grill with 12 fowl roasting, 11 cooks a-tortilla-patting, and 10 waiters scurrying. Dark palette and lots of wood set the tone. Large portions, but rather expensive. Half chicken with potatoes 14,500 pesos. Open Wed.-Mon. 11am-9:45pm.

Restaurante Aquarius, Gastelum 167. Green-and-white tiled floor. Mickey Rourke would feel at home here. *Enchiladas con carne* or ham and eggs 7000 pesos. Open daily 7am-10pm.

Sights and Activities

Seeing Ensenada requires more than a quick cruise down Mateos. Climb the **Chapultepec Hills** for a view of the entire city. The steep road leading to the top of the hill begins at the foot of Calle 2. Any number of dirt paths also wind over the nearby hills, which afford a pleasant ocean view. Watch out for broken glass and pack sunscreen and refreshments.

The English-language *Baja Times* is full of bureaucratic propaganda and upcoming event announcements. Enormous quantities of low-quality curios are for sale along Mateos, but the **FONART** government store, Mateos 1306 (tel. 915-36), next to the tourist office at Espinoza, has high-quality authentic work. Most things you see are produced in southern Mexico, where they are available for less. Bargaining is not allowed. (Open daily 9am-2pm and 3-6pm.) Baja's free-port status makes Ensenada a good place to purchase imported goods. Try the various shops along Juárez, including **La Joya,** at Ruíz.

The mild, dry climate of Northern Baja's Pacific coast has made it Mexico's prime grape-growing area, and **Bodegas de Santo Tomás,** Miramar 666 (tel. 678-25-09), produces 5000 cases of wine every year. The Bodegas have been in business since 1888. Tours (US$2) are conducted Monday through Saturday at 11am, 1pm, and 3pm and include winetasting with bread and cheese.

The **Vapor Catalina,** a tycoon's old cruise ship that has been converted into a floating mall, is tethered to the docks at the end of Av. Riviera. There are two restaurants on board (the informal San Valentín, on deck, serves Mexican/American cuisine; below, the semi-formal Restaurante Catalina specializes in nouvelle cuisine) as well as a disco, a snack bar, several curio shops, and a tourist office booth (tel. 832-22).

Entertainment

Most of the popular hangouts along Mateos are members of that common hybrid species, the restaurant/bar/disco. In most, food and drink are served only until 6pm or so; they turn into full-fledged discos after 8pm. The best of these is **Bananas,** at Mateos 477 (tel. 820-04). Cover charges here average US$3.50 and apply only on weekend nights. Get there before 8pm and you won't have to pay. Some of the more popular places include: **Confetti's,** Alvarado at Paseo Costero; **El Osito,** Blancarte near Mateos, at the Travel Lodge; **Valentino's,** Blancarte at Paseo Costero; and **Las Cazuelas,** General Agustín Sanguines at Las Dunas.

Better known than Ensenada itself is **Hussong's Cantina,** on Ruíz between Mateos and Calle 2. A vastly overrated, overcrowded, and overpriced hangout, its main claims to fame are the Hussong's bumper stickers and T-shirts which crop up all over the Baja. When you tire of the pencil drawings and continuous stream of *mariachi* musicians, cross the street to **Papas and Beer.** This upscale, glitzy restaurant/bar/disco fills with San Diegan weekend warriors, who swill huge margaritas (9100 pesos) and spend corresponding amounts of cash. (Open daily 11am-2am.)

Near Ensenada

Visitors to Ensenada concentrate on shopping, eating, and partying, since the town's beaches suffer from their proximity to a major fishing port. About 11km north lies **Playa San Miguel.** About 8km to the south are **Playas Santa María** and **Estero.** All are sandy and clean, but the hyperactivity might drive you crazy. Farther south you'll find incredible beaches: try **San Quintín,** two hours south of town by car. Locals make their way to the Bahía San Quintín for three reasons: the cool climate, the lack of tourists, and the large clam population near the *Molino Viejo,* near El Presidente 6km south of the city of San Quintín.

The highway leading into San Quintín winds through a bizarre landscape of immense granite boulders, yucca trees (which look like pineapples on stilts), scraggly cholla and *octillo,* the mythic "organ pipe" cactuc, and elephant trees (twisted, 2m-tall bushes with thick trunks and red leaves). The *cirios,* of "Boojum" trees, that also pop up along the road may take you back to your salad days; named after a character in Lewis Carroll's *Hunting of the Snark,* these unusual 13m-tall cones are topped by small tufts of vegetation. Rosario, another modest beach town, lies 58km south of San Quintín on the Transpeninsular Hwy.

La Bufadora, the largest geyser on the Pacific coast, is 30km south of Ensenada. On a good day, the "Blowhole" shoots water 40m into the air. Share the spectacle with the local sea lions. **Agua Caliente** hot springs (admission 12,500 pesos) are 35km east on Rte. 3. **San Carlos** hot springs, accessed by a dirt road 16km south of town, are less expensive (admission 10,000 pesos) but unclean. Both are hot.

The road south from Ensenada is uninspiring. Drivers can exit a few kilometers north of Colonia Guerrero to reach **Parque San Pedro Mártir/Observatorio San Pedro.** Two hours of driving on this graded dirt road will take you high into the Sierra San Pedro Mártir, where pine forests, meadows, and the **Cerro de la Encantada** (3078m) await. Climbers should ask at the Pemex in San Telmo (a few kilometers up the road from the turn-off) if they will be able to pass up to the high country—occasional washouts temporarily close the road. This is one of the most challenging journeys in Baja, but any car with good tires and clearance should make it. Bring water for your radiator; the grades in the mountains are steep and sustained.

San Quintín

Bahía de San Quintín is one of the finest areas for clams in Baja, but humans can't enjoy it unless willing to pay at least US$25 a night. The area is touristed for its cool climate and access to the last Pacific Coast beaches that you can get to without four-wheel drive. South of town, there are primitive but good camping spots north and south of km 29, and at km 35 and 38, where 30m sea cliffs drop to a stone beach. In the middle of town, south of the army base, a dirt road leads 16km west to **Playa San Quintín,** which is not bad, but slightly dirty. There are always a fair number of locals here. Clams inhabit **Molino Viejo,** 6km south of town near the El Presidente.

The town of San Quintín itself is a mere pit stop on Rte. 1; it consists of several unattractive buildings loitering on the side of the highway. Stick to the beach or skip San Quintín altogether.

Without a car, you'll be immobile because the public transit system is extremely limited and does not reach the better beaches beyond town. If you're southbound, take a good look at San Quintín's trees, because except for scattered palms and the occasional Zócalo specimens, they are the last you'll see in Baja. After Rosario, 58km to the south, Rte. 1 climbs inland into the first of Baja's many deserts. This is a bizarre landscape of granite boulders, yucca trees (look like pineapples on stilts), scraggly cholla and octillo, the mythic "organ pipe" cacti, and elephant trees—twisted, 2-meter-tall bushes with foot-thick trunks and red leaves. Most interesting of all are the *cirias,* or "Boojum" trees, named after a character in Lewis Carroll's *The Hunting of the Snark*—13-meter-tall cones with little tufts of vegetation at the very tip. The whole scene will inspire *dèjá vu* in those raised on Dr. Seuss. Keep film in your camera and water in your canteen.

Accommodations and Food

About 1½km north of the army base, just past the bridge, are the **Motel Los Cirios** (tel. 520-80) and the **Motel Chávez** (tel. 520-05), the only affordable places in town. The better of the two is Los Cirios, a few hundred meters back from the road, with cactus gardens and low-beamed ceilings in the rooms. Watch for the sign on the main road. (Singles and doubles 34,900 pesos.) On the road immediately following the bridge, Chavez beckons to those hungry for the comfort of a stereotypical motel: clean, relaxing, and utterly without character. (Singles 39,500 pesos. Doubles 54,000 pesos.) There's also the **Motel Las Hadas,** the army's northern neighbor. Spend the night here if you enjoy sleeping to amplified marital music on mattresses of dubious history. (Doubles 16,300 pesos, with bath 32,000 pesos.) Since San Quintín is a prosperous agricultural town, the food is better than any you'll see between here and La Paz. There are several markets, bakeries, and fruit stands in the center of town, so stock up. (Remember that meal stops on the bus are short and often unappetizing.)

Baja California Sur

Guerrero Negro

Twenty degrees cooler than the bleak Desierto de Vizcaíno to the southeast, Guerrero Negro (Black Warrior) will earn a soft spot in the heart of heat-weary northbound travelers. Situated about halfway between Tijuana and La Paz, Guerrero Negro is the place to spend a cool night if you'd like to break up the killer 25-hour trans-Baja bus trip. If you're heading south, stock up on cold drinks; several hundred miles of sweltering terrain await you.

Guerrero Negro was founded about 40 years ago, when a North American company began a salt export business here. Thanks to low rainfall, sheltered harbors, and strong winds, the lagoons around the town evaporate quickly, making them ideal for salt production. The Exportadora de Sal has since been nationalized, with Mexico owning 51% of the company.

Unless salt evaporation techniques turn you on, Guerrero Negro can be extremely uninteresting. Some excitement is generated between December and early March, when thousands of gray whales make the annual 6000-mile trip from the Bering Sea to the lagoons here to reproduce; unfortunately, when the whales leave for the summer, they take all traces of civilization with them.

Orientation

Guerrero Negro is several miles off Rte. 1. All Baja buses pit stop here, making *de paso* tickets readily available. There is a *de local* bus for La Paz (40,000 pesos) at 4pm, which drops passengers off in La Paz at 3:30am. A bus for Santa Rosalia leaves at noon (1 hr., 5000 pesos), and several depart for Tijuana (39,000 pesos) every day.

Guerrero Negro cleaves into two main sections. One is the neighborhood **Fraccionamiento Loma Bonita,** situated along the access road to the highway. It begins about 3km in from the exit and ends at the bridge by the salt processing plant, 2km farther west.

The other is the town proper, which lies beyond the bridge. The main road becomes **Avenida Baja California** at this point, and intersects **Avenida Madero** 2 blocks down. Av. Baja California ends here in a T-intersection but resumes about 150 ft. south. **Cuartos Sánchez-Smith** is at Av. Comercial and Francisco Madero, 1 block south.

The highway south of Guerrero Negro is one of the worst on the entire peninsula. Deep potholes mar the painfully narrow pavement, guaranteeing speeders the need for a front-end alignment down the road. Cultivated fields flank the highway just outside Guerrero Negro. Since this region receives only 3 in. of rainfall per year, a subterranean water supply (deposited thousands of years ago when Baja was contiguous with a steamy mainland jungle) is tapped for irrigation. The Desierto de Vizcaíno yields briefly at the oasis of **San Ignacio,** where 1000 people pant collectively in the shade of date palms near a small freshwater lake. The reconstructed **Misión San Ignacio** borders the shady Zócalo. These spots are worth seeking out for relief from cacti and sand, but there are no inexpensive accommodations between Guerrero Negro and Santa Rosalía, past the **Volcán de las Tres Vírgenes** and the windy roads leading to the coast.

Practical Information

Currency Exchange: Bánamex, Baja California (tel. 705-57), in front of the salt processing plant 100 yd. south of the bus station. Open Mon.-Fri. 8:30am-1pm.

Post Office: Baja California at 5 de Mayo, 4 blocks west of the salt plant. Open Mon.-Fri. 9am-1pm and 3-6pm. **Postal Code: 23940.**

Telephones: Comercial (tel. 705-65), near Madero. International collect calls 1500 pesos. Open daily 8am-8pm. Spanish-speakers should dial the international operator (tel. 09) from the free phone in the bus station and avoid the charge for collect calls.

Telegrams: 5 de Mayo, in a hut about 100 yd. from the post office. Open Mon.-Fri. 8am-noon and 2-5pm, Sat. 8-11am.

Pharmacies: Farmacia San Martín, several hundred yd. north of the Clínica Hospital along the access road. Open Mon.-Sat. 8am-8pm, Sun. 8am-noon. **Farmacia Santa Mónica,** across from the bus station. Open daily 9am-1pm and 3-9pm.

Medical Emergency: ISSTE Clinic, Obregón at Niños Héroes (tel. 702-33 or 704-33). All-night emergency service also available from **Servicio Médico,** Madero between Baja California and Comercial.

Police: (tel. 702-22), on the main road near the bus station.

Accommodations

Most of the town's motels cling to the eastern end of the access road and are rather expensive. **Motel Cabañas Don Miguelito** (tel. 702-50), across from and to the right of the bus station, has very clean rooms with TV, but large cows roam the bathrooms. (Doubles 70,000 pesos.) Also across from but to the left of the bus station is **Motel El Morro,** on Blvd. Emiliano Zapata. The newly remodeled rooms are in better shape (surprise!) than those in the old section. (Singles in old secion US$12, in new US$16. Doubles in old section US$14, in new US$20. Pesos accepted.) Clean rooms with cement floors, pine furniture, and tepid hot water await you in the **Motel San Ignacio,** across from and to the left of bus station. (Singles and doubles 35,000 pesos.)

Food

Meals are universally expensive here, yet widely variable in quality. A number of grocery stores along the access road sell fresh fruit and junk food. **Disco Taco,** Carretera Transpeninsular, at the fork in the highway. Sit under *palapas,* listen to Mexican music, and down tacos for 2000 pesos. (Open. Mon.-Sat. 8am-3pm.) **Cafeteriá Los Pinos,** Apdo. 14, is a tiny joint with matching yellow ceiling and tablecloths. Management claims to speak English, but "adioós, friend" is all the cashier could muster. Hotcakes'll cost you 12,000 pesos; the filet of fish 15,000 pesos. (Open daily 7am-9pm.) **Marcelo's,** at the bus station, stocks candy bars (2000 pesos) and instant noodles in an elegant styrofoam cup with half a lime (3500 pesos). (Open 24 hr.)

Sights

Watch the whales in the **Parque Natural de las Ballenas Grises,** on the **Laguna Ojo de Liebre,** formerly a deep-water port facility of the Exportadora company. In the early morning, whales swim right up to the docks, and during the rest of the day you can ascend a tall observation tower to view the 100-odd whales who temporarily inhabit the estuary.

No public transportation is available to the park. To get there head south on Rte. 1 toward Santa Rosalía for 8 to 15km. A sign points out the 30km dirt road to the *laguna.* Mario Rueda, the administrator of the park, sometimes leads whale-watching tours in early January and February.

On the main road of Guerrero Negro, across from the gates of the Exportadora de Sal, is a road that leads to **Laguna Guerrero Negro** (2 small signs show the way). The 8km road cuts through flat salt marshes, home to several bird species. This lagoon was discovered by William Scammon, a 19th-century Yankee whaling captain and unknowing naturalist who first happened upon the breeding sanctuary of the gray whales. The only people living near the lagoon are local fishing people.

Mulegé

Veteran beachcombers claim that heaven on earth is the 48km arc of rocky outcrops and shimmering beaches in Southern Baja known as the **Bahía de Concepción;** millions of shells in the area will keep you busy for days and vastly expand your collection. Sport fishing people appreciate the variety and sheer size of the specimens caught here, and divers fall under the spell of Mulegé's underwater sights. Located 136km north of Loreto on Hwy. 1, Mulegé owes its splendor to the Santa Rosalía river, regionally renowned for both fishing and water sports.

Practical Information

Tourist Office: Hotel Las Casitas Madero 50 (tel. 300-19). The unofficial tourist office for the area. Information is fairly reliable, but objectivity is questionable because of the hotel's economic interests in town.

Currency Exchange: Bánamex, 1 block north of the plaza. Open Mon.-Fri. 8:30am-1pm.

Post Office: On the north side of the plaza. Open Mon.-Fri. 9am-12:30pm and 3-6pm, Sat. 9am-noon. **Postal Code:** 23900.

Telephones: Abarrotes Padilla, General San Martín at Zaragoza, 1 block north of the plaza. Doubles as a long-distance *caseta.* International collect calls 2000 pesos. If you speak Spanish, try calling from the free phone on the north side of the plaza. Open Mon.-Sat. 8:30am-8pm, Sun. 8am-noon. **Telephone Code:** 685.

Bus Station: A sheltered white bench about 5m wide just past the turnoff to Mulegé from Rte. 1. All buses out of Mulegé are *de paso,* which means they inevitably arrive late and full. Southbound buses are scheduled to leave at 10am, 11am, noon, 8:30pm, and 9:30pm; north-bound buses depart at 1am, 4am, 6am, 4pm, and 7pm. To: Loreto (7000 pesos); La Paz (26,000 pesos); Tijuana (53,000 pesos); Mexicali (62,000 pesos); Ensenada (46,000 pesos).

Laundromat: Lavamática Claudia (tel. 300-57), beside Hotel Terraza. Wash 3300 pesos, dry 1400 pesos, soap 800 pesos. Open Mon.-Sat. 8am-6pm.

Pharmacy: Farmacia Mulegé (tel. 300-23), on Zaragoza near General San Martín. Open daily 8am-9pm; 24 hr. service by phone.

Hospital: Centro de Salud B, Madero 28 (tel. 302-98). Also referred to as the ISSTE clinic or the Puesto Periférico. Open 24 hr.

Police: Delegación Municipal de Seguridad y Tránsito, Madero 30 (tel. 302-48), next to the hospital.

Accommodations

The recent influx of tourists has driven up prices in Mulegé, but good deals can still be found, though not quite as readily as good shells.

Hotel Terrazas (tel. 300-09), 2 blocks north of the plaza. Expensive, but modern and comfort-able. Clean rooms with soft beds, A/C, and hot water. Singles 50,000 pesos. Doubles 60,000 pesos. Triples 70,000 pesos.

Hotel Rosita (tel. 302-70), on Madero just east of the plaza. The best bargain for a group, especially one with sleeping bags. Rooms are enormous suites with living rooms, kitchens, and A/C. Singles and doubles 60,000 pesos. Triples and quads 70,000 pesos.

Hotel Vieja Hacienda, Madero 3 (tel. 300-21), next door to the Hotel Rosita. Tree-filled courtyard and spacious rooms. Hang out at the VCR bar under the cranking A/C. Singles 30,000 pesos. Doubles 40,000 pesos.

Casa de Huéspedes Nachita (tel. 301-40), 50m down the left branch of the fork as you enter Mulegé. Identifiable by its electric-red doorframes. Box rooms with cot-sized beds. Commu-nal bathrooms win no prizes, nor does the cluttered courtyard. Staff works diligently to main-tain the semi-clean state of rooms. Singles 15,000 pesos. Doubles 20,000 pesos.

Food

A good meal in Mulegé is hard to find. Grocery stores equipped to feed nomadic beach bums are plentiful, and a few unremarkable restaurants cluster near the bus station. **Azteca,** located in the Hotel Terraza, has edible, even somewhat memorable entrees, with prices starting about 10,000 pesos. **Patio El Candil,** just north of the plaza, is also good (breakfasts 8000-9000 pesos, *antojitos* 8000 pesos, fish with garlic sauce 13,000 pesos). **La Purísima,** on the same street as El Candil, serves the best ice cream in the Baja (2500 pesos).

At night, most senior *norteamericanos* in the area meet at the bar of the **Hotel Las Casitas** for drinking and dancing. The last watering hole to close each night is the bar at the **Hotel Vieja Hacienda.**

Sights

The most spectacular cave paintings in Baja are two hours by four-wheeler from Mulegé, in the **Cuevas de San Borjita.** Unfortunately, the caves are on private property, and some enterprising soul has acquired the only permit to them. He'll only make trips from October to June, and the price is US$40. If you have your own car, you'll probably be able to talk him down a bit. Ask at the **Hotel La Casita** (tel. 300-19), on Madero 1 block east of the plaza, for information. They can also arrange sport fishing expeditions on 22-ft. boats (US$32.50).

Mulegé's **mission** sits on a hill to the west, down a lane shaded by bananas and palms, and past the bridge south of the Zócalo. The mission is not a museum: services are still held every Sunday. On a hill east of town, the old **territorial prison** decays slowly.

Near Mulegé: Santa Rosalía

The wooden houses, general stores, and saloons along Santa Rosalía's streets recall the town's previous incarnation as the base for a French 19th-century copper operation that mined the surrounding hills. The spectacular prefabricated cast-iron **Iglesia Santa Bárbara,** at Obregón and Calle 1, truly makes the town shine. Designed by Gustave Eiffel (of Tower fame) and installed in the 1890s, this church was one of four destined for missions in Africa before the company that commissioned forgot to pick up their order. French mining concessionaries spotted the iron church at the 1889 *Exhibition Universal de Paris,* and decided Santa Rosalía couldn't do without it.

The town's only other draw is the northernmost ferry connecting Baja to the mainland. The boat leaves Santa Rosalía for Guaymas Sunday, Tuesday, and Thursday at 11pm from the Transbordadores terminal on Rte. 1 (tel. 200-13), just south of town. Tickets for the seven-hour crossing are sold at the dock from 4:30 to 10:30pm before each ferry; arrive early. Since demand for passenger seats is high, check at the ferry office between 8am and 2:45pm for the latest updates as soon as you set foot in town. On Saturdays, no tickets are sold but the office is open for information dissemination. To get from the ferry to Obregón, Santa Rosalía's main strip, turn right as you leave the ferry compound; Obregón is your second left.

Santa Rosalía offers nothing that would justify an extended visit, and the heat during the summer will drive you out of town with your tail between your legs. Southbound buses to La Paz (21,500 pesos) via Mulegé (3500 pesos) leave at 2am, 4:30am, 5am, 9am, and 8pm; northbound buses to Ensenada (33,100 pesos) and Tijuana (36,000 pesos) leave at 2am, 5am, 5pm, and 7pm.

Mulegé to Loreto

The Bahía de Concepción, 8km outside Mulegé, is lined with the beaches that Mulegé proper lacks. Hitching from Mulegé to the beaches poses no problem; every camper and RVer on the Bahía shuttles to and from Mulegé at least once per day.

Playa Punta Arena, 16km south of Mulegé, is the most attractive beach in the area. Connected to the highway by a 2km rutted dirt road barely passable by car, this stretch of sand is distant enough from the traffic that the roar of the waves drowns out the noise from muffler-less trucks. A dozen palm-frond *palapas* line the beach (hammock hookups US$1 per night), with sand-flush toilets behind them. The Paleolithic people who once inhabited the caves on the hillside south of the beach left behind millions of shells. The biggest cave is of some interest to sightseers for its collection of stones worn smooth from grinding.

The next beach down is **Playa Santispac,** whose tranquil shores are overrun with RVs. Tent-pitching is also permitted; a man comes around once per day to collect the US$2 camping fee. Both of these lodging options are also available at nearby **Playa el Coyote.** Yachts and sailboats bob in the harbor at Santispac, making it the most picturesque, and certainly the liveliest, of the beaches on the bay. The restaurant at the end of the beach sells water to boats and campers as well as breakfasts and dinners (burritos 3500 pesos, quesadillas 2500 pesos). The bakery next door practices the ancient art of daily bread-baking. Santispac is directly on the highway; those hitching will find it more convenient than Punta Arena.

Fifteen kilometers farther down the road, at primitive **Playa Resquesón,** a beautiful spit of sand broadens into a wide beach. The next beach south, small and undeveloped except for a lone toilet, is the last beach before the highway climbs into the mountains separating Mulegé from Loreto.

Mulegé Divers, on Madero 45, down the street from Hotel Las Casitas, rents scuba equipment and organizes boat trips. The day-long scuba-diving excursion, including boat, guide, and all necessary equipment, costs US$38 per person; the skin-diving excursion costs US$18 per person. Make reservations one day in advance. (Open June-Sept. Mon.-Sat. 4-6pm; Oct.-May Mon.-Sat. 10am-1pm and 4-6pm.)

Loreto

Settled by the Spanish in 1697, Loreto was the capital of Baja until a hurricane wiped out the town in 1829. Recent construction has done little to restore it to its former glory. From the hills just south of town, you can see a maze of roads and sidewalks, palm trees, sprinklers, and street lights, but no buildings. Years ago, the Mexican government began to lay the groundwork for a major resort, but funds were diverted to other projects. Loreto thus remains a simple town, despite its three luxury hotels. Most of the foreigners in town are senior *norteamericanos* who have come to fish the spectacular waters off Loreto's coast. The **Dirección de Fomento Turístico** (tel. 306-89) can help prospective anglers and other tourists. Their office on the plaza has brochures and tips for your stay in Loreto and Baja California Sur. (Open daily 9am-3pm and 5-8pm.)

The only sights in town are the fishing boats pulled up on the beach, at the end of Salvatierra on the Malecón, and the **Museo de las Misiones,** inside the beautiful mission next to the plaza. The museum has exhibits on the discovery and conquest of the Baja. (Open Tues. and Thurs.-Sun. 9am-4pm. Admission 500 pesos.)

Budget accommodations are rare in Loreto. **Motel Salvatierra,** at Salvatierra and Márquez de Leon (tel. 300-21), is clean, relatively cheap, and has A/C. (Singles 35,000 pesos. Doubles 42,000 pesos.) Loreto's most affordable eatery is **Restaurant Cuadros,** on Salvatierra across from the Pescador supermarket. Fishing people off to an early start fill their stomachs here. (Eggs any style 4500 pesos. Meat and fish entrees 10,000 pesos. Open daily 5am-8pm.) The **Cafe Olé,** Madero 14, across from Bancomer 1 block off Salvatierra, is more touristy but still affordable. Service is quick and friendly. (Open Mon.-Sat. 7am-10pm.) A coupon for a 10% discount at Olé is available at the tourist office.

The bus station is 1 block before the cobblestone section of Salvatierra, in front of the Restaurant Don Luis. All buses (routinely 2 hr. late) are *de paso,* which makes seats virtually impossible to come by. If you don't relish the thought of standing for five hours to La Paz, ask the ticket agency if you can grab any seats vacated in Ciudad Insurgentes or Constitución, 1½ hours away. Try to be the last passenger on board; this way, you can sit in the front and breathe the freshest air. **Tres Estrellas de Oro** and **Autotransportes Aguila** run south to La Paz (8 per day, 5 hr., 19,000 pesos). Buses run north eight times per day to Mulegé (7000 pesos), Tijuana (60,000 pesos), Mexicali (69,000 pesos), Ensenada (53,000 pesos), and Guerrero Negro (21,000 pesos).

Farmacia Salvatierra is next to the Restaurant Cuadros. The **post office** is on the plaza in the maroon-and-white building with the sign proclaiming the city "Capital Histórica de las Californias." (Open Mon.-Fri. 8am-1pm and 3-5pm, Sat. 9am-noon.) The **postal code** is 23880. You can exchange currency at **Bancomer,** on the plaza. (Open for exchange Mon.-Fri. 8:30am-noon.) If you arrive after bank hours, visit the *casa de cambio* at Salvatierra 75.

North of Loreto, the road passes the beautiful **Bahía de Concepción** on its way to Mulegé. South of Loreto, the road winds away from the coast into rugged mountains and the Planicie Magdalena, an intensively irrigated and cultivated plain. The striking white stripes on the first hillside beyond town consist of millions of shells left by the region's Paleolithic inhabitants. This whole area is strewn with clam, conch, oyster, and scallop shells. Some caves on the hillside, inhabited as recently as 300 years ago, contain shells and buffed stone.

La Paz

For most of the 453 years since Hernán Cortés founded it, La Paz has been a quiet fishing village chiefly noted for the extraordinary pearls off its shores. Accessible only by sea, La Paz was cut off from the rest of the world, and its boats to the mainland loaded with iridescent treasure were favorite targets for pirates. John Steinbeck set *The Pearl* in La Paz, depicting it as a tiny, unworldly fishing village whose bays glittered with the semi-precious globules. In the 1940s, La Paz's oysters mysteriously sickened and died, wiping out the pearl industry. With the institution of the Baja ferries and the completion of the Transpeninsular Highway in the 60s, however, tourists and new industries discovered La Paz, and the city's population rose to its present figure of 200,000.

As night approaches, locals and *viajeros* alike flock to the beach for a front-row view of La Paz's exquisite sunsets.

Orientation

La Paz sits on the Bahía de la Paz, on the Baja's east coast, 222km north of Cabo San Lucas and 1496km southeast of Tijuana. The Transpeninsular Hwy. (Rte. 1) connects La Paz to all major cities and towns on the Baja. Ferry is by far the cheapest way to get from La Paz to the mainland, but for those with a car, procuring a ticket is nearly impossible; these ferries carry mostly commercial trucks and the few slots for other vehicles sell out far in advance. If you ask the La Paz tourist office about procedures for getting your car across, they'll scare you with so much red tape that you may consider pushing your heap off the nearest pier and swimming across the Sea of Cortés.

The ferry is now operated by the **Sematur Company,** with an office located at Reforma and Prieto. Buses running down Obregón make the 18km trip to the ferry dock in Pichilingue (every hr. 8am-6pm, 1500 pesos). Catch the bus at the makeshift bus terminal on Obregón between Independencia and 5 de Mayo. A new company right on the pier, **Baja Express,** will take you to Los Mochis or Mazatlán twice as quickly as the regular ferry for about double the price.

During holidays, ferry demand is great. Except for the Baja Express, ferries are not a tourist service but a means of food supply. Rules and regulations for purchasing ferry tickets are in constant flux. But if you reach the office early, you should have no problem acquiring *salón* tickets. The Sematur office is open daily from 8am to 2pm; be there at 7am for a prime place in line. Although you can actually *buy* tickets only on the day of departure, you can make reservations in advance. Tourist cards, necessary to leave Baja California Sur by ferry, are available at **Servicios Migratorios** (tel. 204-29), on Obregón between Allende and Juárez. (Open Mon.-Fri. 8am-3pm.)

Maps of La Paz depict perfect rectilinear blocks around a tiny enclave of disorder on the waterfront. Since the city's metamorphosis from fishing village to minor resort, this waterfront disarray has emerged as the downtown area, home to most tourist services and budget hotels. The main streets for travelers are **Obregón,** which follows the waterfront, and **16 de Septiembre,** which runs south. On some maps, the stretch of Obregón near the tourist office is called **Malecón.**

La Paz is easy to navigate: the only possible source of confusion concerns the compass points used in directions. It would be a logical assumption that the waterfront faces east, since La Paz is on the eastern side of the peninsula. In fact, in a twist of nature only a contortionist would understand, the waterfront faces northwest.

The municipal bus system in La Paz serves the city sporadically. In general, city buses run daily from 6am to 10pm every half hour (1000 pesos). Flag them down anywhere, or wait by the stop at Degollado and Revolución, next to the market.

Practical Information

Tourist Office: Obregón at 16 de Septiembre (tel. 211-90), in a pavilion on the water. Excellent city maps and information about Baja Sur as well as mainland Mexico. English-speaking staff. Open Mon.-Fri. 8am-8pm, Sat. 9am-1pm.

Currency Exchange: Bancomer, 16 de Septiembre, ½ block from the waterfront. Other banks cluster nearby and on Degollado. **Internacional,** at 5 de Mayo and Revolución, borders the Zócalo. All open Mon.-Fri. 8:30am-1pm.

Immigration Office: Servicios Migratorios (tel. 204-29), on Obregón between Allende and Juárez. You must stop here if you entered Mexico via Baja and are mainland-bound. In an emergency, you may be able to get a permit at the ferry office or the airport, but don't count on it. Open Mon.-Fri. 8am-3pm.

Post Office: Revolución at Constitución (tel. 203-88). Open Mon.-Fri. 8am-7pm, Sat. 9am-1pm. **Postal Code:** 23000.

Telephones: Casetas Benavides, across from the post office. Open Mon.-Fri. 8am-8pm. **Operadora de Viajes,** on Obregón next to Okey Disco, has 3 phones for long distance (2000-peso fee plus a 7500-peso charge for unaccepted collect calls). English spoken and dollars changed. Open Mon.-Fri. 9am-1pm and 3-7pm, Sat. 9am-1pm. **Telephone Code:** 682.

Telegrams: In the post office (tel. 203-22).

Airport: West of La Paz. Taxi fare 25,000 pesos. Served by **Mexicana** (tel. 200-57), Obregón between Muelle and Tejada; **Aeroméxico;** and **Aerocalifornia.** Tickets available through any of the travel agencies by the waterfront and the plaza. To: Los Mochis (US$45); Tijuana (US$115); Mexico City (US$125); Mazatlán (US$52); Guadalajara (US$115); and Los Angeles (US$170).

Bus Station: Independencia at Jalisco, about 20 blocks west of downtown. Municipal bus "Central Camionera" (1000 pesos) runs between the bus station and the public market at Degollado and Revolución. Buses are infrequent (every hr. 6am-8pm), however, and the walk is long, so consider a taxi (5000 pesos). Five bus companies operate out of the terminal, among them **Tres Estrellas de Oro, Autotransportes Aguila,** and **Norte de Sonora.** Buses from La Paz to Tijuana (79,000 pesos) leave daily at 10am, 1pm, 4pm, 8pm, 10pm, and midnight, stopping in all major cities along the way. To: Loreto (19,000 pesos); Mulegé (26,000 pesos); Santa Rosalía (29,000 pesos); Guerrero Negro (40,000 pesos); Mexicali (88,000 pesos).

Ferries: See Orientation above. To Mazatlán (daily at 5pm, 16 hr., *salón* 36,000 pesos, *cabina* 108,000 pesos, *especial* 144,000 pesos, cars (up to 5m) 264,000 pesos, motorcycles 34,000 pesos). To Topolobampo (Sun., Tues., and Wed. at 8am, 8 hr., *salón* 24,000 pesos, *turista* 48,000 pesos, *cabina* 72,000 pesos, *especial* 96,000 pesos, cars (up to 5m) 161,000 pesos, motorcycles 34,000 pesos).

Registry of Vehicles: (tel. 261-89), on Domínguez between Navarro and 5 de Febrero. If you want to bring a car to the mainland, you must have your car permit stamped here. Open Mon.-Fri. 8am-3pm.

Bookstores: Biblioteca de las Californias, on 5 de Mayo between Madero and Independencia. Books about Baja. **Librería Contempo,** on Arreola just off the waterfront, has a section of English-language books, magazines, and newspapers.

Laundromat: Lavamatica, 5 de Mayo at Rubio (tel. 220-00), across the street from the stadium. Wash 3000 pesos, 5-min. dry 300 pesos, detergent 700 pesos. Open Mon.-Sat. 7am-9pm, Sun. 9am-2pm.

Red Cross: (tel. 211-11) on Reforma between Isabel la Católica and Félix Ortega.

Pharmacy: Farmacia Baja California, Independencia at Madero (tel. 202-40), facing the plaza. Open daily 7am-11pm.

Hospital: Salvatierra, Bravo at Verdad (tel. 207-81).

Police: Colima at México (tel. 220-20). Open 24 hr.

Accommodations

There are a number of good, cheap hotels within 4 blocks of the shore. Except during the humid summer months, air conditioning isn't necessary; fans are adequate for La Paz and most other coastal towns.

Pensión California, Degollado 209 (tel. 228-96), between Madero and Revolución. Jungly courtyard, friendly management, and a refrigerator stocked with Pepsi. Fantastic, massive paintings of mythological beasts watch over the lobby. Rooms with fans and private bathrooms. Singles 15,000 pesos. Doubles 22,000 pesos.

Hostería del Convento, Madero 85 (tel. 235-08), at Degollado. Run by the same folks as the California: more blue paint, but less dirt and fewer decibels. Most beds mounted on cement blocks; bathrooms rather cramped. Rooms have ceiling fans. Singles 15,000 pesos. Doubles 22,000 pesos.

Hotel Lorimar, Bravo 110 (tel. 538-22), at Madero. Nice location, clean rooms, and firm beds make this a good deal. The *gringo* manager likes to show off the courtyard. Singles 40,000 pesos. Doubles 45,000 pesos. Triples 50,000 pesos.

Hotel Yeneka, Madero 1520 (tel. 203-35), between 16 de Septiembre and Independencia. Clean rooms with white paint, checkerboard floors, and fans. Graceful, white-tiled bathrooms. Huge leafy fronds shade the courtyard. Singles 25,000 pesos. Doubles 35,000 pesos.

Hotel La Purísima (tel. 234-44), on 16 de Septiembre, between Revolución and Serdán. Identical hallways with identical doors lead to identical rooms. Clean and pleasant, with spotless private showers, color TVs, A/C, fans, and good beds. Singles 55,000 pesos. Doubles 65,000 pesos. Triples 75,000 pesos.

Hotel San Carlos, 16 de Septiembre at Revolución (tel. 204-44). Don't be intimidated by the fluorescent hallway—the rooms are pleasant, with large bathrooms and fans. Singles 18,400 pesos. Doubles 20,700 pesos. Triples 23,000 pesos.

Posada San Miguel, Belisario Domínguez 1510 (tel. 218-02), just off 16 de Septiembre. More like the Posada Keith Partridge. Right in the heart of downtown, but the only noises emanate from the frolicking toddlers in the courtyard. Clean rooms, leafy courtyard, mellow management. Toilets not always functional. Watch out for low ceiling fans. Singles 15,000 pesos. Doubles 20,000 pesos. Triples 30,000 pesos.

Food

On the waterfront you'll find decor, menus, and prices geared toward tourists. Good, cheap meals are available next to the main municipal bus station: the selection is wide and entrees cost as little as 2000 pesos. The public market, at Degollado and Revolución, offers an unremarkable selection of dirt-cheap fruits and vegetables. There are supermarkets on Zaragoza, just west of 16 de Septiembre, and at Hidalgo and Madero, 1 block north of the post office.

La Fábula Pizza, Obregón 95, near 16 de Septiembre. Funky restaurant with records hanging from ceiling and the B-52's blasting from the speakers. Service is slow, but the pizza tastes great. Discount of 30% granted to couples on Thurs. Bilingual menu. Medium pizza with ham 8000 pesos. MC, Visa accepted.

Restaurante El Yate, on the pier near the tourist pavilion. Because of its unrivaled view of the bay, this is a great place for drinks at sunset. Expensive entrees. Lobster salad 35,000 pesos. Open Tues.-Sun. 10am-midnight. MC, Visa accepted.

Restaurante El Quinto Sol, Domínguez at Independencia, near the plaza with the church. Some call it the best vegetarian restaurant in western Mexico; clean, cool, and pleasant. Sells books on nutrition. Alfalfa *agua fresca* 1500 pesos. Cornflakes with milk and banana 4600 pesos. Entrees from 7500 pesos. Avoid the English menu unless you want to pay *gringo* prices. Open Mon.-Sat. 8am-10pm.

Café Olimpia, 16 de Septiembre, across from Hotel La Purísima. Countertop establishment dishes out *big* servings to customers on beautiful orange stools. Lame hot sauce. Three hotcakes and eggs 4000 pesos. Open daily 7am-11pm.

Rostizería California, on Serdán between Degollado and Ocampo, just south of the public market. Family restaurant with a 3-dish repertoire: roast or fried chicken with salad and tortillas, and chicken soup. Whoever roasts the chicken has perfected the art. Half-chicken (more than a meal) 9000 pesos. Whole chicken (for that army you've been waiting to feed) 19,000 pesos. Also sold by the piece. Open daily 8am-3:30pm.

La Revolución, on Revolución, between Reforma and Independencia. Spacious, white-walled dining room more satisfying than the food. This is no hole in the wall, but the food tastes like it came from one. Eggs 5500 pesos. Bland but filling *comida corrida* (served noon-6pm) 8500 pesos. Open daily 8am-midnight.

Nony's Helados, on Belisario Domínguez, down the street from Posada San Miguel. Another Nony's across from the bus terminal. *Tortas de pierna* 5000 pesos. Root beer from a barrel 2000 pesos. Booths for smoochin' in the back. Open daily 7am-11pm.

Antojitos La Pirámide, 16 de Septiembre 220, three doors to the left of La Purísima. Filled with locals enjoying cheap food from the menu scrawled on the front window. Open Mon.-Sat. 7am-1am.

El Campanario, Obregón at La Paz, above the Okey disco. An excellent place to watch La Paz's spectacular sunsets. Butcher-block tables, hanging plants, and ceiling fans. Classy and expensive. Happy Hour 7-9pm. Entrees 12,000-30,000 pesos. Open daily noon-1am.

Sights and Activities

Beaches in La Paz and much of eastern Baja are not your usual long, curving expanses of wave-washed sand. Instead, they snuggle into small coves sandwiched between cactus-studded hills and calm, transparent water: this is prime windsurfing turf.

The best beach near La Paz is **Playa Tecolote** (Owl Beach), 23km northeast of town. A quiet extension of the Sea of Cortés laps against this gorgeous stretch of gleaming white sand, backed up by tall, craggy mountains. Even though there are no bathrooms, Tecolote is terrific for camping; you'll need to drive or hitch here because of the distance from town.

Other beaches worth visiting include **Playa de Balandra** (watch out for the vicious bugs), **Playa de Pichilinque** (a favorite among the teen set, who dig its eatery and public bathrooms), **Playa del Tesoro** (vacant), and **Playas El Coromuel** and **Palmira** (kiddie heaven). These are all a hefty hike or a short ride away. Closer to town, there's fine swimming in the placid waters east of the tourist office, but the farther you venture from La Paz, the better it gets. City beaches are crowded day and night with swarms of adolescents.

For a clear view of the astounding underwater life, rent a mask, snorkel, and flippers (17,500 pesos per day) from **Deportivo La Paz,** Obregón at La Paz, across from and to the right of the tourist office. (Open Mon.-Fri. 9:30am-5pm, Sat. 9am-2pm and 4:30-7pm.) If you plan to stay a few days, it may be cheaper to buy snorkeling gear at **Deportivo Ortiz,** on Degollado between Madero and Revolución. (Masks from 30,000 pesos. Open Mon.-Sat. 9am-1pm and 3:30-8pm.) The **Baja Diving Service,** Independencia 107-B (tel. 218-26), just north of Domínguez, organizes scuba and snorkeling trips to nearby reefs, wrecks, and islands, where you can mingle with hammerheads, manta rays, giant turtles, and other exotica. (Scuba trips US$60 per day, snorkeling trips US$30 per day; both prices include equipment.) The service also offers windsurfing (US$12 per hr., US$50 per day) and waterskiing (US$30 per hr.).

If you tire of the ocean and wish to escape the blistering sun, take a break at the **Museo Antropológico,** 5 de Mayo and Altamirano (tel. 201-62), which displays local art and reproductions of pre-Conquest cave paintings, as well as exhibits on the Baja's biological and geological past. (Open Tues.-Sun. 9am-1pm and 4-7pm. Free.)

On the south side of Constitución Square (the main plaza) soars the **Misión de Nuestro Señora de la Paz** (Our Lady of La Paz Mission), on Revolución between Independencia and 5 de Mayo. This cathedral was founded by Jesuit missionaries in 1720.

Entertainment

Every Sunday evening, La Paz denizens attend concerts under the enormous kiosk on the plaza east of the tourist office. Called "Sunday in the Park with Tecate," these weekly parties are popular with both Mexicans and *gringos.* If you decide to stroll down the pier to stargaze afterward, keep an eye out for missing floorboards.

In the Zócalo's kiosk, *mariachi* bands occasionally sing until dawn. These concerts are less frequent, less crowded, and more spontaneous than the Sunday jams.

At night, a small but enthusiastic crowd supports a handful of discos. **Okey Laser Club,** Obregón at La Paz, widely acknowledged as the most popular hangout, has a sultry bar and a dancing area that is sporadically illuminated by whirling orange lights and incomprehensible videos. (Open daily 9:30pm-5am, but dancing doesn't start in earnest until after 11pm. Cover 10,000 pesos.) **El Bucanero,** about 2km west off Obregón (toward the water at the sign for El Molino steak house), is bigger and glitzier. (Open daily 9pm-3am.) Both play U.S. Top-40 music. In summer, all discos are open only Thursday through Saturday.

South of La Paz: Los Cabos

South of La Paz, the highway splits: one branch travels along the Pacific Coast and the other twists high up into the mountains. The Pacific route, or *vía corta,* passes Todos Santos and Pescadero before arriving in Cabo San Lucas. Barren desert mountains cascade into alluring azure seas, craggy cliffs tower over crashing waves, and ribbons of virgin white sand filter out of the parched desert. One hundred fifty tortuous kilometers after La Paz, the mountain route, or *vía larga,* descends to San José del Cabo. The southern coast of the Cabos is one long, glorious beach, broken by occasional rocky headlands and pounded by enormous waves. Snorkelers and anglers both enjoy (in different capacities) the loads of fish off the coast. If you don't interfere with the manta rays and baby sharks, they won't interfere with you.

The region has only two sizeable towns, San José del Cabo and Cabo San Lucas. A decade ago, both were isolated fishing villages; recently, the Mexican government realized that with the addition of a few luxury hotels, these beautiful, deserted, and perpetually sun-caressed beaches would attract foreign tourists and foreign *dinero.* Cabo San Lucas, teetering on the brink of world-class resort status, is now a virtual *norteamericano* colony with restaurants such as "The Giggling Marlin," "The Happy Shrimp," "The Zealous Clam," and "The Axe Murderer."

It would be easy to bypass the only two towns on 150km of isolated southern coast, but you'd be missing some of the prettiest spots on the Baja. Camping is fairly easy if you have a car or the nerve to rely on unpredictable rides in the hottest part of the peninsula.

Along the *vía corta,* numerous dirt roads lead from the paved highway to stretches of unspoiled sand, where sea lions and crabs are your only company. Watch out for the surf here; the waves will give you the thrashing of your life if you're not careful. The beaches between San José and Cabo San Lucas are more accessible and visible from the highway, thus less secluded. **Sierra de la Laguna National Park** is tucked under a string of 2500m peaks along the coast. A rough road out of Pescadero leads up to the park, which hides deer, pumas, and pine forests among the mountain crevices. The park is terrific for hiking; plan on a three-day trip if you want to make it to the top of the mountains. The highway past Todos Santos may look like it's partly dirt, but it's completely paved and in good condition.

San José del Cabo

Here you'll find more character and less glitz than elsewhere on the coast. The Transpeninsular Hwy. to the west and Av. Mijares to the east connect the town with San José's broad swatch of beautiful beach 2km away. Hitching a ride to the beach with any of the cars bumping down Av. Mijares is possible, if you have a thumb. Local businesses distribute maps; the cathedral and the Zócalo are conspicuous landmarks on Zaragoza, the main strip, which runs perpendicular to Mijares. The Presidente and other luxury hotels convenient to the beachfront have air-conditioned lobbies in which you can cool off.

The most popular beach in town is **Mirador Point,** 1km south of the Brisa del Mar trailer park. It has three- to five-foot waves and four different breaks of great interest to veteran surfers. You can usually hitch or persuade the bus driver to let you off there; ask first, though, in order to avoid being driven all the way to Cabo San Lucas.

The **Hotel Ceci,** on Zaragoza 1½ blocks west of Mijares, has comfortable rooms with private showers and table fans. The Ceci is the only budget hotel in town, so check in as early as possible. (Singles 30,000 pesos. Doubles 35,000 pesos.) You could also crash on the beach near the **Trailer Park Brisa del Mar,** just off the highway when it reaches the coast. It's free, and will save you the long, hot walk or hitch to the beach. If you have a hammock or a tent, you might try to get a reduced rate at the trailer park, which has a bar, a pool, showers, ping-pong tables, and a restaurant.

A pleasant place to have lunch is **Restaurante/Bar Diana,** at Zaragoza 30. Full meals are a bit expensive, but the service is attentive and the tostadas (9000 pesos) are excellent. Several Mexican restaurants on Zaragoza, Doblado, and the streets linking the two serve a *comida corrida.* For a change of pace, try the chef salad (9000 pesos) at **Marco's Pizza,** on Hidalgo between Doblado and Zaragoza. (Open Tues.-Fri. 4-11pm, Sat.-Sun. noon-11pm.) At night, the most popular disco is the **Cactus,** next to the Hotel Presidente. Boogie on its big strobe-lit dance floor. (Open daily 8pm-3am. Cover 6000 pesos.)

The bus station is on Doblado, about a 10-min. walk from Mijares and 1 block south of Zaragoza. Buses travel to La Paz (13 per day, 3 hr., 11,000 pesos) and Cabo San Lucas (16 per day, ½ hr., 2000 pesos). One bus leaves for Tijuana daily at 4:30pm (26 hr., 90,000 pesos). Most buses are *de paso,* and therefore may be behind schedule. Down the hill ½ block from the bus station is a *caseta* where long-distance phone calls are possible for 2000 pesos. (Open Mon.-Fri. 8am-8pm.) There is a public phone in the plaza, on Zaragoza ½ block before Mijares. San José del Cabo's **telephone code** is 684.

Also on Zaragoza, you can find a supermarket (3 blocks from Mijares) and several banks. The **post office** is at the end of the plaza in a large, two-story building at Zaragoza and Mijares. (Open Mon.-Fri. 8am-1pm and 3-6pm, Sat.-Sun. 9am-1pm.) In an emergency, call the **police** (tel. 203-61) or the **Red Cross** (tel. 203-16).

Cabo San Lucas

Cabo San Lucas, until recently a peaceful fishing village, is likely to become one of the largest resorts in all of Mexico; presently there are more buildings under construction than complete. Luxury hotels, having gazed into the future, are squeezing into every available lot within a reasonable distance of the beach. However, Cabo San Lucas has yet to develop facilities for the budget traveler. The few inexpensive hotels in town have seen better days (like before the Revolution), and the prices at most eating establishments are high, even by U.S. standards.

Budget travelers would do best to visit Cabo San Lucas only for the day or to camp out on the beach and treat the town solely as one big supermarket.

Practical Information

The bus station is at Zaragoza and 16 de Septiembre, 2 blocks east of the marina. Buses run to San José del Cabo (16 per day 6:45am-8pm, 2000 pesos); La Paz (13 per day 6am-6pm, 13,000 pesos); and Tijuana (at 4:30pm, 92,000 pesos).

A helpful map of the city can be found inside the *Los Cabos News* bulletin, available for free at the front desk of many hotels. **Banca Serfín** at Cárdenas and Zaragoza, and **Bánamex** at Cárdenas and Hidalgo, are open for exchange Monday through Friday from 9 to 11:30am. Pharmacies line both Morelos and Cárdenas. Supermarkets are on Hidalgo, at the end of Lázaro Cárdenas, near the banks, and along Morelos. In an emergency, call the **police** (tel. 304-25). A *caseta* at Cárdenas and Hidalgo allows collect calls (2000 pesos) Monday through Friday from 8am to 10pm. Cabo San Lucas's telephone code is 684.

Accommodations

Make reservations early for the winter vacation period, and be prepared to pay considerably higher prices than you would during the summer.

Las Margaritas Inn, Cárdenas at Zaragoza (tel. 304-50). Convenient to the beach and shopping. Magnicifent new suite hotel is a bargain for large groups. Spacious rooms include a full kitchen. One-bedroom suites have a pull-out couch and easily sleep four. One-bedroom suites US$40. Two-bedroom suites US$60. US$5 each additional person. Weekly and monthly rates available. MC, Visa accepted.

Hotel Dos Mares, Zapata at Hidalgo (tel. 303-30). Sparkling clean, with A/C and fan. Cramped bathrooms probably warded off most of the tourists. Singles and doubles 50,000 pesos. Triples 58,000 pesos.

Hotel Mar de Cortés (tel. in U.S. (408) 375-4755), on Cárdenas between Matamoros and Guerrero. Nice furniture in and around the backyard pool. Fully stocked bar on the deck induces pool-side antics. Clean rooms. Singles US$27-36. Doubles US$31-40.

Hotel Casa Blanca, Revolución at Morelos (tel. 302-60), 4 blocks east of the marina. Clean bathrooms allow guests successfully to pull off the old do-everything-at-once-trick. Ceiling fans cool rooms. 10,000-peso towel deposit. Singles 40,250 pesos. Doubles 51,750 pesos. Triples 61,200 pesos.

Hotel Freddy, Morelos at Obregón, above the market. All 8 rooms are clean, with ceiling fans and 2 beds. No nightmares here. Singles and doubles, 50,000 pesos.

CREA Youth Hostel (tel. 301-48), a hot 10-min. walk down Morelos and a hotter 5 min. to the right on Av. de la Juventud. You can see the huge, red-lettered sign from the junction of the two roads. Sometimes uncomfortable in the intense summer heat as communal rooms and bathrooms, though clean, lack hot water and fans. Breakfast 5750 pesos. Lunch 6950 pesos. Dorm bunk-beds 12,000 pesos. Singles 21,000 pesos. Doubles 30,000 pesos. Camping 6000 pesos.

There is a trailer park at Blvd. Marina and Matamoros. Hookups average US$12.

Food

Cabo San Lucas's cheap, friendly restaurants congregate on Morelos and cater to locals.

Taquería del Cheef, Morelos at 20 de Noviembre. English-speaking proprietor José's collection of customers' hats never ceases to entertain. His famous 10-in. burritos (3500 pesos), made with any of 8 possible ingredients, are fantastic. Half-pound hamburgers 8000 pesos. Open daily 7am-3pm and 4pm-midnight.

Miguel's American Bar and Grill, Cárdenas at Zaragoza. Succulent teriyaki burger US$5.50. Two-for-one Happy Hour 3-6pm. Open daily noon-midnight.

Rosticería El Pollo de Oro, Morelos at Cárdenas. White patio furniture is perfectly placed for watching the locals inside and outside the restaurant. Roasted half-chicken with rice and salad 15,000 pesos. Three tacos with the fixins 8500 pesos.

Cafe Petisa, across from the Hotel Mar de Cortés, on Cárdenas between Matamoros and Guerrero. Run by an entertaining Italian polyglot. Excellent but expensive pizzas. Small pizza 8000 pesos. Open daily 8am-noon and 5-10pm; winter daily 8am-10pm.

Pollo Sinaloense, Zaragoza at 20 de Noviembre. Nourish your famished body here without exhausting your budget. Quarter-chicken 8000 pesos. Open daily 8am-10pm.

No Name Restaurant Bar, on the beach. Most reasonable eatery at which you can wiggle your toes in the sand. Big plate of *chiles rellenos* with rice and beans 9400 pesos. Breakfast served all day.

Nightlife

Three gold mines have cornered Cabo's nighttime market. **El Squid Roe,** Cárdenas and Zaragoza, is a Carlos 'n' Charlies establishment which attracts a college-age crowd with moderately priced drinks and a tricky (after a few brews) sign above the bar proclaiming "Free Beer Tomorrow." Drinks cost 6000 pesos. (Open daily noon-2am.) All non-tippers are hung ruthlessly by their ankles from the rafters of **The Giggling Marlin,** Cárdenas at Matamoros. Here, great piña coladas go for 7000 pesos. **Cabo Wabo Cantina,** Guerrero and Cárdenas, is Van Halen's latest acquisition. The middle-aged crowd still remembers how to party. Drinks cost 9000 pesos.

Sights

Cabo San Lucas's best beach is the **Playa del Médano,** on the bay around the corner from the marina, near the Hotel Hacienda. If you forgot your umbrella, seek shade in one of the beach's three or four restaurants or many *palapas*. The waters of the Playa del Médano are alive with buzzing jet-skis, parasailers, and motorboats full of lobster-red, beer-guzzling vacationers. The shack in front of the Hotel Hacienda rents snorkel equipment. Glass-bottom boats leave from the beach and from near the ferry terminal: for 22,000 pesos per person they'll take you on a half-hour ride to see the famous **Rock Arch** of Cabo San Lucas. On the beach, try to make a deal and get one price for the whole boat. Dividing that price by six or seven people, it becomes fairly cheap, and the trip is worth it for the view of volcanic rocks and diving pelicans. Lucky sightseers will spot sea lions sunning themselves on the rocks. For landlubbers, **Ramon's Horse Rentals** lends "well-cared-for and gentle" four-leggeds at US$10 per hour. Located at the Hotel Hacienda, Ramon's also runs three-hour guided tours to the Old Lighthouse (US$25 per person/horse) that begin at sunset.

The beaches on the Pacific side are farther away than those by the marina, and the tide is so ferocious that they are unsuitable for swimming. Seclusion seekers, however, will find these spots especially suitable.

JALISCO AND COLIMA

Guadalajara

Location, location, location: whoever developed this real-estate axiom, stressing central location as the key to success, obviously never talked to the citizens of Jalisco's capital, Guadalajara. *Tapatíos,* as they like to be known, saw their town swell into a wealthy city because of its position at the edge of civilization. Violent revolutionary unrest shook the streets of Mexico City during the early 19th century, forcing many Spanish colonists to flee northwest to then-remote Guadalajara. Here they coined the culture famed today for the introduction of tequila, *mariachis,* and the universally loved hat dance.

With its four large central plazas, stately Spanish architecture, and jacaranda-lined streets, Guadalajara is a beautiful vision for those arriving from the northern deserts. Fortunately, city planners had enough foresight to realize the value of the city's history, creating building preservation programs and enforcing strict ordinances limiting the amount of new construction.

The theaters and museums that have arisen in their prescribed sites have made Guadalajara the cultural center of northern Mexico, and an excellent introduction to Mexico's history and culture. *Gringo* retirees find the combination of modern amenities and colonial charm attractive; the largest group of U.S. citizens living outside the States do so around Lake Chapala, 40km south of town.

Guadalajara's ability to display its sophistication without forsaking its past—along with prosperity and a mild climate—has made its reputation as the Republic's best tourist spot.

Orientation

Guadalajara lies 650km west-northwest of Mexico City. Hourly buses in all directions, several trains per day, and daily planes to all points in Mexico and many U.S. cities ensure that Guadalajara remains readily accessible.

From Guadalajara's airport, **Aeropuerto Internacional Miguel Hidalgo,** a *combi* will drop you anywhere downtown for 7000 pesos if full and up to 30,000 pesos if under capacity. A taxi costs up to 40,000 pesos, depending on the time of day; be sure to settle the fare before getting taken for a ride.

To get to the airport from town, flag a taxi. Unless you are calling from a private home, a *combi* (tel. 19-02-13) will not come to get you, and you may miss your flight trying to catch one on the main avenues.

A new bus station, the *Nueva Central Camionera,* has arisen in the town of Tlaquepaque, southeast of Guadalajara on the highway to Mexico City. The sprawling monster looks more like O'Hare Airport than a bus terminal, but it is well-organized. Seven terminal buildings, each representing up to six bus carriers, surround a U-shaped drive. To get downtown, catch a bus (300 pesos), *combi* (300 pesos), or taxi (10,000 pesos) directly in front of any terminal.

To reach the station from downtown, catch a bus on Av. Revolución, just off Independencia Sur. Both the red bus #275 and a green bus marked "Nueva Central" will take you there. In a taxi, be sure to specify the *new* bus station, since some drivers may zip you to the old station and then make you pay extra to go to Tlaquepaque.

The train station lies at the foot of Independencia Sur. To get from the station to the heart of Guadalajara, at the intersection of Independencia and Juárez, take a taxi (10,000 pesos) or bus #18 or 216. You can also walk to Independencia, only

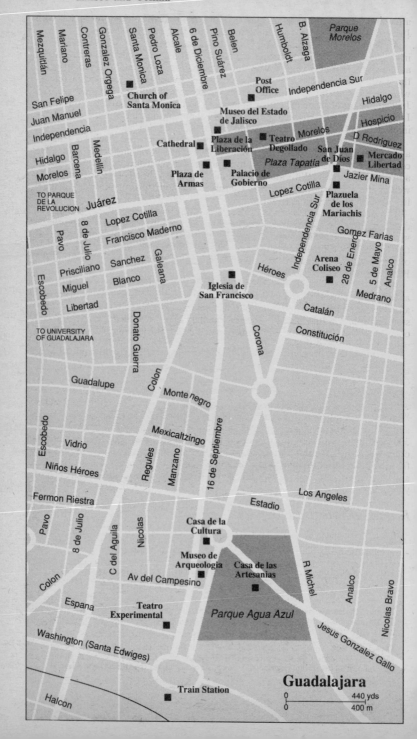

Guadalajara

Mezquitlán
Mariano
Contreras
Gonzalez Orgega
Santa Monica
Pedro Loza
Alcale
6 de Diciembre
Pino Suárez
Belen
Humboldt
B. Alzaga
Parque Morelos

San Felipe
Juan Manuel
Independencia
Hidalgo
Morelos
Barcena
Medellin

Church of Santa Monica

Post Office
Independencia Sur
Hidalgo
Hospicio

Museo del Estado de Jalisco

Cathedral
Plaza de la Liberación
Teatro Morelos
Degollado
Plaza Tapatía
San Juan de Dios
D Rodriguez
Mercado Libertad

Plaza de Armas
Palacio de Gobierno
Lopez Cotilla
Jazier Mina

TO PARQUE DE LA REVOLUCION
Juárez

8 de Julio
Pavo
Escobedo
Prisciliano
Miguel
Libertad

Lopez Cotilla
Francisco Maderno
Sanchez
Blanco
Galeana

Independencia Sur
Plazuela de los Mariachis
Gomez Farias
Arena Coliseo
28 de Enero
5 de Mayo
Analco
Medrano

Héroes

Iglesia de San Francisco

Catalán
Constitución

TO UNIVERSITY OF GUADALAJARA

Donato Guerra
Colon

Guadalupe
Monte negro

Corona

Escobedo
Vidrio
Niños Héroes
Regules
Manzano
Mexicaltzingo
16 de Septiembre

Fermon Riestra

Los Angeles
Estadio

Pavo
8 Julio 8
Colon
Espana

C del Aguila
Nicolas

Casa de la Cultura
Museo de Arqueologia
Casa de las Artesanias
R Michel
Analco
Nicolas Bravo

Av del Campesino

Teatro Experimental

Parque Agua Azul
Jesus Gonzalez Gallo

Washington (Santa Edwiges)

Halcon

Train Station

Guadalajara

0   440 yds
0   400 m

a few minutes from the station, and take bus #45 north to the intersection with Juárez. To return to the train station, take bus #62 to the last stop.

A plethora of street signs makes Guadalajara easy to navigate. Most intersections in the compact downtown district are clearly marked, and only a few streets run at odd angles. Finding your way around outside the *centro* is more difficult because the streets change names at the borders between Guadalajara's four sectors (clockwise from the north: **Libertad, Reforma, Juárez,** and **Hidalgo**). For example, Av. Juárez, one of the principal east-west arteries, becomes Av. Vallarta when it leaves Libertad and enters Hidalgo. Guadalajara's shopping district centers around the intersection of Av. Juárez and **Avenida Alcalde/16 de Septiembre.**

The **Plaza Tapatía** lies just north of the intersection between **Avenidas Hidalgo** and **Moreno,** two east-west thoroughfares. This extensive oblong area contains the cathedral, the **Teatro Degollado,** many churches and museums, broad open spaces, and countless stores. With many of the most expensive hotels and restaurants, as well as the university and the U.S. Consulate, the most prosperous part of town lies west of Pl. Tapatía.

The Andrew Dice Clay of the city's streets (filthy and loud) is **Calzada Independencia** (referred to as Independencia Sur in the part of town of interest to travelers), which divides Guadalajara on a northeast-southwest axis. To the west lies Pl. Tapatía. To the east are Mercado Libertad, Plazuela de los Mariachis, and the hotels of Javier Mina. At the southern end of Independencia lie the train station and the Parque Agua Azul.

A map of Guadalajara is essential. The one handed out at the state tourist office at Morelos 102 in Pl. Tapatía (1 block east of the Teatro Degollado) is confusing and oversimplified. The best maps of Guadalajara cost 15,000 pesos in such bookstores as **Librería Ediciones de Cultura Popular,** López Cotilla 255 (tel. 13-57-56; open Mon.-Sat. 9am-9pm). English-language maps for sale along Alcade and Hidalgo cost only 10,000 pesos.

The poorer *colonias* (suburbs) could be dangerous at any time of day. Check with the tourist office before venturing far from the affluent parts of town. Throughout Guadalajara, it is wise to stick to lit streets after dark and to take taxis after 11pm.

The city's extensive bus system runs far, wide, and often. Bus #45 may become a buddy because it covers the length of Independencia Sur. Electric buses labeled "Par Vial" run along Av. Juárez/Vallarta to the western edge of the city and back along Hidalgo, parallel to and 3 blocks north of Av. Juárez/Vallarta. All buses cost 300 pesos and run every five minutes from 6:30am to 11pm. For information on other bus routes, consult a schedule available at most newsstands. Faster but less frequent than buses, *combis* follow the same routes for 300 pesos. Taxis drop you anywhere in the city for 15,000-20,000 pesos. Remember to establish the fare before you hop in.

Practical Information

State Tourist Office: Morelos 102 (tel. 58-22-22), in the Pl. de la Liberación, next to the Pl. Tapatía. Very informative, with a few simple maps. Some English spoken—ask for Ernesto, the wonder worker. Open Mon.-Fri. 9am-9pm, Sat. 9am-1pm.

Federal Tourist Office: Degollado 50 (tel. 14-83-71), around the corner from the state tourist office. Sketchy information on Guadalajara, but they have free information on every Mexican state. Open Mon.-Fri. 9am-3pm.

Tours: Panoramex, Federalismo 948-305 (tel. 10-51-09). A wide range of trips, including Ajijic, Chapala, Tlaquepaque, and Tonalá, for budgets of all sizes. More information available at the state tourist office.

Consulates: U.S., López Cotilla 1393 (tel. 25-27-00; in an emergency, call 26-55-53). Open Mon.-Fri. 8am-2pm. **U.K.,** Gonzalez Gallo 1897 (tel. 35-89-27). **Canada,** Fiesta Americana Hotel, Local 30 (tel. 15-86-65, ext. 3005). For other countries, try the **Oficina de la Asociación Consular** (tel. 15-55-55).

Currency Exchange: Banks are open for exchange Mon.-Fri. 9am-1:30pm and there are several on the 300-400 block of Juárez. First-class hotels exchange at a less favorable rate. The money-changers on López Cotilla between Corona and Independencia Sur sometimes give a few pesos above the official rate per U.S. dollar. Most money-changers open Mon.-Fri. 9am-2pm and 4-7pm, Sat. 9am-2pm.

American Express: López Mateos 477 (tel. 30-02-00), at Justicia. Take the "Par Vial" bus to the end of the line and then walk several blocks up López Mateos. Mail pick-up and currency exchange services. Open Mon.-Fri. 9am-6pm, Sat. 9am-1pm. **Refund Office,** 16 de Septiembre 730B (tel. 14-70-62).

Post Office: On Carranza, between Juan Manuel and Calle de Independencia (not Independencia Sur), 1 block north of the Teatro Degollado. Expect a wait for stamps in the morning. Lista de Correos not posted, but available upon request. Open Mon.-Fri. 8am-7pm, Sat.-Sun. 9am-1pm. City mailboxes rumored to be unreliable. **Postal Code:** 45120.

Telephones: Long-distance office, Donato Guerra 72, between Moreno and Juárez. No charge for successful collect calls, but it will cost you 8000 pesos if there is no answer or your call is not accepted. Required deposit 10,000 pesos. Open daily 7am-8:30pm. Orange public phones are for local calls and take 50- or 100-peso coins. Blue phones are for long distance and take 1000-peso coins. **Telephone Code:** 36.

Telegrams: Palacio Federal, Alcalde and Juan Alvarez (tel. 13-99-16); and at the airport. Open Mon.-Sat. 9am-3pm.

Airport: 17km south of town on the road to Chapala. Served by: **Aeroméxico** (tel. 89-02-57); **Mexicana** (tel. 49-22-22); **American** (tel. 89-03-04); ; and **Delta** (tel. 30-35-30).

Train Station: At the foot of Independencia Sur, south of the *centro.* Train #302 to Irapuato (5 hr., 6000 pesos) at 7:30pm. Train "Colimense" to Manzanillo (at 7am, 8 hr., 25,000 pesos) and Mexico City (at 9am, 12 hr., 14,100 pesos). Train "Tapatillo" (at 8 and 9pm) gives you special first-class seating to Mexico City for 43,000 pesos or 80,000 pesos per berth. Unlike most train rides in the Republic, the overnight to Mexico City is comfortable and enjoyable. Tickets should be secured in advance and can be purchased from 8am to 9pm at the station. A separate desk marked "Trenes del Pacifico" sells tickets for northbound trains (open Mon.-Fri. 9am-1pm, Sat. 9:30am-noon, Sun. 9:30-11am). You can buy tickets for Train Tapatillo at the **Macull Travel Agency** (tel. 14-70-14), next to the Hotel Universo at López Cotilla 163.

Bus Station: In Tlaquepaque (see Orientation above). **Tres Estrellas de Oro** (tel. 57-72-25), **Transportes del Pacífico** (tel. 57-46-68), and second-class **Camiones de los Altos** (tel. 57-60-30) are among the 31 companies serving Guadalajara. Direct service anywhere in the northern half of Mexico. Tres Estrellas, in terminal #3, offers the most extensive first-class service. To: Mexico City (every ½ hr., 8 hr., 30,000 pesos); Puerta Vallarta (12 per day, 6 hr., 19,500 pesos); Colima (5 per day, 4 hr., 12,000 pesos); Armería (2 per day, 4½ hr., 12,000 pesos); Tecomán (2 per day, 5 hr., 12,000 pesos); Manzanillo (6 per day, 6 hr., 16,500 pesos). Camiones de los Altos to: Mexico City (18 per day, 8 hr., 26,000 pesos)—evening buses are *directo;* Guanajuato (7 per day, 6 hr., 12,500 pesos); Querétaro (5 per day, 8 hr., 17,000 pesos); Acapulco (3 per day, 15 hr., 45,000 pesos); Durango (6 per day, 12 hr., 29,000 pesos); Zacatecas (every hr., 6 hr., 16,000 pesos); Aguascalientes (every hr., 4 hr., 10,000 pesos).

Car rental: Most places are on Niños Heroes or at the airport. Try **Budget,** Niños Heroes 934 (tel. 13-00-27); **Avis** (tel. 13-90-11); **Hertz** (tel. 14-61-39); **National** (tel. 14-71-75). U.S. citizens need a U.S. driver's license, a major credit card, and 21 years under their belt. Prices hover around 135,000 pesos per day with unlimited mileage or 63,000 pesos per day plus 500 pesos per km.

English Bookstores: Sandi Bookstore, Tepeyac 718 (tel. 21-08-63), in Colonia Chapalita. Take bus #50 from Garabaldi. Extensive selection of new books and American newspapers. Open Mon.-Fri. 9:30am-2:30pm and 3:30-7pm, Sat. 9:30am-2pm. Also in Colonia Chapalita, **Happy Tiger Bookstore,** La Ermita 1319 (tel. 22-63-87), sells used books. Open Mon.-Sat. 10am-2pm. The Hyatt carries day-old copies of *The New York Times.*

Ben Franklin Library: Paseo del Hospicio 65 (tel. 17-05-93), 3rd floor. Back issues of *Tiger Beat* and *The New York Times.* Also may let you borrow books. Open Mon.-Fri. 10am-7pm.

Cultural and Arts Information: Departamento de Bellas Artes (tel. 13-20-24, ext. 112), next to the state tourist branch office at Juárez 638. Publishes a seasonal calendar of events. Open daily 9am-9pm. Also look for copies of *Guadalajara Weekly, The Colony Reporter, About Magazine,* and *Welcome Magazine,* available at tourist offices, hotels, and newsstands.

Laundromat: Lavandería San Antonio, López Cotilla 1234, not far from the Bazar de la Salud. Wash and dry 6000 pesos; soap 1000 pesos. Bring a book; you could wait up to 1½ hr. Open Mon.-Sat. 8:30am-7:30pm, Sun. 8:30am-1:30pm.

Missing Persons: LOCATEL (tel. 24-80-00).

Red Cross: Accqui and Juan Manuel (tel. 14-56-00), near the Pl. Tapatía. **Green Cross Hospital:** Tel. 14-52-52.

Pharmacies: Farmacia de Descuento, Pedro Morena 518; **Farmacia Guadalajara,** Javier Mina 221 (tel. 17-85-55). Both open 24 hr.

Hospitals: Hospital del Carmen, Tarascos 3435 (tel. 47-48-82). **Nuevo Hospital Civil,** Salvador Quevedo y Zubieta 750 (tel. 18-93-62). If your *turista* gets really bad, most hotel managers know a doctor who speaks English.

Police: Independencia Nte. 840 (tel. 17-60-60).

Academics

Several universities and institutes in Guadalajara sponsor programs for international students in a variety of disciplines. The quality varies, so eschew arriving in town with the intent of blundering your way into a program. You stand a better chance of getting into a good one and receiving credit for your work if you make arrangements before you leave. The University of Arizona runs a large and highly regarded summer school, which offers sociology, intensive Spanish, and Hispanic literature, among other subjects. For more information, write **Guadalajara Summer School,** Douglas Bldg. #315, University of Arizona, Tucson, AZ 85721 (tel. (602) 621-7551).

Accommodations

Although the thousands upon thousands of tourists who pass through the city every year have jacked up accommodation prices in downtown Guadalajara, hotels in the 15,000-25,000 peso range are better than their counterparts elsewhere in Mexico; the hot water is more or less consistent, the beds are usually comfortable, and the bugs keep a low profile. Many hotels in Guadalajara offer a rarely publicized 10% discount for stays of one week or more.

A good alternative to budget hotels is the *posada. Posadas* are small, family-run establishments that, for a few extra pesos, provide large and better-furnished rooms, and frequently include meals as well. The drawbacks are slightly less privacy and less freedom to stay out late. There are only a few *posadas* in Guadalajara, and they are often full. Check at the tourist office for a list.

Outside of the *posadas,* reservations are only necessary in February, when the city plays host to a large cultural festival.

Near the Plaza Tapatía

Hotels within a few blocks of the Pl. Tapatía have several drawbacks. They are expensive, offer no escape from Guadalajara's traffic, and tend to have few vacancies. The convenience of centrality, however, may make the shortcomings bearable. If it's simply the price and not the noise that bothers you, try the hotels along Javier Minas.

Posada San Pablo, Madero 218 (tel. 13-33-12). Big, slightly tattered rooms with nice furniture. A few canaries in the lovely central atrium try in vain to smother traffic noise. Pleasant owner. Cross your fingers and say a prayer to the *dios* when turning on the hot water tap. Singles 28,000 pesos. Doubles 38,000 pesos.

Hotel Maya, López Cotilla 39 (tel. 14-54-54). A mish-mash of stairways provide many nooks for jugs of *agua purificada,* which are a welcome sight to the traveler arriving from the northern deserts. Blue-interiored, decent rooms, some with closets. Close to the Pl. Tapatía. Singles 23,000 pesos. Doubles 29,000 pesos.

Hotel Universo, López Cotilla 161 (tel. 13-28-15). Not exactly a bargain, but this hotel offers a lot for the dough. The English-speaking manager has TVs and phones in every room, anticipating every need of the worn-out budget traveler. Suites available for extra *dinero*. Singles 40,000 pesos. Doubles 50,000 pesos.

Posada Regis, Corona 171 (tel. 13-30-26). A very sedate establishment. Gorgeous courtyard packed with huge plants. Personable manager offers a discount for multiple-night stays. Singles and doubles 41,000 pesos, but only 31,000 pesos if you stay more than 1 night.

Hotel Nueva York, Independencia Sur 43 (tel. 17-33-98). A large, pink hotel that caters to Mexicans, but welcomes the odd gringo as well. The Flintstones (in Spanish) greet guests on the lobby TV. Watch out for *cucarachas!* Parking lot in back. Singles 20,000 pesos. Doubles 25,000 pesos for 1 bed, 30,000 pesos for 2 beds.

Hotel Hamilton, Madero 381 (tel. 14-67-26). The metal vault-like doors hide unspectacular rooms—no special features but no real drawbacks, either. Doubles are a bit cramped. Singles 20,000 pesos. Doubles 26,000 pesos.

Hotel Occidental, General Villagómez 17 (tel. 13-84-06), off Independencia Sur and Huerta. A good clean deal with the added bonus of ceramic ashtrays in the each room for the smoker. Spacious singles 17,000 pesos. Doubles 21,000 pesos.

Hotel Sevilla, Sánchez 413 (tel. 14-90-37). Not a bad joint at all. Phones, TVs, and the basics to boot: soft beds and clean bathrooms. Singles 35,000 pesos. Doubles with 1 bed 43,000 pesos, with 2 beds 48,000 pesos.

Hotel Latino, Sánchez 74 (tel. 14-44-84). The mattresses are too soft but otherwise similar to those in the Sevilla, only cheaper. Singles 30,000 pesos. Doubles with 1 bed 35,000 pesos, with 2 beds 40,000 pesos.

Hotel Las Américas, Hidalgo 76 (tel. 13-96-22). Unimaginative but comfortable. Traffic noise could be an annoyance, but lodgers must pay some price for the great location: right across the street from Pl. Tapatía. Singles 30,000 pesos. Doubles with 1 bed 35,000 pesos, with 2 beds 40,000 pesos.

East to Javier Mina

The following hotels are clustered within a few blocks of each other, near Independencia Sur on the edge of the poorer section of town. The prices are lower, but the neighborhood is not very safe at night; besides the questionable people, the trash from the Mercado Libertad attracts masses of nocturnal street rats. On the other hand, accommodations here are a short and pleasant daytime stroll from the Pl. Tapatía. If you plan on participating in the nightly festivities on the Pl. de los Mariachis, stay here to avoid the spooky walk across town late at night.

Hotel Ana Isabel, Javier Mina 164 (tel. 17-79-20). Set on the 2nd floor above a small café, Ana Isabel is the best Javier Mina has to offer. Rooms are clean, pleasant, and very comfortable. Quiet open-roof courtyard provides a refuge from the busy streets. Singles 24,000 pesos. Doubles 30,000 pesos.

Hotel Imperio, Javier Mina 180 (tel. 17-50-42). A yellow color scheme and a very polite staff brighten the central courtyard. The bathrooms seem to be approaching the century mark, but everything still works. Singles 20,000 pesos. Doubles 25,000 pesos.

Hotel San Jorge, Javier Mina 284 (tel. 17-79-97). Big windows flood the clean but basic rooms with lots o' light. Some have closets; those on the street are quite noisy. Singles 20,000 pesos. Doubles 25,000 pesos.

Hotel México 70, Javier Mina 230 (tel. 17-99-78). A clone of Hotel San Jorge, complete with identical signs at the desk. Less busy and therefore quieter. All rooms have 2 beds. Singles 20,000 pesos. Doubles 25,000 pesos.

Hotel Azteca, Javier Mina 311 (tel. 17-74-66). Somewhat dark rooms have functional ceiling fans and radios with two stations: on and off. Parking available. Singles 30,000 pesos. Doubles 40,000 pesos. 5000 pesos extra for TV (guess how many stations . . .).

West to University

It could be that the administrative employees of the university are simply trying to instill good study habits in the students, or that they are just too busy running a large university to make much noise, but the area eight long blocks west of Pl. Tapatía is considerably more peaceful than the rest of the *centro*. There are no students, crowds, or traffic—the *posada* here wants to keep it that way and discourages younger, backpacking travelers.

Hotel del Parque, Juárez 845 (tel. 25-28-00), across from the university. If you're looking for the Ritz, this ain't the place for you—but the owners give it the good old Mexican heave-ho. The large rooms contain color TVs, phones, and Servi-Bars. Rental cars also available (tel. 26-60-98). Singles 46,000 pesos. Doubles 57,500 pesos.

Hotel La Paz, La Paz 1091 (tel. 14-29-10), near Donato Guerra. If this is peace, let's go to war—the hotel is old, noisy, and the dirty rugs do nothing to redeem the fact that it's far from the *centro.* Singles 25,000 pesos. Doubles 35,000 pesos.

Posada de la Plata, López Cotilla 619 (tel. 14-91-46). An old mansion run by a *dueña* who takes little joy in accommodating picky young people. Being polite may pay off here; on the other hand, it might be a waste of breath. Singles 28,000 pesos. Doubles 35,000 pesos.

South to Train Station

If you are attracted to noise and dark streets, just love being around choo-choos, and feel at home in cheap, greasy restaurants, stay here. Otherwise, spend the night in this area only if you must catch an early train. Remember that the station is only 15-30 minutes away from the *centro* on foot, depending on your load. The bus takes 10 minutes or less, depending on traffic.

Hotel Flamingos, Independencia Sur 725 (tel. 19-99-21), 4 long blocks from the train station. Small, noisy, and dark but relatively cheap. Pleasant cafeteria in lobby. Singles 19,950 pesos. Doubles with 1 bed 23,000 pesos, with 2 beds 27,600 pesos.

Hotel Estación, Independencia Sur 1297 (tel. 19-00-51), across from the station. Although the small rooms are clean, the highlight of this hotel is the associated café. Phones in all rooms. Watch out for the randomly placed ashtrays on the hallway floors. Singles 30,000 pesos. Doubles 35,000 pesos.

Far West to Minerva

Lots of not-so-great motels are located in this area, which boasts several tasty restaurants. If your interest lies in the downtown scene, don't stay here as the connection via bus is tenuous at best.

The **Motel Guadalajara,** Vallarta 3305 (tel. 47-83-89), next to the Tequila Sauza Bottling Plant, is a two-bus trip from the center (take "Par Vial" to the end of the line, then #130 from Hotel Fiesta Americana). No one knows what lurks in the pool of this run-down motel. Bathrooms are acceptable but rooms undeservedly expensive. (Singles 40,000 pesos. Doubles 45,000 pesos.)

Food

There is a Guadalajaran restaurant for almost any budget—if you don't mind sticking to Mexican dishes. Peso-happy budget blasters will be thrilled to find that Guadalajara is packed with high-class French, Italian, and Japanese restaurants. Expensive places fill the pages of *About Magazine,* available at tourist offices. As a general rule, prices rise as you move west of Independencia Sur.

All sorts of bacteria swarm in the food and water in Guadalajara; even locals fall victim to the microscopic creatures. A program has been launched by the state of Jalisco to improve the hygiene in food establishments, however, and the average Guadalajaran will insist that the food quality has improved. Restaurants and cafeterias should be safe, but avoid sidewalk stalls and the food in Mercado Libertad.

If you want water you should drink your fill at the hotel, because not all restaurants have *agua purificada*; imbibe only when you can see the cooler whence it came.

Near Plaza Tapatía

Unless you love eating shoes there aren't tons of places to get a full meal downtown, but many small snack counters interrupt that all-important clod-shopping spree.

La Terraza, Hidalgo 438, 2nd floor. Two merits to this place: the great view, and 2-for-1 *cervezas* from 1-5 pm. Burgers 5000 pesos. Live music 6-9pm. Open daily 1-9:30pm.

Néctar, Hidalgo 426, 1 block from the cathedral. Good place for juice or yogurt. Medium yogurt 2200 pesos. Open Mon.-Sat. 8:30am-8:45pm, Sun. 9:30am-8:45pm.

El Farol, Moreno 466, 2nd floor. Decent food at decent prices. Two prized tables overlook the street. Entrees 7000-12,000 pesos. Chili and beer 10,500 pesos. Open daily 9am-1am.

La Playita, Moreno 470. The smells in this crowded café are divine though the surroundings resemble purgatory. A Guadalajaran standard. *Lonche* 4300 pesos. Burgers 5000 pesos. Open daily 9am-2am.

Los Sanbrillas, on Pl. de la Universidad at Colón between Moreno and Juárez. This restaurant serves a very American-tasting burger, if you're craving that flavor (7000 pesos). You can watch all the plaza action from your table. Open daily 9am-8:30pm.

Pancho's S.A. Paco Jaurequi, Maestranza 179, 2 blocks east of Av. 16 de Septiembre. Popular bar-restaurant with obscure cognomen serves a largely gay clientele. Houses a "museo taurino": macho bullfighter posters and photographs plaster the walls. Friendly waiters but a somewhat rough scene. Entrees 5000-10,000 pesos. Open daily 9am-2am.

Las Yardas Bar, Juárez 37. A fun, music-filled bar with a few simple dishes. Eclectic decor. Quesadillas 4000 pesos. During happy hour (Mon.-Thurs. 7-9pm) enjoy the 2-for-1 beer special. Open daily 1-11pm.

La Chata, Corona 126. The gaudy tablecloths are hard on the eyes, but the food is easy on your stomach. *Sabroso pollo frito* with *papas fritas* 10,900 pesos. Entrees 7000-12,000 pesos. Open daily noon-11:30pm.

Restaurant Aquarius, Sánchez 416, across from Hotel Sevilla. New Age (as in healing crystals) Mexi-style. Wear your finest peasant shirt and you'll fit right in. Freshly squeezed orange juice (2000 pesos) brings about a personal harmonic convergence. Entrees 7000-8000 pesos.

East to Javier Mina

Restaurants near Javier Mina won't tickle your palate, but they will fill your stomach.

Dacero's, Pl. de los Mariachis. Great Mexican food in the center of the plaza, surrounded by pleasant commotion. Chicken tacos 6000 pesos. Open daily 8am-midnight.

Restaurant Nuevo Faro, López Cotilla 24. Quick and filling, but not much more. Good breakfast dishes: *omeleta mexicana* 6000 pesos. Entrees 7000-12,000 pesos. Open daily 7:30am-11pm.

Restaurant Hermanos Reyes, Independencia Sur 164, in the Hotel de los Reyes. Denny's just might be able to win a copyright infringement suit. The bar stocks all sorts of crazy drinks. Huevos a la Mexicana 10,000 pesos. Open 24 hr.

West to University

Like students the world over, University of Guadalajara kids just dig pizza. They also enjoy the finer things in life—specifically the specialty restaurants in the area.

Café Madoka, 78 Enrique González Martínez, just north of Juárez. Only during soccer season will you catch afficionados yelling at the 2 TVs, but there is always a hot domino game going on in back (men only). Breakfast 3500-5000 pesos. Lunch 5000-8000 pesos. Open daily 8am-11:30pm.

Restaurant Naturalissimo, 8 de Julio 138, near López Cotilla. Family-run place gets relatively crowded during dinner time. The soybean hamburger is a masterpiece. Also various yogurt concoctions and ginseng tea. Open Mon.-Sat. 1-8pm.

Restaurant La China Poblana, Juárez 887, across from the university. *Así-Así* Mexican food in aggrandized Mexican atmosphere. Entrees 15,000-18,000 pesos. Large selection of wines and beers. Open Mon.-Sat. 9am-10pm, Sun. 9am-6pm.

Café Gardel, Juárez 8678, near the Hotel del Parque. The coffee is black as night, but don't expect to find luminous food here. The few dishes are bland. Open Mon.-Sat. 7am-9:30pm.

Luvier, Vallarta 1056, first stop on "Par Vial" after the university. Almost too good to be true, this bakery pleases the eye, nose, and stomach. Cookies 400 pesos. Baguettes 300 pesos. Open daily 7am-9:30pm.

West to Chapultepec

The restaurants in this area, unlike those downtown, are widely spaced. If you are on foot this can be a pain, but the fare is worth the hike. Just remember that the walk burns off calories.

Lüscherly, San Martín 525 (tel. 52-05-09), just north of Niños Heroes. Call for reservations. A lush oasis for your scorched palate, with various international dishes. Try the mushroom Bechamel and ham crepe (9000 pesos)—so tender, it cuts with a fork. Other entrees 17,500-21,000 pesos. Open Tues.-Sat. 1:30pm-midnight, Sun. 1:30-6pm.

Los Itacates Fonda, Chapultepec Nte. 110 Fancy *típico* restaurant with an extensive menu of many Mexican delicacies. Reasonable prices, tasteful art, and attractive tile floors. Breakfast buffet served daily 8:30am-noon (9500 pesos). Entrees 7000-13,000 pesos. Open Mon.-Thurs. 8am-11pm, Fri.-Sat. 8am-midnight, Sun. 8am-7pm.

La Hacienda de Jazo, Justo Sierra 2022, just off Chapultepec Nte. In a courtyard so quiet you'll forget you're in the city. Live piano daily 3-6pm; at all other times, Lionel Richie et al. are piped in. Meat and fish entrees 12,000-18,000 pesos. Open Mon.-Sat. 1-8pm.

Las Margaritas, López Cotilla 1477, just west of Chapultepec. The best vegetarian food in town. Middle-eastern motif. Menu includes 13 salads and 19 sandwiches, priced under 12,000 pesos. Open Mon.-Sat. 8:30am-9pm, Sun. 8:30am-6pm.

Mariscos La Cabaña, López Cotilla 1394, across from the U.S. Consulate. Ordinary seafood but you may catch some down-home English as consular employees often eat here. Entrees 4000-15,000 pesos. Open daily 6:30am-4pm.

Bazar de la Salud, López Cotilla 1295, 1 block east of U.S. Consulate. Decent food and a friendly atmosphere, but no reason for a special trip. Carrot juice 2500 pesos. Open Mon.-Fri. 9am-4pm.

Los Rusitos, Chapultepec 191. An ordinary sidewalk café with above-average food. Look out for the ice pick that iced Trotsky. Mexican entrees 8000-10,000 pesos. Open Mon.-Fri. 8am-5:30pm, Sat. 8am-3:30pm.

Café y Arte, Chapultepec 209 at Libertad. Coffees and desserts. A great place to revive your sleepy bones after siesta; the Angel's Kiss (Kahlua, coffee, and eggnog) will add some zip to your day for 2800 pesos. Open daily 10am-2pm and 5-10pm.

Recco, Libertad 1973, just off Chapultepec. Delicious food in an elegant milieu; those in T-shirts or shorts will feel underdressed. Seafood fettucine 17,500 pesos. Entrees 17,000-30,000 pesos. Open daily 1-11:30pm.

La Trattoria, Niños Héroes (tel. 22-18-17), near López Mateos. Call for reservations or face the prospect of a long wait. Probably the most popular Italian restaurant in Jalisco. Pasta 9000-11,000 pesos. Open Mon.-Sat. 1pm-midnight, Sun. 1-8pm.

Guadalajara Grill, López Mateos 3711 Sur, at Conchita. Sign in front reads "We don't understand English, but we promise not to laugh at your Spanish." Margaritas (3500 pesos) don't get any better than this. Live and loud *norteña* and *mariachi* music around the clock. A mix of well-dressed Muppies (Mexican Urban Professionals) and tourists decked in shorts and T-shirts. BBQ ribs, shrimp, and steak served alongside Mexican *antojitos* and mango crepes. Entrees 6000-18,000 pesos. Open Mon.-Sat. 1:30pm-midnight, Sun. 1:30-5pm.

Sights

Guadalajara's museums are the best introduction to Mexican culture and history outside Mexico City. Many visitors also take pleasure in strolling the streets, conversing in cafés, riding through town in a horse-drawn carriage (35,000 pesos), or hitting local hangouts in the evening.

Downtown

The four plazas in downtown Guadalajara provide a wide-open refuge from the otherwise packed streets. The spacious **Plaza de la Liberación,** with its large, bubbling fountain, is surrounded by the cathedral, Museo Regional, Palacio de Gobierno, and Teatro Degollado.

The **Palacio de Gobierno,** built in 1774 on the plaza's south side, is a Churrigueresque and Neoclassical building graced by yet another mural by Orozco. Here the artist used the surface of the stairwell ingeniously: the sight of Hidalgo's feverish eyes looking down from the wall strikes fear in the heart of many an unsuspecting visitor. (Open Mon.-Sat. 9am-3pm and 6-9pm.)

The imposing **cathedral** faces the Teatro Degollado across Pl. de la Liberación. Begun in 1558 and completed 60 years later, this edifice whirls in a vertigo of architectural styles. An 1848 earthquake destroyed the original towers, and overambitious architects replaced them with much too tall ones. Fernando VII of Spain donated the eleven richly ornamented altars in appreciation of Guadalajara's help during the Napoleonic Wars. One of the remaining original altars is dedicated to Our Lady of the Roses; it is this altar, and not the botanical beauties, that gave Guadalajara its nickname, "City of Roses." To the left of the main altar lies St. Inocencia Mártir, a young girl whose remains were brought to the church from the Roman catacombs. A *fiesta* in her honor takes place on the first Sunday after the 14th of November.

The doors to the sacristy are usually, but one of the attendants will likely let you in. A sign warns women not to enter wearing shorts or other revealing clothes; one should assume that this restriction applies to men as well. Inside the sacristy rests the *Assumption of the Virgin,* by famed 17th-century painter Bertolemé Murillo. The towers, known as the "cornucopias," are being renovated. Ask if you can make the 60-meter climb for the best view in town. (Church open Mon.-Sat. 8am-8pm; tourists unwelcome on Sunday.) On the cathedral's west side lies the arboreal **Plaza de los Laureles;** on the north, the **Plaza de los Mártires** commemorates *tapatíos* who died in various wars.

A building constructed in 1696 on the north side of the Pl. de la Liberación houses the **Museo Regional de Guadalajara.** Also known as the Museo del Estado de Jalisco, Liceo, e Hidalgo, this museum chronicles the history of western Mexico. The first floor is devoted to the country's pre-Hispanic development and includes meteorites, woolly mammoth bones, metalwork, petrified Aerobies, jewels, and some Aztec art depicting the Spanish Conquest. Collections of colonial art, modern paintings, and an exhibit about the history of the Revolution occupy the second floor. (Open Tues.-Sun. 9am-3:45pm. Admission 10,000 pesos, students free. Free to all on Sundays. Movies, plays, and lectures in the museum auditorium. Call 14-99-57 for information.)

Attend the Ballet Folklórico on Sunday mornings to get a good look at the **Teatro Degollado,** a Neoclassical structure on the Pl. de la Liberación's east end. The interior features gold and red balconies, a sculpted allegory of the seven muses on the pediment, and Gerardo Suárez's depiction of Dante's *Divine Comedy* on the ceiling. You can visit any time when there is no performance scheduled (tel. 13-11-15).

The **Plazuela de los Mariachis** lies on the south side of San Juan de Dios, the church with the blue neon cross at Independencia and Javier Mina. The "plazuela" is really a glorified alley, lined with bars and budget restaurants where flashy *mariachis* hustle inebriated *gringos.* As soon as you sit down, someone will try to separate you from 7500 pesos for a song. The daily festivities continue late into the night.

If you've heard the promotional hoopla for the **Mercado Libertad,** at Javier Mina and Independencia, you might be disappointed by reality. Mexico's largest daily market offers three floors of surprisingly low-quality knicknacks, blankets, fresh bananas, and home-cooked treats similar to those found in any border town; the prices here are much lower and the shopkeepers less frenzied, however, making it possible to browse in relative tranquility. Just don't eat here—most of the food has been sitting out all day and may not be clean. (Open daily 9am-8pm, but some merchants do not open on Sun.) A more authentic and fascinating market is **El Baratillo** on Javier Mina, approximately 15 blocks east of Mercado Libertad. El Baratillo lasts all day Sunday and sometimes stretches for 30 or 40 blocks. Everything imaginable is peddled here, from hot tamales to houses. From M. Libertad, walk two blocks to Gigantes and catch bus #37 or 38 heading east.

From the Pl. Tapatía, you can see the dome of the **Hospicio Cabañas** at the corner of Hospicio and Cabañas, 3 blocks east of Independencia. An orphanage until recently, art classes are now given in this 190-year-old building by the Instituto Cultural de Cabañas. It was here that Padre Hidalgo signed his proclamation against slavery in 1811. In the main chapel, Orozco painted a series of murals in 1938-39, which some regard as his best work; the dome holds Orozco's frightening rendition of the Four Riders of the Apocalypse. *Espejos* (mirrors) are available free for those who don't want to strain their necks, or you can lie down on one of the many benches set up for reclined viewing. The hospicio also houses a collection of Orozco drawings and lithographs recently moved from his home in west Guadalajara, as well as other rotating exhibits. (Open Tues.-Sat. 10:30am-6pm. Admission 500 pesos.)

South

Almost everything inside the **Casa de las Artesanías de Jalisco** on González Gallo (the street which bisects Parque Agua Azul) is for sale. Pottery, jewelry, furniture, and clothing cost more here than they do on the back roads, but the quality is extraordinary. (Open Mon.-Fri. 10am-7pm, Sat. 10am-4pm, Sun. 10am-2pm.)

A large, fenced-in tract of woods and gardens with numerous fountains and statues, **Parque Agua Azul** provides a haven for those tired of the noise of south Guadalajara. (Open daily 8am-7pm. Admission 500 pesos.) The **Museo Arqueológico del Occidente,** at Pl. Juárez west of Parque Agua Azul, is smaller than the regional museum downtown, but still preserves a fine collection of figurines and tools from the states of Jalisco, Nayarit, Colima, Michoacán, Guerrero, Sinaloa, and Guanajuato. (Open daily 10am-noon and 4-7pm. Admission 200 pesos.)

West

The University of Guadalajara, founded in 1791, is one of Latin America's best. Classrooms are scattered throughout the city, and the main administrative buildings line López Cotilla and Tolsá. For a good view of the city, take the elevator to the 12th floor of the university's skyscraper on Juárez.

Guadalajara's **Zona Rosa,** the upper-class shopping district, centers on Chapultepec, west of the university. Cultural activity in the city's wealthier areas focuses on the **Plaza del Arte,** 1 block south on Chapultepec from its intersection with Niños Héroes. Local artists strut their stuff on a rotating basis in the plaza's **Centro de Arte Moderno.** (Open daily 8am-2pm and 4-7pm.) The **Galería Municipal,** on the Pl. del Arte, also showcases local painters. Stand-up comedy and performance art periodically enliven the premises. Watch for notices on the blackboard at the Departamento de Bellas Artes, in the Ex-Convento del Carmen.

The **Tequila Sauza Bottling Plant,** Vallarta 3273 (tel. 47-66-74), on the outskirts of Guadalajara, is surely a shrine for serious tequila fans. Pay homage here to the golden elixir of life. (Free tours Mon.-Fri. 10am-noon. Take the "Par Vial" bus west to the end of the line then catch *combi* #130 in front of the Hotel Fiesta Americana. The plant is just before the overpass. Bus #45 will take you back into town.)

Entertainment

This city never sleeps, and nighttime revelers crowd the streets in many spots. Take a taxi home when your evening finally ends.

The **Ballet Folklórico** has toured the world, entertaining audiences with stage antics and the famed Mexican hat dance. There are two troupes in Guadalajara, one affiliated with the University of Guadalajara and the other with the state of Jalisco. The former, reputedly better, performs in the Teatro Degollado on Sunday at 10am (followed by the **state philharmonic orchestra** at noon). Tickets (25,000-45,000 pesos) are sold the day before the show at the Teatro Degollado ticket office (open daily 9:30am-5:30pm). Spend the extra pesos for a front seat, and arrive a half-hour before the show because seats are not reserved within sections, and performances nearly always sell out. The state troupe performs Wednesdays at 8:30pm in the theater of the Hospicio Cabañas (tickets 15,000 pesos). Call 17-44-40 (ext. 22) for more information.

University facilities, scattered throughout the city, have created a market for high culture on a low budget. The **Departamento de Bellas Artes,** in the Ex-Convento del Carmen, Juárez 638, coordinates activities at a large number of stages, auditoriums, and movie screens across the city. The best source of information on cultural events is the blackboard in front of the Ex-Convento, which lists each day's attractions.

The two principal dramatic stages are the **Teatro de Guadalajara** and the **Teatro Experimental** (tel. 19-37-70), across the street from each other at Pl. Juárez, on the west side of Parque Agua Azul. While the works at the Experimental can be recommended only for those proficient in Spanish, the program at the Teatro de Guadalajara includes more easily understood comic and popular works.

The bandstand next to the cathedral hosts state orchestra concerts Sunday afternoon and band concerts on Thursday at 7pm.

The **Instituto Cultural Cabañas** presents live music on an open-air stage in the Hospicio Cabañas at least once a week (tickets 15,000 pesos, students 12,000 pesos). Drop by the Hospicio Cabañas ticket counter (see Sights above), or look for flyers with the Cabañas insignia (a building with pillars) for current schedules. Each October, Guadalajara hosts a month-long festival of cultural and sporting events with fireworks and special displays representing each state in the Republic.

For Luis Buñuel retrospectives and other rare screenings, head to the cinema at Bellas Artes. The **Cine Cinematógrafo,** at Vallarta 1102 just west of the university, is a repertory film house that changes its show weekly (tickets 2500 pesos).

For live jazz, try the **Copenhagen,** at Américas and López Mateos near the statue of Columbus, or **La Hosta,** at México and Rubén Darió.

Many lively discos and bars bedeck Guadalajara. **Elipsis,** at Otero and López Mateos, is the most popular disco, attracting a wealthy Guadalajaran clientele as well as many tourists (cover 20,000 pesos). **Osiris** (10,000 pesos), at Jardines de los Arcos near Lázaro Cárdenas, receives rave reviews from locals. It's private, but if you convince the bouncers of your foreign origin (it shouldn't be hard), they'll let you in. Another popular but less acclaimed disco is **Ciros,** in the Pl. del Sol shopping complex. The Osiris and Ciros are packed on Friday and Saturday night. (Cover at both 10,000 pesos.) All places are best reached by taxi, and any driver should know the names. **Terraza del Oasis,** Hidalgo 436, occasionally has live bands, and **Las Yardas,** Juárez 37, serves drinks under the only *palapa* roof in the city.

Gay men support more nightlife here than in any other city outside the Federal District. The upscale Zona Rosa along Chapultepec is a favorite gathering place. The best-known gay disco is **Unicornio,** López Mateos. Other hangouts include **S.O.S.,** La Paz 1413 at Escoza, which incredibly vibrant drag shows; and **Monica's,** Alvaro Obregón 1713, popular with the young crowd.

People of all sexual orientations enjoy the **Jesse James,** Ramos Millan 955, a honky tonk complete with country-and-western music. A mixed crowd also frequents **Chivas López Cotilla** and **Degollado.**

Sports

Bullfights take place in the Pl. de Toros almost every Sunday from October to April. Posters throughout the city tout each contest. The bullring is at Nuevo Progreso on the northern end of Independencia. Take bus #45 or 62 (300 pesos) north. The ticket and information office is at Morelos 229 (tel. 13-55-58). Guadalajara also features **charros** (rodeos), held in Parque Agua Azul every Sunday.

Soccer games draw the biggest crowds in this city. The *Chivas,* a professional team, is the crowd favorite and a powerful contender for the national championship each season. Don't even think about pronouncing the name of the team's arch-rival from Mexico City (the *Pumas)* or you might find yourself engulfed in a riot. Matches are held from September through May in Jalisco Stadium, at the University of Guadalajara and at the Universidad Autónoma. Guadalajara also supports several other teams. Check the paper or ask the nearest fan for more details.

Ice skating is possible year-round at the Hyatt Regency on Pl. del Sol (tel. 22-59-32). You can rent skates for around 10,000 pesos. (Open Mon.-Thurs. 5-7pm and 7:30-9pm, Fri.-Sun. 4:15-6:15pm and 8:15-9:45pm.)

Public swimming pools in Guadalajara are filthy. If you've got to get wet, try one of the private sports clubs (at least 10,000 pesos), but many no longer permit non-members. People have been known to sneak in to the Hyatt's pool. The easiest option may be an extended shower at your hotel.

Near Guadalajara

Excursions from Guadalajara are prime opportunities for souvenir-hunting. East of the city, Tlaquepaque and Tonalá peddle high-priced artisanry; to the north Zapopan *indígena* craftwork sells at the Casa de Artesanías de los Huichol; on the shores of Laguna Chapala, 40km to the south, the villages of Chapala, Ajijic, and Jopotlán welcome tourist excursions and an expanding population of North American retirees.

Had it with shopping? Head to **Parque Mirador,** at the northern end of Independencia. The park's main attraction is its proximity to the 670-meter gorge of the Río Santiago, where a dozen waterfalls cascade over the cliffs during the rainy season. Refreshment stands sell fruit and drinks to the gaping onlookers. (Open daily 9am-7:30pm. Admission 400 pesos. Take bus "Parque Mirador" north along Independencia.)

Northwest of the city is the town of **Zapopan,** site of the **Basílica de la Virgen de Zapopan,** a giant edifice erected in the 16th century to commemorate a peasant's vision. The walls of the church are hung with many decades' worth of *ex-votos,* small paintings on sheet metal honoring the Virgin's intervention in diseases and accidents. Pope John Paul II visited the shrine in 1979, and a statue of him holding hands with a beaming *campesino* boy now stands in the courtyard in front of the church. *Dios* aside, the **Casa de Artesanías de los Huichol,** a museum and crafts market for Huichol handwork, remains Zapopan's chief point of interest. Clothing, *ojos de dios* (god's eyes), and *makrames,* colorful designs of yarn on wood, are sold at bargain prices. To get there, catch the #275 bus on the Av. 16 de Septiembre and de-bus at the big church. (Open Mon.-Fri. 10am-1:30pm and 3:30-6pm. Free.)

Shoppers who don't mind riding a bus for a while to find a beautiful area shouldn't miss Tlaquepaque (TLA-kay-pa-kay). Pick up the #124 or 275 bus ("Nueva Central") on the corner of 16 de Septiembre and Madero. The ride is slow and rather tedious, but the 300-peso price beats the 10,000 pesos it takes to hire a taxi.

Those who don't trust their fiscal willpower had better stay away from central Tlaquepaque, called El Parían; there are more shops and enticing goods on which to unload needed pesos than you can shake a stick at.

If you decide that you need two days to see all of Tlaquepaque's jewelry, handicrafts, clothing, leather, and hand-blown glass, then plan on staying at the **Posada en el Parían,** Independencia 74 (tel. 35-21-89). Fortunately this small hotel is fairly nice, as there is no other budget hotel in town. The generous owner will let up to three people sleep in the fairly clean rooms for only 20,000 pesos. The *posada* is located on the El Parían, a huge block of restaurants. A bandstand in the center of the block hosts *mariachi* music Monday and Wednesday through Sunday from 3:30 to 9:30pm. Bands will perform at your table for a hefty 25,000 pesos.

There are several restaurants from which to choose in Tlaquepaque; walk around the square and peruse the menus. One fine choice is the **Salon Imperial,** where a quarter chicken goes for 11,500 pesos. That old boring dish, pig skin in vinegar, costs a mere 5000 pesos. (Open daily 10am-1am.) Other places in the Parían with similar hours include **Moctezuma, Beto's, Paco's,** and **Monterrey.**

For something tangible to take back from Guadalajara, Tlaquepaque is a good place to start looking. Just don't visit on Sunday, when almost every shop closes its doors. One place you shouldn't miss is **Sergio Bustamente's,** Independencia 236. His papier-mâché is beautiful enough to view and drool over if you can't afford it. Fish motifs prevail. Another fun if touristy spot (few Mexicans tote camcorders) is **La Roja de Cristal,** Independencia 252, where artisans blow glass by hand Monday through Friday 9:30am to 2:30pm and Saturday 9:30am to 12:30pm. Their goods are then sold Monday through Saturday from 10am to 7pm. Other interesting regional art, including a coven of ceramics, resides at the **Museo Regional de las Cerámicas y los Artes Populares de Jalisco.** Some pieces are for sale. (Open Mon.-Sat. 10am-4pm, Sun. 10am-1pm. Free.)

When you want to return downtown, hop on a #275 bus at the corner of Niños and Independencia. You need only have saved 300 pesos to return downtown by bus or *combi*.

Tonalá is a scaled-down version of Tlaquepaque, mainly because it's harder to reach. Visit Tonalá on Thursday or Sunday, when the town briefly awakens from its near-perpetual siesta. Tonalá specializes in inexpensive, conservatively decorated ceramics. While Tlaquepaque offers greater variety, Tonalá has made fewer concessions to the tourist industry and retains more of its natural charm. You can still find *indígena* women weaving beautiful, multi-colored dolls, and patient ceramics merchants painting personalized messages onto their products. In Tonalá, people take the time to converse with you without making you feel obligated to purchase something.

Tonalá has the added benefit of letting you visit an authentic rural village while allowing you the safety of a long *combi*-shaped lifeline back to the more comfortably urban Guadalajara. Bus #103 and 104, which run through downtown Guadalajara along Moreno, are the best way to reach Tonalá.

Forty km south of Guadalajara lies **Lago de Chapala,** Mexico's second largest lake. The towns of **Chapala, Ajijic,** and **Jocotepec** along the northern shore of the lake present a harmonious mix of Mexican tourists, North American retirees, artists, and would-be artists from around the world. While living in Ajijic in the 1940s before industrial development rendered swimming in the lake impossible, D.H. Lawrence wrote *The Plumed Serpent*. Stark mountains still haunt the lake's opposite shore, keeping the setting beautiful. English-speakers will feel at home in Chapala and Ajijic: there are so many expatriates around that half of the signs are in English and the other half are bilingual.

You can get to Chapala from the Antigua bus station (every ½ hr., 5200 pesos round-trip). There are two acceptable options for anyone wishing to stay near the lake. In Chapala, the **Hotel Nido,** Madero 202 (tel. 521-16), has a nice courtyard with a restaurant and clean, ordinary rooms. (Singles 28,000 pesos. Doubles with 1 bed 36,000 pesos, with 2 beds 45,000 pesos.) In nearby Ajijic, the **Posada Ajijic** is run by a Canadian couple who will give you good sightseeing advice. The rooms are clean and the bathrooms are a joy. (Singles 33,000 pesos. Doubles with 1 bed 45,000 pesos, with 2 beds 54,000 pesos.)

For food try **Beto's,** right next to the Hotel Nido. The food is generally decent, and the pace relaxed: entrees 8000-14,000 pesos. Beer is by far the most popular item on the menu, but the chilly maragaritas go down easy as well. For a great lunch in Ajijic, try **Danny's,** located just off the highway. Great burgers, *lonches,* and sandwiches run from 4000-7000 pesos. (Open Mon.-Sat. 8am-5pm, Sun. 8am-1pm.)

Chapala can be reached from the Nueva Central bus station; the Guadalajara-Chapala line is in terminal #5 (3600 pesos round-trip). The bus (600 pesos) that leaves from the corner of Madero and de Velasco in Chapala will drop you off in Ajijic. The crowds from Guadalajara hit Chapala mostly on the weekends; if you want the place to yourself, go during the week. Tours are also available; call Panoramex (tel. 10-51-09).

Puerto Vallarta

In 1956, tabloid headlines touted Puerto Vallarta as an unspoiled paradise. While on location shooting *Night of the Iguana,* Richard Burton and Elizabeth Taylor had a torrid affair, leaving tourists and moviegoers with an impression of Puerto Vallarta as the world headquarters of sensuality. Back then, neither highway nor telephone wire connected it to the outside world; since that time, Puerto Vallarta has undergone a radical facelift. Thirty-five years and millions of dollars later, Puerto Vallarta is a world-class resort with stunningly groomed beaches, luxurious hotels, and gorgeous mansions.

The local economy is wholly dependent on tourism. The dollars sunk into Puerto Vallarta have rendered it quaint—white stucco, red ceramic tile, and cobblestones fill every square inch—but the effect rubs both ways. Some find that a graceful ambience prevails; others find it a bit like Mexican Disneyland.

Those who come to "Party Vallarty" in search of a unique cultural experience will probably go insane: the town is a huge mall, and the main activity is, of course, shopping. If you left your electronic foot massager at home, don't fret; most *tiendas* sell three models. Happy hunting and *Caveat Emptor.*

Orientation

Running west to the shore, the **Río Cuale** bisects Puerto Vallarta before emptying into the ocean. The southern half of town maintains a more authentic Mexican identity, and contains virtually all the cheap hotels, best beaches, budget restaurants, and frantic dance clubs. The stodgy area north of the river could be mistaken by its looks and its clientele for any U.S. beach resort, but it houses nearly all of the city's tourist services.

The main streets in the southern half are **Insurgentes** and **Vallarta,** which run north-south 2 blocks apart, and **Lázaro Cárdenas,** which runs east-west. A park 2 blocks south of the western end of Lázaro Cárdenas serves as a bus and *combi* terminal; you'll find it at the northern end of Olas Altas and Playa de los Muertos, the waterfront area. Insurgentes and Vallarta run north from Lázaro Cárdenas to the two bridges that link the south and north sections.

The main streets in the north are **Morelos,** the continuation of Vallarta, and **Juárez,** 1 block east. Four blocks north of the Vallarta bridge is the **Plaza Mayor,** whose cathedral, with its crown of open metalwork, serves as a good landmark. The ritzy waterfront between the Pl. Mayor and 31 de Octubre, called the **Malecón,** contains overpriced restaurants and cheesy T-shirt shops. North of the Malecón, Morelos becomes Perú and runs through a working-class neighborhood before joining the coastal highway. North along the highway lie the airport, the marina, and the ferry terminal.

A fleet of cab drivers is eager to help you navigate this straightforward city. They charge about 6000 pesos to travel between the Playa de los Muertos and the entrance to the highway. It's cheaper to master the municipal bus system, which operates daily from 6am to 10:30pm. Buses cost 350 pesos, *combis* 300-600 pesos. All northbound buses and *combis* originate at the park on Olas Altas and run up Lázaro Cárdenas to Insurgentes, across the Insurgentes Bridge, west on Libertad a few blocks, north on Juárez, and onto the highway.

Practical Information

Tourist Office: In the Presidencia Municipal (tel. 202-42), on the northern side of the Pl. Mayor. Enter on Juárez. Centrally located and loaded with maps and other information. Excellent English spoken. Open Mon.-Fri. 8:30am-8pm, Sat. 9am-1pm. Closed holidays (except Easter and New Year's).

U.S. Consulate: Miramar at Libertad (tel. 200-69), just north of the Río Cuale. Open Mon.-Fri. 9am-1pm.

Currency Exchange: Several large banks around the Pl. Mayor change currency, but many only between 9 and 11am. **Banca Promex,** Juárez 386, changes money Mon.-Fri. 9:30am-12:30pm. *Casas de cambio* have worse rates but are open longer, typically Mon.-Sat. 9am-2pm and 4-8pm.

American Express: Centro Comercial Villa Vallarta (tel. 268-77), a few blocks north of the Sheraton. They hold mail for 30 days, and have a well-equipped travel agency with English-speaking clerks. Open Mon.-Fri. 9am-6pm, Sat. 9am-1pm. Open for check cashing Mon.-Fri. 9am-2:30pm and 4-5pm.

Post Office: Morelos 444 (tel. 237-02), at Mina 2 blocks north of the Pl. Mayor. Lista de Correos. Open Mon.-Fri. 8am-7pm, Sat.-Sun. 9am-noon. **Postal Code:** 48300.

Telephones: Long-distance phones at **Tres Estrellas de Oro,** Insurgentes 210. Open Mon.-Fri. 9am-3pm and 5-10pm. Also at Juárez 124, just north of the Río Cuale. Collect calls 6000 pesos. Open Mon.-Fri. 9am-2pm and 4-8pm, Sat. 9am-6pm. **Telephone Code:** 322.

Telegrams: Hidalgo 569 (tel. 202-12), near Corona. Open Mon.-Fri. 8am-1pm and 3-7pm, Sat. 8am-1pm.

Airport: 8km north of town via the coastal highway. Buses labeled "Ixtapa" or "Juntas" pass the airport; you can catch either on Lázaro Cárdenas or Insurgentes 6am-10:30pm. Taxis to the airport cost 6000 pesos. **Aeroméxico,** at the airport (tel. 210-55), **Mexicana,** Juárez 202 (tel. 250-00), and other airlines have frequent flights to: Guadalajara (131,500 pesos); Mexico City (235,000 pesos); Los Angeles (US$178.50); and New York (US$345.50).

Bus Station: There is no central bus station in Puerto Vallarta, but all major bus lines have stations within ½ block of Madero and Insurgentes, except **Transportes del Pacífico,** 2 blocks south at Insurgentes 282. Nearly all bus lines have similar prices and destinations. **Transportes del Norte de Sonora,** on Madero ½ block west of Insurgentes, serves the most cities, including: Tepic (at 10:45am, 3½ hr., 8200 pesos); Guadalajara (at 3:30, 11, and 11:45pm, 6½ hr., 17,500 pesos); and Mexico City (at 3:30pm, 15 hr., 41,000 pesos). **Tres Estrellas de Oro,** Insurgentes 210 (tel. 210-19), sends buses to Colima (at 9am, 6 hr., 13,000 pesos) and Manzanillo (at 9am, 5 hr., 18,000 pesos).

Ferry: Terminal Maritima, 4½ km north of town off the coastal highway. The government has indefinitely suspended all long-distance ferry service to and from Puerto Vallarta. The terminal now launches only bay cruises, and nobody has a clue about the fate of the long-distance service. If you desire to be Baja-bound, call the terminal at 204-76 to check, but don't get your hopes up. To reach the terminal, take bus #12; catch it on Lázaro Cárdenas or Insurgentes (see Getting Around). Cab fare to the terminal is 8000 pesos.

English Bookstore: Most timely selection in **Super Mercado Gutiérrez Rizo** (known as "GR"), at Constitución and Serdán (books 18,000-25,000 pesos). Open daily 6:30am-10pm. Cheaper, used books in a nameless store at Olas Altas 370. Open daily 8am-11pm.

Laundromats: Delfines Lavandería, Madero 357. 3kg load 8000 pesos. Takes 2 hr. Open Mon.-Fri. 8am-2pm and 4-8pm, Sat. 8am-4pm. **Lavandería Elsa,** Olas Altas 385 (tel. 234-65). Pay per article (shirts 1000 pesos, pants 1000 pesos). Open Mon.-Sat. 8am-2pm and 3-7pm.

Pharmacy: Farmacia CMQ, Basilio Badillo 367, ½ block inland from Insurgentes. Open daily 7am-11pm.

Hospital: CMQ Hospital, Basilio Badillo 365 (tel. 235-72). English spoken. Open 24 hr.

Police: Iturbide at Morelos (tel. 201-23 or 216-10).

Accommodations and Camping

Puerto Vallarta's sleeping options conveniently queue up in ascending economic order from the beach south of town (as free as the waves) to the Sheraton in the north. The best cheap hotels are south of the Río Cuale, on or near Madero. These places are more expensive than the average Mexican budget establishment, but are also slightly nicer. Clean rooms and pleasant courtyards are standard.

In general, hotels do not accept unpaid reservations. Go room-hunting between 10am and noon for prime spots because most hotels fill by midday. Larger hotels don't mind storing even the grungiest of backpacks for the day, usually free of charge.

Hotel Yasmin, Basilio Badillo 168 (tel. 200-87), 1 block from the beach. A verdant courtyard leads to clean, airy rooms with fans, desks, and spotless bathrooms. 35,000 pesos per room.

Hotel Villa del Mar, Madero 440 (tel. 207-85), 2 blocks east of Insurgentes. Best of the rest, if farther from the water. Clean rooms cooled by strong fans, and bathrooms warmed by hot water. The yellow courtyard and elegant lobby make good hangouts. All this, plus no bugs. Singles 28,000 pesos. Doubles 35,000 pesos.

Hotel Azteca, Madero 473 (tel. 227-50). Huge wooden key chains will probably keep you afloat if the need arises. Rooms sport wicked oyster shell ashtrays. Singles 26,000 pesos. Doubles 32,000 pesos.

Hotel Analiz, Madero 429 (tel. 217-57). White walls with orange trim outside match the bright orange bedspreads which may fluoresce at night. Weeny bathrooms. Singles 28,000 pesos. Doubles 35,000 pesos.

Hotel Lina, Madero 376 (tel. 216-61). No screens on the windows, and harsh fluorescent lighting is an interior decorator's worst nightmare. Not unlike a hospital room. Clean bathrooms. Singles 26,000 pesos. Doubles 32,000 pesos.

Hospedaje Hortencia, Madero 428 (tel. 224-86). Grand white rooms with lime-green tiled bathrooms are opened by a key on a sea-horse chain. Fans, desks—even chairs on the balconies. Singles 31,000 pesos. Doubles 39,000 pesos.

Hotel Cartagena, Madero 428. Some fans don't work but the bathrooms are big, blue, and clean. As a whole, the rooms could comprise a decent art gallery. Singles 26,000 pesos. Doubles 32,000 pesos.

Hotel Posada Don Miguel, Insurgentes 332 (tel. 245-40). The lobby is immaculate and the rooms are huge. After a cool dip in the pool, a hot-water shower awaits. Rates rise about 30% for the winter season. Singles 35,000 pesos. Doubles 50,000 pesos.

Posada El Real, Madero 285 (tel. 205-87). A bare concrete tunnel leads to dark rooms without screens, but rooms are clean and the owner is friendly. Singles 25,000 pesos. Doubles 35,000 pesos.

Hotel Posada Roger, Basilio Badillo 237 (tel. 206-39). Sumptuous courtyard has more flowers than the entire city of Guadalajara, and pool sparkles like a diamond in the sun. Rooms no larger than in most cheaper places. Brick ceilings try to impress. Singles 45,000 pesos. Doubles 55,000 pesos.

Hotel Belmar, Insurgentes 161 (tel. 205-72). Strange fabric mobile hanging in the main lobby courtyard has puzzled travelers for years. The sink is outside the bath, but the rest of the room is standard, with a bed and small desk. Singles 35,000 pesos. Doubles 55,000 pesos.

Hotel Central, Juárez 170 (tel. 249-66). Nothing attractive except the price and location. The bathrooms are grimy and the paint is peeling like a 3rd-degree sunburn. Singles 15,000 pesos. Doubles 23,000 pesos.

Tacho's Trailer Park is on the highway en route to Pitillal, a village 2km north of town. Head north toward the airport on bus #12 ("Pitillal"), which will turn right at the sign for Pitillal about 1km from Puerto Vallarta.

Officially, Puerto Vallarta frowns on shiftless beach bums, but most travelers encounter no problems. Even the local dogs are friendly. Some beachfront clubs have night guards, who often cast a protective eye on campers if you request their permission before bedding down. Many people dig into the sand behind the Hotel Los Arcos or the Castle Pelicanos, which is government property, or the open space between the John Newcombe tennis courts and the Sheraton.

Food

Puerto Vallarta's Malecón specializes in French and North American cuisine and corners the market on superficial atmosphere. Cheaper, down-home places are numerous on the south side, near Insurgentes, and in the market on the north side, where Insurgentes crosses Río Cuale. The market is open Monday through Saturday from 8am to 10pm. Super Mercado Gutiérrez Rico ("GR"), at Constitución and Serdán, provides a huge array of foodstuffs (open daily 6:30am-10pm). Many taco and quesadilla stands prosper south of the river, near the cheap hotels.

South

Los Parados, Insurgentes 203, at Madero. Fast food and plenty of atmosphere. The grill-master clones tostadas (1000 pesos) at lightning speed: Order sextuplets for a filling meal. Pay first, snag a drink, and grab a seat at the counter. Open daily 10am-1am.

El Dorado, on Pulpito, at the beach. Great seafood 21,000-35,000 pesos. Jumbo shrimp 35,000 pesos. More affordable is the "Chick Sandwich" at 8500 pesos. *Mariachis* provide entertainment and the beer comes in chilled mugs. Open daily 8am-9:30pm.

Le Gourmet, Serdán 242, in the Hotel Posada Río Cuale at Vallarta, set around the hotel pool. If this is gourmet, Taco Bell is the Platonic ideal. The dinner entrees hover around 30,000 pesos, but good chicken tacos cost only 9000 pesos. Poolside sights include a huge inflatible *purple cow.* Open daily 8am-midnight.

North

Me Gusta, Domínguez 128, just east of Díaz Ordaz. This open-air spot pleases all. Beer comes in enormous ceramic mugs and the burgers are juicy half-pounders. Bacon burger 16,000 pesos. Sweeping view of the pelicans swooping over the ocean. Open daily 9am-10:30pm.

Restaurant Villa Vallarta, Morelos 478, just north of Mina on the 3rd floor. Good food at reasonable prices, no mean feat in this part of town, but the reason to chow here is the stunning bay view. Breakfast (2 eggs, ham, beans, rice, tortillas) 9000 pesos, lunch and dinner entrees from 10,000 pesos. Chicken *mole poblana* 12,500 pesos. Open daily 9am-10pm.

Pizza Nova, Díaz Ordaz 674. Don't expect the pizza to taste authentically Italian, but judging by the tourist-dominated crowd, it comes pretty close. Small "Pizza Le Mexicana" 22,000 pesos. Open daily noon-midnight.

El Pollo Vagabundo, México 1295, a few blocks south of the Sheraton. The sign out front—"Eggs at your election"—indicates that English-speakers are welcome, maybe even desperately needed. A local morning hangout: breakfast special 6500 pesos. Roasted half-chicken 10,000 pesos. Open daily 8am-9:30pm.

Frutilandia, Díaz Ordaz 520, on the waterfront. Serves both healthy snack food and traditional Mexican fare. Huge caged parrot lords over the tiny room. Mango juice 4000 pesos. Eggs with sausage 6500 pesos. Open daily 8am-midnight.

Helado Bing, Juárez 280, 1 block from the tourist office; another at Lázaro Cárdenas and Constitución, south of the Río Cuale. Give in to Bing's alluring candy stripes. Cool, open patio dripping with hibiscus flowers. One scoop 1800 pesos, 2 scoops 3000 pesos, sundae 4500 pesos. Order blackberry, cherry, or *cajeta* (butterscotch). Open daily 10am-10:30pm.

Sights

To get the most out of Puerto Vallarta, develop an eye for the merits of its 40km coastline. Some of the least crowded and most gorgeous beaches stretch along the coast south of town on the road to Mismaloya (see Near Puerto Vallarta). The best beach in Puerto Vallarta itself, **Playa de los Muertos** extends south from Muelle de los Muertos in the southern part of town. Named for the victims of a conflict between pirates and *indígenas,* the beach has withstood attempts to rename it a cheerier Playa del Sol. To get there, walk all the way west on Lázaro Cárdenas, and then south on Olas Altas.

Various water sports generate a lot of activity during the morning hours but trickle off by mid-afternoon. Parasailing (US$30 a shot) is particularly popular; parachutes are scattered on the beach across from the square where the *combis* leave, and their owners will descend upon you if you look even remotely interested. **Chico's Dive Shop,** Díaz Ordaz 772, rents scuba equipment for 55,000 pesos per day, and mask, snorkel, and fins for 12,000 per day. They also run boats to Los Arcos and Quimixto. (Open daily 9am-9pm.)

On the northern beach, around the Sheraton, the currency of choice is the U.S. dollar—in bulk. Parasailing is even more popular in this area (same price—US$30 per ride), and waterskiing is possible as well at US$20 per hour. The patio of the Sheraton bar allows a straight shot to the pool, but keep a very low profile; poolside guards will toss you out if they catch you because the Underhills of Room 437 have already had too many pool guests this week.

Municipal efforts to render the **Río Cuale** a cosmopolitan waterway meet with mixed success for about ¼ mi. inland, and fail completely thereafter. Walk inland along the riverbank to get an idea of the town's layout. Women alone should be careful when walking this stretch of the river, and should avoid doing so altogether after dark. **Isla Río Cuale,** between the two bridges, supports small stores selling simple baubles, bangles, and *botanas.* The **Museo del Cuale,** at the seaward end of the island, has a changing one-room exhibit. (Open Tues.-Sat. 9am-4pm, Sun. 10am-3pm. Admission 1000 pesos.) There is a tourist information booth nearby.

The river can also be reached from the north via Zaragoza, which merits a casual meander. Stairs lead up the mini-mountain beginning behind the Church of Guadalupe, breaking out amid bougainvillea and hibiscus into the wealthy Zaragoza neighborhood, known locally as **Gringo Gulch.** The prominent bridge spanning the apex of the street connects Elizabeth Taylor's humble *pied-à-terre* with Richard Burton's. Other ritzy cliff dwellings accompany Zaragoza on its descent to the river.

In the square from which *combis* leave, three-hour horse rentals go for 55,000 pesos; bargaining may work here.

Entertainment

Puerto Vallarta proffers something for everyone, whether it's a cocktail in the moonlight, or a dance through never-neverland. Most of the upscale action occurs along Díaz Ordaz on the northern waterfront, where clubs and restaurants cater to suntanned professionals holding pricey rum drinks and bopping to American Top-40 dance tracks. Down south, and at Carlos O'Brian's, the crowds of young teeny-boppers are aware of the latest New Kids' hit but not much else. Discos cater to those who can spring a 20,000-to 30,000-peso cover charge and pay 6000 pesos per beer. If you just *have* to spend a mindless evening on the town, try to get free passes from the condo hawkers who lurk around the Malecón. Most discos aren't worth visiting until 11pm or midnight; the time is well-spent drinking in cheaper bars.

Carlos O'Brian's Bar & Grill & Pawnshop, Díaz Ordaz at Pipila. O'Brian's attempts successfully to be the biggest party in town: block-long lines wrap around the building all night, waiting to enter the 3 bars, 2 dining rooms, and 1 large dance floor. There's nothing Mexican about this place except the Corona served up in buckets; by the 8-oz. bottle it costs 4500 pesos. Usually chock-full of fluffy-headed young Americans slamming lots o' Tequila Poppers. No cover. Entrees 20,000-40,000 pesos. Open daily noon-1am.

Ciro's Disco and Bar, Díaz Ordaz at Allende. A glitzy alternative for Carlos O'Brian's burnouts, who come in with free passes. Fantastic sound system and a giant video screen hang over the dance floor. Cover 20,000 pesos. No cover during Happy Hour (10-11pm). Starts hopping around midnight. Open daily 10pm-4am.

Andale, Olas Altas 425. Excellent video bar with the motto: "There's no strangers here, only people we haven't met." Teeming crowd of *norteamericanos* and Mexicans of all ages at the bar downs shots to collective shouts of "Andale!" Margaritas 5000 pesos, beer 3000 pesos. Open daily 10am-3am; most crowded 7pm-2am.

Cactus Club, Vallarta 399. Done up like a cave, complete with glowing cacti. Youngsters dominate with a few older people mixed in for texture. Corona 5000 pesos. Cover 25,000 pesos. Open daily from 10pm.

Sundance's, Lázaro Cárdenas 329. Popular with locals. Very chic furnishings. The light and sound system rivals that of Ciro's, and its dance floor is acres bigger—take your pick. Cover 20,000 pesos (includes 2 drinks). Open daily 10pm-4am.

Franzi, on Isla Río Cuale, at the foot of the Vallarta Bridge. Find a table on the shady patio, order a margarita, and listen to the jazz. Entertainment gets no mellower than this. Promotes itself as a "twilight" spot. Cheapest drinks 5000 pesos. Live music Fri.-Sun. 8-11pm.

Gay men are generally accepted in Puerto Vallarta. Lesbians, however—as in most of Mexico—meet with a less understanding reception. Two bars in Vallarta are frequented primarily by gay men.

Los Balcones, Juárez 182, on the second floor. Loads of balconies. Proud of its international clientele. Beer 5000 pesos, wine 6000 pesos. Minimum charge 7000 pesos. Happy Hour 9-10pm. Open daily 9pm-3am.

Piano Bar, Morelos 490. Dark red lights and open-air patio create a Mediterranean atmosphere. Livens up around midnight with raunchier dance music and more people. Drinks about 6000 pesos. Open daily 10:30pm-5am.

Near Puerto Vallarta

Puerto Vallarta's best beaches start a few kilometers south of town. The first two or three you come across are monopolized by resorts and condos, but they're still nicer and quieter than the ones left behind. Farther down the coast lies **Los Arcos.** Any southbound car, boat, or bus cops a view of these rock islands, hollowed out at many points by pounding waves. Similar rocks litter much of Mexico's Pacific coast, but the waves of Bahía de Banderas render these formations most impressive. The coastline here lacks sand, but it still serves as a platform from which to start the 150m swim to the inner rocks. Make sure to bring a mask or goggles—it would be a shame to miss the underwater reef. Be careful where you step; the coral is sharp enough to draw blood.

Another popular jaunt south ends at **Mismaloya,** a crescent beach recently encircled by condos. Best known as the setting of *Night of the Iguana,* the area still harbors *el set,* as well as the hotel that hosted Elizabeth Taylor, Richard Burton, and John Huston, the director. Burton starred with Eva Gardner in the film (which dramatized, in part, the origins of tourism in Mexico), but the real action took place off screen between Burton and Taylor. To reach Mismaloya, catch *combi* #2 (600 pesos) at Insurgentes and Badillo.

The last place to check out on the southern road is **Chico's Paradise,** about 5km inland from the Boca de Tomatlán. The huge and airy *palapas* of this restaurant/bar, on the boulders overlooking the waterfalls of the Tomatlán river, affords a grand view.

You may want to venture even farther out to sea to enjoy the natural environment. To do so, you must sign up with one of the ritzy cruises that leave from the marina with guides and a boatload of *gringos.* Cruises generally cost 35,000-105,000 pesos. One of the most popular daytrips is the eight-hour cruise to **Las Animas,** a remote stretch of white sand. The boat leaves the pier at 9am and returns at 5pm (105,000 pesos), allowing you several hours to bask on the isolated beach. Boats also float to the village of **Quimixto.** During the three-hour stay, you can either bake on the beach or venture through the surrounding jungle to a small waterfall and rock slides (1 hr. by foot or ½ hr. by rented mule). This full-day cruise costs 105,000 pesos per person. Both cruises include lunch. *Chico's Dive Shop* also runs scuba and snorkeling trips to Quimixto (2 per week, 8½ hr., snorkeling US$30, scuba US$52) and to Los Arcos (4 per week, 4½ hr., snorkeling US$18, scuba US$40). Prices include food and drink. More expensive booze cruises cover both routes; ask at any large hotel.

Those who take the popular boat ride to **Yelapa** soon realize that this supposedly secluded, peasant fishing village is a fraud. Yelapa's seemingly simple *palapa* huts were designed by a *norteamericano* architect whose definition of rustic encompassed interior plumbing and hot water. Daily boats for Yelapa leave from the marina north of town on the coastal highway at 9am and return at 5pm (35,000 pesos). Sunset cruises and more elaborate tours of the bay are also available.

For about four times the price of a day-cruise to Yelapa, you can rent a *palapa* there for a month. Seems a small group of North Americans has colonized the area; with waterfalls and nude bathing upstream, and poetry readings downstream, nobody's ready to leave.

If you are over 25 (in some cases 23), gainfully employed, and have a major credit card, all of the activities listed above can become significantly cheaper if you act like you're in the market for some real estate. Lots of new developments, condos, and resort facilities offer freebies to potential buyers. The most common deal is an invitation to eat a free breakfast or lunch at the resort, spend a few hours enjoying its facilities, and then buy tickets, usually at half-price, to any or all of a list of popular tours and cruises. The catch is that you have to listen to their ultra-high-pressure sales pitch, and although you place yourself under no obligation whatsoever, their speech can make the trip unpleasant. If by some fluke the salespeople overlook you, you can find them in booths on the Malecón. While you're at it, try to scrounge a few free disco passes off these rather unsavory characters.

Pitillal does not appear on any list of hotel-organized daytrips because there's nothing much to do in this *pueblito* 2km north of Puerto Vallarta. But if being surrounded by tourists jangles your nerves, Pitillal is a relatively easy escape to a Mexico where Spanish is the language of choice. You can catch the bus labeled "Pitillal" along Juárez. The bus arrives at the edge of the Pl. Mayor, where friendly games of soccer and volleyball occur around a raised gazebo, the plaza's centerpiece. The major church is still under construction, but at dusk its bell rings vigorously for the daily *paseo*. Many residents of Pitillal's small valley work in Puerto Vallarta, and the result is an unusually high standard of living for a small Mexican village.

Hitching is fairly easy around Puerto Vallarta, but unaccompanied women should use other forms of transportation. In general, women traveling alone should be careful in this region. Always know exactly where you're going and how you're going to get there and back; never depend on finding a ride once you are far from your starting point. Should you find yourself stranded, walk quickly in the direction of the nearest bus stop or village, looking confident and purposeful, instead of standing around hoping to arouse the humanitarian instincts of some passerby.

Jalisco Coast

North of the Bahía de Navidad, the highway swings toward the sea to reach the **Bahía Tenacatita**, fringed with idyllic beaches. The larger villages of **Tenacatita** and **La Manzanilla** offer a stray hotel or two, but most visitors prefer camping on the beach. Farther north, on the **Costa Careyes**, budget travelers are as rare a species as the *careyes* (turtles) for which the area is named. Steep cliffs and rocky shoals render most of the "Turtle Coast" inaccessible, and what little isn't might as well be. Club Med in one secluded cove, and a newly spawned hotel-and-condo complex in the next are both prohibitively expensive. If you wish to exercise (discreetly) your right to public beach, share the sand in front of the **Hotel Careyes** with its well-to-do Mexican clientele. A tame pelican and a beautiful pool should satisfy the fussiest of moochers. Buses travel all along this coast—just tell the driver where you want to hop off.

The **Bahía Chamela** seems to have been completely overlooked by the tourist circuit. The lack of development is no fluke; ruthless resort magnates have met their match in the Mexican armed forces, who control most of the beach and have squelched almost all plans for development in the area. Large, forbidding signs label army property "off-limits," but they are flagrantly disregarded by knowing locals who use the beaches regularly. Soldiers stationed in the area seem to enjoy the company, and readily grant unofficial camping permits when people ask them. The military personnel may even offer advice on where best to camp, but don't pound in any stakes before requesting permission.

The beaches here are some of the coast's finest. Gradually sloping white sand meets waves whose irregular patterns result from the offshore islands. Schools of flying fish taunt cruising pelicans, and the diving birds provide entertainment until the sunset assumes that role. Well-marked access roads lead to the local favorites, **Playas Pérula, La Fortuna,** and **Chamela.**

Hitching conditions along the highway are excellent during the day. Hitching to a specific beach is easiest if you travel with the flow of people (beachward at dawn, homeward at dusk).

However, under no circumstances should a single traveler attempt to get to the beaches. Several local people have disappeared from this area; women should go in a group of no less than three.

Services face the highway in elusive **Chamela,** which is more a cartographical expression than a true community. A few ramshackle stores and restaurants (no more than four) cluster on the inland side of the highway near San Mateo in the middle of Chamela. The only alternative to camping is a seven-room hotel run by Señor Pío Nogales, known locally as Don Pío. The rooms, on the second floor of his house, are quainter than your average budget accommodations and include private bathrooms. Don Pío and pals congregate out front, and a stunning view of the nearby bay makes the second story charming. To find this out-of-the-way place, take the bus to San Mateo, and ask for Don Pío. (His house is 2 blocks up the dirt road on the inland side of the highway. Look on the right for the conch-studded domicile.) Two-bed rooms go for 30,000 pesos, three-bed rooms for 35,000 pesos. The chances of a vacancy are pretty good, but the house has no phone, so a trip to San Mateo should hold some suspense.

Bahía de Navidad

Guadalajara and Puerto Vallarta are well-known spots, but the third point of Jalisco's "tourist triangle" remains a hidden treasure. Poised on the north and east banks of the Bahía de Navidad, the towns of **San Patricio** and **Barra de Navidad** are best viewed as one sprawling resort.

In Mexico, a postulate of the dreaded Heisenberg Uncertainty Principle holds true; tourists can't observe a town without irrevocably altering it. Thankfully, the streets of Barra de Navidad are trodden on by few visitors, leaving intact its Mexican character, which may or may not appeal to you. Barra de Navidad may be prettier than its neighbor—its narrow, winding, and shady streets stand in contrast to San Patricio's dusty, garbage-strewn boulevards—and Barra has the better restaurants, but San Patricio's size makes it feel more like a real town. Cheap hotels exist in both areas, and which beach you choose is a matter of taste: San Patricio's is cleaner and usually less crowded, but Barra's has bigger waves.

Orientation

San Patricio and Barra de Navidad are 55km northwest of Manzanillo on Rte. 200, or 240km southwest of Guadalajara on Rte. 54. The towns lie 2km apart over the beach and 5km apart by highway.

San Patricio's excuse for a bus station is a low, dirt-floored, thatched-roof hut on Carranza, a few feet inland of Gómez Farías, the main drag, which runs parallel to the beach. From the bus station, turn left on Gómez Farías and walk 2 blocks to reach **López Mateos.** Another left turn takes you to the town plaza. López Mateos and **Hidalgo,** 1 block beyond, are the main cross streets heading to the ocean.

Barra de Navidad's valiant attempt at a bus stop is at Veracruz 228, on the corner of Nayarit. Veracruz runs roughly parallel to **Legazpi,** the main street that shadows the beach. Turn left on Veracruz from the bus station to get to *el centro.* After 5 blocks, Veracruz is joined by Morelos and skirts the edge of the **Laguna de Navidad.** At the extreme south end of town, Veracruz joins Legazpi and disappears on the sandbar that separates the lagoon from the ocean. Hourly buses run to and from Manzanillo (2200 pesos) and Guadalajara (13,500 pesos) daily from 7:15am to 10:15pm, and 11 buses run to Puerto Vallarta (6350 pesos) daily between 7am and 8:15pm.

Buses (700 pesos) connect the two towns on the half hour, leaving from the northeast corner of the plaza in San Patricio and from the bus stop in Barra. Of course, the 30- to 40-minute walk along the beach between the towns is the true budget option; don't go alone as some women have been harassed along this stretch, and take a cab after dark.

Practical Information

San Patricio

Currency Exchange: Bánamex, López Mateos between the plaza and the ocean. Open for *cambio* Mon.-Fri. 9:30am-noon. Hotel rates are unfavorable.

Post Office: Morelos 44 (tel. 702-30), on the plaza at López Mateos. Lista de Correos. Open Mon.-Fri. 9am-1pm and 3-6pm, Sat. 9am-noon. **Postal Code:** 48980.

Telephones: Morelos 52 (tel. 723-24), northeast of the plaza. Collect calls 2000 pesos. Open Mon.-Sat. 7am-2pm and 4-9pm, Sun. 8am-2pm and 5-9pm.

Bus Station: on Carranza (see Orientation). For long-distance, first-class travel, go to the office of **Tres Estrellas de Oro,** on Gómez Farías just west of López Mateos.

Market: on Ramón Corona, between Hidalgo and López Mateos. Open daily. The *tianguis* on Clemente Orozco is open Wed. 7am-3pm.

Public Facilities: At the obtrusive trailer park on the beach at Gómez Farías and López Mateos. Bathrooms 500 pesos, showers 3000 pesos.

Pharmacies: Farmacia Central, López Mateos 43 (tel. 700-32), south of the plaza. Open daily 9am-2pm and 4:30-9pm. **Farmacia Melaque,** López Mateos 30 (tel. 702-05), also south of the plaza. Open daily 8am-2pm and 4-9pm.

Hospital: Centro de Salud, Cordiano Guzmán 52, between Corona and Gómez Farías.

Red Cross: (tel. 823-00), 15km away in Cihuatlán.

Police: (tel. 700-80), on López Mateos north of the plaza.

Barra de Navidad

Tourist Office: Sonora 15 (tel. 702-37). Maps of Barra and San Patricio. Depending on who is working, some or quite a bit of English spoken. Open Mon.-Fri. 9am-8pm, Sat. 9am-1pm.

Travel Agency: Agencia de Viajes Viacosta, Veracruz 204 (tel. 702-58). Plane tickets only. Open Mon.-Fri. 9am-8pm, Sat. 9am-6pm, Sun. 10am-noon.

Currency Exchange: Banco Mexicano Somex, Sinaloa at Veracruz. Changes dollars Mon.-Fri. 10-11am only. Seaside hotels offer rates as skimpy as Jeff Richter's Speedo, as abysmal as Sadam Hussein's conscience, and as poor as *Let's Go* editors. So there you have it.

Post Office: Guanajuato 100, 1½ blocks inland from Veracruz on the cross street that forms the south side of the maritime monument, near the bus station. Lista de Correos posted around 10:30am. Open Mon.-Fri. 9am-2pm and 3-6pm. **Postal Code:** 48987.

Telegrams: Veracruz 96, on the corner by the plaza. Open Mon.-Fri. 9am-3pm.

Pharmacies: Farmacia Zurich, Legazpi 156. Open daily 9am-10pm.

Police: Veracruz 179 (tel. 820-23).

Accommodations and Camping

San Patricio

With many rich tourists visiting San Patricio, a clean, cheap room is hard to find. The beachside establishments on Gómez Farías are strictly for those with deep pockets; prices drop a block or two inland. In high season (Dec.-May), prices often rise 15 to 30% and vacant rooms become scarce. If you don't want to camp, start your quest for a room early in the day.

Hotel Hidalgo, Hidalgo 7 (tel. 700-45), halfway between the plaza and the beach. A family affair, with an especially friendly English-speaking proprietor. Fourteen clean rooms (with chests of drawers and spotless bathrooms) surround the courtyard, which works overtime as a living room, kitchen, and laundry room. Ask the management to turn on the fan, since there are no switches in the room. Singles 28,000 pesos. Doubles 35,000 pesos.

Hotel San Nicolás, Gómez Farías (tel. 700-66), ½ block west of López Mateos. The walls are clean and bright and some rooms have small balconies above the street. Hot water and fans. Noisy location. Singles 30,000 pesos. Doubles 40,000 pesos.

Hotel Flamingo, Vallarta 59 (tel. 701-96), 1 block inland from Gómez Farías. Some of these light, airy rooms have balconies, and some are unclean. An acceptable option. Singles 25,000 pesos. Doubles 35,000 pesos.

Bungalows Villamar, Hidalgo 1 (tel. 700-05), just off the beach. With a manager who speaks English well and large clean beachside bungalows, this is a deal for groups of 4 or more. Full kitchen and large common area. Call in Guadalajara (tel. 38-99-91) for Dec.-Jan. reservations. Four people 91,000 pesos. Eight people 147,000 pesos.

Vista Hermosa, Gómez Farías 110 (tel. 700-02). Tidy accommodations on the beach, but the price is sky-high and the courtyard amplifies street noise. Slick green tile covers rooms. Singles 50,000 pesos. Doubles 60,000 pesos.

The gaudy **Playa Trailer Park** (tel. 700-65), which mars the beach at Gómez Farías and López Mateos, has 45 lots with electricity, water, and access to bathrooms and showers. (Trailer or camping site for 2, 35,000 pesos; each additional person 15,000 pesos.)

Wild trailer parking and camping are best at the far western end of San Patricio, between the sandy beach and rock formations. The beach nearby is one of the best in the area, with several popular restaurants just steps away. About halfway between the two towns, separating the beach and jungle, is a small land-locked lagoon; pitch your tent on the oceanside or crash among the crabs in one of the deserted or semi-completed beach houses between San Patricio and the lagoon. But look before you sleep: at least one landowner has posted a "no camping" sign.

Barra de Navidad

The more active nightlife in Barra makes up for its smaller number of hotels. The Delfin is your best bet by far if you can afford the few extra pesos. The other hotels here are comparable in price and cleanliness to those in San Patricio.

Hotel Delfín, Morelos 23 (tel. 700-68). Immaculate rooms with large bathrooms and a sink outside the shower room. All guests have access to a balcony overlooking the pool and lagoon. Office loans recent bestsellers. Discount for multiple nights. Singles 42,000 pesos. Doubles 52,000 pesos.

Hotel San Lorenzo, Sinaloa 7 (tel. 701-39), ½ block inland from Veracruz, about halfway between the bus station and sandbar. Small buggies that squeeze through the ripped screens seem to find the bathroom acceptable, even pleasant. Fans. Singles 32,500 pesos. Doubles 40,200 pesos.

Posada Pacífico, Mazatlán at Michoacán (tel. 703-59), 2 blocks from the beach. Generic rooms, but exceptional toilet seats and shower curtains. The young staff is energetic and helpful. Singles 28,000 pesos. Doubles 35,000 pesos.

Bungalows Karelia (tel. 701-87), on Legazpi at the beach next to the Hotel Bogavante. A good deal for 3 or more. Suites contain refrigerator, table, chairs, stove, and fan. Unfortunate bugs which fly into the bathroom are knocked unconscious by the stench and fall to the floor, writhing in agony. Veranda faces the ocean. Singles 28,500 pesos. Doubles 35,500 pesos. Each additional person 8000 pesos.

The best spot to camp or park your trailer in Barra is at the extreme south end of town, on the sandbar near the breakwater. Join the locals in using the lagoon side of the cement building as a latrine, or use the toilet (500 pesos) and the shower (2000 pesos) in one of the nearby sand-floored eateries. (Look for the hand-lettered signs that read "Sanitario/Regadera.")

Food

During the summer, restaurants ship in shrimp from the north, but in high season local fishing boats catch everything that is served on the waterfront. Lobster here is trapped illegally, so help the endangered crustacean's cause by ordering oysters instead.

San Patricio

Although the restaurants on the beach are consistently more expensive than those around the plaza, a few deserve mention.

Los Pelícanos, in the row of *palapas* on the beach 50m beyond Hotel Melaque. The proprietor, New Yorker Philomena ("Phil") García, considers herself the fairy godmother of the way-worn *gringo* and publishes a newspaper called the *Pelican's Pouch*. The walls are covered with colorful yachters' graffiti. Breakfast (around 5000 pesos) and great seafood (18,000 pesos) will cure most cases of homesickness. Open daily 8am-11pm; off-season daily 11am-7pm.

Restaurante Pyrámide, a *palapa* connected to the Hotel Club Náutico. Great breakfasts: *huevos rancheros* 6500 pesos, and pancakes 4500 pesos. Bar conveniently open for breakfast. Open daily 8am-10pm.

The more authentic Mexican restaurants lie around the beautiful (sic) central plaza; dine with the locals here. **Pollos Al Carbón Estilo Mario,** López Mateos at Juárez, sits at the plaza's southwest corner. Soccer is on the set and Mario cooks cheap chicken in the corner while you feast. Steak and frijoles 9000 pesos. Beer's a bargain at 2000 pesos. (Open daily 10am-1am.)

Cheaper still are the nameless, dirt-floored eateries in the *mercado* and near the bus station, or the sidewalk food stands that materialize after the sun sets and the plaza awakes from its heat-induced slumber. As always, watch out for the amoebas that hang out in *mercados*.

Barra de Navidad

In Barra, forgo the expensive seaside restaurants in favor of those that line the lagoon on Veracruz. Note early closing hours.

Restaurant Eloy, Yucatán 47, jutting out into the lagoon, but no Gilligan or Skipper in sight. Small and colorful. Try the great red snapper *a la casa* (15,000 pesos). Open daily 8am-9pm.

Restaurant Mozoka, Veracruz 60, just down the lagoon shore from Eloy. Enjoy your 12-year-old waiter and watch local men play poker. Fish dishes 12,000-18,000 pesos. Full breakfasts 5000-7000 pesos. Open daily 1-8pm.

Pancho's, Legazpi 53. Eat littorally on the beach. The same entrees served at the Eloy and Mozoka but for *menos* pesos. Fine view of the setting sun, and a bard that will play anything for a price are the sole attractions. Open daily 7am-7pm.

As in San Patricio, there are cheaper restaurants inland, so save a few pesos by chowing far from the ocean.

Sights and Activities

The best section of San Patricio's beach is west of the Hotel Melaque. This stretch is the least crowded and offers the best view of the offshore rock formations as well as access to the good beachfront restaurants. When rough waves deposit piles of rocks on this prime swath of sand, however, the more populated beach at the end of Hidalgo and López Mateos should be adequate.

The slightly larger waves of Barra de Navidad are seldom big enough for surfing, but the crowd here tries admirably. **Mariner,** Legazpi 154, across the street from the church, rents surfboards, boogie boards, skindiving equipment, and bicycles (all of these 5000 pesos per hr. plus deposit of passport or credit card; open daily 9am-10pm).

While the short trip across the lagoon to the village of **Colimilla** makes a pleasant diversion, the steep price for small groups is considerably less than pleasant. For

20,000 pesos round-trip, a *lancha* will deposit up to eight passengers amid Colimilla's palms, pigs, cows, and open-air restaurants. For 40,000 pesos per hour, zoom off in the same *lancha* full of equipment for tuna, sailfish, or marlin fishing. Big catches are most common June through December. *Lanchas* and their friendly, talkative owners congregate at the small pier on the sandbar at the south end of town. Their gathering is as much for business as for pleasure, however, since cooperation makes price competition unlikely.

A source of religious pride for Barra is the **Iglesia de San Antonio,** on the corner of Jalisco and Veracruz, 4 blocks south of the bus station. The church, a modern structure, holds a different attraction for visitors than the stately colonial architecture prevalent in Mexico's touristed places of worship. Inside hangs *El Cristo del Ciclón* (Christ of the Hurricane): its arms, instead of being extended to form the traditional crucifix, are bent and, still attached to the body, droop groundward as if in a shrug. When Hurricane Lilly furiously struck the bay at dawn on September 10, 1971, a young girl burst into the church begging the icon for help, causing Christ's arms to detach from the crucifix in order to hold the hurricane back and save the town from destruction. (Church open daily 7am-8pm.)

Though devoid of Irish pubs and four-leaf clovers, San Patricio's **Fiesta de San Patricio** (March 10-17) is a celebration unmatched by any on the Emerald Isle. After filling yourself with Jalisco's finest tequila, dancing to *salsa* until your legs feel like *mermelada,* and watching fireworks while riding the bucking bronco, try not to pass out until after you've attended Philomena García's Sunday mass (9am), the blessing of the fleet, and the all-day procession. Philomena's bash the night before, rumor has it, keeps the residents across the bay awake with its commotion. Drop by her restaurant, Los Pelícanos (see Food), to get in on it.

There are at least four discos in the San Patricio/Barra area. Fanciest is **Discotheque Mar y Tierra,** on the beach in Barra de Navidad, on Legazpi across the street from the maritime monument. Also in Barra is the new **Aladdin,** just down the street from the Delfín Hotel. Both clubs rock from about 10:30pm on into the morn; cover ranges from 5000-12,000 pesos. San Patricio's dance floors are more basic: **Discotheque Albatros** is a half-block inland from the *Zócalo;* **Discotheque Hollywood,** on Ramón Corona, lies 2 blocks east of Hidalgo. Cover at the bawdy pair ranges from 5000-10,000 pesos.

Manzanillo

Residents of Colima state proudly point to Manzanillo as the home of its finest beaches and keystone to its economic future. In their delirious efforts to transform Manzanillo into the next Cancún, however, these worshippers of the Tourist God have overlooked the undeniable fact that a working port can never become a world-class resort. The workhorse of Mexico's Pacific coast, Manzanillo attracts ships from as far away as the Soviet Union. A navy repair station faces the city's main plaza, and *el centro* is a sweaty, workaday place unappealing to the beachgoing tourist.

Needless to say, most tourists avoid central Manzanillo altogether. They stay at glossy resorts on Manzanillo's two bays of golden-brown sand to the north and west of town, where life is good because of a fortuitous combination of currents and latitude which keeps Manzanillo cooler in summer than Acapulco and Puerto Vallarta. The reasonably priced hotels of Manzanillo, however, all lie in the midst of the loud and brazen port action. A 20-minute bus trip (700 pesos) or a 10,000-peso taxi ride separates *el centro* from the beaches. If all you seek is sand and surf, you'd do better to repair to some secluded village, such as Cuyutlán, or Barra de Navidad, where there is no metropolis between your hotel and the Pacific. If, instead, a real city with nearby beaches is your *taza de té,* Manzanillo will extend a warm greeting. Many restaurants have bilingual menus, and almost as many shop doors read "open" in place of "abierto."

Orientation and Practical Information

Manzanillo lies 96km west of Colima and 355km south of Guadalajara. The main bus station lies on the outskirts of town between Laguna Cuyutlán and the ocean.

The local bus labeled "Centro" runs from the station to the corner of 21 de Marzo and Hidalgo. If you decide to make the 15-minute walk, turn left from the station and head down Hidalgo, then turn right onto Jesús Alcaraz. Walk a couple of blocks down Alcaraz and turn left on Niños Héroes, which follows the shoreline and runs into Morelos at the train stop. A few blocks down is Jardín Obregón. The bus ride, which passes more stops than street corners, lasts at least 15 minutes longer than the walk. A taxi (tel. 323-20) from the bus station to the center of town costs 5000 pesos.

The best orientation point in town is Manzanillo's plaza, the **Jardín Obregón.** The plaza faces north onto the harbor, but boxcars often obstruct the glorious view of Pemex tankers. **Morelos** runs along the north (waterfront) edge of the plaza, **Juárez** along the south. **Avenida México,** Manzanillo's main street, runs south from the plaza. Most hotels and services are nearby.

Tourist Office: Juárez 244 (tel. 200-00), in the government building on the southeast corner of Jardín Obregón. Some English spoken. Pick up the simple map which indicates hotel locations. Open Mon.-Sat. 6am-midnight, Sun. 6am-3pm.

Currency Exchange: Bánamex, on Mexico, near the intersection with 5 de Mayo. Open Mon.-Fri. 9am-1:30pm. Many banks line Mexico. As a last resort, accept the less favorable rates at one of the downtown shops.

Post Office: (tel. 200-22), on 5 de Mayo between Juárez and Morelos, east of the Jardín. Lista de Correos. Open Mon.-Fri. 8am-7pm, Sat. 9am-1pm.

Telephones: Conasuper, a half-block east of the plaza on Morelos. Collect calls 2000 pesos. Open daily 8am-8pm.

Telegrams: On Juárez, on the 1st floor of the government building southeast of the plaza. Open Mon.-Fri. 9am-1pm and 3-5pm, Sat. 9am-noon.

Airport: In Playa de Oro, on the highway between Manzanillo and Barra de Navidad. Most flights are charters. **Mexicana,** Mexico 382 (tel. 217-01), is open Mon.-Fri. 9am-7pm, Sat. 9am-2pm. **Aeroméxico,** in the Centro Comercial, Carillo Puerto 107 (tel. 212-67), is open Mon.-Sat. 9am-6pm.

Train Station: On Niños Héroes, near Morelos east of the plaza. Two trains per day; the 6am train takes less time, but the 1pm makes fewer stops. To: Colima (1½ hr., *primera especial* 7300 pesos, *primera regular* 2000 pesos); Ciudad Guzmán (5 hr., 13,900 and 3800 pesos); Guadalajara (7 hr., 25,900 and 7100 pesos). Tickets for the 6am train cannot be purchased before 5am on the day of departure. Tickets for the 1pm on sale Mon.-Sat. 10:30am-3pm, Sun. 10:30am-1pm.

Bus Station: Hidalgo, about 1km east of downtown. **Soc. Coop. de Autotransportes** offers buses every 15 min. to: Armería (2000 pesos); Tecomán (2500 pesos); Colima (4000 pesos). **Tres Estrellas de Oro** has service to: Guadalajara (6 per day, 5½ hr., 16,500 pesos); Puerto Vallarta (1 per day, 12,500 pesos); Mexico City (1 per day, 14 hr., 26,100 pesos). Other lines offer more extensive service. **Autobuses del Occidente** sends 16 buses per day to Guadalajara; **Autocamiones de Pacífico** sends 13 per day to Puerto Vallarta and intervening points such as Barra de Navidad.

24-Hr. Pharmacy: Farmacia Manzanillo, Juárez 10, facing the plaza.

Hospitals: Hospital Civil, (tel. 210-03), on the San Pedrito circle. **Hospital de Seguro Social,** (tel. 201-42), on Calle 10.

Red Cross: 10 de Mayo and Bocanegra (tel. 200-96).

Police: In the Presidencia Municipal (tel. 210-04).

Accommodations

Finding a cheap room in Manzanillo is no great feat, but if you can smell the surf, you will pay through the nose. Should those listed below not work out, you'll have to choose between the grungier hotels near the bus station and the more expensive ones near the plaza or on the beach. Don't voluntarily stay near the bus station unless you're coming in at night and leaving the next morning. The hotels in town are cleaner and many are just as cheap. Even under these circumstances, women traveling alone should consider taking a cab to a hotel in the center. The neighborhood around the bus station can get a bit *peligroso* after dark.

Some restaurants on Miramar may let you camp on their beaches. But be careful: if women ask male proprietors whether camping is possible, the latter may assume their guests want company.

Hotel Flamingo, Madero 72 (tel. 210-37), 1 block south of the Zócalo. No flamingos here, but there are real shower curtains! A great deal, but often booked. Singles 24,750 pesos. Doubles 29,900 pesos. Reservations recommended.

Hotel Emperador, Dávalos 69 (tel. 223-74), 1 block west of the plaza's southwest corner. No hot water but clean bathrooms. Above a restaurant whose aromas make the mouth water. Bug-free. Singles 25,000 pesos. Doubles 30,000 pesos.

Hotel Miramar, Juárez 122 (tel. 210-08), just east of the plaza. Big clean rooms lurking behind a gaudy façade. Interesting, twisty stairways. Singles 25,000 pesos. Doubles 35,000 pesos.

Casa de Huéspedes Petrita, Allende 20 (tel. 201-87). A bunch of leather chairs and a washing machine greet you. Some of the small rooms have thumbnail-sized windows. Singles without bath 20,000 pesos. Doubles with bath 35,000 pesos.

Food

If you are hanging out in the plaza and want a quick snack, try one of the numerous taco and hot dog stands, but stay away from proffered ice cream bars and fruit drinks. Otherwise, uninspiring economical meals are found a few blocks south of the plaza on México. There is a **Conasupo** supermarket a half block east of the plaza on Morelos. The **Restaurante Chantilly,** on the plaza at Juárez and Moreno, is a very popular breakfast spot (waffles 4000 pesos) with great prices on fair food. Avoid the so-called burgers. (Open daily 7am-10pm.) The **Restaurant Emperador,** Dávalos 69 (tel. 223-74), is good for a quick meal of fried chicken (7500 pesos). Meat dishes go for 8000-9000 pesos. (Open daily 8am-10pm.)

Beaches

Two nearby bays, **Bahía Manzanillo** and **Bahía Santiago** serve Manzanillo's beach needs. The former has more expensive hotels, and its sands are a cleaner gold than its neighbor's, but its beach slopes more steeply, creating a large undertow. The beaches at Bahía Santiago, though twice as far from *el centro,* are more popular among *aficionados.*

The closest good beach on Bahía Manzanillo, **Playa Las Brisas,** has a few secluded spots, but parts of the beach are crowded with luxuriant hotels and bungalows. To get to Las Brisas from downtown Manzanillo, take a taxi (10,000 pesos) or the "Las Brisas" bus (750 pesos). Catch the bus on Alcaraz or on the highway going toward the airport and Barra de Navidad. Alternatively, catch the "Miramar" bus and ask the driver to let you off at the *crucero.* From the crossroads, turn left toward populated shores or stake out a private section of beach right at the junction.

If you stay on the "Miramar" bus, you will turn away from Las Brisas at the junction. The bus heads west of Península Santiago toward other excellent beaches on Bahía Santiago. The bay here is not used for shipping, and thus the water is cleaner than at Las Brisas. The "Miramar" buses (1000 pesos to the Bahía) leave from the train station, 3 blocks east of the plaza on Niños Héroes, every 15 minutes. The best place to get off is where everyone else does—at Miramar Beach, where a footbridge crosses the highway. This is the most crowded section of the beach, but it has the best beachfront restaurants and a man who rents boogie boards and surfboards. Crowds disappear 20m east or west of the beach club that owns this stretch of sand. The waves are great for boogie boards and bodysurfing; if you can figure out a way to use a surfboard here, you should move to Waikiki and give lessons. For tranquility, head for **La Avedencía,** a calm cove on the west side of the peninsula, or get the bus to stop just before it turns away from the coast after the footbridge. The bus ride from Manzanillo to Miramar takes 45 crowded, gear-grinding, clattering minutes.

For those who insist on the virtues of hiking to a beach, **Playa San Perdido** is an easy 1km jaunt north of the city center. **Playa Azul,** a residential area, is farther, but its long beach is within sight of a port that attracts international sailing regattas year-round.

Armería

Armería is an unavoidable junction en route to the secluded coves of Cuyutlán and Paraíso, but the sensible new arrival will keep the encounter brief and catch the next bus to the beach. Armería's problem is not that it's smaller, grimier, or more sweltering than most other Mexican towns—although it may well be. It's just that Armería has all the drawbacks and none of the attractions that redeem so many other squalid locales. A small tourist kiosk stands appropriately vacant in the center of town, and locals react to inquiring *gringos* with the same surprise they would show upon meeting the ghost of Benito Juárez.

Should the fates tie a knot in your lifethread and force you to spend the night in Armería, you have two alternatives. **Hotel México,** Netzahualcoyotl 31 (tel. 424-66), has clean rooms arranged around a brightly painted courtyard and bathrooms down the hall. (Singles 15,000 pesos. Doubles 20,000 pesos.) **Hotel San Antonio,** Mexico 17 (tel. 401-66), 2 blocks behind the main bus stop, charges less for its Alcatrazian rooms, but the common bathrooms and showers are dirty. (Singles 8000 pesos. Doubles 10,000 pesos.) Inflation has only mildly affected this place.

There's no real bus station in Armería, but there are two important intersections for catching buses. The main bus stop is on Netzahualcoyotl, Amería's main street, at its intersection with Velásquez/Alvarez. Buses to Manzanillo (every 15 min., 2000 pesos) stop at the intersection's northwest corner, on the Alvarez side of Netzahualcoyotl. Buses to Tecomán (every 15 min., 600 pesos) stop at the intersection's southeast corner, on the Velásquez side of Netzahualcoyotl. These buses run daily 5:30am-10:30pm.

Buses also run to the nearby beach towns of Paraíso (600 pesos) and Cuyutlán (800 pesos). Running every 40 minutes from 6am to 7:30pm, these buses stop at the corner of Netzahualcoyotl and 5 de Mayo, 4 blocks west of the main bus stop and across the street from Restaurant Camino Real. If you need to exchange currency before leaving, there is a **Banco Mexicano Somex** on Velásquez, just south of the intersection with Netzahualcoyotl (open 10-11:30am).

Paraíso

Paradise just might look better than Paraíso. But even with its self-indulgent name, Paraíso is close enough to nirvana after hellish Armería. A well-paved road connects the two towns, cutting through 7km of banana and coconut plantations before it dead-ends into the black sands that surround Paraíso's thatched, beachfront restaurants. Several weathered fishing boats litter the shoreline and lend credence to the *enramadas'* claims of fresh seafood.

Just before the main road becomes the beach, you'll see Paraíso's only other street, which runs along the back of the beachfront restaurants. A left turn here will take you past the village's three hotels. The **Hotel Paraíso** (tel. 429-10), is light years ahead of the other two. The extra cash buys you extra-nice owners, a pool, and a squeaky-clean room with shower. (Singles and doubles 40,000 pesos.)

For the more religious, the **Hotel Villa del Mar** boasts a shrine to the Virgin Mary in the entry room. Rooms are plain with small windows; bathrooms are on the miniscule side. (20,000 pesos for 2 beds, up to 4 people.) **Posada Ramírez** has a great laid-back feel, but can't seem to keep out the dirt. Unhinged cab doors line the halls, and some of the rooms have microscopic windows. The many cats about make each step a possible squealer. Cubicular, messy bathrooms make showering unpleasant. (Singles 15,000 pesos. Doubles 20,000 pesos.) In high season (especially Dec. and April) there may be rooms available in private Paraíso houses, so ask around.

Restaurants run the slim gamut from rustic *enramadas* to dirt-floored *comedores*. The best bet is the eatery at the Hotel Paraíso which, though its menu is average, simply looks nicer, and acts as the beach's social center.

Buses (600 pesos) run to and from the vestibule in Armería every 45 minutes from 6am to 7:30pm. Later, you'll have to get Charon, in the form of a taxi driver, to deliver you back from hell. He only charges 8000 pesos. Hitching is not a good idea because the road is dark and lonely and there Virgil won't appear to guide you.

Cuyutlán

If you're hungry for peace and silence, then Cuyútlan is a wonderful place to visit especially in the off season. Local residents of this sleepy town do little in the way of concerts in the Zócalo, leaving entertainment to the natural attractions. In fact, during that time, the Zócalo is usually as deserted as the beaches, where you'll have the beach chairs all to yourself.

Within the high season (Dec.-May), lifeguards and a well-planned *malecón* make the dark-brown sands even more attractive for the domestic tourists who come in droves. During the summer months, the wild blue waves pound the shore's dark sand *sans* audience.

Cuyutlán's most unusual distinction is the renowned **green wave,** a phenomenon that occurs regularly in April or May. Quirky currents and phosphorescent marine life combine to produce 15m swells that glow an unearthly green.

There is a long-distance *caseta* at Hidalgo 47, 1 block inland from the Zócalo. (Open Mon.-Sat. 9am-1pm and 4-8pm, Sun. 9am-1pm.) Buses to Armería (800 pesos) leave every 45 minutes from 6:30am to 7:30pm. A taxi to Paraíso or Armería costs 12,000 pesos. There is no direct public transportation between Paraíso and Cuyutlán.

Accommodations and Food

Although you may be the only *viajero* in town, bargaining is ineffective as all of the hotel owners charge similar prices.

Waves lap at the doorsteps of all the hotels listed below. If you arrive in Cuyutlán during a crunch period (e.g. Christmas or *Semana Santa*) you may have to try one of the inland hotels, such as **Posada San Antonio,** Hidalgo 139, 1 block seaward from the plaza. If you'd rather camp, a trek 200m to the west (right) of Cuyutlán's hotels will lead to a private patch of black sand. Or string up a hammock in one of the *palapas* east (left) of the hotels—most of them are vacant in summer. Campers and daytrippers can use the toilets (1000 pesos) and showers (1500 pesos) at Hotel Morelos.

Hotel Colima, Veracruz 22 (tel. 5). Clean rooms with 4 beds and private bathrooms line a high-roofed, breezy corridor. Ask for one of the 5 rooms with an ocean view. Singles 20,000 pesos. Doubles 30,000 pesos.

Hotel Fénix, Hidalgo 201 (tel. 100-47). Not a bad place to stay if you don't mind a few bugs. The restaurant is questionable: smiling *cucarachas* have been spotted leaving, apparently full. Bathrooms are clean but lack seats. Fans in every room. 20,000 pesos per person.

Hotel Morelos, Hidalgo 185 (tel. 7), across the street from the Fénix. Flowers galore and a gift shop greet newcomers. The square, clean rooms have fans. 20,000 pesos per person (but you can feed their noisy birds for free).

If for nothing else, the restaurants of Cuyutlán's *playa* are distinguished for their uniformity. Even their menus seem to have been copied from the same master. The only thing that distinguishes **Restaurant Morelos** (part of the Hotel Morelos) from the clones is its color scheme: decor includes orange and green tablecloths, flowers, stuffed parrots hanging from the ceiling, and 4 real talking parrots. As befits a beach town, seafood dominates the menus, with a variety of lobster (25,000 pesos), shrimp (20,000 pesos), and fish (12,000 pesos) dishes. Steaks go for as little as 6000 pesos. For cheaper nourishment, try one of the little restaurants near the Zócalo, where *tortas* set you back only 2000 pesos.

Tecomán

Tecomán is a city with a question, and that question is: *Why?* The land is flat. The land is hot. The land is boring. Tecomán's Zócalo is something out of Walt Disney's nightmares, with a lime green cathedral surrounded by hundreds of garbage cans with plastic lion heads for lids. *Why?* Because Tecomán is proximate to the under-developed beaches of Colima's southern coast, providing surfers and sun-worshippers with services after sundown, when the city's garishness fades into the night.

Orientation and Practical Information

Tecomán lies 329km south of Puerto Vallarta on the coastal highway. There is no central bus station, but all city-to-city buses leave from Progreso by the market. When you get off the bus (facing the market), turn left, walk 2 blocks and then right diagonally onto **López Mateos,** the main drag. Three blocks farther and you hit the Zócalo (notice the lions).

Local buses leave the market around the corner, on Lázaro Cárdenas, for the beaches at Boca de Pascuales and El Real between 7am and 6pm (every hr., 800 pesos). The taxis on the other side of the market can have you instantly beach-bound for a mere 15,000 pesos.

Currency Exchange: Bánamex, López Mateos at Hidalgo, 1 block northwest of the Zócalo. Open Mon.-Fri. 9am-1:30pm. **Bancomer,** López Mateos at Progreso. Open Mon.-Fri. 9am-noon.

Post Office: Ocampo 199 (tel. 419-39), at Vicente Guerrero 2 blocks north and 1 block east of the church. Lista de Correos. Open Mon.-Fri. 8am-7pm, Sat. 8am-2pm. **Postal Code:** 28100.

Telephones: Farmacia Guadalupana, López Mateos 179 (tel. 405-99). International collect calls 3000 pesos. For collect calls, open daily 8am-10pm. **Telephone Code:** 332.

Bus Station: Buses stop at Progreso by the market. **Autobuses del Occidente** office on Progreso opposite the market. To: Guadalajara (5 hr., 12,000 pesos); Mexico City (13 hr., 32,000 pesos); Lázaro Cárdenas (5 hr., 12,500 pesos). **Transportes del Norte de Sonora** office on 5 de Mayo just off Progreso. To Tijuana (40 hr., 112,200 pesos). Buses also leave every 15 min. 5:30am-10:30pm to: Colima (45 min., 1800 pesos); Armería (20 min., 600 pesos); Manzanillo (1 hr., 2500 pesos). Stand on Progreso by the market and listen for your destination; the *sobregargos* (pursers) call them out.

Hospitals: Clinica de Especialidados Sagrado Corazón, 18 de Marzo 89 (tel. 405-33); **Clinica Santa Maria,** Aldama 351 (tel. 420-93); **Clinica Santa Teresita,** Matamoros 4 (tel. 410-32).

Red Cross: Emiliano Zapata at Morelos (tel. 413-00).

Police: República at Jávier Mina (tel. 401-69).

Accommodations

Although there are many cheap rooms south and east of the Zócalo, these three are the best of the bunch.

Hotel Catlina, Balvino Dávalos 42 (tel. 402-47), 2 blocks north of the Zócalo. Visitors welcomed by smiling children in Wonder Woman Underoos who lead you to the room after their mom hands them the key. Rooms have beds and chairs, but not much else except fans. Bathrooms are clean. Singles 18,000 pesos. Doubles 25,000 pesos.

Hotel María Inés, Constitución 253 (tel. 403-74), behind the church. Ancient furniture and pillows doing a good rock imitation. All rooms with fans and seats on the toilets. Singles 20,000 pesos. Doubles 30,000 pesos.

Hotel Tecomán, 20 de Noviembre 639. From the bus station, turn left on Lázaro Cárdenas, go 3 blocks, then turn left on 20 de Noviembre—it's on the right. Not for the fashion-conscious: bright orange-and-yellow hallways, deep blue doors, and pink rooms. Adequately clean rooms are small and, with their hard metal benches, don't feel like home unless you jumped parole to take your Mexican vacation. Soap, towels, and fans, but no toilet seats. Singles 20,000 pesos. Doubles 30,000 pesos.

Food

The cheapest food is available in and around Tecomán's two markets. Examine the art of tortilla-making at the **Mercado Lázaro Cárdenas,** on Progreso between Lázaro Cárdenas and 5 de Mayo. **Mercado Cuauhtémoc,** just southeast of the plaza through the pedestrian mall, sells fruit, fish, cold cuts, and that indispensable staple, Tupperware. Both markets are loaded with cheap juice stands and *fondas,* whose amiable owners will try to coax you into a chair at their counter. The going price for a full chicken dinner at a market *fonda* is 5000 pesos. If you crave sugary cereal, packaged cookies, or 6-packs of Budweiser, walk west of the plaza to **Conasuper,** 20 de Noviembre at Matamoros. (Open daily 8am-8pm.)

Los Faroles, on López Mateos just northwest of Progreso. Mainly a bar with a few broiled meats for 10,000 pesos. Quesadillas 3000 pesos. Live music from 8pm-midnight attracts a crowd. Open daily 1pm-midnight.

La Palapa, Colegio Militar 101, at Progreso. Big *palapa* roof with gaggles of tables underneath. Many caged birds and even a squirrel hang along the walls. Tasty U.S.-cut steaks (23,000 pesos) and ordinary seafood (15,000 pesos). Not too crowded. Open daily 2pm-midnight.

Restaurant Coty, on Colegio Militar. Filling Mexican food, plain and simple. Four *tacos pollo* for 4000 pesos. Open 24 hr.

Near Tecomán: The Coast

South of the resort towns of Cuyutlán and Paraíso, the coast becomes much less inviting. Beachfront *enramadas* empty out at afternoon's end, and buses stop running at dusk. Anyone spending the night on the beach will feel extremely isolated and not at all comforted by the occasional stray dog or carload of drinking buddies out for a rowdy time.

Still, several excellent beaches are close enough to Tecomán to warrant daytrips. **Boca de Pascuales** (13km) and **El Real** (15km) are the most popular. Take the bus from Tecomán (800 pesos). Farther down the coast, Tecuanillo, La Manzanilla, and Boca de Apiza also assuage beach addicts.

Colima

The capital of Colima state is hardly a tiny village, but it manages to maintain a small-town friendliness—men and women sit around and chat all afternoon on the benches of the *Zócalo,* and locals smile as they give directions to tourists. The central plazas are as picturesque now as they were when the city was founded in 1523, but modern civilization has not left Colima unscarred; serenades in the Zócalo on Sunday afternoons must now contend with the unmuffled roar of cruisers in cars with names like Beast o' Fantasy. This isolated city rewards those few who stray from the well-trodden coastal route with a gratifying change of scenery and a good place to shake the sand from those shoes.

Orientation

A string of plazas runs east to west across downtown Colima. The arcaded **Plaza Principal,** flanked by the cathedral and the Palacio de Gobierno, is the business center of town. Colima's two main streets, **Madero** and **Reforma,** are the plaza's northern and eastern boundaries. Reforma becomes **Constitución** north of the plaza, and Madero becomes **Quintero** west of it. On the other side of the cathedral and palacio is the smaller, quieter **Jardín Quintero.** Three blocks farther east on Madero is the large, lush **Jardín Núñez,** the other significant reference point in town. Many tourist services are on **Hidalgo,** the southern boundary of Pl. Principal and the Jardín Quintero.

Practical Information

Tourist Office: Hidalgo 75 (tel. 240-60), 1 block west of Pl. Principal. Staffed by very helpful young'uns. Good advice as well as maps of Colima and other parts of the state. Some English spoken. Open Mon.-Fri. 8:30am-3pm and 5-9pm, Sat. 9am-1pm.

Travel Agency: Avitesa, Constitución 43 (tel. 269-70). Can make plane reservations. Open Mon.-Sat. 9am-2pm and 4-8pm.

Currency Exchange: Bánamex, on Hidalgo, 1 block west of Pl. Principal. No commission and a good rate, but hell might freeze over as you wait in line. Open Mon.-Fri. 9am-1:30pm.

Post Office: Madero at Revolución, on the northeast corner of the Jardín Núñez. Lista de Correos. Open Mon.-Sat. 8am-6pm.

Telephones: Constitución 109, north of the Pl. Principal. 4000-peso charge if not accepted. Long line. Open Mon.-Fri. 8am-1:30pm. Also **Farmacia Colima** (see below); 10,000 pesos if call not accepted. Open daily 9am-9pm. **Telephone code:** 331.

Telegrams: Madero 247, at the post office. Open Mon.-Fri. 9am-12:30pm and 3-5:30pm, Sat. 9am-noon.

Train Station: At the southern end of town. Service to Guadalajara (at 2:45pm, 6 hr., 19,000 pesos) and Manzanillo (at 2:25pm, 2 hr., 7300 pesos). Tickets can be purchased at the station (open Mon.-Sat. 11:30am-4:30pm, Sun. and holidays 1-4:30pm).

Bus Station: On Nícolas Bravo. Frequent buses rumble to: Tecomán (8 per day, 2000 pesos); Armería (1 per day, 3000 pesos); Manzanillo (10 per day, 3200 pesos); Guadalajara (5 per day, 12,000 pesos); Mexico City (3 per day, 30,000 pesos); Puerto Vallarta (1 per day, 17,000 pesos); Aguascalientes (1 per day, 25,000 pesos).

Laundromat: Lava Fácil, Herrera 123. 3½kg wash 3000 pesos. Dry 2500 pesos. Soap 800 pesos. Open Mon.-Sat. 9am-8pm.

Red Cross: Aldama at Obregón (tel. 214-51).

Pharmacy: Farmacia Colima, on Madero at the northeast corner of the Pl. Principal. Open Mon.-Sat. 9am-9pm.

Hospitals: Hospital Civil, San Fernando at Ignacio Zandoval (tel. 202-27); **Centro de Salud,** Juárez at 20 de Noviembre (tel. 200-64 or 232-38).

Police: Juárez at 20 de Noviembre (tel. 218-01).

Accommodations

The Hotel Ceballos is *the* place to stay in Colima. Right on the Pl. Principal in a 19th-century structure, it has an elegance lacking in Colima's other cheap accommodations. Those on a stricter budget will survive but not flourish in the other establishments.

Hotel Ceballos, Portal Medellín 12 (tel. 244-49), on the north side of the Pl. Principal. Sparkling tiled halls with high ceilings lead to your room. All the bedrooms are clean, some have desks and A/C, and there is plenty of *agua* in big jugs. Singles 46,000 pesos. Doubles 50,000 pesos.

Hotel Gran Flamingo, Rey Colíman 18 (tel. 225-25). Rooms with balconies are breezy, but the fake marble sinks have to go. Singles 35,000 pesos. Doubles 40,000 pesos.

Hotel Núñez, Juúrez 88 (tel. 270-30), on the western side of Jardín Núñez. If lots of cement blocks and the color yellow turn you on, stay here. Fans in the room keeps them smelling fresh. Singles 15,000 pesos, with bath 22,000 pesos. Doubles with bath 27,000 pesos.

Casa de Huéspedes, Morelos 265 (tel. 234-67), just off the southeast corner of Jardín Núñez. The matron who runs this house keeps a dog, a cat, and a parrot. Reminiscent of Grandma's House in the story of Little Red Riding Hood. Old furniture in immaculate rooms. Singles 20,000 pesos. Doubles 30,000 pesos.

Hotel Cuyutlán, Morelos 132. Only for the desperate. Bare, somewhat clean rooms, but bathrooms are scruffy and the puddle next to the shower is the Loch Ness Monster's home away from home. Singles 15,000 pesos. Doubles 20,000 pesos.

Food

Although none of the restaurants in Colima are spectacular, several serve appetizing fare. Most of these are clustered around the Pl. Principal. Breakfast at Los Naranjos is a particularly good way to start your day.

Giovanni's, Constitución 50. Chicago it ain't, though the pizza is pretty good. Avoid the salty *salchichas* topping. If you're not hungry, go in for a beer and just soak in the aroma of pizzas (10,500-25,000 pesos). Open daily 1-11pm.

Los Naranjos, Barreda 34. The place to be in the morn. Great toast with lots of butter. Sunlight splashes all over the bright orange tablecloths. Ham and eggs 6500 pesos. Open daily 8am-11:30pm.

La Taba, Medellín 9. If you were wondering what happened to Air Supply, wonder no more: they're playing here. Wall decorations are Argentine (see Maradona score), and the plywood awaits your graffiti. Entrees 15,000-26,000 pesos. Open daily 11am-midnight.

Jugolandia, on Madero between the Pl. Principal and Jardín Quintero. A great place for a natural cool beverage amid lots of orange plastic. *Licuados* 2500 pesos. Freshly squeezed juices 2400-3000 pesos; try the Pineapple y Orange.

Sights

In Colima's well-maintained **Plaza Principal,** white park benches surround a gazebo and several decorative fountains. The double arcade around the plaza encompasses the Museo de Historia, the Hotel Ceballos, and a handful of stores and sandwich shops. The commercial establishments continue along the pedestrian malls, which radiate from the plaza's corners.

On the east side of the plaza, much of the state government is housed in the **Palacio de Gobierno.** An inviting building with breezy courtyards, the palacio also contains a four-wall mural, completed in 1954 by Jorge Chávez Carillo in honor of the bicentennial of Hidalgo's birth. The intricate mural, covering the walls of the staircase closest to the Pl. Principal, moves counterclockwise through Mexico's tumultuous history.

Adjoining the municipal complex is a renovated colonial **cathedral.** The Spanish first built a church on this spot in 1527, but an earthquake destroyed the original structure of wood and palm, and fire consumed its replacement. Even the building's consecration as a cathedral in 1894 did not rescue it from natural disaster. To this day the paintings of the evangelists bear scars from the earthquakes and volcanic eruptions of 1900, 1932, and 1941. The cathedral is still the most striking building in Colima, and the fading paint of its dome and towers does little to decrease their grandeur. The neoclassical interior glitters with gilt paint, chandeliers, and polished marble. In the pulpit designed by Othón Bustos rests a statue of San Felipe de Jesús, the city's patron saint. Guided tours of the cathedral include a precarious journey up the right tower's winding stairs for a view of every other church in Colima. (Open daily 9am-1pm. For a tour, inquire at the church office between the cathedral and the palacio.)

Colima's smaller churches sulk under the *primavera* trees, which bloom yellow in March. Of particular note are **San Francisco,** on the northern edge of town (open 10-11:30am and 5-8pm), the first church erected in Colima by the Spanish; **San José,** on Madero to the north, the focus of a well-to-do residential section; and **El Sagrado Corazón,** on the corner of 27 de Septiembre and Aldama, known for its beautiful interior.

Beyond the city to the southeast (also visible from the top of the cathedral) rises **Colina La Cumbre.** The chapel on its summit is open to "the entire brotherhood of man" (women included)—but only on the eighth day of each month. The chapel and its grounds are a popular site for picnics. If the climb to the chapel wears you out, park it on a shaded bench in the Jardín Quintero next to the chapel. Three blocks east of the Jardín Quintero is the Jardín Núñez, which runs for a long block with an old unused fountain in the middle. Shoe-shiners and hot dog salesmen populate the fringe; the center is deserted except for a few palm trees.

The grimy auto parts shop 1 block south of Templo la Merced on Revolución is a front for Colima's least-expected but most fascinating sight. The **Colección de Automóviles Antiguos** houses over 350 antique cars dating from 1884, in various states of repair (or disrepair) and under assorted coats of dust. The collection's owner, 75-year-old Señor Francisco Zaragoza, is also a poet who will give you a copy of his hand-printed book if you strike him as the sort who would appreciate it. Ask for Señor Zaragoza in the Refraccionaria Zaragoza, Revolución 79. (Open Mon.-Sat. 9am-9pm, Sun. 9am-4pm. Free.)

Pre-Columbian art is displayed at the **Museo de Cultura y Arta Popular,** part of the Universidad de Bellas Artes (tel. 229-90) at 27 de Septiembre and Gallardo Azmoro. The best exhibits are of the brightly-colored, symbolic costumes, used by *indígenas* for ritual purposes. (Open Tues.-Sat. 9am-2pm and 4-7pm. Free. Catch the Sur or Nte. bus across from the Gran Flamingo and get off on the corner of 27 de Septiembre and San Fernando.) Colima's newest museum, the **Museo de Historia,** is at 16 de Septiembre and Reforma on the south side of the Pl. Principal. (Open Tues.-Sat. 10am-2pm and 4-8pm, Sun. 5-8pm. Free.)

Near Colima

In Nahuatl, Colima means "place where the old god is dominant." The old god is **El Volcán de Fuego** (3820m). Recorded eruptions date back to the pre-Conquest era, and today El Fuego emits frequent puffs of smoke and steam to assert its status as the only active volcano in Mexico. El Nevado de Colima (4240m), stands taller than its neighbor, but is dormant and not much fun at parties. Buses run daily from Colima's bus station to Atenquique, 58km away (1800 pesos). From here, a 27km unimproved dirt road runs to the summit of El Fuego. The trip can only be recommended for four-wheel-drive vehicles. Fortunately, logging trucks based at the factory in Atenquique make trips up this road to spots near the summit. For best results, instead of hitching, try asking politely at the factory for a ride. Almost at the top of El Fuego is the **Joya Cabin,** which lacks all amenities except a roof.

A small colony of *indígena* artisans thrives 9km north of Colima in **Comala,** the small town that is said to have inspired Juan Rulfo to write *Pedro Páramo.* Comala's **tianguis** (*indígena* market) sells bamboo baskets, clocks, and wooden furniture on Mondays from 8am to 3pm. The town's **church,** at Degollado and Madero on the Zócalo, supports a thriving colony of bats who have free run of the nave. Buses to Comala leave Colima's bus station every 15 minutes from 6am to 10pm (700 pesos).

If you don't mind a few insects and just have to get away from it all, think about going to **Laguna Carizalillo,** 12km north of Comala. Take the 7am or 4:30pm bus (2000 pesos) from the station in Colima. Visitors come to sit in the pervading peace and listen to birds rather than to fish the lake. Bungalows with kitchens and fireplaces are available. (Doubles 20,000 pesos. Triples 25,000 pesos. Quads 30,000 pesos.) **Laguna La María** is larger, closer to the volcanoes, and less visited. (*Cabañas* for 4 people 32,000 pesos, for 6 44,000 pesos. Simple shelter for 6—no kitchen—21,000 pesos.) Buses for La María leave Colima daily at 7am, 1pm, and 5pm, returning to Colima at 3pm and at other fluctuating times (2000 pesos). To make accommodations reservations at Carrizalillo or La María, ask for Senñora Lety or Adriana at the Colima tourist office (tel. 240-60).

Soak it hot at **Agua Caliente,** a mere 17km west of Colima on the highway to Jiquilpan. In the same region, the thermal waters at **El Hervidero** are said to have medicinal properties. One or two buses run daily from Colima to *el crucero* (17km) that accesses Agua Caliente. From here, you have to walk or hitch a ride 1km down a dirt road to the springs. The same bus continues to **Puerta de Anzar,** 29km from Colima (3000 pesos), which is *el crucero* for Hervidero. From this stop, a 6km hitch or (more likely) hike separates you from soothing heat.

MICHOACÁN DE OCAMPO

The Aztecs dubbed the lands surrounding Lake Pátzcuaro "Michoacán," or "country of fishermen," for nearly all of the region's indigenous Purépeche subsisted by the rod and net. The Purépeche empire, which at one point controlled most of western Mexico, was one of the few *indígena* civilizations to thwart Aztec expansionism. In fact, the Purépeche diverge from other Mesoamericans in more than just their fighting prowess: their language, culture, and even their terraced agricultural plots have led archeologists to believe that they originally emigrated from what is now Peru—and are thus culturally closer to the Incas than to any of their neighbors in Mexico.

The Purépeche hegemony lasted from around 800 AD, when they first settled Michoacán, until the Spanish expedition arrived in 1522. The conquistadors enslaved the Purépeches and forced their conversion to Christianity, but some cultural traditions persisted. Purépeche music, dances (such as *la danza de los viejitos*), and art were insuppressible. Their language, which you may hear spoken in Janitzio and the smaller villages around Lake Pátzcuaro, also survived intact. Local *indígenas* refer to themselves as Tarascos, and thousands of stories exist to explain how they came to be known by this name. The most plausible relates that the last Purépeche lord, cowardly Tangaxhuán II, turned over the whole empire to ruthless and gold-hungry conquistador Nuño de Guzmán in 1530. In the transaction, the Purépeche lord gave his four daughters to Nuño and the other Spanish officers. Some witty Purépeches started calling the Spaniards *tarascues* (sons-in-law), and the linguistically inclined conquistadors in turn used the term when addressing the Purépeches.

Michoacán is also notable for its role in the struggle for independence: it spawned no less than three separate conspiracies and revolts, of which Morelos's attempt was the most significant. The state played a very small role in the 1910 Revolution, but its inhabitants are nonetheless proud of their tradition of rebellion against injustice, as shown by the official name of the state, Michoacán de Ocampo; recently appended, the suffix honors Melchor Ocampo, a leader in the wars for independence.

A combination of mild weather, fertile soil, and abundant water has ordained Michoacán's role from the colonial period to the present day as one of Mexico's leading agricultural centers. The surrounding forest-covered mountain ranges also attract a great number of hunters and wildlife enthusiasts. Large parts of the state still maintain their pristine natural character, untouched by modern civilization. But Michoacán is by no means simply mile after mile of *maíz* and pigs. The state also offers urban sophistication, especially in Morelia, with theaters, discos, and high fashion romping in the town plazas.

Morelia

Morelia is, above all, Morelos (Jose María Morelos de Pavón, the champion of Mexican independence). A dedicated priest, Morelos was serving two parishes on the coast of Michoacán state when another priest, Miguel Hidalgo, appointed him lieutenant and head of the insurgent forces in the south. Morelos wrested the states of Michoacán and Guerrero from the royalists and, after Hidalgo's execution, guided the Republican movement to victory, earning him the nickname "El Caudillo" (Chief). He chaired the first free congress of the Republic before the enemy overtook him in Tezmalca. Excommunicated and found guilty of treason, Morelos

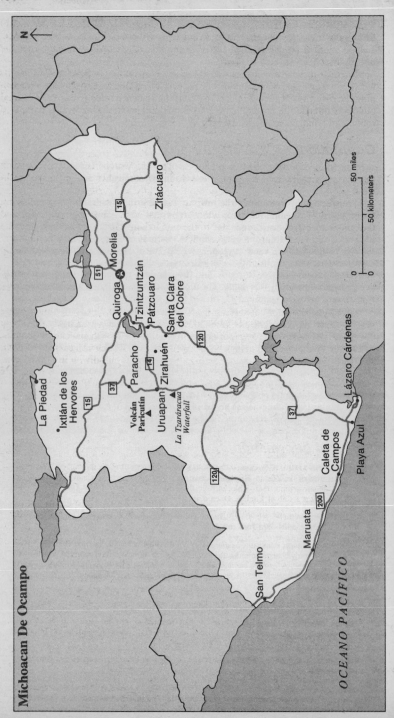

Michoacan De Ocampo

was executed in Ecatepec, Mexico state, on December 22, 1815. After his death, he became the ultimate hero and most poignant symbol of Mexican independence. The second state legislature voted in September, 1828, to name the city after the martyr Morelos.

Morelia is a showcase of exquisite colonial architecture. Baroque façades line its long main street, Av. Madero. Multiple red-white-and-green Mexican flags, overlapping the rosy glow of carved pink stone, lend the avenue a solemn majesty. Colonial buildings outside the center flaunt pink stone and whitewashed walls, parapeted roofs, and windows as big as doors.

Orientation

Situated 309km west of Mexico City via Rte. 15, Morelia is the largest city on the southerly route from the capital to Guadalajara, another 340km to the northwest.

The streets in Morelia cover the town in a large grid. Most interesting points are on or south of **Avenida Madero,** which runs east-west. Parque Cuauhtémoc and the colonnades of the aqueduct rise to the east, where Madero splits into **Avenida México,** leading to Charo, and **Avenida Acueducto,** which becomes the highway to Mexico City. North-south street names change at Madero, and east-west street names change every other block; Madero never forsakes its name.

To get downtown from the bus depot, go left (east) as you leave the building, take a right at the first street, walk two blocks, and then make a left on Madero—the Zócalo is 4 blocks ahead.

It would be a gracious concession to Morelia to say that its metropolitan transit system is terrible. All of the city's 500,000 inhabitants either permanently ride about on the too-few buses and *combis* or are trying to squeeze into them. The large buses, or *urbanos,* are cheap (300 pesos), but as packed as Arnold Schwarzenegger. *Combis* (500 pesos) are more pleasant but as risky as Acapulco cliff-diving in a hurricane; always ask where they are going before you get in. Taxis (3000-4000 pesos) are the best choice, but finding one could prove as difficult as Hercules's labors. After all this, however, and luckily for you, most sights are well within walking distance of the Zócalo. For large groups, the State Tourist Office (see below) can arrange a guide for a walking tour of the city.

Practical Information

State Tourist Office: Nigromante 79 (tel. 326-54), at Madero Pte. in the Palacio Clavijero, 2 blocks west of the Zócalo. Extremely clear maps of the center of town and more sketchy ones of the areas more than 5 blocks from the Zócalo are distributed by a friendly, young staff that takes a stab at English. Open daily 9am-2:30pm and 3:30-8pm.

Federal Tourist Office: (tel. 205-22), on Acueducto. All *combis* running east on Madero pass the office. Open daily 9am-2pm and 4-8pm.

Currency Exchange: Banks line Madero east of the cathedral. Most are open Mon.-Fri. 9am-1pm, but will only change dollars until noon; the sole exception is **Bancomer,** which changes until closing time. A *casa de cambio,* Ocampo 178 (tel. 284-48), at Zaragoza, doesn't have great rates but is open Mon.-Fri. 9am-2pm and 4-6:30pm, Sat. 9am-2pm.

Post Office: Madero Ote. 369 (tel. 246-20), 5 blocks east of the cathedral. Open for Lista de Correos and stamps Mon.-Fri. 8am-8pm, Sat.-Sun. 9am-1pm. **Postal Code:** 58000.

Telephones: 24-hr. long-distance service in the bus station. For international collect calls (13,000 pesos) try the Restaurante Paraiso, Galeana Portal 103, on Madero across from the cathedral. Open daily 9am-10pm. **Telephone Code:** 451.

Telegrams: Madero Ote. 371 (tel. 206-81), next to the post office. Open Mon.-Fri. 9am-8pm, Sat. 9am-noon.

Airport: Aeropuerto Francisco J. Mugica, (tel. 367-80), on Carretera Morelia-Cinapecuaro at km27. Get **Aeroméxico** and **Mexicana** information and tickets at **Wagons-Lits Viajes,** Portal de Matamoros 10, on the western edge of the Zócalo.

Train Station: (tel. 639-65) On Av. del Periodismo. To Mexico City (at 11pm, 9 hr.) and Uruapan (at 7:30am, 3 hr.).

Bus Station: Ruíz, at Gómez Farías (tel. 256-64). Served by first-class **Tres Estrellas de Oro** (tel. 211-86), as well as second-class **Flecha Amarilla** (tel. 255-03) and **Autobuses de Occidente** (tel. 206-00). Hardly a bus leaves late. Be on your guard or be the last in line. First-class fares listed; second-class lines cost about 10% less. To: Mexico City (every ½ hr., 14,000 pesos); Pátzcuaro (every ½ hr. 5am-6:30pm, 2500 pesos); Guadalajara (6 per day, 15,000 pesos); Tijuana (every ½ hr. 5am-10:50pm, 123,000 pesos). Also in-state bus lines.

Red Cross: Ventura 27 (tel. 451-51), at the end of Banuet, next to the Parque Cuauhtémoc.

Laundromat: Laundería Automática Ivon (tel. 431-58), on the Circuito de Campestro. 2500 pesos per kg. Open Mon.-Sat. 8:30am-8:30pm.

Pharmacy: Farmacia Moderno, Corrigedora 566 (tel. 291-99). Open daily 9am-10pm.

Police and Transit Police: (tel. 222-22), on 20 de Noviembre.

Accommodations

Despite a multitude of budget hotels south of Madero and just west of the cathedral, rooms can be hard to find during the university summer session (July-Aug.). At other times, something is sure to be available. None of the hotels are outstanding bargains, but all budgets and tastes are covered.

CREA Youth Hostel (IYHF), Chiapas 180 (tel. 331-77), at Oaxaca. Take a taxi or walk west on Madero Pte. and turn left on Cuautla. Continue south on Cuautla for 7 blocks, then turn right on Oaxaca and continue 2 blocks to Chiapas. A good deal if you don't mind sacrificing a little privacy and freedom. Cleaner than most CREAs, with a ping-pong table to boot. 6000 pesos per person. IYHF members receive a 10% discount. Breakfast 3500 pesos, lunch or dinner 4500 pesos.

Posada Don Vasco, Vasco de Quiroga 232 (tel. 214-84), 3 blocks east and 2 blocks south of the cathedral. Damp, but the blue-tiled bathrooms are tolerably clean and the carved wooden dressers shine. Downstairs rooms seem to collect stray noises, but from them you can literally roll into the great, cheap restaurant for breakfast. Singles 15,000 pesos. Doubles 25,000 pesos.

Hotel d'Atilanos, Corrigedora 465 (tel. 333-09), at Rayón. Great rooms include phones, TVs, high ceilings with solid wooden beams, and spotless bathrooms. Singles 36,000 pesos. Doubles 45,000 pesos.

Hotel Mintzicuri, Vasco de Quiroga 227 (tel. 206-64), across from the Posada Don Vasco. The origin of the interesting name is unknown, but an awesome mural gracing the walls of the lobby in back of some local *indígena* masks may provide a clue. Brown carpet covers the floor in all rooms, clashing monumentally with the green phones. Gleaming bathrooms gush round-the-clock hot water. Central location. Singles 29,000 pesos. Doubles 51,000 pesos.

Hotel Vallarta, Madero Pte. 670 (tel. 240-95), 4 blocks west of the Zócalo. If you get bored listening to the toilet drip, there are always video games in the lobby. Dark hallways, and the ceiling showerhead transforms a shower into a light drizzle. Singles 25,000 pesos. Doubles 35,000 pesos.

Hotel El Carmen, Ruíz 63 (tel. 217-25), 3 blocks north of Madero between Juárez and Morelos. Clean rooms are empty spare the bed, but there is a tub in the bathroom. Rooms overlook a covered courtyard with chairs and a coffee table commandeered by a ceramic swan. Singles 16,000 pesos. Doubles 40,000 pesos. Towel deposit 5000 pesos.

Hotel San Jorge, Madero Pte. 719 (tel. 240-67), across from the Hotel Vallarta. Rooms much more pleasant than the cramped lobby and restaurant would lead you to believe. Wide halls equipped with chairs for that afternoon read. Singles 28,000 pesos. Doubles 38,000 pesos.

Hotel Colonial, 20 de Noviembre 15 (tel. 218-97). The nicest courtyard in Morelia, with graceful stone arches and pillars. Unfortunately, the rooms are marred by damp bathrooms, exposed wiring, and horror of horrors, lumpy pillows. Singles 22,000 pesos. Doubles 25,000 pesos.

Hotel Central, Abasolo 282 (tel. 201-39). Stay here only as a last resort. Tall rooms with furniture that looks like it took part in the firefights of the Revolution. A bare bulb dangles from the ceiling. Communal baths smell unpleasant. Singles 12,000 pesos. Doubles 20,000 pesos.

Food

Good inexpensive meals require a 3-block walk from the Zócalo in any direction. Numerous food stands on the colonial porch around **Plaza Agustín** dish up afternoon *comida corridas* for as little as 3000 pesos. Taco booths in front of the bus station are open until the witching hour. Unless you're willing to burn some serious pesos, avoid the scenic café-restaurants which open onto the Zócalo. **Café Casino,** however, does offer several nice breakfasts for under 6000 pesos.

Restaurant-Bar La Huacana, Aldama 116, at Obeso. The gargantuan oil painting behind the stage makes a nice backdrop for the large dining area. Stone walls provide great acoustics for the *mariachis* who play Mon.-Sat. 3-5pm and 9-10pm. *Pollo ranchero* 8000 pesos. Open Mon.-Sat. 9am-11pm, Sun. 9am-5pm.

Pizza Real, Muñiz 158-B. Big, tasty pies smothered in sauce served by friendly, talkative folks. Spiffy establishment. Individual pizza 7000 pesos, double 12,000 pesos, and group-sized 18,000 pesos. Special ingredients and combos available. Wash it all down with a beer (2000 pesos) or a *refresco* (800 pesos). Open daily noon-11pm.

Pollo-Coa, Madero Ote. 890, by the Tarascan fountain. Fowl fanatics squawk about the Coa. Inside, star-shaped lamps from flea markets across the Americas dimly illuminate unembellished chairs and stable tables. *Filete Milaneza* 12,000 pesos. *Orde de Pollo-Coa* 9500 pesos. Open daily 9am-12:30am.

Restaurant El Torito, Madero Pte. 867, 1 block west of the Hotel San Jorge. Would someone please lasso the kitschy organist? When he's not playing, this local favorite is a good spot to eat and rest your weary feet. *Queso Mexicana* 7000 pesos. *Bistec de Cerdo* 8000 pesos. Open daily 8am-midnight.

Café Morelos, Corregidora 258, near Abasolo. The only ornament in this restaurant is the dusty plastic rose bush Morelos left behind when he stepped outside to grab a mango with his buddy Hidalgo. He never came back and legend has it that the number of plastic petals left on the bush corresponds to the number of Mexican towns without a street named Morelos. *Comida corrida* 6000 pesos. *Tortas* 3000 pesos. Open Mon.-Sat. 10:30am-10pm.

Restaurant "Super Pollos," Madero Ote. at Silva, 2 blocks east of the post office. Cheap oil paintings and an even cheaper wine- bottle clock are the only things to look at here. Great chicken; cheaper and closer than the Coa. *Comida corrida* 7000 pesos. *Pollo placero con enchilada* 9000 pesos. Open daily 8am-9pm.

Sights

In Morelia's **Plaza Central,** large, carefully trimmed trees around the fountains and kiosk provide shade without obscuring the surrounding architecture. *Morelianos* sit, talk, rest, and buy fruit and *nieve* here.

Construction of the **cathedral** overlooking the Pl. Central dragged on for over a century (1640-1744). The massive structure combines the neoclassical idiom with earlier Baroque and *herreriano* (named for the architect of El Escorial, outside Madrid) styles. In the 19th century, a bishop removed the elaborate Baroque filigree from the altarpieces and frescoes, and renovated the church's interior in the symmetric and sober Doric neoclassical style. *Indígenas* sculpted the *Señor de la Sacristía,* the oldest treasure of the church, out of dry corn cobs and orchid nectar. In the 16th century, Felipe II of Spain donated a gold crown to top off the masterpiece. (Open 9am-8:30pm.)

In 1822, after independence was secured, an artist chipped away the shield of Valladolid on the cathedral's Baroque façade and chiseled in the emblem of the Republic. The elaborate central relief—represents the Transfiguration of Jesus, who appears between the apparitions of Abraham and Moses with the three awe-struck apostles at their feet. The evolution of styles is more evident in the two massive towers; the bases follow the *herreriano* style of straight lines and heaviness, while the second levels are built in 17th-century four-sided Baroque style, and their octagonal tops features multiple columns in the neoclassical style of the mid-18th century.

Morelos's residence now contains the **Museo de Morelos,** Morelos 232 (tel. 326-51), 1 block east and 2 blocks south of the cathedral. The museum displays El Caudillo's sable, religious vestments, military ornaments, and uniform, as well as other mementos of the surge for independence, such as armaments, carriages, and documents. Some of his famous sayings, as well as those of Vicente Guerrero, Nicolás Bravo, and other celebrities, sprinkle the exhibits. (Open daily 9am-2pm and 4-8pm. Free.)

Now a museum as well, the **Casa Natal de Morelos** (Birthplace of Morelos) stands at Corregidora 113, 1 block south of the cathedral. Glass cases display his war cartography, communiques, letters, and additional paraphernalia in two halls emblazoned with murals by Alfredo Zalce. The birthplace also has a public library, an auditorium, and an audiovisual projection room (see Entertainment below). Next to the projection room, a torch burns eternally to commemorate Morelos's birth on September 30, 1765. His brigade banner, the first flags of the Republic, and the modern red- white-and-green standard fly over the house. Outside, the martyr's stern bust surveys a rose garden. (Open daily 9am-2pm and 4-8pm. Free.)

On its 100th anniversary in 1986, the **Museo Michoacano,** Allende 305 (tel. 204-07), 1 block west of the cathedral at Abasolo, underwent a complete renovation. Museum exhibits are now divided into five categories: ecology, archeology, the colonial period, the struggle for freedom, and independent Mexico. Among the most important exhibits is a huge, anonymous painting completed in 1738, *La Procesión del Traslado de las Monjas.* Notes by Diego Rivera explain the relevance of the canvas as a ground breaking work of profound realism, in an era when religious themes still dominated art. It depicts colonial society with encyclopedic attention to each social group and its relative importance. Religious oils by Miguel Cabrera and his students are also worth a look, as are those by a trio of indigenous 19th-century artists—Manuel Ocaraza, Felíx Parra, and Jesús Torres. Finally, a powerful mural on the stairway, by Alfredo Zalce portrays those who have affected Mexico's history and criticizes Mexicans' blind admiration of U.S. mass culture. (Open daily 9am-2pm and 4-8pm. Free.)

The **Museo Casa de las Artesanias,** at Humbolt and Juan de San Miguel, is a huge craft museum and retail store. Inside, the first halls display photographs of artisans working at their pottery furnaces, metal anvils, textile machines. Actual examples of the crafts are organized by the town of their origin; on display are colorful macramé *huipiles,* straw airplanes, and guitars. Other crafts include geometrically decorated pottery from workshops in Patambán, painstakingly carved white wood furniture, and clay biblical vignettes. The back of the market exhibits the winners of craft and textile competition. The *mercado* is impressive, but better prices await you in Pátzcuaro. (Open Mon.-Sat. 10am-5pm.) Outside the market, the **Plaza Valladolid** marks the site of the 1541 founding of the city of Valladolid. But don't be fooled; this plaza—as colonial as it looks—was built in 1968.

The **Palacio Clavijero,** at Madero and Nigromante, 2 blocks east of the plaza, was founded in 1660 as a Jesuit school headed by Francisco Javier Clavijero. After the Jesuits were expelled, the palacio held a sucession of mundane jobs. Then, in 1970, the palacio got its big break, undergoing extensive remodelling in order to accommodate the public library and several state offices, including Michoacán's tourist headquarters. Its west balconies hold a small food and craft market. (Building open daily 6am-9pm.)

On the east end of Madero, the **Fuente de las Tarascas** is a source of local gossip. The fountain is a copy made in 1968: some say the original was taken to France by a rich woman to dignify her front garden, while others insist that it is still on the city fairgrounds. Regardless of what happened to the original, the replacement stands next to a park at the endpoint of Morelia's aqueduct. The fountain's waters sparkle and leap around a tripod of half-naked Tarascan women who hold a giant basket of fruits and vegetables, the produce of the irrigated earth. At night, the fountain, park, and aqueduct take on romantic splendor thanks to expert illumination.

Built to alleviate the city's pressing water needs, the aqueduct was finished in 1788. A pedestrian avenue adjacent to the duct invites evening strolls. Here Madero veers off the park's paved avenue to become the highway to Mexico City.

On a well-lit plaza next to the aqueduct, the equestrian monument to José María Morelos depicts the hero strutting into battle. His rear faces the aqueduct, which has become the main entrance to the plaza, but an uncompromising rendering of Liberty on the back of the pedestal diminishes the embarrassment. Liberty also breaks the chains of serfdom in front, and bronze reliefs of the Anahuac Congress and Morelos's charging troops appear on the pedestal's flanks. Finished in 1913, this monument was commissioned during the Díaz dictatorship and inaugurated by the revolutionary forces that toppled him.

Entertainment

The Museo de Morelos projects excellent international art and history movies during the week, at different times in the early evening (call 326-51 for more information). The Cine-Club, sponsor of the films, alternates movies weekly and organizes Eastern European and contemporary Mexican film festivals. Admission is free; the only problem is getting a seat. **Cinema Victoria,** at Madero Pte. 944-C (tel. 243-10), 2 blocks west of the Hotel San Jorge, features Hollywood's latest (admission 3000 pesos). For older North American movies, check out **Sala Eréndira** (tel. 212-87), on Santiago Tapia behind the Palacio Clavijero.

Theater fans attend plays at 8pm on Wednesday night in the ISSTE Morelos theater (tel. 292-36), on Madero in the western part of the city. The theater's university and amateur groups perform picaresque plays, pantomime, and—hold on to your black garters—a Spanish version of *The Rocky Horror Picture Show.*

For a wilder night out, try the **Disco Molino Rojo,** in front of the Plaza Las Américas shopping center in the far easter reaches of town. At the **Baron Rouge,** in the Plaza Rebullones's basement, next to Parque Cuauhtémoc, the young rowdies are more interested in drinking than dancing. Cover at both 10,000 pesos; domestic drink prices about 5000 pesos. (Both open Sun.-Thurs. 8pm-1am, Fri-Sat. 8pm-2am.)

Gyrovago's Laser Disco, 1 block from the Molina Rojo, is the latest trendy nightspot, but only male-female couples are admitted. (Cover 10,000 pesos, drinks 4000 pesos. Open Sun.-Thurs. 9pm-1am, Fri.-Sat. 9pm-2am.) The ultra-chic **Aurum,** in front of the Hotel Morelia Misión provides some of Morelia's best bar action. Party with the university kids in the **Club XO,** at Calzada Capistre and Acueducto. (Cover 10,000 pesos. Open Thurs.-Sun. 9pm-2am.) Also popular but a smidgen more sedate is **Bambalina's,** Escutín 225 at Lazáro Cardenas. (Cover 15,000 pesos. Open Thurs.-Sun. 9pm-2am.)

Children might enjoy the zoo in the **Parque Benito Juárez.** To get there, take the "Guenda" *combi* from the corner of Allende and Galeano. (Open daily 11am-6pm. Admission 2000 pesos.)

Morelia holds several large annual festivals; among them the **Birthday of José María Morelos de Pavón** (Sept. 30), the **Anniversary of the City's Founding** (May 18), and the **Agriculture and Artesanía Fair** (May 21).

Pátzcuaro

Ordained priest and bishop at the age of 75, in 1540, Vasco de Quiroga established his episcopate in the former Purépeche capital, Pátzcuaro. Four years later, Pátzcuaro was selected as the capital of Michoacán state. Inspired by the humanitarian ideals of Thomas More, Bishop Quiroga defended the Purépeche people from landowners and mining magnates. He taught the residents of each Purépeche village around the Lago de Pátzcuaro a different craft, thereby stimulating community trade and economic health.

Long before Vasco showed up, the Purépeches demonstrated artistic talent in their music, dance, and crafts which they bartered in the markets. Today, visitors to Pátzcuaro come to buy beautiful traditional handmade woolens from slightly more modern shops and market stalls. The city also makes an excellent base for excursions to smaller villages like Janitzio, an island-town capped with a grand monument to the father of Mexican independence.

Orientation

Route 14 leads into the city of Pátzcuaro from Morelia (70km) and Mexico City, first crossing Quiroga and Tzintzuntzán to the north and nearby Tzurumútaro to the east, before continuing on to Uruapan, 67km to the southwest.

To reach the center of town from Pátzcuaro's bus station, turn right as you leave the access road to the station, and then cross the road that you are walking along—Av. Circunvalación. Take the first left on an unnamed, small, rough cobblestone street, and walk 3 blocks until you hit pavement. Continue 2 blocks, and then turn right on Ibarra. You will be heading east down Ibarra, and will hit the northwest corner of the Pl. Vasco de Quiroga in a few blocks. From that point, the Pl. Gertrudis Bocanegra is 1 block to your left along Mendoza. Another option is to take the bus (300 pesos) that picks up passengers in front of the station.

The city of Pátzcuaro encompasses two distinct parts. Downtown perches on a hill about 5km south of the lakefront, an area which is primarily residential. To reach the lake from downtown, jump on a public bus labeled "Lago," "San Pedro," or "Sta. Ana," which pass by the Pl. Gertrudis Bocanegra, Portal Regules, and Portal Juárez about every five minutes from 6am to 10pm (300 pesos). These buses rattle down the hill along Av. de las Américas and will brake long enough to drop you off at the restaurant-lined docks, from which *lanchas* (boats) depart for the island of Janitzio and other points around the lake.

To reach towns on the shores of the lake other than Janitzio, take a bus from the second-class terminal (usually 1500-3000 pesos). Boats to these towns leave only when enough people request a ride, and charge up to 28,000 pesos for destinations such as Tzintzuntzán.

Practical Information

Tourist Office: Portal Hidalgo 9 (tel. 218-88), on the west side of the Pl. Quiroga. Knows the specifics and stocks a good map. Open Mon.-Sat. 9am-2pm and 4-7pm, Sun. 10am-2pm.

Currency Exchange: Banco Serfín, Portal Morelos 54 (tel. 215-16), on the north side of the Pl. Quiroga. Open Mon.-Fri. 9am-1pm. The *casa de cambio* at Mendoza 12 (open Mon.-Fri. 9am-4pm) has good rates.

Post Office: Obregón 13 (tel. 201-28), ½ block north of the Pl. Bocanegra. Open Mon.-Fri. 8am-7pm, Sat.-Sun. 9am-1pm. **Postal Code:** 61600.

Telephones: Hotel San Agustín, Iturbide 1, on the Pl. Bocanegra. International collect calls 4000 pesos. Open Sun.-Fri. 8am-10pm, Sat. 2-4pm. **Telephone Code:** 454.

Telegrams: Títere 15 (tel. 200-10), 1 block east and 1 block south of the library. Open Mon.-Fri. 9am-6pm.

Train Station: (tel. 208-03), at the bottom of Av. de las Américas near the lakefront. To Mexico City (second-class at 9:05am, 5700 pesos; first-class at 9:40pm, 29,500 pesos, sleeper 51,200 pesos). Buses between the town center and the lakefront stop here before continuing on to the lake shore.

Bus Station: Off of Circunvalancion, south of town first-class **Tres Estrellas de Oro** (tel. 214-60), **Autobuses de Occidente** (tel. 202-52), and **Flecha Amarilla** (tel. 209-60). To: Mexico City (7 hr., 15,500 pesos); Guadalajara (4 per day, 5½ hr., 12,500 pesos); Morelia (every hr., 6am-10pm, 1 hr., 2800 pesos); Uruapan (every 20 min. 6am-9pm, 1 hr., 2500 pesos).

Laundromat: Lavandería Automática, Terán 14 (tel. 218-22), 2 blocks west of the Pl. Quiroga. 3kg wash and dry 7500 pesos) takes 3-5 hr. Open Mon.-Sat. 9am-2pm and 4-8pm.

Pharmacy: Farmacia San Rafael, Mendoza 27 (tel. 203-32). Open daily 10am-3pm and 5-9pm.

Hospital: Romero 10 (tel. 202-85).

Emergency: Cuerpo de Rescate, Pl. Quiroga, booth 79 (tel. 218-89). 24-hr. service.

Police: Hidalgo 1 (tel. 200-04), on the western edge of the Pl. Quiroga next to the tourist office.

Accommodations

Several hotels in the budget range surround the Pl. Bocanegra, but the rooms aren't stupendous and, though they promise 24-hour hot water, you may have to wait that long to get some. For better economic and aesthetic deals, look to the hotels away from the plazas.

Posada de la Salud, Serrato 9 (tel. 200-58), 3 blocks east of either plaza, ½ block past the basilica on its right. The best budget place in town. Spotless and almost brand-new. Beautiful courtyard, gorgeous carved furniture from Cuanajo, and cloud-soft mattresses. Hot water 24 hr. Singles 22,000 pesos. Doubles 24,000 pesos.

Hotel Valmen, Lloreda 34 (tel. 211-61), 1 block east of the Pl. Bocanegra. Nicer than anything on the plaza. Beautiful Aztec tile and squawking birds fill the courtyards. Well-lit rooms made complete by complimentary postcards. Singles 15,000 pesos. Doubles 25,000 pesos.

Posada Imperial, Obregón 21 (tel. 203-08), a few doors down from the post office. *Better Homes and Gardens* would never approve of the glaring hot-pink bedspreads and matching curtains, but the rooms are dirt-free and well furnished; each has a cabinet stocked with snacks and liquor. Baths large, clean, and tiled. Singles 25,000 pesos. Doubles 30,000 pesos.

Hotel El Artillero, Ibarra 22 (tel. 213-31), 2 blocks west of the Pl. Quiroga. The lobby may remind you of a distant, dingy basement in an ordinary modern building (in other words, home to *Let's Go* editors), but the rooms are sanitary. Decaying bathrooms do function. Singles 20,000 pesos. Doubles 30,000 pesos.

Hotel San Agustín, Portal Juárez 27 (tel. 202-42), on the western side of the Pl. Bocanegra. Yellow is the operative word here. Clean rooms adjoin the bathrooms that smell musty. No flaws, no draws. Singles 25,000 pesos. Doubles 41,000 pesos.

Hotel Concordia, Portal Juárez 31 (tel. 200-03), on the Pl. Bocanegra. The rooms do little to compensate for the curt manager. Ask for a room that overlooks the plaza—the ones that don't are dark around the clock. Upon arrival, the desk equips you with soap and a towel; after that, you're on your own. The windows are covered only by shutters, so watch out for insects. Singles 28,000 pesos. Doubles 35,000 pesos.

Food

Once considered a delicacy, seafood from the lake is now the staple of the Pátzcuaro diet. *Pescado blanco* is far and away the most plentiful and popular dish. *Charales* (smelts), served in the restaurants along Pátzcuaro's lakefront and on Janitzio, are small sardine-like fish fried in oil and eaten whole by the fistful. Try to overcome initial squeamishness; they're tasty and cheap (a plastic baggie stuffed with them, lime, and salsa is 3500 pesos and makes terrific snack for the boat ride to Janitzio). *Caldos de pescado* bubble in large clay vats outside open-air restaurants, particularly on Janitzio. These spicy soups, loaded with fish and sometimes shrimp, crab, and squid, are a meal in themselves.

Most of the small restaurants by the docks close daily at 7pm. Of the restaurants on Muelle, the dockside pedestrian strip, the ones toward the end are quieter and have better views of Janitzio and the rest of the lake. It seems the prices at all the restaurants on Muelle and Janitzio are the same—*pescado blanco* goes for 15,000 pesos, fish soup 6000 pesos. Should such figures wound your wallet, head back to the town market, where portions are smaller and not as well prepared, but one-quarter the price.

Restaurant El Patio, Pl. Vasco de Quiroga 19, on the south side of the plaza. The sophisticated decor blends still lifes, empty wine bottles, and pillars of rough stone. Read your menu by the light of locally crafted hanging lamps. Good food. Breakfasts-around 5000 pesos. Steaks 10,000-17,000 pesos. Open daily 8am-9pm.

Super Pollo Loco, Portal Lerdo 15, on the east side of the Pl. Bocanegra. Juicy chickens grilling in the front serve as beacons to the hungry traveler. A whole chicken (18,000 pesos) should pacify the barbarian in you. The mixed platter of salad, beans, and a quarter-chicken costs 10,000 pesos. Open daily 11am-10pm.

Restaurante El Escudos, on the west side of the Pl. Quiroga, in the hotel of the same name. A *gringo* with surprisingly excellent food that more than compensates for the jungle of plastic plants. Entrees 12,000-20,000 pesos. *Comida corrida* 15,000 pesos. Open daily 8am-9:30pm.

Restaurant El Pollito, Portal Juárez 27, on the Pl. Bocanegra beneath the Hotel San Agustín. A noisy pit, popular with both locals and flies from the market next door. Plastic tablecloths ensure that all spilled liquids flow right into your lap. Well-prepared Mexican favorites include *chuleta de puerco* and *caldo de pollo.* Entrees 5000-8000 pesos. Open daily 7:30am-9pm.

Sights

Pátzcuaro's unique handcrafts, such as hairy Tócuaro masks, elegant Zirahuén dinnerware, and luxuriant textiles are sold in the Pl. Bocanegra's market and in small shops along the passage next to Biblioteca Gertrudis Bocanegra. Bargaining is easier when you buy more than one item, but don't expect a deal on the arrestingly handsome wool articles: thick brown-and-cream sweaters; thin, brilliantly colored *saltillos* and *ruanas* (stylized ponchos); rainbow-colored *serapes;* and dark shawls. The retailers stubbornly stick to their prices, however beseechingly you may plead. Still, these items are far from expensive. Sweaters usually sell for the equivalent of US$12-13, *ruanas* US$20, *saltillos* for US$23; *serapes* and ponchos according to size (US$8 for the smallest). The haphazard piles of woolens in the market may conceal more treasures than the boutique displays. Shops carry both *pura lana* (pure wool) and *media lana* (half wool), plus polyester and acrylic. Differences in quality are easy to detect.

When Vasco de Quiroga came to Pátzcuaro in 1540, he initiated not only social change, but bold architectural projects as well. Quiroga conceived the **Basílica de Nuestra Señora de la Salud,** at Lerín and Serrato, as a colossal structure with five naves arranged like the fingers of an extended hand. Each finger represents one of Michoacán's cultures and races, and the center of the palm, the altar, symbolizes be the Catholic religion. Although construction began in 1554, civil opposition to the ostentation of the building and repeated earthquakes prevented all but the first nave from being opened until 1805. Later, two more earthquakes and a fire forced the church to shut down and undergo reconstruction several times. (Open daily 7am-8pm.)

Today the basilica features a grandiose Romanesque altar. Intricate parallel stripes of frescoed arabesques cross the high, concave ceiling of the church, forming impressive vaults. An enormous glass booth with gilded Corinthian columns and a dome protects the Virgen de la Salud sculpture; when Vasco de Quiroga asked a few Tarascos to design an image of the Virgin in 1546 they complied by shaping her out of *tatzingue* paste made from corn cobs and orchid honey. Tata Vasco added the final touch when he put the inscription "salus infirmorum" (healer of the ill) at the image's foot. On the eighth day of every month, pilgrims from all over Mexico crawl from the plaza to the basilica on their knees to beg the Madonna to perform.

Down the street from the basilica, on Lerín near Navarette, is the **Casa de Artesanías.** Originally a convent for Dominican nuns, called the Casa de los Onces Patios in the 18th century, this complex now contains non-clerical craft shops, a small gallery of modern Mexican art, the tourist office, and a mural depicting Vasco de Quiroga's accomplishments in the region. The Casa de Artesanías sells superb musical instruments (guitars, flutes, and *güiros*), and cotton textiles. For woolens, the market is still your best bet. (Open daily 9am-2pm and 4-7pm.)

The **Museo Regional de Artes Populares,** on the corner of Lerin and Alcanterillas, 1 block south of the basilica, was once the Colegio de San Nicolás Obispo, a college founded by Tata Vasco in 1540. This fantastic museum displays pottery, copperware, and textiles produced in the region. Particularly appealing are the *maque* and *laca* ceramics collections. (Open Mon.-Sat. 9am-7pm, Sun. 9am-3pm. Admission 550 pesos, free Sun.) Next to the museum building, Tata repeated Moses' Sinai Desert miracle by finding among rocks a spring, which supplied abundant fresh water for Pátzcuaro until 1940. A stone shrine to the Virgen de la Salud on top of the exhausted spring serves as reminder of Tata's big feat.

Statues of Pátzcuaro's two most honored citizens stand vigil over the town's two principal plazas. The ceremonious, banner-bearing Vasco de Quiroga inhabits the plaza that bears his name. Vast and well-forested, the Pl. Quiroga feels more like a city park than a Zócalo. The massive, Amazonian, bare-breasted Gertrudis Bocanegra looks out from the northwest corner of **Plaza Gertrudis Bocanegra.** A martyr for Mexican independence, Bocanegra was executed by a Spanish squadron in October 1817, in the Pl. Quiroga. People say bullet holes still mark the ash tree to which she was tied. Calle Zaragoza spans the two blocks that separate the two plazas.

Biblioteca Gertrudis Bocanegra, on the plaza of the same name, occupies the former site of a temple to St. Augustine. The library's multicolored mural by Juan O'Gorman illustrates the history of the Purépeche civilization from pre-Conquest times to the Revolution of 1910. You can borrow material, if you leave identification and the name of your hotel. (Open Mon.-Fri. 9am-7pm.) When the next-door. **Teatro Caltzontzín,** once part of the Augustinian convent, became a theater in 1936, an as-yet-unfulfilled prophecy was uttered: one Holy Thursday, the theater will crumble as punishment for the sin of projecting movies in a sacred place. In the main hall, murals depict Purépeches planting, dancing, and acting, with Janitzio in the background. You can peek at it in the afternoons, Monday through Saturday. If you dare to test the prophecy, catch a flick (2500 pesos for both Mexican and U.S. comedies and dramas); check the posted schedule.

Three kilometers east of the city, at the end of Av. Benigno Serrato, is **El Humilladero** (Place of Humiliation), where the cowardly king Tangaxhuán II surrendered his crown, dominions, and daughter to the sanguinary Cristóbal de Olid and his Spanish troops. Two peculiar features distinguish this chapel: on its altar stands a rare monolithic cross, undoubtedly older than the date inscribed on its base (1553); and on the facade are images of gods which represent the sun and the moon—used to lure Purépeches to Catholicism.

Entertainment

After 10pm, Pátzcuaro launches into its numbingly realistic imitation of a graveyard. The town has no dance floors and few good movie theaters; such urban eccentricities are not tolerated here. The Pátzcuaro Cine Club shows films Tuesdays at 7:30pm in the Escuela Vasco de Quiroga (next to the Museo de Artes Populares). Inquire at the tourist office for details.

Seasonal Events

The town hosts several fiestas during the year. An animated post-Christmas tradition in Pátzcuaro is the pair of *pastorelas,* celebrated on January 6 to commemorate the Adoration of the Magi, and on January 17 to honor St. Anthony of Abad. On both occasions, the citizens dress their domestic animals in bizarre costumes, ribbons, and floral crowns. Pátzcuaro's Semana Santa attracts people from all across Mexico. Particularly moving is the *Procesión del Silencio* on Good Friday, when a crowd marches around town mourning Jesus' death in silence. The biggest celebration is the **Feria Artesanal y Agrícola,** held at the beginning of December to honor the Virgen de la Salud. This festival includes craft contests, *big* plant sales, and fireworks shows. **Noche de Muertos** (Nov. 1-2) holds special importance for the Tarasco community; expect the typical festivities at a magnified level.

Near Pátzcuaro

Visited daily by hundreds of sightseers, the island of **Janitzio** has assimilated a large number of shops and restaurants. Despite the dismaying number of tourists, the boat ride on the lake and the great fish dinners should still prove enjoyable. Full of children, Purépeches, and pigs, Janitzio is a lovable tourist trap.

From the lake, Janitzio resembles a Mediterranean village, all red tile roofs and white walls, but with an added touch—the gigantic statue of Morelos that juts skyward above the small island.

Once ashore, make your way behind the shops and tourists and climb the paths to the **Monumento a Morelos.** In monumentality, historical significance, and posture, this statue is a rough equivalent of the famous one in New York Harbor. But instead of a torch of liberty, Morelos holds up a liberty-demanding finger. The statue is most impressive from the surface of the lake, because Morelos's features are virtually indiscernible up close. Inside, numerous murals give a detailed account of Morelos's life. (Admission 1000 pesos.)

Janitzio is inhabited exclusively by Tarascan *indigenas* who speak the Purépeche dialect. **Restaurant Ishi'r Hua'pa** (Son of the Lake), like its competitors, serves such delicacies as *pescado blanco, tacos de charales, carpa,* and *trucha.* Shops sell butterfly-net and canoe souvenirs, Tarascan folk records, and colorful, hand-woven cotton shirts.

To get to the island, first hop on a bus labeled "Lago," "San Pedro," or "Sta. Ana" at the corner of Portal Regules and Portal Juárez at the Pl. Bocanegra. The bus (300 pesos) rambles to the docks, where you'll stand in a long but fast-moving line to get a ferry ticket (round-trip 2600 pesos). Ferries leave when they fill up (every 15 min., 9am-6pm, ½ hr.). Check the time of the last boat, since Janitzio does not accommodate the stranded. From the boats, the serene towns of Jarácuaro, Nayízaro, Puácuaro, and Ihuatzio, are visible along the verdant lake shore. A guitar trio sometimes plays on board and will ask for tips when you disembark. Before docking, the boats are inundated by Janitzio's fishing people, who paddle out in canoes and briefly demonstrate the use of their butterfly-shaped nets in hopes of earning a small contribution. The ferry then circles the island before dropping passengers off at the town.

To reach the other towns around the lake, take a second-class Flecha Amarilla bus. (See Practical Information.)

Santa Clara del Cobre, 16km south of Pátzcuaro, was a copper-mining town in its heyday. After the mines closed down, the village devoted itself exclusively to crafting copperware. Every single store in this town sells copper plates, pans, bowls, and bells. Prices here are only slightly better than elsewhere in Mexico, but the quality and variety are vastly superior. For a quick look at some of the more exotic pieces, step into the **Museo de Cobre,** close to the plaza. If it doesn't look open, hang around inside the courtyard and someone will come out to let you in. Santa Clara is also known as Villa Escalante—in honor of General Salvador Escalante, a native of Morelia and sub-prefect of Santa Clara, who, supporting the Madero revolutionaries, fought Porfirio Díaz in 1911. There is little to see in Santa Clara beyond *artesanías;* this side trip requires only a couple of hours.

The lake at **Zirahuén** makes another scenic daytrip or a good spot for camping. Not as large a lake as Pátzcuaro, Zirahuén (Where Smoke Rose) is more open, unobstructed by marshes and islands, and considerably cleaner. If you want to camp, hike up one of the ridges that border the lake and set up in any one of the numerous spots that overlook the water; the landowner—if there is one—may ask you to pay a few pesos. Heavy afternoon rains during June and July can turn summer camping into a drenching experience.

The colonial town itself, with its woodwork shops, also merits a visit. To get there, take the bus from the second-class station in Pátzcuaro. If you have wheels, take the road to Uruapan and look for signs to Zirahuén. From Santa Clara del Cobre you can hike about 11km along a dirt road that traverses the wooded slopes to Zirahuén, or catch a ride with people headed to Uruapan from Pátzcuaro.

Tzintzuntzán (Place of the Hummingbirds) was the last great city of the Tarascan empire. In the middle of the 15th century, the great Purépeche lord Tariácori, on his deathbed, divided his empire among his three sons. When, some years later, Tzitzipandácuari reunited the empire, he chose Tzintzuntzán as the capital; the old capital, Pátzcuaro, became a dependency. Not quite the city it used to be, Tzintzuntzán is but a tiny town now famed for its delicate multi-colored ceramics displayed on tables along Calle Principal.

A peculiar pre-Conquest temple, the Yácatas, sits on a hill 1km outside the city. The base of each *yácata*—all that remains today—is a standard rectangular pyramid. The missing parts of the *yácatas,* however, are what made them unique: each was originally crowned with an unusual elliptical pyramid constructed of shingles and volcanic rock. The pyramids are situated along the long edge of an artificial platform 425m long and 250m wide. Each building represents a bird. This vantage point commands a view of the Lago de Pátzcuaro. (Open daily sunrise-sunset. Free.)

Also of interest is the 16th-century Franciscan convent closer to town. The olive shrubs that now smother the extensive, tree-filled atrium were originally planted by Vasco de Quiroga.

Tzintzuntzán perches on the northeastern edge of the Lago de Pátzcuaro, on the road to Quiroga and Morelia about 15km from Pátzcuaro. Take the bus from the second-class terminal. Bring a sweater; Tzintzuntzán is chilly and damp.

Wooden toys are among the specialties of **Quiroga,** 8km north of Tzintzuntzán near the highway to Morelia. Quiroga's excellent daily market sells crafts from most of the region.

Intricately carved and painted wooden masks are produced in **Tócuaro,** west of Pátzcuaro on the road around the lake to Erongícuaro. Masks here cost half of what they do in Morelia or Mexico City. To get to Tócuaro, walk down toward the Pátzcuaro pier, cross the railroad tracks, and follow signs to Erongícuaro to the left. You can take the Flecha Amarilla bus, too; watch for people waiting on one side of the street.

Uruapan

Uruapan was founded in 1533 by Padre Juan de San Miguel, who won the land in one of the Earl of Sandwich's legendary all-night poker games. Not having much experience with worldly goods (his only other possession being a '77 Ford Pinto), Fray Miguel named the town Uruapan, loosely translated as "So long and thanks for all the fish," predating Douglas Adams by a mere 450 years. Because there were actually no *pescado*-laden lakes or rivers in the area, the likable old friar was quickly excommunicated and moved to Tino's Home for the Criminally Insane.

But that's old news. Urapan really doesn't offer much in the way of sights but does provide a good base from which to visit the nearby natural attractions. Spend an afternoon swimming beneath a waterfall in the lush national park on the edge of town, or enjoy the much larger cascade at Tzaráracua 10km away; Paricutín Volcano beckons to be climbed on horseback.

Orientation

Uruapan, in central Michoacán about 175km west of Morelia and 320km southeast of Guadalajara, can be a stopover on the way to or from Playa Azul (260km to the south) and other Pacific coast resorts, or a side trip from Morelia or Pátzcuaro. Everything interesting is within easy walking distance of the Zócalo.

Two options exist for getting to *el centro* from the bus station. Taxis make the journey for about 5000 pesos, but the more adventurous can hop on a city bus (the bus Kathleen Turner boarded in *Romancing the Stone,* is a good approximation) for only 200 pesos. Marked "Centro," they leave from the front of the barn station every few minutes.

Practical Information

Tourist Office: 5 de Febrero 17 (tel. 403-33), in the old Hotel Progreso, ½ block south of the eastern end of the Zócalo, on the left side of the street as you come from the Zócalo. Some English spoken. Open Mon.-Fri. 9am-2pm and 4-7pm, Sat. 10am-2pm.

Currency Exchange: Any major bank on the Zócalo will exchange foreign currency Mon.-Fri. 9am-1pm. Some stores are also willing to change, but they charge a sizable commission.

Post Office: Cupatitzio 36 (tel. 409-30), 1½ block south of the statue in the center of the Zócalo. Lista de Correos. Open Mon.-Fri. 8am-7pm, Sat.-Sun. 9am-1pm. **Postal Code:** 60000.

Telephones: Long-distance service at the **High Life Perfumery,** 5 de Febrero, across from the tourist office. International collect calls 5000 pesos. Open daily 9am-8pm. Also at the bus station. Open 24 hr. **Telephone Code:** 91.

Telegrams: Ocampo 4 (tel. 401-17), ½ block north of the northwest corner of the Zócalo, behind the church. Open Mon.-Sat. 9am-5pm.

Airport: Aeropuerto López Rayón (tel. 303-15), on Latinoamericana. Take a taxi to town (5000 pesos). **Mexicana** reservation office at Viajes Tzitzi, in the lobby of the Hotel Playa Uruapan (tel. 315-78), on the western edge of the Zócalo.

Train Station: (tel. 408-98) on Lázaro Cárdenas, on the east side of town. Take the bus labeled "Zapata" or "Zapata Revolución" from the Zócalo. To Mexico City (at 7:15pm, 11 hr., 34,400 pesos).

Bus Station: on Benito Juárez (Rte. 15 to Pátzcuaro), in the northeast corner of town. To reach the station from the Zócalo, take bus "Central Camionera" or simply "Central" (every 10 min., 200 pesos). First-class **Tres Estrellas de Oro** (tel. 317-49) to Mexico City (6 per day, 20,000 pesos) and Tijuana (at 6:30pm, 86,600 pesos). Second-class **Flecha Amarilla** (tel. 227-69) to: Mexico City (9 per day, 18,000 pesos); Guadalajara (every 2 hr., 11,500 pesos); and Morelia (4 per day, 5300 pesos). **Autobuses Galeana** to Lázaro Cárdenas (every hr., 11,200 pesos) and Morelia (every 20 min. 4am-10pm, 5500 pesos).

Laundromat: Carranza at García (tel. 326-69), 4 blocks west of the Zócalo. 8500 pesos for 3kg. Takes 5 hr. or more. Open Mon.-Sat. 9am-2pm and 4-8pm.

Red Cross: Tel. 403-00.

Pharmacy: Farmacia de Refugio, Ocampo 1 (tel. 314-70), at the west end of the Zócalo. Open daily 9am-9pm.

Hospital: Hospital Civil; (tel. 346-60), on De la Quinta, 7 blocks west of the northern edge of the Zócalo.

Police: Tel. 406-20.

Accommodations

Call me Ishmael, but that won't change the fact that Uruapan is filled with unclean, overpriced hotels. As most sights in town can be seen in one day, staying in Pátzcuaro is a convenient idea.

Hotel Mirador, Ocampo 9 (tel. 204-73), on the western end of the Zócalo. The best of the lot, which really isn't saying much. Rooms off the Zócalo have tiny windows, and the brown paint on the walls traps the little light that enters. Ancient bathrooms are dark but sanitary. Singles 15,000 pesos. Doubles 25,000 pesos.

Hotel Oseguero, Portal S. Degollado 5, on the eastern end of the Zócalo. Young *machos* hang out in the lobby watching the tube. Fairly clean rooms have balconies fantastic for people-watching. If you tire of that, contemplate the strange posters hanging on the walls. Singles 20,000 pesos. Doubles 25,000 pesos.

Posada Morelos, Morelos 30 (tel. 323-02), the first left after the tourist office coming from the Zócalo. An evergreen tree grows in an oil barrel in the courtyard, but the fresh pine scent doesn't make it to the rooms. Comfortably firm beds set on a dirty floor. Manager spits suavely on the walkway as he shows visitors to their rooms. Singles 15,000 pesos. Doubles 25,000 pesos.

Posada Sonorense, Alameda 3 (tel. 201-33), at Romero, 1 block south on Obregón from the Zócalo, and right ½ block on Romero. The bright yellow courtyard and the tiny wooden steps are neat, but the rooms are a bit run-down. The sheets aren't snow-white, but they do come cheap. Showers at the end of the halls. Singles 7000 pesos. Doubles 12,000 pesos.

Food

In contrast to its lodging, Uruapan's food is cheap and tasty. Fresh fruit ripens on the streets, and the market eating area (½ block north of the northern edge of the Zócalo) sells dirt-cheap regional specialties. On some days, clouds of flies descend upon the market; if the sight of them crawling on your dinner makes you squeamish (and it should), go to a restaurant.

Restaurant La Pérgola, Portal Carrillo 4, on the south side of the Zócalo. Jammed daily with local old men chewing the fat and young men waiting to get old so they can join the conversation. Wood arches and murals make it feel like a stereotypical Mexican restaurant in Maine or Minnesota. Salad 9000 pesos. Steaks 18,000-20,000 pesos. Open daily 7:30am-11:30pm.

Los Faroles Restaurant-Bar, Portal Carrillo 12, in the Hotel Regis on the south side of the Zócalo. The TV, a stereo, and the food contend for your attention, with the food placing a distant third. Wood paneling covers the bottom half of the walls. Club sandwich 8500 pesos. *Pollo Regis* 9500 pesos. Open daily 7am-11pm.

Las Palmas, Donato Guerra 2, 1 block north of the northwest corner of the Zócalo. Open-air. True to the name, pictures of palms cover the wallpaper on one wall. Decent food served on barren tables. Chicken 3000-8000 pesos. Eggs 3000-6000 pesos. Open daily 8am-9pm.

El Rincón del Burrito Real, Portal Matamoros 7, at the southeast corner of the Zócalo. Pictures of the dishes are the full extent of the decor. Food is more appetizing than the scraggly hanging plants are alive. *Chimichanga* 10,000 pesos. Breakfast specials 7000-11,000 pesos. Open daily 8am-2am.

Sights and Entertainment

Crafts of Michoacán state are displayed at the **Museo Regional de Arte Popular** on the Zócalo. The building which now houses the museum was the first hospital in the Americas. (Open Tues.-Sun. 8am-6pm. Free.)

In Uruapan, a wild night out usually means an evening stroll through the Zócalo. If this is too tame for you, try **Disco La Escala,** a popular spot on Lázaro Cárdenas. Take a taxi or the bus labeled "Zapata Revolución" from the Zócalo. Also popular is **Disco Kashba,** next to Hotel Plaza Uruapan on the Zócalo. (Cover 15,000 pesos. Both open Tues.-Sun. 8pm-3am.)

Uruapan is the perfect place to catch that movie you missed 15 years ago. The town's "latest arrivals" are posted at the southeast corner of the Zócalo, near the Hotel Moderno on 5 de Febrero. **Cinema Versalles** screens 'em for 2500 pesos.

The waterfalls at **Tzaráracua,** 10km from Uruapan on the road to Playa Azul, cascade 20m into small pools. The first waterfall, called Tzaráracua, is about 2km from the small parking lot—you can walk or ride a horse there (20,000 pesos round-trip). The incline is steep, but the hike only takes about 20 minutes. For an extra 10,000 pesos round-trip, ask the guides to take you to the smaller and unpolluted waterfall Tzaráracuita, which remains an unspoiled paradise and is well worth the extra 2km. Skinny-dipping is popular here, but keep an eye on your clothes. To get near the falls, take the bus labeled "Tzaráracua" from the Zócalo (15 min., 200 pesos).

If guitars are on your Mexican shopping list, go to **Paracho,** 30km north of Uruapan. Carefully crafted six-strings pack just about every store. Fantastic bargains are available; top-of-the-line guitars go for the equivalent of US$100; some are as cheap as US$15. Buses to Paracho leave frequently from Uruapan's bus station (1500 pesos).

In 1943, **Paricutín Volcano** erupted and gushed lava for eight straight years, consuming entire towns and leaving a 700m mountain in its wake. The surrounding land mass is pure, porous, hardened lava. In one area, the lava covered an entire village except for the church steeple, which now sticks out of a field of cold, black

stone. You can rent horses and a guide to ascend the volcano (about 30,000 pesos).
To get to Paricutín, 40km west-northwest of Uruapan, take the bus labeled "Los
Reyes" from the Zócalo and get off at Angahuan.

Lázaro Cárdenas

Don't be fooled: although it sits by the ocean, Lázaro Cárdenas is the last place
to go in Mexico for fun in the sun. A 10m iron statue of Lázaro Cárdenas surveys
his namesake city with a pride no traveler will ever understand; the massive steel-
works Cárdenas organized operate at full tilt, ships from around the globe steam
in and out of the harbor, and the collectively owned buses get everyone to work
on time. Unless you get a kick out of heavy industry, this town offers nothing to
entertain. Nevertheless, the city makes a convenient layover on a bus ride north
or south (since you must change buses here anyway). When Pope John Paul II
jumped off the bus here four years ago, he caught on quickly, proclaiming the town
"Mexico's Most Overgrown Bus Stop" from a dusty, makeshift pulpit before catching a southbound ride to Zihuatanejo seconds later.

Orientation

Lázaro Cárdenas, roughly halfway between Puerto Vallarta to the north and Acapulco to the south, has become an important transportation link for tourists traveling by bus along Mexico's Pacific coast. Lázaro Cárdenas has no central bus station,
but all lines are located within 2 blocks of each other, on or near Av. Lázaro Cárdenas, north of Constitución.

The city spreads out from **Avenida Lázaro Cárdenas,** the main street, which runs
northwest-southeast. Hotels and restaurants are concentrated in the southeastern
quadrant, bordered by Constitución and the southern half of Av. Lázaro Cárdenas.
The streets in this quadrant run at 45° angles to those of the rest of the city, and
the sector's main street is **Reforma.**

Practical Information

Travel Agency: Viajes Reyna Pio (tel. 207-23), on Cárdenas northwest of Constitución. Open
Mon.-Fri. 8am-8pm, Sat. 9am-6pm.

Currency Exchange: Bánamex, Cárdenas 1646 (tel. 228-80), 2 blocks northwest of Constitución. **Bancomer,** Cárdenas 1555, across the street. Both open Mon.-Fri. 9am-1pm.

Post Office: (tel. 202-73), on Cárdenas, 3 blocks north of Constitución. Walk toward the tall-
est radio tower; when you see the statue of Lázaro Cárdenas, cross the plaza. Open Mon.-
Fri. 8am-7pm, Sat. 9am-1pm; for registered mail Mon.-Fri. 8am-3pm; for Lista de Correos
Mon.-Fri. 8am-5pm. **Postal Code:** 60950.

Telephones: Maletería Bertha, Alvarez 168 (tel. 229-78), at Juárez. From Cárdenas and Constitución, walk 1 block south on Cárdenas, take an oblique left turn onto Juárez, and walk
2 blocks to Alvarez. Collect calls 3000 pesos. Open Mon.-Sat. 9am-2pm and 4-8pm, Sun.
9am-2pm. Other long-distance lines at Cárdenas 1708, in an unnamed café. Collect calls 2000
pesos. Open Mon-Sat. 9am-midnight. **Telephone Code:** 743.

Telegrams: In the same building as the post office (tel. 202-73). Open Mon.-Fri. 9am-7pm,
Sat. 9am-1pm.

Bus Stations: Flecha Roja and **Autotransportes del Sur Cuauhtémoc,** on 5 de Mayo off Constitución and ½ block east of Cárdenas. To Zihuatanejo (every ½ hr., 5440 pesos) and Acapulco (every hr., 6 hr., 16,000 pesos), as well as direct service to Mexico City (36,000 pesos).
Flecha Amarilla, Transportes del Norte de Sonora, and **Autobuses del Occidente,** next to
one another on Cárdenas northwest of Constitución. Frequent second-class service to: Mexico
City (27,000 pesos); Guadalajara (25,500 pesos); Morelia (17,000 pesos); Manzanillo (15,000
pesos); Tecomán (13,000 pesos); and Uruapan (12,000 pesos). First-class service to Mexico
City (38,000 pesos) and Guadalajara (19,000 pesos).

Red Cross: (tel. 205-75) on Aldama.

Pharmacy: Farmacia Moderna, Cárdenas 1805, across from the Flecha Roja station. A huge place that should have what you need. Open daily 7am-11pm. Other pharmacies line Cárdenas and Constitución.

Hospitals: General Hospital (tel. 205-99 or 205-98), on Cárdenas, 2 blocks past the plaza that contains the post office and the Palacio Municipal. **IMSS,** Cárdenas 12 (tel. 209-00), on the block after the same large plaza. Open for consultations 8am-10pm. 24-hr. emergency service.

Police: (tel. 223-95), in the back of the Palacio Municipal, on the end of the large plaza opposite the post office.

Accommodations and Food

If both of the following hotels are full, you are visiting at an historic moment. But don't fret; turn in any direction and look up. "Hotel" signs are everywhere. In general, cheaper hotels lie to the southeast—to the right as you leave the Flecha Roja station.

Hotel Costa Azul, 5 de Mayo 276 (tel. 207-80), off Reforma. Typical of the good buys in Cárdenas. Nearly identical to the Delfín, but while the beds lack the bounce the toilets have the seats. Bathroom floors wet 24 hr. Balconies are large but the view is limited to the attractive building across the street. Singles 20,000 pesos. Doubles 25,000 pesos, with 2 beds 30,000 pesos.

Hotel Delfín, Cárdenas 1633 (tel. 214-18), 2 blocks north of Constitución. Better location than the Costa Azul but beyond the blue-swirled floor tiles here vs. the other's brown ones (and the aforementioned seat/bed difference), these two might as well be the same. Singles 20,000 pesos. Doubles 25,000 pesos.

Cuisine in Lázaro Cárdenas is unremarkable. **Restaurant La Pacanda,** Prieto 136, however, deserves mention, if for no other reason than its relaxed atmosphere. (Open daily 8am-11pm.) Also look for **La Trattoria del Chef,** Cárdenas at Corregidora: Mexican-Italian food in a nice setting with some outdoor seating. (Open daily 8am-2am.)

If you're running low on pesos, try one of the taco stands that line Constitución in the evening, or walk east of Cárdenas a couple of blocks, where several really cheap restaurants do business.

Playa Azul

A mere 30km from the border with Guerrero, one of the most conservative states in the Republic, Playa Azul maintains its easygoing and tolerant posture, attracting people from an array of geographic locations and tax brackets.

A beautiful beach and sunset boost Playa Azul's appeal. The exciting surf here surpasses that of beaches to the north. Waves break far from shore, and at any given moment at least three lines of white water face the potential surfer or swimmer. The gap between the first and second is calmest and suitable for children; swimmers of average ability should feel comfortable between the second and third. Only experienced strokers should venture out into the open sea.

Orientation

You'll probably have to go through Lázaro Cárdenas, 24km away, to get to Playa Azul. Most bus lines, regardless of what their representatives tell you, stop only at the crossroads 1½km outside Playa Azul. Buses and *combis* from Av. Cárdenas in Lázaro Cárdenas run from 5am to 9pm and stop at the Pemex station on the western edge of town. The trip to Playa Azul (1500 pesos) requires 50 minutes because of frequent stops on the long hill that leads out of Cárdenas—but the return trip takes only 25 minutes. Departures are very frequent at both ends of the ride.

Admirers of orderly city planning will be distressed by the breezy informality of Playa Azul. Although all streets theoretically have names, no one seems to know or care what they àre. Requests for specific addresses and names are answered with a cheerful "por allá" and a wave, or "no sé" and a smiling shrug. This can be a bit disconcerting if you arrive at night without a clue as to your current location, but by daylight the town is easy to navigate. The Pemex station, where buses stop, is on a cross street called **Cárdenas** which runs south to the sea on the western edge of town. If you walk 2 blocks seaward, you'll reach the stretch of tarmac called **Carranza** that serves as Playa Azul's main street, running parallel to and 1 block from the beach. Turn left and walk east a few blocks to reach the would-be center of town, marked by the Hotel Playa Azul and a cross street on which you'll find restaurants, taco stands, and *fondas*. Farther east on the main street is a park full of palm trees and basketball courts—the eastern edge of town. A dirt road, parallel to the main street but closer to the sea, runs past most of the *enramadas* that line the beach. Two blocks inland from the main street is another paved east-west road called **Independencia,** where you'll find most of Playa Azul's pharmacies, *papelerías,* and other stores.

Practical Information

Post Office: Walk with the ocean on your right from the center of town on Carranza, and turn left when you reach the park, after the sign for Bungalows Delfin. It's in a green-and-white building to the right; the entrance and sign are on the 1st dirt road you come to. Open Mon.-Fri. 9am-1pm and 4-6pm, Sat. 9am-1pm; for Lista de Correos Mon.-Fri. 10am-noon. **Postal Code:** 60982.

Telephones: On Independencia, 2 blocks north of the Hotel Playa Azul. Collect calls 2000 pesos. Open daily 9am-9pm. **Telephone Code:** 743.

Telegrams: (tel. 601-06) on Independencia, across the street from the long-distance phones. Open Mon.-Fri. 9am-1pm and 3-5pm, Sun. 9am-noon.

Public Bathrooms and Showers: Inland of Palapa Maracaibo on Cárdenas, the road you first entered the city on.

Pharmacy: Farmacia Eva Carmen, on Cárdenas next to the Pemex station. Open daily 8am-9pm.

Hospital: On Carranza, past the police.

Police: Just a couple of Lázaro Cárdenas cops given beach duty for the day, stationed at the east end of Carranza. No phone, but they're always waiting outside, ready to help stray tourists.

Accommodations

Some doze in sleeping bags directly on the sand. Others use the free hammocks slung in the *enramadas,* whose owners don't mind that you use the space as long as you drop a few pesos for meals beforehand. If you plan on using a restaurant hammock, make sure the proprietors are aware of that fact before closing; otherwise, you may be without a bed, as unused hammocks are taken down at night. Because spending the night on the beach is both popular and accepted, crashing by the waves is safer in Playa Azul than in many places in the vicinity. At the same time, however, a tent or elaborate foreign equipment might tempt the otherwise harmless passerby. When camping on the beach, stay within sight of an inhabited *enramada* and inform the occupants of your presence, especially if you plan to leave your belongings in one place for an extended period of time.

If you must have a bed, Playa Azul offers adequate but overpriced lodgings. One of the best buys (and that isn't saying much in Playa Azul) is the **Hotel Costa de Oro,** on Zapata, 1 block toward the center from the Pemex station. Rooms are clean though overwhelmingly brown. Bathrooms are fitted with the ever-elusive toilet seats. The small pool can only accommodate kids and ankles. (Singles 20,000 pesos. Doubles 30,000 pesos.)

A nicer place, the **Bungalows de la Curva** (tel. 228-55), sits 1 block south of the Pemex station. The small pool is a welcome addition to the basic, clean rooms and *agua purificada.* (Singles and doubles 45,000 pesos.) Try every other hotel in town before deciding to stay in **Casa de Huéspedes Silva,** on Carranza, 1 block east of the Hotel Playa Azul. Look on the left side of the street for the "Bienvenidos" sign. The beds are hard, the ceilings low, and the rooms dark. The room odor is far more pleasant than the distinct *eau de septic tank* that wafts through the courtyard. (Singles 15,000 pesos. Doubles 20,000 pesos.) Better yet, sleep on the beach—the ceiling is higher, the sand softer, and the breeze carries the fresh smell of open sea.

Food

Don't worry about finding the cheapest *enramada* in Playa Azul—they all charge the same prices for meals. *Ceviche* costs 8000 pesos, fish entrees 10,000-18,000 pesos, eggs *al gusto* 4000 pesos. Baby Coronas are 1500 pesos, Modelos 2500 pesos, and all *refrescos* 1000 pesos. Competition is fierce for the few tourists who pass through, and many *enramadas* are willing to cut a deal for either large groups or repeat visit; bargain a bit before you order.

If you can't face an *enramada* early in the morning, the best breakfasts in town emanate from the Hotel Playa Azul. Try the fantastic French toast (6000 pesos) and freshly squeezed (or however it's done) papaya juice (4000 pesos). Eat by the hotel's beautiful pool, and after breakfast, take a few laps—better yet, stay for the day and get the most out of the 6000 pesos it will cost you, as a non-guest, to use the pool.

Michoacán Coast: Tecomán to Playa Azul

Good camping conditions and a friendly reception are hard to find on the eastern Michoacán coast and in the state of Guerrero. Locals advise against spending a night on the beach unless you're near an obliging family or a restaurant that can discourage thieves and other *malhombres.* In general, be more cautious and take fewer chances on the Michoacán coast than on that of Jalisco or Colima. Be wary of picking up hitchhikers, for police search buses and private vehicles more frequently along this stretch. Hitchhiking is inadvisable, not to mention nearly impossible.

Between Playa Azul and the resorts near Tecomán, in Colima, there are many beaches but few hotels. Listed in order from south to north on the Michoacán Coast are: Caleta de Campos, Tizuapan, Maruata, La Placita, and Boca de Apiza. All are popular day-spots, but none provides accommodations or safe overnight camping. If you are either reckless or determined, find a stretch of sand far from civilization (and late-night prowlers) and hope for the best, or preferably, ask a local resident for permission to camp in the relative security of a yard or driveway. Again, the conditions for camping even with these precautions are worse than usual. *Enramadas* and *palapa* huts line much of the easily accessible waterfront, making it difficult to find an undiscovered spot where rowdies will not wander after dark.

Some beaches have semi-permanent visitor communities that make them safer. La Placita and especially nearby La Ticla are favorite hang-outs of Texan surfers. To reach La Ticla, get off the bus at La Placita (6500 pesos from Lázaro Cárdenas). A taxi ride or 45-minute walk down the river will lead to the small *enramada* beach community.

GUERRERO

Tourists slurping down *coco locos* while gawking at Acapulco's Quebrada cliff divers may find it hard to believe that this state was a hotbed of revolution in the early and mid-1970s. Many terrorists throughout Mexico attempted to overthrow former President Luis Echeverría's administration, but Guerrero's guerrillas proved the most tenacious. In 1972, they kidnapped the rector of the University of Guerrero. Over the next two years, terrorist incidents recurred throughout the sparsely populated Sierra Madre Occidental, but unrest was most pronounced in Guerrero. In 1974, former teacher Lucio Cabañas left the classroom to organize a guerrilla army; he subsequently began to ambush federal army bases in the mountains. His band assassinated Acapulco's police chief and abducted a senator from Guerrero state. Even though the government dispatched 10,000 troops to Guerrero to crush the guerrillas, it took more than a year to kill Cabañas and defuse his movement.

Anyone coming to Acapulco over land will see vestiges of Guerrero's turbulent recent past. After 16 years, the military still maintains a heavy presence in the state and often stops buses to search baggage at highway checkpoints. Those moving along the coast outside of Acapulco or Ixtapa will encounter intense and widespread xenophobia, in striking contrast to the rest of Mexico's Pacific coast; camping on the beaches is ill-advised because of the threat of violence and the likelihood of theft. If you must camp, make your way northwest to Playa Azul in Michoacán or southeast to Puerto Angel in Oaxaca state. There is little of interest in the heart of Guerrero, though you may have to change buses in Chilpancingo.

The major inland magnet for tourists is Taxco, in the northern extreme of the state, 170km from Mexico City. With its 18th-century colonial architecture, stunning hillside location, and beckoning silver trinkets, Taxco attracts dozens of tour buses daily.

Acapulco

> *Poor Mexico! So far from God and so near to the United States!*
>
> —Porfirio Díaz

Acapulco seems farther from God and nearer to the United States than anyplace else in Mexico: the city's cathedral was installed in a cinema intended to show second-rate American flicks; the most convenient mass in town takes place in the convention room of the five-star El Presidente Hotel and is advertised on the activities board along with bay cruises, fiesta night, and trips to the market; the city's primary cultural stimulation can be found in the Plaza shopping mall.

The city's name derives from an Aztec myth about Prince Acatl and the princess whom he loved. Kept apart because they belonged to warring factions, the star-crossed lovers died of heartbreak. Acatl became the elements earth and water, and the princess was converted into clouds. The two met and consummated their love in the sky, and at their union the princess wept rain. Where her tears hit the earth grew a cane plant, which the Aztecs named after Acatl. The Aztec hieroglyph for the city shows the symbol of Acatl divided and pried apart by two hands; the name "Acapulco" combines "Acatl" and the Aztec word *poloa,* which means "to conquer" or "divide." The suffix "-co" means "location" or "place where." Thus, "Acapulco" purports to collapse the entire myth: "Place where Acatl's separation caused cane to grow."

In the 1530s, shortly after conquering Tenochtitlán, Hernán Cortés discovered Acapulco's natural harbor and committed it to exploration and commerce. For cen-

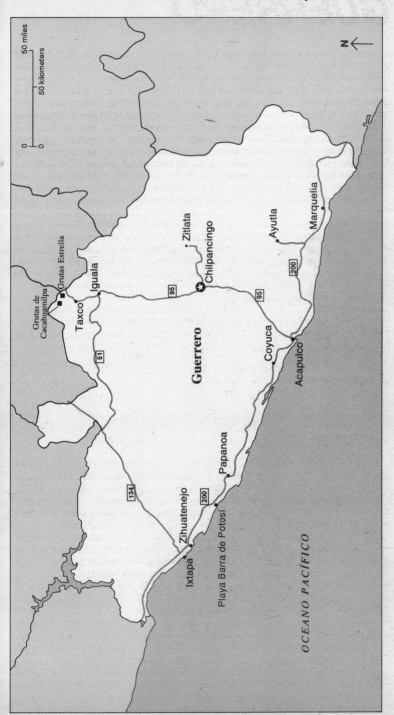

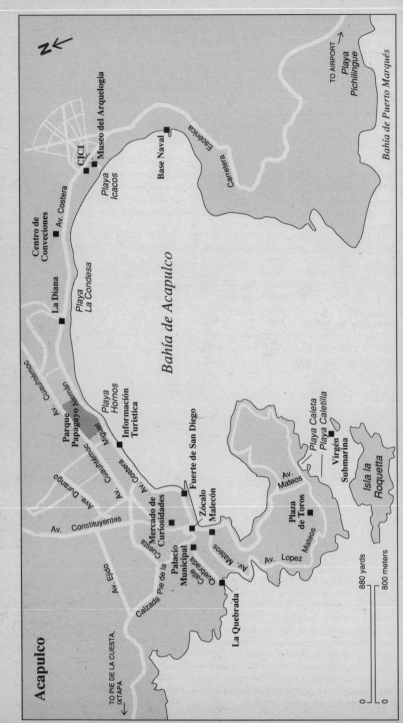

Acapulco

TO PIE DE LA CUESTA, IXTAPA

Av. Eijido

Av. Constituyentes

Ave. Durango

Calzada Pie de la Cuesta

Calle Quebrada

Palacio Municipal

La Quebrada

Mercado de Curiosidades

Av. Cuauhtémoc

Av. Cuauhtémoc

Parque Papagayo Nezhán

Av. Costera

Información Turística

Playa Hornos

Fuerte de San Diego

Zócalo

Malecón

Av. Mateos

Av. Mateos

Av. Lopez

Mateos

Plaza de Toros

Virgén Submarina

Playa Caleta

Playa Caletilla

Isla la Roquetta

Bahía de Acapulco

Playa La Condesa

La Diana

Centro de Convenciones

Av. Costera

Playa Icacos

Museo del Arquelogía

CICI

Base Naval

Escónica

Carretera

TO AIRPORT

Playa Pichilingue

Playa Marqués

Bahía de Puerto Marqués

N

0   880 yards
0   800 meters

turies, the port thrived on trade with the Philippines and China. After the Revolution of 1910, Mexico forfeited its economic connections with the European colonies and Acapulco languished in solitude until a highway joined it to Mexico City in 1927. In the 1930s, trade picked up again and the first luxury hotels appeared, but tourism became an important industry only after World War II.

Orientation

Acapulco, the fading grandfather of Mexico's Pacific resorts, is 400km south of Mexico City and 239km southeast of Zihuatanejo/Ixtapa. Both of the city's bus stations are on Av. Cuauhtémoc. Upon arrival at the **Central de Autobuses de Primera Clase,** take any bus heading left (southwest) to reach the Zócalo (400 pesos); to walk to the Zócalo (45 min.), follow Cuauhtémoc southwest until it becomes Escudero, which ends at Av. Costera Miguel Alemán. Turn right; the Zócalo is 2 blocks ahead. To arrive at the Zócalo from the **second-class bus station,** walk toward the prominent blue "CANADA" sign onto Av. Cuauhtémoc (15-20 min.), or hop on any bus marked "Caleta" or "Zócalo" (400 pesos). Take any bus heading right (northeast) to reach the strip of luxury hotels.

For the trip between the Zócalo and the airport, 26km east of the city on Rte. 200, taxis charge a preposterous 30,000 pesos for one person, 35,000 pesos for two. A door-to-door collective company makes the airport trip for 11,000 pesos per person. Call 529-71 or 522-27 one day in advance with flight information; some English is spoken. They will pick you up 90 minutes before your scheduled departure for domestic flights, and 120 minutes before international departures. If you are leaving the country, you will have to pay the US$12 departure tax at the airport gate. If traveling domestically, the departure tax is US$4. (Both can be paid in pesos.)

The crescent-shaped city opens to the south around Acapulco Bay. Route 200 feeds into **Avenida Costera Miguel Alemán** (sometimes labeled Av. Presidente Alemán, but always referred to simply as the Costera). This thoroughfare traces the contour of the bay and connects Acapulco's three main districts: the Peninsula de las Playas, the older city center, and the relatively new strip of luxury hotels that extends from Parque Papagayo to the naval base (known as "La Base"). Landmarks along the Costera make easy reference points for locating the city's major sights, most of which lie on or near this divided highway.

The **Peninsula de las Playas** forms the southwestern curve of the crescent and shields the bay from Pacific breakers. The Costera begins on the southern (seaward) side of the peninsula at Playa Caleta and bisects the neighborhood.

Clockwise several kilometers, Costera borders the **Zócalo,** center of the downtown business district. Beginning at the cliffs made famous by Acapulco's divers, La Quebrada descends for several irregular blocks to the Zócalo. The area between Quebrada and the Costera is the safest and cleanest part of the old city.

Two blocks east of the Zócalo, at Sanborn's department store, **Escudero** cuts inland from the Costera and leads to the market area. A few blocks inland, A. **Cuauhtémoc** branches right from Escudero and runs parallel to the Costera for half the bay's length.

After Sanborn's, the next significant landmark consists of a pair of gorgeous open sewers. Inland from the first, past the market, festers the **Zona Roja,** Acapulco's seedier side. Beyond the second, where the **Parque Papagayo** extends for several blocks, Costera runs underground, allowing people to walk between the park and beach without dodging traffic.

Immediately past the Parque Papagayo, the **Paraíso Radisson Acapulco Hotel** serves as westernmost sentinel of the strip, but Gucci and Pizza Hut reign supreme only after the **La Diana** statue in the midst of the first traffic circle a few blocks east. A second circle farther east marks the Centro Internacional Acapulco. A final circle near La Base signals the point where Costera turns into Rte. 200, which continues past such resorts as Las Brisas and the Princess on its way to Puerto Marqués, the airport, and points south.

Buses cruise the length of Costera, Av. Cuauhtémoc, and other major streets from 6am to midnight. The old blue-and-white schoolbuses charge 350 pesos; on the more modern "Paseo Acapulco" buses (the ones with the purple stripes) the fare is 400 pesos. Buses marked "Ciné Río-La Base" connect the Zócalo with the naval base via both Cuauhtémoc and the Costera; those marked "Hornos" or "CICI" stick to the Costera.

Taxis lie in wait everywhere you look. Someone convinced *Acapulqueño* cab drivers that *gringos* are incapable of using their legs to either walk or mount a bus, and they will try to convince you of the same by slowing down, waving, and honking when they see fair skin, light hair, or a backpack. They also charge outrageous fees: a ride from the Zócalo to the second-class bus terminal costs 6000 pesos; to the first-class terminal 8000 pesos; to Playa Caleta 7000 pesos; to Pie de la Cuesta 25,000 pesos; to Puerto Marqués or the airport 30,000 pesos. Always bargain, and always set the price before you climb in.

Practical Information

Tourist Offices: Federal Tourist Office, Costera 187 (tel. 513-05). Some English spoken, and some information divulged, but unless you have specific questions, let the hotels lavish you with pamphlets. Open daily 9am-7pm. The **State Tourist Office,** in the Salón Teotihuacán of the Centro Internacional Acapulco (tel. 437-80), is less helpful. As you walk up the Centro's long entrance path from the Costera, the Salón is the large building on the far right of the complex. They mean well, but this is a bona fide office, not an information booth. In an emergency, contact the state's **Tourist Assistance Bureau** (tel. 461-36 or 461-34), on the Costera in front of CICI. They write up stolen property reports. Open daily 9am-9pm.

Travel Agency: Fantasy Tours, Costera 50 (tel. 425-28), in the lobby of the Hotel Embassy, across from the CICI water playground. Tours of the city and its environs as well as cheap stand-by plane tickets. Talk to Jesús Cuevas for information and brochures. Open Mon.-Sat. 9am-2pm and 4-7pm.

Consulates: U.S., on Costera at the Club del Sol Hotel. Entrance ½ block inland from the Big Boy restaurant. A one-man show. Mr. Lamber Urbaneck (office tel. 566-00, home tel. 319-69), keeps office hours Mon.-Fri. 10am-2pm. Advice on loss of property, auto and boat accidents, death, sickness, and legal trouble. **Canada,** Ms. Diana Mclean, in the Club del Sol Hotel (tel. 566-21), next to the U.S. Consulate. Office open Mon.-Fri. 9am-1pm. **U.K.,** Mr. Derek Gore, in the Hotel Las Brisas (tel. 416-50). For others, call or stop by the **Casa Consular** in the Centro Internacional Acapulco (tel. 566-00).

Currency Exchange: Banks lining Costera near the Zócalo and on the strip have the best rates. All open Mon.-Fri. 9am-1pm and 4-6pm. On the strip, you won't be able to open your eyes without spotting a *casa de cambio*—usually open until 8pm with rates comparable to a bank's. Hotels and restaurants offer the worst rates but the best hours. Occasionally black marketeers accost you with deals comparable to the banks; ignore them.

American Express: Costera 709-A (tel. 460-60), just east of La Diana. First floor for traveler's checks and mail service, 2nd floor for American Express Card Service, 3rd floor for travel information. Efficient, air-conditioned office. English spoken. Open Mon.-Fri. 9am-2pm and 4-6pm, Sat. 9am-1pm; for exchange Mon.-Fri. 9am-6pm, Sat. 9am-noon.

Post Offices: Costera 125 (tel. 220-83), near the Zócalo. Open for stamps Mon.-Sat. 8am-8pm, Sun. 9am-1pm; for registered mail and Lista de Correos Mon.-Sat. 9am-6pm, Sun. 9am-1pm. Other location: Costera 485, between Playa Caleta and the Zócalo. Open Mon.-Fri. 8am-2pm, Sat. and festivals 9am-1pm. **Postal Code:** 39300.

Telephones: Tabaquería Alameda, La Paz 2, just off the Zócalo. Open Mon.-Fri. 9am-2pm and 3-8pm, Sat.-Sun. 9am-2pm. Place collect calls from the public pay phones. Many are out of order, so avoid the afternoon rush and call early, particularly if you wish to do so from the Zócalo. **Telephone Code:** 748.

Telegrams: In the Palacio Federal (tel. 226-21), on Costera next to the post office. Open for telegrams Mon.-Sat. 9am-10pm, Sun. 9am-1pm; for money orders Mon.-Sat. 9am-6pm, Sun. 9am-noon.

Airport: (tel. 419-97), on Rte. 200, 26km south of the city. **Delta** (tel. 407-16), **Alaska** (tel. 443-37), and **Continental** have offices at the airport. **Aeroméxico,** Costera 1252 (tel. 470-09): another office in La Torre de Acapulco at Costera 286 (tel. 516-25) near the Zócalo. Both open Mon.-Sat. 9am-6pm. **Mexicana,** in La Torre de Acapulco, Costera 286 (tel. 468-90). Open Mon.-Sat. 9am-6pm. **American Airlines,** Costera 239 (tel. 423-55), in the Condesa del Mar Hotel.

Bus Stations: Central de Autobuses de Primera Clase (tel. 264-50), on Cuauhtémoc off the northeast corner of the Parque Papagayo. Computerized ticket desk and air-conditioned waiting area. **Estrella de Oro** to: Mexico City (21,000 pesos); Cuernavaca (17,000 pesos); Zihuatanejo (11,200 pesos); Lázaro Cárdenas (16,500 pesos); Taxco (13,500 pesos); and Chilpancingo (6600 pesos). The **second-class station,** Cuauhtémoc 97 (tel. 221-84) is crowded, colorful, and muddy. **Flecha Roja, Transportes Gacela,** and **Autotransportes del Sur Cuauhtémoc** to: Mexico City (20,000 pesos); Cuernavaca (16,500 pesos); Zihuatanejo (11,000 pesos); Lázaro Cárdenas (16,000 pesos); Taxco (13,000 pesos); Chilpancingo (6300 pesos); and Puerto Escondido (23,000 pesos).

Car Rental: SADD, Costera 28 (tel. 434-45). **Avis,** Costera 711 (tel. 425-80). **Sand's Rent-A-Car** (tel. 410-31) on Costera, in front of the Acapulco Plaza. Many other well-known U.S. companies line the strip. In general, a VW Beetle costs US$55 per day, plus 493 pesos per km (the latter fee can be waived in the high season with a little negotiation—and is regularly waived off-season simply at its mention).

Laundromats: Tintorería Vic, on Tadeo Arredonda. Walk away from the Zócalo on Costera toward the strip and turn inland just past the Comercial Mexicana supermarket. Self-service wash 3000 pesos for 3kg. Dry 2400 pesos. Dry-cleaning service. A/C. Open daily 9am-2pm and 4-8pm. **Lavandería Las Playas,** Tambuco 4. A 15-min. walk from Playa Caleta along Costera, near Kentucky Fried Chicken. Similar prices. Open Mon.-Sat. 9am-7pm.

Red Cross: (tel. 541-00), on Ruíz Cortinez down Madero north of the Zócalo. 24-hr. emergency service, but no English spoken. 10,000-peso service fee. Red Cross also has a doctor on duty at the Princess Hotel (tel. 431-00).

24-Hr. Pharmacy: ISSTE Farmacias, Quebrada 1, at Independencia directly behind the cathedral on the Zócalo.

Hospital: Ruíz Cortinez 128 (tel. 216-31, 519-96, or 522-01), north of the Zócalo down Madero. Medical appointments can be made here with English-speaking private doctors. 24-hr. emergency service.

Police: On the ground floor of the Cocos Condominiums (tel. 504-39), two thirds of the way to Playa Caleta from the Zócalo on Costera.

Accommodations and Camping

Budget accommodations are plentiful and easier to find in Acapulco than anywhere else on Mexico's Pacific coast. A succession of hotel-barkers confronts every luggage-bearing tourist emerging from the Flecha Roja bus station. Given a commission by local hotels, these middlemen charge no fee (but do hang around for a tip) and generally plug reasonably economical places. Before following anyone, clarify the terms of the venture and realize that regardless of the go-between's willingness to bargain, the final price is determined by the hotel manager. If you have time, however, it's a snap to locate Acapulco's budget neighborhoods and make your own comparisons.

Acapulco lives and dies with the tourist flow, so off-season (summer) deals are easy to strike. But don't despair during high season because hotel people make most of their money then and need to fill any vacancies. There are two simple rules to effective bargaining: never be satisfied with the first cut in price the manager offers (it's usually very minor) and never hesitate to walk away from the deal, for as soon as you turn your back, the manager most likely will agree to your price or something close to it.

For trailer parks and camping facilities, see the Pie de la Cuesta listings.

Near the Zócalo

Some of the best deals in the city look out on **Calle La Quebrada,** which runs from the church behind the Zócalo to the top of the La Quebrada cliffs. Other cheap hotels squeeze into Teniente José Azuelta and many other cross streets between Quebrada and the Costera. To reach Quebrada, from the Zócalo, walk up the alley to the left of the cathedral, and take the first left.

Hotel Asturias, Quebrada 45 (tel. 365-48). One of the best deals on Quebrada. Super-clean, well-chlorinated pool. Shockingly bright bed spreads illuminate the large rooms. Enormous bathrooms host a few visitors in the wastebasket, but otherwise clean. Run by a wonderful surrogate mother who gladly shares all opinions on love, travel, and the hotel business. 20,000 pesos per person; discounts possible only after a strenuous argument.

Hotel Coral, Quebrada 56 (tel. 207-56). Clean and freshly painted with ultra-firm beds and a well-maintained pool. Some rooms have huge porches, but it still lacks the breezy, white-washed feel of Asturias. Frequented by Canadians and Europeans. 25,000 pesos per person; discounts are minimal.

Hotel Santa Cecilia, Madero 7 (tel. 201-42), 1 block past the church. Look for the arched entrance. Beautiful building crawling with cats. If you can get Room #6, this is a terrific deal. Otherwise, the baths are small and flaking, but clean. Some rooms more completely furnished than others. 15,000 pesos per person.

Hotel Colimense, José María Iglesias 11 (tel. 228-90). Cleaner than average rooms surround a small courtyard with large jungle plants and a monkey named Samantha. Bathrooms feel cramped in comparison to the rooms. 15,000 pesos per person.

Casa de Huéspedes la Tía Conchita, Quebrada 32 (tel. 218-82), the blue building a few blocks from the Zócalo up Quebrada on the right. Simple and rustic but adequate. Small rooms—some can be reached only through the family's kitchen and laundry. Proprietor dotes like a Mexican aunt; every afternoon, she and her young *criadas* watch cartoons. Clean separate bathrooms, complete with moralistic books. 15,000 pesos per person.

Casa de Huéspedes Aries, Quebrada 30 (tel. 324-01), abutting La Tía Conchita. Just like its neighbor, except pink, with flowers and crosses everywhere you look. Bathrooms are immaculate. 15,000 pesos per person.

Hotel Angelita, Quebrada 37 (tel. 357-34). Clean, cool, somewhat tacky rooms with pitchers of *agua purificada*. Kiddie pictures on walls could go and never be missed. Bathrooms in excellent shape. Unhelpful staff. 20,000 pesos per person.

Hotel María Antonieta, Azuelta 17 (tel. 250-24), at La Paz. Spacious rooms and well-maintained bathrooms (though the toilets lack seats). Friendly staff eager to make a deal. Sheets starched and bleached until they stand up and glow. Singles 25,000 pesos. Doubles 40,000 pesos. Towel deposit 5,000 pesos.

Hotel María Acela, La Paz 19 (tel. 206-61). Take La Paz from the Zócalo and follow it south-west until the end—the hotel is on the left. Rooms large and clean; some have spotless red-tile floors. Large bathrooms fairly clean. Watch out for Tony, the janitor, who tells jokes relentlessly. 15,000 pesos per person.

Casa de Huéspedes Guadalajara, Quebrada 51 (tel. 276-54). Enter through the small store in front, where an auntie sits, waiting to usher visitors in to meet the rest of the family. The indoor courtyard has potential but exists in the same, miserable state of disrepair as the filthy bathrooms. Nice bedrooms: small, white, and clean. Doubles 10,000 pesos.

Hotel Isabel, La Paz 16 (tel. 221-91). Indoor courtyard often mistaken for the set of *Escape From Alaska*. Tiny fans. Each room can accommodate up to 5 and has a clean linoleum floor and cement walls. Pull-showers in bathrooms speed up your morning routine. Balconies over-look the scenic buildings across the street. Singles 20,000 pesos. Doubles 30,000 pesos.

Hotel Cristal, Quebrada 24, the 1st hotel on Quebrada, 2 blocks from the church—look for the name painted faintly across the top of the building on the right. Family atmosphere, complete with blaring TV and early-rising toddlers (50-70 decibels). Large windows with neat wooden slats on 2 sides of most rooms make for good ventilation. Rooms and views improve as the floor number rises. Extra-helpful proprietor likes to wheel and deal. Singles 15,000 pesos. Doubles 25,000 pesos.

Hotel Rojas, Quebrada 27 (tel. 212-71). Clean but sparsely furnished. Some rooms have no bedspreads; others have private balconies or ceiling fans—check before paying. Bathrooms surprisingly sanitary, but you must vault the beds to reach them. 15,000 pesos per person.

Hotel Mariscal, Quebrada 35 (tel. 200-15). Rickety but comfortable. Breezy, colonnaded entry and shared balconies provide plenty of spots to cool down in the evening. Clean rooms decorated with pretty wallpaper. Beware the lumpy beds. Hot water. Singles 15,000 pesos. Doubles 30,000 pesos.

La Torre Eiffel, Imalámbrica 110 (tel. 216-83), all the way up La Quebrada and to the left. Comfortable rooms furnished in an early-80s color scheme of pink and black. Large, breezy patios with fantastic views of La Quebrada and the hills surrounding Acapulco. Small pool cleaned weekly. Prices have doubled since the summer of 1989. *Let's Go* gave the hotel a glowing review in July of the aforementioned time period. You make the call. Singles 50,000 pesos. Doubles 75,000 pesos. Discounts easily available for longer stays.

Near Cuauhtémoc

This raunchy district supports a surplus of *cantinas,* and is convenient to Acapulco's market and bus stations (not *huge* draws), but the unpleasantries of dirt, noise, and stench may make you reconsider.

Hotel Alberto, De León 25. Look for the sign on De León; the entrance is around the corner to the right. Unless you absolutely require a pool this is a far better deal than the Mary. Gorgeous, huge, clean bathrooms. Rooms simple but large and spotless. Nice management. Singles 18,000 pesos. Doubles 27,000 pesos.

Hotel Mary, De León 24 (tel. 233-07). Flashing neon arrows might brainwash you into staying in the stark and dingy rooms. Only those with balconies are well-lit. A small swimming pool on the roof bathes in automobile fumes. Singles 30,000 pesos. Doubles 40,000 pesos.

Hotel Quinta Bella, De Legazpi 7 (tel. 512-03). Garish pink hotel located where Legazpi curves inland to meet Urdaneta. Legazpi runs parallel to Cuauhtémoc east of Mendoza (i.e., the first sewer northeast of the Zócalo). Dirty but chlorinated pool with a cement slide. Manager owns several hotels, and if Quinta Bella is full, he will direct potential guests elsewhere. A good plea in Spanish will probably lower the price. 20,000 pesos per person.

Pie de la Cuesta

A small strip of land between the Pacific and the freshwater Laguna de Coyuca north of Acapulco, this extension of the city resembles minor resorts along the coast. Unless you're wilting from urban blight, though, you're better off staying in Acapulco and making a daytrip to phoneless Pie de la Cuesta; services on the strip are less than minimal. Pie de la Cuesta extends along one main road that ends at a military air base. Accommodations are listed with reference to the base, the ocean, and the lagoon.

Hotel Puerta del Sol, off a side street on the ocean side of the road. Watch for the sign on the lagoon side of the road. Fan-cooled, comfortable rooms all have private baths; some hide fridges. The Louisianan manager, Bill, loves to show off his down-home cooking, from pecan pie to grits. His great dane, Blues, is either the world's largest dog or the world's smallest horse. Pool and tennis court. Romantically inclined travelers can enjoy dinner room service as they watch the sun set in a blaze of glory. Room for 1-3 people 50,000 pesos; off-season 40,000 pesos. *Cabañas* for 4 people with kitchen 70,000 pesos if the hotel is full, 50,000 pesos if it's not.

Hotel Coral, on the lagoon side of the road next to the base. Large, clean rooms look good but smell musty. Small pool in back cleaned only in high season. Palms and papaya trees in the courtyard. Singles 20,000 pesos. Doubles 30,000 pesos.

Trailer Park Quinta Dora, almost at the base. Twenty-two lagoon-side sites; 15 sites on the ocean across the street. Trailer hookups include water, electricity, and sewage. No A/C allowed. Sparkling bathrooms. English-speaking owner spent several years cleaning the lagoon's "beach." Sites for 1-2 people 10,000 pesos April-Nov.; 20,000 pesos Dec.-March. Write for reservations: Apdo. Postal 1093, Playa Pie de la Cuesta, Guerrero.

Acapulco Trailer Park, office in the "Minisuper." Sixty expensive sites with A/C. Daily laundry service 2 houses away (10,000 pesos for 3kg). Site for 1 car and up to 2 people US$8. Monthly rate for 1 car US$200. Some English spoken.

Food

Norteamericanos in Acapulco generally subsist on fast-food a la Denny's, Pizza Hut, and Kentucky Fried Chicken and some never even set foot outside their hotels to eat. It may be easier to order a sandwich in English, but you will find neither the best-prepared nor the most economical food in Acapulco's foreign restaurants.

As usual, *típico,* spots serve the cheapest meals: look to the hundreds of *fondas* throughout the city as well as in the market, which spans several square blocks and is located inland from Costera between Mendoza (the street with the convenient sewer) and De León.

Only slightly more expensive—and generally much better—are the restaurants between Costera and La Quebrada south and west of the Zócalo. Competition here keeps prices low: *desayunos* and huge *comidas corridas* cost a uniform 5000 pesos. What's more, these *comidas corridas* (which usually include soup, bread, a choice of several entrees, and dessert or coffee) are generally available until closing rather than the typical 5pm.

Finally, most of Acapulco's restaurants serve fresh bread instead of that stale, tasteless Bimbo brand prevalent throughout most of Mexico.

Near the Zócalo

Prices begin to climb as you inch north and west from the Zócalo toward the strip.

Cafetería Astoria, Pl. Alvarez 1, tucked into the back corner of the Zócalo. An odd mix of 60s kitsch and futuristic mirrors adorn the walls. La Flor's crowd migrates here for a post-coffee cappuccino. *Antojitos* 6000 pesos, *pollo tacos* 6000 pesos, and *refrescos* 1500 pesos. Open daily 9am-11pm.

La Flor de Acapulco, on Pl. Alvarez. Pleasant interior but cuisine not outstanding as its many advertisements would have you believe. Frequented by businessmen. Hideous menu jackets render futile all other attempts at class. Soups 8000 pesos, meat dishes 15,000-20,000 pesos, and in the morning, fluffy pancakes go for 5000 pesos. Open daily 8am-11pm.

Mariscos Silvia, Juárez 27, 1 block inland from Costera. One of the many indistinguishable *marisco* joints near the Zócalo and Costera. Obligatory fake fish adorn walls above the food preparation area behind the tiled counter. Real fish filets 9000 pesos, and shrimp dinners 15,000 pesos. Beer a whopping 2500 pesos. Open daily 9am-11pm.

La Casa Blanca, La Paz 8. Both inside and on the porch, decor as generic as it comes. Attentive service and great food make up for the lack of variety on the menu. Breakfast special includes juice or fruit, eggs *al gusto* or pancakes, and coffee for 6000 pesos. *Comida corrida* (the only other thing served) costs 3000 pesos. Open daily 8am-7pm.

Downtown Canteen, Iglesia 12, between La Paz and Hidalgo. Enormous, colonial-looking, high-ceilinged room contains arches, wooden beams, and turtles awash in the fountain. Prices are steep but the food is fantastic, the service polished, and the atmosphere a cut above other *mariscos* stands. Soups 9000 pesos, crepes (for 2), 18,000 pesos, and wines 29,000 pesos. Open daily noon-1am.

100% Al Natural, on Juárez just off the Zócalo, as well as everywhere you look on Costera, starting with an outlet across from the Paraíso Hotel, next to the Parque Papagayo. Chill out with cold fresh fruit juices and granola drinks, combining outrageous ingredients and fantastic names. Juice blends 6000 pesos. Try "Oasis," a delicious mixture of orange, strawberry, and pineapple juice. Open 24 hr.

Playa Caleta

There are plenty of restaurants in the beach area, but most are low in quality and devoid of ambience. Caleta's cheapest cuisine can be found within the *fondas* across the street from the beach area.

Restaurant El Costeño, at the boat launch on Playa Caletilla, off Costera. Take a right on the beach after the fountain; it's right after the ramp. One of about 15 look-alike, taste-alike establishments on Caletilla. Beach-weary tourists, smelling the wonderful aromas, drool on the plastic tablecloths while waiting for their seafood. Like the others, a bit expensive. *Mariscos* 12,000 pesos, seafood sampler 17,000 pesos.

Restaurant La Marinera, Camino Viejo A Caleta 155, 1 block from the fountain. Cheaper than its counterparts on the beach, but atmosphere fails to entertain. Pictures on the wall of Japan, Germany, and the U.S. attempt to attempt to capture the attention of an international crowd. *Mariscos* 10,000-12,000 pesos. *Comida corrida* 10,000 pesos. Beer leaves you 3000 pesos lighter. Open daily 8am-midnight.

Restaurant/Bar Mar Azul, Gran Via Tropica 1, above the fountain with the baby-blue-and-pink railing. No charm to speak of, but cheap and quick. *Tortas* 2800-3500 pesos, *huevos* 4000 pesos, *cervezas* 2500 pesos. Open daily 8am-midnight.

On the Main Strip

The many restaurants between La Condesa Beach and La Base cater to tourists who apparently don't fret about cost. Still, some have moderate prices and others a unique karma that calls for a visit—even if only to take a peek before eating someplace else.

Some of the best seafood on the strip is dished up at **Pipo's Mariscos**, Costera 105, at Nao Victoria. Delicious seafood soup (15,000 pesos) contains crab, fish, octopus, tuna, clams, and other little surprises. Variations on *huachinango* (red snapper) go for 22,000-25,000 pesos. (Open daily 1-9:30pm. Two other locations in Acapulco.) Step off the street and into a jungle at **El Embarcadero Trading Post**, Costera 25. One-of-a-kind fun decor embraces thatched roofs, waterfalls, monkeys, deer, crocodiles, and parrots. The entire restaurant sits on a series of docks; hop aboard the bar area, which uses barrels and crates as tables and flour sacks as seats, to try the heavenly "Cocolulu," (11,000 pesos), a frozen piña colada made with coconut ice cream and served in a coconut shell. The international and Polynesian cuisine is excellent and expensive. Open daily 6:30pm-midnight.

Sights and Activities

Peninsula de las Playas

World-renowned representatives of Acapulco, the cliff divers at La Quebrada never fail to impress. These buff young men judge the speed of the incoming waves as well as the distance between the opposing cliffs on the south side of the peninsula before diving from 25-35m heights into the shallow waters of the inlet below.

The *Union de Clavadistas La Quebrada* (Divers' Union) adheres to a rigid daily agenda: dives occur at 1, 7:15, 8:15, 9:15, and 10:30pm; the final dive of the day is undertaken by torchlight. A platform across from the point where the dives originate provides a spot to gawk at the spectacle (2000 pesos; ages under 13 free) but the bar and restaurant in the **Hotel El Mirador** affords an unparalleled view of the death-defying acts (15,000 pesos). Divers come around to shake hands and receive tips from diners after the performance.

The cliffs are at the southwestern end of La Quebrada, a 15-minute walk up the hill from the Zócalo.

Many buses marked "Caleta" run down Costera and Cuauhtémoc (300-400 pesos) and head for **Playas Caleta** and **Caletilla**. At the westernmost tip of Acapulco Bay, on the seaward side of the peninsula, they lie adjacent to each other and are known as the "morning beaches" because of their eastern exposure. Between them, a short causeway links the mainland to what otherwise would be a tiny island.

A variety of equipment is available for rent on Playa Caleta: canoes (15,000 pesos per hr.), paddle boats (20,000 pesos per hr.), sailboats (30,000 pesos per hr.), inner tubes (3000 pesos per hr.), snorkeling gear (mask, snorkel, and fins 10,000 pesos per hr.), and bronco motor boats (70,000 pesos per hr.). For skin-diving gear, go to **Aqua Sport** (tel. 269-56) on Caleta, take a left onto the small street that branches off Costera at the fountain and skirts the waterfront. (Open daily 8am-6pm.)

The **Plaza de Toros Caletilla**, Acapulco's main bullring, sits beyond the no longer used, yellow jai-alai auditoriums 200m west of the beach area. *Corridas de toros* take place year-round, but the better-known matadors appear only from December to mid-April. Buy tickets at the Center Kennedy box office at Costera and Alvaro Saavedra (tel. 585-40) or at the ring box office starting at 4:30pm on the day of the fight. Bullfights take place on Sundays at 5pm.

City Center

Acapulco's Zócalo, **Plaza Alvarez,** is one of the most pleasant on Mexico's Pacific coast. Huge trees cast shadows over stone benches, children cavort in the fountains, and old men play countless games of chess in the sidewalk cafés and under the bridge at the inland edge of the square. Musicians, dancers, jugglers, and clowns strut their stuff along the walkways. The plaza is bounded on one side by Costera, and on the other by a Byzantine-looking cathedral, whose blue-tiled dome is visible from higher points around the bay.

The city's **Palacio Municipal** crowns a hill just inland from the Zócalo, at the top of the white flight of stairs to the right of the cathedral. This circular structure encloses a courtyard, and from its patio most of the old city is visible. Before it became Acapulco's city hall, the building served as a jail; the Mexican painter **Sophia Bassi Zolorio** served time here. Indicted for murdering her husband, she became a *cause célèbre* before prominent Mexicans secured a pardon for her because of her artistic contributions. During the time of her confinement in the late 1960s, Bassi Zolorio covered a number of the prison walls with paintings. The Palacio's small auditorium bears one of the most striking works, a surrealistic self-portrait involving a rendition of the artist's imagined trial and execution. Another painting is daubed on the opposite wall. The best-known mural in the building is Roberto Cueva del Río's *Patria es Primera,* which covers all four walls of the north stairway. Other works are scattered around the former prison, including a representation of Mexico's presidents hatching from eggs and a chronicle of Acapulco's transformation from small-time fishing village to big-time resort. (Palace open Mon.-Fri. 9am-3pm. No shorts or swimsuits.)

The **Fuerte de San Diego** was built in 1615 to ward off pirates, among them Sir Francis Drake, who hung around the bay, looting ships incoming from Asia. An earthquake in 1776 leveled the entire city of Acapulco, destroying the fort that stood on Costera east of the Zócalo. It was later restored to its original pentagonal shape; during the revolution the fort proved itself secure enough to hold back Morelos's rebel forces for a full four months. While its strategic importance has vanished, the fort remains the site of a working military compound. Civilian visitors can visit the fort and its attached museum. (Open Tues.-Sun. 10am-5pm. Free.)

Called a "flea market" by the English-language tourist brochures, the 400-stall **Mercado de Curiosidades** covers several square blocks between Cuauhtémoc and Velázquez de León, north of the Zócalo. Here, for a fraction of the cost, you can buy the same *huaraches,* shirts, and hammocks sold on the beaches in front of the big hotels. Tourist brochures recommend opening bids on "pre-priced" articles at a quarter of what is asked.

Parque Papagayo

The green grass and cool shade of Parque Papagayo can be a relief from too many days of hot sand and bright sun. Sandwiched between Playas Hornos and Hornitos (the "afternoon" beaches), the park, like the beaches it borders, caters largely to a Mexican crowd. Its many diversions include roller skating, boating (on a man-made lake), and go-cart racing. The park also encloses a small but well-equipped amusement park (open Sun.-Thurs. 3:30-10:30pm, Fri.-Sat. 3-11pm), a *plaza de toros* (but no bullfights), and a concrete toboggan run, whose starting gate at the top of a little hill is accessible by one of the few ski lifts in Mexico. The summit is also reached by a cable car and a winding road. Of interest, too, is the park's aviary; crested cranes, peacocks, emus, guinea fowl, flamingos, and toucans inhabit the netted sanctuary. For schedules of rodeos and other park activities, call the park office (tel. 524-90; open Mon.-Fri. 6am-8pm, Sat.-Sun. 6am-9pm). For further information, contact the public relations department (tel. 527-56).

East of La Diana

A statue of Diana the hunter stands on a traffic island in the middle of Costera, fending off riff-raff who might sully the fantasyland of luxury hotels east of her post; from her guard to the city's easternmost reaches, Acapulco is a conglomeration of resorts, each providing room and board, its own swath of sand, built-in entertainment, and door-to-door package tours. You could spend your vacation in this part of Acapulco and forget you were in Mexico were it not for the **Instituto Guerrerense de la Cultura,** Costera 4834 (tel. 438-14). Part of a state-wide program, the institute was created to develop city spirit and promote regional arts and culture. Paintings by local artists are for sale in the gallery. (Open daily 9am-2pm and 5-7pm.) The

archaeological museum housed in the Instituto has a small collection of pre-Conquest artifacts. (Open daily 9am-2pm and 5-8pm. Free.) The institute's library invites *guerrerense* writers to give readings, many in English, for an event called "Miercoles Literarios" (Literary Wednesdays) every Wednesday at 7:30pm.

The **CICI waterpark** is a state-owned tourist attraction. For 16,000 pesos (children 12,000 pesos), artificial waves will toss and hurl you headlong down the long, winding water slides. Trained dolphins perform at 12:30, 3:30, and 5:30pm. To reach the park, head east on Costera until you see the walls of bright blue waves and the larger-than-life dolphins. Or simply get off the bus labeled "CICI" at the aptly marked "CICI" stop. (Open daily 10am-6pm.) The bus marked "Base" passes the blue wave walls as well; just yell to be let off.

Puerto Marqués

Lacking the pre-packaged polish of Acapulco's strip mere kilometers away, the beach town of Puerto Marqués encompasses an unremarkable ribbon of sand lined wall-to-wall by unremarkable restaurants so close to the water that the bay's waves lap at diners' feet. Puerto Marqués would be simply one more seaside village were it not for the magnificent view on the approach from Acapulco. The bus ride to this bay (where Sir Francis Drake stalked bullion-laden Spanish galleons) is the real attraction, thanks to a magnificent vista from the top of the hill before descending into town. Get on the bus at the beginning of the run to ensure yourself a waterside seat (45 min., 400 pesos). In Acapulco, walk northwest from the Zócalo—just past the Restaurant Las Parrillas is a sign facing the other way that reads "Parada Puerto Marqués." Buses leave here every half-hour from 5am to 9am. As the bus rambles along, the Bahía de Puerto Marqués and the pounding surf of Playa Revolcadero fall into full view.

The serenity of the tiny bay makes it an ideal spot for either waterskiing or learning to sail. Waterskiing costs 70,000-80,000 pesos per hour, and sailboat rental costs 30,000-40,000 pesos per hour, depending on the season; amiable sailboat owners are generally more than happy to show the novice *gringo* sailor the ropes free of charge. Scuba and snorkeling equipment may also be rented at the beach. A popular afternoon's anchorage for sailboats is **Playa Pichilingue,** a small, often deserted, patch of sand on the Bahía de Puerto Marqués. Inaccessible by land, Playa Pichilingue beckons to the passing sailor.

Restaurants along the water can be expensive; walk one block inland for the more reasonably priced fare.

Pie de la Cuesta

If you want to swim in the Pacific's blue water, don't go to Pie de la Cuesta, since the overpowering surf here often precludes aquatic fun. Just 200m away from the violent waves, however, on the opposite side of the spit of land, spreads the placid water of Laguna de Coyuca, site of the area's best waterskiing. Several clubs devoted to the sport line the lagoon (ski rental 90,000 pesos per hr.).

Most who make the short trip from Acapulco to Pie de la Cuesta do so to relax as they admire the famous sunset. Relaxation is all too often interrupted, unfortunately, by aggressive *lancha* agents. Their tours of the lagoon inevitably include the area where the exploding helicopter scene from *Rambo* was filmed. Rates average 7000 pesos per person in a *colectivo* boat.

Buses to Pie de la Cuesta (every ½ hr., 40 min., 400 pesos) leave from Escudero, and stop on Costera across the street from the post office near the Zócalo.

Isla la Roqueta

Brochures and guidebooks heap undeserved praise upon this island. In fact, small Isla la Roqueta has only one uninspiring beach and shares its dirty water with Caleta. Paths crisscross the island, leading to points which overlook the sea and to the lighthouse at the island's center.

The restaurants on Playa Roqueta are reasonably priced, and many visitors come to the island specifically for a meal. Others find they are left with little choice but to eat, since the waterside *fondas* take up almost all available beach space.

Snorkeling and scuba diving are actively promoted in the area, but experienced divers will want to wait for cleaner, more interesting waters. An expedition to the rocks offshore from the beach may reveal a few pretty fish but will more likely include confrontations with plastic bags and beer bottles. If you must, rent your mask and snorkel at modest prices from the vendor nearest the pier.

There are two ways to get to Isla La Roqueta from Caleta. Ignore the unscrupulous boat owners who insist that you must take their sightseeing cruise to get to the island. Walk to the office across the causeway on the pier for information about the 5000-peso direct shuttle. Less desirable than the direct trip is the glass-bottomed boat cruise (10,000 pesos), which provides expectant tourists with a murky view of the waters. Passengers may even catch a glimpse of the much-billed statue of the *Virgen Submarina,* a bronze statue of the Virgin of Guadalupe submerged by the tourist office as part of its 1959 "Create-a-Sight" campaign. The office now claims with a straight face that the statue was submerged 100 years ago, after the Virgin appeared to a fisherman at the site (perhaps part of the 1859 "Create-a-Miracle" campaign). *Lanchas* from two boat companies leave roughly every half-hour from 10am to 5:15pm for the island; they charge the same fares but do not honor each other's return tickets. Save ticket stubs for the trip back.

Entertainment

Dinner is traditionally served late in Acapulco, and many visitors spend a lot of time and money on the final meal of the day. Restaurant decorations are lavish, from Japanese gardens and waterfalls to jungle animals and lagoons. Those up for shaking some booty at meal's end head for either the chic discos on the strip or in the Zona Rosa. Remember that loud music is no sure proof of a large crowd; try to look inside before paying the cover. Be warned that many of Acapulco's larger, glitzier discos (like **Fantasy** and **Extravaganza**) require reservations on Friday and Saturday nights and, without them, no amount of pleading and name-dropping will get you inside. If you intend to be sexually active with strangers during your stay, keep in mind that Acapulco is one of the cities with the most reported AIDS cases in Mexico; condoms are always a good idea, anyway. End of public service announcement, and party on.

Baby O (tel. 474-74), at the intersection of Costera and Nelson, 5 minutes from La Base, is considered by many to be the best of Acapulco's discotheques. It is also the farthest out along Costera and attracts a younger crowd than the high-tech Fantasy and Extravaganza. In its huge, cave-like interior, videos and the latest dance tunes rock the willing. (Cover 40,000 pesos. Drinks 8000-12,000 pesos. Open daily 10:30pm-5am.) The also popular **Boccaccio's,** Costera 5040 (tel. 419-00), one block from Baby O, attracts a slightly older crowd with a smaller dance floor and glistening black-and-gold ceilings. (Cover 30,000 pesos. Open daily 10pm-4am.) These and other discos at the east end of town—such as **Magic,** at Costera and Yucatán (tel. 488-15), one block toward the Zócalo from Boccaccio's (cover 40,000 pesos; open daily from 10:30pm)—are notorious for picking and choosing their crowd; bouncers first admit single women, then male-female couples, and finally, if room permits, single men. If you find this practice offensive or prohibitive, you may wish to frequent discos farther west. **Le Dome,** on Costera (tel. 433-99), across from the Holiday Inn on the 2nd floor of Fiorucci, lives up to its name, from the vaulted ceiling inside to the shaved head of the bouncer at the door. (Cover 35,000 pesos. Open daily 10pm-5am.) According to the tourist office brochure, **Eve** (tel. 447-77) attracts "politicians, stars, business people, and international tycoons," but the budget traveler can have a good time as well. (Cover 30,000 pesos with open bar, but no cover from 7-10pm. Open daily 10pm-5am.)

Acapulco is still an extremely popular homosexual destination. Although the government has lately taken a harsher stance, tourists mean business and are seldom harrassed. **Gallery,** De los Deportes 11 (tel. 434-97), 1 block inland from the Calinda Quality Inn, is popular for its famous female impersonators, which attract a mixed crowd to both the 11pm and 1am shows.(Cover 30,000 pesos. Dancing begins daily at 10pm.) **Les Girls,** Costera 1545 (tel. 402-24), also features female impersonators nightly at 11:30pm and 1:30am. (Dancing begins daily at 10pm.)

Taxco

After silver was discovered here in 1534, Taxco (pronounced TAHS-co) exploded into a tangled confusion of cramped, cobbled *callejones* (alleys) that twist, turn, and slope precipitously through rolling green hills nearly 2000m above sea level. Pedestrians and cars squeeze past each other in the narrow alleys. Tourists, attracted by countless highly touted silver shops that sell necklaces, charms, medallions, and bracelets, swarm through town.

Beneath it all lies a dwindling reserve of silver. Tlahuicas, Chichimecs, Olmecs, and Chantales had alternately dominated the area until the Aztec empire absorbed it in 1440. Huitamila, the Aztec lord of Tetelcingo, handed over the land and mines to the delighted Spaniards, who changed the city's name to Taxco, a corruption of the Nahuatl term for ballgame, *tlachco.* Their discovery of silver brought fortune seekers, merchants, artisans, and *arrieros* (people who directed the burros which carried the mineral out of the mines) in increasing numbers, and the chaotic city prospered amid the sharp, inhospitable mountains.

Among the many whose fortunes were made in Taxco, Don José de la Borda—the man who built the Jardín Borda in Cuernavaca—stands out. He arrived from Spain in 1716, a dejected 16-year-old, to work for his miner brother. Twenty-seven years later he struck one of the richest veins in Taxco's history. Borda became a great philanthropist, giving the city, among other things, its most outstanding building and landmark, the Cathedral of Santa Prisca. An inscription above Borda's porch read "God gives to Borda and Borda gives to God."

After Borda, tranquility reclaimed the town until 1928, when isolated Taxco was connected to the outside world by a paved road stretching from the city gates to Acapulco. Soon after, the Mexican government declared Taxco a national monument and decreed that all new buildings be built in colonial style and all new streets be cobbled. Little more than lip service was paid, however, to the city's sterling past until about 1932, when Professor William Spratling, "Don Guillermo" to locals, gave up teaching and opened a silver workshop in Taxco. He taught the silversmith's craft to locals, and his jewelry quickly gained international repute. Others soon followed suit, and today over 300 silver shops operate in the area, attracting a staggering number of North American tourists: a Mexican comedian once quipped that he couldn't join his friends in Taxco because he didn't speak English.

Orientation

Taxco is at the northern end of Guerrero state, only 185km southwest of Mexico City. **Avenida J. F. Kennedy,** the principal artery, traverses town from its eastern to its northern borders. Outside of designating Kennedy as a main thouroughfare, it would be a waste of paper to try to explicate the layout of the rest of town, for you need know only one thing: from any spot in the city, to get to *el centro* look for the highly visible **Catedral de Santa Prisa** atop the hill and work your way up to it on any of the many small alleys.

Taxco's most interesting sights and shops center around the cathedral and adjacent Zócalo (also called the Pl. Borda). Parking spots available at the plaza disappears quickly in the morning. *Combis* run along three main routes: from Los Arcos (the north entrance to town where Av. Kennedy begins) down Kennedy to the south end of town; from Los Arcos up La Garita, through the center and out Cuauhtémoc-San Nicolás-San Miguel; and along the Panorámica, another avenue bordering Taxco on the west. *Combis* are often full halfway through town; if you manage to squeeze into one, you can go virtually anywhere in the city for a mere 300 pesos. (After 5pm, *combis* cost 350 pesos.) If not, hop in one of the countless empty white taxis that bump along every street (3000-4000 pesos).

Practical Information

Tourist Offices: Federal Tourist Office, Kennedy 28 (tel. 215-25), on the right as you walk north up Kennedy. Extremely knowledgeable staff, though no English spoken. Sketchy maps of the city help somewhat. Open daily 9am-7pm. The other two offices are *casetas* which border the town in the north and south. The northern *caseta,* Kennedy 1 (tel. 207-98), at De la Garita, is next to the Pemex gas station. Flawless English, but no handouts. The southern *caseta,* on Kennedy at Capilinta (tel. 219-86), is 4km south of the Estrella de Oro bus station. Both *casetas* open daily 9am-6pm.

Currency Exchange: Banca Confia, on the Zócalo, **Mexican Somer,** Cuahtémoc 5 (the street leading off the Zócalo), and **Bancomer,** at the intersection of Cuauhtémoc and Pl. San Juan. All open Mon.-Fri. 9am-1:30pm. *Casas de cambio* are ubiquitous. Most silver and crafts shops offer better rates than the *casas de cambio,* but you of course must buy something before the salesperson will "change" your dollars or traveler's checks.

Post Office: Juárez 6 (tel. 205-01), down the street from the Pl. de Bernal. Open for general services Mon.-Fri. 8am-7pm, Sat. 9am-1pm; for registered mail Mon.-Fri. 8am-6pm, Sat. 9am-1pm. **Postal Code:** 40200.

Telephones: Long-distance service in **Farmacia de Cristo,** Hidalgo 12 (tel. 200-23), down the road from the Pl. de San Juan. Collect calls abroad (4000 pesos) are possible when the owner is present (most of the time). Open daily 8am-10pm. Also in **Farmacia Oscarin,** Kennedy 47-B (tel. 218-75), across from the Flecha Roja station. Collect calls (only until 8pm) 8000 pesos. Open Mon.-Sat. 9am-9pm, Sun. 10am-2pm. Collect calls are not possible from pay phones.

Telegrams: Veracruz 17 (tel. 200-01). Open Mon.-Fri. 9am-3pm, Sat. 9am-noon.

Bus Stations: First-class **Estrella de Oro,** Kennedy 126 (tel. 206-48), at the southern end of town. Only 2 routes. To Mexico City (4 per day, 3 hr., 7700 pesos) and Acapulco (4 per day, 5 hr., 13,500 pesos). The Acapulco buses stop at Iguala and Chilpancingo; the 6pm bus also stops at Zihuatanejo. Second-class **Flecha Roja** (tel. 201-31), at the middle of Kennedy, straight downhill from the cathedral. "Station" is a misnomer: more like a mud pit decorated with a ticket shack. To: Acapulco (7 per day, 5 hr., 13,000 pesos); Mexico City (11 per day, 3 hr., 7200 pesos); Toluca (7 per day, 4 hr., 9500 pesos) via Ixtapan (2 hr., 4800 pesos). Crowded *servicio ordinario* buses to Iguala (every 45 min. 5am-11pm, 1 hr., 1900 pesos) and Cuernavaca (every 20 min. 6:30am-7:20pm, 2 hr., 3700 pesos) make many stops but neither ride is lengthy and the mountain views are unbeatable.

Pharmacy: Farmacia de Borda, Celso Muñiz 4 (tel. 206-46), in the alley to the left of Santa Prisca. Open daily 8am-10pm. Also try the central **Farmacia de Lourdes** (tel. 210-66), in the Zócalo. Open daily 8am-10pm.

Hospital: Kennedy 19 (tel. 237-77 or 201-21), to one side of the Hotel Misión. Serves Taxco's welfare community.

Police: Pajaritos 6 (tel. 200-07).

Emergency: Radio Brigada de Auxilio, Kennedy 28 (tel. 239-20). Open 24 hr.

Accommodations

The sparkle of silver has encouraged the proliferation of expensive hotels in Taxco; that elusive vein of low-budget lodgings has yet to be discovered. Luckily, most visitors prefer the upper-class lodgings, so the few cheap rooms in town are usually available. You may have to do some walking, though, and reserve in advance for Semana Santa (beginning of Nov.), Día de San Miguel (end of Sept.), or the Feria Nacional de la Plata, a two-week celebration of silver (late Nov.-early Dec.).

Casa de Huéspedes Arellano (tel. 202-15), 3 stores down from Cuauhtémoc, in the market. Take the alley to the right off Cuauhtémoc (beside the cathedral) down a few steps until your first left, then walk left and down 2 levels; the *casa* will be on your left when you hit the next street. It doesn't get much lower than this in Taxco, both in quality and in price. Rooms graffitied, very green, and equipped with extra beds. Communal bathrooms emit an incredible stench but the showers provide a generous water flow. Nice terrace on 2nd floor for sun and conversation with the backpacking clientele. Singles 20,000 pesos, with bath 25,000 pesos. Doubles 25,000 pesos, with bath 30,000 pesos.

Posada Santa Anita (tel. 207-52), on Kennedy 1 block to the left along the avenue as you leave the second-class station. Small, plain rooms are far enough off the highway to be quiet. A slight septic smell permeates the private bathrooms, which probably are not worth the extra 10,000 pesos. Beds are comfortable and clean. Furniture attacks you from all angles. Bottled water is provided on the patio. Singles 20,000 pesos, with bath 30,000 pesos. Doubles 30,000 pesos, with bath 40,000 pesos.

Hotel Casa Grande, Pl. San Juan 7 (tel. 201-23), on the small plaza down Cuauhtémoc from the Zócalo. Rooms on the upper floor of an old Mexican movie house. Large beds fill small, stucco rooms. The top floor proffers a good view, but microscopic bathrooms on both floors lack toilet seats. Singles 32,000 pesos. Doubles 35,000 pesos.

Hotel Los Arcos, Alarcón 12 (tel. 218-36), across the street from Los Castillos. Handsome whitewashed rooms (larger than Los Castillos's) with brick floors, original artwork, and solid wood furniture. Beautiful stairways and outdoor courtyard. Rooftop terrace provides a great view of the town and surrounding hills. Bar and restaurant downstairs serve a fantastic breakfast (10,000 pesos). Singles 45,000 pesos. Doubles 60,000 pesos.

Hotel Los Castillos, Alarcón 3 (tel. 213-96), just northeast of the Pl. Borda. Even before the viny bathroom walls get a chance to impress, the hand-carved wood furniture in the bedrooms should bring a smile to your face. Indoor courtyard comes complete with fountains, murals, and statuettes. Kindly proprietor sells trashy novels (5000 pesos) at the desk. A true pleasure. *Agua purificada* available. Singles 40,000 pesos. Doubles 50,000 pesos.

Hotel Melendez, Cuauhtémoc 6 (tel. 200-06), 50m south of Santa Prisca church in the Zócalo, toward the small plaza. Before entering the rooms, don your sunglasses or risk being blinded by the hot pink bedspreads. Spotless if sterile-smelling rooms and bathrooms. Beds creak, but are nicely made up. A terrific restaurant beckons from the lobby. Singles 40,000 pesos. Doubles 50,000 pesos.

Food

Prepare to drop your doubloons if you want atmosphere to accompany your meal. The cheaper *taquerías* are outnumbered by Taxco's tourist restaurants, but they multiply as you move away from the Pl. Borda. Eating at the market stands entails a considerable sacrifice in hygiene, but *perros calientes* (literally, hot dogs) are generally safe.

Cold breakfasts are the specialty of the *neverías*—plentiful in town alleys—which sell coffee, *licuados,* pastries, delicious pieces of *pan de queso* (custard-like Mexican cheesecake), and other goodies. Be sure to choose carefully among *neverías,* since some charge sterling prices.

Bora Bora Pizza, on the Pl. Borda opposite the cathedral. Not long on atmosphere (just a few tourists, a few Taxco residents, and a few piñatas), but a great view and, honest to Juárez, the best pizza this side of the Yucatán. Huge helpings of spaghetti smothered in cheese cost 11,000 pesos. The small pizzas (10,000-15,000 pesos) will easily feed 2. Open daily 1pm-midnight.

Restaurant Al Fonda, Cuauhtémoc 6, inside the Hotel Melendez. The dining area is beautifully tiled and the view from the outdoor deck quickens the pulse. Friendly service. Delicious 5-course *comida corrida* costs 15,000 pesos, and a full breakfast goes for 10,000 pesos. Open daily 11:30am-4pm and 7-10pm.

Restaurant El Patio, Pl. Borda 1, on the Zócalo. The cheapest meals in Taxco. Large, open courtyard with coffee tables. Order at the glorified magazine stand on your right as you enter, and wait for the tired workers to prepare your meal. Good burgers 4500 pesos, sandwiches 2500 pesos, cool and smooth *licuados* 2500 pesos. Open daily 10am-11pm.

Restaurant Ethel, Pl. de San Juan 14, east of the fountain. Mertzy roadside restaurant decorated with cute ferns and squat clay figurines that preside over your meal. Large sandwiches 5000 pesos, *cerveza* 3000 pesos. Roasted meats dominate choices for the *comida corrida* (served 1-5pm, 15,500 pesos). Open daily 9am-9pm.

Restaurant La Plazuela, Plazuela de Bernal 1 (tel. 230-96), around the corner from the post office. Small, nondescript restaurant serving a variety of *mariscos,* as well as *bertas,* a tasty tequila Taxco specialty (2000 pesos). *Comida corrida* 11,000 pesos. Open daily 7am-11pm.

Restaurant Santa Fe, Hidalgo 2, down to the left from the Pl. San Juan. Flower-bedecked, big, and cheap: the most economical of the fancier restaurants. Popular despite slow service. Try the scorching *pollo a la Mexicana* (12,000 pesos) or the delicious *plátano jugo* (banana juice; 2500 pesos). English menu. Open daily 8am-11pm.

Restaurant Cielito Lindo, Pl. Borda 14, next to Bar Güiri-Güiri. Fake balconies make you feel like you're on the set of a B-movie. Chintzy plastic star-shaped lights and walls half-painted with dopey *indígena* drawings are sure signs of a tourist trap; the prices back up that thought. Cheeseburger 12,500 pesos, entrees 20,000-25,000 pesos. On the other hand, the food is good. Open daily 10am-10pm.

Vicky Helados, Juárez 19 (tel. 230-77). One of the best ice cream shops near the *centro.* One scoop 1700 pesos, 2 scoops 2800 pesos. Open daily 10am-2pm and 4-9pm.

Sights

Taxco's main sights sparkle on sales tables in a zillion silver shops around town. Although one must beware of bargain sellers and cheating craftspeople who pass off *alpaca* (fool's silver) or *plateados* (silver-plated metals) as the real McCoy, Taxco's enormous selection of silver and silver-related crafts is its forte. Larger pieces, such as necklaces and bracelets, are consistently striking, and even *alpaca* belt buckles maintain the shine of the artisan's careful handiwork. Ceramic crafts and leather products abound, as do fashionable beach clothes and sandals. Many proprietors speak English and accept U.S. currency, but stick with Spanish and talk pesos while bargaining, or risk being charged tourist prices. In general, the farther one walks from the Pl. Borda, the cheaper the beginning quotes become. Bargain at stores with silver workshops by dodging the clerk and going straight to the artisan. Most shops have two prices: *menudeo* (retail) and *mayoreo* (wholesale), the latter for those profit-oriented people who load their bags with silver in Taxco to resell at lofty prices back home. Remember that only the official ".925" stamp on the object's side guarantees that your shiny new charm is indeed silver: Inspect merchandise carefully before purchase.

To see examples of original silver craft, stop at the **Los Castillos** shop (tel. 206-52), at the Pl. Bernal 1 block down from the Zócalo. Like many renowned Taxco families with great traditions in silverwork, the Castillo family keeps its workshop (right on top of their store) open for tourists to visit. *Lapidería* (stone mounting), metal pane cutting, *baño de plata* (silver coating), and hammering take place in one long room full of machinery, tools, and benches. Polishing is done downstairs. Most of the silverware Los Castillos produces is just silver-coated—only a few piece of the jewelry are pure silver. Among their most interesting wares are products of a technique said to be inherited from the Aztecs—decorative silver pieces laced in *malaquita* (malachite), and *trabajo de plumas,* which are copper- or silver-coated sheets with shapes and silhouettes cut into them and bright feathers pasted behind the openings. (Open Mon.-Sat. 9am-7pm, Sun. 10am-3pm.)

If silver weighs too heavily on your purse, head to the **Market of Artesanías** off Veracruz just behind Santa Prisca for browsing, bargaining, people-watching, and snacking. Merchants sell everything from silver to pomegranates to painted ashtrays. The market is open daily from 10am to 5pm but most crowded during the aftenoon siesta, when confused *gringos* (instead of sleeping) hit Taxco's version of a mall.

A major attraction is the Zócalo's **Catedral de Santa Prisca,** with its beautiful Baroque façade of pink stone. Intense white light illuminates the 40m towers until 9pm in the evenings. On foggy nights the towering nave and blue-tiled dome are illuminated as well. Don José de la Borda hired two Spanish architects, Diego Durán and Juan Caballero, to design and build the church for Borda's son Manuel, a priest. Begun in 1751, the church took only seven years to complete. Among the shapes, designs, and figures on the façade, the outstanding features are the Churrigueresque *interestípite*—decorative inverted columns with a Corinthian flourish at the bottom. Inside the church, a canvas by renowned 18th-century Mexican artist Miguel Cabrera depicts the martyrdom of Santa Prisca, who was tortured and killed by Roman guards in the first century for defending Christians. Cabrera also painted the picture on the altar of St. Sebastián, the town's patron, as well as one of the world's many paintings depicting a pregnant Virgin Mary. English-speaking tour guides gladly usher you around the church for 20,000 pesos per hour. But if you speak Spanish, go with the children, who have digested the booklet sold in front of the entrance for 30,000 pesos and regurgitate it in front of tourists for a scanty donation. (Open daily 6:30am-8:30pm.)

The **Museo de Arqueología Guillermo Spratling,** Delgado 1 (tel. 216-60), down the street to the right of Santa Prisca, displays pre-Conquest art on its top two floors, mostly from cultures along Mexico's west coast. William Spratling, a *norteamericano* collector, donated his ceramics and figurines to the museum. Downstairs is a pictorial mining history consisting of tools, ore, and photographs. (Open Tues.-Sun. 10am-5pm. Admission 1000 pesos, Sun. and holidays 100 pesos, children always free.)

The **Casa Humboldt,** Alarcón 6, down the street to the left of the Hotel Los Castillos, one of the oldest colonial homes in town, has unusual bas-reliefs in Moorish *mudéjar* style on the front. This was the temporary home of South American explorer Alexander von Humboldt, whose bust still oversees the interior. The carefully restored house now contains a silver gallery. (Open daily 9am-8pm. Free.) The **Convento de San Bernandino,** in the Pl. del Convento, was built in 1592 as a Franciscan monastery. A fire destroyed the building two centuries later, and in 1823 it was reconstructed in neoclassical style. The struggle for independence officially ended within the walls of this ex-convent when the Plan of Iguala, written by Iturbide, was signed here in 1821. Now, a local school convenes under its roof. (Open daily 10am-5pm. Free.)

Taxco has given more than silver to the world: **Don Juan Ruíz de Alarcón,** the 18th-century playwright, spent his youth in the town. A miserly plaque, on the house where he was born at the bottom end of Alarcón, is the only tribute to him. Inside the Palacio Municipal's post office is a mural by Luciano Cabrere of an inspired Alarcón at work.

Another Cabrere mural graces the front entrance wall of the post office. Like Rivera's mural at Cortés's palace in Cuernavaca, this too shows Mexican colonial history in all its hair-raising color, but doesn't stop at the revolution; the historical depiction continues until 1965, when Cabrere completed the mural.

Entertainment

Taxco's already crowded streets somehow manage to accommodate a huge influx of tourists during its two major festivals. The **Feria Nacional de la Plata,** a national contest of silverworkers sponsored by the President to encourage silver artisanship, runs from November 19 to 26, and **Semana Santa** festivities are even more popular in Taxco. On Good Friday, hooded *penitentes*—men who volunteer their bodies and spirits but not their identities—carry huge logs made out of cactus trunks on their shoulders or subject themselves to flagellation in order to expiate their own sins and those of the town.

After silver shops close, most of Taxco's locals and visitors converge on the **Plaza Borda** in front of the illuminated façade of Santa Prisca. If you are still up for dancing after a day of hiking Taxco's relentless hills, two choices exist. In the **Tropica Disco Bar,** Pl. Borda 2 (cover 10,000 pesos; open Fri.- Sun. 8pm-3am), great music has plenty of locals jitterbugging and drinking. **La Lechusa,** Pl. del Torril 3, to the right of Santa Prisca, plays rock music and serves plenty of Mexican drinks (6000 pesos). (Open Fri.-Sun. 8pm-3am; minimum purchase 2 drinks). At video-bar **Güiri-Güiri** (pronounced Gwiddy-Gwiddy), Cuauhtémoc 2 (open Fri.-Sun. 7:30pm-1:30am; minimum purchase 2 drinks), video games and folk art complement the modern wood-paneled bar, and a large video monitor shows typical MTV clips. The outdoor terrace affords an earth-shattering view of Santa Prisca, the *ex-convento*, and much of eastern Taxco. (Occasional live music 9pm-midnight.) Fight tequila bouts at the **Restaurant/Bar Paco**, Pl. Borda 12. *Mariachis* play during the afternoon and excellent guitarists sit at your table at night to perform romantic classics. The "Pepe"—vodka, *rompope*, and grenadine (6000 pesos)—is the specialty of the house. (Open daily noon-midnight.) Boards around the plaza announce the day's movies at Taxco's three theaters. The **Casa de la Cultura** features an excellent art-film series on Saturday and children's matinees on Sunday; check at the tourist office.

Near Taxco: Grutas de Cacahuamilpa and Iguala

The caves at **Cacahuamilpa** are a spectacle of awesome nature and ugly tourism. Believed to have been a site for *indígena* rites in pre-Conquest times the 2km-long caverns have lost much of their enchantment to overpromotion by the tourist office. Nevertheless, the beauty of this natural phenomenon manages to shine through the commercial veneer.

According to legend, the cavern was a hiding place for runaway *indígenas,* freedom fighters, and revolutionaries. A Tetipac chief is said to have regained his lost throne by having his daughter emerge from the cave disguised as a deity and pronounce the return of the former chief to power. Another story tells of the first European explorer of the caves who lost his way in the darkness and eventually expired, but not until his dog went out whining for help, to no avail. The loyal hound came back to die by her master's side.

Equally legendary historical personalities also came to admire the caves. Empress Carlota, wife of Maximilian, left some mundane graffiti in the Salón de las Palmeras (Hall of the Palm Trees) when she visited the cavern: "María Carlota was here." Mexican President Lerdo de Tejada was slightly more clever in 1872 when he added his own inscription beneath Carlota's uninspired attempt at immortality: "Sebastián Lerdo de Tejada went beyond this point." Here in 1881, Porfirio Díaz threw a great banquet, which Alexander von Humboldt described in his famous travel log. Moreover, the caves have proffered inspiration to many poets, including Chilean Nobel Prize winner Gabriela Mistral.

All of this occurred before the fateful February of 1970, when President Díaz Ordaz inaugurated the visitors center and numerous parking spaces at the caves' entrance. Today, the site floods daily in a tide of families, excursion groups, boy scouts, and uniformed summer-camp troops. Outside, shops sell T-shirts, pamphlets, posters, postcards, and caps. Once swallowed by the cave's mouth, however, the outside world fades into an unpleasant memory. Twenty huge *salones* (halls) dazzle the visitor with their stalactites, stalagmites, and rock formations of fancy shapes, sizes, and colors. The columns and ceilings taller than those of any church (some as high as 85m) are all the work of that great subterranean stream that developed into the Río San Jerónimo.

Tours leave on the hour from the visitors center and afford little opportunity for traipsing about on your own. Guides use a lamp to indicate rock formations that have become famous for uncanny resemblances to lions' heads, chickens, a flock of sheep, and elephant trunks, among other whole and partial animals. Tours move quickly and, when the group passes from one hall to the next, the guide turns off the light of the former, so pay close attention to each exhibit as it is presented.

Charter tours bring their own English-speaking guides to the caves. Some guides employed by the caves speak English, but only for a good-sized group of *gringos*. (Open daily 10am-5pm. If enough people stay after 5pm, they'll give an extra tour. Admission 3000 pesos, children 1500 pesos.)

A little past the Grutas de Cacahuamilpa are the **Grutas Estrella,** about 1½km from the highway. (You'll see signs on the *carretera* on the left.) Here there are no tour guides, no tourists, and no public transportation; leaving visitors to enjoy the beauty in solitude.

To get to Cacahuamilpa from Taxco, take the bus to Toluca or Ixtapán from Taxco's Flecha Roja bus station (check bus listings for scheduled runs). Buses run about once every two hours and the last one returns to Taxco at 6pm. The bus will drop you at the crossroads, where you also catch the return bus. Take a right down the street; the cave entrance lies just after the curve. Pullman de Morelos and Flecha Roja buses from Cuernavaca's Autos Pullman station leave every half hour. Cacahuamilpa is 30km north of Taxco, 36km south of Ixtapán, 69km southwest of Cuernavaca, and 149km from Mexico City.

An hour south of Taxco, on the road between Mexico City and Acapulco, sits a small town that to foreigners may seem little more than a dreary dustbin ringed by high mountains. Ignored by most travelers, **Iguala** possesses rich meaning for the nation as the spot where independence was proclaimed on February 24, 1821.

When Vicente Guerrero finished reading the Plan de Iguala, which listed the ideals of the newly created Republic, he gave *igualeño* José Magdaleno Ocampo one day to design the new flag. Within 24 hours, the tri-colored Flag of Independence had been woven. The banner flew first on the flagpole of the Ayuntamiento (city hall) after the Spanish flag was lowered and burned; the central plaza in front of the Ayuntamiento has been called the **Plaza de la Bandera** (Plaza of the Flag) ever since. Other cities in Mexico adopted surnames of heroes in the years following Independence and the Reform: Dolores, in Guanajuato state,, became Dolores Hidalgo, Oaxaca became Oaxaca de Juárez, and so on. But Iguala has been known since 1835 as Iguala de la Independencia.

The tranquil town keeps a low profile most of the year, but beginning eight days before Independence Day, and continuing eight days after, Iguala celebrates the **Feria de la Bandera Nacional** (Celebration of the National Flag), the largest non-religious *fiesta* in the country.

The Plaza de la Bandera, is the focal point of the city, with vast groomed lawns, paved cross-hatching paths, giant tamarind trees, caged exotic birds, and a beautiful church towering in the east. Park benches are usually occupied, especially in the evenings; *novios* quickly seize the opportunity to share intimate moments with each other. But a sunny walk through the park fends off the heat of the streets and gives you a chance to have the dust shined off your shoes at one of the innumerable infant-run stands.

If your're arriving at the Estrella de Oro station, take a right onto Cortínez as you exit the station. Stay on Cortinez for 6 blocks and you'll hit the Zócalo—impossible to miss as it's the only vegetation in Iguala. From Flecha Roja take a left onto Galeana and go straight for 7 bocks to come upon the greenery. There is no tourist office, but Sr. Miguel Romero, the **Director de Obras Publicas,** on the 2nd floor of the Palacio Municipal (tel. 200-01), 1 block east of the Zócalo, can answer specific questions about the area. You can change money at **Bahamex** on the northwest corner of the Zócalo at Juárez and Constitución. (Open Mon.-Fri. 9am-1:30pm.)

Iguanas in Iguala? Dead right—literally. The restaurant **Iguana Loca** (tel. 215-41), on the Carretera Club de Leones, serves up the tasty critters (9000 pesos) under a huge *pulapa* roof daily from 1 to 8 pm. Wash 'em down with the fruity-cool drink "El Convento" (5000 pesos), comprised of such "little mothers" as rum, tequila, lime, orange juice, and other pulverized fruits. The restaurant is a sweaty 45-minute walk from the zócalo; the cab ride (3500 pesos) is well worth the extra cash.

Iguala is served by the first-class **Estrella de Oro,** at the intersection of Rte. 95 and Cortínez, and second-class **Flecha Roja,** at Galeana and Salazar. Estrella de Oro departs for Taxco (3 per day, 1700 pesos) and for Acapulco (11 per day, 11,600 pesos). Flecha Roja duplicates both routes on the half hour for a few hundred fewer pesos. Both companies run frequently to Iguala from Taxco, Acapulco, and Mexico City.

Chilpancingo

Everybody seems to go by the title of professor in Chilpancingo. Not surprising, since the University of Guerrero, together with other institutions in the city, requires refresher courses for teachers and professors in both summer and winter. The economy of the city benefits from all the academics, but when school is in session, tourists must hunt high and low for lodgings.

Do not skip class to visit this one, kids: though nestled among scenic rolling hills, tranquil, squeaky-clean Chilpancingo does not warrant a special trip.

Orientation

Chilpancingo is 133km north of Acapulco and 280km south of Mexico City on Rte. 95. Acapulco-Mexico City express buses, which must stop in Chilpancingo, leave both Mexico and Acapulco at least every half hour. Express buses between 10pm and 4am often stop on the main street next to the market instead of at the bus terminal. Be careful if you board here: some bus drivers going from Mexico City to Puerto Escondido, but not scheduled to stop in Chilpancingo, may pick you up here, charge you a bit less than the full fare, and could pocket the money for themselves. This saves you cash, but the deal does not include a boarding ticket, which will be problematic at required stops like Pinotepa Nacional if the supervisor asks to see your stub.

To reach the Zócalo from the Estrella de Oro bus station, take a left onto Juárez as you exit the station, and continue straight for 7 blocks (don't be fooled by the Parque Alameda that comes before the Zócalo; you've still got a few blocks to go).

Practical Information

Tourist Office: Secretaría General, Juárez 1 (tel. 222-87), in the Ayuntamiento on the Zócalo. City officials will tell you about the town, nearby villages, and *balnearios* to which townfolk retreat on weekends. No city maps or brochures and no English spoken. Open Mon.-Fri. 8am-3pm.

Currency Exchange: It's hard not to find a bank if you're anywhere near the Zócalo. **Bancomer** and **Bánamex** sit side by side on Zapata, facing the church. Both are open Mon.-Fri. 9am-1:30pm.

Post Office: Hidalgo at 5 de Mayo (tel. 222-75), 3 blocks east of the Zócalo. Open Mon.-Fri. 8am-7pm, Sat. 9am-1pm; for Lista de Correos Mon.-Fri. 10am-3pm. After 5pm, only stamps are sold.

Telephones: Long-distance *caseta* in **El Puerto de Veracruz,** 5 de Mayo 3 (tel. 222-70), a drugstore 1 block behind the Parroquia de la Asunción. International collect calls 10,000 pesos. Open daily 8am-2pm and 4-8pm. Also at 16 de Septiembre 16, about 3 blocks west of the church. Open Mon.-Fri. 8am-5:30pm. **Telephone Code:** 747.

Telegrams: Guerrero 33 (tel. 220-17), on the way to the university from the Zócalo. Open Mon.-Fri. 9am-2pm and 4-6pm, Sun. and holidays 9am-noon.

Bus Stations: First-class **Estrella de Oro,** Juárez 53 (tel. 221-30), behind the gas station, next to the statue of Morelos where the main street leading to the Zócalo divides into two smaller streets (both of which bring traffic to the Zócalo). Frequent service to Acapulco (6300 pesos) and Mexico City (14,500 pesos). Also to Taxco (at 11:15am and 1:30pm, 6700 pesos) and Iguala (at 12:15pm, 6600 pesos). Second-class **Flecha Roja** (tel. 220-51), on Roberto Masera, close to the north entrance to town behind the big *mercado*. To Acapulco, Mexico City, Tixtla, Chilapa, Tlapa, Tlacotepec, Zumpango, and Tierra Colorada.

Red Cross: Juárez at Ignacio (tel. 265-62 or 265-14), next to the Parque Alameda. 24-hr. emergency service.

Pharmacy: Farmacia Conchita, Zapata 8 (tel. 220-23), on the Zócalo. Open daily 9am-10pm.

Police: Juárez 24 (tel. 220-62), about 4 blocks from the Zócalo toward the Estrella de Oro station.

Accommodations and Food

Moderately priced hotels congregate within a 3- to 4-block radius of the Zócalo.

Hotel Muñiz, Ramírez 23 (tel. 220-34), on the southeast corner of the Zócalo. Juárez turns into Ramírez at the Zócalo. Rooms are clean, but the paint is peeling, the fans are filthy, and the bathroom mirrors are rusting around the edges. If you're lucky enough to get a room in the younger section of the building, the screaming pink spreads might keep you up at night. The cluttered courtyard is home to a friendly dog that yips to welcome guests. 15,000 pesos per person.

Hotel Laura Elena, Madero 1 (tel. 230-12). Views of a corrugated metal roof or the building across the street await. Some rooms floored with ugly carpets, others with garish tiles, but all wear new peach paint with baby blue trim. You wouldn't want to live in the bathrooms, but they're bearable for a few minutes at a time. *Agua purificada* available. Singles and 1-bed doubles 25,000 pesos. Doubles with 2 beds 35,000 pesos. There are only 3 singles; if you're alone and plan to arrive on a weekend, reserve a room.

Fruit, torta stands, and flies abound in the market in front of the Flecha Roja station. Your stomach will be happier if you take it to the inexpensive restaurants downtown, which serve typical Mexican food.

La Parroquia, Dragón 2 (tel. 229-28), next to the Palacio de Gobierno on the Zócalo. Large menu accommodates any urge. A favorite for early breakfasts as the rainbow-hued tablecloths will open all eyes. Eggs, any style, plus ham and frijoles 3500 pesos. Open Mon.-Sat. 7:30am-10pm.

Restaurant Laurel, Apreza 4 (tel. 231-04), up the street from La Langosta, behind the Red Cross. Cheerily buzzing place of good repute throughout town. Excellent cuisine at reasonable prices. The house specialty, *cabrito asado* (roasted goat), serves 2 for 10,700 pesos. Open daily 8am-9:30pm.

Zihuatanejo/Ixtapa

Before Zihautanejo achieved its world reknown as a quiet haven of idyllic beaches and souvenir shops, it was nothing but a pier on which to unload the day's catch. Centuries before that, its pre-Conquest matriarchal society gave the town its original name—Cihuatlán, from the Nahuatl words *cihuatl* (woman) and *an* (place). When the Spanish arrived, they put men in charge, developed the harbor, and corrupted the name to Zihuatanejo. In the 19th century, larger ports such as Manzanillo and Acapulco assumed Zihuatanejo's trade with Asia, and the city reverted to a fishing village.

The recent remodeling and development of the area, including the creation of the tourist complex at Ixtapa, was masterminded by the Bank of Public Works and Services, contracted by the Mexican government to provide tourists with "a picturesque town on the shore of a small, peaceful bay." Even though the cold hand of urban planners can often be felt in Ixtapa, the development scheme seems to have worked, as witnessed by the planeloads of tourists from around the world that arrive daily; given the resort's awesome beaches, the developers could hardly have gone wrong.

Although designed by the same people, the beach resorts of Zihuatanejo and Ixtapa have absolutely nothing in common. Ixtapa is little more than a line of expensive hotels along an unbelievable beach, burst full-grown from the collective mind of its developers. Ixtapa has no public services, no downtown, no residential district, and no cheap anything. Zihuatanejo, the area's commercial center and the only base for budget travelers, fills these voids. All of Zihuatanejo's ritzy hotel complexes operate outside town; cheap hotels, open-air restaurants, and boutiques cram the small downtown area. In fact, downtown Zihuatanejo looks like a small fishing village in which everyone simultaneously decided to open a souvenir shop. The combination of cheerful informality and frenetic activity makes it one of the Pacific coast's premier vacation spots.

Orientation

Zihuatanejo and Ixtapa rise from the Pacific coast, 115km southeast of Playa Azul and Lázaro Cárdenas and 250km northwest of Acapulco. Second-class **Flecha Roja** and first-class **Estrella de Oro** buses provide the most frequent service to the two towns, stopping in Zihuatanejo. Flecha Roja's is so convenient that you don't have to plan ahead unless you're going to Mexico City. Theoretically, Estrella de Oro's attraction is its seat reservation system, but seeing that passengers leaving Zihuatanejo on second-class buses almost always get seats, you might as well take cheaper Flecha Roja.

Both bus companies have stations northeast of the downtown area. To reach Flecha Roja from the center of town, walk north to Paseo Zihuatanejo (also called Morelos) and turn right; when the road divides, stay to the left, and you'll approach the station almost immediately. No signs mark the station, so look for the few buses parked in the lot behind the station. To get to Estrellas de Oro, follow the directions to Flecha Roja but stay to the right when the road divides, and follow Paseo del Palmar. When it forks again, bear right; the station is on the first corner. To get to the center of town from either station, walk west (right from Flecha Roja, left from Estrellas de Oro) on Paseo Zihuatanejo, and turn south (left) on Juárez. The walk takes five minutes from Flecha Roja and 10 minutes from Estrellas de Oro; taxi fare from either station to the center of town is 2000 pesos.

Jet-setters start their vacation at Zihuatanejo's international airport, 16km south of the city on the highway to Acapulco. Taxis from Zihuatanejo cost 16,000 pesos. Mexicana and Aeroméxico provide the most extensive service.

Downtown Zihuatanejo forms a rectangle of about 25 square blocks bounded by the major streets Paseo Zihuatanejo (or Morelos) to the north, Juárez (whose signs sometimes say "Paseo del Cocotal") to the east, Paseo del Pescador (a.k.a. the waterfront) to the south, and 5 de Mayo to the west.

Ixtapa consists of a single access road, Boulevard Ixtapa, which parades past a phalanx of huge luxury hotels and terminates abruptly after the last resort. A smaller road off the boulevard continues to the northwest beaches. Buses shuttling between the two cities leave from the intersection of Juárez and Morelos in Zihuatanejo, and from various bus stops on the boulevard in Ixtapa (every 15 min. 6am-11pm, 15 min., 700 pesos). Cab fare between the two towns is 8000 pesos.

Practical Information

If the address is not on Boulevard Ixtapa, the office or place of business is in Zihuatanejo.

Tourist Office: In the big, white Palacio Municipal on Paseo de la Pescador to the left of the small town square as you face the beach (tel. 420-01). Maps and basic information handed out, but no English spoken. Open Mon.-Fri. 9am-3pm and 5-8pm. There is also a state tourist office *caseta* on the boulevard in Ixtapa with piles of maps and pamphlets. Officially open Mon.-Fri. 9am-9pm, but it's usually closed 1-4pm (*siesta*, you know . . .). Back in Zihuatanejo, a real-estate office runs an information *caseta* at the intersection of Bravo and Guerrero. English spoken, but no maps available. Open daily 10am-2pm and 5-7pm.

Currency Exchange: Multibanco Comermex, Ramírez at Guerrero, doesn't extract a commission. Open Mon.-Fri. 10am-noon and 4-6pm. **The Money Exchange,** on Galeana between Ascencio and Bravo (signs in your face all over town). Rates around 100 pesos less than the banks on the dollar, but they charge no commission. Open daily 8am-9pm. Gift shops also change money; snoop around for the best rates. **Bancomer,** on Boulevard Ixtapa, in front of the Centro Comercial La Puerta. Open for exchange Mon.-Fri. 9:30am-noon and 4-6pm.

Post Office: Cuauhtémoc 73 (tel. 433-38). Walk inland on Cuauhtémoc, past the small plaza, and follow the pink statues to the right. Open Mon.-Fri. 8am-7pm, Sat. 9am-1pm. **Postal Code:** 48800.

Telephones: Ascencio at Galeana, in the ice cream shop. Collect calls to the U.S. cost 3000 pesos. Also, the ice cream shop at Altamirano 6 and Guerrero will connect collect calls for 2000 pesos. Both open daily 8am-9pm. **Telephone Code:** 743.

Telegrams: Altamirano 10 (tel. 421-63), ½ block west of Guerrero, in an unmarked white building on the north side of the street; sign says "Entrada Pública." Open Mon.-Fri. 9am-1pm and 3-8pm, Sat.-Sun. 9am-noon.

Airport: On the coast to the south (tel. 421-00). **Mexicana,** Bravo at Guerrero (tel. 422-08). Open Mon.-Sat. 9am-5:30pm, Sun. 9am-3pm. **Aeroméxico,** Alvarez 34 (tel. 420-22). Open daily 8am-6:30pm. Together, the 2 serve more than 30 destinations in Mexico and the U.S.

Bus Stations: Flecha Roja, Paseo de Zihuatanejo/Morelos (tel. 422-89). Second-class service to Acapulco (every 30 min. 6am-4pm, 5 hr., 11,000 pesos). Direct service to: Acapulco (14 per day, 4 hr., 11,000 pesos); Lázaro Cárdenas (every hr. 5:45pm-8:30pm, 2 hr., 6000 pesos); Mexico City (5 per day, 11 hr., 31,000 pesos). **Estrella de Oro** (tel. 421-75), on Paseo del Palmar. First-class service to: Acapulco (5 per day, 11,790 pesos); Lázaro Cárdenas (7,100 pesos); Mexico City (32,690 pesos).

English Bookstore: Byblos, Alvarez 7. A few English-language books, mostly from the upper reaches of the literary spectrum. Open daily 10am-1pm and 5:30-9pm. The unmarked, nameless *librería* on Bravo, between Galeana and Guerrero, has a selection of cheap used English-language cheap thrillers and romances.

Laundromat: Super Clean, Galeana 11, at Gonzalez. 8000 pesos per 3kg (takes 2-4 hr.). Open Mon.-Sat. 9am-6:30pm.

Red Cross: (tel. 420-09), on the right side of Av. de las Huertas as you leave town. 24-hr. emergency service.

Pharmacy: Farmacia Ejido, Ejido at 5 de Mayo, across from the Centro de Salud. Open daily 8am-2pm and 4-8pm. Several pharmacies in town rotate 24-hr. duty; call 420-08 to find out which is open.

Medical Assistance: Centro de Salud, Ejido at 5 de Mayo (tel. 420-38). Open for consultations Mon.-Fri. 9am-2pm. 24-hr. emergency service. **English-speaking physician,** Dr. R. Grayeb, at Bravo 18 (tel. 426-91 or 425-22), across from the Torito Restaurant. Open daily 9am-2pm and 4-9pm. There is also a private hospital with an English-speaking staff on a little side street off the eastern end of Bravo (tel. 439-91 or 430-70). Open 24 hr.

Police: Alvarez at Cuauhtémoc (tel. 420-40), behind the tourist office in the Palacio Municipal.

Accommodations and Camping

Zihuatanejo supports a youth hostel not too far from the center and a load of reasonably priced hotels smack downtown. Dirtier, cheap hotels cluster along Bravo, the western end of Alvarez, and Morelos; cleaner, slightly more expensive establishments line the streets that run between Bravo and the waterfront.

The tourist office frantically discourages unofficial camping, possibly because they believe *gringos* can't do without the amenities of a five-star hotel, but most likely because they hate to see tourist dollars slip away. If you choose not to heed their warnings, try the point beyond and to the northwest of Playa Las Gatas on the Bahía de Zihuatanejo; ask anyone in sight for permission, and they'll most likely grant it. Better yet, empty sand awaits northwest along Ixtapa's Playa Palmar away from the hotels.

Villa Deportiva Juvenil (tel. 446-62), on Morelos. From Playa Municipal, take 5 de Mayo north until you hit Paseo de Zihuatanejo. Turn left and follow the curve—it's on the right (a 15-min. walk). From either bus station, hike west on the Paseo de Zihuatanejo for 15-20 min. Basic rooms have 4 bunks cooled by 1 tiny fan. Clean communal bathrooms lack hot water but enjoy a monopoly on the area's toilet seats. 9000 pesos per person. All meals below 6000 pesos.

Casa de Huéspedes Juve, Ascencio 3 (tel. 425-41), at Ramírez, 1 block from the waterfront. A tropical, family-run place. Large, clean, cement rooms (in which more water leaks through the roof than comes out of the shower head), big ol' beds, and fans that are slow to begin but adequate once they get up to speed. The few assorted cockroaches, bugs, and other *animales* will stay out of your way. No hot water (and no water at all in room 17). Singles 15,000 pesos. Doubles 30,000 pesos. Small discounts for longer stays.

Hotel Casa Aurora, Bravo 27 (tel. 430-46), between Guerrero and Galeana. Pink flamingos in lobby serve as fair warning of the tacky decorating scheme in the musty but clean, basic rooms. Large, hot-water-less bathrooms often lack toilet seats. Hot, even with the good fans. 20,000 pesos per person.

Posada Citlali, Guerrero 3 (tel. 420-43), near Ascencio. Great stucco rooms paneled with wood. Creaky rocking chairs in front of each room, on the tranquil inner courtyard, are fantastic for afternoon naps. Firm beds, wonderful fans, and hot water, repeat, *24-hour* hot water—no excuses. Singles 40,000 pesos. Doubles 50,000 pesos.

Casa Bravo, Bravo 11 (tel. 425-28), west of Juárez. Potted palms in the open-air lobby sway in the breeze as the manager naps in his hammock; an almost elegant scene. Rooms are also attractive, though they don't live up to the lobby's example. Strong ceiling fans, and spruce bathrooms with no hot water but huge bars of soap. Balconies in some rooms overlook the street; jugs of *agua purificada* await in every room. Singles 50,000 pesos. Doubles 60,000 pesos. Mention a discount during off-season, and the rates start to fall. This hotel has gone through a period of *Let's Go* inflation: after a good write up in the 1990 edition, management, in a non-related move, raised their prices by a factor of two. Oh, the coincidence of it all.

Food

Most hotels in Ixtapa include meals in the price of a room. For this reason, the resort has failed to spawn the swanky restaurants so common in Acapulco and Puerto Vallarta. In Zihuatanejo, however, you should have little trouble finding a budget meal. In general, restaurants farther inland are cheaper, less polished, and more likely to offer something besides seafood.

Pollos Locos, Bravo 15, next to the Casa Bravo. The prototypical beachside chicken joint complete with high tin roof and roaring open barbecue—the only thing missing is the beach. Once the fire cranks up, the inviting smell of barbecued chicken (9000 pesos) wafts around the block. Vegetarians can enjoy the *sopes* (corn pancakes with beans and cheese) for 4500 pesos. Open daily 1-10pm.

Panificadora El Buen Gusto, on Guerrero, a ½ block down from Ejido towards the water. Fantastic french pastries and breads. A chocolate doughnut (750 pesos) and a fruit juice (1000 pesos) make a perfect snack any time of day. Open Mon.-Sat. 7am-10pm, Sun. 8am-11:30am.

Café Marina, Paseo del Pescador 9, near Cuauhtémoc, to the right of the small plaza and basketball courts as you face the ocean. Come in and chat with El Gringo Loco, Joseph, a California surfer transplanted to Mexican soil. Ché Guevara, Emiliano Zapata, and the *Far Side* hang on the wall. Limited menu includes pizza, yogurt, cake, cookies, and the best *tortas* in Zihuatanejo. Totally delicious. Dude. Small *Pizza Hawaiana* 10,000 pesos. The yogurt plate with fruit, honey, and granola (6000 pesos) makes a healthy dessert. After the meal, and before hitting the surf, do a little reading in the in-house library, or take a thriller to the beach for 3000 pesos. Open Mon.-Sat. noon-9pm.

Casa Elvira, Paseo del Pescador 8, on the waterfront near the municipal pier across from a thatched souvenir shop. No sign, just an orange lifesaver outside with "Casa Elvira" written on it. The best of the waterfront restaurants serves whale-like portions. For a break from seafood try the guacamole (5000 pesos). Seafood 14,000 pesos. Open Wed.-Mon. 2-10pm.

Kapi Kofi, Ascencio 12, near Galeana. Blue-and-white (*faux* ocean) walls adorned with swordfish. Great burgers by Mexican standards. *Gringos* make up most of the clientele. Also cooks tasty breakfast specials (6000-7500 pesos), and the *comida corrida* (8000 pesos, served Mon.-Fri. 1-5pm) is one of the few in town. Open daily 8am-10pm.

Beaches

Neither Zihuatanejo's self-conscious charm nor Ixtapa's flawless panache could every eclipse the area's natural beauty. In Zihuatanejo, four stretches of sand line the water: they are, in clockwise order from the municipal pier, Playa Principal, Playa La Madera, Playa La Ropa, and Playa Las Gatas. Ixtapa overlooks the unbroken white stretch of Playa del Palmar on the Bahía del Palmar, but the most beautiful beaches lie beyond Laguna de Ixtapa: Playa Quieta, Playa Linda, and, at the bay's western edge, Isla Ixtapa.

Unless you're interested in playing alongside El Gringo Loco (Joseph) in a pick-up game of basketball at 6:30pm on the court overlooking the Playa Principal, downtown Zihuatanejo's beach is the most uninteresting of the area's sands. **Playa La Madera,** named after the wood once exported from its shores, is slightly more attractive. To reach it, walk 15 minutes east on one of the trails along the shoreline (some scrambling over rocks is involved), or walk east along the canal on Paseo de la Boquita, cross the canal at the bridge, and follow the signs to Playa La Madera.

Zihuatanejo's two best beaches are Playa La Ropa and Playa Las Gatas, neither of which can be reached by walking along the bay's shores. **La Ropa** (clothing) takes its name from the silks and other garments that washed ashore following the shipwreck of a trading vessel from Asia. Protected from the rough Pacific by the shape of the bay, La Ropa's crescent of sumptuous white sand attracts tourists from the hotels on the surrounding cliffs. The stretch is quite long and wide, making La Ropa the least crowded of Zihuatanejo's beaches. Several adequate seaside restaurants are close at hand.

To get to La Ropa, follow Paseo la Boquilla along the canal, cross over, and head toward the airport, as if going to La Madera. Bypass the Madera access road and follow the signs to La Ropa. The 20- to 30-minute walk, which can be uncomfortably hot even at night, affords a view of the bay that makes the drudgery worthwhile. The shortest route to the beach requires an immediate right turn into the drive of Playa Club La Ropa after passing the small park that has benches and flower pots. Hotel Catalina Sotavento's access road also leads to La Ropa. Make your way through the multi-tiered experience of a hotel complex and down the stairs to the bay. The imposing gate at the foot of the stairs is often locked at night, but a large gap underneath permits access to beach bums of all shapes and sizes.

Las Gatas was named for the sharks that once inhabited the waters close to shore. Long before the Spanish conquistadors settled the area, Tarascan King Caltzonzín built an artificial breakwater to create a safe swimming space for himself and his daughters; the sharks had to search elsewhere for sustenance. Since then, a natural reef that supports an abundance of marine life has grown over the original stone barricade.

Because of its reputation as an isolated, exotic spot, Las Gatas is one of the area's most crowded beaches. Actually quite small, the beach fills quickly as boatload after boatload of tourists descend upon it like bees to honey. Thankfully, an army of restaurateurs stands ready to anchor them to wicker chairs away from the water with potent *coco locos* in hand. Crowds notwithstanding, Las Gatas's white sands and excellent snorkeling make it worth the trip.

To get to Playa Las Gatas, walk along the shoreline from Playa La Ropa. In several spots you must use your hands, but the hike isn't terribly difficult. Follow the dirt road as far as Restaurant-Bar Capricho del Rey (look for the pink flags); from there, strike out across the rocks. Ten minutes later you'll be lounging on a beach chair at Las Gatas, *refresco* in hand. A road accesses Playa Las Gatas, but the strenuous walk from La Ropa takes well over half-an-hour.

A less tiring and more popular way to reach Las Gatas is to pile into one of the *colectivo* boats from Zihuatanejo's municipal pier (every 15 min. 9am-5pm, roundtrip 6000 pesos). Buy tickets at the base of the pier at the western end of Paseo del Pescador; the boats leave from halfway down the pier. Save your ticket stub for the trip back.

Jean-Claude, the Frenchman who owns **Carlo Scuba** and plays the best tunes on Las Gatas, will take divers of any experience level on a one-tank dive for US$30 or a two-tank dive for US$45; a second dive costs US$15. He also rents snorkels, masks, and fins (5000 pesos each per day; 10,000 pesos for all 3). Windsurfers cost US$10 per hour, and boogie boards 15,000 pesos per day. Waterskiing, is possible only in high season. Next to Jean-Claude's shop, at **Oliviero's Scuba,** Oliviero arranges a one-tank dive for US$25 or a two-tank dive for US$40. **Antonio,** a newcomer to Playa Las Gatas, doesn't have Jean-Claude's or Oliviero's fancy scuba gear, but he does offer a bargain or two. For US$15 per person (or a mere 10,000 pesos per person if you can scare up a group of 10), he'll shuttle the beginning snorkeler to Isla Ixtapa, provide gear for the day, and give a snorkeling lesson. Snorkeling gear alone costs 10,000 pesos per day. Try bargaining, especially in off-season.

For gear closer to town, Juan Manuel, a marine biologist turned scuba instructor works out of **Zihuatanejo Scuba Center,** Paseo del Pescador 4 (tel. 421-47), at the foot of the pier. He'll conduct a one-tank dive for US$40 or a two-tank dive for US$60, and will make snorkeling trips for groups of 4 or 5 for US$120 and night dives for US$50.

While most of Zihuatanejo's crescent beaches are protected from the waves, 3-footers pound Ixtapa's endless stretches of sand. Ixtapa would be beach-bum heaven were it not for one unfortunate fact: It's difficult to purchase any food or drink without selling off the family jewels first. All of Ixtapa's hotels are four- or five-star, and all of its restaurants, beachfront and otherwise, cater to the same clientele. But by no means should the budget traveler avoid Ixtapa. Buy some food and drink in cheaper Zihuatanejo and take the bus to paradise. Stride into a glittering hotel lobby as if you owned the place. Window-shop the latest designer fashions. Walk bare footed on a lush, manicured lawn or two. Swim in the huge, elaborate, crystal-clear pools. In a swimsuit—having shed backpack, grimy jeans, and your copy of *Let's Go*—you look like any other mundane tourist.

Ixtapa's **Playa del Palmar** measures in as the resort's longest beach and one of the most beautiful stretches of sand in the world. To the southeast, chaise lounges invite loiterers, and parasailers make circuits during daylight hours until gas and demand run out (35,000 pesos). To the northwest, past existing hotels and the foundations for new condominium projects, the beach becomes even more pristine. The beauty of the spot is enhanced by perfectly sloping sands, deep blue water, and waves custom-designed for body surfing. In the morning hours particularly, the beach is delightfully deserted. To get to Playa del Palmar, take the bus from Zihuatanejo, get off in front of any hotel, and walk through the lobby. To reach the northwestern end of Del Palmar, drive down the Boulevard until it dead-ends by Laguna de Ixtapa or walk (15 min.) along the beach or road.

To the northwest of Ixtapa are **Club Med, Playa Quieta,** and **Playa Linda,** less crowded and more stylish than the beaches at Ixtapa or Zihuatanejo. To drive here from Ixtapa, follow the boulevard northwest beyond most of the hotels and turn right at the sign for Playa Linda. If you're driving from Zihuatanejo, the access road from Rte. 200 is more convenient; go past the exit for Ixtapa in the direction of Puerto Vallarta and take the next left, marked Playa Linda. The road skirts Laguna de Ixtapa and hits the beach farther northwest. A taxi to Playa Linda or Playa Quieta costs 8000 pesos from Ixtapa, 11,000 pesos from Zihuatanejo.

Crystal clear water and bodysurfing waves await at **Playa Cuatas,** across the street from the tennis courts at Club Med on Playa Linda. Bring a lunch; there are no services here.

Some claim that, of all of the area's beaches, the most picturesque are those on **Isla Ixtapa,** about 2km offshore from Playa Quieta. Though activity picks up in a few shoreside restaurants by day, the island's 10 acres remain uninhabited at night. Boats to Isla Ixtapa leave from the municipal pier in Zihuatanejo at 11:30am, starting their return journeys between 4 and 4:30pm (round-trip 17,500 pesos). Three stretches of beach ring the island and the two with northeastern exposure sustain crowds, small restaurants (no bargains), and snorkel gear booths. The third is prohibitively rough and therefore generally deserted. Several dealers on the island rent scuba equipment. Prices are higher than at Las Gatas, and snorkeling conditions are worse because of the choppy water.

Entertainment

Not surprisingly, Ixtapa also provides the area with its best night-time entertainment. For dinner, drinks, and beachside dancing, the ever-popular, omnipresent, always crowded **Carlos 'n' Charlie's,** Paseo de Palmar S/N (tel. 300-85), is the place to visit. Just ask one of the drunken tourists taking swigs from the wandering *sangria* server. Great tortilla soup costs 7000 pesos. Entrees run 20,000 to 25,000 pesos. Head to the dance floor with a generous 12,000-peso margarita. (Open daily 7pm-1am.)

After Carlos 'n' Charlie's closes a pack of partiers migrates to Ixtapa's most popular disco, **Christine's,** Blvd. Ixtapa 429, in the Hotel Kristal. One of Mexico's prettiest discos, with tiered seating and hanging vines, it has a small, wooden dance floor on which *gringos* hoping to get lucky stomp the night away. (Cover 35,000 pesos. Open daily 10pm-4am.)

Costa Grande: Zihuatanejo/Ixtapa to Acapulco

The Guerrero coast north of Acapulco is often called the "Costa Grande" to distinguish it from its smaller counterpart (Costa Chica) to the south. Trade with Asia centuries ago left some of the area's inhabitants with Polynesian features. Of specific interest are Barra de Potosí, 20km southeast of Zihuatanejo, and Papanoa, another 60km farther along Route 200.

Barra de Potosí

For the *gringo* whose head is spinning from ruins, cathedrals, and souvenirs, there is no better tonic than a spell at **Playa Barra de Potosí.** Life here could not get more *tranquilo;* both residents and tourists alike have trouble enough lifting themselves from hammocks, let alone exerting their bodies to stroll on the impressively deserted stretch of sand and watch the breaking waves. Now and then someone bothers to roll out of the hammock for a bit of fishing. The owners of the 20 or so open-air *enramadas* that constitute "town" are proud of Playa Potosí's laid-back friendliness—and its cheap prices. In keeping with the casual spirit of the place, no restaurant seems to have a menu; they'll whip up whatever you want and then pull an amount out of the blue only after you remind them about your *cuenta.* You shouldn't have to pay more than 3000 pesos for a full breakfast, 10,000 pesos for fish, or 12,000 pesos for shrimp or other *mariscos. Refrescos* are 1000 pesos, *cerveza* 2000 pesos. Friendly beyond the call of duty are the folks at **Enramada Bacanora** (the second *enramada* on the beach as you enter the *enramada* area); by the time you finish your breakfast conversation with the proprietor and Miguel the fisherman (who prefers swinging in a hammock at the Bacanora to fishing), it may be time for lunch.

There are no hotels at the tiny village of Barra de Potosí. Visitors are expected to sleep in the hammocks that adorn each *enramada.* The owners don't care if you sack out in their hammocks forever—as long as you buy a meal from them every now and then. *Baños,* too, are free of charge. Don't worry about your pack—leave it in the *enramadas* for as long as you like, with the owners' blessing. The mosquitoes, however, are not so kind, so bring plenty of repellent.

If you simply *must* exert yourself (which the locals may not understand or appreciate), your only option is to hike the dirt road to the lighthouse on top of **Cerro Guamiule** (2000m), the nearby peak that guards the southern entrance to the bay. After a half-hour walk, you will be rewarded with a view of the bay and its 20km of beaches.

From Playa Potosí, the southernmost beach on the bay, walk north along the shore to aptly named **Playa Blanca** (3km). You will pass **Playa Coacoyul** (8km), **Playa Riscaliyo** (19km) and pebbly **Playa Manzanillo** (24km) before reaching another lighthouse (26km), which overlooks the northern edge of the bay. All beaches are free of tourists.

To reach Playa Potosí, get off a second-class bus at **Los Achotes** (from Zihuatanejo 1000 pesos, from Petatlán 750 pesos). The microbuses that run between Zihuatanejo and Petatlán also pass by Los Achotes, which is little more than a *crucero.* From Zihuatanejo, the microbus trip costs 800 pesos, and leaves frequently from Juárez. Look for the buses with the purple stripe. From *el crucero,* hop on one of the fairly frequent *camionetas* (flatbed pickup trucks) that travel the dirt road to the playa (every hr., ½ hr., 1500 pesos). Hitching with one of the friendly residents is easy as well. The last *camioneta* returns to *el crucero* at 5pm. From there, try to flag down a second-class bus. Buses won't always stop, though; a better bet is the Zihuatanejo-Petatlán microbus. From *el crucero*, with your back to the beach, Zihuatanejo is to the left and Petatlán to the right.

Papanoa

North of Pie de la Cuesta in Acapulco, Rte. 200 curves inland to skirt Lagunas Coyuco and Mitla before coming in contact with the coast once more at Papanoa. Small-time resorts, with cabañas on the beach and fresh seafood in the restaurants fill this part of the coast.

Club Papanoa caters to those who want to spend a day or two on the less-traveled circuit. The expensive rooms would break your budget, but the friendly management usually allows camping on the grounds for 15,000 pesos per person, particularly during low season or in an off year. The club sits on a point in the Bahía Papanoa, between two often deserted, white-sand beaches. An *enramada* on the beach serves excellent seafood; from the hotel, walk toward the ocean and to the right. The seaside site beats the club's in-house restaurant for price and atmosphere. For reservations at the club, write Felix Aventón at Hotel Club Papanoa, Cayaquitos, Guerrero (local tel. 13). You can reserve by phone in Mexico City (tel. 753-06-25).

To reach the club, get off the first-class bus in the city of **Papanoa** (80km southeast of Zihuatanejo), 3km from the club, because the bus won't stop any closer. Most second-class bus drivers will drop you off at the entrance to the hotel, but none will pick up passengers there again. From the first-class station, the club is to the right as you exit; from the second-class station, it's to the left. The walk along the highway isn't strenuous but takes 30 minutes. Taxis are stationed close to both bus stops and will make the trip to the club for 3000 pesos. Collective flat-bed pickups pass frequently, and will drop you off at the club for around 450 pesos. To catch a *colectivo* from the club back into town, walk left on Rte. 200 (toward Zihuatanejo) for about ½ km. On the inland side of the highway, there is a small shaded lot where *colectivos* stop to make pickups. However, a wildly gesticulating tourist is bound to get the *colectivo* drivers to stop anywhere along the highway. Drivers to Club Papanoa should look for km155 on Rte. 200.

Costa Chica: Acapulco to Puerto Escondido

Acapulco's history as an international harbor has left indelible traces on the southern coast of Guerrero. Slave ships bound for Acapulco sometimes foundered, enabling their passengers to flee to freedom and take their chances with the rough Pacific and *indígena* population. Today the region is inhabited by both black and indigenous people.

No cities or interesting beaches exist between Oaxaca's Puerto Escondido and Acapulco. **Pinotepa Nacional,** 144km northwest of Puerto Escondido, is the largest and best of many poor places to break up the grueling journey. Pinotepa is dusty, hectic, beachless, and unfriendly to outsiders: Get out quicker than a greased pig on the Fourth of July. If you're forced to stay overnight here, the **Hotel Marissa** along the main street, 2 blocks south of the Zócalo, is the least disagreeable choice. The bus station is on the same street, several blocks north; a few cheap restaurants lie across the way. The market, on the south side of the Zócalo, is also inexpensive.

Cuajinicuilapa, 52km farther north, is the *indígena* capital of the region and has a market that may prove interesting. Farther north, you'll find **Copala** and **Marquelia,** 127km and 145km south of Acapulco, respectively. Both have nearby beaches and a few budget accommodations.

OAXACA

Upon conquering the valley of the Mixtecs, the Aztecs named it Huaxyacac, which translates from the Nahuatl as "In the Nose of the Guaje Tree." Although the Aztec warriors were tops in their field, their scholars had not yet arrived at the conclusion that trees lack noses; the misguided nomenclature is therefore forgivable. The Spanish, who could find no such potrusion on the area's trees, later corrupted Huaxyacac to Oajaca, and when the Mexicans gained control, it became Oaxaca (pronounced wa-HA-ka).

Several *indígena* civilizations and more than 200 tribes, including the Mixtec and the Zapotec, have occupied the valley over the past two millennia. Over one million *oaxaqueños* still speak the ancient *indígena* languages, and more than a fifth of the state's population speaks no Spanish whatsoever. This language barrier, and the cultural gap behind it, has long exacerbated problems between the Oaxacan government and its native population.

After the Spanish Conquest, in an attempt to eradicate paganism, Catholic missionaries inseminated Oaxaca with Catholicism by constructing magnificent Baroque cathedrals to overwhelm the *indígena* religious edifices. In an attempt to maintain the old way of life, the small villages around the city of Oaxaca did what they could to continue production of the folk arts for which they were previously famed; many of them are crafted to this day: the magnificent hand-dyed and hand-stitched *alfombras* (carpets) made on foot-pedaled Spanish looms in Teotitlán del Valle; the leather belts woven by hand in Santo Tomás Jalietza; the dresses embroidered in San Antonino; the inscribed silver hunting knives forged in Ejutla; and the exquisite black pottery thrown in San Bartolo Coyotepec. Weavers turn out vibrantly colored *huipiles* (blouses) and other clothing, and enterprising families whittle blocks of wood into intricate figurines.

Little of this culture is evident once you cross the Sierra Madre del Sur to the coastal resorts of Puerto Escondido and Puerto Angel. The attraction of these two beautiful towns is not the opportunity to experience another way of life but the chance to relax, and perhaps to digest what you've seen on the other side of the mountains. Until recently, these small towns were unknown to all but the most resourceful tourists; word of their charm has spread like wildfire among both travelers and developers, and the tourist zone of the Oaxaca coast, which now stretches east of Puerto Angel, is ablaze with expansion. The Bahías de Huatulco—nine magnificent, once isolated bays—are receiving a dose of *desarrollo turístico,* (development) including a brand-new Club Med and Sheraton.

Oaxaca de Juárez

Deep in the highlands of Sierra Madre del Sur, on a giant plateau that gracefully interrupts the terrain's descent into the Oaxaca Valley, Oaxaca City has gripped Spaniards and visitors ever since Hernando Cortés built his beloved (but unfinished) private estate here in 1535. Nicknamed "City of Jade" after the many buildings inlaid with the emerald gem, Oaxaca glows to a year-round average temperature of 70°F (21°C). Despite its well-deserved popularity among travelers, the state capital maintains a small-town atmosphere. Even locals patronize the colonnaded cafés on the Zócalo, where prices are high but not out of control. Miraculous, too, is the absence of any large international hotel.

During the last two decades, the city of Oaxaca has expanded from insider's secret to major travel destination. For years, Oaxaca lured *norteamericanos* with the potent "shroom," which *indígenas* cultivate in the surrounding hills. More standard attractions include Oaxaca's several markets and its unusually large Zócalo, one of the most amiable in the Republic. Unlike most Mexican *centros,* the entire area

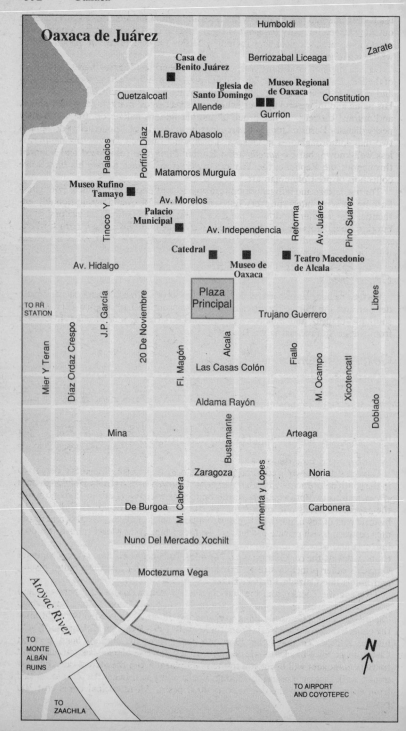

is a pedestrian mall punctuated by tall trees and pots of flowers. Just a short distance outside Oaxaca lie many *indígena* villages, and, in the hilly environs, a number of outstanding archeological sites including Mitla, Yagul, and Monte Albán—all of which make great daytrips.

Oaxaca has nurtured quite a few Mexican celebrities. Benito Juárez, champion of the Reform era, was a poor Zapotec *indígena* born in the nearby town of Guelatao and raised in Oaxaca by a wealthy *ladino* family who lived on Calle García Vigil. His name and image pop up everywhere: on street signs, markets, bus lines, shops, and murals. Citizens are less proud of another famous native son, the notoriously pesky dictator Porfirio Díaz. His name may be unloved, yet it nonetheless designates two major thoroughfares in Oaxaca. Local son Francisco Toledo, the painter, is less well-known, but *oaxaqueño* artist Rufino Tamayo is recognized and honored throughout the Republic; the Tamayo museum in Oaxaca houses his impressive collection of pre-Columbian art.

Tourist culture and indigenous culture coexist and interact in Oaxaca. Foreigners flashing cameras interrupt every few steps, but this Mexico is unquestionably authentic. The sweater vendors in the Zócalo may depend entirely on visitors' *pesos,* but these merchants are greatly outnumbered by the knife-sharpeners, corn-huskers, coffee-grinders, and grasshopper-eaters who go about their business as if Oaxaca were just another mountain town.

Orientation

Oaxaca de Juárez rests in the Oaxaca Valley, between the towering Sierra Madre del Sur and the Puebla-Oaxaca range—523km southeast of Mexico City, 435km south of Veracruz, and 526km west of Tuxtla Gutiérrez. Principal access to Oaxaca from the north and east is via Rte. 190.

Getting Around

Oaxaca isn't huge, but orienting yourself can be difficult as many streets change names when they pass the Zócalo. Most streets follow a perfect east-west, north-south grid. The large maps posted around the Zócalo clearly mark all sights in English.

The Zócalo, on Hidalgo (one of the few streets that does not change names in the center of town), consists of two squares: the main one lies between Hidalgo and Trujano/Guerrero, and the Pl. Alameda de León just to the north is sandwiched by Hidalgo and Independencia.

Oaxaca's downtown is circumscribed by a busy expressway called the Periférico in the south before acquiring other names as it loops north. **Avenida Hidalgo** divides *el centro* into two principal areas: the budget district lies south of Hidalgo while the expensive hotels and restaurants cluster around the Zócalo on Hidalgo. The historic part of town, north of Hidalgo, contains most of Oaxaca's sights and museums between lavish private residences. **Avenida Macedonio Alcalá** splits downtown into east and west sections, serving for a few blocks north of the Zócalo as a pedestrian walkway, the *corredor turístico.* **Morelos, Independencia,** and **García Vigil** are Oaxaca's other principal streets. Farther north, the more luxurious clubs, discos, and hotels line **Calzada Porfirio Díaz.**

To reach the Zócalo from the first-class **ADO** station, take a left at the exit and walk 2 blocks west on Chapultepec to the bus stop at Juárez. Take a bus labeled "Santa Rosa" or "Centro" (300 pesos) and get off on 20 de Noviembre right after the church of San Felipe Neri. From there, walk 1 block east on Hidalgo and you'll hit the Zócalo. To make the 20-minute walk from the station, head west on Chapultepec for 6 blocks to Alcalá and turn left. Twelve blocks past churches and tourist colonnades will bring you to the main plaza. From the second-class bus terminal, walk east on Truano for 8 long blocks and you'll reach the Zócalo. A taxi from either station to the *centro* costs 4000 pesos. All municipal buses cost 300 pesos.

Hiking from one end of town to the other takes no more than 45 minutes, and walking on the pedestrian mall at night is safe. Though petty crime has surged in Oaxaca with the influx of tourists, it rarely escalates above pickpocketing; still, it's a good idea for travelers to take taxis if crossing town late at night. A taxi ride from the Zócalo to a downtown hotel costs 4000-8000 pesos, depending on the time of day (cabbies charge extra under 11pm-5am, under cover of the night).

Practical Information

Tourist Office: Centro de Amistad Internacional, Independencia 607 (tel. 638-10), in the Palacio Munciipal just across from Alameda de León, the section of the Zócalo between the post office and the cathedral. Excellent maps and pamphlets (many in English) describing surrounding villages and archeological sites. Extremely helpful staff speaks English, offers lists of accommodations, restaurants, and services, and sells tickets for the Guelaguetza dances in July (60,000-90,000 pesos). Also serves as a liaison in case of emergency by contacting lawyers and consulates for tourists who have suffered accident or robbery. Open daily 9am-8pm.

State Tourist Office: Dirección General de Turismo, Morelos at 5 de Mayo (tel. 648-28). Staff much less helpful than at the Centro de Amistad. Also sells tickets for the Guelaguetza festival. Open Mon.-Fri. 9am-8pm, Sat. 9am-noon.

Federal Tourist Office: On 5 de Mayo near Morelos, next door to the state tourist office. As is the norm across Mexico, the feds offer much less than the other offices; worth a visit only if you need information on those distant spots in Mexico that you've come to Oaxaca to visit. Open Mon.-Fri. 8am-3:30pm.

Consulates: In an emergency, go first to the Centro de Amistad Internacional (see above), whose staff will scare up consular assistance. **U.S.,** Sra. Roberta French, Crespo 213 (tel. 606-54), hidden under an arched doorway. Office open Mon.-Fri. 10am-1pm. **Canada,** Sra. Valery Sommers, Fortín 128 (tel. 646-88). **West Germany,** Sr. Wolfgang Westphal (tel. 656-00). Open Mon.-Sat. 9am-1pm.

Currency Exchange: Herds of banks encircle the Zócalo; all are open Mon.-Fri. 9am-1:30pm, but hours for currency exchange vary. **Bancomer,** García Vigil 120 (tel. 676-43), at Morelos. Open for exchange Mon.-Fri. 9-11am. **Bánamex,** Hidalgo 821 (tel. 659-00), just off the Zócalo. Open for exchange Mon.-Fri. 9-11am and 4-5pm. **Banco Serfín,** Independencia 705 (tel. 628-55), on the north side of the Zócalo. Open for exchange Mon.-Fri. 9am-2pm. *Casas de cambio* trade at less favorable rates: Try **La Estrella,** Alcalá 201. Open Mon.-Sat. 9am-1:30pm and 4-7pm. On Sun., try the hotels around the Zócalo.

Post Office: (tel. 626-61), in the Pl. Alameda de León (the Zócalo annex). Lista de Correos. Open Mon.-Fri. 8am-9pm, Sat. 9am-1pm. **Postal Code:** 68001.

Telephones: Long-distance collect calls are best made from telephone booths on the street. If the lines are too long, you can try a long-distance office, although they have only self-service for collect calls (i.e., they provide you with a phone and you dial 09 for the international operator yourself). The one in **Hotel Mesón del Rey,** Trujano 212 (tel. 601-99), 2 blocks west of the Zócalo, has extra cables; usually less than a 5-min. wait. Open Mon.-Sat. 7am-8:30pm. Another at **Farmacia Hidalgo,** 20 de Noviembre at Hidalgo (tel. 644-59), 1 block west of the Zócalo, sprouts long lines at 8:01am. Open daily 8am-10pm. **Telephone Code:** 951.

Telegrams: Independencia at 20 de Noviembre (tel. 642-55), next to the post office. Open for telegrams and money orders Mon.-Sat. 9am-6pm.

Airport: Aeropuerto Juárez, on Rte. 175 8km south of the city. Taxis to the airport cost 12,000-15,000 pesos. You can also arrange transportation to the airport through **Transportes Aeropuerto,** Alameda de León G. on the Zócalo (*colectivo* 4000 pesos, *especial* 12,000 pesos). Give them advance notice and they'll pick you up at your hotel. Open Mon.-Sat. 9am-2pm and 4-7pm. **Mexicana,** Independencia at Fiallo (tel. 684-14, airport tel. 623-37), to Mexico City (3 per day, 50 min.). **Aeroméxico,** Hidalgo 513 (tel. 671-01, airport tel. 628-44) flies to Mexico City, Acapulco, Tapachula, and the Bahías de Huatulco. **Aerovías Oaxaqueños,** Armenta y López 209 (tel. 638-33), shuttles vacationing families to Puerto Escondido (4 per day).

Train Station: Ferrocarriles Nacionales de México (tel. 648-44), in an ancient building at the western end of Madero (the extension of Independencia), across the Periférico from downtown. Service to Mexico City (2 per day, 14½ hr.), Puebla (2 per day, 10 hr.), and a few villages south of Oaxaca via Ocotlán.

Bus stations: Only partial listings are given; it is possible to go literally anywhere in the Republic at any time of day or night. **First-class station,** Niños Héroes de Chapultepec 1036, about 10 blocks north and 5 blocks east of the Zócalo. Clean and well-organized. From the station, **ADO** (tel. 517-03) runs to: Mexico City (21 per day, 9 hr., 25,000 pesos); Puebla (6 per day, 7 hr., 18,271 pesos); Veracruz (2 per day, 10 hr., 24,000 pesos); Tuxtepec (at 6pm, 9 hr., 25,000 pesos); Córdoba (3 per day, 7 hr., 18,000 pesos); Yanhuitlán (4 per day, 2½ hr., 4400 pesos); Matamoros (3 per day, 5½ hr., 16,000 pesos). **Omnibus Cristóbal Colón** (tel. 512-14) to: Salina Cruz (6 per day, 5 hr., 12,000 pesos); Tehuantepec (7 per day, 5 hr., 11,200 pesos); Villahermosa (2 per day, 10 hr., 34,000 pesos); San Cristóbal (at 7am, 11 hr., 30,000 pesos); Tuxtla Gutiérrez (3 per day, 10 hr., 26,000 pesos). The **second-class station,** next to the Central de Abastos (big market), across the Periférico from the western end of Trujano or Las Casas. The large number of regional bus lines—many without signs or ticket windows—make the set-up rather confusing. Frequent service to every small town near Oaxaca. In general, each town is served by only one line; the staff of each line knows who goes where, so don't be bashful. Most rides cost less than 3000 pesos. To: Zaachila (every 20 min., 30 min.); San Bartolo Coyotepec (every 15 min., 15 min.); Ocotlán (every 15 min., 30 min.); Ejutla (every 30 min., 1 hr.); Cuilapán (every 20 min., 15 min.); Santa María El Tule (every 15 min., 40 min.); Teotitlán del Valle (every hr., 1 hr.); Mitla (every 20 min., 1 hr.). A few buses make longer trips toward the Pacific coast. **Oaxaca Pacífico, Solteca, Oaxaca Istma,** and **Fletes y Pasajes** send buses to Puerto Angel (7 hr., 8000 pesos); Puerto Escondido (10 hr., 22,000 pesos); and Salina Cruz (5 hr., 7800 pesos). The most convenient way to get to Puerto Angel is to transfer at Pochutla. The **Hotel Mesón del Angel bus stop,** Mina 518, between Mier y Terán and Díaz Ordaz, serves as a third bus station. Buses to Monte Albán leave here (every hr. 8:30am-3:30pm, 4 per day off-season; 3000 pesos round-trip with return 2 hr. after arrival, 1000 pesos extra to return on a later bus). "Tourist-class" buses depart from this lot and cover the ground between Oaxaca and Puerto Escondido in record time (at 8am and 10:45pm, 6 hr., 24,000 pesos).

Car Rental: Avis, Alameda de León 1 (tel. 650-30), on the Zócalo. Must be over 24 and hold a driver's license and credit card. VW Bugs rent for around US$40 including unlimited mileage. **Budget,** 5 de Mayo 300 (tel. 503-31), in the Hotel Presidente, has similar prices and rules.

Auto Repair: Auto Camiones de Oaxaca, Hidalgo 104 (tel. 606-42). Prefers Fords, but repairs all makes. Open Mon.-Fri. 9am-2pm and 4-7:30pm, Sat. 9am-2pm.

Bookstore: Librería Universitaria, Guerrero 104 (tel. 642-43), off the southeast corner of the Zócalo. Good selection of used paperbacks in English (2500-3500 pesos), and a number of English-language books about Mexico. Also sells posters and paper supplies. Open Mon.-Sat. 9:30am-2pm and 4-8pm.

Laundromat: Lavandería Automática, 20 de Noviembre 605 (tel. 623-42), 3½ blocks south of the Zócalo. Clothes ready by noon if you bring them in at 9am; ready by evening if in by noon. 6000 pesos per 3½kg. Open Mon.-Sat. 9am-8pm.

Red Cross: Armenta y López 700 (tel. 620-56), between Pardo and Burgoa. Free medical and ambulance service. Some doctors and nurses speak English; all are helpful and knowledgeable. Open 24 hr.

Pharmacies: Farmacia Del Centro, Portal Marqués del Valle 8 (tel. 611-22), under the arcade on the Zócalo. Open daily 8am-11pm. **Farmacia Zarate,** Hidalgo 411 (tel. 642-80), 2½ blocks west of the Zócalo; second store around the corner at Garciá 100 (same phone). Both open daily 7am-midnight.

Hospitals: Hospital Civil, Porfirio Díaz 400 (tel. 537-25), gives free medical service to all. Private hospitals include **Seguro Social,** Chapultepec 621 (tel. 520-33), and **Hospital Vasconcelos,** Morelos 500 (tel. 636-52), at Padre Angel.

Police: Aldama 108 (tel. 611-55 or 622-44), between Miguel Cabrera and Bustamante. Some English spoken. Open 24 hr.

Accommodations

Oaxaca's accommodations confirm its charm and resistance to development. There are few pushy advertisements or rip-offs, and even the most expensive hotel in town, the **Hotel Presidente,** occupies a small and unassuming *ex-convento.* Because of Oaxaca's status as a trading center, most of the budget hotels draw their greatest income from marketeers from nearby villages. High-quality budget lodgings appear on nearly every street corner, especially in the southern part of town.

Several trailer parks lie outside the downtown area. The **Trailer Park Oaxaca,** Violetas 900 (tel. 527-96), is near the Zona Militar in the northeast part of town. To get there, take the "Colonia Reforma" bus from the stop on García just north of Hidalgo. The **Trailer Park San Francisco,** Madero 705, in the northwest part of town, is accessible on the "Santa Rosa" bus from the same stop as above. This bus also will take you to the more distant **Trailer Park Rosa Isabel,** on Carretera 131 to Mexico City, km539.

North

The northern part of town is more prosperous, residential, and tranquil than the south; hotels are relatively expensive, but sequestered away are some of the best values in town. Cleanliness is universal here.

Casa Arnel, Aldama 404 (tel. 528-56), at Hidalgo in Colonia Jalatlaco, 2 blocks east and 7 short blocks south of the ADO station, across the street from a greenish colonial church with kids playing in the steeples. Immaculate courtyard packed with exotic plants, sculptures, and giant parrots—an alluring backdrop to the hotel's restaurant, which serves excellent cheap fare. (Restaurant open daily 7:30-10am and 7:30-10pm.) Social atmosphere; *Let's Go* users the world over congregate around a family-sized table in the courtyard. Cozy and spruce rooms with colorful bedspreads served by 24-hr. hot water. An in-house "travel agency" arranges transportation to nearby sights. The only catch is the distance from the Zócalo; it's quite a hike. Staying here means experiencing the quietly residential Oaxaca rather than busy, hyper-historical one. A few rooms available with communal baths, at about two-thirds the cost. Singles 27,000 pesos. Doubles 34,000 pesos.

Hotel Central, 20 de Noviembre 104 (tel. 659-71), between Independencia and Hidalgo, 1 block from the Zócalo. About as close to the Zócalo as budget hotels get. Nice courtyard with TV. All rooms have private bath. Singles 19,000 pesos. Doubles 25,000-28,000 pesos.

Hotel Virreyes, Morelos 1001 (tel. 651-41), 4 blocks from the Zócalo at Reforma. Very comfortable, commodious pink rooms adjoin way-cool private bathrooms. Phones and large mirrors in all rooms, charming balconies off some. Colonial-style courtyard brims with arches. Singles 14,400 pesos. Doubles 18,000 pesos.

Hotel Reforma, Reforma 102 (tel. 671-44), 4 blocks from the Zócalo above a row of stores. Extremely quiet and popular with schoolteachers on vacation. Well-furnished rooms have luxurious bedspreads, phones, and private baths, some of which are rather unsanitary. Singles 28,000 pesos. Doubles 35,000 pesos.

Hotel Pombo, Morelos 601 (tel. 626-73), between Vigil and Díaz, just around the corner from the Zócalo. Proprietor has the right attitude: "What's important is that the people are happy here." Rooms are clean but vary greatly in size; singles without baths are just larger than this book. Some "private" bathrooms are a short walk down the hall from the bedroom. Ask to see a room, then ask for a bigger one. Prime location. Singles 15,000 pesos, with bath 17,000 pesos. Doubles with bath 22,000 pesos.

Hotel Santo Tomás, Abasolo 305 (tel. 638-00), 7 blocks from the Zócalo. A bit of a walk, and probably not worth the extra pesos unless you're starved for silence. Exterior, courtyards, and rooms are plain but neat. Metal beds and sparse furniture remind many guests of college dormitory days. All rooms have private bath. Helpful friendly staff. Singles 41,000 pesos. Doubles with 2 beds 51,000 pesos.

South

Most budget hotels sit south of the Zócalo; often four or five share the same block, particularly along Díaz Ordaz. Because of the proximity of the market and second-class bus terminal, many of these hotels occupy dirty, noisy neighborhoods. Reservations are necessary during *fiesta* weekends (particularly during the Guelaguetza). Arrive in the early afternoon, since these hotels fill quickly.

Hotel Pasaje, Mina 302 (tel. 642-13), 3 blocks south of the Zócalo. Spotless rooms with well-equipped (i.e. shower-curtained) private bathrooms. Desks and art posters, art posters and desks. Courtyard features Lorenzo the parrot who shouts, cries, whistles, and sometimes sings the blues. The amount of soap handed out each day suggests the owner is a majority shareholder in a Mexican pumice company. Singles 20,000 pesos. Doubles 30,000 pesos.

Hotel Vallarta, Díaz Ordaz 309 (tel. 649-67), 3 blocks west of the Zócalo's southwest corner. Courtyard and freshly-painted halls make for a cheerful atmosphere. Simple, comfortable munchkin rooms shine; all have private baths. Singles 20,000 pesos. Doubles 40,000 pesos.

Hotel Lupita, Díaz Ordaz 312 (tel. 627-15), across from the Hotel Vallarta, and less expensive. Freshly painted rooms are now colorful stone cells. Fairly clean bathrooms enjoy hot water service 6:30-9am. Singles 15,000 pesos, with bath 17,000 pesos. Doubles 20,000 pesos, with bath 25,000 pesos.

Hotel La Cabaña, Mina 203 (tel. 659-18), 3 blocks south of the Zócalo's southwest corner near Cabera. Fifty small, tidy rooms show off a variety of orange bedspreads, most more cheery than the ugly brown-and-yellow tiled courtyard. Only a few rooms without private bath available—too bad for all you exhibitionists. Reasonably clean communal baths. Singles 18,000 pesos, with bath 25,000 pesos. Doubles 22,000 pesos, with bath 30,000 pesos. Two-bed doubles with bath 40,000 pesos.

Hotel Aurora, Bustamante 212 (tel. 641-45), 1½ blocks south of the Zócalo's southeast corner. Friendly management and wide courtyard. Soft beds covered by tattered sheets. Bathrooms (some communal) are clean but the water pressure is as low as a well in Death Valley. Some recently built huge rooms in back are neat but naked. Singles 15,000 pesos. Doubles 20,000 pesos. Triples 20,000 pesos.

Hotel Guelaguetza, Rayón 215 (tel. 656-91), between Fiallo and Armenta y López. A gaudy green-and-blue building with tacky Guelaguetza designs near the entrance. The courtyard features a viny, Winnie-the-Pooh-style tree. Soft beds, dusty rooms, moldy bathrooms, and vanishing toilet seats. Great prices. Singles 12,000 pesos, with bath 15,000 pesos. Doubles 15,000 pesos, with bath 18,000 pesos.

Hotel Bahena, Armenta y López 416, near Rayón, 1 block east and 2 blocks south of the Zócalo. Musty, uncomfortable cement rooms of various shapes and sizes. Singles are generally so small your foot could wedge between the bed and any of the walls. Acceptable bathrooms either lack doors or are located next door. Singles 15,000 pesos. Doubles 25,000 pesos.

Food

Eating well in Oaxaca is as easy as falling off a log; nearly every side-street café and tourist hotspot serves fresh, well-prepared meals at reasonable prices (most *comidas corridas* cost only 5000 pesos). Oaxaca specializes in *mole* and also in exotic (but often not sweet) pastries and ices. When sampling sweets on the streets, exercise caution. Most pastry vendors cover their goodies with glass or plastic, but some don't, and huge flies tend to descend upon unattended delicacies. Most frozen sweets (*nieves*) are made from water and are closer to sorbet than to ice cream.

The many mesmerizing cafés around Oaxaca's Zócalo retain reasonable prices and are especially good for breakfast; *huevos a la oaxaqueña* (scrambled eggs in spicy tomato soup) is a great way to start the day. The best of several large markets, the **Benito Juárez produce market,** occupies the block bounded by 20 de Noviembre, Aldama, Cabrera, and Las Casas. Try the large, white, beet-shaped fruit called *jicama* (often seasoned with spicy powder) or a bag of *nísperas* (custard apples). Vendors also sell peeled and sliced fruit on the street. You'll pay more for this prepared fruit, but 1000 pesos for a mongo mango is surely worth it.

Cafeteria Alex, Díaz Ordaz 218. A cozy joint packed with locals enjoying huge bowls of soup and fruit salad. Nothing over 5500 pesos. Tasty *comida corrida* with soup, meat, rice, 2 drinks, and dessert is a steal at 5000 pesos. Open Mon.-Sat. 7am-9pm, Sun. 7am-noon.

Fondo de Cultura Oaxaqueña, Trujano 213, a few blocks west of the Zócalo's south side. Clean family restaurant with wooden chairs and blue-checkered tablecloths. Tasty breaded fish. *Comida corrida* has 2 entree choices (5000 pesos). Open daily 7am-9pm.

Restaurant Quickly, Alcalá 101, 1½ blocks from the Zócalo. The name may irk, but the decor is colorful and the food both good and cheap. Breakfasts 3000-8500 pesos. "Autentica-mente gringas" hamburgers 3900-5500 pesos. Feast on the *parrillada,* a platter of grilled vegatables smothered with cheese and your choice of toppings (7500-10,000 pesos). Also 3 *comidas corridas:* regular 5500 pesos, vegetarian 7500 pesos, and luxury 8500 pesos. Open daily 8am-10pm.

El Arca de Emmanuel, Chapultepec 1023, at Aldama across the street from and 1 block east of the ADO terminal. Excellent vegetarian cuisine amid elegant decor. Delicately spiced soups and exotic entrees. *Queso fundido con chapiñones* (melted cheese with mushrooms for 2) 7900 pesos. Fantastic wheat bran pizza (medium 19,500 pesos) easily feeds 2 as well. Vegetarian *comida corrida* 12,000 pesos. Occasional live music. Open Tues.-Sat. 9am-8pm, Sun. 1-6pm.

Restaurant El Oaxaqueño, Bustamante 409, at Artega 3 blocks south of the Zócalo. New family-run restaurant with white walls and red tables. Small portions of tasty regional food served with huge flour tortillas. *Comida corrida* 5000 pesos. Open daily 8am-10pm.

Café El Sol y La Luna, Murguía 105, between 5 de Mayo and Reforma. The classiest, artsiest place in town. Excellent gallery in back exhibits local graphic artists and photographers. Guitar and folk music daily 9pm-midnight (8000-peso cover) Food somewhat overpriced: good pizza 15,000 pesos, crepes (for 2) 10,000 pesos. Crowded on weekends. Open Mon.-Sat. 7pm-1am.

Restaurant Lichita, Fiallo 5-D, between Arteaga and Rayón. Filthy floors, clean tables, and delicious home-cooked food. Family-run kitchen so familiar to locals that there is no menu and nary a *gringo*. Huge breakfasts and *comida corrida* both 5000 pesos; fancy *mole oaxaqueño* 3000 pesos. Open daily 8am-9:30pm.

Restaurant Los Danzantes, 20 de Noviembre at Trujano, 1 block west of the Zócalo's southwest corner. Bright and festive, with beautiful *oaxaqueño* wool wall-hangings and candlelit tables. Multilingual menu describes *típico* cuisine. Huge *botana oaxaqueño* serves up to 5 people (30,000 pesos). *Comida corrida* 7500 pesos. Open daily 8am-1:30am.

Pizzería Alfredo da Roma, Alcalá 400, on the *corredor turístico*. Popular student hangout serving great pizza; both dining rooms always full. Red-checkered tablecloths. Small pizza 9500-19,000 pesos, pasta dishes around 12,000 pesos. Open daily 1:30-11pm.

Restaurant Plaza Gourmet, Morelos 509, next to the Museo Rufino Tamayo. Vegetarian-restaurant-turned-variety-restaurant still serves some tasty meatless dishes. Soups 3000 pesos. *Camarones al gusto* (shrimp cooked to taste) 15,000 pesos. Pizza built for two (13,000 pesos). Open daily 7am-11pm.

El Biche Pobre II, Calzada de la República 600, at Hidalgo. Popular with local families. Pretty tablecloths and wood-paneled ceilings. Excellent service. *Mariachis* meander between the tables in the mid-afternoon. Order the *botana surtida*—2 big plates (served one at a time) juggling bits of *oaxaqueña* cuisine (11,000 pesos). Try El Biche Pobre I at Rayón 1133 if II is full. Open daily 1:30-6pm.

Gino's Pizza, Independencia 503, just down the street from the post office. The in place for students pardner: Wild West decor includes swinging barroom doors, steer horns, piles of hay, and signs proclaiming "Grand Saloon" and "Far West City." Small (and rather bland) pizza 9000-12,000 pesos; beer more satisfactory (1500-2000 pesos). Open daily 2-11pm.

Maderas, Aldama 509, 2 blocks south of the Zócalo. Schizophrenia rules. A pseudo-Swiss hamburger grill with Cajun side orders; a mural of Reichenbach Waterfall, where Sherlock Holmes threw Moriarty to his death, on the side wall. English menu has a section for kids and a few regional dishes. "Tell 'em Sybil sent you." Breakfasts 4000-6000 pesos, *comida corrida* 5000 pesos. Open daily 8am-8pm.

Sights

Oaxaca's **Zócalo,** composed of two plazas, is always congested with people. Early in the morning, vendors set up expensive, exotic pastry stalls, women sell fruit from baskets, and toy dealers push huge multi-colored balloons and demonstrate the workings of mechanical Batman figures to passersby. Every evening between 7 and 9pm, live concerts shake the square. Local rock groups, *marimba* performers, and the state brass band alternate to keep the people dancing. By 10pm, however, foreigners dominate the Zócalo.

Throughout Oaxaca's streets, vendors push knitted cotton blankets, *sarapes,* jade bookends, *oaxaqueño* guitars (always out of tune), wooden letter openers, masks, and straw baskets. Make clear from the beginning whether you intend to buy or not; entrepreneurs become indignant if they think you're just stalling to fetch a better price. A quarter of their asking price for *sarapes* and half for musical instruments is not too low for starters. Eavesdropping on the final price other tourists pay is usually useless, since most shell out more than twice the bargain rate. On Saturdays, be sure to visit the *tianguis* setup in Oaxaca's biggest market, the Central de Abastos (across the Periférico from the western end of Mina), where virtually every resident of Oaxaca state is either buying or selling food, art, or crafts. The market divides into categories, so you'll find immense areas selling only baskets, only peppers, only bread, or only rugs, for example. Everyone hawks with vigor. Come in the morning, because pickpockets in Oaxaca seem to rise and shine around lunchtime. During the rest of the week, the market is much more subdued.

The **Catedral de Oaxaca** and the Palacio de Gobierno (not to be confused with the Palacio Municipal, which incorporates the tourist office) sit on opposite sides of the Zócalo. Originally constructed in 1535, the cathedral was damaged and finally destroyed by a series of earthquakes before being rebuilt in the 18th century with *oaxaqueño* green-brown stone and ornamented in filigree. The ornate bishop's seat, in the central altar, provides the focus of attention. (Open daily 6am-8pm.)

Inside the **Palacio de Gobierno,** on the south side of the Zócalo, a mural by García Bustos presents an informative collage of *oaxaqueño* history. The center panel is dominated by Benito Juárez, his wife Margarita Masa, and one of his much-repeated phrases, "Respect for the rights of others brings peace."

On the wall to the right (as you ascend the staircase) is a portrait of Sor Juana Inés de la Cruz, the poet, theologian, and astronomer. Often considered Mexico's first feminist, she penned a diatribe against misogynists called *Hombres Necios* (Foolish Men). After impersonating a man for several years in order to attend the university in Mexico City, Sor Juana eventually made her way onto the front of 1000-peso bills.

Walking north from the Zócalo on Alcalá—the *corredor turístico*—you arrive first at Oaxaca's newest museum, the aptly named **Museo de Oaxaca**, Alcalá 202 (tel. 684-99), inaugurated in 1986. The museum's colonial building is known as the Casa de Cortés, although historians insist that it is not in fact Cortés's Oaxaca estate. Inside, a sketchy exhibit on the history of Oaxaca fronts the more interesting galleries which include a permanant exhibit of Miguel Cabrera's paintings and several rooms of contemporary art. (Open Tues.-Sun. 9am-9pm. Free.)

Farther up Alcalá, 6 blocks north of the Zócalo, the **Iglesia de Santo Domingo** has perhaps the most stunning internal decoration of any church in the Republic. Around the arches, on the ceiling vaults, and above the altars and chapels, waves of ornamented stucco form elegant arabesques. Time has somewhat eroded the church's façade of rose and green-gray stone. Construction on the church began in 1575, the consecration came in 1611, and improvements and artistic work continued after that. Built 2m thick as protection against earthquakes, the walls served the convent well when it saw service as military barracks for both sides during the Reform wars and the Revolution. (Open Mon.-Sat. 9am-1pm and 4-7:30pm, Sun. 7am-1pm and 4-8pm.)

The ex-convent next door was converted in 1972 into the city's prestigious **Museo Regional de Oaxaca.** The frescos, paintings, and especially the stucco work on its walls have withstood a century of military abuse. The museum fastidiously organizes its archeological and ethnographic exhibits into sections focusing on each of the state's *indígena* peoples. The superb exhibits cover every facet of *indígena* life, even the *teohanacatl* (hallucinogenic mushrooms) used by the Mixtecs. The most outstanding archeological hall displays Mixtec jewelry found in Tomb 7 at nearby Monte Albán. This treasure might be the largest ever unveiled in a tomb in the Americas: its elaborate working of gold, silver, and copper chains, brooches, and rings, some set with fine jewels, demonstrates the sophistication of Mixtec metalworkers. (Open Tues.-Fri. 10am-6pm, Sat.-Sun. 10am-5pm. Admission 10,000 pesos. Free for students and teachers, and on Sun.)

Another renowned museum, the **Museo Rufino Tamayo,** Morelos 503 (tel. 647-50), at Díaz 3 blocks north of the Zócale, shows off the *oaxaqueño* artist's personal collection of pre-Conquest objects from all over the Republic. The figurines, ceramics, and masks that Tamayo collected were selected for their aesthetic value as well as for anthropological interest. Pieces are arranged in roughly chronological order rather than by culture. (Open Mon. and Wed.-Sat. 10am-2pm and 4-7pm, Sun. 10am-3pm. Admission 10,000 pesos, domestic students 5000 pesos.)

For a glimpse of more modern artwork, stop in at the **Instituto de Artes Graficas,** Alcalá 507, opposite Santo Domingo church. Many small rooms display prints and graphic art from around the world. (Open Wed.-Sat. 10am-2pm and 4-7pm, Sun. 11am-5pm. Admission 1000 pesos.)

Five blocks north of the post office on García Vigil is the **Casa de Benito Juárez,** García Vigil 609 (tel. 618-60). This may look like the house of a poor, 19th-century Zapotec *campesino,* and with good reason—it's not. It all started when Benito's older sister left the Juárez home in Guelatao to come to Oaxaca as the domestic servant of the wealthy Masa family. The Masas were *paisanos* from Spain and good friends with the equally wealthy Salanueva family. The Salanuevas took a keen interest in young Benito, adopted him, and brought him to Oaxaca. His subsequent education and upbringing qualified him to marry the Masas's daughter, Margarita, and to embark on a career in law, then politics, and finally the Reform. His memorabilia kill the first room on the right. The rest of the house—living room, bedrooms, kitchen, well, and "bookbinding/ weaving shop"—is a model of 19th-century upper-middle-class *oaxaqueño* life. (Open Tues.-Sun. 9am-7pm. Admission 1000 pesos, free Sun.)

The **Teatro Macedonio Alcalá,** on 5 de Mayo at Independencia, 2 blocks east of the Zócalo, is one of the most beautiful buildings in Oaxaca and an illuminating example of the art and architecture that flourished in Mexico under Porfirio Díaz. Díaz's regime had a serious case of *afrancesamiento,* the taste for French art and French intellectual formulas. Oaxaca, the birthplace of Díaz, remained a favorite of the dictator, and his support was instrumental in this theater's construction, which began in 1904. On the ceiling, scantily clad Muses float above the giant candelabra. (Usually open for shows Mon.-Sat. at 8pm, Sun. at 6pm; it is possible to take a peek immediately before shows.)

Entertainment

Nightlife in Oaxaca is a bit livelier than in most towns south of Mexico City. Many discos and bars are open throughout the week, though usually more crowded on Friday and Saturday nights. The most popular disco in town is **Yonkee,** Jalisco 15, in the Hotel San Felipe Misión at San Felipe. A cab ride there costs 8000-10,000 pesos. A large video screen keeps people on their feet for hours on end. The cover is 15,000 pesos Saturday nights, 10,000 pesos Fridays and Sundays, and free the rest of the week. (Open Tues.-Sun. 9pm-3am.) In a more spectacular setting and nearly as popular is the disco at the **Hotel Victoria,** behind Auditorio Guelaguetza atop the hill. Its wood-paneled bar and veranda overlook the entire city. (Cover 15,000 pesos. Open Mon.-Sat. 9pm-2am.) **Kaftan,** at Díaz 102, in the Misión de Los Angeles Hotel, jangles partiers with loud Mexican pop for a cover of 15,000 pesos Saturday nights, 10,000 pesos Friday nights, and 7000 pesos the rest of the week. (Open Mon.-Sat. 9am-3am.) The conveniently located **Los Arcos,** 20 de Noviembre between Hidalgo and Independencia, attracts young gangs; you may be better off footing the cab bill to hit the hotel clubs, all three of which draw a mix of locals and tourists. Women alone are less conspicuous in Oaxaca than in some other Mexican cities, but it's still a good idea to party with others.

Oaxaca's cinemas are superb. The **Alameda,** at Independencia and 20 de Noviembre (tel. 640-07), shows recent North American and European films four times per day in a beautiful modern theater. The **Reforma,** at Trujano 1 (tel. 655-30), ½ block from the Zócalo, also shows U.S. movies with Spanish subtitles. Several blocks north at Juárez and Berriozábal, **Arte-Cinema Ariel 2000** (tel. 652-41) probably has the best selection of films in town. Those interested in Mexican popular culture should head to **Cinema Oaxaca,** Morelos 701 (tel. 636-96), 2 blocks north of the Zócalo. Most of the films here are "Hecho en México." Most theaters charge 2500 pesos.

Even bigger stars come into focus at Oaxaca's **Canuto Muñoz Mares Observatory** and the **Nundenui Planetarium,** on Cerro del Fortín (tel. 524-35), the hill overlooking Oaxaca from the northwest. To get there, climb the stairs from Crespo at the corner of Quetzalcóatl. If you plan to walk along the unlit road to the observatory, leave early in the evening, because night traffic can be dangerous. Buses cost 2500 pesos round-trip and leave from the Hotel Mesón del Angel on Mina, between Díaz Ordaz and Teran, whence the buses to Monte Albán also depart. Planetarium shows (1000 pesos) happen Tuesday through Sunday at 6:30pm (the bus leaves at 6pm and returns at 7:30pm) and 8pm (the bus leaves at 7:45pm and returns at 9pm). (Observatory open Tues.-Sun. 10am-2pm and 6-9pm, when the sky is clear; admission 1500 pesos.)

Oaxacan summer and fall *fiestas* occur in wild splendor. The biggest summertime festivity is **La Guelaguetza** or **Los Lunes del Cerro** (Mondays of the Hill), when costumed hoofers from different *oaxaqueño* tribes perform fantastic regional dances in Oaxaca City's largest amphitheater. The festival is held on the third and fourth Mondays of July. Front-section tickets cost 90,000 pesos, mid-section tickets are 60,000 pesos, and the back section is free (arrive 2-3 hr. early to secure a seat.) In early November, *oaxaqueños* celebrate **El Día de los Muertos** (Day of the Dead), with ritual dances and raucous parties. The **Night of the Radishes** in late December outshines the colossal carnival in mid-February as well as the altars erected for the Day of the Dead; there seems to be no limit to what structures can be carved out of or dishes cooked with the sublime vegetable.

Near Oaxaca

Zaachila and Cuilapán

An interesting local market is held each Thursday 18km south of Oaxaca in Zaachila, the last political capital of the Zapotecs after they abandoned their ceremonial center at Monte Albán. The Zaachila market vends exotic treats such as preserved bananas, which look and taste remarkably similar to fried grasshoppers. Even more interesting than the market is Zaachila's archeological site, barely 100m from the basket stands. Until 1962, the locals prohibited excavations on the grounds that their Zapotec heritage should not be dissected by outsiders. Few potential sites have since been explored, but two Mixtec tombs with well-preserved architecture and jewelry have been uncovered. To the right of the church, across from the market, follow the path uphill to the site. The first tomb's interior is decorated with what were once colorful stucco carvings. The treasure of gold, turquoise, jade and bone artifacts that distinguished the second tomb has long since been removed to local museums, leaving the uninspired architecture abashedly unadorned. From the mound you can look across the valley to see the cupola of the ex-convent at Cuilapán and even the hill on which Monte Albán is built. (Open daily 10am-6pm. Admission 1500 pesos.) In addition to second-class buses, *colectivos* also service Zaachila, leaving every 20 minutes both from the Central de Abastos, southeast of the second-class bus station, and from Armenta y López, 4½ blocks south of the Zócalo, in front of the Red Cross (1000 pesos). Just north of Zaachila on the highway back to Oaxaca, you can stop to visit the ex-convent visible from the archeological site. The Cuilapán ex-convent was one of the first built by the Spanish in Oaxaca Valley. Its plan is nearly identical to that of the Yanhuitlán ex-convent to the north. The structure is renowned for its "open" *capilla,* and some of the original 16th-century frescos stand first on the interior walls. (Open daily 10am-5pm. Admissión 800 pesos.)

San Bartolo Coyotepec

Fifteen kilometers south of Oaxaca on Rte. 75, the tiny town of San Bartolo Coyotepec was, until 1934, just another of the numerous villages in the valley called Coyotepec. In that year, a strong-willed woman named Rosa discovered a unique way to mold the dark gray clay that lay underground nearby. Two nearly flat bowls, one inverted upon the other, substitute for the traditional potter's wheel in the process still followed by Doña Rosa's family. The successful *alfarería* (pottery factory) she founded 45 years before her death in 1979 continues to produce distinctive black pottery. You can buy these vases, flutes, and candlesticks in almost any of the market towns around Oaxaca, but only here can you watch the potters at work, and sometimes even try your hand at it. Signs along the main road direct visitors to the potters' houses. Doña Rosa's place is 2½ blocks away from the field next to the Palacio Municipal, east on Juárez. (Workshop/store open daily 9am-6pm. Free.) *Colectivos* supplement the second-class bus service to San Bartolo; they leave from the corner of Bustamente and Zaragoza, 4 blocks south of the Zócalo.

Guelatao

Twenty-four years ago, the *pueblito* of Guelatao, 57km north of Oaxaca, became a national monument: on March 21, 1967, the centenary of the victory of Mexican Reform forces over the French occupation, President Díaz Ordaz ordered the construction of a civic plaza, a museum, statues, and a mausoleum in Guelatao to honor Benito Juárez, Guelatao's native son. Guelatao now seems less a living town than a memorial park, high adrift in the Cuenca del Papaluapan mountain range. Should you catch it between national holidays, political campaigns, and TV docudrama filmings, you will find Guelatao empty and peaceful.

Guelatao's civic plaza separates the one-room Museo Benito Juárez from the town's Palacio Municipal. A bust of Benito's wife, Margarita Masa de Juárez, sits near the museum behind the stark, four-legged mausoleum containing the remains of Juárez and his son. Closer to the *palacio* stands an elegant statue of Benito. On the shore of the well-lit lake, which was cleaned up as part of the memorial overhaul, a smiling bronze statue depicts Benito as a child; the wooden buildings around the shore belong to a bilingual educational center that teaches Spanish to Papaluapan people.

The **Palacio Municipal,** besides serving as Guelatao's governing office, hoards Juárez paraphernalia. Before you leave, sign the log book where Mexican and foreign presidents and other Juárez admirers have inscribed their respects. Once you've scribbled your thought, you'll be handed a small pamphlet containing the most interesting comments left through the years. (Office hours vary.)

The grape-sized **Museo Benito Juárez** delineates Juárez's life. The museum balcony commands a view of Guelatao's rugged landscape. (Open Mon.-Sat. 9am-2pm and 5-7pm. Free.)

To get from Oaxaca to Guelatao, take a Benito Juárez bus, the line farthest to the right as you enter the second-class terminal. Get an early start for this trip; the 2½-hour ride is rough. The Papaluapan cliffs are very steep and bridges few; even towns visible from Oaxaca on the side of the mountains take a long time to reach. The crowded bus back to Oaxaca passes every two hours until 5pm.

Monte Albán

Monte Albán, the most popular tourist spot in the Oaxaca Valley, towers atop one of the green mountains surrounding Oaxaca. Only 10km southwest of Oaxaca, across Río Atoyac, this was the greatest capital left by the Zapotecs, whose descendants now constitute the fourth-largest language group in Mexico. The ancient city, one of 260 Zapotec cities in the Oaxaca Valley, once spread over six square km. Most of its huge complex of tombs, pyramids, platforms, and temples of worship has been expertly reconstructed.

Throughout its multicultural past, elite classes have populated Monte Albán. Famous kings and exalted priests of Zapotec (and later, Mixtec) blood took up residence in this city of pyramids. The Zapotecs designed and built the city before the Mixtecs appropriated its fields and tombs.

Monte Albán is not merely the spiritual storehouse of the Zapotecs. This site has interested archeologists over the past half-century, because all of the civilizations of the Oaxaca Valley have left a piece of their heritage here. Archeologists have identified five different stages in Monte Albán's history.

Elaborate pottery, hieroglyphic writing, a calendar system, and written numbers date from about 500 BC. Objects from this period, known as **Monte Albán I,** generally show Olmec influence, as in the sculptures of dwarfs, or figurines with deformities, or facial representations that incorporate features of the jaguar. By the end of Monte Albán I, the city was the largest and most important community in Southern Mesoamerica.

Monte Albán II lasted approximately from Christ's death to 300 AD. During this time, the Zapotecs consolidated their empire and expanded their commercial trading routes. The Maya borrowed the calendar and writing system already in use at Monte Albán and constructed a drainage system to channel water during the rainy season into a storage vat for later use in relieving the frequent droughts. The first of the funerary urns and four-legged vessels, which usually represent gods, also come from the site.

By **Monte Albán III** (300-750 AD), the population of the valley had peaked. Almost all of the extant buildings and tombs as well as several urns and murals of *colanijes* (richly adorned priests) come from this period. Burial arrangements of variable luxury and size among the different tombs show the tripartite social division of the period between priests, clerks, and laborers.

The Zapotec citadel decayed during **Monte Albán IV** (750-1000 AD). Construction ceased, and political control of the Zapotec empires shifted from Monte Albán to other cities such as Zaachila, Etla, and later Mitla. The quality of pottery, ceramics, and jewelry all fell. During this period, the Mixtec people invaded from the northwest and took over many of the Zapotec cities.

Late Mixtec culture flourished during **Monte Albán V,** from 1000 AD to the arrival of the Spaniards. By then, Monte Albán functioned as both a fortress and a sacred necropolis. The Mixtec nobility buried its own in the Zapotec tombs. Mixtec tombs were elaborate, treasure-filled chambers; when the most noteworthy, Tomb 7, was discovered in 1932, the treasure found within more than quadrupled the previously identified number of gold Mixtec objects.

A visit to Monte Albán today can be as startling as it was for the conquistadors who first walked across the **Central Plaza.** At the northern end of the plaza, to the right as you enter the site, lies the **Northern Platform,** with temples on both its eastern and western sides. The southern boundary of the temple on the eastern side has a number of stones engraved with the famous "dancers," so named because of their animated poses. In front of the stairway leading to the North Platform stands **Stela 9**—one of the most important architectural and artistic pieces in Monte Albán. The south side is worn, but the long stairway has protected its other side, where serpents and a man with a great headdress are clearly visible. Although the most recently rebuilt, the buildings on either side of the altar are in poor condition. The North Platform dates from Monte Albán III.

Bear left as you enter the site, and walk along the eastern boundary of the Central Plaza; you'll pass first the ballcourt, then a series of aligned substructures, and then two pyramids. The inclined walls that seem like flights of narrow steps were originally flat, covered with stucco and frescoes.

Building P, the first of the two pyramids, fascinates archeologists because of its inner stairway feeding into a tunnel to the central structures a few meters away. The tunnel apparently allowed priests to pass into the central temples unseen by the public. The second pyramid here, the **Palace,** is a wealthy Zapotec's residence with a patio-courtyard surrounded by several rooms. A cruciform grave was discovered in the center of the garden.

Directly outside the porch are the four central monuments of the plaza. **Monuments G, H,** and **I** are attached and together constitute what was likely the principal altar of Monte Albán. To the east of the central group were the old marketplace, ceremonial center, and site of political activities and festivities.

Directly to the east, between the central Monument H and Building P, is the small, sunken **Adoratorio** where archeologists dug up an intricate jade bat mask. This is Monte Albán's oldest structure, dating from Monte Albán II. A sacred icon and the most famous piece from this period, the bat mask contains 25 pieces of polished, forest-green jade. Slivers of white conch shell form the teeth and eyes. Unfortunately, the mask has flown to a new perch in the Museo Nacional de Antropología in Mexico City.

The fourth of the central structures, **Monument J,** is one of the strangest of all pre-Conquest buildings in Mexico. Formed in the bizarre shape of an arrowhead on a platform, the structure is riddled with tunnels and vaults. Moreover, unlike any other ancient edifice in Mexico, it is asymmetrical, and built askew to the other edifices around the plaza—its walls run neither parallel nor perpendicular to the others: a sole iconoclast amid the perfect grid of Monte Albán. The broad, carved slabs belong stylistically to Monte Albán II and suggest that the building is one of the oldest on the site. Many of the glyphs have an upside-down head below a stylized hill, thought to represent a place and a name. According to archeological speculation, this indicates a conquest, the upside-down head representing the defeated tribe and the name identifying the region conquered; others insist that Monument J was an astronomical observatory.

Behind the arrowhead stands the huge **Southern Pyramid,** of which only the staircase, rising from the plaza, remains visible; the rest has yet to be excavated. On both sides of the staircase on the plaza level, to the right of the platform, are a number of rain-god and tiger stelae. The top of the Southern Platform affords a glorious view of the plaza to the north. One of the two mounds atop the platform is currently being excavated and reconstructed; yet another pyramid rises from this great height. To the left of this upper pyramid, an overgrown path leads to a smaller group of buildings named the **Seven Deer System** after a clear lintel glyph found there.

Along the western border of the Central Plaza are the foundations of **Building M,** followed by the **Platform of the Dancers,** at the foot of Building L. The low platforms in front of Building M were designed to correct the plaza's asymmetry, caused by the need to build around inconveniently located rock formations. The "dancers" on the platform, among the most interesting examples of pre-Conquest sculpture, date from about the 5th century BC—almost identical to contemporary Olmec sculptures along the Gulf Coast. Many are accompanied by glyphs and number schemes indicating mastery of a system of writing and of calendrical records. The arrangement of the stone dancers is believed to represent historical or mythical events related to the founding of Monte Albán. The two tunnels cutting into **Building L** date only from the 1950s, when archeologists decided to display some of the earlier sections of the building.

Branching off from the road between the Central Plaza and the entrance to the site, a clearly-marked path leads down a ravine to **Tomb 104** and the **Northern Cemetery.** The mirror-wielding guard at the tomb reflects sunlight to illuminate a stunning portrait of the handsome noble buried here. (Tomb 104 closed Sun.)

At the entrance to the site, the expensive gift shop and cafeteria attract more visitors than does the small museum. The interesting artifacts from the site have long since been carted off to museums in Oaxaca and Mexico City, but the museum at least gives a chronological summary of Monte Albán's history (in Spanish), and displays sculpted stones from the site's earlier periods. (Site open daily 8am-5pm. Admission 4000 pesos, free Sun. and holidays.)

Buses to Monte Albán leave from the Hotel Mesón del Angel, Mina 518, between Mier y Terán and Díaz Ordaz in Oaxaca (see Oaxaca Practical Information above). The site is only 10km away, but the ride through mountainous terrain takes 30 minutes. The normal procedure is to buy a round-trip ticket, with the return fixed two hours (about right for a full perusal) after arrival at the site; if you want to stay longer you can pay an extra 1000 pesos to come back on one of the later buses. Buses from the hotel leave daily every hour from 8:30am to 3:30pm during high season, and four times per day during low season (3000 pesos round-trip). Travel agencies around the Zócalo arrange special excursions to the ruins—some with English-speaking guides—at considerably more expense than the do-it-yourself option.

Yanhuitlán

The gargantuous **Ex-Convent of Santo Domingo de Yanhuitlán,** on Rte. 190 just north of the town of Nochixtlán (100km northwest of Oaxaca), was erected by Dominican missionaries sometime in the 16th century to convert the vast Mixtec kingdom that populated Valle Yanhuitlán. In the early 17th century, an epidemic transmitted from Europe by the monks killed half the population and forced the other half to emigrate south. The priests eventually left, too, in search of more *indigenas* to enlighten. The church and convent stood unattended until the mid-19th century, when French forces used it as headquarters during the occupation; Maximilian's supporters thoughtfully ransacked the place. Later, armies and rebel bands sporadically used the convent as a barracks until 1928. Far from any urban center, the tall church and convent now stand completely isolated.

The first hall stores the few relics left after the convent was turned into a museum. A map of Oaxaca points out the *indígena* areas in which Dominican priests built monumental churches. Dominicans converted the Mixtec tribes of Teotongo, Loixlahuaca, Tlaxiaco, and Yanhuitlán, and the Zapotec hamlets around Ixtlán, Guilapan, Tlacolula, and Oaxaca (the Augustines were assigned to the city and state of Mexico, while the Franciscans christianized Puebla).

Although the huge convent is believed to have sheltered 300 priests, the second floor consists of only 16 chambers for resident monks. Each room has an emblem carved in stone above the door: a hand holding the model of a church, a Dominican cross, a hand holding tulips, an eagle, a skull, a star, a pair of keys, and crosses of all shapes. In a hall to the rear, 16 toilets line a square corridor, four on each side.

Unfortunately, some of the best sights at Yanhuitlán lie behind locked doors, but the guards may sometimes be cajoled into opening them. A large door off the courtyard leads to the massive **church.** The ceiling looms some 30m overhead, and the altar also reaches a comparable height. Three dense rows of ornate gold arabesques and statues of Dominican saints aspire to the ceiling vault. This spectacular altar served as the model for the altar in the church of Santo Domingo in Oaxaca. Perhaps the best reason to find a way in, however, is to climb 40m to the top of the bell tower. Once you've ascended the narrow spiral staircase, you can scramble all over the convent's roof for a view of the surrounding countryside.

The façade of the convent is carved out of unembellished pink stone. The shield of St. Domingo—a black-and-white cross—and the Dominican symbol—a faithful dog sitting on a book and lighting the globe with a torch held in its mouth—adorn the base of the columns. (Convent open daily 10am-6pm.) A garden, with a fountain and violet shrubs, flourishes behind the church, providing an idyllic spot from which to take in the towering arches and the sheer rear wall of the Yanhuitlán church.

To visit the church and the Ex-Convent of Santo Domingo de Yanhuitlán, take the bus from Hajuapan or Oaxaca and ask the driver to stop at the church. Buses in both directions pass about every hour until 8pm, and they'll stop if you flag them. If you need to spend the night, stay at the **Hotel Yanhuitlán,** just to the right as you face the convent. Lodgings are also available in the nearby town of Nochixtlán.

Oaxaca to Mitla

A number of interesting stops tempt the thorough traveler on the Pan American Hwy. (Rte. 190) east from Oaxaca to Mitla, a distance of 46km. All of these sights can be reached by buses that leave every 20 minutes from Oaxaca's second-class bus station; fare is roughly 1000 to 2500 pesos. If consulted ahead of time, the driver of the bus to Mitla will let you off anywhere. Most people visit these sites on daytrips, but if you'd like to stay overnight, inquire at the Oaxaca tourist office for information on guest houses. Street vendors sell virtually the only food available to non-residents.

Santa María El Tule

Just 9km outside Oaxaca, the roadside attraction of Santa María El Tule awaits. One of the largest, oldest trees on earth stands in the courtyard of the church, just a few meters off the highway. Called **El Tule**, it is an *ahuehuete,* a relative of the cypress; neither as tall as the redwoods nor as old as some of the white pines, El Tule lays claim to the greatest girth—160 feet in circumference. In the crags around its trunk, visitors can identify likenesses of deer, fish, lions, as well as Grandma Patsy. The fence around the tree and the vendors selling El Tule paraphernalia detract from its majesty. To catch a bus back to Oaxaca, hang out on the highway and wave your souvenir.

Tlacochahuaya

The walls of the **Iglesia de San Jerónimo Tlacochahuaya** display the application of Zapotec decorative techniques to Catholic motifs. At the end of the 16th century the Dominicans built this church and convent 21km east of Oaxaca, far (in those times) from worldly temptations. (Church open daily 7am-noon.) To visit Tlacochahuaya, take the Mitla bus from the second-class terminal in Oaxaca; it will drop you at the crossroads leading into town. Locals can give you a ride to the church, but if nobody passes by, the walk is enjoyable because of the scenic *maguey* and corn fields and surrounding rocky hills.

Dainzú and Lambityeco

The **Dainzú** ruins, just off the road branching to Macuilxochitl, 22km east of Oaxaca, probably belonged to a merchant in Monte Albán's final pre-Conquest epoch. At the base of the tallest pyramidal monument, a series of figures magnificently carved in relief represents ballplayers in attitudes similar to the "dancers" at Monte Albán. Two humans and two jaguars, gods of the sport, supervise the contest. To the west of the pyramid is Group B. Up the hill from the pyramid, another ballgame scene is hewn in the living rock. (Open daily 10am-6pm. Free.) The Tlacolula or Mitla buses from Oaxaca drop off and pick up passengers here, but be sure to introduce yourself and your desires to the driver beforehand.

Teotitlán del Valle

Roughly 20km from Oaxaca, a turn-off leads north to Teotitlán del Valle, the original Zapotec city (called Xaguixe). Today the source of most of the beautiful woolen *sarapes* produced in Oaxaca, the town's 200 to 300 families earn their livelihood spinning and weaving for the most part. Many allow tourists to visit their homes or workshops, and a live demonstration impresses more than any museum exhibit ever could. Frequent buses run directly from Oaxaca to Teotitlán del Valle (1000 pesos).

Tlacolula and Yagul

About 33km east of Oaxaca, a southerly turn-off leads to **Tlacolula,** an ancient village that hosts a lively market every Sunday morning. Merchant action spreads beyond the official roofed market to the rest of the town; nary a street is without temporary stalls. A large influx of tourists extends each week, but the presence of outsiders has not dimmed the *indígena* nature of the event; every other woman is still carrying a basket on her head. Plenty of items might interest travelers—*sarapes* and *tapetes* (rugs), baskets and pottery—but much more fascinating are the things you wouldn't take home if they paid you. Many vendors sell live pigs and goats as well as varieties of carved wood oxen yokes. The market drags on until 6pm, but the activity starts to wind down around 2pm.

Yagul, 38km east of Oaxaca, was a Mixtec city contemporary to Mitla, built in two distinct sections on the skirt of a large rock outcrop. Most of the buildings and tombs are in the acropolis, the area closest to the parking lot (about 2km north of the highway). Here, the Court of the Triple Tomb, the ballcourt, the Palace of the Six Patios, and the Council Chamber have all been thoroughly excavated and reconstructed. Farther up, on top of the hill, await the second section, the Great Fortress, the natural watchtower around to the right, and the unusual stone bridge built to reach it.

The four temples of the Court of the Triple Tomb include a huge sculpted animal ensconced in the lower section of the eastern temple. You can enter the Triple Tomb itself through an opening near the altar in the center of the plaza. Past the door with glyphs on both sides, the tomb has a façade with two majestic stone heads.

The ballcourt here is the largest of all those in the Oaxaca Valley. The only clue to the nature of the game is a stone snake's head that was found attached high on the southern wall of the ballcourt and now nibbles at the glass of a small case in the Museo Regional de Oaxaca.

Still farther north, the Palace of the Six Patios was a private residence. The rooms around the patios are floored with red stucco; at one time the walls were similarly covered. A ruined throne crumbles in the patio in the northeast corner. Site open daily 8am-5pm. Admission 5000 pesos.)

Buses between Oaxaca and Mitla (2000 pesos) stop about 2km from the entrance to Yagul.

Mitla

When the Spanish arrived in southern Mexico, Mitla, 46km directly east of Oaxaca, reigned as the largest and most important of the Mixtec cities. Earlier Mixtec cultures centered around cities farther north, such as Montenegro, a contemporary of Monte Albán I, and Yucuñudahui, contemporary with Monte Albán II. These, however, have bequeathed relatively few artifacts to modern society.

Mitla is significantly smaller than Monte Albán, but the decorations on the palaces here are unique in pre-Conquest art and architecture. Of the five groups of buildings, only two have been excavated to reveal the stone mosaic that have aroused interest in Mitla since colonial days.

Walking through the village, you arrive at the doorstep of the Catholic church (after which the Church Group is named) and the entrance to the official archeological zone. This fenced-in area encloses the **Group of the Columns,** by far the most interesting of the site's several "Groups." After entering, you approach two small quadrangles joined at one corner.

The tombs of the pyramids form a cross: for years, the Spaniards thought this proved that the Mixtecs somehow knew the story of Jesus. Engineers have since discovered that the shape of the tombs, which corresponds to a complex vector formula, enabled the structures to endure the huge earthquakes that were common at the time of their construction. The main temple rises on the north side of the first quadrangle. A raised triple doorway leads into a long gallery whose roof rests on six columns. Beyond a protective passageway is an inner patio with narrow rooms on either side. A mosaic of small stones for which Mitla is famous, covers the rooms and patio; they called the designs of repeating geometric forms *xicalcoliuhqui.* Tens of thousands of stones had to be cut to perfect size before they were affixed to the stone-and-mud wall.

On the second patio in the Group of the Columns, two tombs in the temples to the east and north of the courtyard are accessible to visitors. In the east temple, fairly large stones feature the characteristic mosaic patterns. The roof of the tomb in the north temple rests on a single huge column, still referred to as the Column of Life by local *indígenas.* Some make a pilgrimage here each year to embrace the column; in exchange for the hug, the column tells them how much longer they will live.

A set of three patios comprise the **Group of the Church.** One of the patios is almost completely buried by the Catholic church; only a few of the original palace walls remain visible. Many of the building blocks of the church belonged to nearby

Mixtec structures before being reappropriated by the missionaries. Walk to the right around the church to arrive at the central patio to the north. Through a passageway in the northern wall of this patio, you can enter an interior courtyard, at the far end of which you'll find the last surviving band of Mixtec decorative paintings. A few figures can be barely discerned through the dusty red, the accompanying glyphs were calendar references and place names.

The other groups of pre-Conquest structures at Mitla have not yet been excavated and as a result hold little interest. On the road back to town, you can veer off to the right to climb the pyramid of the **Adobe Group,** whose crowning temple was converted into a Catholic shrine to the Madonna. From here, the Church Group, the Group of the Columns, and the **Arroyo Group** are visible below. (Site open daily 8am-6pm. Inquire about informative guided tours. Admission 8000 pesos, free Sun. and holidays.)

Between the Group of the Columns and the Church Group, a daily bazaar mainly concerned with *típico* clothing takes place. Although prices are high, bargaining is expected, and the selection is extraordinary large. On the way back to the village, you can see *sarapes* and *rebozos* (women's scarves) being woven in the shops which line the road.

On the central plaza back in town, the **Frissel Museum** contains thousands of figurines from Mitla and other Mixtec sites. Arranged around a beautiful courtyard papered with posters and newspaper articles, some descriptions are in English. Although the printed guide to the museum has been out of stock since 1980, the curator speaks impeccable English and loves to answer questions. (Open daily 8am-5pm. Donations appreciated.) In town, you are likely to hear Zapotec, not Spanish, spoken. There's no reason to stay in Mitla overnight, but if circumstances conspire, **Hotel La Zapoteca,** 5 de Febrero 12 (tel. 26) on the main road to the ruins (a 10-min. walk away) rents slightly dirty rooms around a spacious, sunny courtyard. (Doubles 50,000 pesos.)

Buses to Mitla leave Oaxaca's second-class terminal every 20 minutes all day (2000 pesos).

Oaxaca to Puerto Angel

By bus, six arduous but beautiful hours separate Oaxaca from Puerto Angel. With little more than weekly markets to interest tourists, the tiny villages on the way provide only very limited services.

Ocotlán

Forty-five minutes from the capital, the town of Ocotlán hosts, every Friday, the largest and most diverse market in Oaxaca Valley except for that in Oaxaca itself. In a bizarre marriage of technology and tradition, outdoor public-address systems attract buyers' attention to curative herbs and black, gray, and white *rebozos* that wrap the newly bought as well as the newly born. Ocotlán's market puts up fine cattle for auction, and sells works of local artisans, including *hojalatería* (tin and metal works) and *talabartería* (leather goods). The lacquered pottery from Atzompa, the *sarapes* from Teotitlán del Valle, and the *típico* clothing from all over are as plentiful and cheap at Ocotlán as at any market in the valley. (Market open Fri. 6am-7pm; most active 10am-5pm).

Depending on the season, Ocotlán also serves the best selection of exotic local dishes such as *nopal* (cactus leaves marinated in a salty sauce), small *níspera* fruits, water drinks made from the pumpkin-like *chilacayota,* and *tejate,* a soupy drink pounded out of the cacao and its flower. Notorious for its *cohetes,* firecrackers that children set off all afternoon, Ocotlán also knows how to slumber quietly, as it does on non-market days.

Buses heading north to Oaxaca and south to Ejutla and Miahuatlán pass every half hour until about 8pm.

Ejutla

Artisans in Ejutla, 60km south of Oaxaca, once made strong alloy knives, both decorative and durable, for the local *campesinos*. Nowadays, tourists supply the demand, and quality has plummeted. (Market day is Thurs.)

On the other hand, the people of Ejutla pride themselves on the production of *mezcal*, the strong liquor *ejutlanos* call "Mexican cognac." Bottles of homemade *mezcal* sell briskly in Ejutla's streets on both market and non-market days. *Ejutlanos* accuse national distributors of adulterating the drink to stretch quantities and increase profits. The real stuff, they argue, is found only in Ejutla: the farther from Ejutla *mezcal* is produced, the less body and punch it has. You can take a taxi or walk to the villages near Ejutla to witness the distillation of the celebrated spirits.

The most popular sport in Ejutla is *pelota mixteca*, a variation of the Mixtec ball game. Teams of five players, wearing 5½ kg cowhide gloves rimmed with metal caps, hit a *maguey* ball on a 25m-long field. The object of the game is to keep the ball in the air as long as possible.

On non-market days, Ejutla bores. The monument to Porfirio Díaz in the Zócalo praises the infamous dictator as "gran patriote, gran soldado, gran presidente," and then, "EJEMPLO MORAL" (moral example). Across from the plaza stands the colonial Templo de Ejutla, whose interior gold altar pales next to the electric sign proclaiming "AVE MARIA." To the left of the church, the Mercado Díaz Ordaz feeds as many flies as customers with its fruits and vegetables.

There are no hotels or *posadas* in Ejutla. Locals suggest taking the bus to Miahuatlán or unfolding your sleeping bag near the porch of the Ayuntamiento, guarded all night and obviously the safest place in town. There was once a hotel in Ejutla, and residents also used to open their homes to sleepy *viajeros*, but several scandals involving drugs and foreigners forced the hotel to close down and led *ejutlanos* to distrust strangers. Nonetheless, most citizens remain friendly.

Buses head both north to Oaxaca and south to Miahuatlán every half hour until about 8pm.

Miahuatlán

The region around Miahuatlán, 39km south of Ejutla, is also renowned for its *mezcal*. Market day (Mon.) brings textiles of all types, tall wood *pilones* (for pounding corn or other seeds into tortilla flour), and *huaraches* (sandals) made out of strips of salvaged car tires. Miahuatlán, the biggest village on the way to the coast, is the best place to stay overnight if you must go somewhere.

The **Hotel Mansión Real**, 2 de Abril 201, on the second floor of a building across from the police station, is a comfortable establishment of wide corridors and clean rooms with private bathrooms which lack toilet seats. (Singles and doubles 20,000 pesos.) The **Casa de Huéspedes David**, 3 de Octubre 203 (tel. 201-03), 2 blocks down from the Zócalo, has plainer rooms and spotless, stone-floored communal bathrooms also without toilet seats. Some rooms are separated by a wall that doesn't reach the ceiling; if your neighbor snores like a bulldozer, it could be a long night. (Singles 15,000 pesos. Doubles 25,000 pesos.)

The **Bánamex** on the Zócalo changes money Monday through Friday from 9am to noon. At other times, go to the **Mueblería Miahuatlán**, 3 de Octubre 105, 1 block from the Zócalo. The **post office** is at 3 de Octubre 215, 2 blocks down from the Zócalo. (Open Mon.-Fri. 8am-7pm, Sat. 9am-1pm.) Not only the Zócalo (Parque Porfirio Díaz) honors the dictator: Miahuatlán itself has been officially renamed Miahuatlán de Porfirio Díaz. The second- and third-class **bus station**, on Mariano Escobedo, offers a schedule so inexact that even the station employees are unable to give precise information; buses head both north to Oaxaca and south to Pochutla about every half hour until around 12:30am. Some of the buses to Pochutla continue to Puerto Escondido, but most of the time you'll have to transfer in Pochutla for either Puerto Angel or Puerto Escondido.

Pochutla

Known for its black coral jewelry, Pochutla is important more for its proximity to Puerto Angel than for anything else. Unlike its chaise-potato beach-bumming neighbor to the south, at least Pochutla changes currency and sells stamps. It also provides decent accommodations for those arriving late at night, although if you have energy and means to do so you may as well go the rest of the way to Puerto Escondido or Angel. The *tianguis* (*indígena* market) falls on Mondays. Other days, a large market on Cárdenas, visible as you enter town from the north, operates until sunset.

Those who choose to stay in Pochutla should do so at **Hotel Pochutla,** Madero 102 (tel. 400-33), 1 block from the Zócalo. Its rooms aren't huge, but they're clean and exude comfort. Nothing except bone china could be finer than the private bathrooms. (Singles 20,000 pesos. Doubles 25,000 pesos). At Cárdenas 88, the **Hotel Santa Cruz** (tel. 401-16), is the next-best bet, but you'd better hope your neighbors don't snore or frolic loudly, because, like the David in Miahuatlán, the walls between rooms don't reach the ceiling. (Singles 18,000 pesos. Doubles 24,000 pesos.) Across from the Conasupo, the **Hotel Izala,** Cárdenas 59 (tel. 401-15), has a pretty courtyard and inflated prices. Toilets spit out fluid instead of sucking it in, and the light switches in the bathrooms often shock their users—proceed with caution. (Singles 25,000 pesos. Doubles 35,000 pesos.)

You will find plenty of food in the market behind Bancomer. In addition, restaurants line Cárdenas all the way from the market to the bus station at the other end of town. All are about the same: very small, cheap, and usually family-run. The nicest location in town belongs to **Restaurante La Esmeralda de la Costa,** Constitución 2, on the second floor, with a terrace overlooking the Zócalo. Meat entrees are 7000-8000 pesos, *antojitos,* 3000-5000 pesos. (Open daily 7:30am-11pm.) The **Cafetería Los Arcos,** Cárdenas 74, across from Madero, plays loud rock on the stereo all day, jiggling your morning eggs (4000 pesos). (Open daily 7am-5pm.)

Lázaro Cárdenas is the main street in Pochutla. Buses and taxis from nearby towns will drop you off on this street; any place you'll need to visit will be either visible from the street or within walking distance of it. The **post office** is behind the Palacio Municipal, 2 blocks from Hotel Pochutla. (Open Mon.-Fri. 9am-1pm and 3-6pm, Sat. 9am-1pm.) Pochutla's **postal code** is 70900. There are two banks in town, but only **Bancomer,** Cárdenas at Allende, near the market, changes money. (Open for currency exchange Mon.-Fri. 9:30-11am.) The **bus station** (tel. 401-38), on Cárdenas, toward the southern end of the street, frequently dispatches buses to: Puerto Angel (every 30 min. 6am-8pm, 20 min., 800 pesos); Puerto Escondido (every hr. 6am-8pm, 1 hr., 2500 pesos); Huatulco (every hr. 6:30am-7:30pm, 1 hr., 1400 pesos); Salina Cruz (every hr. 5am-9pm, 4 hr., 6000 pesos); and Oaxaca (10 per day, 6 hr., 7500 pesos).

Puerto Angel

Without post office, bank, or newsstand, Puerto Angel draws a crowd of urban escapists to its shores. A glut of unsullied beaches, tasty lobsters, fishing fanatics, vagabonds, and vacationing Mexicans awaits the traveler who makes the trek to Puerto Angel and nearby Playa Zipolite. A decade ago, this secluded fishing village approximated a beachside Eden, but, despite its skimpy facilities, the town has developed considerably since then. Hotels now overshadow palm trees and *palapas* infringe on the Zipolite dunes.

Puerto Angel has evolved into a popular destination for sun-seekers. It is not, as many concerned travelers insist, a dangerous hippie drug town where police wait in ambush to bust the next foreigner who roams unsuspectingly onto its shores. However, the spirit of the 60s is alive, smoking, and often nude on the beham-mocked sands of fun-loving Zipolite Beach—a paradise only partly fallen whose beauty isn't diminished by the few who crash near its waves.

Orientation

Puerto Angel caps off a southward bulge in Oaxaca's coastline, 240km south of Oaxaca de Juárez via Rte. 200, before the shore recedes to form the narrow Istmo de Tehuantepec. Pochutla, 12km north of Puerto Angel, provides stamps, pesos, and an egress from this part of the world, and is readily accessible by bus (every 20 min. 8am-7pm, 500 pesos). Puerto Escondido, 68km to the west on Rte. 200, is easily reached by bus from Pochutla (every hr. 5am-8pm, 1 hr., 3000 pesos).

Taxis provide a second link between Puerto Angel and Pochutla for 1000 pesos *colectivo* or 5000 pesos *especial*. Do whatever you can to get the *colectivo* rate, and don't let drivers con you into paying extra baggage-carrying fees.

The road from Pochutla turns into Puerto Angel's main drag at the edge of town. **Avenida Principal** curves around Playa Puerto Angel past the municipal pier and military base, becoming **Boulevard Virgilio Uribe.** The thoroughfare then turns inland again to avoid a large hill separating the two halves of town. Soon after leaving the first half of town, the road branches off to the left, leading to private houses and sheer cliffs. The main road crosses a creek and forks at a sign for Hotel Angel del Mar; the upper, right-hand road rambles farther down the coast to Zipolite, and the lower, left-hand road heads for the Playa Panteón. The only significant side street in town climbs the hill directly across the street from the pier on Playa Puerto Angel; it starts out as **Vasconcelos,** then curves to the left and becomes **Teniente Azuela.** Few hotels or restaurants in Puerto Angel have addresses with street names or numbers, and none have phones. The Spanish word for address is *dirección,* and in this town the word couldn't be more appropriate: the only way to find a place is to ask directions every few feet. In general, no street lights illuminate Puerto Angel's winding dirt roads, and finding your way at night can be a challenge without a flashlight.

Except during high season (Sept.-March), buses to Zipolite (1000 pesos) are few and far between and taxis cost an arm and a leg. Try to bargain the cabbies down from the 10,000-peso asking price before embarking; otherwise, car pool or set out on the 45-minute hike prepared to encounter a few stray dogs, pigs, and donkeys along the way. During high season, *colectivos* make the trip for 2000 pesos. All fares increase 2000 pesos from sunset until dawn, and when roads are muddy.

Practical Information

Services in this town are less than minimal; most supplies and snatches of information are gleaned in nearby Pochutla.

Currency Exchange: None. Near Pochutla's market, **Bancomer,** Lázaro Cárdenas 113-B (tel. 400-53), on the opposite end of town from the bus station, is open for exchange Mon.-Fri. 9-11am. Don't go on Mon. or you'll languish in line for hours, and don't have money wired. If you're desperate, some restaurants and hotels in Puerto Angel change money at awful rates.

Post Office: None. The nearest one is in Pochutla at Progreso 17, behind the municipal building off the Zócalo. Open for regular service Mon.-Fri. 9am-1pm and 3-6pm, Sat. 9am-1pm. Anything mailed to you during your stay in Puerto Angel should be sent to the Lista de Correos in Pochutla. If you are mailing out of Puerto Angel, be sure to bring stamps. **Postal Code:** 70900.

Telephones: Long-distance *caseta* at Vasconcelos 3 (tel. 403-98), opposite the pier. Open Mon.-Sat. 7am-10pm, Sun. 2-9pm. Collect calls 3000 pesos Mon.-Fri. 7-9am and 2-4pm. If you need to make collect calls on Sat., go to Pochutla; a long-distance *caseta* is on Constitución, the street extending southeast from the Zócalo. Collect calls 2000 pesos Mon.-Sat. 7-9:30am and 2-4pm. **Telephone Code:** 958.

Telegrams: Take Azuela up the hill and turn left on the dirt path at the top. Open Mon.-Fri. 9am-3pm.

Buses: Service to Pochutla every 20 min. 8am-7pm (500 pesos). From Pochutla, **Estrella del Valle** (tel. 401-38), on the right side of Lázaro Cárdenas coming into town, sends a bus to Puerto Escondido every ½ hr. 5am-8pm (3000 pesos) and to Oaxaca (5 per day 5am-11pm, 6 hr., 10,500 pesos). **Lineas Unidas del Sur Flecha Rosa,** Hidalgo 6 (tel. 401-93), sends a direct bus to Acapulco at 9am and 10pm; the *ordinario* leaves 5 times per day (26,000 pesos).

Also to: Huatulco (6 per day 6:45am-7:15pm, 2000 pesos); Puerto Angel (at 9:15am, 2:15pm, and 5:15pm, 1000 pesos); Mexico City (at 5pm, 45,600 pesos).

Supermarket: Tienda Sedemar, on Azuela, on the inland side of a dirt road across from the naval base. Food and liquor. The cheapest snacks and *refrescos* in town. Open daily 7am-8pm.

Pharmacy: Farmacia Angel, up Vasconcelos on the right, opposite the road to the Centro de Salud. Open daily 8am-10pm. After hours, knock at the door.

Police: None, but naval officers everywhere around the base stand in for police. Otherwise, trek to Pochutla to the municipal building on the Zócalo for serious inquiries and emergencies. Open daily 9am-3pm and 6-9pm. The **Agency of Public Ministry** (tel. 401-81) will contact the police in emergencies.

Medical Emergency: Centro de Salud, up Vasconcelos/Azuela, on the same dirt path as the telegram office. Open for basic services Mon.-Fri. 9am-2pm and 5-8pm; for emergencies 24 hr. This health center is staffed by a sequence of young doctors each of whom stays for a year, making the schedule subject to slight change. For problems too serious to be treated here, take a taxi to the **Clínica San Pedro,** at Las Avillas and Galeana in Pochutla, behind the cinema, or the **Centro de Salud,** on Lázaro Cárdenas by Pochutla's bus station. Both open 24 hr.

Accommodations

Although many travelers come here only to sleep and sunbathe on the beach in nearby Zipolite, Puerto Angel supports a slew of cheap, charming hotels and *casas de huéspedes.*

Budget lodgings are strung along the hills on the inland side of the town's main road between the two beaches. Hammock spaces are inexpensive and fill up quickly. Only the expensive hotels have hot water.

Pensión Puesta del Sol, across the *arroyo* (creek) on the road to Playa Panteón. You'll see the signs on the right; hike up the steep hill. Don't be alarmed by the construction in front: beautiful rooms with concrete floors and private patios for breakfast (3000 pesos) are downhill from the rubble. The large, clean communal bathrooms are beautifully tiled. Run by a hospitable German-Mexican couple. Singles 20,000 pesos. Doubles 25,000 pesos.

Casa de Huéspedes El Capy, on the right side of the main road to Playa Panteón, after the fork. Each spacious room includes fan, large desk and mirror, bug-netting, and private bathroom. Ocean view from top-floor terrace. Tasty, cheap restaurant downstairs. Singles 15,000 pesos. Doubles 20,000 pesos.

Casa de Huéspedes Gundi y Tomás, up the hill from the military base. A sign across the road from the base points the way through the woods. Halfway up the hill, the cement stairwell rises to your left. A short hike, but the rooms are as big as some local restaurants, and the stone-and-tile common bathrooms are spotless. The whole place smells pleasantly of soap. Friendly proprietor. Hammock spaces 6000 pesos. Singles 18,000 pesos. Doubles 20,000-25,000 pesos.

La Posada Cañon Devata, a short walk from Playa Panteón. From the center of town, walk down the road to Playa Panteón, make a left past the tombstones at the base of the road, and follow the sign to "Hotel Angel del Mar." Bear right around Hotel Las Cabañas—the *posada* sign will be on your left and the inn off to your right. Convenient to the beach. A cool, shady complex owned by a gracious Mexican-American family. Lanterns illuminate the wooden bridges at night. The *posada* rubs elbows with a gourmet vegetarian restaurant and an expensive crafts shop. New fans in all rooms. *The* place to blow some *dinero.* Closed May 1-June 30. Singles 25,000-45,000 pesos. Doubles 35,000-55,000 pesos. Hilltop bungalows with 2 double beds 55,000 pesos.

Casa de Huéspedes Alex, on Calle de La Buena Compañía. On the right after you follow the signs to La Buena Vista. The ocean is out of sight but raucously loud. Photos of hotel's Michigan-born namesake adorn stuffy downstairs rooms. All rooms have bathrooms and fans, but the cement floors and the seatless toilets make for a hard existence. Singles 20,000 pesos. Doubles 25,000 pesos.

Posada Rincón Sabroso, Domicilio Conocido, on the high hill near the bus station where Uribe curves inland for the first time. Large sign at base of hill points to the steep staircase leading to the inn. Cozy, clean, and convenient. New blue bedspreads and sparkling baths. Panorama of Playa Puerto Angel from the beautiful, tiled terrace adjoining all rooms. Singles 25,000 pesos. Doubles 30,000 pesos.

La Buena Vista, on Calle de la Buena Compañía. Look for the sign advertising rooms "*confortables y tranquilos*" at the right after the *arroyo*. Scenic walk off the main road if you manage to stay out of the way of the stampeding pigs. Charming, family-run establishment. Firm beds, stone walls, and tile floors; all rooms have fans and clean bathrooms with unusual sinks and short showers. Great terrace with chairs overlooks red clay roof, trees, and the big blue ocean beyond. Singles 25,000 pesos. Doubles 35,000 pesos.

Hotel La Cabaña de Puerto Angel, across from the row of restaurants facing Playa Panteón, at the end of the main dirt road. Pretty, clean rooms, each with a handwoven wall tapestry and spotless tiled bathrooms with hot-water shower. Fans and ventilators. Large terrace for gazing at the ocean. Singles get snatched up fast, so arrive early. Singles 35,000 pesos. Doubles 45,000 pesos. Triples 55,000 pesos.

Hotel Soraya, up Vasconcelos (across from the pier), then right up the hill where the sign says "Soraya." A modern, luxurious (the luxuries being towels and toilet paper) hotel that hardly belongs in this town. If you're lucky, the beach will be visible from your balcony; otherwise, enjoy the parking lot view. Somewhat overpriced. Singles 40,000 pesos. Doubles 50,000 pesos.

Food

Food in Puerto Angel is usually fresh and filling. Do not spend much time or money in the small shacks along the dirt road; in many, the fare is as old and dirty as the structure. Reasonable prices and excellent seafood make the beachfront *palapa* restaurants attractive to budget travelers. As in most small Mexican resort towns, closing time is flexible—don't expect to be served if you appear at the last minute, but on the other hand, don't fret about getting kicked out if you feel like sitting around and talking into the night. Many *palapas* on Zipolite will let you cook your own fish.

Restaurant-Bar Brico y Cordelia, the first restaurant on the sands of Playa Panteón. Excellent food at good prices. Tables are available both on the beach and under a giant *palapa*. Lobster dishes expensive, but delicious fish platters cost only 8000 pesos. Don't miss their special seasonal dessert *plátanos flameados* (flaming bananas, 6000 pesos). Happy Hour daily 7-9pm. Open daily 8am-10pm.

Restaurant Cañon Devata, in the *posada* of the same name. A tranquil spot in the woods. Excellent multi-course vegetarian dinner with soup, salad, entree, homemade bread, fruit juice, pie, and coffee for 15,000 pesos. You're welcome to come for dinner at 7pm, even if you're not staying at the *posada;* just let the cook know by 11am. During the day, plenty of vegetarian face-stuffers: delicious soyburgers 5000 pesos, fruit salad with yogurt 5000 pesos. Open Mon.-Sat. 7:30am-4pm and from 7pm until dinner conversations end.

Restaurant El Capy, downstairs from the Casa de Huéspedes of the same name, on the dirt road between the 2 beaches, to the right as you descend to Panteón. The proprietor-fisherman catches everything El Capy serves. A hangout for international beach bums. Delicious sea fare: shrimp in garlic 10,000 pesos, *pescado* from 7000 pesos. Open daily 8am-noon and 2-9pm.

Restaurant Susy, on Playa Panteón next to Brico y Cordelia. Slightly cheaper than its neighbor, but (except for the parrots) lacks the flair. Tasty lobster 15,000 pesos. *Pescado empapelado* (fish stuffed with veggies for 12,000 pesos) is out-of-the-ordinary. Open daily 8am-10pm.

Beto's, to the right midway up the hill past the *arroyo* on the main road, behind a small, crowded flower garden. Romantic Mexican hits serenade patrons in stereo. Looks dark and dumpy, but looks deceive: it's hygienic and homey. Cheapest fish filet in town (6500 pesos). Open daily 4:30-10pm.

Sights

Of Puerto Angel's two beaches, the smaller **Playa Panteón,** on the far side of town, is also the better. Its name derives from a pantheon marking the entrance of a nearby cemetery. The water is calm and warm, the coves great for exploring. To rent a boat at Playa Panteón, inquire at Restaurant El Amigo del Mar, Restaurant Susy, or any of the beachside restaurants. The asking price is 70,000 pesos per hour; bargaining works wonders off-season. You can also rent snorkeling equipment at Restaurant Susy (5000 pesos per hr.) The beach nearer the pier, **Playa Puerto Angel,** has become somewhat polluted and dirty, but people still take the plunge. **Elias Tarias,** the small, white-roofed restaurant on the side of the pier away from Playa Panteón rents boats for 40,000 pesos per hour. Visitors renting boats can pay with part of their catch.

Nightlife in Puerto Angel is comatose, save for a few *fiestas* at the beach cafés along Playa Panteón's moonlit shoreline.

Near Puerto Angel: Zipolite

Zipolite, "beach of the dead" in Xenpoaltec, is named more for the visitors who give up their former lives convinced that they have found paradise than for those who have drowned in the unforgiving surf. The long smooth stretch of powdery gold sand is endowed with a row of humble *palapas* (fresh fish 8000 pesos; some places let you cook your catch) and a carefree hippie crew, but no hotels and precious few showers. Waves break dramatically offshore, crashing over the beach-mongers who frolic naked in the surf. Always exercise caution when swimming: the undertow is fierce and can quickly exhaust the strongest of swimmers.

String up your hammock (3500 pesos) next to 20 of your newly acquired friends or rent one (4500 pesos) at any of the *palapas*. Prices vary slightly from place to place. **Gemini's** always draws a crowd and serves the only pizza on the beach. Zipolite is plagued by theft, and anything left out overnight can be kissed goodbye; leave valuables locked up with proprietors of the *palapas*.

If communal bonding isn't your thing, **Posada Lulu** offers barren rooms on the hill behind the road (15,000 pesos per night for a cot and 2 hammocks). On the far end of the beach, **Shambhala** has even more rustic accommodations improved by a gorgeous view. Rickety cabañas with cement floor and a *palapa* roof (bring your own sleeping mat) go for 10,000 pesos and overlook the entire beach and surrounding hills. A cabaña with space for just one hammock costs 5000 pesos; a hammock spot alongside other people in a large room goes for 3000 pesos, 5000 pesos if you aren't toting your own. Shambhala also runs the most formal restaurant in Zipolite, with vegetarian dishes for 5000 pesos. May and December are the busiest months in Zipolite; during the summer months the beach is yours for the taking.

A few kilometers east of Puerto Angel sprawls **Playa Estacahuites** (a-STACK-a-WHEAT-eez), a nudist beach popular with the port's international daytrippers. In a small, secluded cove ideal for snorkeling, Estacahuites attracts enough visitors to its gentle shore that beach thefts are common; keep an eye on your stuff. **Roberto's Bar/Restaurant,** behind the beach, serves excellent shellfish and costly drinks. Taxis run to Playa Estacahuites from Puerto Angel for 2000 pesos *colectivo,* and 9000 pesos *especial;* prices rise when roads are muddy or skies are dark.

Pochutla, the town 12km to the north, is famous for its black coral jewelry, hand-crafted by prisoners in the local jail. Mexican prisoners are not granted the luxury of rations, and for many, jewelry is the sole source of bread money. The line of buyers outside the jail on Av. Constitución is usually long; when you get to the front, name your price.

Puerto Escondido

At Puerto Escondido you either hang out or hang ten. Less than two decades ago, Puerto Escondido was a quiet *indígena* fishing village where visitors had to wheedle overnight lodging from a local family. Today, the Pacific surf rages beneath droves of stocky surfers who break at the crack of dawn for Playa Zikatela. Surf-seekers usually arrive via Acapulco, whose playful pools and mild climate are poor primers for the pounding heat and surf of Puerto Escondido.

Its increased popularity has rendered obsolete Puerto Escondido's former reputation as an obscure outpost of wild *norteamericano* and European decadence. Yet this fabulous stretch of beach between two majestic outcroppings of rock still plays host to an amiable international company. Where only a handful of scantily clad *extranjeros* used to romp, hotels now outnumber hippies, drug use has dwindled, and naked means naughty. Rife with many of the conveniences and exciting night-spots lacking in Puerto Angel, Puerto Escondido is a different kind of escape: a place to get away from inland life, but one that establishes its own fast pace between the peak tanning hours. People strut up and down the main strip here partaking of the thriving consumer culture along the roadside. Excellent food, exotic drink, and cheesy trinkets all compete for the pedestrian's pesos and lend the *paseo* an urban air.

The fact that the port was not built for tourists shows in the tangle of unnamed, congested streets converging on Pérez Gasga, the main beachside thoroughfare. The crowding is so tight that at night music from other restaurants fills the air when your restaurant's band is on break. The best of Puerto Escondido lies beyond Pérez Gasga, along the grassy dunes where the tiny *cabañas* make Gilligan's *palapa* look like a Hyatt.

Orientation

Like all self-respecting seaside villages should, Puerto Escondido has its own air-port. It is also connected to the outside world by land: a long, treacherous road winds through the Sierra Madres to Oaxaca City, and a beautifully paved coastal road twists through ramshackle fishing towns and coastal forests on its path to Aca-pulco.

The Carretera Costera (coastal highway), often called Rte. 200, separates the well-marked perpendicular streets of uptown Puerto Escondido from the maze of walkways to the beach. Route 131, from Oaxaca, crosses Rte. 200 and becomes Pérez Gasga. The airport is 3km east along Rte. 200, a difficult walk or short cab ride (5000 pesos) to the center of town.

Bus stations cluster around the intersection of Rte. 131 and Av. Miguel Hidalgo y Costilla, 2 blocks north of Rte. 200, and are the only reason for visitors to stray this far from the beach. To get from the stations to the center of town, walk down Hidalgo to Rte. 131, then left (downhill) across Rte. 200 (this intersection is known as *el crucero*). Your first left (once again downhill) leads to Pérez Gasga, which is blocked off to vehicles at sea level, transforming it into a wide pedestrian mall.

Cabs from *el crucero* transport the weary traveler downtown or to the *playas* for about 3000 pesos. To leave town, hike the steep hill to *el crucero,* or take a cab from the chained-off entrance to Pérez Gasga. Taxis in Puerto Escondido are outra-geously priced for the short distances they cover. Unless your surfboard is weighing you down or it's 105°F (both eminently possible), the walk is easy.

Practical Information

Tourist Office: Hidalgo 120 (tel. 203-58), at Oaxaca, on the 2nd floor of the building occupied by the Super Estrella grocery store at the intersection near the bus station. Maps of Puerto Escondido, Puerto Angel, and Oaxaca. Will call the **Centro de Amistad Internacional** in Oa-xaca de Juárez if you are robbed or run into other trouble. Open Mon.-Fri. 9am-2pm and 5-8pm, Sat. 10am-1pm.

Currency Exchange: Money Exchange (tel. 205-92), on Pérez Gasga across from Farmacia Corts, exchanges at the official rate. Open Mon.-Sat. 9am-2pm and 5-8pm.

Post Office: 7a. Calle Nte. at Oaxaca, 5 blocks north of Hidalgo on Rte. 131 and to the right. Lista de Correos. Open Mon.-Fri. 8am-7pm, Sat. 9am-1pm.

Telephones: (tel. 204-87) on Pérez Gasga across from Farmacia Cortés. Collect calls 5000 pesos. Open Mon.-Sat. 9am-1pm. **Telephone Code:** 958.

Telegrams: (tel. 202-32) next door to the post office. Open Mon.-Fri. 9am-9pm, Sat. 9am-noon; for money orders Mon.-Fri. 9am-5pm, Sat. 9am-noon.

Airport: 3km west of the *centro* on Rte. 200. Taxis to downtown 5000 pesos. **Aerovías Oax-aqueñas** (tel. 201-32), on Pérez Gasga across from the bank on the far end of the street. Office open Mon.-Sat. 8am-1:30pm and 4-7pm. Daily flight to Oaxaca (at noon, 45 min., 172,555 pesos). **Mexicana,** Pérez Gasga 302 (tel. 200-98). Office open Mon.-Sat. 9am-6pm. Daily flight to Mexico City (at 3:50pm, 50 min., US$63).

Bus Stations: Puerto Escondido has no central bus terminal, but the offices and stops of all lines gravitate around the intersection of Rte. 131 and Hidalgo, 3 blocks north of Rte. 200. **Lineas Unidas del Sur** and **Transporte Gacela,** at Rte. 131 and Hidalgo (tel. 204-27), send out the most buses. To: Acapulco with *servicio ordinario* (18 per day, 7½ hr., 23,000 pesos) or *servicio directo,* which makes only one stop (at 10:30am, 1:30pm, and 10:30pm, 6 hr., 23,000 pesos); Mexico City (at 7:30 and 8pm, 13 hr., 43,000 pesos); Pochutla (10 per day, 1 hr., 3000 pesos), where you can transfer to Puerto Angel; and Huatulco (10 per day, 5000 pesos). In the *palapa* across the street is the office of **Autotransportes Oaxaca Istmo,** Hidalgo 102 (tel. 203-92). To Pochutla (5 per day, 1 hr., 3000 pesos) and Salina Cruz (5 per day, 5 hr., 10,500 pesos). Two blocks to the east on Hidalgo, **Líneas Unidas Estrella del Valle y Oaxaca Pacífico** (tel. 200-50), sends buses to Oaxaca with *servicio ordinario* (at 9am, 3:30pm, 10pm, and 10:30pm, 9 hr., 14,000 pesos) or *servicio directo* (at 8am and 10:45pm, 6 hr., 16,500 pesos) and Salina Cruz (15 per day, 5 hr., 10,100 pesos).

Taxis: Tel. 200-26. Rates go up after 11pm.

Car Rental: Hertz, Pérez Gasga 3 (tel. 200-35). VW sedan 63,485 pesos per day plus 493 pesos per km, plus insurance; 138,725 pesos per day with 200km free, insurance included. Open Mon.-Sat. 8am-7pm.

English Bookstore: El Acuario (tel. 201-27), on Pérez Gasga downhill from and opposite Casa de Huéspedes Las Dos Costas. Doubles as a stationery store. A few *norteamericano* bestsellers plus a wide selection of *gringo* magazines. Open Mon.-Sat. 8:30am-2pm and 4-8pm, Sun. 9am-2pm.

24-Hr. Pharmacy: La Moderna, Pérez Gasga 203 (tel. 205-49), toward the top of the hill.

Hospital: Seguro Social, 5 de Febrero at 7a. Calle Nte. (tel. 201-42). Open 24 hr. **Centro de Salud,** Pérez Gasga 409, below and across from the Hotel Virginia. Small medical clinic open for emergencies 24 hr. Some English spoken.

Emergency: Agencia Municipal, in the Palacio Municipal on Peréz Gasga (tel. 201-18). For lost property and other non-medical crises. Open Mon.-Sat. 8am-3pm.

Police: Pérez Gasga In the Palacio Municipal on Pérez Gasga (tel. 201-11). Open 24 hr.

·Accommodations

The beach here is not safe for camping, particularly in the more secluded spots, but a multitude of hotels downtown cater to every budget. Unfortunately, beach-front and budget are mutually exclusive, unless sharing a stark cabaña with several species of insects is up your alley.

On the Hill

Hotel San Juan, Felipe Marci 158 (tel. 203-36), 1 block down Pérez Gasga from *el crucero* and left, with a big painted sign visible only from the downhill side. The best value in town. The terrace, with plenty of chairs and a stunning view of the beaches and ocean below, is so pleasant that you won't even make it to the beach if you're the least bit lazy. Comfortable rooms with fans. Excellent bathrooms. Singles 24,000 pesos. Doubles 30,000 pesos.

Casa de Huéspedes Las Dos Costas, Pérez Gasga 302 (tel. 201-59), halfway down the hill from *el crucero,* on the right. Look for the glass doors. A new twist on traditional lodging proportions: small bedrooms complement the huge bathrooms. Fans are cool consolation, as is the price. Singles 15,000 pesos. Doubles 25,000 pesos.

Hotel Castillo de Reyes, Pérez Gasga 300 (tel. 204-42), on the right, as you descend from the hilltop. The sign is almost hidden by overgrown trees. Beautiful rooms, white stucco walls, pink tile roof, a courtyard filled with large ferns, and tables cut out of tree trunks. Very clean bathrooms. Singles and doubles 30,000 pesos.

Casa de Huéspedes Naxhiely, Pérez Gasga 301, across from Las Dos Costas. Clean, stuffy, plain rooms. Singles 20,000 pesos. Doubles 30,000 pesos.

Hotel Virginia, Camino Alfaro 104 (tel. 201-76), off Pérez Gasga. Coming down the hill, take the dirt road to the right after Restaurant Selina. Big sign. Although the view is beautiful, its terrace isn't quite the San Juan's: get out your binos to watch the water action. Bathrooms could use a scrub. Singles 25,000 pesos. Doubles 40,000 pesos. Triples 45,000 pesos.

Hotel Alderate, Hidalgo 211, near the bus stations. The farthest from the beach. Friendly family proprietors and fans in every room (which weren't designed by Ralph Lauren), but the common bathrooms feel a bit grungy. Nary a toilet seat in sight. Singles and doubles 20,000 pesos, with bath 25,000 pesos.

On the Beach

Aldea Marinero, on Marino. From the beach, hang a left between Neptuno and Zihuaraya. Technically not on the beach but you can hear the surf a-pounding. Friendly owner has been known to greet guests in his underwear. Ten well-constructed cabañas share a green lawn. Rooms come with mosquito netting. Singles 10,000 pesos. Doubles 15,000 pesos.

Casas de Playa Acali (tel. 202-78), past the rocks close to the beginning of the surfing beach. In a different league than the other *cabañas:* each comes with fan, refrigerator, stove, clean private bathroom, hot water, and screened windows. An excellent deal for 3 or more people. Singles 25,000 pesos. Doubles 30,000 pesos. Triples 35,000 pesos. Don't let them give you A/C unless you want to shell out 120,000 pesos.

Cabañas Zihuaraya, on the beach next door to Cabañas Playa Marinero. *Cabañas* on the cement roof of a restaurant-bar. *Palapa* huts contain 2 double beds (including sheets and bedspreads) and light bulbs. Communal bathrooms are adequate but toilets lack seats. Cleaner, cooler, safer, and friendlier than its neighbor. Lack of screens ensures a barrage of bugs. Beautiful restaurant in front. Singles 8000 pesos, overlooking the beach 10,000 pesos. Doubles 15,000 and 20,000 pesos.

Cabañas Playa Marinero (tel. 203-27), on the beach, 100m past the fleet of fishing boats. *Palapa* huts on cement platforms, each with 2 single beds. Light bulbs function only after 6pm. Common bathrooms soggy and dirty but functional. Bring a sleepsack and inspect your hut for insects. Nice beachfront restaurant and young international clientele. 10,000 pesos for 1-2 people.

Camping

Trailer Park Carrizalillo (tel. 200-77), in Puerto Angelito. From *el crucero,* go up Rte. 200 ½ km in the direction of Acapulco, left on the dirt path Hidalgo, and right at the decaying white "Pepsi" sign, where a smaller sign points to "Trailer Park." Bear left until you reach Posada Carrizalillo, then left to the park. A 20-min. walk from the center. Water, electricity, cooking grills, and a seasonal swimming pool. Bathrooms are clean. Only the women's toilets have seats. Near a cliff overhanging beautiful, secluded Playa Carrizalillo. Office open daily 10am-2pm and 4-8pm. Site for 2 people and 1 car 20,000 pesos. Each additional person 5000 pesos. A/C 5000 pesos.

Trailer Park Neptuno (tel. 201-22), on Pérez Gasga beyond the center of town on the beach side of the road. Turn right at Banana's. Sign points to large complex. Plenty of palm trees for hammocks. Bathrooms have no toilet seats, and only some are clean. Tent site 6000 pesos per person. Parking 6000 pesos for compact cars.

Food

If dinner is a long time in coming, it's probably because they're having a tough time catching it. Puerto Escondido's fishers net huge amounts of snapper, lobster, shrimp, and octopus, all deliciously prepared in the restaurants along the pedestrian mall. Menus, prices, and decor differ inconsequentially. A crowd is the best indicator of who netted the prize fish of the day.

Los Crotos, on Pérez Gasga, across the street from Hotel Rocamar at the end of a below-sidewalk path toward the beach. The service is stiff but very attentive. Seafood brochette with lobster, shrimp, and octopus served with piping hot bread for 12,000 pesos. Bananas *flambé* without the flames 4000 pesos. Open daily 7am-11pm.

Restaurant Spaghetti House, Pérez Gasga 703, on the beach straight back from Banana's. A spacious Italian-Caribbean outpost; red-and-white checkered tablecloths under a *palapa,* with a view of the breakers. Even the menu reads Italian: Try the delicious *pizza del mare* (14,000 pesos). Spaghetti with meat sauce 9000 pesos. Open daily 7:30am-8pm.

El Marisquero, on Marina Nacional, 2 blocks off Pérez Gasga to the right. Earth-shaking view of Puerto Escondido's entire circuit of beaches through red brick archways. Breakfasts 3500-4500 pesos, filet mignon or shrimp cocktail 8000 pesos, fish 7000-8000 pesos. Open daily 7am-8pm.

Restaurant Alicia, across from the Farmacia Cortés on Pérez Gasga. Beachfront access only. Six tables, 18 indígena masks, and at least 100 flies. Not the best fish you'll ever have, but it swam yesterday, it's cooked now, and it's the cheapest in town at 6000 pesos. Shrimp in garlic sauce 7000 pesos. Open daily 7am-11pm.

Banana's, the last restaurant on the beach side of Pérez Gasga. Look for the unmistakeable jungle entrance en route to the beach. Listen to great music, have an intimate conversation with friends, and play ping-pong or backgammon under the palm trees. Upper deck affords a great view. *Crepas de chocolate* 6000 pesos. Big drinks 6500 pesos. Homemade ice cream 5500 pesos. Open daily 8am-1am.

Resturante Loli's, on Pérez Gasga, on the inland side of the *carretera*. A few whirring fans are the only concession to aesthetics. Lots of locals, but fishing for tourists with a big sign on the highway. Shrimp or octopus 9000 pesos. Breakfast omelettes come with beans, avocado, tomato, and tortillas for 4000 pesos. Open 24 hr.

Restaurant Selene, Pérez Gasga 402, opposite the Centro de Salud. Small, family-run place with a small, reasonably priced menu. Shrimp dishes 7000-10,000 pesos, *mole oaxaqueño* 9000 pesos. Open daily 6:30am-11pm.

El Son y La Rumba, Andador Marisol at Pérez Gasga, a few steps uphill. Extensive drink list includes "vampires" and margaritas (5000 pesos). Wooden donkey with bad hips at the door. The specialty is *paella* (15,000 pesos per person) and the fish (9000 pesos) is delicious. Open 6pm-midnight.

Cheko's and Willie Lobster House and Tacos, Pérez Gasga and the *carretera*. Though squashed between 2 major roadways, its small deck set slightly below ground makes meals pleasant. Tacky cowhides and rodeo posters adorn the walls. The cheapest tequila around (2000 pesos per shot). Reasonable *menú del día* includes fish (8000 pesos). A la carte entrees are unreasonably priced. Open daily 7:30am-midnight.

El Padrino, Hidalgo 205, 2½ blocks west of Pérez Gasga. Huge *palapa* hut far from the tourist zone. The 8-yr.-old bartender has been working for 3 yrs., and he's already better than most 20-yr. veterans. Big portions of fresh fish at low prices; try their special *filete al Padrino* (breaded marlin, 8500 pesos). Open daily 7am-midnight.

Restaurant Vegetariano, Pérez Gasga, on top of the hill. A plain, clean shack with grain-bedecked shelves. Granola, yogurt, and fruit 5000 pesos, entrees (including *ceviche de soya* and *botana vegetariana*) 3500-9000 pesos. Open daily 8am-10pm.

Sights and Activities

There isn't much to do here except relax, eat fish, and contemplate the tireless erosive efforts of the surf. But then again, that's why most people come here in the first place.

A rock outcrop southwest of town divides the main beach at Puerto Escondido into two parts. The southern half, **Playa Zikatela,** faces the open sea and has rough waves ideal for surfing; spectators on the long white beach enjoy the antics of the daredevils in the breakers. This is not a place for beginners—rarely does a day pass without at least one injury to an experienced surfer. **Choy's Surf Shop,** on Pérez Gasga across from Loli's, rents low-quality boards for 20,000 pesos per day. (Open daily 8am-2pm and 4-10pm.) Early morning surfers can make arrangements the night before. **Central Surf,** a few doors down on Pérez Gasga across from Farmacia Cortés, offers a similar deal (5000 pesos per hr. or 20,000 pesos per day; open daily 9am-2pm and 5-9pm).

Playa Marinero, the town's quieter beach, harbors the local fishing fleet. An angling trip can be arranged on the sands or with one of the seaside restaurants for 50,000 pesos per hour, with the average trip lasting three hours. To avoid the dirty work, arrange in advance for your catch to be cleaned and cooked as part of the original fee.

Nearby **Puerto Angelito** fosters a more tranquil environment better suited to snorkeling. A boat from Puerto Escondido will take you there for 10,000 pesos, or a taxi for 3000 pesos, but the distance is short enough to hoof it. Walk down Rte. 200 in the direction of Acapulco and turn left on Hidalgo, away from Padrino's. At the faded "Pepsi . . . *es lo de hoy*" sign, turn left and pick a path at the fork. The left-hand branch descends steep rocky terrain to **Playa Manzanillo.** Beneath the calm surface of its waters, coral makes wading a bit treacherous but snorkeling very interesting. The path to the right of the Pepsi sign is wider and leads to **Playa Puerto Angelito,** opposite Manzanillo. Both of these beaches are small enough to seem crowded when even a few people are present; their days as secluded coves are irretrievable.

When the sun goes down, beachmongers slip into the restaurants and pubs on the strip. **La Taberna,** on Pérez Gasga, rocks to Jimmy Buffet and serves a gaggle of margaritas and tequila shots to tourists with wandering eyes (4000 pesos). (Open daily noon-midnight.) Go bonkers at **Banana's** during Happy Hour, daily from 6 to 10pm. For loud *salsa* and *mambo,* hike up the port's largest beachside hill to **Disco Le Dome,** Av. Juárez 506. To get there, retreat 1 block toward the center from the roadblock on Gasga next to La Taberna; hang a right up the 10 steep flights of stairs until you reach the *carretera,* and then keep climbing past the noisy crickets and whining stray cats to the summit. An outdoor terrace overlooks the beach and the town, and inside are an inviting floor thumping to a *salsa* beat, flashing colored lights, and occasional transvestite entertainment. Although most of the patrons are locals and Mexican tourists, some *extranjeros* are usually on hand. Beer costs 3000 pesos, a cup of wine 4000 pesos. (Open Tues.-Sun. 9pm-2:30am. Cover 3000 pesos, 6000 pesos when acts are scheduled.)

Tehuantepec

The only city on the Istmo de Tehuantepec unconquered by industry, Tehuantepec lies roughly halfway between its bigger, more grotesque siblings Salina Cruz and Juchitán. An enormous outdated sign near the Zócalo proclaims Tehuantepec to be the "spiritual center of the isthmus," but this center does not hold spirit now, let alone physical attractions that might captivate the casual visitor.

A thousand years ago, this riverside town was the site of the Zapotec capital. The ruins of its ceremonial center, Guien-Gola, were discovered some 15km away but have not yet been fully excavated. An intense rivalry between Tehuantepec and Juchitán to the northeast has lasted for centuries; the bloody battles of bygone days have given way to today's ferociously competitive partying. Around *fiesta* times, you can see women stitching together the long dresses of dark velvet that they wear despite the intense heat. The two weeks leading up to Christmas and Semana Santa are the best times to catch the street festivities.

Sight-seeing in Tehuantepec is easy: park yourself on a bench in the Zócalo. The bronze statue in the center of the Zócalo is of Doña Cata, a local peasant whose 30 years of extramarital activities with the nationally despised, also-married dictator Porfirio Díaz earned her the love and respect of the townspeople. In addition, she is credited with attracting the railroad to Tehuantepec at the turn of the century. The only other form of sight-seeing is a stroll through the market, to the left of the post office on the Zócalo. In the filthy restaurant stalls upstairs, Tehuanas serve turtle meat, armadillo, and iguana.

Orientation and Practical Information

Tehuantepec lies 18km north of Salina Cruz on Rte. 200/185 and 40km southwest of Juchitán on the same road. Rte. 190 from Oaxaca joins Rte. 200/185 in Tehuantepec on its way down the coast. Although Rte. 200/185 passes just west of the Zócalo, all buses arrive at and depart from a depot—actually a dusty parking lot—on the northern edge of town. Immediately upon arriving, investigate departure schedules and prices and save yourself a special trip later. To reach town from the station, take a *colectivo* (500 pesos) or the bus marked "Centro/Estación"; it's far too long to walk. Taxis charge 2000 pesos for the trip. Two of the four cardinal directions correspond to prominent landmarks—the Palacio Municipal to the south and the market to the west—making the rest easy. Two major streets run north-south on either side of the Zócalo; to the west in front of the market is Romero, and east of the Zócalo is Juárez.

Currency Exchange: No banks will exchange traveler's checks. **La Espera,** Juárez 10 (tel. 500-42), on the east side of the Zócalo, extracts a 5000-peso commission per transaction.

Post Office: Hidalgo at 22 de Marzo (tel. 501-06), on the Zócalo. Lista de Correos. Open Mon.-Fri. 8am-7pm, Sat. 8am-noon. Packages must be sent from Salina Cruz. **Postal Code:** 70760.

Telephones: Long-distance *caseta* (tel. 508-02) on Dominguez Local 1 in the natural food store to the right of the Hotel Donaji. Collect calls 5000 pesos. Open daily 8am-9:30pm.

Telegrams: on Hidalgo at 22 de Marzo (tel. 501-59), on the Zócalo next to the post office. Open for telegrams and money orders Mon.-Fri. 9am-9pm.

Train Station: (tel. 504-14) on Av. de Ferrocaril, 1km north of the Zócalo. One train departs daily at 7:45am to Coatzacoalcos.

Bus Stations: Cristóbal Colón (tel. 501-08), on Rte. 200/185. To: Mexico City (at 6:30pm and 8:30pm, 42,000 pesos) via Puebla (at 6:30pm, 36,000 pesos) or Cordoba (at 8:30pm, 27,000 pesos); Tuxtepec (at 8:30am, 20,000 pesos); Villahermosa (at midnight, 20,500 pesos); Salina Cruz (8 per day, 900 pesos); Tonalá (at 2am and 8:45pm, 8900 pesos); San Cristóbal de las Casas (at noon and 1:30pm, 17,000 pesos); and Tuxtla Gutiérrez (4 per day, 13,000 pesos). **Second-class station,** on Guerrero 2 blocks past the Colón station. To: Salina Cruz (19 per day); Oaxaca (every hr.); Tuxtla Gutiérrez (4 per day); Arriaga (4 per day); Tuxtepec (3 per day); Juchitán (every hr.). **Transportes Oaxaca** buses leave from Salina Cruz for Puerto Escondido via Pochutla (5 per day, 10,500 pesos) and for Oaxaca (4 per day, 11,000 pesos).

Red Cross: (tel. 502-15) on Av. de Ferrocaril. Ambulances and 24-hr. emergency service.

Pharmacy: Farmacia de Istmo, Juárez 19 (tel. 501-72). After hours, knock or ring the bell. Open Mon.-Sat. 8am-9pm.

Hospital: Sanatorio San Francisco, Domínguez 1 (tel. 509-23), at Romero away from the Zócalo past the Hotel Oasis. 24-hr. emergency service.

Police: In the Palacio Municipal (tel. 500-01), on the Zócalo. No uniforms, no English spoken, just a bunch of the guys protecting their extended lunch hour. Open 24 hr.

Accommodations

Hotel Oasis, Ocampo 18 (tel. 500-08), 1 block south on Romero from the Zócalo. A monkey on a rope, a caged parrot, *aqua purificada* at the front desk, and a shady courtyard—no wonder it's the most popular in town. Make sure to see the room before paying. Forceful ceiling fans. Singles 20,000 pesos. Doubles 30,000 pesos, with 2 beds 35,000 pesos.

Hotel Donaji, Juárez 10 (tel. 500-64), 2 blocks south of the Zócalo. A beautiful interior courtyard, not matched by the rooms. All have ceiling fans; most open onto a balcony overlooking the street. Adequate restaurant on the 2nd floor. Some guests get free viewings of the B-movies showing next door. Singles 20,000 pesos. Doubles 30,000 pesos, with 2 beds 35,000 pesos.

Casa de Huéspedes Istmo, Hidalgo 31, 1½ blocks from the Zócalo. Entrance unambiguously marked "Hotel." Places a distant third despite its tranquil courtyard with a bougainvillea arbor. Decaying rooms and bathrooms. 20,000 pesos per room.

Food

Café Colonial, Romero 66, 2 blocks south of the Zócalo. A romantic amalgamation of starry-eyed couples, pretty tablecloths, bright paintings, and a brick archway. Unusual gourmet Mexican selections, most notably *huevos motuleños* (8000 pesos), a tortilla and egg dish stuffed with peas, fried bananas, and ham. Open daily 8:30am-10pm. MC, Visa accepted.

Restaurante Mariscos Rafa, 22 de Marzo 35, a few doors from the post office. Fans, conversation, and a large local crowd exacerbate the noise level of the already bustling Zócalo location. Excellent, though expensive, seafood. Small shrimp or oyster cocktail 7000 pesos. Open daily 7am-8pm.

Restaurant La Carreta, 22 de Marzo 23, on the Zócalo, across from the post office. The smell gives it away as yet another seafood restaurant. Superb fish. *Ceviche* entrees 10,000 pesos. Non-seafood *antojitos* 5000 pesos. Open daily 7am-10pm.

Near Tehuantepec

A visit to the Huave villages near Salina Cruz could be a welcome diversion from the polluted Istmo. The Huaves migrated north to this region only a few centuries before the Spaniards arrived, and continue to this day to practice the closest thing to matriarchy in Central and North America. Men do the domestic sewing as well as the artisanry, while women take care of trading and local politics.

The only Huave communities left are those around the Lagunas Superior and Inferior, affectionately called Diuk-guialoni and Diuk-guialiat. San Dionesio del Mar and San Francisco del Mar are across the lakes from Salina Cruz and are accessible from Juchitán via Niltepec. Huazontlán, upriver toward Tehuantepec, and San Mateo del Mar and Santa María del Mar, along the peninsula to the east, can be reacged from Salina Cruz. The most interesting of the villages is the largest, **San Mateo.** Several buses leave from Salina Cruz every day; the ride takes less than an hour by bus to San Mateo and another two hours by passenger truck from there to Santa María. You can catch the bus about a block up from the market in Salina Cruz, on Guaymas. Hitching is easier the earlier you leave.

Tuxtepec

On the Papaloapan River, between Veracruz and Oaxaca, the town of Tuxtepec attracts travelers in transit between Mexico City and the Yucatán by virtue of the interesting settlements in the region.

Although downtown Tuxtepec is surrounded on three sides by water, it is more a market town than a fishing village. The hand-crafted products sold here blend *veracruzano* and *oaxaqueño* cultures, but shop owners also proudly display fine imports like Miller beer (3970 pesos per can). The Zócalo is lush and unusually quiet, and the small park at the corner of Independencia and Allende, behind the Palacio Municipal, acts as a social center for local marketeers.

Orientation and Practical Information

Tuxtepec occupies the tongue of land created by a sharp bend in Río Papaloapan (also known as Río de las Mariposas) about 130km south of Veracruz and 200km west-southwest of the Tuxtlas. The drive from Mexico City to Tuxtepec along the road to Veracruz takes approximately nine hours, the return via Jalapa only seven hours.

The first-class **ADO** bus station is at 1 de Mayo, off Sebastián Ortiz on the outskirts of town. To reach the center, turn left as you leave the station on Ortiz and walk to the intersection with Libertad; turn left on Libertad, right on Aldama, and continue until Independencia in the middle of downtown. Taxis to downtown cost 3000 pesos. **AU,** the second-class bus line, has its station on Libertad, several blocks west of the center. To reach the center, turn right upon leaving and right again on any major cross street.

The only available Tuxtepec map beautifies a wall in the small public park overlooking the river at the corner of Independencia and Allende. The map shows Río Papaloapan making a hairpin turn whose opening faces west. The peninsula of land cut off by the river is gridded with streets running east-west, starting with Independencia in the south and continuing north with 20 de Noviembre, 5 de Mayo, Libertad, and Carranza. The most important north-south streets begin with Matamoros in the west, and continue east with Aldama, Morelos, Arteaga, Juárez, Rayón, Hidalgo, and Allende.

The city's most active area centers on **Independencia,** along the north shore of the southern stretch of river. Scattered further west are the town's inordinate number of smaller bus stations, each serving particular towns in the area. Stations include **Terminal de Tuxtepec,** Matamoros 248; **Transportes Tuxtepec,** Libertad 1440B (tel. 515-51), at Ocampo; and **Autotransportes Rápido,** Carranza 800 (tel. 524-18), at Aldama.

Tuxtepec has no tourist office. The only source of detailed information on the area is the state tourist office in Oaxaca City.

Currency Exchange: Bánamex, on Independencia 1 block from the Zócalo. Get there when the doors open to avoid long lines. Open Mon.-Fri. 9am-1:30pm.

Post Office: Independencia at Hidalgo. Open Mon.-Sat. 9am-noon and 3-5pm.

Telephones: A long-distance *caseta* at Juárez 6, between Libertad and 5 de Mayo, allows only national calls. Open daily 8am-11pm; for collect calls 8am-8pm. For international calls, go to Juárez 63, between Independencia and 20 de Noviembre. Open Mon.-Sat. 8am-9:30pm, Sun. 8am-3pm; for collect calls Mon.-Sat. 10am-1pm and 4-7pm. **Telephone Code:** 287.

Bus Stations: ADO (tel. 504-73), on 1 de Mayo. First-class buses to: Mexico City (5 per day, 7½ hr., 17,100 pesos); Puebla (2 per day, 6 hr., 13,500 pesos); Veracruz (5 per day, 4 hr., 7000 pesos); Oaxaca (1 per day, 9300 pesos); Jalapa (2 per day, 10,200 pesos). **AU,** on Libertad. Second-class buses to Veracruz (4 per day, 6000 pesos) and Cordoba (4 per day, 5400 pesos).

Market: Independencia at Juárez. The indoor *Arcado Central* contains pottery, flowers, shoes, fresh fruit, and handmade *oaxaqueño* products. Many outdoor food vendors congregate across Independencia. Open daily 6am-7pm.

Medical Emergency: Clínica Benito Juárez, 5 de Mayo 557 (tel. 506-76), between Juárez and Rayón. Emergency 24-hr. ambulance service. No English spoken.

Police: 5 de Mayo at Allende (tel. 500-39), on the Zócalo. No English spoken. Open 24 hr.

Accommodations

Hotel Mirador, Independencia 985-A (tel. 505-00). Large, plentifully furnished rooms with fan or A/C and phones. Bright, tiled bathrooms. Fantastic river views at sunset. Singles 27,600 pesos. Doubles 34,500 pesos, with A/C 48,600 pesos.

Hotel María de Lourdes, 5 de Mayo 1386 (tel. 504-10), at Degollados 2 blocks west of Matamoros. Not centrally located. Fair sized rooms and small, dark baths are clean but painfully plain. Extra-holy *agua purificada* available; all rooms have fans. Singles 25,000 pesos. Doubles 30,000 pesos.

Hotel Central, Independencia 565 (tel. 500-65). Small rooms with fans and baths set around a courtyard reminiscent of Alcatraz, in stark contrast to the cute crocheted bedspreads that came straight from grandma's house. *Agua purificada.* Singles 15,000 pesos. Doubles 20,000 pesos.

Hotel Catedral, Guerrero 295 (tel. 507-64), between Libertad and 5 de Mayo, ½ block north of the Zócalo. If this cathedral represents *your* religion, convert. Tiny, damp rooms separated from bathrooms by a low wall. Roach-infested and not pristine. Singles and doubles 15,000 pesos.

Food

Tuxtepec suffers from a dearth of restaurants, but what the chosen few lack in competitive suspense, they make up for in sheer pleasantness and solid cuisine.

Restaurant and Grill Manhattan, Independencia 256 (tel. 518-90), 2 blocks east of the market. Grab a table with a river view or just enjoy the interesting decor. Delicious meals served by attentive waiters. Entrees 10,000-20,000 pesos. Live guitar Fri.-Sat. 7-11pm. Open daily 1-11pm.

Restaurant La Jardín, 5 de Mayo 1386, attached to Hotel María de Lourdes. This outdoor restaurant's courtyard is insulated from the commotion of 5 de Mayo by a barrier of shrubbery. Barbecued *pollo* (9000 pesos) sometimes grilled before your eyes. Open daily 8am-10pm.

Pizza Viva, Libertad at Ortiz, 3 blocks west of Matamoros. Always lively, even late into the night. Medium-sized pizza 9000 pesos. Open Mon.-Sat. 6pm-2am. Also at 5 de Mayo 598.

Near Tuxtepec

To the west of Tuxtepec lie the Chinantec villages of **Ojitlán** and **Jalapa de Díaz** as well as the **Presa Miguel Alemán,** a reservoir formed by the dam at Temaxcal. The road south to Oaxaca City passes through many small towns and provides access to swimming holes on the **Chiltepec River,** the **Monte Flor** archeological site and cold springs, and **Guelatao** (see Near Oaxaca), the birthplace of Benito Juárez. The key to reaching neighboring villages is the second-class bus line, **Autobuses Unidos (AU),** which navigates the nearby mountain roads around the clock.

CHIAPAS

Chiapas is simply gorgeous. The Sierra de Chiapas exemplify Cortés's answer to the question of what Mexico looked like: he crumpled a piece of parchment and laid it on the table. Through these rugged green mountains, buses career around hairpin turns above deep valleys and before hurtling down to jungles on rutted roads. One of Mexico's most enchanting cities, San Cristóbal de las Casas, rests high in the mountains. If leaving Mexico City for Oaxaca or the Yucatán, consider a detour to Chiapas. If you'd planned on striking out for Guatemala and points south along the speedy but uninteresting coastal route, meander instead through the inland mountains.

Chiapas is close to the Mayan heartland—the Guatemalan Petén—and the huge Lacandón Rainforest, in the eastern part of the state, hides spectacular ruins, notably Bonampak, Yaxchilán, and Palenque. It took a long while for the descendants of these cultures to mesh peacefully with the invading *ladinos,* and their relationship is still edgy to this day. Throughout Mexico's southernmost state, you are likely to hear diverse languages and find markets and other public places filled with *indígenas,* but *mestizos* own most of the land and run the businesses in villages where they themselves do not live. The descendants of the conquerors are not as brutal as in times past, but they still have the upper hand in *chiapaneco* society.

Chiapas's many different *indígena* cultures were already at war with one another in 1523 when the conquistador Luis Marín entered Chiapas. The Spaniards took advantage of this discord by pitting the groups against one another. In 1528, Diego de Mazariego founded present-day San Cristóbal de las Casas as Ciudad Real. The "Royal City" was an administrative center for the *encomiendas* (huge plots of land awarded to Spanish soldiers in lieu of pay). Each *encomendero* also received a group of slaves to till the land; after being branded, the *indígenas* were worked to an early death. One of the few defenders of the *indígenas* was a friar of the powerful Dominican order, Bartolomé de las Casas, who arrived in 1545. Largely through his efforts, chattel slavery was abolished by royal decree in the 1550s. Exploitation and abuse continued for centuries, however, with equally grotesque but different systems of forced labor such as the *repartimiento,* which required adult males to leave their villages several times a year to work for Spaniards.

In 1712, a young Tzeltal girl in the village of Cancuc had a vision of the Virgin Mary promising relief to the *indígenas* if they would attack the Spanish minority. The ensuing rebellion was quelled at Ocosingo and Huixtán. The only other major show of resistance occurred a century-and-a-half later. In 1867, Agustina Gómez discovered some *piedras hablantes* in the Tzotzil village of Tzajalhemel. These "talking stones" attracted followers in such villages as San Juan Chamula, Chenalhó, Pantelhó, Tenejapa, and San Andrés. Soon the stones advised the people to rise against the Spaniards, and the Rebellion of 1869 began. The *indígena* forces were no match for the *ladinos,* who quickly crushed the uprising, killing many participants in the process. It was not until 1936, under the guidance of President Lázaro Cárdenas, that the *indígenas* of Chiapas received a measure of autonomy with the establishment of the *ejido,* a system of communal land titles.

Today, relations between *indígena* people and the *ladino* and *mestizo* neighbors they call *kashalán* are steadily improving, as trade in coffee, sugar, cattle, and artisanry brings prosperity to the region. A new source of tension, however, is the increase in tourism. Some villagers don't take kindly to gawking foreigners, and they particularly object to photography as a rape of the subject's soul. Two tourists were murdered a few years ago for taking pictures in the church in Chamula. In *indígena* areas, keep cameras packed away; buy postcards instead.

Outsiders who wear *indígena* clothing may offend natives here, since the patterns and styles of garments are invested with social meaning. If you buy clothing at a *tianguis* (*indígena* market), don't wear it until you've left the region.

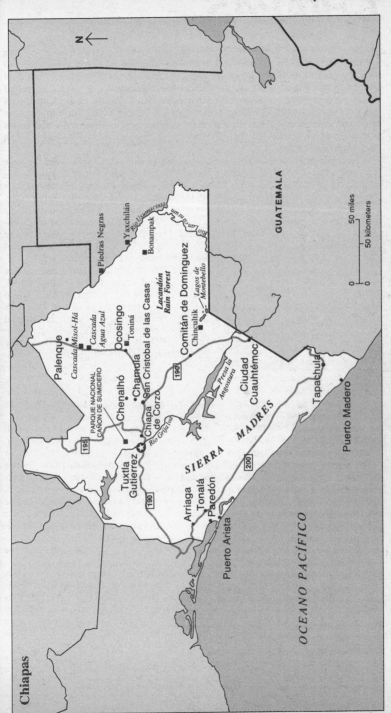

Chiapas

A second caution regarding clothing: *Chiapanecos,* especially in indigenous areas, are very conservative in dress. Keep shorts and other revealing garments in your backpack until you can feel the ocean spray on your face.

San Cristóbal de las Casas

If San Cristóbal isn't on your list of must-see spots, make a new list. Swept up into the lush, cloud-bedecked mountains around the Valley of Hueyzacatlán, high in the Sierra de Chiapas, San Cristóbal de las Casas outdoes virtually every other town in the Republic in terms of sheer beauty, and here, *indígena* and European influences merge more successfully than anywhere else. Trendsetters fill the city's elegant cafés, while barefoot Tzotzil women fill downtown streets; local merchants, dressed in bright patterns which have not changed in centuries, hawk their traditional goods at the Sunday market.

The architecture of San Cristóbal is all-out colonial, and those buildings not constructed by the Spanish are artful imitations of the tile-roofed structures that the *conquistadores* wove around courtyards and gardens. Some *indígena* men have switched from their traditional trousers to Western clothing, but most women continue to wear brilliantly embroidered skirts, *huipiles* (blouses), and grand *rebozo* scarves which complement the bright ribbons braided into their long hair. Most of the indigenous people of the *chiapaneco* highlands speak the Mayan tongues of Tzeltal or Tzotzil, although Chol, Tojolabal, and sometimes Zoque or Lacandón are also heard.

Founded by the *conquistadores* in 1528, San Cristóbal de las Casas was once the colonial capital of the region. Three-fifths of its name honors the 16th-century bishop Fray Bartolomé de las Casas, the "Protector of the Indians," who fought the oppression of indigenous peoples. Today, the city is often referred to (especially on bus schedules) simply as "Las Casas."

Orientation

San Cristóbal de las Casas rests in a valley 2100m above sea level, 84km east of Tuxtla Gutiérrez, 87km northwest of Comitán, 90km west of Ocosingo, and 204km west of the ruins of Palenque. **Route 190,** the Pan American Highway, cuts east from Tuxtla Gutiérrez, touches the southern edge of San Cristóbal, and then heads southeast to Comitán and Ciudad Cuauhtémoc at the Guatemalan border.

The first- and second-class bus stations are on the Pan American Hwy. at the southern edge of town. The most convenient route to *el centro* is along Av. Insurgentes. From Cristóbal Colón, the Zócalo is 7 blocks to the right of the exit. From either of the second-class bus stations, walk east 2 or 3 blocks on any cross street and turn left on Insurgentes.

Since San Cristóbal is a popular destination for tourists, most of whom travel by bus, book seats as far in advance as possible during the Christmas season and Semana Santa. At other times, reservations one day in advance are sufficient.

Buses and *combis* reach many of the nearby *indígena* villages and leave from the lot 1 block past the market at Utrilla and Honduras. Destination signs next to the buses are only occasionally accurate; always ask drivers where they're going. Prepare to rub shoulders with the other passengers.

Most of San Cristóbal's clearly labeled streets fall into a neat grid. The **Zócalo,** also known as Pl. 31 de Marzo, is the city center, and the four cardinal directions are indicated by prominent landmarks around town: the church and former convent of Santo Domingo to the north, the blue-trimmed Templo de Guadalupe on the hill to the east, the Cristóbal Colón first-class bus station to the south, and the Templo de San Cristóbal on the mountaintop to the west. **Avenida Insurgentes** connects the town center to the Pan American Hwy., and becomes Av. Utrilla past the main market. It is helpful to think of the city as four quadrants, since all streets change names when crossing imaginary north-south and east-west axes centered at the Zó-

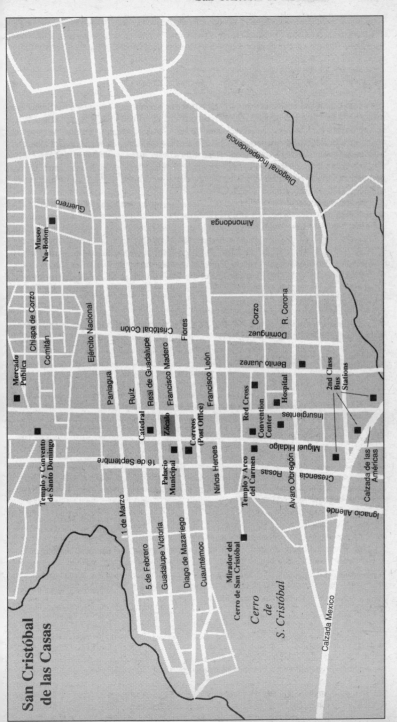

San Cristóbal
de las Casas

calo. Taxis (tel. 823-96) line up along the north side of the Zócalo by the cathedral. Standard fare within town is 2500 pesos; prices to nearby *indígena* villages are negotiable. In town, you probably won't need a taxi unless you're carrying leaden bags.

Practical Information

Tourist Office: (tel. 804-14) on the western edge of the Zócalo under the Palacio Municipal. The well-informed staff speaks English and distributes maps of San Cristóbal. Information available about nearby *indígena* villages. They also sell postage stamps. Open Mon.-Fri. 8am-2pm and 3-8pm, Sat. 9am-2pm and 3-8pm, Sun. 9am-2pm.

Currency Exchange: Bancomer (tel. 812-43), on the Zócalo, as well as **Multibanco Comermex,** Utrilla 5 (tel. 814-67), 1 block north of the Zócalo. Open for exchange Mon.-Fri. 10-11am and 10-11:30am, respectively. You can also change cash and traveler's checks at **Casa de Cambios Lacantun,** Real de Guadalupe 12-A (tel. 825-87), 1 block east of the Zócalo. Open Mon.-Sat. 8:30am-2pm and 4-8pm, Sun. 9am-1pm.

Post Office: Cuauhtémoc at Crescencio Rosas (tel. 807-65), 1 block southwest of the Zócalo. Packages can be mailed Mon.-Fri. 8am-6:30pm, Sat. 9am-1pm. Open Mon.-Fri. 8am-7pm, Sat.-Sun. 9am-1pm. **Postal Code:** 29200.

Telephones: Collect calls can be placed from public pay phones at the Palacio Municipal. Dial 09 for the international operator, 02 for the national version, and M for murder. For direct dial long-distance or domestic service, a *caseta* at Autotransportes Tuxtla charges 7000 pesos per min. to the U.S. Open Mon.-Sat. 8am-9pm, Sun. 8am-2:30pm. The *caseta* at Mazariegos 19 (tel. 834-79), on the right side of the street 2 blocks west of the Zócalo, charges 10,000 pesos per min. to the U.S. Check rates in advance. Open Mon.-Sat. 9am-9pm, Sun. 9:30am-2pm.

Telegrams: Mazariegos 28 (tel. 816-71), 2½ blocks west of the Zócalo. Open for telegrams Mon.-Fri. 8am-midnight, Sat. 9am-9pm, Sun. and festivals 9am-noon; for money orders Mon.-Fri. 9am-1pm and 4-5:30pm, Sat.-Sun. 8am-noon.

Bus Stations: Cristóbal Colón, Pan American Hwy. at Insurgentes (tel. 802-91), 7 blocks south of the Zócalo. Station open daily 6am-9pm. Public toilets. Frequent first-class service to: Tuxtla Gutiérrez (14 per day, 2 hr., 3800 pesos); Comitán (10 per day, 1½ hr., 3900 pesos); Pochutla (at 7am, 11 hr., 27,000 pesos) via Tehuantepec (8 hr., 17,000 pesos) and Huatulco (10 hr., 26,000 pesos); Cuauhtémoc (3 per day, 3 hr., 7800 pesos); Tapachula (at 8am, 9 hr., 22,000 pesos) via Arriaga (5 hr., 10,700 pesos); Tonalá (6 hr., 12,000 pesos); Huixtla (8 hr., 20,000 pesos). Also to: Cortzagoalios (at 7:30am, 10 hr., 26,000 pesos); Villahermosa (at 10am, 7 hr., 14,500 pesos); Mexico City (at 6:30pm, 18 hr., 56,000 pesos) via Córdoba (14 hr., 40,000 pesos). The only bus to Oaxaca leaves at 4:45pm and is usually packed; buy tickets 1 to 2 days in advance (12 hr., 30,000 pesos). Second-class **Autotransportes Lacandonia,**Piño Suarez 11 (tel. 814-55), on the Pan American Hwy. 2 blocks west of Insurgentes; enter by the sign for "Fonda Chonita." Open daily 4am-8pm. To: Ocosingo (17 per day, 2½ hr., 4000 pesos); Mérida (at 6pm, 14 hr., 33,000 pesos); Villahermosa (at 7am, 8 hr., 15,000 pesos); Palenque (6 per day, 5 hr., 9000 pesos); and to neighboring villages. Second-class **Autotransportes Tuxtla** (tel. 805-04), on Ignacio Allende 1 block north of the highway, 3 blocks west of Insurgentes. To: Ocosingo (10 per day, 3900 pesos); Palenque (7 per day, 9100 pesos) via Agua Azul (6500 pesos); Tuxtla (every ½ hr. 6am-9pm, 2 hr., 3800 pesos); Comitán (every hr. 6am-9pm, 2 hr., 3800 pesos); Tapachula (at noon and 5pm, 8 hr., 14,800 pesos); Yajaloon (at 9:30am, 2:30pm, and 8pm, 6400 pesos). Baggage storage (1500 pesos per hr.) open daily 8am-7pm.

English Bookstore: Librería Soluna, Real de Guadalupe 24-D, 1 block east of the Zócalo, has a miniscule rack of used English books. They trade 2-for-1. Open Mon.-Sat. 9:30am-1:30pm and 4:30-8pm, Sun. noon-8:30pm.

Laundromat: Lavandería Automática, Crescencio Rosas 12, (tel. 820-87), 1 block west and 2½ blocks south of the Zócalo. 7000 pesos to wash and dry 3kg. Open Mon.-Sat. 8:30am-6pm. **Casa de Huéspedes Margarita,** Real de Guadalupe 34. Wash and dry 2500 pesos per kg.

Markets: 7 blocks north of the Zócalo, between Utrilla and Domínguez. Open daily 6am-2pm. Best selection on Sat.

Hospital Civil: Insurgentes 24 (tel. 807-70), 4 blocks south of the Zócalo, by the Church of Santa Lucía in Parque Fray Bartolomé. Emergency room open 24 hr.

LET'S GO Travel

1991 CATALOGUE

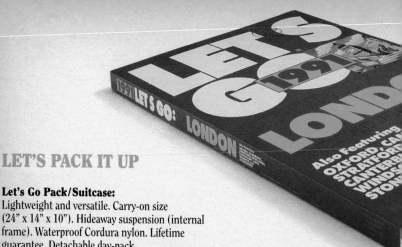

LET'S PACK IT UP

Let's Go Pack/Suitcase:
Lightweight and versatile. Carry-on size
(24" x 14" x 10"). Hideaway suspension (internal
frame). Waterproof Cordura nylon. Lifetime
guarantee. Detachable day-pack.
Navy blue or grey.
10014 Suitcase   **$144.95**
Free shoulder strap and
Let's Go travel diary.

Let's Go Travel Books:
Europe; USA; Britain/Ireland;
France; Italy; Spain/Portugal/Morocco; Gre
Israel/Egypt; Mexico; California/Hawaii; Pac
Northwest; London; New York City.
1016 Specify USA; Europe   **$1**
1017 Specify Country   **$1**
1018 Specify New York or London   **$**
This is $1.00 off the cover price!

International Youth Hostel Guide for
Europe and the Mediterranean:
Lists over 3,000 hostels. A must.
10015 IYHG   **$1**
FREE map of hostels worldwide.

Passport/Money Case:
Zippered pouch of waterproof nylon.
7 1/2" x 4 1/2". Navy or grey.
10011 Passport Case   **$6.50**

Sleepsack: (Required at all hostels)
78" x 30" with 18" pillow pocket. Durable
poly/cotton, folds to pouch size. Washable.
Doubles as a sleeping bag liner.
10010 Sleepsack   **$13**

Undercover Neck Pouch:
Ripstop nylon and soft Cambrelle. 6 1/2" x 5".
Two separate pockets. Black or tan.
10012 Neck Pouch   **$6.95**

Fanny Pack:
Pack cloth nylon. Three compartments.
Charcoal or Marine Blue.
10013 Fanny Pack   **$13.95**

LET'S G🖐® Travel
We wrote the book on budget travel

1991-1992 American Youth Hostel Card

(AYH): Recommended for every hosteler, this card is required by many hostels and brings discounts at others. Applicants must be US residents. Valid internationally.

10022	**Adult AYH (ages 18-55)**	**$25.00**
10035	**Youth AYH (under age 18)**	**$10.00**
10023	**Plastic Case**	**$0.75**

FREE directory of hostels in the USA.

S SEE SOME I.D.

ternational Student
cation Card (ISIC): Provides
s on accommodations, cultural events,
and, this year, increased accident/
insurance. Valid from 9/1/90–12/31/91.

ISIC **$14.00**
nternational Student Travel Guide"
rance information.

ternational Teacher Identification
TIC): Similar benefits to the ISIC.

TIC **$15.00**
nternational Student Travel Guide" and
e information.

uth International Education
ge Card (YIEE): Similar benefits
IC. Available for non-students under
f 26. Valid by calendar year.

YIEE **$14.00**
iscounts for Youth Travel."

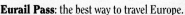

Eurail Pass: the best way to travel Europe.

First Class

10025	15 Day	**$390.**
10026	21 Day	**$498.**
10027	1 Month	**$616.**
10028	2 Months	**$840.**
10029	3 Months	**$1042.**

Flexipass

10030	5 Days within 15	**$230.**
10031	9 Days within 21	**$398.**
10032	14 Days in 1 month	**$498.**

Eurail Youth Pass (Under 26)

10033	1 Month	**$425.**
10034	2 Months	**$560.**
10036	15 days in 3 months	**$340.**
10037	30 days in 3 months	**$540.**

Child Passes (age 4-12) also available.

All Eurail Pass orders include FREE: Eurail Map, Pocket Timetable and Traveler's Guide.

LET'S GO® Travel
One source for all your travel needs

LET'S GET STARTED

PLEASE PRINT OR TYPE. Incomplete applications will be returned.

International Student/Teacher Identity Card (ISIC / ITIC) application enclo

❶ Dated proof of current FULL-TIME status: letter from registrar or administ
   or copy of transcript or proof of payment.
❷ One picture (1½" x 2") signed on the reverse side.
   Applicants must be at least 12 years old.

Youth International Exchange Card (YIEE) application enclose:

❶ Proof of birthdate (copy of passport or birth certificate).
   Applicants must be age 12 – 25.
❷ One picture (1½" x 2") signed on the reverse side.
❸ Passport number _____ ❹ Sex: M

Last Name_____First Name_____

Street_____
             Continental U.S. Addresses only. We do not ship to P.O. Boxes
City_____State_____Zip Code____

Phone ( )_____—_____Citizenship_____

School/College_____Date Trip Begins_____/_____/___

ITEM NUMBER	DESCRIPTION	QUAN-TITY	UNIT OR SET PRICE		TOTAL
			Total Price		
			Total Shipping and Handling		
			Optional Rush Handling (add $9.95)		
			Mass. Residents (5% sales tax on Gear, Books & Maps)		
				TOTAL:	

Shipping and Handling
If your order totals: Add
Up to 30.00 $2.00
30.01 to 100.00 $3.25
Over 100.00 $5.25

Please allow 2-3 weeks for delivery.
RUSH ORDERS DELIVERED WITHIN
ONE WEEK OF OUR RECEIPT.
Enclose check or money order payable to
Harvard Student Agencies, Inc.

Harvard Student Agencies, Inc. Thayer Hall–B Cambridge, MA 02138
(617) 495-9649   1-800-5LETSGO

Red Cross: Ignacio Allende 57 (tel. 807-72), 3 blocks south of the Pan American Hwy. 24-hr. emergency service.

Pharmacies: Central Farmacia (tel. 819-96), on the south side of the Zócalo. Open daily 8am-2pm and 3-8pm. **Farmacia San Martín,** Real de Guadalupe 16 (tel. 801-39), east of the Zócalo. Open Mon.-Sat. 8:30am-9pm. Pharmacies rotate 24-hr. duty; consult the notice board outside the Palacio Municipal on the west side of the Zócalo.

Police: In the Palacio Municipal (tel. 805-54), on the west side of the Zócalo. Open 24 hr.

Accommodations and Camping

Because San Cristóbal has long attracted impecunious Europeans and vacationing Mexican families, inexpensive hotels fill the streets. The cheapest are on Insurgentes, south of the Zócalo and near the bus stations. More expensive and convenient lodgings are farther north on Insurgentes, near the Zócalo, and on Real de Guadalupe east of the Zócalo. At this altitude, there are few bugs, but blankets are necessary as nights can be very cold.

Posada El Candil, Real de Mexicanos 7 (tel. 827-55), 2 blocks west of the Iglesia de Santo Domingo. San Cristóbal's best value includes hot water. The large rooms (better upstairs than down) surround an uninteresting courtyard, but budget travelers from around the globe provide plenty of company. Curfew 11:30pm, but knock after hours. Singles 10,000 pesos. Doubles 12,000 pesos. Triples 18,000 pesos.

Casa de Huéspedes Margarita, Real de Guadalupe 34 (tel. 809-57), 1½ blocks east of the Zócalo. Slightly overpriced, but still San Cristóbal's most popular budget hangout. An old mansion featuring a colonial-style courtyard with patio tables, sofas, and a convenient restaurant. Beds come with 2 wool blankets. Bathrooms shared but spotless; limited hot water; shower early and quickly. Dormitory bunks 9000 pesos. Singles 15,000 pesos. Doubles 20,000 pesos. Triples 27,000 pesos. Quads 36,000 pesos.

Posada Insurgentes, Insurgentes 73 (tel. 824-35), 1½ blocks north of the first-class bus station and 5 blocks south of the Zócalo. Barren rooms off a vacant courtyard exude minimal signs of life. Big beds piled high with blankets. The communal baths shine. 10,000 pesos per person.

Posada Lupita, Insurgentes 46, 6 blocks south of the Zócalo. Work your way through the banana-colored labyrinth to find the lovely garden in back. The world's thinnest person would have trouble squeezing into the singles. Generous supply of newspaper in the bathrooms. 8000 pesos per person.

Posada Cerrillo, Domínguez 27. From the Zócalo, take Real de Guadalupe east 1 block to Domínguez, then 3½ blocks north; the *posada* is on the right. Dark rooms around a yellow courtyard off a quiet street. Smelly common baths, but 24-hr. hot water and nice sheets and spreads. Singles and 1-bed doubles 14,000 pesos. Doubles with 2 beds 16,000 pesos.

Posada Tepeyac, Real de Guadalupe 40 (tel. 801-18), near Cristóbal Colón, a few blocks east of the Zócalo. Many clean, dark rooms with low ceilings and wooly-mammoth blankets. Dense vegetation makes the maze-like courtyard even more confusing. Some baths much cleaner than others. Singles 10,000 pesos, with bath 15,000 pesos. Doubles 15,000 pesos, with bath 20,000 pesos. Triples 20,000 pesos, with bath 25,000 pesos.

Posada Capri, Insurgentes 99 (tel. 830-18), 1 block north of the first-class bus station. Modest rooms around a vacant ballpark-sized courtyard. Street outside sounds like the Yankee Stadium parking lot after a game. Dirty bathrooms. Not a great deal but convenient if arriving in town late at night. Singles 10,000 pesos. Doubles 16,000 pesos. Triples 22,000 pesos.

Rancho San Nicolás (tel. 800-57), on the extension of Francisco León 1km east of town. Camping and trailer park in a quiet, farmland setting. Bathrooms with 24-hr. hot water and trailer sewage hook-ups. Trailer parking 8000 pesos per person. Camping 2000 pesos per person with tent. 5000 pesos per person for small wood cabins.

Food

Thousands of villagers flowing in and out of the city every day buoy a street-vendor economy. The street food is cleaner than in most Mexican towns, but proceed with caution nonetheless. Pastries, chili popcorn, fresh mango, coconut slices, and all kinds of *pasas* (pickled fruits) are available on the Zócalo. Corn on the cob is popular, both boiled and roasted, usually drowned in mayonnaise and *salsa pi-*

cante. If these offerings don't inspire you, a few excellent restaurants in town specialize in granola cuisine.

The *fondas* near the Pan American Hwy. and the bus stations, and in San Cristóbal's *mercado,* serve those with few pesos to spare.

Peña Real del Diez, Real de Mexicanos 10, 2 blocks west of the Iglesia de Santo Domingo. Little House on the Prairie meets Picasso. Tree stumps for benches, fires on cool nights, and modern paintings along the walls. Many entrees can feed 2. Pizza 8000-17,000 pesos. Stuff your face with *El Rancheros:* tacos, quesadillas, beans, guacamole, and tortillas (10,000 pesos). Live music on weekends. Open Tues.-Sun. 8am-10:30pm.

Restaurante Madre Tierra, on Insurgentes at Domínguez, 2½ blocks south of Zócalo. Beautifully carved wood cabinets and classical music generate a civilized image that copmlements the excellent array of international dishes. Quiche lorraine 4000 pesos, and *pollo en curry* 10,000 pesos. Generous servings include homemade wheat bread. Breakfasts 5000-7000 pesos. Open daily 8am-9:45pm. Bakery next door open Mon.-Sat. 9am-8pm, Sun. 9am-2pm.

Restaurant El Bazar, Flavio A. Paniagua 2, 3 blocks north of the Zócalo, and to the right on Paniagua. Bohemian coffeehouse with extensive menu covering dishes from Mexico and the whole wide world. Choices include yogurt with fruit, whole-wheat sandwiches, and superb *tamales* in season. Breakfasts from 4000 pesos, along with a multitude of coffee concoctions (2000-3000 pesos). Meat dishes 10,000 pesos. Ancient waist-high stack of *Newsweek* magazines awaits excavation. Open daily 8am-11pm.

La Familia, Utrilla 12-A, just north of Paniagua. Resembles Madre Tierra but to the tune of Bob Marley and the Wailers: live folk music every evening at 8pm. Granola with fruit and yogurt 4900 pesos. Vegetarian omelette 4800 pesos. Open daily 8am-11pm.

Restaurante Leti, Real de Mexicanos 7-B, next to Posada El Candil. A hole in the wall that serves consistently good food to good company. Some of the cheapest meals around. Three chicken tacos go for a mere 1500 pesos. Large breakfast including eggs, cheese, beans, and ham 3000 pesos. Open daily 7am-9pm.

Cafetería y Lonchería Palenque, Insurgentes 40, 1½ blocks from the bus station. Relax, sip coffee (800 pesos), and watch TV; during commercials check out the local goods on display. *Huevos rancheros* 4000 pesos. Sandwiches 2000-3500 pesos. U.S. dollars and Guatemalan quetzales accepted. Open daily 8am-10:30pm.

Restaurante El Teatro, 1 de Marzo 8, upstairs, north of the cathedral. Candlelit dining room looks out upon roofs and mountain peaks. French and Italian cuisine. Mushroom crepes (3 for 10,500 pesos), chocolate crepes (4500 pesos), and pizza (10,000-15,000 pesos). Live music Fri.-Sat. at 8pm. MC, Visa accepted. Open Mon.-Sat. 1-9:30pm.

Super Pollo, Domínguez 3, 1 block east of the Zócalo. Eat in or take out. Exceptionally tasty fowl. Roasted quarter-chicken 5000 pesos. The Purple Cow says, "Chow, dude." Open daily 7am-10pm.

Ziggley's Palacio, 16 de Agosto 20, at the end of the narrow alley to the right of the cathedral. A vegetarian's most hell-bound nightmare: burgers, burgers everywhere, and not a leafy, green thing in sight. Stout stools of dark oak surround solid sterling tables. The ever-witty waiters, Cristóbal, Jaime, and Mikeykay, aim to please. Oregon rules. Open Fri. 5pm-2am.

Sights

Ever since the Spanish built it in the 16th century, the **Zócalo** has been the physical and spiritual center of town. Colonial buildings border the plaza on three sides, and the **cathedral,** its patterned wooden roof supported by white Corinthian columns, overlooks the fourth. Consecrated 10 years after it was built in 1528, the building now tends a flock of the devout among its pews and a flock of chirping birds in its rafters. The cathedral's Baroque façade rises on one side of a small pedestrian park. (Open Mon.-Sat. 6am-8pm, Sun. 4-8pm.)

Utrilla and Real de Guadalupe, the two streets radiating from the northeastern corner of the Zócalo, contain colorful shops which sell *típico* attire for less than the market stands or neighboring villages. On Saturday mornings, locals do their weekly shopping. Watch, listen, and learn: these shrewd experts wrote the book on bargaining.

North on Utrilla, beyond the **Iglesia de la Caridad,** sits the **Iglesia y Ex-convento de Santo Domingo.** Gold leaf covers the interior of the Santo Domingo, running in elaborate patterns up walls, around portraits, and over the exquisite pulpit in the left nave. The church's intricate Baroque façade, though faded, stands out from the rest of the unremarkable exterior. A pair of two-headed eagles form the crest of the Spanish empire on the façade.

Stashed in Santo Domingo's *ex-convento* is **Sna Jolobil** ("House of Weaving" in Tzeltal), a cooperative of 700 weavers from 20 Tzotzil and Tzeltal villages in the *chiapaneco* highlands. The members' objective is to preserve and revitalize their ancestral weaving techniques. High-quality woven and embroidered items are sold in Sna Jolobil's showroom. Over the surrounding cobblestone paths and grassy areas, dozens of Tzeltal and Tzotzil clothing merchants spread their wares, weaving or spinning wool as they await the next sale. (Cooperative open daily 9am-2pm and 3:30-7:30pm.)

Next door to Sna Jolobil, the **Instituto Nacional de Antropología e Historia Centro Cultural de Los Altos de Chiapas** mounts exhibitions on the history of San Cristóbal and the neighboring villages. (Open Tues.-Sun. 9am-2pm. Admission 1100 pesos.)

San Cristóbal's most famous museum is **Na-Bolom,** on Guerrero at the end of Chiapa de Corzo, in the northeastern section of the city. The name of the museum stems from a Lacandón mispronunciation of the last name of Gertrude (Trudy) Blom and her late husband, archeologist Franz Blom. "Na" means "house" and "Bolom," with the extra "o," is Lacandón for "jaguar," considered the most powerful animal in the jungle. For many decades the Bloms worked and studied among the dwindling *indígena* population in the Lacandón Rainforest along the Guatemala border. Since the death of her husband in 1963, Trudy Blom has continued their work and won acclaim as an ethnologist and photographer. Her latest book, *Bearing Witness* (University of North Carolina Press, US$22), is a photographic study of the Lacandóns.

Even when the 89-year-old Trudy is absent from Na-Bolom, as is often the case, volunteers who live with her at the home-turned-research-center conduct tours of the library, the gardens, and the Bloms' personal museum. The library's manuscripts concentrate on Mexico and Central America, with numerous periodicals, news clippings, and rare papers dealing with rainforest ecology and the plight of Guatemalan refugees. The collection also documents the Bloms' own lives and achievements. Library materials can be perused by the public on the premises. The building was originally intended as a seminary; a small ornate chapel now serves as a gallery of post-Conquest *chiapaneco* religious art created by *ladinos* and *indígenas* alike. Other rooms in the main house are devoted to archeological finds from the nearby site of Moxviquil, religious artifacts from the Lacandón Forest, and the work of artists in residence. The best available map of the Lacandón Rainforest, drawn by Franz Blom, can be purchased here.

The house and museum of Na-Bolom does triple-duty as a guest house for those with a genuine interest in the Bloms' work (about US$50 a night; proceeds support the work of the center). Inquire before you arrive, since rooms are always in demand. Enormous, ranch-style meals, included in the price, served around a monstrous table. Dinner (15,000 pesos) at 1:30pm and supper (12,500 pesos) at 7pm sharp are shared with non-overnight guests. Make reservations one day in advance and ascertain that Trudy will attend. In the extensive gardens behind the house, several buildings are reserved exclusively for visiting Lacandóns, who extend to Trudy and other Na-Bolom affiliates similar hospitality on their visits to the villages. Na-Bolom accepts volunteers for a six-month stay at the museum. (Museum open to the general public by guided tour Tues.-Sun. at 4:30pm. Tours in English and Spanish 3000 pesos. Library open Mon.-Sat. 9am-1pm. For guest-house reservations or information concerning the volunteer program, write or call Na-Bolom, Vicente Guerrero 33, tel. 814-18.)

The hill on the east side of town is capped by the **Iglesia de Guadalupe.** To reach the church from the Zócalo, follow Real de Guadalupe east and climb the long flight of baby-blue stairs. The church is open only for festivals and mass but the panorama from the summit justifies the hike. Although not as impressive as the daytime view, a nighttime peek at the neon crown over the Virgin's head raises the eyebrows of pilgrims and tourists alike.

Easily visible from Guadalupe, but almost a kilometer away in the opposite direction, the **Iglesia de San Cristóbal de las Casas** requires an even more arduous ascent. The church rewards pilgrims with a better view. Behind the church stands a 20-ft. crucifix built of license plates that gives the neon crown of Guadalupe a stiff run for its money in the annual "Chintziest *Chiapaneco* Religious Symbol" contest. To reach the foot of San Cristóbal's steep stairs, walk 3 blocks west from the Zócalo on Mazariegos, and turn left on Ignacio Allende. (Church open daily 9am-4pm. Beware of those who haunt the trails surrounding the church; women have been harrassed here, especially in the afternoon and evening.

Three blocks south of the Zócalo on Hidalgo, the distinctive tower of the **Templo del Carmen** surges skyward. The adjoining courtyard is defined by three buildings, which together sponsor more cultural events every year than the rest of Chiapas combined. The polygonal structure on the courtyard's north side is the auditorium of the Casa de la Cultura, which hosts concerts of classical and folk music nightly. (Peformances often but not always free. For details, contact the tourist office, consult the list posted on the auditorium door, or call 823-49. Auditorium open Mon.-Sat. 9am-2pm and 6-8pm.) The **Instituto de las Bellas Artes,** on the east side of the courtyard, gives instruction in the visual and performing arts. On the south side, San Cristóbal's **Casa de la Cultura** houses traveling crafts exhibits as well as permanent displays of local art. Amid the spectrum of snapdragons, lilies, and rosebushes in the central courtyard, a discreet picnic may go undisturbed.

Exceptionally colorful clothing and people jam San Cristóbal's daily morning market, at the northern end of Utrilla. Cheap veggies and fruit abound, but the *indígena* clothing for sale can often be had for less elsewhere in the city. Theoretically restricted to one square block, the market spills over into the nearby side streets. (Market open daily 4:30am-4pm.)

Entertainment

A soporific silence pervades the streets of San Cristóbal after 10pm. If your biological clock tends to tick on past this witching hour, plan ahead. A few restaurants have live folk music and a lively cocktail scene late at night. **La Galeria,** Domínguez 22 (tel. 216-22), stays open until 11pm and has a band on tap every night except Wednesday. When the music stops there, head across town to **La Peña Real del Diez,** where the owners and other locals play improvisational folk music when they're not scampering from table to table topping off everyone's beer. Check posters around town and in front of the tourist office for other options. If the folk scene isn't lively enough for you, shake your booty at **Disco Princess** or **Disco Crystal,** across the street from one another on the Pan American Hwy., 300m toward Comitán from the Cristóbal Colón bus station. One or both of these discotheques is open every night from Thursday through Sunday, and the music doesn't stop until 5 or 6am. The cover is 6000-10,000 pesos depending on the night of the week. On Sunday evening, the Zócalo fills with townspeople who come out for an after-dinner *paseo* (stroll).

Horseback riding is extremely popular on the trails around San Cristóbal. The villages of San Juan Chamula and Zinacantán, both about 10km to the northwest across cornfields and back roads, are good excuses for taking a ride. The route to the villages proceeds along a gravel surface for a stretch before cutting through some beautiful farm country. El Arcotete, a natural arch and rock formation 4km east of town, and the Grutas de San Cristóbal, 10km to the southeast (see Near San Cristóbal), are also worth a gallop. Horse rental prices and departure points fluctuate with the weather and the animals' health. If you are concerned about the latter, check for sores under the horses' saddles. For rental information, check at the city's travel agencies or drop by the Casa de Huéspedes Margarita, which charges 40,000 pesos per person for a five-hour trek.

Many hiking trails twist through the lush hills around San Cristóbal. One of the most convenient hikes leads from the village of Chamula 7km to the village of Zinacantán. The walk winds through rolling *milpas* (cornfields) and typical thatched-roof *indígena* dwellings, concluding with a stunning view from the ridge above Zinacantán. The journey from Chamula to Zinacantán is less strenuous than the hike in the opposite direction. The trail out of Zinacantán starts at the sharp turn in the road, about ½km out of town toward San Cristóbal. From Chamula, follow the dirt road that ascends the hill across the Zócalo from the church. For a longer hike, cover the segment between San Cristóbal and Chamula on foot, which adds another two hours; the route runs uphill the whole way.

Another full-day option is a round-trip trek to a secluded waterfall on a small river east of town. Follow Francisco León east from Insurgentes, past the San Nicolás campground, and across a larger highway until you reach the river. Travel four hours upstream through farmland and forest; it is polite to ask permission (almost always granted) before crossing private property. Break out the obligatory picnic and take a well-deserved dip upon arrival. No signs mark the way and tourists frequently get lost; leave early and allow some time for aimless wandering.

For the more sedate adventurer, an hour or two at **Baños Mercedarios** merits consideration. Reach these steam baths, at 1 de Marzo 55, by walking 2 blocks north of the Zócalo on Utrilla and then left on 1 de Marzo for 4 blocks. (Open daily 6:30am-7:30pm.) Steam baths cost 5000 pesos, Turkish baths (dry heat) 3000 pesos, and hot showers 3000 pesos. For a small fee the baths will provide every possible accessory (towels, shampoo, soap, razors, etc.).

Seasonal Events

San Cristóbal's Semana Santa is rather *tranquila*. Many business establishments close their doors, and the processions and cultural events that do take place are of a decidedly reverent mood. On Easter Sunday, however, Semana Santa gives way to the week-long **Feria de la Primavera y de la Paz.** Before the riotous revelry really gets going, a local beauty queen is selected to preside over the festivities, which include concerts, dances, bullfights, Aerobie tosses, rooster fights, and baseball games. Hotel rooms for either week must be reserved several months in advance.

One of the most exotic of regional festivals is Chamula's **Carnaval** (Mardi Gras). The celebration begins when about 40,000 *indígenas* pack this small village one week before Miércoles de Ceniza (Ash Wednesday). The event happens to coincide with Lent, but has its origins in an ancient Mayan ritual concerning the five "lost" days at the end of the 360-day agricultural cycle. During the festivities, men don monkeyskin hats, and sing and dance while religious leaders run through fires to purify themselves.

In San Cristóbal and the many villages in its vicinity, hardly a week goes by without some kind of religious festival; consult the detailed list at the tourist office.

Near San Cristóbal

On Sunday morning, the action moves from San Cristóbal to the markets of nearby villages. However, bad roads and infrequent bus service make visiting more than one village in a single morning almost impossible. Buses do not connect the towns directly; all service is via San Cristóbal. The exception to this maddening scenario is Chamula, 10km from San Cristóbal on a well-paved road. Chamula's market lasts into the afternoon (although selection is poorer later in the day), and a trip here can follow a visit to Zinacantán's morning-only market.

Many of the town populations are divided between the *mestizos,* who own and run the businesses, and *indígenas,* who live on the surrounding farmland and show their faces in public only on market day. Each *indígena* group has its own distinctive clothing patterns and colors; this part of Chiapas is one of the few regions in Mexico where people maintain traditional dress codes. Photographers should be particularly cautious, since many of the people are violently opposed to photography on account of their religious beliefs. An indiscreet barrage of camera-clicking tourists has stirred up an appreciable degree of hostility in the nearer, more visited villages. Anger climaxed several years ago when two tourists ignored warnings expressly forbidding photography in Chamula's church and were stoned to death by an outraged populace. Consider leaving all camera equipment in San Cristóbal and buying postcards upon return. Visitors should pay particular attention to their own dress and conduct: revealing clothing (including shorts) is coldly received in these communities, as are abuses of regional dress. For instance, women should not wear the broad, ribboned hats reserved in most villages for men.

Many *indígena* villages still uphold the *cargo* (burden) tradition. After years of accumulating wealth, prospective *cargo*-holders place their names on a list of political positions ranging from minor village posts to the mayor's office. The election is held on the eve of the new year; new officials must then assume the *cargo,* which means that they foot the bill for the new year's *fiestas.* Tradition places *cargo*-holders under intense pressure to make the year's festivals the biggest and best ever. Major *cargo*-holders spend themselves and their relatives into debt for fireworks, liquor, Aerobies, and decorations. In return, they receive unparalleled prestige; the waiting lists for such positions are often filled seven to eight years in advance. Power is handed to the new leaders at noon on December 31, amid much pomp and celebration that lasts until midnight. Check the tourist office for dates of festivals for each village.

San Juan Chamula

San Juan Chamula is the largest and most touristed of the villages around San Cristóbal. Chamulan men wear white or black wool *sarapes* tied with thick leather belts. Designs decorating the sleeves of their white tunics indicate their *pueblito* or *colonia.* Only village officials or elders drape ribbons over their large "10-gallon" sombreros. The women often fold their red-fringed, deep blue or black wraps into a square on their heads and twist colored ribbons into their long braids. Chamula is a fascinating place, but the town has seen so many tourists in recent years that it has ceased to be friendly; the 25,000 inhabitants have earned a reputation for hostility to outsiders.

Before entering the brightly painted church (open daily 5am-8pm), you must obtain a permit (2000 pesos) from the tourist office on the Zócalo and the permission of the guards inside the church. Under no circumstances should you take pictures. Chamulans believe that a part of their soul is captured in every snapshot, and they must go through extensive healing ceremonies to regain it. The Chamulan healing ceremonies, performed inside the church, are the same as those practiced by the ancient Maya, with a few interesting variations. The Catholic idols introduced by the Spaniards have merely assumed the position of the pre-Conquest idols as manifestations of the Mayan gods. The *espejos* (mirrors) hung around each saint's neck help the saint identify the person offering the prayer; in order not to confuse the saints, Chamulans pray one at a time to the effigies.

Chamulans believe that every mote of our material world has its counterpart in the spiritual world, represented by the mountains encircling the community. When a babe is born, a corresponding guardian animal is born at the same time in the spiritual mountains. The pine needles covering the floor of the church, the flowers, and the burning incense are intended to bring sufferers closer to the spiritual mountains, and thus to the interceding gods. You may notice bottles of Coca-Cola and Pepsi in the shaman's medicine kit on the floor. Over the past 10 years, soft drinks have gradually replaced water and fruit juice as the ingredient mixed with *posh,* a slightly alcoholic drink made from sugar cane. Chamulans drink *posh* to reach a state of ecstasy from which they recall all of their sins and then are cleansed. This ceremony can grow dangerous during festivals when overly purified villagers walk through fire and set off fireworks into the large crowds.

Chamulans stubbornly resist both religious and secular Mexican authority. Catholic bishops are allowed in the church only for baptisms. The government medical clinic to the north of the Zócalo goes practically unused.

Outside and to the left of the church, Chamula's *cargo*-holders sit in a circle every Sunday from 8am to noon—the minor holders on the outside, major holders on the inside, and the *presidente* in the middle. Villagers approach to discuss business, and small crowds often assemble while the mayor dispenses justice.

In addition to Chamula's Carnaval (see Seasonal Events above), the **Fiesta de San Sebastian** (Jan. 20), the **Fiesta de San Mateo** (Sept. 21-22), and the **Fiesta de San Juan Bautista** (June 22-24) warrant a trip to the village. **Combis** to Chamula (½ hr., 1000 pesos) leave when full (every ½ hr. 6am-5pm) from Utrilla by the market in San Cristóbal. To reach Chamula by car, drive west from the Zócalo on Guadalupe Victoria and bear right after crossing the small bridge on Diagonal Ramón Larraínzar. At the fork, bear right for Chamula, which is at the end of an 8km stretch of paved road.

Zinacantán

Close to Chamula is the smaller village of Zinacantán, whose citizens' short, almost triangular hot-pink *sarapes* stand out like sore thumbs. On both men and women, tassles of deep red and purple fly in the breeze, and the men often top their straw hats with colored ribbons as well: long ribbons designate a man's married status. During *fiestas,* Zinacantecans maintain ancient Mayan custom by wearing high heel-guards on their *huaraches* (sandals). Their biggest *fiestas* are **Semana Santa,** the **Fiesta de San Lorenzo** (August 8-11), and the **Fiesta de San Pedro Mártir** (March 29).

Unlike Chamula, this village has accepted the Catholic clergy. The handsome, whitewashed church is used exclusively for Catholic worship, while the small, white convent at its side is a separate facility for ritual healing and pre-Conquest forms of worship. Both the convent and the church hold services on Sunday mornings. To visit the church you must pad the clerical coffers (1000 pesos); tickets are available inside, but it's best to report to the Presidencia Municipal (town hall) first. Tourists who step inside the convent are expected to drop a small donation into the *limosna* box. Zinacantán does not tolerate picture-taking here or anywhere else in the village.

Combis to Zinacantán cost 1000 pesos and leave San Cristóbal from the lot near the market as they fill (6am-8pm). To drive to Zinacantán, follow Guadalupe Victoria west from the Zócalo and turn right after crossing the small bridge on Diagonal Ramón Larraínzar. At the fork, turn left toward the "Bienvenido a Zinacantán" sign.

San Andrés Larraínzar

San Andrés Larraínzar, 26km northwest of San Cristóbal and 16km from Chamula, is more difficult to reach than most other villages, making its citizens much friendlier toward the outsiders who do make the trip. Mexicans refer to the village as Larraínzar, but local Tzotziles prefer the name San Andrés. Since many of the villagers refuse to carry their produce for an hour and a half over bumpy terrain to San Cristóbal, the market (open until 1pm) is better stocked here than at Chamula or Zinacantán, but goods are bartered rather than sold.

Combis make several trips on Sunday to San Andrés from the San Cristóbal market, the first leaving at 7am. The last returning *combi* leaves San Andrés at 11am. Hitching is possible but difficult. To reach San Andrés by car, take the road northwest from San Cristóbal to Chamula and continue past the village on the unpaved road. On a curve some 10km later, a prominent sign announcing "S.A. Larraínzar" points left to a road climbing the steep side of the valley; the village lies approximately 6km beyond the fork. The entire journey from Chamula takes roughly half an hour at top speeds of 35-40km per hour.

Chenalhó

Even farther beyond Chamula, Chenalhó seems far more remote than its 36km from San Cristóbal would indicate. *Norteamericanos* are a rare enough sight here to cause some small children to burst into tears at their appearance and to arouse a friendly interest on the part of almost everyone else.

In Chenalhó, typical dress for men varies from white or black ponchos worn over pants and bound with heavy belts, to very short, light, white tunics, to Budweiser T-shirts and other such garb. Women who have not adopted more current fashions dress uniformly in dark blue *naglas* (skirts) and white *tocas* (shawls) embroidered with bright orange flowers. One small store behind the enclosed market supplies almost all the ready-to-wear clothing for the town. The market spreads out into the plaza in front of the church on Sunday and sells mostly foodstuffs, including *chiche,* a potent drink made from fermented cane. Villagers enthusiastically wave visitors into **San Pedro,** the church in the town's center, which is a secular as well as religious meeting place; the main aisle often shimmers with the light from candles riding on waves of incense. Chenalhó residents celebrate the **Fiesta de San Sebastián** (June 13), the **Fiesta de San Pedro** (May 27-30), and the **Fiesta de Jesús de la Buena Esperanza** (Aug. 6).

You'll find Chenalhó's most respectable restaurant and its only hotel, run by Señor Albert, at 16 de Septiembre 49, parallel to the main street away from the river and toward Chamula. The quiet, clean restaurant is open daily from 8am to 7pm.

Autotransportes Fray Bartolomé de las Casas operates buses to Chenalhó and the even more remote town of Pantelhó. The San Cristóbal bus leaves from the station on Utrilla north of the market at 7am and 1pm (3000 pesos) and returns to San Cristóbal at 5am and 3pm. Bus trips take two hours. Driving to Chenalhó can cut transit time in half, but only at a teeth-chattering speed of 35-40km per hour on the dirt road northwest of Chamula.

Tenejapa

Tenejapa, 27km from San Cristóbal across several small mountain ranges, is one of the area's most picturesque *indígena* settlements. Also one of the poorest villages in the region, Tenejapa has experienced many internal problems in recent years, including debates over the collectivized price structure of *artesanía* goods. Furthermore, several tourists reportedly have been assaulted here over the last several years: to ensure your safety, keep your camera out of sight and pick up a tourist ticket in the Palacio Municipal.

Occasional problems notwithstanding, Tenejapa is a simple, quiet village, where the men usually wear black knee-length tunics and ribboned hats and women don colorful *huipiles.* Tenejapa's only paved street doubles as the market.

The trip from San Cristóbal to Tenejapa takes an hour and costs 3000 pesos. *Combis* and buses leave daily every half-hour or so between 7am and 2pm from the lot near the market. Take an early bus (8am at the latest) to the village and leave by noon, since it's sometimes difficult to find a returning *combi* later in the afternoon. To drive the 27km to Tenejapa, head east on Francisco Madero from the Zócalo toward the blue-and-white Church of Guadalupe, and turn right before the road comes to a dead end. After passing Periférico, turn left at the fork. A good distance out of town, a road branches left to Pantelhó; bear right for Tenejapa.

Grutas de San Cristóbal

Ten kilometers southeast of San Cristóbal off the Pan American Hwy., the Grutas de San Cristóbal is one large cave extending deep into a mountain. A slippery boardwalk penetrates ½km into the illuminated cavern, past some jaw-dropping stalactites and stalagmites. The cool, moist air is very refreshing on warmer days.

When asked, second-class buses en route to Comitán or smaller villages will drop off passengers at the sign for the *grutas* on the Pan American Highway (1500 pesos). The beautiful, short walk to the site through the tall pines of the Parque Recreativo

Grutas de San Cristóbal is a delight in itself. (Cave admission 1000 pesos.) Buses leave San Cristóbal from 9am-5pm. Be sure to leave the caves before 5pm to catch the last returning bus.

Chiapa de Corzo

Legend has it that when the Spaniards came to Chiapa de Corzo in 1528 asking for the town keys, they were warmly greeted by masses of *indígenas* jumping to their deaths from the treacherous cliffs of Cañón El Sumidero. The *chiapanecos* chose that sacrificial path over the option of slavery to the conquistadors. Nowadays, this small town greets the few *extranjeros* who pass through in a more hospitable manner; the lone hotel and breezy riverside restaurants provide shelter and nourishment for those whose main interest lies in boat trips through the encompassing canyon.

Orientation and Practical Information

Chiapa de Corzo sits on the Río Grijalva, 10km east of Tuxtla Gutiérrez and 74km west of San Cristóbal de las Casas. Most points of interest lie on or near the sizable Zócalo (also called Pl. Angel Albino Corzo), which is bounded on the north by 21 de Octubre, on the east by La Mexicanidad, on the south by Julián Grajales, and on the west by 5 de Febrero. One block south of the plaza are the city's cathedral and market; beyond them flows the river. Boats to Cañón El Sumidero leave from the *embarcadero* (dock) at the end of 5 de Febrero, 2 blocks south of the Zócalo. The Cristóbal Colón station is on 21 de Octubre 1 block east of the plaza; buses and *combis* to and from Tuxtla Gutiérrez stop ½ block from the plaza, in an alley on the north side of 21 de Octubre.

Chiapa de Corzo does not offer many services to the tourist. Fortunately, metropolitan Tuxtla Gutiérrez is only a half-hour, 700-peso *combi* ride away.

Bus Station: Cristóbal Colón, 21 de Octubre 26, 1 block east of the Zócalo. Unfortunately, all buses are *de paso* from Tuxtla with only a few seats set aside for Chiapa de Corzo pickups. As a result, tickets are often sold out a day in advance. Either buy early or, better yet, backtrack to Tuxtla for your connection. People will tell you to take a local bus to the *crucero* (crossroads) and then catch the bus to San Cristóbal. The *crucero* bus, however, is no less crowded than the one that leaves from the station; it's better to wait in town. To San Cristóbal (6 per day 6:30am-2:45pm, 3100 pesos). *Combis* go to Tuxtla Gutiérrez (every 15 min. 6am-8pm, ½ hr., 700 pesos). Service on Sunday and during festivals depends on demand.

Post Office: Cenobio Aguilar 234 bis (tel. 602-35), 1½ blocks north of the Zócalo. Open Mon.-Fri. 8am-6pm, Sat. 9am-1pm. **Postal Code:** 29160.

Telephone Code: 961.

Market: 1 block from the Zócalo on La Mexicanidad, to the left of the cathedral. Teems with high-quality produce and baked goods. Open daily 4am-6pm.

Pharmacy: Farmacia San Marcos, 21 de Octubre 102, on the northeast corner of the Zócalo among other pharmacies. Open daily 8am-2pm and 4-8pm.

Police: In the Palacio Municipal (tel. 602-26). Open 24 hr.

Accommodations and Food

Hotel Los Angeles, Julián Grajales 2 (tel. 600-48), at La Mexicanidad on the southeast corner of the Zócalo, is the only game in town. Fortunately, it's also cheap, clean, and attractive. Get an edge on the Mexican motorists competing for the few rooms by calling ahead. Guests enjoy a colonial courtyard, clean tiled bathrooms, spacious rooms with headboards on every bed, and French windows that open onto the street. (Singles 25,000 pesos. Doubles 30,000 pesos.)

Restaurants in Chiapa de Corzo are pleasant, but don't quite qualify as bastions of culinary innovation; the seafood *palapas* lining the docks are the best bet.

Sights

Most visitors look past Chiapa de Corzo's colonial comeliness, viewing the town as the departure point for boat tours of the nearby **Cañón El Sumidero.** The two-hour, 47km trip down the Río Grijalva and back provides a dramatic view of the immense cliffs on both sides, as well as of the alligators and exotic birds that live in the Grijalva's murky green waters and encroaching forest.

Speedboats journey through the canyon along the tranquil waterway formed by the recently completed Netzahualcóyotl Dam. From Chiapa, boats head up the river, passing under the road to Tuxtla Gutiérrez on the way. After the bridge, the banks of the river grow steeper, the cornfields and grazing land disappear, and the Grijalva fills the narrowing chasm. The voyage includes brief sojourns inside caverns and under waterfalls. The most spectacular waterfall, the *Arbol de Navidad,* plunges over a series of rock terraces and dissipates into a fine mist that envelops the boat.

Boats leave from Chiapa's *embarcadero* daily from 7am to 4pm. Cruises cost 10,000 pesos per person for groups of six or more, 80,000 pesos per boatload when fewer than six people take part. Usually, at least 10 people pack into each *lancha.* You can also take boats up the canyon from Cahuaré, where the highway to Tuxtla Gutiérrez crosses the river near the island *balneario* of the same name. A *colectivo* boat also runs from Cahuaré with similar prices. The trip is popular year-round, especially during Semana Santa and Christmas holidays, but it's best to go at the height of the rainy season in August, when all four waterfalls gush hardest.

Most of Chiapa de Corzo's rich architectural treasures date from the city's colonial period. The **Zócalo** contains two colonial structures: a small clock tower and a fountain shaped like the crown of Queen Isabel of Spain. This famous Moorish fountain, often called **La Pila,** brought the town fresh drinking water during an epidemic in 1562. The fountain taps 5km of underground waterways. Inside the fountain, tile plaques recount some of the area's colonial history.

The red-and-white **Catedral de Santo Domingo** (open daily 6am-2pm and 4pm-6:30pm) sits 1 block south of the Zócalo near Río Grijalva. The most famous of the four bells dangling in its tower, Teresa de Jesús, is named after a mystic Spanish saint and bears a mysterious inscription. When most of the writing had long been worn away, legally blind locals swore they could still discern the Spanish words "My name is María Teresa; I weigh 100 *quintales,* and anyone who doesn't believe it can lift me up and see." Only after a visit in 1916 by the literate Don Guillermo Gugelman of Switzerland did it become clear that the words, the only legible one of which was "María," were actually in Gothic, not Roman letters, and that the writing was in Latin, not Spanish. The bell's inscription was merely an elaborate "Hail Mary." You figure it out.

The **Palacio Municipal's** main entrance, on the Zócalo, displays the Chiapan coat of arms, granted by Carlos I of Spain (Holy Roman Emperor Karl V) soon after the Conquest. Upstairs by the balcony, a map of the city diagrams the Battle of 21 de Octubre, in which revolutionary Colonel Urdina led local forces against Don Juan Ortega. The mural on the wall of the central stairway gives an interesting account of the battle.

Used as forts by the revolutionaries, the three churches portrayed in the mural overlook the city and are a hop, skip, and a jump away. **San Gregorio** is visible from the edge of the Zócalo farthest from the river; take any road uphill from the Zócalo and bear right toward the white church for the best overview of the town. Facing the river, the ruined **Convento de San Sebastián** and the dome of another large, colonial church loom to the left. Visit the convent in early morning, before the masses arrive. Because San Gregorio is seldom attended and San Sebastián has been abandoned altogether, both have become popular as late-night partying spots.

Chiapa de Corzo is well known for its lacquerwork; the **Museo de la Laca** on López, bordering the Zócalo, celebrates this handicraft. The museum has some interesting festival masks and pottery, and serves as a refuge during the afternoon *siesta* or summer rains. (Open Tues.-Sun. 9am-7pm. Free.) Lacquering lessons (materials and tools included) are offered here free of charge, Monday through Friday from 4 to 7pm.

Chiapa's **Fiesta de San Sebastián** (Jan. 16-22) is most famous for "Los Parachicos": men in heavy costumes and stifling masks dancing dawn-to-dusk under the hot Chiapas sun. The fiesta's *gran finale* is the mock **Combate Naval** between "Spaniards" and "Indios." More a beauty contest than a battle, the *combate* features elaborately decorated boats, costumed sailors, and fireworks. All the action passes by the *embarcadero*.

Tuxtla Gutiérrez

When the Zoque founded a village near the remains of an ancient settlement known as Acala, they dubbed it Coyatocmo ("land of rabbits"). After the Aztec invasion, Coyatocmo was renamed Tuchtlán. And when the marauding Spaniards arrived, they "castilianized" the Aztec name to Tuxtla and scared off all the hares.

In the middle of the 19th century, a fresh struggle for power brought about yet another name change. Joaquín Miguel Gutiérrez, son of a Spanish-born merchant, was named governor of Chiapas immediately the conservative *centralistas* gained control of Mexico. The liberal took up arms against the new government, but the centralist forces soon overwhelmed Gutiérrez and his men, who valiantly held out in a local church. Some say Gutiérrez was then betrayed, killed by one of his own men, and dragged through the streets. According to other accounts, Gutiérrez wrapped himself in the Mexican flag and jumped from the church tower rather than submit to the *centralistas*. In any case, he died a dramatic death in his native Tuxtla in 1838, and 14 years later the city was renamed Tuxtla Gutiérrez in his honor.

Today, Tuxtla Gutiérrez is the capital of Chiapas state and the transportation and commerce center for much of southern Mexico. Though renowned for its gold filigree and carved amber, Tuxtla now supplies the Republic with most of its molded plastics. The city's rapid commercial success has given it a modern gloss, but Tuxtla has endeavored to stem the tide of cinderblock construction with parks, museums, an excellent zoo, and other cultural and recreational facilities.

Orientation

Just west of the center of Chiapas state, Tuxtla Gutiérrez lies 289km south of Villahermosa via Rte. 195 and 190, and about 160km east-northeast of the Pacific coast via Rte. 190. San Cristóbal de las Casas is 84km east on Rte. 190.

Several bus stations and two airports serve Tuxtla Gutiérrez. To get to the *centro* from the **ADO** station, go left (north) on 9 Pte. for 5 blocks to Av. Central. Turn right and the Zócalo is 9 blocks ahead. The first-class **Cristóbal Colón** bus station stands at 2 Nte. and 2 Pte. To get to the Zócalo, go left on 2 Nte. Pte. for 2 blocks. The Zócalo is 2 blocks to the right on Calle Central. The second-class **Autotransportes Tuxtla Gutiérrez** station is in a cul-de-sac near 3 Sur and 7 Ote. From the station, turn right and then right again into the walled-in alley that doubles as a market. Make the first left onto 2 Sur, and continue west to Calle Central—the Zócalo is 2 blocks to the right. Travelers from Chiapa de Corzo often disembark at a small station on 3 Ote. between 2 and 3 Sur. As you face the street from the bus stop, head left for Av. Central, then left again for the Zócalo.

If you're heading on to San Cristóbal (often referred to as Las Casas on bus schedules) or Comitán, buy your ticket as early as possible. Both first- and second-class buses tend to fill up quickly, especially in the afternoon and evening. Cristóbal Colón limits tickets to the number of seats; if they leave you out in the cold, head over to the second-class station.

Streets are labeled in Mexico's infamous numeric/geographic system. **Avenida Central** (sometimes called Av. 14 de Septiembre) is the city's east-west axis. Perpendicular to this is **Calle Central** (called Central Nte. above Av. Central and Central Sur below). Streets on either side of Calle Central are numbered beginning with

1 and increasing away from Central. These north-south streets are designated Ote. or Pte. depending on whether they are east or west, respectively, of Calle Central. Street numbers on streets running east-west increase progressively away from Av. Central and are designated Nte. or Sur. Occasionally, a street address will include two directions (e.g. 5 Sur Pte.), which locates it in one quadrant of the city. Expect to be confused.

Note that Av. Central changes its name. To the east of Calle Central it is Central Ote., to the west Central Pte: about 15 blocks west of the center of town it becomes Blvd. Dr. Belisario Domínguez, and 11 blocks east Blvd. Angel Albino Corzo. Calles 11 and 12 Ote. are major routes that extend beyond the immediate urban area. South on 12 is the zoo; north on 11 is Parque Madero.

The downtown area focuses on the Zócalo at the intersection of Av. Central and Calle Central, a huge expanse of tile, manicured trees, and dozens of benches occupied by shoe shiners and exhausted shoppers. You will also find government offices, the cathedral, and much of the city's nightlife here.

Municipal buses (250-300 pesos) operate from 5am to 10pm. Major lines run west on 2 Sur, east on 1 Sur, north on 11 Ote., and south on 12 Ote. Buses post destinations on their windshields. *Colectivos* (300 pesos) run frequently through the city from 6am to 10pm, but are sometimes difficult to catch. To snag one, stand on one of the corners with a blue *colectivo* sign and hold out fingers to indicate the number of passengers in your party. If the vehicle fails to stop, don't despair, because it's probably already full. If it does stop, jump in fast; otherwise, locals will do so, leaving you waiting despondently on the corner to hail a taxi (2500 pesos).

Practical Information

Federal Tourist Office: Domínguez 950 (tel. 255-09), 4th floor, 17 long blocks west of the Zócalo just past the huge Bancomer building on the north side of the street. The best place to launch your tour of Chiapas. Has photocopied town maps in English unavailable in the towns themselves plus useful information on Bonampak and Yaxchilán. Extra-helpful staff. Some English spoken. Open Mon.-Fri. 8am-8pm.

Currency Exchange: Bánamex, 1 Pte. 141 (tel. 200-14), at 1 Sur, and **Bancomer,** Av. Central 214 (tel. 282-51), at 2 Pte., change currency Mon.-Fri. 10am-noon. Some local businesses may also change currency. Try **El Gran Cheffe** Av. Central Pte. 238 (tel. 208-07), next to Hotel Avenida. Open daily 7am-midnight.

Post Office: 1 Nte. and 2 Ote. (tel. 204-16), in the large building on the northeast corner of the Zócalo. Open Mon.-Fri. 8am-7pm, Sat.-Sun. and *festivos* 9am-1pm.

Telephones: Place collect calls from the public pay phones. Dial 02 for the international operator. *Casetas* scattered throughout the city handle direct calls only; the one nearest the Zócalo is at 2a. Sur Ote. 669. Look for the "Yumi" sign. All *casetas* open daily 9am-10pm. **Telephone Code:** 961.

Telegrams: (tel. 202-81) on the Zócalo next to the post office. Open for money orders Mon.-Fri. 9am-noon and 3-7pm, Sat. 9am-2pm; for telegrams Mon.-Fri. 9am-9pm, Sat. 9am-5pm.

Airports: Aeropuerto Llano San Juan (tel. 206-01), about 35km west of the city on the Pan American Hwy. *Colectivos* (7500 pesos) run daily 7:30am-12:20am to the airport. **Mexicana,** Av. Central Pte. 206 (tel. 200-20), at the corner of 1 Pte. Daily nonstop flights to Mexico City at 11am and on Mon., Wed., Fri., and Sun. at 1:50pm. Office open Mon.-Fri. 8am-7pm, Sat. 9am-2pm. **Aeropuerto Teran** (tel 229-20), on the Pan American Hwy. **AeroCaribe,** Domínguez 180 (tel. 220-22), in the Hotel Bonampak. Daily flights to Cancún via Mérida and Villahermosa depart at 4pm; to Oaxaca at 2:45pm. Office open Mon.-Fri. 9am-2pm and 4-7pm, Sat. 9am-2pm. **Aviacsa,** 1 Nte. Pte. 1026 (tel. 309-18). To: Tapachula (daily at 6:30am and Mon.-Fri. at 2:30pm); Mexico City (daily at 9:30am); Oaxaca (Mon.-Fri. at 11am and Sat.-Sun. at 10am); Villahermosa (daily at 2pm and Mon.-Fri. at 10am); Palenque (Mon.-Sat. at 8am); Huixtla (Mon., Wed., Fri., and Sun. at 10:30am); and Manititlán (Mon., Wed., Fri., and Sat. at 7am). Office open Mon.-Fri. 9am-2pm and 4-7pm, Sat. 9am-2pm.

Bus Stations: Cristóbal Colón,, 2 Nte. 221 (tel 226-24), near 2 Pte. First-class service to: Comitán (every hr. from 6am, 3½ hr., 5500 pesos) via San Cristóbal (2½ hr., 2700 pesos); Tapachula (14 per day, 7 hr., 12,750 pesos) via Tonalá (3½ hr., 5600 pesos) and Arriaga (3 hr., 4900 pesos); Villahermosa (5 per day, 7 hr., 9800 pesos); Veracruz (Tues. and Fri.-Sun.

at 8:45am, 21,800 pesos); Oaxaca (at 11:30am and 11:15pm, 10 hr., 17,200 pesos); and Mexico City (5 per day, 17 hr., 38,000 pesos). **Autotransportes de Oriente (ADO),** 9 Pte. at 5 Sur (tel. 287-25). To: Mexico City (at 9am and 4:15pm, 34,700 pesos); Oaxaca (Tues., Fri., and Sat. at 8:30pm, 17,200 pesos); Puebla (at 6pm, 30,400 pesos); Veracruz (Mon., Wed., Fri., and Sun. at 8:45pm, 21,800 pesos.) **Autotransportes Tuxtla Gutiérrez,** 3 Sur 712 (tel. 202-30). Long lines—arrive early. Second-class service to: Villahermosa (3 per day, 12,000 pesos); Chetumal (at 3:15pm., 15 hr., 36,000 pesos); Mérida (at 1:30pm., 17 hr., 39,000 pesos); Oaxaca (4 per day, 22,000 pesos); San Cristóbal (every ½ hr. 4am-9pm, 3800 pesos); Comitán (every hr. 4am-5pm, 7600 pesos); Comalapa (every hr. 4am-5pm, 12,000 pesos); Tapachula (5 per day, 16,000 pesos); Yajaloon (at 12:30pm, 10,100 pesos); Arriaga (every hr. 7am-10pm, 3200 pesos); Tonalá (4 per day, 7100 pesos); and Palenque (at 5am, 13,000 pesos). The **regional station,** on 3 Ote. between 2 and 3 Sur, has service to Chiapa de Corzo (every 15 min. 4am-10:30pm, ½ hr., 700 pesos).

Laundromat: Gaily II, 1 Sur Pte. 575 (tel. 234-52), 5 blocks west and 1 block south of the Zócalo. 9000 pesos for 3kg. Open Mon.-Sat. 8am-2pm and 4-8:30pm.

Red Cross: 5 Nte. Pte. 1480 (tel. 204-92), on the west side of town. City-wide ambulance service. Open 24 hr.

Pharmacy: Farmacia Regina, Av. Central 112 (tel. 211-26), at Calle Central across the intersection from the Zócalo. MC, Visa, AmEx accepted. Open 24 hr.

Hospital: Centro de Salud, 2 Ote. Sur 1092 (tel. 201-78). Open for consultations Mon.-Fri. 7:30am-noon. 24-hr. emergency service.

Police: In the Palacio Municipal (tel. 216-76), at the north end of the Zócalo. Go to the left upon entering the building. Open 24 hr.

Accommodations and Camping

People scramble for moderately priced rooms in Tuxtla, and its hotels thrive regardless of season. Unfortunately, the relentless demand gives them little incentive to make beds, chase bugs, provide free Aerobies for guests, or de-mildew towels. Always check the room before you accept. The best deals are on the outskirts of town. Because it may take some time to find an acceptable vacancy, check your bags at the second-class bus station (200 pesos per hr.) before beginning the hunt.

Hotel Avenida, Av. Central 244 (tel. 208-07), 1½ blocks from the Zócalo. Clean, soothing rooms with pink walls and seaside murals. Within earshot of the cathedral chimes and traffic jams on Av. Central. A step up from the others, and more centrally located. Ask for a room off the street. Singles 25,000 pesos. Doubles 30,000 pesos.

Casa de Huéspedes La Posada, 1 Sur Pte. 555 (tel. 229-32), between 4 and 5 Ote. Close to the second-class bus station on 2 Sur. Orderly courtyard. Very clean, comfortably furnished, and popular. Because many rooms are under construction, you should make sure your room is away from banging hammers. Some rooms have private baths. Singles 20,000 pesos. Doubles 30,000 pesos, with 2 beds 40,000 pesos. Triples 45,000 pesos.

CREA Youth Hostel (IYHF), Corzo 1800 (tel. 334-05), next to yellow footbridge. Take a *colectivo* east on Av. Central/Blvd. Corzo. The entrance to the complex is on Corzo; the entrance to the hostel proper is to the left of the youth center and café. Bunk beds in immaculate single-sex dorms. Lockers and large communal showers. Pool (1000 pesos) open Tues.-Sun. 10am-2pm. Ballfields out back perfect for a quick Aerobie toss. Student ID rarely requested. Curfew 11pm. 6000 pesos per person. Towels, sheets, and pillowcases included.

Casa de Huéspedes Ofelia, 2 Sur 643 (tel 273-46), near 5 Ote. Perhaps the best bargain in town if you appreciate cleanliness, but not likely to have rooms available; ask specifically about rooms all the way upstairs if staff says they're booked solid. Home-cooked meals served downstairs. Limited water available. Singles 7500 pesos. Doubles 15,000 pesos. Triples 22,000 pesos.

Casa de Huéspedes Muñiz, 2 Sur Ote. 733 (tel. 211-29), adjacent to the second-class bus station. Only worth it if you must catch a bus at 6am. Small, musty rooms. The air in a select few is pushed around by weak ceiling fans. Guests compelled to pray for good health should visit the downstairs chapel complete with Madonna. Singles 10,000 pesos. Doubles 12,000 pesos. Triples 14,000 pesos.

Hotel Santo Domingo, 2 Nte. 259-A (tel. 348-39), between 1 and 2 Pte. across from the Cristóbal Colón station. Dangerously low and wobbly ceiling fans. Mind your pate while descending the low-ceilinged staircase. Secure door locks, but little solitude. A good place to crash if your bus out leaves early. All rooms have baths. Singles 20,000 pesos. Doubles 25,000 pesos. Triples 30,000 pesos. Hard hats 2000 pesos.

Hotel María Teresa, 2 Nte. 259-B (tel. 301-02), next to the Santo Domingo. The spittin' image of its neighbor. Lie low. Singles 20,000 pesos. Doubles 25,000 pesos. Triples 30,000 pesos.

Gran Hotel Olimpo, 3 Sur Ote. 215 (tel. 202-95) at 1 Ote. across from the market. A shabby 187-room colossus with paint peeling before your eyes. Some rooms rent by the hour. Singles 23,000 pesos. Doubles 30,000 pesos.

La Hacienda Hotel Trailer Park, Belisario Domínguez 1197 (tel. 279-86), a hefty 25 blocks from town. Take a westbound *colectivo* on Av. Central (300 pesos). 20 full hookups. Grassy area, but right off a busy highway. Amenities include bathrooms with hot water, a pool, and an adjoining cafeteria. Plenty of space; avoid the expensive rooms of the main building. Trailer with full hookup 20,000 pesos. Tent site 20,000 pesos for up to 2 persons, 5000 pesos each additional person.

Food

If you're fed up with *frijoles* and tortillas, Tuxtla will snatch Mexican cuisine from the jaws of your wrath. There are plenty of budget eateries around town, plus a number of superb restaurants. Tuxtla's numerous juice bars serve *licuados* with such delectable ingredients as alfalfa leaves, spinach, soy flour, and *taxcalate.*

The marketplace *fondas* provide, as always, a penny-pinching alternative. The main market, cleaner and better-lit than most, is 2 blocks directly south of the Zócalo. Another market with plenty of food stands is on 11 Nte. Ote., near Parque 5 de Mayo.

Las Pichanchas, Av. Central Ote. 857, about 8 blocks east of the Zócalo. This *palapa* serves outstanding Mexican food in an elegant setting at moderate prices. Live *marimba* band Tues.-Sun. 2-5pm and 8-11pm. Three tacos or enchiladas 9000 pesos, chicken and meat dishes 9000-11,000 pesos. Large fresh fruit plate with honey 6500 pesos. Open daily 2pm-midnight. MC, Visa accepted.

Restaurante Forteza, Av. Central Ote. 433. Cheap food, friendly service, and a garden out back. Exotic rice, beans, potato and meat combo 7000 pesos. Egg breakfasts 1800-3500 pesos. Open daily 8am-10pm.

Restaurant Tuxtla, Calle Central Nte. 263, 1 block from the Zócalo. Less polished than its counterparts, but good food and service. You'll be the only *gringo* in sight. Two pancakes 4000 pesos. Three quesadillas 6000 pesos. Open daily 7am-5pm.

Restaurant Jow-Hua, la. Nte. Pte. 217. An authentic, family-run Chinese restaurant. Huge portions feed 2. Chicken dishes 12,000 pesos. Multi-course dinner for 3 or more 15,200-18,300 pesos per person. Enormous liquor selection 4000-6000 pesos. Open daily 8am-10pm. MC, Visa, AmEx accepted.

Restaurante Vegetariano Nah-Yaxal, 6a. Pte. 724, just north of Av. Central. Read about the fiber content of the meatless tacos and tortillas (3000 pesos) while you dine. *Clorofila* and alfalfa *licuados* 2500 pesos. Open Mon.-Sat. 7:30am-9pm. Smaller Nah-Yaxal *kiosko* hides behind the cathedral.

Restaurante Los Arcos, Av. Central Pte. 806. Low arched doorways, funky wood chairs, and dimness: the pleasant atmosphere packs 'em in. Three-course *comida corrida* 10,000 pesos. Breakfasts 6000-7500 pesos. Open daily 7:30am-11pm. MC, Visa accepted.

Sights

Downtown Tuxtla is much more hectic than its smaller counterparts throughout Chiapas. Unyielding traffic, crowded buses, and polluted streets ward off many tourists. There are several escapes within and around the city, however, that preserve one's sanity in the heat and noise. Regional animals in their native habitats make the **Miguel Alcarez del Toro Zoo** famous throughout Central America. You could easily spend an afternoon roaming through the cool vegetation and admiring the unusual animals and colorful birds. (Open Tues.-Sun. 8:30am-5:30pm. Free.) To get to the zoo, take the "Cerro Hueco" bus, which leaves roughly every half hour from 1 Ote. between 6 and 7 Sur (20-30 min., 300 pesos). The bus traces an indirect and sometimes unbearably slow route to the zoo's front gate. To return to the center, catch a bus at the park's entrance.

The **Parque Madero** unfurls in the northeast part of town, at the intersection of 11 Ote. and 5 Nte. Its focal point is a large and modern theater, the **Teatro de la Ciudad Emilio Rabasa.** Films by Latin American directors and Ballet Folklórico shows dominate the schedule. Check monthly bulletins at the theater. To the east of the theater, a tree-lined walkway bisects a large children's recreational park, complete with rides and a miniature train. (Open Tues.-Fri. 9:30am-8:30pm, Sat.-Sun. and holidays 9:30am-9:30pm.) The 13m water slide, which empties into a well-kept public pool, is visible through the trees directly in front of the theater. (Pool open Tues.-Sun. 9am-7pm. Free.) A broad concourse, demarcated by fountains and bronze busts of famous Mexicans, leads west of the theater past the **Museo Regional de Chiapas,** which primarily displays regional archeological finds. (Open Tues.-Sat. 9am-4pm. Free.) Farther down the concourse, at the **Jardín Botánico Dr. Faustino Miranda,** you can stroll through colorful arrangements of Chiapan flora. (Open Tues.-Sun. 9am-2pm and 4-6pm. Free.)

If you're interested in the ruins at Bonampak, visit the **Hotel Bonampak,** Domínguez 180. Its reproductions of the famous Mayan murals from the Lacandón jungle ruin site are infinitely clearer and brighter than the originals. In fact, many of the postcard photographs of the murals are actually taken here rather than at the site itself. The hotel is always open; to get there, walk or take a *colectivo* west on Av. Central until it becomes Domínguez past the federal tourist office—the hotel is on the right.

Near Tuxtla Gutiérrez

Head north on Calle 11 Ote. Nte. toward a string of five lookout points over **Cañón El Sumidero,** one of the world's most spectacular canyons. Called *miradores,* the sites are named, in order: La Ceiba, La Coyota, Los Tepehuajes, El Roblar, and Los Chiapas (also called La Atalaya after the restaurant there). La Coyota commands the most awesome view. For transportation, inquire at the office of Combis Cañón del Sumidero, la. Nte. Ote. 112, at Av. Central and Calle 11 Ote. *Combis* to the lookouts cost 2500 pesos. Micbrobuses charge 4000 pesos, and two or three depart daily on request.

The excursion from Tuxtla to the **Cascadas de Aguacero** is popular among domestic tourists. Buses heading west to Ocozocoautla will drop you off at the access road for the waterfalls; a half-hour hike brings you to a stairway, which ascends to the beautiful Patersonian cataract. Visitors to the secluded spot often bathe nude in its cold water.

Arriaga

Arriving in Arriaga at night, you may feel you've been deposited in a scene from Borges: clumps of passengers wait patiently at bus stops, only to dash off en masse at the news that the bus has arrived on another block. The helpless newcomer suffers a barrage of misinformation offered so convincingly that it almost seems malicious. Some of the nightmarish qualities are alleviated (for those who actually stay through the night) by the dawning of day and the knowledge that Arriaga's streets have been renamed, following a system so complicated that even the locals can't say for sure where anything is. The bus drivers seem equally confused, and despite meticulously updated bus schedules, appear to leave whenever they have a mind to, as often as not from some dark, back alley with their lights off and mirrors askew. Taxis contradict the destinations clearly marked on their sides, and will pick up passengers only at some unmarked, predestined place, stonily bypassing wildly gesticulating tourists.

Since Arriaga is chiefly a transportation hub for travelers headed toward Guatemala or the Yucatán, such confusion does not bode well for its future as a stopover. You would do better to set aside enough time to arrive in smaller, more accommodating towns such as nearby Tonalá, the beachside Puerto Arista to the south, or Tehuantepec to the north, where hotels are more inviting and streets more comprehensible.

Orientation

Arriaga is in far western Chiapas state, 148km from Tuxtla Gutiérrez and 232km from San Cristóbal de las Casas, on the Golfo de Tehuantepec. Both Rte. 200 to Guatemala and Rte. 190 west to Oaxaca or east to Tuxtla Gutiérrez access the town.

Arriaga conforms (if unconventionally) to the fairly common Mexican grid system in which streets and avenues are laid out according two major axes, and change names upon crossing either one. In Arriaga, the axes are **Calle Central,** which runs north-south along the side of the park, and the railroad tracks, which run east-west just south of the park. Streets running north-south are called *calles,* and those running east-west are called *avenidas.* Not desiring to be readily understood, Arriaga abides by one more rule: All *calles* east of Central are *números nones* (numbered odd), while those to the west are *pares* (even). The same is true of *avenidas* south and north of the railroad tracks, which are odd and even respectively. Thus, for example, the corner of Calle 2 Pte. and Av. 3 Nte. does not exist, since the first runs only in the northwest quadrant of town, while the latter is confined to the northeast. But in the end, this is all just trivia—even locals are puzzled by the system. When in doubt, ask.

Both bus stations are on 2 Ote., 3 blocks east of El Parque. The most visible landmarks in Arriaga are the several Pemex signs; the one at 2 Ote. and 3 Nte. is easily spotted from either station. The Zócalo is 2 blocks beyond it.

Practical Information

Currency Exchange: Bancomer, Central Nte. 2 (tel. 211-54), across from Roxy ice cream on the northwest corner of the Zócalo. Open for exchange Mon.-Fri. 10am-noon.

Post Office: Calle 5 Nte. 15 (tel. 206-97). Facing away from the Zócalo, take the first right after the Cristóbal Colón station. Lista de Correos. Open Mon.-Fri. 8am-6pm, Sat. 8am-noon. **Postal Code:** 30450.

Telephones: 7 Nte. at 2 Ote. (tel. 212-46). International collect calls 2500 pesos. Open Mon.-Sat. 6am-10pm, Sun. 6am-2pm. **Telephone Code:** 966.

Telegrams: Av. 2 Pte. 7 (tel. 207-89), ½ block west of Calle Central Nte. Open Mon.-Sat. 9am-1pm and 3-7pm.

Bus Stations: Cristóbal Colón, 2a. Calle Ote. 35 (tel. 201-77), 1 block west of the Pemex station on the same side of the street. First-class buses to: Oaxaca (at 10pm, 8 hr., 21,000 pesos) via Tehuantepec (3 hr., 8000 pesos); Mexico City (*de local* at 5:30, 7:50, and 9:20pm, 13 hr., 47,000 pesos); Tuxtla Gutiérrez (11 per day, 3 hr., 6800 pesos); San Cristóbal de las Casas (at 1:30pm, 5 hr., 6600 pesos); Villahermosa (at 9pm, 12 hr., 25,000 pesos); Tapachula (8 per day, 4 hr., 11,200 pesos). Also **second-class** service to: Mexico City (at 3:30, 4, and 6:30pm, 13 hr., 40,000 pesos) via Puebla (11 hr., 34,000 pesos) and Cordoba (10 hr., 26,000 pesos); Coatzacoalcos (5 per day, 9 hr., 15,500 pesos); Tehuantepec (at 11:30am, 3 hr., 7100 pesos); Salina Cruz (3½ hr., 7900 pesos); Tapachula (6 per day, 5 hr., 10,100 pesos); Veracruz (at 8:30am, 11 hr., 25,000 pesos). **Autotransportes Tuxtla Gutiérrez,** 2a. Calle Ote. 34 (tel. 201-30), across from the first-class station. To: Oaxaca (at 4am, 9:30am, 4:30pm, and 9pm, 9 hr., 17,500 pesos); Tuxtla Gutiérrez (15 per day 5am-midnight, 6200 pesos); and Tapachula (8 per day 4am-11pm, 4½ hr., 10,000 pesos).

Taxis: At 2 Ote. and 3 Nte. 2000 pesos takes you anywhere in town.

Red Cross: (tel. 204-88) on Zaarabia 1km from *el centro* on the way to Tapachula, across from the Pemex station. Ambulances and 24-hr. emergency service.

Pharmacy: Farmacia Cristal, 3a. Calle Nte. 24. Open daily 8am-10pm.

Police: 2a. Av. Pte. at Central Nte. (tel. 200-02), in the Palacio Municipal on the northwest corner of the park. Open 24 hr.

Accommodations and Food

Hotel Albores II, 3a. Calle Nte. 30. Walk toward the Pemex sign from the bus station and take the first right. An improvement on the original. Freshly poured concrete, clean rooms, and even cleaner baths. Dull, gray courtyard reminiscent of a rainy day in Portland. Singles 20,000 pesos. Doubles 35,000 pesos.

Hotel Colonial, Av. del Ferrocarril 2 (tel. 208-57), ½ block south of the Colón bus station. Clean rooms each with fan and private bath. Attentive front-desk service. Singles 15,000 pesos. Doubles 20,000 pesos.

Hotel Albores, Calle 4 Nte. 17 (tel. 203-96) Walk toward the Pemex sign from either of the bus stations and take the first right onto Calle 3 Nte., then make the first left. A treacherous javelin hanging above the entry scares away *cucarachas*. Ancient rooms have ceiling fans and shockingly bright lights. Ask for an upstairs room with a window. Singles 20,000 pesos. Doubles 25,000 pesos.

Hotel Colón, Calle 3 Nte. 5 (tel. 201-20), the first left walking from either bus station toward the Pemex sign. Large, black-and-white sign on institutional green building. Ugly colors inside and out. Adequate rooms with working fans; bathrooms could use a scrub. Singles 23,000 pesos, with A/C 33,000 pesos. Doubles 28,600 pesos, with 2 beds 35,200 pesos, with A/C 45,100 pesos.

Café Tupinamba, Av. 2 Ote. 29, a few doors from the first-class bus station. The best food in town is easy on the wallet. Well-prepared oyster and shrimp cocktails or *huevos rancheros* 4000 pesos. Open 24 hr.

Restaurante Barkley, 4a. Calle Nte. 2. Take the first right from either bus station toward the Pemex sign, then 1 block on the right. Clean, well-lit, and friendly. No menu; just ask for the daily special. *Comida corrida* 6000 pesos. Entrees 7000-9000 pesos. Open daily 7am-9pm.

Restaurante Playa y Sol, Calle 1 Nte. 6, 1 block west (toward the Zócalo) past Pemex then 1 block to the left. Locals like it here. Good *sopa de mariscos* 9000 pesos. Entrees 8000-12,000 pesos, beer 1500 pesos. Open daily 8am-6pm.

Beaches

Even fewer tourists go to **La Gloria** and **Balneario Santa Brijada** (both 15km from Arriaga) than go to Puerto Arista and Boca del Cielo near Tonalá. There are almost no waves, and zero formal accommodations; you'll just have to suspend your hammock between two palm trees. The several food stands serve fresh seafood and *antojitos*.

To get to either of these beaches, take a local bus (2000 pesos), leaving from Arriaga's *mercado* at 8 and 10am and returning at 2 and 4pm.

Tonalá

There are times of year when flocks of screeching *golondrinas* (bigmouthed swallows) invade Tonalá's Zócalo, nesting on the plaza's incomprehensible bush sculptures and providing free entertainment for the town. The cessation of your amusement at the crazy cackles (maybe after 20 minutes) should serve as a signal to catch the next bus out of town. Tonalá's attractions and citizenry can hardly ever match the birds' proficiency for sustaining a modicum of intrigue.

Tonalá is the major beachbum crossroads in Chiapas, with connections to Paredon, Puerto Arista, and Boca de Cielo. On Sundays and holidays, Chiapan families arrive en masse at these beaches; during the week, however, the completely deserted expanse of gray sands and crashing surf is conducive to meditations on the meaning of life and Crazy Jamie's indelible optimism for which those around him are truly indebted.

Orientation

Tonalá lies 223km northwest of Tapachula along Rte. 200, 180km southwest of Tuxtla Gutiérrez on Rte. 190, and 26km from Arriaga. The town is served by frequent buses and daily trains along the southern Pacific line to the Guatemalan border. Both bus stations are on Hidalgo, the main drag, which passes the Zócalo. From the first- and second-class bus stations, walk 6 blocks left (east) from the entrance to the Zócalo; all local buses from Tapachula stop on Hidalgo 3 blocks before the Zócalo. Local *colectivos,* taxis, and buses from small, neighboring towns may stop near the market (2 blocks southeast of the Zócalo), on the Zócalo, or nowhere in particular; ask directions to *el Zócalo* when you disembark.

Most of Tonalá's important points hover around **Avenida Hidalgo,** which runs east from the stations, past the post office, the Zócalo, the Palacio Municipal, and a half-dozen hotels and restaurants before continuing to Tapachula and Guatemala as Rte. 200. Matamoros parallels Hidalgo 1 block south of the Zócalo, passing several more hotels and restaurants as well as the market.

Practical Information

Tourist Office: In the clock-crowned Palacio Municipal (tel. 301-01), on the Hidalgo side of the Zócalo. Excellent map of Chiapas and several informative pamphlets. No English spoken. Open daily 8am-8pm.

Currency Exchange: Bancomer, Hidalgo at 21 de Marzo, 1 block east of the Zócalo. Open Mon.-Fri. 10:30am-noon.

Post Office: Hidalgo 148 (tel. 306-83), at Zambrano 2 blocks west of the Zócalo. Lista de Correos. Open Mon.-Sat. 8am-7pm; for registered mail Mon.-Fri. 8am-6pm. **Postal Code:** 30500.

Telephones: Cafetería La Diligencia (tel. 301-88), on Independencia off Hidalgo east of the Zócalo. Open daily 8am-2pm and 6-8pm. **Telephone Code:** 966.

Bus Station: Cristóbal Colón (tel. 305-40), on Hidalgo 6 blocks west of the Zócalo. Open 24-hr. First-class service to: Mexico City (at 7:30 and 9pm, 13 hr., 48,000 pesos) via Puebla (10 hr., 42,000 pesos); Tapachula (5 per day, 3½ hr., 10,100 pesos); Tuxtla Gutiérrez (6 per day, 3 hr., 5800 pesos); Oaxaca (at 9:30pm, 10 hr., 22,000 pesos); Veracruz (at 11:30pm, 10 hr., 32,000 pesos). Second-class buses headed toward Arriaga (1100 pesos) and Tapachula can be flagged at the Colón station and at the intersection of Hidalgo and Independencia, near the Zócalo.

Taxis: Catch 'em at the Zócalo or near the *mercado.* Taxis run *colectivo* to Arriaga from the east side of the Zócalo (2000 pesos).

Market: On Matamoros, several blocks southeast of the Zócalo. Walk east on Hidalgo 1 block and right on Independencia to Matamoros. Dirty and dark. Open daily 4am-4pm.

Health Care: Centro de Salud, Madero 56 (tel. 300-31 or 306-87), on the west side of the Zócalo. No English spoken. Open 24 hr. for emergencies; for consultations Mon.-Fri. 8am-2pm.

Red Cross: Hidalgo 177 (tel. 301-20). Ambulance service. Open 24 hr.

24-Hr. Pharmacy: Clínica de Especialidades, Hidalgo 127 (tel. 312-90), at Independencia east of the Zócalo. No English spoken.

Police: (tel. 301-03) on 12 de Octubre 2 blocks west of the bus station and 1 block to the right at the group of yellow school buildings. Easy to miss the faded sign. No English spoken. Open 24 hr.

Accommodations

Tonalá's hotels are rather expensive and let *cucarachas* run wild, a one-two punch that may have you clamoring for a spot on the bus.

Hotel El Farro, 16 de Septiembre 24 (tel. 300-33), 1 block south of the Zócalo at Matamoros. If not for the insects, this run-down 19th-century hotel could almost be classy. Spacious quarters with high ceilings, strong fans, and private bathrooms (just don't kick over the garbage can). Singles and 1-bed doubles 25,000 pesos. Doubles with 2 beds 35,000 pesos.

Hotel Thomas, Hidalgo 103 (tel. 300-80), 3 blocks east of the Zócalo. Look for the building with "Motel Restaurant Motel" painted on its façade. Bring your own air-freshener and ask for a discount. Singles 20,000 pesos. Doubles 25,000 pesos.

Hotel Galilea, Hidalgo at Callejón Ote. (tel. 302-39), on the east side of the Zócalo. An expensive, rather fancy motel. Attentive staff and good restaurant. A/C in rooms may merit high prices. Singles 36,000 pesos. Doubles 45,000 pesos.

Hotel Tonalá, Hidalgo 172 (tel. 304-80), 4 blocks west of the Zócalo and 2 blocks east of the bus station. Don't fall for the semi-modern exterior; rooms are old and gritty. Elvis would feel at home on the velour bedspreads. Singles 30,000 pesos. Doubles 40,000 pesos, with A/C 45,000 pesos.

Food

In Tonalá, cheap meals are more common than gators in Okeefenokee. Inexpensive restaurants cluster around the bus station, a row of taco stands marks the western edge of the Zócalo, and the *mercado's* fresh produce beckons incessantly.

Restaurante Nora, Independencia 10, just north of Hidalgo and 1 block east of the Zócalo. Any more pink and customers will puke. Mexican breakfasts (3000-6000 pesos) popular with locals. Chicken entrees 8000 pesos. Open Tues.-Sun. 7am-10pm.

Cafetería y Restaurant Samborn's, Hidalgo 1 at Madero, the yellow-and-orange place on the southwest corner of the Zócalo. Decorator graduated from the Nora Neon School of Design. Good *ensalada de camarón* 12,000 pesos. Large selection of *antojitos.* Open daily 7am-1am.

Restaurante Hotel Galilea, Hidalgo at Callejón Ote., on the east side of the Zócalo. Delicious sandwiches with an assortment of vegetables cooked in vinegar. Easy-going staff. Expensive by taco-stand standards, but worth it if *chiles* and *frijoles* are getting you down. All *tortas* under 4000 pesos. Open Thurs.-Tues. 8:30am-11pm.

Beaches

The coast near Tonalá stretches from El Mar Muerto west of town, along the enormous sandspit extending southeast from Paredón, and past Puerto Arista to its endpoint—a peninsula containing a small beach and the village of Boca de Cielo.

Among these settlements, the most popular is **Puerto Arista,** 18km from Tonalá on a paved road served by public transportation. While Puerto Arista cannot compare with the beauty or facilities of Puerto Angel or Escondido farther north in Oaxaca, it makes a good daytrip for travelers heading south (who won't encounter another decent beach for miles).

Along the 16km of dark gray beach at Arista, the undertow is so strong that few swimmers venture more than a few meters from shore. In several spots, *canales* (forceful channels or currents) can take you on a one-way trip far out to sea; ask about dangerous spots before diving in.

Puerto Arista's points of interest and import line the road that parallels the beach. The paved highway from Tonalá dead-ends into this road near a white lighthouse; to the right, another paved road continues up the coast, and hammock-hanging spots hover above the tide line. To the left, the road is unpaved. Arista's only reasonably priced hotels and bungalows are in this direction, but the waterfront abounds with restaurants. There is little to see after you pass the lighthouse.

Sleeping on Arista's beach is fairly safe but there are few palms to provide shelter at night; a few restaurants on the beach have covered poles on which to hang hammocks, and most eateries rent hammocks (5000 pesos). The space is free as long as you order meals at the same establishment. If you don't have a tent, you'll be especially glad you forked over the few extra pesos when it rains (not an uncommon occurence in summer). If you want slightly more privacy and comfort, march left down the beach. There are two or three places toward the end that rent rustic *ca-*

bañas with thatched-roof rooms and sand floors. The privacy is minimal, however, since pigs, chickens, and brats wander through the *cabañas* day and night.

Just before Puerto Arista, a sign on the left of the road points down a dusty trail to **Boca de Cielo,** 20km south. This resort is for the reclusive, inhabited by only a few fishing families and visited by even fewer tourists. There is a restaurant here, but no formal hotel, so bring a sleeping bag, hammock, or tent. Swimming at Boca de Cielo can be a relatively safe and viable option. A large sandbar tames the waters close to shore; on the sea side, beware of rough surf and dangerous currents.

Paredón, a tranquil town northwest of Puerto Arista and 15km from Tonalá, attracts a steady stream of sport fishers, and the waters off the coast of El Mar Muerto are perfect for waterskiing.

Beach Transportation

Buses, *colectivos,* minibuses, and taxis connect Tonalá wth the nearby beaches. In the early evening, when *colectivos* and buses stop running, taxis become the only means of public transportation; it's best not to travel at this time, since fares go up as cabdrivers enjoy their few hours of monopoly.

Buses make the half-hour journey to Puerto Arista every hour from 5am to 8pm (1500 pesos), departing from the corner of 5 de Mayo and Juárez, just east of the market. *Colectivos* (2000 pesos) run more frequently and often later than buses, leaving from the same corner or from Matamoros.

Only buses (2 per day, 60-90 min., 2500 pesos) make it to Boca de Cielo, shoving off from the corner of 5 de Mayo and Juárez. The 11am bus returns to Tonalá at 5pm the same day, and the 3pm bus stays overnight, returning from Boca de Cielo at 9am the following day.

Combis and taxis leave for Paredón from the corner of Madero and Allende, south of *el centro.* They run from 5am to 10pm, but taxis are more frequent. To reach the intersection from the Zócalo, walk west on Hidalgo, turn left (south) on Madero, and continue 3 blocks over a white bridge that spans a riverbed full of trash until you reach Allende. *Combis* charge 1500 pesos, *colectivo* taxis 1000 pesos.

Tapachula

Four thousand meters below the majestic volcano Tacaná, a fertile river basin drains the southernmost part of the Mexican Republic on its run to the Pacific Ocean. Tapachula rises out of a clearing in the jungle which still nurtures jaguars, pumas, and packs of *peccaries* (akin to pigs) and *chakalakas* (turkey-like fowl). Topiary trees, their leafy crowns trimmed square and joined to one another, form a green canopy over the Zócalo's 2 square blocks. Relaxing outdoor cafés provide sanctuary from the activity and *marimba* music that define the big city.

Primarily a business center, Tapachula attracts its share of tourists bound for Guatemala or the north. If you must stay for more than a brief layover, you can always escape via bus from the second-class station, (every 20 min. 5:30am-7pm, 45 min., 1000 pesos) to the beach at **Puerto Madero,** 27km away. Though not spectacular (locals describe the beach as "dirty"), it provides ample opportunity to enjoy sand and surf either before or after a long bus journey.

Orientation

Tapachula is 18km from Talismán at the Guatemalan border on Rte. 200, and 303km west-northwest of Guatemala City. The first-class Cristóbal Colón bus station is on 17a. Calle Ote./Rte. 200 at 3a. Av. Nte., 7 blocks north and 6 blocks east of the main plaza. From the station, turn left on 17a. Calle and left again on Av. Central Nte. Continue 6 blocks to Calle 5 Pte. and the Zócalo is 4 blocks to the right. At night, take a taxi to the center (2000 pesos per person). The main second-class bus station is closer to the Zócalo, at 7a. Calle Pte. between 2a. Av.

Nte. and Av. Central Nte. From here, go right along Calle 7 Pte., turn left on 6a. Av. Nte., and walk 1 block.

Combis shuttle between the airport and 2a. Av. Nte. between 7a. and 9a. Calle Pte. The 7000-peso fare is much lower than a private taxi's (25,000 pesos).

Tapachula's streets are organized in a clear-cut if confusing manner. *Avenidas* run north-south, and *calles* run east-west. *Calles* north of Calle Central are odd-numbered; those south of the central axis are even-numbered. Similarly, *avenidas* east of Av. Central are odd-numbered, and those west have even numbers. Thus, an address's number (odd or even) and its single direction (Sur, Nte., Pte., or Ote.) places it in a specific quadrant of the city. But unlike most *chiapaneco* cities, Tapachula's main plaza is not located at the intersection of Calle Central and Av. Central, but at 3a. Calle Pte. between 6a. and 8a. Av. Nte., northwest of the center.

Practical Information

Guatemalan Consulate: 2a. Calle Ote. 33 (tel. 612-52), between 7a. and 9a. Av. Sur. U.S. and Canadian citizens need only a passport to acquire a visa (see Guatemala for more information regarding entrance requirements). Visas usually take less than ½ hr., but arrive early and be persistent or you may wait all day. Open Mon.-Fri. 8am-4pm. Ring the bell after hours for emergencies.

Currency Exchange: Bánamex, Av. Central Nte. 9 (tel. 629-24). Open for exchange Mon.-Fri. 9am-1pm. **Casa de Cambio Tapachula,** 1a. Calle Pte. near 4a. Av. Nte. (tel. 651-22), across from Bánamex. Changes U.S. dollars (cash and traveler's checks) and Guatemalan quetzales at good rates. Open Mon.-Sat. 8am-7pm. Another branch with same hours at 4a. Av. Nte. and 3a. Calle Pte.

Post Office: 1a. Calle Ote. 32 (tel. 639-22), between 7a. and 9a. Av. Nte., beneath the large red-and-white radio antenna. Lista de Correos. Open Mon.-Fri. 8am-6pm, Sat.-Sun. and festivals 9am-noon. **Postal Code:** 30700.

Telephones: Long-distance *casetas* are located at 17a. Calle Ote. 1 (tel. 630-71), 1 block west of the Cristóbal Colón bus station. Collect calls 8000 pesos. Open daily 8am-10pm. The *caseta* at 3a. Calle Ote. 31 (tel. 639-63) only charges 2000 pesos for a collect call. Open daily 7am-9:30pm.

Telegrams: (tel. 610-97) next to the post office. Open Mon.-Fri. 8am-midnight, Sat. 9am-8pm.

Airport: On the road to Puerto Madero, about 17km south of town. To Mexico City (at 12:35pm, US$101). For information, go to **Aeroméxico,** 2a. Av. Nte. 6 (tel. 647-94). Open Mon.-Sat. 9am-6pm.

Train Station: Av. Central Sur 150 (tel. 525-98), at the end of the *avenida* behind a miniature plaza and a small market. Slow, cheap, unreliable service to Mexico City (at 3pm, 36 hr., 14,000 pesos) via Veracruz (24 hr., 9400 pesos), Oaxaca (12 hr., 5000 pesos), Arriaga (7 hr., 3500 pesos), and Ixtepec (1½ hr., 4500 pesos). Also to Ciudad Hidalgo (at 1pm, 1½ hr., 500 pesos).

Bus Stations: Cristóbal Colón, 17a. Calle Ote. at 3a. Nte. No office; buses depart from the terminal to Huixtla (every ½ hr. 10am-midnight, 7000 pesos). **Second-class Station,** 7a. Calle Pte. 5, between Av. Central Nte. and 2a. Av. Nte. Served by **Social Cooperativa y Transportes San Francisco Belisario Domínguez, Transportes General Paulino Navarro,** and **Gutiérrez,** among others. To: Arriaga (every 2 hr. 4am-7pm, 5 hr., 10,200 pesos) via Tonalá (10,000 pesos); Tuxtla Gutiérrez (4 per day, 7 hr., 16,000 pesos); Comitán (4 per day, 7 hr., 10,800 pesos); San Cristóbal de las Casas (2 per day, 14,500 pesos). Inquire at the ticket window for more complete schedule.

Transportation to the Border: Autobus Union y Progresso leaves every 10 min. from 5a. Calle 23 to Talismán. Buses from **Cristóbal Colón** leave every ½ hr. 4am-10pm (2000 pesos). From the second-class bus station, **Paulino Navarro** sends buses every 20 min. 5am-8pm (2200 pesos) to Ciudad Hidalgo and **Tuxtla Gutiérrez** departs 4 times per day to La Mesilla (4 hr., 10,000 pesos). If need be, take a taxi from the Zócalo to Talismán for 25,000 pesos: Refuse to pay higher rates.

Red Cross: 9a. Av. Nte. at 1a. Calle Ote. (tel. 535-06), across from the post office. 24-hr. ambulance service.

24-Hr. Pharmacy: 8a. Av. Nte. 25 (tel. 506-90), on the northeast corner of the Zócalo. No English spoken. Delivery to anywhere within the city available 7am-11pm.

Hospital Civil Carmen de Acebo: 4a. Av. Nte. at 19a. Calle Pte. (tel. 601-55). Open 24 hr.

Police: In the Palacio Municipal, at 8a. Av. Nte. and 3a. Calle Pte. (tel. 610-93). Open 24 hr.

Accommodations

As befits a major transportation hub, there are scores of hotels in Tapachula—just about one on every block.

Posada Rochester, 2a. Av. Nte. 6 (tel. 614-06), near 1a. Calle Pte. The fresh interior improves upon the tacky, tiled exterior. Huge bathrooms and immaculately clean rooms. Popular. Singles 18,000 pesos. Doubles 20,000 pesos.

Hotel Tabasco, Av. Central Nte. 123, at 17a. Calle Ote. Near the Colón station. So new, the mattresses still have plastic on them. Peachy interior. Singles 15,000 pesos. Doubles 25,000 pesos. Triples 40,000 pesos.

Hospedaje Las Americas, 10a. Av. Nte. 47 (tel. 627-57). Good value: very clean rooms with fans and slightly less clean but tiled bathrooms. Resident wild animals sulk in the courtyard. An amorphous rabbit greets guests at the front desk. Singles 15,000 pesos. Doubles 20,000 pesos.

Hotel Fénix, 4a. Av. Nte. 19 (tel. 507-55), between 1a. and 3a. Calles Pte., 1 block west of the Zócalo. More expensive than the others, but a quantum leap ahead in quality. Worth the extra pesos if you're recuperating from Guatemala or can't stand the Tapachulan heat. Excellent service with fans, telephones, and private baths. Parking available. Singles 41,000 pesos. Doubles 53,000 pesos, with A/C 63,000 pesos.

Food

A moderately priced meal is not hard to come by in Tapachula—but don't expect a feast. The four restaurants on the Zócalo are pricey; better meals can be had on the streets just off the plaza. Cheap taco stands line 10a. Av. Nte., 1 block west of the Zócalo. Tapachula supports many Chinese restaurants, but the Sino-Mexican hybrid is often appalling.

La Parilla, 8a. Av. Nte. 20, on the west side of the Zócalo. Fluorescent lights, cafeteria tables, and huge birds perched on the wall. Large Mexican breakfasts 6000 pesos. *Frijoles,* enchiladas, and tamales 2000-6500 pesos. Four-course *comida corrida* 7000 pesos. Open daily 8am-10pm. MC, Visa accepted.

La Posta del Cazador, Av. Central Nte. at 13a. Calle Pte. Tapachula's only attempt at decor, humble as it is. Stuffed baby crocodiles mounted on paneled walls have scared off many a potential patron. Lunch-sized *comida corrida* 3500 pesos. *Antojitos* 2500-3000 pesos though selection is scarce at night. Open Mon.-Sat. 11am-11pm.

Helados Irma, Av. Central Nte. 3 at Calle Central. Unusually good ice cream: Gorge on banana splits and sundaes (2500 pesos). Fresh yogurt 6000 pesos per liter. Open daily 9:30am-10pm.

Comitán de Dominguez

Most travelers are so intent upon crossing into Guatemala or visiting the national park at the Lagos de Montebello that they don't stay in Comitán longer than it takes to get a Guatemalan visa or change buses. Indeed, Comitán doesn't merit a special trip. But should you find yourself stranded here for a day or two, make the most of this genially active city whose crowded Zócalo seems to breed raucous *marimba* bands alongside a small, sedate anthropology museum in the Casa de la Cultura.

Orientation and Practical Information

Comitán is the last major town on the Pan American Hwy. before the Guatemalan border (85km away). The city is 171km southeast of Tuxtla and 86km from San Cristóbal de las Casas. Rapid growth has transformed once-tiny Comitán into a maze of tangled streets: *avenidas* run north-south, *calles* east-west. Calle Central and Av. Central intersect at the Zócalo, breaking the town into four quadrants. *Calles* are numbered away from Calle Central, and given two directional designations based on the quadrant in which they lie. Calle 1 Sur Pte. is thus 1 block south of the Zócalo and west of Av. Central, while Calle 1 Sur Ote. lies south of the Zócalo and east of Av. Central. *Avenidas* are similarly numbered by quadrant, except that Ote. or Pte. comes before Nte. or Sur in an address (e.g. Av. 1 Pte. Nte.).

Comitán's bus stations are conveniently (not) located on the outskirts of town. To reach the Zócalo from the first-class station, turn left outside, walk downhill to the third right, and go straight to the Zócalo from there (25 min.). From **Autobuses de la Costa,** take a left out the door and turn right at the end of the street. The Zócalo is 6 blocks ahead. From **Autotransportes Tuxtla Gutiérrez,** walk 3½ blocks left on Calle 4 sur Pte. and then left again. Those arriving at night may want to call for a taxi (tel. 201-05).

Tourist Office: (tel. 200-26) first office on the left inside the Palacio Municipal. City maps available: Grab one. English-speaking staff makes your day. Open Mon.-Sat. 8am-8pm, Sun. 9am-2pm.

Guatemalan Consulate: 2a. Av. Pte. Nte. 28 (tel. 226-69), 2½ blocks north and 2 blocks west of the Zócalo; look for the blue-and-white Guatemalan flag. Visas free for holders of U.S. and Canadian passports; citizens of most European nations do not need a visa at all (see Guatemala). Warm and fuzzy staff. Open Mon.-Fri. 8am-2pm and 3-5pm, Sat. 8am-2pm.

Currency Exchange: Bánamex, Av. 1 Ote. Sur 10 (tel. 207-99), just south of the Zócalo. Open for exchange Mon.-Fri. 9am-12:30pm. **Bancomer** (tel. 202-10), across the street from the Casa de la Cultura. Open for exchange Mon.-Fri. 9-11am. After hours, **Farmacia Boulevard,** Domínguez 79, on the Pan American Hwy., changes U.S. dollars—and Guatemalan quetzales—at a poor rate, and traveler's checks even less favorably. Open Mon.-Sat. 8am-9:30pm, Sun. 9am-2pm and 5-9:30pm. Several shops and restaurants downtown accept dollars and quetzales; some might even change small amounts of cash. If you ask nicely.

Post Office: Av. Central Sur 47 (tel. 204-27), between Calles 2 and 3 Sur. Open Mon.-Fri. 8am-7pm, Sat. 9am-1pm. **Postal Code:** 30000.

Telephones: Long-distance *caseta* at Av. 1 Pte. Sur 2-C (tel. 208-00), off Calle Central Pte. International collect calls 2000 pesos. Open daily 8am-8pm. Scores of public pay phones scattered throughout Comitán; if you speak Spanish and find one of the few phones that work, dial 09, deal with the international operator, and save 2000 pesos. **Telephone Code:** 963.

Telegrams: Next door to the post office. Open Mon.-Fri. 9am-8pm, Sat. 9am-noon.

Bus Stations: Cristóbal Colón, Domínguez 43, on the Pan American Hwy. southwest of *el centro.* Eleven buses per day run to San Cristóbal (2 hr., 3900 pesos) and Tuxtla (3½ hr., 7700 pesos), 10 of which pass through Chiapa de Corzo (3 hr., 7000 pesos). A bus leaves at 3pm to Mexico City (59,000 pesos); buy your ticket a day in advance. Also service to Cuauhtémoc (see below). **Autobuses de la Costa,** Calle 6 Pte. Nte. 55 (tel. 219-59), sends 4 buses per day from 4:30-8:30am to Tapachula (10,000 pesos) via Huixtla (9000 pesos) and Comalopa (4500 pesos). Also to Cuauhtémoc (3500 pesos). **Autotransportes Tuxtla Gutiérrez,** Calle 4 Pte. Sur 53 (tel. 200-14), between Av. 3 and 4 Pte. Sur. Second-class service to: Tuxtla (14 per day 5am-9:30pm, 7600 pesos); Motozintla (6 per day, 6600 pesos); Chicomuselo (at 1pm, 5400 pesos); Tapachula (at 2 and 6pm, 10,800 pesos); Comalapa (at 4 and 5pm, 3000 pesos.) **Linea Comitán-Montebello** (tel. 208-75), Av. 2 Pte. Sur between Calles 2 and 3 Pte. Sur. Service to Lagunas de Montebello and beyond (every ½ hr. 5am-4pm, 2700 pesos); the last bus returns at 3:30pm. *Combis* to Lagunas de Montebello leave when full (about every 15 min. 5am-4pm, 2500 pesos).

Transportation to the border: First-class service to Ciudad Cuauhtémoc (at 6am, 8am, 11am, and 3pm; 4000 pesos) from the **Cristóbal Colón** station. **Autotransportes Tuxtla Gutiérrez** sends *de local* buses to Cuauhtémoc (13 per day, 2400 pesos). Ciudad Cuauhtémoc is about 5km from the Guatemalan immigration facilities; after you've visited the Guatemalan Consulate (if you need a visa) and the Mexican immigration office in Cuauhtémoc, hop on one of the many trucks heading up the hill toward the Guatemalan side of the *frontera* (1000 pesos).

From here, buses (Q10) leave at 2, 4, 6, 8, and 10am, noon, and 11pm. First-class buses (Q15) leave at 2:45, 7, 7:30, and 9am.

Markets: Mercado Primero de Mayo, Calle Central Ote. at Av. 2 Ote. Nte. **Mercado Municipal,** Calle 11 Sur Pte. and Av. 5 Pte. Sur. Both open Mon.-Sat. 5am-6pm, and Sun. 5am-1pm.

Red Cross: 5a. Calle Nte. Pte. (tel. 218-89). 24-hr. emergency service.

Hospital María Gandulfo: 9a. Sur Ote. 3 (tel. 201-35). Ambulance service available. Open 24 hr.

Medical Assistance: Dr. Rafael Gullen Utrilla, Calle 1 Sur Pte. 9 (tel. 205-44). English spoken. Open Mon.-Sat. 9am-2pm and 4-8pm.

Police: (tel. 200-25) on Av. Central. Open 24 hr.

Accommodations

Hotel rooms in Comitán range from pseudo-prison cells (without the bread and water) to classy, modern *cuartos*. Plenty of cheap, dark, and grungy *hospedajes* lie within a few blocks of the Zócalo. Start your search west of the plaza.

Hospedaje Montebello, Calle 1 Nte. Pte. 10 (tel. 217-70), 1 block north and 1 block west of the plaza. A cut above the cheap alternatives, but still only a minimal attempt at decor. Dim lights and low ceilings can induce cabin-fever. Miniscule but clean and tiled bathrooms. Singles 6000 pesos, with bath 16,000 pesos. Doubles 12,000 pesos, with bath 18,000 pesos.

Hospedaje Primavera, Calle Central Pte. 4. Large rooms around a colonial courtyard with pillars and tiled walkway. Bathrooms are orderly and clean. Singles 10,000 pesos. Doubles 12,000 pesos, with 2 beds 15,000 pesos. Triples 20,000 pesos.

Posada Las Flores, Av. 1 Pte. Nte. 17 (tel. 233-34), between Calles 2 and 3 Nte. Pte., 1 block west and 2 blocks north of the Zócalo. Rooms dark and shabby but clean. The tiled floor, striped wallpaper, and plaid spreads in some rooms launch quite an assault on your optical nerves. 12,000 pesos per person.

Posada San Miguel, Av. 1 Pte. Nte. 19 (tel. 211-26). Clean and cheap. Narrow rooms would overlook a barren courtyard with ample parking space, if they had windows. Save your shower for another day. Singles 6000 pesos. Doubles 10,000 pesos. Triples 18,000 pesos.

Hotel Internacional, Av. Central Sur at Calle 2 Sur (tel. 201-10), 1 block south of the Zócalo. Fairly modern building with granite hallways and spacious, immaculate rooms. A good place to rest after emerging from the jungle. Singles 32,000 pesos. Doubles 36,000 pesos.

Pensión Delfín, Domínguez 9 (tel. 200-23), on the west end of the Zócalo. Best location imaginable. Large rooms have tasteful wood paneling, but bathrooms are smelly and dirty; demand hot water, towels, and toilet paper. Upstairs rooms have a lovely view of the drained pool. Black-and-white TV in the lobby. Parking available. Singles 20,000 pesos. Doubles 30,000 pesos.

Food

Fear not should you find your wallet thin and your stomach empty. But if your palate is sensitive, you've found trouble. Most restaurants and cafés are concentrated around the Zócalo; straying from it will bring you little luck.

Café Gloria, Av. Central Nte., next to the *casa de cambio*. Waiters break a sweat running from table to table, delivering small plates of authentic Mexican cuisine to a packed house. A la carte items are cheap and it takes but 2 tamales (1200 pesos each) to make a meal. Quesadillas 1000 pesos. Open daily 11am-11pm.

Restaurante Nevelandia, on the northwest corner of the plaza. One of but 4 restaurants in Comitán to be granted "Tourist Quality" status by the state tourist office. The uniformed waiters may claim that this justifies the high prices. Simple breakfast 5000 pesos. If you're going to be around all day, invest in their 3-meal plan for 17,000 pesos. "Video Bar El Tapanco" upstairs is *the* place for that first date. Open daily 7:30am-midnight.

Restaurante Los Gallos, Carretera Internacional 1259, heading south on the highway out of town. People come here from miles around to sample some of the best regional food in Chiapas. No menu; the only choice is a large plate loaded with *chiapaneco* specialties. A rare gustatory experience. 20,000 pesos per person. Open Tues.-Sun. noon-5pm.

Restaurante Acuario, Domínguez 9, on the west side of the Zócalo. The typical *comiteco* eatery; one in a line of nearly identical restaurants under the plaza's western arcade. Basic: *pollo* or *carne* dishes 6000 pesos. Two tamales 2500 pesos. Attentive service doesn't seem to be on the menu. Open daily 9am-9:30pm.

Cafetería Casa de la Cultura, on the porch of the Casa de la Cultura, overlooking the Zócalo. The most sophisticated establishment in Comitán, serving only beverages and desserts, as is the fashion. Open daily 7:30am-midnight.

A spare hour can be well spent at the **Casa Museo Dr. Belisario Domínguez,** Av. Central Sur 29, ½ block south of the Zócalo. Domínguez, a native son of Comitán, studied medicine in France in the early part of this century before gaining respect throughout Mexico for his medical knowledge and service to Comitán's poor. In 1913, President Madero appointed him Senator from Chiapas. After Madero's assassination, Domínguez delivered an eloquent speech to a full Senate, decrying the authoritarian and illegitimate tactics of Huerta. Almost as soon as he stepped off the podium, he too was assassinated. The museum occupies the house where Domínguez grew up and later treated his patients. It contains a fascinating turn-of-the-century pharmacy and doctor's kit, and provides a slice of aristocratic life at the time. The text of Domínguez's famous speech (in English and Spanish) is distributed at the door. (Museum open Tues.-Sat. 10am-1:45pm and 5-6:45pm, Sun. and holidays 9am-12:45pm. Admission 300 pesos, tour included.)

The **Museo del Arte Hermillo Domínguez,** Av. Central 51 (tel. 201-40), near Calle 3 Sur Ote., exhibits the work of modern painters from the area such as Rufino Tamayo, known for his fruity still lifes, and José Luis Cuevas. (Open Tues.-Sat. 10am-1:45pm and 5-6:45pm, Sun. and holidays 9am-12:45pm. Admission 300 pesos.)

Near Comitán: Lagunas de Montebello

Sixty-eight lakes are scattered among pine-covered hills in the national park at Lagunas de Montebello. Unfortunately, rather than prevent development, Mexico's park administration seems to encourage it. The marked path is beaten severely, although the hills above it and river valleys below it remain untrammeled. At the lakeside areas where the bus drops off passengers, such as **Laguna Monte Azul** or **Laguna Montebello,** there are picnic tables, assertive restaurateurs, taxis, and public toilets. The last bus back leaves at 3:30pm.

Hike a few minutes off the highway that connects Comitán and the lakes to the Mayan ruins at **Chinkultic.** Perhaps more interesting than the 6th- and 7th-century structures themselves are the diminutive *cenote* (natural well) and the striking view of the lake region from the hilltop. Hikers can also venture to **Grutas El Paso del Soldado,** about 1km beyond Laguna Monte Azul (called Laguna Bosque Azul by locals).

Between Laguna Monte Azul and the youth hostel on Laguna Tziscao, a path traverses 15km of forest. Along the way from Monte Azul (4km from the security office at the intersection of the road from Trinitaria and to the path to Tziscao) to Tziscao, Lagunas Ensueño and Agua Tinta on the left as well as Laguna Encantada (attached to Laguna Monte Azul) and Esmeralda. After a left turn at the intersection, a 4km walk (muddy in rainy season) leads to another dirt road that continues downhill and left toward Laguna de Montebello. One kilometer farther down the main track, a badly rutted dirt alley on the left winds 3km down to Las Cinco Lagunas. After yet another kilometer on the main track, Laguna Rojos turns up (about 1km to the left), with Laguna Yalpech soon following. From here, the road continues 5km to Las Dos Lagunas and on to the small *pueblitos* clinging to Mexico's border with Guatemala. The right turn here through the cleared fields leads to the village of **Tziscao,** on the long lake of the same name.

To reach the **youth hostel,** walk through the tiny town toward the lake, and keep to the path on the left. The tall building is past the lakeside. Don't count on its being open. The bathrooms are spotless and the beds, stacked three high, seem to be made of reinforced concrete. (5000 pesos per person.) Except at the slowest times of year, the hostel chaperons groups across the lake to a cave that used to be a Mayan sanctuary. The trip takes several hours on small outboards. The boats themselves (without guides) are also available for rent.

Back on land, the hostel managers claim to have found several abodes of the rare *quetzal* bird that ruled the jungle between Mexico and Guatemala in days of yore. They cannot guarantee a sighting of this sacred, legendary bird, but any opportunity to glimpse one is worth the gamble.

Restaurante Orquídea, on the park road between the immigration *caseta* and the ranger's office, rents *cabañas* for 8000 pesos per person. Ask the bus driver to let you off at the "Orquídea" or "La Casa de Doña María" (the owner).

Popular with locals but more obscure than Montebello is the **Cascada de Chiflón,** a 250m waterfall 45km from Comitán. The lake is safe (albeit cold) for swimming, but don't venture too close to the waterfall, or you may take a once-in-a-lifetime plunge. There are some nice places to camp here, but no facilities. To get to Chiflón, take a *combi* (700 pesos) from Av. 2 Ote. Nte., directly east of the Zócalo, to La Mesilla. *Combis* leave every half hour. Taxis charge 1900 pesos for the trip. From La Mesilla, the waterfall is a 5km walk.

Ocosingo

Although often mentioned in the same breath as the *indígena* villages near San Cristóbal, Ocosingo belongs in a different category. The citizenry is a mix of *indígenas* and *mestizos,* whose clothing is more likely to have come from Sears than the handloom. In addition, handsome colonial architecture elevates Ocosingo above its neighbors. *Gringos* are still a rarity here, so expect more than a few curious stares.

The town of Ocosingo has little to interest travelers moseying down the "*gringo* trail" between San Cristóbal and Palenque. All the same, the excellent (though seldom visited) archeological site nearby deserves a slot on every Mayaphile's itinerary.

Orientation

Ocosingo is 68km from San Cristóbal de las Casas and 118km from Palenque. The highway between San Cristóbal and Palenque follows a ridge west of town, and bus lines serving both cities have stations on or near this road. Avenida 1 Nte. runs downhill from Autotransportes Fray Bartolomé de las Casas on the highway, past Autotransportes Tuxtla Gutiérrez and Autotransportes Lacandonia, ending a block north of the Zócalo at Calle Central.

The town is laid out on the customary compass grid, but it's small enough that one can almost ignore street names. From the Zócalo, cardinal directions are marked by the Hotel Central to the north, the Iglesia de San Jacinto to the east, the Palacio Municipal to the west, and nothing much to the south.

Within town, taxis (2000 pesos) are unnecessary. Hiking to the ruins, however, is discouraged; in spite of the locals' assurances to the contrary, they are simply too far away to be reached on an enjoyable stroll. Plan ahead and catch one of the *colectivo* pickup trucks that run in the morning.

Practical Information

Currency Exchange: Change money before you go to Ocosingo. Bánamex and other banks will *not* change U.S. dollars.

Post Office: 1 Ote. Nte., 4 blocks north of the Zócalo. Open Mon.-Sat. 9am-2:30pm. **Postal Code:** 29950.

Telephones: Long-distance *caseta* (tel. 300-54) in the pink building on 1 Ote., 1 block north of the Zócalo on the left. International collect calls 1000 pesos. Open Mon.-Sat. 9am-9pm, Sun. 9am-1pm. **Telephone Code:** 967.

Bus Stations: Autotransportes Tuxtla Gutiérrez, Av. 1 Nte., 1 block south of the highway. To: Tuxtla Gutiérrez (8 per day, 5 hr., 7700 pesos) via San Cristóbal (2 hr., 3900 pesos); Palenque (7 per day, 3 hr., 5250 pesos) via *el crucero para* Agua Azul (1½ hr., 2600 pesos). Only the 6am buses to both locations are *de local* and can guarantee a seat. Tickets go on sale the day before at 5:30pm. Open daily 5:30am-7pm. **Autotransportes Lacandonia,** Av. 1 Nte., uphill from the Tuxtla Gutiérrez station, behind the cinderblock wall with the white, hand-lettered sign. To San Cristóbal (every hr. 5:30am-4pm, 4000 pesos). **Autotransportes Maya,** same office as Lacandonia. *De local* buses to Palenque (at 5:30am, 7am, 9am, noon, 3pm, and 4:30pm, 4000 pesos). **Autotransportes Fray Bartolomé de las Casas,** on the highway at the end of Av. 1 Nte. To San Cristóbal (5 per day, 3300 pesos).

Market: Two blocks south and 3 blocks east of the Zócalo. Open daily 5am-7pm.

Pharmacy: Cruz Blanca, Calles 1 Ote. and 2 Sur, 1 block south of the Zócalo. Open daily 7am-9pm.

Medical Emergency: Instituto Méxicano de Seguro Social (IMSS) (tel. 301-52), 1km south on Callejón del Panteón Municipal. Open 24 hr.

Emergency and Lost Property: Comandancia Policía (tel. 301-13), on the highway 600m south of town.

Accommodations

Ocosingo offers a simple economics lesson: large supply plus tiny demand results in low prices. Most of these places, however, put out at the same level they take in; hot water remains the only sign of life in many local lodgings.

If the hotels listed below are (by some cosmic coincidence) full, you should have no trouble finding a cheap *hospedaje* within 2 or 3 blocks of the Zócalo in any direction. You can camp or park a trailer on the town's small airstrip if you obtain permission from the Presidente Municipal (on the 2nd floor of the Palacio Municipal).

Hotel Central, Av. Central 1 (tel. 300-24), on the north side of the Zócalo. Small but inviting rooms with pretty bedspreads, fans, and clean, tiled bathrooms in an arcaded colonial-looking building. Slightly overpriced. Ask for a room with a view. Singles 25,000 pesos. Doubles 35,000 pesos. Triples 40,000 pesos.

Hospedaje San José, Calle 1 Ote. 6 (tel. 300-39), ½ block north of the northeast corner of the Zócalo. Family-run place where women should feel safe. Rooms dark, shabby, and musty, but moderately clean. Bathrooms of the wet-cement-floor variety; no hot water. Certainly in the "dive" category, but tolerable, even strangely comfortable. Singles 7000 pesos. Doubles 10,000 pesos, with bath 12,000 pesos, with 2 beds and bath 15,000 pesos.

Posada Agua Azul, Calle 1 Ote. 127, 2½ blocks south of the Zócalo—through iron gates on left side of street. Feels a bit like a jungle lodge, complete with caged animals gazing into the infrequently cleaned pool. Singles 15,000 pesos. Doubles 25,000 pesos. Triples 25,000 pesos.

Hotel San Jacinto, Av. Central 13, 1 block east of the Zócalo. Look for the fabulous blue-tiled exterior. Thirteen clean, concrete, poorly lit rooms open onto a dreary courtyard. Beds come with a single tattered sheet. Chac would cherish the wet bathroom floors. Singles 8000 pesos, with bath 10,000 pesos. Doubles 16,000 pesos, with bath 20,000 pesos. Triples 24,000 pesos, with bath 30,000 pesos.

Food

Scores of cheap restaurants jostle for space in the streets of Ocosingo. The ones listed below have an iota of atmosphere; even less expensive fare is served on practically every street corner.

Restaurant La Montura, Av. Central 5, in the Hotel Central on the north side of the Zócalo. Somewhat overpriced, but the outdoor tables with colorful tablecloths under the arcade are the most pleasant in town. Chicken and beef dishes 10,000-12,000 pesos, *enfrijolades* 4500 pesos. Staff will make sandwiches for your picnic at the ruins. Open daily 7am-11pm.

Restaurant Los Portales, Av. Central 19, on the northeast corner of the Zócalo. Old pillars and tile floor. This Homey-the-Clown restaurant is a blessing to the poor and hungry. *Huevos rancheros* 5000 pesos. *Comida corrida* 7000 pesos. Open daily 7am-5pm.

Restaurante San Cristóbal, Av. Central 22, 1 block west of the Zócalo. Look for the lime green exterior. Animal pelts, snake skins, turtle shells, and stuffed birds from the Lacandón Rainforest make the place look busy even when there isn't a soul around. *Comida corrida* with soda 7000 pesos.

Flights

For those with little time and money to burn, **Taxis Aereos Ocosingo** operates a number of one-day whirlwind tours of Chiapas's archeological sites. If you don't mind bopping into and out of small jungle airstrips, this top-of-the-line excursion comprises Yaxchilán, Bonampak, Palenque, and Agua Azul—all in one day (2-4 passengers US$500, 5 passengers US$550.) They also offer the more traditional Yaxchilán/Bonampak tour (2-4 passengers US$320, 5 passengers US$400), as well as other combinations of sites. A single flight to just about any airstrip in Chiapas runs US$200-300.

Taxis Aereos Ocosingo's office (tel. 301-88) is at the Aeropuerto Municipal, on 2a. Av. Sur, east of the Zócalo just past the market. (Open Mon.-Fri. 8am-6pm, Sat.-Sun. 8am-2pm.)

Near Ocosingo: The Ruins of Toniná

The ruins of Toniná rarely surface on a list of can't-miss sights in Mexico, but they are larger and more interesting than overbilled Bonampak and as impressive as many better-known sites in the Yucatán. Toniná's glyphs and artwork are well-maintained and relatively unweathered. Located 25 to 30 minutes from Ocosingo, the ruins remain difficult to reach and virtually untouristed; travelers without a car can dole out a steep taxi fare, prepare for days of walking, or catch a morning *colectivo.*

The Toniná complex, encompassing 15 acres of ruins, was a religious and administrative capital for the Mayan city-state that flourished from 300 to 1000 AD. Unlike the symmetric ruins of Monte Albán or Chichén Itzá, the structures at Toniná are dispersed and lack an astrological floor plan. Many statues have lost heads and feet to decay and neglect, and the pyramids can never be fully restored since the governor of Ocosingo took stones from the site to build roads around the turn of the century. The entrance path, which leads across the river east of the ruins and up a small gully, emerges on the **Plaza of War,** the first artificially terraced level of the site. Trees and grass have overgrown a pyramidal mound on the left; nearer the river is the grassy depression of the unexcavated **main ballcourt,** beyond which lies a sacrificial altar.

Toniná's chief ruin is a massive pyramid which towers 60m above the plaza. The seven tiers corresponded to the city's different social strata, from the general populace flush with the plaza to the high priests, whose four temples rest on the seventh level. Well-preserved panels and sculptures survive from almost all of the levels, but many have been removed to the museum on the premises and to Mexico City.

The ruins of a smaller ballcourt lie forgotten at the back of the plaza, by chunks of statues and panels scattered near the fence. Extensive glyphs on the back of these figures relate to the scenes on the front, often giving the *fechas fatales* (birth and death dates) of the prominent characters. Three animals—the bat, the snake, and the jaguar—appear together repeatedly. Each was revered for a different kind of natural force: the serpent for the sharp teeth with which it drew blood in self-sacrifice, the bat for its nocturnal perspicacity, and the jaguar for being the most powerful denizen of the jungle. The three stelae at the foot of the first level commemorate the inauguration of new governments.

The pyramid's **central stairway** leading up to the third level was used solely by priests and governors; others used the minor set of stairs on the right. An impressive throne balances on the third level.

The fourth level is uninteresting, but in the center of the fifth level gapes a royal grave. Here archeologists found a stone sarcophagus, made of a single piece of limestone, which held the king's body and two unidentified corpses. To the left of the grave on the same level is a shrine to Chac, the Mayan rain god. The stone originally above the figure, carved in 300 AD, is now in the museum on the premises. The **Altar de Monstruo de la Tierra** is on the right of the sixth level.

The seventh level was Toniná's religious focal point, and it supports four large pyramids dedicated to the forces of city life and prosperity. The lowest and least impressive is the **Temple of Agriculture,** on the far right of the terrace. This now crumbling, pyramidal building contained private rooms for the high priests and governors. Considerably higher, the **Pyramid of Life and Death** rises to the left of the Temple of Agriculture, slightly nearer the pyramid's summit. Archeologists believe this mound once housed the king and the royal family.

Side by side behind the Pyramid of Life and Death tower Toniná's two most important temples. The **Pyramid of War** on the right, which served as an observatory to patrol the countryside, is higher and clearly more important than its neighbor, but the **Pyramid of Finances** adds a satisfying touch of symmetry to Toniná's huge mountain site. A climb to the top of either provides a brilliant view and a cooling breeze. Below the Pyramid of War is a newly excavated statue of **King Zotz-Choj** (the jaguar-bat king), with a giant headdress depicting an eagle, serpents and the symbols for wind, smoke, and fire.

Below, the museum at the head of the footpath is painted yellow, red, blue, and white to represent the four seasons and cardinal directions. Though small, the museum possesses some 50 pieces of detailed stone work, statues of priests and slaves, and several round calendar stones with Mayan numbers and mathematical signs along their circumferences. The large, symmetrical holes in some statues show where precious and semi-precious stones were once lodged. (Site and museum open daily 9am-4pm. Admission to both 700 pesos.) A guide is usually available at the entrance for the one-to two-hour free tours; the guides are paid by the government, but a tip is customary.

Taxis from Ocosingo's Zócalo charge an outrageous 60,000 pesos for the trip to Toniná and back, with a one-hour stop at the ruins. Instead, catch a *colectivo* pickup truck to Guadalupe (2000 pesos), a village 1km from the site. A bus to Guadalupe (**Unión de Vehículos de Pasaje y Carga "Mixta" Ocosingo**) leaves from the front of the market in Ocosingo at 9 and 11am, returning at 9:30am and noon. To drive or walk to the ruins, follow Calle 1 Ote. south out of town, past the clinic on the right. Bear right past the radio station on the left. Follow the signs for "Toniná ruins" to the Rancho Toniná, which encompasses the site. The road to the left of the gate leads to the museum and ruins. Inquire at the ranch about camping.

The Lacandón Rainforest

La Selva (Forest) Lacandona once covered most of the state of Chiapas, but after centuries of incursions by agricultural interests, less than 15% of the original jungle remains. The Lacandón people have been the most isolated of the country's many *indígena* groups ever since small Mayan clans from different parts of northern Mesoamerica fled deep into the jungle to avoid the Spanish conquistadors. Calling themselves "Hachack-Winick" (The True People), they developed a common dialect and cultural bond, despite their dispersal over a large area. Their isolation continues to this day, and many still live on family *milpas* (cornfields) rather than in villages.

The Lacandón culture has experienced its share of change, however. A single missionary based at Lacanjá began converting *indígenas* in the 19th century, one *milpa* at a time. The Lacandones have since fused Christianity with their ancient Mayan beliefs.

Commerce with *ladino* civilization has made the Lacandones the wealthiest *indígenas* in Mexico: they sell timber rights to multinational companies that harvest mahogany from the vast tracts of jungle, using these revenues to facilitate their entry into other markets such as chicken-farming. But as the ethic of expedience and fast profit takes hold, the Lacandones' way of life is changing once again. Short-sighted lumber companies burn swaths of forest, destroying whole acres of wood and leaving only the mahogany booty standing. From the air you can see the blazing fires and resulting wasteland. Lacandón reforestation efforts have been fighting a losing battle against such pillage. The jungle ("Reserva Integral de la Biósfera Montes Azules" in government jargon), once the Lacandones' source of security and livelihood, now dwindles toward nothing.

Earlier this century, the Lacandones' practice of burning incense in clay "godpots" in each family's religious center (or "godhouse") and then leaving them at Mayan ruin sites in the rainforest, led archeologists to such hidden cities as Bonampak. Today, only the northernmost group of Lacandones around the city of Naja exercises the old custom. Visitors occassionally witness early morning rituals at Yaxchilán.

Practical Information

The Na-Bolom museum in San Cristóbal is responsible for the best of the few available maps of the Lacandón jungle. The map is as old as the hula hoop, but marks most settlements. Roads lead to three of the four most popular destinations in the rainforest, but a more exciting, if riskier, method of transport is by *avioneta* (small airplane) to Naja or Lacanjá, the jungle's most accessible towns, or the Bonampak and Yaxchilán ruins (the latter not accessible by road at all). Flights to these areas are available from Comitán, Palenque, Tenosique, and Ocosingo. Logging and petroleum firms constructed the roads that do exist, and since repairs are made infrequently, travel is restricted to four-wheel-drive vehicles and buses. During the rainy season, roads are often impassable; at other times of year one should carry machetes and chains.

Línea de Pasajeros Comitán Lagos de Montebello runs buses as far as San Javier, 13km from Bonampak. Montebello also provides bus service to such remote locations in the Lacandón Rainforest as Pico de Oro and Benemérito. For further information, inquire at the bus stop across the street from Palenque's market on Velasco Suárez.

No public transportation directly serves Frontera Echevarría (also called Corozal) on the Río Usumacinta, 25km farther down a mangled dirt road from San Javier. You can take a bus to the San Francisco *crucero*. From there, hike to Frontera Echevarría (bring overnight supplies and plenty of water); some hitch rides with the occasional trucks. Some private homes in Frontera Echevarría rent beds for the night. From here, launches run down the Río Usumacinta to Yaxchilán. Locals operate the boats and charge about 12,000 pesos per person for the two-hour trips. Boat trips to Yaxchilán (50,000 pesos per boat) can also be arranged with the Lacandones at Bonampak.

Bonampak

The ruins of Bonampak, the "City of Painted Walls," lie on the northern side of the Valle Río Lacanjá, on the slopes of a small mountain range that separates the Lacanjá and Usumacinta river basins. This ceremonial center, like many in southern Mexico, coalesced during the Mayan Classical period (200-900 AD). Most of the buildings of Bonampak extant today were built during the 300-year period before 700 AD, with legible inscriptions dating from 605 to 792.

The excitement about Bonampak owes to its ancient murals, which relate a large number of previously unknown details of Mayan daily life. But because many of the murals have deteriorated almost beyond recognition, the site is unimpressive to most tourists. Yaxchilán, Chinkultic, Toniná, and Palenque are of more interest to the layman.

Unless arranged through an agency, tours of Bonampak are given in Spanish only. The pamphlet distributed on arrival is also in Spanish, but it contains a small map helpful for identifying the more decayed buildings. There are no facilities at the ruins, so take an ample supply of water, some food, and small change for tipping guides.

The few buildings standing at Bonampak surround a rectangular plaza with an approximate north-south orientation. The skewed position of the foundation of Building 15 to the north suggests that there was once an extension of the plaza, adjacent to the main one but with a slightly different orientation. The buildings on the north, east, and west sides of the main plaza have been reduced to rubble. To the south, the site's major attraction is a huge hill of calcite rock, the abruptly rising front of which has been skillfully modified into a series of walls, terraces, stairways, and temples.

With the exception of one lintel and a panel on the south side, the sculptures at Bonampak narrate historic events. The most important monument concerns conquest and religious celebrations, in which most of the population took part. The enormous stela at the foot of the terraced hill represents the warrior-king Hatach Huiñic, Bonampak's most powerful ruler, who led the city-state to victory over the Olmecs. Two more stelae are protected against the elements on the stairs rising to the south of the plaza; Chac is on the left, while the right illustrates the Mayan conception of a bloodthirsty sun god claiming a sacrificial victim with a mighty stroke of his battle axe.

In the center of the first level, Building 2 remains unexcavated, while Buildings 1 and 3 at the right and left extremes respectively, have survived more or less intact and are typical examples of Classical Mayan architecture. Building 3 contains several stones used for sacrifices and provides some respite from the jungle heat after the climb from the plaza. Anthropologist Agustín Villagra has called **Building 1** the "Sistine Chapel of the Americas." Intricate murals begin at the doorjambs and cover all four walls of three separate rooms. These murals are significant because they treat aspects of daily life comprehensively and in detail, instead of covering the more esoteric religious rituals usually recorded. Musicians, warriors, prisoners, nobles, dancers, and magicians are all portrayed—a total of 270 human figures, most 85-92cm high. Just as unusual are the accompanying glyphs, which describe the scenes and gossip about various characters.

Because of their blatantly two-dimensional nature (almost all figures appear in profile), the murals have often been compared to Egyptian paintings, and have given rise to a number of theories connecting the two cultures. The Maya have also been positively identified as the Lost Tribe of Israel, the survivors of Atlantis, and the instigators of the Bigfoot myth.

In the 12 centuries since the murals were completed, tropical rains have left thick calcium carbonate deposits on the walls. While experts have created faithful reproductions of the murals, which hang in all three rooms, the originals remain woefully obscure. On the east wall of the building's first room, partial cleaning has rendered sections of the murals visible once more. Larger-scale reproductions of the murals are on view in Tuxtla Gutiérrez and Mexico City: a graphic scene from the central chamber chills guests of the Hotel Bonampak in Tuxtla Gutiérrez, and the Museo Nacional de Antropología in Mexico City has a complete set of reproductions.

Unlike those of the first level, the eight smaller buildings atop the southern monument have architectural features unique to Valle Río Lacanjá. The buildings are on a more modest scale than most Classical Mayan constructions, in part because the familiar false arch has here been diminished or eliminated completely in favor of a simple sloped ceiling. These buildings are also distinguished by their cylindrical stone altars.

Bonampak can be reached by plane or bus (see Practical Information above). Launches leaving from Piedras Negras, Yaxchilán, and Tenosique sputter down Río Usumacinta to the ruins; inquire at the bus station in front of the market in Palenque or outside Tenosique on the river for more information.

Yaxchilán

Yaxchilán ("green stones") takes its name from the banks of a nearby stream and, more than most Mayan ceremonial centers, took its shape and character from the site on which it was constructed; the Maya found it impossible to impose their typical geometric configuration near the tortuous channel of the Río Usumacinta and the stubborn hills of calcite rock on its bank. Instead, they built Yaxchilán on and around swells in the terrain created thousands of years earlier by the wandering river. Although the architectural features here resemble those of other sites in the region, closer inspection reveals altered proportions and adaptations to the topography. The overall effect is more organic than monumental.

Yaxchilán gained prominence during the four centuries of the Maya's golden age; all buildings bear dates between 514 and 807 AD. Two powerful governors who ruled during the city's 8th-century heyday appear in many of Yaxchilán's glyphs and carvings. Archeologists believe that the first governor, Escudo Jaguar (Jaguar Shield), migrated from present-day Guatemala before assuming control of Yaxchilán. His glyph, a jaguar in profile, smatters Buildings 23, 33, and 34, all built during his reign. After a successful period of territorial expansion, one of Escudo Jaguar's three wives took over for a short time. She was replaced by Escudo's son, Pájaro Jaguar (Bird Jaguar), who continued to augment the city's holdings through matrimonial alliance and military conquests from 752 to 770 AD. Many of the buildings on the main plaza were constructed during this epoch. Pájaro Jaguar's favorite glyph consists of a slightly smaller jaguar profile with a horizontal bird as the forehead. Often juxtaposed with Escudo Jaguar on stelae and panels, Pájaro Jaguar is distinguished by the feathers on his back.

A rocky path cuts through the jungle from the airstrip, emerging at two crumbling pyramids. Four entrances in the second pyramid lead into what is commonly referred to as the Labyrinth, a series of twisted pitch-black passageways and chambers which exits on the southern side of the building amid several round stones once used for human sacrifice. Facing away from the building, the ruins of the main plaza are on the left, and a small temple on a raised terrace is to the right.

An overgrown path climbing up a hill behind the temple to the southeast terminates at Building 33, which was constructed by Escudo Jaguar. Panels along the building's base illustrate a ballgame play by play.

As impressive as this temple is, farther up the hill you'll find still taller and larger monuments that are usually left off guided tours. Be insistent if you want to see these uppermost temples. The set is not visible from the plaza, and many tourists take a farewell photograph of the ruins from the departing plane, only to realize through the telephoto lens that their US$100 tour was incomplete. **Building 41,** the largest of the three, is also the backdrop for several stelae from the time of Escudo Jaguar. From this height, the lay of the land and the full extent of the site become clear.

To the right of the stairs leading out of Building 33, several residential structures lie in shambles. Restoration is underway, however, on the promising stelae at the foot of the stairs and the four buildings to the left and right. The two more interesting buildings are to the right. **Building 21,** excavated in 1983, contains a very clear stela of a woman offering a sacrifice. In **Building 20,** a lintel depicts two men discussing the death of a third; the dead man's spirit emerges from the speaker's mouth, in keeping with Mayan beliefs about death and the afterlife. The same scene appears less clearly on the lintel of the second doorway.

In the middle of the plaza in front of the stairs, statues of a crouching jaguar and a life-sized crocodile flank another well-preserved stela. A bit farther northwest, on the river side of the plaza, an unexcavated ballcourt lies beneath two sloping mounds. Tours generally do not cover the docks and piers along the river or the extensive unexcavated areas southeast up the river, but you can easily explore them without a guide.

The pamphlet handed out to visitors is in Spanish and includes an adequate map of the site. Compare buildings on the map with those you see on the tour and ask about conspicuous omissions. The unremarkable Building 33, for example, is often maliciously pawned off as Building 41, the site's highest structure. Since tours usually only advertise two hours at Yaxchilán and demand is great, it may be difficult to change a set routine or allow enough time to strike out on your own. People arriving by foot or whitewater raft from the Río Usumacinta have the freedom to stay longer and explore in greater detail. Carry enough water for the visit and the sometimes stifling plane ride. You should also bring food, flashlights, an Aerobie, and change to tip the guides.

Guides allow travelers to hang hammocks or camp under the large tin-roof shelter near the dock for free. The mosquitoes are not as gracious; bring a mosquito net or tent. When not occupied by archeologists, a small cabin with two beds is rented out for a small fee. To reach Yaxchilán, take a boat from Fontera Echeverría, Bonampak, Piedras Negras, or Tenosique. The site is free and always open.

Naja and Lacanjá

These two villages, on the edge of the once huge Lacandón Rainforest, are the most accessible of the Lacandón villages, a few hours from Palenque by car. Caught in a cultural transition, both towns still attempt to abide by traditional dress codes: women usually wear brightly colored feathers and seed jewelry. Some elders are making a last-ditch effort to pass on ancient religious traditions to their grandchildren who are more impressed by automobiles, guns, and economic opportunities. The Lacandón language, however, still dominates; few women speak Spanish. The traditional *balché* drink, made from fermented sugar cane with a tasty bark flavor, is easy to find in any of the huts lining the dirt streets. At the same time, the Christian cross, planted outside homes to protect them, is steadily replacing the ancient cross symbolic of the cardinal directions and their corresponding colors (white for north, red for east, yellow for south, black for west). As yet another freak of modernity, many Lacandónes are purchasing radios, TVs, and household appliances even before acquiring electricity.

Buses (modified trucks) to the villages run irregularly, sometimes only every other day. Inquire across the street from Palenque's market for more information. If you hitch, be patient; there are long periods when no vehicles pass to Naja. To be safe, bring water, insect repellent, a poncho during the rainy season, and a hammock and light sheet for nighttime warmth. Buses to Naja take at least nine hours to maneuver along the treacherous path; Lacanjá is only six hours away on a much better road.

Río Usumacinta

The river that forms the border between Chiapas and Guatemala flows past nature at its best and humanity at its gravest. Ruins and wildlife speckle the riverbanks, and those who brave the white water between Frontera Echeverría and Tenosique may see wild bands of monkeys as well as rabid bands of Guatemalan guerrillas. Interspersed are refugee camps, exotic orchids, fighter planes and helicopters, black panthers and pumas, and completely deserted villages of a far more recent vintage than the ruins of Yaxchilán or Piedras Negras. Plates and silverware have been left uncleared in some of these hastily evacuated towns, and a surreal air pervades the whole area. Because of the warfare, a trip here could be more of an adventure than you can handle. It is advisable to consult your embassy, consulate, or other government authority knowledgeable about the border region's status before making plans. Travel in parts of the region is often officially restricted (see Guatemala).

Two important archeological sites and several less interesting Mayan ruins perch upon the banks of the Usumacinta. Ancient docking facilities and extensive excavation make it easy to spot Yaxchilán, which is close to Frontera Echeverría. Unless you hire a guide, **Piedras Negras** is extremely difficult to locate. On the Guatemalan side of the river, it is one of the oldest Mayan sites known, built during the pre-

Classical period. Though the ruins were explored and at least partially excavated earlier in this century, the Guatemalan jungle has voraciously reclaimed the ancient city and obscured the site completely. The ruins lie in a protected canyon near the Usumacinta, and though completely overgrown with forest and underbrush, provide a vision of the Mayan past as archeologists encounter it.

Palenque

The ruins of Palenque straddle a magnificent 300m-high *palenque* (natural palisade) in the foothills of the Altos de Chiapas. Dozens of thundering waterfalls tumble into the yellow-green savannah, and the vast tropical rainforest blankets the surrounding region in emerald humidity. Most visitors, wide-eyed even without the aid of the hallucinogenic herbs and fungi that flourish in the moist shadows of the forest, easily understand why the ruins have, for centuries, been revered as magical.

Eight kilometers from the ruins lies the sleepy town of Santo Domingo—called simply "Palenque" after the crumbling temples that are its lifeblood. Tourism may sustain the town of Palenque, but it hasn't made it attractive. Fed on visitors' dollars, the once small, poverty-stricken village has undergone uncontrolled sprawl. Though no one would bother to visit the city just to visit the city, Palenque serves as an adequate base for excursions to the nearby ruins.

A potent hallucinogenic mushroom ("hongos" in Spanish) grows in the fertile countryside around Palenque. State police occasionally offer rewards for turning in *jipi-drogistas*. Remember: the ruins are fantastically more interesting than the damp walls of the local cell block.

Orientation

Palenque is in the northeastern corner of Chiapas, 315km from Tuxtla Gutiérrez. From the west, it lies at the end of a rough and winding five- to six-hour journey on dirt roads that lead to San Cristóbal via Ocosingo. To the east, the Yucatán awaits, within easy reach on excellent paved roads that pass through Chetumal. Arriving on the Rte. 186 bus that connects Chetumal and Villahermosa, get off at Catazala, from which *combis* and taxis will take you to Palenque. The last *combi* (2000 pesos) leaves at 7:30pm. After that, hitch a ride or find a group to split the 15,000-peso taxi fare for the 23km trip into town.

Palenque lacks the rational layout of most of Chiapas's settlements, although some semblance of order does exist: streets running east-west are labeled "Avenidas," and those running north-south "Calles." The main avenue, **Avenida Benito Juárez,** links Palenque's Zócalo to the highway and the ruins. Running north-south, **Calle Independencia** borders the Zócalo on the west. To get to the Zócalo from the bus station, walk 4 blocks uphill on Juárez.

Practical Information

Tourist Office: In the Palacio Municipal, on the north side of the Zócalo. English spoken, but useful maps of Palenque are available only once in a blue moon. Open Mon.-Fri. 8am-8pm, Sat. 8am-1pm. Another office beckons 28km from town on the road to Villahermosa. Same hours.

Travel Agencies: Palenque's travel agents can arrange some exciting (if expensive) excursions. **Viajes Toniná,** Juárez 105 (tel. 503-84), near Allende, organizes a 2-day trip to Bonampak and Yaxchilán for US$85, 6-person minimum. Fee includes a *lancha* trip on the Río Usumacinta, 5 meals, and camping equipment. Also sends *combi*-loads to the remote *indígena* villages of Lacanjá and Naja (400,000 pesos each village for up to 6 people) and to Agua Azul (15,000 pesos per person, 7-person minimum). **Anfitriones Turísticos de Chiapas** (tel. 502-10), on Allende just north of Juárez, offers a 2-day excursion to Bonampak and Yaxchilán (nearly identical to those offered by Viajes Toniná) for US$75, 6-person minimum. A 4-day trip to Guatemala's Tikal ruins costs US$400, 2-person mimimum. Fee includes *lancha* on the Río San Pedro, hotels, and all meals. A daytrip to the ruins of Toniná near Ocosingo costs US$120 for up to 7 people.

Currency Exchange: Bancomer, Juárez 40 (tel. 501-98), and **Bánamex,** next door. Both are west of the Zócalo, and both exchange only traveler's checks Mon.-Fri. 10am-noon. Exceptionally slow lines. After hours, many hotels and travel agencies will change cash and sometimes traveler's checks.

Post Office, Independencia at Bravo (tel. 501-43), around the left side of the Palacio Municipal, north of the Zócalo. Lista de Correos. Open Mon.-Fri. 9am-1pm and 3-6pm, Sat. 9am-1pm. **Postal Code:** 29960.

Telephones: Long-distance *caseta* (tel. 500-00) at the ADO station. Collect calls 5000 pesos. Open daily 8am-2pm and 4-9pm. Another *caseta* at Heladería Holandesa in the Hotel Palenque is open daily 7am-2pm and 5-9pm. Same rates. **Telephone Code:** 934.

Train Station: Just past the Cabeza Maya 6km north of town. Train to Mérida via Campeche, scheduled daily at 9:30pm, is often 2-6 hr. late for a 24-hr. trip. The 10am Mexico City train usually takes much longer than 30 hr. Tickets on sale 1 hr. before departure time. Second-class passage only. Taxis to the station charge 1000 pesos.

Bus Stations: ADO, 5 de Mayo at Juárez (tel. 500-00), about 4 blocks west of the Zócalo. First-class service to: Mexico City (at 6pm, 14 hr., 49,000 pesos) via Orizaba (35,000 pesos); Villahermosa (6 per day, 2½ hr., 6700 pesos); Macuspana (at noon and 7pm, 1½ hr., 4300 pesos); Catazajá (5 per day, ½ hr., 1300 pesos); Campeche (at 7:15pm, 16,000 pesos) via Escarcega (9200 pesos). Luggage storage to the left of the station (1000 pesos) open daily 6:30am-7pm. ADO station open daily 6am-7pm. **Autotransportates Tuxtla Gutiérrez,** Juárez 159 (tel. 503-69). Second-class buses to: Tuxtla Gutiérrez (5 per day, 8 hr., 13,000 pesos); Agua Azul (at 8am, 2 hr., 2000 pesos); Ocosingo (5 per day, 3 hr., 5200 pesos); Chiapa de Corzo (5 per day, 7 hr., 12,300 pesos); San Cristóbal de las Casas (5 per day, 5 hr., 9000 pesos). Luggage storage costs 700 pesos per piece per day. **Transportes Dag Dug** occupies a hole in the wall a few doors west of Autotransportes Tuxtla Gutiérrez on Juárez. Second-class buses to: Tuxtla Gutiérrez (at 8am, 18,000 pesos) via Villahermosa (6200 pesos); Mérida (at 5pm, 9 hr., 24,000 pesos). The Mérida-bound bus usually sells out by the morning of departure; purchase your ticket a day in advance.

Taxis: Tel. 501-12. Easy to find around the Zócalo, transportation stations, and the ruins.

Transportation to the ruins: ADO bus runs daily at 10:30am (500 pesos). Quicker and more frequent are the *combis* operated by **Transportes Chambalu,** at Hidalgo and Allende, 1 block north of Juárez (every 15 min. 6am-6pm, 1000 pesos). **Transportes Palenque,** on 20 de Noviembre, operates during the same hours and charges only 500 pesos. Look for the red sign in the window. The last bus leaves the ruins at 6pm. Board *combis* at the office, or anywhere on Juárez west of Allende.

Laundromats: Lavandería Bolaños, on 5 de Mayo across from the ADO station. Wash and dry 8000 pesos for 3kg. Open Mon.-Sat. 8am-2pm and 4-7pm.

Hospital: Clínica Palenque, Velasco Suárez 33 (tel. 502-73). 24-hr. emergency service.

Police: In the Palacio Municipal (tel. 501-41). Open 24 hr.

Accommodations

Hotel prices in Palenque are high and rooms uniform. You can try to bargain, but even Palenque's dives often have their rates clearly posted behind the reception desk, rendering them immutable. The best bet is to cough up the extra pesos and console yourself with the fact that you only need spend a night or two here, anyway.

Staying in one of the several hotels en route to the archeological site makes it easier to get to the site itself but more difficult to get to a cheap restaurant or to the market. Although most of these roadside hotels are quite expensive, the notorious **Mayabell Trailer Park and Camping** ("Shroomland") allows guests to string up a hammock or put down a sleeping bag under a *palapa* roof for 4000 pesos. Electricity, water, and sewage facilities are available for trailers (8000 pesos). This laidback hippie hangout is a great place to snag travel tips. The campground's **Restaurant Yaxché** serves nothing over 6000 pesos. The campground is 6km from town, 2km from the ruins. The best way to get there is by *combi.*

Palenque is not the safest place for wild camping, since locals have figured out that foreigners often carry dollars and other valuable tidbits.

Hotel Vaca Vieja, 5 de Mayo 42 (tel. 503-77), at Chiapas 3 blocks east of the Zócalo, in a quiet part of town; so named when the owner sold his last cow to buy the place. Spotless modern rooms and bathrooms. Comfortable beds. Dangerously powerful ceiling fans. Excellent restaurant. Singles 25,000 pesos. Doubles 35,000 pesos. Triples 45,000 pesos.

Hotel Lacroix, Hidalgo 10 (tel. 500-14), just to the left of the church from the Zócalo. The oldest hotel in Palenque (founded in 1956) is beginning to show its age. Many famed archeologists have stayed here through the years. Their graffiti concerning the ruins cover the exterior of the hotel. Semi-clean rooms with ceiling fans. Often full. Singles and doubles 25,000 pesos. Triples 30,000 pesos.

Hotel Santa Elena, on Domínguez, off Juárez 2 blocks west of the bus station. Comfortable rooms with large, clean, tiled private bathrooms. Low, cozy beds, fans, and colorful bedspreads. Off the beaten path yet still close to the bus station. Singles 20,000 pesos. Doubles 25,000 pesos. Triples 51,000 pesos.

Posada Santo Domingo, 20 de Noviembre 119 (tel. 501-46), near the bus station. A friendly, busy place with booming TV at front desk. Private bathrooms with towels and soap. Rundown but fairly clean bedrooms have fans, no sheets. Check rooms carefully before paying because some "beds" are really cots. Singles 15,000 pesos. Doubles 20,000 pesos. Triples 30,000 pesos.

Casa de Huéspedes Alicia, Velasco Suárez 59, across the street and west of the municipal market, northwest of the center of town. Look for the "House Boarding Alice" sign. Fans can't air out smelly communal bathrooms. Not well-maintained. Cheap, but a 10-15 min. walk from *el centro*. Singles 14,000 pesos, with bath 15,200 pesos. Doubles 20,000 pesos, with 2 beds 25,000 pesos.

Food

Palenque has cheap restaurants, but most are completely devoid of atmosphere and appetizing fare. If you spend the day at the ruins, you might want to brown-bag it, since the sole on-site eatery is a souped-up snack bar. In town, several small grocery stores line Juárez. For a good selection of cheap fruits and vegetables, try the market on Velasco Suárez, 4 blocks west and 4 blocks north of the Zócalo. You can also grab a cheap meal at any of the several marketplace *fondas*.

Restaurant Yunuen, 5 de Mayo 42, at Chiapas in the Hotel Vaca Vieja, 3 blocks east of the Zócalo. Small, friendly place with fancy service and reasonable prices. Breakfast specials 4000-6500 pesos. Feast on the *pollo a la Palencana*—potato, fried bananas, 2 cheese tacos, rice, beans, salad, and chicken for only 11,000 pesos. Open daily 7am-10pm.

La Escondida, 20 de Noviembre 96, 2½ blocks west of the Zócalo. Friendly, English-speaking owner advises caution on Sunday afternoons when the local crowd gets rowdy. Dinner special of soup, salad, and spaghetti with fish or chicken 8000 pesos. Four chicken tacos 4500 pesos. Open daily 8am-9pm.

Restaurant Maya, Independencia at Hidalgo, on the west side of the Zócalo. Large place patronized by more *viajeros* than locals. Service is less than five-star, but the food is good. *Pollo a la Palenque* (cooked in beer) 9900 pesos. Breakfast 4800 pesos. Open daily 7am-11pm.

Restaurante Las Tinajas, 20 de Noviembre 41, at Abasolo. Lanterns, hardwood floors, and high-backed chairs. Pricey, but excellent service and generous portions. Meat 14,000 pesos. Open daily 8am-11pm.

Café Centenario-100% Puro, Juárez 187, a few blocks south of the Zócalo. Excellent Chiapan coffee: toasted, ground, and brewed on the premises (500 pesos). Open daily 6am-2pm and 4:30-9pm.

Piccolino's Pizza, on Juárez near Allende. Swallow outrageously expensive pizza in exceptionally small and uncomfortable chairs. Large pizza (enough for 2) 20,000 pesos. Mexican pizza (with sausage, peppers, avocado and tomato) 28,000 pesos. Open daily 7am-11pm.

Sights

One of Palenque's ancient names means "Place of the Sun's Daily Death," for this was one of the westernmost cities of the Mayan territory. When settlement began in the 3rd century, the Maya had only the slightest notion of other communities, occasionally coming into contact with the Olmecs; for the most part their jungle civilization flourished in isolation.

Palenque owes much of its spectacular architecture, including the finest examples of stucco bas-relief sculpture anywhere, to its most famous ruler, the club-footed King Pakal (615-683 AD), who is often referred to in glyphs by a sun and shield. More than 8 square kilometers were landscaped for dwellings, platforms, and plazas under the guidance of Pakal and Ahpo-Hel, the sister he married. One of the inscriptions carved around the time of Pakal's death indicates that he lived into his fifth *katun* (20-yr. period), when his son Chan-Bahlum succeeded him. Chan-Bahlum, represented by the jaguar and serpent glyphs, celebrated his accession by building his father a crypt in the pyramid (now called the Temple of Inscriptions). He also ordered the construction of the Sun Plaza group and placed stone tablets inside each of the temples there. These are the only narratives found on such large tablets in Mexico (usually messages appear on smaller, upright stelae).

Although the inscriptions include self-explanatory pictures of the main characters, props, and actions, less than a fifth of the thousands of Mayan glyphs have been deciphered. While experts pore over these tablets, visitors to the ruins marvel at the wall murals and the stucco sculpture. The "cement" is a concoction of bark, clay, and stone, in which intricate details were molded while the mixture was still wet.

Indígena men dressed in all-white gowns sell bows and arrows at the entrance to the ruins. These Lacandones from Lacanjá are amiable and willing to discuss their culture. In contrast to most other *indígena* groups, it is the men among the Lacandón who continue to wear the traditional garb, while women sport Western dresses and hairstyles.

Upon entering the site, you pass the tomb of Alberto Ruz Lhuillier, an archeologist so devoted to Palenque that he insisted on being buried beside the restored ceremonial plaza. To the right rises the steep **Temple of Inscriptions,** named for the magnificent tablets inside, the earliest inscribed for Chan-Bahlum in 692. Although the outer stucco reliefs are rapidly deteriorating, the inner sanctum still harbors the inscribed tablets. In 1949, Ruz discovered a secret stairway beneath a few slats in the inner sanctum floor and later uncovered the royal tomb where Chan-Bahlum laid his father to rest in 683, the first such burial place found anywhere in the Americas. Visitors can climb down the many slippery stone stairs and peer through a window to see the crypt. The perfectly preserved, elaborately carved sarcophagus weighs five tons. (There is a copy in the small museum on the premises.) Inside the sarcophagus, food, stone sculptures, rings, necklaces, a mask, bracelets, and a crown were stored beside the body. Archeologists at first referred to the dead leader as the "jade king," because the mineral was found in his mouth, hands, and strewn about the tomb. Outside the royal crypt was another tomb for the young men sacrificed to serve Pakal on his voyage through the afterlife, during which they would carry his dishes, jade and pearl jewelry, red shells, and other necessities. A tubular duct was built between the royal tomb and the stairway hall to allow communication between Palenque's priests and their dead king. Unlike the rest of the ruins at Palenque, the tomb inside the Temple of Inscriptions is only open daily from 10am to 4pm.

A trail leads up the mountainside to the left of the Temple of Inscriptions. About 100m along this trail, on the right, is the **Temple of Jaguars.** If you descend the stairwell inside the structure, you will come upon the 7-ft. well to the left of the temple, where a few faint traces of paint are losing the battle against the green slime of the jungle. The trail continues up the hill before reaching the tiny *indígena* village of Naranjo. The difficult but oddly refreshing hike takes 90 minutes and passes through territory that would make Tarzan wax nostalgic. Bouts of malaria have broken out in this village, so before setting out check with the Palenque tourist office.

At the center of the ceremonial plaza, next to the Temple of Inscriptions, a complex consisting of four patios of various sizes called the **palace** forms a trapezoid on a stepped platform. Detailed stucco reliefs ornament the walls, and the northern courtyards conceal scaly monsters. All of this is visible from the unique, four-story astronomical tower in the center of the complex. On the inner wall of the eastern patio are several 3m-tall statues standing shoulder-to-shoulder, pledging allegiance to a long-forgotten god. A steam bath and ancient latrines have also been excavated.

The path between the palace and the Temple of Inscriptions forges the Río Otolum before leading to the Sun Plaza, another landscaped platform. The first building here is the **Temple of the Sun,** with the smaller **Temple 14** next to it. The **Temple of the Cross,** up a narrow rocky path, is the largest of the temple-pyramids in the Sun Group. The outer layer of blue-tinted stucco has worn away, but the inner sanctum protects a large sculpted tablet and reliefs on either side of the door.

About to be swallowed again by the jealous jungle, the **Temple of the Foliated Cross** lies across the plaza from the Temple of the Sun. Despite the overgrown path, the inner sanctum here, too, contains a surprisingly clear carved tablet. The temple takes its name from the unusual tree or cross with branches remarkably similar to that found on a temple at Angkor-Wat, Kampuchea, but nowhere else in the Americas.

To the south, through the wall of trees, several more unreconstructed temples surround the uncleared Plaza Maudslay. North from the Temple of the Inscriptions, past the palace, the vestige of a ballcourt is on the right, and on the left is the Temple of Frederick, Count of Waldeck, who lived here while studying the ruins in the 1830s. Beyond and to the right of this temple are the remains of the North Group.

The museum near the North Group has a few items on display, all from the Palenque archeological investigations. The few placards do only a cursory job of explaining the exhibits in Spanish. Just steps behind the museum a trail leads to the **Queen's Bath,** a beautiful set of waterfalls crashing through a steep, shady ravine. As the name implies, Palenque's queens once bathed here. Waterfall enthusiasts should also visit **Cascada Motiepa.** About 600m before the entrance to the ruins, a small sign marks the path to the waterfalls. A short jaunt through the jungle delivers you to this aquatic nirvana.

The archeological site is open daily from 8am to 5pm. The museum is open from 10am to 5pm and the crypt from 10am to 4pm. Admission to the site is 10,000 pesos, with student ID 4500 pesos.

Near Palenque: Cascadas Agua Azul and Misol-Ha

Both of these large *cascadas* (waterfalls) have overflowed with tourists of late. And for good reason. **Agua Azul,** 62km south of Palenque, breathtaking from the mountain ridge above, is even more so from its rocky shores. Over 500 individual falls lead to rapids, whirlpools, and calmer swimming areas in between. The Río Yax slams into limestone bedrock, but toward the end of the rainy season the silt turns the water to murky coffee.

One safe swimming area is 1km upstream from the falls. Even strong swimmers should still be cautious; the five crosses near the falls stand in memoriam of more than 100 deaths caused by the whirlpools and tremendous underwater currents. Rely on a buddy system if the falls aren't already teeming with tourists.

Since the 4km walk down (and up!) from *el crucero* is tiresome with any baggage, it's best to spend only the day at the falls, returning to Palenque in the afternoon. It's possible, though, to get hammock or sleeping space at the campground here for 3000 pesos.

The falls at **Misol-Ha** are 24km from Palenque and only 2km from the highway crossing. There is only one large cataract here, but the swimming area is clean. The small restaurant has a few good dishes at reasonable prices.

Buses between Palenque and Ocosingo or San Cristóbal will stop at the crossroads for either falls, to pick up or discharge passengers (3000 pesos to Palenque). Since few buses pass after 4pm, leave the falls in the early afternoon. Reliable pickup truck traffic makes hitching relatively easy. Entrance to the falls costs 2000 pesos per person or 5000 pesos per carload.

The most painless way to visit Agua Azul and Misol-Ha is aboard one of Transportes Chambalu's *combis* (25,000 pesos). Arrive at the Palenque station at Hidalgo and Allende by 9:30am; *combis* leave daily at 10am. After a 15-minute photo stop at Misol-Ha, the van continues to Agua Azul (no need to hike—passengers are dropped off right by the falls) for a two-hour swimming session. You should be back in Palenque by 3:30pm.

TABASCO

Gateway to the Mexican southeast, the state of Tabasco is a lush, flat plain, criss-crossed by rivers and dotted with lakes and swamps. By one explanation, Tabasco's name springs from the *indígena* word "Tlapalco," meaning "moist land." With good reason, too: the jungle here is even more dense, hot, and humid than its northern counterpart. To attract tourists, Villahermosa has launched an enormous image-changing drive. The government has relocated most of the state's archeological treasures to new museums near downtown Villahermosa. These efforts notwithstanding, most people still come to Tabasco for business rather than pleasure.

The Olmec culture, Mexico's oldest and arguably most influential, flourished in the area now within Tabasco's boundaries. Travelers in Tabasco will soon become familiar with the Olmec style of sculpture and carving, including the colossal stone heads that cover the state's tourist posters and brochures.

Because few Olmec artifacts exist, their civilization remains shrouded in mystery, but archeologists do know that the Olmecs worshiped the jaguar as a divine creature. Manifest reminders of this passion for the powerful cat remain in many of the Olmecs' monumental stone carvings, in which man and jaguar inseparably intertwine. The Olmecs' art, architecture, astronomy, and calendar were adopted and refined by the later Mayan and Toltec cultures.

The combined efforts of the state and Pemex (in its quest for oil under the jungle; the area is possibly the largest untapped reservoir of oil in the world) have made Tabasco's tourist sites remarkably accessible. The most important remains of the Olmecs' principal city, La Venta, have been moved to a park in Villahermosa's newest cultural complex, **Center for the Investigation of Olmec and Mayan Cultures (CICOM)**. Tabasco's most important set of Mayan ruins, Comalcalco, lies only an hour from the capital, easily reached by bus or car. Many tourists stay in Villahermosa to visit the ruins of Palenque in Chiapas state, two hours away. A few determined to see Mexico's less accessible ruins fly from Villahermosa or Tenosique into the Lacandón Rainforest of Chiapas to explore Bonampak and Yaxchilán.

The highway system in Tabasco and the Yucatán consists of haphazardly connected local routes, which allow coherent travel if you trust the posted destinations and not the route numbers. Route 180 cuts east across Tabasco from Veracruz to Villahermosa, after which it crosses into Campeche state and connect to Ciudad del Carmen. Route 186 heads southeast toward Palenque before turning north to cross the Río Usumacinta and the Campeche border. The mostly paved road from Catazaja on Rte. 186 passes through Palenque and Ocosingo on its way to the Pan American Hwy., San Cristóbal de las Casas, and Comitán. Faster and more heavily traveled, Rte. 195 shoots south from Villahermosa to Chiapas and joins the Pan American Hwy. roughly halfway between Tuxtla Gutiérrez and San Cristóbal.

Villahermosa

Weary of defending the coast against British and Dutch pirate raids, the Spanish colonists of this area migrated inland up the Grijalva River to found Villahermosa (at first a fishing town called San Juan Bautista) in 1596. Over the course of the next few centuries, Villahermosa developed slowly into a minor agricultural and commercial center; transport to and from the capital was fluvial until the late 1940s, when a short connection to Teapa linked Villahermosa by rail to the rest of the nation. Since then, the oil industry has transformed Villahermosa from backwater to boomtown. Satellite antennae, luxury hotels, and Pemex apartment complexes have sprouted virtually overnight, and what was once a pock-marked swamp has become a cluttered urban metropolis.

Drowning in oil revenue, the state invested billions of pesos to improve the capital with new museums, monuments, bus stations, libraries, and parks. In its archeological park and anthropological museums, Villahermosa safeguards the remaining artifacts from the region's ancient Olmec culture. Another development success, the Tabasco 2000 complex, includes government buildings, a planetarium, and a sparkling shopping center. Yet shedding an old identity and fabricating a new one will take Villahermosa some time. Less than six years after its opening, the complex's large department stores seem more like museums than shops. Locals stick to the noisy Zona Remodelada shopping area downtown and to the city's open-air market on Pino Suárez.

Orientation

Tabasco's state capital lies in the central third of the state, only 20km from the border with Chiapas state. Escárcega, the major crossroads for Yucatán-bound travelers, lies 298km east of Villahermosa via Rte. 186; Coatzacoalcos, where the Mexican isthmus tapers to its narrowest, lies 169km to the west via Rte. 180, and Tuxtla Gutiérrez, capital of Chiapas, lies 293km to the south, 34km west on Rte. 190 after the end of Rte. 293.

Villahermosa has grown in an expansive maze of winding, heavily-trafficked streets. Most areas of interest lie downtown, though the city claims residents in 95 outlying *colonias*. First- and second-class buses depart from the city's eastern edge. An international airport lies northwest of the city, 14km from the downtown area; taxis shuttle between the airport and downtown (20,000 pesos *especial,* 4500 pesos *colectivo.*)

To reach downtown from the first-class **ADO** station, walk 2½ blocks south on Mina to Méndez. From there, take a *combi* (300 pesos) labeled "Tierra Colorada Centro-Juárez," and get off a few minutes later at the Parque Juárez. You can find most hotels south of the park on Madero or its parallel cousin Constitución. Walking from the station to the Parque Juárez takes 15 to 20 minutes; upon exiting the terminal, head straight ahead (east) across Mina and down Fuentes or Merino 5 blocks to the Parque de la Paz. On the far side of the park, turn right (south) on Madero; you will reach the Parque Juárez and the hotel zone after 6 blocks. Taxis from the first-class station to anywhere in the city cost 3000 pesos.

From the **second-class bus terminal,** cross Grijalva on the pedestrian bridge to the left of the station exit and jump on a bus labeled "Indeco Centro" (300 pesos). De-bus at the Parque Juárez on Madero; the hotels stand to the south. To make the 25-minute walk from the station, cross the bridge and continue away from the station (east) on Grijalva (away from the station) until you reach Madero, which runs 14 blocks south to the Zócalo, passing many hotels on the way. Consider taking the taxi (3000 pesos) to avoid the bus hassle or the long walk from the second-class station.

Those driving from the north will enter Villahermosa on the road that merges with the southbound Universidad. Turn left off Universidad onto Grijalva just before the toll bridge over the river, then right onto Madrazo, which bypasses the center about 14 blocks to the south. Those coming from the east should cross the toll bridge over the river and head left as soon as possible for 14 blocks along the river to the Zócalo. Arriving from Tuxtla Gutiérrez, Teapa, or points south, after entering the city in the southeast corner, cars should head right (north) on the Cámara Freeway, which turns into Madrazo as it approaches the center. Coming from Cárdenas, Coatzacoalcos, or points farther west, you should enter via Grijalva, make a right on Tabasco, and continue to the river—the center is 3 blocks to the left.

Downtown Villahermosa lies between the Río Carrizal to the west and the Río Grijalva to the east; the large Laguna de las Ilusiones winds its way through the northern half of the city. The **Zócalo** and city center are on the west bank of the Grijalva, south of the rest of the city. Madrazo runs roughly north-south, following the Grijalva's west bank, and Blvd. Grijalva acts as a *periférico,* making an extended

S-shape across the city. **27 de Febrero,** which meets Madero to form the spine of the downtown area, and **Paseo Tabasco,** which winds past the Tabasco 2000, see most of the downtown action. Tabasco intersects 27 de Febrero in front of the cathedral.

To reach Tabasco 2000, make the half-hour walk or catch the "Tabasco 2000" bus from the city center by the Parque Juárez to the end of Tabasco. The same trip costs 3000 pesos by taxi.

The state tourist office and major hotels provide excellent city maps, which afford a general overview of the metropolis and a clear picture of the downtown area. Villahermosa's many one-way streets are not indicated as such on the map, nor is a concise summary of the thorough urban bus system available, but passersby will most likely be willing to give directions to any destination. *Saetas* (public buses) are usually painted green and white and cost 300 pesos; *combis* cost 300 pesos as well.

Practical Information

Because Villahermosa is spread over a large area, always get specific directions to your destination and find out if it is served by public transportation.

State Tourist Office: Tabasco 1504 (tel. 506-94), in the new state office building across from the Palacio Municipal in the Tabasco 2000 complex. Walk halfway into the arcade and go up the staircase to the right. Loaded with maps and glossy brochures. Large, English-speaking staff. Open Mon.-Fri. 9am-3pm and 6-8pm, Sat. 9am-1pm.

Federal Tourist Office: Tabasco 1504 (tel. 628-91), in the same office as the state office above. Some English spoken. Open Mon.-Fri. 9am-3pm.

Tourist Information Booths: In the airport (tel. 272-55). Open daily 7am-1pm and 2-9pm. In the first-class bus station; open daily 7am-9pm. At the Museo La Venta; open daily 9am-3pm.

Currency Exchange: Bancomer, Juárez at Zaragoza (tel. 237-00), 1 block west of Madero. **Bánamex,** Reforma at Madero (tel. 289-94), 3 blocks north of the Zócalo. Similar rates. Both open Mon.-Fri. 9am-1:30pm. Expect to wait in lines for 45 min.

Post Office: Saenz 131 (tel. 210-40), at Lerdo, 3 blocks west of Madero and 1 block south of Zaragoza. Open for stamps Mon.-Fri. 8am-7pm, Sat. 9am-1pm; for all other services Mon.-Fri. 8am-5:30pm, Sat. 9am-noon. Branches at the ADO station supposedly open Mon.-Fri. 8am-6pm, but often closed in actuality. **Postal Code:** 86000.

Telephones: Long-distance calls are best made from pay phones on the street, since many *casetas* do not allow collect calls or don't exist at the locations indicated on the tourist office's map. **Café La Barra,** Lerdo 608, up the stairs by the main telegram office, does allow calls. Open Mon.-Sat. 7am-2pm and 3-9pm. **Telephone Code:** 931.

Telegrams: Lerdo 601 (tel. 224-94), uphill from the post office at Saenz, 3 blocks west of Madero and 1 block south of Zaragoza. Open for money orders Mon.-Fri. 8am-5:30pm, Sat. 9am-noon; for all other services Mon.-Fri. 8am-midnight, Sat. 9am-1pm. Branch at the ADO station (tel. 237-51) open Mon.-Fri. 9am-3pm.

Airport: (tel. 243-86), on Cametera Rovirosa. **Aeroméxico,** Periférico Carlos Pellicer 510 (tel. 211-64). Open daily 9am-7pm. To Mérida (at 8:15pm, 1 hr., 190,000 pesos) and Mexico City (at 8:10am, 1 hr., 245,000 pesos). **Mexicana,** Av. 4 at Calle 13 (tel. 350-44), in the Tabasco 2000 complex. Open Mon.-Fri. 9am-7pm, Sat. 9am-1pm. To Mexico City (2 per day, 1 hr., 167,264 pesos). Fares 25% lower for those under 21. **Aerocaribe,** Tabasco at Mina (tel. 432-02), serves Oaxaca, Cancún, and Mérida.

Bus Stations: ADO and **Cristóbal Colón,** Mina 297 (tel. 221-91), at Merino, in the northeast corner of the city. Walk 11 blocks from the center north on Madero to the Parque de la Paz, turn left on Merino, and walk 6 blocks to the station. Get to the station as far in advance as possible to buy tickets; it's not unlikely that lines at ticket counters will be 2 hr. long. First class service to: Campeche (14 per day, 7 hr., 14,350 pesos); Coatzacoalcos (11 per day, 3½ hr., 5550 pesos); Comalcalco (3 per day, 1½ hr., 2800 pesos); Mérida (12 per day, 9 hr., 20,500 pesos); Mexico City (12 per day, 13 hr., 42,000 pesos); Oaxaca (3 per day, 14 hr., 34,000 pesos); Palenque (2 per day, 2 hr., 4750 pesos); Paraíso (3 per day, 2½ hr., 3400 pesos); Puebla (9 per day, 10 hr., 25,600 pesos); Puerto Ceiba (4 per day, 3 hr., 3650 pesos); Salina Cruz (2 per day, 21,500 pesos); San Andrés Tuxtla (13 per day, 6 hr., 13,000 pesos); San Cristóbal (1 per day, 14,500 pesos); Tapachula (1 per day, 36,000 pesos); Teapa (5 per day,

1 hr., 1905 pesos); Tenosique (7 per day, 4 hr., 6650 pesos); and Veracruz (12 per day, 8 hr., 15,550 pesos). **Central de Autobuses de Tabasco,** Grijalva/Cortínez, 3 blocks inland from the river in the northeast corner of town. Tickets not usually sold in advance, so arrive at least a ½ hr. early. Second-class service to Teapa (every hr., 1 hr., 3000 pesos). Service also to Comalcalco, Paraíso, Mexico City, San Cristóbal, and many other points.

Taxis: Tel. 369-30. Almost any trip in Villahermosa costs 3000 pesos, but be sure to settle the price before you get in.

Supermarket: Bonanza, Madero at Zaragoza (tel. 422-80). Cheap beer, wine, and bulk foods. Open daily 8am-9pm.

Car Rental: National Car Rental, Reforma 304, at the Miraflores Hotel, in the Zona de la Luz. Open Mon.-Sat. 8am-2pm and 4-7pm. Also in the Villahermosa Hyatt. Open Mon.-Sat. 7-9am and 1:30-9:30pm. **Tabasco Auto Rent,** Méndez 507 (tel. 235-05), 2 blocks off Madero.

Laundromat: Lavandería Automática, Reforma at Constitución. 6500 pesos per 3kg for next-day service. 4-hr. service worth the additional 1500 pesos. Open Mon.-Sat. 8am-8pm.

Red Cross: (tel. 335-93 or 334-39) on General Sandino in the Colonia 1 de Mayo. Take the "1 de Mayo" bus from Madero. 24-hr. emergency service and ambulance service to any point in the city. No English spoken. A good clinic is the **Sanatorio Santa María,** Zaragoza 1202 (tel. 250-00 or 251-99). English-speaking staff. Open daily 7am-8pm.

Pharmacy: Farmacia Canto, Madero 602 (tel. 220-99), at Sanchez Marmol. Member of large pharmacy chain that accepts major credit cards. Knowledgeable chemist on duty daily 3-5pm. Open daily 7am-10pm.

Police: 16 de Septiembre at Periférico (tel. 319-00). No English spoken. Open 24 hr.

Accommodations

Many rooms in Villahermosa hover around 15,000 pesos. Budget hotels line Madero and Constitución, and quite a few congregate in the nearby Zona Remodelada. Madero offers shopping, noise, and close proximity to the Zona, while Constitución is less elegant and a bit farther away from the action. Reservations are generally unnecessary since the city has not yet blossomed into the tourist magnet it aspires to be.

Hotel Madero, Madero 301 (tel. 205-16), near 27 de Febrero. An old Spanish building that could use some maintenance. Handsome pink staircase leads to small, immaculate rooms. Firm mattresses, bathrooms with hot water, and fans make for a comfortable existence. Manager asks after your health, stores packs, and gives good directions. Singles 25,000 pesos. Doubles 30,000 pesos.

Hotel Oviedo, Lerdo 303 (tel. 214-55), the 1st hotel on the pedestrian walkway off Madero. Grape-sized square rooms off a maze of dark hallways. Mattresses sag so much as to totally cut off the breeze created by the furious fans. Street-side rooms are noisy. Singles 12,000 pesos. Doubles 20,000 pesos.

Casa de Huéspedes Teresita, Constitución 224 (tel. 224-53). Ten small, cozy rooms off an upstairs lobby where the cheerful manager dances to piped-in music. Singles and doubles 15,000 pesos.

Hotel Cristóbal Colón, Constitución 1001 (tel. 242-64), at Magallanes. Surrounded by blue walls and covered by high ceilings, mattresses lie contentedly on concrete blocks decorated with bathroom tiles. Friendly management keeps place spic and span. All rooms have fans and hot water. Singles 10,000 pesos. Doubles 15,000 pesos.

Hotel Don Carlos, Madero 422 (tel. 224-99). Costly contemporary class. Beautiful, well-maintained rooms and lobby, purified water on every floor. All rooms have phone, TV, A/C, and hot water. Respectable restaurant. Singles 63,000 pesos. Doubles 70,000 pesos. Reservations accepted.

Hotel Miraflores, Reforma 304. Large, Holiday Inn-like hotel with restaurant, parking garage and A/C in lobby. Cool rooms adorned with *agua purificada* and TVs. Strong showers. Singles with bath 63,000 pesos. Doubles 70,000 pesos. Triples 77,000 pesos.

Hotel Buenos Aires, Constitución 216 (tel. 215-55), between Lerdo and Reforma. Like a gloomy funhouse—walk through the pink-and-blue hallways then duck your head past the curvy mirrors to enter the small *habitaciones*. Grimy bathrooms don't amuse. Offers the bare minimum of facilities at rock-bottom prices. Singles and doubles 15,000 pesos.

Hotel Oriente, Madero 425 (tel. 211-01), between shops in the arcade north of 27 de Febrero. Dark and musty rooms off nice hallways reminiscent of elementary school. *Agua purificada* in lobby, and a restaurant on the ground floor. Singles 20,000 pesos. Doubles 25,000 pesos.

Hotel Providencia, Constitución 210 (tel. 282-62), between Lerdo and Reforma. Look for the "Hotel P" sign with an eye inside a triangle. Low prices for decent accomodations, including fans, *agua purificada*, and cold showers. Large, lumpy-as-bad-porridge beds with clean sheets usurp most of the space in the tiny rooms. If you can fit in the bathrooms, you'll find sanitary facilities and toilets with entertaining flushing systems. Singles and doubles 12,000 pesos.

Hotel Grijalva, on Zaragoza between Pino Suárez and Constitución. Two young men rent 2nd-floor rooms that have that cement basement feel. Dark, musty bathrooms won't win any prizes for cleanliness. Singles 15,000 pesos. Doubles 20,000 pesos.

Trailer parking is allowed in small **La Choca Park** in Tabasco 2000 but camping is not.

Food

Despite booming development and a desire to attract tourism, Villahermosa cooks up paltry few pleasures for the budget traveler's palate. Cafés, *torterías,* and frozen yogurt shops permeate the Zona Remodelada, and the restaurants that line Madero rarely rise above the ordinary. The main produce market operates off Pino Suárez near Zozaya, a few blocks from Puente Grijalva.

El Torito Valenzuela, 27 de Febrero 202, at Madero. The friendliest and cleanest of the numerous downtown *taquerías;* eat on the bumpy cafeteria bar and attempt to finagle a souvenir hat out of the waiters. Quesadillas 2200 pesos, *tortas* 4000 pesos. Open daily 8am-midnight.

Los Jinetes, Mina 119, at Arboleda near the first-class bus station. Wooden chairs, plaid tablecloths, and rock music cranked up to 11. Sip a beer while watching your meat roast on the grill. Extremely tender and tasty *brocheta de filetes* (shish-kebab) worth the 18,000 pesos. Variety of steaks 10,000-15,000 pesos. Open Tues.-Sat. 2-11pm.

Cafe Bar Impala, Madero 421. Fun hangout serving great *tamalitos de chipilín,* a regional specialty (1000 pesos). *Panuchos* and tacos 800 pesos each. Colorful tiles surround the interior, and loud Mexican pop music fills the air. Great for people-watching. Open daily 8:30am-8:30pm.

La Playita Restaurant-Bar, Constitución 202, with a riverfront entrance as well. Spruce, casual family restaurant popular with the local crowd. *Sopa de mariscos* 15,000 pesos, 10 varieties of chicken (even Wade Boggs would drool) 10,000 pesos each. Open Mon.-Sat. 8am-8pm.

Restaurant Oriente, Madero 425, in the arcade north of 27 de Febrero. A hotel cafeteria that attracts locals as well. Tropical bird prints embellish white cement walls. Simple chicken quesadillas 8000 pesos. Roast beef 11,000 pesos. Open daily 8am-8pm.

Capitán Beulo, on Lerdo, floating on the river. Villahermosa's most interesting dining option. Originally a banana boat and later a floating medical clinic for towns along the river, the captain's barge now serves meals as it cruises down the Grijalva River. Entrees moderately priced (from 11,000 pesos); price includes passage. Leaves the dock Tues.-Sun. at 1:30, 3:30, and 9:30pm.

Ric's, on Mina, in the Las Galas shopping center next to the ADO station. Cushioned booths and simply *wonderful muzak.* Fruit salad 4800 pesos, sandwiches 7000-11,000 pesos. *Menu del dia* 15,000 pesos. Open daily 8am-10pm.

Los Tulipanes, in the CICOM complex. Elegant restaurant with beautiful river view. Good service, tasty food, and high prices. Breakfasts 4000-10,000 pesos. Simply yumsters *tortuga en sangre* (turtle in blood) goes for 25,000 pesos. Open daily 8am-1am.

Restaurant Geminis, Madero 704, between Méndez and Magallanes. Mediocre local budget dishes served on sticky plastic placemats. An almost indecipherable mural depicts unhappy gods or possibly New Kids on the Block after Donnie cut his chin. Breakfast specials 4400-7500 pesos. *Enchiladas Geminis,* a curious combination which includes a chicken leg, costs 12,800 pesos. Open daily 7am-9:30pm.

Sights

While exploring a ruin site at La Venta, Tabasco, in the early 1940s, U.S. archeologist M.W. Sterling discovered six massive sculpted stone heads. Further studies indicated that La Venta—in the middle of a swampy region of contemporary western Tabasco—had been a principal ceremonial center of the Olmecs. In the late 1950s, the monumental pieces were moved to an archeological park in Villahermosa designed especially for the artifacts, the Parque-Museo La Venta.

In 1800 BC, the Olmecs formed the matrix culture of Mesoamerica. At the height of their civilization (between 800 and 200 BC), the Olmecs numbered only 250,000, but their distinctive artistic style influenced groups from the Ríos Sinaloa and Panuco in northern Mexico to the Península Nicoya in Costa Rica. Most nearby cultures adopted their belief in the jaguar as a divine creature and the creator of the peoples of the world. In honor of the cat, sculptors at La Venta produced numerous beautiful jade carvings of the jaguar, but the animal's artistic influence far exceeds that: the Olmecs even gave their carvings of people what has been called a "jaguar mouth," symbolizing the intermingling of the jaguar and the human, the divine and the mortal. These colossal sculptures range from 2m to 10m in height. Each of the spherical heads wears a war helmet and has the thick eyelids, wide nose, and prominent lips of the Olmecs, yet each expression is distinct. The stern, disembodied heads weigh heavily on low mounds of dirt, evoking images of a thick neck, great torso, and powerful legs reaching far into the bowels of the earth.

The beautiful **Parque-Museo La Venta,** on Laguna de las Ilusiones 3km north of the city center, displays five of these giant heads as part of a self-guided tour. Stop briefly at the small museum just inside the entrance (off Grijalva) to study a large-scale model of the actual La Venta site. Difficult-to-spot concrete footprints lead the way past nearly three dozen large stone sculptures. There are no labels, but descriptive pamphlets (1000 pesos) are sometimes available at the entrance. Better yet, pick up the pamphlets at the tourist office for free.

To get to the *parque-museo,* take the "Tabasco 2000," "Circuito #1," or "Parque Linda Vista" bus (300 pesos) from Madero in the center to the intersection of Tabasco and Grijalva. Walk northeast on Grijalva for five minutes until you reach the "La Venta" entrance. (Site open daily 8am-4:30pm. Admission 2500 pesos. Light-and-sound show in Spanish Tues. and Thurs.-Sat. at 7 and 8pm, weather permitting. Tickets 3000 pesos.) Return to Paseo Tabasco through the **Parque Tomas Garrido Canabal,** which also lies on the Laguna de las Ilusiones and surrounds the Parque-Museo La Venta. Landscaped alcoves hide benches and fountains. Climb the 40m *mirador* for an excellent view of Villahermosa, and look for the manatees that reside in the *laguna* below. (Main entrance at the corner of Tabasco and Grijalva. Open daily 8am-9pm. Free.)

Farther northwest on Tabasco, away from the city center and Río Grijalva, lie two more city parks. **Tabasco 2000** is a long strip of sparkling new buildings that includes the city's ultra-modern Palacio Municipal, a convention center, several fountains, a shopping center, and a planetarium whose Omnimax shows are made in the U.S. and dubbed in Spanish. (Shows every hr. Tues.-Sun. 4-8pm. Admission 3500 pesos, half-price with student ID.) **Parque La Choca** is the site of Villahermosa's annual livestock and crafts fair, an eight-day event held in the last week of April. During the rest of the year, the park is a pleasant place to picnic. (Open daily 8am-9pm. Free.) To reach Tabasco 2000 and the Parque La Choca, take the "Tabasco 2000" bus from the city center.

The great instigator behind the creation of the Parque-Museo La Venta was Carlos Pellicer Cámara, Tabasco's most famous poet. His name graces the **Museo Regional de Antropología Carlos Pellicer Cámara,** the main attraction at Villahermosa's new CICOM complex. The museum's well-presented material describes archeological sites near Villahermosa including Palenque and Comalcalco. The first floor concentrates on the life, times, and arts of the two tribes that successfully dominated the region, the Olmecs and the Maya, while the top floor includes representative pieces from all of Mexico's indigenous tribes.

From the Zona Remodelada, the museum is best reached by a 20-minute walk south along the Grijalva River. The crowded "#1" and "CICOM" buses pass frequently. (Open daily 9am-8pm. Admission 1000 pesos.)

The CICOM complex also houses the second-most important library in Mexico, in a modern stone building at Carlos Pellicer 107 (tel. 421-24). For a cool afternoon stop in and enjoy the theater, the musical equipment, the cafeteria, and of course, the books. (Open Mon.-Sat., 8am-9pm, Sun. 9am-5pm.) The management at the **Teatro Esperanza Iris,** next door to the library, enjoys showing off their beautiful, modern theater. Ballet, orchestra, and other performances take place at the theater twice per month; tickets cost up to 20,000 pesos. Call 259-59 for information. The complex also contains the Los Tulipanes Restaurant, a craft shop, and an expensive bookstore.

Attractions for children in Villahermosa include the **Parque de Convivencia Infantil,** next to the Parque-Museo La Venta and north along Cortínez. Attractions include an aviary and petting zoo, and play space for local children. The park is least crowded on weekday mornings when school is in session. (Open Tues.-Sun. 9am-5pm. Admission 500 pesos, ages under 12 free.)

Entertainment

Villahermosa presents two basic nightlife options: either frequent the discos in the luxury hotels or attend one of the many cultural activities sponsored by the Instituto de la Cultura.

Keep your nose in the air at the most popular disco in town, **Snob,** Juárez 106, in the Hyatt. A sweltering mix of locals and tourists jams all night long to U.S. rock, *salsa,* and tropical music. (Open Tues.-Sun. from 10pm. Women free Thurs.) **Estudio 8,** Grijalva at Mina, in the Hotel Maya Tabasco, also packs 'em in. (Open Mon.-Sat. 10pm-3am.) A more mature crowd watches shows and dances at **La Troje,** Tabasco at Grijalva in the Hotel Viva. (Open Mon.-Sat. 10pm-3am.) The Hyatt and Viva are both near Tabasco 2000, while the Maya Tabasco lies closer to the center. Cover charges will set you back roughly 20,000 pesos.

For mellower diversion, head for **Galería El Jaguar Despertado,** Saenz 117, near Reforma in the Zona Remodelada. The café in back features live classical music nightly. (Open daily 10am-10pm.)

The **Instituto de la Cultura,** in the Edificio Portal del Agua on Magallanes (tel. 279-47), publishes a monthly calendar of musical, theatrical, and other cultural events. Look for it in museums and major hotels.

Near Villahermosa

Two daytrips within Tabasco state offer impressive sights and an escape from the heat of the capital. The Mayan ruins at Comalcalco, with their unique architecture, make a stimulating prelude to the nearby beach. Or head inland to Teapa to visit the vast caverns of Coco005n and spend a lazy afternoon in the pools of the nearby El Azufre spa. Both sights are accessible by public transport, although you should start early in the day and expect to transfer a number of times.

Comalcalco

Whereas La Venta documents Tabasco's Olmec past, Comalcalco demonstrates the Maya's dominance over the area in the later Classic period (200-700 AD). One of the northernmost Mayan settlements, Comalcalco grew contemporaneously with Palenque in nearby Chiapas and has yielded evidence of contacts with other Yucatecan Mayan settlements, as well as with the Toltecs, Mexica, and Totonacs. The site's most distinctive feature is its architecture; unlike those of other Mayan cities, the pyramids and buildings of Comalcalco were constructed from packed earth and clay and later covered with stuccoed oven-fired bricks. Eroded but still imperial, the constructions contrast dramatically with the grass slopes and the jungle backdrop. Do not climb the temples, since Uzi-toting guards are serious about the "no subir" signs.

With 10 levels, the hulking 25m-high pyramid to the left of the entrance to the site is Comalcalco's best-known landmark. The north face bears traces of the elaborate stucco carvings that once completely covered the structure's sides. Behind the pyramid stretches the north plaza, surrounded by a series of ruined minor temples and mounds whose dilapidated state allows a closer look at Comalcalco's brickwork and oyster-shell mortar.

From the plaza, a well-worn path leads up the side of the acropolis area and passes a group of three temples on the way (from right to left, Temples 22, 13, and 12). As with the main pyramid, vestiges of elaborate decorative carvings can be seen on each of these temples.

Farther up the acropolis, turn right to reach the **Tomb of the Nine Knights of the Night,** named after the nine bas-relief figures on the walls of the tomb. Visible from the acropolis, three sides of Comalcalco's ballcourt (to the left) remain unexcavated and covered with tropical vegetation. Several temples and administrative buildings, including one known as The Palace, stand in pieces atop the acropolis against a backdrop of tall, square brick columns and several roofless rooms. (Site open daily 10am-5pm. Admission 1170 pesos; free Sun. and holidays.)

The archeological zone lies 55km northwest of Villahermosa near the town of Comalcalco (2km away) and can be reached by the bus that travels to Paraíso via Comalcalco (see Villahermosa Practical Information). Get off at Comalcalco and walk back a block on Méndez to its major intersection with Rte. 187. From this corner catch a green-and-white *combi* (1000 pesos) and ask the driver to let you off at the access road to the *ruinas.* From here, the walk to the site is a pleasant 1km. You can also take a taxi (*especial*) directly to the site from the Comalcalco bus station (5000 pesos).

Tabasco Coast

In terms of natural beauty, the beaches of the Tabasco Coast pale in comparison to those of the Pacific or those on the other side of the Yucatán Peninsula; furthermore, oil drilling has had no salutary effect on the coastal ecosystem. Generally speaking, however, Tabasco beaches are clean and good for swimming.

Most of the small resort towns offer budget accommodations, and all are adept at preparing delicious seafood. The westernmost resorts on the coast near Villahermosa, **El Paraíso** and **El Limón,** can be reached by bus from the inland town of El Paraíso. From Villahermosa and El Paraíso, buses also run daily to the resort at **Puerto Ceiba,** where you can rent boats to explore its lagoon. From there, you can reach a number of other small towns on Laguna Mecoacán. These settlements are not beach towns, but rather fishing villages that owe their livelihoods to oysters. Farther to the west, **Pico de Oro** and **Frontera** both bask on the sandy shore and provide possibilities much the same as those at the closer El Paraíso and Limón.

The town of El Paraíso is a brief 20-minute drive north on Rte. 187 from Comalcalco. To catch a bus after visiting the ruins, wait where the access road intersects Rte. 187 and flag down a blue bus or green-and-white *combi* marked "Paraíso." Many first- and second-class buses leave El Paraíso for Villahermosa. Check out the return times at the corresponding Villahermosa bus stations.

Teapa

An hour's drive south of Villahermosa, along roads flanked by banana groves, Teapa attracts visitors to its sulphuric spa and impressive caverns. Only 9km apart, the two sites together comprise a full daytrip from Villahermosa. Teapa itself, however, is hot and dingy, understandably receiving few visitors, although recent efforts by the state government to woo tourists have resulted in the improvement of a few hotels and restaurants.

El Azufre Spa, 5km west of Teapa, flaunts two large pools, a picnic area, and a modest restaurant. Ignore the dilapidated facilities: the mountain setting is striking and the waters superb. The first pool is cool and only mildly sulphuric, the second warm, bubbling, and loaded with the malodorous mineral. Should you become addicted to the suave waters, the site provides rustic, dirty bungalows for stays at 20,000 pesos for one or two persons, 25,000 pesos for three. (Site open daily 6am-6pm. Admission 2000 pesos; use of picnic facilities 4000 pesos per group.)

Las Grutas Coconá were discovered around 1800 by the Calzada brothers during a hunting trip, as several youngsters will recount in unison at the site's entrance. The truly impressive caverns plunge several kilometers into a hillside. When a large enough group has assembled, a Spanish-speaking guide launches into a half-hour locution explicating the cool, moist caverns. The guide will also point out tons of animal likenesses in the rocks that only he can see, as well as a lagoon containing purportedly blind fish (they don't wear dark glasses). Every two hours, if the machines are working, a sound-and-light show bounces colored beams off the huge stalactites. Chances of catching a tour and a show are best on Sundays, when the caves are filled with visitors. Chances of hitching a ride back to town are greater on Sunday as well; if you plan to wait for the *combi*, bring insect repellent because the large bloodsucking bugs are insatiable. (Open daily 10am-5pm. Admission 1000 pesos.)

Those journeying by car to El Azufre or Las Grutas can avoid Teapa altogether. To get to the spa, stay on Hwy. 195 from Villahermosa, and do *not* take the "Teapa" exit after the railroad tracks. The spa is 4km farther down the road. To reach the caves, cross the bridge and soon bear left for the 2½km ride to the caves.

Getting to Teapa from Villahermosa via public transport is easy: catch a first-class Cristobál Colón bus (4 per day, 5500 pesos) or a more frequent second-class Transportes Villahermosa-Teapa bus from the Central Camionera off Grijalva. Be sure to arrive a half-hour early to ensure seating. The second-class *directo* (26 per day, 1 hr., 3000 pesos) is nearly as fast as the first-class bus. The Transportes Villahermosa-Teapa bus lets you off at Teapa's main bus terminal on Méndez, from which local buses whisk you to either the spa or the caves. If you arrive by Cristóbal Colón, walk ½km up Romas toward the town's center; the local terminal sits on the right.

To reach El Azufre from Teapa, take the Pichucalco bus (every hr., 500 pesos) and ask the driver to let you off at the short access road to the spa. To return to Teapa, walk back to the highway and flag down a returning bus or hitch a ride. To reach the *grutas* from the Teapa terminal, look for the frequently departing *combi* van marked "Grutas" (500 pesos), which leaves from Méndez in front of the station. Taxis cost 5000 pesos to the *grutas* and 10,000 pesos to the spa, although rates are very flexible. Be sure to schedule a return time.

Teapa has adequate facilities to accommodate an overnight stay. The most expensive and by far the nicest hotel in town is the **Hotel Quintero,** E. Bastar 108 (tel. 200-45). Clean rooms off a palm-studded courtyard have A/C, patterned bedspreads, and sparkling bathrooms. To get there from the main bus station, turn right and walk up Méndez for about 10 minutes; the hotel is on the right. (Singles 36,000 pesos. Doubles 46,000 pesos.) Nearby, the **Hotel Jardín,** Av. Plaza de la Independencia 122 (tel. 200-27), at the end of Méndez, offers less attractive dim blue rooms. Laundry hangs in the courtyard in a blatant attempt at a down-home atmosphere. All rooms have fans and baths. (Singles 25,000 pesos. Doubles 30,000 pesos.) The cheapest accomodations in town are found at the **Casa de Huéspedes Miye,** Méndez 215. Tiny, bright rooms face a cramped courtyard. (Doubles 20,000 pesos, with bath 25,000 pesos.) Dining options are scarce, but try **El Jacalito,** Méndez 113, just past the Palacio Municipal, an indoor/outdoor café that serves generous chicken and beef dishes for 12,000-13,000 pesos.

La Venta Archeological Site

"This place has changed a lot since the time of old Queen what's-her-name" is an old travel guide cliché, and La Venta is no exception. Especially after 2500 years.

In 600 BC La Venta thrived as the capital of the Olmecs, who were ancestors of the Maya, predecessors of the Aztecs, and founders of modern Mexico. Today, La Venta contains one hotel, a few restaurants, and two streets. The polestar around which these miniscule attractions revolve is the stellar **Museo Arqueológico de La Venta,** paradoxically situated on the edge of the city.

Under a high thatched roof, the museum's single room holds exhibits about Olmec daily life, several large stone artifacts, and a few precision jade pieces. An outdoor trail circles the hill that once was the pyramid in the center of the city, but most of the artifacts that once surrounded the hill have been moved to La Venta Park in Villahermosa. The climb to the top of the hill is arduous in the heat of the day, and the disheartening view from the crest encompasses acres of empty countryside. (Museum open Mon.-Sat. 9am-4pm. Free.)

To reach the museum, turn right as you leave the ADO station and head down Benito Juárez, La Venta's main thoroughfare. The street curves to the right around the Olmec head in the large plaza. Keep going until you reach the large thatched roof on your right. Two Olmec heads flank the entrance to the museum. From the AU station, take a right and head 1 block uphill to Juárez and the plaza; turn left; the museum is ahead and to the right. La Venta makes a daytrip from either Coatzacoalcos or Villahermosa. **ADO** runs one first-class bus (2600 pesos) per day to La Venta from Coatzacoalcos at 2:30pm. The last ADO bus leaves La Venta for Coatzacoalcos at 7:30pm, and for Villahermosa (6000 pesos) at 5:35pm. **AU** runs three buses per day from Coatzacoalcos (2300 pesos), all before 11:20am.

If it is too hot to make the 10-minute walk across town to the *museo,* you should hail one of the golden-brown cars with the upside-down triangle and the word "Tabsi" (loosely translated as "Taxi") on the side. They are stationed at the town's cross street.

After visiting the museum, leave La Venta. If you must spend the night here, the **Hotel Selene,** across from the ADO bus station on Juárez, has acceptable (because they're the only game in town) rooms with mostly operable fans and baths. (Singles 20,000 pesos. Doubles 37,000 pesos.) A simple restaurant right before the plaza, at the corner of Juárez and the town's other main street, has no menu but offers low prices and friendly service.

Tenosique

There are but two reasons to set foot in Tenosique: to make a bus connection via the Río San Pedro or to catch a cheap flight to the ruins of Bonampak or Yaxchilán.

Orientation and Practical Information

Tenosique lies near the Río Usumacinta, about 25km from the Guatemalan border and 58km south of the nearest Mexican interstate highway, Rte. 186, which connects Villahermosa and the Yucatán.

In Mexican fashion, Tenosique's planners mapped out its grid "by the numbers" and wrapped the entire mathematics around a Zócalo. Even-numbered *calles* run roughly north and south, odd-numbered ones east and west. The Zócalo is bounded by Calle 21 on the north, Calle 23 on the south, Calle 28 on the west, and Pino Suárez (Tenosique's main drag, also called Calle 26) on the west. Everything, with the exception of the bus and train stations, is within spitting distance of the Zócalo. The **post office** is 1 block past the Zócalo on Calle 28 (**Postal Code:** 86900); the **telegram office,** 1 block past Calle 26 on Calle 21. There is a long-distance *caseta* on the corner of Calles 23 and 22, 1 block from the Zócalo. **Bancomer** (tel. 201-85) sits on the corner of Calles 26 and 23, behind the Zócalo (open Mon.-Fri. 9am-1:30pm), **Bánamex** on the corner of Calles 26 and 27 (open Mon.-Fri. 9am-2pm and 4-6pm). Banks in Tenosique won't change traveler's checks, but **Ortiz y Alverez,** Calle 28 #404, will (open Mon.-Fri. 9am-1pm and 5-8:30pm).

Tenosique is serviced by first-class **ADO** buses from the station on the corner of Calles 42 and 55 (tel. 200-39), about 8 blocks from the Zócalo. Buses go to: Villahermosa (10 per day, 9400 pesos); Macuspana (4 per day, 7000 pesos); Catazajá via El Zapata (5 per day, 4000 pesos); and Mexico City (at 5pm, 52,000 pesos) via Cordoba (37,000 pesos) and Puebla (46,000 pesos). Those traveling to Palenque should take a bus to the Catazajá crossing; from there, microbuses depart to Palenque every half hour until 8pm (2000 pesos). To get to *el centro* from the station in Tenosique, turn right, walk 2 blocks to Calle 28, and turn right again.

Second-class buses operated by **Transportes Dag Dug, Transportes Macuspana, Autobuses de Jalapa, Autobuses del Sur,** and **Union de Camineros de Yucatán** leave from the corner of Calles 26 and 31, across from the church. Purchase tickets in advance in the small office on Calle 31 beside the church. (Open daily 5-9am, 11:30am-1:30pm, and 2-6pm.) Six buses run daily to Villahermosa (8500 pesos) and points en route, including Catazajá (3600 pesos). Two per day, at 8am and 6pm, head to Mérida (24,000 pesos).

Tenosique is also tenuously connected to the outside world by an unreliable train service. To Merida (at 8:30 and 11 pm, 12 hr., 7000 pesos) and Mexico City (at 8am, 24 hr., 15,000 pesos). If you value your health, avoid the cesspool (signs mistakenly label it a "train station") that lies 2km from the Zócalo on Calle 20. *Colectivos* (500 pesos) pass by frequently on their way to *el centro*.

Accommodations and Food

Tenosique has few hotels, and those the Public Health Bureau permits to function overcharge for their uninspiring rooms. As always, late-night knocks at your door should go unanswered. **Hotel Rome,** Calle 28 #400 (tel. 201-51), has moderately clean rooms and baths. (Singles 17,000 pesos. Doubles 21,000 pesos. Triples 23,400 pesos.) If you mention that you were referred to the hotel by Nicholas Valenzuela from the wharf in La Palma, Rome will knock the price down a few thousand pesos. At the **Hotel Azulejos,** directly across from the church on Calle 26, the upstairs rooms are well-ventillated. (Singles 18,000 pesos. Doubles 22,000 pesos. Triples 25,000 pesos.) Cheaper still are the unsavory *casas de huéspedes* within 1 or 2 blocks of the Zócalo.

Tenosique has few restaurants for a community its size, and all are unappealing. Rejoice if you succeed in satisfying your stomach, and don't complain when it begins to systematically empty itself.

To Guatemala via the Río San Pedro

After ages spent smashed between chickens, children, and cabbage on an interminable bus ride, you might vow to sell your soul for a few hours on an uninhabited (save the alligators) river. If so, rest easy; the alternative river route into Guatemala will set you back little more than one night at a hotel. It begins with a bus to **La Palma,** caught in Tenosique at the gas station on Calle 28, about 3 blocks south of the Zócalo. Buses (2500 pesos) leave at 6am, 9am, 1pm, and 4pm. Passengers on the 1pm bus spend the least amount of time waiting for the *lancha* at La Palma, which departs at 2pm. From La Palma, boats charge 35,000 pesos or Q50 per person for the trip down the Río San Pedro to **El Naranjo** in Guatemala. Expect a thorough baggage search at the border. From El Naranjo, buses (Q10) travel to Flores at 2am, 3am, and 1pm. Faced with spending the night in El Naranjo, you have two options: stay in a toad-infested hotel near the dock (Q5) or a swing in a hammock by the river at **Comedor San Pedro** on the far end of town (Q2). Heading the other way, only the 5am bus from Flores will get to El Naranjo before the launch departs to La Palma at 1pm. Buses from La Palma depart from 8am to 5pm (2500 pesos) to Tenosique, where there are no connections to Palenque until the following morning (see Tenosique).

Flights to Bonampak and Yaxchilán

Pedro Joaquin Mandujano Quintero is the only pilot in Tenosique who offers flights to the ruins of Bonampak and Yaxchilán, but he doesn't charge monopolistic fares. In fact, flights to these sites from Tenosique are much cheaper than from more conventional stops on the *gringo* trail. Sr. Mandujano charges US$270 to take up to five passengers to Bonampak, US$250 to Yaxchilán, US$300 to both. The plane remains on the ground for one hour at Bonampak and two hours at Yaxchilán. Such visiting periods are negotiable, however, as are prices. Travelers whose Spanish is good should remind the amiable Sr. Mandujano that a low-paying customer is better than no customer at all.

Tenosique's **airport** is about 2km out of town on the road toward La Palma (i.e. the continuation of Calle 28). Municipal buses labeled "Batallon" pass by about every half hour (300 pesos). A taxi from the Zócalo costs 3000 pesos. If Sr. Mandujano is not at the airport (try there before 9am or at night), talk to his mechanic or call him at home (tel. 200-99).

YUCATÁN PENINSULA

Too engrossed in a hunt for slaves to watch where he was going, Hernández de Córdoba of Cuba mistakenly ran aground on the southern tip of Mexico in 1517. The *indígenas,* when asked the name of the land by the freshly disembarked sailors, replied "Tectetán," meaning: "we do not understand you." Misinterpreting the Maya's reply, Córdoba dubbed the region Yucatán before shoving off again. This anecdote distills the essence of the Yucatán's history: misunderstood by outsiders and never fully conquered, but continually molested. Today, the peninsula's culture remains essentially Mayan, but foreign influence fights on. Maya is still the first language of most of the inhabitants, nature worship continues (if with a Catholic veneer), and fishing, farming, and hammock-making overwhelm big industry and large-scale commerce. Burgeoning tourism, however, is threatening the traditional *yucateco* way of life: as travelers from around the world discover the peninsula's fine beaches, beautiful colonial towns, and striking Mayan ruins, more workers are drawn into the funnel of the tourism industry; many of those not working in the hotels or restaurants of one of the tourist magnet towns find themselves weaving hammocks for *viajeros* in Mérida, fishing lobster for visitors to Cancún, or driving tour buses to ruin sites.

The peninsula's geography consists mostly of flat limestone scrubland or rainforest dotted with an occasional *cenote* (natural well). Because of the highly porous limestone subsoil, there are no above-ground rivers in Yucatán. Poor soil and the lack of water make farming difficult; corn is still the all-important subsistence crop. The prominence of the rain god Chac at most Mayan ruins testifies to the eternal importance of the seasonal rains, which fall from May to early summer.

Since the Maya conquered the peninsula around 500 BC, Yucatán has known several masters. Many of the buildings in the Maya's illustrious city of Chichén Itzá are the creations of Toltecs, built after the tribe took the peninsula in the 11th century. Spanish imperialists landed first at Quintana Roo but did not attempt to penetrate the region until landing again at Campeche, which was taken and lost several times before being secured with fortifications and a half-dozen forts during the mid-16th century. The Montejo family orchestrated the Spanish conquest in the Yucatán, establishing Mérida on the site of a Mayan village in 1542 and later installing additional colonial strongholds such as Valladolid. More recently, other European influences have shaped Yucatán's new cities—most notably in Mérida, where the Paseo Montejo imitates the Champs Elysées of Paris.

Colonialism brought more than just forts and stone cathedrals, however. Spanish settlers received vast land grants and convinced displaced *indígenas* to labor on their estates. Oppressed and humiliated, the *indígenas* rebelled against the white *ladino* overlords in 1546, 1585, 1610, and 1624. After gaining independence from Spain, *ladinos* stepped up their exploitation of Mayan peoples and lands. Thousands of Mayans were conscripted as debt laborers on the expanding *henequen* plantations. In 1847, Mayan discontent exploded in a bloody racial struggle, known as the Caste War, which enveloped the peninsula. At the height of the Mayan advance a year later, only the cities of Mérida and Campeche remained in *ladino* hands. A sovereign rebel Mayan community survived in eastern Yucatán until 1901, decades after Mexican troops had retaken most of the peninsula.

Yucatán's most recent culture shock resulted from the completion of Rte. 180, which links the peninsula with mainland Mexico. Desiring to maintain their historical isolation from the rest of the Mexican Republic, *yucatecos* originally resisted the federal highway plans. Despite new competition in shipping and transportation

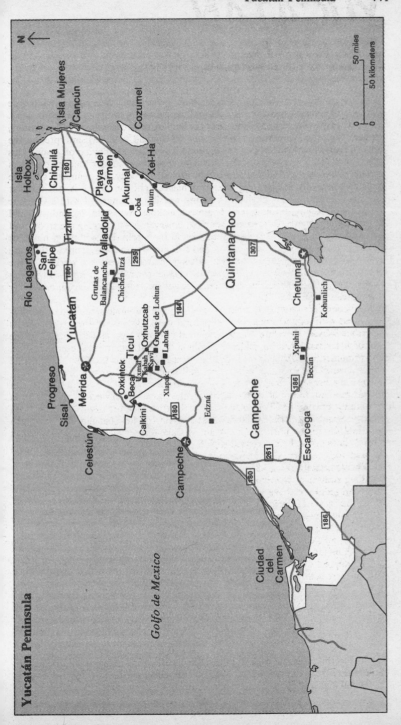

Yucatán Peninsula

from the south and the ongoing invasion of sun- and ruin-seeking foreigners, Yucatán retains its distinctive character: *yucatecos* have held on to their native drawl, and more importantly continue to brew the dark beers considered to be the nation's finest.

Mayan culture thrives in the peninsula's small towns, where the only evidence of Western influence arrives weekly in the form of Coca Cola vendors. In the expanses between the touristed archeological sites, *yucateco* women continue to carry bowls of corn flour on their heads and wear embroidered *huipile* dresses. In large cities like Campeche and Mérida, the stability of Mayan culture manifests itself more subtly in the citizens' unpretentious hospitality.

The Yucatán Peninsula divides into three states: Campeche, on the Gulf Coast, forms the peninsula's western side; Yucatán constitutes the center; and Quintana Roo, on the eastern side, faces the Caribbean Sea. "The" Yucatán refers to the region, not the state; Yucatán without the article can refer to either entity.

Yucatán and Campeche

Although the highlights of Yucatán state are the ruins—Chichén Itzá, Uxmal, and the triad of Sayil, Kabah, and Labná—the colonial cities also deserve a spot on your itinerary. Mérida and Valladolid are both appealing urban centers, the first bustling with international visitors and one of Mexico's finest markets, the second drowsing in the backwater of Yucatán's history.

Campeche state languishes in its relaxed colonial ambience, but has fewer sights of every type. The state's famous archeological site, Edzná, is easily reached from the capital of the same name, and more remote Mayan cities may tempt you to wander through other corners of the state.

Route 186 connects the Yucatán to mainland Mexico, entering Campeche State from Tabasco. At the crossroads town of Escárcega, Rte. 186 heads east past remote ruins en route to Chetumal and Quintana Roo. Route 261 heads north from Escárcega and meets the shorter coastal Rte. 180 at Champotón shortly before reaching the capital. Several roads encircle Campeche, but all converge on the two routes from Campeche to Mérida.

Campeche

Campeche once served as the major port on the Yucatán Peninsula's Gulf Coast. Vicious winds persisting for days at a time drove trade ships to seek shelter in Campeche, and their cargos tempted pirates who sought the wealth that Campeche's inhabitants derived from the logwood dye business. After countless incursions by Dutch and English corsairs between the 16th and 18th centuries, the Spanish decided to construct protective walls around Campeche; the stark stone bulwarks and high fortifications successfully terminated the pirate raids.

After the Bourbons came to power in Spain in the 18th century, Campeche lost its monopoly over peninsular trade. Ciudad del Carmen, a deep-water port on the state's southern coast, quickly replaced Campeche as the center of regional trade. Despite the recent, massive influx of petroleum profits, which have revitalized flagging Campeche state, the capital city has changed little. Parts of the fragmented stone wall stand today, as do several of the original *baluartes* (bulwarks). Like the fortifications, many of Campeche's buildings date from the 17th century. In the northeast section of the walled city, high sidewalks with narrow steps descending to the street bear the impressions of 300 years of *campechano* footsteps.

Modern Campeche exerts as much energy attracting *extranjeros* today as it did repelling them some centuries ago. The recent construction of an airport outside town and a highway from Mérida has made Campeche more internationally and domestically accessible; results, in the form of increased tourism, are starting to show. Three gargantuan hotels and a tourism complex have arisen between the old town and the waterfront, and construction is underway on many more.

The effects of these changes, however, are difficult to perceive. Lazy streets still flood at the first hint of rain, and *aguadores* with mule-drawn carts sell collected rain water door-to-door. Adventurous swashbucklers can tackle a few mid-jungle ruin sites in the vicinity, but most modern-day invasions will be brief, staged on the way to or from greater exploits in Yucatán.

Orientation

A convenient 252km southwest of Mérida and 444km northeast of Villahermosa, Campeche is a popular stopover on the trek east and north from mainland Mexico to the northern Yucatán. The city, along the main Yucatán thoroughfare, is served by many bus, train, and air routes.

The most direct link between Mérida and Campeche by car is Rte. 180. Recent improvements to the pavement have shortened the trip to two hours. Route 261 is longer, leading almost directly south from Mérida through Muna, Uxmal, Kabah, and Hopelchén before swinging west to Campeche, passing the access road to Edzná en route. (See Campeche to Mérida below.) From the south, take coastal Rte. 180 from Ciudad del Carmen, which merges at Champotón with Rte. 261 from Escárcega. Watch out for speed bumps throughout the area; because of them, the narrow, curving 66km stretch of Rte. 180 between Champotón and Campeche is excrutiatingly slow.

All major routes into the city intersect the peripheral highway that encircles it; this highway's name changes frequently, particularly along the city's western edge, which borders the waterfront. A smaller circular road with only two names—Circuito Baluartes on the three island sides and Avenida 16 de Septiembre along the Gulf—falls within the outer highway, circumscribing the old city. All main roads cross the Circuito near the city center. **Avenida Gobernadores** leads in from the Mérida highway northeast of the city, crosses the peripheral highway, and joins the Circuito at Baluarte San Pedro. Gobernadores accesses the train station, airport, and bus terminal.

To reach the Zócalo from the first- and second-class bus terminal, 4 blocks northeast of the city walls on Gobernadores, catch the "Gobernadores" bus (500 pesos) at the front of the station. There are no fixed stops; ask the bus driver to let you off at Baluarte de San Francisco. Turn right into the old city and walk 4 blocks on Calle 57 to the Zócalo. If you'd rather make the 15-minute walk from the station, head left on Gobernadores for a few minutes and bear left as it becomes the large divided Circuito Baluartes. Three blocks later, turn right on Calle 57, and walk 4 blocks to the Zócalo. From the train station, the "Sureste" bus (500 pesos) takes you to the market; from there, walk 3 blocks south down Circuito Baluartes to Calle 57, turn right, and walk 4 blocks to the Zócalo. Taxis from the airport to the Zócalo cost 15,000 pesos.

Campeche once fit into the 40 square blocks marked off by the still-standing set of seven *baluartes*. Sightseers in Campeche usually find nothing of interest outside this compact area. Most *campecharos* live in large, suburban areas north of the old city.

In the old city, odd-numbered streets run east-west (perpendicular to the sea) from 51 in the north to 65 in the south. Even-numbered streets run north-south, beginning with Calle 8 in the west, 1 block inland from Av. 16 de Septiembre, and continue through Calle 18 in the east. The Zócalo lies near the sea, bordered by Calles 8, 10, 55, and 57. Excellent city maps are available at the tourist office, hotels, and a small information stand inside the ADO bus station.

A confusing network of buses links Campeche's more distant sectors to the edge of the old city; fare on all buses is 500 pesos. The market, at the point where Gobernadores becomes Circuito Baluartes, serves as the hub for local routes. Any market vendor knows which bus stops where. Buses sometimes stray from their routes and have no established stops; it is possible to flag them down at almost any point on their route. No buses are permitted within the old city; you must disembark at the periphery and enter on foot. Buses run between 6am and 11pm, and crowd to the point of suffocation in early afternoon and evening. Car rentals are worthwhile for groups planning tours of the nearby but hard-to-reach ruins.

Practical Information

State Tourist Office: (tel. 660-68), on Pl. Moch-Couoh between 16 de Septiembre and Ruíz Cortínez, the coastal highway. Inside a low, pyramidal building; the hard-to-see entrance faces southwest. Information provided on tours of the city and the nearby ruins. Students on the staff are friendly but know little more than the information transcribed on the city maps they provide. Open Mon.-Fri. 9am-2:30pm and 4-9pm, Sat.-Sun. 9am-2pm.

Federal Tourist Office: Circuito Baluartes at Calle 14 (tel. 673-64), in the Baluarte de Santa Rosa. Better for help with problems than for general information. Open Mon.-Fri. 9am-3pm.

Tours: Sr. Antonio Romero, Tzalan 13 (tel. 614-54). An extremely knowledgeable and enthusiastic man who gives tours of the city, the coast, and nearby ruins. He'll also take you to all the ruins along the Campeche-Mérida route, except for Hochob during the rainy season (June-Sept.). Sr. Romero speaks some English.

Bus Tours: Several travel agencies peddle one-day guided sightseeing trips to the Edzná ruins and tours of Campeche's city walls. Try the **Viajes Programados (VI-PS)** in the Edificio Belmar behind the Ramada Inn (tel. 683-33), or **Viajes Jaina,** Ruíz Cortínez 51 (tel. 116-19), in the Ramada lobby. Both offer similar tours in buses with A/C; English-speaking guides available if you call a day in advance. Edzná tours (40,000 pesos) leave at 9am, picking up passengers at the larger hotels, and return at 1pm. Campeche tours (35,000 pesos) leave at 4pm and return at 8pm.

Currency Exchange: Bancomer, Calle 59 #2-A (tel. 666-22), at 16 de Septiembre opposite the Baluarte de la Soledad. Open Mon.-Fri. 9am-1pm. **Bánamex,** Calle 53 #15 (tel. 652-51). Open Mon.-Fri. 9am-1:30pm and 4-5pm. For longer hours but lower rates, there is a *casa de cambio* at the western edge of the Plaza Commercial A-Kin-Pech, in the northwestern corner of the city.

Post Office: 16 de Septiembre at Calle 53 (tel. 688-60), in the Edificio Federal. Open for stamps, registered mail, and Lista de Correos Mon.-Fri. 8am-8pm, Sat. 9am-1pm; for international service and packages Mon.-Fri. 8am-1:30pm. Difficult to send packages since customs office is in neighboring town. **Postal Code:** 24000.

Telephones: Long-distance **Caseta El Travieso,** Gobernadores 519 (tel. 660-10), on 2nd floor of the building 1½ blocks from bus terminal as one heads towards the old city. International collect calls 1000 pesos. Open Mon.-Sat. 7am-9pm, Sun. 9am-2pm. **Telephone Code:** 981.

Telegrams: Edificio Federal, 16 de Septiembre at Calle 53 (tel. 643-90), in the Edificio Federal (the post office building), to the right upon entering. Open for money orders Mon.-Fri. 8am-midnight, Sat. 9am-noon; for telegrams Mon.-Fri. 8am-midnight, Sat. 9am-8pm, Sun. 9am-noon.

Airport: (tel. 614-38), on Porfilio, 10km from the city center. **Mexicana,** Calle 10 #365 (tel. 618-93), between Calles 65 and 67. To Mexico City (4 per week). **Aeroméxico,** at the airport (tel. 666-56). To Mexico City (daily at 12:35pm).

Train Station: Nacozari 26 (tel. 651-48), 2km northeast of the city center. Make reservations a week in advance for first-class service. Best to arrive 1 hr. before departure to reconfirm time and purchase tickets; trains either arrive late or never rumble in. To Mexico City (daily at 12:30am, 30 hr., 20,000 pesos) and Mérida (at noon, 3000 pesos). Open for tickets daily midnight-3pm. For security reasons, the tourist office strongly discourages taking trains.

Bus Station: First- and second-class buses at terminal on Gobernadores between Calles 47 and Chile, 4 blocks northeast of the city wall. The first-class ADO terminal, with baggage check, waiting room, and so-called restaurant faces Gobernadores; the second-class terminal lies behind it (access via first-class terminal or the side street Chile). **ADO,** Gobernadores 289 (tel. 628-02), sends first-class buses to: Ceiba Playa (2 per day, ½ hr., 1600 pesos); Mérida (25 per day, 2½ hr., 8700 pesos); Mexico City (8 per day, 18 hr., 62,000 pesos); Puebla (1 per day, 16 hr., 56,000 pesos); San Andrés (5 per day, 12 hr., 35,000 pesos); Villahermosa (5 per day, 7 hr., 20,500 pesos). **Second-class** buses run more frequently to a larger slate of destinations. To: Edzná (Sat. and Sun. at 8am, 1½ hr., 2500 pesos); Iturbide, for the Dzibilnocac ruins (5 per day, 3 hr., 6500 pesos); Bolonchen, near the Grutas de Xtacumbilxunaan (5 per day, 2 hr., 5500 pesos); Kabah ruins (5 per day, 3 hr., 6000 pesos); Santa Elena (5 per day, 3 hr., 6500 pesos); Uxmal (5 per day, 3½ hr., 7000 pesos).

Taxis: Tel. 652-30. Three stands: at the intersection of Calles 8 and 55, to left of the cathedral; the intersection of Calle 55 and Circuito, near the market; and at the intersection of Gobernadores and Chile, near the bus terminal. Basic rate for intra-city travel 5000 pesos.

Car Rental: Auto Rent (tel. 627-14), between Calles 10 and 12. Open Mon.-Sat. 8am-1:30pm and 4-7pm. Similar rates quoted in the lobby of the Hotel Baluartes at Ruíz Cortínez and Calle 59. Open Mon.-Sat. 8am-1pm and 4-7pm.

Laundromat: Lavandería y Tintorería Campeche, Calle 55 #22. 4000 pesos per kg. Same-day service if they don't have much else to do. Open Mon.-Sat. 8am-4pm.

Market: At Gobernadores and Circuito, beyond the city wall. Unexceptional handicrafts and cheap food, including many *chiles.* Open daily sunrise-sunset.

Supermarket: Super Diez (tel. 679-77), in the Pl. Comercial A-Kin-Pech on 16 de Septiembre. Large, modern supermarket with a bakery, bookstore, and clothing boutique, next to a small shopping complex. Open daily 8am-9pm. Credit cards accepted.

Red Cross: (tel. 606-66), on Resurgimiento near the market. Free 24-hr. emergency service.

Pharmacy: Farmacia Canto Surcursal Lanz, Calle 10 #7 (tel. 652-48), at Calle 55. Good selection of shampoos for dry, damaged, oily, or normal hair. Open daily 8am-1:30pm and 4:30-9pm.

Medical Assistance: Seguro Social (tel. 618-55), on López Mateos south of the city. Designed and subsidized for affiliates, but legally required to help anyone in an emergency for a small fee. Good service but often overcrowded.

Police: (tel. 636-35), on Resurgimiento, ½km south of the old city, at the intersection of the coastal highway with López Mateos and across from the *balneario.* No English spoken. Open 24 hr.

Accommodations and Camping

The limited number of budget accommodations in Campeche is due in part to the presence of three waterfront luxury hotels: the Baluartes, Alhambra, and Ramada Inn. In a city often overlooked by tourists, few middle-range establishments have survived the competition, and many of the cheaper places have sunk to unusually low levels of cleanliness and maintenance.

For some travelers, the youth hostel may be a tempting alternative, but its distance from the city center (3km) is daunting. It is, however, the safest option for camping; they rent tents as well. Campers often exercise their other option and stay at the **Trailer Park Campeche,** on Agustín Melgar past the youth hostel in a low-income area with potential for danger. Hookups for trailers plus good bathroom and shower facilities for campers are a bonus, but the 3½km walk from the city center is a drag; to reach the campground, walk south on the coastal highway from the Zócalo, turn left at Agustín Melgar, and follow the signs past the hostel and the university.

Villas Deportiva Juvenil (tel. 618-02), on Agustín Melgar, several blocks east of the water and the coastal highway. From the Zócalo, take the "Campeche Lerma" bus south along the coastal highway to the intersection with Melgar, and walk the remaining few blocks. Spotless bunk beds, with rooms segregated by sex. As appealing as institutions get, with a large pool and decent, cheap cafeteria food. No reservations accepted, but Campeche rarely receives tourists, anyway. Also has camping and trailer park facilities. Bunk rental (includes towel, blanket, and pillow) 5000 pesos per night. Camping 2500 pesos; tent rental 10,000 pesos. Breakfast 3500 pesos, lunch or dinner 4500 pesos.

Hotel Posada del Angel, Calle 10 #307 (tel. 677-18), across from the cathedral. Beautiful balconied establishment with an enthusiastic manager and a panoply of plants. Wooden doors lead to a charming lobby with flowered chairs. Large, well-maintained rooms are carpeted and decked out in wood. Hot water and fans. Singles 28,000 pesos. Doubles 35,000 pesos. A/C 10,000 pesos extra.

Hotel América, Calle 10 #252 (tel. 645-88), between Calles 59 and 61. A broad staircase leads up to three stories that overlook a peaceful colonial courtyard. Dark wood accents cream-colored walls; bathrooms shine. Popular, so get here early. Rooms have fans, phones, and hot water. Singles and doubles 35,000 pesos. Extra person 10,000 pesos.

Hotel Colonial, Calle 14 #122 (tel. 622-22), between Calles 55 and 57, 2½ blocks from the Zócalo. Typical colonial building includes quaint courtyard. Small rooms crowded with green furniture (including a rocking chair). Clean, neat, and orderly. Rooms have fans, phones, and hot water. Singles 30,000 pesos. Doubles 35,000 pesos, with A/C 40,000 pesos.

Hotel Castelmar, Calle 61 #2 (tel. 651-86), between Calles 8 and 10, 3 blocks south of the Zócalo under a large sign visible from the coastal highway. What a bargain! Colonial building and courtyard with a weighty feeling of antiquity. Huge, musty rooms have rather dirty bathrooms but gushing showers. Fans, hot water, and hammock hooks in rooms. Singles 16,000 pesos. Doubles 21,000 pesos.

Hospedaje Teresita, Calle 53 #31 (tel. 645-34), between Calles 12 and 14 in a quiet residential part of the old city, 3 blocks northeast of the Zócalo. Run by a pleasant woman and her large dog. Tattered sheets don't completely cover the grungy mattresses, and showers need scrubbing. Badly. Before they organize and demand more money. Rooms have fans, but no hot water. Singles 15,000 pesos. Doubles 20,000 pesos.

Food

Campeche garners rave reviews for its seafood, and the market is amply stocked with sea creatures from the tranquil Bahía de Campeche. Sadly, the market places, taco stands, and street food don't make up for the dearth of sit-down establishments in a city of this size. A few places dish up excellent seafood, notably shrimp and *pan de cazón* (baby shark wedged between two corn tortillas and black beans), but all too often the gourmand must choose between high prices and questionable hygienic conditions. The few budget eateries cluster on Calle 8 south of the Zócalo, and on Calle 57 in front of the plaza. Mangos and papayas are excellent in Campeche; try the *aguas de frutas* from any of Campeche's snack shops, or pick up some fresh fruit at the city market. Peel the mangos yourself; to avoid Bacteria Bill, stay away from the bags of mango slices sold by street vendors. The large **Conasuper San Martín** supermarket, at the corner of Calles 10 and 49, sells a variety of fresh fruits. (Open Mon.-Sat. 9am-9pm, Sun. 2-8pm.)

Restaurant La Parroquia, Calle 8 #267, in front of the sea gate. Campechan family food in a large, new restaurant with bar upstairs. Small shows of music or ballet occur every night on the stage. Breakfast specials (served Mon.-Fri. 7-10am) 3500-7000 pesos. *Comida del día* 9000 pesos, *pescado veracruzano* 13,000 pesos. Open 24 hr. MC, Visa accepted.

Restaurant Campeche, Calle 57 #2, on the Zócalo. Plain cafeteria in the birthplace of Justo Sierra, who founded the national university in Mexico City. Diners' eyes usually riveted to a fuzzy black-and-white TV. Cheapest seafood in town: try the tasty shrimp cooked in garlic (13,000 pesos). Also a good selection of chicken and meat dishes; *pollo a la catalana* with a heap of cooked vegetables and bacon 6500 pesos. Open daily 7am-11pm.

Restaurant Del Parque, Calle 57 #8, at Calle 8 on the Zócalo. Cool fuschia chairs, lots of plants, and Mexican rock music. Serves light fare: soups, sandwiches, desserts, and giant-sized alcoholic and non-alcoholic drinks. Fish soup 5000 pesos. *Pie de queso* (cheesecake), 2800 pesos. Freshly squeezed orange juice 4000 pesos. Open 24 hr.

Naturo 2000, Calle 12 #160, at Calle 59. Campeche's first vegetarian restaurant. Four-table joint serves delicious frozen mango yogurt (1300 pesos) and the house specialty, soy *tortas*. The *bomba*, made of fruit, honey, and granola (4200 pesos), pleases even the earthiest Birkenstock wearers. Open daily 8am-4:30pm.

Restaurant Miramar, Calle 8 at 61. The nicest reasonably priced restaurant in the center. Elegant room with wood paneling, stone arches, and linen tablecloths fills with local lunchtime crowd. Changing daily menu of seafood and *comida típica*. A good place to feast on shrimp: *camarones empanizados* (breaded and fried) 20,000 pesos. Miramar soup 14,000 pesos. Open Mon.-Fri. 8am-midnight, Sat. 8am-1am, Sun. 11am-7pm. Credit cards accepted.

Marganzo, Calle 8 #261. A pleasant cafeteria, where waiters wearing black and white tend the plastic bouquets on the tables. Fish prepared several different ways for 11,000 pesos; breaded shrimp prepared one way 18,000 pesos. Open Mon.-Sat. 7am-10pm, Sun. 8am-4pm.

Sights

Campeche was a crucial gateway into Mexico for the first Spanish people in the Yucatán. After the Mayan tribes resisted the advances of Córdoba, Grijalva, and Cortés, the Montejos managed to establish a beachhead at Campeche in 1540, building on the site of the Mayan village of A-kin-pech (serpent-tick). The Spanish corrupted "Kin-pech" to "Campeche." From here, Montejo began his conquest of the Yucatán as Cortés, having fled west to Veracruz, marched on the Aztecs who were in the central highlands. During the colonial era, Campeche became an important port city, and until well into the 18th century, Veracruz and Campeche were the only ports in New Spain permitted to conduct trade. The city attracted British, French, and Dutch pirates who resented the Iberian claim to exclusive sovereignty over the Americas. Openly supported by their governments, these buccaneers regularly raided affluent Campeche.

Campeche's city government meticulously maintains a series of museums in the wall fragments as well as at various other points within the old city. You can visit several of the pirate-repelling *baluartes* simply by following the Circuito Baluartes around the old walled boundaries. In the **Baluarte de la Soledad**, across from the Zócalo off Calle 8 near Calle 57, the **Museo de Estelas Maya** has a small but worthwhile collection of Mayan stelae and reliefs taken from sites in Campeche state. Informative texts in Spanish and pictographs reveal details about each piece, and a friendly old caretaker lives to answer questions. Visitors may also climb the walls of the fort, which is surrounded by a park. (Open Tues.-Sat. 8am-8pm, Sun. 8am-1pm. Free.)

The tourist office is rightfully proud of the **Museo Regional de Campeche,** Calle 59 #36 (tel. 691-11), between Calles 14 and 16. Downstairs rooms contain well-documented exhibits describing the nearby ruins and displaying the jewelry, pottery, and funeral artifacts of the Campeche region Maya. Highlights include an exquisite jade mask and a large phallic sculpture. Upstairs (open Tues.-Sat. 9am-2pm), the history of the city of Campeche is laid out. A collection of colonial swords, crossbows, and cannons transforms images of the tranquil fortresses into scenes of combat, and a large-scale model of colonial Campeche reveals how little the old city has changed in two centuries. The museum inhabits an 18th-century building known as the Casa del Teniente del Rey (King's Lieutenant's House). (Open Tues.-Sat. 9am-8pm, Sun. 8am-1pm. Admission 1500 pesos.)

In the **Fuerte Santiago** at the northern corner of the city, the **Jardín Botánico Xmuch Haltun,** Calles 8 and 51, makes an inviting stop on a hot day or night. Over 250 labeled species of plants thrive amid shade trees and fountains in a pleasant, open-air courtyard, complete with walkways and benches. It only takes 10 minutes to walk through the garden, after which you will emerge with a relaxed smile on your face. If more than five people arrive at once, a guide will lead a special tour. (Open Tues.-Fri. 8am-2pm and 4-9pm, Sat. 9am-1pm and 5-8pm, Sun. 9am-1pm. Admission 500 pesos.)

In the heart of the Zócalo rises the **cathedral,** site of the first mass conducted on the American continent. Don Francisco de Montejo ordered its construction on October 4, 1540, but builders did not finish the job until 1705. The main attraction is its façade, which includes human figures and obscure carvings. Inside, you'll find the *Santo Entierro* (Holy Burial), a sculpture of Christ in a carved mahogany sarcophagus with silver trim. (Open daily 6am-noon and 4-8pm. Free.)

Removed from the center of town, the **Iglesia de San Román** deserves a visit to see *Cristo Negro,* an object of great veneration among *campechanos*. St. Roman is Campeche's patron, and two weeks of both religious and secular festivities, starting September 15, celebrate his feast. (Open daily 6am-noon and 4-8pm. Free.)

Two high stone forts on the outskirts of town offer panoramas of Campeche that become postcard-perfect at sunset. **Fuerte San José El Alto** is a few kilometers north of the center and near one of the oldest lighthouses in the Americas. If you don't have a car, take the "San José El Alto" bus from the market or make the long walk. Head north on Gobernadores, turn left on Cuauhtémoc, left on Calle 101, and right on Calle 7. Señor Herrero, a metalworker near the fort, will let you in if the gates are closed. A permanent guard has charge of **Fuerte de San Miguel,** a few kilometers south of town near the youth hostel. Walk, or preferably drive, south along the oceanfront road then turn left on Carretera Escenico just after Melgar. A short jaunt inland will take you to San Miguel.

Playa Bonita, the best beach in the immediate area for swimming, accessible by the "Lerma-Playa Bonita" bus from the market, has lockers and a restaurant and fills with locals on weekends. Another swimming option is 30km away, at **Playa Payucán,** 2km from a small town called Ceiba Playa (accessible by first- and second-class buses). Here the sand is cleaner and more abundant than at Playa Bonita, but the beach lacks basic amenities. Payucán also offers good snorkeling and scuba diving areas—if you own equipment: rentals, like bathrooms, are unavailable.

Entertainment

Campeche's active tourist office and city government sponsor free outdoor musical events and *ballet folklórico* in the Zócalo (Pl. Principal) each Thursday at 7pm. Campeche traditionalism emerges in the Zócalo every Friday and Saturday evening, when local musicians in *campechana* costumes perform folk songs. Half the city turns out for these shows, which begin around 7pm.

The luxury hotels provide the most modern nightlife, but you must pay for the privilege of fun. **Atlantis,** in the Ramada Inn, boogies into the wee hours on weekends. (Cover 15,000 pesos. Open Thurs.-Sun. 10pm-4am.) The small **Jet Set** video bar, near the Super Diez supermarket, is the newest rage among local sonic youth. (Open Thurs.-Sat. from 10pm.)

Near the youth hostel, on López Mateos, the lounge **Cine Alhambra** plays both foreign and Mexican movies. Other cinemas in town include **Cine Colón,** Calle 59 #8, at Calle 12, and **Cine La Cruz,** Calle 8 at 51. Both charge 1400 pesos and show a variety of movies.

Near Campeche

While in Campeche, a jaunt to the nearby ruins of **Edzná** (House of the Grimaces) is easy and worthwhile. At the site, the huge **Acropolis,** a pyramid of five stories, towers over a large plaza among more than 200 mounds covering many square kilometers. Sixty-five steps lead to the five-room temple that crowns the pyramid. During the Mayan heyday, when the area was called Itzna, standing atop the monument one could see the network of irrigation canals criss-crossing the valley close to the Río Champotón, more than 20km to the west. Like the huge stone pyramids, the canals were built without the use of wheels, metal tools, or domesticated animals. Nearby, among the many "hitchhiker" thistle bushes, lie the remains of a ballcourt and several other temples of a central plaza, presently being excavated by Guatemalan refugees and Mexican archeologists. Also on display are some of the 19 stelae found at Edzná, one crafted as early as 672 AD, others dating closer to the 10th-century evacuation of the ceremonial center. Campeche's state tourist office has further details on the ruins.

The 90-minute bus ride to Edzná leaves Campeche at the crack of dawn. Go to the station in advance for details, as schedules change often. Ask the driver to let you off at the access road to the ruins; the site is 500m down this road. Only one bus returns to Campeche; ask at the Campeche station and on the bus en route to Edzná. Alternatively, take one of the guided tours that leave from Campeche every morning (see Campeche Practical Information under Tours). Either way, a canteen of water is a must. (Site open daily 8am-5pm. Admission 1000 pesos; pay at the caretaker's hut to the left as you enter.)

Campeche to Mérida (Short Route)

Two routes link Campeche to Mérida. The long route (see below), passing several major archeological sites is far the more interesting of the two. The short route (193km along Rte. 180) crosses small villages such as Pomuch (69km from Campeche), with houses built of materials from Mayan ruins, and Calkini (101km from Campeche), where a 16th-century monastery recalls the early days of the Spanish Conquest.

In **Hecelchakán** 76km from Campeche between these two towns, the small **Museo Arqueológico del Camino Real** displays representative pieces uncovered at the many archeological sites in Campeche to which visitors are not admitted. Most interesting are the clay figurines and jewelry found in some of the 1000 tombs discovered on the Isla de Jaina, off the peninsula's western coast. (Open Tues.-Sat. 9am-1pm and 5-8pm. Admission 1500 pesos.)

Several unexcavated, undeveloped Mayan sites in the area around Hecelchakán may satisfy the traveler who yearns for more than the familiar museum tours. To uncover your own exhibits, however, you'll have to hire a guide and a jeep for the trip to Kocha, Xcalumkin, Holactun, Cumpich, and Almuchil.

Closer to Mérida, past Calkini and almost at the Yucatán state border, lies the tiny town of **Becal,** the center of the panama hat trade. The town's zealous vendors will show you the underground workshops of artisans, who laboriously handweave sombreros from the leaves and off-white flower buds of the *jipijapa* palm tree. The hats must be made *sub terra* because the moist earth naturally maintains the correct temperature and humidity. High-quality hats have fine, tight weaves, and retain their proper shape no matter how cruelly you stuff them in your pack.

First-class buses automatically take this short route from Campeche to Mérida, and most drivers cruise by the villages of interest without so much as a wave. Second-class buses plying the short route stop in the above locations, as well as many others along the way. Though you must forgo air-conditioning, the extant Mayan villages unique to the Yucatán deserve a visit; get to the bus station half an hour early to secure a seat.

Campeche to Mérida (Long Route)

The long route (Rte. 261; 254km) between Campeche and Mérida, sometimes called the **Ruta Maya,** traverses the Puuc Hills, an area that was densely populated in Mayan times, playing home to about 22,000 people during much of the Classic period (4th to 10th centuries). Decimated by Spanish diseases and climatic changes, the Maya eventually surrendered most of their cities and ceremonial centers to the jungle until the 18th century, when the Mayan population began a recovery. Today, most Puuc Maya live in towns with paved roads, but many women continue to wear traditional embroidered *huipiles,* and Maya remains the dominant language in the majority of villages.

Only a few ruin sites have been excavated and opened to the public; of these, Uxmal receives the most visitors, while Hochob's remote location keeps most tourists at bay. Many of the sites remain closed during the rainy season (usually July-Aug.) when muddy roads render them inaccessible. Check with the Campeche or Mérida tourist office.

Uxmal, Kabah, the Grutas de Xtacumbilxunaan, and Dzibilnocac can be reached by public bus (the first three from both Campeche and Mérida, the last from Campeche only). Ask the driver to let you out as close to the sites as possible. The return trip can be tricky. Find out in advance when buses or *combis* will pass the site and wave your arms wildly to flag down a ride, but don't expect full vehicles to stop.

For a guaranteed ride back, rent a car or go on an organized tour. In Campeche, the state tourist office will refer you to Antonio Romero, who will take you on a private tour to any of these sites (see Campeche Practical Information under Tours).

It's best to take three or four people to split costs. From Mérida, the cheapest secure way to see the sites is to take the special ADO "Ruta Puuc" bus that leaves daily at 8am. The bus stops for about 45 minutes at each of the sites of Uxmal, Kabah, Sayil, Xlapak, Labná, and Loltun, returning to Mérida at 3pm. The fare is 20,000 pesos, a rootin' tootin' bargain even though it doesn't include admission to the ruins. The state tourist office in Mérida also dispenses information on tours organized by travel agencies. Most offer standard daytrips to Uxmal/Kabah and to Chichén Itzá (see Mérida Practical Information under Tours). Agencies will also organize private tours to all sites on the peninsula. Poor road conditions can create significant delays, especially when it rains, but inclement weather often means that you will have the site to yourself.

Most sites harbor at least a small gift shop that sells *refrescos,* but hotels and restaurants are scarce. The sole exception is Uxmal; those who cannot afford the sky-high rates here have two options: base yourself in Campeche or Mérida, or take advantage of the cheap accommodations and dining in **Ticul,** just 15km away off Rte. 261.

Edzná is the closest ruin to Campeche (see Near Campeche). Dzibilnocac and Hochob lie 88km south of the highway at Hopelchén, which in turn is 41km from Campeche. Two-and-a-half kilometers after passing from Campeche into Yucatán state through a 19th-century archway, a road veers east. Sayil (5km from the crossroads), Xlapak (13km), Labná (17km), and three Mayan ruins in the Puuc style lie along the road before it terminates at the Grutas de Loltun (36km). This road is paved, but the ruins themselves are often quite swampy in the rainy season. Continuing north on the highway after the turnoff to Sayil, Kabah is 5km down the road; 22km past Kabah lies Uxmal.

Dzibilnocac

Dzibilnocac and Hochob (see below) are unique in the sense that they seldom receive visitors; this alone makes them worth a trip. Whereas most archeological sites on the Yucatán's *gringo* trail have fences, gates, guards, portable potties, and ticket offices, these have only the jungle as protection against tourists. Dzibilnocac is easier to reach from Campeche, but Hochob is more enticing.

Although many overgrown pyramidal mounds at Dzibilnocac are visible in the forest and *milpas* near the road, the only excavated buildings are a set of three temples in various states of decay.

In the worst condition, the nearest temple has only one wall standing atop a once-symmetrical structure. Roots in the crumbling mortar slowly pull apart the temple's stones. The middle temple looks at first glance like nothing more than a pile of rocks topped by a tuft of trees and bushes; closer examination, however, reveals two corbel-arched, cave-like rooms partially filled with rubble.

The third temple is Dzibilnocac's prize. A tall, narrow building with rounded corners, it has rooms on several stories and still retains part of its stucco façade. Climb to the highest level for a closer view of a gruesome mask of the raingod Chac. At the middle levels, observe simpler and more primitive reliefs executed without perspective or dimensions, in the style of cave paintings. From the top of this temple, larger pyramidal mounds are visible nearby, bulging under the thick underbrush.

The actual site extends for miles—for those who insist on exploring, several roads and paths connect farms and cornfields. Very often, smaller ruins or pyramids rise from the middle of an otherwise cleared corn field. Temples in the area tend to fall to pieces faster than they would at nature's hands alone, since local farmers find the stones from ancient Mayan buildings both cheaper and classier building materials than those available at the local TruValu hardware store. Beware of the undergrowth's dangerous thorns and spines, and make sure your legs are completely covered because the poisonous snakes in this area are not always afraid of, nor happy with, intruders. (Site open daily 8am-4pm. Free.)

The Dzibilnocac ruins hide some 61km off Rte. 261, near the small town of **Iturbide.** To reach this village by car, exit Rte. 261 at Hopelchén and drive south toward

Iturbide. You'll soon reach a prominent sign at a fork pointing the way (straight on, *not* to the right) to Iturbide. Well-marked "km" signs are posted all along the road. When you reach the village, bear right around the Zócalo, passing Iturbide's small, yellow church, and continue out of town on a slightly worse, if less rocky, road (treacherous in rainy season, when it's better to walk). Fifty meters into the forest, the right branch of the fork in the road ends at the ruins. If you don't have a car, take the bus from Campeche to Iturbide via Hopelchén (5 per day, 3 hr., 6500 pesos). The last bus leaves Iturbide for Campeche at 3:30pm. If you miss it, you can attempt to hitch back to Hopelchén on Rte. 261, where buses run later into the afternoon.

Dzibalchén, between Iturbide and Hopelchén, has no hotels, but stranded travelers can spend the night here in a tent or hammock. Ask at the Palacio Municipal for bathroom facilities and hammock hooks. Small restaurants around the Zócalo are open during daylight hours. Buses to Campeche leave Dzibalchén early each morning.

Hochob

Hochob is the perfect place to experience ruins in silence and solitude, and campers will be hard-pressed to find a more deserted yet equally accessible site. But traveling to Hochob is ill-advised in the rainy season, when access roads do their fantastic mud-pit impersonation.

Arranged like a Greek acropolis, the three temples at Hochob cluster around a central plaza at the area's highest point, which swells modestly from the flat rainforest. Upon entering the plaza, you'll see several small heaps of rubble on the immediate left. Ahead and to the right, deep-relief geometric patterns molded in stucco cover a well-preserved one-room temple. The entire front of the building once resembled an enormous mask of Chac, with the large door serving as mouth for the gaping rain god.

Climb the ruined pyramid immediately to the left of the temple for a good view of the elevated site. To the right of the temple, at the corner of the plaza, a small path leads to a perfect camping spot in a clearing above the otherwise unbroken green rainforest.

At the far end of the plaza from the entrance road, a ruined façade still bears traces of its geometric motifs. Facing this ruined building, you can see Hochob's highest building, a spire-topped temple resting on a steeply sloping pyramid, to the right. The floor plan of the ruined building to the right of the temple is still evident in surviving walls and foundations. Beyond this, a high but decayed pyramid and wall rise to face the temple on the opposite side of the plaza.

Although Hochob, like Dzibilnocac, spreads for miles, the hilltop ceremonial center is the most thoroughly excavated and most interesting area for visitors. Near the sight, the right branch of the road has deteriorated to a point where its only value is its view of the highest buildings and the main temple's well-preserved roof comb. (Site open daily 8am-4pm. Free.)

The Hochob ruins lie closer to the town of Dzibalchén than do the ruins of Dzibilnocac, but they are more difficult to reach without a car. Take the road out of Dzibilchén for about 1km toward Campeche, then follow the sign pointing left to the town of Chencoh, 9km down a rough but still passable dirt road. In "town," take a left at the second intersection of roads lined with stone walls. After passing a small elevated concrete platform on the right and a barnyard full of pigs and turkeys (1 block or so), turn left again, and follow the dirt track some 4km into the jungle. Because of its many potholes, this road becomes especially dangerous in heavy rain. Just after most visitors throw in the towel, the road forks. Bear left, and soon the outline of temples will appear against the sky. Park at the small *palapa* hut below Hochob's hilltop site and continue up the road on foot.

There is no public transportation from Dzibalchén (or anywhere else) to Chencoh, and vehicles pass even less frequently here than on the stretch of road to Iturbide. To catch a ride, ask your driver to let you off at the access road to Chencoh, 1km before Dzibalchén.

Grutas de Xtacumbilxunaan

Along the main highway, 31km past Hopelchén, follow a turn-off to the left to reach the Grutas de Xtacumbilxunaan (Caves of the Hidden Girl), which sit 1km off the highway. A custodian leads a tour past deep *cenotes* (natural wells) that once supplied all of the water for Bolonchén, 3km away, and points out the various barely discernible shapes on the cavern's walls and ceilings. Although these caves compare poorly to the grand ones at Loltún, even novice spelunkers will have a good time poking around. (Tours in Spanish given only during daylight hours. Free, but tour guide expects a tip.)

The Grutas lie 1km down a well-marked access road that crosses Rte. 261 2km south of Bolonchén. Second-class bus drivers usually drop passengers at the access road.

Sayil

Sayil, the "Place of Red Ants," offers enough fascinating structures to make the prospect of facing the onslaught of ants worthwhile. The magnificent **Palace of Sayil** contains over 50 rooms on three terraced stories. Eight elegant, second-floor chambers open onto pleasant porticos, each graced by two bulging columns. Walls between porticos are carved with two rows of four slender colonnettes, which together with the open spaces and thick columns, create an interesting visual rhythm. From atop the palace, the Puuc Hills form the horizon. Behind the palace sits a *chultún* (plastered catch basin), that ancients used to collect rainwater for the dry season.

After descending the palace stairs, follow a path to the right, which leads to **El Mirador** (lookout), a temple with grandiose columns. Follow the path to the left to find the **Stela of the Phallus**, now protected by a thatched (and questionably effective) thin roof. A few other temples on the site appear as mounds covered with jungle growth. (Site open daily 8am-5pm. Admission 2000 pesos, free Sun.)

The only public transportation to Sayil is the ADO "Ruta Puuc" bus (20,000 pesos) that leaves Mérida daily at 8am and stops at several other ruin sites as well. (See above, Campeche to Mérida: Long Route.) Buses do run, however, from Mérida to Kabah, 10km away on the main highway (see Kabah); hitching from Kabah to Sayil is possible. Tourist vans operate from Uxmal, but drivers rarely negotiate the high fare; it's usually better to solicit a lift from enthusiastic four-wheeled travelers at either Uxmal or the Grutas de Loltún (see below).

Xlapak

Chac still rules at Xlapak (shla-PAK), where the raingod's image smothers a ruined 20m-long palace that has undergone partial restoration. Of the three sites on this road, Xlapak is least important and the most painless to miss if you run short on time or insect repellent.

Entering from the north, after giving your autograph to the caretaker walk 200m south to reach the palace. In Puuc style, the lower-floor façade is plain, punctuated only by doorways, but the building is beautifully proportioned. Masks of Chac and various fretted patterns adorn the cornice. The evolution of Mayan architecture over the centuries is evident in the contrasting styles of the western and eastern sides of the buildings. The government will soon open many more structures on the site. The only public transportation serving Xlapak is the ADO "Ruta Puuc" bus (see above, Campeche to Mérida: Long Route). (Site open daily 8am-5pm. Free.) See Kabah for information on buses from Mérida to Kabah, 18km northeast of Xlapak.

Labná

Labná may have been established as early as the 8th century, when the Puuc cities were connected by a *sacbé* (white road), a trace of which runs nearby. Raised above the surrounding land, this causeway was of great use during times of flooding. Water shortages were a problem, as witnessed by the three dozen huge *chultunes* (catch basins) found at Labná alone. The *chultunes* served the same purpose as *cenotes* (natural wells) did in northern Yucatán in more than one respect. They collected not only water (up to 8000 gallons in each), but also the bodies of the poorest Mayans, who were given simple burials. It seems unlikely, however, that the receptacles were used for both domestic and religious purposes simultaneously.

Labná is famed for its arch of stone, a span over 3m wide and 6m high, with an ornate mosaic façade on the west and a geometric design on the east. On either side of its base is a room with a cornice carved in a zigzag design and second-floor stone latticework. Once part of a building that stands between two plazas, the arch stands at the rear of the site, by the southern group of buildings, and now more closely resembles a gate.

Labná's other well-known attraction, the palace, lies on the northern side of the site. The largest edifice in the Puuc region, construction of the palace continued over the course of several centuries but was never actually completed. Labná's palace is similar in design to the one in Sayil, with separate apartments and porticos on the second floor (where there is also a *chultún*). The ornate second-floor cornice culminates at the eastern corner of its façade with the sculpture of a serpent head, its open mouth chomping on a human head. The eastern wall bears an unusually large, stylized mask of Chac in astonishingly good condition. Nearby remains of mosaics depict the palm huts in which most people lived; stone palaces were a privilege of the aristocracy.

East of the arch, on the unrestored base of a pyramid, stands **El Castillo,** also called the Temple-Pyramid and El Mirador (lookout). The "castle's" notable façade rises over the box-like structure and bears sculptures attached by tenons or dowels. The terracing around the temple contained many *chultunes.*

Labná, less restored than nearby sites, is 5km farther east along the road to Xlapak, a total of 17km from the Campeche-Mérida highway. The ADO "Ruta Puuc" bus stops at Labná (see Campeche to Mérida: Long Route, above, but see Kabah for other transportation information; site open daily 8am-5pm. Admission 2500 pesos, free Sun.)

Grutas de Loltún

After descending from the dense jungle of mahogany, *sapodilla, ceiba,* and gumbo-limbo trees, you enter a 1½km maze of enormous caverns and narrow alleys. Graced by Mayan sculptures, the caves themselves are the carvings of nature, fashioned long before humans ventured inside. The Maya settled in the area to take advantage of the water and clay in these caves. Any detailed exploration of Yucatán should include the *grutas* along the Sayil-Labná road, 19km east of Labná and 27km east of the Campeche-Mérida highway.

The name "Loltún" (Flower of Rock) seems to refer to the group of petal-shaped rooms off the central vestibule at the end of the tour. This cavern is called the "Room of the 37 Inscriptions," many of which are still visible. Other rooms include the Na Cab (House of the Bees), where you can see the *ka'ob* (grindstones) left by the Maya; the slippery Gallery of Fallen Rocks, where the Maya removed the curtains of stalactites at their tips for use as spears and arrows; the Gallery of the Five Chultunes, where a sculpted jaguar head drips water into cisterns, while a huge warrior and eagle look on; and the Cathedral, the palatial room that hosted Mayan feasts during which clay plates were ceremonially smashed against the walls in a sign of satisfaction. The guides may also point out a shadow that resembles the image of former Mexican president Díaz Ordaz, the "air-conditioned" cubicle through which cool drafts flow, the discotheque of reflected lights, and the open pits from which the Maya mined red clay for pottery. Among nature's own sculptural achievements are camels, *volcanitos,* the Virgin of Guadalupe, and an assortment of protrusions identifiable as body parts.

Technically, entrance to the caves is allowed daily only at 9:30am, 11am, 12:30pm, 2pm, and 2:30pm and then only with a guide. There are usually enough tourists, however, to persuade guides to leave as soon as large groups assemble. If you don't understand Spanish, it's worth waiting for an English-speaking group to gather, because the guides relate entertaining anecdotes. (Admission 3000 pesos, plus a tip of at least 1000 pesos.)

The difficulty in touring the caves is getting to the entrance. If you don't take the ADO "Ruta Puuc" package bus from Mérida (see Campeche to Mérida: Long Route, above), you'll have to catch a bus to Oxkutzcab (at the intersection of Rte. 164 and the road from Labná) and proceed from there. Cabs (often pickup trucks) that cluster on the market side of the Zócalo work in collusion, and routinely refuse to travel the quick 7km for anything less than 8000 pesos. Alternatively, either hitch with travelers coming from Uxmal or one of the other ruins, or pick up a *camión* (passenger truck) from the road facing the market entrance. These converted minitrucks, crammed with standing passengers, chickens, and blocks of ice, spend more time stopping than advancing, but they pass every hour and cost only 300 pesos. The custom is to ask the price only at journey's end. You will be the only *extranjero* on the truck.

The **Restaurant El Guerrero,** at the exit for the *grutas* (½km from the entrance), has a limited menu of interesting local dishes such as *papadzules* and *poc-chuc* (8000 pesos each). Whether or not you eat here, the restaurant is a good place to solicit rides when you can't bear to wait for the sardine truck back to Oxkutzcab.

Kabah

Codz Poop Temple, up the grassy slope to the right of the Kabah site, reveals a labor of extraordinary effort. Nearly 300 masks of Chac, each a sculptural mosaic composed of 30 carved pieces, cover its long façade. The site probably served as a judicial court, in which specially appointed justices settled disputes with the help of the gods. The elaborate mats they plopped down upon explains the palace's Mayan name, "Rolled Mat."

Codz Poop shows the influence of the Chenes style, a design not often found in the area; two of its neighbors to the east, **El Palacio** (a 25-meter pyramid) and **Las Columnas,** were designed in the plainer and more common Puuc fashion. Several other monuments in the vicinity remain submerged in jungly growth.

Across the highway from the main site beyond the parking area, a short dirt road leads in three directions: an unrestored group of temples lies to the right, the nearly camouflaged West Group to the left, and a beautifully sculpted arch directly ahead. The arch marks the beginning of the ancient *sacbé* (paved, elevated road), which ended at a similar arch in Uxmal. (Open daily 8am-5pm. Admission 200 pesos, free Sun.)

Kabah is 153km from Campeche and 101km from Mérida along the Campeche-Mérida highway. Uxmal lies 22km northwest, and the road to Sayil, Xlapak, Labná, and Loltúm 5km south. Because of its location on Rte. 261, Kabah is easily accessible by bus.

In addition to the special ADO "Ruta Puuc" buses (see Campeche to Mérida: Long Route, above), public buses to Kabah leave from Mérida's main bus station, Calle 69 #544 (tel. 24-90-55), and go on to Campeche. Buses from Campeche leave the ADO station, Gobernadores 289 (tel. 628-02). Buses will stop at Kabah only if a passenger notifies the driver beforehand or if the driver sees a person wildly gesticulating on shoulder of the highway. Since almost all the tourists who come here have cars, it's also possible to hitch a ride back to Uxmal or to the other ruins and the Grutas de Loltún in the Puuc hills. There are no services at Kabah.

Uxmal

The most famous archeological site along the Ruta Puuc, Uxmal (oosh-MAL) emanates both grandness of stature and beauty of detail. The finely-sculpted reliefs and immense masks impress even more when one remembers that the Maya didn't have the service of metal tools. Unfortunately, most of the stone sculptures are absent from the site, now sitting the museums (such as the "Governor of Uxmal") or in the hands of thieves (such as the phalli that once ensured the fertility of the ancient city). The *chultunes* and *aguadas,* lime-covered cisterns used to store rain, have been eroded and carried off by the flood of years. All that remains is the monumental shell of the ancient city that the modern Maya call Oxmal, "thrice-built," which guides will quickly point out was actually built five times.

Uxmal receives deserved attention from the government, which has provided a tourist center and a good deal of glossy hype. The ruins make for a pleasant daytrip or the anchor of a two-day tour of the many less-accessible ruins in the area.

Orientation and Practical Information

Uxmal sits on Rte. 261, the main highway between the state capitals of Mérida (79km north) and Campeche (175km southwest). The road to the smaller sites at Sayil, Xlapak, and Labná branches east off the main route 27km south of Uxmal.

Second-class buses connect Uxmal (as with Kabah) with Mérida and Campeche. Five buses per day travel in each direction (see Campeche and Mérida listings for details). Ask the driver to stop at the access road to the *ruinas.* To return, catch a passing bus or one of the many *combis* from anywhere along the highway. The last bus to Mérida passes at 7:30pm; the last bus for Campeche comes at 6:30pm.

Try to arrive at Uxmal early in the morning, before the sun is high and the cattle-cars of tourists arrive. The large site is poorly shaded; wear sunscreen and carry a water bottle.

A stunning tourist center containing a small museum, a restaurant, a gift shop, and a photographic supply shop, greets you at the entrance to the ruins. The Kit Bolon Tun theater, also in the tourist center, features melodramatic but informative half-hour video presentations about the Yucatán's archeological sites and the peninsula's enduring environmental and cultural riches. (Two shows in Spanish and 2 in English daily. Free.)

Accommodations and Food

No modern village has arisen at Uxmal; the array of hotels and their clientele constitute the region's population. Prices at these hotels are, as usual, inversely proportional to their distance from the ruins; in this vein, the only true budget accomodations are in the somewhat distant town of Ticul, a half-hour drive from Uxmal. Travelers without wheels can either take a series of *combis* and buses to the site from Ticul (see below) or choose from the luxurious arm-and-leg establishments abutting the ruins.

The **Hotel Villas Arqueológicas** (tel. 24-70-53), an affiliate of Club Med, sports a huge complex with pool, boutique, lounge areas, and a large cage of spider monkeys. Their beautiful, air-conditioned rooms will set you back a bundle. (Singles 128,000 pesos. Doubles 146,000 pesos.) **Hacienda Uxmal,** (tel. 24-71-42), on Rte. 261 400m from the entance to the ruins, has smaller rooms off an expansive jungle of a courtyard and oasis of a pool. Rooms with fans and bathrooms are fit for Chac. (Singles and doubles 120,000 pesos.) Uncomfortably far from the ruins (2½km north on the highway), the **Hotel Misión Uxmal** (tel. 24-73-08), offers goitrogenic rooms with red-tiled floors, fans, and a gorgeous view of the ruins among the hills. Chac rules. (Singles 126,000 pesos. Doubles 136,000 pesos.)

Cheaper accommodations, camping, and trailer facilities are available at **Rancho Uxmal** (tel. 201-82), 4km north of Uxmal toward Mérida. Rooms come with tile bathrooms, hot water, and strong ceiling fans. (Singles 52,000 pesos. Doubles 60,000 pesos.) The friendly owner also permits campers to pitch tents or sling hammocks in the large gravel driveway area. (Sites 5000 pesos per person, including use of bathrooms and showers.) To shuttle between the ruins and Rancho Uxmal, use the buses and *combis* passing along the highway (every ½ hr., 1000 pesos).

For food at Uxmal, your best bet is the new air-conditioned **Restaurant Yax Beh** by the complex's entrance. Entrees here are on the expensive side (simple sandwiches go for 13,000 pesos), but substantially cheaper than the pricey, gourmet cuisine in the three nearby hotels. (Open daily 8:30am-9:45pm.) Though somewhat distant, Rancho Uxmal serves moderately priced pork, chicken, and fish dishes (*poc chuc* 20,000 pesos) under a large *palapa.* Drink beer with the locals and the skinflints from the luxury hotels from 9am to 9pm. The budget-conscious should also take advantage of small-town prices in nearby Ticul.

Sights

As with many of the Mayan ruins, the story of the people who once occupied Uxmal is incomplete. Popular legends give more detailed and amusing explanations of Uxmal's history than archeologists provide; these stories, however, are literature, not history. Most of the structures visible today date from the Classic period (7th century). Uxmal's style, unlike Chichén Itzá's, is purely Mayan Puuc without Toltec influence.

According to the **Chilam Balam,** a Mayan historical account written in phonetic Spanish, Ah Suytok Xiu invaded with his warriors from the Valley of Mexico around the end of the 10th century. The Xiu dominated until civil warfare toppled the League of Mayapán and ended Uxmal's prosperity in the 12th century. The last ruler of Uxmal was Ah Suytok Tutul Xiu, whose descendants still live in the Puuc region and in the village of Oxkutzcab. Because his priests foretold the coming of the white, bearded men from the ocean, the Xiu put up no resistance against the conquistadors. At Tutul Xiu's baptism as an old man, his godfather was none other than Francisco de Montejo, conqueror of the Yucatán.

The near-pyramid visible upon entering Uxmal is the **Temple of the Sorcerer,** built by a dwarf-magician who supposedly hatched from a witch's egg and grew to maturity in only one year. These events rightfully struck terror in the heart of the governing lord of Uxmal, so he challenged the fledgling dwarf to a contest of building skills. The dwarf's pyramid easily outclassed the governor's Great Pyramid, still visible to the right of the Governor's Palace. Grasping at straws, the spiteful ruler complained that the dwarf's pyramid was actually elliptical at the base instead of square or rectangular. In the ensuing struggle, the dwarf's magical strength prevailed over the governor's superior geometry and the deposed ruler landed in the Cemetery Group to the east of the Temple of the Sorcerer and the Nunnery Complex.

Archeologists claim that the 30m-tall pyramid contains at least five superimpositions built at different times. To the west of it, the **Nunnery Complex** consists of four buildings around a quadrangle measuring 65m×45m. Here, the folklorists come closer to the truth than the archeologists. The latter have adopted the name the Spanish gave to the group when its 74 rooms reminded them of the convents in the 16th-century Spain they had left behind. Meanwhile, the Maya told of the buildings' construction by the "Hand of the Heavenly Worker." Excavations revealed ceiling handprints, often associated with the god of the sky and sun, Itzamná. Many frieze sculptures, mostly of Chac (but some of Krac, Chac's half-brother and the black sheep of the family), ornament the plaza. The rain god usually appears as a triple mask with a long hook nose.

On the way to the other reconstructed buildings, a path divides the two platforms of the ballcourt. In contrast to many other ballcourts found in Mesoamerica, this one is simple and poorly preserved. The two rings through which the players tried to pass the solid ball of hardened rubber bear hieroglyphic dates only one day apart from each other.

Emerging from the ballcourt, the path breaks off to the right and runs a few hundred meters to the **Cemetery Group,** which consists of a plaza bounded by a small pyramid to the north, a temple to the west, and two other ruined structures. Stones that once formed four small platforms in the plaza bear haunting reliefs of skulls and crossbones. These "gravestones" have given the group its name, although excavations have revealed no human remains.

From the ballcourt, the path branching to the right reaches the **Dovecote,** easily recognizable by the eight triangular sections of cresting pierced by lizardholes. Ahead through the façade of the Dovecote lies the base of the **Chenes Temple.** The pyramid today is a huge mass of jungle-covered rubble, of which only the uppermost crest of the temple that stood atop the pyramid has been excavated. It is best seen from the House of Turtles (see below). To the northeast lies the **Great Pyramid,** built by the governor in his contest with the dwarf and today one of the better-restored structures at Uxmal. Only the front steps and the first platform can be scaled; guards will not permit you to climb any farther.

The House of Turtles and the Palace of the Governor top an escarpment east of the Great Pyramid. Three buildings comprise the **Palace of the Governor.** Over 100m long and built on several concentric landscaped terraces, the palace is typical of the Puuc style. The pediment is plain but 103 masks of Chac, laid out in a line which undulates like a serpent, decorate the eastern frieze. After the governor's defeat at the hands of the dwarf-magician, laborers filled the many rooms of the palace with stones in preparation for a superimposition that was never completed. The small **House of Turtles,** on the northwest corner of the escarpment, may not initially impress, yet archeologists consider it one of the most aesthetically pleasing structures in Mesoamerica. The House is adorned with an intriguing series of sculpted turtles—still venerated by the Maya—along the upper frieze of the two-story structure.

From the Palace of the Governor, you may be able to spot the **House of the Old Woman** lies to the east. According to legend, the dwarf imprisoned his witch-mother in the kitchen cabinet of this now completely overgrown pyramid. About 400m south of the House of the Old Woman lies the **Temple of the Phalli.** Phallic sculptures hang from the cornices of this ruined building and spurt rain runoff from the roof. Locals believe this house helped the witch-mother hatch the dwarf. This temple seems to date from the Toltec-Xiu period.

Outside the hotels, Uxmal's only nightlife consists of a tacky but entertaining sound-and-light show. While you sit in the Nunnery bleachers, staff members flip switches for colored lights and play a tape that dramatically lauds Mayan culture. The Spanish version (3700 pesos) begins at 7pm and ends after the last of the Mérida or Campeche buses pass Uxmal, but hitching a ride with other spectators is relatively easy. The English version (5000 pesos) begins at 9pm. (Site open daily 8am-5pm. Admission 10,000 pesos, free for adults on Sun. and for ages under 12. Parking 8am-10pm 2000 pesos.)

Ticul

A small town off the Campeche-Mérida highway, Ticul is an ideal base for exploring Uxmal, Kabah, Sayil, Xlapak, Labná, and the Grutas de Loltún. Mere minutes from these sights, Ticul draws few tourists, despite its two cheap hotels and inexpensive restaurants.

"Ticul" could well translate to "land of the bicycle," for bicycles outnumber both pedestrians and cars on Calle 23, the town's main east-west artery. In the evening, resting bikes surround the Zócalo and pedal-thumping youths cruise the streets, irritatingly joined by more obstreperous motorcycles. The town's three-wheeled taxis place passengers on a bench above the axle, while the driver pedals behind. (Fare 1000 pesos.)

Although Ticul works well as a base for covering the ruins, it holds nothing of interest itself. In the afternoon, most of the bicycles disappear and Ticul turns into a ghost town. A regional center for red clay pottery (one of the children's parks oddly pays sculptural tribute to six clay vases), Ticul's artisans inflate their prices as much as 100% for tourists; it's cheaper to make purchases in Mérida.

Streets in Ticul fall in a grid, with the main street, Calle 23, passing through the center. Even-numbered streets run north-south. Most of the towns' commercial activitiy takes place between Calles 26 and 32, a block in either direction from Calle 23.

An amiable old woman with insider tips on the ruins' transportation system hangs out at Ticul's **post office,** Calle 28 #202 (tel. 200-40; open Mon.-Fri. 9am-1pm and 3-6pm, Sat. 9am-1pm). **Banco de Atlántico,** Calle 23 #214 (tel. 200-06), off the Zócalo, changes U.S. dollars (in traveler's checks or cash) Monday through Friday from 9am to 1pm. **Farmacia 24 Horas,** Calle 26 #199-B, faces the Zócalo and provides daily necessities 'round the clock. The town's long-distance *caseta,* Calle 23 #210 (tel. 200-00), at Calle 28, makes international collect calls for a refreshingly cheap 2000 pesos. (Open Mon.-Sat. 8am-1pm and 4-8pm, Sun. 8am-1pm.) **Lavandería Burbujas,** Calle 28 #117, has one-hour service for 2000 pesos per kg. (Open Mon.-Sat. 8am-5pm, Sun. 8am-1pm.) **Police** headquarters are just off the Zócalo on Calle 23 at 24a. Calle (tel. 202-10; open 24 hr.).

Ticul has two hotels and several good restaurants. Three blocks from the Zócalo, the **Hotel San Miguel,** Calle 28 #213 (tel. 203-82), is clean, cheap, and sunny. Rooms have hot water and fans, and the staff is obliging. (Singles 15,000 pesos. Doubles 20,000 pesos, with 2 beds 25,000 pesos.) The newer **Sierra Sosa,** Calle 26 #199-A (tel. 200-08), right off the Zócalo, somehow appears dirtier: all rooms in the guest house have hot water and fans, but the walls bear suspicious yellow stains. (Doubles 28,000 pesos.) Ticul's best dining option is **Los Almendros,** Calle 23 #207, between Calles 24 and 26. Rustic handpainted wooden chairs and family photos fill the air-conditioned Andalusian palace. Most entrees, such as roast chicken and *poc chuc,* cost 12,000 pesos. (Open daily 8am-8pm.) **Los Delfines,** Calle 23 #208 at Calle 30, specializes in surf 'n' turf dishes. High-backed upholstered chairs compensate for the lack of air conditioning. *Chile relleno con camarones,* stuffed with shrimp, goes for 15,000 pesos. (Open daily 8am-1pm and 5-11pm.) Next to the Sierra Sosa, the **Restaurant El Colorín,** Calle 26 #199-B, serves sandwiches, burgers, and yogurt for 1500-3000 pesos. The café is packed by 3pm for the hearty 7000-peso *comida corrida.* (Open daily 8am-11pm.)

Public transportation from Ticul makes it fairly easy to reach Uxmal, Kabah, and the caves of Loltún. To get to Uxmal and Kabah, take the *combi* to Santa Elena (just off the Campeche-Mérida highway) from the intersection of Calles 23 and 28 (15 min., 700 pesos). From Santa Elena, *combis* head north to Uxmal; ask the driver to let you out at the ruins (15 min., 700 pesos). Campeche-bound buses stop in Santa Elena every two hours; take one of these to reach Kabah 8km to the south (15 min., 500 pesos) or to return from Uxmal. If you have trouble in Ticul finding a *combi* to Santa Elena, you can also go the long way to Uxmal and Kabah via the small town of Muna at the intersection of Rte. 184 and 261. Buses leave Ticul for Muna every two hours (20 min., 1000 pesos); from there, buses heading south stop in Muna every half hour (700 pesos to Uxmal).

Reaching Loltún from Ticul also requires changing buses. The first leg of the journey involves a *combi* from Ticul to Oxkutzcab that leaves from the intersection of Calles 23 and 28 (15 min., 700 pesos). In Oxkutzcab, from a lot across from the giant market "20 de Noviembre," *combis* leave for Loltún 7km southwest. Tell the driver to drop you off at the "grutas," because everyone else on board is most likely bound for the agricultural cooperative 3km farther down the road (10 min., 500 pesos).

Mérida

Hub of the Yucatán Peninsula and capital of Yucatán state, Mérida centripetally attracts cultural resources from miles in every direction. Built atop the ruins of the ancient Mayan capital of T'ho, the city is a rich amalgamation of proud *indígena* history, powerful colonial presence, and modern-day international flavor. The stones of the fortress-like cathedral bear imprints of the Mayan temples from which they came and the Mayan labor which moved them. The Maya called it the "place

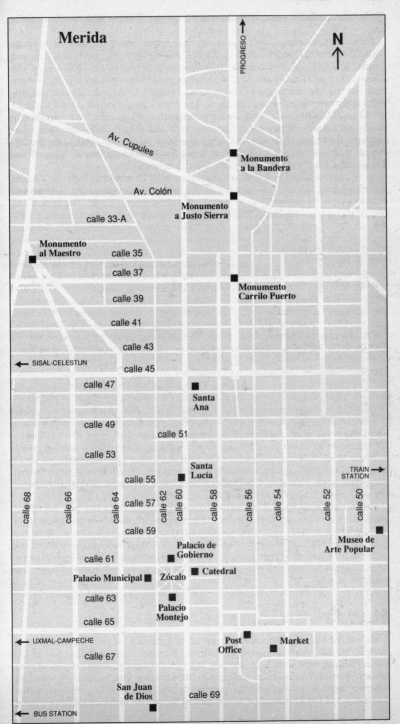

of the fifth point," placing it at the dead center of their universe, bounded by the four points of north, south, east, and west.

Now, Mérida serves as the region's commercial center. Thousands of shops line the narrow streets and flood the sidewalks. Panama hats, made from the leaves of the *jipijapa* plant and the *guano* palm, come from Becal in the neighboring state of Campeche; hammocks arrive from the nearby *pueblito* of Tixcocób; and the raw, stripped *henequén* is trucked to Mérida's industrial zone from all over Yucatán before being exported as hemp.

Old World influences emanate from the 25,000 *meridaños* of recent Lebanese and Syrian descent; a small French community is responsible for Mérida's version of the Champs-Elysées, the Paseo Montejo; and increasing numbers of American expatriates also call Mérida home. A newly discovered focal point for travelers from around the world, Mérida plays host to planeloads of tourists who arrive to spend days museum-hopping and market-shopping, and to pass romantic evenings in music-filled parks. Mérida, the largest city on the Yucatán Peninsula, has yet to succumb to big-city indifference. Street cleaners busily maintain its reputation as "The White City," intimate conversations whisper in Zócalo loveseats, and every Sunday draws hordes of strolling families to enjoy "Mérida en domingo."

Orientation

All roads lead to Mérida. Route 180 arrives from Cancún (300km) and Valladolid (160km) to the east, becoming Calle 65 which passes through the busiest part of town 1 block south of the Zócalo.

Those approaching on Rte. 180 from Campeche 153km to the southwest end up on Av. Itzáes (also called Av. de la Paz), which runs north-south, or on Calle 81, which feeds into the north-south Calle 70. Both intersect Calle 59, the best access to the center of town, running east to a point 1 block north of the Zócalo. Paseo Montejo begins at Calle 47 and passes some of Mérida's finer homes, continuing north as Rte. 261 to Progreso and the coast.

Buses arrive and depart from Mérida to every city on the Yucatán Peninsula and in the rest of Mexico. To find the Zócalo from the main terminal, turn right (east) from the entrance, walk 3 blocks, turn left (north), and the Zócalo is 3 blocks ahead. From the train station, either take a taxi (6000 pesos) or walk the lonely 6 blocks west on Calle 55 and 3 blocks south on Calle 60.

Mérida's international airport lies 7km southwest of the city on the highway to Campeche (Rte. 180). Bus #79, called "Airport," runs between the terminals and a midtown bus stop at the corner of Calles 67 and 60 (every 20 min. 5am-9pm, ½ hr., 500 pesos). **Transporte Terrestre** vans leave from the airport for the Zócalo as soon as they fill (500 pesos). A taxi to the airport costs 14,000 pesos.

Mérida's consistent grid of one-way streets is easy to navigate. Excellent maps, with Mérida on one side and Yucatán state on the other, are available at large hotels and tourist offices. Odd-numbered streets run east-west, with street numbers increasing toward the south; even-numbered streets run north-south, and street numbers increase toward the west. Using the streets which border the Zócalo as rough directional axes, numbers greater than 500 usually lie west or south, smaller than 500 north or east. Addresses in Mérida are given using an "x" to separate the main street from the cross streets and "y" ("and" in Spanish) to separate the two cross streets if the address falls in the middle of the block. Thus "54#509 x 61 y 63" reads "Calle 54 #509, between Calles 61 and 63."

Mérida's municipal buses (500 pesos) meander along idiosyncratic routes to arrive at predestined neighborhoods. You can go to tourist information booths or the main office for exact information, but the city is small enough that a bus headed in the right direction will usually drop you off within a few blocks of your desired location. Locals and tourists alike tend to catch them at their boarding points, usually in the center, a few blocks from the Zócalo. City buses run daily from 5am to 11pm.

Taxis do not roam the streets soliciting business. You must call for one or have your hotel or restaurant call for you. Taxis blanket the city, with stands along the Paseo de Montejo and at the airport. Fares are exorbitant; expect to pay at least 5000 pesos for a trip of more than a few blocks.

Car rental agencies in Mérida operate north of the Zócalo on Calles 60 and 62, near the cross streets of 59 and 57. A few more line Paseo Montejo, and well-established operators have offices at the airport. It is unnecessary to rent a car for trips to Chichén Itzá and Uxmal, since day tours of the sites departing from Mérida are numerous and relatively inexpensive, but a car provides the easiest access to the hard-to-reach ruins at Xlapak, Sayil, and Labná.

Practical Information

Federal Tourist Office: In the Peón Contreras Theater (tel. 24-92-90), on Calle 60 between Calles 57 and 59. Excellent maps and knowledgeable bilingual staff. Disperses large numbers of colorful pamphlets, the most useful of which is *Yucatán*, a seasonal guide listing practical information and local events. Open Mon.-Sat. 8am-9pm, Sun. 8am-8pm.

State Tourist Office: Calle 86 #499-C (tel. 23-85-47), on the top floor of the new Museo de Antropología. Not worth the long walk from the Zócalo unless you're headed to the museum anyway. Free Mérida posters. Open Mon.-Fri. 9am-3pm.

Tourist Information Booths: At the airport (open daily 8am-8pm), and on the first-class side of the main bus station (open Mon.-Sat. 8am-8pm, Sun. 10am-4pm). English spoken.

Travel Agents: Yucatán Trails, Calle 62 #482 (tel. 28-25-82), near Calle 59. Canadian owner Denis LaFoy is a genial source of insider information on Mérida and the Yucatán. Open Mon.-Fri. 9am-2pm and 4-7pm, Sat. 9am-2pm. **Turismo Planeta** (tel. 28-15-60), on Calle 59 between Calles 60 and 62, and **Turismo González** (tel. 24-86-87), in the bus terminal and on Calle 59 near Calle 56, have marginally cheaper rates on daytrips to the ruins. Daytrips to Chichén Itzá and Uxmal hover around US$45.

Consulates: U.S., Montejo 453 (tel. 25-50-11 or 25-54-09), at Av. Colón. Call first to determine hours for visas. Open for general business Mon.-Fri. 7:30am-4pm. **U.K. and Belize** (Honorary Consulate), Calle 58 #498 (tel. 28-39-62). Information about travel to Belize. Open Mon.-Fri. 9am-1pm. **West Germany,** 1d. Calle #217 (tel. 311-11), between Calles 20 and 20a.

Currency Exchange: Banks center on Calle 65 near the Zócalo and are open Mon.-Fri. 9:30am-1:30pm. *Casas de cambio* trade at slightly lower rates than banks but keep longer hours. Most are open until 4pm, and are scattered among the banks on Calle 65. Lines run out the door everywhere.

American Express: Paseo de Montejo #495, office #106 (tel. 28-43-73), between Calles 43 and 45. Travel agency, lost traveler's check service, and general advice. Open Mon.-Fri. 9am-1pm.

Post Office: On Calle 65 between Calles 56 and 56a., 3 blocks southeast of the Zócalo in the Palacio Federal. Open for Lista de Correos and stamps Mon.-Fri. 7am-7pm, Sat. 9am-noon; for packages Mon.-Fri. 7am-6pm. *Surcursales* (branches) at Calle 58 between Calles 49 and 51, at the airport, and at the main bus station open for stamps only Mon.-Fri. 8am-6pm. For regulations, call 23-89-07. Postal Code: 97000.

Telephones: International collect calls cannot be made from *casetas* in Mérida. Instead, dial 09 for the international operator from a public phone: if he or she is on *siesta*, which is usually the case, the national operator at 02 can transfer the line. Highway robbery rates (30,000 per min. to the U.S.) are charged for long-distance calls made from the *caseta* in the **Edificio Condesca,** Calle 59 at 62. (Open Mon.-Fri. 8am-1:30pm and 3:30-6:30pm, Sat. 8am-7pm.) Other branches are at the airport (open daily 8am-9pm) and the main bus station (open daily 8am-10pm). **Telephone Code:** 99.

Telegrams: In the same building as the main post office (tel. 21-37-03), on Calle 65. Open Mon.-Fri. 8am-midnight, Sat. 9am-8pm.

Airport: On Rte. 180 7km southwest of the city. Post office, telegram office, long-distance telephone, and car rental available. **Aeroméxico,** Paseo Montejo #460 (tel. 27-94-55), at Calle 37, and at the airport (tel. 24-66-65). **Mexicana,** Calle 61 #500 (tel. 24-67-76), at Calle 58, and at the airport (tel. 23-69-86). **Aerocaribe,** Paseo Montejo #500-B (tel. 24-95-00), at Calle

47. **Aviateca,** Paseo Montejo at Calle 37 (tel. 26-42-75). The carriers listed above reach most cities in Mexico, across the southern U.S., and limited destinations in Europe.

Train Station: (tel. 23-59-44) on Calle 55, between Calles 46 and 48, 8½ blocks northeast of the Zócalo. Open daily 7am-10pm. Double check train status at the information booth, and buy tickets at least 2 hr. before departure (you must buy tickets on the day of departure). Busy during Semana Santa, summer, and Christmas. Second-class service only to: Mexico City (at 8pm, 37 hr., 17,200 pesos); Palenque (at 8pm, 12 hr., 6000 pesos); Valladolid (at 4pm, 3 hr., 1700 pesos); Tizimín (at 8pm, 3 hr., 1900 pesos).

Bus Stations: Calle 69 #544 (tel. 24-37-43), between Calles 70 and 72, 6 blocks southwest of the Zócalo. Check departures ahead of time since changes are frequent and complete schedules are often not posted. First-class service to: Mexico City (6 per day, 24 hr., 71,000 pesos); Puebla (1 per day, 20 hr., 65,000 pesos); Jalapa (1 per day, 20 hr., 56,000 pesos); Veracruz (2 per day, 16 hr., 51,000 pesos); San Andrés (5 per day, 14 hr., 44,000 pesos); Coatzacoalcos (3 per day, 12 hr., 30,000 pesos); Villahermosa (14 per day, 9 hr., 29,000 pesos); Campeche (30 per day, 3 hr., 8700 pesos); Playa del Carmen (7 per day, 5 hr., 18,000 pesos); Valladolid (4 per day, 2½ hr., 7500 pesos); Cancún (17 per day, 6 hr., 15,000 pesos); Chichén Itzá (1 per day, 2 hr., 5300 pesos); Escárcega (5 per day, 4 hr., 15,500 pesos); Chetumal (1 per day, 22,000 pesos); and Ticul (6 per day, 1½ hr., 3800 pesos). Second-class service to: Chetumal (20,000 pesos); Carillo Puerto (12,500 pesos); Tulum (3 per day, 18,500 pesos); Playa del Carmen (6 per day, 6 hr., 16,600 pesos); Valladolid (2½ hr., 6500 pesos); Chiquilá (2 per day, 13,000 pesos); Kabah (4 per day, 2 hr., 2600 pesos); Uxmal (4 per day, 2 hr., 2000 pesos); Ticul (20 per day, 1½ hr., 3500 pesos); and Oxkutzcab (20 per day, 2 hr., 3800 pesos). There is a bus station serving many **local routes** at Calle 62 #524 (tel. 24-89-91), between Calles 65 and 67, 1½ blocks south of the Zócalo. Buses to: Dzibilchaltún (7 per day, ½ hr., 1000 pesos); Progreso (every 15 min. 5am-9pm, 45 min., 1700 pesos, round-trip 3200 pesos)—as this is a popular trip, expect to wait an hour after you buy your ticket to board; Tixcocób (every 15 min., 1 hr., 1200 pesos). **Autotransportes del Sur,** Calle 50 #531 (tel. 24-90-55), at Calle 67, 7 blocks southeast of the Zócalo runs to Celestún (7 per day, 2 hr., 3300 pesos). **Autotransportes del Noroeste** (tel. 24-11-43), on Calle 52 between Calles 63 and 65, runs to: Río Lagartos (3 per day, 2 hr., 9000 pesos); Las Coloradas (3 per day, 2½ hr., 9000 pesos); and San Felipe (4 per day, 2 hr., 1500 pesos).

Car Rentals: Mexico Rent-A-Car, Calle 60 #495 (tel. 27-49-16), between Calles 57 and 59. The cheapest place in Mérida; VW Beetles US$32 per day. Open daily 8am-1pm and 6-8pm. **Max Rent-A-Car,** Calle 60 #480 (tel. 24-76-06) between Calles 55 and 53. Open daily 8am-1pm and 5-8pm. **Budget** (tel. 28-27-50), on Calle 60 between Calles 55 and 57. Open Mon.-Sat. 8am-1pm and 4-8pm. Branch at the airport (tel. 24-97-91). Prices increase by about 50% during high season (July-Aug.) at nearly every agency.

Bookstore: Hollywood, Calle 60 #496 (tel. 21-36-19), near Calle 59. A small collection of English travel guides and paperback novels. Open Mon.-Sat. 8-10am and 1-5pm, Sun. 8:30-10am.

Laundromat: Lavandería Santiago, Calle 59 #580-B, at Calle 72, 6½ blocks northwest of the Zócalo in the *barrio* of Santiago. Excellent, inexpensive service. Same-day service if clothes dropped off in the morning. Wash and dry 7500 pesos per 3kg. Open Mon.-Fri. 8am-6pm.

Market: Covers more than 4 blocks south of Calle 65, behind and on either side of the Palacio Federal on Calle 56. Convenient to the post office for shipping home. Crowded and particularly fun on the weekends. Open daily sunrise-sunset.

Red Cross: Calle 68 #533 (tel. 21-24-45 for emergencies, 21-68-13 for information), between Calles 65 and 67, 4½ blocks southwest of the Zócalo. 24-hr. emergency and ambulance services. No English spoken. **Hospital O'Horan,** on the city's western edge, also has 24-hr. ambulance service; dial 23-87-11 or 21-30-56.

Pharmacy: Congreso Farmacia, Calle 58 #488 (tel. 24-49-57), at Calle 59. Home delivery service available. Open Mon.-Sat. 8am-8:30pm.

Medical Assistance: Centro Médico de las Américas, Calle 54 #356 (tel. 27-31-00), at Av. Pérez Ponce. Many of Mérida's private physicians speak English.

Police: (tel. 25-25-55) on Reforma (also called Calle 72) between Calles 39 and 41. Take bus "Reforma." 24-hr. emergency service. No English spoken.

Accommodations

Mérida's hotels are more expensive than Campeche's, but a bargain compared with *gringo* magnets Chichén Itzá and Cancún. Inexpensive hotels near the Zócalo are particularly good places to meet budget travelers from the U.S. and Europe, who may join you to rent a car for longer trips to ruins. None of the hotels listed are outside of the city center, but for the sake of convenience, they have been split into two groups, using Calle 65 as the north-south divider.

North

Hotel Reforma, Calle 59 #508 (tel. 179-20), between Calles 60 and 62. A stone's throw from the Zócalo. Peaceful tiled courtyard, clean pool with bar, and beautiful high-ceilinged rooms with fans and hot water. Attentive management (room-service *agua purificada*). Singles 40,000 pesos. Doubles 55,000 pesos. A/C 5000 pesos extra.

Hotel Dolores Alba, Calle 63 #464 (tel. 21-37-45), between Calles 52 and 54. Handsome old building in excellent condition. Friendly management and Homey-the-Clown rooms with patterned quilts and wooden headboards. Cement courtyard includes plain square pool and flat parking area. Water comes as you like it: cold, purified, or hot. Singles 40,000 pesos. Doubles 50,000 pesos. Triples 55,000 pesos.

Hotel Trinidad, Calle 62 #464 (tel. 21-30-29), between Calles 55 and 57. Unique. Antique furnishings and ultra-modern paintings by Mexican artists decorate this restored colonial mansion. Twelve clean rooms with dark wood dressers and old-fashioned fans overlook a verdant garden. Each room decorated differently; prices vary accordingly. Lobby moonlights as a café and art gallery, and the large screen in the bar displays satellite TV and movie videos. Singles with communal bath 25,000-45,000 pesos. Doubles 30,000-60,000 pesos.

Trinidad Galeria, Calle 60 #456 (tel. 21-09-35), at Calle 51. Less charm and more mosquitoes than its sister, Hotel Trinidad. Large, leafy swimming pool. Modern art and eclectic antique collection. Single with communal bath 30,000 pesos. Doubles 45,000 pesos.

Hotel El Caribe, Calle 59 #500 (tel. 24-90-22), set back in a park 1 block from the Zócalo. Immaculate pint-sized rooms with arches over beds, fans, phones, and hot water. Rooftop pool. *Muzak* piped into each room, but you *can* turn it off. Singles 55,000 pesos. Doubles 65,000 pesos. A/C and TV 10,000 pesos extra.

Gran Hotel, Calle 60 #496 (tel. 24-77-30), in the park. The high ceiling, majestic staircase, and large courtyard lobby crammed with antiques make this building beautiful. French cedar doors lead to rooms furnished in art deco a la *Batman*. Rooms with A/C lack balconies. All rooms have fans but no hot water. Singles 60,000 pesos. Doubles 70,000 pesos.

Hotel Margarita, Calle 66 #506 (tel. 21-32-13), between Calles 61 and 63, 1½ blocks west of the Zócalo. A good buy, and slightly closer to the bus station than the other hotels. Rooms a smidgen stuffy and unclean, but they do have fans, hot water, and toilet seats. Doubles considerably more spacious than singles. Singles and 1-bed doubles 28,000 pesos. Doubles with 2 beds 32,000 pesos. A/C 5000 pesos extra.

Hotel Janeiro, Calle 57 #435 (tel. 23-36-02), at Calle 48. Large, modern complex distant from the Zócalo but only 1½ blocks from the train station. Quiet rooms off a pleasantly obscure hallway have deep-green patterns on curtains and beds to match the leaves floating in the pool below. Fans and hot water. Singles 35,000 pesos. Doubles 40,000 pesos. A/C 10,000 pesos extra.

Hotel Kristal (tel. 24-33-76), on Calle 55 between Calles 48 and 50, 8 long blocks from the Zócalo and 1 block from the train station. Mattresses on concrete blocks in miniscule rooms on concrete blocks. Most come with balconies, but they only overlook the noisy, smoggy street; all have hot water and fan. Spotless bathrooms lack doors. Singles 25,000 pesos. Doubles 30,000 pesos.

South

Casa de Huéspedes Peniche, Calle 62 #507 (tel. 21-32-35), between Calles 63 and 65. The least expensive option near the Zócalo. Beautiful, disintegrating colonial building with engraved glass and wooden doors that don't lock. Tolerable communal showers, baths, and fans. Best for those with their own locks, towels, and trusting hearts. Singles 16,000 pesos. Doubles 25,000 pesos.

Hospedaje Bowen, Calle 66 #501 (tel. 21-81-12), at Calle 65 halfway between the main bus station and the Zócalo. Green, well-tended courtyard surrounded by white, colonial columns. International guests mingle around the arcaded patio. Some rooms enjoy kitchenettes (1 burner and fridge), but all rooms are hooked up with fans and hot water. Singles 27,000 pesos, with kitchenette 30,000 pesos. Doubles 31,000 pesos, with kitchenette 35,000 pesos.

Hotel Peninsular, Calle 58 #519 (tel. 23-69-96), between Calles 65 and 67, 2½ blocks southeast of the Zócalo. Distinctive green awning and brown colonial façade accommodate several stores as well as the hotel entrance. Tiny, shimmering pool in a grassy atrium. Huge yellow cement rooms are quiet but have few windows. Fans and hot water. Singles 37,000 pesos. Doubles 45,000 pesos. A/C 10,000 pesos extra.

Hotel Sevilla, Calle 62 #511 (tel. 23-83-60), at Calle 65 1½ blocks south of the Zócalo. Elegant colonial building deteriorating quickly. Handsome lion statues flank the stairs leading out of the courtyard. All rooms have hot water, phones, and fans. Singles 33,000 pesos. Doubles 36,000 pesos. Triples 40,000 pesos.

Hotel México, Calle 60 #525 (tel. 24-70-22), between Calles 65 and 67, 1½ blocks south of the Zócalo. Clean rooms off an institutional hallway equipped with fans, phones, and hot water. Low wall separates bed from bath. Singles and doubles 50,000 pesos. TV 5000 pesos extra. Microwave 3000 pesos extra. Frozen burritos downstairs.

Hotel El Caminante, Calle 64 #539 (tel. 23-67-30), between Calles 65 and 67. Sanitary green rooms with barred iron doors not unlike a prison's. Fans and hot water. Snappy snack shack in the lobby. Singles 30,000 pesos. Doubles 35,000 pesos.

Hotel Oviedo, Calle 62 #515 (tel. 21-36-09), between Calles 65 and 67. Old building with high ceilings and attractive courtyard. Austere rooms have fans, hot water, closets, and dirty walls. Purified water. Singles 33,000 pesos. Doubles 36,000 pesos. 4000 pesos per extra person.

Hotel Del Prado, Calle 50 #454 (tel. 24-94-33), at Calle 67. Ornate fans cool the lobby, off which dark hallways lead to comfy rooms. Shower curtains and toilet seats beautify the bathroom. What would be a deep pool is usually bone dry. Singles 32,000 pesos. Doubles 36,000 pesos. A/C 10,000 pesos extra.

Hotel Del Mayab, Calle 50 #536 (tel. 21-09-09), at Calle 65. Crumbling cement blocks spill into the courtyard and filterless pool. Neat rooms have fans and hot water. Often full. Singles 33,000 pesos. Doubles 36,000 pesos.

Hotel María Teresa, Calle 64 #529 (tel. 21-10-39), between Calles 65 and 67. Run-down, with mildewy baths and flaking cement. Rooms vary in size, so ask to see several; all of them have fans and hot water. Voracious mosquitoes swarm the halls during the rainy season. Singles 28,000 pesos. Doubles 30,000 pesos. Triples 36,000 pesos.

Food

Mérida's diverse population demands a wide variety of food. Look for *yucateco* specialties and international cuisine, as well as the standard selection of *huevos rancheros,* enchiladas, and *flan.*

Travelers wary of over-seasoned *chiles* and weary of avoiding water should note two things. Generally, you can safely explore unknown stews and sauces because the local scorcher, the *chile habanero,* does not lurk within dishes but instead waits patiently in a garnish bowl or in a shaker on the table blended with tomatoes. And the fruit and vegetable *aguas* you've been avoiding elsewhere are made with the city's purified water, so indulge. Mérida's excellent specialties include: *sopa de lima* (frothy lime soup with chicken and tortilla bits); *pollo pibil* (chicken with herbs baked in banana leaves); *poc-chuc* (pork steak with onions doused in sour Seville orange juice); *papadzules* (chopped hard-boiled eggs wrapped in corn tortillas served with pumpkin sauce); *huevos motuleros* (refried beans, fried egg, chopped ham, and cheese on a tortilla garnished with tomato sauce, peas, and fried banana); and *horchata* (a Mayan rice drink flavored with vanilla, honey, and almond).

The cheapest food in town fills the market that stretches south from Calle 65 2 blocks east of the Zócalo. Stands overflow with fruits, vegetables, and *antojitos.* For more substantial nourishment, head to the market's second level off Calle 56 at Calle 67. Almost 40 small *puestos* (restaurants), offering a variety of *yucateco* dishes for 6000-9000 pesos cram this cavernous area. (Restaurant complex open Mon.-Sat. 8am-8pm, Sun. 8am-5pm.)

La Prosperidad, Calle 56 at 53, and **El Tucho,** on Calle 60 between Calles 57 and 55, are two restaurant/afternoon cabarets popular with both locals and tourists. While singers, musicians, and comedians entertain you, troupes of waiters ferry trays of free *botanas* (tacos and hors d'oeuvres) between customers. As long as you keep drinking, the *botanas* keep coming. (Both open daily 1-8pm.)

El Patio Español, Calle 60 #496, at Calle 59 in the Gran Hotel. Classy, tranquil, hip, and inexpensive. A great place to sample *yucateco* specialties: *pollo pibil* 9000 pesos; Yucatecan pork 11,000 pesos. Tortillas or hot bread and butter accompany meals. Open daily 7am-11pm.

Restaurant Express, Calle 60 #509, at Calle 59 across from the Hotel El Caribe. Local coffee-breakers and tourists pack the fleet of wooden tables so full the waiters can't keep up. Eleven ways to cook eggs for 2500-5000 pesos. Sandwiches 2000-5000 pesos. *Comida corrida* 13,000 pesos. Open daily 7am-11pm.

Los Almendros, Calle 50 #493, between Calles 57 and 59, by the Pl. de Mejorada. Huge and popular, with 6 branches in Ticul and Cancún. Serves all native specialties. The combination (16,000 pesos) affords a sampling of *yucateco* dishes: *poc-chuc, longaniza* (grilled sausage), *cocherita* (baked pork), and *escabeche* (turkey with black pepper, cloves, garlic, and onion). Entrees 10,000-14,000 pesos. Open daily 11am-11pm.

Restaurant Mérida Internacional, Calle 62 #493, 1 block from the Zócalo. The cheapest restaurant around the Zócalo. Wooden chairs, plastic tablecloths, and photos of Chichén Itzá on the walls. Tasty regional *yucateco* specialties, with several pork and beef dishes (6000 pesos). Salads 2000 pesos, *comida corrida* 5000 pesos. Open daily 6:30am-11:30pm.

Patio de Las Fajitas, Calle 60 #467 (tel. 28-37-82), between Calles 55 and 53. Every imaginable combination of savorous *fajitas* cooked out on the palm-lined patio of this colonial building. Try the beef, pork and chicken combo (20,000 pesos). Open Tues.-Sun. 1-11pm.

Pop Cafetería, Calle 57 #501, between Calles 60 and 62. Cool, comfortable black-and-white snack joint. Mural of 3 brooding men puts a damper on the happy tone created by the college students who file in from across the street. Few substantial dishes (chicken in *mole* sauce 8000 pesos) or worthwhile sandwiches (5000-10,000 pesos); stick to the drinks and tempting ice cream concoctions. Sundaes 5000 pesos. Open daily 7am-midnight.

Pancho's, on Calle 59 between Calles 60 and 62. Paunchless Pancho Villa look-alikes in pseudo-1890 atmosphere show off their incendiary techniques with flaming dishes and wild cocktails. Eats are good but expensive. The outdoor disco in the back is jam-packed with strident *gringas* and hopeful *mexicanos* twisting the night away under *palapas*. Entrees 20,000-35,000 pesos. Three-drink minimum at the disco (no cover). Open daily 6pm-2am.

La Jungla, Calle 62 #500, between Calles 59 and 61, on the corner of the Zócalo. Wade through the gift shops to the 2nd-floor dining area, a long hall overlooking the Zócalo. An Italian restaurant with hanging papier-mâché parrots and murals of the Tower of Pisa. Wafer-thin pizzas (small cheese 5500 pesos), sandwiches (5500 pesos), and spaghetti (6000 pesos). Wafer-thin after-dinner mints not available. Open daily 11:30am-11:30pm.

El Cedro de Libano, Calle 59 #529, between Calles 64 and 66. Tasty Lebanese food but depressingly bland decor. Try *berenjena con tehina* (*baba ghanoush* or eggplant pâté) for 7000 pesos. *Alambre* is akin to shish-kebab, and *labna con crema de ajo* is a yogurt-like dish with a thick, delicious garlic sauce. Entrees 11,000-17,000 pesos. Open daily 11am-11pm.

Cafe La Guaya, Calle 60 #472, between Calles 53 and 55. Small vegetarian café with a wide array of juices, salads, and entrees (9000-12,000 pesos), and genuine espresso. Talented regional cook prepares nutritious meals. Open Mon.-Sat. 4-11pm.

El Louvre, Calle 62 #499, between the Palacio Municipal and the Palacio de Gobierno. Big, affordable cafeteria where locals talk politics. Service is prompt but curt. Entrees, including brain, tongue, and satisfying sandwiches, cost 3000-5000 pesos. Filling *comida corrida* (6800 pesos) is a bargain. Open 24 hr.

Wini Cafetería, at both Paseo de Montejo 466 and Calle 60 #491. A/C, E-Z listening versions of Manilow and Mangione tunes, and bland food: close your eyes, click your heels, and return to the Topeka Denny's. Still, good for a safe snack with the office lunch-hour crowd. Sandwiches 8000-12,000 pesos. Enchiladas 11,000 pesos. Open daily 7am-noon and 6pm-midnight at Montejo; daily 7am-11:30pm at Calle 60.

El Trapiche, Calle 62 #491, between Calles 59 and 61. A student pizza hangout, best for lunch. Pizza ranges from plain cheese (small 6000 pesos) to the extravagant Hawaiian with *jamón y piña* (small 8000 pesos). Also serves delicious *jugos* and *aguas*. Open daily 7am-11pm.

Pizzeria de Vito Corleone, Calle 59 (tel. 23-68-46), between Calles 60 and 62. Near the university. The best (and maybe only) bubble gum pizza you'll ever eat (small 6500 pesos). Students lean close together over small tables, nibbling pepper pizzas (small 7500 pesos) and garlic bread. Seats upstairs cooled by a phalanx of fans. Large pizzas 12,000-16,000 pesos. Open daily 10am-11pm.

Yannig Restaurant, on Calle 62 between Calles 57 and 59. Elegant French restaurant with a chef from Brittany. Good service and delicious meals. Fish almondine 17,000 pesos. Entrees 14,000-22,000 pesos. Open Mon.-Tues. and Thurs.-Sat. 5-11:30pm, Sun. 1-10:30pm.

Messina's, Itzáes at Calle 31. Out of the way. Authentic Italian food and pizzas served *al fresco.* Inexpensive, generous entrees, with bread and pasta, from 7000 pesos. Open daily 6pm-midnight.

Panadería Modelo, Calle 65 #502-A, near the Zócalo. This bakery whips up fresh wine breads (1200 pesos) and cakey *pan de nara* (1500 pesos). Open daily 6am-10pm.

Sights

Mérida's salon, the **Zócalo,** inspires animated discussions upon *confidenciales* (loveseats with the halves facing in opposite directions). If you speak Spanish, you can easily join or strike up a conversation.

Almost all of Mérida's larger historic buildings are within easy walking distance of the Zócalo, but don't restrict yourself to the downtown area. Pocket-sized parks and fading colonial arches throughout town reward the ambulatory traveler. The twin spires of the yellow *catedral* loom over the eastern side of the Zócalo. The three Corinthian doors of solid wood with brass nails and the stark, windowless façade recall, with their fortress-like presence, the bitter centuries of struggle between the Maya and missionaries. The stone blocks were themselves stolen from the Mayan temples of T'ho. Inside, unlike almost all other Mexican cathedrals, opulence is conspicuously absent. Since mobs denuded this and other buildings during the revolution, little has been restored. (Open to visitors daily 5-11am and 4-7pm, except during Sun. services. Free.)

As you leave the cathedral, the **Palacio de Gobierno** stands to the right, along the northern edge of the Zócalo. Each of the great walls of this century-old colonial-style palace is graced by a huge painting in a series celebrating the social evolution of the Yucatecan people. Fernando Castro Pacheco, still a Mérida resident, created these works for the city over the course of a quarter-century. The soft colors bleed into one another, lending a timeless quality to the traditional Mayan symbols. Maize dominates the stairwell mural, and the *Popul Vuh,* one of the only books by and about the Maya, reigns over the next layout. The History Chamber upstairs recounts the story of the priest Diego de Landa, who tried to burn every written relic of the Mayan religion and succeeded in destroying all but three of the priceless codices.

Taken together, the murals evoke the protracted, brutal conquest of the Maya by the conquistadors and the peaceful triumph of the elements of Mayan culture that have persisted and influenced modern Yucatecan culture. The History Chamber also contains books on Yucatecan history and Mayan culture. (Open Mon.-Sat. 8am-8pm, Sun. 9am-5pm. Free.)

Continue along the Zócalo until you stand in front of the **Palacio Municipal,** across from the cathedral. A jail until the 18th century, it was rebuilt in colonial style in 1928 in accordance with its new function. Concerts and classes in *jarana,* the Yucatecan colonial dance, now take place here; schoolgirls and grandmothers pass afternoons tapping their sturdy white shoes rhythmically against the tile floor.

On the southern side of the Zócalo, the Palacio Montejo arose in 1549 seven years after the conquest of T'ho, complete with a carved façade intended to boast about the conquest of the Maya. The expressions on the faces of the soldiers have faded, but the anguish of the four Mayan heads on which they stand remains clear. The carving conforms to the Toltec tradition of representing warriors standing on the heads of their conquests. Interjected are the coats of arms of the King of Spain and the Montejo family. The building now houses a bank.

Celebrating the crafts and craftspeople of Mexico, the **Museo de Arte Popular** lies 6 blocks east of the Zócalo on Calle 59, between Calles 48 and 50 behind the Convento de la Mejorada. The ground floor displays a wide array of Yucatecan handiwork, from costumes and masks to pottery, weavings, and *huipile* embroidery. Upstairs you'll find a varied collection of handicrafts from all of Mexico's states. The room of sculpted skeletons (you'll see two of them as you climb the stairs) frightens and amuses. (Open Tues.-Sat. 8am-8pm. Free.)

Mérida's most impressive museum is the **Museo de Antropología,** recently moved to the western edge of the city. The Instituto de Antropología maintains this extensive tribute to Mayan history, on Calle 86 at the end of Calle 59. Archeological finds illustrate the *indígena* history of Yucatán, and extensive anthropological information in Spanish accompany the artifacts. Geology, horticulture, linguistic history, demography, religion, and daily life are covered thoroughly. Even if you don't read Spanish, the museum will fascinate. Grimace at the holes drilled in teeth for jewelry stones, stare in awe at the head-flattening devices applied to the craniums of the infants of upper-class families, and learn to recognize the *chac-mool* (Mayan for "red fingernails") form of sculpture prevalent in the Yucatán. If you plan to visit any archeological sites, the shop downstairs sells comprehensive English-language guidebooks for much less than the price charged at the ruins themselves. (Museum open Tues.-Sun. 8am-8pm. Admission 2000 pesos, free Sun. Shop open Tues.-Sat. 8am-3pm.)

One block from the Museo de Antropología, on Calle 59 at 84, lies the small **Museo de Historia Natural.** This limited yet ambitious collection goes about explaining the history of life from the origin of the universe through the emergence of species. Housed in a beautiful 19th-century *hacienda,* the museum merits a stop en route back into town. (Open Tues.-Sun. 9am-6pm.)

Mansions and boutiques line **Paseo Montejo,** which culminates to the north with the **Monumento a la Patria.** Sculptor Rómulo Rozo in 1956 imitated Mayan stone carving style in forming major figures from Mexican history. An eternal flame and a filthy fountain stand guard. After the half-hour walk up Paseo Montejo, rest in the **Parque de las Américas,** Calle 20 at Colón, just southwest of the monument, so-named for its collection of trees from each of the countries of Central and South America.

The many parks, churches, and statues scattered throughout the center also warrant exploration. The eastern limit of the city was once marked by the **Arco de los Dragones** and the **Arco del Puente,** both colonial structures on Calles 61 and 62, between Calles 48 and 50. Nearby, much of the **Convento de la Mejorada,** on Calle 59 between Calles 48 and 50, has been converted into apartments, though the church still serves its original purpose. The old gate behind the **Parque** and **Iglesia de San Juan de Dios,** on Calle 69 between Calles 62 and 64, marks the southern limit of the center, while the **Iglesia de Santa Lucía,** on Calle 60 between Calles 53 and 55, and its park surrounded by colonial arches, stand north of the Zócalo. In between sits the **Universidad de Yucatán,** on Calle 57 between Calles 60 and 62. This Hispano-Moorish complex dates from 1938, though the university was founded in 1618.

Shopping

Mérida, the commercial center of the Yucatán Peninsula, attracts some of Mexico's finest produce, flowers, and handicrafts to its four square blocks of *mercado,* which opened in 1909 and peddles everything from toothpaste to parakeets. Its streets have been paved with bottle tops pounded in by millions of passersby. The market is a major tourist attraction—expect to receive friendly attention from multilingual sandal sellers and piñata pushers.

The main market occupies the block southwest of the Palacio Federal, spreading outward from the corner of Calles 65 and 56. Shops, awnings, and tin-roofed shacks ramble for a good many blocks both east and west behind the *palacio.* The only border is busy Calle 65 to the north, but even here colorful stands spill over onto the other side of the street and around the small square formed by Calles 65, 56, and 56a. across from the Palacio Federal.

Facing the Palacio Federal, the main building in the market complex lies to the left. Many tourists are directed to the second-story "artisans' market," part of a modern building behind and to the right of the Palacio Federal, but food, *huaraches,* hats, and clothing sell at far better prices in the market surrounding the building. Sandal shops face the easternmost edge. Sandal-makers (*fabricadores*) in the market will often custom-make sandals upon request; this service can require a few hours or a day, and costs about 60,000 pesos before haggling. In general, the lowest prices and largest selections of sandals, jewelry, and hammocks found in their *fábricas* (factories); ask around to locate the various factories hidden within the market.

Mérida's market is the best place in the Yucatán to buy *piñatas;* a huge selection of shops congregate on Calle 65 between Calles 54 and 56. *Piñatas* range from 2500 to 10,000 pesos, depending on the size and design, and weigh next to nothing because they are stuffed with newspaper. Neighboring stores sell bags of candy in bulk so that desperate fun-seekers can have a *piñata* party on the spot. Most hats in the market are imported from Campeche. The panama hats are woven in underground caverns at precise humidities in Becal, Campeche, from the leaves of the *jipijapa* plant and the *guano* palm tree.

Several large, government craft shops carry a wide selection of artisanal goods in one place at only moderately inflated prices. These include the **Museo Regional de Artesanía,** and another located in the Fonapas Building (the **Agora-Dif**), at Calle 63 between Calles 64 and 66. Quality here is good, prices fair, and the range of works enormous.

White *huipiles,* with colorful embroidery skirting the neckline and hem, adorn most local women and shop windows. The same is true for the maroon, silky *rebozo,* which resembles a shawl. Men wear the *guayabera,* a short-sleeved shirt with four pockets, plentiful buttons, and distinctive vertical columns of very tiny double-stitching as decoration. **Kary's** on Calle 64 between Calles 65 and 67 stitches and exhibits a good selection of *guayaberas.* A somewhat more expensive factory, which also carries women's regional clothing, is **Jack's,** on Calle 59 between Calles 60 and 62: finely made *guayaberas* cost up to 25,000 pesos. Make sure to check the fabric content.

Jewelry stores pepper the downtown area, offering excellent buys on silver. Prices are almost always fixed and designs vary little between stores. Bargains can be found at the bazaar on Sundays in front of the Palacio Municipal, although the quality of the silver may not be consistent. **Margarita,** on Calle 60 between Calles 59 and 57, offers terrific bargains on original designs; all of their jewelry goes for 3000 pesos per ounce. A sister store, **Mar Del Plata,** around the corner on Calle 59 between Calles 60 and 62, also carries a huge selection including brass and shell designs. Another popular shop is **Sonrisa del Sol,** on Calle 62 #500, a second-floor handicrafts store sharing space with a pizza parlor. Bypass the tacky ceramics and head for the extensive jewelry cases.

Travelers should be wary when approached by Mexican children who want to give a "free" shopping tour. Although you may feel overwhelmed and disoriented in the sprawling market, it's best to go it alone; the kids often receive a commission from the shops, which jack up their prices accordingly.

Hammocks

Hammock-seekers have many options in what has become the hammock mecca of Mexico and the world. A whole hierarchy of vendors exists: the opportunists who assault tourists with their wares in the Zócalo, restaurants, and churchyards; the established stores that have better quality merchandise at higher prices; the market vendors who seem to enjoy bargaining over their merchandise more than they do selling it; and the suppliers, both in the city and in the villages around Mérida.

All establishments sell hammocks ranging in quality from the finest (good cotton; tight, triple weave) to what locals refer to as *basura* (trash), a flimsy, loosely woven net pawned off on unsuspecting *norteamericanos* as a top-of-the-line hammock. Avoid buying from the walking vendors on the Zócalo and in other city parks, if only because they have a poor selection. Established stores are at the other extreme;

most have a wide variety of merchandise in enormous storerooms. While the prices are relatively high, customers can see exactly what they are purchasing, with assurance of quality and size.

Behind and to the right of the Palacio Federal spreads a series of interconnecting shops and shacks covered by awnings, sheets, and corrugated tin that plays home to the market's largest concentration of hammock vendors. Larger stalls offer a wide variety of colors, sizes, and qualities, but prices are never predictable; purchasing in quantity always helps deflate the cost. Both retail and wholesale stalls exist within the market; the retail sale shops usually have a better selection, but the wholesale places sell hammocks for less. The few hammock outlets outside the market are often just as cheap. Although many stalls such as **La Rablana, El Aguacate, El Campesino,** and **La Bodega** are frequently mentioned by locals, those in the know go to **El Hamaguero,** Calle 58 #572, between Calles 69 and 71. They have 30 years of experience, a wide selection, and a try-out room; those who ask to test the hammocks are escorted to a back room and treated with more respect than the average *joe norteamericano*. The owners are pleasant, and since they make the hammocks in-store, prices are reasonable.

If you're still unsatisfied after a visit to the market and nearby stores, enture to the villages around Mérida, particularly **Tixcocób** (buses leave from the Progreso station during the day), where you may find better bargains than in the city.

Entertainment

Mérida's fast-paced nightlife finds locals dancing outdoors in the evenings. A few of the expensive hotel complexes include discos, after-hours bars, and live entertainment, but the availability of these depends on the seasonal ebb and flow of foreign feet. Lack of interest occasionally forces nightspots to close before 9pm (around the same time most *cantinas* close). **Bin Bon Bao,** Calle 29 #97, at Calle 18, in Mérida's poshest neighborhood, provides the local elite with a stomping ground. (Open Fri.-Sat. 9pm-3am.) Also popular is **L'Disco,** in the Holiday Inn on Colón between Calle 60 and Paseo Montejo. (Open daily 10pm-3am.)

Mérida thrives on constantly rotating nightly activities. Large posters glued to walls about town announce upcoming events. Keep an eye out for the student theater posters near the university. The **Teatro Peón Contreras** (tel. 24-38-42), on Calle 60 near Calle 57, hosts special events and frequent concerts. The *ballet folklórico* performs "Roots of Today's Yucatán" every Tuesday night at 9pm. (Tickets 15,000 pesos at the door or from travel agencies.)

A number of cinemas scattered throughout downtown Mérida show flicks for a steady 2200 pesos. **Cine Cantarell,** Calle 60 #488, plays primarily popular U.S. movies. A mixture of Mexican and U.S. movies runs nightly at 5, 7, 9, and 11pm at **Cine Fantasio,** Calle 59 at Calle 60.

A number of restaurants sponsor musical and other tableside entertainment. El Tucho and La Prosperidad (see Food above) stay open until 8pm, and along with two or three drinks come enough *botanas* (appetizers) to make a full meal. For similar nocturnal diversion, **Tulipanes,** Calle 42 #462-A, between Calles 45 and 47, features non-stop music, *yucateco* dance, and even a chilling re-enactment of a Mayan sacrifice—a Bloody Mary will get you into the swing of things. (Open daily noon-2am.)

The municipal government provides a never-ending series of free musical and dance events in the city's parks. On Mondays, the folklore ballet and the police *jaranera* band perform at 9pm in front of the Palacio Municipal. Classical musicians play Tuesday nights at 9pm in Santiago Park at Calles 72 and 59. The **Mayab Culture House,** on Calle 63 between Calles 64 and 66, sponsors romantic poem readings and guitar trios on Wednesdays at 8pm. Thursday nights (at 9pm) feature a "Yucatecan Serenade," with romantic music and folk dance in Santa Lucia Park, Calle 60 at 55. On Fridays at 9pm, students perform regional dances from all areas of Mexico at the University of the Yucatán, at the corner of Calles 60 and 57. Mérida's Zócalo enchants on Sundays, when streets are blocked off by 10:30am for the festive

"Mérida en domingo" (Mérida on Sunday). A Yucatecan orchestra performs at 11am, followed by a re-enactment of a *mestiza* wedding at 1pm in front of the Palacio Municipal. The city's other parks feature *marimba* concerts and *jarana* demonstrations throughout the day.

Near Mérida

Two popular package tours from Mérida are daytrips to **Chichén Itzá** and **Uxmal/Kabah** (about US$35 each). Packages usually include an air-conditioned bus, a guide, site admission, lunch, and tax. Standard package trips to **Cuba** are also available at most Mérida travel agencies. The six-day packages (US$295) include air travel, visa, first class hotel, and two meals per day. The trips leave several times weekly and are open to citizens of all nations—just book 3 days in advance, and bring your passport.

Celestún

A popular weekend retreat, Celestún lies 92km west of Mérida on the southern tip of a kilometer-wide strip of land, which separates Río Esperanza from the Gulf of Mexico. Celestún is a sleepy town with excellent, inexpensive fresh seafood and a large sanctuary for exotic flora and fauna. 50,000 flamingos share Celestún's estuary with pelicans and toucans. Interested tourists hire local fishing people to take them from the dock (1½ km from town) around the river to see the enormous pink and red clouds of flamingos. The 1½ hour trip drains your purse of 70,000 pesos. Find other interested tourists at the beach, and you can split the cost. Although the flamingoes are the main attraction, the clear water of the Gulf of Mexico is worth a dip; stick to the beaches in front of the hotels, because the morning's fishing rejects lie rotting on the remote parts of the beach.

Sleeping on the beach offends no locals, but may be uncomfortable without a tent because of windblown sand. Some of the restaurants along the beach have hooks for hanging hammocks. For more standard accommodations, **Hotel Gutiérrez** (tel. 24-63-48) makes the most sense. Take a left as you hit the beach from the bus stop. This pink-and-white building has huge, clean rooms, some with a beautiful view of the water. All rooms have fans and hot water. (Singles and doubles with bath 25,000 pesos.) **Hotel San Julio,** in town on Calle 12 #92, offers cheaper accommodations. From the bus station, walk toward the beach and take the last right; it's the small green building past the Restaurant Avila. Large rooms come with clean baths. Waves break just a few meters from your door. (Singles and doubles 20,000 pesos.)

The shoreline holds a strip of low-priced, stuccoed seafood places. The best of the beachside bunch is **La Playita,** where octopus, snails, shrimp, and other sea beasts are served at bargain prices. (Entrees 6000-12,000 pesos; open daily 8am-6pm.) Also reasonably priced, the **Restaurant Avila,** at Calle 12 #101-B, serves *pescado frito* with tortillas and *salsa* for 6000 pesos. Cocktails go for 7000 pesos. (Open daily 9am-6pm.) While waiting for the bus, treat yourself to a mixed seafood cocktail (6000 pesos) at the **Cocteleria Giomara,** on Calle 11 in the strip of small stands next to the *palapa* bus station. (Open daily 8am-5pm.)

The street bounding the Zócalo on the side opposite the church is Calle 10. Calles 12 and 14 run parallel between the Zócalo and the ocean. Facing the church, Calle 7 is to the right, Calle 9 to the left. Buses drop off passengers in front of the market alongside the Zócalo. Neither the market (open daily until 1pm) nor the plaza is remarkable, except for three large trees and the obligatory bust of Juárez. Buses to Mérida depart daily every hour from 5 to 10am and every two hours from 10am to 8pm. The trip takes just over 90 minutes and costs 5200 pesos.

The **Banco del Atlántico** transacts at Calle 12 #103. (Open for exchange Mon.-Fri. 9am-noon.) The **post office,** on Calle 15 between Calles 10 and 12 in an unmarked hut, doubles as a private residence. To get there, walk along the beach past the Hotel Gutiérrez, turn left, and walk 1½ blocks; it's on the left. The clerk provides full service out of his living room while watching "I Love Lucy" re-runs. (Open Mon.-Tues., Thurs., and Sat. 8am-noon.)

The national telegram office is located at Calle 11 #98, next to the *mercado* (open daily 9am-1pm and 3-6pm). A telephone *caseta* sits at Calles 9 and 12, diagonally across from the Zócalo (open Mon.-Sat. 4-6pm). **Police** occupy Celestún's Palacio Municipal on Calle 7.

Dzibilchaltúm

Hidden behind the tiny village of the same name north of Mérida, the ruin site of Dzibilchaltúm spreads over more than 25 square mi. of barren scrubland. The oldest city continuously used by the Maya as a ceremonial and administrative center, Dzibilchaltúm (Place Where There Is Writing on Flat Stones) flourished from approximately 2000 BC until the Conquest. While Dzibilchaltúm's importance and continuous influence on Mayan culture is of great interest to archeologists and historians, the excavated site now open to tourists is less impressive and accessible than other ruins near Mérida.

The ruins lie some 20km north of Mérida off an access road from Rte. 273, the extension of Paseo Montejo. Watch for the sign indicating the turn-off. The road from the entrance leads past several foundations and partly restored structures to Dzibilchaltúm's *cenote,* **Xlacá,** which served both as a source of water and as a sacrificial well similar to those at Chichén Itzá. National Geographic Society divers have recovered ceremonial artifacts and human bones from the depths of the 44m-deep *cenote.*

Intersecting the road to Xlacá, a dirt track to the left passes through an almost unrecognizable plaza. Farther along this road, Dzibilchaltúm's showpiece, the fully restored **Temple of the Seven Dolls,** possesses a harmony of proportion and style lacking in other temples. This is also the only known Mayan temple with windows. The seven clay "dolls" discovered here are believed to represent different illnesses or deformities, and along with various artifacts from the site and human bones taken from the *cenote,* are now on display in the museum.

Mounds and hills marking ancient buildings and temples dot the surrounding countryside, but archaeological excavations have disinterred little of interest to the layperson. Even so, Dzibilchaltúm has all the trappings of a tourist attraction, including a modern museum, a refreshment stand, and porta-potties. For just 500 pesos (free Sun.), you can explore the museum and the ruins. (Both open daily 8am-5pm.)

To return to Mérida, take one of the three daily buses, or go out to Rte. 273 and attempt to persuade a bus coming from Progreso to stop. Second-class buses rocket by every hour or so. Hitching is possible, but often slow on the 4km access road from the highway to the ruin entrance. Early risers should be able to catch a bus to the site, see the ruins, and walk or take a bus back to the highway by noon to catch a bus to Progreso and the beach.

Progreso

Just seconds away from oily tan bodies relaxing on the town's wind-blown beaches, skinless hanging meat carcasses bang against each other in Puerto Progreso's frantic market. During the summer months, Progreso proves a popular retreat for the citizens of Mérida, who make the 33km jaunt northward to enjoy the clean, quiet beachfront, the gulf waters, and the famous surreal green sunset.

Puerto Progreso was built in the mid-19th century to replace Sisal (40km to the southwest) as Yucatán's major port and *henequén* distribution center. The leaves of the blue-gray *henequén* plant yield strong fibers, used in twine- and rope-making. Progreso-bound buses pass through denuded fields which once sprouted with the sharp, spiked leaves. *Henequén* production peaked with the proliferation under Díaz of the *hacienda* system: prisoners, entire villages from other parts of Mexico, and Yaqui people from faraway Sonora were imported as *peones* and often forced to work in shackles on the *haciendas.* Post-WWII discoveries of synthetic fibers have strangled world demand for *henequén,* but the century-old mansions built with yesteryear profits still stand as testimony to Progreso's past. From the bus station, walk east along the Malecón to see the moguls' residences.

Although history is admittedly man's noblest concern, visitors flock to Progreso to fry on the beach. The calm ocean laps upon sands which are usually deserted, except during a few school holidays and the *temporada* (the busy season of July-Aug.) Lately, however, the quiet season has been busier than usual: in September 1988, Hurricane Gilbert wreaked thousands of dollars worth of damage on a number of Yucatecan seaside towns, including Progreso. The boardwalk and many beachfront homes were destroyed; reconstruction of the Malecón is finally nearing completion, and beachside hotels have a breath of windy freshness to them.

Unfortunately, the development of Progreso from quiet port town to large-scale resort is also well underway. In 1985, the federal and state governments decided to market Progreso's natural beauty to North American beach devotees. Yucatán state hopes to lure cruise ships and sun-worshippers to a massive hotel-condominium complex (called "Nuevo Yucatán") near Progreso. Covering more than 2.2 square miles, this massive project threatens to become a small city unto itself, with a marina, shopping areas, sports facilities, and private residences. These may be the last years to enjoy the untainted beaches and small-town familiarity of Progreso before Nuevo Yucatán sweeps it up in a push to outdo Cancún.

If progress on this project is already too successful for your taste, seek the more isolated beaches to the west and east. Chelém lies 8km west, a quick bus ride away from Progreso. To reach the port of Sisal or the fine beaches of Celestún to the west or Río Lagartos to the east, you'll have to backtrack to Mérida.

The custodian of the lighthouse El Faro, at Calle 80 near Calle 27, welcomes visitors during the day if he is not too busy. A spiral *caracol* (snail) staircase leads to a single 1000-watt bulb and an array of reflectors. The 2km *muelle* (pier), which clings precariously to the sandy beach, facilitates great fishing in the early morning and evening.

Progreso's bus station is on Calle 80 between Calles 27 and 29. Buses returning to Mérida (½ hr., 1900 pesos) leave every 15 minutes from 5am to 9:45pm. To reach the deserted Zócalo from the terminal, turn right and walk 2 blocks on Calle 80. The Zócalo lies at the intersection of Calle 80 (which is sometimes called Calle 30) and Calle 31, the main drag through town. If you want to hit the beach immediately from the bus station, turn left on Calle 80 and walk 4 blocks to its end. For a taxi, call 501-71.

Progreso's **tourist office,** Calle 80 #176, at Calle 36, has a friendly and somewhat helpful staff and small maps of the town. (Open Mon.-Fri. 9am-1pm and 4-8pm.) The **Banco del Altántico,** Calle 80 #144 (tel. 501-78), is open for currency exchange Monday through Friday from 10am to 1pm. **Bánamex,** Calle 80 #136 (tel. 508-31), at Calle 27, changes currency Monday through Friday from 10am to 2pm. The **post office,** Calle 31 #153 (tel. 505-65), at Calle 78, is open Monday through Friday from 8am to 7pm, Saturday from 9am to 1pm. (**Postal Code:** 97320.) The **telegram office** is in the same building. (Open Mon.-Fri. 9am-8pm, Sat. 9am-4pm.)

Lavanderia La Vista is on Calle 31 near Calle 6. **Farmacia Yza,** open 24 hr., sits on Calle 29 at Calle 78. The **police station** (tel. 500-26), is on the Zócalo at Calle 82.

Many of the beautiful hotels along the beach fill on weekends; rates run higher around Easter week and in July and August. Cheaper accommodations are available closer to the town center. **Tropical Suites,** Malecón at Calle 20 (tel. 512-63), on the beach, is the most popular and expensive option in Progreso. Clean rooms have beautiful ocean views, fans, and hot water. The hotel is a 10-minute walk from the Zócalo along the beach, but close to the best restaurants. (Singles and doubles 40,000 pesos, with kitchen 75,000 pesos.) With commodious hot water-spouting rooms and attached kitchenettes, the **Hotel Playa Linda,** Calle 19 at 76 (tel. 511-57), before Tropical Suites on the beach, is a comfortable place. For some reason, however, the owners have deemed furniture an unnecessary pleasantry. (Singles and doubles 50,000 pesos.) Rooms in the **Río Blanco,** Calle 27 #148 (tel. 500-66), across from the market, have schizophrenic fans and dim lights off a balcony that overlooks a dirty, laundry-filled courtyard. (Singles 20,000 pesos. Doubles 35,000 pesos). **Hotel Miramar,** Calle 27 #124 (tel. 505-52), between Calles 24 and 26, offers fairly comfortable rooms that include fans, immaculate bathrooms, and hot water. (Singles 23,000 pesos. Doubles 35,000 pesos.)

Progreso's best restaurants are well worth the 10-minute walk down the Malecón from Calle 80. **Capitán Marisco** on Malecón between Calles 60 and 62, the traditional favorite, occupies prime oceanside real estate where the mansions start. Pamper yourself with good service and delicious seafood. *Pulpo en sutinta* costs 22,000 pesos, and fish in garlic sauce goes for 16,000 pesos. (Open daily 9am-8pm.) **Las Velas Restaurant/Bar,** on Malecón 2 blocks before Capitán Marisco, is the raucous newcomer to the Progreso beach scene. This indoor/outdoor restaurant has a splendid view of the beach, live *marimba* music, and jovial waiters sporting Popeye outfits. Spinach guacamole and tortilla chips precede the memorable seafood dishes. (Entrees 11,000-18,000 pesos. Open daily 11am-11pm). In town, **El Cordobé's** Calle 80 #150 on the Zócalo, has attracted crowds since 1900. Join the fishing folk for breakfast and admire the paintings of Progreso. Soups go for 3500 pesos and a wide variety of fish entrees cost 12,000 pesos. (Open daily 6am-midnight.)

Chichén Itzá

For two hours each day, Chichén Itzá becomes a writhing mass of foreign invaders, as camera-toting aliens from another space and time infest its innards, spouting newly-acquired misinformation, videotaping every last *chac-mool*, and chasing errant sunhats across the central plaza. For the other 22 hours, the most extensive, well-preserved, and beguiling remnants of any *indígena* culture in Mexico stand in peace. Unfortunately, the site is closed at night and several of the major buildings have limited opening hours. With a little foresight and planning, however, the intelligent traveler can imbibe Chichén's heady draught without sharing the cup with thousands of tourists.

Chichén Itzá well deserves its status as a tourist magnet. El Castillo is breathtaking from the bottom and harrowing from the top; the ballcourt sports elaborate carvings of the players and wholly intact rings left from original games; the sacrificial *cenote* has yielded enough bones and artifacts to reconstruct the stories of hundreds of human victims; and the observatory attests to a level of astronomical understanding far beyond that of Old World contemporaries.

In order to see all the ruins at a comfortable pace, spend the night near the site and enter when the gates open at 8am. Avoid visiting around noon, when the sun scorches, and it seems that the entire population of Cancún beachmongers has descended upon the ruins. Buy a guide booklet, carry a water bottle, and don a hat.

Orientation

There isn't a travel agency on the Yucatán that doesn't hawk Chichén Itzá packages to newly arrived travelers, but these tours usually arrive at midday, along with the brunt of the heat and the rest of the masses. Budget travelers should have no problem reaching Chichén Itzá early in the day by bus or car for about one-fifth the cost.

Chichén Itzá abuts Rte. 180, the highway that connects Mérida (121km west) to Cancún (213km east) via Valladolid (43km east). The town of Pisté, 2½km west of the ruins, provides travelers with basic services. Ample public transportation to Chichén Itzá makes arriving easy, although few buses travel the 1½km access road that leads to the gates of the ruins.

Two first-class buses leave for Chichén Itzá daily from Mérida (5500 pesos), and several depart from Cancún (11,000 pesos). Many second-class buses also connect Chichén Itzá to Mérida and Cancún, but most zip past the access road to the ruins and stop only in Pisté, east of the Zócalo. If you can finagle a ride back to Pisté after seeing the ruins, you will have a better chance of catching the next bus to Mérida or Cancún. Headed for Mérida, buses pass Pisté's Zócalo approximately every half hour from 5:30am to 9pm and cost 5200 pesos; for Valladolid and Cancún, they pass every half hour from 7:30am to 10pm and cost 9500 pesos. A few buses stop at the entrance to the ruins; ask at the front desk for information.

Taxis between Pisté and Chichén Itzá cost 5000 pesos; walking takes a half hour on a new, raised sidewalk designed to protect hikers from snakes and other local surprises, although harmless giant iguanas have no problem clambering across it. Except during the winter, the jungle quickly turns muggy under the strong sun, so make the hike early in the morning. To hitch a ride to Mérida, stand at the gas station 1km west of Pisté. To hitch to Cancún, stand at the main division between Chichén Itzá and Rte. 180.

Practical Information

The first stone edifice confronting visitors at Chichén Itzá is the space-age **visitors complex** (open daily 8am-10pm) at the site's western entrance. Buy your ticket in the complex, and turn right around the corner to reach a small information booth. If you clear your throat seven times, a Spanish-speaking agent will appear to provide useful information about transportation and lodging; specific questions about the ruins are referred to official guides. There is a long-distance telephone in the booth as well, though it is only for national calls except in an emergency (tel. 627-24; **telephone code:** 985). The booth is theoretically open Monday through Saturday from 8am to 10pm and Sunday from 8am to 3pm.

The visitors complex also houses a first aid station, restrooms, gift shops, a restaurant, a bookstore (which sells Aerobies and guides to the ruins in Spanish and English from 8300 pesos), a theater, and a small museum (see Sights below).

A **Bánamex**, in central Pisté near the Cunanchén Hotel, opens for currency exchange Monday through Friday from 9am to 1:30pm. Some of the larger hotels in the area, including the Misón Inn, exchange after hours at a slightly worse rate. Pisté's one *caseta* (tel. 626-71), next to the pink Xaybé Handicrafts Bazaar on the main street, has international collect service for 5000 pesos. (Open daily 8am-9pm). **Farmacia Bonny**, across from Restaurant Nicté-Há, is staffed by English-speaking doctors. (Open Mon. 3-9pm, Tues.-Sat. 9am-9pm.) **Clínica Promesa**, off Rte. 180 beyond the Cunanchén Hotel, is open 24 hr. for medical problems.

Accommodations

A few luxury hotels snuggle right up to the ruins, but most economical options exist in and around Pisté, where the water supply at some hotels doesn't run from 8pm to 8am. Either plan to bathe at other times or verify 24-hr. service with the management. If you are camping or sleeping in your vehicle, try the **Pirámide Inn Trailer Park**—the fee gives you glorious access to the hotel pool. You can also take advantage of the plentiful budget options in Valladolid and make the 40km commute to the ruins.

Dolores Alba, about 2½km past the ruins towards Cancún (not in Pisté!). Beautiful rooms set around a social *palapa* and clean pool. All abodes have fans and some have A/C. Inconveniently far from the site, but to compensate, the friendly proprietor transports guests to the ruins; take a bus or taxi for the return. Make reservations at the hotel of the same name in Mérida (tel. 21-37-95). Singles 40,000 pesos. Doubles 45,000 pesos. Triples 50,000 pesos.

Stardust Inn, on Rte. 180 2km past the ruins toward Pisté. Decor orange on the outside, green on the inside. What is this, a technicolor pumpkin? Sparkling rooms have A/C, sleep up to 4, and receive 82 TV channels via satellite. Nice restaurant, bar, and pool. 100,000 pesos per room.

Pirámide Inn and Trailer Park, on Rte. 180 1½km west of the ruins at the edge of Pisté. Trailer park fee provides electricity, *agua purificada,* and access to showers and the large hotel pool. 20,000 pesos per vehicle. Tent camping is also available: 1 person 10,000 pesos, 2 people 15,000 pesos. The inn's hotel rooms include A/C, hot water, and tacky wall hangings of Chichén Itzá. Singles 80,000 pesos. Doubles 85,000 pesos. Triples 90,000 pesos.

Posada Olalde, 150m down an unmarked dirt road across the street from the Carousel Restaurant in Pisté. Friendly family rents 7 huge cement rooms with arched doorways. Fans in summer, hot water in winter. Singles 20,000 pesos. Doubles 25,000 pesos.

Posada Poxil, Calle 15 #52, in central Pisté past the Centro de Salud. Big hotel has plain, acceptably clean rooms with fans and hot water. Dingy cement pool and large cafeteria-style restaurant downstairs. Singles 30,000 pesos. Doubles 50,000 pesos.

Posada El Paso, Calle 15 #89, a yellow, L-shaped building in the middle of Pisté. Second-floor rooms are enormous, with beds to match. Slightly dismal atmosphere, but fans, hot water, and sanitary bathrooms even things out. Singles 20,000 pesos. Doubles 25,000 pesos.

Misión Inn, on Rte. 180 2km west of the ruins. The most elegant hotel in Pisté, with sparkling pool and beautiful restaurant. Must have borrowed large quantities of leftover orange paint from the Stardust Hotel. Non-guests can swim in the pool if they first buy a few drinks at the bar. Singles 115,000 pesos. Doubles 120,000 pesos.

Food

Centuries after the sacrifice of their Mayan ancestors, local restaurant owners now attempt to massacre foreigners' wallets. Even the ice cream shop in the Chichén Itzá complex joins in the bloody rite; tiny tidbits of ice cream cost 3000 pesos. Once again, stick to Pisté, where the *mercado municipal* (open daily 8am-2pm) across from Cunanchén allows you to avoid restaurants altogether. All Pisté restaurants listed are located on Calle 15, the main drag in town. Many provide swimming pools for their diners, which non-customers can use for a small fee.

Restaurant Ruinas de Chichén Itzá, in the Chichén visitors complex. Convenient, air-conditioned, and exorbitant. Club sandwich 14,000 pesos, fish filet 15,000 pesos. The soft drinks that go for 2000 pesos can be had for 50% less at the small stands in rear corner of parking area. Open daily 7:30am-5pm.

Restaurant Xaybé, across from the Misión Inn. Pisté's nicest restaurant attracts a parking lot full of tourist *combi* vans. Excellent service, a swimming pool, and "international" (mostly *norteamericano*) food. Baked chicken 16,000 pesos. Tasty breakfast specials 8000 pesos. Open daily 7:30am-9pm.

El Carrousel, in central Pisté. A large thatched *palapa*—watch your head going in. Regional food, at lower prices than other budget restaurants in town. Entrees 8000-12,000 pesos. Open daily 6am-9pm.

Nicté-Há, in central Pisté. A local bar-like hangout decorated with shiny murals of cheeseburgers, shrimp cocktails, and beefy Amazonians. Serves sandwiches, tacos, and quesadillas from 4000 pesos. Open daily 10am-4pm and 7-10pm.

Restaurant Poxil, Calle 15 #52, in the hotel of the same name. Huge cafeteria-bar with an army of flowered plastic chairs. *Comida corrida* 15,000 pesos. Breakfast special (eggs, juice, tortillas, coffee) 8000 pesos. Open daily 7am-10pm.

Parador Maya, in central Pisté, just down the street from the Xaybé. Yellow picnic benches covered by a *palapa* roof. Help is so busy bantering with you they almost forget to serve the food. Cute "Hogar, Dulce Hogar" (Home, Sweet Home) placemats. Fair chicken, pork, and beef dishes 12,000 pesos. Open daily 7am-4pm and 6:30-11pm.

Restaurant Sayil, Calle 15 #55, near the Stardust Inn. Cheap food inside a plain white building. *Pollo pibil* (chicken cooked in banana leaf) 6000 pesos. Open daily 8am-9pm.

Sights

As the Mayan name Chichén Itzá (Mouth of the Well) implies, the earliest inhabitants chose to settle here because of two nearby freshwater *cenotes* (springs). Pottery shards tell the story of these first sedentary people from 2000 BC to the beginning of the current era. The *Chilam Balam,* one of the few pre-Hispanic Mayan texts to survive the early missionaries' book-burnings, describes the construction of the oldest buildings which now constitute of the current site. Between the years 500 and 800 AD, construction was purely Mayan. The Maya never developed the true curved arch; because of this, the rooms in these structures are long and narrow beneath lines of corbeled arches, stepped upward and outward from the walls.

At its height in the 7th century AD, the Mayan city was inexplicably abandoned as its populace migrated to Chaacanputún, today's Champotón. Chichén was not repopulated for over 300 years and was never again purely Mayan. Sometime before 1000 AD, the Toltec tribes of Tula, in what is now Hidalgo state, infiltrated the Yucatán and easily dominated the peaceful Mayan communities. They brought with them the cult of Quetzalcóatl, the plumed serpent, as well as a new breed of soldier—the politician. When the Toltecs arrived at Chichén, its second "Maya-Toltec" phase of growth began. Chichén was fortified for the first time, and in the wake of regional imperialism became the most important *yucateco* city.

The distinctive Toltec architectural influence can be seen in the round building and pyramid. Their trademark plumed serpents and warrior images grace many pillars and columns, as do jaguars and eagles, markings of their military order. The Toltec death cult glorified human sacrifice, making the *chac-mool* the predominant altar. After high priests ripped out the hearts of their sacrificial victims, they placed the still-pumping organs on the abdomens of the reclining figures flanking the altar for the crowd to see.

In 1461, Chichén Itzá was abandoned for a second time, but religious pilgrims continued to visit the site until well after the Spanish Conquest. Today, the relentless flow of curious tourists ensures that Chichén Itzá will never again stand in solitude.

The Ruins

Pause in the visitors complex at the entrance to Chichén Itzá for an overview of the site. On the terrace, a scale model artfully lays the ruins at your feet. A small museum traces the history of Chichén Itzá and displays a sampling of sculptures and objects removed from the sacred *cenote*. The air-conditioned Chilam Balam Theater shows videos daily (4 in Spanish, 3 in English) that gush about the state's archeological sites and modern-day tourist attractions. Before 10am and during low tourist season, the theater and museum are often closed due to lack of interest.

Hiring an official guide at the entrance is unnecessary. If you carry a guide book (or even just a map) and read the explanatory captions (in Spanish, English, and French) on plaques at each major structure, you can appreciate the ruins inexpensively and at your own pace. If you can opt for a guide, check at the information booth for the current regulated tour price. Tours generally last 2½ hours and cost 70,000 pesos. Roaming guides offer their services at the ruins as well as at the visitors center. It is often easier to bargain with "guides" outside the complex, but these may not be reliable. Before joining their tour, ask to see identification, which indicates guide certification and tested foreign language ability.

From the main parking lot and visitors center, the first group of ruins is up the gravel path and to the left. As the trees give way to the huge cropped lawn, the largest pyramid at Chichén Itzá, El Castillo, appears straight ahead.

El Castillo, Chichén's most famous and intriguing sight, rises in perfect symmetry from the vast green fields, culminating in a temple supported by pillars in the form of serpents. Its striking appearance, however, was not the only aspect that earned the pyramid international fame (and a ubiquitous presence on placemats throughout the land). El Castillo testifies to the astronomical genius of the Maya as well: the 91 steps on each of the four faces plus those on the upper platform total 365, representing the number of days in the year; the 52 panels on the nine terraced levels equal the number of years in a Maya calendar round; and each face of the nine terraces is divided by a staircase, yielding 18 sections equivalent to the 18 Mayan months.

The axes are so perfectly aligned with the four cardinal directions that during the semi-annual equinox, the shadow of the rounded terraces falls on the embankment of the north staircase, and the silhouette of an undulating serpent, whose head is sculpted at the bottom of the staircase, becomes visible. In March, the serpent appears to be sliding down the stairs precisely in the direction of the Sacred Cenote, while in September the motion is reversed. The exact equinox dates and times vary slightly from year to year, but tend to cluster around March 21 and September 21. People from all over the world converge on Chichén to see this event. At those times, all accommodations will be full, but keep in mind that the snake can still be seen for a few days before and after the actual equinox. A less well-known but equally impressive supernatural event can be experienced at El Castillo when Jupiter is high and Capricorn is rising over Venus: the entire pyramid resonates in perfect synch, emitting faint traces of Elvis Costello's *Watching the Detectives.*

El Castillo was built on an early Toltec temple, the inner chamber of which can be entered through a door at the bottom of the north staircase, behind the serpent's ears. (Open daily 11am-3pm.) An interior set of narrow, slippery steps ascends to a ceremonial chamber with a grimacing *chac-mool* sculpture and a rust-red, jaguar-faced sacrificial throne encrusted with jade stones and flint fangs.

Just to the left of the entrance (behind you if you're walking toward El Castillo), the **ballcourt** competes for attention with the huge pyramid. The enormous playing field is bounded by two long, high, parallel walls and a temple beyond either end zone. This is the largest ballcourt in Mesoamerica; amazingly, people speaking at the Temple of the Bearded Man at the north end of the court can be heard clearly 140m away at the southern wall. The Toltec called the ballgame "Tlachtli"; the Mayan translation is "Pok-Ta-Pok," and the object seems to have been to knock a solid ball made of rubber-like chicle through the stone rings still visible high up on the long walls. The game had a religious dimension as well: in the rare event of a goal, members of one of the teams (archeologists do not agree on whether it was the winners or the losers) were honored as the next sacrificial victims. The famous reliefs at the base of the walls on either end and in the center clearly depict many ceremonially dressed, smiling players, and several freshly beheaded victims.

The sculptures in the **Temple of the Bearded Man** at the north end of the ballcourt and the paintings inside the **Temple of the Jaguars** on the eastern wall confirm the importance of sacrifice in fertility rites. On the ground level of the temple facing the plaza, another room with murals also merits a visit. The inner chambers of these two structures are open daily from 10 to 11am and from 3 to 4pm.

A short distance from the ballcourt toward the grassy open area is the **Tsompantli,** Aztec for "Platform of the Skulls." When the Spaniards conquered the Aztecs, they were aghast not just at the ritual of human sacrifice but also at the racks in Tenochtitlán designed to display the skulls of the sacrificed. This purely Toltec design at Chichén served a similar purpose. Now, eerie rows of skulls in bas-relief decorate the platform's walls.

Just to the side of the long, low Tsompantli is the **Platform of Jaguars and Eagles,** named after the military orders who took the names of these ferocious animals and whose social role was to obtain prisoners for human sacrifice. To either side of the feathered serpent heads on the balustrades of the staircases, reliefs of jaguars and eagles clutch human hearts in their claws. These beliefs and architecture are solely Toltec.

The dirt path leading north (away from El Castillo) over the ancient Mayan *sacbé* (roadway) links the ceremonial plaza with Chichén Itzá's most important religious center, the **Sacred Cenote,** 300m away. The roughly circular well, perhaps 60m across, induced vertigo in the sacrificial victims perched on the reviewing platform before their last plunge into the murky depths. The rain-god Chac supposedly dwelt beneath the water's surface and needed constant gifts to grant good rains. Young children and occasionally a jewel-bedecked virgin were thrown into the *cenote* at sunrise. If, by some miracle, they survived the fall and could keep afloat until noon, they were then fished out and forced to tell what they had witnessed during the ordeal.

Beyond El Castillo, at the far edge of the central plaza, the **Temple of the Warriors** and **Group of the Thousand Columns** present an impressive army of elaborately carved columns which at one time probably supported a roof of perishable material. On the temple itself, in front of two great feathered serpents and several sculpted animal gods, reclines one of the best-preserved *chac-mools* at Chichén. The ornamentation of this building is largely Toltec; in Tula, capital of the Toltecs far to the west, stands a nearly identical structure. The Temple of the Warriors marks the end of Chichén's restored monuments and the beginning of an overgrown area extending behind and to the right of the pyramid. Standing at the walls nearest the pyramid, you can see several rubble walls and smaller, ruined pyramids to the southeast. Dirt paths and roads lead from the columns to these ruins. If you follow the paths to the southernmost end of the semicircle (opposite the Temple of the Warriors), you'll reach Chichén Itzá's market complex, which consists of several buildings with intact walls and columns.

A red dirt path on the south side of El Castillo leads to the less popular South Group of ruins, once misnamed Old Chichén. Just beyond the green building with toilets, this path leads past a refreshment stand. The first pyramid along the path on the right is the **Ossuary,** or **High Priest's Grave,** barely recognizable as a pyramid. A natural cave extends from within the pyramid 15m down into the earth. The human bones and votive offerings found in this cavern are postulated to be those of an ancient high priest.

Past the Ossuary, the road forks, presenting two different routes to the clearing of the second set of ruins in the South Group. The most interesting structure in this group of ruins is the **Observatory,** the large circular building to the left of the Ossuary. This ancient planetarium consists of two nested rectangular platforms with large west-facing staircases and two circular towers. Because of the tower's interior spiral staircase (not open to the public), this structure is often called El Caracol (the Great Conch). In Mayan times, the slits in the dome of the Observatory could be aligned with the important celestial bodies and cardinal directions, making the building the Maya's principal astrological center. El Caracol was built in several stages by Mayan and Toltec architects. Diagrams in front of the ruin explain the plans.

Walking due south from El Caracol, toward the nunnery at the other end of the clearing, you first pass the tiny ruins of a sauna and then the **Temple of the Sculptured Wall Panels** behind it. On the exterior walls of this temple, you can still discern the sculptures for which it is named. Though difficult to decipher, the panels contain representations of Toltec warriors—jaguars, eagles, and serpents—in three rows.

The largest structure in this part of Chichén is the **nunnery,** on the south side of the quadrangle. Although it was probably a royal palace to the Maya who built it, the many stone rooms reminded Spaniards of a European convent. After several superimpositions and some decay, the building is now almost 20m high on a base 65m long and nearly 35m wide. To the left as you face the staircase, you can see a smaller annex to the nunnery at an angle. Its many sculpted masks of Chac and its lattice motif are in the Chenes style, usually found only in northeastern Campeche, as at Edzná.

Diagonally across from the nunnery annex is the church, its upper walls intricately ornamented with many masks of the hook-nosed Chac. Both to the left and to the right above the door are representations of the four *bacabs* (animal deities who hold up the sky).

A poorly-maintained path (which may be closed during rainy months) runs about 130m east from the nunnery group, past the chapel to the long **Akab-Dzib.** The oldest parts of this structure are believed to be Chichén's most ancient constructions. The two central rooms were built around the 2nd or 3rd century; the annexes on either side and to the east were added later. The simple ornamentation is purely Mayan. Inside the rooms it is still possible to make out small rose-red hand prints on the ceiling near the doors. These were supposedly the hands of the sun-god Itzamná.

The **Cenote Xtoloc** lies past the South Group ticket office inside the site and behind the observatory. To reach it, walk 6m past the ticket hut and turn right in the sand driveway—the small path may be obscured, but believe you me, it's there. This *cenote,* once the source of all Chichén's drinking water, is little more than a deep, muddy pool. The small, ruined temple of Xtoloc, the lizard god, pleases the eye nearby. The walkway down can be extremely slippery in the rainy season. Swimming is prohibited here because of dangerous underwater currents.

The entire site of Chichén Itzá is open daily from 8am to 5pm; the visitors complex from 8am to 10pm. Authorities are diligent about protecting the site, and those who try to sneak in before or after these hours may find themselves paying a hefty fine to get out of the Pisté jail. Admission is 3500 pesos (free Sun. and holidays). Baggage check and parking (open 8am-10pm) cost 2000 pesos each.

As if the natural spectacle weren't enough, after hours the latter-day priests of illumination prepare the **Sound and Light Spectacular.** The monuments, awash in red, blue, green, and yellow light, fail to look more ancient, but the show makes for an impressive evening. A booming voice details the history of the site (Spanish version daily at 7pm, 2000 pesos; English version daily at 9pm, 2700 pesos.) To avoid the nighttime walk from Pisté over steps and reptiles, you may want to take a taxi to and from the show (5000 pesos each way).

Chichén Viejo

Chichén Viejo, set about 2km apart from the rest of Chichén, is for rugged or well-informed visitors only, and the paths that lead to the site are difficult to follow in the rainy season (May-Oct.). Ask some of the merchants at Chichén if they know someone who would be willing to serve as guide for a fee determined in advance. The unlicensed and under-age but cheap guides can tell Spanish speakers nearly as much about these less accessible ruins as their better-paid counterparts can about the main section of Chichén Itzá. Bring food and water.

A dirt path lies to the right of the nunnery as you face the great staircase. A 15-minute walk down the path will take you past an intersection of other dirt paths to a couple of huts around a well. Walk through the smaller hut and continue to follow the tracks of the old narrow-gauge *tranvía* (donkey-drawn trolley). Soon the rocky trail enters a clearing with a cluster of ruins called the **Date Group,** dominated by the **House of the Phalli.** The **Date Lintel,** a block upheld by two layered columns, carries the only dated inscription in all of Chichén Itzá. In both classical and abbreviated hieroglyphic calendars appear the dates "10.2.9.1.9, 9 Muluc 7 Zac" and "10.2.10.0.0, 2 Ahau 13 Chén," both corresponding to the year 879. The rest of the temple has been destroyed.

The path continues into the jungle behind the right of the House of the Phalli. Another 15- to 20-minute walk leads either to the **Principal Group of the Southwest** or to the **Lintel Group.** On the right, the Southwest Group contains a ruined pyramid, **Castillo de Chichén Antigua,** and the **Jaguar Temple,** where only a few Atlantean columns remain to salute the ancient military order of the Jaguars. On the left, the **Temple of the Lintel** is barely recognizable, since the sculptured lintel has long since collapsed.

Turning to the right through the jungle from the Southwest Group, you may stumble upon the **Bird Cornice Group, Temple of the Turtle,** and **Temple of the Sculpted Jambs.** The cornice has a strip of carved birds, the Temple of the Turtle once yielded a turtle-shaped stone, and the jambs of the last temple are molded into human figures.

Near Chichén Itzá

There are a few worthwhile sites in the region around Chichén Itzá. To reach the ones on the main highway (Rte. 180), take a second-class bus and when you get on, tell the driver where you want to be let off.

Grutas de Balancanche

Although the soft limestone of the Yucatán has in many places been carved into subterranean labyrinths by underground streams, the Grutas de Balancanche has always been held in particular regard by the local population. In 1959, a severe storm dislodged the boulder that hid an undiscovered inner cave. An archeologist who had been working at Chichén Itzá cleared the rubble and began to poke around.

Further exploration opened a 300m path, which runs past stalactites carved to resemble leaves on the ceiling and a huge tree-like stalactite surrounded by dozens of votive vessels with ghoulish masks. Archeologists came to believe that the cave was a center for Mayan-Toltec worship of the gods Chac, Tlaloc (the Toltec rain god), and Kukulcán during the 10th and 11th centuries. For unknown reasons, subterranean worship in Balancanche stopped at the end of this period, and the offerings of ceramic vessels and stone sculptures rested undisturbed for eight centuries. Artifacts aside, the impressive stalactites and a strikingly clear underground river make the cave worth a visit.

One more light-and-sound show dramatizes the cave's history and recounts Mayan legends, keeping up with the tour group via a series of hidden speakers. A guide, available for questions, paces the group through the chambers along the 1km path. Self-guided tours are not permitted.

The grottos lie about 6km from Chichén toward Cancún and about 2km from the Dolores Alba Hotel. You may want to take a taxi and then walk up the long driveway, as getting buses to stop at the driveway can prove difficult. Tours cost 3200 pesos (free Sun. and holidays). The small museum and garden complex are open daily from 9am to 5pm. Tours in Spanish begin at 9am, 10am, noon, 2pm, and 4pm; tours in English at 11am, 1pm, and 3pm. No tour leaves with more than 30 or fewer than six people.

Mérida to Chichén Itzá

Travelers can hitch or take short bus rides from one Mayan village to another along the busy road between Mérida and Chichén Itzá. If hitching, remember to tote water—waits can be long and shade sparse. Second-class bus drivers stop anywhere if requested to do so, but a new fare is charged for each trip. After leaving Mérida, the highway passes near the five private *henequén haciendas* known as San Pedro, Teya, Ticopó, San Bernardino, and Holactún. Next come the villages, each dominated by a main plaza and an oversized church. First are Tahmek and Hoctún (47km from Mérida). From Hoctún, you can turn left for a detour to **Izamal**, 24km north of the highway, although second-class buses do not make the detour. This tiny town contains the largest church plaza in Mexico, ringed with rows of yellow arches around the church and convent, and some of the earliest Spanish buildings, dating from 1533 and built from the boulders of the Mayan pyramid that they replaced. Since almost all the buildings in Izamal are yellow, the city is sometimes referred to as Ciudad Amarilla (Yellow City). Its Mayan name, derived from the god Itzamná, means "Dew of Heaven." The ancient *cenote* of Ixcolasc is only 1km away.

Upon returning to the Mérida-Chichén-Valladolid highway, you arrive at Kantunil (68km from Mérida). Xocchel, the "Place Where the Chels Read," is an attractive town along the highway 17km back from Mérida. Next is Holca, then Libre Unión (94km from Mérida), with a sizable *cenote*. During squabbles between the territories of Yucatán and Quintana Roo, the town found itself smack on the border. Rather than split in two, the city voted to stick together and become part of the state of Yucatán. "Libre Unión" means "free union" in Spanish.

Valladolid

In the middle of the Mérida-Cancún route and only half an hour from Chichén Itzá, Valladolid ought to be jammed with tourists hopping down the *gringo trail*. After all, while most towns have only one grand church, Valladolid boasts six; while others may offer a *balneario* or windswept beach, Valladolid harbors a pair of edenic *cenotes*, nature's breathtaking improvement on swimming pools.

A history of struggle, rebellion, and suffering has generated a deep community spirit in Valladolid. In 1543, Francisco de Montejo, the nephew of the Spanish conquistador of the same name, was sent to the Mayan town of Zací to convert the population and begin a Spanish enclave. After constructing his home with Mayan stone and labor, he was driven away by their animosity and the sweltering jungle heat. A second Francisco de Montejo (*son* of the Spanish conquistador) came to take his place, succeeded where his cousin had failed, and built many churches in celebration of his conquest.

Some 250 years later, cut off from the rest of New Spain by dense jungle, *vallisoletanos* challenged the authority of local Spanish rule. In 1809, a cabal of Mayan leaders, clergy, and disaffected military personnel devised a revolutionary plot; their scheme was uncovered and the leaders imprisoned, but a rebellious spirit persisted. When Mexico finally resolved itself to independence, a good number of *vallisoletanos* led the fight.

Interracial conflict between the elite *ladinos* and oppressed *indígenas* erupted once again in the Caste War (1847-48), during which machete-wielding Mayan rebels besieged Valladolid for two months. The Maya eventually took the city, sending 10,000 *ladinos* fleeing to Mérida. In ensuing years, the caste schism has healed but slowly. Today, Valladolid is a vigorous metropolitan center. *Indígena* women deal hammocks and fruit in the Zócalo, eight-year-olds agressively push chewing gum to passersby, and loud trucks nearly crush pedestrians' toes at every corner. Visitors to the city enjoy the commotion of the artisanal fair and the nearly-free provisions at the food market, then seek out the bat-enhanced tranquility of Valladolid's grand colonial churches and beautiful *cenotes*.

Orientation

Rte. 180 skewers Valladolid on its way from Mérida to Cancún, 150km from each city. Valladolid falls into a grid with streets aligned in the four cardinal directions. Even-numbered streets run north-south, with the city center bordered by 26 on the east and 60 on the west. Odd-numbered streets run east-west and start with 27 in the north, ending with 53 in the south. The Zócalo, enclosed by Calles 39, 40, 41, and 42, sits literally at the center of Valladolid. Everything of interest is within easy walking distance of the Zócalo; the Franciscan church lise to the south. All the hotels on the Zócalo (the San Clemente, Mesón del Marqués, and María de la Luz) hand out green maps of the city center. To get to the Zócalo from the bus station, walk 2 blocks east on Calle 39.

Practical Information

Tourist Information: A clearly-marked booth on the Calle 41 side of the Zócalo is open when the information agent has nothing better to do. **Hotel Mesón del Marqués,** Calle 39 #203 (tel. 620-73), politely and unofficially answers questions about the city and the region. Desk open daily 6am-midnight.

Currency Exchange: Banks proliferate on the Zócalo and on Calle 41. Open Mon.-Fri. 9am-1:30pm.

Post Office: In an unmarked yellow building on Calle 43, between Calles 40 and 42. Open Mon.-Fri. 8am-7pm, Sat. 9am-1pm. **Postal Code:** 97780.

Telephones: Calle 42 #193-B (tel. 628-49), between Calles 37 and 39, ½ block north of the Zócalo. Best time for international collect calls (4000 pesos) 6-8pm. Open daily 8am-8:30pm. **Telephone Code:** 985.

Telegrams: (tel. 621-70) on Calle 40, through an unmarked doorway on the Zócalo. Open Mon.-Fri. 9am-8pm, Sat. 9am-noon.

Bus Station: On Calle 39, between Calles 44 and 46. Both first- and second-class service. No luggage check. First class operates out of the left ticket window. All buses arrive *de paso*. To: Mérida (23 per day, 2 hr., 7500 pesos); Cancún/Puerto Juárez (15 per day, 2 hr., 7500 pesos); Playa del Carmen (6 per day, 3 hr., 10,200 pesos). Second class to: Mérida (23 per day, 3 hr., 6500 pesos); Cancún/Puerto Juárez (10 per day, 3 hr., 6000 pesos); Playa del Carmen (8 per day, 4 hr., 9300 pesos); Carillo Puerto (3 per day, 2½ hr., 6000 pesos); Chiquilá (3 per day, 2½ hr., 6300 pesos); Tizimín (14 per day, 1 hr., 2200 pesos).

Taxis: Tel. 620-46. Available in front of the bus station and on the Zócalo (3000 pesos through town).

Bike Rental: On Calle 44, between Calles 39 and 41. The outer *cenote* is reached most easily on bike, but tall people will feel clownish on the small, rickety frames. 1500 pesos per hr. Open Mon.-Sat. 8am-1pm.

Market: Food market bordered by Calles 35, 37, 30, and 32; 5 blocks northeast of the Zócalo. Artisans' market occupies the sidewalks near the intersection of Calles 39 and 44. Both open daily 6am-6pm.

Supermarket: Super Economía Vidal, on Calle 46 near Calle 39, across from the bus station. Open Mon.-Sat. 7:30am-1:30pm and 4:30-8:30pm, Sun. 7:30am-1:30pm.

Pharmacy: Farmacia San José, Calle 39 at Calle 44 (tel. 622-71). Good selection at discount prices. Open Mon.-Sat. 8am-9pm, Sun. 8am-1pm.

Red Cross: Calle 40 #212 (tel. 624-13), 1½ blocks south of Zócalo. Open daily 8am-1pm and 4-8pm. If closed, try 24-hr. **Clínica Santa Anita,** Calle 40 #221 (tel. 628-11), farther down the street from the Zócalo.

Police: Calle 41 at Calle 40 (tel. 621-34), around the corner from the Zócalo in the Palacio Municipal. No English spoken. Open 24 hr. for emergencies.

Accommodations

Hotel Zací, Calle 44 #191 (tel. 621-67), between Calles 37 and 39. Huge, well-kept complex built around a beautiful garden and courtyard. Iron railings on the beds and palatial bathrooms make you feel like a monarch. Singles 27,000 pesos, with A/C and TV 33,000 pesos. Doubles 33,000 pesos, with A/C and TV 42,000 pesos.

Hotel María Guadalupe, Calle 44 #188 (tel. 620-68), between Calles 39 and 41. Excellent budget hotel: spotless, freshly painted rooms with fans and hot water. *Agua purificada* available. Baths have either toilet seat or shower curtain, but not both. Singles 25,000 pesos. Doubles 32,000 pesos.

Hotel María de la Luz, Calle 39 at Calle 42 (tel. 620-71). Advantageous location on the northwest corner of the Zócalo. Plain courtyard includes a pool. Simple rooms with fans and hot water are almost elegant; *agua purificada* yours upon request. Doubles 45,000 pesos, with A/C 55,000 pesos.

Hotel El Mesón del Marqués, Calle 39 #203 (tel. 620-73), on the Zócalo. Simply the best hotel in town, this restored colonial mansion now boasts a fancy pool. All rooms have A/C. Singles 60,500 pesos. Doubles 66,000 pesos.

Hotel Mendoza, Calle 39 #204 (tel. 620-02), opposite the bus station. The low prices draw 'em in, but the dingy, dim rooms can't keep 'em for long. Fans valiantly attempt to drown out street noise. Acceptable bathrooms. Singles 20,000 pesos. Doubles 30,000 pesos.

Hotel Lily, Calle 44 #192. Informal management rents out inexpensive, reasonably clean rooms. Low wall separates bath from bedroom. Noisy at night. Singles 15,000 pesos, with bath 20,000 pesos. Doubles with bath 25,000 pesos.

Hotel Don Luis, Calle 38 at Calle 39 (tel. 620-24), 1 block east of the Zócalo. Clean, modern hotel sans ambience. Palms on the patio shade a well-maintained pool. Friendly management. *Agua purificada.* Phones, fans, and parking. Singles 42,000 pesos. Doubles 48,000 pesos. A/C 5000 pesos extra.

Hotel Maya, Calle 41 #231 (tel. 620-69), between Calles 48 and 50. Inconveniently distant from the Zócalo and bus station, and decorated like a tacky Polynesian restaurant. Clean, modest rooms have fans, hot water, and baths. Singles 18,000 pesos. Doubles 20,000 pesos. Triples 25,000 pesos. A/C 10,000 pesos extra.

Hotel Alcocer, Calle 38 between Calles 44 and 46, across from Hotel Mendoza. The cheapest place in Valladolid brings you dirty sheets, tattered curtains, and scummy baths. Hang a hammock to sleep away from the crawling insects. On the bright side, no room is without a fan or hot water. Singles 10,000 pesos. Doubles 15,000 pesos.

Food

Several dishes are native to the Valladolid region. *Lomitos de Valladolid* are small cuts of pork in a tomato sauce. *Escabeche oriental de pavo* is a hearty and delectable turkey soup prepared with onions, garlic, and spices. *Panuchos,* sold in the bus station, are small tortillas piled with various combinations of meat, beans, lettuce, and tomato. *Longaniza* (sausage) is wonderfully greasy, tasty, and filling.

Satisfying *tamales,* sold for 800 pesos on most street corners near the bus station and the Zócalo, are sometimes accompanied by *pozole,* served in the half-shell of a coconut-like fruit.

El Bazaar, Calle 39 at Calle 40, on the Zócalo. Not a restaurant, but a pink open-air courtyard supporting cafés and juice bars under shady arcades. Great for a cheap meal and people-watching. At least one café open daily 6am-1am. **La Rancherita,** closest to the Zócalo, opens earliest and throws together an unbeatable fruit salad (3000 pesos). Later in the day they cook soft chicken *panuchos* (1000 pesos) and a variety of *Yucateco* entrees. **Sergio's** makes an interesting pizza without tomato sauce (small 6000 pesos). **Doña Mary** scoffs at the concept of a turkeyburger, serving instead juicy hamburgers (3000 pesos) and other 100% red meat dishes.

Restaurant San Bernadino de Siena, Calle 49 #227, 3 blocks southwest of the Zócalo near the church of the same name. Excellent regional dishes and huge jugs of juice at good prices under a large *palapa.* Try the tasty *poc chuc,* a thin slice of grilled pork (7000 pesos). Open daily 6:30am-10pm.

Casa de los Arcos, on Calle 39, between Calles 38 and 40. Iron arches define this stylish yet reasonably priced restaurant. Tasty local specialties (with unusually good tortillas) from 9000 pesos. Open daily 7am-10pm. Credit cards accepted.

Restaurant Los Cupules, Calle 42 #206, on a porch across from the cathedral. Hotel restaurant with high-backed wooden chairs and cheap regional specialties. Often empty. Delicate *pollo pibil* (chicken cooked in a banana leaf) 8500 pesos. Ham and cheese sandwich 2000 pesos. Open daily 7am-9pm.

Cenote, on Calle 36, between Calles 37 and 39, overlooking Cenote Zací. After dreaming of a quick dip (see Sights below), sit back, relax, and chow in this lovely thatched-roof restaurant. Elegant decor and background music. Excellent liquor selection, including locally produced Xtabentun. Grilled meat entrees 10,000-12,000 pesos. Open daily 8am-7pm.

Mesón del Marqués, Calle 39 #203, on the Zócalo. Sharp service and beautiful decor make the high prices more bearable. Chicken Valladolid-style, the cheapest dinner, sets you back 10,000 pesos. Lobster fresh from Río Lagartos 40,000 pesos. Open daily 7:30am-10pm.

María de la Luz, on Calle 39, in the hotel of the same name on the northwest corner of the Zócalo. Targeted at vacationing families. Unremarkable presentation of local specialties, with some *norteamericano* items tossed in for good measure. *Comida corrida* 9000 pesos. Open daily 10am-10pm.

Paletería La Michoacana, Calle 40 #90, right off the Zócalo. A marvelous aquamarine ice cream parlor (though in need of a serious paint job) that quivers to the jukebox's Mexican Top 40. Small portions of flan, jello, and ice cream 700-1300 pesos. Open daily 6am-9pm.

Sights

Resented by *indígenas* for the imposition of Christianity and despised by laymen for their control of large tracts of land, Franciscan monks in Valladolid built their churches as stoutly as fortresses for security's sake. Not even these bastions, however, could hold back the masses during the Caste War and the Mexican Revolution, when raiders looted the valuable ornamentation that encrusted the churches. The most interesting churches are **Santa Lucía,** at Calles 27 and 40; **Santa Ana,** at Calles 41 and 34; **San Juan,** at Calles 49 and 40; **San Roque** (now a branch of the Museo de Valladolid), at Calles 41 and 38; and **La Candelaria,** at Calles 35 and 44. (All open Mon.-Fri. 8am-1pm and 5-9pm. Donation expected.)

The most famous of Valladolid's churches is **San Bernardino de Siena** with the **Ex-Convento de Sisal,** 41a. Calle, 3 blocks southwest from the intersection of Calles 46 and 41. Built in 1552, they are the oldest clerical buildings in the Yucatán and possibly in all of Mexico. The monks abandoned the convent in the 18th century, when the Franciscans and other religious orders in Mexico were obligated to turn their property over to the secular church. Interior decoration today is minimal because of theft and vandalism during the Caste War. On the altar at the rear of the church is a large image of the Virgin of Guadalupe, brought from Guatemala. Outside, the colonial irrigation system for the vegetable garden and the 17th-century horse-drawn well is being restored. The entire complex (chapels, gardens, and cemetery) was built over a tremendous *cenote* known to the Maya as Sis-Ha (cold water). As was the norm, the Spanish linguists mangled the name before bestowing it on the *barrio* and church. Poke around for hidden staircases and ladders up to the stone roof for a commanding view of Valladolid. (Open Mon.-Sat. 9am-1pm and 3-6pm, Sun. 8am-noon. Free.)

The **Catedral de San Gervasio,** built near the Zócalo around a peaceful garden, is unremarkable except for an old story recounted by Eligio Ancona in his *Historia de Yucatán.* According to the author, two men took sanctuary in the church at the beginning of the 18th century after being accused of a crime. An angry mob discovered and brutally murdered them. When the bishop learned of the event, he closed up the church immediately and had it destroyed. To atone for the blasphemy, he had workers rebuild the church to face south on Calle 41, instead of west on Calle 42, its original orientation.

Cenote Zací (pronounced sa-KEY), on Calle 36, 3 blocks from the Zócalo between Calles 37 and 39, draws tourists today just as it fascinated the *indígenas* centuries ago. Walk down the worn, stone stairs and the cavernous hollow will half surround you. Above, bats beat their wings against ghastly stalactites; below, *chinha* (lake lettuce) floats on murky jade-colored water. *Vallisoletano* youths periodically dive in to clean the water, but tourists are forbidden to swim because of the sly underwater currents. To the right of the path leading down to the *cenote,* two small huts constitute the **Museo de Valladolid,** which displays local handicrafts and a collection of photographs. Captions are in Spanish. (*Cenote*/museum/restaurant open daily 8am-7pm. Admission 1000 pesos.)

More spectacular, though farther away, the **Cenote X-kekén** (pronounced chay-kay-KEN), plunges into the ground near the town of **Dzitnup.** It can be reached by a half-hour bike ride, a 12,000-peso taxi trip, or with an importunate plea to a Mérida-bound bus driver to drop you at the access road (a 20-min. walk from the *cenote).* To get to it on foot, take Calle 41 west out of town, past the Hotel Maya and the Coca Cola plant. At the highway, turn left, and then left again at the sign for the *cenote.* Swimming is permitted and a profound experience when alone. Change clothes in the tiny restroom or behind a boulder, and descend the narrow, slick staircase into the cave. If school is out, roving packs of eight-year-old boys will offer to guide you to the natural pool. The luminous turquoise water reflects pendant stalactites and the single brilliant sunbeam emanating from a small hole in the ceiling, 40m above the surface of the pool. The best time to swim is at 7am, before the whole gang arrives, but the spectacle of ricocheting light is most awesome at noon. (Open daily 7am-5pm. Admission 1000 pesos.)

Valladolid is home to Xtabentun, one of the most popular liquors on the peninsula. Observe the production of the anise- and honey-flavored drink at the factory on Calle 42, at the intersection with Calle 47. The Sosa family, who have been making the product for 50 years, sell their entire line here at great discounts (Xtabentun 8000 pesos per bottle). You'll get free samples and a tour if you ask politely and they're not too busy watching the Celtics on TV. (Factory open Mon.-Sat. 8am-1:30pm.)

Entertainment

Valladolid doesn't bend over backwards to entertain visitors. **Cine Díaz,** on Calle 40 between Calles 41 and 43, just off the Zócalo, shows Mexican and American films in a vintage 1950s movie emporium. On Calle 51, between Calles 38 and 40, the fully air-conditioned **Cine San Juan** projects double features nightly at 7:30pm (2000 pesos).

If you prefer live entertainment, keep your eyes peeled for occasional functions sponsored by the **Club de Leones** (Lions Club), whose dances, cookouts, and bake sales are announced in the Zócalo. Even more lively are the *cantinas,* especially **Barracuda** and **El Pedregal,** both on Calle 42 near Calle 45, where conversation and beer flow freely. The cheapest and perhaps most rewarding hangouts are the El Bazaar café complex and the Zócalo itself, where *vallisoletanos* and visitors alike linger until the witching hour. **Discoteque Friday,** on Calle 40 between Calles 37 and 39, delivers *salsa* on Friday and Saturday evenings from 10pm. (Cover 3500 pesos.)

Between January 26 and February 2, the Fiesta de la Candelaria entails daily bullfights and evening dances in honor of Valladolid's patron, la Virgen de la Candelaria.

Near Valladolid

Tizimín

Passengers on northbound buses from Valladolid to Chiquilá or Río Lagartos inevitably stop in Tizimín. Although the urban center of a large agricultural area, Tizimín is less cosmopolitan than Valladolid. Trucks burdened with bleating sheep roll past the Zócalo; farmers in cowboy hats and shit-kickers suck on evening *cervezas* in the cantinas.

Five blocks northwest of the Zócalo on Calle 51, the **Parque Zoológico de la Reina,** established in 1974 to commemorate a visit from Queen Elizabeth II, is a brisk 20-minute walk from the bus stations. Although the zoo has declined since the Queen's visit (the 8 snake tanks have but 3 residents), the diverse collection of animals in the large park might entertain bored travelers. Many of the zoo's denizens—including iguanas, pink flamingos, pisots, and peacocks—are native to Yucatán. (Open Mon.-Sat. 9am-noon and 3-6pm, Sun. 9am-6pm. Free.)

The huge **Discoteca Extravaganza** (tel. 320-49), on the outskirts of town, has been rated one of the five most happening discos in Mexico, drawing pelvis-grinders from as far as Valladolid. The only way to get there is by taxi (10,000 pesos from the Zócalo). (Open Fri.-Sat. from 10pm. Cover 10,000 pesos, women free on Fri.)

All hotels, restaurants, and other services in Tizimín are near the verdant Zócalo, which residents call "el parque." To get there on foot from the bus stations turn (10 min.), walk 2 long blocks down the hill on Calle 47, passing the market. Turn left on Calle 50 and walk west 1 block toward the large cement church. The **Banco del Atlántico** (tel. 320-05) on the Zócalo is open for exchange Monday through Friday from 9am to 1:30pm. The **post office** is stashed away in a yellow building at Calle 43 #417. To get there, walk 3 long blocks on Calle 50 (to the right of the Palacio Municipal) away from the Zócalo, then turn left and walk 3 blocks on Calle 43. (Open Mon.-Fri. 8am-6pm, Sat. 9am-1pm. **Postal code:** 97700.) A long-distance telephone *caseta* (tel. 325-13), on Calle 50 just off the Zócalo, connects international calls after 3pm for 5000 pesos. The rarely open **telegram office** faces the Zócalo, as does **Farmacia Tizimín** (open daily 8am-1pm and 4-8:30pm). The **police** station, where 10 uniformed men drink Coke and play poker, is located in the Palacio Municipal on the Zócalo.

Two bus lines in adjacent terminals serve Tizimín. **ADO,** at Calle 46 and Calle 47, sends one first-class bus daily to Mérida (at 11:30am, 3 hr., 8600 pesos). Second-class buses go to Cancún (3 per day, 3 hr., 8600 pesos); Valladolid (2 per day, 45 min., 2200 pesos); and Playa del Carmen (at 11:30am, 4 hr., 11,700 pesos). **Autotransportes del Noreste** (tel. 320-34), on Calle 46 near Calle 47, has first-class service to Mérida (7 per day, 3 hr., 8500 pesos); Río Lagartos (3 per day, 1 hr., 2600 pesos); and San Felipe (2 per day). Second-class buses run to Valladolid (2 per day, 45 min., 2300 pesos); Chetumal (2 per day); Río Lagartos (5 per day, 1 hr., 2000 pesos); San Felipe (4 per day, 2000 pesos); and Kantunil (2 per day).

Tizimín has three large hotels. Conveniently located on the Zócalo, the **Hotel San Horge** provides Homey-the-Clown rooms with mismatched colors and neat green bathrooms. (Singles 25,000 pesos. Doubles 30,000 pesos. A/C an additional 20,000 pesos.) The **Hotel San Carlos,** Calle 54 #407 (tel. 320-94), is the newest sheriff in town, located 2½ blocks off the Zócalo. It has clean, comfortable rooms (with curtains hung backwards) facing a cement courtyard pool. (Singles 25,000 pesos. Doubles 35,000 pesos. A/C an additional 10,000 pesos.) Also on the Zócalo, the **Hotel Tizimín** (tel. 321-52), has acceptably clean rooms with fans and narrow, sagging mattresses. (Singles 20,000 pesos. Doubles 30,000 pesos, with A/C 35,000 pesos).

Good restaurants play hard to get in Tizimín. You would be wise to purchase fruits, vegetables, and bread at the market on Calle 47 (14 shoe stores market their wares here in case your soles give out) and eat in the beautiful Zócalo. The most popular eatery is the air-conditioned **Restaurant Tres Reyes,** on the Zócalo. Friendly management will get up from their own meal to serve you hearty portions of impressively mediocre food. Fish, beef, and pork entrees cost about 12,000 pesos, soup 5000 pesos. (Open daily 7:30am-11pm.) **Cesar's Pizzas,** on Calle 53 next to the Hotel Tizimín, makes spaghetti (5200 pesos) and layers unusual combinations of toppings on top of deliciously thin crusts. A small pepper, onion, pineapple, and cheese pizza costs 6800 pesos. (Open daily 5:30pm-11:30pm.)

Río Lagartos

A great pink and red carpet covers a pale beach, backed by lush jungle vegetation. As a boat of admiring visitors strays too near, the carpet suddenly dissipates into individuval strands, each flying low across the lagoon. Almost every visitor to Río Lagartos comes just to catch a fleeting glimpse of this flamingonic spectacle. The local base of the *Phoenicopterus ruber,* a spectacularly scarlet species of flamingo, awaits 16km east across the lagoon from Río Lagartos; the birds are most numerous from May to August, but the site is inhabited year-round. Locals claim that the site serves as breeding ground for the entire flamingo population of the Yucatán Peninsula.

On the northern coast of the Yucatán Peninsula, Río Lagartos still derives more income from fish than tourists. Hotel Nefertiti sees few visitors, and its disco is un-crowded if not altogether empty on Saturday nights. The traveler seeking relaxation could do worse: Río Lagartos has blue waters, colorful birds, and deserted beaches up its sleeve.

Río Lagartos lies 52km north of Tizimín and 103km north of Valladolid, at the end of Rte. 295. Three first-class buses and five second-class buses arrive daily, stopping just south of the Zócalo and the docks. To reach the Zócalo, take a right from the station to the center of the horseshoe of water that defines the town. Behind a stunted obelisk rises the Palacio Municipal, the cream-colored building bordering one side of the Zócalo. The municipal president's office inside is open for questions and problems Monday through Friday from 8am to noon and 4 to 8pm. On the left side (when facing its front) of the building sits the town **police** station, which opens whenever the one-man squad comes in.

The **Hotel Nefertiti,** Calle 14 #123 (tel. 14-15), 4 blocks to the right if you face the Palacio Municipal on the Zócalo, maintains a monopoly on Río Lagartos's small tourist trade. The resulting steep prices for institutional rooms include baths and fans. (Singles 30,000 pesos. Doubles 40,000 pesos.) Guests receive free admission to **Los Flamingos,** a disco *extraordinaire.* (Cover for non-hotel guests 5000 pesos for women, 8000 pesos for men. Open Sat. 10pm-1am.) During the rest of the week, the disco serves as a restaurant with a wide selection of seafood entrees from 8000-12,000 pesos.

More economical accommodations can be found in a two-story house on Calle 10, 1 block from Restaurant Los Negritos toward the Zócalo. Decorated with wagon wheels on the outside and cowboy trappings on the inside, the house has three small, clean, carpeted rooms, and one communal bath. (Singles and doubles 25,000 pesos.) For campers and travelers with hammocks, there are two open-air *palapa* huts donated by the government for free lodging. Unfortunately, they are hidden along a remote stretch of beach; your best bet is to ask a fisherman for a ride or to ask to be dropped off after a flamingo tour.

The best eatery in Río Lagartos is the screened-in **Restaurant Los Negritos,** located on the second floor above the bus stop. Their specialty, *Tin Quin Xic,* consists of a big fish laden with tomatoes, onions, and spices (20,000 pesos) and makes a meal for two. Shellfish soup goes for 6500 pesos. **Restaurant Económica** is across the street from the Hotel Nefertiti on Calle 14. Crowded with fishing folk in the afternoon, the restaurant serves heaping portions of *ceviche* (6500 pesos) and fried fish (8000 pesos).

For flamingo-watching tours, the Hotel Nefertiti (the large pastel edifice on your right as you enter town) offers the best deals. The most elaborate safari visits the particularly dense flamingo population outside **Las Coloradas**. Leaving at 7am, and including a stop at the beach on the island across from Río Lagartos, the three-hour tour costs 80,000 pesos for up to 5 people. Rumor has it that this is the same three-hour tour on which Gilligan and his buddies embarked on that fateful day years ago; bring supplies accordingly.

If you arrive during the middle of the day, you will probably encounter enough fellow travelers to make a chartered boat tour from a local fisherman worthwhile; you might even convince him to throw in a fresh fish lunch. Fishing boats will also ferry passengers across the lagoon to the beach (30,000 pesos round-trip). The gulf side of the island, off Río Lagartos or Las Coloradas, makes the best swimming area, while the lagoon off Río Lagartos is less pleasant for aquatic frolic. Don't even think about a dip in the lagoon which the flamingos inhabit; shark sightings are frequent enough there to make the wait for other areas bearable. For a swimming hole closer to downtown, try the **Chiquilá Spring.** From the shore opposite the Hotel Nefertiti, turn right and walk 1km along the water to two thatched huts beside the sparkling freshwater pool.

Going directly to Las Coloradas by ground transport is possible, but picking up a boat in Las Coloradas to take you to the flamingos may be difficult. Check at the Hotel Nefertiti first to see if boats in Las Coloradas are available. If approaching Las Coloradas by car, turn east at the crossroads 1km before the town of Río Lagartos; follow this road for roughly 14km, cross the only bridge that spans the river in the vicinity, and continue 2km to Las Coloradas. Hitching along the road to Las Coloradas is very easy at the well-marked crossroads.

Two buses run daily from Río Lagartos to Las Coloradas, leaving from the front of Restaurant Negritos. Seven first-class buses to Mérida depart daily (12,000 pesos). Second-class buses leave for Tizimín (7 per day, 2500 pesos); San Felipe (at 11:30am and 9:30pm, 700 pesos); and Las Coloradas (at 1 and 3pm, 1000 pesos).

San Felipe

San Felipe belongs to a beachless part of the northern Yucatán that holds little of interest for the traveler. Across the channel from San Felipe, however, a series of tangled mangrove islands and seaweed-strewn sandbars stretches across the horizon. On the closest of the islands unfolds a long, seashell-covered swath of sand called **Playa El Dragado.** Shallow, turquoise water extends 50m from the fine sand before dropping precipitously into blue depths. During Semana Santa, and throughout July and August, a stand on the beach sells beer, soft drinks, and fried fish. Camping is best along the exposed beach, but the island's vegetation affords limited shelter from the squadrons of mosquitoes; bring a tent or net of some sort. Although a nearby lagoon dredge groans most of the night, Playa El Dragado still furnishes seclusion unknown in Cancún or Cozumel. Camping from October to March, however, is dangerous due to sudden *nortes,* storms that can stir up gnarly, beach-flooding waves.

A 12km road leads to San Felipe from an intersection 1km south of Río Lagartos. To reach San Felipe's main drag, which parallels the ocean, turn right at the well-marked fork near the village and continue past the quaint graveyard on the outskirts of town. Buses stop in front of Cinema Marrufo, 100m or so off the ocean. One first-class bus leaves San Felipe daily at 5:30am for Mérida (11,000 pesos). Four second-class buses go to Tizimín daily (2500 pesos), and two buses reach Río Lagartos (1000 pesos).

The man to know in San Felipe is Miguel Archangel Marfil Medina, garrulous president of the Tourist Committee of San Felipe. Miguel can be found at the pier or at home in the blue house to the left of Hotel Marrufo, Calle 10 #48. He also has an office at the Palacio Municipal (tel. 320-89). For 3000 pesos per person, Miguel will shuttle visitors to Playa El Dragado for the night and return for them in the morning. In the event of a *chubasco* (sudden storm), he will rescue stranded campers. He also runs a three-hour tour (75,000 pesos) of the nearby island beaches, the estuaries on the mainland, and the partially excavated Mayan ruins at **Cerrito**, a small island west of San Felipe. Because of the many narrow channels weaving through the islands and the reportedly good fishing, you may wish to rent a boat from Miguel (25,000 pesos per hour for up to four people, tackle included).

Options are limited for non-campers who wish to stay overnight. In 1988, Hurricane Gilbert demolished the town's hotel and cinema. Three reasonably clean rooms and a communal bath survived *el ciclón,* but only one has mosquito netting. They are located in the large blue building across from the Palacio Municipal and next to the Cinema Marrufo façade. (Singles and doubles 15,000 pesos). Ask about room availability at the red convenience store, Tienda Floresita, across the street. If you decide to prolong your stay in San Felipe, renting a house is an inexpensive option. Although a minimum stay of 15 days is the norm, shorter leases are negotiable. Bare houses start at 20,000 pesos per day (bring a hammock); furnished houses cost 40,000 pesos per day. Again, talk to Miguel.

Restaurant El Payaso, Calle 8 #55, is well hidden but worth searching for. Inside, huge portions of good seafood are traded for few pesos: fantastic *camarones mantequilla* (shrimp in butter sauce) cost 11,000 pesos. The *filete de relleno* is large and thick (8500 pesos). (Open daily 8am-6pm). From the central street, walking away from the water, turn left at the Tienda Floresita. Walk 1½ blocks and turn right on Calle 8. The Payaso is on the right. The **Restaurant Bar La Playa,** 200m west of the pier, does not clown around: though the food is not as pleasing to the palate, the prices mimic those at El Payaso, and the building is much easier to locate. Locals pack this corner hangout after work to watch the sunset over the ocean and to down the *camarones mantequilla* (11,000 pesos). (Open daily 10am-6pm.)

Chiquilá and Isla Holbox

Although these towns are in the Yucatán's neighboring state of Quintana Roo, the only public bus service to Chiquilá and Holbox leaves from Tizimín. (See Near Cancún.)

Quintana Roo

For decades after industrialization introduced the rest of Mexico to noise, pollution, and other manifestations of modernity, Quintana Roo's picturesque coastline and lost ruins lounged unnoticed and unspoiled beneath the Caribbean sun. In fact, the region did not even achieve statehood until the 1970s. Then, with brutal suddenness, Quintana Roo was discovered by government bureaucrats who designated Cancún, on the Quintana Roo coast, as Mexico's paradise. After pouring money into constructing resorts as awesome as the beaches, the transformation from tropical idyll to tourist trap was swift; spendthrift Americans realized that Quintana Roo was a mere puddle-jump from the southern U.S., and Cancún became the primary beachhead for marauding *norteamericanos.* Isla Cozumel fell next, with Isla Mujeres and Tulum close behind.

Small fishing villages along the coast south of Playa del Carmen still possess their *indígena* soul. The "biosphere reserve" of Sian Ka'an, a protected jungle and marine habitat for thousands of rare flora and fauna species, comprises a large part of Quintana Roo. The area's natural beauty is more impressive in person than on any of the many promotional packages that the mega-resorts mail out. Untamed landscapes and Caribbean coastline provide the backdrop for many adventures. Small wonder that the region remains one of the most alluring vacation spots in the world.

Cancún

Miles of magnificent white beach sparkle against the steely-blue Caribbean at Cancún. It would make a perfect isle of solitude, with its fine sand, rich undersea life, and eternal warm weather. But all tranquility vanished when merchants learned (from the Mexican government) how to cash in on Cancún's beauty.

Now more popular than Acapulco and Puerto Vallarta, Cancún is a frightening success story. The L-shaped island was selected by computer in 1967 to become an international resort, and construction began in 1970. The mainland city of Cancún was given space to grow and plenty of housing for hotel workers, and the Hotel Zone (Zona Hotelera) was built with every conceivable tourist need in mind. The Mexican government installed a water-purification system to provide the Hotel Zone with pure tap water, declared all of its beaches public, and instituted strict zoning laws to prevent a scourge of skyscrapers. Begging was banned on the streets of Cancún to minimize tourists' exposure to the poverty of local workers. While wealthy vacationers cruise in taxis to classy restaurants and discos downtown, hotel employees are packed like lemmings into lurching diesel buses that ferry them home to *colonias* north of the city. Ciudad Cancún grows even more explosively than the Zona Hotelera, as thousands, from as far as Mexico City, arrive looking for work.

Cancún's attractions are obvious. Here, in mid-winter, you can parasail and scuba dive, shop in chic boutiques, and slam tequila at rowdy Tex-Mex bars . . . all the while speaking English and spending dollars. But if you have fewer greenbacks to throw around and are searching for traditional Yucatán, abandon the mega-resort and seek enjoyment at nearby Playa del Carmen or Isla Holbox.

Orientation

At the easternmost tip of the Yucatán Peninsula, Cancún lies 321km east of Mérida via Rte. 180 and 360km north of Chetumal and the Belizan border via Rte. 307.

The resort has two sections: **Ciudad Cancún,** center of shopping and services, and **Isla Cancún,** home of the **Zona Hotelera** and the pure white beaches. Both are accessible from the airport south of the city by *colectivos* in the form of white-and-yellow vans (6500 pesos).

Private green taxis criss-cross Cancún, looking to shuttle tourists from the beaches to the stores and back again in time for sundown (7000 pesos, but settle the price before getting in). Buses marked "Hotels" (1000 pesos) run through the hotel strip from 5am to 10pm along **Avenida Tulum,** the city's main street. Follow the example of the locals by pounding hard on the wall: this signals the *kamikaze* drivers to slow down enough that you break only a few bones when jumping off. Many places rent mopeds, which are useful for reaching Club Med at the end of the Zona Hotelera.

Practical Information

Most services are along Av. Tulum, easily accessible from the Zona Hotelera by bus.

Tourist Office: Several offices and booths all over town open daily 8am-1pm and 4-8pm. Main office at the **Palacio de Gobierno** (tel. 300-94), on Tulum. Open Mon.-Fri. 9am-3pm. English spoken. More knowledgeable is the staff of **Cancún Tips** (tel. 413-42), in Pl. Pariana near the Hotel Zone's Convention Center, and in Pl. Caracol (tel. 304-47). The firm publishes *Cancún Tips,* a free English-language magazine with invaluable maps and practical information. A more frequent publication, *Cancún Scene,* is available at the office and in most pharmacies.

Consulates: U.S., Cobá at Tulum (tel. 424-11). Open Mon.-Fri. 9am-2pm and 3-6pm. **West Germany** (tel. 309-58), in the Club Lagoon. **Italy** (tel. 321-13). **Spain** (tel. 418-95), at Flamingos Real Estate. **Sweden** (tel. 411-75), at Rentautos Kankun.

American Express: (tel. 419-99) on Bonamapak next to Hotel América, the first hotel hit when coming from the Zona Hotelera. Personal checks cashed, money wired (2-3 days from the U.S.), and mail held (up to 6 mo.; P.O. Box 1320) for cardholders only. Open Mon.-Fri. 9am-1pm and 4-5pm, Sat. 9am-1pm.

Currency Exchange: There are many *casas de cambio* along Tulum, but the best rates are given in banks. **Bánamex, Banco Surfin,** and **Bancomer** on Tulum will provide cash advances on major credit cards. Banking hours are Mon.-Fri. 9am-1:30pm and 3-5pm. Bánamex has a Cirrus money machine and a special adjacent money exchange annex open Mon.-Fri. 9am-6pm.

Post Office: (tel. 414-18) on Sun Yax Chén several blocks beyond the intersection with Yaxchilán. From Tulum, cut through any side street to Yaxchilán and head up Sun Yax Chén. Open for stamps and Lista de Correos Mon.-Fri. 9am-6pm. **Postal Code:** 77500.

Telephones: Cheapest international collect calls (3000-peso service charge) at **Caseta M-28** in Mercado 28 (tel. 437-67), behind the post office; and the air-conditioned **Caseta Uxmal** (tel. 711-38), on Yaxchilán (tel. 711-38). Both open daily 8am-10pm. **Club Verano Beat** near the youth hostel provides 24-hr. long-distance service (5000 pesos). **Telephone Code:** 988.

Telegrams: (tel. 415-19) at the post office. Open daily 9am-6pm.

International Airport: (tel. 490-80) on Rte. 307 just south of the city. Taxis monopolize transport to the airport (8000 pesos from Ciudad Cancún, 13,000 pesos from the Zona Hotelera). Airlines: **Aerocaribe** (tel. 421-33), to Cozumel and Merida; **Mexicana** (tel. 414-32), to Mexico City, Guadalajara, and major U.S. cities; **Lasca** (tel. 424-14), to Central America; **American** (tel. 429-47); **Continental** (tel. 425-40); **Northwest** (tel. 409-46); **United** (tel. 428-58).

Bus Station: First- and second-class station (tel. 308-72) on Uxmal, near Tulum beyond the main shopping area. There are 2 different bus lines at this station. **First-class** service every hr. 6am-midnight to: Valladolid (2 hr., 7500 pesos); Chichén Itzá (3 hr., 9000 pesos); Mérida (5 hr., 15,000 pesos). Also to Playa del Carmen (5 per day, 1 hr., 4000 pesos) and Mexico City (4 per day, 85,000 pesos). **Second-class** service every hr. 6am-midnight to: Mérida (13,000 pesos); Valladolid (6500 pesos); Chichén Itzá (8200 pesos); Tizimín (8600 pesos). Also to: Puerto Morelos (6 per day, 1600 pesos); Playa del Carmen (6 per day, 3100 pesos); Xel Ha (6 per day, 4000 pesos); Tulum (6 per day, 5200 pesos); Carrillo (6 per day, 6465 pesos); Balacar (6 per day, 9900 pesos); Chetumal (6 per day, 10,870 pesos). Hours for the second-class buses vary; check at the station.

Ferries: To Isla Mujeres, take bus #8 or a van with "Pto. Juárez" on the destination display to the 2 ferry depots north of town (Punta Sam for car ferries, Puerto Juárez for passenger ferries). Passenger ferries (3000 pesos) leave 9 times per day. Ferries to Cozumel (5000 pesos) leave from Playa del Carmen, accessible by bus from the terminal in town.

Car Rental: Cars are readily available in Cancún, though bargains are not. Expect to pay about US$36 per day for a VW Beetle, plus 25¢ per km. Try **Avis,** at Viva Hotel (tel. 308-28), or **Budget,** at the Convention Center (tel. 308-50).

Moped Rental: Hotel Las Perlas (tel. 320-22) or **Hotel Carrousel** (tel. 302-39), both on Kukulkán; in the Hotel Zone on either side of the CREA; and in several shops along Tulum near Uxmal. No bargains: about US$10 per hr., US$30 per day. At the edge of the mainland, less expensive moped rentals are available at **Motos del Caribe** in the Hotel America (tel. 418-26). US$20 per day; deposit US$30. All open daily 9am-5pm.

English Bookstore: Multiservicio Don Quixote, Uxmal at Margarita, across from the bus station. International newspapers, magazines, and trashy beach books. Open daily 8am-10pm.

Laundromats: Lavandería María de Lourdes, Orquideas off Yaxchilán. Do it yourself or they'll do it for you (in 1½ hr.) for 3000 pesos per kg with a 9000-peso minimum. Open Mon.-Sat. 7am-11pm. **Lavandería y Tintorería Americana,** Sun Yax Chén 31 (tel. 421-13). High-class, with prices to match: shirt 3375 pesos, dress 8750 pesos, pants 5380 pesos.

Supermarket: Super San Francisco, Tulum next to Bánamex. Down-home grocery store with a large selection of fresh tropical fruit at affordable prices. Open Mon.-Sat. 8am-10pm, Sun. 8am-9pm.

Red Cross: Dial 06 in case of emergency. For routine medical services, call 416-16. Free medical service for tourists downtown at Yaxchilán 156 and in the Hotel Zone next to Villas Marlin.

Pharmacies: Several along Tulum and Yaxchilán, the largest and most reasonable being **Farmacia Paris,** Yaxchilán 32 (tel. 401-64). Open 24 hr. In the Zona Hotelera, try **Farmacia Don Quijote** (tel. 300-27) on Kukulkán at the Convention Center. Open daily 8am-10pm.

Police: Tel. 411-07. Most speak English.

Accommodations and Camping

Cancún is a chic international resort, where a US$100 room is a bargain to people used to paying US$200 per night. Budget travelers either stay in the CREA hostel or avoid the Zona Hotelera altogether, but even downtown spots cost at least US$20 for doubles. You can camp at the CREA (see below) or on the beach beyond the Sheraton (an increasingly difficult option as new construction devours the remaining open spaces). Several trailer parks lie close to Cancún. **Meco-Loco,** near Punta Sam north of Cancún, has a beach, unlike the park 2km south of the airport.

CREA Youth Hostel (IYHF) (tel. 313-77), on Kukulkán close to the mainland. Huge: 712 beds in single-sex dorms. Tolerable bathrooms. Friendly (especially if you speak some Spanish), mostly Mexican student crowd with a sprinkling of European hippies. Small beach and tiny pool are evening hangouts because most use the resort hotel beaches during the day. Lock your valuables when showering. Lockers, sheets, towels provided. 18,000 pesos per person, plus 20,000-peso deposit. No ID required.

CREA Camping Area, next to the youth hostel on an uneven semi-grassy lot. Not very nice, and no facilities except those in the hostel. Locker included. 9000 pesos per person, plus 20,000-peso deposit.

Hotel Canto, Punta Tonchactalpen at Yaxchilán (tel. 412-67). An excellent budget hotel loaded with amenities. Clean rooms have A/C, color TV, hot water, and closets. *Agua purificada* in the halls. Singles and doubles 55,000 pesos.

Hotel Colonial, Tulipanes 22 (tel. 415-35), off Tulum. Central location and clean, large rooms off a plant-filled courtyard with a bubbling fountain. Comfortable. Singles and doubles with fan 50,000 pesos, with A/C 60,000 pesos.

Hotel Cotty, Uxmal 44 (tel. 413-19), near the bus terminal. The rooms inside this glorified cement block attached to Lou's Bar and Grill are not as nice as Hotel Canto's, but they do have comparable amenities: A/C, TV, and hot water. No reservations. Singles and doubles 55,000 pesos.

Hotel Villa Rossana, Yaxchilán 68 (tel. 419-43). Small, dark lobby leads to uninspiring and noisy rooms, all with bathrooms and hot water. Singles 40,000 pesos. Doubles 50,000 pesos.

Hotel Bonampak, Bonampak at Sayil (tel. 402-80). Call before making the trek. New hotel with spacious lobby, large pool, and spotless rooms with terraces, A/C, and marble sinks. Singles and doubles 45,600 pesos. Triples 57,100 pesos.

Hotel Coral, Sun Yax Chén 30 (tel. 420-97). Squeezed behind palm trees on a busy street. Bright, spacious rooms have A/C and hot water. Purified water in halls. Shallow pool overrun with neighborhood kids. Singles and doubles 50,000 pesos.

Food

In Cancún, the epic battle between Mexican culture and tourism has turned into an epic slaughter by the forces of tourism. As a result, Cancún's food is overpriced and under-spiced. In the Zona Hotelera, "cheap" and "restaurant" are mutually exclusive. Head to Ciudad Cancún to dine inexpensively and buy picnic fixings for the beach.

In Ciudad Cancún, open-air **markets** proffer the least expensive chow. (For best selection, go between 9am and 2pm.)

Mercado 28, behind the post office and circumscribed by Av. Xel-Ha, is the largest food market. Numerous budget cafés are located in its western courtyard. Try the tasty, thin soups and meat sauces that come with thick wheat tortillas at **Restaurant Veracruz** (*comida corrida* 7500 pesos, choice of 5 entrees). A more hearty *comida corrida* can be had at **Restaurant Margely** for the same price. Two stalls away, **La Chaya** serves vegetarian meals, including tofu tacos, at comparable prices. All Mercado 28 cafés are open daily from 7am to 6pm.

If you want to avoid tourists altogether, walk or take a bus north on Tulum, where you'll find the smaller **Mercado 23** nestled between Tulum and Uxmal.

Throughout the city, taco shops, *abarrotes* (mini-supermarkets), and *panaderías* (bread stores) offer greater convenience and reasonable prices. For tacos, stick to **Avenida Cobá,** where three taco joints stand at attention: **El Tacolate, Tako's,** and **D'Leos.**

The CREA hostel has a diner upstairs, but the food is disappointing; most guests snack on supermarket fare. (Breakfast 5750 pesos, served daily 8-9:30am. Lunch and dinner 7000 pesos, served daily 2-3:30pm and 7:30-9pm, respectively.)

Except for Carlos 'n' Charlie's, all the restaurants listed below are in Ciudad Cancún.

Restaurant Los Delfines, Sun Yax Chén 44. Give your wallet a break and your stomach a treat in this plain indoor/outdoor café. Prints and posters reveal latent francophilia. Grilled beef and pork dishes 7000-10,000 pesos. Open daily 8am-6pm.

Cafe Super San Francisco, Tulum 18, in front of the namesake supermarket. Plain but air-conditioned, and great for a snack before shopping or going through the exchange ordeal at neighboring Bánamex. BLT 5000 pesos, soup of the day 4500 pesos. Open daily 8am-9pm.

El Rincón Yucateco, Uxmal 24. Authentic *típico* specialties dished up under a thatched porch that opens onto the street clamor. Simple burrito 6500 pesos, chicken 7500 pesos. Open daily 7am-10pm.

Mandarin House, Sun Yax Chén 52, across the street from the Hotel Coral. *Gringo* chef prepares tasty, Cantonese-style dishes. Elegant beige linen and dark wood chairs. A/C, but no fortune cookies. Cantonese chicken 11,500 pesos. Open Thurs.-Tues. 1-10:30pm.

100% Natural, Sun Yax Chén 6. Three veggie meals a day served on an airy, verdant porch with framed art on the wall. Nice 'n' clean. Burritos 8000 pesos, mouthwatering tropical shakes, 4500-6500 pesos.

Blackbeard's, Av. Tulum 107), at Av. Tulipanes. Gaudy but popular Tex-Mex restaurant where tequila shots are *de rigueur* (all drinks 7000 pesos). Restaurant converts to disco nightly at 9:30pm (free admission with meal or purchase of 1 drink). Exchange rate (customers only) better than at banks. Entrees from 15,000 pesos. Open daily 10am-1am.

Carlos 'n' Charlie's, across from the Casa Maya Hotel in the Zona Hotelera. Fun, loud, and expensive. "Members and Non-Members only" sign seems clever after a few drinks. Restaurant to the left and outdoor bar/disco to right (cover 10,000 pesos). Rowdy atmosphere a stronger draw than the food. Entrees 20,000-30,000 pesos. Open daily noon-midnight. Disco open from 9pm.

Sights

Cancún's powder-fine sand and shimmering blue waters delight even ultra-bronzed global beachtrotters. If you stay inland in Ciudad Cancún, you should still take advantage of the well-groomed beaches behind the luxury hotels in the Zona Hotelera. All beaches are public property, and you can often discreetly use hotel restrooms, fresh water showers, and lounge chairs. Deserted strips of shoreline south of the Sheraton Hotel are accessible by city bus (1000 pesos).

The beach at the **Sheraton Hotel** is one of the safest and the most pleasant. The sand is clean, the water transparent, and the waves active. Organized beach activities include volleyball, cake-eating contests, and beer races. Rent boogie boards at the shack 100m north of the lifeguard tower. (Boards US$5 per hr., US$10 per day. Open daily 10am-6pm.)

To avoid that unsightly tan line, head out to the nude beaches by Club Med. Remember that public bus lines don't extend that far, making hitching or a taxi the only options. For large waves, try **Playa Chac-Mool** in front of the Miramar Misión Hotel in the Zona Hotelera. **Playa Linda,** a 5-minute walk east from the CREA hostel, affords mellow swimming in calm water.

With more marinas than sand crabs, Cancún facilitates water-sport adventures. Snorkeling is the cheapest way to cavort with the multicolored denizens of the Caribbean. Two shallow reefs (*arrecifes*), accessible from the beach, invite skin diving.

El Camino Real, at Punta Cancún behind the Camino Real Hotel, is the smaller of the two. The rocky cove surrounding the reef serves as the hotel beach. (Snorkel rental in the hotel US$6 for 2 hr., US$10 per day. Open daily 9am-5pm; water is usually calmer in the early morning.) Distant **Club Med** has a bigger reef, and also rents snorkel gear. Full-day snorkel trips (US$25-30) to several offshore reefs are available through most dive shops and travel agents and include guide and lunch.

If you'd rather not get wet, board a **Nautilus** (tel. 332-16) from the San Marino dock next to the hotel of the same name. These passenger boats have glass viewing areas below the water line that allow you to sit and gape at exotic fish. Cruises (US$20 including drinks) last 1½ hours and leave every two hours from 10am to 4pm.

For those who desire a more up-close and personal look at the sea creatures, scuba opportunities are pervasive but expensive. The standard half-day two-reef tour includes guide and all equipment for US$48. Novice divers can take a two-hour resort course for US$12 to qualify for the trip. **Neptuno Dive Shop,** behind the Hotel Verano Beat near the CREA hostel, has a particularly helpful, qualified staff.

Boat rental establishments cater expressly to moneyed *norteamericanos*. You'll pay at least US$10, US$14, and US$25 per hour respectively for windsurfer, Sunfish, and Hobie Cat sailboat rentals. Parasailing costs US$20 for an eight- to 10-minute ride.

Other daytime distractions include shops and museums, although those in Cancún are quite bland compared to those elsewhere in Mexico. The shops are overpriced (it's better to buy in Mérida), but **Plaza Caracol** is a pleasant, air-conditioned modern mall with yet another Benetton. Other shopping centers within five minutes of Pl. Caracol include **El Parian, Mayfair Gallery,** and **Plaza Flamingo.** Cancún also has its very own Museo de Antropología, but damage from Hurricane Gilbert closed the museum "until further notice" late in 1988. Check for re-opening.

Cancún even has its own ruins. The Sheraton encompasses some small-scale ruins on the highest point in Cancún, affording shuriken-like views in all directions. Other ruins in the immediate vicinity include **El Rey,** between the Sheraton and Club Med. This site supposedly a regal burying ground, consists of a small pyramid and vestiges of Mayan painting. Large, hungry iguanas usually outnumber visitors at El Rey. (Open daily 8am-5pm. Admission 2000 pesos.) The **Pok-Ta-Pok** golf course (tel. 308-71) also contains a small, well-preserved archeological site near the 12th hole, which was discovered during sand-trap construction. (Open daily 6am-6pm.)

Entertainment

Cancún's most tangible advantage over nearby Isla Mujeres and Playa del Carmen is its steamy nightlife. Discos and restaurant/bars ooze partiers every night of the week. Restaurant workers in the Zona Hotelera are good at pointing out which spots are hot. If you feel like dressing up, head for one of the popular discos in the Zona Hotelera, which open nightly at 10pm and charge a US$10 cover. **Christine,** at the Hotel Krystal, draws lines of people into its maze of flashing lights, as does **La Boom,** a 10-minute walk east from the CREA hostel. **Aquarius,** at the Hotel Camino Real, cools dancers with blue geometric designs and lets ladies in *gratis* Tuesday night.

For cheaper, less formal nighttime diversion, try a disco bar. Next to its chic disco, **La Boom** has a raucous bar with an outdoor dance area. Tango on the tables with the mixed Mexican and American crowd. (Drinks 9000 pesos. Open daily 8pm-2am.) **Carlos 'n' Charlie's** (cover 7000 pesos) in the Hotel Zone and **Blackbeard's** (entrance free with 1 drink) downtown both switch from restaurant to dance club after sundown.

A more expensive entertainment option is the **Ballet Folklórico** (tel. 301-99) at the Convention Center in the middle of the Hotel Zone. (Performances Mon.-Sat. 7-10pm. Tickets US$37, including dinner, 1 drink, and the show.) The **Cine Blanquita,** Margaritas 32, shows Mexican and American movies nightly. **Cine Royal,** on Tulum, and **Cine Duplex,** on Xcaret, feature English-language films more frequently; check movie schedules printed in the Quintana Roo daily newspaper, *Nove-dades.* Most movie theaters are a short taxi ride from the intersection of Kukulkán and Tulum.

Bullfights are performed 'round the calendar, every Wednesday at 3:30pm, in the bullring next to the gas station on Paseo Kukulkán in Ciudad Cancún. Tickets (75,000 pesos) are available at large restaurants and travel agencies on Tulum.

Near Cancún

Chiquilá and Isla Holbox

Undiscovered on a tourist-trodden peninsula, Isla Holbox (pronounced ol-BOSH, meaning "dark well" in Mayan) remains literally uncharted and safely out of reach of Cancún's tour buses. Two thousand people live here, catching fish, cooking fish, and eating fish as they contentedly grow old. Schoolmates become life-long friends, and rarely do residents make the one-hour boat ride and two-hour drive to Tizimín, the nearest large city; news and B-movies from the outside world arrive primarily via satellite dishes that gather North American waves. Groups of tourists who drop by for two-hour visits to Holbox's quiet beaches are generally ignored. But the few who venture to find a room and spend some time on the island rarely leave without having made new friends.

Chiquilá is the unfortunate embarkation point for passengers ferrying to the secluded beaches of Isla Holbox. The small settlement will not menace in-transit tourists, but after the last ferry chugs out to sea, late arrivals usually prefer to head back to civilization for a meal and a bed because at dusk mosquitoes strike fear into even the locals' hearts. The only businesses in this *pueblito* are a general store beneath a thatched roof where the bus stops (open daily 7am-8pm), and a modest food store diagonally across the street. The manager of the general store grudgingly rents out buggy, bedless rooms with hammocks for 9000 pesos per person. He also supplies incense (mosquito repellent) on request. **Restaurant La Conchita,** on the left as you enter town, has the only seats to accompany food. Its breezy *palapa* overlooks a stumpy swamp. Mediocre entrees (6000 pesos) come with an endless supply of fresh tortillas. (Open daily 6am-8pm.)

Campers must usually choose between the mudflats and the town's concrete pier when settling down for the night. The pier's pebble-strewn expanse of oil-stained hardness is uncomfortable and even dangerous—the cars and buses that come to park here during the night may harm inconspicuous (or even very obvious) campers. Set up camp at the far end, near the edge of the pier. A slightly more appealing area faces the ocean from the pier; follow the dirt path through *palapas* and low brush to a dry, open space 100m or so from town. You are as safe sleeping here as anywhere else in the open, although you will be closer to the local dogs who sometimes terrorize strangers crossing their territory after sunset. The mangroves along the path are the best public toilet facilities.

Perhaps a better option for those who missed the last ferry to Isla Holbox is **Posada Leti** in the town of **Kantunil Kin,** 43km south of town on the Chiquilá access road. The managers of the *posada* may even show you how to make a household pet of one of the town's many *cigarras* (locusts). Unexcavated ruins surround Kantunil Kin; Sr. Olegario at the Escuela Gabina Barreda (available Mon.-Fri. 8am-noon) provides information and guided tours.

Transportation to and from Holbox must be planned in advance, as buses and boats are few and far between. Buses leave Tizimín for Chiquilá at 5:30am, 10am, and 5pm. From Valladolid they depart at noon and 2:30am (in order to arrive at dawn), stopping briefly at Ideal before turning north on the highway to Chiquilá. There are no direct buses from either Puerto Juárez or Cancún to Chiquilá. Ask the driver of a Valladolid-bound bus from Cancún (of which there are many; see Cancún listings) to let you off at Ideal on Rte. 180, next to the customs office. From here, catch one of the Chiquilá-bound buses from Valladolid. If you arrive at Ideal to find you have missed the bus, take a taxi to Kantunil Kin (10,000 pesos) and either catch Tizimín-Chiquilá bus or stay in Posada Leti (see Chiquilá listings above). From Chiquilá, buses leave for Tizimín at 6am, 1pm, and 3:15pm.

A ferry leaves Chiquilá for Isla Holbox punctually at 8am and 3pm. The 5:30am and 10am buses from Tizimín are the only ones that will get you to Chiquilá in time to catch the ferries for that day. Ferries return to Chiquilá from Holbox at 5am and 2pm. Regardless of which ferry you take, be at the pier at least 30 minutes before departure, because the captains sometimes leave before scheduled times. The one-hour ride costs 4000 pesos per person. Cars are neither necessary nor advisable on the island, and difficult to transport there in the first place. If you miss the boat and don't want to wait, launches will speed groups of up to five across the strait for a mere 80,000 pesos.

Ciudad Holbox occupies a small part of the elongated island's western side. The town's unpaved main street, Juárez, leads north from the pier and traverses the width of the island, passing by the Zócalo before ending on the beach. Beginning farther inland and to the west, Palomino parallels Juárez to form the other side of the Zócalo. Nearest the ocean side of the Zócalo, Igualdad runs east-west and, 1 block south, Díaz parallels it.

Holbox's **post office** (tel. 434-65) is on Díaz, between Palomino and Juárez (open Mon.-Fri. 8:30am-noon and 3-6pm). The **telegram office** on the second floor of the Palacio Municipal, on the Zócalo, will literally tap out your messages Monday through Friday from 9am to 1pm and 3 to 5pm. There is a public telephone *caseta* on Igualdad, ½ block west of the Zócalo (open Mon.-Sat. 8:30am-noon and 4-8pm). The one-man **police** force lazes in his office on the Zócalo at Díaz at Juárez (open daily 8am-8pm). The island's **Centro de Salud,** on the right side of Juárez in the blue building, is open 24 hr. for emergencies.

The main attraction of Holbox is not the town itself but rather the uninhabited coast enclosing the narrow island. There is plenty of space for the recluse to stretch and relax, or for the peace-seeking camper to brush aside a few thousand conch shells and pitch a tent. At this northernmost outpost of the Yucatán Peninsula, the waters of the Gulf of Mexico and the Caribbean mix; and though decomposing seaweed can leave the shallows silty and brackish, patches farther out to sea flash shades of steel-blue. You can wade or stroke out to the pure waters, as the sea is shallow enough for standing as far as 100m offshore. Isla Holbox's waterline is a wilderness, not a domesticated playground; flamingos and pelicans wet their ankles in the sea, sand billows along the beach, and when the wind drops (particularly in summer) the mosquitoes attack without mercy.

Exploring the overgrown, swampy interior can be a blast for the enthusiastic bushwhacker, but in the damp months, insects are even fiercer here than on the exposed beach. Aside from meandering walks along the beach, the best way to see Isla Holbox (and the only way to see its smaller neighbors) is by boat. The police station gives information about renting fishing boats, but this option is extremely expensive; arranging a tour with a local fisherman proves much more economically advantageous. Strike up a conversation with a fisherman, and see if you might ride along in his *lancha* on a daily outing (they leave 7-8am). Even better, strike up a longer conversation and maybe he'll offer you a special tour on the weekend or in his spare time. Then you'll have a chance to see the **Isla de Pájeros,** called Isla Morena by locals, where nearly forty species of birds feed and nest.

Non-campers can choose from among three types of lodging on Isla Holbox. The town has two official hotels. **Hotel Holbox,** immediately to the right off the pier, is far from the Zócalo and beach but perfect for taking the 5am ferry. The small, fresh rooms have private baths and ceiling fans. (Singles and doubles 20,000 pesos.) **Posada Amapola,** an unmarked pink house on the east side of the Zócalo, rents spotless, green-and-white rooms with good beds, window screens, private bathrooms, and ceiling fans. (Singles 15,000 pesos. Doubles 30,000 pesos.) There are also several people in Holbox who rent out extra rooms or hammock hooks. **Don Joaquín Avila,** who lives in a white house on Igualdad near Palomino, rents hammock hooks and communal baths for 10,000 pesos per person. Ask nicely, kids, and he might lend you a hammock. And don't forget to say thanks. **Donña Caridad Argueyas,** owner of a green-and-white house on Igualdad facing the basketball courts, has two simple cement rooms with hammocks and a primitive toilet for 5000 pesos per person.

The best area for camping is the oceanside of Holbox, on the long expanse of deserted beach extending east of town. If you begin to feel at home in Holbox and would like to stay longer, there are several family-size *palapa* huts for rent along the beach. Tirzo Juan "Chico" Cáceres Correa has a *palapa* near the Hotel Holbox with living room, two bedrooms, kitchen, bath, and laundry facilities which he rents out for 30,000 pesos per night, making the spot ideal for a long-term or group vacation.

If you are dining on a budget, the buy-before-you-fry principle applies to Holbox's beaches. The town bakery, fruit store, and tiny **Tienda Dinorah** off the Zócalo are far more expensive than their mainland counterparts. Stock up in Kantunil Kin en route to Chiquilá.

For the catch of the day, try **Restaurant Luis Ocho,** in an unmarked but often crowded *palapa* off Juárez, about 100m before the Zócalo. The staff cooks fulfilling portions of fresh fish to order. Try the *pescado al mojo de ajo* (fish in garlic sauce; 10,000 pesos). (Open daily 9am-10pm.) Two doors down on Juárez, **Restaurant El Campanario de San Telmo,** the clearly marked and garishly decorated *palapa,* serves a 3500-peso *comida corrida,* as well as reasonably priced fish, tacos, tostadas, and *salbutes.* (Open daily 9am-11pm.) Neither restaurant serves alcohol, so procure beer for your meal at the liquor store next door. **Lonchería El Parque,** off the Zócalo two doors down from Tienda Dinorah, serves decent fried fish and a wide range of snacks (tamales 2000 pesos, ham and eggs 4000 pesos). (Open daily 8am-11pm.)

On the weekends, Holbox's younger crowd amuses itself at **Cariocas Restaurant and Disco,** on Igualdad 2 blocks east of the Zócalo. Rock, *salsa,* and lambada shake the covers on the colored lights. (Cover 5000 pesos. Beer 1500 pesos. Open Sat.-Sun. only.)

The city's **baseball field** hosts visiting teams from the mainland every other Sunday. Local players are still looking for a good pitcher to duel with former L.A. Dodger Steve Howe, who throws for one of the two Cancún teams. Any strong-armed hurler could become the next local legend.

Isla Mujeres

Dozing in the Caribbean Sea a short boatride away from Cancún's northern port is a small strip of land which, although composed of the same substance as Cancún, is nothing like its southern neighbor. Isla Mujeres is blessed with powdery sand, crystalline waters, and colorful aquatic reef-dwellers, but even though thousands of tourists arrive daily to enjoy these attractions, "La Isla" somehow retains its fishing-village aura. Seafood-laden bicycles bump down cobbled streets, young men play basketball in the Zócalo, and town *fiestas* call people to dance in the streets every month.

Three stories circulate to explain the island's name, "Island of Women." The first claims that Francisco Hernandez de Cordova, sailing from Cuba in 1517, named the island for its many paintings and statues of Ixchel, the Mayan fertility goddess. Another says that when the conquistadors arrived, the men of the island were on a long fishing expedition, leaving their womenfolk behind. A third myth supposes that during the 17th century, pirate bands regularly left their women on the island while they roamed the Caribbean. But it could be that the island is a token enclave of feminist empowerment in an otherwise tenaciously patriarchal hemisphere.

Despite new condominiums, a first-class hotel, and upscale residences, Isla Mujeres remains a budget traveler's paradise, with a sizable fan club whose members originally intended only short visits, but often stay mesmerized for months or return like clockwork, year after year.

Orientation

The island lies 11km northeast of the northern coast of Quintana Roo. Passenger ferries (9 per day, 1 hr., 4500 pesos; fare collected on the boat) depart from Puerto Juárez, 2km north of Ciudad Cancún, the mainland section of the Cancún resort. Puerto Juárez is a 10- to 15-minute ride from Ciudad Cancún on any bus labeled "Puerto Juárez" (1000 pesos), which can be picked up along Av. Tulum. The bus lets you off at the dock; the modern building to your left subsumes the amiable tourist office. Taxis from Ciudad Cancún to Puerto Juárez cost 5000 pesos. A car ferry (4000 pesos per person, 18,000 pesos per car) runs to Mujeres from Punta Sam, 5km north of Puerto Juárez. As bus service from Juárez to Sam is infrequent, this ferry is inconvenient for travelers to Mujeres.

Isla Mujeres is only 8km long and 4km wide, making it possible to get to know a large part of it on foot, bike, or moped. The small town on the northern tip of the island, where the ferries dock, spans a mere 7 blocks in one direction and 4 blocks in the other. The bayside **Avenida Rueda Medina,** runs parallel to **Avenida Hidalgo,** the main drag two blocks north. Both are greater centers of activity than the Zócalo (on the east side of the village), and run the length of the town from Playa Los Cocos in the northwest to the marine base in the southeast. Streets were paved only recently, and most traffic is still limited to either two feet or two wheels. That most streets are unmarked makes navigation challenging. Rough maps and general information are provided by the two local publications, *Islander* and *Isla Mujeres Today,* available in many shops and restaurants. Points of interest outside town can also be reached by bike or on foot.¢The island's major highway leads to the pirate Mundaca's *hacienda* near the island's center, Garrafón National Park on the leeward shore, and Playa Lancheros on the southwest coast. Taxis shuttle the length of Mujeres: you should have no problem catching one unless you are returning from Garrafón at the end of the day. Buses run irregularly from town to the *colonias* on the road to Garrafón but don't go far enough to be of much value to tourists.

Practical Information

Tourist Office: Guerrero 8 (tel. 201-73), by the Zócalo's basketball court. Casual help with specific questions and a useful list of hotels. A crude map of the town is free when available, but the best maps are handed out by the tourist office in Cancún. Some English spoken. Officially open Mon.-Fri. 9am-2pm and 6-8pm, but don't bet the house on it.

Currency Exchange: Banco del Atlántico, Juárez 5 (tel. 201-04). **Banco Serfín,** Juárez 3 (tel. 200-51). Both open Mon.-Fri. 9am-1:30pm; for exchange Mon.-Fri. 10:30am-noon.

Post Office: Guerrero and López Mateos (tel. 200-85), at the northwest corner of town, around the corner from the Poc-Na hostel. Open Mon.-Fri. 8am-8pm, Sat. 9am-noon. **Postal Code:** 77400.

Telephones: Long-distance *caseta* in the lobby of **Hotel María Jose** (tel. 202-44), on Madero just off Rueda Medina. International collect calls 5000-8000 pesos. Open Mon.-Sat. 9am-1pm and 4-8pm. **Telephone Code:** 988.

Telegrams: Guerrero 13 (tel. 201-13), next to the post office. Open Mon.-Fri. 9am-3pm, Sat.-Sun. 9am-noon.

Taxis: Tel. 200-66. Lines form near the docks and at the sights and beaches. Check the list of established rates, posted on the right-hand wall as you come off the dock.

Moped Rental: Shop around; prices vary. All rentals should come with a full tank of gas. Be careful, because the sandy roads in town slippery. The best deal is at **Moto Rent Ciro's** (tel. 203-51), on Guerrero between López Mateos and Matamoros, near the market. Brandnew mopeds go for 20,000 pesos per 2 hr., 40,000 pesos per day; 50,000-peso deposit required. Open daily 8am-5pm.

Bike Rental: Caribbean Tropic, on Juárez near Morelos. Bikes 12,000 pesos for 4 hr., 15,000 pesos for 8 hr.; 30,000-peso deposit required. Open daily 8am-6pm.

Laundromat: Lavandería San Jorge, Juárez 29-A (tel. 201-55), near López Mateos. From the boat dock, walk straight 1 block and then left 4 blocks. 5000 pesos per kg. Open daily 6am-5pm.

Supermarket: Super Betino, Morelos 3, on the Zócalo. Wide selection of dry goods at non-resort prices, and a small pharmacy. Open daily 7am-10pm.

Pharmacy: Farmacia Lily, Hidalgo at Madero, 2 blocks straight off the dock. Open Mon.-Sat. 8am-1pm and 4-9:30pm, Sun 8am-1pm.

Health Care: Centro de Salud, Guerrero at Morelos (tel. 201-17), at the northwest corner of the Zócalo, in a light-blue building. Open 24 hr. In such emergencies as ingestion of green plastic shards, go to **Clínica IMSS** (tel. 200-91), on Carlos Lazo.

Doctor: Sr. Antonio Torres García, Hidalgo at Abasolo (tel. 203-83). English spoken. Open 24 hr.

Police: Hidalgo at Morelos (tel. 200-82), off the Zócalo. Choppy English spoken. Open 24 hr.

Accommodations and Camping

Budget accommodations on Isla Mujeres dent your budget more than in most of mainland Mexico, but they're similarly comfortable and consistently clean. Virtually every hotel raises their rates 20% from December through January: the sole exception is the Poc-Na hostel, a sociable but minimalist option. Camping on the island is legal only at Coco Beach; police search out and destroy campers elsewhere.

Poc-Na Youth Hostel, Matamoros 15 (tel. 200-53), near Carlos Lazo. Popular white-stucco hostel with friendly resident monkey and a busy social *palapa.* Rooms are bare and musty, with a few assorted roaches and mosquitoes. Bunk beds are not segregated by sex. Towel, sheet, and lock rental 2000 pesos per item, plus deposit. Bunk rental with mattress and blanket costs 11,000 pesos (plus passport or 20,000-peso deposit).

Hotel Caracol, Matamoros 5 (tel. 201-50). Spacious, well-furnished rooms in a potent shade of green. Even the bathrooms are comfortable here. Used English paperbacks, including this very book, are lent out for beach perusal. Singles and doubles 35,000 pesos, but only 30,000 pesos if multiple nights are paid for ahead of time.

Hotel Las Palmas, on Guerrero across from the post office. Walk 3 blocks straight off the dock and then 4 blocks left. Clean, airy, well-lit rooms cooled by powerful fans. Prime location near the beach. Doubles 30,000 pesos. Triples 45,000 pesos.

Hotel Rocamar, Guerrero at Bravo (tel. 201-01), straight back from the dock. Shells decorate the curtains, hang over the headboards, and infiltrate the sink tiles of the beautiful bathrooms. Cozy rooms have a view of the ocean. Singles 35,000 pesos. Doubles 50,000 pesos.

Hotel María José (tel. 201-30), on Madero just off Rueda Medina. From the dock, walk 1 block left and turn right. Clean, older rooms include tacky maroon curtains and bedspreads. Noisy. Doubles 30,000 pesos. Triples 40,000 pesos.

Hotel Martínez, Madero 14 (tel. 201-54), just down the street from Hotel María José. Simple, exceptionally clean rooms; those on the 3rd floor afford a fine bay view. Singles and doubles 40,000 pesos. Triples 50,000 pesos. Prices swell more than most during tourist season.

Hotel Caribe Maya, Madero 9 (tel. 201-90), between Hidalgo and Guerrero. From the dock, walk 1 block left and 2½ blocks right. A fancy hotel wanna-be: the low prices and dull decor reveals its true identity. Green-and-pink rooms are fairly clean and comfortable. Singles 26,000 pesos. Doubles 30,000 pesos. Triples 40,000 pesos.

Autel Carmelina, Guerrero 9 (tel. 200-06), at Madero. From the dock, walk 3 blocks straight and 1 block left. The façade crumbles before your eyes, but rooms in the wing to the right are new and immaculate. Patterned bedspreads decorate the other plain cement-box rooms. Powerful fans and *agua purificada* in the lobby. Prices negotiable during low season. Singles 30,000 pesos. Doubles 40,000 pesos.

Food

The fact that many restaurants on Isla Mujeres reveal a dash of international chic hasn't completely overpowered the *típico* Mexican atmosphere or the low prices. In addition to the ubiquitous *pescado* (fish) and *camarones* (shrimp), such exotic delicacies as *caracol* (conch) and *pulpo* (octopus) tempt you from every corner. *Ceviche,* Mexico's famous salad appetizer, made from seafood marinated in lime juice, coriander, and other herbs, is at its best on Mujeres.

Five minutes from the beach, four home-style *loncherías* serve three especially inexpensive meals and two types of snacks at the one market, on Guerrero between Matamoros and López Mateos, just around the corner from the post office. Rainbow-colored menus are painted on the walls of the cafés. At first, the regulars may raise their eyebrows at *extranjeros,* but the atmosphere soon grows open and friendly. **Lonchería Carolina** serves a *comida corrida* for 8000 pesos. (All four *loncherías* open daily 6am-6pm.) When Isla Mujeres's one official bakery, **La Reina,** closes up shop on Sunday, **Porky's** restaurant, at Juarez 5, sells fresh rolls and sweet bread from 5:30pm until they run out.

Cafe Cito, on Guerrero near Carlos Lazo, ½ block from the Poc-Na hostel. An aquamarine-colored gem. Amazing waffles, Kahlua sundaes, and crepes with homemade marmalade (4000-9000 pesos). Popular among *den Deutschen.* Open Tues.-Sun. 9am-noon and 6-11pm.

Restaurante La Peña, on Guerrero, along the Zócalo. An old favorite among the salty vacationers. Pink tablecloths flutter over the sea. Smorgasbord menu features 30 seafood dishes (lobster 22,000-35,000 pesos) as well as pizza and Chinese food. Happy hour times seven (3-10pm) makes for a joyous afternoon. Basic breakfast combos 5000-10,000 pesos. Open daily 7am-midnight.

Chen Huaye, on Hidalgo near Matamoros. Six-table *antojitos* joint a-teeming with locals in the late evening, when tourists are abed. Good *salbutes, burritos,* and *quesadillas,* all for pocket change (1000-4000 pesos). Open daily noon-3pm and 6pm-midnight.

Restaurante Bucanero, Hidalgo 11, between Abasolo and Madero. Exclusively foreign-born crowd lounges on a breezy outdoor patio. Specialties include seafood soup with lobster (12,500 pesos) and enchiladas (8900 pesos). Open daily 11am-11pm.

Restaurant Miramar, Rueda Medina, just left of the dock as you land. Great ocean view compensates for cafeteria decor. Small portions of slightly tough seafood at good prices. Shrimp or *caracol* in butter sauce 12,000 pesos. Open daily 6:30am-9:30pm.

Restaurante Tropicana, Rueda Medina at Nicolas Bravo, to the right of the dock as you face town. No-frills joint often packed with local Mexican families, especially on Sunday. Healthy portions of fried fish or breaded fish 9500 pesos, and beef or pork 11,000 pesos. Open daily 7am-10pm.

El Sombrero del Gomar, Hidalgo at Madero, smack-dab in the center of town. Waiters' flowered shirts clash with the 50 stuffed parrots suspended from the ceiling. Tasty food and drink at tourist prices. Soups 10,000 pesos. Chicken 12,000 pesos. Whopper of a lobster for 50,000 pesos. Open daily 7am-11pm.

Sights and Entertainment

The crystal-clear *agua* lapping at Mujeres's beaches inspired the island's Mayan name, Zacil-Ha ("Sparkling Water"). At **Garrafón National Park,** you can float around in the champagne waters and admire the rainbow schools at point-blank range as thousands of tropical fish rub noses with your snorkel and mask. (Rental in the park; mask, snorkel, and fin sets 10,000 pesos per day, plus a 40,000-peso, passport, or credit card deposit.) Choppy waters and moderate currents detract from Garrafón's snorkeling potential; some say Cozumel offers a better view for both beginners and more serious snorkelers. To reach deeper waters, follow the narrow channel between the coral reefs; the area to the left is most impressive. Be careful, though: brushing against the sharp reefs, which appear dark in the turquoise water, might leave you lacking some skin.

There are lockers (2000 pesos) and free showers at the park. Getting here early, before the schools of two-leggeds arrive from Cancún, is imperative. After your swim, visit the park's miniscule aquarium. (Park open daily 8am-7pm. Admission 5000 pesos.) Garrafón is accessible by bike, moped, or taxi (5000 pesos from the dock) or a tortuous two-hour walk along the leeward coast to the southern tip of the island.

The most popular activity on the Isla, especially on weekends, is suntanning at Coco Beach. Warm azure waters, sand as soft as flour, and a shady palm grove make this the best spot for swimming, people-watching, or gazing at a sunset. Topless bathing is permitted here, although usually practiced only a good distance past the *palapa* restaurants. To get to Coco Beach, follow Guerrero, Carlos Lazo, or Hidalgo away from the Zócalo to their northern end.

Take a time out at the **Hacienda de Fermín Mundaca de Marechaja**. In the mid-19th century, Mundaca, a wealthy pirate and slave trader, built these gardens, archways, and bungalows to woo Prisca Gómez, a Spaniard who vacationed on the island. The more he built, the less interested she became; she eventually married another Isla gentleman. Mundaca went insane, but not before carving his own gravestone (today in the Isla Mujeres cemetery) which reads, "As you are, I was. As I am, you will be." To see the pirate's monument to his unrequited love, follow the coastal road south past the *colonias* on the outskirts of town. Just after you see two signs warning of dangerous curves ahead, the road turns sharply to the right; continue straight for roughly 100m. When the small dirt road splits, take the right fork up the hill to the top (no more than 20m) and the complex sits on the right. You can stroll through the open grounds whenever there is enough sunlight to guide you.

Playa Lancheros, the beach near Mundaca's fort, is notorious for the *tortugas* (sea turtles) and *tiburones* (sharks) that are confined to a filthy underwater cage next to the *balneario* (swimming area). If they're alive at all, the turtles are now barely the shells of what they were in the wild, and the sharks move only to force oxygen into their system. The locals have no fear of swimming in the cage; in fact, the only time the turtles wake up is when someone climbs on their backs. On Sunday afternoons in summer, Playa Lancheros hosts beach parties complete with bands, cold sodas, and grilled fish. The music is free and fun; the fish (10,000 pesos) is less attractive but acceptable.

Across the Laguna de Makax from the populated tip of Isla Mujeres is **PESCA,** a biological research station where scientists study the conservation of marine species. Although the site is not officialy open to the public, you can ask permission to see the plethora of preserved tropical fish. The best time to visit is between 9am and 2pm.

Snorkel gear rentals are fairly cheap in town. **Buzos de México,** Rueda Medina at Madero (tel. 201-31), just to the left of the ferry dock, rents masks, snorkels, and fins for 10,000 pesos per day. They can point you toward alternative snorkeling sites should you want to avoid the tame Garrafón. (Open daily 7am-6pm.)

For scuba fans, Isla Mujeres is a dreamy playground with an infinite number of nooks, crannies, inlets, and reefs to explore. The staff at the dive shops will lend you their expertise with directions to their favorite spots. You'll need a scuba license (and mounds of money) to rent gear. Buzos de México leads scuba trips to Sleeping Shark Cave and several reefs for US$45. **Bahía Dive Shop** (tel. 203-40) on Av. Rueda Medina just off the dock, offers scuba trips that include guide and regulator for US$45. (Open daily 8am-7pm.) Buzos de México runs daily trips (8:30am-4pm) to nearby **Isla Contoy** for US$30; the fee includes snorkeling equipment, lunch, drink, and a chance to spot some of the island's 5000 species of birds.

A Mayan ruin decays on the southern tip of the island, a stone's throw past Garrafón. Francisco Hernández de Córdoba spotted it in 1519 when a storm blew him in from Cuba. Before the eastern and southern walls collapsed into the waves, this temple to Ixchel, the goddess of fertility, had slits facing the cardinal directions for astronomical observations. Small figurines of deformed women that once inundated the temple have long since been stolen or destroyed, and the ruined remains were almost totally wiped out by Hurricane Gilbert in 1988. But the setting is beautiful, especially if you ask permission to climb the lighthouse to view the afternoon sun glistening on the sea. Be careful clambering down the slippery rocks to the shore. To reach the ruins, follow the road until you can see the lighthouse, then walk along the track to the right. As you return from the ruins, Garrafón, Mundaca's fort, and Playa Lancheros are all to the left.

At nightfall, snub the aggressively friendly and overpriced **Bronco's.** Head instead to Coco Beach's popular **Bad Bones Cafe,** next to the North Lighthouse, and jam out in a cave-like cement building (open daily 6-11:30pm). If you want to party on the beach, shimmy to **Buho's,** a restaurant/bar/disco, or **Calypso Bar,** a favorite among local fishermen (beer 3000 pesos, mixed drinks 5000 pesos). For video distraction and the Isla youth scene, amble over to **Video Bar Tequila,** at the corner of Matamoros and Hidalgo. (Beer and soda 4000 pesos. Mixed drinks 6000 pesos. Open Tues.-Sun. 9pm-3am.)

Restaurant Video Bar Disco Casa Blanca (the entrance is on Bravo between Juárez and Hidalgo) provides a wild slew of entertainment choices. Your best bet is the 2-for-1 (plus free snacks) Happy Hour (Mon.-Fri. noon-5pm and 9-11pm). Isla Mujeres's only cinema, **Cine Blanquira** (next to the supermarket on the Zócalo), frequently projects movies in English with Spanish subtitles. Seating for shows (2000 pesos) occurs at 7pm and 9pm in rows of uncomfortable orange plastic seats.

The cheapest and liveliest entertainment is in the **Zócalo.** Virtually every night, townspeople flood the plaza to stroll, play tag, and chat about the day's catch. Volleyball and basketball games sponsored by local businesses start at 8pm. If you happen to be in Isla Mujeres at the right time, you may can add your two cents to one of the many *fiestas* that explode in the Zócalo for days on end; some of the excuses to party include Mardi Gras in February, the yacht regattas in April and May, the birth of the Ziggley deity in August, the international festival of music in October, and the honoring of the town saint in November and December.

Isla Cozumel

Before the Spaniards overran the island, Cuzamil, the "place of the swallows," was a sacred Mayan ceremonial site. Pilgrims often braved the stormy straits in canoes to worship at the shrine of Ixchel, goddess of the Moon and of Love, or at one of more than 40 carvings of swallow deities. Spanish explorer Juan de Grijalva chanced upon the island in 1518, and a year later Cortés stopped here before proceeding to conquer the Aztecs.

The first mass in Mesoamerica was celebrated here by Grijalva, but neither Cortés nor the Montejos could successfully wrest the coveted island from the *indígenas* until 1545; eventually, conquistador brutality and diseases annihilated the native population. As the Spanish colony on the Yucatán grew, Cozumel became a hideaway for such pirates as Francis Drake and Jean Lafitte. Mayan refugees from the Caste War began arriving in the late 19th century.

Attributing strategic importance to the island, the U.S. Air Force built a base here during World War II, and in so doing demolished almost all of what remained of the ancient Mayan city now called San Miguel. In the 1950s, Jacques Cousteau's exploration of Palancar Reef drew international attention to Cozumel's marine life, and the military airfield became the welcome mat for a wave of civilian invaders.

Today, direct flights from the U.S. and Mexico land daily, ships cruise into port from around the world, and boatloads of passengers stumble in from nearby Playa del Carmen and Puerto Morelos. *Norteamericano* tourists are probably outnumbered on the island only by "I love Cozumel" T-shirts, and nearly every island shop and restaurant lists prices in U.S. dollars. The reason for the island's popularity is simple: Cozumel is surrounded by liquid emerald and some of the most beautiful reefs anywhere.

Orientation

The island of Cozumel lies 18km east of the northern Quintana Roo coast, and 85km south of Isla Mujeres. Main access is via ferry from Playa del Carmen to the west or from Puerto Morelos to the north. Ferries from Puerto Morelos transport cars (but only non-rentals) to Cozumel twice in the morning and return twice in the afternoon, docking in the island's only town, San Miguel de Cozumel (nick-named "Cozumel"), in the middle of its mainland side.

Two ferry companies shuttle passengers between Playa del Carmen and Cozumel. The new **Waterjet Mexico** and its sister boat **Mexico II,** equipped with bucket seats, air conditioning, and rock videos, zip across the waterway in 25 minutes. The older, open-air, Madonna-less passenger ferries take almost an hour to complete the same trip. The **Cozumeleño** costs as much as the Waterjet, but the smaller **Xel-Ita** is roughly half the price. If you are prone to seasickness, the Waterjet is the only way to go. You can enjoy a spectacular view of the sunset aboard the 6:30pm ferry to Playa del Carmen.

An alternative to the ferry is the air shuttle operated by **Aerocozumel** (tel. 209-28) from both Playa del Carmen and Cancún, but the small planes and may prove even harder on the stomach than the aged ferry. Numerous international carriers serve Cozumel, including Mexicana, American, and Continental.

At 55km long and 15km wide, Cozumel is Mexico's largest Caribbean island. Although public transportation is virtually nonexistent, downtown streets are clearly labeled and numbered with Vulcan logic. The rest of the island is easily ex-plored by bike or moped.

As you step off the ferry into Cozumel, the dock becomes **Avenida Juárez,** which cuts east-west through town. *Calles* running parallel to Juárez are given an even number if they are north of Juárez and an odd number if they are south of it; num-bers increase in both directions moving away from Juárez. Additionally, *calles* are redundantly labeled "Sur" when they are south of Juárez and "Norte" when north of it. *Avenidas* run north-south, are numbered in multiples of five, and are designated "Norte" if north of Juárez or "Sur" if south. Juárez becomes the Carretera Trans-versal at the eastern edge of town, extending across the island's midsection to the other shore. The road to the airport forms the city's northern boundary. **Avenida Rafael Melgar** runs along the western edge of town next to the sea and leads to the luxury hotels north of town and the uninhabited northern coast. The national park at Laguna Chankanaab and the popular beach at San Francisco are south of town on the western shore; off the island's southern tip lie the Palancar Reefs. The nearly deserted eastern coast dotted by Mayan ruins supports only a few restau-rants.

Practical Information

Tourist Office: On the 2nd floor of the building to the left of Bancomer (tel. 209-72), on the Pl. del Sol. Advice on hotels, services, and transportation, but only sketchy maps. Some Eng-lish spoken. Open Mon.-Fri. 9am-3pm and 6-8pm.

Currency Exchange: Ban País (tel. 203-18), right off the dock. Charges 1% commission on traveler's checks. Open Mon.-Fri. 9am-1:30pm. **Bancomer** (tel. 205-50) and **Banco Atlántico** (tel. 201-42), near the main plaza. Bancomer extracts a smaller commission for traveler's checks. Open for exchange Mon.-Fri. 10am-12:30pm.

Post Office: (tel. 201-56) off Rafael Melgar along the sea (tel. 201-06), just south of Calle 7 Sur. Open Mon.-Fri. 8am-7pm. **Postal Code:** 77600.

Telephones: Caseta Misha (tel. 208-80) Av. 5 Nte., 1 block north of the plaza. International collect calls 11,000 pesos. Open daily 9am-9pm.

Telegrams: At the post office (tel. 200-56). Open Mon.-Fri. 9am-8pm, Sat. 9am-4pm.

Airport: (tel. 204-85) 2km north of town. Take a taxi. **Aerocozumel** (tel. 205-03) to Cancún (every 2 hr. 8am-6pm, 89,000 pesos) and Playa del Carmen (at 9am, 11am, 3pm, and 5pm, 26,000 pesos). Aeroméxico (tel. 202-51) to Mérida (at 4:10pm, 155,000 pesos). Also served by **Mexicana** (tel. 201-57), **American** (tel. 208-99), and **Continental** (tel. 208-47).

Ferries: Depart from the dock at the end of Av. Juárez. Arrive ½ hr. early to secure a ticket. **Waterjet Mexico** and **Mexico II** cruise to Playa del Carmen (10 per day 4am-6:30pm, 25 min., 11,500 pesos). **Cozumeleño** steams to Playa del Carmen (5 per day 6:30am-6:30pm, 1 hr., 11,500 pesos), while **Xel-Ha** chugs to Playa del Carmen (4 per day 4am-8pm, 50 min., 6000 pesos).

Taxis: (tel. 202-36) wander the streets near the docks. Ask to see the list of authorized fares. All fares (except to the airport) cover up to 5 people.

Car Rental: Avis, at the Hotel Presidente (tel. 202-19) and at the airport (tel. 200-99). VW sedan US$52 per day, with unlimited mileage. **National,** Rafael Melgar at Av. 11 (tel. 215-15) and at the airport (tel. 212-12), has similar rates.

Bike Rental: Best deals are at **Rentadora Cozumel** (tel. 211-20), on Av. 10 near Salas. Bikes 10,000 pesos for 24 hr.; credit-card or US$50 deposit required. Open daily 8am-8pm.

Moped Rental: At nearly every corner and in nearly every hotel. Shop around. All mopeds should come with a full tank of gas. **Rentadora Cozumel** charges 70,000 pesos for 24 hr. on a deluxe moped, insurance and tax included; credit-card or 100,000-peso deposit required. Get cheaper, older models at **Erik Motos,** a table in front of the Costa Brava Hotel, Rafael Melgar 601 (tel. 214-53). US $22 per day, plus credit card or US $50 deposit required.

Laundromat: Margarita Av. 20 #285, near Calle 3 Sur. 4000 pesos per self-service wash, 4500 pesos per 20-min. dry. Open Mon.-Sat. 8am-10pm.

Red Cross: Adolfo Salas at Av. 20 Sur (tel. 210-58). Some English spoken. 24-hr. emergency service.

Pharmacy: Farmacia Kiosco (tel. 224-85), on the Zócalo near Hotel López. Open daily 8am-10pm.

Health Care: There are several English-speaking private physicians in Cozumel. For consultations, go to Adolfo Salas 260 (tel. 209-49; 24-hr. emergency tel. 209-12). Open daily 10am-noon and 6-8pm. Otherwise, go to Av. 10 Nte. at Calle 6 Nte. (tel. 203-95; 24-hr. emergency tel. 211-01). For aquatic medical concerns, call **Servicios de Seguridad Sub-acuatica,** Calle 5 Sur at Rafael Melgar (tel. 223-87).

Police: Calle 11 Sur at Av. 5 Sur (tel. 200-92). Open 24 hr.

Accommodations and Camping

Budget rooms in Cozumel are considerably more cheery and cost 5000-10,000 pesos more than those in Playa del Carmen, but because the ferry compounds costs, it makes sense to sleep in Cozumel if you plan on spending more than one day on the island. Hunt down a room before noon, because the few inexpensive lodgings on the island fill quickly.

Campers should register at the naval base on Rafael Melgar, past Calle 7 Sur. (Open 24 hr.) Ask for a free *permiso de acampar.* The police patrols may fine you and send you scurrying to the base to get a permit if they catch you without one. Secluded but safe camping spots in Cozumel are at **Punta Morena** and **Punta Chiqueros,** on the island's Caribbean coast.

Hotel Flamingo, Calle 6 81 Nte. (tel. 212-64), 1 block inland. The best budget hotel in Cozumel offers huge rooms with bright bedspreads, fans, and sparkling bathrooms. Friendly, English-speaking management. Singles 32,000 pesos. Doubles 46,000 pesos.

Hotel Yoly (tel. 200-24), on Calle 1 Sur, 1 block from the beach. Turquoise rooms are small and austere but still pleasant. Fills up as quickly as leaf-clogged gutters in an Oregon rainstorm. Singles and doubles 30,000 pesos.

Hotel López (tel. 201-08), on the south side of the plaza. Good location and cheerful management lessen the sting of the high rates. Chillin' A/C and uncommonly luxurious bathrooms don't hurt, either. Genial bargaining particularly effective in low season. Room #20—a cozy nook on the roof with fan, bath, and view—is the best buy in town (30,000 pesos for 1 person). Singles 40,000 pesos. Doubles with A/C 60,000 pesos.

Hotel Saolima, Adolfo Salas 268 (tel. 208-86), between Av. 10 Sur and 15 Sur. Clean rooms off a plant-filled hall in a slightly dirty but quiet part of town. Friendly manager and son rent bicycles. Singles 30,000 pesos. Doubles 35,000 pesos.

Hotel Flores, Adolfo Salas 72 (tel. 214-29), at Av. 5 Sur. Huge, musty, cement bedrooms with closets and clean bathrooms. Noisy location. Singles and doubles 40,000 pesos.

Hotel Posada Edén, Calle 2 Nte. 4 (tel. 211-66), next to Restaurante Edén. Jovial owner in "My parents went to Cozumel and all I got was this lousy T-shirt" T-shirt speaks some English and rents out rooms whose main decoration is the set of beds. Fans circulate vaguely smoky air. Cold *agua purificada* available. Singles 35,000 pesos. Doubles 40,000 pesos. Triples 50,000 pesos.

Costa Brava, Rafael Melgar 601 (tel. 214-53), across from the naval base. Modern rooms set back from the highway. Three windows allow wonderful cross-ventilation. Cushy sofas in the lobby. Singles and doubles US$20.

Hotel Pirata (tel. 200-51), on Av. 5 Sur just off the plaza. Great location. Bland beige rooms have excellent showers. Laundry service available. Singles and doubles with fan 50,000 pesos, with A/C 60,000 pesos.

Food

Food on Cozumel is expensive, especially when proffered close to the beach or the plaza. Fortunately, there are several moderately priced restaurants a few blocks from the center, as well as small *típico* cafés hiding on side streets. The market, on Adolfo Salas between Av. 20 Sur and 25 Sur, sells the standard meats, fish, and fruits. The five small restaurants outside the market do minimal damage to your wallet in exchange for regional dishes. Each sells a *comida corrida* for only 7000 pesos. (Restaurant complex open daily 6:30am-6:30pm).

Cocina Económica Mi Chabelita, on Av. 10 Sur near Adolfo Salas. Great budget dining in a bright yellow garage, but no Love Bugs in sight. Large fruit salad 4000 pesos. Fried chicken 11,000 pesos. Try the fried bananas (3000 pesos). Open daily 7am-7pm.

Restaurante Costa Brava, Rafael Melgar, south of Calle 7 Sur, across from the naval base. Looks and smells like a tourist spot, but the prices are low. Excellent service. Unbeatable hot breakfast includes eggs, coffee, and juice for 4000 pesos. *Ceviche* 15,000 pesos. Cheapest lobster in Cozumel (39,000 pesos). Open daily 6:30am-11pm.

El Abuelo Gerardo, on Av. 10 between Juárez and Calle 2 Nte. Soothing music and wooden tables transform this garage into a pleasant dining experience. Grandpa Gerard dishes up fish filets of every type (10,000 pesos). Open daily 11am-11pm.

Restaurant El Foco, Av. 5 Sur 13, a few blocks from the plaza. Chic bar-like hangout. Decode the graffiti while waiting for your food. Their hearty main meal (2 tortillas with cheese, beef, sausage, and onions) goes for 12,000 pesos. Open daily 5pm-1am.

La Choza, Rosado Salas 198, near Av. 10. "Typical Mexican cuisine" at resort prices. The outrageously friendly service (hostess, waiters, and cooks play drinking games with the customers) and the 3-sauce nachos make up for the expense. *Comida corrida* 15,000 pesos. Open daily 11am-1am.

The Corner Store and Fruit Bar, Adolfo Salas at Av. 5 Sur. A produce shop with healthy munchies sold at the counter. Yogurt with fruit, granola, and honey 5000 pesos; ham and cheese sandwich 5000 pesos; fresh amaranth muffin 1000 pesos. Open Mon.-Sat. 8am-2pm and 5-9pm, Sun. 8am-1pm.

Sights and Entertainment

Partaking of the beautiful beaches, undersea adventure, and hidden ruins of Cozumel can become an expensive habit. Transportation to outlying parts of the island, tips for guides, scuba classes, master dives, and waterskiing jaunts are amazingly high-priced by Mexican standards. The best bet is to bike or take a taxi to the closer attractions, such as the Laguna Chankanaab or the popular San Francisco Beach, and rent a moped there to explore the farther reaches of Cozumel. Playa Maya and Playa del Sol are two other favorite beaches, although much of Cozumel's windward side is just as attractive and more peaceful. The **Arrecife Palancar** (Palancar Reef) is too far offshore to be seen without a boat, but the **Laguna Columbia,** off the south side of the coastal road, can be reached on foot from the highway.

At the underwater park in **Laguna Chankanaab,** fish and coral stir the water near the shore. Snorkeling in the enclosed lagoon has been discontinued because the suntan lotion from snorkelers was killing the sealife, but you can stand at the rim of the lagoon and ogle the slick survivors. In the open water, snorkeling remains excellent; the water is clearest and calmest early in the morning. Four dive stands rent gear at identical rates (mask and snorkel US$2 per day, fins also US$2), and will usually stash your belongings behind the counter for free. Chankanaab also has a botanical garden, restaurants, and boutiques. To get to the underwater park, take a taxi (14,000 pesos) or rent a moped. (Open daily 8am-4:30pm. Admission 7000 pesos.)

The **Dzul-Ha** reef draws fewer visitors but is a rich snorkeling area as well. To get there, follow the coastal highway 1km north of Chankanaab to the Hotel Club de Sol Cozumel. Stop at the "Dzul-Ha" sign, and swim out about 60m. The reef here only reaches a depth of 6m, and the fish always outnumber the humans. Rent gear and obtain advice from the dive shop in front of the hotel.

If you're a strong swimmer, explore the plane wreck 100 yd. from Hotel La Ceiba's beach, north of Dzul-Ha and just south of town. A 40-passenger Convair aircraft lies upside down on the white sand, sunk for a film by a North American movie producer. To view the wreck, just walk to the back of the hotel and plunge in.

Most of the larger reefs around Cozumel are farther offshore and accessible only by boat. The many dive shops in town (most are on Rafael Melgar near the docks) offer expensive snorkeling trips, scuba trips, instruction, and equipment rentals. One of the most reliable is **Dive Paradise**, Calle 3 Sur 2 (tel. 210-07), near the waterfront. A full-day two-tank scuba trip costs US$40, introduction to scuba or scuba refresher courses US$60, and a full three- to five-day scuba certification course US$325. (Open daily 8am-9pm.) **Blue Bubble Divers**, at Av. 5 and Calle 3 Sur (tel. 218-65), has a mellow, English-speaking staff (employees continually murmur "Blue bubble . . . no trouble") and a choice of 20 reefs to visit. Their two-tank day trips are expensive (US$45-50), but their package deals are within reason. You can rent snorkeling equipment anywhere on the island, including at Laguna Chankanaab and Playa de San Francisco. The standard rate is US$6 plus deposit per 24 hr.

To see the reefs without getting wet, take a one-hour ride on a glass-bottomed boat. Boats leave from Hotel El Presidente daily at 10am, noon, and 2pm. The price hovers around US$6-10. Try to take one of the older open-air boats rather than the modern ones which seat you in the sweltering hold. Call **Fantasia Divers** (tel. 208-50, ext. 941) for the latest information.

Between beach stops and reef dives, you may want to explore the jungle interior of Cozumel and locate its several small ruins. From the lighthouse at **Punta Celerain,** Cozumel's southern tip, you can view the entire island and the bobbing fishing boats. The unreconstructed ruins of the Tumba del Caracol are near the beginning of the road to Celerain.

The route along the east coast passes many secluded beaches that would make good camping spots. Midway along the coast, Carretera Transversal branches west and loops back through the jungle to town. North of Transversal, the unpaved road winds toward **Punta Molas** and its lighthouse. Aguade Grade, Janan, and other small ruins tucked into the jungle on the island's northern tip are difficult to find without a guide, but **Castillo El Real,** just north of the *palapas* of Los Cocos, is hard to miss. This crumbling structure was the largest of the Mayan buildings on the island.

To get to **San Gervasio,** the only extensively excavated and partially reconstructed ruin on the island, take Juárez out of town. After 8km, a dirt road marked by a "San Gervasio" sign branches to the left. Follow this road for another 8km to the ruin site. (Site open daily 8am-5pm. Free.) A green map of the ruins, a better buy than the guides or the group tours, is available all over town.

The small, air-conditioned **Museo de la Isla de Cozumel** (tel. 215-45), on the waterfront between Calles 4 and 6, serves as a sanctuary from the rain, sun, and tourists downtown. Four rooms acquaint you with the island's social and geological history. (Open Sun.-Fri. 9am-1pm and 4-8pm. Admission US$1 pesos, Sun. free.)

Living the nightlife on Cozumel relieves you of lots o' dough. Fancy restaurants routinely charge 8000 pesos per piña colada. **Carlos 'n' Charlies,** on Rafael Melgar just 1 block north of the dock, rocks all day long, entertaining *norteamericanos* with crazy drinks, slammer contests, and arm wrestling matches. (Open daily 5pm-midnight.) The most popular disco is **Disco Neptuno,** on Rafael Melgar about 5 blocks south of town. Smaller, less chic, and almost as popular is **Disco Scara-mouche,** at Rafael Melgar and Salas, on the southern edge of town. The cover charge at discos is 10,000 pesos and the action revs up around 10pm. Drink prices are out-rageous (6000 pesos per beer), so imbibe before you arrive. Six-packs of locally brewed Dos Equis cost 8000 pesos in stores. If you want to catch live *salsa,* head to **Los Quetzales Bar and Grill** on Av. 10 Sur at Calle 1 Sur. Latin American bands play weeknights from 7:30 to 9:30pm and weekends from 10:30 to 12:30am. (Open daily 6pm-midnight.)

Playa del Carmen

For the most part, Playa (as the locals call it) remains a quiet fishing port. But when Cozumel-Playa ferry traffic picks up toward midday, Playa gets more hectic than the floor of the New York Stock Exchange. Though less expensive than Cancún or Cozumel, Playa del Carmen is no longer a budget traveler's haven. Its beaches are beautiful, but no more so than less urban ones farther south. The town's main road connecting highway and beach is being reconstructed to handle a heavier flow, boding ill for the once-tranquil Playa as increasing numbers of visitors tramp through en route to Isla Cozumel.

Orientation and Practical Information

With three main transportation centers concentrated in a small area, Playa liter-ally revolves around sea, land, and air transport. The ferry dock links it to Isla Cozu-mel; the nearby bus stations serve Chetumal, Cancún, and Mérida; and nine-seat prop planes make frequent trips to Cancún and Cozumel from a tiny airfield only 3 blocks southwest of the bus station. (See Isla Cozumel Practical Information for ferry and air shuttle schedules.) **Avenida Quinta** runs parallel to the beach and en-compasses most of the *tiendas* and inexpensive *típico* restaurants. **Avenida Principal,** the main drag, shoots west from the beach to the Cancún-Chetumal highway 1km away. Most of the town's everyday services lie along this road, starting from the bus station/plaza at the intersection with Av. Quinta.

In the first block west of the plaza on Av. Principal, **Banco del Atlántico** bustles with peso-hungry tourists. (Open for exchange Mon.-Fri. 9am-noon). Across the street, hidden in the lobby of Hotel Playa del Carmen, is the town's only long-distance telephone *caseta* (tel. 212-11; open Mon.-Sat. 7am-2pm and 3-9pm, Sun. 7am-noon; international collect calls 6000 pesos). A travel agency next door will grudgingly provide tourist information, but there is no official tourist office. (Open Mon.-Fri. 7am-7pm, Sat.-Sun. 8am-1pm and 4-7pm.) The **post office** is also on Av. Principal, 2 blocks west of the plaza. (Open Mon.-Fri. 9am-1pm and 3-5pm, Sat. 9am-1pm. Lista de Correos. **Postal Code:** 77710.) On the fourth block inland, **Far-macia Lupita** sells regular pharmaceutical goods out of a small garage. (Open Mon.-Sat. 8am-1pm, Sun. 8am-noon.) Electric washing machines in Playa del Carmen have a troubling propensity to breakdown weekly, making it difficult to find a work-ing laundromat. If the machine at the Hotel Playa del Carmen on Av. Principal isn't running, the friendly woman living 1 block south of the ADO station will wash your clothes for 1000 pesos per article.

Bus Stations: Autotransportes de Oriente, in the big bus yard on Av. Principal. First-class service to Cancún (7 per day, 1 hr., 4000 pesos); Valladolid (6 per day, 6 hr., 10,500 pesos); Chichén Itzá (6 per day, 3½ hr., 12,500 pesos); Mérida (6 per day, 6 hr., 18,000 pesos). For longer rides, ADO buses depart from the small *tienda* on Av. Principal 3 blocks west of the plaza. To: Mexico City (7 per day, 82,000 pesos); Villahermosa (6 per day, 40,000 pesos); Veracruz (2 per day, 62,000 pesos); and Puebla (1 per day, 76,000 pesos). Second-class ADO (from the big bus yard) to: Cancún (7 per day, 1 hr., 3100 pesos); Valladolid (7 per day, 3 hr., 9500 pesos); Mérida (7 per day, 6 hr., 16,000 pesos); Tulum (3 per day, 45 min., 2600 pesos); and Cobá (3 per day, 2 hr., 4600 pesos). **Autotransportes de Caribe,** on Av. Principal next to the bus yard, proffers first-class service to Chetumal (10 per day, 4 hr., 15,000 pesos); Cancún (8 per day, 1 hr., 4000 pesos); Tulum (10 per day, 45 min., 4000 pesos). Second class to Chetumal (4 hr., 13,000 pesos).

Accommodations and Camping

Playa's hotels have been bitten by the infectious tourist bug. Prices sky, except at the hostel, while quality bottoms out.

CREA Youth Hostel (IYHF), on a dirt road off Principal, 4 blocks inland from the beach. Turn right 1 block past the Acuario paint store, at the Farmacia Lupita. Walk 1km on a seemingly endless dirt road, before signs direct you to the hostel 100m to the left. This sprawling complex, includes an auditorium, classroom space, and a basketball court. Empty except during July, Aug., Christmas, and Semana Santa. Single-sex dorms. No curfew. A good deal, but inconvenient to the beach. Bunk with sheets 6000 pesos. 5000-peso deposit.

Posada Sian-Ka'an, on Quinta, 1 block north of the bus station. Early morning nearby bus belches disrupt sleep in these clean, comfortable bungalows. Most rooms have a fan, but share common bathrooms. For those interested, the name means "where the sky is born" in Mayan. Singles 30,000 pesos. Doubles 35,000. Room with private bath 50,000 pesos.

Hotel Lilly, on Principal, 1 block west of the plaza. Swell bathrooms attached to small, neat rooms. Convenient but noisy location near the bus stop and ferry ticket booth. Often full. Singles 25,000 pesos. Doubles 30,000 pesos. Triples 40,000 pesos.

Posadas Mar Caribe, to the left of Principal, 2 blocks inland. A small hotel in a quiet neighborhood. Sterile yellow rooms have commodious bathrooms. Singles or 1-bed doubles 35,000 pesos. Two-bed doubles 45,000 pesos.

Campamento La Ruina. Arriving by ferry, follow the beach 200m to the right. Steer clear of the dismal cabins with "cots." Instead, camp right on the beach, and 2 ft. away from the next person. Communal baths have showers. The famed Carmen mosquito show occurs nightly; some audience participation is required. Small tent or hammock 5000 pesos, large tent 9000 pesos.

Food

Good restaurants are rare and costly in Playa del Carmen. A better bet is to nibble on fruit and snacks along Av. Principal.

Huevas del Coronado, on Quinta, 2 blocks north of the bus station. Hearty, if plain, meals served on plates that patrons take to the beach to use as frisbees. Mexican-style chicken 8000 pesos, roast pork 6000 pesos.

Restaurant Nuestra Señora del Carmen, next door to the Autotransportes de Oriente station. No ambience, but close to the buses. Try the *pulpo en escabeche* (Yucatán-style octopus) for 13,000 pesos. Most entrees 8000-15,000 pesos. Open daily 8am-11pm.

Restaurant El Herradero, 1 block west of the terminal on Principal, then ½ block right. Waves of Spanish rock music hold up the small *palapa*. Bland burritos 7000 pesos, and cheap breakfasts to boot. Open daily 7am-midnight.

Belvedere Restaurant, on Principal, almost on the beach. A popular, if expensive, Italian restaurant that laughs late into the night. Lasagna 12,000 pesos. Fish 13,000 pesos.

Playa Caribe, on Quinta, 2 blocks north of Principal. Small portions of uninspiring food in a truck-stop atmosphere. *Pollo asado* with beans and rice (6000 pesos) is the least expensive *comida corrida* in town. Seafood 9000-13,000 pesos. Open 24 hr.

Sights and Entertainment

The beach, free of seaweed and coral for 5km along the coast, beams a natural beauty that many claim is superior to anything in Cozumel or Cancún. Palm trees line the shore and dense jungle extends inland just beyond the town limits. Windsurfers and other gear can be rented from some of the fancier hotels just south of the pier.

After sunning and swimming, there is little else to do in Playa except wander into the shops on Av. Quinta. The prices here are quite reasonable, especially if you bargain jovially with the storekeepers once they invite you into their shops.

The Maya settled here in the 13th century, leaving ruins scattered about the island. Some lie behind the military base, to the left after walking 1 block west of the bus station. The first structure on the right contains three inner chambers and may have been used for sacred rituals. One kilometer farther down the trail parallel to the beach lie the largest ruins in the area. Beware of scorpions lurking between the large palm leaves, and wear shoes. The last two structures in this group of ruins, which may have served as astronomical observatories for determining solstice and equinox dates, reach high enough to provide a view of the ocean and horizon.

No one comes to Playa looking for after-hours excitement, but a few spots in town interrupt the tranquility of the night. The **Tequila Discoteca,** one block south and a half-block west of the bus station, is Playa's premiere dancing spot. (Cover 3000 pesos. Beer 4000 pesos. Open Thurs.-Sat. 9:30pm-4am.) Local kids also hang out into the morning hours at **Aqua Caliente** on Quinta. Music plays for a more mellow international crowd at **Belvedere Restaurant** on Principal near the beach.

Cobá

Deep within the densest part of the Yucatán jungle, 40km northwest of Tulum, Cobá is too inconvenient to attract many tourists. The Mexican government excessively promotes sites like Chichén Itzá and Tulum, leaving the grandeur of Cobá largely unexcavated, unrecognized, and as close to its original splendor as any site in the Yucatán. Few buses pass this way because few people want to board them. If you can endure the steamy jungle heat and the swarming insects, Cobá's isolation provides a therapeutic counterpoint to mainstream tourism.

Buses leave you in the 10-shack village of Cobá, a few hundred meters from the entrance to the ruins. To reach the entrance, take the left fork at the end of the paved road by the lake. A few meters into the park, the main path forks. The right branch leads to the **Grupo Cobá.** The 25m-high **Temple of the Churches** stands here among several ruins and rock mounds. From the top of the temple, you can see the Nohoch Múl pyramid towering to the north and two of the five lakes which attracted the Mayans to this area. Only the front face of the Temple of the Churches has been excavated to reveal several attached corbel-vaulted passageways as well as a few free-standing ones. The Grupo Cobá path ends at Lake Cobá.

The left branch of the main path leads first to the **Conjunto de las Pinturas** (Temple of the Paintings). On the way stand several stelae with hieroglyphs placing the Cobá settlement early in the 7th century. Many of the stelae have been badly eroded by the jungle climate, and the murals lining the temple on top of the pyramid have not fared much better.

Back on the main path from the Temple of the Paintings, you can walk 2½km, hypnotized by history, to the largest of Cobá's monuments. At the outer limits of the site, the **Nohoch Múl** (Big Hill) pyramid, the highest Mayan structure on the Yucatán Peninsula, soars 40m above the jungle. Mayan priests once led processions up the pyramid's 12 stories. The tiring climb, from which you should refrain if susceptible to heatstroke, does afford a spectacular view. All that remains of the carvings on the pyramid are two diving god images similar to those found at Tulum. As you look out from the front of Nohoch Múl, the large mound to the right, once a mammoth plaza, now awaits excavation funds. (Ruins open daily 8am-5pm. Admission 10,000 pesos, free Sun. and when they run out of tickets.)

While you hope and pray for a bus to arrive (see below), you can eat at **Restaurant Bocadito,** 200m before the bus stop, on the right when entering town. At lunchtime, breakfast omelettes cost twice as much as they do in the morning. Avoid the overpriced stands in the parking lot of the site advertising "real" Mayan food. The **Hotel Bocadito** (next to the restaurant) offers budget accommodations for overnight visitors. (Singles 20,000 pesos. Doubles 25,000 pesos.)

Swimming is possible outside the village in the freshwater **Lake Cobá**, but, near the shore, slimy mud covers the bottom. More pristine and expensive swimming is sometimes possible in Hotel Villa Arqueológica's pool, where usage of their pool facilities comes with the steep price of a drink or a meal. Inquire politely at the restaurant or bar.

Two buses leave Tulum daily at 6 and 11am, stopping at Cobá around 7am and 12:30pm before continuing to Valladolid. In the other direction, two buses leave Valladolid at 4am and noon, stopping at Cobá at 6am and 2pm on their way to Tulum. If you don't ask the driver to stop at the ruins, the bus may cruise right by. Also, both buses occasionally steer clear of the Cobá area entirely. For at least a crack at the public transportation designed to serve you, hitch or walk the 3km to the highway, where buses have no choice but to pass. The bus stops on the highway about 150m south of the intersection with the Cobá access road. Buses appear without warning, so arrive early; check at the intersection for up-to-date information. It's considerably easier on your patience, but harder on your wallet, to take one of the taxis from Tulum's parking lot (45,000 pesos, 80,000 pesos round-trip) with two hours at the ruins and a stop at a *cenote* on the way back. If you want to visit the ruins from Cancún or Puerto Juárez, you'll have to take a bus to **X-Can,** an unpleasant truck-stop of a town, on the Yucatán-Quintana Roo border, and then connect with the bus from Valladolid. At Cobá, those not on a set schedule can often arrange rides with other Cobá visitors or friendly guests at the Hotel Villa Arqueológica by Lake Cobá, at the opposite end of the road from the ruins.

Tulum

On the eastern edge of the way-old Etaib (Black Bees) jungle, halfway down the Caribbean coast of the Yucatán, lies the walled Mayan "City of the Dawn." Although the ruins here are less extensive and less detailed than those at Uxmal and Chichén Itzá, their backdrop is stunning: Tulum's graying temples and nearly intact watchtowers on the city wall rise above palm trees and white sand massaged by the steely-blue Caribbean Sea. Perhaps to unite the city of the rising sun with the god of the setting sun, the Maya endowed Tulum with beautiful representations of a god diving into the water, legs up and spread wide. The diving god appears only on the western walls of buildings, struck by the setting sun's rays.

Unlike the Aztecs, who combined their strength with other societies' to form a federation, the Maya had divided into 15 to 20 warring city-states on the Yucatán, of which Tulum was one, by the late post-Classical period. First settled in the 4th century, Tulum was, when the Spanish arrived, the Western Hemisphere's longest continuously inhabited city. After 50 years of sporadic attacks, the Spanish finally defeated Tulum in the 16th century. It was resettled three decades later by Mayan refugees from the Caste War. One of the last areas conquered by the Spaniards, Tulum continues to inspire rumors about the survival of the enigmatic race of the Aluxob (tiny people).

This century's repopulation of the ruins was initiated by the archeologists who study here, living in *palapa* huts provided by the Mexican government. In recent times, the trickle of settlers has become a torrent of camera-toting tourists spilling out of buses for a two-hour visit. Popular tours departing from Cancún and Cozumel stop at Xel-Ha and Tulum. From about 9am until 3:30pm, the ruins teem with sightseers. The archeological site, often called Nuevo Tulum, includes a vast parking lot surrounded by more souvenir shops and high-priced restaurants than in most beach towns. Fortunately, there are some small huts and affordable places to eat on the quiet stretch of sand just south of the ruins. Admire the ruins as the sun rises and try to stick close to the sea, baking in the midday sun, while the tour groups canvass the ruins.

Orientation and Practical Information

The city of Tulum, 42km from Cobá, 63km from Playa del Carmen, and 127km from Cancún, is the southernmost link in the chain of tourist attractions on the Caribbean coast of Quintana Roo. Although few people live here and even fewer visitors stay overnight, Tulum takes up a good deal of space, in three separate venues: *el crucero*, Pueblo Tulum, and the beach adjacent to the ruins. Arriving in Tulum from Cancún on Rte. 307, buses first stop at *el crucero*, the intersection with Rte. 180 to Mérida; here, restaurants, "mini-supers", and the only bona fide hotels in the area band together. The parking lot and the entrance to the ruins spread out 200m east on the well-paved access road. More informal food and lodging can be found at beachside campgrounds 1km south past the ruins along the same access road. Pueblo Tulum, 4km south of *el crucero* on Rte. 307, offers travelers little except a long-distance telephone *caseta* (open Mon.-Fri. 1-4pm).

Try to arrive at Tulum during the day. If you arrive after dark, it's likely that the one hotel at the crossroads will be full, forcing you to take a taxi (2000 pesos) past the ruins to the campgrounds. The peso-less option is to set off on the arduous 25-min. hike down the unlit road, but don't even think of attempting the trek without a flashlight.

Buses provide cheap transportation from Tulum to nearby cities if you can lay your hands on a schedule and are fortunate enough to find a seat on the bus when it arrives. Scheduled stops vary from month to month and are quite brief. Most of the buses pass between 6 and 11am; it's best to arrive early in the morning at the shaded benches 150m south of *el crucero* and ask the locals the status of the next departing bus. Going north to Xel-Ha, Playa del Carmen, and Cancún, buses stop roughly every two hours from 6am; southbound buses to Carrillo Puerto, Bacalar, and Chetumal stop around 6:30am, 10am, 11:30am, noon, 2:30pm, 4pm, 4:30pm, 7pm, and 8:30pm. Two additional buses pause at the crossroads at 6 and 11am on their way to Cobá, 42km into the dense jungle, before continuing on to Valladolid. These buses comprise the only public transportation from the south to the Cobá ruins.

If you aren't able to convince a bus driver to stop, or if you find yourself waiting long hours in the afternoon sun, hitchhiking is a viable option in Tulum. Friendly drivers may even pull over and offer you a lift if you start walking along the highway. Taxis congregate around the ruins and *el crucero*, and will even convey a person to faraway Cancún (about 70,000 pesos) or Cobá (40,000 pesos). Your best bet is to split the cost among a group of four or five.

Accommodations and Camping

Tulum offers two kinds of lodging: hotels and *cabañas*. The sterile hotel rooms around *el crucero* cater to wealthier travelers. The beachside *cabañas* (*palapa* huts with hammocks) are a far better choice if you don't mind minimalist conditions: El Mirador, Santa Fe, and Don Armando are the most popular and enjoyable. Clustered together on the beach 1km from the ruins, these campgrounds and *cabañas* enable you to meet other travelers, perfect your tan on the spectacular beach, and escape the conventional tourism just a short distance away.

Don Armando Cabañas, next to Santa Fe. The best of the bunch. You can't miss the jocular, rotund Don Armando, who once owned Santa Fe but then decided to construct new and better *cabañas*. Cheap restaurant and full-serivce dive shop attached. Bed or hammock, mosquito netting, candle, real showers, and doors with locks for 25,000 pesos (1 or 2 people). A plot of land on which to camp or hang a hammock goes for 8000 pesos.

El Mirador and **Santa Fe Cabañas and Campgrounds,** next to each other, an 8 min. walk south from the ruins on the paved access road. Both establishments are on the beach, but El Mirador is more rustic and less popular, renting cabins with hammocks and access to communal bathrooms for 8000 pesos per person. Camping at El Mirador costs 5000 pesos per person. Santa Fe is luxurious by comparison, although the facilities are still minimal. Friendly management. Hammocks with mosquito netting, purified drinking water, and use of bathrooms and washing well. Snorkel gear 12,000 pesos per day. Cabins for 2 people cost 15,000 pesos. Camping spots go for 6000 pesos per person.

Acuario Motel y Restaurante, on the highway at the Tulum crossing. Although often full, you can avoid a long trek by staying here. Sterile rooms with TVs and acceptable bathrooms. Midnight roar of passing buses can be heard even underwater in the small cement pool. Few singles, but many 5 to 6 person rooms. Doubles 45,000 pesos.

El Paraíso Cabañas, 1½ km from the ruins, a little farther than El Mirador or Santa Fe. "Luxury" cabins with beds, mosquito netting, concrete floors, and private baths. Decently clean, but lifeless compared to Santa Fe and Don Armando. Cabins for 2 people 25,000 pesos.

Cabañas Tulum, near the end of the access road, about 8km south of the ruins. Costly and inconvenient, but tidy and comfortable. Cabins have ceiling fans and private bathrooms. Set on the most peaceful and beautiful beach in the area. Doubles 70,000 pesos.

Food

Despite increasing numbers of visits from tour groups, Tulum's few restaurants retain authentic cuisine and reasonable value. The parking lot establishments (open daily 7:30am-5pm) uphold *típico* menus, atmosphere, and prices. Bury your toes in cool sand at the campground cafés and savor the informality and undemanding prices. At *el crucero,* several restaurants offer more refined and costlier fare.

Restaurant Don Armando, at the campground on the beach. The international backpacking set crowds this large *palapa.* Generous breakfast 4000 pesos. *Comida corrida* 10,000 pesos. Open daily 7am-9pm.

Santa Fe Restaurante, at the campground on the beach. Reggae tunes float through the small *palapa.* Cooking area won't win the 1991 "Most Hygienic in the Yucatán" award. *Comida corrida,* usually including a big local fish, costs 9000 pesos. Open daily 8-11am and 3-8pm.

El Mirador Restaurante, high on a ridge overlooking the beach and *cabañas.* Cheapest campground food. Breakfast (4000 pesos) includes eggs, fruit, yogurt, and toast. Open daily 7am-8pm.

El Crucero Restaurante, in the hotel of the same name at the crossroads. Feels like a comfortable local pub. Small, reasonably priced portions. Chef salad 9000 pesos, fried fish of the day 12,500 pesos. Open daily 8am-10pm.

El Faisán y El Venado, across from El Crucero, at the crossroads. Similar to El Crucero in ambience, but superior in cuisine. Most entrees (12,000-20,000 pesos) come with rice, beans, and guacamole. Chef salad (veggies washed with purified water from Cancún) 11,000 pesos. Real espresso 3000 pesos. Open daily 6:30am-10pm.

Sights

The Ruins

Tulum may be the ancient city of Zamá, Juan de Grijalva's first glimpse of civilization on his voyage from Cuba in 1518. From the parking lot, your first glimpse of Tulum will be of the still impressive, dry-laid walls that surrounded the city center's three landlocked sides. Enter to the right through the western gate. The wall, made of small rocks wedged together, was originally 12m thick and 10m high but has deteriorated over the years. It shielded the city from the aggression of neighboring Mayan city-states and prevented all but priests and governors of Tulum from entering the city for most of the year. After Tulum's defeat at the hands of the Spanish in 1544, the wall fended off English, Dutch, and French pirates and in 1847 gave rebel Mayans refuge from government forces during the Caste War.

Just inside and to the left of the west gate stand the remains of dwelling platforms which once supported huts. Behind these are the **House of the Halach Uinik,** endowed with the typical Mayan four-column entrance; the **House of the Columns,** the largest residential building in Tulum; and the **Temple of the Frescoes,** a good example of post-Classical Mayan architecture. Well-preserved murals inside the temple depict deities intertwined with serpents, as well as fruit, flower, and corn cob offerings. Masks of Itazmná, the Mayan creator, occupy the northwest and southwest corners of the building.

As with many Mayan structures, Tulum's temple was built along astrological guidelines; to this day the inner chamber is illuminated naturally at the two equinoxes. In contrast to the remarkably precise architectural planning and execution of such earlier cities as Chichén Itzá and Uxmal, however, Tulum is held together with massive amounts of mortar. The classic Mayan practice of cutting all stones to exactly the right dimensions, fitting them together without mortar, and polishing the surfaces, was abandoned here.

El Castillo (castle), the most prominent structure in Tulum, looms behind the smaller buildings and over the rocky seaside cliff. Serving as a pyramid and temple, it commands a view of the entire walled city as well as the Caribbean Sea to the east. This may have been the tower mentioned in the reports of Grijalva's expedition. Its walls, like those of many buildings in Tulum, slope outward while the doorposts slope inward. Much of the castle's shape arose from its having been annexed many times over the years.

In front of the temple is the sacrificial stone where the Maya held battle ceremonies. Once the stars had been consulted and a propitious day determined, a warrior-prisoner was selected for sacrifice. At the climax of the celebration, attendants painted the warrior's body blue—the sacred color of the Maya—and broke his spine over the sacrifical rock. After the heart had been cut out and blood poured over the idols in the temple, the body was given to the soldiers below, who through cannibalism acquired the strength to conquer their enemies.

To the right of El Castillo on the same plaza is the **Temple of the Initial Series.** Named after a stela found here, the temple bears a date that corresponded to the beginning of the Mayan religious calendar in the year 761 AD. The **Temple of the Descending God,** with a fading relief of a feathered, armed deity diving from the sky, stands on the other side of El Castillo's plaza. (Site open daily 8am-5pm. Free. Tours in English and Spanish, 10,000 pesos per person.)

The Beach

The beach by the campgrounds makes an attractive conclusion to a day at the ruins. Nude bathing is tolerated here, although it usually takes one brave soul to be the first to bare all. The Mexican Navy drops in every once in a while to tell everyone to get back in uniform, but this situation lasts only until the last patrol boat is out of sight. Managers of the *cabañas* only complain (but then loudly) if you walk through the campgrounds in the buff.

The reef 500m offshore is an extension of the largest reef in the Americas and the second largest in the world. Although the water here is not as clear as at Xel-Ha or Akumal (see the following section), there are just as many species of fish. Low-key Arturo and Fernando manage the beach's only dive shop, between Santa Fe and Don Armando. Prices are high (mask, fin, and snorkel for US$5 per day; scuba tank for US$25; 3-hour boat trip to reef for US$10), but the fellows know the reef well, and are worth consulting even if you don't dive with them. Ask to see their impressive handmade black-coral jewelry. If you snorkel, be sure to get fins, since the 500m swim out to the reef sometimes involves a struggle against a north-south current that becomes easy with fins.

Cenotes, natural swimming holes, punctuate the woods near Pueblo Tulum. One excellent, clear swimming hole is **Cenote Kristal,** 5km south of Pueblo Tulum. Watch for the small patch of gravel, large enough for two cars, on the right side of the road as you head toward Chetumal. From here, follow a rocky dirt path to the *cenote.* You might even see Tulum youths diving Acapulco-style from high tree limbs.

Between Playa del Carmen and Tulum are some of the most spectacular beaches on the peninsula. **Xcacel,** the first beach north of Tulum, has the best waves and the fewest visitors. **Chemuyil,** 8km north of that, is billed as "the most beautiful beach in the world," only a slight exaggeration. This crescent-shaped beach has sparkling, serene waters and warm, fine sand, bordered by a graceful arch of palm trees. You can camp here for 6000 pesos; hammock rentals cost an extra 7000 pesos from the restaurant on the beach. (Open daily 9am-9pm.) Reasonably clean baths and showers are provided by the government at Chemuyil.

Near Tulum: Xel-Ha and Akumal

The clear, semi-fresh waters of the *caletas* (inlets) at Xel-Ha and Akumal were rediscovered only in 1920, when Sylvanus Morley made archeological finds in the area. The road from Tulum to Puerto Juárez, from which they are easily accessible, was not opened until 1972. The water at both is fantastic (75m visibility underwater).

Xel-Ha is the world's largest natural aquarium, an inlet filled with protected tropical fish. The calm waters draw busloads of tourists from Cancún and Cozumel. Like duty-bound ants from a colony, they file through the gates, march along the well-paved paths, and rent snorkels at the hut (mask, snorkel, and fins for 20,000 pesos). Most of the swimmers hover along the edges and near the docks. If you long for peace, search for the altar which was discovered in an underwater cave nearby. It is possible but dangerous to swim into the cave, although the idols have long since been stolen. (Open daily 8am-5pm. Admission 7000 pesos.)

Xel-Ha also maintains a small archeological site across the highway from the inlet entrance. These ruins were only recently opened to the public, and are not extensive. The small Classical and post-Classical ruins, including **El Templo de Los Pájaros** and **El Palacio,** top off an afternoon of snorkeling. (Site open daily 8am-5pm. Admission 8000 pesos.)

The inlet at **Akumal** is much smaller than Xel-Ha, although a resort is evolving in the area; two luxury hotels already operate there. Many tour groups visit both sites, but if you only have time for one, choose Xel-Ha.

Xel-Ha lies 15km north of Tulum, and Akumal is 10km past that. It is a bit difficult to find buses which will stop at either location; ask ahead of time to be let off. Vigorously wave down the bus to return from the site. If you're lucky, a second-class bus will pick you up en route to Tulum or Cancún.

Chetumal

Chetumal, the capital of the state of Quintana Roo, basks on the Caribbean's western shore just minutes north of the Belizan border. No beaches or hidden ruins here, just deteriorating brick streets and hip teenagers perusing the numerous duty-free shops. Mexican and Belizan tourists come to Chetumal to snap up appliances, electronics, and clothes. Since statehood was granted in 1975, customs procedures between Quintana Roo and its neighbors Campeche and Yucatán have become more stringent, but officials continue to wink at domestic tourists smuggling cheap imports back to their home states. For foreigners arriving from Cancún or Cozumel, Chetumal's cheap goods will come as a welcome relief. Otherwise, the town serves mainly as a rest stop between the Yucatán and Tikal.

Orientation

Tucked into the Yucatán's southeastern corner, Chetumal is just north of the Río Hondo, the natural border between Mexico and Belize. There are three principal approaches: Rte. 186 from Escárcega (273km); along the Caribbean coast from Cancún (379km); and from Mérida via Peto (414km) or Valladolid (458km).

The spiffy new **bus station** at Av. de los Insurgentes and Av. Belize is Chetumal's ground transportation hub. **Autotransportes del Caribe** serves the terminal, as do **Batty Brothers** and **Venus** with connections to Belize City.

Travelers passing through Chetumal may wish to check luggage (500 pesos per hr.) at the bus station in the area marked "Lockers," which closes at 9pm. Next to the bus station, **Blanco,** a fully stocked supermarket sells everything from paté to sneakers in air-conditioned comfort (open Mon.-Sat. 8am-9pm).

Take a taxi (2000 pesos) into town, or walk the 15 blocks south along Av. de los Héroes. The thriving shopping district on Héroes begins at the market and extends 1km south to the bay. Along the way, between Aguilar and the bay, Héroes crosses Héroes de Chapultepec, Lázaro Cárdenas, Plutarco Elías Calles, Ignacio Zaragoza, Obregón, O. Blanco, Carmen Ochoa, and 22 de Enero, in that order. This compact commercial area encompasses most of Chetumal's hotels and restaurants. At the southern terminus of Héroes lies Blvd. Bahía, a wide avenue flanked by statues and small plazas that follows the bay for several kilometers. From here you can see part of Belize: it's the long spit of land stretching out to the right as you face the sea.

Practical Information

Tourist Office: On the 2nd floor in the Palacio de Gobierno (tel. 208-55), at Héroes and Carmen Ochoa. A/C alone makes a visit worthwhile. Best to drop by in the morning. Open Mon.-Fri. 8am-2:30pm and 4-10pm. The office's **information booth** (tel. 236-63), on Héroes near Aguilar, is equally helpful but not as cool. Open Mon.-Sat. 8am-1pm and 5-8pm.

Guatemalan Consulate: Obregón Pte. 342 (tel. 230-65). Will happily help you with your Guatemalan jaunt; a picture or photocopy of your passport is the only requirement for a visa.

Currency Exchange: Bánamex, Juárez 51 (tel. 226-56), at Obregón 8 blocks south and 1 block west of the Mercado. Open Mon.-Fri. 9am-1:30pm and 4-6pm. Many banks are on Héroes, close to Carmen Ochoa. All open Mon.-Fri. 9:30am-1pm. If **Baroudi's,** Héroes 39 (tel. 206-16), has money available, he'll change traveler's checks after bank hours. Open Mon.-Sat. until 8:30pm.

Post Office: Plutarco Elías Calles 2A (tel. 225-78), 6 blocks south and 1 block east of the Mercado. Open for stamps and Lista de Correos Mon.-Fri. 8am-7pm, Sat. 9am-12:30pm; for registered mail Mon.-Fri. 8am-6pm, Sat. 9am-noon.

Telephones: Long-distance office on Zaragoza (tel. 211-08). Head south on Héroes and turn left on Zaragoza—the small, unmarked office is 20m in, on the back side of the shopping center. Long-distance collect calls Mon.-Fri. 3000 pesos. Office open Mon.-Sat. 8am-1pm and 5-8pm, Sun. 9am-1pm.

Telegrams: In the same building as the post office (tel. 206-51). Open Mon.-Fri. 9am-9pm, Sat. 9am-5pm.

Airport: (tel. 266-75) 5km south of the city on Aguilar. **Aero Cozumel** serves Mérida (US$65), Cozumel (US$62), and Cancún (US$111). Taxis to the airport cost 6000 pesos.

Bus Station: At Insurgentes and Belize (tel. 207-41). **Autotransportes del Caribe** offers first-class service to: Mérida (8 per day, 6 hr., 22,000 pesos); Excarcéga (10 per day, 4 hr., 12,500 pesos); Cancún (5 per day, 5 hr., 20,000 pesos) via Tulum (2 hr., 11,500 pesos) and Playa del Carmen (3 hr., 14,000 pesos); Palenque (at 9:30pm, 7 hr., 21,500 pesos); Veracruz (2 per day, 16 hr., 48,000 pesos); Mexico City (3 per day, 22 hr., 68,000 pesos). **Batty Bros.** runs to Belize City (7 per day, express at 2pm, 10,000 pesos or BZ$7).

Red Cross: Chapultepec at Independencia (tel. 205-71), 1 block south and 2 blocks west of the bus station, in the back of Hospital Civil Morelos. Open 24 hr.

24-Hr. Pharmacy: At Madero 261-B (tel. 266-97).

Hospital: Hospital Civil Morelos, Aguilar at Juárez (tel. 215-88). Walk-in clinic.

Police: Insurgentes at Belize (tel. 215-00), at the northern end of town next to the bus station.

Accommodations

Chetumal caters to travelers just off the bus who would willingly sacrifice their grandmothers to Chac for a bed and a shower. Most hotels resemble the motor lodges out of the late 70s. Campers and RVers should take advantage of the great trailer park in Calderitas (see below).

CREA Youth Hostel (IYHF), Calzada Veracruz at Obregón (tel. 234-65), pretty far out of town. Student ID not required; no maximum age. Clean, modern single-sex rooms hold 4 or 6 *literas* (bunk beds). You may have a room to yourself off-season. 11pm curfew, but you may get in later if you bang on the door. Bed with sheets, towel, and locker 8000 pesos. 10,000-peso deposit for sheets. Optional skimpy meals: breakfast (8-9:30am) 4000 pesos, lunch (2-3:30pm) 5300 pesos, dinner (7-8:30pm) 5000 pesos.

Hotel Ucum, M. Gandhi 167 (tel. 207-11), close to the market. Often accommodating when others are full. Enormous place built around a broad courtyard. Spotless rooms and bathrooms with good ceiling fans but weak showers. Singles 15,260 pesos. Doubles 19,620 pesos. Triples 22,890 pesos. Quads 30,520 pesos.

Hotel Baroudi, Obregón 39 (tel. 209-22), just east of Héroes. In a sea-green building of modernist pretensions. Some rooms fresh and spotless; others dimly lit, with run-down bathrooms. Look at the room before paying. *Agua purificada* in the hall, and phones in the rooms. Singles 18,000 pesos. Doubles 25,000 pesos. Triples 31,000 pesos. Quads 42,000 pesos.

Hotel Jacaranda (tel. 214-55), Obregón near Héroes. Austere lobby fronts clean rooms that sport fans, hot water, and a balcony with a busy street corner view. Get here early to nab A/C. Singles 20,000 pesos, with A/C 23,500 pesos. Doubles 27,500 pesos, with A/C 33,000 pesos. Triples 35,000 pesos, with A/C 43,000 pesos.

Hotel Brasilia, Aguilar 186 (tel. 20-64). Lobby rooms are a bit musty but the spacious rooms upstairs enjoy a strong breeze. Beds lumpier than bad porridge. Private baths. Singles 17,500 pesos. Doubles 24,000 pesos. Triples 31,000 pesos. Quads 38,000 pesos.

Trailer Park, in Calderitas 9km northeast of Chetumal. Beautiful, windy location overlooking Chetumal Bay. Well-kept with thin grassy lawn and large coconut palms. Electricity, water hookups, and clean bathrooms. Trailers 20,000 pesos, with services 30,000 pesos. Tents 20,000 pesos. Local buses to Chetumal pass park gate every ½ hr. (20 min., 250 pesos).

Posada Familiar América, O. Blanco 216. Toward the bay on Héroes and then right 1 block past the vicious, caged dogs. Uh-oh! Roaches the size of the old wooden beds sighted. A good deal if you want a private bath and don't mind the creepy-crawly company. Doubles 20,000 pesos.

Food

The café-restaurants at the end of Héroes, on 22 de Enero near the bay, are small on atmosphere but even smaller on price. To reach them, however, you must walk through the possibly appetite-squelching meat market; as you pass, keep the ample reward in mind.

Restaurante Pantoja, 16 de Septiembre 181, on the corner across from the market. Extremely popular family restaurant. Chicken 6500 pesos. Wash down large servings of enchiladas (5000 pesos) with gigantic lemonades (1500 pesos). Open Mon.-Sat. 7:30am-9pm.

El Taquito, Plutarco Elias Calles 260, near Juárez. The only place that makes an attempt at atmosphere. Enjoy a meal of 4 or 50 tacos (1200 pesos each) under a huge thatched roof. Crowded and steamy. Open Mon.-Sat. 9am-11pm.

Restaurant Campeche, Obregón 204, near Héroes. Originally a house, dining now takes place in 1 of the 2 bedrooms. Sample a cold *cerveza* (1500 pesos) and *pollo frita* (7500 pesos) while checking out the eclectic crowd. Open Mon.-Sat. 7am-11pm.

Sights

Mexicans and Belizans looking to smuggle cheap imports back to their home states converge on **El Mercado.** In addition to the standard pyramids of fruit, tanks of sugar water, and dusty tacos, you can purchase a prom dress, cheese from Holland, or homemade *salsa* tapes. Outside the market, medicinal snake cures and hammocks brought in from Tixkokob, Yucatán, are available at outrageously low prices.

Nothing else in town is of much interest to strangers. The nearest beach is the *balneario* at **Calderitas,** a 20-minute bus ride from Chetumal. Buses (250 pesos) leave every half hour between 6am and 8pm from Av. Belize between Colón and M. Gandhi. Although the water is turbid and the shores rocky, the beach jams with locals during summer and school holidays.

Much nicer, both atmospherically and for swimming, are the three watering holes near the town of **Bacalar,** 20km away. The local bus to Bacalar (1000 pesos) leaves every hour from Chetumal's bus station; *combis* leave every hour from the corner of Hidalgo and Primo de Verdad in front of the public library (30 min., 1500 pesos). The last bus returns at 8:30pm. The route passes **Laguna Milagros** and **Cenote Azul** before reaching Bacalar. Both have bathing areas, dressing rooms, and lakeside restaurants. The huge dining room by Cenote Azul, though expensive, offers oddly soothing tableside views of a bristly mountain pig and an overly adventurous spider monkey.

Past the uninteresting Fuerte de San Felipe in Bacalar lie the docks of the **Laguna de Siete Colores,** named for the colors reflected in its depths. The fresh water is warm, perfectly clear, devoid of plant or animal life, and carpeted by powdery limestone, making it excellent for swimming. Best of all, it's not yet a tourist attraction; schools of bathing *niños* and novice snorkelers populate the waters. Nearby are bathrooms, dressing rooms, fruit vendors, and expensive dockside restaurants.

Chetumal to Escárcega

The 276km road between Escárcega and Chetumal, rarely traveled by tourists, passes several Mayan ruins that cluster on the Campeche-Quintana Roo border. They are largely unexcavated and undeveloped; instead of majestic, meticulous restorations, the sites are sublime, mosquito-infested piles of rubble. Bus service is poor, and hitching difficult—this trip is not for those who need spoon-feeding. But for ruins as they were before cosmetic surgery, few sites can compare.

Orientation

Consider renting a car in Chetumal or Escárcega (130,000 pesos per day): though there may be a schedulted stop at Xpujil, the 10 buses that supposedly travel the highway daily in each direction often refuse to stop at the ruins, and hitching is unpredictable. From Chetumal, most drivers are going only to Bacalar (a few kilometers west of the city), and any continuing to Escárcega who do stop for thumbers still have to be persuaded what a lark it would be to go ruin-hopping. Do not accept a ride only part of the way to either main city, since there are no services along most of the route. If you gather a large group, a taxi will make the trip for approximately 40,000 pesos. Bring water and snacks in case you get stranded.

Kohunlich

The ruins of Kohunlich (66km west of Chetumal) consist of some 180 mounds, the vast majority of which have yet to be excavated. Plans to turn it into another Chichén Itzá are underway. Ignacio Ek and his son, both local farmers, discovered the site when they unearthed several large clay masks and jars. Nobly, they reported their findings to authorities instead of observing precedent and selling them to foreigners for a fraction of their scientific and aesthetic value. In recognition of his scruples, Ignacio was named custodian of the site, and still serves in that capacity.

The ruins' earlier Mayan name, Kohunrich, which means "Place Where the Date Trees Fruit Richly," was reportedly changed to Kohunlich because a Mexican archeologist thought the old name sounded more Germanic than Mayan. The Eks have begun planting date palms again, to re-create the oasis described in Mayan texts. Aside from this beautiful new growth, take note of the **Pyramid of the Masks.** Of the eight original larger-than-life masks flanking the central stairway, six suffered near-destruction at the hands of looters. The two that remain in good condition represent the sun god. Traces of color related to the East (red) and the West (black) remain on the masks, which have thick features reminiscent of the Olmecs. The Eks sometimes give tours of the site.

The road to Kohunlich branches south off the main highway 58km west of Chetumal; the ruins lie 9km from the highway. No public transport connects the highway with the site; pray for a taxi, or hitch.

Xpujil, Becán, and Chicanná

The ruins of Xpujil, Becán, and Chicanná lie in Campeche state, near the mid-point of the Chetumal-Escárcega highway.

Xpujil presents a face more martial than regal. The three towers of its largest structure, visible from the highway, are topped by lattice-work rims. Very little else has been excavated. Xpujil ruins are 3km east of Becán and 34km west of the Quintana Roo border. Many buses stop in Xpujil for gas. Wait here for the next bus to the ruins, or take your chances hitching.

Becán's name, "Path of the Snake," refers to the moat (nearly 2km long) that encircles the site. Seven bridges once crossed the 16m-wide moat into the walled city center. Built between 650 and 1000 AD, Becán's temples once towered 19-35m above the ground.

Chicanná (House of the Snake's Mouth) was probably named after the many Chenes-style buildings still being excavated here. Their portals are dominated by huge animal figures, most with ornamentally carved, wide-open mouths. Some of these represent the earthly and celestial incarnations of the god Itzamná. Building 2, with foundations for two façade towers, is a superb example of the Río Bec style of Mayan architecture (named after the undeveloped site at Río Bec, about 40km east of Chicanná). Chicanná is on the north side of the highway.

Escárcega occupies the intersection of Hwy. 261 and Hwy. 186. From here, buses go north to Mérida (330km), east to Chetumal (264km), southwest to Villahermosa (301km), and south to Palenque (233km) and Tenosique. **Hotel San Luis,** on the Zócalo in Escárcega, provides spotless, comfortable accommodations just 3 blocks from the bus station. The restaurant downstairs serves good *enchiladas suize*. Usually the bus to Palenque arrives full in Escárcega, so expect to stand for most of the ride to the ruins.

Belize

US$1 = BZ$1.98	BZ$1 = US$0.5
CDN$1 = BZ$1.72	BZ$1 = CDN$0.5
UK£1 = BZ$3.78	BZ$1 = UK£0.2
AUS$1 = BZ$1.68	BZ$1 = AUS$0.6
NZ$1 = BZ$1.23	BZ$1 = NZ$0.8

Mesoamerican surrealism shrouds Belize City. As daylight turns to dusk, youn creole day-laborers wearing New York Mets baseball caps over their Rastafaria dreadlocks blast reggae music from shiny boom boxes while smoking brown-pape joints the size of large cigars. Gospel shrieks from a Seventh-day Adventist reviva meeting mingle with the roar of buses arriving at the station. Red beans and ric replace tortillas and *frijoles* as the specialty of the bus station cafeteria. The Hind taxi driver whizzes through town and drops you off at your hotel, then charges thre times the amount of an equivalent trip in Mexico. You grudgingly hand over th currency, plastered with the likeness of Queen Elizabeth, and head down a stree to the Chinese restaurant for curried chow mein. Hustlers wander in, hawking dop and "Mayan" artifacts. Welcome to Belize.

For many Mayan ruin-hoppers, Belize means little more than a shortcut betwee Tulum and Cobá in Quintana Roo and the magnificent kingdom of Tikal in th Guatemalan Petén. For the American expatriate living in Mexico, Belize enable a biannual renewal of the tourist card, involving only a short, weekday hop from Chetumal to the Mexican Embassy in Belize City. Yet more and more traveler flock to Belize for its own sake. Snorkelers and scuba divers gawk at the second largest barrier reef in the world, just off the coast. Veterans of Cancún thrill to tha endangered species *beachus tropicallus tranquillus* on the island *cayes* and atolls Fans of *Mutual of Omaha's Wild Kingdom* hike through wildlife sanctuaries, in cluding the world's first jaguar preserve. Over 600 Mayan ruins—mostly unexcavat ed—will keep archeologists and ruin-hoppers busy for years to come. Other travel ers are drawn to voodoo and Carib black magic in the southern Dangriga region

A Mayan people flourished here between 300 and 900 AD, and then, for unknow reasons, abandoned their homestead and migrated elsewhere. The Ketchi-speaking descendants of those who remained can be encountered today in the Cayo, Stan Creek, and Toledo districts to the west and south.

In 1638, shipwrecked British sailors established Belize's first European settlemen and were joined by British soldiers and families after the capture of Jamaica from Spain in 1655. Spanish claims of sovereignty and attacks on the British communit (whose main industry was the sawing of logwood for dyes) persisted despite severa treaties, until the British won a decisive victory at the Battle of St. George's Caye in 1798. British Honduras became an official colony in 1862. Although it achieve independence in 1981, Belize's enduring ties to Britain are apparent in the Queen nominated (though Belizan) Governor General and the British garrison stationed here to protect it against foreign attack. Foreign antagonism persists because of ar unresolved Guatemalan claim to sovereignty. The map at the Guatemalan custom at its western border shows Belize as part of Guatemala. Many Belizans resent both the Guatemalan claim and the British presence: Tactfully refrain from calling the country either "British Honduras" or "Guatemala."

Though inflation has boosted the prices of Mexican food and lodging, the cos of living has increased only moderately in Belize, where singles for US$8 or les are the norm. While plane or boat travel is expensive, Belizan buses are not (US$1. to cross the country from north-south), and market or supermarket food is reason ably priced. Since the Belizan-U.S. dollar ratio is fixed and few Belizan banks wan the unstable peso in their coffers, it's best to exchange all of your pesos for Belizar dollars at the border.

English is the official language, but almost half of the country speaks another tongue. In the Corozal, Orange Walk, and San Ignacio districts, Spanish is the language of the majority. In Toledo and Stann Creek districts, some inhabitants' first language is Garifuna or Maya. In the Belize district (around and including Belize City), locals should understand your English with ease, but their creole dialect may throw you for a loop.

Passports are required of all visitors to Belize. U.S. and Commonwealth citizens don't need visas as long as they hold a return ticket; most other citizenries do. Liability insurance, required of those driving into Belize, can be purchased at the border from the Belize International Insurance Company (Belinsco) for BZ$25. Never park your car on the street in Belize City; it almost certainly will be broken into if not spirited away altogether. Instead, find a private, guarded lot, or avoid driving your car into the country in the first place.

Belize City

In contrast to the rest of the country, Belize City lives up to Aldous Huxley's remark that "if the world had any ends, British Honduras would surely be one of them." Streams of sewage flow in the canals that line the streets. Poverty is endemic, and police seem to be conspicuously absent as dealers ply drugs openly in doorways across the city. The introduction of crack has sent many red-eyed hustlers to favorite tourist spots in search of easy cash. The operatives of the so-called "Terror Brigade," headed by three well-known hoodlums, rely on their exotic desirability and the tourist demand for drugs to befriend their unsuspecting prey. Don't even think about giving large sums of money to anyone who claims that the drug deal of the century is waiting to be made. Tuck in your moneybelt while in Belize City, and remove all jewelry; you'll look fine without it, and feel much happier when you still have it back at home. In this lazy town, you should be wary of anyone who moves too quickly. Belize City is especially unsafe after dark; walk with friends along a busy main street or take a taxi in the evening.

Many backpackers come here solely to call home, as Belize City has the cheapest phone rates in Central America, while for others it serves only a departure point for the Cayes or the interior. Those dead-set on passing the day in the city can enjoy a leisurely seafood fest in one of the several fine budget restaurants. The market comes alive on Saturdays, and many small pubs and reggae bars offer late-night backstreet diversion for the more intrepid.

Orientation

Belize City is 154km south of Belize's northern border with Mexico, and 134km east of the western border with Guatemala. The Caribbean Sea virtually surrounds the city, lapping upon the eastern, northern, and southern shores. **Haulover Creek,** which runs southeast to the sea, splitting the city into northern and southern sections, is spanned by the **Swing Bridge.** Most services are within a short walk of the bridge. **Queen Street** runs northeast from the Swing Bridge, and **Albert Street** forms the major thoroughfare south of the bridge. **Town Park,** at Church and Albert St., occupies the center of town and is 2 blocks south of the Swing Bridge.

Taxis, usually monstrous station wagons identifiable by their green license plates, can be flagged down on the street or at the stand in Town Park. The standard fare is BZ$3 per stop within Belize City, plus BZ$1 for each extra person. Always ask the fare before engaging a taxi.

Batty Brothers and **Venus** buses serve northern routes, Orange Walk, Sarteneja, Santa Elena, and Chetumal (8 per day) with an express return from Chetumal at 2pm. **Novelo's** buses go west to Benque Viejo (Mon.-Sat. 5 per day, Sun. 4 per day) and the **Z-line** takes the southern route to Dangriga (5 per day) and Punta Gorda (2 per day). Bus stations are clustered around the pound yard on Orange St., six long blocks from the center of the city.

The **international airport** is located 16km northwest of Belize City on the northern highway. American cash is accepted in Belize, so you need not change money at the airport. Try to share a cab, as the fare will run you BZ$25. A municipal airport in Belize City offers flights to points within Belize, including Ambergris Caye and Caye Chapel (US$35).

Boats coming into Belize must pass through an authorized port of entry: Belize City, Corozal, Dangriga, Ambergris Caye, Barranco, or Punta Gorda. Launches to Caye Caulker leave Belize City daily from Jan's Service Station, 73 N. Front St., near the Swing Bridge (see Caye Caulker below). A ferry to San Pedro leaves once per day from the Bellevue Hotel, 1 block south of the market on S. Foreshore Rd. (Mon.-Sat. at 4pm, Sun. at 1pm, BZ$20). A ferry from Punta Gorda to Puerto Barrios, Guatemala, leaves Tuesdays and Fridays at 2pm. Tickets (US$5.50) are available from Carlos Godoy, Middle Main St., Punta Gorda, or from Chet at Nature's Way. Buy your ticket the day before and be prepared to wait around if the ferry is booked. Placentia can be reached by a ferry from Big Creek or by bus from Dangriga.

Practical Information

Belize Tourist Bureau: 53 Regent St. (tel. 772-13), 7½ blocks south of the Swing Bridge. Offers comprehensive maps of Belize City (BZ$4), the Cayes, and interior. Open Mon.-Thurs. 8am-noon and 1-5pm, Fri. 8am-noon and 1-4:30pm.

Embassies: U.S., 20 Gabourel Ln. (tel. 771-61), at Hutson St. Take Queen St. northeast until it meets Gabourel and turn right—the embassy is the old white house on your left. Open Mon.-Fri. 8am-noon and 1-5pm. **Mexico,** 20 N. Park St. (tel. 301-93), on the waterfront. Pass the U.S. Embassy on Hutson St. and turn right—it's at the end of the block. Unless you want to make the trip from Belize to Chetumal twice in the same day, get a Mexican tourist card in the embassy's consular division before leaving. Travelers without cards have been turned back at the border. Open Mon.-Fri. 9am-12:30pm. **Guatemala** has no diplomatic corps in Belize. Obtain your visa at the border (US$1).

Currency Exchange: Any of the commercial banks clustered around Town Park change money. **Barclay's Bank,** 21 Albert St. (tel. 772-11), does not charge a commission. Open Mon.-Fri. 8am-1pm. The official rate is fixed at US$1 — BZ$1.98 but money is changed 2-for-1 on the street or in many stores in the area. American dollars are widely accepted. A permit must be obtained from the **Central Bank of Belize,** 2 Bishop St. (tel. 772-16), in order to exchange traveler's checks for U.S. dollars. Open Mon.-Thurs. 8am-3pm, Fri. 8am-6pm.

American Express: Global Travel Services, 41 Albert St. (tel. 772-57). Full service office open Mon.-Fri. 8am-noon and 1-4:30pm, Sat. 8am-noon.

Post Office: Queen and N. Front St. (tel. 722-01), near the Swing Bridge. Open Mon.-Thurs. 8am-5pm, Fri. 8am-4:30pm; for registered mail Mon.-Thurs. 8am-noon, Fri. 1-4:30pm. Pharmacies also sell stamps and have mailboxes. To receive mail, address letters: Poste Restante, Belize City, Belize, CENTRAL AMERICA.

Telephones: Many travelers head to Belize just to take advantage of the cheap rates. **Belize Telecommunications Limited,** 1 Church St. (tel. 113), off Albert St., has A/C and private booths. Direct and collect calls (no surcharge). Three min. to the U.S. or Canada BZ$10, to Europe BZ$18. BZ$30 deposit required. Open Mon.-Sat. 8am-9pm (until 10pm for collect calls), Sun. 8am-6pm (collect calls only). Faxes sent at same rate as international calls. **Telephone Code:** 02.

Telegrams: In the same office as the phones (tel. 113). To the U.S. and Canada BZ32¢ per word, to Europe BZ60¢ per word. Open Mon.-Sat. 8am-5pm.

Airports: Belize International Airport, 16km northwest of Belize City. Regularly scheduled flights to Houston on **Continental,** 32 Albert St. (tel. 778-27), departing daily at 12:40pm. Miami, New Orleans, San Francisco and Central Mexico are serviced by **Taca Airlines,** 41 Albert St. (tel. 771-85). In addition to these cities, **Tan Sanasa,** at Queen and New St. (tel. 770-80) in the Valencia Bldg., flies to Panama (Mon.-Tues., Thurs., Sat.) and to Mexico via Honduras. **Tropic Air** (tel. 456-71) flies to Cancún (BZ$205) depart daily from the municipal airstrip. **Aerovias,** 55 Regent St. (tel. 733-56), to Guatemala City (Tues., Fri.-Sun. at 3pm, BZ$156) via Flores. Passengers leaving the country must pay a BZ$20 departure tax. Cheaper flights to the Cayes and the interior depart daily on the following airlines from the international airport and from the **Belize Municipal Airstrip** on the waterfront north of town. **Maya**

Airways, 6 Fort St. (tel. 440-32), flies to San Pedro (½ hr., BZ$39), Punta Gorda (½ hr., BZ$99) via Dangriga (20 min., BZ$45), and Placentia (1 hr., BZ$76). **Tropic Air** has scheduled flights to San Pedro (same price as Maya Air) and Caye Chapel (10 per day, BZ$30). **Taca** goes to Corozal (1 per day, BZ$75).

Bus Stations: Batty Brothers Bus Service, 54 E. Collet Canal (tel. 771-46), is the most comfortable. To Chetumal (every hr. 4-11am, 4 hr., BZ$7). Before leaving Belize City, get your Mexican tourist card at the Mexican embassy. To Belmopan (4 departures before 10am, 1½ hr., BZ$3) continuing on to San Ignacio (3 hr., BZ$4). Only the 6:30am bus goes to Melchor de Mencos, Guatemala (BZ$4.50): there is a pick-up service for the express if you buy your ticket in advance. **Venus Bus Lines,** 2371 Magazine Rd. (tel. 733-54). Take Orange St. 3 blocks west of Collet Canal, then make a right onto Magazine Rd. Afternoon trips to Chetumal (BZ$7), Corozal (BZ$6), and Sarteneja (BZ$8). **Z-line,** same building as Venus (tel. 733-54). To: Dangriga (3 per day, additional 6am bus on Mon., BZ$9); Punta Gorda (Mon.-Sat. at 10:30am, Sun. at 10am, BZ$19); and Independence (BZ$15). **Escalante** sends 3 yellow school buses from the pound yard across the bridge from Batty Bros. to Orange Walk (5:30pm, 1½ hr., BZ$3.50). **Novelo's,** 19 W. Canal (tel. 773-72). Take Orange St. west, turn left immediately after the bridge, and walk 1 block. Service to Benque Viejo (every hr. 11am-7pm, 3 hr., BZ$4) via San Ignacio (BZ$3.75) and Belmopan (BZ$2.75).

Bookstore: The Book Center, 144 N. Front St. (tel. 774-57), near Queen St. Good selection of English novels and magazines. Stock up before proceeding to Guatemala or Mexico. Open Mon.-Sat. 8am-noon, 1-5pm, and 7-9pm.

Supermarket: Brodie's, on Albert St., off Town Park. Everything from groceries to mail-order abdominizers. Open Mon.-Tues., Thurs., and Sat. 8am-7pm; Wed. 8am-12:30pm; Fri. 8am-9pm; Sun. 9am-12:30pm.

Laundromat: Carry's Laundry, 41 Hyde's Ln. (tel. 452-80), near Barracks Rd. Wash and dry BZ$5 each. Open Mon.-Fri. 8am-5:30pm, Sat. 8am-6pm.

Pharmacy: Brodie's, on Albert St., next to Town Park. Pharmacy at rear of store open Mon.-Tues., Thurs., and Sat. 8am-7pm; Wed. 8am-12:30pm; Fri. 8am-9pm; Sun. 9am-12:30pm.

Health Care: Belize City Hospital (tel. 772-51), on Eve St. Outpatient entrance on the corner of Eve and Craig St. Open Mon.-Fri. 8am-4pm. On weekends, go to the casualties entrance, 1 gate to the right. Open 24 hr.

Dentist: Dr. René Hegar, 24 Daly St. (tel. 456-54). Emergency service. Open Mon.-Fri. 8am-noon and 3-6pm, Sat. 8am-noon.

Police: 9 Queen St. (tel. 022-22 or 446-46 for emergencies), at New Rd. Open 24 hr.

Accommodations

Cheap hotels used to be scarce here, but as lodging prices in Mexico soar, Belizan rates increase more slowly, making budget rooms in Belize City only slightly more expensive than in Mexico City or Mérida. Security is of prime importance. Door locks should be solid, with at least one extra chain lock on the inside. Because hustlers swarm to popular hotels, managers lock their main entrances at regular hours each night. Ceiling fans and open windows assure a comfortable stay. Most places serve breakfast of toast, eggs, and coffee for around BZ$3.

Sea Side Guest House, 3 Prince St. (tel. 783-39). Five blocks south of Town Park on Albert St., then left on Prince St. Fred, Mary Jo and 3 hounds offer breezy rooms overlooking the sea, breakfast, maps, and a wealth of information. By far the best deal in this safe and quiet neighborhood. Frequented by businessmen and backpackers alike. Usually full, so call ahead. Beds in a 5-bed dorm BZ$10. Singles BZ$17. Doubles BZ$28. Breakfast BZ$3.

Dim's Mira Rio, 59 N. Front St. (tel. 449-70), across from the North Front Street Guest House. Three austere rooms on the 2nd floor with toilets and wash basins. Rm. #1 offers a fine view of the unsightly creek. Aquarium-like bathtub and shower. Visit the bar downstairs to see the river up close. Laundry service BZ$6. Singles BZ$15.75. Doubles BZ$21-23.

Bonaventure Hotel, 122 N. Front St. (tel. 441-34). Next to the North Front Street Guest House. The front rooms in this clean hotel are the most pleasant. Large communal dining table for breakfast (BZ$4.50) and dinner (rice, beans, and chicken, BZ$6.50). Singles BZ$15. Doubles BZ$28. Triples BZ$30.

North Front Street Guest House, 124 N. Front St. (tel. 775-95), just past Jan's Service Station. Eight claustrophobic, passably clean rooms with grungy communal baths. Breakfast (BZ\$3) and dinner (BZ\$6) served in common room with TV and daily newspapers. Singles BZ\$15. Doubles BZ\$25. Triples BZ\$30.

Deep Roots, 3A Thurton Alley. From Batty Bros. walk 1 block north to Vernon St.; it's ½ block to the right. A few beds and space for hammocks are separated by curtains. Outdoor shower. Run by Creek, a free-spirited Rastafarian who will cook a true Belizan dinner for BZ\$3. Singles and hammock spots BZ\$5.

Glenthorn Manor, 27 Barracks Rd. (tel. 442-12). A bit of luxury before or after the Guatemalan jungle in a beautiful 3-story building with fine grille work. British-educated Caribbean proprietor enjoys international travelers and runs his place like a European pension. Singles with private bath BZ\$60. Doubles with private bath BZ\$79. Triples BZ\$90. Price includes Belizan breakfast of johnny-cakes and fried fish served around a large communal table.

Food

Lunch is the chief meal in Belize, with dinner referred to as tea. Red beans and rice are still staples, but an army of fried chicken stands is overrunning the city. To cool off, fresh lime juice and the domestic Beliken brew (BZ\$1.75 per bottle) are the drinks of choice. Meat pies and fruit tarts are creole specialties that make a good snack. In addition, the multi-ethnic community supports some high-quality Chinese and Indian restaurants. Beware: open sewers are indicative of a low standard of sanitation.

Macy's Restaurant, 18 Bishop St., 1 block southwest of Town Park, between Albert and S. Side Canal St. Homey atmosphere with blues and country music. Outstanding Belizan food cooked with coconut milk and fresh ingredients. Menu changes daily but whole fish, rice, and beans are always available (with coleslaw and fried *plantane* BZ\$7). Open Mon.-Sat. 11:30am-9:30pm.

Dit's Restaurant, 50 King St., between Albert and S. Side Canal St. Café/bakery, undistinguished except for fancy saloon-style fans. Standard rice and bean dishes. Try the *garnaches*, tortillas fried with beans and topped with hot sauce and cheese (BZ35¢ each). Known locally for great pastries, including coconut, custard, and lemon pies. Open Mon.-Sat. 7am-9pm, Sun. 7am-4pm.

Mom's Restaurant, 11 Handyside St., near Queen St. In a dimly lit room with a disturbingly low ceiling. A Belize City institution, popular with locals and globetrotters. Full breakfast BZ\$5-10. Full dinner includes potatoes, salad, bread, and coffee. Conch soup with rice BZ\$7. Open Sun.-Fri. 6am-10pm.

Pop N' Taco, 24 Regent St., 1 block from Brodie's. Neon green storefront, with 4 tables and flashing Christmas bulbs inside. Packed at lunch. Chinese fare on the cheap side. Large serving of seafood soup BZ\$6. Open Mon.-Sat. 8am-9pm, Sun. 11am-3pm and 5-9pm.

New Chon Saan Restaurant, 184 N. Front St., just past the Texaco Station. Great Chinese restaurant serves the best fried chicken in town; the shady neighborhood and questionable characters outside make it all the more popular with locals. The lunch menu combo (chicken soup, egg roll, chow mein, and fried rice for BZ\$8.85) is a hefty meal. Open Mon.-Thurs. 11am-midnight, Fri.-Sat. 11am-1:30am, Sun. 11am-2pm and 5pm-midnight.

Sights and Entertainment

Belize City lacks tourist attractions. The one building worth going out of your way to see is **St. John's Cathedral,** on Albert St. at the southern end of town. Dating from 1826, the building stands as the oldest Anglican cathedral in Central America. The lavish coronations of the kings of the Mosquito Coast took place here. Take a breezy waterfront stroll along **Marine Parade** or **Southern Foreshore** roads, where the city's poshest homes are isolated from its squalor. A few beaches outside of town offer some relief, but the walk back is quite a workout in the heat; it's best to stifle your urge to swim until you arrive at the Cayes. Belizans head to Gillett Beach, 7km out on Western Highway, to picnic. Check local newspapers for the scoop on sporadic outdoor concerts at **Bird's Eye,** located at the southern end of Albert St. A visit to the **Belize Zoo,** 45 minutes west of the city by bus, makes a good daytrip, but leave your pack at the hotel to ease the pain of the mile-long hike into the zoo.

Nightlife is abundant for the adventurous. On Saturday and Sunday, reggae bands draw large crowds to the **Lumba Yaad Bar and Grill,** 1½ miles out on Northern Highway. Locals and tourists dance under thatched roofs on decks overlooking Haulover Creek. (Open Mon.-Thurs. 1:30pm-midnight, Fri. 2pm-midnight, Sat. 3pm-midnight, Sun. 7pm-12:30am.) **The Pub,** 921 N. Front St., caters to a younger crowd and is usually packed. **The Big Apple,** 67 N. Front St., is busy on weekends. A tougher, local crowd dances here alongside neon statuettes of liberty and multi-colored Christmas lights. The **Upstairs Cafe,** a hangout for British soldiers and lo-cals in the know, has live music on Thursdays (Cover BZ$4). The **Hard Rock Cafe,** on the third floor of the building on the corner of Queen and New St., is a more upscale club that some consider the best in town. Dancing and drinking continue until 3am when clubs officially shut their doors, but night owls need only knock to be let in.

The Cayes

The Cayes, Belize's 175 offshore islands, offer spectacular diving and fishing op-portunities for both experienced ocean lovers and recent converts. Because of the natural beauty and increasing tourist demand, investors have been eager to develop the isles. Landing strips and posh hotels already infest **Ambergris Caye** and **Caye Chapel.** The day when all of the *cayes* are converted into clones of Cozumel has yet to come, however, and many of the islands remain uninhabited mangrove swamps.

Most accessible are the *cayes* right off the Belize City shoreline. Flights from the municipal airport take vacationers to Ambergris Caye and Caye Chapel, and regu-larly scheduled launches zip travelers from Belize City to **Caye Caulker,** the less commercialized favorite of budget travelers. Charter a launch to reach the other *cayes* (ask at Jan's Service Station by the Swing Bridge in Belize City). Golf's Caye and English Caye are popular daytrips.

Caye Caulker

The crowded streets of Belize City are a far cry from this island refuge where the most active beings are the gekkos sunning themselves midday, or perhaps the coconut trees swaying in the afternoon breeze. Home to many sun-scorched fisher-men and a few foreigners guarding the secret of their island retreat, Caye Caulker lures tourists in for long stays. Five mestizo families from the Yucatán settled here in 1850 to fish. Their descendants now run modest seaside hotels and restaurants where you can feast on lobster tails (in season July 15-March 15) and beer.

Snorkeling and scuba trips to the reef offer an escape from the heat, pesky mosqui-toes, and sand flies. True, there's no sandy beach, but you won't find jet-skis, T-shirt boutiques, or tequila-crazed teen vacationers on the rampage, either.

Orientation

Zoom from Belize City to Caye Caulker by high-speed launch (45 min., BZ$12). Several islanders make daily round-trips leaving the *caye* promptly at 6:45am and heading back between 10:30 and 11am from **Jan's Service Station,** 73 N. Front St., 2 blocks from the Swing Bridge. Skippers circle like sharks outside the station, try-ing to recruit passengers. Ask inside for a reliable boatman such as **Chocolate,** who runs a mahogany skiff called *Soledad* and is the first to leave in the morning. There are many Chocolates in Belize City: you want the smaller man with a white mous-tache. The other boats leave whenever a group gathers.

If you miss the last regular Caye Caulker boat, you can probably find someone willing to make a charter trip by asking around at Jan's. If you can collect five or more Caye-bound voyagers, you may pay as little as BZ$20 per person. Inspect all crafts before boarding because charter rides on overcrowded boats with puny motors can last up to three soaking hours. To avoid the clamor of Belize City harbor, fly from the international airport to Caye Chapel (BZ$45) and catch a launch from there to Caye Caulker.

In 1961, Hurricane Hattie split Caye Caulker, an elongated isle, into two pieces. The town of Caye Caulker lies on the northern tip of the southern portion. There are no street signs in Caye Caulker—indeed, there are no street names and no addresses. Two parallel dirt roads, known informally as "the front street" and "the back street," run north-south through town. A leisurely walk from end to end takes 15 minutes. A hand-drawn map, on display at most restaurants and guest houses, will help you get your bearings. Landmarks include the police station, on the front street at the center of town, and the two largest piers, which jut out on the east and west sides of the island, a bit south of the police station.

Practical Information

Tourist Information: María Vega, at Vega's Far Inn (tel. 21-42), represents the Belize Tourist Industry Association. Maps BZ$5. Hours vary.

Currency Exchange: None. Most guest houses and restaurants will exchange traveler's checks for clients at poor rates. Try Marin's, open daily 8am-1:30pm and 5:30-9pm.

Post Office: Celi's Mini-Supermarket (tel. 21-01), at the northern end. Mail picked up on Tues. and Fri. Poste Restante available. Open for postal services Mon.-Fri. 8am-noon and 3:30-5:30pm, Sat. 8am-noon.

Telephones: Belize Telecommunications Limited (tel. 21-68 or 21-69), near the soccer field at the north end of town behind Miramar Hotel. Free international collect calls. Open Mon.-Fri. 8am-noon and 1-4pm, Sat. 8am-noon. BZ$40 deposit required. **Telegrams:** same office and hours.

Health Care: (tel. 21-66), 2 blocks from the police station. Clinic open Mon.-Fri. 8am-5pm. After hours emergency only.

Police: (tel. 21-20) in a green and cream-colored house by the basketball half-court on the front road. One-man squad available 24 hr.

Accommodations

Simple hotels, communal showers, cold water, and fans keep the Cancún jet set at bay. Hotel owners often play to the security concerns of their international guests by barring all locals from the premises. Look for a place on the Caribbean side, right on the water; a steady breeze keeps you cool here while giving the cold shoulder to voracious mosquitoes and sand flies. Campers can wander to a desolate part of the isle, or pitch tents at Ignacio's for BZ$3.50 (see below). To minimize attacks by dive-bombing bugs, burn mosquito coil (BZ$1.50) and keep the lights off.

Tom's Hotel (tel. 21-02). Arriving at the island, it's on the far left, close to Celi's Mini-Super, overlooking the Caribbean. Unassuming, cozy rooms with strong ceiling fans. Spiffy communal bathrooms. Young travelers read, rap, and drink rum on the breezy veranda. Towels BZ$2. Singles BZ$13. Doubles BZ$20.

Riva's Guest House (tel. 21-27), at the north end of town, above Aberdeen's Chinese Restaurant. Eight turquoise fan-bedecked rooms off a yellow hall. Pleasant veranda. Singles BZ$10. Doubles BZ$15.

Deisy's Hotel, (tel. 21-50), very close to Celi's, but disadvantageously set back from the water. Six gloomy but clean basement rooms. Genuinely friendly management lives upstairs, past the contingent of half-crazed canines and a hyperactive pet monkey. Doubles BZ$16. Triples BZ$24.

Ignacio's, on the northern beachfront, left of Tom's. Catch Ignacio on a good day and rent your own cabaña with thatched roof and private bath for two (BZ$31.50). Hammock spaces directly on the sandy beach are also available (BZ$3.50).

Food

Caye Caulker's restaurants are legendary for cheap seafood and laid-back (i.e. low) service. Lobster and eggs for breakfast cost just BZ$5.50, but your food may not arrive until lunchtime. To some, the wait is annoying; to others, it's simply an excuse to down a few more beers.

Several homes post signs advertising daily specials, including some of the best pastries and conch fritters on the island. **Miss Gregory,** on the back road, makes delicious lobster burritos.

Marin's Restaurant and Bar, on the back path behind the church. Inside, lights pulse to the reggae beat, while cooler and quieter dining takes place on the back patio. Large servings of fresh fish and potato go for BZ$6.50. Rocky, the bartender, will deny that there is any rum punch left but it's worth the plea (BZ$2.75). Open daily 8am-1:30pm and 5:30-9pm.

Island Yougert, near Sea-hawk. Homemade whole-wheat Belgian waffles with yogurt and fruit (BZ$4.50) served on a pine deck beneath wooden parakeets in cages. Open Mon.-Sat. 8am-noon; in winter Mon.-Sat. 2:30-5:30pm.

Glenda's, behind Syd's. Worth the wait for icy, fresh orange juice (BZ$3 per bottle) and delicious fresh bread and cinnamon rolls (BZ50¢). Four small tables upstairs. Open Mon.-Sat. 7am-4pm.

Syd's, on the back path. Best bet on the Caye for lunch. Tacos BZ25¢, garnaches BZ25¢ and burritos BZ$1. On Saturday night, catch the island-renowned BBQ (BZ$6). Open daily noon-3pm and 6-9pm.

Cabana's, at the northern end of town past Hotel Martinez. Newly remodeled cedar floors and walls make this one of the Caye's most elegant spots. Lobster, eggs, and fryjacks breakfast costs BZ$6. Excellent fresh barracuda in small portions (BZ$8). Open daily 7-10am, 11:30am-3pm, and 6pm-midnight.

Sights and Entertainment

Faintly visible to the east of Caye Caulker, the **Barrier Reef** is a 10-minute launch ride away. The reef is the second largest in the world, bested only by Australia's Great Barrier Reef. Half-day snorkeling trips to the reef's shallow coral gardens and deeper channels are the most popular and economical diving option. Boats leave between 9 and 10am, stop at three snorkeling sites, and return by early afternoon (BZ$10, not including gear rental). Rent fins, a mask, and a snorkel from **Sea-Hawk,** at Island Yougert or **Island Sun,** in front of it. (Rentals BZ$5 plus passport deposit. Both open daily 8am-5pm.)

Captains hang out at the docks soliciting passengers. Before arriving at the docks, ask around for the name of a reliable operator. Be sure to leave your valuables ashore. Chocolate is a reliable informant: ask for him between November and August at **Chocolate's Gift Shop** (tel. 21-51). He also charters day-long river runs through the Maya Mountains (BZ$50). Other local fishermen offer spearfishing trips to the reef (BZ$10-12 per person).

From November to mid-June, you can arrange a relaxing, day-long cruise to San Pedro (BZ$20). The boat leaves between 9 and 10am, and the price includes lunch on Ambergris. You can rent snorkeling gear for an extra BZ$5. Ask at **Sea-Hawk** to find out which boat is going.

Frenchie's, behind Island Yougert, caters to the scuba enthusiast. Two-tank dives cost BZ$75, with gear BZ$100. They also offer night diving for BZ$55. **Belize Diving Services** (tel. 21-43), behind soccer field, offers a four-day NAVI or PADI certification course for US$300. (Open Mon.-Sat. 8:30am-5pm, Sun. 10am-4pm.)

Caye Caulker's only strip of sandy beach lies north of town, where Hurricane Hattie split the island. Would-be tanners beware: insects are especially fierce here because of the heavy vegetation nearby. Opt instead for the piers on the Caribbean side of the island.

For entertainment, islanders and sun-toasted travelers often follow a two-stop circuit. **The Reef Bar** concocts the best, though only mildly alcoholic, rum punch (BZ$3 per glass, BZ$8 per bottle). The bar often shuts down earlier than the stated

midnight closing time. Late-night crowds head to **Pirates,** where an old boat serve
as the bar. Despite the loud reggae tunes, the large dance floor often remains empty
(Open daily 6pm-midnight.)

Ambergris Caye and Caye Chapel

Just 15km north of Caye Caulker, **Ambergris Caye** is Belize's leading tourist des
tination. Although fishing remains a vigorous industry, tourists are fast becoming
the island's most lucrative catch. The main town on the isle, San Pedro, has become
the Atlantic City of the Cayes as North American developers spawn resort hotel
with swimming pools and inflated prices. Golf carts, jet-skis, and sailboards are th
main modes of transportation, and boutiques outnumber budget lodgings here. Try
Rubi's Hotel (tel. 620-63) on the southern side of town. Rubi offers big, airy room
and umbrellas on the beach. (Singles BZ$20, with bath BZ$25. Doubles BZ$40.
If you're only stopping for lunch on the docks, watch the sharks, turtles, and sting
rays play outside the **Tackle Box.**

Ambergris Caye does have a good beach, and because the Barrier Reef runs righ
along the isle's eastern shores, diving is easier here than at Caye Caulker. The **Ho**
Chan Marine Reserve, just south of Ambergris, attracts an assortment of bold fish
that expect stale bread instead of hooks from divers. (Admission BZ$3.)

Several flights depart daily for Ambergris Caye from the international and munci
pal airports in Belize City (BZ$70 round-trip; see Belize City Orientation). A boa
leaving from the Bellevue Hotel in Belize City links the island with the mainland
(BZ$40 round-trip).

Two km south of Caye Caulker lies the answer to every beach freak's prayers
Caye Chapel. Only one resort, with tennis courts and a golf course, interrupts the
natural beauty of the island. A daytrip to Caye Chapel can be arranged at Jan's
Service Station on N. Front St. in Belize City (BZ$20 round-trip). A convenient
alternative is a flight from the international airport in Belize City to Caye Caulker
(BZ$45) and a 10-minute boat ride from there (BZ$5).

Belize City to Guatemala

Belize's Western Hwy. runs 124km from Belize City to the frontier, spanning
grassy savannahs before winding into the Maya Mountains. Although you can
power from Belize City to Tikal in one exhausting day, a few hours of sight-seeing
in western Belize will make the trip far more pleasant. You can visit the Belize Zoo
and tickle a jaguar, or spend the night in San Ignacio (also known as "El Cayo")
and trek through the nearby ruins of Xunantunich or the Mountain Pine Ridge
national forest. From San Ignacio, the great ruins of Tikal in the Guatemalan Petén,
are a hop, skip, and a bumpy three-hour bus ride away.

The Belize Zoo

When the British nature film company she worked for failed in 1983, American
animal lover Sharon Matola opened a zoo. Forty-six kilometers west of Belize City
on the Western Hwy., the menagerie has expanded to house 70 species native to
Belize. Tapir, jaguar, ocelot, monkey—never again will you be so close to such exotic animals.

The zoo is refreshingly unorthodox, without moats, concrete platforms, or cotton
candy. The watchword here is symbiosis. Young guides lead you among the enclo-
sures, pointing out elusive denizens and patiently answering questions. They may
even allow you to pet Gregory and Victoria, a couple of bristly peccaries. Hand-
painted signs drum home a conservationist theme: "We Macaw parrots are as scarce
in this region as rice and beans on the North Pole."

Well worth a stop on the Tikal-Belize City trail, the zoo is easily accessible by car or bus. East and westbound buses on the Western Hwy. pass the 1½km dirt access road about every hour. The fare from Belize City is BZ$2. (Zoo open daily 10am-4:30pm. Admission with ½-hr. tour BZ$10. Buy a distinctive zoo T-shirt for BZ$20 and help support the underfunded park.)

San Ignacio

The village of San Ignacio boomed between 1920 and 1950 thanks to the vigorous exploitation of mahogany and chicle. Eventually the trees dwindled, and Mr. Wrigley found cheap synthetic substances to placate gum chewers. Since the resultant crash, the town has begun a new growth cycle as a center of livestock and agriculture. Today, the Cayo region—of which San Ignacio is the capital—draws increasing numbers of "Eco-tourists," who come to hike, canoe, and ride on horseback through the lush parks and archeological sites. San Ignacio's bank and telephone office, as well as inexpensive food and lodging, make it a good base for exploring the nearby Mountain Pine Ridge forest reserve or the Mayan ruins of Xunantunich (see below) before moving on to Tikal or Belize City.

Entering San Ignacio, you'll pass over the Macal River on Belize's only suspension bridge (built in 1949). To continue toward Benque Viejo del Carmen and Guatemala, make the first left on Old Benque Viejo Rd. and head uphill out of town. To reach the town center, take the first right onto Burn's Av. and drive 2 blocks to Belize Bank. Buses stop near here. **Burn's Avenue,** running north-south, is San Ignacio's commercial strip. For official-as-it-gets **tourist information,** served with beans and rice, consult the staff at Eva's Restaurant, 22 Burn's Av. (Open daily 6am-midnight.)

Belize Bank, 16 Burn's Av. (tel. 20-31), changes money (open Mon.-Thurs. 8am-1pm, Fri. 8am-1pm and 3-6pm). After hours, Bob, the owner of Eva's Restaurant, will exchange U.S. dollars or traveler's checks for Belizan dollars or Guatemalan quetzals.

The town **post office** is on the second floor of the administration building across from the Venus Hotel near the bridge. (Open Mon.-Fri. 8am-noon and 1-5pm.) Downhill on Burn's Av., the **telephone/telegram office** (tel. 220-52), permits free international collect calls. (Open Mon.-Fri. 8am-noon and 1-4pm, Sat. 8am-noon.) If the office is closed, try phoning from Eva's Restaurant. The **telephone code** for San Ignacio is 09.

Several hotels in San Ignacio provide comfortable lodging at comfortable rates. The stately **Hi-Et Hotel,** 12 West St. at Waight St., lacks Hyatt splendor but does have clean rooms with balconies, and the owner may lend you his canoe. (Singles with communal bath BZ$10. Doubles BZ$20.) The **Venus Hotel,** 29 Burn's Av. (tel. 221-86), with its large rooms and immaculate lounge, is the Ritz of the village and worth the few extra dollars. (Singles BZ$20, with bath BZ$35. Doubles BZ$25, with bath BZ$45.) The **Imperial Hotel,** 22 Burn's Av. (tel. 225-82), just upstairs from Eva's, offers a relaxing balcony and clean rooms with fans. (Singles BZ$15. Doubles BZ$20.) If all the rooms are completely full, Bob at Eva's may be able to put you up.

Jungle lodges are popular retreats for "back-to-the-basics" folks and travelers who long for solitude. **Nabitunich** (tel. 323-09), 9km west of San Ignacio, offers ample opportunity for riding, hiking, and canoeing, as well as a view of Xunantunich. From San Ignacio, a *colectivo* costs BZ$2. (Singles US$20, with 2 meals US$45. Doubles US$30, with 2 meals US$60.) Camping is also available (BZ$10). Even farther away from civilization is the **Rancho de Los Amigos** (tel. 322-61), a strenuous 2km hike from the turnoff into San José Succotz directly across from the Xunantunich ferry. An acupuncturist and nutritionist have cleared only enough trees to build two immaculately clean huts and a dining area where all the cooking is done over fire. Two meals are included for US$13. Camping is available.

Low-cost dining abounds in San Ignacio. At **Eva's Restaurant,** 22 Burn's Av., you'll find locals downing brews with their eggs and beans (BZ$4) first thing in the morning. Eva's also stocks a large collection of international postcards and Chicago Cubs posters. The scarcely populated **Serendib Restaurant,** 27 Burn's Av., specializes in Sri Lankan food but also offers a wide variety of steaks (BZ$10) and hamburgers (BZ$4). (Open daily 10am-3pm and 6:30-11pm.)

Great for an afternoon swim after a long bus ride, the **Macal River** flows below the eastern edge of town. Swim from the gravel banks close to town, or find a more secluded spot upstream along the San Ignacio side of the river.

Near San Ignacio: Mountain Pine Ridge and Xunantunich

Mountain Pine Ridge, just south of San Ignacio, is a great daytrip for civilization's discontented, especially if they have a car. Tall conifers, mountains surpassing 1000m, and clear streams grace the large forest reserve, accessible by a road branching off the Western Hwy. just east of San Ignacio at Georgeville. Don't miss the **Hidden Valley Falls** in the park's northwest corner, where a stream plunges 300m into a misty valley. To camp in the reserve, obtain a permit (BZ$15) from the Ministry of Agriculture in Augustine. Contact Mr. Rosado (tel. (22) 10-21-06), Director of the Forestry Department. Remember to bring food, since there are no facilities in the park.

If you do not have a car but want to visit the reserve, you and up to four other people may wish to hire a taxi in San Ignacio (BZ$175 for a full-day tour).

Past San Ignacio on the road to Guatemala, El Castillo, the main temple of **Xunantunich,** towers in the distance to the right. "Maiden of the Rock" in Mayan, Xunantunich was an important city in the late Classic period (700-900 AD) and either a rival or a satellite settlement of Tikal. Only partially excavated and studied, the ruins at Xunantunich are mildly interesting (if disappointing to Tikal veterans); they include an impressive pyramid and a fantastic view of the Belize-Guatemala border area.

Xunantunich rests atop a hill, across the Mopan River and 1½ km up a dirt road from the hamlet of San José Succotz. About 9km from San Ignacio, Succotz is accessible by *colectivo,* several of which shuttle between the Esso station in San Ignacio and the town of Benque Viejo del Carmen on the border (BZ$2). Batty Bros. heads to Benque Viejo from San Ignacio at 9am (BZ50¢) At Succotz take the small cable-drawn ferry across the Mopan. (Operates daily 7:30am-noon and 1-4:30pm. Mon.-Fri. free, Sat.-Sun. BZ$1 per person.) The dirt road leading up to the ruins is rough and steep, making for a vigorous hike or a jangly drive through the jungle.

El Castillo, the tallest edifice (40m) in Belize, dwarfs the other temples and unexcavated mounds. Scamper up the lower portion of the pyramid, which still is engulfed by vegetation, to the partially restored stucco frieze on the eastern corner. Here, two masks depict Kinich Ahau, the sun deity, and Ixchel, the moon god. From El Castillo's reconstructed roof comb, the settlements of Succotz, Benque Viejo del Carmen, and Melchor de Mencos (in Guatemala) are visible from left to right, tucked into the green hills. (Site open daily 8am-5pm. Admission BZ$3.)

To learn about the traditional Mayan bush medicine still practiced in the area, visit the **Panti Trail,** just 3km outside San Ignacio near Cha-Creek. (Trail information book BZ$5. Guide costs BZ$15 per person in groups of three or more.) Be a *mensch* and explore the Macal River by canoe for BZ$25 per day; ask for Toni at Eva's.

Belize/Guatemala Border

Unless you're wearing camouflage or toting ancient Mayan vases, the border crossing should be quick and easy. (Border open daily 6am-9:30pm.) Money changers will approach you on the Belize side, claiming to offer the best rates outside of Guatemala City on U.S. dollars for Guatemalan quetzales. They lie. The **Bank of Guatemala** branches, on the other side of the frontier and in Flores, both convert at substantially better rates. (Open Mon.-Fri. 8:30am-6pm.)

In theory, all passport-carrying citizens of non-communist countries can obtain Guatemalan visas at the border. The length of the visa ranges, apparently in random fashion, from 30 days to several years. Even if you have obtained a visa beforehand, you will be asked to pay a visa fee, ranging from Q5 to US$5, at the border.

Guatemalan buses bound for El Cruce and Flores (last one at 4pm) stop at the border (see Tikal Orientation below), making a stay in **Melchor de Mencos,** the bleak Guatemalan border city, unnecessary.

GUATEMALA

US$1 = 4.50 Quetzales	1 Quetzal = US$0.22
CDN$1 = Q3.92	Q1 = CDN$0.26
UK£1 = Q8.60	Q1 = UK£0.12
AUS$1 = Q3.83	Q1 = AUS$0.26
NZ$1 = Q2.79	Q1 = NZ$0.36

Guatemala spins yarns in over 40 *indígena* languages, as well as in Spanish—of strange politics, Mayan ruins, huge disparities of wealth, lush jungles, and a stunning landscape of volcanoes, rivers, and palms.

The white Ladinos, political and economic rulers of Guatemala, came primarily from Europe and the U.S.; many of them derive their power from *fincas* (plantations) in the countryside, where they grow coffee, sugar cane, and bananas. Although the economy depends heavily on the output of these farms, Guatemala City enjoys urban luxuries such as theaters, a symphony, and many ritzy discos.

Despite Ladino rule, indigenous people constitute more than 80% of the population. Today's Guatemalan *indígenas* are descended from the Maya and for the most part continue their lives as they have for hundreds of years—making and eating tortillas around fires in thatched homes, tilling small plots of land, weaving complicated *huipiles,* and bringing their goods to a market each week.

The rise of the military has forced changes in their life, however; *indígenas* involuntarily make up most of the lower ranks of the army, while rebel *indígenas* join the guerrilla bands. Between the two groups, many of the men have been killed in the last ten years, leaving over 40% of Guatemalan families fatherless. Alcoholism and illiteracy are also challenging problems in this tumultuous country.

Guatemala is still strictly Catholic, but Evangelism is rapidly gaining ground on the Roman Church. Throughout the countryside, many Evangelist churches have sprung up, most of which broadcast their huge and hectic services over public address systems. More aesthetically pleasing are the beautiful cathedrals, such as the one in Chichicastenango, where Catholicism has been imposed on old pagan rituals.

Tourist flow to the area is picking up steam, especially since the political terror of the early 1980s has tapered off. Guatemala provides many excellent places to shop and live extremely well on a tiny budget. The markets are filled with dashing ethnic clothing, leather, pottery, and woven blankets and rugs, all costing a tiny fraction of what they would cost elsewhere. Small woven money purses go for US$0.40; back in the U.S., the same purse commands US$6-8. The budget *viajero* can find excellent meals for the equivalent of about US$2, and a fine hotel room for US$3.

Since gaining independence from Spain in 1821, Guatemala has been governed by a succession of military and civilian dictators. During the 1940s and 1950s Guatemala experimented with a socialist and then communist government led by Arevalo and Arbenz, respectively. Arbenz tried to effect land reform (approximately 20 extended families still own more than 80% of the land in Guatemala). His attempt angered many groups, including the U.S., whose United Fruit Company operated a profitable banana monopoly in the country. In retaliation for the unprovoked attack on the banana crops, the U.S. helped instigate a military coup. Since that time military dictators have run the country; political violence and terror peaked in the mid-1980s. Almost every Guatemalan has friends and family who were killed during this period. Luckily, in the last few years the country has become much more politically stable and safe, under civilian president Vinicio Cerezo, who was elected in 1985. Traveling through the country is now safe for tourists, but guerrilla bands persist and discontent lingers. In the summer of 1989 there was a 2½-month national mail, teacher, and finance strike, with more than 80,000 employees participating. Caution is still called for.

Entering Guatemala

U.S. and Canadian citizens need a visa to enter Guatemala; these may be obtained, free of charge, at any Guatemalan consulate (see Comitán, Tapachula, and Chetumal).

Citizens of the following nations need only a valid passport to enter the country: Austria, Belgium, Denmark, Finland, France, Holland, Italy, Liechtenstein, Luxembourg, Norway, Spain, Sweden, Switzerland, and the Vatican.

Citizens of the U.K.—and often also New Zealand and Australia—may have difficulty obtaining the necessary visa, due to an ongoing dispute with Belize (formerly British Honduras).

The Mexico/Guatemala border crossings at Ciudad Cuauhtémoc, Ciudad Hidalgo, and Talismán are officially open daily from 6am to 9pm, but it is advisable to arrive as early in the day as possible, both to facilitate transportation connections and to avoid delay if the border closes (as has been known to happen) at an unofficially early hour. (For information on transportation from the border to capital, see Guatemala City, Getting There, below).

Food and Health

As in Mexico, one has to be very watchful of one's health while in Guatemala. Diarrhea strikes most foreigners traveling here, and local amoebas love to induce cases of amoebic disentary, generally transmitted through water or by improperly cleaned foods.

The water in Guatemala City and Antigua has been chemically treated and is theoretically safe to drink. Nonetheless, bottled water, *salvavidas,* is a smart idea in the cities, and absolutely necessary in the smaller villages. Also avoid vegetables and fruits that absorb a lot of water, or that can't be peeled, such as lettuce.

You can sanitize vegetables and water by boiling them; soaking greens for 15 minutes in iodine and water also kills nasty amoebas and germs. Most restaurants in Guatemala City and Antigua cater to a foreign crowd and serve safe, delicious *típico* foods.

Additional Concerns

For more information on visiting Guatemala, contact the **Guatemala Tourist Commission,** P.O. Box 144351, Coral Gables, FL 33114.

Guatemala City

Guatemala City is the sprawling center of the Republic, the heart of Ladino culture, and a prime example of the tension between modernization and traditional society. Diesel buses roar down paved avenues, trailing streams of black smog. Men tug wooden carts filled with cucumbers down dirt roads past entrepreneurial *ladinos* meeting over tea before the theater to discuss the latest coffee prices or deregulation policy. Women cook and sell corn tortillas from air-conditioned shacks. Everyone comes to casual and cautious terms with guerrillas and the military; tourists gloat over their new cheap purchases and compare experiences from the countryside and all around Central America.

The city verges on the cosmopolitan. Its *discotecas* pulse to typical *salsa,* and the city supports an active business district, several universities, and a large European and North American contingent. However, the city's center and the majority of its neighborhoods are dominated by *indígenas,* many traditionally dressed in brightly colored woven fabrics.

Few tourists choose to remain in Guatemala City for long. It is large (pop. 1,500,000), polluted, and unsafe for walking alone at night. Nevertheless, the city is not without its charms: it is a comfortable place from which to start exploring, and distills much of what is fascinating about the country.

Orientation

The immense capital divides into 19 "Zonas," but nearly all sights and services of interest to the budget traveler are located in Zona 1, 4, 9, and 10.

Zona 1, Guatemala City's "downtown," is its oldest section. *Calles* run east-west, with street numbers increasing as one moves southward. *Avenidas* run north-south, with numbers increasing as one moves eastward. A building with the address "12a. Calle 6-14," is on 12a. Calle between 6a. and 7a. Av.; the last number in the address simply signifies how many meters the building stands from the end of the block. The major thoroughfare is **6a. Avenida,** which passes the Pl. Mayor (the city's main plaza) in the northern part of Zona 1 and continues south through Zonas 4 and 9.

Zona 4 lies immediately south of Zona 1. Its *calles* also run east-west, and its *avenidas* north-south, but a series of northeast-to-southwest *vías* and northwest-to-southeast *rutas* (with numbers increasing north to south) complicate matters. Fortunately, Zona 4 is too small for you hopelessly to lose your bearings.

Zonas 9 and **10** are Guatemala City's *zonas rosas,* the realm of exclusive boutiques, fancy restaurants, five-star hotels, and elite homes. The southern portion of Zona 10 is the *Zona Viva* (Lively Zone), where the bulk of the city's most expensive nightclubs and discos provide entertainment late into the night. The two Zonas are divided by north-south **Avenida de la Reforma;** Zona 9 is to the west, and Zona 10 to the east.

Dilapidated, crowded *camionetas* (buses) go almost anywhere in the city for 20 centavos. Bus #2 follows perhaps the most useful route, from 10a. Av. in Zona 1, through Zona 4, and down Av. Reforma between Zonas 9 and 10. Returning, it travels north on Av. Reforma, through Zona 4, and up 9a. Av. in Zona 1. The color of the bus number is significant; a bus displaying a red #5, for example, has a slightly different route than one with a black #5. Although the buses are generally safe and orderly, hold on to your valuables.

Micros (vans or smaller buses) observe the same routes as *camionetas,* plus many additional routes, charging 20 centavos as well. Destinations are posted on the windshields. If the one you wish to take arrives already brimming over with passengers, don't fret: there's usually room for one more.

La Aurora International Airport is about 7km south of downtown, in Z.13. It is served by **Pan Am** (tel. 821-81); **Continental** (tel. 31-20-51); **Eastern** (tel. 31-74-55); **Iberia** (tel. 37-39-11); **Mexicana** (tel. 51-88-24); and **KLM** (tel. 37-02-22), as well as several other local airlines. **Aeroquetzal** (tel. 34-76-80), **Aerovías** (tel. 34-53-86), **Tapsa** (tel. 31-91-80), and **Aviateca** (tel. 31-82-22) all fly to Flores (close to Tikal) for about US$100 round-trip. Bus #6 and bus black #5 shuttle passengers between *el centro* and the airport for 20 centavos. A taxi from downtown costs Q25.

Guatemala City's train station is at 9a. Av. 18-03, Z.1 (tel. 830-31). Trains provide slow, uncomfortable, unreliable, cheap service to Tecún Umán and Puerto Barrios several times per week. (To Puerto Barrios Tues., Thurs., and Sat. at 7am; to Tecún Umán Tues. and Sat. at 7:15am.)

Guatemala City has no central bus terminal; dozens of bus companies maintain separate offices across the city. Many buses leave from 19a. Calle between 7a. and 10a. Av. (near the train station in Z.1). Several others leave from the huge combined terminal/market in Zona 4, between 1a. and 4a. Av. and 1a. and 7a. Calles. Few companies have offices here; buses simply idle in one of the two enormous parking lots while crews call out their destinations.

Transportation to and from the Mexican Border

To La Mesilla (Ciudad Cuauhtémoc): El Cóndor, 19a. Calle 2-01, Z.1 (tel. 285-04), leaves for the border at 4, 8, and 10am (7 hr., Q12). **Rutas Lima,** 8a. Calle 3-63, Z.1 (tel. 53-18-28), charges Q15 and stops in Quetzaltenango. Buses to Quetzaltenango (4 hr.) depart at 8am, 2:30pm, 4:30pm, and 8pm. From there, buses head for the border at 5am and 3:30pm, and return to Guatemala City at 4:30am, 10am, and 2pm.

To El Carmen (Talismán): Autopullmans Fortaleza, 19a. Calle 8-70, Z.1 (tel. 51-79-94), sends 18 per day (5 hr., Q14). Autopullmans Galgos, 7a. Av. 19-44, Z.1 (tel. 53-48-68), has 16 per day in each direction (Q15). Rutas Lima buses leave Guatemala City at 6:30am, 2:30pm, 6:30pm, and 8pm and returns at 4:30am, 10am, and 2pm (Q13).

To Ciudad Tecún Umán (Ciudad Hidalgo): Fortaleza sends 6 per day 5:15am-3pm (5 hr., Q12) and Rápidos del Sur, 19 Calle 8-82, Z.1 (tel. 51-66-78), offers more frequent service (19 per day, Q12).

Transportation to Flores, Petén (Tikal)

Fuente del Norte 17a. Calle 8-46, Z.1 (tel. 838-94), dispatches common (see next paragraph) buses (Q25) at 1, 2, 3, 4, and 5am on the 18-hr. trip to Flores. If possible, take the pullmans that leave at 7am and 11pm (Q40); buy tickets in advance for the 11-hr. trip.

Common buses, lamented by some as "mobile chicken coops," are converted schoolbuses that sit three to a bench. The long, rough road between Flores and Guatemala City will dominate your nightmares in years to come if you make the passage in one of these.

There are few if any paved roads in northern Guatemala, and the now-paved Puerto Barrios highway is poorly maintained. Rainy season results in a head-flailing ride; beefy Adrian advises, "See your personal rolfer when you get home." Flying to Tikal is far more expensive, but you should consider trading the family jewels for the comfortable ride (see above for airline information).

Transportation to the Interior

To Poptún: Fuente del Norte passes by en route to Flores and sends a direct bus daily at 9am (Q20).

To Antigua: Lux, America Preciosa, and several other companies leave every 20 min. 6:30am-8pm. Buses (Q2) depart from 15a. Calle 3-63.

To Quetzaltenango: Rutas Limas (see La Mesilla above) and Lineas America, 2a. Av. 18-47 (tel. 214-32), send 5 buses per day each way (Q10), and Galgos sends 7 per day each way (Q10).

To Chichicastenango: Veloz Quichelense leaves every ½ hr. 5am-6pm from the bus terminal in Z.4.

To Panajachel: Rebulli, 3a. Av. 2-36, Z.9 (tel. 51-65-05) leaves every hr. 6:45am-3:45pm.

Consult bus schedules at the tourist office for more information.

Practical Information

Tourist Office: Instituto Guatemalteco de Tourismo (INGUAT), 7a. Av. 1-17, Z.4 (tel. 31-13-33), in the Centro Cívico just south of the Zona 1 border. Staff helpful, knowledgeable, and fluent in English. Maps (US$1.50) of the city and surrounding areas. Open Mon.-Fri. 8am-4:30pm, Sat. 8am-1pm.

Embassies: U.S., Av. Reforma 7-01, Z.10 (tel. 31-15-41 through 31-15-46). Open Mon.-Fri. 8am-noon and 1-5pm. Canada, 7a. Av. 11-59, Z.9 (tel. 32-14-11 or 32-14-13), 6th floor. Open Mon.-Thurs. 8am-4:30pm, Fri. 8am-1:30pm. U.K., 7a. Av. 5-10, Z.4 (tel. 32-16-01), 7th floor of the Centro Financero Torre II. Consult the blue section of the phone book for other embassies (New Zealand and Australia have no embassies in Guatemala).

Consulates: Mexico, 13a. Calle 7-30, Z.9 (tel. 36-35-73), ½ block from Av. Reforma. Get your Mexican tourist card here. Open Mon.-Fri. 8:30am-2:30pm, Sat. 9:15-11am. Arrive as early as possible. If your journey takes you farther south, inquire about visa requirements, etc., at the following Central American consulates. Costa Rica, Av. Reforma 8-60, Z.9 (tel. 32-05-31), third floor. Open Mon.-Fri. 9am-3pm. Honduras, 16a. Calle 8-27, Z.10 (tel. 37-39-21). Open Mon.-Fri. 8:30am-1:30pm). Nicaragua, 10a. Av. 14-72, Z.10 (tel. 37-42-64). Panamá, 5 Via 4-50, Z.4 (tel. 32-07-63), on the 7th floor of the Edificio Maya. El Salvador, 12a. Calle 5-43, Z.9 (tel. 32-58-48).

Immigration: To extend your stay in Guatemala past the limit stamped in your passport, drop by the Guatemalan Immigration Office (Migración), 8a. Av. 12-10, Z.1 (tel. 53-41-58). Open Mon.-Fri. 8am-4:30pm; arrive as early as possible.

Currency Exchange: Banks generally are open Mon.-Fri. 9am-8pm, and are much safer but slower than the *cambistas* on the street. The black market yields a slightly more favorable rate, but traders sometimes rob tourists or pass them funny money. Ask a local to refer you to a reputable money-changer.

Central Post Office: 7a. Av. 12-11, Z.1, in the enormous pink building. Lista de Correos posted in the rooms marked Poste Restante, at the end of the hallway to the left as you enter the building. Open Mon.-Sat. 8am-4:30pm. Guatemala's postal service is plagued by strikes and poor management. If necessary, packages can be sent from **King's Express Carrier** at several locations, including the *tienda* at 7a. Av. 12-39, Z.1, across from Guatel. In the summer of 1990, parcels could not be sent to Europe from Guatemala.

Telephones: Main office of Guatel, the national communications network, is at 7a. Av. 12-39, Z.1. Long-distance calls may also be placed from any of the Guatel branches located throughout the city, including at 7a. Av. 3-34, Z.4; and on 8a. Av. at 12a. Calle, Z.1. Open 24 hr. Phoning is incredibly difficult here, even from Guatel *cabines;* try the more expensive hotels when placing international or domestic calls. Collect calls can be made from any of the city's pay phones free of charge by dialing 190.

Telegrams: Telegrams may be sent from any Guatel office. Open 24 hr.

Bookstores: La Plazuela, 12a. Calle 6-14, Z.9. Large selection of used paperbacks for sale at half the U.S. price. They'll also give you credit for your old books. Open Mon.-Fri. 9am-12:30pm and 3-6pm, Sat. 9am-12:30pm. Guatemala City's best selection of U.S. magazines is at the **Book Nook,** in the Camino Real Hotel, Av. Reforma 14-30, Z.9 (tel. 31-94-31). The latest best-sellers (Q20) and U.S. newspapers (Q9-11) also on sale. Open daily 7am-9pm.

Laundry: El Siglo, 3a. Calle 13-09, Z.1 (tel. 214-69). 3kg wash for Q6. Other locations in the city. Open Mon.-Sat. 8am-6pm.

Red Cross: 8a. Av. at 3a. Calle, Z.1 (tel. 125). 24-hr. emergency service.

24-Hr. Pharmacies: Farmacia Sinai Centro, 4a. Av. 12-74, Z.1 (tel. 51-52-76); **Farmacia Angie,** Av. Elena 16-26, Z.3 (tel. 856-36); **Farmacia de Urgencia,** 7a. Av. 3-20A, Z.9 (tel. 36-79-64).

Ambulance: Tel. 128. 24-hr. service.

Police: 6a. Av. 13-71, Z.1 (tel. 120).

Accommodations

Zone 1 is hardly hurting for cheap hotels, but one must be willing to tolerate the noises and stench of the unmuffled, fire-breathing behemoths that traverse the streets. Even the upscale hotels in this area will only set you back about US$10.

Hotel Chalet Suizo, 14a. Calle 6-82, Z.1 (tel. 51-37-86). "Ambiente Internacional," declares the sign out front, and it is no idle boast: the hotel's luxurious rooms attract true world-travelers. Very popular and often full: Get here early in the day or get lost. Clean rooms and hot water. Singles Q14, with bath Q19. Doubles Q30, with bath Q38. Triples Q33, with bath Q48.

Pensión Meza, 10a. Calle 10-17, Z.1 (tel. 231-77). The best place to overhear travel tips. Play ping-pong in the game room, lounge in the courtyard, or sip a beer in the attached café. Helpful bulletin board. Away from the busy streets. Communal bathrooms. Singles Q15. Doubles Q20. Bed in dormitory Q8.

Spring Hotel, 8a. Av. 12-65, Z.1 (tel. 266-37). Handsome old building. Enormous doors and windows open onto a large, clean courtyard. Popular with adults over thirty and Brady Bunch-types. Guatemologist Darcy oozes praise for the joint: "I'm naming my first kid Spring." Singles Q12. Doubles Q19, with bath Q24. Triples Q26.

Hotel Gran Central, 9a. Av. 15-31, Z.1 (tel. 295-14). Eighty four rooms off a narrow, 2-tiered hallway. Few *gringo* guests, but there's almost always a vacancy. Very basic, fairly clean. Friendly management. Singles Q10, with bath Q16. Doubles Q12, with bath Q17.

Hotel Colonial, 7a. Av. 14-19, Z.1 (tel. 229-55), around the corner from the Chalet Suizo. Gorgeous colonial building with a verdant covered courtyard. Mahogany cabinets and an electric fireplace in the sitting room. Singles Q36, with bath Q45. Doubles Q48, with bath Q60.

Hotel Fénix, 7a. Av. 15-81, Z.1. Achieves that lived-in look: slanted floors, tattered living room, and an ancient restaurant, but very comfortable. Some rooms have carpet. Q9 per person, Q24 per room with bath.

Hotel Ritz, 6a. Av. 9-28, Z.1 (tel. 53-63-46), right on the main drag. Climb the stairs to a surprisingly quiet courtyard. Fairly clean and pleasant rooms with cotton mattresses that do a decent hammock impersonation. Grungy communal baths. Singles Q17. Doubles Q29. Triples Q35. Quads Q41.

Hotel Bilbao, 15a. Calle 8-45, Z.1 (tel. 292-03). Gray rooms and old tiled floors recede from the comfortable, high-ceilinged lobby. Hot water in communal baths. Parking available. Doubles Q17, with bath Q22. Triples Q27.

Hotel Ajau, 8a. Av. 15-62, Z.1 (tel. 204-88). Two floors of cushy rooms and clean bathrooms. Cozy leather couches sprout in the covered courtyard. Singles Q16. Doubles Q22. Triples Q24. Private baths an additional Q5.

Food

Budget travelers (except those heading for Chapter 11), indulge yourself in Guatemala City! The capital is home to *típico guatemalteco,* various ethnic cuisines, rustic outdoor *fondas,* and luxurious five-star establishments. At many moderately priced restaurants, you can enjoy a good-sized, savory meal for little more than *dos dólares.*

Los Antojitos, 15a. Calle 6-28, Z.1, and Av. Reforma 15-02, Z.9, plus several other locations throughout the city. Excellent regional food in an upscale but casual atmosphere. Quick, friendly, and polite service. Enormous *combinaciones típicas* go for Q8. *Viejitos* churn out live *marimba* music nightly. Open Mon.-Sat. noon-10:30pm, Sun. noon-6pm. MC, Visa, and Diners Club accepted.

Las Tertulias, Av. Reforma 10-31, Z.10. Fancy, with a large menu, but its main attraction is the "Super Lunch Ejecutivo": a huge multi-course meal (soup or fresh fruit, excellent bread, 2 vegetables, entree, dessert, and coffee or tea) all for Q8. Similar "Super Cena" Q11. Open daily 9:30am-midnight.

Restaurante y Cafetería Peñalba, 6a. Av. 11-71, Z.1, in the heart of downtown. Popular with travelers and locals, especially for breakfast. Eggs (scrambled or fried), bacon, cereal, toast, coffee, and orange juice Q3-5.50. Large daily lunch specials Q5. Excellent coffee Q1. Open daily 7am-10pm.

Restaurant Bolognia, 10a. Calle 6-20, Z.1. Walk through the brick arch in back and straight into Naples. Tasty pizza Q4-10. Minestroni Q6. Open daily 10am-10pm.

Danny's Pancakes, 12a. Calle 5-54, Z.9, at 6a. Av. in a shopping plaza. Enjoy fluffy American-style pancakes as you thumb through back issues of *Car and Driver.* Short stack (of pancakes, not magazines) with butter and 3 kinds of syrup Q4, with fruit and whipped cream Q5. The miracle cure for those subterranean homesick American blues. Open Mon. 6:30am-Sun. 10pm.

Pollo Campero, 6a. Av. at 15a. Calle, Z.1, and dozens of other locations. Like Kentucky Fried Chicken, but the food outranks the Colonel's. The "Menú Super Campero" includes 3 pieces of chicken, fries, slaw, bread, soda, and coffee all for Q8; for smaller appetites, the "Menú Campero" includes only 2 pieces (Q6). Jam-packed and steamy at lunchtime; arrive early to get a table. Open daily 7am-11pm.

Entertainment

Guatemala City's nightlife gets active, particularly in the newly developed *Zona Viva* (Zone 9). Outside this area it's unsafe to walk alone at night. **Kahlua,** 1a. Av. 13-29, Z.10., is quiet during the week but explodes to the beat of U.S. rock on the weekends. People show up around 10:30 or 11pm and leave around 3am. Drinks range from Q6 to Q14. The DJs and the small dance floor are appropriate for the over-24 crowd. The grown-up wanna-bees head down the street two blocks to **Dash,** in a commercial complex on 10a. Calle. Locals consider the **Tropical Room** (between the Sheraton and a strip joint on 6a. Av., Z.1) a bit sleazy because of the excessive degree of dirty dancing that goes on, but it's a great place to practice your *salsa.*

Sights

La Plaza Mayor (also called Pl. de Armas) hogs a large city block in the northern sector of Zona 1, bounded on the west and east by 6a. and 7a. Avenidas and on the north and south by 6a. and 8a. Calles. Permanently animated by persistent *limpiabotas* (boys who charge your shoes 50 centavos for a fine polish), the plaza provides a forum for scruffy vendors hawking Budweiser T-shirts. Often called "the center of all Guatemala," the plaza never bores the wanderer.

To the east of the plaza rises the beautiful Catedral Metropolitana, constructed between 1782 and 1868. To the north, guarded by dozens of camouflaged and gun-toting soldiers, is the Palacio Nacional, seat of the Republic's often-troubled government. Free tours are given Monday through Friday from 8am to 4:30pm.

A few blocks from here, the Central Market has a fantastic selection of food, crafts, and flowers, with great deals offered in every stall. Unlike those in other towns, such as the square in Antigua, this market caters primarily to locals. (Open Mon.-Sat. 8am-6pm, Sun. 8am-noon.)

The Mercado de Artesanías, 11a. Av. at 6a. Calle, sells textiles, ceramics, and jewelry from each region of the country in a pickpocket-free atmosphere. Located in the museum district of Z.13, it is accessible by either the #6 or black #5 bus, which runs up and down 10a. Av.

The Mapa en Relieve, an enormous horizontal relief map of Guatemala, is ogled by tourists and Guatemalans alike. Viewers mount towers on either side of the map, designed and built in the early 1900s, to look down upon the precise representation of the mountainous country. This immensity is a boon for Guatemalans who cannot afford to travel outside the city, and for others who want to put their travels into perspective. The map is at the end of 6a. Av., about 2km north of the plaza (take bus #1 from 5a. Av. in Zona 1 or the #45 or 46 from 5a. Av. elsewhere).

The Museo Nacional de Arqueología y Etnología, Edificio 5 La Aurora (tel. 72-04-89), on 6a. Calle, Z.9, near the airport, keeps hundreds of Mayan artifacts from all over Guatemala, an excellent 1:200 scale model of the ancient city at Tikal, an exhibit of regional *típico* apparel, and a large collection of ceremonial masks, both pre-Columbian and modern. (Open Tues.-Fri. 9am-4pm, Sat.-Sun. 9am-noon and 2-4pm. Admission Q1.)

Across the street in Edificio 6 is the Museo Nacional de Arte Moderno (tel. 72-04-67). In this corner of the world, "modern" means post-Columbus. On display are several hundred *guatemalteco* paintings and sculptures, of which the oils by Carlos Mérida (1891-1984) are most interesting. (Museum open Tues.-Fri. 8:30am-4pm, Sat.-Sun. 9am-noon and 2-4pm. Free.)

Museo Popol-Vuh, Av. Reforma 8-60, Z.9 (tel. 34-71-21) specializes in pre-Columbian Mayan pottery. (Open Mon.-Sat. 9am-5:30pm. Admission Q3, ages age 10 and under 25 centavos.)

Other bastions of culture include the Museo Nacional de Historia, 9a. Calle at 10a. Av., Z.1 (tel. 53-61-49; open Tues.-Fri. 8:30am-4pm, Sat.-Sun. 9am-noon and 2-4pm; free); the Museo Nacional de Artes e Industrias Populares, 10a. Av. 10-72, Z.1 (open Tues.-Fri. 9am-4pm, Sat.-Sun. 9am-noon and 2-4pm; admission 25 centavos); the Museo de Fray Francisco Vásquez, a collection of religious artifacts and art from the 17th through 20th centuries in the Iglesia de San Francisco, the larger of the two churches at the corner of 13a. Calle 6-34, Z.1 (open Mon.-Fri. 9am-noon and 3-6pm; admission 50 centavos); and the Museo de Historia Natural, 7a. Av. at 6a. Calle, Z.9, across the street from the archeology/ethnology and modern art museums (open Tues.-Fri. 9am-4pm, Sat.-Sun. 9am-noon and 2-4pm; free).

The archeological site of Kaminaljuyú, in Zona 7, several kilometers west of downtown, is closed to the public while excavations continue. Call the Instituto de Antropología (tel. 259-48) for further information. To get to the site take a bus marked "Kaminaljuyu."

Near Guatemala City: Volcano Pacaya

Guatemala's most active volcano receives rave reviews from the hikers who ascend to the summit. Situated between the city Escuintla and the southern tip of Guatemala, it is difficult to reach and a particularly challenging climb during the rainy season. Buses leave Guatemala City from the terminal in Zona 4 to **San Viciente Pacaya**, **El Cedro**, and **San Francisco de Salle**. It's best to stay the night at any of these spots and start the two-hour ascent early the next morning in order to catch the bus back to Guatemala City at noon or 3pm. In El Cedro, **Sr. Rocael Armando Morales** rents out one room (Q10) and offers a guided tour (Q25). From San Viciente, hitch or hike 6km to San Francisco de Salle, then ask for the road to the volcano. From the woods, turn left and follow the narrow road up the mountain. A building halfway up serves as a nondescript landmark.

Be sure to bring warm clothes and plenty of water. Caution is advised, especially for women: two rapes, as well as numerous armed robberies, have been reported. Travel with a group and leave nothing to chance.

Antigua

In 1527, the second capital of Guatemala was built none-too-sagely at the base of the magnificent Volcan de Agua. Twenty years later, the volcano belatedly showed its appreciation by spewing forth enough lava to obliterate the city. By 1543, the Spaniards had laid out another town in the Valley of Panchoz; originally named Santiago de los Cabelleros de Guatemala, the city reigned as capital of Spanish Central America for 200 years before being destroyed by a gargantuan earthquake in 1776.

The quake jostled Antigua from its position as political, social, and spiritual center of the Spanish holdings in the New World, but the city remains a major tourist epicenter to this day. Rugged green mountains encroach upon *colonias* of majestic colonial architecture, providing a beautiful setting for the thousands of students who come to the city to learn Spanish (see Spanish Schools below).

Antigua will, no doubt, remind travelers coming from Mexico of San Cristóbal de las Casas; both are colonial outposts sequestered high in the mountains, deep within *indígena* territory. Yet the southern city enjoys several advantages over its near-twin: Antigua is warmer, the nearby *indígenas* are friendlier to outsiders, and the roving vendors less pesky with their sales pitches. On top of all this, Antigua is cheaper.

Orientation

Antigua is only 45km west-southwest of Guatemala City, but the trip over winding mountain roads requires a whole hour.

Frequent second-class schoolbuses connect the capitals of past and present. **Lux, San Francisco, Reina Antigua, America Preciosa,** and several other lines leave Guatemala City every half hour (see Guatemala City, Transportation to the Interior) and arrive in Antigua at *el mercado* on Alameda Santa Lucia, 3 blocks west of the central plaza. Fare is Q1.20 on weekdays, Q1.50 on Saturday and Sunday.

Though compact, Antigua can prove tricky to navigate. Very few *calles* and *avenidas* are marked, street numbers follow no obvious plan, and many streets look alike. *Avenidas* run north-south and are numbered one to seven beginning in the east. North of 5a. Calle, *avenidas* are designated "Norte"; south of it, they are labeled "Sur." *Calles* run east-west and are numbered one to nine starting in the north. East of 4a. Av., *calles* are named "Oriente"; west of it, they are designated "Poniente." The **Parque Central** is bounded by 4a. and 5a. Calles on the north and south, respectively, and 4a. and 5a. Av. on the east and west.

Practical Information

Tourist Office: In the Palacio de los Capitanes (tel. 32-07-63), on the southeast corner of the Parque Central. Friendly employees are very knowledgeable about Antigua and environs, but slaves to the 5 o'clock bell. Go early and pick up a free city map. Open daily 8am-5pm.

Currency Exchange: Lloyds Bank, 4a. Calle Ote. 2 (tel. 32-04-44) at 4a. Av., on the northeast corner of the Parque Central. Open Mon.-Fri. 9am-3pm. **Banco del Agro,** 4a. Calle Pte. 8 (tel. 32-07-93) on the north side of the park. Open Mon.-Fri. 9am-3pm, Sat. 9am-1pm. Both change cash and traveler's checks.

Post Office: Alameda Santa Lucía at 4a. Calle Pte. (tel. 32-04-85), across the street from the market and the bus stop. Open Mon.-Fri. 8am-4pm. In the summer of 1990, the national post office stopped delivering packages until better rates could be negotiated. For reliable courier service, try **King's Express,** 4a. Calle Pte. 23, near the post office. Q4 for a 1-oz. letter to the U.S. Open Mon.-Sat. 8:30am-12:30pm and 2:30-7pm.

Telephones: Guatel, on 5a. Av. Sur, just south of the southwest corner of the park. Often crowded. Q14 charge for unsuccessful long-distance calls. Open daily 7am-midnight. From pay phones, dial 190 for the international operator.

Telegrams: International telegrams can be sent from **Guatel,** 5a. Av. Sur, just south of the Parque Central. Open daily 7am-midnight.

Bus Station: Behind the market on Alameda Santa Lucia. To get to Chichicastenango or Quetzaltenango, take a bus to Chimaltenango (every hr. 6am-4pm, 75 centavos). At this intersection, **Los Encuentos** buses and *combis* stop on their way to Chichicastenango and Quetzaltenango (Q1).

Laundromat: Posada Refugio, 4a. Calle Pte. 30. Wash and dry 3kg Q7. Same-day service. Open daily 7am-7pm.

Hospital Pedro de Betancourt: 3a. Av. at 6a. Calle (tel. 32-03-01).

Police: Policía Nacional (tel. 32-02-51), on the south side of the Parque Central in the Palacio de los Capitanes Generales. 24-hr. emergency service.

Accommodations

The spigots deliver hot water, the floors are clean, and the company good; in general, Antigua is a city of great budget accommodations. Many families rent out rooms on a weekly basis (Q100), all meals included. Ask at the tourist office for details.

Pensión El Arco, 5a. Av. Nte. 32. Cluttered but clean, with an extremely friendly, relaxed atmosphere. Sparkling floors and small communal bathrooms. Only a few rooms; arrive early. Singles Q8. Doubles Q13.

Hospedaje El Pasaje, Santa Lucía Sur 3, south of the bus stop. Spic-and-span rooms and well-maintained bathrooms with hot water. Extremely amiable staff. If they're full, let them direct you to their annex, 4 blocks away. Q5 per person.

Posada Refugio, 4a. Calle Pte. 30, near the bus stop. Long Antigua's most popular budget hotel, it's not quite as well-preserved or comfortable as some of its competitors. Room quality varies greatly, so inspect carefully before accepting. Get up early for a hot shower: the *agua caliente* doesn't last forever. Doors lock at 1am. Singles Q8, with bath Q10. Unofficial overnight guests pay an extra Q8.

Posada de Doña Angelina, 4a. Calle Pte. 33, near the bus stop. Clean and comfortable. No need for morning coffee: rooms on the 3rd floor afford an eye-opening view of 3 volcanoes. First-floor rooms (Q12) are usually bypassed for the plusher ones upstairs. Singles Q14, but for you, says the friendly proprietor, prices can be arranged.

Posada San Francisco, 3a. Calle Ote. 19, 1 door past Alianca Francesa. No sign hangs outside this newcomer. Loose electrical wiring could make for a scream of a night. Great owners. Singles Q10.

Pensión La Antigüeñita, 2a. Calle Pte. 25, northwest of the Parque Central. The old cots are rock-hard, chickens shuffle in the desolate courtyard, and the showers are a nauseating shade of banana, but the price is right. Curfew 10pm. Doors open at 6am. Singles Q5. Doubles Q7, with 2 beds Q9.

Posada Landívar, 5a. Calle Pte. 23, ½ block southeast of the *mercado.* Very modern and clean with extra perks: soap, towels, big beds, and water jugs in the halls. Q20 per room.

Food

Some only half-jokingly call Antigua "the capital of international budget cuisine"; restaurants here cater to *gringo* taste and the backpacker's budget.

Panadería y Cafetería Doña Luisa de Xicotencatl, 4a. Calle Ote. 12, 1 ½ blocks east of the Parque Central. Fancy hangout for *gringos* and well-to-do *guatemaltecos.* The place to be to find out who is in town. Fabulous breakfasts of yogurt, fruit, and granola (Q7). Pancakes Q4. Large library of English books open Mon.-Sat. 10am-6pm. Restaurant open daily 7am-10pm.

Restaurant Zen, 3a. Av. Nte. 3, 1 block east of the park. Look for the small wooden sign outside. Huge portions of excellent Japanese food. Vegetarian dishes with eggs and rice Q5, with shrimp Q7. Fried ginger chicken Q8. Open daily noon-10pm.

Fonde de la Calle Real, 5a. Av. Nte. 5, ½ block north of the park. Looks tiny from the street, but there's plenty of room upstairs. Tasty *comida típica* in untypically small doses. *Quesos fundidos* with 7 different cheeses Q5-6. Grilled chicken, potato, rice salad, and tortillas Q10. Open daily 7am-10pm.

Casa de Café Ana, 5a. Av. Sur at 9a. Calle Pte. Small, quiet, and off the beaten path. The *menú del día,* a 5-course meal with meat or chicken, pasta, vegetables, soup, and dessert, costs Q11. The best dinner deal in town. Open Thurs.-Tues. 8am-9pm. MC, Visa accepted.

Restaurante San Carlos, under the arcade on the north side of the park. A true Guatemalan joint squatting incongruously in the midst of chic Euro-American restaurants. Food simple but tasty. A superb spot for breakfast or lunch. Breakfast of eggs, beans, orange juice, and coffee Q5. Open daily 7am-10pm.

The biggest party in town is at **Mío Cid Bar,** on 5a. Calle Ote. at 3a. Av. Nte. 1 block east of the plaza, a high-tech hangout popular with European and North American travelers. The music is marvy and the drinks range from Q2 to Q5. Videos every evening before the band sets up. (Open Mon.-Fri. 4pm-1am, Sat.-Sun. 2pm-1am.) **Bianco's,** 6 Av. Nte. 17, jams to a live band almost every night and pours 2-for-1 beers weeknights from 5 to 7pm.

Sights

Antigüeños boast that their **Semana Santa** celebration is the most vibrant (and the most solemn) in the Western Hemisphere. Everyone who's anyone participates in the week's activities: images of the saints, borne on the shoulders of the faithful, bob through a dignified, torturously slow procession; *velaciones* (wakes) last long into the night in many of Antigua's 25 candle-lit, incense-filled churches; carpet-weavers spend days making *alfombras;* and celebrants craft intricate designs of brilliant flower petals on the city's cobblestone streets.

The spectacle begins on **Domingo de Ramos** (Palm Sunday). Each day of the following week brings at least one—and often several—processions or *velaciones,* culminating on **Viernes Santo** (Good Friday). During Semana Santa, Antigua is inundated with pilgrims and tourists, both Guatemalan and foreign; make accommodations arrangements as many months in advance as possible. The best chance for a bed if you arrive without reservations is in a private home.

Sure, Semana Santa is a spectacle; but Antigua is by no means ordinary the rest of the year. The entire city—with its colonial churches, secular buildings, and mountain setting—qualifies as a sight; several places merit special visits. The **Parque Central** serves as a comedic classroom for frenetic foreigners practicing their *español* with patiently enduring locals. The central fountain, *Llamada de la Sirenas* (The Siren's Call), built in the 1730s, and the park's stone benches are prime places to pick up new *amigos.* On the north side of the plaza is the **Palacio del Ayuntamiento;** to the south is the **Palacio de los Capitanes;** to the east is Antigua's **cathedral.**

The **Museo de Santiago,** in the Palacio de Ayuntamiento, exhibits colonial furniture, tools, coins, clothing, paintings, and weapons. (Open Tues.-Fri. 9am-4pm,

Sat.-Sun. 9am-noon and 2-4pm. Admission 25 centavos.) In the same building you'll find the **Museo del Libro Antiguo** (Old Book Museum), which examines the history of New World printing and bookmaking, plus 17th-century books and manuscripts. (Open Tues.-Fri. 9am-4pm, Sat.-Sun. 9am-noon and 2-4pm. Free.) Among the city's other museums are the **Museo de Arte Colonial,** on the old campus of the University of San Carlos on 5a. Calle Ote. 5 east of the park (open Tues.-Fri. 9am-4pm, Sat.-Sun. 9am-noon and 2-4pm; admission 25 centavos), and **Casa K'ojom,** Recoletos 55, behind the bus stop, which doubles as a study center for indigenous music (museum open Mon.-Sat. 9:30am-12:30pm and 2:30-5pm; admission 50 centavos; slide shows and live music demonstrations Tues. at 3pm and Wed. at 10:30am).

Guatemala has been rocked by several serious earthquakes. Such tremors caused the capital to be relocated in the early 1700s. One of the most interesting colonial earthquake casualties is the ruined **Iglesia y Convento Santa Clara,** 2a. Av. Sur 27 at 6a. Calle Ote. Wander through the cloister, infirmary, and "chapel" (more like a huge sanctuary) of this former convent and church. Its stunning semi-restored grassy courtyard gushes with brilliant flowers. (Open Tues.-Sun. 9am-5pm. Admission 25 centavos.)

Don't miss the churches **La Merced,** 1a. Calle Ote., at the northern end of 51a. Av., and **Iglesia de San Francisco,** 7a. Calle Ote. and Calle de los Pasos, where one wall is covered with letters of gratitude to "Hermano Pedro" (Pedro de San José Bethancourt), a Catholic saint interred in a sepulchre there. (Both open daily 6:30am-7:30pm.) Also of interest is **Casa Popenue,** 5a. Calle Ote. and 1a. Av. This 17th-century house, including its first bathroom and kitchen, has been restored to its original condition. (Open to the public for guided tours Mon.-Sat. 3-5pm. Admission Q1.)

Spanish Schools

Antigua attracts many students to its language institutes; at present, nearly 30 schools teach Spanish to foreigners from around the globe. All schools offer individual instruction, most at flexible times (usually 4-7 hr., 5 days per week). In a one-on-one situation, the skill of the individual teacher is the crucial factor. The weekly payment plan makes it easy to switch instructors.

Schools encourage potential students to make written reservations well in advance. It may be better, however, to arrive in Antigua without specific arrangements and then shop around to find a *simpático* teacher. Given the large number of schools in town, finding an opening should pose no problem; stop by the tourist office or peruse restaurant bulletin boards for information.

Tuitions (including room and board with a local family) are fairly uniform, and prices drop about Q10 after the first week. **Escuela de Español Arcoiris,** 7a. Calle Ote. 19, charges Q200 per day for four hours of instruction, Q300 for six. Room and board cost Q90 per week. **Centro Experimental de Español Centroamérica,** Santa Lucía Nte. 33, charges US$40 per week for four hours of daily instruction, US$65 including a local homestay. **Academia Nahual,** 5a. Av. Nte. 31, gives four hours of instruction per day for US$53 per week; with room and board, the package costs US$80. The six-hours-per-day deal costs US$63, and weekly room and board is an extra US$27. **Escuela de Español Tecún Umán,** 6a. Calle Pte. 34, charges US$45 for four hours and US$55 for six, with room and board an extra US$25. In addition to the above schools, the following have received the very unofficial recommendation of the tourist office staff: **Instituto Antigüeño de Español,** 1a. Calle Pte. 33; **Centro Lingüística Antigua,** 6a. Av. Nte. 25; and **Escuela de Español Jiménez,** 1a. Calle Pte. Because North Americans tend to equate high prices with quality, some schools jack up their prices to entice such *extranjeros;* if you are of (or feign) European origin, quoted prices will plummet.

Near Antigua

Several of the *pueblitos indígenas* near Antigua make excellent daytrips. **Ciudad Vieja,** an even earlier former capital of Guatemala, is 5km from Antigua. Only a few ruined colonial buildings remain. Buses for Ciudad Vieja leave from Antigua's market every half hour from 9am to 5pm and charge 40 centavos. After passing through Vieja, buses continue to **San Antonio Aguas Calientes,** a weaving center 9km from Antigua. The last bus returns to Antigua at 5:30pm. Another village reached by frequent buses from Antigua (7am-5pm), **Santa María de Jesús,** marks the origin of the trail leading to the summit of **Volcán de Agua** (3766m). Ask locals for directions to the trail: once out of Santa María, it is easy to follow and most hikers need four to five hours to follow it to the top. The last bus back to Antigua leaves at 4:30pm, but there is a pension in the village in case you have to spend the night.

Other nearby volcanoes, more arduous a climb than Agua, are **Acatenango** (3975m) and **Fuego** (3763m). Most climbers tackle these two peaks from Finca de Soledad. (Buses from Antigua to Acatenango will drop you off at the Finca *crucero.*) For best results, climb Acatenango first, spend the night at the hut in the saddle that connects the two volcanoes, and in the morning, scamper to Fuego's summit.

Camping gear for volcano climbs is available for rental in Antigua at **Casa Andin- ista,** 4a. Calle Ote. 5-A. Sleeping bags or tents go for Q10 per day; boats, stoves, or backpacks for Q5 per day. All rentals require a hefty deposit. Detailed maps (which may be photocopied for a small fee) and guidebooks are available for pur- chase. Experienced climbers recommend bringing much water and warm clothes, especially for sleeping near the summit. One last bit of useful information: Fuego is an active volcano which emits sulfur fumes, and occasionally spews out a large quantity of molten lava, giving the climb an added dash of danger.

Lake Atitlán

A multitude of volcanoes and foothills splashed with heavy vegetation encircle the icy waters of Lake Atitlán, 116km west of Guatemala City. Small villages popu- late the shore; roads lead to some, but most are accessible only by boat. Some *pueb- los* remain strongholds of *indígena* culture and hotbeds of political resistance, while others have peacefully surrendered to tourism and westernization.

Panajachel

Thanks to a highway linking it to Guatemala City, Panajachel plays host to swarms of tourists. The *pueblo's* streets are filled with *típico* vendors selling bananas, bracelets, and peanuts to charmed visitors. If watching the moon rise and the sun set over the surrounding crags isn't enough nighttime entertainment for you, bars and fine restaurants line Calle Principal.

Practical Information

Panajachel has yet to be introduced to the high-tech concept of street signs, but a 20-minute walk covers the entire town. Most everything (with the exception of the beachfront luxury hotels) lies along **Calle Principal** which connects Panajachel with Sololá, or **Calle Santander,** which branches off to the right at the bank. The public beach is to the left at the end of this street. Although the town is not serviced by phones, you can make long-distance calls at **Guatel,** halfway down Principal. (Open daily 7am-midnight.) Change currency at **Banco del Argo** on Principal (open Mon.-Thurs. 9am-3pm, Fri. 9am-3:30pm), or in the barber shop to the left of the bank (open daily 7am-9pm). The **tourist office** (open Wed.-Sun. 8am-noon and 2-

6pm, Mon. 8am-noon), on Principal before the bank, posts a bus and launch schedule after hours on the door.

Launches to surrounding villages (Q3) depart from the front of **Hotel del Lago** near the public beach to Santiago (5 per day, 1 hr., last return to Panajachel at 3pm), and San Pedro (6 per day, 1 hr., last return at 5pm). A San Pedro-Santiago-San Antonio excursion departs at 9am and returns at 3pm (Q20). Transportation to other lakeside villages can be negotiated at the docks.

All buses depart from and arrive at the tourist office. **Rebuli** buses go to Guatemala City (8 per day 5am-2:30pm, 3 hr., Q5). Get off at Chimaltenango to make a southbound connection to Antigua. Four buses depart for Quetzaltenango between 5:30am and 2:30pm (2 hr., Q4). To reach the southern border, change at the Quetzaltenango station for a direct bus to Tapachula. Buses to Chichicastenango leave daily at 6:45, 7:45, 8:45, and 9:45am (1½ hr., Q2.50) and return at 12:30, 1, 2, and 3pm. All buses pass through Los Encuentros; connections can be made there to all points.

Accommodations

Pana, as locals affectionately dub it, is more expensive than Antigua or the capital. Cheaper *huéspedes* enable you to save a few quetzales to drop later in the well-stocked markets. If you're planning on an extended stay in town, consider renting a house for US$30 per week.

Casa de Huéspedes Santander, in a little alley off Santander 1 block from the bank. The quietest, cleanest, and best game in town. Dense garden shields guests from the nightly merrymaking in the village. Simple rooms with tiled floors. Singles Q14. Doubles Q20. Triples Q26.

Mario's Rooms, on Santander past Guatel. Incredibly comfortable beds, coal-stuffed pillows, and hot water before noon. Rooms of varying vintages. Restaurant in front serves the cheapest breakfast in town (Q3). Singles Q13. Doubles Q20.

Hospedaje Santa Elena, on Principal, down the alley across from the tourist office. Chickens and dogs run rampant in front of this grungy hotel. Roosters will make sure you rise with the rest of civilization in the morn. Despite the sagging mattress and damp bathrooms, it's not cheap. Singles Q13. Doubles Q17.

Hotel Fonda del Sol, on Principal before the tourist office. Several rooms, in a colorful assortment of ages and prices. Singles Q14-20, with bath Q35. Doubles Q24, with bath Q44. Triples Q39, with bath Q54.

Food

If *plátanos* and peanuts don't appeal to you, fear not. Panajachel's gourmet restaurants are sure to pacify the palate.

Deli, on Principal, 2 blocks past the bank; the restaurant is hidden behind a few trees on the right. The best breakfast in town hands down. Three whole-wheat pancakes with fruit Q5. Bottomless cup of Guatemalan brew Q2. Bagel sandwiches Q6-8. Open daily 8am-7:30pm.

Amigos, on Santander, halfway to the lake. Beer flows freely, served with enamel-cracking tortilla chips and salsa. Owner rushes around placating the masses. Arrive early to try the ginger tofu (Q9) or the gigantic burrito (Q10). Open daily 9am-7pm.

Chisme, on Los Arboles. Bear left from Principal after the bank, and walk 1 block. A favorite of Pana's long-term visitors. Good place to get trekking advice or a ride to a nearby market. Baked eggs with herb cream sauce Q7, banana crepes Q5. Waffles and fruit Q5. Open daily 7am-11pm.

Near Panajachel

Santiago Atitlán, directly across the lake from Panajachel, remains indifferent to the recent tourist onslaught. Women still wear traditional *nim pots* and most men don *indígena* garb. Santiago is perhaps most famous for its worship of Maximón, a wooden idol dressed in *típico* clothes, a cigar drooping from his pursed lips. On

Wednesday of Semana Santa, Maximón is paraded through the village, and worshipers pay their respects by chomping on unlit stogies as the icon passes.

An overnight visit gives a more genuine impression of the community. An immaculate hotel, *Chi Nim Ya's*, lies up the hill and left of the dock. Two spacious floors of shelter are frequented by laid-back travelers. (Q7 per person, Q10 for a room with a private bath.) Another option is **Posada Rosita**, to the right of the Catholic Church, which is equally clean but more desolate. Balcony rooms face the Volcano San Pedro. (Q6 per person.) The **Gran Sol**, straight ahead as you leave the dock, has a patio and serves a large *desayuno típico*, eggs, beans, fried *plátano*, cheese, cream, and tortillas for Q4. (Open daily 7am-9pm.)

Launches from Santiago to Panajachel (Q3) leave daily between 5:30am and 3:30pm.

Several other villages are less than one hour from Panajachel by boat. **San Pedro**, to the west of Santiago, accommodates overnighters. **Pension Chausinahi** and **Hotel Villa Sol**, in the big cement block complex to the right of the docks, have clean, comfortable rooms for Q8. To the far right, by the mailboat dock, the **Johanna Hotel** attracts international travelers to its budget café, where nothing costs more than Q5.

On Thursdays and Sundays, **Chichicastenango** (37km north of Panajachel) becomes a blur of pigments, looms, and textiles as indigenous artisans descend from the hills to sell their goods in Guatemala's most colorful and extensive market. A few hours of browsing through the *típico* clothing will stain hands yellow and purple and eyes green with envy as travelers nearing the end of their trip load bags with cheap goods. Bargain for the best deals on Saturday night when vendors are just setting up and crowds are sparse. The market closes around 4 or 5pm. The last bus back to Panajachel or Antigua (changing at Quetzaltenango) leaves at 3:30pm.

Tikal

Tikal is probably the most fascinating archeological site in the Americas. In northern Petén 670km north of Guatemala City, the ruins encompass over 3000 different Mayan stone constructions, including six towers, of which two are entirely excavated. You'll need at least two days to explore the complex center and the surrounding **Parque Nacional Tikal** (222 square mi.). Those fortunate enough to witness a full moon rising over Temple IV and the encroaching jungle often cite it as one of the most memorable sights of their life. Arguably, the jungle is as intriguing as are the ruins themselves: falling fruit is a tell-tale sign of spider monkeys overhead, remote paths hide wild parrots, peacocks, lizards, iguanas, and early risers occasionally spot a jaguar slinking through the undergrowth.

Orientation

Most bus connections are made through Flores, one hour outside Tikal. Overland routes connect Tikal with Tenosique (Mexico), Guatemala City, and Belize City. The Belize route is the most comfortable and popular of the three. Buses from Belize City run daily to the Guatemalan border (see Belize City to Guatemala above). Buses to Flores leave the border from 5am to 4pm (4½ hr., Q5). The intersection two-thirds of the way to Flores at El Cruce is **Ixlu crossing**; from here a bus runs to Tikal at 6:30am and 1:30pm, and microbuses (Q10) run all day. Few cars go to Tikal in the afternoon, making hitching difficult. Buses from Flores directly to Tikal (1 hr., Q5) leave at 6am and 1pm from Hotel San Juan near the causeway. Microbuses leave from most hotels at 6, 8, and 10am (45 min., Q10) returning at 2, 4, and 5pm.

Four airlines shuttle daily between Guatemala City and **Santa Elena**, 60 minutes by bus from Tikal, 45 minutes by microbus. (Bus fare Q5, microbus Q10.) Buy your ticket in the capital or Santa Elena, and book at least one day in advance. The planes leave Guatemala City at 7am, returning at about 4pm (1 hr., US$55). Charter flights from Mexico and Belize also serve Santa Elena.

Not surprisingly, buses from Guatemala City are cheaper than planes, but by land you'll suffer through the 280km of jarring dirt roads between Morales and Santa Elena. Should you decide to brave the bus, take the first-class Pullman, which has shock absorbers and doesn't make rest stops to relieve the chickens (10 hr., Q40). The regular bus takes at least 13 hours (Q17). A Pullman leaves Fuente Del Norte (see Transportation to Tikal in the Guatemala City section) at 10pm and arrives in Flores around 8am. Microbuses here will transport you to Tikal.

To keep up with the Indiana Joneses, the wildest alternative is a two-day boat and bus odyssey from Tenosique, Mexico. This involves a four-hour cruise up the Río San Pedro to El Naranjo, Guatemala (expensive at Q50, but fun). From El Naranjo you'll bounce seven hours east over dirt roads to Santa Elena (Q10).

Passing into Tikal National Park, officials will relieve you of Q5 at a checkpoint 17km from the site itself. Save the ticket; you'll need it to enter the ruins. If you plan to stay in the ruins past 5pm, have an inspector stamp it so that you can stay for the sunset and until 8:30pm.

Practical Information

As a small jungle outpost, Tikal offers minimal services. The **post office** (open Mon.-Fri. 8am-noon and 2-5pm) is to the left of the **visitors center**. The **dispensary**, next to the museum, cares for minor medical problems. (Open the first 22 days of each month 7am-noon and 2-5pm.) For full medical service, go to Flores via Santa Elena.

Accommodations and Food

Tikal has one good campground and two moderately priced hotels. The popular camping complex, set in a vast grassy field, consists of large concrete platforms with thatched roofs. Less amiable than your fellow backpackers are the scorpions and tarantulas. Communal bathrooms have showers, but lockers are not available. Most campers sleep in hammocks rented from the caretaker. (Camping Q5 per person. Hammock rental Q5.) **Hotel Jaguar Inn** has a few tents out back, each with two mattresses (Q25). For a real bed, electric light, and screened windows, beautiful bungalows are available at Q70 per person, which includes three large meals. The only other budget option is a bed (Q20) in a four-bunk room at the **Jungle Lodge.**

Two fly-infested restaurants and a mini-mart face the visitors center. These mid-range restaurants have identical menus and prices: eggs and beans for Q2, chicken and beans for Q5.50, beans and beef for Q5.50; the daily bean special goes for Q4. (Open daily 6am-9pm.) The **Restaurant Jaguar Inn** caters to the wealthy crowd, with bean prices set accordingly. A full breakfast (pancake, eggs, fried bananas, homemade bread, and coffee) costs Q10. Complete lunches and dinners are Q18. Bean quiche is a bargain at Q7. (Open daily 7am-8:30pm.) The **Café Restaurant del Parque,** can be as bland as it wants to be; it's the only place that serves filet mignon (Q20) or fettucini Alfredo (Q14). (Open daily 7am-8:30pm.)

Sights

Tikal protects its history. Ceramic shards prove that ancient Maya settled the site at least as early as 600 BC, and seashells from the Pacific Coast and jade from the highlands testify to Tikal's extensive role in the Mesoamerican trade network. Architectural details and artifacts from several tombs suggest that Tikal was influenced by distant Teotihuacán, near modern Mexico City. Most of the temples and other constructions at Tikal date from the late Classic period (550-900 AD), when Tikal may have had over 20,000 inhabitants. It thrived longer than any other ancient civilization, but like Palenque and other important Mayan lowland centers, Tikal collapsed mysteriously at the end of the Classic era. Theories of its downfall include war with the Aztecs, a fast-spreading plague, and the famous Rosen Theory of beancrop failure. While post-Classic descendants of the original population continued to live and worship at Tikal, they did little of significance but pillage the tombs. By 1000 AD, the jungle was the final usurper of Tikal's civilization. The modern world did not rediscover Tikal until 1848, when Guatemalans Modesto Mendez and Ambrosio Tut stumbled upon the site. It was left undisturbed for another 58 years, when excavation exposed layers upon layers of platforms and monuments.

Begin your tour at the **Great Plaza,** Tikal's geographic and ceremonial heart, 2km west of the site entrance. Facing north in the plaza, the terraced North Acropolis lies ahead. To the right and left are the symmetrical Temples I and II. The Central Acropolis is behind, exhibiting the spiritual importance of the number nine; Mayans believed in a world beneath the earth ruled by the Nine Lords of the Night.

Temple I, or the Temple of the Great Jaguar, towers 145 ft. above the Grand Plaza. Built around 700 AD, this structure, the modern-day symbol of Tikal, has nine sharply ascending terraces supporting a three-chambered temple on top. The first seven steps have been restored to their original state, but the stairs to the top are well-worn, making them slippery when wet (Bonjovistic, if you prefer). Its westward orientation (toward the setting sun) and the fact that the other temples face it, emphasize its importance among Tikal's constructions. Only a few carved lintels remain in the upper chambers, but the view is fantastic. Many of Tikal's artifacts were removed to museums in Europe and the U.S. years ago.

Across the plaza, **Temple II** is shorter and easy to scale. Excavations at the **North Acropolis,** a partially restored complex of temples, have revealed at least 10 levels of construction dating from progressively earlier eras, as well as several stelae and rich burial tombs. Descendants of the Mayans now leave their mark on the acropolis in brightly colored spray paint. The ballcourt, just south of Temple I, used to host a game akin to soccer but played with a hard rubber ball. Unlike in soccer, ritual decapatation awaited the losers. Rulers occupied the Great Plaza, burying their dead in large pyramids, while commoners lived in thatched huts outside the area, laying their dead to rest under the kitchen floor.

One kilometer west of the Great Plaza, on Tozzer Causeway, is **Temple IV** (dating from the 8th century), the tallest construction in pre-Columbian America. (Teotihuacán's Pyramid of the Sun was probably loftier, but nothing remains of its uppermost temple.) Two hundred twelve feet from base to roof comb, the pyramid is almost completely shrouded in jungle growth. Clamber up the tangle of roots and ladders at the structure's northeast corner to the summit, where the humongous view compensates for the temple's lack of detail.

Temple V faces east, 500m south of the Great Plaza. The 190-ft. temple has a small chamber at the top, accessible only by a daring ascent up metal scaffolding. At the subterranean **Palace of the Masks,** ½km southwest of Temple V, bas-relief carvings depict a number of gods and pregnant women. Ornate hieroglyphs cover the towering roof comb of the **Temple of the Inscriptions,** 2km southeast of the Great Plaza. Most visible at dawn, the monumental symbols record the Mayan date 9.16.15.0.0 (766 AD). Ancient graffiti at **Maler's Place** tells of the Mayan practice of squashing the head of a ruling class infant between two boards to create the admired flattened skull. At **Group G,** the walls depict a human sacrifice with the victim spread over an altar to facilitate the removal of his heart. The walls are channeled, to allow orderly outflow of freshly liberated blood.

The small **Museum of Tikal,** at the entrance to the site, displays a collection of ceramics, stelae, jade offerings, and carved and painted bones. Richly detailed Stela 31 depicts "Stormy Sky," a 5th-century AD governor of Tikal. Peer down at the reconstruction of Tomb 116, which contains a full skeleton accompanied by shells and ceramics, as well as 16 pounds of jade. (Museum open Mon.-Fri. 9am-5pm, Sat.-Sun. 9am-4pm. Admission Q2.) The **Stelae Museum** by the visitors center is free.

Visit the ruins at dawn or dusk, when the air is cool and the animals most active. Bring mosquito repellent and a flashlight (for exploring dark corners and finding your way out at nightfall). The site is officially open daily from 6am to 6pm (admission Q5), but you can stay until 8:30pm if you get the back of your ticket stamped in advance at the administration building (left up a small slope at the site entrance). The ticket must be renewed each day.

To sightsee intelligently, invest in a handbook to the ruins or hire a guide; a quick study of the scale model by the museum provides a good introduction to Tikal but won't suffice. Tikal's major attractions are dispersed over a 4 square-kilometer area, and few signs point the way. A useful map of the site (Q2), which quickly goes limp in the tropical humidity, is available at the museum. Better yet, pick up William Coe's *Tikal,* the classic guide to the ruins, with a large pull-out map, beautiful illustrations, and tiresome text (Q40). Tours range in price, depending on the linguistic ability and the historical knowledge of your guide (some of the "most studied" guides have merely memorized Coe's handbook). **Yolanda,** who can be contacted at the **Jungle Lodge Hotel,** offers an informative tour (Q80-100 per group) that emphasizes the flora and fauna of Tikal. Other guides are available at the entrance to the site. Tours leave around 10am and last for three hours.

Flores

If making a bus connection in Santa Elena entails spending the night in Flores, don't despair. Buses stop in Santa Elena's dusty market, just a few hundred meters across the causeway. Stock up for long hauls here, then head across the lake to the island town of Flores. If you need cash after hours, several luxury hotels change money. Beyond the causeway, walk left on Central America and bear right at the end of the street. **Hotel Petén,** on the left, offers a fair exchange rate. The **Banco de Guatemala,** on the far side of the island, is open Monday through Thursday from 8:30am to 2pm and Friday for an extra half hour. Most hotels in Flores serve thick walleted guests, but there are a few cheapies. The **Petén Anexo,** on Central America behind Casa Azul, has singles for Q10, doubles for Q15, and triples for Q21. **El Tucan,** Central America 45, on the far end of the avenue, hides a pet monkey and several overly friendly toucans amid the dense patio vegetation (Q22 per room). Prices plummet across the causeway in Santa Elena. **Hotel Jade,** Calle 62, 10m past the causeway, has clean but fanless rooms and an amiable old owner. Next door, the **Mesón de Don Quijote** has high ceilings and low beds. (Singles and doubles Q8, with bath Q25.) The only alternative to the pricey restaurants are the numerous *comedores* that line the street. They offer standard fare of eggs and (memories of Tikal) beans for Q2.50. Beans and chicken or meat go for Q6.50. If you're craving inauthentic nachos and burritos, shell out the Q12 for a modest serving at **El Tucan.** (Open Mon.-Sat. 9am-10pm.)

The **post office** is in the center of Flores on Av. de Reforma (open Mon.-Fri. 8am-4:30pm). First-class **Fuente del Norte** buses leave Santa Elena from a yellow building on the right 3 blocks through the market. Buy tickets in advance to Guatemala City (at 11am and 11pm, 12 hr., Q40) via Río Dulce (Q40). Tickets to the Belize border (at 5am, 4 hr., Q5) and to El Naranjo (at 5am and 12:30pm, 7 hr., Q10) can be purchased at the **San Juan Hotel** near the causeway. **Pinita** buses, which depart from the center of the market, go to El Naranjo (at noon, 7 hr., Q7) and Poptun (4 per day, 5 hr., Q5).

INDEX